A GOD LIKE NO OTHER

A GOD LIKE NO OTHER

Depaganizing the God of the Hebrew Bible

David A. Brondos

Comunidad Teológica de México
Ciudad de México

Theological Community of Mexico
Mexico City

2024

A GOD LIKE NO OTHER:
DEPAGANIZING THE GOD OF THE HEBREW BIBLE

Comunidad Teológica de México/Instituto Internacional de Estudios Superiores
Av. San Jerónimo 137
San Ángel
01000 México, CDMX
México

Cover image/Imagen de la portada: Catie Radney, "Generations," © 2019.

Cover and interior design/Diseño interior y de la portada: theBookDesigners

First edition/Primera edición: 2024

Hardback ISBN: 978-607-98034-9-0
Paperback ISBN: 978-607-98034-8-3
eBook ISBN: 979-8-218-47159-0

Printed in the U.S.A./Impreso en los Estados Unidos de Norteamérica

*For
Alicia, Michael,
and Max*

Contents

Introduction 1

Chapter 1. The Repaganizing of a Depaganized God 13

Chapter 2. The God Who Began with an End 53

Chapter 3. A God of Loving Demands and Demanding Love 103

Chapter 4. Delivering Justice from the Hand of the Oppressor 165

Chapter 5. The Healing Chastisements of an Unrelenting God 221

Chapter 6. The Wrath of a God Burning to Save 285

Chapter 7. Giving Life by Taking It 349

Chapter 8. Purging a Paganized God from the Sins of His Interpreters ... 393

Chapter 9. Consecrating a People Set Apart for Solidarity 463

Chapter 10. The God Who Plans to Bless 523

Chapter 11. A Stubborn Love for a Stubborn People 583

Chapter 12. Bringing a Stiff-Necked People to Their Knees 639

Chapter 13. Proclaiming a Passion that Refuses to Die 687

Conclusion 741

Abbreviations 755

Bibliography 757

Index of Scripture and Ancient Literature 763

Index of Authors 773

Index of Subjects 775

Contents by Chapter

Introduction 1

Chapter 1. The Repaganizing of a Depaganized God 13

The Pagan Gods of Antiquity 17

The Gods of the Enuma Elish 23

The Gods of Homer's Iliad *and* Odyssey 28

The God of Israel and the Hebrew Scriptures 37

The Character of Israel's God 39

The Desires and Objectives of Israel's God 41

The God of Israel according to Walter Brueggemann 45

Chapter 2. The God Who Began with an End 53

Creation and God's Sovereignty 53

Creation and God's Goodness 57

Creation and God's Love 63

God's Love as Unconditional 68

The Objectives of God's Love 73

Suffering, Sin, and Evil in God's Creation 78

Seeking to Bring Good out of Bad 81

Sin and Evil Elsewhere in the Opening Chapters of Genesis 91

Seeking Good in Evil 98

Chapter 3. A God of Loving Demands and Demanding Love 103

God's Plan through Abraham 104

The Law That Gives Life 109

The Torah and Shalom 113

The Commandments as a Means to Promoting Well-Being for All 116

Instilling Obedience through Purity, Sacrifice, and Worship 123

Rejecting the Gods Who Bring Death 126

The Many Evils of Idolatry 128

Prohibitions Designed to Protect 133

Finding Meaning in Commandments That Seem Anything but Good 140

The Inherent Goodness of the Torah and Its Observance 149

The Torah as an Instrument of Blessing 149

The Law and the Love of God 157

Chapter 4. Delivering Justice from the Hand of the Oppressor 165

Justice, Righteousness, and the Deliverance of the Oppressed 166

Judging to Save 168
Justice as Love and Compassion 173
Contrasting Justice in Hebrew and English 178
Justice in the Pagan Worldviews of Antiquity 182
The Justice of the Gods 182
Upholding an Unjust Order in the Name of Justice 190
The Oppressive Justice of Empire 199
The Subversive Justice of the God of Israel 208
Establishing an Order That Is Truly Just 208
Restoring a Justice That Saves 217

Chapter 5. The Healing Chastisements of an Unrelenting God 221
Demanding an Obedience That Brings Blessing 223
The Intrinsic Consequences of Obedience 228
Rethinking Reward 230
Healing Disobedience through Chastisements 234
Punishment as Chastisement, Discipline, and Correction 236
The Return of Repentance 241
Grace That Punishes as It Forgives 243
The Harrowing and Healing Chastisements of Leviticus 26 and Deuteronomy 28 ... 247
A God Who Curses? 250
Finding Love and Purpose in the Depths of Despair 255
Loving and Serving a God Whom One Fears 261
Chastisement and Healing in Israel's Narrative 268
The Frustrated Love of a Frustrated God 269
Salvaging a Righteous Remnant through Destruction 278

Chapter 6. The Wrath of a God Burning to Save 285
The God Who Seeks Nothing but Justice 287
Deserving Help That Is Undeserved 287
Confessing Sin to Seek Salvation 294
The Gratitude Born out of Goodness 299
A God Who Seeks Sacrifice While Spurning It 301
Desiring Sacrifice from Those Who Refuse to Give It 301
Reclaiming Sacrifice by Rejecting It 307
The Causes of God's Wrath 310
Giving Vent to God's Rage 313
The Anger and Hatred of God's Love 318
A God of Vengeance? 325
Rediscovering the Love of Vengeance 326
Translating Vengeance in a Way That Avoids It 334
Visiting Sinners and Their Sins 342
The Terrible Evils of God's Love and Goodness 347

Chapter 7. Giving Life by Taking It 349
Sacrifice in the Pagan Worldviews of Antiquity 349
Sacrificing to the God of Israel 353

Sacrifice as Offering and Prayer 358
The Offering of Gifts as the Offering of One's Self 365
   The Transforming Power of Sacrificial Offerings and Rites 371
   Finding Meaning and Purpose in the Offering of Sacrifice 377
Promoting Justice and Righteousness through Sacrifice 382

Chapter 8. Purging a Paganized God from the Sins of His Interpreters 393
Seeking Favor and Forgiveness from the Pagan Gods of Antiquity 394
Sacrifices for Sin in the Hebrew Bible 398
   Purification and Expiation through Sacrificial Rites 400
   Distinguishing Holiness from Purity 403
Finding a Need for Sacrifices for Sin 404
Satisfying the Demands of God's Justice through Sacrifice 407
   Questioning Punishment and Propitiation 412
   A God Held Captive by His Nature 415
   Substituting Sacrifice for Obedience 419
   Trying to Make Sacrifice Work 421
   Reconsidering Atonement as a Biblical Concept 425
Satisfying the Need of a Holy God for Purity 427
   Pollution, Purification, and the Power of Sacrificial Blood 428
   The Dangers of a Holy God 434
   Protecting Israel's God from the Perils of Pollution 437
   Giving Substance to the Metaphor of Impurity 442
   Attempting to Reconcile Symbol with Reality 451
Defusing the Dangers of God's Holiness 455

Chapter 9. Consecrating a People Set Apart for Solidarity 463
Putting Away Sin through Sacrifice 463
   Reconsidering Expiation, Propitiation, and Atonement 467
   The Cleansing of Yom Kippur 473
Bearing Sin and Iniquity 477
The Servant Who Takes Away Sin by Bearing It (Isaiah 53) 480
Sacrificial Blood and the Offering of Life 489
A Holiness to Be Embraced 496
   Setting Apart a People for Justice 503
   Commanding Respect for the Symbols of God's Presence 509

Chapter 10. The God Who Plans to Bless 523
The Intentions of the Gods in Ancient Pagan Thought 523
The Blessing of Israel in God's Plan 525
   The Challenge of Bringing Blessing 526
   Blessing a People to Be a Blessing for All 528
A God for the Nations 533
A Covenant Designed for Blessing 541
   The Covenant as Faithfulness and Commitment 548
   Israel as God's Treasured Possession 556
A God Concerned for His Name 565

Rejoicing in the Blessings Sure to Come 571
   Blessing David to Bless Israel 577
   Judging the Nations for Good 580

Chapter 11. A Stubborn Love for a Stubborn People 583
Setting the Stage for Sinai 584
   Engendering Trust to Beget Obedience 586
   Hardening Hearts in Pursuit of Justice 596
Sin, Seduction, and Sedition at Sinai 599
   Bordering on the Edge of Destruction 601
   Putting God's Wrath to Rest 608
Delving Further into Distrust and Disaster 612
   Pushing a Patient God to the Limits 613
   Breaking the Yoke of a People Bent on Rebellion 619
A Final Plea for Deaf Ears to Hear 626
Laying to Rest a Prophet Like No Other 631

Chapter 12. Bringing a Stiff-Necked People to Their Knees 639
A Fresh Start for a Polluted Land 640
   Contending with the Carnage of a Conquest 640
   Taking Possession of a Promise 649
Sinking Back into a Cycle of Chaos 653
The Ascent and Descent of Israel's Kings 659
   A King after God's Own Heart 662
   The Glories of a Kingdom Soon to Fade 668
   Dragging a People Down to Destruction 672
   A Wrath with No Remedy 676
Putting a Broken People Back on Their Feet 679

Chapter 13. Proclaiming a Passion that Refuses to Die 687
Pining for a Wayward People 688
Pursuing the Lusts of an Adulterous Heart 696
The Struggle to Save a People from Themselves 701
A Love That Will Not Be Scorned 707
   Peering into Eyes Fixed for Evil 711
   The Ravages of a Wrath Unleashed 716
   Striving to Make Sense of Terror and Torment 720
Sowing Hope in the Midst of Heartache 728
   A Return to Rejoice In 731
   Pondering a Future for Israel and the Nations 735

Conclusion 741

Abbreviations 755

Bibliography 757

Index of Scripture and Ancient Literature 763

Index of Authors 773

Index of Subjects 775

INTRODUCTION

"His steadfast love endures forever!" Readers of the Hebrew Bible or Old Testament will search in vain for a phrase describing the God of Israel that appears more frequently in the biblical texts than this one. In principle, it is a wonderful phrase that celebrates God's unceasing love and grace as well as his immense goodness and mercy.

While very few readers of the biblical texts would acknowledge it openly, however, in the minds of most that phrase is at best a half-truth, if not an outright lie. Although in many passages the Hebrew Scriptures portray the God of whom they speak as good, gracious, kind, and merciful, in others they present him as anything but loving. He is a God who is frequently said to be filled with wrath and threatens to pour out that wrath without pity or mercy, as he seems to do in the account of the flood in Noah's day, the story of Sodom and Gomorrah, and countless other passages in which he inflicts death and destruction on human beings. He is explicitly called a God of vengeance and is even said to hate certain people. At times he acts with great cruelty and violence, lashing out to harm and even kill those who stand in his way or rebel against him. He describes himself as a God who punishes children for the iniquity of their parents down to the third and fourth generation and has Moses tell his people Israel: "the Lord your God is a devouring fire, a jealous God" (Deut 4:24). Even when he is said to love people, when they refuse to do as he commands or anger him in some other way, that love can turn to rage, fury, and devastation at any moment. If such is the case, then it would appear that his love is *not* steadfast and does *not* endure forever. On the contrary, it depends on people doing what he tells them to do, and it lasts only as long as they obey him and submit to his will in the way he commands.

Yet precisely because so many passages from the Hebrew Bible insist that the steadfast love of God *does* endure forever, any who wish to speak of God in a manner that is faithful to the biblical texts cannot dismiss such a claim outright simply because other portrayals of God found in those texts seem to contradict it. The fact that the biblical texts themselves hold together these apparently conflicting conceptions of God makes it necessary for those who wish to take those texts seriously either to attempt to reconcile those conceptions of God with one another or else to explain how they came to stand alongside one another in those texts despite the inconsistencies or contradictions reflected in them.

Over the centuries, most interpreters of the biblical texts have opted for the first of these two alternatives. For the most part, the manner in which they have reconciled these apparently conflicting conceptions of God to one another is by affirming that although God's love is steadfast and enduring, that love must be seen in conjunction with other attributes of God, including especially his justice, righteousness, and holiness. Because by nature God is just, righteous, and holy, he cannot simply overlook or tolerate sin and evil but must demand that those who practice these things be punished and kept out of his presence. While he loves human beings and in principle would like to show his grace, kindness, and favor to all of them, his nature demands that certain conditions be fulfilled in order for him to do so. In particular, those who wish to obtain his acceptance and forgiveness must repent of their sins, ask his forgiveness, and make atonement for the wrongs they have committed.

Rather than reconciling God's love to these other attributes of God, however, such a portrayal of God sets his love *in opposition* to those attributes. Human beings are said to experience either God's love or else his wrath, judgments, and condemnation, but they do not experience both of these things at the same time because God's just, righteous, and holy nature prevents him from showing love and favor to those who do not fulfill the demands of that nature. Precisely for that reason, however, God's love can hardly be considered steadfast and enduring. Instead, it depends on the manner in which sinful human beings respond to it. If they reject God, rather than experiencing his love, they will experience his rejection, since he will withhold his love from them and reject them as they have rejected him. At best, his love will be steadfast and enduring only for those whose love for him is *also* steadfast and enduring. For those who do not love him in that way, what will be steadfast and endure forever is not his love but rather his wrath, judgment, condemnation, and punishments.

For many biblical scholars and interpreters, such an understanding of God's steadfast love is not considered problematic. In fact, it is common to observe that all of the deities of antiquity were thought to relate to human beings in this same way. They loved those who loved them and hated those who spurned and scorned them. The comparative studies done by biblical scholars over the past couple of centuries have identified many similarities and parallels between the manner in which the God of Israel is portrayed in the biblical texts and the manner in which the gods are described in the texts of other peoples from antiquity known to us. Those studies have revealed that many other ancient sources speak of the gods loving and caring for human beings while at the same time portraying those gods as wrathful and vindictive. The love attributed to those gods is not unconditional or undeserved but is simply a form of self-interest. They show favor to those who obey and serve them faithfully but deny that favor to those who disobey them and refuse to submit to them. On that basis, those scholars conclude that when the biblical texts speak of God's love, they are merely ascribing to him the same type of behavior that was characteristic of other gods of antiquity. He is kind and gracious to those who are careful to do what he commands but punishes severely any who rebel against him in the same way that the other gods of antiquity known to us did.

The problem with such an interpretation of the biblical texts is that it seems to run contrary to what we find in those texts rather than representing faithfully the conception of God reflected in them. Those texts repeatedly insist that the God of Israel was fundamentally different from the other gods of antiquity and in some ways was even radically opposed to them. The affirmation that God's steadfast love endures forever, in fact, seems to have been intended to convey the idea that his love for human beings is *distinct* from the type of love that other gods were said to show for human beings. Unlike the love of those gods, which was *not* steadfast and did *not* endure forever, the love of the God of Israel knew no bounds or limits and was unconditional. It did not depend on the manner in which human beings responded to it but instead remained constant independently of whether they accepted that love or rejected it. His love was a free and gracious gift rather than something that human beings had to deserve or merit by means of their conduct. It was precisely this understanding of God's love that set him apart from all of the other gods of antiquity. In large part, in fact, the reason why the biblical texts prohibited so strongly the worship of other gods was that their worship led human beings to treat others in the same way that those gods did, "loving" those who loved them in the sense of giving them what they needed and wanted for their own sake but hating those whom they considered their enemies and seeking to do them harm. If the God of Israel related to human beings in this same way, he was just like all of the other gods of antiquity known to us.

Rather than attempting to reconcile the allusions to God's steadfast love in the biblical texts with other affirmations that appear to contradict them, many biblical scholars and interpreters would instead maintain that we should not expect those texts to portray God in ways that are entirely consistent with one another. These scholars would point out that the research done over the past couple of centuries has made it clear that the Hebrew Bible incorporates a wide range of perspectives regarding God that are often in tension and conflict with one another. Whereas prior to the rise of critical biblical research in the eighteenth and nineteenth centuries it was common to suppose that God alone was responsible for the content that appears in the Bible as the one who had revealed to the biblical authors all that it contained, that research has made it increasingly evident that most of the books of the Hebrew Bible underwent a lengthy and complex process of redaction and editing before they reached the form in which they exist today. Those who have studied the Hebrew Bible in academic settings, for example, are well-acquainted with what is known as the Documentary Hypothesis, according to which the first five books of the Bible or Pentateuch incorporate material from sources known as the Yahwist (J), the Elohist (E), the Deuteronomist (D), and the Priestly tradition (P).

Most biblical scholars today now regard this hypothesis as overly simplistic and maintain that the books of the Pentateuch are the result of a process that was much more complex.[1] According to these scholars, many different sources were brought together to form these books, and the period during which they continued to be reworked and edited lasted for several centuries. Many scholars also agree that they did not exist in the form in which we know them today until the fourth, fifth, or sixth century BCE. It is widely recognized that most of the other books of the Hebrew Bible underwent the same type of editorial process, including especially longer books such as Isaiah, Jeremiah, and the Psalms.

Once it is recognized that the books of the Hebrew Bible are the product of a long process in which many different sources and traditions were incorporated into the biblical texts and those texts underwent repeated revisions, affirmations that are seen as conflicting with one another or appear to contradict one another can be attributed to this process. Because those sources and traditions originated in different historical contexts and were developed in order to respond to different situations and realities, they reflect a wide variety of perspectives that can hardly be expected to agree fully among themselves. In each of those contexts, it was necessary to emphasize different ideas and concepts in order to address the problems and concerns that were particular to them. Because each of the different sources and traditions also developed over a long period of time and was the result of a complex process in which their content was repeatedly revised and reformulated, when those sources and traditions were brought together and placed alongside of one another in the biblical texts, it was inevitable that affirmations and concepts that were not fully compatible with one another and at times even contradicted one another would be found in those texts.

Those who stress the diversity of sources and traditions that have been incorporated into the biblical texts also tend to insist that rather than seeking to identify and reconstruct the theology or worldview found in those texts, it is necessary to stress the diversity of beliefs and perspectives present in them and speak in the plural of the *theologies* and *worldviews* reflected in them. This manner of viewing the texts contrasts sharply with traditional conceptions of the Bible, according to which it was impossible for there to be

---

1. On this point and what follows, see especially Konrad Schmid, *The Scribes of the Torah: The Formation of the Pentateuch in Its Literary and Historical Contexts*, AIL 45 (Atlanta: SBL, 2023), 17-20, 109-26, 151-204, 681-702; Jaeyoung Jeon, "Introduction: The State of Pentateuchal Research," in *The Social Groups behind the Pentateuch*, ed. Jaeyoung Jeon, AIL 44 (Atlanta: SBL, 2021), 3-27 (3-12); Christoph Levin, "The Pentateuch: A Compilation by Redactors," in *The Formation of the Pentateuch: Bridging the Academic Cultures of Europe, Israel, and North America*, ed. Jan C. Gertz, Bernard M. Levinson, Dalit Rom-Shiloni, and Konrad Schmid, FAT 111 (Tübingen: Mohr Siebeck, 2016), 579-87; Benedikt Hensel, "Who Wrote the Bible? Understanding Redactors and Social Groups behind Biblical Traditions in the Context of Plurality within Emerging Judaism," in *Social Groups behind Biblical Traditions: Identity Perspectives from Egypt, Transjordan, Mesopotamia, and Israel in the Second Temple Period*, ed. Benedikt Hensel, Bartosz Adamczewski, and Dany Nocquet, FAT 167 (Tübingen: Mohr Siebeck, 2023), 11-23.

tensions, conflicts, or contradictions in the biblical texts because everything in them had been communicated to their authors by direct revelation from God. If that was the case, then by definition there could be no discrepancies in those texts because God could never contradict himself. Once it is recognized that the biblical texts as we now have them incorporate material from a wide variety of different sources and traditions, however, then the task of biblical scholars is understood to consist of identifying those sources and traditions and understanding each of them on its own terms and in its own historical context. If some passages in the Hebrew Bible affirm that God's steadfast love endures forever and others speak of God hating or rejecting certain human beings and pouring out his wrath on them in order to avenge himself, therefore, it is likely that these conflicting portrayals of God arose in different historical contexts and are grounded in different sources or traditions. For that reason, each of those affirmations must be read and interpreted from within the particular context in which it was originally made and cannot always be expected to be in harmony with affirmations that originated in other contexts.

The problem with this manner of resolving the difficulties raised by the portrayals of God in the biblical texts that seem to conflict or clash with one another is that it assumes that those involved in the process of redacting and editing those texts and bringing them together in a single collection chose simply to let conflicting conceptions and ideas stand alongside one another without making any attempt to reconcile or harmonize them with one another. Those who brought together the different writings that now form part of the Hebrew Bible, however, must have established and adhered to certain criteria when they accepted some writings into that collection but rejected others. Among these criteria would have been the conception of God that appears in them. If they considered that certain writings contained passages that were in conflict with the conception of God reflected in the other writings that formed part of that collection, it seems safe to assume that they would either have excluded those writings from the collection or else would have made revisions and modifications to them in order to bring them into harmony with the other writings in the collection. Even though the diverging perspectives that were evident in the different writings included in the collection would not be suppressed or eliminated entirely, there would be limits as to the degree or extent of the disagreement among them that would be regarded as acceptable.

The same observations would apply to the process of editing and revising each of the writings that formed part of that collection. Those who chose to make changes in the texts that had been passed down to them or bring them together with other texts in order to form a new text would undoubtedly seek to ensure that there was consistency and harmony in the new and revised text. When they incorporated material from other sources into the texts that they possessed, they would either choose to incorporate only material that was already compatible with those texts or else would alter and edit the material they took from other sources in order to make it compatible and harmonious with everything else that was contained in those texts.

If such was the case, then one would expect that those involved in the editorial process who sought to stress and celebrate the enduring nature of God's steadfast love would have altered or suppressed at least to some extent any affirmations regarding God that they regarded as conflicting with their conception of God and his love or as contradicting it. What we find in the biblical texts, however, is that affirmations that from our perspective seem to be conflicting or mutually contradictory stand alongside one another in those texts. Thus, for example, in one of the sayings that is used to describe God in two key texts from the Pentateuch that characterize him as "abounding in steadfast love," it is said not that God does not get angry but that he is "slow to anger" and also that he forgives iniquity while at the same time refusing to clear the guilty and visiting the iniquity of the parents upon their children down to the third and fourth generation (Exod 34:6-7; Num 14:18). Here there appears to be a clear contradiction, since if God does not leave sin and guilt unpunished or put away his anger entirely when people sin, then it is by no means evident how it can be said at the same time that he is a God of steadfast love who consistently *forgives* iniquity. Even if these apparently conflicting affirmations regarding God had their origin in different sources or contexts, it hardly seems possible that when they were brought together as parts of the same saying no attempt was made to reconcile or harmonize them with one another. If those who redacted and edited the biblical texts left these affirmations to stand alongside one another in the same saying, it seems much more logical to assume that they did not regard them as contradicting one another or being in conflict with one another.

In light of these observations, if we are to make sense of the repeated affirmations regarding God's steadfast love and its enduring character that appear in the biblical texts, those texts themselves make it clear that neither of the two alternatives just outlined can be considered acceptable. Rather than setting God's steadfast and enduring love in opposition to his justice, righteousness, and holiness as well as his wrath, judgments, condemnation, and punishments, the biblical texts hold together all of these apparently con-flicting ideas and seem to reject the idea that they contradict one another or are incompatible with one another. They also appear to reject the idea that God's love is conditional upon the manner in which human beings respond to it in the way that the love of other gods of antiquity was thought to be. At the same time, both the biblical texts themselves as well as the manner in which they were brought together in a single collection seem to presup-pose that running throughout those texts there is a conception of God that is uniform and consistent with itself rather than a variety of conflicting and contradictory conceptions of God that cannot be fully reconciled and har-monized with one another.

If we wish to reconstruct faithfully that conception of God and grasp it properly, therefore, we must begin by assuming not only that it is present throughout the biblical texts as a whole but also that in important ways it is fundamentally distinct from other conceptions of the deity that existed in antiquity as well as conceptions of God that set his steadfast love in opposition to his justice, righteousness, and holiness and regard his anger, judgments, and punishments as contrary to his love. These are the assumptions that constitute the basis and starting-point for the present work. If these assumptions are correct, then the affirmation that the steadfast love of the God of Israel endures forever must be seen not only as being fully in harmony with everything else that is said of that God throughout the Hebrew Bible but also as one of the claims regarding that God that distinguishes him most from other gods in antiquity and from the God of whom many biblical scholars and interpreters speak today.

In order to reconstruct the conception of God that runs throughout the biblical texts, for the most part it will be sufficient to examine those texts themselves and ask certain questions of those texts. What do they say about the God of Israel and how do they portray him? What assumptions concerning God are reflected in those texts? What ideas and conceptions regarding God are implicit in them? What motives do they ascribe to him when he is presented as acting in human history? It is important to stress that to approach the biblical texts with questions such as these does not involve reading ideas back *into* those texts but seeking only to read *out* of those texts ideas that are assumed and implicit in them. Such an approach involves attempting to understand the texts on their own terms.

Because my focus here will be on the biblical texts themselves, throughout most of this volume I will not be referencing the work of biblical scholars. Most of the scholarly literature on the Hebrew Bible is aimed at reconstructing the original meanings of the biblical texts by means of comparative studies as well as historical reconstructions of the contexts out of which those texts emerged. What interests me here, however, is not the intended meanings of the texts in their original contexts but the manner in which they were read and interpreted by those who put them in the form in which they now exist and brought them together in a single collection, as well as the readers and hearers for whom that collection of texts was originally intended. Rather than inquiring as to the meanings or ideas that the authors of these texts intended to convey to those for whom they wrote, I wish to explore the question of how those who read the texts in the form in which they now exist would have understood them in light of the collection of texts as a whole. While of course we do not have direct access to the interpretations of those who brought those texts together in a single collection and those who originally read those texts as part of that collection, by looking at those texts alongside one another from within that collection in the same way that they did we can gain a fairly clear understanding of how they would have been read and interpreted.

In fact, one of the assumptions made by those who preserved the biblical texts and brought them together in a single collection was that those texts could stand on their own and be understood properly simply by being read within the context of the collection as a whole. Nevertheless, in order to understand them today, some general knowledge of the historical contexts in which they were composed, edited, and brought together as a collection is necessary. For that reason, the scholarly reconstructions of those historical contexts cannot be ignored entirely if we are to seek to understand them in our own contemporary contexts. It is also self-evident that those texts must be translated from the Hebrew in order to be read and understood by English speakers today, and the task of translating them would be impossible to carry out without the work of biblical scholars.

Yet while the reading and interpretation of the biblical texts would not be possible without the work of biblical scholars, that work must also be subjected to critical analysis if it is to represent and reflect faithfully the meanings and ideas present in those texts. For that reason, when seeking to understand the biblical texts, at the same time that one draws upon the work of biblical scholars to interpret those texts one must also constantly look to those texts to ask whether the interpretations and assumptions made by those scholars are in fact grounded in those texts and have been read *out* of those texts rather than being read back *into* them. As I have already noted above, throughout the present work there are two assumptions commonly made by biblical scholars that I am especially interested in challenging, namely, that the same type of love ascribed to the gods of other peoples and nations in the ancient texts we possess can be ascribed to the God of Israel as he is presented in the Hebrew Scriptures and that running throughout these Scriptures we find conceptions of God that are sharply at odds with one another and even contradict one another rather than a conception of God that at its root is uniform and consistent with itself.

These assumptions can only be challenged, of course, by looking at the writings of other peoples and nations of antiquity in order to consider the manner in which the gods are portrayed in those writings and by examining as well the conceptions of the God of Israel that biblical scholars find in the Hebrew Bible on the basis of the traits and characteristics that they regard him as having in common with those gods. For the reasons mentioned above, however, rather than looking for *similarities* and *parallels* between the conceptions of the deity found in other ancient texts and the conception of the God of Israel that runs throughout the Hebrew Bible, I will look primarily for *dissimilarities* and *differences* in order to *contrast* Israel's God with the gods of other nations in the same way that the biblical texts themselves do both explicitly and implicitly. Because the comparisons I wish to draw are for the most part relatively simple, straightforward, and self-evident, it will not be necessary to do an exhaustive survey of the writings of other peoples in antiquity in order to make those comparisons. Instead, I will focus on several representative texts. In a similar manner, rather than attempting to offer a general survey of works by contemporary biblical scholars in which the assumptions and interpretations that I wish to challenge appear, I have chosen to limit myself to examining more closely a small but representative sample of scholarly writings in which those assumptions and interpretations are especially evident.

Because many of these same assumptions and interpretations are at times evident in the English translations of the Bible as well, and also because in many of the passages from the Hebrew Bible that I will be citing I wish to bring out certain points that are not readily apparent in most English translations of the biblical texts, throughout the present work I have chosen to provide my own translations of the passages cited from the Hebrew Bible. At the same time, however, in order to take into consideration the work of scholars and translators whose knowledge of biblical Hebrew far exceeds my own and to avoid interpreting the biblical texts on the basis of ideas that might be considered foreign to them, I have followed closely the translations that appear in several of the English versions of the Bible that are most widely respected among biblical scholars. These include especially the Revised Standard Version (RSV), the New Revised Standard Version (NRSV), and the updated edition of the New Revised Standard Version (NRSVue), but also the English Standard Version (ESV), the New American Standard Bible (NASB), the 1995 edition of the NASB, and the New International Version (NIV).[2] Because the NRSVue is the most recent of these translations and is also the version that is preferred in many scholarly circles, for the most part I have followed the reconstructions of the Hebrew text on which it is based as well. For reasons that have to do primarily with the length of this volume, I have also departed from the common practice of formatting passages that contain Hebrew poetry differently than those that are written in prose. For abbreviations of the biblical books and other ancient sources cited as well as the transliterations of Hebrew and Greek, I have followed the guidelines of the second edition of *The SBL Handbook of Style*.[3]

Throughout the present work, I will be focusing primarily on the writings that form part of the Hebrew Bible due to the normativity and authority ascribed to these writings in the Jewish and Christian traditions. It is

---

2. The copyright information for these versions is as follows: Revised Standard Version of the Bible, © 1946, 1952, 1971 by the Division of Christian Education of the National Council of the Churches of Christ in the United States of America, Washington, DC; New Revised Standard Version of the Bible, © 1989 by the National Council of the Churches of Christ in the United States of America, Washington, DC; New Revised Standard Version Updated Edition, © 2021 by the National Council of the Churches of Christ in the United States of America, Washington, DC; The Holy Bible, English Standard Version, © 2001 by Crossway, Wheaton, IL; New American Standard Bible, © 1960, 1971, 1977, 1995, 2020 by The Lockman Foundation, La Habra, CA; New American Standard Bible 1995, © 1960, 1971, 1977, 1995 by The Lockman Foundation, La Habra, CA; New International Version of the Bible, © 1973, 1978, 1984, 2011 by Biblica, Palmer Lake, CO.

3. *The SBL Handbook of Style*, 2nd ed. (Atlanta: SBL, 2014).

important to stress, however, that the process of bringing these writings together into a collection that came to be regarded as sacred scripture was a gradual one that took place throughout most of the period of the Second Temple, which is generally dated from around 515 BCE to 70 CE. As already noted above, as these writings were brought together into a single collection, they were subjected to a process of editing and revision that sought to shape them into a whole that was greater than the parts. As a result of this process, they also ceased to be viewed and read in isolation from one another as separate books or writings and came to be regarded not only as a single collection of sacred texts but in some sense as a single book, text, or Bible as well.

As this process took place, both those who did the final editing of the texts that were incorporated into the collection of writings and those who originally read and viewed these writings as a single collection understood them to be in harmony with one another and to convey ideas, truths, and convictions that were consistent with one another. Both those who shaped them into a single collection and those who first read them as a collection of writings also believed that there was a clear and consistent logic underlying them. It is that logic that I wish to examine and reconstruct here.

Of course, even when the various writings had been brought together and shaped into a single collection, during the Second Temple period there was as yet no clear consensus as to which of those writings were to be considered part of that collection and were to be regarded as normative or authoritative. There can be no doubt that the books of the Pentateuch were given special status within that collection from the beginning and that most of the books that are now considered part of the Hebrew Bible also formed part of the collection of writings that most Jews viewed as sacred scripture throughout the last several centuries of the Second Temple period. Many Jews, however, also considered other writings as sacred or divinely inspired in some sense. In fact, because there were many different Jewish groups in the Second Temple period, in a sense it would be improper to speak of the Hebrew Bible as existing in the Second Temple period, both because there was no absolute consensus among Jewish groups in antiquity as to which writings were to be regarded as normative and authoritative and also because many of the writings that were viewed in this manner were either translations of Hebrew writings into other languages, including especially Greek, or else writings that were composed in those languages. These writings include the books that are generally referred to as the Apocrypha and Pseudepigrapha, some of which appear in the Bibles used by many Christians today.

Throughout the present work, I have chosen to speak of the Hebrew Bible or Hebrew Scriptures in order to refer to the collection of texts that Christians call the Old Testament and many Jews refer to as the Tanakh. Biblical scholars often debate which of these designations is to be preferred and in some cases even prefer other designations, such as First Testament. All of these designations are problematic for different reasons.[4] Because certain portions of several of the books that now form part of the Hebrew Bible were composed in Aramaic rather than Hebrew and also because most Jews in the Second Temple period did not know Hebrew and had to read those books and others that they regarded as sacred scripture in other languages, many biblical scholars prefer to avoid referring to the books of the Old Testament or Tanakh as the Hebrew Bible or Hebrew Scriptures. I would argue, however, that even though these books were generally read in languages other than Hebrew and portions of some of them were written in Aramaic, they may nevertheless be regarded as Hebrew writings in the sense that they reflect the Hebrew worldview and modes of thought of those who originally composed and preserved them and brought them together in a single collection.

Because I will be focusing on the manner in which the writings of the Hebrew Bible would have been understood among those who formed them into a collection of sacred texts and those who first read them as part of that collection, throughout the present work I will also be looking at other Jewish writings of the Second Temple period. These include not only the books of the Apocrypha and Pseudepigrapha but also the writings of Philo of Alexandria and Flavius Josephus. Strictly speaking, of course, the works of Josephus fall outside of the Second Temple period, since they were composed following the destruction of Herod's Temple by the Romans in the year 70 CE, yet because most of the beliefs reflected in those works date back to the period in which the Second Temple was still standing they can be regarded as belonging to that period. All of these Jewish writings are especially helpful and relevant for addressing the question of how the biblical texts were originally understood by those who brought them together in a single collection and those who first read and viewed them from within that collection because they provide us with the earliest interpretations we have of those texts. The Greek translation of the Hebrew Bible known as the Septuagint is also helpful in this regard, since it too offers insights as to how the writings of the Hebrew Bible were being read and interpreted in the Second Temple period.

When all of these different writings are viewed in conjunction with the biblical texts and with one another, it becomes clear that they reflect the same assumptions that run throughout the Hebrew Scriptures as a whole, namely, that the God of Israel is indeed a God who is fundamentally different from all of the other gods of antiquity known to us and that one of the primary characteristics that sets him apart from those other gods is that his love is indeed steadfast and endures forever. If such is the case, then rather than seeking to reconcile such a conception of God with the countless passages from the

---

4. On this discussion and the process by which the books of the Hebrew Bible came to be regarded as sacred scripture by Jews and Christians, see especially T. C. Vriezen and A. S. van der Woude, *Ancient Israelite and Early Jewish Literature*, trans. Brian Doyle (Leiden: Brill, 2005), 53–70; Stephen B. Chapman, "Collections, Canons, and Communities," in *The Cambridge Companion to the Hebrew Bible/Old Testament*, ed. Stephen B. Chapman and Marvin A. Sweeney (New York: Cambridge University Press, 2016), 28–54.

Hebrew Bible that appear to conflict with it or contradict it, we must seek to discern the manner in which those who arrived at that conception of God took it as a basis and starting-point for everything that they came to affirm regarding the God of whom the biblical texts speak. This must involve not only capturing more fully the understanding of God's steadfast love that is assumed throughout those texts but also questioning our own understandings and assumptions regarding the nature of God's steadfast love, its unconditional and enduring quality, and its relation to God's justice, righteousness, and holiness as well as the wrath, judgments, condemnation, and punishments that the biblical texts also attribute to the God of Israel. Only as we let the biblical texts speak for themselves and call into question our own assumptions and the interpretations of those texts that have been passed down to us is it possible for these objectives to be accomplished.

CHAPTER 1

THE REPAGANIZING OF A DEPAGANIZED GOD

In many ways, the God of Israel as we encounter him in the Hebrew Scriptures was no different than the gods of other nations in antiquity. Like those gods, he had a name, which in Hebrew was written with four consonants, YHWH. He was associated with a particular people and a particular land as other gods were, yet like most of them he was also thought to transcend space and time by dwelling and moving in the air or sky and enduring throughout countless generations without aging or dying in the way that human beings do. While for the most part he could not be seen and heard, like other gods he was able to observe what took place in the world and to hear the prayers of those who invoked him. Those who worshiped the God of Israel presented him their sacrificial offerings and sought his blessings in the same way that other peoples of antiquity implored the favor of their gods by worshiping them and offering them gifts and sacrifices. Just like other gods in antiquity, the God of Israel was thought to become angry with those who refused to submit obediently to his will and at times to punish them by subjecting them to various types of sufferings and afflictions.

At the same time, however, the writings that we now know as the Hebrew Bible portray the God of Israel as a god who in important ways is fundamentally distinct from the gods of other nations. As the creator of all that exists, he possesses powers and knowledge that far exceed those of any other being, human or divine. In some sense, in fact, he alone is God in a way that merits distinguishing him from other gods by using the capitalized form of the term "god" in English to refer to him. While some of the people known as *Yehudhi* or Jews who lived in the period following the construction of the Second Temple in Jerusalem in approximately 515 BCE may have believed that other divine or semi-divine beings existed in some sense, they would not have understood those beings to be comparable to YHWH the God of Israel.[1] If such beings did in fact exist, they derived their existence from Israel's God as their creator and were subject to him as their Lord and sovereign.

In the centuries that have passed since the period in which the writings of the Hebrew Bible were composed and brought together as parts of a single collection, those who regard those writings as sacred scripture have

---

1. On Jewish beliefs in heavenly and divine beings other than God in the Second Temple period, see Larry W. Hurtado, *Ancient Jewish Monotheism and Early Christian Jesus-Devotion: The Context and Character of Christological Faith* (Waco, TX: Baylor University Press, 2017), 163-76; Paula Fredriksen, "Philo, Herod, Paul, and the Many Gods of Ancient Jewish 'Monotheism'," *HTR* 115 (2022): 23-45.

continued to conceive and speak of the God whom they portray in ways that distinguish him from the gods of other peoples and nations. By the late fourth century of the Common Era, both the Jews who worshiped the God of Israel and the Christians who adopted the Jewish Scriptures as their own were using the term "pagan" to refer not only to those who worshiped other gods but also to those gods themselves. While in one sense it would be improper and anachronistic to use this same term to refer to peoples of previous centuries and the types of gods they worshiped from time immemorial, in another sense such a usage is entirely appropriate, given that virtually all of those gods were seen as possessing certain traits that made them similar to one another and distinct from the God of whom the Hebrew Scriptures spoke. In many ways, in fact, the gods worshiped by the peoples of ancient Europe, Asia, and Africa who eventually came to embrace Christianity were no different than the gods worshiped by peoples such as the Egyptians, Greeks, and Romans in biblical times, as well as those of the peoples who inhabited the regions of Mesopotamia and the ancient Near East for several millennia prior to the composition of the biblical texts. For that reason, many historians and biblical scholars consider it appropriate to use the adjective "pagan" to refer to the gods of these peoples as well, as I will do throughout the present work.

Yet while the preservation and ongoing use of the writings of the Hebrew Bible among Jews and Christians in the centuries following their composition and formation into a single collection led members of both groups to continue to conceive of God in ways that made him different from the gods of other nations and peoples, it would be a mistake to suppose that their conception of God remained entirely uniform and unchanged over that period of time. For at least three or four centuries prior to the beginning of the Common Era, in fact, the vast majority of Jews who adhered to the Hebrew Scriptures as their own had no longer been able to read or understand those Scriptures in the language in which they had been written and preserved. The main reason for this was that by that time the number of Jews throughout the world who continued to speak and communicate in Hebrew had dwindled to a relatively small minority. In addition, however, the primary means of access that most Jews of the Second Temple period had to their Scriptures consisted of the oral traditions that had been passed down to them by their ancestors and the translations made of those Scriptures into other languages, including especially Aramaic and Greek. It can hardly be doubted that both the new social, political, and religious contexts in which the Jewish people came to find themselves and the loss of Hebrew as the everyday spoken language of most Jews had at least some impact on the manner in which they conceived and spoke of the God of Israel, not only because they were inevitably immersed in the worldviews of the peoples among whom they inhabited but also because they had to define and live out their faith in languages and contexts that in many ways were different from those of their ancestors.

The destruction of the Jewish temple in Jerusalem in the year 70 CE, the increase in the number of Jews living outside of Judea following the Jewish revolts against Rome in the first and second centuries, and the rise of Christianity also led to changes in the manner in which those who read the biblical texts understood the God of whom they spoke. No matter how fervently and faithfully they sought to remain grounded in those texts, both the Jews and the Christians who regarded them as sacred scripture were constantly forced to define and redefine their understanding of the God in whom they believed in dialogue with other peoples and worldviews. In most places, those Jews who preserved their faith and identity lived as small minorities among other peoples and thus had no choice but to interact extensively with persons whose ways of thinking and speaking were distinct from their own. Whether they realized it or not, over time many aspects of those ways of thinking and speaking became their own. Among Christians, the influence of pagan conceptions of the gods on their own view of God was much stronger, primarily because the overwhelming majority of those who embraced Christianity came from pagan backgrounds themselves. Even when they renounced their previous beliefs in order to embrace the God of whom the Bible spoke, they could not entirely avoid conceiving of that God in many of the ways in which they had conceived of the pagan gods whom they had worshiped previously. Beginning in the late fourth century, in fact, most of those who were baptized as Christians became so to some extent only in name, both because many did not do so out of sincere conviction and because even those who did generally found it impossible to leave behind completely the beliefs and worldviews that had been ingrained into them and their ancestors for centuries prior to their conversion.

Of course, among both Jews and Christians there were many different groups who read and interpreted the biblical texts in ways that distinguished them from other groups that claimed to confess the same God and the same faith. From the very beginning, the claim that in Jesus the God of Israel had sent his Son into the world and had constituted him as the Messiah or Christ of whom the Jewish Scriptures spoke led those Jews who came to be followers of Christ to conceive of that God in ways that distinguished them from those Jews who did not accept that claim. Eventually those Jews and the large number of non-Jews who became Christians came to view and designate the Jewish Scriptures as the Old Testament and set those Scriptures alongside a collection of writings that were unique to them, which they labeled the New Testament. While Christians thus read the Jewish Scriptures or Old Testament through the lens of the New, most Jews came to read their Scriptures through the lens of the rabbinic writings that began to circulate and rise to prominence in the second century CE.

Although in most ways the manner in which both Jews and Christians understood the Hebrew Scriptures and the God of whom they spoke remained constant over the following centuries and into the modern period, in many

Jewish and Christian circles the rise of biblical scholarship in the nineteenth century led to significant changes in the way in which those Scriptures were read and interpreted. Biblical scholars and historians dedicated themselves to the task of reconstructing not only the texts themselves but also the contexts in which they had been composed and collected. On the basis of these reconstructions, they came to view differently not only the biblical texts themselves but also the beliefs reflected in those texts. It became clear that beliefs regarding the God of Israel had evolved a great deal in the centuries preceding the Common Era and that a variety of views regarding God and his relation to Israel and humanity in general could be discerned in the biblical texts. It also became evident that the beliefs of other peoples in antiquity had influenced in important ways the beliefs regarding God that developed among those who identified as Jews and as members of Israel. For these reasons, many biblical scholars and historians would now reject the notion that there is a single, uniform, and fully consistent conception of God running throughout the biblical texts.

While to some extent those scholars and historians can be considered justified in rejecting such a notion, it must also be recognized that there is a sense in which it would be correct to claim that throughout the biblical texts we encounter a manner of conceiving of the God of Israel that is in fact uniform and consistent. Those texts, for example, consistently use masculine pronouns when referring to God. Nowhere do they speak of Israel's God having a female consort or engaging in activities such as eating, drinking, sleeping, or having sexual intercourse. On the contrary, they consistently present him as not being subject to needs of the type that human beings experience. They also repeatedly describe him in terms that convey the idea that, as the creator of all that exists, he sees and knows all things, including the thoughts and intentions that arise in human hearts and minds. The biblical texts agree in ascribing to the God of Israel other characteristics that distinguish him from the gods of other nations as well and in claiming that he had been active in certain moments and events in the history of Israel and the world in order to carry out his sovereign will.

Precisely when, where, and how this manner of understanding the God of Israel arose is of course a subject of ongoing scholarly debate and will undoubtedly remain so for many years to come. Intimately related to that debate are similar questions concerning the manner in which the biblical texts as we now have them came to be composed, edited, transmitted, and brought together as parts of a single collection that we now call the Hebrew Bible or Old Testament. In the present work, however, I will not address such questions or engage in those debates. For that reason, for the most part I will not be referencing the scholarly literature that examines the biblical texts on the basis of those questions and debates.

What I propose here is something distinct from what most scholarly works on the Hebrew Bible attempt. Rather than seeking to reconstruct the original meanings of the biblical texts on the basis of historical considerations,

I simply wish to engage those texts as they now stand in order to examine basic elements of the conception of Israel's God that runs throughout them and the manner in which that conception of God is reflected in the traits and activities that those texts ascribe to him. This involves taking what is known as a synchronic approach to the texts rather than a diachronic approach.[2] Whereas a diachronic approach attempts to examine the various stages in the formation of a text, a synchronic approach analyzes a text in the final form in which it now stands. Even those scholars who analyze the biblical texts from a synchronic perspective, however, generally address questions regarding the historical contexts in which those texts are thought to have reached their present form. For the most part, I will not be addressing such questions here.

My reason for approaching the biblical texts in this manner is grounded in the argument that I will be developing in the present work. What I will argue is not merely that there are certain traits that the writings of the Hebrew Bible consistently ascribe to the God of Israel but also that for centuries interpreters of the Hebrew Bible have failed to understand properly those traits because they have instead read back into the biblical texts beliefs and ideas that are grounded in pagan conceptions of the deity and are therefore foreign to those texts. As a result, it may be said that the God of whom those interpreters speak is no longer the God of the Hebrew Bible but a God who has been paganized.

The claim that for centuries the God of the Hebrew Bible has been paganized presupposes that there are certain ways of conceiving of the divinity that can be labeled pagan. Such a presupposition can lead one to overlook the fact that many different conceptions of the gods existed in antiquity. Nevertheless, there are certain characteristics that were commonly ascribed to most of the gods known to us. It is these that interest us here.

THE PAGAN GODS OF ANTIQUITY

Despite the differences among them, most of the accounts of the origins of the gods and the world known to us from antiquity share a number of common traits. In virtually all of these accounts, known as theogonies and cosmogonies, the gods and the world are simply said to exist from the beginning, usually in some type of unordered or chaotic form. Strictly speaking, neither the plurality of gods nor the cosmos are said to have been created and are not seen as having arisen out of nothingness as the result of a conscious and deliberate decision on the part of some personal deity or sovereign power to bring them into existence. Most of the gods are said to have their origin in other primordial gods who procreate or generate them in some way. These primordial gods are often associated with some foundational reality, substance, or matter that is either identified with them or else constitutes the

---

2. On this distinction and its history in the area of biblical studies, see especially Paul R. Noble, "Synchronic and Diachronic Approaches to Biblical Interpretation," *JLT* 7 (1993): 130-48; Koog P. Hong, "Synchrony and Diachrony in Contemporary Biblical Interpretation," *CBQ* 75 (2013): 521-39.

source from which they emerge. The existence of this primordial matter and the primordial gods associated with it is simply assumed from the outset and is not thought to be preceded by a time in which nothing existed at all.

In the Babylonian account of the origins of the gods and the world known as the *Enuma Elish*, for example, the two primordial gods Apsu and Tiamat are said to have existed in the form of water from the very beginning. After they have engendered other gods from within themselves, they are separated into salt water and fresh water. Subsequently the heavens and earth as well as animals and human beings are fashioned from the bodies of the gods themselves or from the same primordial reality.[3] The ancient Egyptian theogonies and cosmogonies known to us also speak of water as the source from which everything else emerged, including the first gods.[4] In his *Theogony*, the Greek writer Hesiod speaks of four primordial gods, Chaos (the chasm), Gaia (the earth), Tartarus (the underworld), and Eros (desire), yet he does not offer any explanation regarding their origin. The rest of the gods are said to have descended from these gods.[5] According to all of these conceptions of the origins of what now exists, the gods are composed of the same basic substance, matter, or reality as the world itself.

This manner of understanding the origin of the gods and their relation to the world is significant for a couple of reasons. First, neither the gods nor the world are viewed as existing for some reason or purpose. They are not brought into being in order to accomplish some objective. Instead, they simply exist for their own sake. And second, even though the gods possess a great deal of power that enables them to exert control over the forces of nature, at the same time to some extent they are themselves subject to many forces of nature. In some cases, in fact, the gods are identified with the forces of nature or natural realities such as the sun, the stars and planets, or the sea. This means that they are generally regarded as being subject to certain laws that limit them and define what they can or must do. Even when they are seen as personal beings who exist independently of the natural order, they generally must still do things such as sleep, rest, and eat. They also tend to be driven by passions and desires that are similar to those that human beings experience. These include not only sexual passions but also the desire to receive praise, honor, and recognition from others.

---

3. See the first six tablets of the *Enuma Elish*, also known as the Babylonian Epic of Creation or Babylonian Creation Myth, especially I.1-32, IV.93–140, VI.1-34.

4. On the different types of ancient Egyptian theogonies and cosmogonies that posit water as the source of the primordial gods, see Gordon H. Johnston, "Genesis 1 and Ancient Egyptian Creation Myths," *BSac* 165 (2008): 178-94 (180-81). Johnston notes there that the four major Egyptian cosmological texts in which this idea is found are the Pyramid Texts, the Coffin Texts, the Book of the Dead from the New Kingdom period, and the so-called Shabaka Stone. See also George Hart, *Egyptian Myths*, The Legendary Past (Austin, TX: University of Texas Press, 1990), 9-28.

5. On the origin of the gods and the world in ancient Hellenistic thought and mythology, see Richard Caldwell, *The Origin of the Gods: A Psychoanalytic Study of Greek Theogonic Myth* (Oxford: Oxford University Press, 1989), 126-45; Carolina López-Ruiz, *When the Gods Were Born: Greek Cosmogonies and the Near East* (Cambridge, MA: Harvard University Press, 2010), 84-129.

These same needs, passions, and desires define what the gods are said to want and seek from human beings. If the gods did not need or desire anything from human beings, they would simply ignore them. They would have no reason to respond to prayers or petitions that human beings present to them or concern themselves in any way in human affairs. In principle, human beings might offer the gods gifts or favors in an attempt to obtain something from them, yet because the gods would neither need nor desire what human beings offer them, they would simply remain uninterested in those offerings and indifferent to them. Conversely, human beings would have no reason to present petitions or offerings to the gods, since they would never receive any type of benefit or response from the gods by doing so. As a result, the gods and human beings would simply live in their own separate realms, unconcerned with what happened in the realm of the other.

Of course, this is not the reality we encounter in the belief systems of the peoples of antiquity who worshiped pagan gods. In all of those systems, the gods take at least some interest in the activities and petitions of human beings. They receive gifts and offerings from human beings and respond to those gifts and offerings by bestowing favors on them. When those human beings fail to present to the gods the gifts and offerings they desire or need, the gods become angry and respond by inflicting various types of suffering on human beings as punishment.

While the gods are consistently presented as desiring gifts and offerings from human beings in these belief systems, the question of precisely *why* they desire these things is rarely raised or addressed in the ancient texts known to us. In some cases, it is maintained that the gods actually consume the food and drink presented to them as offerings, if not physically at least in some spiritual or ethereal sense. In other cases, it is the aroma of what is offered that pleases them. When the offerings are burnt on an altar so as to rise up to the heavens in smoke, they are generally thought to be converted into a form in which they can actually ascend to the gods in order to be received by them.

In those belief systems in which the gods are not thought to consume what is offered to them, they are seen as desiring gifts and offerings for some other reason. In virtually every case, this reason is that they wish to be revered, worshiped, and held in high regard by human beings. They long for recognition, acclaim, and adulation. Because they regard such things as ends in themselves, they are viewed as being motivated by vanity and are generally regarded as egotistical or egocentric. Many of the offerings said to be presented by human beings to the gods are not food items but things such as precious metals and stones, jewelry, or other items of great value. If the gods are pleased by such offerings, it cannot be because they need them or wish to consume them, but simply because they desire from human beings the type of veneration and worship that those offerings are intended to express and convey.

It is important to stress that the gods are invariably thought to desire these things *for their own sake*. When they demand sacrificial offerings, they are not seeking the well-being of human beings or wishing to benefit them in some way. The relationship between the gods and those who worship them is one of *do ut des*, which is Latin for "I give (to you) so that you may give (to me)": the gods give human beings what they want in exchange for receiving from those human beings what they want for themselves. What motivates the gods is not love for human beings or any kind of genuine concern for their well-being or happiness. Rather, those human beings serve as a means by which the gods obtain what they desire for themselves. If the gods want human beings to enjoy peace and well-being, it is only so that those human beings can dedicate themselves to serving the gods without being impeded by any type of hardship, conflict, or obstacle.

Of course, because human beings are especially dependent on the gods and their favor, they are thought to be under obligation to present offerings to the gods and express their gratitude and allegiance to the gods by means of those offerings. The gods are therefore entitled to receive gifts and offerings, which are said to be due to them. If human beings do not fulfill their obligations in this regard, the gods have a right to demand from them the offerings owed to them and to punish those human beings until they receive those offerings. They may also require that those human beings who have angered and offended them by failing to give them what is theirs by right atone for their offenses by presenting offerings aimed at appeasing them and by carrying out other actions that demonstrate contrition for having failed to fulfill their obligations to the gods.

It is also important to stress what such gods do *not* demand or expect. As long as they receive the offerings due to them, it does not matter to them whether or not those offerings are given out of a spirit of sincere love, devotion, and gratitude. What the gods want is not merely verbal or sentimental expressions of love or affection but concrete gifts and offerings as ends in themselves. In fact, because the relationship between the gods and human beings is based on the principle of *do ut des*, it is generally recognized that those who present the gods offerings do so, not to express heartfelt love and thankfulness, but because they wish to receive something from the gods in exchange for their gifts. Those who offer the gods gifts therefore do so out of self-interest, motivated by the same type of egocentrism and concern for themselves that characterizes the gods.

For the most part, the gods are also unconcerned about the ethical behavior of those who present them the offerings due to them. It matters little to them if the offerers practice justice and kindness in their daily life, care for the needy, or oppress the weak. Nor does it generally matter to the gods if the gifts presented to them have been stolen or plundered from other human beings through acts of violence or injustice. In fact, the gods themselves may send and empower those who worship them to ravage and pillage other peoples in order to receive more gifts for themselves, and when their worshipers are successful in such endeavors, it is expected that they will express their gratitude to the gods for having enabled them to obtain what they have plundered by offering a considerable portion of it to them.

For this reason, while human beings may be said to offend or anger the gods or transgress against them, it would not be entirely accurate to speak of human beings *sinning* against the gods. In English, to sin generally involves violating some ethical norm or committing some type of wrongdoing. What moves the gods to demand gifts and offerings and to become angry if they do not receive them, however, is not any kind of concern for ethical conduct or the practice of what is good and right, but simply their desire to receive such gifts and offerings for their own sake.

In fact, for the most part the gods themselves are uninterested in practicing what is good and right or engaging in ethical behavior, except as such behavior promotes their own ends. In many cases, they actually do the opposite, acting with cruelty and violence out of spite and hatred or seeking to satisfy their lusts and passions through sexual encounters that many human beings would even consider illicit. They may overlook injustice or even promote it and be pleased by it. At times, of course, they may be moved to pity when they observe human beings in pain, distress, and afflictions, yet even in those cases they tend to be motivated not by love but simply by an aversion to seeing pain and suffering, especially when those who are enduring such things are thereby prevented from giving them the offerings and worship they desire. At the same time, the gods tend to be capricious and moody, acting amicably one moment while becoming consumed with rage the next, often for no apparent reason.

Ultimately, what interests the gods is to be able to dwell in peace and tranquility, unmolested by any kind of trouble or conflict so that they may enjoy the pleasures of their blissful existence. The gifts and offerings they receive from human beings help make this possible. The praise and adulation that human beings offer up to them also contribute to their enjoyment and bliss. Human beings are often seen as fulfilling the role of entertaining the gods. They do this not only by dancing, singing, and playing music for the gods but also by means of other activities that arouse their interest, including competitions and games as well as warfare and bloodshed.

Naturally, those human beings who please the gods the most by satisfying their needs and desires and entertaining them in ways that they find especially pleasing are objects of their special favor. The most important gods show preference for those human beings who are wealthy and powerful, primarily because such human beings are able to present them with gifts that are more lavish and abundant. They also favor those who are physically strong, gifted, and attractive because such individuals are more entertaining and pleasant to gaze upon. These gods are especially interested in the affairs of kings and rulers due to the power and influence that they have over other human beings and also have special regard for the priests who are dedicated to presenting them the offerings they wish to receive. In contrast, such gods tend to show little concern for the common people, the weak, and the needy, since such people have little to offer them and thus are scarcely considered worthy of their time and attention.

While human beings generally look to the gods for salvation in the sense that they seek the gods' assistance in order to accomplish their objectives and overcome any hardships or difficulties they encounter, including especially opposition from their enemies, in many cases the gods represent the *problem* for human beings rather than the *solution* to their problems or plight. Because they must do whatever is necessary not only to obtain the gods' favor but also to avoid arousing their wrath, in a sense it can be said that human beings must be saved not only *by* the gods but *from* them as well. They must constantly be concerned to keep the gods satisfied and content by offering them whatever they desire and serving their interests in other ways. To some degree, therefore, human beings live in slavery and bondage to the gods, since they have no choice but to do the gods' bidding in order to survive in the world and have success accomplishing any ends of their own.

The superiority of the gods over human beings also results in relationships that are defined in terms of dominance and submission. All seek to gain power over others in order to obtain from them what they want by imposing their will on them. These relationships are therefore characterized by constant conflict and violence. The gods engage in conflicts with one another until the most powerful are able to establish themselves in a position of supremacy over the rest. The same is true among human beings, who also tend to be constantly engaged in struggles for dominance over one another. Because relationships are defined in terms of superiority and inferiority, they are invariably hierarchical. The only way in which conflict can give way to peace is for all to accept their place in the hierarchical order. This peace is understood in terms of a lack of conflict, yet it does not involve equity or a well-being that all are to enjoy equally. Instead, this peace favors and benefits those who are in positions of power and supremacy, since those who are inferior to them are forced to dedicate themselves to serving their needs and satisfying their desires over their own.

Although many myths and stories regarding the gods from antiquity might be cited to illustrate all of the characteristics just considered, for our purposes here that objective can be accomplished merely by examining three of the writings that were most widely known among people in the Mediterranean basin and the area of Mesopotamia in the Second Temple period, namely, the *Enuma Elish* from Babylon and the two epic poems of Homer known as the *Iliad* and the *Odyssey*. Scholars generally agree that the *Enuma Elish* in the form in which we know it today was composed some time before the first millenium BCE, while Homer's poems are usually dated to the late eighth or early seventh century BCE.[6] While some knowledge of these writings on the

---

6. On the dating of the *Enuma Elish*, see James B. Pritchard, *Ancient Near Eastern Texts Relating to the Old Testament*, 2nd ed. (Princeton: Princeton University Press, 1955), 60: "There is as yet no general agreement as regards the date of composition. None of the extant texts antedates the

part of readers would be helpful for understanding the discussion that follows, it is not essential in order to grasp the points I wish to stress. Nor is it necessary to enter into a detailed consideration of these accounts.

The Gods of the Enuma Elish

As noted briefly above, at the outset of the *Enuma Elish*, two primordial gods are said to exist in the form of water prior to the formation of the heavens and the earth, namely, the male god Apsu and the female goddess Tiamat. These two gods engender another group of gods who in turn engender even more gods. The account seems to assume that these gods are brought into being as a result of sexual relations that are similar to those in which human beings engage, motivated by a bodily desire or urge rather than a deliberate desire to procreate offspring. Nowhere are the gods presented as making a conscious choice to engender children in order that they may love them, care for them, or show them affection once they have been born. In fact, it is not long before Apsu seeks to destroy the lesser gods that he has engendered with Tiamat.

What leads Apsu to become angry at the gods that he and Tiamat have brought into being is that their constant dancing and merrymaking will not let him sleep at night or rest during the day. For that reason, he determines to have them destroyed (I.22-40). Apsu tells Tiamat: "Their behavior has become displeasing to me, and I cannot rest in the day-time or sleep at night. I will destroy and break up their way of life, that silence may reign and we may sleep" (I.37-40).[7]

Initially, Tiamat stands opposed to the destruction of these gods, even though she too is bothered by their raucous and rowdy behavior. When one of the gods named Ea learns of Apsu's intentions, however, he recites an incantation to put Apsu to sleep and then kills him. He even makes a dwelling for himself out of Apsu's corpse (I.41-78). Subsequently, Ea's wife Damkina gives birth to Marduk, whose strength, beauty, and wisdom are said to surpass by far those of any of the other gods (I.81-100). Angered by the slaying of Apsu, Tiamat makes plans with her new consort Qingu and some of the other gods to destroy Ea and those gods who have sided with him. The account portrays Tiamat as a hideous monster who brings into existence other monstrous beings to assist her. When all of the gods whom Tiamat seeks to destroy are intimidated by her, Marduk rises up as their champion and vows to defeat her if the gods who have taken his side establish him as king over them (I.109–III.138).

---

first millenium B.C. On the internal evidence, however, of the context and the linguistic criteria, the majority of the scholars would assign the epic to the Old Babylonian period, i.e. the early part of the second millenium B.C."

7. Quotations from the *Enuma Elish* are taken from W. G. Lambert, *Babylonian Creation Myths*, MC 16 (Winona Lake, IN: Eisenbrauns, 2013), 45-134. References in parentheses throughout this section are to the tablet and the line numbers of the text of the *Enuma Elish*.

Once these gods submit to his rule, Marduk proceeds to fulfill his vow. He pierces Tiamat with an arrow, tears open her entrails, binds her up, throws her corpse to the ground, and smashes her skull with a mace. He then severs her arteries and cuts her body in two in order to fashion the heavens and the earth from her corpse. Marduk forms the heavens by stretching one half of Tiamat's body over the other and uses various parts of her body to form rivers, mountains, springs, and the landscape in general (IV.101-4, 127-40; V.47-64). He treats the gods who had allied themselves with Tiamat with the same type of cruelty. Marduk then orders the world he has fashioned in the way that pleases him, assigns to each of the remaining gods a place in that order, and tells them that they must submit to him as lord if they wish to enjoy prosperity and abundance (V.1-114). Those gods gladly acknowledge Marduk as their lord out of self-interest and even kiss his feet (V.86). In addition, Marduk commands that a luxurious dwelling place be built for him in Babylon so that he may reign from there forever. After decreeing that Babylon is to be home for the other gods as well, he prescribes the celebration of festivals and the offering of sacrifices to them and to himself at the temples that are to be built in their honor there (V.117-38).

Marduk then decides to fashion human beings from the blood of Qingu. He has Qingu slain in his presence before having his arteries cut in order to drain the blood from his body (VI.1-34). The purpose for which Marduk brings human beings into existence is that they may perpetually serve him and the other gods. This is stated explicitly in several passages. He tells the god Ea: "I will create Lullû—man, on whom the toil of the gods will be laid that they may rest" (VI.5-8). At Marduk's command, Ea is said to have "created [hu]mankind, on whom he imposed the service of the gods, and set the gods free" (VI.32-37). Elsewhere it is affirmed that Marduk created humankind to spare the gods from having to do any kind of work (VII.25-29). What Marduk desires and demands of human beings, therefore, is that they serve him and the other gods obediently so that those gods may live in luxury together with him, relaxing and enjoying themselves. In essence, human beings are to submit to the gods as their slaves.

Once Babylon with its temples and shrines has been built and the gods have taken up the places assigned to them by Marduk, they all gather to drink and feast there (VI.39-76). The newly-formed human beings are commanded to submit to Marduk as their king by presenting him and the other gods with lavish offerings and even kissing Marduk's feet. They are also told that Marduk will reward them with life, abundance, assistance, and prosperity if they serve him and the other gods faithfully and obediently, but that he and the other gods will punish and destroy any who rebel against them and refuse to fulfill their duties to them (VI.95-146). From that point on, if human beings wish to be shown mercy by Marduk rather than being forced to endure his fierce rage and fury, they must submit fully to his rule and constantly learn and remember his words as the one who possesses the truth and is the source of all wisdom (VII.25-56, 140-60). For their part, the lesser gods are happy to submit to Marduk because he makes it possible for them to enjoy a life of luxury and pleasure. Like Marduk, they want human beings to hold celebrations and festivals in their honor and offer up to them lavish sacrifices. They are therefore pleased that Marduk has fashioned human beings and has placed them under the gods as their servants or slaves.

From this summary of the *Enuma Elish*, it is clear that the relation between the gods is one of animosity, conflict, and violence from the start. Moved solely by a concern for his own comfort and interests, Apsu wishes to destroy the gods who will not let him rest undisturbed, and from that point on all of the gods fight to subjugate and destroy one another in order to establish their dominance over those who survive. Ultimately, because nature has endowed him with a power and a wisdom that are superior to those of the other gods, Marduk is able to establish himself as king and lord over all in order to rule over them as he wishes and order the world in the way that pleases him most. The gods who submit to him celebrate his victory and sing his praises out of the same type of self-interest that is reflected in him due to the benefits that they derive from his reign. What they all desire is the same thing that Marduk desires, namely, to live in luxury and splendor, feasting, relaxing, and enjoying themselves as they are served and honored by the human beings that Marduk has created as their slaves. While the gods also serve one another's interests, they cannot truly be said to love one another in the sense of selflessly desiring the well-being of all. Much less do they love human beings as their inferiors.

In his role as lord and king, Marduk is presented as the one who provides abundantly and generously for the needs of all, including not only the other gods but human beings as well. He is portrayed as a shepherd who "supplies pasturage and watering, making the stables flourish," as well as "the god of the pleasant breeze, lord of success and obedience, who produces bounty and wealth, who establishes abundance, [and] who turns everything scant that we have into profusion. . . ." (VI.124; VII.20-22). The reason that Marduk does these things, however, is not that he truly loves others and cares for them but because it is in his own best interest to do so. As long as he keeps the other gods content and at ease, they will continue to submit to his reign, which he intends to last for all eternity. At the same time, he must also keep human beings as happy and healthy as possible, because if their living conditions become too dire and difficult, they will not only be unable to serve the gods but will also be moved to rebel against them and the order that Marduk has established. Great emphasis is therefore laid on the idea that Marduk is the benefactor of human beings as well, even though he created them for the sole purpose of serving the gods with their gifts and offerings, since human beings will not wish to serve the gods unless they too are convinced that doing so is in their own best interest.

In a sense, of course, human beings know that they have no choice but to submit to Marduk and the other gods if they wish to survive and prosper within the limits laid out for them. If they refuse to serve the gods faithfully, Marduk promises to inflict tremendous sufferings and hardships on them and even destroy them. The poem repeatedly stresses not only Marduk's tremendous power but also his intense anger and rage at those who disobey him, as well as the extreme cruelty and great violence with which he treats all who oppose him. Its purpose is clearly to warn any human beings who might dare to disobey and oppose him of the terrible consequences that they will endure if they do so.

While the *Enuma Elish* does not refer explicitly to the establishment among human beings of the same type of hierarchical relationships that exist among the gods, it clearly presupposes such relationships. If human beings are to dedicate themselves to producing food and other goods to give to the gods as offerings, some of them must be dedicated to organizing and overseeing the production of these things and their presentation to the gods as offerings. Those who read the *Enuma Elish* in antiquity would also have been aware that the priests and the elites in Babylon retained the goods that were offered to the gods and thus were able to exert control not only over those goods themselves but over the population that depended on those goods as well. It was also generally maintained that gods such as Marduk had assigned to certain individuals and groups the place that they occupied in the social order they had established. In particular, the kings and rulers had been designated by the gods to reign over others as their subjects. Of course, all who rose to positions of power and privilege by imposing their will over others would claim that they had done so as a result of the gods' favor and approval and that the gods had chosen them personally to occupy those positions. Thus the relations between human beings would constantly be characterized by the same type of conflict, violence, and cruelty that the *Enuma Elish* ascribes to the gods, since human beings would similarly strive to establish their dominance over others in order to subjugate them and be served and obeyed by them.

Even though human beings are condemned to serve perpetually the gods and those whom the gods establish to rule on earth if they wish to avoid becoming the objects of their wrath, they are also commanded to praise and honor the gods, and especially Marduk. The final section of the *Enuma Elish* is dedicated almost completely to extolling the great power and accomplishments of Marduk in order to exhort all to acclaim and worship him as lord over all (VI.95–VII.162). Marduk is called by fifty names or titles, each of which points to some outstanding quality that he possesses or some benefit that he confers on others, and on that basis all are called to serve and glorify him: "Let men command that his praises be constantly uttered, let them offer worship to him" (VII.24). If human beings fulfill this command, however, they do so not out of genuine love and affection but out of self-interest and fear. They know that they can obtain what they want from him and enjoy his favor only if they render obeisance to him in the way he desires, and that if they fail to honor him with their sacrifices and offerings they will be subjected to his wrath and fury.

Although Marduk is presented as being cruel and ruthless by nature, he is also described as good, merciful, and forgiving. In part, these attributes are ascribed to him because those who must be convinced to serve him and submit to him cannot be motivated solely by fear if they are to do so willingly and enthusiastically. They must also be drawn to be faithful and loyal to him by his favors and kindness. Nevertheless, they know very well that if Marduk does show them kindness and mercy, it is not because he truly cares for them and is concerned for their well-being as an end in itself, but only because it is in his own best interest to treat them in that manner. For this reason, the poem states: "On the peoples that he created, the living beings, he imposed the service of the gods and they took rest. Creation and annihilation, forgiveness and exacting the penalty occur at his command, so let them fix their eyes on him" (VI.129-32). The idea here is that Marduk will do whatever suits his purposes best in order to be served by human beings. At times, this involves showing them kindness and forgiveness, yet at other times it involves punishing them and even annihilating some of them so that those who remain will submit slavishly to his will out of fear.

While human beings must praise and serve Marduk to remain in his favor and avoid his wrath, when those of lower rank wish to receive some type of favor from the gods, they will generally invoke the lesser gods rather than Marduk himself. The reason for this is that, because they have little to offer Marduk personally, they are generally not worthy of his time and attention. Such human beings will therefore have a greater chance of obtaining whatever they seek if they approach the lesser gods with their petitions and offerings. Within the hierarchical order of the deities as Marduk has established it, the rank of the gods whom the different groups of human beings invoke should therefore correspond roughly to their own rank within the hierarchical order that exists among human beings themselves.

Several passages from the *Enuma Elish* speak of Marduk as one who upholds what is right and true and preserves order by punishing those who do wrong. He is called "the destroyer of crooked enemies" who actively searches out sin and transgression, extirpates the wicked, and does not let evildoers escape (VI.154; VII.34-36, 156; cf. VII.48-52). "He made truth to prosper, he uprooted perverse speech, he separated falsehood from truth" (VII.39-40). Marduk is even referred to as "the pure god, who cleanses our character" (VI.156). It must be recognized, however, that all of these qualities are defined in relation to the hierarchical order or system established by Marduk. While to some degree any understanding of what is true and right must be grounded in the nature of reality, ultimately it is Marduk and the gods who determine what is to be accepted as true, right, fair, and just. They also determine what rewards and punishments human beings are to receive in response to their behavior. Whatever poses a threat to the established order must be regarded as a sin or transgression and must be labeled false, perverse, and evil. Any who oppose that order are wicked and must be treated with violence as its enemies.

What actually concerns the gods, however, is not the well-being of all but upholding the order that Marduk has established, an order that benefits the gods as well as those human beings who enjoy positions of power and privilege. Naturally, it is claimed that this order or system must be preserved perpetually for the good of all, since otherwise chaos would ensue, yet in reality that order or system is not designed to promote the well-being of all equally. Even though those in power claim that the only alternative to the established order is chaos, the reality is that other forms of organizing the relations between human beings might also avoid chaos and promote greater equity and justice. Because public discourse is controlled by those in positions of power and authority, however, this possibility is not acknowledged openly.

What concerns Marduk and the gods, therefore, is not that human beings practice what is good, right, or just for their own sake but that they maintain the order that benefits the powerful and privileged and keeps them in a position of supremacy. Furthermore, whatever rights and duties exist are defined by Marduk and the gods and exist in relation to them rather than in relation to their subjects, who have no choice but to accept whatever the powerful determine to be good and right and submit to whatever obligations and duties are imposed on them. While the gods and those in positions of authority generally acknowledge that they have some obligation or duty to protect and defend those who are under them, they are also free to suspend any such obligations or duties as they see fit and can always claim to do so in the name of the common good that they are supposedly in charge of defining, promoting, and preserving.

The Gods of Homer's Iliad *and* Odyssey

Many of the same traits associated with the deities of whom the *Enuma Elish* speaks are displayed by the gods and goddesses that appear in Homer's *Iliad* and *Odyssey*. Like the gods of Babylon, the Greek gods wish to spend their time feasting, drinking, relaxing, and enjoying other luxuries and pleasures, including sexual relations. They are surrounded in splendor and virtually everything they possess and use is made of gold and other precious materials. They engage in laughter and gaiety and listen to heavenly music at their banquets until they are filled and satisfied and then, after the sun goes down, they go to their mansions and doze off to sleep (*Iliad* 1.597-611). Olympus is described as a place where there is no rain, snow, or strong wind: "there the blessed gods dwell in endless sunshine, illumined forever by a peaceful and radiant light" (*Odyssey* 6.41-46).[8] It is said that they constantly take great delight in their festivities and prosperity (*Od.* 11.603). The gods are also happy to travel to other places such as Ethiopia in order to attend the feasts and sacrifices that the inhabitants of those places offer in their

---

8. Translations from the *Iliad* and the *Odyssey* are my own and are based on the text of volumes 104, 105, 170, and 171 of the Loeb Classical Library (Cambridge, MA: Harvard University Press, 1911–).

honor (*Il.* 1.423-24; *Od.* 1.22-24; cf. *Od.* 5.99-102). They especially enjoy the music and entertainment that their worshipers provide for them as well as the games and competitions held on their behalf. However, because such an idyllic and blissful existence can at times become tedious and monotonous, the gods also get involved in human affairs. In fact, they often become so interested and engrossed in those affairs that some of them engage personally in the conflicts and fighting among different peoples and on occasion even end up getting struck and wounded themselves.

When the Olympian gods do get absorbed in human affairs, they show interest only in those human beings who are worthy of their attention. These include especially powerful kings and mighty warriors such as Odysseus, Agamemnon, Hector, and Achilles, as well as important peoples such as the Trojans and the Achaeans or Greeks. Rarely do the gods ever concern themselves with the individual lives of common people. Such persons must turn to deities of lesser rank and inferior power for assistance in obtaining what they seek, since they are not worthy of the attention of the mighty Olympian gods.[9] The gods also show little concern for people of nations other than those who serve them, except of course as those nations relate to those whom they watch over and protect.

Precisely why the gods favor some individuals and peoples and not others is not always clear. Generally, the gods and goddesses show favor to those who are their children or descendants, independently of whether they are immortal or human, although occasionally the gods may repudiate and even loathe their offspring. Of course, they show special regard for those who build them temples and regularly offer them sacrifices. They also want those offerings to be as lavish and abundant as possible.[10] Naturally, only the rich and powerful are able to provide such sacrifices and build great temples for the gods. The gods are also attracted to those human beings who are particularly intelligent and clever or who display qualities such as beauty and charm. In the *Odyssey*, for example, while the goddess Athena does not give any explicit reason for being so concerned about the well-being and safe return of Odysseus, she is presented as admiring his wisdom and intelligence (*Od.* 1.48, 65-66). She also tells him that she cannot leave him because he is "soft of speech, keen of wit, and prudent" (*Od.* 13.331-32). Above all, however, the gods tend to be enamored of those who are powerful in battle and perform heroic feats that they find admirable and awe-inspiring. It is generally that admiration that leads them to come to the aid of the great figures around whom the *Iliad* and the *Odyssey* revolve.

In many cases, the gods are presented as being capricious, favoring some human beings over others for no clear or apparent reason. This is particularly true of Zeus, the greatest and most powerful of the gods who stands at the top of the hierarchical order as a result of his superior might and wisdom. In the

---

9. See, for example, *Il.* 2.398-401.
10. See, for example, *Il.* 1.436-74; 10.291-98; *Od.* 3.379-84, 418-63.

Odyssey it is said that Zeus "gives good and evil as he chooses, for he can do all things" (*Od.* 4.236-37). Elsewhere the poem affirms that "it is Zeus himself, the Olympian, who gives prosperity to all people, whether good or bad, in whatever way he sees fit" (*Od.* 6.188-89). This passage implies that Zeus does not take into account whether human beings do good or evil when he chooses whether or not to grant them good fortune. The same idea is expressed more clearly toward the end of the *Iliad* in a passage that also underscores the gods' blissful existence on Olympus: "The immortal gods know no care, yet the life that they spin for miserable mortals is full of sorrows. On the floor of Zeus's palace there stand two urns, one filled with evils and the other with good things. If Zeus, the hurler of thunderbolts, mixes these together, a person meets with both good and bad fortune. But if Zeus decides to take only from the urn full of evils, he makes a person an object of scorn, and the cruel hunger of famine forces that person to wander all over the face of the earth, dishonored by gods as well as mortals" (*Il.* 24.525-33).

In a sense, it may at times be said that the gods love certain human beings. They may even be enamored of particular individuals or care for entire cities or peoples. Once again, however, this is generally because they are related to those persons or people or find in them the qualities that please them. Chief among these qualities is the obedience of human beings to their will. They love those who do what they want yet despise and punish those who refuse to do so. According to the *Iliad*, "the gods gladly give ear to the prayers of those who obey them" (*Il.* 1.218). Their "love" for certain people therefore tends to respond to their own self-interest or self-centeredness. It is also conditional upon the faithful and loyal submission of human beings to their desires and commands.

What the gods especially desire, of course, is sacrifice. Toward the end of the *Iliad*, for example, Zeus tells his wife Hera: "Among all the mortals in Ilios, Hector was most loved by the gods and also the dearest to me, for he never failed to offer me gifts to my liking. My altar has never yet gone without the sacrifices that we claim by right, the drink offerings and the fragrant smell of burnt offerings" (*Il.* 24.66-70; cf. *Il.* 22.168-72). Here Hector is the "most loved" of Zeus because of the generosity and regularity of his sacrificial offerings. Likewise, in the *Odyssey*, Zeus is presented as showing favor to Odysseus because he has faithfully offered sacrifices to Zeus and "beyond all others has given sacrifice to the immortal gods" (*Od.* 1.60-62, 65-68). In fact, throughout both of Homer's poems, whenever human beings want something from the gods, they invariably point to their faithfulness in presenting the gods the offerings due to them or else promise to honor them by offering them sacrifices and building them temples in the future.

Conversely, when human beings arouse the wrath of the gods, the way in which they attempt to appease them is by presenting them sacrificial offerings. Numerous passages from the *Iliad* and the *Odyssey* affirm explicitly that the gods are appeased by sacrifice when they become angry.[11] Perhaps the clearest

---

11. See, for example, *Il.* 1.142-47, 442-44; 6.379-80; *Od.* 1.60-62; 3.144-45; 4.581-83.

affirmation of this idea is found in Book 9 of the *Iliad*, where the horseman Phoenix tells Achilles: "Even the immortal gods can be appeased; their might and honor and majesty are greater than ours, yet with incense and reverent vows and drink offerings and the sweet smell of sacrifice human beings can turn them from their wrath with supplications whenever they have sinned and transgressed" (*Il.* 9.499-501). The frequent allusions to these ideas makes it clear that the basis upon which human beings are ultimately accepted or rejected by the gods is not their practice of what is good, right, and kind or their moral qualities and behavior, but their sacrificial worship of the gods.

Neither the *Iliad* nor the *Odyssey* portray the gods actually consuming the sacrificial offerings presented to them, though they are said to take pleasure at the odor of the smoke from the burnt offerings that rises up to them. What pleases them, therefore, is not simply the sacrifices themselves but the honor, devotion, and reverence of which they are an expression. Numerous passages stress that the gods are especially concerned for their own honor, fame, and renown. In a couple of passages from the *Iliad*, such an idea is stated explicitly. In the context of allusions to the feasts, drink offerings, and burnt offerings offered to them at their altars, Zeus's wife Hera and subsequently Zeus himself refer to "the worship that is owed to us" (*Il.* 4.48-49; 24.68-70). Here it is said not only that the gods *desire* to receive worship or honor but that it is *due* to them as their *right*.

When human beings are suffering hardships or tribulations, they generally suspect that they have angered the gods, especially by not giving them the offerings they desire and demand. The reason for this is that they know that the gods are vengeful and do not tolerate any type of disobedience or failure to give them what is owed to them. At the outset of the *Iliad*, when Apollo rains down arrows on the Achaeans in wrath, they seek a seer who can tell them "for what reason Phoebus Apollo has become so angry, if it is because he blames us for some unfulfilled vow or hecatomb that we have failed to offer, and whether he can be convinced by the fragrant smoke of lambs and the sacrifice of unblemished goats to lift the plague from us" (*Il.* 1.64-67). Elsewhere in the *Iliad*, Aeneas suspects that some god is angry with the Trojans about their sacrifices and for that reason is setting himself against them (*Il.* 5.176-78). Later on, the goddess Artemis is said to have become upset with the Aetolians and to have "sent a plague upon them in anger because Oeneus had not offered her the first fruits of the harvest of his bountiful orchard; the rest of the gods had been given the sacrifices due to them for them to feast upon, but he had failed to offer anything to this daughter of great Zeus." She takes out her wrath on Oeneus by sending a wild boar to destroy his orchard lands (*Il.* 9.533-42).

The gods become angry not only when they do not receive the sacrificial offerings to which they are entitled but also when human beings seek to deprive them of what is theirs by right. These may be material possessions, including especially animals from their flocks and herds. The reason why

Odysseus must suffer throughout the *Odyssey* in order to arrive back to his home in Ithaca is that Zeus and the other gods became angry after Odysseus's men ate the cattle of the sun-god Hyperion when they were stranded on the island of Thrinacia.[12] Although they had been warned through Odysseus that they would be destroyed if they ate the cattle, when the men were starving and had nothing left to eat, they preferred to take their chances eating the cattle and hoped to appease the gods by vowing to build a great temple to Hyperion when they returned home and promising to fill it with lavish gifts and offerings (*Od.* 12.345-57). Nevertheless, led by Zeus, the gods destroyed all of Odysseus's men and left Odysseus adrift at sea. It did not matter to them that Odysseus's men had been desperate and at the point of starvation, nor were they concerned to show mercy to Odysseus and his men by providing them with something else to eat or assisting them in some other way. The only thing that they cared about was that human beings not take from the gods that which was theirs—in this case, Hyperion's cattle.

The plight of Odysseus and his men is said to have begun after they had committed a similar offense against Polyphemus, a monstrous, one-eyed Cyclops who is said to be the son of Poseidon and to reign over the other Cyclopes as their king on the island they inhabit. When Odysseus and his men wander into Polyphemus's cave and eat some of the cheese he elaborates there, Polyphemus discovers them and seals off the entrance to the cave with a great boulder so that they cannot escape. He then begins to devour Odysseus's men two at a time with great savagery whenever he becomes hungry. Finally, desperate to escape with their lives, Odysseus and the men who remain drive a sharp pole into the eye of Polyphemus when he is asleep in order to blind him. In this way, they are able to sneak out of the cave unseen by Polyphemus (*Od.* 9.307-445). Once Odysseus and his men are back on their ship out of the reach of Polyphemus, Odysseus climbs up a mast and shouts back at Polyphemus in order to gloat over him and to boast that he had been able to make his own will prevail over that of the gods by escaping from him (*Od.* 9.502-5). This angers Polyphemus even more, and as a result he cries out to his father Poseidon to avenge what Odysseus has done (*Od.* 9.528-35). Poseidon then takes out his wrath on Odysseus by destroying his ship and doing everything in his power to prevent Odysseus from returning home to Ithaca. Because Odysseus enjoys the favor of Zeus and especially Athena, however, Zeus does not allow Poseidon to kill Odysseus as he would like.

This story illustrates several other points that are important to understand the nature and character of Homer's gods. First, even though Odysseus had been forced to blind Polyphemus in order not to be devoured by him, from the perspective of the gods, he deserved to be punished for having done harm to one of their lot. While Odysseus had no doubt transgressed against Polyphemus by entering into his cave and eating some of his cheese, Polyphemus had also treated Odysseus and his men with much greater cruelty than they deserved

---

12. See *Od.* 1.6-9; 12.260-453; 19.273-77; 23.329-32.

by eating some of them alive. In the narrative, in fact, it is suggested that according to the accepted norms of conduct, Polyphemus should have shown hospitality to Odysseus and his men and that Zeus himself took vengeance on Polyphemus for his monstrous and unjust behavior by allowing Odysseus to blind him (*Od.* 9.265-71, 477-79). In spite of Polyphemus's behavior, however, Odysseus had no right to do him harm because mortal human beings are never justified in acting against the gods, whom they are always to treat as their superiors.

A second point of importance is that the god Poseidon is angered and outraged by Odysseus's blinding of Polyphemus not only because Odysseus is a mere mortal but also because Polyphemus is his son. No matter how inexcusable Polyphemus's behavior may have been, as his father Poseidon is obliged to defend him and seek to destroy any who do him harm. According to this logic, loyalty to one's own family and people takes precedence over a commitment to what is good, right, and just. Even when a member of one's family or people has done something that is wrong and unacceptable, the other members of the family or people must take sides with him or her. For that reason, Poseidon is fully justified in seeking to destroy Odysseus and attempting to make his return home as torturous and miserable as possible after Zeus has prohibited him from taking Odysseus's life. At the same time, because Zeus also owes loyalty to his fellow gods, even though he favors Odysseus, he feels obliged to allow Poseidon to harass and oppress Odysseus for what he has done to Polyphemus, despite his prohibition against Poseidon killing him.

A third point illustrated by this story is that mortal human beings deserve to be punished for depriving the gods not only of their sacrifices and property but also of the honor and respect that is due to them. For that reason, from the perspective of the gods, Odysseus's boast that he can make his will prevail over that of the gods is intolerable. The gods are extremely jealous for their honor and will not stand by idly when human beings have the audacity to compare themselves favorably to the gods or claim to be superior in some way. Those human beings must be put in their place in order to preserve the order established by the gods and to keep human beings in subjection under the gods' power and authority.

This principle is emphasized elsewhere in the *Iliad* as well. When the Achaeans arouse the admiration and awe of the gods by building a great wall and a trench with tremendous speed, for example, Poseidon becomes upset that the size and scope of their wall has outdone and overshadowed a large wall that he had built together with the god Apollo. On that basis, moved by envy and jealousy, he asks Zeus to allow him to tear down the Achaeans' wall (*Il.* 7.451-53). Poseidon is also upset that the Achaeans did not sacrifice to the gods or seek their approval before constructing the wall and trench, since he fears that human beings might conclude that in the future they can carry out their projects without consulting the gods or offering them sacrifices (*Il.* 7.446-50). Further on, when the inhabitants of Phaeacia act contrary to

Poseidon's will by assisting Odysseus and taking him home, Poseidon seeks Zeus's permission to wreck their ship and destroy their city, claiming that he will lose the respect of both gods and human beings if the Phaeacians are left unpunished. When Zeus grants him his petition, Poseidon takes out his wrath in full on the Phaeacians, despite the fact that both they and Odysseus offer him sacrifices in an attempt to appease him (*Il.* 13.98-193; 23.274-81).

The logic behind all of these examples is that, in order to preserve their position of power and privilege, the gods cannot allow human beings to do anything that might call into question their superiority, rival them, or undermine their authority. For that reason, any human beings who fail to submit humbly and obediently to the gods and show them the deference, respect, and honor due to them must be severely punished. While they undoubtedly desire sacrifice, the gods will not be appeased by the sacrifices of those who dare to oppose their will and challenge their supremacy. The idea that the gods reject the sacrifices of those human beings who disobey them is reflected in other passages as well. Before Odysseus's men eat the cattle that belong to the sun-god Hyperion, for example, they offer up sacrifices (*Od.* 12.339-48). They do the same before eating Polyphemus's cheese (*Od.* 9.231-32). Such sacrifices are unacceptable, however, because those who present them are not respecting the property and honor of the gods and are not asking the gods for permission ahead of time for the things they intend to do.

These narratives and others found throughout Homer's epic poems also serve to illustrate another important point, namely, that what angers and offends the gods is not the injustice and cruelty that human beings show to one another but simply their failure or refusal to submit to the gods as they should. In other words, what concerns the gods is not the manner in which the behavior of human beings affects human beings themselves but the manner in which it affects them as gods, whether directly or indirectly. If the gods prohibit certain actions or behaviors, they do so not because those actions or behaviors undermine or destroy the well-being of human beings themselves but because they deprive the gods of what they desire and claim as their own by right.

This principle is evident as well from the fact that in the *Iliad* and the *Odyssey*, the gods are said to respond favorably to those who ask for their assistance in taking vengeance on their enemies.[13] Just as the gods are ruthless in exacting revenge on any who dare to disrespect or injure them, even if those who do so are acting in accordance with justice or merely seeking to survive, under certain conditions they are also willing to give support to those human beings who wish to inflict pain and suffering on others motivated purely by spite and a desire for revenge. Similarly, just as the gods themselves constantly lust for greater wealth, power, and glory, they may lend their assistance to human beings who lust for the same things. They often respond favorably to the petitions of those who seek their approval and help in attacking the cities of other peoples in order to plunder and destroy them and take many of their

---

13. See, for example, *Il.* 1.35-43; 2.411-18; 3.351-54; *Od.* 17.49-60.

inhabitants captive as their slaves, especially if those human beings promise to offer to the gods a portion of what they pillage and steal.

If the gods are willing to assist human beings who carry out acts of violence motivated by greed, thirst for power, and a spirit of revenge, it is obvious that the condition upon which they accept favorably the prayers and sacrifices offered to them is not the practice of what is just, kind, good, and right. Nowhere in the two poems of Homer are the gods said to refuse sacrificial offerings and worship on that basis. Instead, the principle that serves as the basis for their relationship to human beings is that of *do ut des*. The gods are generally willing to grant human beings what they ask and desire, whether it be good or evil, as long as those human beings will give them what they demand and desire, namely, the gifts, offerings, and worship that please and honor them. It is also important to note that the gods do not care whether or not the human beings who give them the gifts, offerings, and worship they desire do so with a spirit of sincere affection, gratitude, and dedication. Because the gods demand the offering of sacrifices and worship for their own sake and regard these things as ends in themselves, as long as human beings fulfill that demand, it does not matter to the gods if they do so willingly or reluctantly, out of love or out of fear. Nor do they care whether the human beings who give them what they desire and demand treat their fellow human beings with kindness or cruelty or whether they obtain the things they offer fairly or unjustly through acts of violence or deception.

For the most part, the Greek gods do not make any moral demands on human beings. In fact, the gods themselves practice deceit, commit adultery and fornication, take the lives of human beings for no good reason other than that they derive satisfaction from doing so, and are driven by things such as envy, revenge, lust, and other selfish passions. They also incite human beings to wage war and engage in violent conflicts against other peoples, not because these peoples have done anything unjust or oppressive, but simply because for whatever reason the gods do not like them. In many cases, when human beings are engaged in conflict, the gods actually take different sides. This demonstrates that their preference for some persons and groups over others has nothing to do with favoring those who practice what is good, just, and right over those who do not. They either act arbitrarily in giving preferential treatment to some over others or take the side of those who will offer them the worship and sacrifices they desire and demand.

Among the adjectives that Homer uses to describe the Olympian gods are cruel, hateful, deceitful, malicious, and envious.[14] Zeus is said to take delight at watching the gods quarrel among themselves and at seeing human beings be made to suffer (*Il.* 19.270; 21.389-90), while the goddess Aphrodite enjoys beguiling feeble women (*Il.* 5.348-49). At the same time, the gods incite the same types of behavior among human beings, stirring up strife among them and putting evil in their hearts.[15]

---

14. See, for example, *Il.* 2.348-49; 8.360-61; 9.17-22, 158-59; 15.14; *Od.* 5.118-19; 22.201-2.
15. See, for example, *Il.* 3.414-17; 9.636-38; *Od.* 3.136-37.

Undoubtedly, the gods of Homer generally expect human beings to respect certain norms of behavior and observe certain rules, such as offering hospitality to strangers and keeping their word when they make vows and treaties. In order to preserve peace and order in the world, they must enforce justice and demand that human beings treat one another with honesty and a certain degree of respect. In fact, the gods themselves are expected to adhere to basic moral principles in their dealings with one another and with human beings. As sovereign arbiters of what is good, right, and fair, however, the gods are often free to bend the rules and even suspend them as they see fit.

At the same time, however, there are certain natural forces that even the Olympian gods must respect. In Homer's poems, these forces are often personified as gods, as if they had a will of their own. Sleep, Death, Morning, and Night are presented in this way, for example, as are Strife, Tumult, and Fate.[16] While at times the Olympian gods can exert control over these forces, to some extent they must also be subject to them. Sleep, for example, can overcome Zeus, yet Zeus may also punish Sleep if he wishes (*Il.* 14.247-62). These personified natural forces generally play the role of preserving order and equilibrium in the cosmos. Therefore, even if those who violate the unwritten ethical code can avoid arousing the wrath of the gods, sooner or later these natural forces will act to restore order and justice and to set right whatever is wrong. Because of these forces, actions that are good or evil can be said to have consequences that are natural, intrinsic, and ultimately unavoidable as well, even when those actions are not rewarded and punished by the gods personally.

This distinction between the desires of the Olympian gods and the forces of nature affects the manner in which sin and transgression are understood in Homer's poems. While the gods regularly punish human beings for failing to give them the honor, respect, and worship that they regard as their due, they rarely inflict punishments on human beings for their violations of moral or ethical norms. Because what ultimately interests the gods is not the practice of what is good and right among human beings but the offerings and reverence that they demand from them, those who do not fulfill that demand do not sin in the sense of acting immorally, doing evil, or committing wrongdoing. Their failure to obey the gods may therefore be labeled an offense or transgression, yet strictly speaking it is not a sin in the sense in which that word is generally understood today. Human beings can also transgress the laws of nature in various ways, yet in these cases it is not gods such as the Olympians who punish them but the forces of nature themselves. Despite the fact that these forces are often personified as gods, when they punish those who disobey the laws of nature they do not act out of anger or because they have been offended. They simply bring upon human beings the intrinsic consequences of their actions.

When human beings violate the laws of nature, there is usually nothing that they can do to avoid suffering the consequences of their actions. As noted above, however, when they offend and anger the gods, they are generally able

---

16. See, for example, *Il.* 8.1; 11.4; 14.231, 261; 16.829; 19.1, 136.

to appease or propitiate the gods by offering sacrifices and pledging to avoid in the future the behavior that has displeased the gods.[17] Although by means of their offerings and vows they express implicitly their remorse for having offended the gods, strictly speaking this remorse is not the same as heartfelt repentance, since the only reason they may regret what they have done is that it provoked the wrath of the gods and resulted in suffering and punishment at their hands. For the most part, the gods do not care if those who have angered them and seek to be restored to their favor are sincerely sorry for what they have done, since they are concerned only with what human beings actually do and not what is in their heart.

Ideally, what human beings would like is to be able to act in any way they please without having to fear any type of punishment or consequences at the hands of the gods. If they can escape notice by the gods, who are not all-seeing or omniscient, human beings can often get away with disobeying them. For the most part, however, if they wish to be blessed by the gods and avoid falling under their wrath, they have no choice but to treat the gods in the way they demand and seek their permission and approval in all that they do.

Ultimately, then, the gods of Homer's poems respond favorably to the prayers and offerings presented to them only when they consider it in their own self-interest to do so. If the gods want there to be peace, justice, and well-being among human beings, it is not for the sake of human beings themselves but only because in that way human beings can dedicate themselves to giving the gods what they desire and not disturb them as they devote themselves to enjoying their idyllic existence. For their part, human beings must strive to keep the gods content and satisfied because only in that way can they obtain from them what they desire for themselves and also keep them at a distance so as not to be threatened or bothered by them. As noted above, therefore, while at times human beings must be saved and delivered *by* the gods, they must continually be saved and delivered *from* them as well.

THE GOD OF ISRAEL AND THE HEBREW SCRIPTURES

Throughout the Hebrew Scriptures, we encounter a God who in many ways is radically and fundamentally different from the type of gods just considered. While he is undoubtedly viewed as possessing certain traits that were characteristic of other gods in antiquity, there are two attributes in particular that set him apart from them, namely, his sovereignty as creator and Lord of all that exists and his unconditional love for all of the human beings and creatures that he has made.

As we have seen in the opening section of the present chapter, precisely how and when this conception of God developed among the people of Israel in the centuries leading up to the final redaction and compilation of the books

---

17. See, for example, *Il.* 1.99-100, 146-47, 442-44; 6.379-80; *Od.* 3.143-45, 418-20; 4.581-84; cf. *Od.* 1.60-62; 8.508-10.

of the Hebrew Bible as we know them today is by no means clear. That process was no doubt a long and complex one and involved the transmission of stories, ideas, and texts in both oral and written form from one generation and group of people to another. Over time those stories, ideas, and texts underwent changes and were gradually shaped, edited, and reformulated in various ways before they came to take the form in which they now exist. At some point during the period of the Second Temple, however, that process came to an end and the biblical texts became fixed in their present form, even though minor variations in those texts continued to exist in different times and places and among the different communities that looked to them as authoritative. Although there were no doubt a number of criteria that were employed in the process of editing and revising those texts in order to bring them into harmony with one another and shape them into a whole that was greater than the parts, one of the most important of these criteria was the conception of God reflected in them. The persons and communities that were responsible for fixing the texts in the form in which they exist today clearly did their best to ensure that the conception of God that appears throughout their pages was uniform and consistent.

Biblical scholars and careful readers of the biblical texts can, of course, still discern traces of earlier conceptions of the God of whom those texts speak. Thus, for example, Psalm 82 begins by affirming that God takes his place in the council or assembly of the gods that are gathered together (v. 1). In this verse, while the god that is identified with the God of Israel stands supreme, other lesser gods exist alongside of him. The idea of an assembly of divine or semi-divine beings may also be reflected in other passages from the Hebrew Bible, such as those that present God consulting and speaking with other beings in the opening chapters of Genesis when he creates human beings and decides to exclude them from the garden after they disobey him (Gen 1:26; 3:22). Traces of earlier conceptions of God may be evident elsewhere in the biblical texts as well.[18]

Earlier conceptions of God may also be reflected in the fact that the term used in Hebrew for God is generally *'elohim*, which is a plural noun. The biblical texts also provide evidence that at some point in the history of the people that became known as Israel the ancient god El came to be associated and identified with the god YHWH. Scholars continue to debate the origins of the belief in the god YHWH, yet it is hardly to be doubted that beliefs in this god evolved over time, as did beliefs regarding the god El. Archaeologists have also found evidence that at least in some places and times the god YHWH, like the god El, was said to have a female consort. It would be a mistake,

---

18. On the passages from the Hebrew Bible that suggest a belief in the existence of other divine or semi-divine beings alongside YHWH the God of Israel, see especially Michael S. Heiser, "Monotheism, Polytheism, Monolatry, or Henotheism? Toward an Assessment of Divine Plurality in the Hebrew Bible," *BBR* 18 (2008): 1–30. On this subject as well as the points that follow below, see Thomas Römer, *The Invention of God*, trans. Raymond Geuss (Cambridge, MA: Harvard University Press, 2015).

however, to assume that beliefs regarding YHWH and El were uniform among all the people in the region at any given time. There can be little doubt that at different stages of the history of those who believed in and worshiped YHWH and El there were many different conceptions of these gods as well as the god into which both came to be fused, just as there was a great deal of diversity and evolution throughout the history of the people who eventually came to be known as Israel. In large part, this was because for a long period of time there was no central authority that had the power to establish throughout the peoples in the land the uniformity of beliefs regarding YHWH and El that is reflected in the biblical texts as they now stand.

At some place and time unknown to us, however, the full and definitive fusion of YHWH and El or Elohim that we find in the biblical texts took place among at least some of the people known as Israel, as did the final redaction and collection of those texts as they have been preserved for us. Throughout the present work, it is the final and definitive conception of the God of Israel that runs throughout the biblical texts that will interest us. For that reason, the approach taken here will be exclusively synchronic and questions regarding the manner in which the biblical texts and the beliefs that appear in them evolved over time will not be addressed.

The Character of Israel's God

The biblical texts are remarkably consistent in ascribing certain characteristics and attributes to the God of Israel. While those texts as we have them today generally write his name as YHWH, at times they use the abbreviation YH. Other forms of his name may have existed in antiquity as well. There is evidence that the letters YHWH were pronounced as Yahweh, yet there may have been some variation in the pronunciation of this name from one time and place to another. By the third century BCE, many Jews had stopped pronouncing God's name due to the biblical prohibition against misusing it (Exod 20:7; Deut 5:11). Among many it became customary to substitute the title "lord" for the name YHWH when referring to God (Hebrew: *'adon* or *'adonay*, "my lord"; Greek: *kyrios*). English versions of the Bible that use this title when translating the Hebrew YHWH generally use three small uppercase letters at the end of the word to indicate that this title is being substituted for God's name, thus writing it as Lord, as I will do in the present work. As just mentioned above, the biblical texts also use the term *'elohim* to refer to God, and Jews in antiquity continued to use that designation as well. For our purposes here, however, for the most part it will be sufficient to refer to God (with an uppercase G) or the God of Israel when referring to him.

What distinguishes the God of Israel from the gods of the other nations of antiquity, however, is much more than his name. In some sense, he alone can truly be called God. If some Jews of the Second Temple period believed that other divine or semi-divine beings existed in addition to the God of Israel, the vast majority would have regarded these beings as subservient to the one true God YHWH. This is in fact the view taken with regard to other spiritual or heavenly beings mentioned in the biblical texts, such as angels, cherubim, seraphim, Satan, and the demons or evil spirits. What made the God of Israel supreme and placed him over all other beings was that he is the sole creator of all, including whatever spiritual or heavenly beings were thought to exist. According to this conception, any deities other than YHWH who might be called gods were not truly God in the same sense that YHWH was and would have been thought to have had their source and origin in him.

This did not mean, however, that the other gods and living beings in the world were actually thought to share in God's own being, essence, or substance. They had not been born of him or generated from him in the same way that gods such as Tiamat and Apsu were formed of water and engendered other gods. Instead, all of the beings and realities that existed in the world were thought to be of a different nature, essence, or substance than the God who had created them. Given that the biblical texts never refer explicitly to anything such as the nature, essence, or substance of God, it might even be thought that it was inappropriate to employ that type of terminology when speaking of God. Furthermore, just as the one true God had created all of the other beings that existed, he could destroy them or will them out of existence at any time if he so desired. In this regard, then, the God of Israel was fundamentally distinct from any of the other gods of antiquity known to us.

Other characteristics also made Israel's God unique. The biblical texts consistently portray him as one for whom nothing is impossible. This claim is closely tied to the belief that he is the creator of all things. Because he brought all things into existence, he is sovereign over all in a way that no other gods in antiquity were thought to be. Unlike other gods, he was not in any way subject to nature or its forces. He did not need to eat or sleep, nor was he subject to passions and desires in the same way that they were. He controlled whatever type of destiny was thought to exist rather than being determined by it. He was also present throughout his creation and was not confined to any location. While he might make himself present in a special way at his sanctuary or at a particular place such as Bethel or Mount Sinai, even then he continued to be able to see all things in the world and remained present everywhere. For that same reason, he knew all things, including the thoughts of human beings and the desires of their hearts and minds. All of these things set him apart from the other gods of antiquity, who were not believed to be all-powerful and all-knowing in the way that the God of Israel was.

The commitment of the God of Israel to what was good, right, just, and merciful also distinguished him from other gods in antiquity. He practiced justice and righteousness and demanded that human beings do so as well. Injustice and oppression were never acceptable to him. This concern for justice and equity also led him to care especially for the needy, the poor, the weak, and the disadvantaged. He did not show favoritism to the rich and powerful but instead demanded that they too act justly and mercifully toward others and assist those who were in need, such as orphans, widows, and foreigners. While there were undoubtedly other gods in antiquity who were concerned for justice and mercy, none of the ones known to us were thought to be as insistent and uncompromising in their demand for these things as the God of Israel. As we shall see further on, he was even said to reject sacrificial offerings if those who presented those offerings were not fully committed to justice, righteousness, and mercy in the way that he was.

The God of Israel was also said to reject many of the customs and practices that were associated with other peoples. These included things such as adultery, fornication, drunkenness, and other behaviors that are regarded as immoral in the biblical texts. Among other peoples, these behaviors and others such as prostitution, the celebration of games and competitions, and even child sacrifice were associated with the worship of their gods. Such things were strictly prohibited by the God of Israel, however.

The Desires and Objectives of Israel's God

As noted at the outset of this chapter, while there were important differences between the manner in which the pagan gods of antiquity and the God of Israel were conceived of and viewed, there were also many similarities. The biblical texts present him as wishing to be obeyed and being moved to anger by disobedience to his will. He is also said to bless and prosper those who do what he commands but to punish and even curse those who refuse to do so. These punishments include things such as plagues, famines, natural disasters, defeat in battle, and oppression at the hands of enemies. Like the other gods of antiquity, he desires to reign over others as their lord and king and demands that people submit to his rule and authority. He shows mercy and kindness to those who serve him faithfully but is said to take action against those who oppose him and rebel against him. Even though at times he is said to show no favoritism, he chooses Israel as a people of his own and his "treasured possession," while promising to make them the most blessed of all peoples (Exod 19:5; Deut 7:14). He orders his people to build him a sanctuary in which he may be said to dwell and commands that they offer him there their sacrifices and gifts.

The question that must be asked when considering the passages that portray the God of Israel in these terms, however, is whether he seeks such things and behaves in those ways *for his own sake* or rather *for the sake of the human beings he has created* and the world in general. In principle, for example, he might pour out blessings on people, not in order to obtain something from them, but simply because he wishes for them to be happy and enjoy what he gives them. He might also give them commandments and punish those who disobey those commandments, not out of a concern for himself, but solely out of a concern for their well-being. Similarly, he might wish to reign over human beings, demand that they submit to him, and wish to receive their worship, not in order to obtain something that he desires for himself, but because their submission and obedience to his will and their acknowledgment of him as God will promote among them a way of living that will allow them to experience well-being, wholeness, and happiness.

In principle, of course, the idea that God seeks the well-being and happiness of human beings and the idea that God seeks something for himself in his dealings with human beings are not mutually exclusive. On the contrary, it might even be argued that God's own well-being and happiness depend in some way on the well-being and happiness of the human beings he has created and therefore that God cannot seek his own well-being and happiness without seeking theirs as well. When God is understood to be the sovereign creator and originator of all that exists, however, priority is generally given to God's own desires and interests. According to such an understanding of God, he created the world and human beings *for his own sake* rather than *for theirs*. In fact, to claim that God created human beings for their own sake can be seen as implying that God himself exists for the sake of human beings and therefore in a sense subjects himself to them in order to dedicate himself to serving *their* desires and interests over and above *his own*. This would make God subservient to the world and the beings he has created.

Such a conception of God and his relation to the world and to human beings seems to run contrary not only to logic but also the biblical texts. For that reason, biblical interpreters over the centuries have commonly supposed that God created the world and human beings *for his own sake* rather than theirs. In reality, however, this involves claiming that the God of the Bible behaves in the same way as the pagan gods of antiquity were thought to do and is motivated by the same concerns. What he seeks is to satisfy some need or desire to which he is subject.

Because in biblical thought there is nothing above God or superior to him, the needs and desires to which he is said to be subject are generally associated with God's own being or nature. While God is not said to have been driven to create the world because he stood in need of it or because he depends on the world and human beings in some way in order to exist or be whole, the fact that he freely chose to create the world and also wills that it continue to exist makes it clear that its existence responds to some desire on his part. In that case, while he does not need the world or human beings in themselves, he can be said to need or want something from them in order to satisfy the desire that led him to create them and moves him to continue to will that they exist.

According to this manner of interpreting the biblical texts, if the creation and ongoing existence of the world serve to satisfy some desire on God's part and this desire revolves around God himself, then even though in many respects he is different from the pagan gods of antiquity, ultimately he is motivated by the same type of concern for himself that was thought to be characteristic of those gods. Because this desire cannot be rooted in any type of physical or material need, it has commonly been understood to consist of a desire to be worshiped, honored, served, and glorified. Like the gods of other nations in antiquity, the God of Israel would have created human beings in order to receive from them the praise, honor, and obedience he desired for himself for his own sake.

While such an idea is commonly assumed among biblical scholars and theologians, rarely is it stated explicitly. There is one tradition, however, in which that idea is expressly regarded as a central tenet of the biblical faith. That is the Reformed tradition. At the outset of the first catechism that he wrote for the Church of Geneva in 1538, John Calvin affirms that "all human beings have been born for religion" and explains this idea thus: "all of us have been created in order to acknowledge our Creator's majesty and to receive it and esteem it, once acknowledged, with all fear, love, and reverence."[19] Several years later, in the Latin version of the *Catechism of the Church of Geneva 1545*, Calvin begins by affirming that the chief end of human life is "to know God by whom human beings were created" and then continues: "he created us for this, and placed us in the world, that he might be glorified in us. And it is certainly proper that our life, of which he is the beginning, be directed to his glory."[20] Calvin also spoke of the purpose of the creation and life of human beings in terms of rendering God the honor due to him and frequently understood sinfulness in terms of desecrating, diminishing, and violating God's honor or robbing God of the honor to which he is entitled.[21]

Other Reformed writings stress the same ideas. In his commentary on the *Heidelberg Catechism*, of which he was the chief author, the sixteenth-century Reformed theologian Zacharias Urinus wrote: "The glory of God is, therefore, the chief and ultimate end for which man was created. It was for this purpose that God created rational and intelligent beings, such as angels and men, that knowing him, they might praise him forever. Hence, man was created principally for the glory of God. . . ."[22] The affirmations of the renowned Dutch Reformed theologian Herman Bavinck reflect the same ideas:

> Christian theology almost unanimously teaches that the glory of God is the final goal of all God's works. Although in its early years theologians especially featured the goodness of God as the motive for creation, still the honor of God as the final end of all things is not lacking. . . . [T]he Reformed tradition made the honor of God the fundamental principle of all doctrine and conduct, of dogmatics and morality, of the family, society, and the state, of science and art. . . . God can rest in nothing other than himself and cannot be satisfied in anything less than himself. He has no alternative but to seek his own honor. . . . Inasmuch as he is the supreme and only good, perfect itself, it is the highest kind of justice that in all creatures he seek his own honor. . . . Voluntarily or

<hr>

19. I. John Hesselink, *Calvin's First Catechism: A Commentary* (Louisville: Westminster, 1997), 7.

20. John Calvin, *Calvin: Theological Treatises*, trans. J. K. S. Reid, LCC 22 (Philadelphia: Westminster, 1954), 91.

21. See Marijn de Kroon, *The Honour of God and Human Salvation: A Contribution to an Understanding of Calvin's Theology according to His Institutes* (Edinburgh: T & T Clark, 2001), 26-39.

22. Zacharias Ursinus, *The Commentary of Dr. Zacharias Ursinus on the Heidelberg Catechism*, trans. G. W. Williard (Grand Rapids: Eerdmans, 1954), 28. Ursinus (1534-1583) was the principal author and interpreter of the *Heidelberg Catechism*, which dates to 1563.

involuntarily, every creature will someday bow his knee before him. Obedience in love or subjection by force is the final destiny of all creatures.[23]

In Reformed thought, to affirm that the purpose for which human beings were created is that they might glorify and honor God and acknowledge his majesty is by no means to deny that God also desires the well-being and happiness of human beings. The seventeenth-century *Westminster Larger Catechism*, for example, begins by affirming both of these ideas: "1. Q. What is the chief and highest end of man? A. Man's chief and highest end is to glorify God, and fully to enjoy him forever."[24] Nevertheless, as is evident here, while the enjoyment of God is spoken of as one of the ends for which human beings were created, it is clearly subordinated to the glorification of God.[25] If human beings are to enjoy God, they have no choice but to glorify him.

There can be no doubt that the God of Israel as he is presented in the biblical texts is concerned for the happiness and well-being of the human beings he has created and thus seeks to establish justice in the world out of love for all. In this regard, he is fundamentally distinct from the pagan gods of antiquity. Nevertheless, the idea that the primary and ultimate purpose for which God created human beings was that they might praise, serve, obey, and glorify him seems to portray the God of Israel as similar to a pagan deity in the sense that he is concerned primarily for himself and his own honor, glory, and worship. These things take precedence over human happiness and well-being. In fact, if God responds in wrath against those who fail to offer him the praise to which he is entitled and punishes them for robbing or depriving him of the honor and glory that is rightfully his alone, it would seem difficult to maintain that he is acting out of love for them and a concern for their well-being. Instead, it would appear that he cares more for his own glory, majesty, and honor than he does for human beings. While he may love them, this love seems to be conditional upon their giving him what he wants for his own sake. Likewise, although it can be argued that human beings can find happiness and well-being only by serving, honoring, and worshiping God as the one for whom they exist, God's punishment of those who refuse to do these things can hardly have their happiness and well-being as its goal if it is aimed at compelling them to do these things against their will or simply involves sentencing those who do not give him what he needs or desires to eternal torments and condemnation.

The biblical affirmations regarding the holiness, purity, and justice of God have also commonly been understood as reflecting the idea that God's primary concern is for himself rather than for human beings. Supposedly, God's holiness, purity, and justice make it impossible for him to tolerate human sin.

---

23. Herman Bavinck, *Reformed Dogmatics*, vol. 2: *God and Creation* (Grand Rapids: Baker Academic, 2004), 433-34. Bavinck (1854-1921) continues to be revered as one of the most important theologians of the Reformed tradition.

24. See Johannes G. Vos, *The Westminster Larger Catechism: A Commentary*, ed. G. I. Williamson (Phillipsburg, NJ: R & R Publishing, 2002), 3.

25. On this point, see Ursinus, *Commentary*, 29; Bavinck, *Reformed Dogmatics*, 2:431-45.

For that reason, he must keep sin and impurity at a distance from himself or else cover these things up from his view. Similarly, God's justice is understood as preventing him from overlooking or forgiving human sin without punishing it. Because this inability to tolerate sin and impurity is considered to be inherent to his holy and righteous nature, if God wishes to have any type of communion with sinners or accept them into his presence, he has no choice but to deal first with their sinfulness and impurity by eliminating it, punishing it, or removing it from his sight.

The God of Israel according to Walter Brueggemann

The idea that the primary concern of the God of the Hebrew Bible is for himself, his own desires, and the demands of his holy and righteous nature is especially evident in the work of Old Testament scholar Walter Brueggemann, who is clearly influenced by the Reformed tradition to which he belongs. In his monumental work *Theology of the Old Testament*, Brueggemann argues that the Hebrew Scriptures portray Yahweh the God of Israel as one who is driven primarily by what he calls "self-regard," that is, a concern for his own sovereignty.[26] According to Brueggemann, this self-regard on the part of Yahweh is particularly evident in the passages from the Hebrew Scriptures that speak of Yahweh's concern for his own glory and his holiness as well as those that present him as jealous. As sovereign, what Yahweh ultimately wants is to be glorified and honored as sovereign and for all to submit to him. In this regard, he is essentially no different than the pagan gods of antiquity:

> Yahweh, the God of the First Commandment, is a God who intends to be fully sovereign, who will brook no rival, who practices intense self-regard, and who will not tolerate those who detract from this self-regard. In this aspect of Yahweh's life, Yahweh does indeed practice "common theology"—that is, the way of "being god" that was everywhere available in the ancient Near East. In that propensity, Yahweh imposes an order (moral, political, or otherwise), guarantees the order's system of benefits, and deals with rigorous sanctions toward those who violate the order. To some extent, Yahweh conducts Yahweh's life like any god known in this way (283).

For Brueggemann, this self-regard and concern for his sovereignty is manifested first and foremost in Yahweh's demand that all respect his right to be acclaimed and acknowledged as God over all. Yahweh is a "God who takes with savage seriousness Yahweh's right to be worshiped, honored, and obeyed" (272). While Yahweh undoubtedly is concerned for the needs of human beings, including especially those of his people Israel, this concern takes a back seat to his concern for his own reputation as sovereign. Brueggemann thus speaks of

---

26. Walter Brueggemann, *Theology of the Old Testament: Testament, Dispute, Advocacy* (Minneapolis: Fortress, 2005). Due to the large number of references to this book in the section that follows, I will refer to the pages cited and referenced by enclosing the page numbers in parentheses rather than using footnotes. I will also be using pronouns of masculine gender to refer to God, even though Brueggemann avoids this practice throughout his work.

"the extreme measures to which Yahweh will go for the sake of Yahweh's own reputation, without reference to Israel's need" (202). In other words, Yahweh values his sovereignty and honor more than he values his people Israel. Therefore, if he is forced to choose between preserving his reputation and satisfying his people's needs, he will opt for the first of these two alternatives.

Intimately related to Yahweh's concern for his sovereignty is his desire to be glorified by human beings. As their sovereign creator, he has the right to demand this from human beings. In passages such as Isaiah 42:8 and 48:11, where Yahweh insists that he will give his glory to no other in the context of allusions to Israel's return from its exile in Babylon, Brueggemann claims to find the idea that Yahweh "is a God who is supremely self-confident, who is entitled to all the glory, and who is eager to be recognized as such" (284). For Brueggemann, Yahweh's concern for his glory is particularly evident in the narratives regarding his struggle with the Pharoah on behalf of Israel's liberation. There his desire to manifest his power and glory even takes precedence over his desire to free the Israelites from their bondage in Egypt: "Israel's cause is subordinated to Yahweh's self-agenda" (284). This self-agenda involves demonstrating his power so that he may be given the praise and glory he longs for: "Yahweh emerges as more powerful than Egypt, and so is entitled to be honored, worshiped, and obeyed as the true sovereign of the realm" (284).

For Brueggemann, these passages and others demonstrate clearly the priority of God's concern for his own glory. As a result of the power he manifests when delivering the Israelites from the hand of Pharoah and bringing them out of their exile in Babylon, "Yahweh is known to be the real sovereign power in the earth to whom other powers must submit. From these two narrative recitals, Israel generalizes to assert that Yahweh everywhere and always is the true possessor of glory" (284). Brueggemann identifies the same concern in passages from the Psalms in which other gods and peoples from among the nations attribute glory to God: "all the other gods recognize in (or assign to) Yahweh the rightful claim of glory and all the authority, power, honor, and dignity that go with it" (285). Those passages thus "make visible and compelling the rightful claim of Yahweh to glory," as well as "the right to wield authority over all rivals" that is his alone (285).

Brueggemann insists that the same concern for Yahweh's self-regard is behind the repeated allusions to his holiness in the biblical texts, as well as his repeated insistence that human beings regard him as holy. Due to his intolerance of any type of contamination or pollution that might result from human sin, he will withdraw his presence from human beings when they threaten to create disorder through their impurity: "those zones of life that are inhabited by Yahweh in an intense way must be kept pure and uncontaminated" (192). Behind this demand for purity and his commands that his people be holy is ultimately a concern not for them but for himself: "The holiness commands evidence the claims that God's preoccupation is with God's own life, which must remain protected from all profanation. . . . God is also jealously *for God's own self* and takes with dreadful seriousness every threat of profanation to God's own life (cf. Ezek 36:22-23)" (193). According to Brueggemann, this concern for Yahweh's own self and holiness is greater than his concern for Israel and the nations: "In the end, the notion of Yahweh's holiness suggests that Yahweh cares most about Yahweh's own name, reputation, and character—even more than Yahweh cares for Israel. Yahweh does indeed penultimately care about Israel, and so the Holy One comes to save Israel. Some texts—the more decisive texts, I believe, related to this notion of holiness—make clear that finally Yahweh cares most about Yahweh's own self" (290). This concern for his name, identity and reputation derives from "Yahweh's special uncompromising character," which will not allow his name to be debased, profaned, or diminished (290).

Brueggemann sees the repeated allusions in the Hebrew Scriptures to Yahweh's jealousy as reflecting the same concerns. Because his claim to honor is uncompromising, he responds to any challenge to that claim with fury, rage, and destruction:

> Yahweh is a jealous (*qn'*) God. We add the claim of jealousy to those of glory and holiness in our study of Yahweh's profound self-regard. While the terms *jealous* and *jealousy* may be carefully nuanced, their meaning is the one we commonly connect to the English term *jealous*, for they refer to Yahweh's strong emotional response to any affront against Yahweh's prerogative, privilege, ascendancy, or sovereignty. Thus the terms assume Yahweh's singular preoccupation with self, and the expectation that Yahweh will be fully honored and readily obeyed in every circumstance (293).

According to Brueggemann, this concern to be honored and obeyed as sovereign is the driving force behind much of the behavior ascribed to Yahweh in the Hebrew Scriptures. While he seeks the praise and worship of human beings by demonstrating to them his power and glory in different ways, Yahweh also threatens with his "destructive fury" those who would fail to ascribe to him the glory to which he is entitled (294). His self-regard and jealousy lead him to act in "savage propensity" against any who offend, disobey, or affront him:

> Indeed Yahweh's name is Jealous (Exod 34:14)—that is who Yahweh is. In the indignation and emotion that guard Yahweh's peculiar claim to honor, Yahweh is uncompromising. Yahweh acts in fury and rage, sometimes destructively. . . . This aspect of the character of Yahweh admits of no taming or minimalization. It witnesses to Yahweh at the extremes of love and anger. The extremity of Yahweh's passion will be turned against any who affront Yahweh, and Yahweh will act without restraint or discipline. That passion may be turned against Yahweh's own people, if Yahweh's self-regard is sufficiently affronted or Yahweh's claim for sovereignty is excessively disregarded (293-94).

Brueggemann notes that numerous passages from the Hebrew Bible also speak of God being jealous for Israel as his people. He insists, however, that even this jealousy "is in the service of Yahweh's self-regard" (294). The reason that Yahweh is jealous for his people Israel is that they are the people who are known by his name. By protecting and defending them, therefore, he is ultimately protecting and defending his name. Nevertheless, because he values his name and sovereignty above all else, including his people themselves, he will not hesitate to act destructively toward them if it is necessary to do so in order to defend his holy name. On the basis of several texts from the prophetic writings, Brueggemann argues that if Yahweh is forced "to choose between self-regard and engagement on behalf of Israel," he will consistently opt for the former: "Yahweh will characteristically choose self-regard, even if to do so requires destructiveness toward Israel" (295).

Brueggemann concludes his analysis of the biblical allusions to Yahweh's glory, holiness, and jealousy by stressing how all of these concepts revolve around Yahweh's concern that, as sovereign God, he be given the worship, honor, and obedience that are due to him. While Yahweh is committed to Israel, this is because Israel is the means by which he manifests his sovereignty to the world. Therefore his commitment to Israel is in reality a commitment to his own sovereignty, which is what matters to him most:

> The collage of texts concerning the glory, holiness, and jealousy of Yahweh leave one astonished at the largeness and roughness of the claim made for Yahweh, and the power and intensity with which that claim is made. This is a God who will be taken seriously, who will be honored and obeyed, and who will not be mocked. The nations are warned; and Israel is also on notice. Yahweh must be taken in full capacity as sovereign; there is no alternative (295).

Because even the most minimal disregard for Yahweh's honor and glory can provoke him to intense anger, Brueggemann notes the "hovering danger" that at any moment Yahweh may act as a "loose cannon" and vent his rage in destructive ways (280, 296). Even though his people may be confident of his love for them, this unpredictability on the part of Yahweh makes the people's relationship with him a source of constant anxiety for them, since they never know when his rage will erupt (282). On this basis, Brueggemann argues that in the Hebrew Bible Yahweh's concern for his own self and his sovereignty is often seen as standing in opposition to his love and compassion for human beings, that is, his pathos: "This self-regard may emerge as unsurprising moral claim, or it may emerge as a kind of wild capriciousness, as sovereignty without principled loyalty. It is this propensity in Yahweh, Yahweh's determination to be taken seriously on Yahweh's own terms, that precludes any final equation of sovereignty with covenantal love or with pathos" (303). While Yahweh undoubtedly loves Israel, therefore, that love often stands in conflict with his love for his own self. For Brueggemann, "Yahweh's self-regard and Yahweh's regard for Israel and the world are in tension with each other" (307).

In fact, Brueggemann even claims to find in several biblical texts the idea that God's steadfast love for Israel is actually not truly a love for Israel but a love for himself and his sovereignty, that is, his self-regard.[27] In these passages, Yahweh's compassion for Israel is "only an inescapable by-product of Yahweh's self-regard," since the reason he saves Israel is ultimately not because he loves Israel but because he wishes to uphold his name and sovereignty, which are linked to Israel: "Yahweh acts, not in the interest of Israel, but in Yahweh's self-regard. . . . The ground for Yahweh's saving activity is completely Yahweh's self-regard" (307). In Brueggemann's words:

> In these texts it is clear that viewed per se, Yahweh has no positive regard for Israel and is not moved by its plight. Nor, for that matter, does Yahweh mind saving Israel, for it is no special inconvenience for Yahweh. Yahweh in effect has no interest in Israel, but Israel is a convenient, ready-at-hand vehicle for the assertion and enactment of Yahweh's self-regard. This is no bad thing for Israel—but it is not the same as "steadfast love," and it ought not to be construed as such. Yahweh has long since been linked to Israel and must continue to act on that basis. But the action of Yahweh is fully, without reservation, for the enhancement of Yahweh (308).

According to Brueggemann's reading of the biblical texts, it was this same concern for himself and his own glory that led Yahweh to choose Israel as his people and enter into a covenant relationship with them. What he sought above all else was a people who would be dedicated to serving and honoring him in the way he desired: "The covenant generated for Yahweh a people who would endlessly seek to obey Yahweh's commands and sing Yahweh's praises, and thus enhance Yahweh's sovereignty" (297). At the same time, however, Brueggemann points to passages that from his perspective affirm that God may choose to terminate the covenant relationship with his people if they do not fulfill faithfully the role he has assigned to them: "Indeed it is the relentless thought of the prophets of Israel that Yahweh may indeed terminate Israel in an exercise of sovereign self-regard. . . . This act of abandonment of the partner by Yahweh is rooted in Yahweh's uncompromising self-regard. . . . Yahweh's self-regard permits—perhaps requires—such termination as a defense of Yahweh's glory, holiness, and jealousy" (297-98). In the end, however, Brueggemann notes that the biblical texts never present Yahweh taking such a step.

Despite the priority he assigns to Yahweh's concern for his own sovereignty in his interpretation of the biblical texts and his claim that this concern often stands in tension with Yahweh's love for human beings, Brueggemann by no means overlooks the stress on Yahweh's concern for social justice, righteousness, and equity that also runs throughout those texts. On the contrary, he regards this concern as lying at the core of Yahweh's being. Brueggemann rightly notes that the biblical texts consistently speak of Yahweh as one who cares deeply for all of his people, but especially those who suffer greatest need: "The justice that is proposed and for which concrete implementation is provided, moreover, is a social practice in which the maintenance, dignity, security, and well-being of every member of the community are guarded in concrete

---

27. These texts are Exod 34:6-7, Num 14:11-12, 19-21, and Ezek 20:41-44; 36:22-32; 39:25-29.

ways" (189). According to Brueggemann, however, rather than standing in opposition to Yahweh's self-regard, this concern for justice, righteousness, and well-being among human beings is grounded in Yahweh's concern for himself and is an expression of that concern:

> The substance of that righteousness is the well-being of the world, so that when Yahweh's righteousness (Yahweh's governance) is fully established in the world, the results are fruitfulness, prosperity, freedom, justice, peace, security, and well-being (*shalôm*). Because Yahweh in righteousness wills good for creation, there is a complete convergence of Yahweh's self-regard and Yahweh's commitment to Israel and to creation (303).

While for Brueggemann Yahweh's concern for himself and his concern for social justice and human well-being converge, this does not mean that they are equally important or constitute one and the same thing. Ultimately, Brueggemann insists that Yahweh's concern for justice and well-being among his people is subordinate to his concern that the people ascribe to him the glory and honor that are due to him and fulfill properly their role of enhancing his sovereignty. Pointing to Isa 45:21-25, where God invites people of all nations to turn to him to be saved before adding: "To me every knee shall bow, every tongue shall swear," Brueggemann writes:

> Yahweh's righteousness is engaged in the work of well-being. Israel has benefited from this gift of Yahweh's righteousness, and the nations are invited to participate in the same. But neither Israel nor the nations can receive such transformative activity unless they are among those who bend the knee and swear with the tongue to the sovereignty of Yahweh (306).

Although Brueggemann's claim that Yahweh's concern for justice, righteousness, and well-being in the world is secondary in relation to his concern for his own reputation, sovereignty, and glory may seem to set these two concerns at odds with one another, in reality such is not the case. The reason for this is that, in Brueggemann's thought, even though Yahweh wants there to be justice, righteousness, and well-being in the world, ultimately he wants these things *for his own sake*. According to this logic, the well-being of human beings is not an end in itself but a means toward another end, namely, allowing Yahweh to be content, satisfied, and at rest as he contemplates the good creation he has made for himself and receives the praise, honor, and obedience of those who inhabit it. Any disturbance in that order upsets and displeases him because it deprives him of the peace, worship, and glory that he desires above all else. Similar to the manner in which the primordial god Apsu in the *Enuma Elish* is angered when the lesser gods will not let him rest and be at peace, apparently Yahweh becomes upset when the practice of injustice and oppression provokes discord and disorder in the world he has created and thereby undermines his sovereignty. While Brueggemann never goes so far as to claim that the reason that Yahweh cares for the poor and oppressed is that their suffering and cries of pain are bothersome to him and prevent him from enjoying the worship and praises being offered to him by others without being disturbed, one might argue that such a conclusion is by no means incompatible with his portrayal of the God of Israel and may even be regarded as following logically from it.

From Brueggemann's perspective, therefore, even though Yahweh cares deeply about human beings, what he cares about even more is the honor, praise, and obedience that they owe to him. In fact, it was for the purpose of receiving these things from human beings that he created them and subsequently chose Israel as his people. Because he cares for himself above all else, what concerns him is not the effect that human behavior has upon human beings themselves, but rather the effect that their behavior has *on him*. For that reason, if human beings fail to practice justice and righteousness and instead oppress one another, what upsets God the most is not the harm that such behavior does to human beings themselves but rather the fact that it deprives him of the glory, praise, and honor that he desires above all else.

All of these assertions of Brueggemann, therefore, provide the basis for his claim that as the God of Israel Yahweh practices "the way of 'being god' that was everywhere available in the ancient Near East" by imposing on human beings the order he desires and conducting his life in the same way as the other gods known to us from antiquity (283). While there are certain traits and characteristics that distinguish the God of Israel from the gods of other nations, in essence he behaves in the same way that they do and for the same reasons, namely, that he is concerned for himself, his self-regard, and his own honor, holiness, and glory. Like those gods, his relation with human beings is based on the principle of *do ut des*: he will grant human beings his blessings and give them what they want and need, but only on the condition that they serve and obey him, acknowledge his lordship over their lives, and give him the reverence, respect, and praise that he desires as an end in itself.

Many scholars of the Hebrew Bible or Old Testament, of course, would take issue with numerous aspects of Brueggemann's reading of the biblical texts. For the most part, however, the same assumptions made by Brueggemann can be found in the work of biblical scholars and theologians in general. Brueggemann merely makes explicit a concept of God that other biblical scholars and interpreters take for granted. In the minds of these scholars and interpreters, the God of the Hebrew Bible was never fully depaganized but instead was thought to retain many of the same fundamental traits that were believed to be characteristic of the gods of the other nations of antiquity. What we shall see throughout the remainder of the present work, however, is that the God of whom biblical scholars and interpreters speak today is no longer the depaganized God of the Hebrew Scriptures but a repaganized God who has been read back into those Scriptures for centuries.

CHAPTER 2

THE GOD WHO BEGAN WITH AN END

The question of what God wanted when he created the world is never addressed explicitly in the Hebrew Bible. The biblical texts clearly presuppose, however, that he wanted *something*. The reason for this is that they present the creation of the world as an act of God's free and sovereign will. Because God is not seen as depending on the created order in any way and is never said to have been compelled or forced by anything or anyone to create what he did, it is clear that he was not thought to have done so in order to satisfy some type of personal need. If he had freely chosen to create the world and all that is in it and had not done so out of any type of necessity or compulsion that was either external or internal to him, therefore, he must have done so for a reason. Even though the biblical texts never state precisely what that reason was, by asking the right questions and examining carefully certain ideas that are implied and presupposed in those texts, we can discern in broad terms how those who composed and read them would have answered the question of what God wanted when he created the world.

CREATION AND GOD'S SOVEREIGNTY

The creation account in Genesis 1 opens with the simple affirmation that in the beginning God created the heavens and the earth, and that the earth was without form and void or empty, covered by darkness (Gen 1:1-2). Many contemporary translations of the Hebrew text add the word "when" after the initial phrase "in the beginning" so as to reflect more clearly the idea present in the Hebrew, namely, that the earth existed in that condition "in the beginning, *when* God created the heavens and the earth." On the basis of this idea, biblical scholars often claim that the opening verses of Genesis do not speak of God creating the world out of nothing (*creatio ex nihilo*), contrary to many traditional interpretations of these verses.[1]

It must be recognized, however, that the Hebrew phrasing in this first verse of Genesis is ambiguous. While it can be understood in the sense that the earth *already* existed in that condition when God began to create or fashion it together with the heavens, the Hebrew text can also be understood as implying that when God began to create the earth together with the heavens, he originally made the earth to be formless, void, and covered with darkness.

---

1. On this discussion, see especially John Day, *From Creation to Abraham: Further Studies in Genesis 1–11* (London: T & T Clark, 2022), 1-4.

This is, in fact, the way in which the earliest interpretation of these verses known to us understands them, namely, the interpretation of the translators of the Septuagint (LXX), the Greek translation of the Hebrew Scriptures that was begun in the third century BCE. There the opening verse of the passage reads: "In the beginning God made the heaven and the earth." In the Greek text, this affirmation is also a separate sentence from the sentence that immediately follows: "But the earth was invisible and unformed, and darkness was over the face of the abyss" (Gen 1:2 LXX).

Whether or not those who heard and read the opening words of the Genesis account in the Second Temple period would have understood them as implying that God created the world out of nothing, there is nothing in the text that would have suggested to them that God had not been free to create or fashion the world in whatever way he desired. Even if they did read the text as implying that God had fashioned the heavens and the earth out of some preexistent matter or substance, they would probably have seen this preexistent matter or substance as having had its source in God himself as its originator rather than having existed independently of him for as long as he had himself existed. The reason for this is that both in the Genesis account and elsewhere throughout the Hebrew Scriptures, God is consistently portrayed as having full control over the heavens and the earth and all that exists. Just as he can create, so also can he destroy. As we noted in Chapter 1, the God of the Hebrew Bible is not viewed as being subject to the created order or as depending on it in any way. He is never said to emerge from some type of preexistent matter or substance in the way that the gods of Babylon, Greece, and other nations were believed to have done, nor is he ever understood to have his source or origin in anything that existed prior to him. In biblical thought, therefore, it was God who had defined the world rather than being defined by it in some way. For the same reason, the created order was not believed to have been defined by any power or force independent of God or to have defined itself on its own. Rather, God alone was thought to have defined everything in the created order in the way he thought best.

Undoubtedly, certain passages from the Genesis account and other writings in the Hebrew Bible and in Second Temple Jewish literature seem to convey the idea that there were other beings already in existence alongside God when he created the heavens and the earth.[2] While some of these beings are called gods, others are described as existing in the form of angels or as evil spirits opposed to God. These other beings, however, would almost certainly have been thought to have been created by God either before he created the heavens and the earth or at the same time that he created everything else. In any case, these beings are consistently presented as being inferior to God and subject to him. At no time is it ever said or suggested that any of them have some power or authority over God or that his will is subject to theirs in any way. If any of these beings were believed to have participated in the creation

---

2. See especially Gen 1:26; 3:22; Ps 82:1; 86:8; 95:3.

of the world and human beings, as Gen 1:26 may imply ("Let us make man in our image, after our likeness"), they would have been thought to have done so in an auxiliary role to God at his command and initiative.

Although the biblical texts never state explicitly that God created the world in accordance with some type of design or plan that he had conceived ahead of time, they clearly presuppose such an idea. God would hardly have been thought to have created and fashioned the world as he did without having first contemplated what he wanted that world to look like. This design or plan would also have been understood to be God's own rather than having its source in someone or something else.

Because in biblical thought the world as it exists was both designed and created by God, it must also be seen as existing separately from him. God may be present throughout his creation, yet that creation is not thought to form part of God's being and is not an extension of God. The same is true of the people and things that are found in the world. None of them can be identified or equated with God in any sense.

The biblical texts never discuss the question of the origin of God. They do, however, seem to assume that he has no beginning. In Ps 93:2, for example, the Psalmist tells God: "Your throne is established from of old; you are from everlasting." A number of passages use the phrase "from everlasting to everlasting" (*me'olam, 'ad-'olam* or some variant) in connection with God, thereby implying that he not only exists from time immemorial but will also continue to exist forever into the future: "Before the mountains were brought forth, or ever you had formed the earth and the world, from everlasting to everlasting you are God" (Ps 90:2).[3] Other passages from the Hebrew Scriptures speak in similar terms.[4]

All of these ideas reflect the conviction that the God who created all that exists is fully sovereign over everything he created. This sovereignty includes several aspects. Chief among these is God's omnipotence. The biblical texts and Second Temple Jewish writings in general suppose that God is able to do all things and that nothing is impossible for him.[5] While the terminology of omnipotence does not appear explicitly in the Hebrew Bible in relation to God, it is significant that the Septuagint repeatedly refers to God as *pantokratōr*, that is, the "almighty one" or the one "powerful to do all things." If God created all that exists simply with his word, it follows that he possesses the ability to alter that creation and intervene in it in any way he sees fit. Furthermore, if he existed prior to that creation and independently of it, he can exist without it and therefore does not depend on it or have need of it in any way.

The God of the Hebrew Scriptures is sovereign not only in the sense that he has full power over the created order and does not need anything that he

---

3. See also Ps 41:13; 103:17; 106:48; 1 Chr 16:36; Neh 9:5.

4. See, for example, Gen 21:33; Isa 40:28.

5. In the Hebrew Bible, see, for example, Gen 18:14; Job 42:2; Ps 115:3; 135:6; Jer 32:17, 27; Dan 4:35.

has created in order to exist, but also in the sense that everything that he has created belongs to him. What he has created is *his*. This includes not only the world as a whole but all of the things and living beings that are *in* the world as well. In fact, because all people and things are understood as belonging to God as their sovereign creator, there was nothing that anyone might give to him that was not already his own. Furthermore, because everything God has created is his own, he can do whatever he wants with his creation. Just as he fashioned it in the way he desired from the beginning, he can continue to fashion and shape it as he desires in the present and future.

Strictly speaking, however, it would not be accurate or correct to affirm that, as the creator of the world and all that it contains, the God of the Hebrew Bible has the *right* to do whatever he wishes with his creation.[6] Such a claim must be seen as reflecting an idea that is foreign to the biblical texts. This is because it presupposes that there is some principle of what is just and right that is superior to God and grants him certain rights, such as the right to rule over creation or the right to be worshiped and obeyed by those whom he has created. In biblical thought, God is not subject to any type of laws or rules that govern what he can or must do or that prohibit him from carrying out whatever he desires and intends. He does not need to justify his actions to anyone or anything that stands above him. For that reason, he cannot be said to have rights, and much less to be within his rights or alternatively to exceed his rights when he does certain things or acts in certain ways.

For the same reason, God does not need to justify his actions to human beings, who might look to some law or principle that is above God in order to judge whether he is acting in conformity with that law or principle and on that basis determine whether he is acting properly or justly. Undoubtedly, in biblical thought there are certain laws and norms that God himself has established and chooses to respect, just as he expects those whom he has created to respect them. Human beings may therefore make certain appeals to God on the basis of those laws and norms and even question whether God himself is actually respecting them as well, yet their basis for doing so is not that God is subject to such laws and principles by nature but that he is the one who has established them.

All of these ideas clearly distinguish the God of Israel's Scriptures from the type of pagan gods described in the belief systems of other peoples from antiquity known to us. None of those gods was conceived of as having the type of sovereignty over the world that is attributed to the God of Israel in the Hebrew Scriptures.

---

6. Jack Cottrell, for example, claims to find such an idea in the biblical texts: "God's authority, his legitimate and deserved right to absolute Lordship, is his by virtue of creation. God has the right to do with his creation whatever he wishes because he owns it; and he owns it because he created it. . . . [T]he Creator—and the Creator alone—has both the power and the right to rule in whatever way he desires" (*What the Bible Says about God the Ruler*, vol. 2 of *The Doctrine of God*, Eugene, OR: Wipf and Stock, 2000, 270).

CREATION AND GOD'S GOODNESS

In the creation account that appears in Gen 1:1–2:4, no point is stressed as strongly as the idea that everything that God made was good. At the end of each of the six days of creation, God is presented as looking upon all that he has made and concluding that it is good. On the final day, after he has created human beings, he even observes that all that he has created is "exceedingly good" (Gen 1:31). Both that passage and the one that follows in Gen 2:5-25 describe a paradisiacal world full of beautiful things that bring great pleasure to human beings. God places the human beings he has created in a garden, where they will be able to find delight in the trees that are "pleasant to the sight and good for food," and also pronounces a blessing upon them (1:22, 28; 2:9). At the same time, nothing that is considered *not* to be good is said to exist, other than the initial solitude of the man whom God had created (2:18). God quickly resolves that problem, however, by forming from one of his ribs the first woman as his partner (2:21-23). All of these things convey the idea that God intended for the human beings he had created to be happy and find companionship, friendship, affection, and intimacy as well.

The repeated insistence that everything that God created was good would have been understood as implying a number of related ideas. Above all, it would have led to the same conclusion about God himself, namely, that God is good in every way and that there is nothing bad or evil about God. If all that God had made was good, it also followed that God had desired nothing but what is good for his good creation from the very beginning. Before he had created the world, he must have envisioned that creation as something that would be "exceedingly good" and thus would be thought to have designed it in the best way possible. If throughout the first chapter of Genesis God is presented as being pleased that all the things that he has created are good, this can only be because he is himself good and desires only what is good for his creation.

It is also important to stress that the repeated affirmation that everything that God created was good communicates the idea that it was good *in itself*. According to this idea, that goodness does not exist solely in relation to some greater end or objective. Neither the world nor human beings are viewed as having been created to serve some function or end related to God or anything else beyond or above them, such as God's own enjoyment or praise. Contrary to what we find in the *Enuma Elish*, for example, neither in the Genesis account nor elsewhere in the Hebrew Scriptures are human beings ever said to have been created for the purpose of serving God or satisfying some need or desire on his part concerning himself and his own well-being or happiness. The only commands that God gives the first human beings in Genesis 1–2 are to be fruitful and multiply, to fill and subdue the earth and exercise dominion over it, and to refrain from eating certain things (Gen 1:28-30; 2:16-17). In Gen 2:15, it is also said that God put the man he had created in the garden "to till it and keep it," yet this seems to be an activity that the man is to enjoy rather than something that causes him pain and suffering, as it will later on (3:17-19). Nowhere does God demand that the human beings he has created present him with gifts and sacrifices, or even that they praise and worship him, and nothing in the Genesis account suggests that they initially did such things or were expected to do them. This same vision of the creation appears in Psalm 8, in which the Psalmist admires the glory and majesty of all that God has created, including human beings themselves, and repeats the idea that God has placed the human beings he created over everything he has made.

By presenting God in these terms, in fact, the Genesis account conveys the idea that what God has created is *for human beings and their enjoyment* rather than constituting something that responds to some personal end or need found in God himself. As already noted above, in biblical thought God does not need anything that he has created or depend on it in any way. If he subjects all the things he has created to human beings, he must have created those things *for their sake* rather than his own. And because all of those things are good, he must have wanted only good things for those human beings from the start.

At the same time, given that all the things that God has created are good, God's command to human beings to subdue all of those things and exercise dominion over them carries implicitly within it the idea that they are to do these things *for good* and *in a good way*. In this context, the idea of bringing other things and beings into subjection and exercising dominion over them cannot be understood in terms of abusing or misusing them, doing harm to them, or relating to them in ways that are *not* good either for those things and beings themselves or for the human beings that have dominion over them. In other words, as they relate to the things and beings that God has placed under them, human beings are to see and treat them as good and thus care for them in the way that God intended so that they *continue* to be good. Human beings are also to see themselves and one another as good and therefore are to treat themselves and one another as good as well, in the same way that God does.

The Genesis account thus implies that, even though human beings are created as good alongside many other things and beings, unlike those other things and beings, God does not regard human beings as a means to a greater end but *as an end in themselves*. By placing all things under them and also surrounding them with good and pleasant things in the way that the Genesis account describes, God is simply seeking their happiness and well-being as an end in itself. He does not ask anything of them for himself but only asks of them what is for their own well-being and happiness. In fact, according to Gen 1:28, the first thing that God does after he creates the man and woman is not to give them commands but to *bless* them (cf. 5:2). This can be seen as God's primary will or desire for them: that they be blessed. If God treats human beings as ends in themselves, therefore, by definition he is seeking something good *for them* rather than attempting to obtain or receive something from them solely for himself.

Although the Genesis narrative does not affirm explicitly that God was pleased or content with all that he created, the repeated affirmation that when he observed the things that he had created he considered them good clearly implies such an idea. If that is the case, then God would be said to derive enjoyment from his creation. Given that in biblical thought God does not experience any type of need in the way that the beings he created do, it would seem inappropriate to speak of God enjoying well-being or wholeness in the way that human beings may do. By nature, God is always well and whole, and nothing can change or affect this. The biblical texts, however, do imply that God experiences emotions, including happiness and contentment when things are well in his creation and those whom he has created enjoy well-being.

The affirmation that God considered all that he had made to be good thus implies not only that he desired that everything that he had created experience and enjoy that goodness but also that when that happens he is pleased and content. In that case, when human beings enjoyed happiness and well-being, together with all of the other living beings he had created, God would also be happy and rejoice. The idea that God enjoyed his creation and also wished to enjoy spending time in the presence of human beings seems to be suggested in Gen 3:8-9, which describes "the sound of the Lord God walking in the garden at the time of the evening breeze" and then presents him calling out to the man to ask where he was. These verses appear to present God not only deriving pleasure from the garden and the calm evening breeze but also seeking out the company of the human beings he had created in order to spend time with them in the garden, although this is not stated explicitly. Other verses in the first three chapters, of course, also speak of God talking with the man and woman, giving the impression that there was some type of ongoing or regular conversation between God and the man and woman.

As noted briefly above, the only passage in the first two chapters of Genesis in which God is presented as observing something that does *not* please him appears in Gen 2:18, where God observes that "it is not good that man should be alone." Here God notices that the man he has created is not yet whole or complete in the way he desires. He thus realizes that he must do something else to give the man the wholeness that he desires for him. Just as God can be pleased with the goodness of what he has created, he can also be displeased when he sees that something good is lacking in that creation. This verse portrays God as experiencing displeasure or discontent because the man has no one else like him to share his life with or enjoy as a partner. The fact that God is said to have created a woman for the man clearly conveys the idea that God did not want the man to feel lonely or suffer solitude.

The affirmation in Gen 2:18 that God made the woman to be the man's helper has often been seen as implying some type of subordinate role for the woman in relation to the man, as if she were merely to serve him. Such an interpretation is problematic for several reasons. First, it takes the verse out of context. What God is seeking when he creates the woman from the man's rib is not that the man have someone to serve his needs but merely that he not be alone or lonely. His intention is to provide the man with someone who can keep him company. The passage nowhere speaks of the woman serving the man in any way. Furthermore, if God's purpose is that the man not be alone, then he would be concerned not only that the man have someone to enjoy his company but also that the woman enjoy the company of the man. The man would hardly derive joy from the company of the woman if she did not also enjoy his company and did not desire to spend time with him. Second, as many interpreters have noted, the idea that God forms the woman from the man's rib suggests some type of unity and equality with him. She is to be by his side rather than being subject to him or over him. Third, to refer to someone as another person's helper is not necessarily to place that person in a subordinate role. The same Hebrew noun is repeatedly used throughout the Hebrew Bible to refer to God as the helper of human beings, and in no way does he do so from a position of inferiority.[7] On the contrary, the person who assumes the role of helper is able to do something for another person which that person is incapable of doing for himself or herself. And finally, the verses that speak of the woman as helper would have been read against the background of Gen 1:26-27, where God is said to have made both the man and the woman in his own image.

In any case, what is important in these verses is that *God does not want the human being he has created to be alone or suffer solitude*, and that when he observes that happening, he acts to remedy the situation. This action expresses unequivocally a concern for the happiness of the human beings God has created as an end in itself, as well as a desire that those human beings not suffer any type of need. At the same time, these verses imply that God is unhappy when he sees human beings lacking something they need to enjoy life and well-being and that he is committed to providing for them whatever they lack. The passage clearly conveys the idea that God does these things *for their sake* and not merely for his own.

While the Genesis creation account clearly presents God as desiring the happiness and well-being of human beings as an end in itself, however, it also implies that God derives enjoyment and satisfaction when human beings are content and have everything they need to enjoy the good things he has placed under their dominion. In that case, God's happiness is linked to that of the living beings he has created, including especially human beings. When they are happy and are able to rejoice in the good things he has given them, God himself will be happy and rejoice. Yet because as sovereign creator God has made all things in accordance with his will and design, if God's happiness is linked to that of human beings, it can only be because *God himself has determined that it should be so*. In other words, God himself has chosen to link his own happiness to that of the human beings he has created.

---

7. See, for example, Exod 18:4; Deut 33:7, 26, 29; Ps 33:20; 70:5; 115:9-11; 121:1-2; 124:8; 146:5.

To make such an assertion is not, however, to regard the happiness and well-being of human beings solely as a means to God's own happiness and not as an end in itself. Once the happiness of human beings and that of God are inseparably linked to one another, one cannot take place without the other. God cannot seek and desire his own happiness without seeking and desiring the happiness of human beings. God's happiness and human happiness are not two separate ends that might be sought independently of one another but constitute one and the same end. In addition, this end is *an end in itself* rather than a means toward another end.

For the same reason, even if God is said to have created all that he did not only for the enjoyment of human beings but also for his own enjoyment, this cannot be regarded as a selfish or self-centered act on God's part. Because he has linked his own happiness to that of human beings, God cannot be concerned with his own self without also being concerned for them. Even though God certainly desires his own happiness, his happiness has become inseparable from that of the human beings he has created. This means that, by definition, once God has linked his own happiness to that of human beings, it is impossible for God to act selfishly or concern himself only with his own desires. God cannot enjoy the good world he has created if the creatures in that world are not happy and content as well, enjoying the good things he has shared with them. On the contrary, he will be displeased at their unhappiness, just as he was displeased when he saw that the man he had created was alone and lacked companionship. God cannot pursue his own happiness and contentment by doing anything that does not at the same time promote the happiness and contentment of his creatures. He cannot abuse or mistreat them or use them selfishly for his own ends because that would undermine or destroy their happiness as well as his own, which is inseparably linked to theirs.

For that reason, even though the God of the Hebrew Bible can be said to have created the world for his own enjoyment, in no way does the biblical narrative view such an action as egotistical or self-serving on his part. He was not seeking to be entertained or amused by what he had created, precisely because he had linked his own happiness to that of his creatures so as to make their happiness inseparable from his own. In contrast, those who seek to be entertained or amused by others are generally understood to be seeking something for themselves rather than for others. What concerns them is their own amusement rather than the well-being of those who entertain and amuse them as an end in itself. For that reason, those who merely wish to be amused and entertained by others may even take pleasure at seeing them suffer or experience pain and difficulties. Such is by no means the case with the God of the Hebrew Bible. What he seeks from the world and from human beings is not to be entertained or amused, as if he wished to bring into existence something such as a zoo or circus. Rather, he seeks the well-being of all so that all may rejoice and be content and so that he may rejoice and be content with them, because their happiness and his own are one and the same.

It is important to add, however, that by linking the happiness of the human beings he has created to his own, God has also linked the happiness of each human being to that of every other human being. If some human beings act in ways that make others unhappy, God will not be happy, nor will those human beings be able to be happy in the way God desires. The reason for this is not simply that God will be displeased with them and treat them with displeasure, but that the well-being of each individual depends on the well-being of others. If everything that God has created is good, as the Genesis creation account stresses, then if something in that creation ceases to be good, the creation itself as a whole loses part of its goodness and is no longer entirely good. If there is something that is not good, it can no longer be said that *everything* is good. And if the beings that God has created are to enjoy all of the good he desires for them, then it is necessary for all of those beings to experience the well-being God desires for all. If any of them do not experience that well-being, the rest will be affected negatively in some way. For that reason, in biblical thought human beings must seek the well-being of others together with their own if they are truly to attain that well-being in its fullness as God desires. Once they isolate their own well-being and happiness from the well-being and happiness of others, they undermine not only the well-being and happiness of others but their own as well.

To some readers, it may seem that many of the ideas just stated go far beyond what we find in the Genesis account. I would argue, however, that all of these ideas are implicit in that account and follow logically from it. To affirm that everything that God made was good is to claim that nothing that he made was bad. It also involves making numerous assumptions. To draw out those logical conclusions and assumptions and make them explicit, therefore, is not to read ideas *into* the biblical text but to read them *out* of the text.

A number of the ideas just considered, in fact, are stated explicitly elsewhere in the Hebrew Bible. Numerous passages, for example, affirm that everything in the world as well as the world itself belong to God as his own because he is the one who created all that exists. "The earth is the LORD's and all that is in it, the world, and those who live in it; for he has founded it on the seas, and established it on the rivers" (Ps 24:1-2). "The heavens are yours, the earth also is yours; the world and all that is in it—you have founded them" (Ps 89:11). "In his hand are the depths of the earth; the heights of the mountains are his also. The sea is his, for he made it, and the dry land, which his hands have formed" (Ps 95:4-5; cf. 1 Chr 29:11-14; Ps 115:6). The idea that what God has made brings him happiness and joy is affirmed explicitly in Ps 104:31, which speaks of God rejoicing in his works. That idea is suggested as well in Prov 8:22-31, in which God's wisdom is personified and said to have been present with God before he created the heavens and the earth, acting alongside him "like a master worker" to guide him as he set everything in order. This passage describes wisdom as God's delight, "rejoicing before him always, rejoicing in his inhabited world and delighting in the human race"

(vv. 30-31). The author of Psalm 8 not only recalls that God has given human beings dominion over all that he has created but also marvels that God is mindful of human beings and cares for them in the way that he does (vv. 3-8). These and other passages from the Hebrew Bible, therefore, draw out from the Genesis creation account ideas that are implicit in the narrative.

There is, however, one other important idea that seems to be implied by the biblical affirmation that everything that God created was good. If all that God did and made was good at the time of creation, when everything still depended solely on what God had chosen to do and not what anyone else would do, it would seem to follow logically that everything that God would *continue* to do and make would *also* be good. If from the beginning, when all was fully under his control alone, God's desire was *only for good* and his intention was that *everything be good*, there is no reason to think that God's desire and intention would ever come to change. It would seem illogical for a God who desired only what was good suddenly to *cease* to desire only what was good. Furthermore, to affirm that after he has created a world in which everything is good and nothing is bad God will *continue* to do and seek only what is good and not what is bad would seem to lead to the conclusion that everything that God will do in the future after creating the world must also be considered good.

Given the many terrible things that God is said to do and command in other parts of the Hebrew Bible, at first glance such an affirmation may seem to be entirely implausible and even contrary to biblical thought. Unlike the other assumptions and logical conclusions considered in this section, the idea that all that God has done and will continue to do is good does not necessarily follow implicitly from the biblical text itself, since it is possible that a God who initially desired and made only what is good later came to desire and make what is *not* good of his own free will. Most interpreters would maintain that much of what God is said to do elsewhere in the Hebrew Bible is *not* good, and certainly there is a sense in which that is true. It can nevertheless be asked, however, if there is also a sense in which it *is* true that the biblical texts continue to see everything that God does after creating the world as good in some way. That question can only be addressed after we have looked at the biblical texts as a whole and therefore must be considered further on in this study.

CREATION AND GOD'S LOVE

While God's desire for good is evident throughout the creation account in Genesis, nowhere in that account is God explicitly said to love the world he has created or the human beings under whose dominion he places his creation. Nevertheless, when combined with the idea that all that God created was good, the belief that God was in need of nothing and had created all people and things simply because he had freely chosen to do so would have inevitably led readers of that account to conclude that God's creation of the world and human beings was an act of love. In order to speak of God's love, however, it is important to define the manner in which that term is to be understood.

Among most English speakers, love is associated particularly with a sentiment and is understood to involve the expression of affection. To love is to experience a certain feeling or emotion in relation to someone else and to treat that person with kindness, warmth, and affection. It often involves physical contact, such as embraces and caresses. The Genesis account of creation does not explicitly speak of God loving human beings in these ways. It never mentions any feelings or sentiments experienced by God, although as just noted above, that account does imply that God was pleased when he contemplated the goodness of his creation. Similarly, because the God of the Hebrew Bible is a spiritual being, he does not manifest his love and affection through physical contact in the way that human beings do.

Several things in the Genesis creation narrative, however, do suggest a desire on God's part for some type of communion, fellowship, or friendship with the human beings he creates. His concern that the man not be alone but have a partner implies that God values companionship as something good, important, and desirable. The female companion he makes for the man can also be seen as an expression of God's love for him. The fact that God converses with the man, places him in a garden filled with delightful things, and gives him the task of assigning a name to each of the animals alongside which he will live in the world also suggests the image of a God who wishes to share good things with others and desires fellowship and friendship with human beings. As noted above, this same image is reflected in Gen 3:8-9, where God is presented as walking in the garden in the evening breeze and seeking out the man and woman he had created, presumably to enjoy their company. One can hardly imagine gods such as Marduk, Zeus, or Poseidon wishing to go for a pleasant evening stroll with human beings in a luscious garden, enjoying their companionship as they walk amicably alongside one another.

These implicit allusions to the idea of companionship and fellowship are perhaps the closest that the Genesis account comes to suggesting some type of purpose or reason for God's creation of the world and human beings. The notion that God does not want the human beings he has created to live in isolation or solitude can be seen as implying that they are designed to live in communion not only with one another but with God as well. If all of the beings and things that God has created are good in themselves, they must also have been designed and intended to be good in relation to one another. They are to complement one another in the way that the woman and the man are to do. In a sense, however, they also complement God. The fact that God is presented as continuing to relate closely to all of the people and things that he has created after he fashions them indicates that he is a God who seeks to be involved in the lives of the beings that form part of his good creation.

While in some places the Genesis narrative suggests that God loves human beings in the sense of feeling warmth and affection for them and seeking some type of fellowship with them, that narrative leaves no doubt that

God loves the human beings he created in the sense of being committed to filling their lives with good things. He provides for their needs, giving them food and companionship and placing under their dominion all of the good things he has made. Rather than consisting merely of sentiments or expressions of affection, therefore, God's love takes the form of doing everything in his power to make it possible for the human beings he has created to enjoy true happiness and well-being.

When referring to God's love for human beings, English versions of the Bible generally use the word "love" to translate two different Hebrew nouns, *ḥesed* and *'ahabah*, the second of which is derived from the verb *'ahab*. While for the most part both of these terms convey the same basic meaning as the word "love" in English, they tend to focus on concrete actions rather than sentiments alone. Thus, for example, when the verb *'ahab* is used to command the people of Israel to love God with all their heart, soul, and strength in Deut 6:4, the idea is not merely that they are to experience some favorable sentiment toward God but that they are to dedicate themselves actively to doing all that he desires and commands. In most English versions of the Bible, the noun *ḥesed* is translated as lovingkindness or steadfast love. When used in relation to God, *ḥesed* particularly stresses the unconditional nature of God's love, that is, his faithfulness to those whom he loves and the enduring character of that love. It is a love that is constant, reliable, and unending.

Although the Genesis account of creation does not use the vocabulary of love to describe the way in which God relates to the world and the living beings he has created, numerous other passages in the Hebrew Bible do speak explicitly of God's love for his creation. Most of these passages are found in the book of Psalms. The idea that God's *ḥesed* or steadfast love extends throughout all of his creation is repeated a number of times. "The earth is full of the steadfast love of the LORD" (Ps 33:5; cf. 119:64). "For your steadfast love is as high as the heavens; your faithfulness extends to the clouds" (Ps 57:10). In Ps 136:4-9, the Psalmist recounts one by one God's wondrous works in creation and after mentioning each of them adds: "for his steadfast love endures forever." A portion of Psalm 36 especially extols God's *ḥesed* and equates it with his justice and righteousness, that is, his saving activity:

> Your steadfast love, O LORD, reaches up to the heavens, your faithfulness to the clouds. Your righteousness is like the mountains of God, your judgments are like the great deep; you save humans and animals alike, O LORD. How precious is your steadfast love, O God! All people may take refuge in the shadow of your wings. They feast on the abundance of your house, and you give them drink from the river of your delights. For the fountain of life is with you; in your light we see light. O continue to grant your steadfast love to those who know you, and your salvation to the upright of heart! (vv. 5-10).

While all that God has created is said to manifest God's love, that love is also associated with everything that God continues to do in relation to his creatures. God is said to inspire awe and wonder at the way he loves and cares for his creation and fills it with abundance and joy.[8] The author of Psalm 107 sees God's steadfast love manifested in "his wonderful works to humankind; for he satisfies those who are thirsty and fills those who are hungry with good things" (vv. 8-9). According to Psalm 139, God continues to be involved in the formation of each human being from the moment of conception: "For it was you who formed my inward parts; you knit me together in my mother's womb. I praise you, for I am fearfully and wonderfully made" (vv. 13-14). Psalm 104 dedicates over thirty verses to describing how God remains active in various ways throughout creation: he cares for everything he has made, provides animals and human beings with food, and enables their hearts to be filled with gladness. Perhaps the most explicit affirmation of God's constant love for all peoples of the earth is found in a passage from the Wisdom of Solomon, which probably dates to the first century BCE:

> But you are merciful to all, for you are able to do all things, and you overlook people's sins to bring them to repentance. For you love all the things that exist and detest none of the things that you have made, for you would not have made anything if you had hated it. How could anything have endured if you had not willed it? Or how could anything not called forth by you have been preserved? You spare all things because they are yours, O Lord, you who love the living (Wis 11:23-26).

Many of the Psalms speak not only of the immensity of God's love for his creation but also of the tremendous and unbridled joy which that love inspires in all who experience it. The goodness and steadfast love that God manifests for his creation are described as evoking expressions of admiration, wonder, and praise, not only in human beings but also in God's works themselves. Often these works are personified so as to be presented as singing God's praises and admiring his glory and power as if they were living beings. "The heavens declare the glory of God, and the firmament proclaims the work of his hands. . . . Their voice goes out through all the earth, and their words reach to the end of the world" (Ps 19:1, 4). "The heavens proclaim his righteousness, and all the peoples look upon his glory" (Ps 97:6). Of course, human beings are also said to respond in the same way to God's marvelous works throughout creation, including not only all the nations but their kings as well: "There is none like you among the gods, O Lord, and there are no works like yours. All the nations you have made will come and bow down before you, O Lord, and will glorify your name. For you are great and do wondrous things; you alone are God" (Ps 86:8-10). "All the kings of the earth will praise you, O Lord, when they have heard the words of your mouth. They will sing of the ways of the Lord, for great is the glory of the Lord" (Ps 138:4-5). "They will celebrate the fame of your abundant goodness, and will sing aloud of your righteousness. The Lord is gracious and merciful, slow to

---

8. See Ps 65:5-13; 111:2-7; 146:5-7; 147:7-9.

anger and abounding in steadfast love. The LORD is good to all, and extends his compassion over all that he has made" (Ps 145:7-9).

In passages such as these, the response of praise and admiration that God's works throughout creation are said to evoke is presented as something that occurs spontaneously and of its own accord. In other passages, however, God's creatures exhort one another to join together with them in order to sing God's praises and glorify him. While Psalm 96 in its entirety exemplifies this idea, several verses in particular stand out: "O sing to the LORD a new song; sing to the LORD, all the earth! Sing to the LORD, bless his name; tell of his salvation from day to day! Declare his glory among the nations, his marvelous deeds among all the peoples! . . . Let the heavens be glad, and let the earth rejoice! Let the sea roar, and all that fills it! Let the field be jubilant, and everything in it! Then shall all the trees of the forest sing for joy before the LORD" (vv. 1-3, 11-13; cf. Ps 89:5-16). "Make a joyful noise to God, all the earth! Sing the glory of his name; give to him glorious praise! Say to God, 'How awesome are your deeds! Because of the greatness of your power, your enemies cringe before you. All the earth worships you; they sing praises to you, sing praises to your name'" (Ps 66:1-4). "Make a joyful noise to the LORD, all the earth! Break forth into joyous song and sing praises! . . . Let the rivers clap their hands; let the hills sing together for joy" (Ps 98:4, 8). In each verse of the lengthy canticle attributed to the three young men in the blazing furnace that appears in the deuterocanonical version of Daniel, the many different works of God throughout his creation are told to bless the Lord and "sing praise to him and highly exalt him forever" (Pr Azar 28-65).

In many of the other Psalms, it is human beings who exhort one another to praise God for his steadfast love and kindness. "Praise the LORD, all you nations! Extol him, all you peoples! For great is his steadfast love toward us, and the faithfulness of the LORD endures forever. Praise the LORD!" (Ps 117:1-2). In the context of allusions to the manner in which God comes to the aid of all who are in need and look to him for help, Psalm 107 repeatedly exhorts human beings to "give thanks to the LORD for his steadfast love, for his wonderful works to humankind" (vv. 8, 15, 21, 31). After exhorting all the earth to make a joyful noise to God and worship him with gladness and singing, the author of Psalm 100 recalls that "it is he who made us, and we are his," before concluding: "For the LORD is good; his steadfast love endures forever, and his faithfulness stretches to all generations" (vv. 1-3, 5). The idea that God reigns over all the earth and judges it also serves as a basis for exhorting all peoples throughout the earth and the earth itself to rejoice and sing God's praises.[9] In Psalms 103 and 148, not only are human beings and the works of God's hands throughout the earth called to praise God, but the angels and heavenly host as well (Ps 103:19-22; 148:1-14; cf. Ps 29:1-2).

---

9. See Ps 47:5-9; 95:1-5; 97:1-2; 113:1-9; 145:1-13; cf. Ps 93:1-2; 99:1-5.

God's Love as Unconditional

When considering all of the passages from the Hebrew Bible that speak of God's steadfast love for his creation and the response of love, joy, and praise that his love evokes in his creatures, it is important to note that these passages never speak of any conditions that must be fulfilled in order for human beings and creation as a whole to be loved by God. Nowhere in these passages is God said to love the living beings he has created only if and when they behave in certain ways or give him certain things that he desires for his own sake. Nor is he presented as making any kind of demands upon the living beings he has created and telling them that if they do not fulfill those demands he will withhold his love from them. On the contrary, these passages and others describe a love that is completely *unconditional* on God's part. He seeks the happiness and well-being of all that exists as an end in itself and not because he hopes to receive something in exchange for his love and blessings. In fact, the tone of these passages suggests that there could never be anything that might lead God to *stop* loving all the peoples and creatures he has made. This is how the affirmation that "his steadfast love endures forever" should be understood: his love never ceases or wavers but remains constant and persistent for all time, independently of anything that human beings might do or fail to do. That love is resolute, unfailing, and unshakable.

The type of love attributed to God in these passages is fundamentally different from the type of love that was thought to characterize the pagan gods of antiquity. Those gods were not thought to love human beings unconditionally in the sense of seeking their well-being as an end in itself. Rather, they granted their favors and blessings in exchange for the things they desired to receive from human beings, such as their worship and praise. The idea that such gods might love and care for the natural order and all that it contained, such as the plants and animals and the seas and mountains, was also foreign to most of the ancient worldviews known to us.

For the same reason, in the non-Jewish and extra-biblical texts from antiquity known to us, it is rare for human beings or other living beings and realities in the natural world to be portrayed as breaking out in spontaneous praise and worship for such gods in the way that they do in the passages just considered and as expressing the kind of profound love and sincere affection for them that those beings and realities are said to manifest for God in the biblical texts. While those who worshiped the pagan gods of antiquity often expressed their praise, adulation, affection, and reverence for those gods in an energetic and effusive manner, they generally did so in exchange for the favors and blessings that they hoped to receive from those gods. The logic was that of *do ut des*: they gave the gods the praise and honor they desired in order to receive from them the things they desired for their own sake.

The biblical idea that God's love for human beings is unconditional rules out the possibility that human beings might obtain some type of favor or blessings from God in exchange for their expressions of love, praise, and worship, since God is already fully committed to blessing them and show-ing them his love and favor independently of anything they may do. If God already loves the human beings he has created and wants only good things for them, what more could they hope to obtain from him by means of their praises? Because they can seek or ask for nothing greater than the infinite and unconditional love that is already theirs as a gracious gift from God, by definition they cannot be acting out of self-interest or attempting to obtain something more from God when they praise and worship him. They cannot get God to love them more by praising and glorifying him, nor will he love them any less if they fail to do so. Of course, that love will not always take the form of giving them everything they desire and ask of him, since in his love and sovereignty God may determine that what is best for them is something other than what they desire and ask for. In fact, as we shall see further on, in biblical thought God's love often takes the form of chastisements that are aimed at correcting people and bringing them to live in ways that promote their well-being instead of undermining and destroying it.

In principle, of course, it might still be argued that God bestows his blessings and favors on human beings and his creation in order to obtain the worship, honor, and reverence that he desires for his own sake, even though such an idea is never affirmed explicitly in the biblical texts or even implied there. In that case, however, the God of the Hebrew Bible would be essen-tially no different from the pagan gods of antiquity or the God described by Walter Brueggemann in the previous chapter. His primary concern would be that human beings acknowledge his sovereignty, sing his praises, and ascribe to him glory and honor. While he would no doubt care for human beings and want there to be peace and justice among them, these things would be less important to him than his self-regard and would interest him only to the extent that they contributed to the fulfillment of his own self-interests. Although he might be said to love human beings, this love would be condi-tional upon receiving from them the worship, honor, and praise he desires and demands for his own sake and would quickly turn into wrath and pun-ishment if they withheld these things from him. His relationship to human beings would be defined on the principle of *do ut des*: he would be willing to bless and prosper human beings in the way they wanted, but only in exchange for the worship, submission, and obedience that he wanted from them for himself. In that case, expressions of praise, love, and affection for God such as those found in the Psalms and the other biblical texts just considered would constitute the objective that God sought in all his works, while the blessings he bestowed on his creation and the living beings within it would constitute the means by which he sought to attain that objective.

If such were the case, however, God could not truly be said to love all the people and things he has created in the sense of seeking their happiness and well-being as an end in itself. Instead, he would be using them to obtain what he wanted for his own sake. For the same reason, neither the natural order nor the living beings within it could truly be said to love God in a genuine and disinterested sense. Whatever praise and affection they expressed for him would be an expression of self-interest, aimed at receiving from him what they wanted for their own sake and attempting to stay on his good side so as to avoid his wrath and punishments. In the same way that God would seek to manipulate them for his own ends, they too would seek to manipulate God for their own ends. Rather than brimming with spontaneous joy and enthusiasm in response to God's love and goodness, they would in essence behave as sycophants, pretending outwardly to celebrate his kindness and compassion and rejoice at the manner in which he cares for them while inwardly cowering in fear over the manner in which he might react should they fail to manifest the exuberance he desires and demands to see in them.

While such an interpretation of biblical passages such as those just considered must be considered problematic in light of the apparent spontaneity and sincerity of the expressions of love and adoration for God reflected in them, that interpretation becomes even more problematic when it is remembered that in biblical thought God is able to look inside of human hearts and minds to see what is in them.[10] In this regard, the God of Israel was distinct from the other gods of antiquity. Because God could examine people's hearts and minds and view the thoughts and sentiments present there, he could determine whether or not the worship, praise, and adoration that they expressed for him was sincere or feigned. If they were simply seeking to manipulate him by outward expressions of love and adulation that were not genuine or heartfelt, he would perceive this immediately.

For that reason, if the God of the Hebrew Bible is viewed as desiring the worship and praise of the living beings he created for his own sake and as an end in itself, he cannot be thought to desire the sincere and heartfelt love of those beings at the same time. On the contrary, it would be necessary to claim that it does not matter to God if those who ascribe to him the power, glory, and honor he craves for his own sake do so purely out of self-interest in an insincere manner. Such a God would simply be unconcerned about what people really thought about him and whether they truly cared for him or not, as long as they *told* him that they cared for him and honored him for his greatness and majesty. When they gave him thanks, it would not matter to him whether they were genuinely thankful or appreciated his kindness, as long as they *said* that they did. He would be indifferent to what he actually saw in their hearts and minds as they expressed outward joy and enthusiasm at his goodness and sang exuberantly of his wonders and magnificence. Hypocrisy and mere lip service would be ignored by him as long as those who expressed their love and appreciation for him *appeared* to be sincere as they worshiped and bowed down before him. In fact, if this were all he wanted, God could obtain it by threatening human beings with suffering

---

10. On this idea in the Hebrew Bible, see especially 1 Sam 16:7; 1 Kgs 8:39; 1 Chr 28:9; Ps 7:9; 19:14; 26:2; 44:21; 139:1-4, 23-24; Prov 17:3; 21:2; Jer 11:20; 17:10; 20:12; Ezek 11:5.

and violence if they refused to give him the worship he desires and inflicting punishments on them until they felt that they were left with no option but to praise him. In that case, it would even be pointless or superfluous for God to bless people in order to receive their worship and praise, since those threats of punishment would be sufficient for him to obtain these things from them by force and compulsion.

If, however, God *does* want those who praise, worship, and glorify him to do so with genuine love and sincerity, then he cannot bring them to do this merely by bestowing his blessings on them and granting them favors. Any favorable reaction he would receive in response to those blessings and favors would simply be an expression of self-interest on the part of the recipients rather than sincere love. They would praise and thank him only as long as they continued to obtain from him what they wanted, motivated solely by a desire to receive more. Their praise and gratitude might be sincere to some extent, yet as soon as he stopped pouring out his blessings and favors they would no longer have any reason to praise and thank him. They might even become angry at him and feel as if he had merely been manipulating them to receive from them the praise and thanksgiving he wanted for his own sake.

For similar reasons, God cannot *compel* human beings to praise and worship him with genuine love and sincerity, since these things must be voluntary. Genuine love for another is not something that can be imposed on anyone by force. It is not brought about by coercion or compulsion, nor is it something that can be bought through gifts or bribes. The only way in which people can be brought to love others with a love that is sincere, genuine, and heartfelt is by experiencing such love themselves in their own life.

In biblical thought, therefore, if human beings are to offer God expressions of thankfulness and praise that are sincere, genuine, and heartfelt, they must first be convinced that he truly and genuinely loves them. They must believe in their heart that he sincerely cares for their well-being *as an end in itself* rather than regarding them and their well-being merely as a means to obtaining from them what he wants for himself, motivated solely by his own self-interest. In other words, they must be fully convinced that he seeks their well-being and happiness *for their sake rather than for his own*, that is, *that he truly loves them unconditionally and unreservedly and will always continue to do so, no matter what may happen in the future*. Anything less than that is not truly love. To affirm that God lays down conditions for loving human beings in the sense of seeking their well-being is in reality to deny his love for them, since in that case he will seek their well-being only as long as they continue to fulfill those conditions. Love that is not unconditional is not truly love.

In fact, the idea that God wishes to receive from human beings the same type of sincere and genuine love that he has for them must be seen as excluding the possibility that he created human beings in order to be glorified by them and receive from them their worship and praise. If God truly desires to be loved in the same way that he loves human beings, he cannot obtain that love by offering them rewards and threatening them with punishments, since any favorable response he receives from them in return will be an expression of self-interest on their part rather than sincere love. Those who do certain things that please him only in order to obtain rewards for themselves are acting purely out of self-interest, as are those who refrain from doing certain things only in order to avoid punishments. One cannot obtain the love of others through rewards and punishments alone. By definition, therefore, a God who seeks to obtain the praise and worship of human beings through rewards and punishments cannot be seeking to be truly loved by them.

Once this is understood, it becomes clear that *the only way that God can truly be loved by human beings is by loving them sincerely and genuinely in the sense of being fully and unconditionally committed to their well-being and happiness*. Only genuine love can produce and evoke genuine love in others. At the same time, if God genuinely loves human beings, what will interest him is *not receiving their praise and worship but receiving their love*. Any praise and worship that is not an expression of sincere love will not interest him and may even provoke him to anger if it is an attempt to manipulate him or purchase his favor.

It must also be stressed, however, that if the God of the Hebrew Bible wishes to be loved in a sincere and genuine manner, *it is not merely for his own sake but for the sake of the human beings whom he loves*. Because as sovereign creator of all that exists God stands in need of nothing, he has no need to receive the love of the human beings he has made and does not depend on them in any way to provide anything on which his existence might depend. If his only desire is to see those human beings happy, whole, and fulfilled due to his love for them and his longing to see their lives filled with good things, then he will want nothing else than for them to desire and seek the very same things for themselves. This will happen as they love him and dedicate themselves and their lives to him and his service, since what he asks, seeks, and demands of those who love him is that they love themselves and one another unconditionally in the same way that he does. If they love him with a genuine and sincere heart and live for him by presenting their lives to him, they will love themselves as those whom he loves and live for themselves and one another by sharing their lives with all of the other beings and creatures he has made. Due to his love for them and all of his creation, this will fill God with joy and contentment, since this is what he longs to see above all else. If God wishes to be loved, therefore, and not merely praised and worshiped, he does so because the love of his creatures for him will lead them to love all of his creation in the same way that he does. Similarly, if he wishes to be praised and worshiped for his love, it is so that all people everywhere may come to know that love and rejoice in it as they experience the good things he wishes to give to all.

The Objectives of God's Love

Of course, God's unconditional love for human beings does not guarantee that those human beings who experience that love will respond to him with the same love. They may even reject his love. However, while God's unconditional love for them does not guarantee that they will love him with the same type of love in return, what is certain is that if God does *not* love them unconditionally, they will never be brought to love him in that way. Instead, they will merely pursue their own self-interests in relation to him in the same way that they believe that he is pursuing his own self-interests in relation to them.

While the love of God for human beings will take the form of caring for them and seeking their well-being, their love for him cannot take the same form, since God has no needs and his existence does not depend on anything human beings might give to him or do for him. In fact, because everything belongs to God, including human beings themselves, there is nothing that they can actually give him that is not already his. One of the forms that the love of human beings will take, of course, is the type of worship, praise, and adoration that the biblical texts regard as an expression of that love. However, if what God ultimately desires is the well-being and happiness of his creatures, then the manner in which they will fulfill that desire is by being committed to seeking their own well-being and happiness in the same way that he is. What will make God happy is that human beings dedicate themselves to doing what is necessary for them to enjoy the well-being that he desires for all without exception, and also that they care for his creation as a whole and all of the creatures that form part of it.

At first glance, it may seem somewhat surprising to affirm that the manner in which human beings will manifest their love for God is by loving themselves unconditionally in the same way that God loves them. Although it may seem selfish for them to do so, in reality such is not the case. The reason for this is that, as we have seen above, in biblical thought God has not only linked himself in love to human beings but also has linked them to one another together with himself. Therefore, as long as they continue to link themselves to one another in love for one another, all those who seek their own well-being will at the same time be seeking the well-being of others, which is inseparable from their own. Because they are dedicated not only to themselves but to all of their fellow human beings as well, by caring for themselves they will also be caring for others. Conversely, by doing what is necessary for others to experience the well-being God desires for all, by definition they will also be doing what is necessary for them to experience that same well-being themselves, since the well-being of each individual is inseparably tied to the well-being of all other individuals as well as God's creation as a whole.

The idea that human beings must be convinced that God loves them unconditionally in order for them to love him and one another in the same way and thereby attain the well-being and happiness he desires for all naturally raises the question of what is necessary for them to become convinced of that truth. In some way, it must be communicated to them. According to the biblical texts, God does this especially through his prophets, as we shall see further on. However, passages such as those just considered above regard this task as something that God also accomplishes through the works that he has created. Their beauty, splendor, and glory serve as the most magnificent and convincing expressions of God's tremendous love for all. The logic of these passages is that only a God who truly cares for all of the beings he has created and is fully committed to their well-being and happiness would have created a world that is full of such wonderful and delightful things.

Once this is understood, it becomes clear why the biblical texts seem to present God as being pleased when human beings and his creation sing his praises and marvel at his power and glory. In biblical thought, God does not desire these things *for his own sake*. God already knows how marvelous and magnificent the things and beings that he has created are. He therefore does not need to be told of that truth or constantly reminded of it by means of the praise of human beings. Much less does he wish to be extolled because he seeks adulation for his own sake and is pleased when his creatures flatter him and gratify his ego. Rather, what he wants is for his creatures to know of the immensity of his love for them so that they may be brought to love themselves and one another in the same way. He wants them to acknowledge his power and glory, not *for his sake*, but *for theirs*. Only in that way will they continue to draw near to him and seek him out so that he may continue to care for them, provide amply for their needs, and help them when they require his assistance and support. Likewise, if he wishes to be loved by them, even that wish must be grounded in a concern *for them* rather than for himself alone. It is they who will benefit from loving him and others since that love will transform them and fill them with the joy and satisfaction that come from giving of themselves to and for others. It is this that God ultimately desires.

In biblical thought, it is for that reason that God is pleased when human beings and the works he has created sing his praises and glory and tell of his wondrous works. He wishes human beings themselves to be reminded constantly of his love for them and the power he possesses in order to help them and provide for their every need. When they sing of his glory and might and call on others to do the same, they grow not only in their own love for him but also in their love for one another, since the manner in which they manifest their love for him is by loving and caring for one another and his creation as a whole. While he might tell them of his love for them directly, when his creatures tell one another of that love and his glory and might, they serve as witnesses to these things. In that way, it is they who convince one another of God's love for all rather than God himself who must convince them of his love on his own.

For these same reasons, the idea that those who fail to acknowledge God or sing his praises rob or deprive him of the glory and honor due to him must be considered foreign to the biblical texts. As we shall see further on, nowhere do those texts ever speak in such terms, nor do they present God becoming angry or upset that human beings have not offered him the praise and worship that is supposedly his due. The notion that God is entitled to receive worship from human beings and that such worship constitutes his right as something that is due to him must also be regarded as foreign to biblical thought. The reason that God's creatures are said to worship him is not that they have a duty or obligation to do so, as if they were under compulsion, but that the goodness and kindness he shows them evokes spontaneously their joyous response of praise and blessing.

Conversely, when those who have experienced his love respond by praising and blessing him, what will please God will not be that praise or worship per se but the sincere and genuine love of which it is an expression. In order to understand this difference, we may return to Walter Brueggemann's interpretation of the words attributed to God in Isa 45:20-25, a portion of which we have already considered in the previous chapter:

> Assemble yourselves and come together, draw near, you survivors of the nations! They have no knowledge—those who carry about their wooden idols, and keep on praying to a god that cannot save. Declare and present your case; let them take counsel together! Who told this long ago? Who declared it of old? Was it not I, the LORD? And there is no other god besides me, a righteous God and a Savior; there is none besides me. Turn to me and be saved, all the ends of the earth! For I am God, and there is no other. By myself I have sworn, from my mouth has gone forth in righteousness a word that shall not return: "To me every knee shall bow, every tongue shall swear." Only in the LORD, it shall be said of me, are righteousness and strength; to him shall come and be ashamed all who were incensed against him. In the LORD all the offspring of Israel shall triumph and glory.

According to Brueggemann's reading of this passage, which we considered in Chapter 1, what God seeks when he offers to save people is that they acknowledge his sovereignty and worship him by bowing their knee to him: "Israel has benefited from this gift of Yahweh's righteousness, and the nations are invited to participate in the same. But neither Israel nor the nations can receive such transformative activity unless they are among those who bend the knee and swear with the tongue to the sovereignty of Yahweh."[11] God's saving activity is therefore a means by which he attempts to obtain something for himself. What ultimately concerns him is not the well-being or salvation of human beings but the worship and praise he desires to receive from them. For that reason, if they do not give him what he desires, he will either refuse to save them or else will punish them in some other way in an attempt to compel them to do so. In one way or another, however, he will bring them to bend the knee before him so as to obtain from them the worship for which he longs. In the words of Herman Bavinck, also cited in the

---

11. Walter Brueggemann, *Theology of the Old Testament: Testament, Dispute, Advocacy* (Minneapolis: Fortress, 2005), 306.

previous chapter: "Voluntarily or involuntarily, every creature will someday bow his knee before him. Obedience in love or subjection by force is the final destiny of all creatures."[12]

Such ideas must be considered entirely foreign to the thought reflected in this passage, however. If God's love for people throughout the earth is understood as his commitment to seeking their well-being and happiness and in that sense saving them, then it is that love that motivates him to call out to all the nations inviting and exhorting them to turn to him so that he might save them. What he seeks is not to manipulate them into being subject to him by saving them in order to place them in debt to himself or obligate them to acknowledge his sovereignty. Rather, God's hope is that, in the same way that the works of creation are said in the Psalms to break forth spontaneously in joyful song to him when they experience his goodness, people throughout the world may one day fall down before him in praise and worship out of genuine and heartfelt love for him as a result of having come to experience the salvation he brings.

This understanding of God's intentions in the passage is evident from several of the ideas that appear there. First, when God expresses his desire for all to turn to him, he states his purpose not in terms of wanting to be praised and honored but in terms of *wanting all the ends of the earth to be saved*. The imperatives that appear in the passage are not: "Bow every knee to me and make every tongue swear," but: "Turn to me and be saved." What God is said to seek is not the worship of human beings but their salvation. That worship will only follow his salvation as its natural consequence. Second, the reason for which God insists that there is no god but he and calls on the people to cease to worship other gods is precisely that *those gods cannot save*. Therefore, those who serve and worship such gods cannot attain the salvation that Israel's God desires for all, not for *his* sake, but for *theirs*. Third, the same desire for the salvation of all is behind the desire he expresses that all bow down to him and proclaim his justice, righteousness, and strength, since only if they are convinced of that justice, righteousness, and strength will they draw near to him to attain the blessings and life he desires for them. And fourth, the idea that those who were incensed against God will be ashamed and come to him expresses a desire not to impose his will on all by force and take vengeance on those who have not served him but rather his willingness to forgive those who rejected him and bring them to find salvation in him as well. Even though they were incensed with him, he is not angry at them but still desires their salvation. His hope is that they will feel ashamed when they realize that the one against whom they were incensed loves them and desires their well-being and that their feelings of shame will bring them to approach him with a humble and contrite spirit so that he may receive and save them.

According to this passage, therefore, if God wants every knee to bow and every tongue to swear before him, it is not *for his sake* but for the sake of those

---

12. Herman Bavinck, *Reformed Dogmatics*, vol. 2: *God and Creation* (Grand Rapids: Baker Academic, 2004), 433-34.

whom he wishes to bless and save. As they experience his goodness and love, people will acknowledge him as God and commit themselves to serving him voluntarily and gladly out of love for him and also seek to make that goodness and love known to others so that they may experience these things as well. And the way in which they will serve and love him is not by giving him anything, since he needs nothing, but by serving and loving those whom he loves, namely, themselves and others.

The hope expressed in these verses, therefore, is that all will come to God so as to be saved by him. When that happens, out of sheer joy and thanksgiving they will be brought to bend the knee and express with their tongue their love for God, not because they will feel *obliged, forced*, or *compelled* by him to do so, but because the kindness and goodness that they have experienced from God will fill their hearts with the desire to do so spontaneously. If anything can be said to compel them to respond in the way that the passage describes, it is the inexhaustible love and compassion that they will have been shown by God, which will overwhelm them and move them so deeply that they will not be able to restrain themselves from rejoicing in him and singing his praises with all their heart. It is this that will please God and make him rejoice as well.

For all of these reasons, the expressions of love, praise, worship, and adoration for God that are attributed to human beings and God's works in creation throughout the Psalms and in other passages of the Hebrew Bible and Second Temple Jewish literature should be understood as spontaneous and sincere expressions of love and thanksgiving to God for his immense goodness and kindness. The unconditional love that God manifests for his people and his creation as a whole generates in them the same type of love toward him. Nothing else could move them to love him in that way and devote themselves to him gladly and joyously with their whole heart, mind, and strength in the same way that he is devoted to them. To understand those passages in any other way is to misunderstand them entirely, given that the God of the Hebrew Bible would hardly be honored and pleased to receive praise and worship from those who offer him these things unwillingly, insincerely, or hypocritically, purely out of fear of punishment and self-interest.

In light of these observations, it becomes clear that Bavinck's affirmation that creatures will either have to obey God in love or else be subjected to God by force is entirely untenable. If God seeks to compel people to obey him by means of the promise of rewards and threats of punishment, they will not obey him out of love but only out of fear, selfishness, or self-interest. Conversely, if God intends to use force to subject human beings to himself and compel them to bend the knee before him against their will, then God is not interested in being loved by those human beings but merely receiving from them a servile obedience and worship that will also be an expression of fear, selfishness, and self-interest rather than love. Rather than being a good and loving God, a God who relates to human beings in that way will ultimately be just like the pagan gods of antiquity, pursuing his own desires and interests purely out of a concern for himself and selfishly using the human beings he has created as a means to gratifying those desires and satisfying those interests. Such a God is not the God of the Hebrew Bible.

SUFFERING, SIN, AND EVIL IN GOD'S CREATION

Almost immediately after describing the manner in which God created the world and the human beings that inhabit it and characterizing that creation as "exceedingly good," the Genesis account recounts the disobedience of the man and woman created by God to his command not to eat of the fruit of the tree of the knowledge of good and evil at the instigation of the serpent, as well as the consequences of that disobedience (Gen 3:1-24). Readers of this account in antiquity would have found many elements of the narrative just as enigmatic and problematic as they are for readers today. Precisely because of its enigmatic nature, this passage lends itself to having many different ideas read back into it. For that reason, when considering how it would have been read in antiquity, it is important to be aware of the many assumptions and inherited interpretations that have influenced the manner in which this passage has been read over the centuries in order to question to what extent those assumptions and interpretations are actually faithful to the text. Thus, for example, nowhere in Genesis 3 do words such as "sin," "punishment," or "fall" appear, nor is the serpent identified with a being such as Satan or the devil, even though traditional readings of the text associate all of these ideas with the narrative.

The allusion to the tree of the knowledge of good and evil in vv. 9 and 17 of Genesis 2 brings us to the first of many problems with the common English translations of the biblical texts that we shall see throughout the present work. The Hebrew word in this phrase that is generally translated as "evil" is *ra‘*, which is an adjective rather than a noun. Generally, this adjective simply refers to something that is bad or not good. It can be translated in many different ways. One widely-respected Hebrew lexicon, for example, lists the following definitions ahead of the definition "evil": "of bad quality, inferior"; "disagreeable, unwholesome"; "bad, of no value, contemptible."[13] The same lexicon also includes definitions such as "displeasing," "undesirable," "annoying," "objectionable," "harmful," and "adverse." In Jeremiah 24, for example, this adjective is used to refer to figs that are not good in the sense that they are of such poor quality as to be inedible and perhaps spoiled or rotten as well.

The problem with translating *ra‘* as "evil" in the verses that refer to the tree whose fruit God forbids to the man and woman is that in English this word conveys certain ideas that may not be present in the text, especially due to its extensive use in theological contexts. Evil is often understood as an active force that is opposed both to God and to what is good. In many cases, to call something evil is to consider it not only profoundly immoral or wicked but

---

13. "*ra‘*," *A Concise Hebrew and Aramaic Lexicon of the Old Testament*, ed. William L. Holladay, (Leiden: Brill, 1971), 341-42.

even vicious, malevolent, depraved, or diabolic. To do evil is not merely to do harm to others but to do so intentionally and deliberately, usually motivated by a desire to see them suffer. Often it involves acting with cruelty and vindictiveness out of spite, hatred, and malice. In contrast, to call something or someone bad simply involves affirming that the thing or person is not good in some sense. A bad decision is not necessarily an evil decision. A bad plan is not necessarily an evil plan. Bad behavior is not necessarily evil behavior. While that which is evil is always bad in some sense, that which is bad is not always evil.

Similar observations can be made with regard to the English term "wicked," which is often used to translate the same Hebrew adjective. A wicked person is not someone who merely makes bad decisions or devises bad plans but one who seeks to inflict harm and suffering on others, often on a persistent basis. To be wicked is generally synonymous with being sinister, vile, perverted, depraved, or fiendish. Complicating matters even further is the fact that in English the noun formed from the adjective "bad" is "badness," yet this noun is rarely used in English. For that reason, English translations of the Bible generally use either "evil" or "wickedness" to translate *ra'* when it is used as a noun, yet in some cases this can be misleading. In the book of Proverbs, for example, we find sayings such as: "Do not be wise in your own eyes; fear the LORD, and turn away from evil" (3:7), and: "The wise are cautious and turn away from evil, but the fool throws off restraint and is careless" (14:16). While these sayings may certainly be interpreted in the sense that one should turn away from the deliberate and conscious practice of what is evil or wicked, in principle they can also be understood in the sense of turning away from what is merely bad, unhealthy, unprofitable, or injurious in some way. This difference in meaning is evident if we translate the phrase "turn away from evil" as "turn away from what is bad." In principle, this last phrase might even be translated as: "turn away from what is bad *for you*." Similarly, when in the Bible people are called to put away their "badness" or bad behavior, in some cases this may simply involve putting away behavior that is harmful, damaging, or detrimental to their well-being but not necessarily evil or wicked in a moral sense.

Even though the narrative in Genesis 3 never refers to the decision of the man and the woman to disobey God's command as bad, it can be helpful in illustrating the difference in meaning. When they ate of the fruit of the tree that God had forbidden to them, the man and woman certainly did something bad, yet most interpreters would probably not affirm that what they did was evil or wicked. They appear to have acted somewhat naively and perhaps out of ignorance as well, yet they did not act out of malice, spite, viciousness, or enmity. In contrast, most interpreters would probably characterize the behavior of the serpent as evil or wicked, since the serpent deliberately sought to do harm by deceiving the man and woman in order to corrupt them.

On the basis of these observations, it should be noted that according to a literal translation of the Hebrew text, the tree whose fruit God had forbidden to the man and woman was the tree of the knowledge of what is good and *bad* rather than what is good and *evil*. As we shall see further on, this distinction is important in that the behavior that is condemned in many passages of the Hebrew Scriptures is not always evil or wicked in a moral sense but at times can simply be considered bad in the sense that it is harmful and detrimental to human well-being. To make such an observation is by no means to overlook the fact that much of the behavior that the biblical texts repeatedly describe and condemn as bad is indeed evil, wicked, and perverse, yet in some cases the reason for condemning certain behaviors is not any evil intent underlying them but merely the harm they do to those affected by them. While it is therefore possible that the phrase "good and bad" used in the Genesis narrative in relation to the tree was intended to convey what we understand as "good and evil" and would have been understood in this way by readers in antiquity, this must not be assumed and cannot be determined from the Hebrew text itself.

The narrative in Genesis 3 is problematic for other reasons as well. It also raises many questions. It is not clear why God had forbidden the man and woman to eat of the fruit of that particular tree or exactly what God meant when he said that they would die on the day in which they ate of it, especially since they did not die in a literal sense on that day after they had eaten of it. God's affirmation that the man and woman would die if they ate of the fruit can be taken either as a threat of punishment or as a warning regarding the dire consequences that would follow naturally and intrinsically from eating of the tree, yet nothing in the text provides a clear basis for opting for one or the other of these interpretations. The narrative does not explain where the serpent came from and how it had come to oppose or question God, given that in Genesis 1 all of the beings said to have been created by God are called good. No motive is ascribed to the serpent's deception of the woman, nor is it clear how the serpent could speak and why it approached the woman rather than the man. In what sense the man and woman came to know what is good and bad after eating of the forbidden fruit is also left unexplained. The narrative describes some type of change taking place in them immediately after they eat, yet while this change involves becoming aware of their nakedness and coming to know what is good and bad, it appears to involve something more profound within their being as well. These and numerous other considerations make the narrative extremely difficult to interpret.

It is not necessary to address all of these questions, however, in order to grasp the points that are relevant for the discussion here. What is clear is that the woman and the man willingly disobeyed God's command regarding the fruit of the tree. While in the narrative they are not presented as mentioning why they chose to eat of the forbidden fruit, their decision to do so must at the very least be interpreted as a lack of trust in God's sovereignty and his love. If they had been fully convinced that as their creator God knew what was best for them and had also been equally convinced that he truly loved them and cared for them, they would have believed that when he prohibited them from eating of the tree, he did so motivated solely by his love for them and a concern for their well-being. In that case, they would have had no reason to question or disobey his command. On the contrary, even if they had not understood why God had prohibited them from eating of the fruit of the tree, they would have concluded that since God loved them and knew what was in their best interest as their sovereign creator, what he had prohibited must be bad or harmful for them. In the serpent's words to the woman, the serpent not only claims that God is deceiving them by telling them that they will die if they eat of the forbidden fruit but also questions God's motives and seems to affirm that God's prohibition was motivated by a desire to prevent them from gaining equality with himself: "You will not die; for God knows that when you eat of it your eyes will be opened, and you will be like God, knowing good and bad" (Gen 3:4-5). For whatever reason, the woman ends up believing the serpent rather than God, although it is not clear from the narrative whether the woman had learned of God's prohibition from God directly or only indirectly through the man. In either case, however, the word that the serpent questions is that of God rather than that of the man. By his own disobedience to God's command, the man would be seen as having demonstrated the same lack of trust in God's sovereignty and goodness that the narrative implicitly attributes to the woman.

Among the ideas that the narrative would have communicated to the readers, then, was that things began to go badly for the man and woman from the moment they ceased to trust in God's sovereign wisdom as their creator and in his love for them. In addition to feeling uncomfortable and ashamed on account of their nakedness, the man and woman are subjected by God to certain measures in response to their disobedience. Those measures include especially the pain of childbirth for the woman and her subjection to the rule of her husband from that point on, the pain that the man will experience when toiling to obtain food to eat, and finally the expulsion of both from the garden (Gen 3:16-19, 22-24). Outside of stating that their expulsion from the garden will prevent them from eating of the tree of life so as to live indefinitely, no purpose for imposing these measures is given in the text.

Seeking to Bring Good out of Bad

While the account of the sin of the first human beings in Genesis 3 can be interpreted in many different ways, on the basis of what we have seen up to this point, those interpretations can be divided into two types. The first of these takes as its starting point a concept of God that attributes to him ways of thinking and acting that are characteristic of the pagan gods of antiquity. The second type of interpretation involves understanding the narrative on the basis of the concept of God described in the previous sections of the present chapter.

According to the first of these two types of interpretation, what had led God to prohibit the man and woman from eating of the tree of the knowledge of what is good and bad was a concern of the kind attributed to him by the serpent. In this case, God was concerned for his sovereignty in a way similar to that described by Walter Brueggemann in the passages from his work cited in the previous chapter. He wished to retain his position of superiority over the man and woman and prevent them from doing anything that might challenge or undermine his authority over them or place them on an equal level with himself. To repeat Brueggemann's words, the God reflected in the narrative is one "who takes with savage seriousness Yahweh's right to be worshiped, honored, and obeyed," that is, "a God who intends to be fully sovereign, who will brook no rival, who practices intense self-regard, and who will not tolerate those who detract from this self-regard."[14] Because the Hebrew term for God is the plural *'elohim*, the words attributed to the serpent in v. 5 of the narrative can be translated either as: "you will become like God," or: "you will become like gods." In either case, this phrase can be interpreted in the sense that the serpent was claiming that eating of the fruit would enable the man and woman to attain some type of equality with God. If this was what concerned God, then he had prohibited them from eating of the fruit because he wanted to prevent them from usurping his power and authority so that he might remain in a position of superiority over them, apparently for his own sake. This type of concern was generally attributed to pagan gods such as Marduk, Zeus, and Poseidon in antiquity. As we have seen in Chapter 1, when mortal human beings such as Odysseus claim to be equal or superior to them in some way, the gods become angry and seek to punish or destroy those human beings in order to keep them in their place and make it clear to them that they must continue to be subservient to them.

Of course, what leads the gods to punish or destroy human beings when those human beings disobey them is not always a concern for their own sovereignty. Often what concerns and angers them is merely that those human beings are taking from them something that they regard as rightfully theirs or are not giving them something that they want or need for themselves. In some cases, the gods simply regard the disobedience of human beings as a lack of respect for them and a lack of submission to their authority, and for that reason they feel compelled to punish those human beings who dare to disobey them. For their own sake and for the sake of their supremacy over all, they cannot and will not tolerate disobedience among human beings but will act swiftly and decisively to do whatever is necessary to put an end to that disobedience and seek to prevent its recurrence.

If the Genesis account is understood on the basis of these ideas, then God had originally prohibited the man and woman from eating of the tree of the knowledge of what is good and bad, not because they would be harmed or affected directly in any way by doing so, but out of a concern for his sovereignty. Perhaps they would in fact gain some type of knowledge that would threaten his sovereignty. Alternatively, God may simply have wanted to test

---

14. Brueggemann, *Theology*, 272, 283. It is important to note that Brueggemann is not referring explicitly to this passage from Genesis 3 when he portrays God in these terms.

their obedience or teach them to obey him by giving them some command in order to see whether they would remain subject to him. If they did not, he would punish them in order to make it clear to them what he will do to any who challenge his authority. Given that God is also presented as spending time in the garden, he may have wanted to enjoy their presence, but only as long as they continued to submit to him. By means of his prohibition, he would be able to discern whether they would in fact remain dedicated and loyal to him and make it clear to them that if they dared to disobey him, he would no longer be able to tolerate them in his presence. It might even be argued that God wanted to preserve the fruit on the tree for his own enjoyment and thus prohibited the man and woman from eating it for the same reasons that had led gods such as Hyperion and Polyphemus to become angry with Odysseus and his men for for taking their animals and their food without their permission in the *Odyssey*.

God's response to the disobedience of the man and woman would then be understood in terms of inflicting pain, suffering, and hardships on them in order to demonstrate to them that he will not overlook any failure or refusal to submit to his sovereign will. By expelling them from the garden, he accomplishes that objective and also sets them at a distance from himself so that they will not disturb or pollute his presence with their sinfulness and disobedience. God might also be seen as acting out of a concern for his beautiful garden, which he wishes to keep pure, unsullied, and unstained from the type of behavior that defiles and debases it. A similar reason might be given for his decision to impose death on them by making them mortal. Because such a measure is definitive and apparently irreversible, by imposing it on them he either wished to keep them out of his immediate presence definitively or simply wished to subject them to such a fate eternally for having dared to challenge his sovereignty and for having offended him in the way that they did.

Although at first glance such interpretations of the passage might seem feasible, upon closer examination they present numerous problems. While the narrative affirms that the man and woman do in fact acquire the knowledge of what is good and bad as a result of their eating of the tree, this is not presented as something that benefits them but rather as something that does them harm. They become conscious of their nakedness as something that is bad and attempt to cover it up, apparently because it causes them some type of shame or displeasure. As a result, they hide from God's presence. What leads them to do so, however, is not their fear of punishment or a sense of guilt at having disobeyed God, but their nakedness itself. The reason that the man gives for being afraid is not that he has provoked God to wrath by disobeying him but that he has realized that he is naked (Gen 3:10). In that case, what he fears is God's rejection on account of his nakedness rather than his punishment. Similarly, God responds to the man not by accusing him of having disobeyed but by asking him who told him that he was naked. He then concludes that the man must have eaten from the tree, not because he saw that fruit was missing, but because the man was now aware of his nakedness. Evidently, God knew that this awareness of his nakedness could have come about in the man only if he had eaten of the forbidden fruit. In that case, what concerned God was not that the man had disobeyed him by taking the fruit but that the man now felt naked and ashamed in God's presence, evidently because of the new knowledge that he had attained by eating of the fruit. It was this feeling of shame and the consciousness of his nakedness that resulted from the man's disobedience that God had wished to avoid rather than the loss of fruit from his tree or that disobedience in and of itself.

According to the narrative, therefore, it is not God who can no longer tolerate the presence of the man in the garden and distances him from himself, but rather the man who hides from God's presence. At the same time, it is not God who is affected in any way by what the man and woman have done but the man and woman themselves. Other than allowing them to know what is good and bad as God does, eating of the forbidden fruit did not make the man and woman like God. When the man and woman eat of the fruit, even though they are said to gain some type of knowledge regarding good and bad that they did not possess previously, they do not become like God in the sense of obtaining the same type of power or supremacy that God possesses over the created order, as if that power or supremacy had been denied them prior to their eating from the tree. Their disobedience does not cause any type of injury to God, nor does it undermine or diminish his sovereignty over them and the created order. The man and woman do not come to pose any type of threat to God as a result of their disobedience. Nor does that disobedience take from God something that he wished to retain for himself alone. The man and woman are not presented as having done any type of damage to the garden, polluting it in some way or lessening its beauty. If God wishes to enjoy the garden, nothing that the man and woman did prevents him from doing so. God is not harmed by their disobedience, just as he was not initially benefited in any way by their obedience.

Undoubtedly, when the serpent tells the man and woman that God does not want them to eat of the fruit of the tree of the knowledge of what is good and bad because by doing so they will become like God, the serpent's words seem to imply that God wishes to prevent this from happening. However, the story clearly suggests that the reason that God had desired that they not obtain the knowledge that would result from their eating of the forbidden fruit was that, once they had come to possess that knowledge, they would no longer enjoy the same type of happiness, bliss, and well-being that had been theirs up to that point. According to the logic of the story, therefore, contrary to what the serpent affirms, God's command for the man and woman not to eat of the fruit of the tree of the knowledge of what is good and bad had been given, not out of any type of selfishness or self-interest on God's part, but solely out of a concern for their own well-being and happiness. In that case, what displeased God was not the disobedience of the man and woman per se but the negative effect that their disobedience came to have *on them*. While he wanted to be obeyed, he desired this for *their* sake rather than his own.

For all of these reasons, the story makes more sense if interpreted on the basis of the idea that God's concern throughout the narrative is not for himself or his own sovereignty, honor, or glory, but rather for the well-being of the human beings he has created. While it is by no means clear why God had placed the tree of the knowledge of what is good and bad alongside the tree of life in the garden and why he had prohibited the man and woman from eating of its fruit, when they disobey God and obtain the knowledge of what is good and bad, it is *they* who are harmed rather than God. They become aware of their nakedness and cover themselves because for some reason their nakedness now causes them to experience shame and discomfort. According to the logic of the narrative, because this shame and discomfort will be permanent and irreversible in the same way that their knowledge of what is good and bad will now be, God must do something to mitigate the consequences of what they have done. His gift of loincloths made from animal skin in order to replace the loincloths they had made from fig leaves must be understood as an act of kindness aimed at providing them with a piece of clothing that would be more durable and of better quality to cover what would continue to make them feel ashamed and uncomfortable (Gen 3:7, 21).

The story clearly suggests, therefore, that the reason that God had desired that the man and woman not obtain the knowledge that would result from their eating of the forbidden fruit was that, once they had come to possess that knowledge, they would no longer enjoy the same type of happiness, bliss, and well-being that had been theirs up to that point. Contrary to what the serpent affirms, God's command for the man and woman not to eat of the fruit of the tree of the knowledge of what is good and bad had been given, not out of any type of selfishness or self-interest on God's part, but solely out of a concern for the well-being and happiness of the man and woman themselves. While the account clearly seems to portray God as being displeased at the disobedience of the man and woman, he is not said to become angry at them. What displeases God is not any type of personal loss or injury but simply seeing his good purposes for the man and woman thwarted. It might even be supposed that their disobedience evoked in God the same reaction attributed to him a few chapters later, where upon contemplating the destructive behavior of human beings he is said to have become grieved or saddened rather than angry (Gen 6:5-6).

Although the curse to which the serpent is subjected is understood as a punishment for its deliberate deception of the woman, which was rooted in a desire to do her harm, the purpose for which God imposes on the man and woman the measures mentioned in the narrative is not entirely clear. The account presupposes that the pain and suffering that the man and woman will now experience at different moments of their life will contribute in some way to their good. Because those measures are definitive and irreversible and will not be altered by the manner in which the man and woman behave from that point on, and also because those measures will not affect in any way the knowledge of what is good and bad that the man and woman have obtained, those measures cannot be seen as having a purely corrective purpose. Even if the man and woman correct or improve their behavior, they will continue to be subject to the measures dictated by God and those measures will not be made less severe or less permanent if the man and woman behave in a certain way. They may serve to remind the man and woman and their descendants of what had happened as a result of their disobedience, yet this reminder would only serve to instruct them with regard to the past and perhaps lead them to recall some important truth, since those measures will not be affected by their future obedience or disobedience. Nowhere in the narrative does God threaten to subject the man and woman to measures that are even more severe if they continue to disobey him, nor does he offer to reverse the measures he has imposed on them if they mend their ways by becoming obedient to him once more. This suggests that God does not impose those measures on them in an attempt to deter them from continuing to disobey him.

It may therefore be preferable to interpret the measures imposed by God as preventative rather than corrective. By making their life painful in different ways, God will attempt to minimize in some way the negative consequences that will follow from the knowledge of what is good and bad that they have obtained as a result of their disobedience. If that pain serves as a reminder of what took place, it will remind them not merely of the tragic consequences of their disobedience but also of the fact that God initially desired only what was good for them and that it was only their disobedience that prevented them from obtaining that good. In that case, even though the measures imposed by God would be painful, those measures would remind them of God's love for them, not only because God had chosen to inflict sufferings on them rather than destroying them entirely but also because they would be led to recall the truth that whatever God commanded them was an expression of his sovereign love and care for them and his desire for their well-being. If he had not wanted them to know what is good and bad, it had been *for their sake* rather than his own.

Now that the man and woman had obtained that knowledge, however, in some way the suffering that God imposed on them over and above the suffering or discomfort that they already began to experience immediately after eating of the forbidden fruit would lessen or perhaps even remedy to some extent the harm that resulted intrinsically from the knowledge of what is good and bad that they had obtained. That suffering might help prevent the knowledge that was now theirs from bringing them to do even greater harm to themselves or might also limit the harm done to them by that knowledge, since the sensation of pain and suffering would deter them from using that knowledge in ways that were not in their best interest. It might even encourage them to do something good with that knowledge rather than something even more harmful and destructive. In any case, the painful measures imposed by God would somehow counteract or limit the harm done to them by their acquisition of the knowledge of what is good and bad and perhaps even bring something positive to come out of the acquisition of that knowledge. The account provides no basis for supposing that God simply wished to impose suffering on the man and woman as an end in itself out of spite for having disobeyed him or because he wished to avenge himself on them in some way.

While it is by no means clear how the condition of mortality that the man and woman come to possess as a result of their disobedience would benefit them, at the very least it would serve to bring to an end at some point the pain and suffering that would now be theirs as a result of their knowledge of what is good and bad. Because their living forever would not harm God or affect him negatively in any way, there is no reason to suppose that his decision not to allow this was motivated by jealousy toward the man and woman or a concern to prevent them from attaining some type of equality with him. Rather, that decision would be seen as fulfilling some objective in relation to human beings rather than God himself. In some way, it would limit the suffering that human beings would experience as a result of their acquisition of the knowledge of what is good and bad and God's response to that acquisition. Some interpreters of the biblical text would eventually come to regard the condition of mortality to which the man and woman are subjected as a result of their disobedience as making it possible for them to be transformed into a new and more blessed condition following their death rather than having to remain forever in a condition that would be characterized by pain and suffering. While there is no hint of this idea in the Genesis account, it is important to stress once more that the biblical narrative sees the measures imposed by God as a response, not to the disobedience of the man and woman per se, but to their acquisition of the knowledge of what is good and bad. Ultimately, it is this knowledge that does them harm rather than the measures taken by God in and of themselves. Those measures must therefore be regarded as an attempt to minimize or mitigate in some way the harm that they will do to themselves and the pain that they will endure as a result of the knowledge of what is good and bad that they have obtained.

This conclusion also seems to follow from the affirmation that God expelled the man and woman from the garden so as to prevent them from eating of the tree of life (Gen 3:22-24). Nothing in the Genesis account provides any basis for maintaining that the man and woman would have posed some threat to God or his sovereignty had they come to live forever. In fact, the notion that eating of the tree of life would make the man and woman immortal in and of itself suggests that what concerned God from the beginning were the intrinsic consequences that would follow from eating not only of that tree but also of the tree of the knowledge of what is good and bad. In that case, what had led God to prohibit the man and woman from eating of the tree of the knowledge of what is good and bad was his loving concern for their well-being, which would be diminished in some way if they ate of its fruit. Now that they had come to the knowledge of what is good and bad, however, it was apparently in their best interest that they not become immortal by eating of the tree of life as well, not because of any adverse effect that their immortality would have on God but rather because for some reason that immortality would do them more harm than good, perhaps by making their condition of pain and suffering interminable.

It should not be overlooked that the narrative in Genesis 3 ends with a threat of violence. God is said to place cherubim at the entrance of the garden with a flaming sword in order to prevent the human beings from reentering it (vv. 22-24). Because it would have been God's concern for the human beings or his creation that led him to prohibit the man and woman from reentering the garden once they had been expelled from it rather than any concern for himself or his own sovereignty, this threat of violence would be seen as being ultimately motivated by a concern for the well-being of those human beings and the creation of which they form part. It is important to note, however, that the disobedience of human beings has made it necessary for God to threaten them with violence in order to promote and preserve their well-being as best as possible. Just as God must inflict pain and suffering on them in an attempt to bring them to live in ways that will limit and mitigate the pain and suffering that will result intrinsically from their acquisition of the knowledge of what is good and bad, so also God must threaten them with violence in order to prevent them from doing even more harm to themselves. Unfortunately, as a result of their disobedience and the condition to which that disobedience has led, God has no choice but to threaten them with violence and at times even make use of violence if he is to continue to seek their well-being.

Rather than portraying a God who behaves in the same way and for the same reasons as the pagan gods of antiquity, therefore, the account regarding the expulsion of the man and woman from the Garden of Eden in Genesis 3 should be understood as presenting a God who seeks that the human beings he has created obey him for their own good and responds to their disobedience by imposing measures aimed at limiting the harm that they do to themselves by means of that disobedience. Ultimately, what leads to the pain and suffering that the man and woman will now experience together with their descendants is not what *God* does but rather what the man and woman do to themselves by disobeying God and failing to trust in his love, sovereignty, and goodness. It is not God who puts an end to their blissful existence but the man and woman themselves by failing to do what God had commanded them for their own good. For that reason, when God is presented as telling the man that he will die if he eats of the tree of the knowledge of what is good and bad in Gen 2:17, his words should be understood primarily as a loving but serious warning of the consequences that would follow upon eating of the tree's fruit rather than as constituting a threat of punishment. Nevertheless, because it was God who established death as the consequence that would follow upon their disobedience and also because he does not act to reverse that consequence after they disobey him, their death can be seen as a punishment imposed by God as well.

At the same time, the fact that God does not destroy or abandon the man and woman after they transgress but continues to relate to them and their descendants must not be overlooked. The account seems to presuppose that God will not only attempt to minimize the harm and suffering that they and their descendants will endure as a consequence of the new condition to which their disobedience has led but also that he will attempt to do something in the future to restore human beings to the condition of happiness and well-being that he originally intended for them. In some way, the measures God has taken in response to their disobedience will contribute to the accomplishment of that objective. If such were not the case, then both those measures themselves as well as the ongoing existence of the man and woman and their descendants would be pointless. If the good that God intended for the human beings he had created could no longer be attained as a result of the disobedience of the man and woman, then God would simply have done away with them or let them continue to go their own way without him so as to do themselves even greater harm by behaving in ways that were not in their best interest.

Despite the measures that God is said to have imposed on the man and woman, therefore, the Genesis account clearly conveys the idea that God still intends for them to live and to prosper. They will still fulfill his command to be fruitful and multiply. They will also continue to enjoy God's blessings and the good things he has created, even though they will not enjoy them as fully as they would have had they not disobeyed. The text seems to leave no doubt that God still cares deeply for them and wishes only good things for them. While they will suffer in life and eventually die, by no means will their life be reduced merely to pain and hardships. On the contrary, in many ways their life will continue to be good and enjoyable. This view of human life stands in contrast to the notion that human beings are condemned to live their lives as servants or slaves for the gods, dedicating themselves perpetually to the demanding task of providing for all of the needs and desires of the gods in the way that the *Enuma Elish* describes.

What the account in Genesis 3 seems to stress most strongly, however, is that if the human beings God has created are to attain the happiness and blessings God desires and intends for them, they must submit obediently to God and acknowledge his sovereignty over their life. They must renounce any desire or attempt to "be like God," especially by seeking to define good and bad on their own, and instead must submit to him obediently.

This idea is stressed repeatedly elsewhere in the Hebrew Scriptures and Second Temple Jewish literature. Toward the end of the first century CE, the Jewish writer and historian Flavius Josephus interprets the account found in Genesis 3 in the following terms: "The serpent, living in the company of Adam and his wife, grew jealous of the blessings which he supposed were destined for them if they obeyed God's commands, and believing that disobedience would bring calamities upon them, he maliciously persuaded the woman to taste of the tree of knowledge, telling her that in it resided the power of distinguishing between what is good and bad, the possession of which would result in their leading a blissful existence not inferior to that of a god" (*Ant.* 1.41-42).[15] Then, after relating the disobedience of Adam and Eve to God's command and affirming that the fruit they had eaten had "sharpened their intelligence" and had deceived them into thinking that they were now happier than they had been before, Josephus presents God telling them: "I had decreed for you to live a life of bliss, unmolested by any type of affliction and free of any care that might vex your souls; through my providence, all things that contribute to enjoyment and pleasure were to spring up for you spontaneously, without any toil or distress for you; blessed with these gifts, old age would not soon have overtaken you and your life would have been long. But now you have frustrated this intention of mine by disobeying my commands" (*Ant.* 1.46-47). These passages from Josephus make it clear that in the eyes of at least one Jewish interpreter of the Genesis account in antiquity, God had wanted only what was good for the first human beings, the "blissful existence" of which Josephus speaks. Their disobedience, however, had frustrated those good intentions.

As we shall see below, the account in Genesis 3 undoubtedly raises many theological problems that are extremely difficult to answer in a satisfactory manner. On the basis of what we have seen here, however, that account seems clearly to have been designed to communicate at least two points. First, whatever suffering and evil exists in the world was not originally intended by God but is instead a result of human decisions. God wanted only what was good for human beings, yet what has prevented them from attaining only what is good is not anything that God did but what those human beings did in disobedience to God and contrary to his will. And second, while God imposes pain and suffering on the man and woman in response to their disobedience, in reality it is their disobedience itself to God's good and loving will that is the cause of their pain and suffering and not the measures taken by God. What motivates God to take those measures is not any type of ill will toward human beings or a desire to harm them for having disobeyed him, but his desire to see them attain as much as possible the good he originally intended for them in a situation in which their own actions have made it impossible for them to enjoy fully that good. For that reason, those measures are an expression, not of spite, vengeance, or hatred, but of God's love, care, and concern for the human beings he created.

---

15. Citations from the writings of Josephus are based on my own translation of the Greek text of his works found in volumes 186, 242, and 281 of the Loeb Classical Library (Cambridge, MA: Harvard University Press, 1911–).

Sin and Evil Elsewhere in the Opening Chapters of Genesis

The problem of how a good, loving, and all-powerful God is to respond to the disobedience, evil, and destructive behavior of human beings lies at the heart of several of the narratives that appear in the following chapters of Genesis. In Gen 4:1-16, both Cain and Abel offer sacrifice to God. According to the narrative, they do so entirely at their own initiative and not because God has asked them to do so or has even suggested that such a thing would please him. When God accepts Abel's sacrifice but not that of Cain, Cain becomes very angry. Although the text does not affirm explicitly why God found Abel's sacrifice acceptable but had no regard for that of Cain, God's words to Cain in v. 7 suggest that the reason had to do with Cain's behavior or motives: "If you do well, will you not be accepted? And if you do not do well, sin is lurking at the door; its desire is for you, but you must master it." Because these words make it clear that the condition for being accepted is to do what is good and avoid what is bad, it can be concluded that the reason that God had no regard for Cain's offering was that in some way he was not doing what was good.

In his anger, Cain then murders his brother Abel. When God hears Abel's blood crying out to him, he tells Cain: "What have you done? Listen! The voice of your brother's blood is crying out to me from the ground. And now you are cursed from the ground, which has opened its mouth to receive your brother's blood from your hand. When you till the ground, it will no longer yield to you its strength; you will be a fugitive and a wanderer on the earth" (Gen 4:10-12). Depending on how the Hebrew word *'avon* is translated, Cain responds to God by telling him either that his punishment is too great to bear or that his crime is too great to be forgiven.[16] In order to protect Cain, God decrees that "anyone who kills Cain will be punished sevenfold" and then decides to place a mark on Cain "so that no one who came upon him would kill him" (4:15).

This narrative clearly reflects God's ongoing concern for the well-being of the human beings he has created. His initial words to Cain indicate that he wants them to do what is good and that the refusal to do so is unacceptable to him. By stressing this point to Cain, God not only explains to Cain why he is not pleased with Cain's conduct and offering but also implicitly encourages him to think and act differently. Obviously, God's concern is for Cain rather than for himself. In this regard, the God of whom the narrative speaks is very different from most of the pagan gods of antiquity. What interested those gods was not that human beings do what is right and good but that they present them with the sacrificial offerings they desired for their own sake. The sentiments with which those human beings presented those offerings was of no importance to them, nor did the spirit or attitude with which

---

16. Although translations such as the NRSVue present Cain referring to his "punishment" at God's hands in Gen 4:13, in reality the Hebrew text speaks of Cain referring to his iniquity or guilt (*'avon*). The Septuagint translation of this verse reads: "My crime is too great for me to be forgiven."

those offerings were made matter to them. One can hardly imagine such gods rejecting the sacrifice of Cain, unless of course they thought it was of poor quality and should have been more lavish and abundant than it was. In contrast, the God of whom the narrative speaks is interested not in the offerings themselves but in the conduct and the heart of those who present them. His concern is not for himself but *for them.*

It is this concern that leads God to react in the way that he does to Cain's murder of Abel. If God continues to care for the human beings he has created, he cannot merely overlook or ignore what Cain has done, since that would involve not only tolerating destructive behavior but also encouraging it by remaining indifferent to it. At the same time, if God simply allows human beings to kill one another, such violent behavior will gradually spiral out of control (see Gen 4:23-24). Of course, God might simply put to death those who murder others and practice other forms of violence. If God chooses either of these last two alternatives, however, it will not be long before the entire race of human beings is extinguished from the earth.

In the face of Cain's deed, therefore, the form that God's love takes is that of punishing Cain while nevertheless protecting him from becoming the object of further violence himself. While in a sense God subjects Cain to a curse, strictly speaking it is the ground that is said to curse Cain as a result of the blood of Abel that has been poured out on it (Gen 4:11). This suggests that God has designed the world in a way in which the created order itself will not tolerate passively the practice of hatred, violence, and evil. In any case, the curse to which Cain becomes subject serves a purpose in relation not only to Cain himself but also to the rest of humanity. Those human beings who observe the manner in which Cain has been cursed will be led to refrain from killing others, since they will conclude that they may become subject to the same type of curse if they do what Cain did. The afflictions to which Cain is subjected will also constantly remind both Cain himself and the rest of humanity of the consequences of the type of destructive behavior into which Cain had fallen and hopefully lead them not only to refrain from such behavior but also to live in constructive ways that will benefit all instead of doing people harm.

It is important to stress, however, that underlying the measures that God takes against Cain is a concern for the well-being of Cain and that of other human beings as well. Nothing in the account indicates that God is punishing Cain because God's justice will not allow him to tolerate sin and evil, as if God's concern were to satisfy a need internal to himself to exact retribution for violations of his just and holy will, such as that committed by Cain. On the contrary, the measures that God takes should be understood as being rooted in his desire and insistence that human beings act in ways that contribute to their own well-being and avoid behaviors that destroy that well-being. God's ongoing concern for Cain and his desire for Cain's well-being are evident from the manner in which he acts to protect Cain by placing a mark upon him and threatening any who might kill him with even greater punishments. In addition, by making Cain a fugitive and wanderer, God not only punishes Cain but also keeps him at a distance from other human beings, both for their protection from Cain as well as for the protection of Cain from them. It is also worth noting that God is not said to become angry at Cain when imposing these measures on him, even though the narrative suggests that God is outraged and horrified at what Cain has done. While God's response to Cain's deed can undoubtedly be understood as an expression of anger, any anger on God's part would be motivated by his desire that human beings live in ways that promote their own well-being rather than a concern for the inviolability of his own justice, holiness, or righteousness.

The murderous deed of Cain sets the stage for the account of the flood in Genesis 6–9. At the beginning of that account, God is said to regret having made human beings due to their sinfulness: "The LORD saw that the wickedness of humankind was great on the earth, and that every inclination of the thoughts of their hearts was only evil continually. And the LORD was sorry that he had made humankind on the earth, and it grieved him to his heart. So the LORD said, 'I will blot out from the earth the human beings I have created—people together with animals and creeping things and birds of the air, for I am sorry that I have made them'" (Gen 6:5-7). Several verses later, the same idea is repeated: "Now the earth was corrupt in God's sight, and the earth was filled with violence. And God saw that the earth was corrupt; for all flesh had corrupted its ways upon the earth. And God said to Noah, 'I have determined to make an end of all flesh, for the earth is filled with violence because of them; now I am going to destroy them along with the earth'" (6:11-13). At the same time, however, rather than making an end of humanity as a whole, God preserves Noah and his family due to Noah's righteousness and blamelessness (6:8-9). God tells Noah: "I have seen that you alone are righteous before me in this generation" (7:1).

While the adjective *ra'* and the noun derived from it are used here to characterize both human beings as a whole and the inclination of their hearts as bad, the allusion to corruption and violence clearly conveys what is involved. The Hebrew communicates the idea that the violence of human beings has ruined the earth as well as human beings themselves. In this case, the language of evil and wickedness certainly seems appropriate.

The love of God for human beings is reflected in the affirmation that God was grieved in his heart at seeing the persistent wickedness and violence that had filled the world and for that reason regretted having made human beings. Once again, it is important to note that God is not said to become angry. Instead, he is saddened or grieved. This indicates a sense of pain on God's part. It is important to stress, however, that the cause of this pain and sadness is not anything that human beings do or fail to do in relation *to God* but what they do *to one another*. For that reason, what moves God to sadness is not any concern for himself but rather his love for human beings and his desire that they enjoy well-being and happiness. Their behavior does not harm God but rather harms human beings themselves by preventing them from attaining the good that God desires for them in his love.

This account presupposes an idea that runs throughout the biblical texts and is vital to understanding them, namely, that God cannot bring human beings to leave behind their destructive and violent behavior by force or by an act of divine omnipotence. He cannot simply produce some type of mysterious transformation in them that will make them choose to do good rather than evil. Were that possible, then God could make the problem described in the narrative go away merely by changing the inclination of the hearts of all so that they would love one another rather than destroying one another. In that case, in fact, God could have avoided that problem from the very beginning. If he had the ability to make human beings live in love and do what is good of his own accord, one can assume that he would have done so from the moment in which he created the first man and woman. Had he done so, they would never have disobeyed him in the first place. The biblical texts consistently assume, however, that God cannot force human beings to live in ways that will enable them to enjoy the well-being he desires for all or unilaterally bring about in them such a life of their own free will. If he could, he would have done so.

The biblical text also reflects a second presupposition that is equally important and vital for understanding the narrative here and throughout the Hebrew Bible. Because the well-being and happiness of human beings depends on their living in ways that promote that well-being among them, God cannot bring about that well-being on his own simply by filling their lives with good things. If they refuse to live in love and instead practice evil and violence, they will take the good things God has given them and use them to do one another harm. Their failure to do what is good and right will make it impossible for them to attain the good that God desires for them. No matter how badly God wishes them to experience well-being in its fullness and how zealously he pursues that objective, their destructive and self-destructive behavior will not allow God's good purposes to be accomplished in them. Those purposes can be achieved only if they obey God and submit to his loving will for them. If God wants them to obey him, therefore, it is for *their* sake rather than this own.

By describing the situation as one in which "every inclination" of the hearts of human beings collectively was "only evil continually," the biblical narrative implicitly raises the question of how God is to respond to the persistent evil or bad behavior of the human beings whose good he seeks. Because the situation is so dire, God cannot simply ignore or overlook what is happening. If he did, the violence, wickedness, and destructive behavior of human beings would only intensify and spread even further as they continued to populate the earth. His love will not allow him to remain idle or simply abandon human beings to such a fate. At the same time, if human beings can attain the well-being and happiness God desires for them only by living in accordance with God's will, but they adamantly refuse to do so and cannot be brought to do so unilaterally by God, it is by no means clear what form God's love for human beings is to take. There is no option or alternative left open to God that can be considered good. For that reason, if God hopes to change the situation, he must do something that is in some ways bad. If he does so, it will be reluctantly and with the same type of pain and sadness attributed to him in the narrative. In the face of the situation described, however, his love leaves him no choice but to take some type of action to put an end to it in the hope of bringing about a new situation in which his loving will for human beings may ultimately be accomplished.

In principle, God might attempt to bring the human beings who have fallen into such persistently destructive behavior to abandon that behavior by inflicting some type of punishment on them. He might demand that they change their ways and threaten them with severe hardships and afflictions if they do not. In that case, however, even if they did alter their behavior, they would do so out of fear of punishment rather than out of a sincere conviction that it is in their own best interest to live and behave differently. As soon as the punishments and afflictions came to an end, they would simply go back to their destructive behavior. While there seem to be other approaches to the problem that God might take in addition to inflicting punishment, in the biblical narrative he chooses to take a much more drastic measure. He decides to destroy humanity and cleanse the earth by means of a flood in order to make a fresh start with the righteous Noah and his family. The logic appears to be that, because Noah is righteous and blameless, those who descend from him will hopefully follow in the same path, living in ways that allow them to experience the well-being God desires for all rather than destroying that well-being. The obedience that Noah demonstrates by doing everything that God asks of him seems to offer a basis for hoping that what God intends can indeed be accomplished through him.

It is important to stress, however, that the destruction of humanity by means of the flood is not a form of *punishment* but rather a *purification*. Punishments have the purpose of bringing about some type of change of behavior either in those who are punished or in others who observe the punishment and are thereby deterred from engaging in the conduct that led to the punishment. In this case, however, by destroying all human beings with the exception of Noah and his family, God is not seeking to alter their behavior. Nor is he seeking to make those human beings suffer or sentencing them to death in order to satisfy his justice, lay down an example, or exact retribution or vengeance. Rather, he is simply seeking to cleanse the earth from evil and violence by washing away the mass of humanity that has fallen into these things in order to start over with Noah and his family, hoping that this time things will turn out differently. This is how the flood narrative is interpreted by Philo of Alexandria, for example, who speaks of the flood in Noah's days not as a punishment but as a purification (*katharsis*) of the earth from evil (*Moses* 2.64).

The last part of the flood narrative conveys the idea of a fresh start by presenting God as giving some of the same commands to Noah and his children that he had originally given to the first man and woman immediately after creating them. He tells Noah and his children to be fruitful and multiply and to fill the earth, as well as prescribing for them what they are to eat (Gen 9:1-7). For the first time he gives human beings permission to eat meat, as long as they do not consume the animal's blood with it. At the same time, perhaps due to the pain and sorrow that the destruction of the human beings he loves caused him, God promises never again to destroy human beings or cleanse the earth in that manner (9:11-17). The pleasing odor of the sacrifice that Noah offers him and God's realization that from the time of their youth the inclination of the heart of human beings is bad or evil are also said to lead God to make such a promise (8:21-22). It is not clear whether God arrives at the decision never to destroy humanity in that way again because he discovered that it was not the best way to accomplish his purposes, because he realized that such a measure was futile or overly painful for him, or for some other reason. The fact that he is presented as being pleased by the odor of Noah's sacrifice indicates that he sees that there are still good things in the world and that not all is bad. In any case, it is clear that God wishes for human beings and the world to continue to exist, despite the fact that things have not turned out in the way he had originally hoped and intended when he created the world.

After God brings the flood to an end, it is not long before human beings return to the same type of behavior that had characterized them previously. Noah becomes drunk and curses the descendants of his son Ham when Ham sees his nakedness as he lies uncovered in his tent (Gen 9:21-27). Once human beings have multiplied into many different nations, they join together to build a tower that will reach up to the heavens in order to make a name for themselves, yet God responds by confusing their language so that they no longer understand one another (11:1-9). The concern that is attributed to God in this passage is that if those constructing the tower are allowed to finish it, nothing will be able to stop them from doing even greater things and accomplishing everything they propose (v. 6). This affirmation need not be understood in the sense that God is concerned and fearful for his sovereignty for his own sake, however. Rather, what may be seen as concerning God is the type of oppressive behavior associated with the mindset that led to the construction of the tower. If that behavior and mindset remain unchecked and are allowed to propagate further, they will lead to great oppression for the majority of human beings who are not in positions of power over others. The name of Babel given to the tower and the description of the preparation of bricks to build it seem to anticipate the oppression that many peoples and nations will suffer at the hands of great empires such as those of the Babylonians and the Egyptians.

Several chapters later in the Genesis narrative, the wickedness of human beings reaches new heights. God is presented as hearing the outcry of many against Sodom and Gomorrah for their great sin and descending to observe for himself what is happening there (Gen 18:16-22; cf. 13:13). When the two angels that he has sent into Sodom enter into Lot's house, they are surrounded by the men of the city who seek to force themselves on them sexually. However, the angels prevent them from doing so by rescuing Lot from their midst and striking the men with blindness (19:1-11). The next day, God rains down sulfur and fire to destroy the city, saving only Lot and his wife and daughters, although Lot's wife is turned into a pillar of salt (19:18-29).

This story illustrates the same basic points as the story of the flood and raises the same question regarding the form that God's love is to take in the face of extreme wickedness such as that which is attributed to the inhabitants of Sodom and Gomorrah. For God to have done nothing would have involved ignoring the outcry of those who were suffering at the hands of the cities' inhabitants, which is said to be very great due to the gravity of the sin of those inhabitants (Gen 18:20; 19:13). Once again, therefore, he must take action to put an end to the violence and oppression. He does so by destroying the two cities and their inhabitants.

It is important to note, however, that the narrative does not suggest in any way that this action on God's part is simply an act of vengeance against the inhabitants of Sodom and Gomorrah. Nor does the narrative suggest that what moved God to destroy these two cities was the manner in which their behavior was affecting him personally. On the contrary, because God's purpose in destroying those inhabitants is to deliver others from the type of violence and oppression attributed to them in the narrative, ultimately that purpose must be seen as grounded in a loving desire on God's part to save the oppressed from their oppressors. Once again, while the Genesis narrative appears to present God as being outraged and horrified by the behavior of the human beings he ends up destroying, God is not said to become angry or to act out of wrath. Although that idea does appear in Deut 29:23, which speaks of "the destruction of Sodom and Gomorrah, Admah and Zeboiim, which the LORD destroyed in his fierce anger," God's objective in the account is clearly to deliver those who are suffering at the hand of those who have fallen into such wicked and violent behavior. By destroying the wicked, he will also prevent such behavior from continuing and spreading further and communicate to human beings elsewhere that he will not tolerate such wickedness and violence in the future. By destroying Sodom and Gomorrah, then, he is not acting *in opposition* to the well-being of human beings but *in favor* of that well-being, even though his actions result in the destruction of many human lives. In addition, it is important to stress that the narrative does not speak of the violent behavior of the inhabitants of the two cities affecting God in any way but refers only to the effect that such behavior has on those being oppressed by them, as well as the threats they present to Lot and those dwelling in his house. God is therefore seen as acting, not for *his own* sake or for the sake of his own justice, but for the sake of those who need to be delivered and protected from such acts of violence and oppression.

While the measure that God takes in response to the behavior of the inhabitants of Sodom and Gomorrah is no doubt drastic and extreme, the narrative justifies it not only by stressing the outcry of those being affected by the violence perpetrated by the inhabitants of Sodom and Gomorrah and the gravity of their sin but also by the account of Abraham's intercession on behalf of the two cities (Gen 18:23-33). When Abraham tells God that it would not be good or right to destroy the righteous with the wicked, God agrees with him. The fact that God destroys the cities after having promised Abraham that he would not do so if he found ten righteous persons in them thus indicates that the two cities in their entirety had become corrupt, wicked, and violent. Among those righteous persons would have been Lot, his wife, and his two daughters. Had there been at least a handful of righteous persons in the two cities, there might have been some hope that the way of life that God desires to see in all for their own good might still prevail among at least some of the inhabitants. On their account, God might have been willing to spare the two cities. According to the logic of the narrative, however, if any hope of righteousness among the inhabitants had disappeared, then nothing could be gained by sparing the two cities, since the wickedness that had overtaken them would only grow worse and expand further if God did not act to extinguish it for good.

SEEKING GOOD IN EVIL

The Genesis account of the origins of human beings and their subjection to sin and death raises a number of theological questions and problems that are nowhere discussed or even acknowledged in the text. Precisely how those who composed, collected, and preserved the biblical texts would have attempted to resolve these questions and problems is not clear.

One of the main points that the Genesis narrative seems intended to convey is that God did not intend for there to be anything bad or evil in his creation. Yet because things such as pain, suffering, violence, and death seem to be an integral and inevitable part of the world as we know it, for readers in antiquity it would have been as difficult to conceive of a world without such things as it is for us today. While the biblical texts regard these things as existing contrary to God's original will, they leave unaddressed questions such as how the world could have existed without such things and how they came into existence. In both the Jewish and Christian traditions of interpretation it has been common to regard the figures of Adam and Eve as responsible for the entrance of sin and death into the world. The narrative never explains, however, why God planted the tree of the knowledge of good and evil in the garden and prohibited the man and woman from eating of its fruit. Nor does it say why the serpent chose to tempt the woman to eat of its fruit, apparently out of a desire to do the man and woman harm. Other questions such as why death should have followed as a consequence of the disobedience of the man and woman to God's command and why God did not want them to live forever are also left unaddressed.

The Genesis narrative also suggests that God did not know what would happen when he created the world. This is especially evident in Gen 6:5-6, where God is said to have regretted having made human beings. After God sends the great flood, his promise never to destroy humanity in that manner again suggests that he realized that such a measure was not the best way to resolve the problem of humanity's sinfulness. Other passages in the opening chapters of Genesis, including especially the account of the disobedience of the man and woman to God's command regarding the fruit of the tree, also seem to make sense only if it is supposed that God did not know fully ahead of time what human beings would do and how he would respond to their actions. The idea that God does not know all of the details of the future ahead of time is suggested elsewhere in the biblical texts as well. While at times the passages that speak in these terms appear to conflict with others in which God does seem to foresee the future, these two ideas do not necessarily contradict each other. If God is all-powerful and knows what he intends to do in the future, then he can have knowledge about many of the things that will happen without necessarily knowing the future in all of its details.

Perhaps the most serious problem reflected in the Genesis narrative regarding the origins of the world is that of theodicy, namely, why a God who is all-powerful and all-loving allows sin, evil, and suffering to exist. If nothing is impossible for God and if he loves all of his creatures, why does he not eradicate sin, evil, and suffering? And why did he not create human beings differently from the start so that they would do his will so as to enjoy the good rather than falling into behavior that was violent and destructive and would result in their death? While the biblical texts never address questions such as these explicitly, the belief in God's omnipotence and goodness reflected in them suggests that from God's perspective he had made the best world possible. If at some point after creation he realized that he should have made the world and human beings differently, he might have destroyed everything with the same power that made it possible for him to create the present world in order to make a better one. The fact that he does not do so seems to indicate a recognition on his part that he could not make a world that is any better than the present one.

As briefly noted above, the fact that God allows human beings to continue existing despite their sinful and destructive behavior suggests that God is convinced that at some point he will be able to alter or correct that behavior and resolve the problem of sin, evil, and suffering in some way, at least in part. It is important to stress, however, that according to the biblical narrative the problem that must be resolved is not one of *forgiveness* but rather the type of violent and destructive behavior described in Gen 6:5-6 and elsewhere in these opening chapters of Genesis. What human beings need in order to attain the well-being that God desires and intends for them is not simply to be forgiven but rather to be brought to leave behind the type of behavior that prevents them from attaining that well-being in order to live in ways that make it possible and promote it. It would do them no good for God simply to ignore, overlook, or pardon their destructive behavior, since the obstacle to their well-being is not located in God, God's justice, or God's inability to forgive wrongdoing, but in the ways of thinking and acting that fill the lives of human beings with pain, suffering, injustice, oppression, and other forms of evil.

According to the logic of the biblical narrative, therefore, if God wishes for human beings to enjoy his blessings and attain the good, he must find a way to bring them to change their ways of thinking, acting, and living so that they stop harming themselves and one another and instead make use of all that he has created in ways that benefit them. In fact, for God simply to pardon, ignore, and overlook their destructive behavior would constitute a *lack* of love and concern for them on his part since it would involve simply allowing that behavior to continue unchecked rather than taking measures aimed at enabling them to change and correct it for their own good.

This belief also sets the God of the biblical texts apart from the type of pagan gods considered in Chapter 1. In addition to the fact that those gods are not concerned with improving human behavior or bringing human beings to live in ways that enable them to enjoy well-being for their own sake, such understandings of the gods suppose that what human beings require is simply to keep the gods as happy as possible and give them whatever they demand in order to placate their anger when they become upset. In other words, what matters is not living in ways that lead to human well-being for intrinsic reasons but gaining and retaining the approval of the gods in all that one does. If the language of salvation is used in this regard, what human beings require in order to be saved is not to live in accordance with what is good and right but to please the gods by giving them what they desire and refraining from what provokes them to wrath. As we have noted previously, human beings need to be saved not only *by* the gods but *from* them. In contrast, in biblical thought human beings do not need to be saved *from* the God of Israel but only *by* him, since what prevents their salvation is not any obstacle lying *in God* but an obstacle lying *in them*, namely, the ways of thinking, acting, and living that prevent them from experiencing the well-being that God in his love desires for all.

Although the biblical texts never address explicitly the reason why God made the world and human beings as he did or offer answers to the question of why a good and all-powerful God allows evil and suffering, the observations just made suggest that those who composed, preserved, and collected the biblical texts might have responded to those questions by claiming that the ways of thinking, acting, and living necessary to experience the well-being that God desires for all cannot be imposed by force but must be brought about and embraced voluntarily. As we have already noted above, the fact that God is presented as responding to the violent and destructive behavior described in Gen 6:5–6 by sending a flood to destroy the vast majority of human beings and provide for a fresh start through Noah and his family clearly conveys the idea and assumption that God is not able to bring about unilaterally in human beings the type of behavior necessary for them to attain the well-being he intended for them. In that case, in order to accomplish his good purposes for human beings and creation as a whole, he had to create the world and human beings in the way that he did and must continue to allow them to exist in spite of the pain, suffering, and evil that has come to characterize their existence.

Affirmations such as these remain problematic for numerous reasons and cannot be thought to resolve the theological problems raised by the biblical texts in a manner that is entirely satisfactory. Nevertheless, in spite of the failure of the texts to provide answers to those problems, the fact that they consistently assume God's love for human beings as well as God's omnipotence over the creation he brought into existence indicates that they also assume that the reason why God has not destroyed the world he created in order to replace it with a better one is that he is convinced that he could not have made a world that is better than this one. At the same time, the fact that in his omnipotence and love for all he lets the world and human beings continue to exist in the condition that the biblical texts describe despite the pain, suffering, and evil that characterize that existence suggests that he believes that the manner in which he can bring about a better world is by remaining active in the present world to transform it rather than destroying it in order to start over by creating a different one.

CHAPTER 3

A God of Loving Demands and Demanding Love

Although the narrative that runs throughout the first eleven chapters of Genesis is clearly designed to convey certain core convictions regarding God and his intentions for human beings and the world in general, it also lays out the problem that God must resolve if those intentions are to be fulfilled. The creation account leaves no doubt that God wants only what is good for his creation and for the human beings whom he has placed over it. Those human beings, however, can attain that good only if they live and behave in ways that allow them to experience and enjoy the well-being that God in his love desires for them. They must care for one another and God's good creation, continually seeking the well-being of all others at the same time that they seek their own. Yet this is precisely what they fail to do. Rather than seeking the good for themselves and one another, they live and behave in ways that undermine and destroy their well-being. They persistently choose the bad instead of the good and are consumed by hatred, jealousy, rivalry, ambition, and selfish lusts and passions. All of these things fill their lives with pain and suffering and make it impossible for the good that God intended for them to be theirs.

According to the Genesis narrative, then, the problem that God must resolve is how to bring human beings to abandon their destructive behavior and instead live in ways that will allow them to attain the well-being and wholeness he desired for them from the start. In the language of Genesis, the reality that he must address is that from the time of their youth, "every inclination of the thoughts of their hearts" is "only evil continually," and as a result the earth has come to be filled with evil, violence, and corruption (Gen 6:5, 11-13; 8:21). The manner in which God will attempt to overcome that problem and accomplish his objective for human beings and the world is spelled out at the beginning of chapter 12 of the Genesis account: by means of the righteous Abraham and the nation that God will bring into existence through him, God will act to bless not only that nation itself but all of the families of the earth together with it. However, because human beings can experience and enjoy God's blessings of well-being and wholeness only if they live in ways that promote these things, God can accomplish his purposes for human beings only if he succeeds in bringing them to live in those ways. In order to bless them, therefore, God must provide them with the guidance and instruction they need to live in a manner that will allow them to enjoy the well-being he desires for them and must also bring about in them the desire and commitment to live in accordance with that guidance and instruction for their own good.

While such a reading of the Genesis narrative may seem relatively straightforward, uncontroversial, and self-evident, the reality is that it is strongly at odds with the interpretations of the biblical text that have held sway in the West for centuries, especially among Christians. The reason for this is that biblical interpreters have ascribed to the God of Israel the same type of motives and concerns that were believed to be characteristic of the pagan gods of antiquity. Supposedly, rather than dedicating himself fully to seeking the well-being of human beings and the created order in general as an end in itself, he was preoccupied with satisfying his own desires and the needs that are grounded in his nature. According to this manner of reading the biblical texts, while God certainly sought to bless human beings, those desires and needs made certain demands on him that had to be met if he was to accomplish his objective of blessing Israel and the nations with life, well-being, and wholeness.

GOD'S PLAN THROUGH ABRAHAM

Following the account of the tower of Babel in Genesis 11 and a list of the descendants of Noah's son Shem, the figure of Abram appears in the biblical narrative, together with his wife Sarai or Sarah. At the beginning of Genesis 12, God says to Abram: "Go from your country and your kindred and your father's house to the land that I will show you. And I will make of you a great nation, and I will bless you and make your name great so that you will be a blessing. I will bless those who bless you but will curse any who disdain you; and in you all the families of the earth will be blessed" (Gen 12:3).[1] This passage, which in many ways lays the basis for everything else that will follow in the biblical narrative regarding Israel, makes it clear that in spite of the sinful and destructive behavior of human beings, God remains firm in his commitment to bless them. In other words, rather than going back on his original intention for human beings or giving up on that intention, he continues to

---

1. The translation of the latter part of Gen 12:3 is problematic for a couple of reasons. First, while many English translations speak of God cursing those who curse Abraham, in reality the Hebrew text does not use the verb for "curse" in the second part of the phrase but instead uses a different verb that means "to make light of" or "disdain." On the translation used here, see Gordon J. Wenham, *Genesis 1–15*, WBC 1 (Waco, TX: Word, 1987), 276–77. Second, in principle the Hebrew phrase that appears at the very end of v. 3 may be translated in three different ways: "in you all the families of the earth will be blessed," "in you all the families of the earth will find blessing," and "by you all the families of the earth will bless themselves." Although many translators prefer the last of these options, the basic idea underlying all three of these translations must be considered essentially the same. As Wenham notes, "even if a reflexive 'bless themselves' is preferred here, it would also carry the implications of a middle or passive. For if those who bless Abram are blessed, and all families of the earth bless Abram, then it follows that 'all families will be blessed/find blessing in him" (278). It should also be noted that the earliest interpretation of this verse that we possess, namely, that of the Septuagint in the third century BCE, uses the passive voice "be blessed" in Greek rather than the middle voice "bless themselves."

desire that "all the families of the earth" attain the good he intended for them when he created the first man and woman and will seek to do whatever is necessary for that objective to be accomplished. Clearly, this can be due only to his unconditional love for all of the nations and peoples that are descended from that man and woman. This desire and intention to see all the families or nations of the earth blessed through Abram, who is subsequently renamed Abraham, is expressed repeatedly in the following chapters of Genesis.[2] There can be no doubt, therefore, that this idea is central to the narrative.

The narrative will eventually make it clear that the "great nation" of which God speaks in Gen 12:3 is the nation descended from Abraham through Sarah and their son Isaac as well as Isaac's son Jacob, who is renamed Israel after he wrestles with the angel of God in Gen 32:22-32. By linking the blessing of all the families of the earth to the blessing of Israel, the Genesis account conveys the idea that the blessing of Israel is not merely an end in itself but also constitutes a means by which God intends to bring blessing upon people of other nations.

Initially, no reason is given as to why God chose Abraham in order to carry out his purposes through him. As the narrative continues, however, that reason gradually becomes evident. When God tells Abraham to leave his homeland and family in order to go where God tells him, namely, the land of Canaan, Abraham immediately obeys (Gen 12:4-6). Given the perils and uncertainties of leaving the security of one's home and family in order to go to a place where one will be a foreigner and have no one to rely on except God himself, Abraham's obedience to God's command must be seen as an expression of profound faith in God. In the following chapters, the narrative consistently presents Abraham as a person who loves God and is committed to practicing what is good, right and just. The first thing that Abraham does after arriving in the land of Canaan is to erect an altar there and invoke God's name (12:7-8). In Gen 13:8-12, Abraham shows kindness and generosity by giving his nephew Lot the choice between two plots of land on which to dwell and put his herds out to pasture, thereby seeking to avoid any type of strife with Lot and his household. He also risks everything he has to rescue Lot and his family and possessions when they are taken captive (14:1-14). When Abraham offers tithes to God by presenting them to Melchizedek, the king of Salem and priest of the most high God, Melchizedek pronounces God's blessing on Abraham (14:18-20). Immediately thereafter, the king of Sodom offers to give him great wealth, yet Abraham refuses to receive it because he does not wish to enrich himself in that way (14:22-24). In Genesis 17, Abraham continues to manifest his faith in God and his promises by obeying God's command to be circumcised along with all the males of his household. The hospitality that Abraham shows when God appears to him in the form of three visitors in Gen 18:1-15 also underscores Abraham's righteousness and his concern for the well-being of others. Subsequently, when God shares

---

2. See Gen 18:18; 22:18; 26:4; 28:14.

with Abraham his intention to destroy the cities of Sodom and Gomorrah, Abraham intercedes repeatedly on behalf of their inhabitants in spite of their sinfulness and depravity, asking God to spare the wicked for the sake of the righteous (18:16-33).

All of these stories convey the idea that Abraham is a good and righteous man who cares for others and responds to God's blessings with gratitude and devotion.[3] According to the narrative, however, the reason why he behaves in this way and obeys God in all that God commands him is that he trusts in God and in God's goodness. While this idea is implicit throughout the narrative regarding Abraham, it is made explicit in two passages in particular. The first of these is Gen 15:6. There, after God has reiterated to Abraham his intention to give him a son through his wife Sarah even though she is far too old to bear children, it is said that "Abraham believed the LORD, and the LORD reckoned it to him as righteousness." Here Abraham is deemed righteous because he trusts and believes God's promise, in spite of the fact that Sarah's age seems to make it impossible for God to bring that promise to pass. It is important to stress that the logic underlying the passage is that God accepts Abraham as righteous not merely because he believes what God tells him but also because Abraham's faith and trust in God will lead him to continue to do all that God commands him. In other words, it is not merely Abraham's faith itself that leads God to view him as righteous but the type of life that will *result* from that faith.

The most outstanding expression of Abraham's faith and his willingness to obey God in all things, however, is the account of the binding of Isaac in Gen 22:1-19. There God tells Abraham to sacrifice his son Isaac to him. In principle, Abraham might have refused to obey God, not only due to the cruelty and inhumanity of such an act but also because Abraham could hardly expect to have another son with the aged Sarah. To put Isaac to death would therefore appear to make it impossible for the promises that God had made to Abraham to be fulfilled through Isaac. Rather than objecting to God's command, questioning God, or wavering in his trust in God's goodness and promises, Abraham does not hesitate to do as God commands. Just as Abraham is about to plunge the knife into Isaac in order to slay him, God calls out to Abraham and tells him: "Do not stretch out your hand against the boy or do anything to him; for now I know that you fear God, since you have not withheld your son, your only son, from me" (vv. 10-12). The story concludes with God telling Abraham: "Because you have done this and have

---

3. Although for the most part the Hebrew Bible does not explicitly describe Abraham as an extremely righteous individual, this idea seems to be assumed there, especially in the Genesis narrative. A variety of Jewish writings of the Second Temple period, however, make explicit mention of Abraham's surpassing righteousness and virtue; see, for example, Sir 44:19-20; 1 Macc 2:52; Pr Man 1:8; Jub. 17:17-18; 18:16; 23:10; Philo, *Abraham* 225-44; Josephus, *Ant.* 1.256. The allusions to Abraham as God's friend in 2 Chr 20:7 and Isa 41:8, as well as the description of Abraham as a prophet in Tob 4:12, can also be seen as implying that Abraham was an extremely righteous individual.

not withheld your son, your only son, I will certainly bless you, and I will make your offspring as numerous as the stars of heaven and as the grains of sand that are on the seashore. And your offspring will possess the gate of their enemies, and by your offspring will all the nations of the earth be blessed, because you have obeyed my voice" (vv. 16-18).

At first glance, it might seem that God's words to Abraham in this latter passage present a stark contrast with the words that God is said to have spoken to Abraham in Gen 12:1-3. Whereas initially God simply promises to bless Abraham, his descendants, and all the families of the earth in him without giving any reason as to why he has chosen Abraham for that blessing or laying down any conditions that must be fulfilled in order for Abraham and his descendants to attain it, in Gen 22:16-18 God affirms that the reason that he will bless Abraham and his descendants is that Abraham has obeyed him by being willing to offer up his son Isaac. In reality, however, this latter passage is merely making explicit what is presupposed in Gen 12:1-3. Just as God had chosen Noah to make a new start because he was a just and righteous man, so also had he chosen Abraham to create a new people through him because he anticipated that Abraham would trust in him and obey him by doing what is good and right. Of course, the narrative seems to assume that God did not know for certain from the start whether Abraham would in fact obey him in all things, yet Abraham's behavior confirms this to be true. While Abraham behaves obediently and righteously prior to receiving the command to offer up Isaac in sacrifice to God, his willingness to obey God by offering up Isaac demonstrates beyond a shadow of a doubt that Abraham will obey God in all things and trust him no matter what God asks of him. It is this that God wants, *not for his own sake*, but because Abraham's faith and obedience provide a basis for hoping that through him God can bring into existence a people who will live in the same type of faith and obedience so as to attain the well-being that God desires for all by practicing the justice and righteousness necessary for that well-being to exist. And once that people has been brought into existence, it will be possible to bring other peoples and nations to live in the same faith, obedience, justice, and righteousness by means of that people.

The idea that Abraham's commitment to justice and righteousness constituted the basis upon which God made to him the promises that he did is also present in Gen 26:3-5. There, following Abraham's death, God tells Isaac: "I will make your offspring as numerous as the stars of heaven, and I will give to your offspring all these lands; and all the nations of the earth will be blessed through your offspring, because Abraham obeyed my voice and kept my charge, my commandments, my statutes, and my laws" (vv. 4-5). These words imply that Abraham's obedience to God's will is the basis for the promises he makes not only with regard to the multiplication of Isaac's offspring but also with regard to the blessing of the nations. In other words, the nations will be blessed or bless themselves as a result of Abraham's obedience to God. The idea is that Abraham's obedience and righteous conduct will bring not only his descendants through Isaac but also people of other nations to live in the same obedience and righteousness so that they may attain the blessings of wholeness and well-being that result from such a way of life.

The hope that Abraham's own obedience and righteousness will make it possible to form from him a people who will be characterized by the same kind of obedience and righteousness is expressed explicitly in Gen 18:17-19. There, as God contemplates his intention to destroy Sodom and Gomorrah due to the wickedness of their inhabitants, he is presented as asking himself: "Shall I hide from Abraham what I am about to do, seeing that Abraham will become a great and mighty nation and that all the nations of the earth will be blessed in him? No, for I have chosen him, that he may charge his children and his household after him to keep the way of the LORD by doing righteousness and justice, so that the LORD may bring about for Abraham what he has promised him." Here it is not merely Abraham's own obedience, justice, and righteousness that will enable God's promises of blessing to Abraham's descendants and the nations of the earth to be fulfilled, but the hope and expectation that those who will descend from him will live in the same type of obedience, justice, and righteousness seen in Abraham.

In Genesis 17, Abraham's faith, obedience, and righteousness are presented as the basis upon which God establishes his covenant with Abraham. The chapter begins with God telling Abraham: "I am God Almighty; walk before me, and be blameless. And I will make my covenant between me and you, and will make you exceedingly numerous" (vv. 1-2). While these verses do not affirm explicitly that the condition upon which God makes his covenant with Abraham is that he walk before him blamelessly, they certainly express that expectation and see it as related in some way to the establishment of that covenant. Of course, Abraham will not be blameless in the sense of being perfectly sinless throughout his life. As the Hebrew Scriptures make clear elsewhere, to live blamelessly is not to be entirely free of sin but rather to be fully committed to living in accordance with God's will. Many readers of the Genesis account, for example, would have considered that Abraham's conduct in concealing his relationship to Sarah in Gen 12:10-20 and 20:1-13 as well as his treatment of Hagar and Ishmael in Gen 21:8-14 was not fully in accordance with the practice of what is good and right.

After God indicates his intention to establish his covenant with Abraham in the opening verse of Genesis 17, he defines the content of that covenant in terms of making Abraham the father of many nations, giving the land of Canaan to his offspring, and being God to them and to Abraham himself (vv. 4-8). God then commands Abraham and his descendants to keep his covenant and to be circumcised as a sign of that covenant (vv. 9-14). As other passages from the Hebrew Scriptures will emphasize further on, this circumcision is to serve as a reminder not only of God's covenant with Abraham but also of the life of faith, obedience, justice, and righteousness that characterized Abraham and is to characterize all of his descendants as well.

The narrative regarding Abraham in chapters 12–26 of Genesis, therefore, makes it very clear what God wants to see happen. Just as he initially blessed the first human beings when he created them, God continues to desire to bless all the families of the earth and intends to do so by means of Abraham and the descendants he will give him through Isaac and Jacob, who will be blessed in a special way. Yet because the happiness, wholeness, and well-being that God desires for all depends on their living in justice and righteousness in accordance with God's will and avoiding the type of violence and destructive behavior described in the previous chapters of Genesis, in order for all of these people to attain and enjoy the blessings God desires for them, they must be brought to live as God desires and commands for the good of all. If they do not, no matter how much God may wish to bless them, he will not be able to do so, since rather than benefiting from his blessings they will use them to harm and destroy themselves and one another.

Even though the Genesis narrative conveys the idea that the faith, obedience, and righteousness of Abraham constitute the basis for his election as the one through whom God will fulfill his promises, it is important to stress that Abraham is not regarded as having earned God's favor and blessings by his obedience and righteousness, as if that favor and those blessings were due to him on account of his obedient and righteous conduct. If Abraham's obedience and righteousness are a condition for attaining God's blessing, this is not because God wants such obedience and righteousness for *his own* sake and therefore promises to bless Abraham in exchange for receiving what he desires, but rather due to the intrinsic relationship between obedient and righteous conduct and the well-being that such conduct makes possible. God's intention to bless Abraham and his descendants and all the families of the earth through them is an act of pure grace on the part of God rather than something merited or deserved by Abraham, yet that grace can accomplish God's purposes only if human beings such as Abraham respond to God's goodness by living in the way necessary for them to enjoy the happiness and blessings that God desires for all. As the story of Abraham illustrates, when people believe and trust in God as one who is both sovereign and good, they do what God commands for their own good out of love for them.

THE LAW THAT GIVES LIFE

To some extent, everything that appears in the narrative that follows in the remainder of the book of Genesis, as well as in the Pentateuch and the Hebrew Scriptures as a whole, can be regarded as aiming toward the fulfillment of the promises God makes to Abraham and his descendants in Gen 12:1-3 and elsewhere in the account of Abraham's life. Nevertheless, for the reasons we have just seen, those promises can be fulfilled only if the people descended from Abraham are brought to practice justice, righteousness, mercy, and love in relation to one another and refrain from oppressing one another and doing one another harm. Only if they come to live in such a manner can they be blessed with well-being.

Although throughout the biblical narrative God is presented as acting in a variety of different ways to bring about such a way of life in his people Israel, the primary means by which he seeks to accomplish that objective is the law or Torah that he gives them through Moses at Mount Sinai following their liberation from slavery in Egypt. While that law is generally understood as consisting of a series of commandments, in reality the Hebrew term *torah* refers to guidance, direction, and instruction. The use of this term conveys the idea that, by means of the commandments he gives, God graciously lays out for his people the way of life that will enable them to enjoy the well-being he desires for them.

This is not to say, however, that it is improper to translate *torah* into English as "law." The use of this English term is suggested by the Septuagint's translation of *torah* as *nomos*, which also tends to be rendered into English as "law" in most versions of the Christian Bible. It should be noted, however, that in ancient contexts *nomos* generally referred to a norm, custom, order, tradition, or convention and not merely a law in the sense in which this word is commonly understood in English.[4] It is likely, therefore, that those who produced and read the Septuagint viewed the collection of prescriptions that the Hebrew calls the Torah as a set of customs or conventions rather than a legal code as we understand it today. In that case, the translation of *torah* as *nomos* should be seen as reflecting the idea that the Torah lays out a particular way of life and a series of norms that serve as a basis for ordering life among God's people Israel. Like the Hebrew term *torah*, the *nomos* or law given by God would be seen as promoting the people's well-being by ordering their life in ways that will benefit them.

This concept of the law or Torah as a gracious gift is comprehensible only if the God who is said to have given it is seen as having done so out of love for his people rather than for his own sake. Such a view of the God of Israel distinguishes him sharply from the pagan gods of antiquity. Because those gods were concerned primarily for their own needs and desires, any laws or commandments they gave human beings were not an expression of love for them or an attempt to promote their well-being as an end in itself but rather an imposition aimed at enabling the gods to obtain what they needed or wanted for themselves, whether directly or indirectly. As such, those laws or commandments constituted a burden for human beings, who had no choice but to fulfill the desires and commands of the gods in order to remain in good favor with them and avoid provoking them to wrath. Undoubtedly, knowledge regarding the will of the gods enabled human beings to obtain blessings from them, since the gods responded favorably to those who obeyed them

---

4. See H. Kleinknecht and W. Gutbrod, "*nómos*," *Theological Dictionary of the New Testament*, vol. 4, ed. Gerhard Kittel and Gerhard Friedrichs, trans. G. W. Bromiley (Grand Rapids: Eerdmans, 1964), 1022-90 (1023-24).

by rewarding their obedience, yet both the gods who gave commands and the human beings who obeyed them were acting out of self-interest, seeking primarily something for themselves rather than pursuing the well-being of others as an end in itself.

The notion that the commandments given to the people of Israel by God through Moses constitute a gracious gift or blessing runs contrary to the manner in which those commandments have been portrayed in much Jewish and Christian thought over the centuries. The reason for this is precisely that the God of the Hebrew Bible has been viewed as acting in the same ways and for the same reasons as the pagan gods of antiquity. According to much traditional thought, God chose Israel as his people and gave them the commandments *for his own sake*, since his purpose was to obtain for himself a people who would satisfy his desire to be worshiped, served, and obeyed. The logic underlying such a conception of God and the commandments is that of *do ut des*: God gave his laws to the people in order that they might give him what he wanted for his own sake, while at the same time those laws enabled the people to obtain from God what they needed and wanted for their own sake by obeying what God had commanded. Rather than being an expression of God's love and his concern for the well-being of his people, God's commandments were a means by which God sought something for himself.

It has also been common to view God's law as an expression of God's just and holy nature. Supposedly, God's justice, righteousness, and holiness do not allow God to tolerate any kind of behavior that is incompatible with his nature. While God wishes to bless and save human beings out of love for them, his righteous and holy nature makes certain demands on him and requires that those demands be met in order for him to be in the presence of human beings, show them his acceptance, or grant them his blessings. By means of the commandments, therefore, God makes known to his people the conditions that they must fulfill if he is to be able to accept, forgive, and bless them. The people are brought to know which actions and behaviors are incompatible with God's nature and thus intolerable for him so that they may avoid those actions and behaviors and thereby obtain from him the good things that he wishes to give them by giving him the obedience he seeks. Those commandments also inform them of the punishments that God's holy and righteous nature will make it necessary for him to impose on them if they disobey him.

According to such an understanding of God and his law, both God and human beings are subject to the dictates of God's nature, which places limits on God and defines what he can and cannot do. It is said that it is impossible for God to act in ways that run contrary to his holy and righteous nature and therefore that God has no choice but to act in conformity with his nature. God's nature compels him to act in certain ways and imposes on him certain conditions and requirements that he must satisfy if he is to exist and to relate to human beings in the way he desires. This manner of understanding God's relation to the world and nature is essentially the same as that which is found in the belief systems of other peoples in antiquity. As we saw in the first chapter of this study, in those systems of thought the gods were viewed as being subject to certain forces or laws of nature that existed prior to them and set limits on them, defining what they could and could not do. They had no choice but to submit to these forces and laws and obey them. To claim that the God of the Hebrew Bible has no choice but to act in conformity with his own holy and righteous nature, therefore, involves subjecting him to certain forces or laws that are inherent to his being and dictate to him what he can and cannot do.

When the commandments given by God are understood on the basis of this concept of God, their purpose is seen in terms of responding to some need on God's part to safeguard his holiness or ensure that his strict justice is satisfied as he relates to human beings. In that case, God gives the commandments *for his own sake*, that is, for the sake of his holiness, justice, and righteousness, which cannot be compromised but must be upheld or safeguarded. While in a sense God's commandments benefit human beings in that their observance makes it possible for God to relate favorably to them in the way he desires, their purpose is not to benefit human beings in and of themselves but to satisfy some requirement found in God's nature that stands in the way of God's desire to bless and save sinful human beings freely. For the same reason, those commandments are not expressions of God's love but rather of God's justice and holiness, which are *in conflict* with God's love in that they place limits and conditions on God and prevent him from manifesting his love for sinful human beings in the ways he desires unless the demands that they make on him are met.

According to this understanding of God's law, while God gives his commandments in order to bring about in his people a life of justice and righteousness, his demand that they lead such a life is ultimately rooted not in a concern for their well-being but rather in his own inability or unwillingness to tolerate unrighteousness on account of his perfectly holy and righteous nature. In other words, what matters to God is not the effect that the behavior of human beings has *on them* but rather the effect that it has *on him*. The reason that people must keep God's commandments is not that the failure to obey them does them harm and prevents them from enjoying the well-being that results intrinsically from their observance but rather that his holy and righteous nature will not let him tolerate or accept them if they behave in ways that are incompatible with that nature. According to this logic, while there is a sense in which it can be said that God wishes for his people to obey his commandments for *their own* sake, the obstacle that must be overcome in order for them to attain wholeness and well-being is found not *in them* but *in God*. They need to live in justice and righteousness, not because the failure to do so harms them directly, but rather because God's nature prevents him from accepting them and granting them his blessings unless their behavior is in conformity with the demands of his nature.

The Torah and Shalom

If there is one Hebrew word that can summarize the blessing that God desires for Israel and all the other nations of the world, it is *shalom*. Although this term is generally translated into English as "peace," in reality it refers to well-being in a much broader sense. The Hebrew noun is derived from the adjective *shalam*, which literally means "complete" or "whole." For that reason, it can be seen as referring to all aspects of life, including physical and emotional health, the satisfaction of basic needs, the absence of any kind of hardship or suffering, and healthy relations with family members, friends, and others within the community. Applied to a society as a whole, *shalom* can be said to exist when there is equity, prosperity, harmony, security, justice, happiness, fullness of life, and well-being for all in both body and soul. In contrast, when any of these things are lacking for any within the society or community, that society or community cannot rightly be said to be whole or to enjoy shalom in the way that it should.

Because God can bless his people with that kind of well-being only if they live in ways that promote it and make it possible rather than undermining or destroying it, however, God's first task must be that of bringing them to live in those ways. It is this that he seeks to do by means of the commandments of the Torah.

At the same time, of course, if the people are to attain that well-being, they must not only receive the instruction and guidance that God provides them by means of his commandments but must also submit willingly and obediently to those commandments. This involves being fully committed to their own well-being in the same way that God is. Obviously, the people cannot enjoy shalom if they are not committed to living in ways that make that shalom possible. Yet because the well-being or shalom of each individual is inseparable from the well-being of everyone else in the community and society of which all form part, the only way in which each individual can truly seek his or her own well-being is by being fully committed to the well-being of everyone else within the community or society at the same time. By definition, however, to be committed to the well-being of others as an end in itself is to *love* them. For that reason, one can love oneself and seek one's own well-being and happiness only if one is committed to loving others by seeking their well-being and happiness at the same time. If God wishes to bless people with well-being and shalom, therefore, he must bring them to love one another in that way, which is the same way in which God himself loves them. In biblical thought, the Torah is the means by which he seeks to accomplish that objective.

In order for the people whom God loves to be brought to live in accordance with the Torah of their own accord, they must be convinced of two truths. First, they must believe that God knows what is best for them and in fact knows better than they do how they must live in order to attain the well-being that he desires for them and that they desire for themselves. This belief depends on another, namely, that God is the sovereign creator of all that exists and therefore possesses an understanding of the world and the creatures he has made that far exceeds their own. That understanding enables him to guide them in the way that they should go for their own good. Second, they must believe that God loves them unconditionally and seeks their well-being as an end in itself. Only if they are convinced of these two things will they believe that the things that God asks and demands of them are truly in their own best interest. If they do not believe that God knows what is best for them, they will not want to obey him but will instead seek to define on their own independently of God the way of life that they believe will truly promote their well-being. Alternatively, if they believe that God is pursuing some end other than their well-being by means of the things that he asks and demands of them, they will not want to do what he commands but will instead choose to follow their own will in an attempt to attain the well-being they desire for themselves.

In principle, of course, even those who are not convinced that God knows what is best for them and that in love he seeks their well-being as an end in itself may still feel compelled to obey what he commands in order to try to keep him content and avoid provoking him to anger. They can hardly enjoy or pursue well-being if their conduct is leading God to inflict suffering and punishments on them because it is contrary to his will. Similarly, because the well-being of a people depends on their receiving from God things that are in large part under his control rather than their own, such as abundant harvests, freedom from sickness and disease, and deliverance from enemies who are more powerful than they, they must strive to obtain and retain his favor by doing whatever he demands of them, even if they believe that his demands are not in themselves aimed at their well-being but instead respond to his own needs, desires, or self-interests.

In that case, however, those who receive God's commandments will constantly be in conflict with them and wish to rebel against them. If from their perspective God's will for them and their own will for themselves are at odds with one another rather than being one and the same, they will continually be forced to choose between doing God's will and their own. They will want to obey what God commands in order to remain under his favor and avoid his wrath, yet at the same time they will want to *disobey* God in order to follow their own desires and pursue what they regard as being in their own best interest. As a result, when they believe that they can escape God's notice or his punishment, they will disregard and disobey God's will in order to do their own will instead. When they find themselves in a situation in which they believe themselves to be under God's scrutiny and feel threatened by God, however, they will submit to his will in order to avoid arousing his wrath and being punished by him. When they obey him, therefore, they will do so reluctantly, motivated primarily by fear of God's punishments.

By definition, any who live and act in that manner cannot be happy or enjoy well-being or shalom. Their fear of punishment will fill them with constant anxiety and prevent them from being at peace. The conflict that they will experience in their interior will be ongoing, since they will continually be forced to choose between behaving in ways that they find burdensome and disagreeable in order to please God and running the risk of provoking God to wrath by disobeying him so as to follow their own desires and impulses instead. Rather than feeling free to act in accordance with their own will as they see fit, they will feel obliged to submit to God's will as if they were his slaves and had no choice but to seek to please him rather than pleasing themselves. In other words, because their own will and the will of God will constantly be in conflict with one another, whether they choose God's will over their own or instead choose their own will over God's, they will suffer.

For these reasons, if God is to bring his people to follow the instruction and guidance he gives them through the Torah gladly and willingly—which is the only way that the Torah can actually be obeyed, since half-hearted and reluctant obedience will not truly be obedience—, he must demonstrate to them that he sincerely loves them and seeks nothing but their well-being. At the same time, he must also convince them that he knows what is best for them. Only in that way will they come to be united in a single will with God, wanting the same things that he wants and making his own will their own voluntarily so as to do whatever he commands with gladness. Rather than considering God's will a burden or imposition, they will see it as something that benefits them and will regard it as the greatest good, since they will be convinced that there is no path that they could follow that would bring them greater happiness and well-being than the one God has laid out for them in his infinite love and wisdom.

According to the book of Exodus, the actions that God takes in relation to his people Israel after they have fallen into slavery in Egypt demonstrate to them precisely the two things just mentioned, namely, that God loves them and that he is sovereign over all people and things. God manifests his love for the people by delivering them from their bondage and oppression at the hand of the Pharoah in order to take them to the good land he had promised to them, where they will be able to enjoy the bounteous blessings he wishes to pour out on them. At the same time, the Pharoah's persistent refusal to let the Israelites go provides God with the opportunity to demonstrate to the Israelites his sovereign power. This he does by means of the ten plagues as well as the parting of the sea and the destruction of the Pharoah's army. By demonstrating to the people both his love for them and his sovereignty, God hopes to gain their trust so that they will believe that whatever he asks and commands of them is in their own best interest and is motivated solely by a concern for their happiness and well-being.

Only when the Israelites have witnessed and experienced both God's sovereignty and his love for them does God take them to Mount Sinai in order to explain to them through Moses his intentions for them. Upon their arrival there, he tells them: "You have seen what I did to the Egyptians and how I bore you on eagles' wings and brought you to myself. Now, therefore, if you obey my voice and keep my covenant, you will be my treasured possession out of all the peoples" (Exod 19:3-5). However, because God can bless the people with the well-being he desires for them only if they live in a way that promotes that well-being rather than destroying it, he must also provide them with the instruction necessary to bring about such a way of life among them. This he does by means of the commandments or precepts that he gives them through Moses.

It is important to stress, however, that the precepts that God lays down for the people do not constitute conditions that they must fulfill in order for God to love them. On the contrary, his love for them is a given, since that love is *unconditional*. Rather than being conditions for obtaining God's love, those precepts are conditions for attaining the well-being that God desires for them in his love. The people cannot enjoy that well-being, for example, if they practice murder, adultery, theft, and falsehood or covet what is not their own rather than seeking to assist and care for one another and to build one another up in love. For that reason, God makes it clear to the people that if they are to live as his own and enjoy his blessings in the land he wishes to give to them, they must commit themselves to acting in ways that will benefit them and avoid behaviors that will do them and others harm. In other words, as Exod 19:3-5 makes clear, the people will be God's treasured possession only if they obey his voice and keep his covenant, not because God will cease to love them if they disobey him, but because only if they trust fully in him will they obey him so as to live as his own.

The Commandments as a Means to Promoting Well-Being for All

For readers of the biblical texts in antiquity, the purpose of most of the commandments that appear in the Torah would have been self-evident. By means of those commandments, God sought to promote justice, peace, equity, and well-being among his people. These things would be seen as resulting both directly and indirectly from the observance of his commandments.

In many cases, the manner in which particular commandments contributed to human well-being was quite obvious. A number of the commandments, for example, clearly had the purpose of promoting and preserving within homes and families relationships that might be healthy and strong. Such was the case with the command to honor one's parents and the prohibition of adultery in the Decalogue or Ten Commandments, as well as the commandments that sons and daughters show respect for their parents and not curse or strike them.[5] The prohibition of incest and other forms of sexual immorality as well as the command that nakedness not be uncovered within the family served the same purpose.[6] Many of these commandments also

---

5. See Exod 20:12, 14; 21:15, 17; Lev 19:3; 20:9; Deut 21:18-21; 27:16.
6. See Lev 18:6-20; 20:10-21; Deut 22:13-30; 27:22-23.

sought to protect individuals from sexual abuse and other forms of mistreatment or neglect, including especially those who were at greatest risk of such abuse, such as young women and girls and women who were pregnant.[7]

Other commandments were aimed at promoting social justice and combating various forms of injustice. In addition to prohibiting stealing and false testimony in the Decalogue, the Torah mandated against any form of deception and dishonesty.[8] Weights and measures were to be fair. No one was to swear a false oath, slander another person, or move a boundary marker so as to wrongly claim a portion of the property of their neighbor as their own. Kidnapping, extortion, and murder by hire were explicitly forbidden as well. The innocent were not to be punished in the place of the guilty and corporal punishment was not to be overly harsh or denigrating for the one receiving it. Special care was to be taken so that legal proceedings would be fair and equitable and any perversion of justice might be avoided. Judges were not to show any type of partiality and were not to receive gifts, since this might influence their decisions or give the appearance that they had shown favoritism in exchange for those gifts. Measures were to be taken so that no one would be convicted of wrongdoing on the basis of false testimony, and special provisions were to be made in order to deal with difficult cases. The principle of "an eye for an eye and a tooth for a tooth" was not generally understood as something to be applied literally but rather had the intention of ensuring that punishments in a judicial setting were neither excessive nor overly lenient. The idea that justice was to reign in all that was done is stressed especially in Deut 16:20, which states: "Justice, and only justice, you shall pursue, so that you may live and occupy the land that the LORD your God is giving you."

Numerous commandments also sought to avoid or minimize damage to people and property.[9] Provisions were made to compensate victims of accidents or of negligence on the part of others. If someone accidentally took the life of another person or their animal, restitution was prescribed. The same was true if someone maimed another person or injured them in some other way, whether intentionally or unintentionally. The roofs of houses were to have parapets around them to keep children and others from falling off. Those who injured their slaves by mistreating them were required to liberate them. Cities of refuge were also provided for those who accidentally killed someone in order to protect them from acts of revenge, although if the killing was intentional the murderer was not to be afforded protection.

In most societies, the rich and powerful tend to dictate laws in their favor and impose their will on the rest of the population in order to promote and protect their own interests. In the Torah, however, one is hard-pressed to

---

7. See Exod 21:8-11, 22; 22:16-17; Lev 19:29; 20:10-14, 17-21; Deut 23:17-18.

8. On this point and those that follow, see Exod 20:13, 15-17; 21:12-25; 22:1-4; 23:1-9; Lev 6:2-3; 19:11-13, 15-16, 35-36; 24:17-20; Num 25:16-34; 30:2; 35:30-33; Deut 5:20; 16:18-20; 17:6; 19:14-21; 24:7; 25:2-3, 13-16; 27:17, 24-25.

9. On this point and those that follow, see Exod 21:18-36; 22:5-15; Lev 24:18-21; Num 5:5-8; 35:9-15; Deut 19:1-13; 22:8.

find commandments that favor the powerful over the weak. On the contrary, throughout the Torah the concern is consistently for the weak and under-privileged within the society.[10] The command not to oppress the poor and the needy is stated explicitly in several passages. Numerous commandments protected widows, orphans, foreigners, slaves, the elderly, and those with physical disabilities. These commandments not only prohibited mistreating and neglecting members of these groups but also required that measures be taken to assist them. Fields were not to be reaped fully so that some of their fruits and grains might be left over for those who were hungry and in need, while a portion of the tithes and offerings were to be shared with the weaker elements of society. Those who had sufficient resources were to lend to the poor at no interest and were not to take away as a pledge the millstone with which they ground their grain. While a cloak might be received as pledge for a loan, the cloak was to be returned to the debtors at night so that they might not go cold. Workers were to receive their wages on the same day that they had labored so that they might be able to meet their needs daily. The book of Deuteronomy tells the people explicitly: "There will be no poor among you" (Deut 15:4). Clearly, this represented an ideal toward which all were to strive rather than constituting an expectation that poverty would in fact disappear entirely in the land if all obeyed God's commandments, yet the care and concern that all were to show for one another would make it possible to approach that ideal to a great extent.

Although the law prescribed many concrete actions that were designed to promote the well-being of all, it also demanded that all of God's people love and care for one another in general terms. In Lev 19:17-18, the people are told: "You shall not hate in your heart anyone of your kin; you shall reprove your neighbor, or you will incur guilt yourself. You shall not take vengeance or bear a grudge against any of your people, but you shall love your neighbor as yourself." These commands cover all aspects of the people's life.[11] In all of their daily dealings with others, they were to seek the well-being of all, do what was good and right, and avoid anything that might do others harm. They were not to practice evil, join in with the wicked, desire ill for others, or act presumptuously. They were also to purge evil from their midst, avoid any type of oppression, and show kindness even to their enemies. Those who had at their disposal resources with which they might assist the poor were commanded not only to provide them with the assistance they needed but to do so generously and willingly. The command for them to reprove their neighbor meant that they were also to demand these same things of others around them by insisting that their fellow Israelites treat one another with love and by acting to admonish and correct them when they failed or refused

---

10. On this point and those that follow, see Exod 22:21-27; 23:9-11; Lev 19:9-10, 13-14, 32-34; 23:22; 24:22; 25:35-37; Deut 10:19; 14:22-29; 15:4-14; 23:7, 19-20; 24:6, 10-22; 26:12-13; 27:18-19.

11. For other commandments prescribing care and concern for others in general terms, see Exod 23:1-2, 6-9; Lev 19:33-34; Deut 10:19; 15:7-11; 23:16; 24:17.

to do so. At the same time, these commands go beyond prescribing outward actions to address what was to be in the people's heart. They were not merely to refrain from doing harm to others in order to offer them instead their help and support but to be committed in their heart to seeking the well-being of all around them and to avoid wishing ill for others, bearing a grudge against them, or desiring to get back at those who had done them wrong by exacting vengeance on them.

While there are few commandments in the Torah that are as general in scope as the command to love one's neighbor, it seems likely that commandments that were more specific in nature were applied in a broad sense to address other areas of life. Whereas in our contemporary world we tend to derive specific laws and regulations from broader principles, such as that of loving one's neighbor, in Jewish tradition it became common to do the opposite by deriving general principles from commandments that addressed explicitly only specific situations. Thus, for example, the commandment to place parapets around the sides of the flat roofs of houses so that no one might fall off of them would be applied in a more general sense to insist that any house or building that was constructed be designed in ways that sought to ensure the safety of all who would use or occupy it (Deut 22:8). The commandment to take back to one's enemy his donkey if one found it going astray would be interpreted in the sense that one should always strive to practice justice and kindness to one's enemies in other situations and contexts as well (Exod 23:4-5; Deut 22:1-4). Similarly, the general principle that one should not take advantage of those who were limited by any kind of physical or mental disability or do them harm but instead help them out in whatever way possible would be derived from the commandment not to pronounce curses on a deaf person or put a stumbling-block in the path of a blind person (Lev 19:14).

It is also important to note that, with few exceptions, the laws found in the Torah apply to all equally. Whereas in antiquity it was generally the rulers and elites who dictated the laws for the people under them, in the Torah it is God alone. The task of seeking justice and equity is presented as belonging to all of the members of the community and not merely to the rulers or elites. Similarly, both the rich and the poor were subject to the same laws. The compensation required if one injured a wealthy person was the same as that required for injuring a poor person, a slave, or a foreigner. Undoubtedly, the Torah anticipated that different social classes would exist among the people. In particular, it allowed for slavery, yet this was commonplace in the contexts of antiquity.[12] While from our modern perspective slavery is certainly oppressive, in antiquity it often served as a means by which those who were destitute could obtain food and shelter for themselves and their family by selling themselves and their labor to someone who could provide them with these things. The Torah also contained commandments aimed at the care and protection

---

12. See Exod 21:1-11; Lev 25:35-46.

of slaves.[13] If they suffered certain injuries at the hands of their owner, slaves were to be freed. Owners who killed a slave were to be punished. Runaway slaves were to be protected as well. In fact, the Torah prohibits returning runaway slaves to their owners.

In the one passage in which prescriptions are given regarding kings, the concern is that of limiting their power and authority rather than protecting their position or interests (Deut 17:14-20). In addition to mandating that any king set over the people be one of their own rather than a foreigner, this passage prohibited the kings from taking many wives and acquiring for themselves many horses and great wealth. The idea is clearly that the king must not be an oppressive figure, enriching himself at the people's expense rather than being concerned for their welfare and well-being above all else. The kings are also commanded to read and study the Torah continually in order to be subject to it and promote its observance among the people. This passage from Deuteronomy thus stresses that the king is not above the law and is also not above the other members of the community. For that reason, he is not to exalt himself over them. Such a vision of the monarchy contrasts notably with the visions of most other peoples in antiquity.

One of the most important commandments that is repeated numerous times throughout the Torah is that which prescribes rest on every seventh day or Sabbath.[14] This commandment applied to all within the society, including not only the rich and the poor but also slaves, foreigners, and even animals. It not only prevented people from being overworked but also allowed them to enjoy life by dedicating themselves periodically to resting and relaxing. This same desire that life be enjoyable is reflected in other commandments as well.[15] Those who had recently built a house, planted a vineyard, or taken a wife, for example, were not to go to war for a year so that they might have some time to enjoy their married life or the fruit of their labors. In fact, in a number of passages the book of Deuteronomy even commands that the people rejoice, generally in the context of allusions to the feasts they were to celebrate as they shared among themselves the portions of their sacrificial offerings that the law assigned to them for their consumption.[16]

In addition to prescribing that animals were to rest from their labors on the Sabbath in the same way that human beings did, the Torah included provisions that were designed to protect them and avoid their suffering.[17] Animals of two different kinds were not to be made to plow together and an ox treading grain was not to be muzzled. Certain types of crossbreeding were forbidden and baby calves were not to be boiled in their mother's milk.

---

13. See Exod 21:20, 26-27; Lev 25:39-43; Deut 15:12-14; 23:15-16.

14. See Exod 20:8-11; 23:12; 31:12-17, 21; 34:21; 35:2-3; Lev 19:3, 30; 23:3; 26:2; Deut 5:12-15.

15. On this point and those that follow, see Lev 19:24; 23:39-40; Deut 20:5-7; 24:5.

16. See Deut 12:7, 12, 18; 14:22-26; 16:11, 14; 27:7.

17. On this point and those that follow, see Exod 21:33-36; 22:19; 23:19; 34:26; Lev 18:23; 19:19; 20:15-16; 24:18; Deut 14:21; 22:6-7, 10; 25:4.

Human beings were not to use animals to gratify their sexual desires. While eggs or baby chicks might be taken from a nest for food, the mother was to be left alone so that she might have other broods again in the future.

The laws concerning the Sabbath applied not only to the seventh day of every week but also to every seventh year as well as the year of Jubilee, which concluded every seventh period of seven years.[18] These laws not only provided for a more extensive period of rest but also sought to restore equity among the people, which would inevitably be eroded over time as wealth gradually came to be concentrated in the hands of a select few while many others fell into poverty and hardships. By periodically returning properties to their previous owners, freeing slaves, and canceling debts, the law sought to ensure that resources be distributed as equitably as possible and offered a fresh start to those who had fallen upon hard times or had lost their freedom or possessions. These laws also prescribed that lands periodically lie fallow so that over time the fields might remain as fertile and productive as possible.

Numerous sanitary measures were also prescribed in order to avoid sickness and plague.[19] Lepers and other persons with diseases that were possibly contagious were to be isolated from the rest of the community. Quarantines were also mandated for those who were in need of special treatment out of the same concern. Care was to be taken when handling corpses and giving proper burial to those who had died. Many of the laws regarding cleansing and purity also had the purpose of promoting good health among the people. Some of the prescriptions regarding diet were probably understood as having the same purpose.

Of course, the Torah also prescribed punishments for the violation of many of the commandments and prohibitions it contains. These were necessary in order to enforce their observance. From a modern perspective, many of these punishments seem excessively harsh and even inhumane, especially those that mandate putting to death those who do things such as commit adultery, worship other gods, take God's name in vain, or fail to respect their parents.[20] Like the laws regarding slavery, however, such punishments seem to have been common in the context of antiquity. In any case, these punishments were not designed to promote any type of vengeance or inflict suffering on wrongdoers as an end in itself but rather were thought to have the purpose of contributing in various ways to the preservation of peace, justice, order, and equity among the people.

While the Torah undoubtedly prescribes *retributive* justice, it should be clear from the overall content of the laws just considered that it stresses much more strongly the notion of *distributive* justice. The primary concern behind the commandments taken as a whole is that there be equity and order among

---

18. On this point and those that follow, see Exod 21:2; 23:10-11; Lev 25:1-55; Deut 15:1-18.

19. On this point and those that follow, see Exod 22:31; Lev 5:2-3; 7:19; 11:27-28, 39-40; 13:1–15:33; 17:15; 22:3-8; Num 5:1-9; 19:11-16; Deut 24:8.

20. See Exod 21:12-36; 31:14-15; 35:2; Lev 19:20; 20:2-27; 24:16-17, 21; Num 35:16-21, 30-31; Deut 13:5, 10; 17:2-7; 21:18-23; 22:21-26; 25:11-12.

the people and that the needs of all within the society be met. Retributive justice is therefore regarded as a means for promoting the distributive justice that constitutes the primary objective of the Torah. Retribution accomplishes this objective in several ways. When possible, it seeks to set right whatever injustices have been committed and provide some type of compensation to those who have been injured or wronged. It is also designed to serve as a deterrent to those who would be tempted to violate certain laws or commandments. In particular, by prescribing that action be taken in response to wrongdoing, retributive justice aims at putting a stop to that wrongdoing and the suffering that it causes for those affected by it, in addition to preventing it from spreading any further. Retributive justice may also serve to correct either the wrongdoers themselves or others who might fall into the same type of destructive behavior.

It is particularly important to note the *intrinsic* relation between the observance of commandments such as those just considered and the well-being of the people that those commandments were intended to promote. *In and of itself*, observance of the commandments to care for one another, defend justice, refrain from injustice and oppression, avoid violence and wrongdoing, and practice what is good and right leads to well-being and happiness among the people. Those commandments would therefore be seen as having been given *for the good of the people themselves*, to bring them to live and behave in ways that were beneficial to all and enabled all within the society to experience the shalom that God desired for each person without exception.

Conversely, of course, disobedience to the commandments given for that purpose generates injustice, oppression, and suffering for many. Throughout the Torah and the Hebrew Scriptures as a whole, God is repeatedly said to be concerned especially for the weak, the needy, and the disadvantaged among the people and for that reason seeks to ensure that they are taken care of as much as possible. When that does not happen, in reality all are affected negatively, since the injustices and inequity that exist generate violence and conflict and do not allow true peace and harmony to reign in the society. In order for all to enjoy well-being, the social fabric must remain strong and all without exception must have what they need. Only when the relationships among all the members of a society are characterized by things such as love, respect, kindness, solidarity, honesty, equity, and justice can all those who form part of that society be healthy, happy, and whole on both an individual and a collective level.

All of the commandments just considered, therefore, would have been understood as having the purpose of promoting in various ways the well-being of human beings rather than responding to some type of need, desire, or self-interest on the part of God. What had led God to give these commandments was not a concern for himself but a concern for his people. This is especially evident with regard to commandments such as those that prescribe certain sanitary measures and rest on the Sabbath. Because such commandments did not benefit God in any way or affect him personally, they can hardly be regarded as having been given for God's own sake. God gained nothing, for example, by prescribing that his people rest every seventh day. While over the centuries it has become customary to dedicate some type of worship or service to God on the Sabbath, the Torah itself does not prescribe or even mention any such activity on the Sabbath. It merely ordains rest. God did not, therefore, obtain greater glory, worship, or honor for himself by means of the people's observance of the Sabbath, nor was he affected personally in any way by its observance or the failure to observe it. If he prescribed severe punishments for violating the Sabbath commandment, it could only be because his concern for the well-being of his people led him to insist on its strict observance for their own good.

Similar observations can be made with regard to the commandments regarding sanitary measures as well as the Jubilee laws. The command to quarantine those who had contagious diseases or were in danger of infecting others in some way clearly had the purpose of helping people remain healthy rather than protecting God in some way or safeguarding his justice or holiness. As noted above, the same concern for the collective well-being of his people and the land they inhabited was behind the Jubilee laws. Neither the observance of these prescriptions nor the punishment of the failure to observe them would have been thought to affect God in any way or satisfy some need in relation to his own nature. What is true of these commandments, then, can be regarded as true of the other commandments considered above: rather than giving those commandments *for his own sake* in order to satisfy some desire or need related to his holiness, righteousness, self-interest, or self-regard, God had given them solely for the sake of his people in order to promote their well-being and happiness out of love for them.

Instilling Obedience through Purity, Sacrifice, and Worship

Rather than addressing relationships within the family and society, many of the commandments of the Torah have to do with questions such as purity and impurity, the sacrificial worship of God at his sanctuary, and the observance of feasts, festivals, and holy days. At first glance, it might seem that most of these commandments do not play any role in promoting and preserving human well-being, justice, or equity. In reality, however, they too are designed for the same purpose. Rather than contributing to the people's well-being in a *direct* or *intrinsic* manner, however, such commandments do so *indirectly*.

To some extent, of course, many of the commandments regarding purity can be seen as contributing directly to the people's well-being by helping to avoid the spread of illness, disease, and various types of pollution and contamination. Those commandments would therefore have been viewed as means by which God sought to bring his people to live in ways that would allow them to enjoy good health and physical well-being. In many cases, however, the purpose of such commandments was not entirely clear. For example, it might be thought that God had given the dietary laws that prohibited the consumption of certain foods because those foods were unhealthy or might cause disease or illness, yet in most cases it was by no means evident that the foods prohibited were actually harmful or detrimental to anyone's health. The cultivation, production, or consumption of such foods might instead be thought to affect the people negatively or undermine their well-being in some other way, yet neither the biblical texts nor Jewish writings of the Second Temple period provide any clear evidence for such a claim.

What the purity and dietary laws did help promote, however, was the idea that *Israel was a special people, distinct from other peoples and nations.* They served as a constant reminder to the people that they were to live differently from other peoples rather than conform to them. This idea is stated explicitly in Lev 20:22-26, where in the midst of a command to distinguish the clean from the unclean, God tells the people: "I have separated you from the peoples. . . . You shall be holy to me; for I the LORD am holy, and I have separated you from the other peoples to be mine." In reality, of course, what was to distinguish Israel from other nations was *the practice of justice and righteousness,* as well as the other traits promoted in the law, such as love for neighbor, mercy, compassion, generosity, hospitality, and care for the weak, needy, and disadvantaged. By prescribing practices with regard to purity and diet that gave the people a special and unique identity and to some extent kept them separate from other peoples, therefore, the law promoted and encouraged among them a way of life that was distinct as well.

The same purpose can be seen with regard to the prescriptions regarding male circumcision.[21] Whether or not circumcision was thought to promote sexual health or to help avoid disease or illness in some way, in the biblical texts it is repeatedly associated with the practice of what is good, right, and just. Israel is told to be circumcised not only in the flesh but in the heart (Deut 10:16; 30:6; Jer 4:4). Those who are circumcised physically but do not practice justice and righteousness are even said to be uncircumcised in a sense.[22] As noted above, when God commands that Abraham and all of his offspring are to be circumcised, he makes it clear that circumcision is to serve as a reminder of the everlasting covenant that he is establishing with them (Gen 17:9-19).

Many of the other commandments that God is presented as giving in the Torah also had the purpose of serving as a constant reminder to the people that they had been set apart by God and were thus to live differently from people of other nations by practicing justice, mercy, and righteousness in all their dealings. In Deut 6:7-9, Moses tells the people: "These words that I am commanding you today are to remain in your heart. You shall repeat them diligently to your children and speak of them when you are at home and when you are away, when you lie down and when you rise. You shall bind them as a sign on your hand, fix them as an emblem on your forehead, and

---

21. See Gen 17:9-14; Lev 12:3.
22. See Lev 26:41; Jer 9:25-26; Ezek 44:7, 9; cf. Exod 6:30.

write them on the doorposts of your house and on your gates" (cf. Deut 4:9; 11:18-21). Further on in Deuteronomy, Moses commands the people to recite their story in a summarized form when bringing their offerings of first fruits to the sanctuary and to read out the entire Torah every seventh year on the Festival of Tabernacles (6:20-25; 26:1-11; 31:10-13). In this regard, it should be remembered that in biblical thought the Torah does not merely include the commandments given through Moses but the entire narrative from Genesis to Deuteronomy as well. The narrative in Deuteronomy also expresses the concern that the people might come to forget all that God has done for them, recognizing that this might lead them not only to forget his commandments but also to forget that they are an expression of his love for them (Deut 4:9-20; 6:10-13; 8:11-18). By reminding the people constantly of all that God had done for them and of the commandments that he had given them out of love for them, God hoped to continue to evoke in the people the type of love that would lead them to love and obey him for their own good.

While in Chapter 7 we will examine in greater detail the commandments related to the sacrificial worship offered to Israel's God and the feasts, festivals, and holy days that the people were to celebrate, in general terms those commandments would have been seen as serving the same purpose of reminding the people how they were to live for their own good and reinforcing that way of life in their midst.[23] By bringing them to recall the manner in which God had brought them out of Egypt to live under him as his own people, for example, the annual celebration of Passover reminded them of their unique identity as well as God's good intentions for them. Among the things they were to remember when they rested on the Sabbath was that God had created the world in six days before resting on the Sabbath. As they did so, the idea that everything belonged to God and was to be used for good in the way that he originally intended was reinforced. Similarly, the Day of Atonement or *Yom Kippur* was a means by which God led his people to examine the manner in which they were living, identify any sinful or unjust behavior that existed among them, and commit themselves to putting away that behavior. Other festivals and special days served the same purpose, thereby promoting among the people a way of life that was essential to their well-being and happiness.

Each of the various types of sacrifices prescribed in the Torah would have been seen as promoting similar values and behaviors.[24] By means of their burnt offerings or holocausts, the people were led to acknowledge God's sovereignty over their life as a whole and were reminded that they were to give of themselves wholly to God so as to live in the way he commanded for their own good. The offering of first fruits and the redemption of the firstborn served as means by which they expressed their gratitude to God for the many

---

23. See Exod 12:1-27, 43-49; 23:14-17; 34:18, 22-25; Lev 16:1-34; 23:1-43; Num 9:1-3; 15:1-31; 28:16-31; 29:1-39; Deut 16:1-17.

24. On the different types of sacrificial offerings and practices mentioned here, see Exod 13:1, 11-16; 22:29-30; 34:26; Lev 1:1–7:38; 17:1-9; 19:5-8; 27:1-33; Num 5:1-10; 6:1-21; 28:1-31; 29:1-39; Deut 15:19-20; 26:1-15; 27:1-8.

blessings he gave them, including especially the gift of life, and also underscored the belief that they belonged to God together with all that he had given them. In that sense, nothing that they possessed was truly theirs. For that reason, they were to dedicate themselves and all that they had to his service by making use of all that they had received from him in the way he had prescribed for the good of all. The offerings of well-being or peace offerings provided an opportunity for the people to come together in God's presence to rejoice and to enjoy the good things God gave them, yet the fact that part of those offerings was presented to God also reminded them that they owed all they had to him and that he was to be present in all aspects of their life. The sacrifices for sin were to serve as a means by which the people acknowledged their wrongdoings and renewed their commitment to serving God. As they did so, they also sought and experienced God's forgiveness and acceptance.

Both directly and indirectly, then, the commandments of the Torah that had to do with purity, sacrifice, festivals, and holy days were thought to promote shalom, justice, righteousness, equity, and a way of life that was in the people's best interest. Because of this, God would have been thought to have given those commandments for the same reason that he had given the commandments that regulated relations within the home, the community, and society in general, namely, that he loved his people and sought their well-being as an end in itself. By strengthening their identity as a people set apart for him to practice justice, love, and righteousness, such commandments reinforced among them the type of life that would allow them to enjoy the blessings that God wished to pour out on them out of love for them.

REJECTING THE GODS WHO BRING DEATH

Throughout the books of the Torah, one of the commandments that appears most frequently is the prohibition against worshiping and serving gods other than the God of Israel. In fact, this prohibition stands at the very beginning of the Decalogue: "You shall have no other gods before me," that is, "in my presence" (Exod 20:3; Deut 5:7). The worship of other gods and idols is considered so grave a sin that it is to be punished by death.[25] A number of passages from the Torah also describe the God of Israel as a jealous God who demands that his people worship and serve him alone.[26]

Biblical interpreters have traditionally understood God's prohibition against serving other gods and the affirmation that he is a jealous God as reflecting a concern for his own glory, worship, and honor above all else. Supposedly, he refused to tolerate the worship of other gods because his righteous and holy nature led him to command that the praise, acclaim, and adoration of his

---

25. On the prohibitions regarding idolatry and idolatrous practices, see Exod 20:3-5, 23; 22:20; 23:13, 24, 32-33; 34:13-17; Lev 18:1-5, 21, 24-30; 19:4, 26-29; 21:10; 26:1; Deut 5:6-8; 6:14; 7:5, 25-28; 11:26-28; 12:1-4, 29-32; 13:1-17; 14:1; 16:21-22; 17:1-7; 18:9-14; 27:15; 29:18-19.

26. See Exod 20:4-6; 34:13-14; Deut 4:23-24; 5:8-10; 6:13-15; 13:4; 32:16-21.

people be reserved exclusively for himself. As we have seen in Chapter 1, in fact, it is commonly claimed that the purpose for which he had chosen Israel as a people was precisely so that he might receive from them the worship and praise he desired for himself. Such an understanding of the God of Israel once more involves attributing to him the type of motivation that was characteristic of the pagan gods of antiquity, who were thought to demand that people worship them and offer them lavish sacrifices and exuberant praise for their own sake.

In reality, however, a careful reading of the biblical texts and other Second Temple Jewish writings makes it clear that the prohibition of the worship of gods other than the God of Israel is grounded in a concern that is very different: such worship inevitably leads to injustice, cruelty, violence, and oppression. Unlike the God of Israel, pagan gods such as those mentioned in the Hebrew Scriptures, the *Enuma Elish*, and Homer's epic poems were not concerned for the well-being of their worshipers as an end in itself. Rather, they saw human beings as a means to the satisfaction of their own needs, desires, and passions and thus sought to use and manipulate them for their own selfish ends. The worship of such gods, therefore, is viewed as leading people to live and behave in the same ways.

While the biblical texts and other Jewish writings of antiquity condemn the worship of gods such as Baal, Asherah, Astarte, Chemosh, and Milcom, their strongest condemnation is reserved for the god Molech, who demanded that the lives and blood of human children be offered to him.[27] The worship of Molech is associated not only with human sacrifice but also with the shedding of innocent blood in general.[28] Obviously, gods who demand that innocent children be put to death in order to satisfy their lust for blood or put away their wrath will not prohibit human beings from shedding the blood of other innocent human beings as well. On the contrary, the worship of such gods will encourage people to practice violence and bloodshed among themselves and treat one another with the same cruelty and inhumanity, motivated by the same type of selfish lusts, passions, and desires that were thought to characterize gods such as Molech.

Although most of the deities worshiped by Israel's neighbors in antiquity did not demand human sacrifice in the way that Molech did, they too were seen as promoting the practice of injustice, oppression, violence, and destructive behavior among those who worshiped them. The most powerful gods such as Assur, Marduk, and Baal valued their own worship above all else and were generally unconcerned about the manner in which the offerings presented to them had been obtained. As we have noted in Chapter 1, in many cases such gods were even thought to sanction violence, oppression, and

---

27. See Lev 18:21; 20:2-5; 2 Kgs 21:6-9; 23:10; 2 Chr 33:4-6; Isa 57:9; Jer 32:35; cf. 2 Kgs 17:17; Ezek 20:31; 23:37-39; Philo, *Spec. Laws* 1.312-13.

28. See Ps 106:36-38; Jer 19:4-5; Ezek 22:3-12; 33:25-26; Wis 12:3-6; 14:23-25; Jub. 1:8-11; 11:4-6.

exploitation on the part of those who were dedicated to their worship and to lend their support to those who robbed, pillaged, and enslaved others in order to provide them with the sacrificial offerings they desired. The empires that conquered other peoples in the name of such gods did so not because they sought the happiness and well-being of those peoples but because they wished to subjugate, exploit, and enslave them for their own ends. Because such gods were commonly thought to be driven by things such as selfishness, jealousy, hatred, a lust for power, and a desire for revenge, their worship led to the same type of attitudes and behaviors among those who dedicated themselves to their service. The gods of the nations were not committed to justice, righteousness, compassion, and care for the poor and needy in the way that the God of Israel was. On the contrary, unless such things contributed in some way to the promotion of their own self-interests, they had little interest in them and were therefore for the most part unconcerned for the practice of those things among their worshipers.

The difference between the God of Israel and the gods of the other nations mentioned in the biblical writings is particularly evident in the story of Elijah and the prophets of Baal in 1 Kings 18. When the prophets of Baal cry out to him to set fire to the wood arranged around the animal victim they have prepared for sacrifice and Baal fails to do so, they begin to cut themselves and draw out their own blood in order to get him to respond (v. 28). According to the logic of such a practice, the only reason why Baal would become attentive to those who did these things rather than continuing to ignore their pleas is that the sight of blood and the cutting open of people's flesh would arouse his interest and capture his attention, evidently because such things fascinated him or brought him some kind of morbid pleasure. If that type of bloodshed was attractive and pleasing to him, then the same would be said regarding the shedding of human blood under other circumstances. In contrast, the God of Israel would never be thought to be pleased if people intentionally cut and wounded themselves or others in order to capture his attention or obtain his favor. On the contrary, such actions would provoke him to intense anger due to his love for his people and his desire for their well-being.

The Many Evils of Idolatry

While the Pentateuch and historical books repeatedly reject and prohibit the worship of other gods among God's people Israel, for the most part they do not state explicitly the reasons for this rejection and prohibition. Numerous passages from these books characterize the worship of idols as abominable or abhorrent and associate it with evil practices and the abandonment of God's law. Although these passages can be understood in the sense that the worship of other gods is itself sinful and abhorrent, many of them also seem clearly to condemn such worship because of the other sins to which it leads. Those who worship idols not only shed innocent blood but also deceive and steal from others, despise and abandon God's good commandments in general, and fall into other forms of wickedness and injustice.[29]

Elsewhere in the biblical texts, however, the relation between the worship of other gods and the practice of injustice, violence, and oppression is made explicit. In Hosea 4, for example, after using extremely harsh and graphic language to condemn the people for sins such as unfaithfulness, swearing, lying, murder, stealing, adultery, and bloodshed and stressing the depravity, greed, lustfulness, and shamelessness with which they have acted, the prophet continues: "My people consult a piece of wood, and their divining rod gives them oracles.... They sacrifice on the tops of the mountains and make offerings upon the hills, under oak, poplar, and terebinth" (vv. 12-13). In this same context, Hosea claims that the people have lost all understanding and accuses them of practicing adultery, prostitution, and harlotry in both a literal and a figurative sense: "Therefore your daughters play the harlot, and your daughters-in-law commit adultery. . . . For the men themselves go aside with harlots and sacrifice with temple prostitutes; thus a people without understanding comes to ruin. . . . Ephraim is joined to idols—let him alone. When their drinking is ended, they indulge in sexual orgies; they love lewdness more than their glory" (vv. 13-14, 17-18). At the same time, all of this leads the people to abandon the one true God: "For a spirit of harlotry has led them astray, and they have prostituted themselves, forsaking their God" (v. 12).

In a similar manner, immediately after affirming that "the righteous perish, and no one takes it to heart," and that "the devout are taken away, while no one understands," the prophet Isaiah accuses the people of being "children of transgression" and "the offspring of deceit" by burning with lust among the trees, slaughtering their children in the valleys, and prostituting themselves with offerings to gods such as Molech (Isa 57:1-10). In Isa 65:2-3, Isaiah presents the people as continuously provoking God to his face by "sacrificing in gardens and offering incense on bricks," while at the same time portraying them as "a rebellious people, who walk in a way that is not good, following their own devices." The idea that the worship of other gods leads the people to go after worthless things that are not good and do them harm rather than profiting or benefiting them also appears in Isa 44:9-20, where Isaiah criticizes the people for calling out to the idols they have fashioned with their own hands from iron and wood: "Save me, for you are my god!"

These same themes are stressed in Jeremiah as well. There the prophet claims that by exchanging the God of Israel for other gods such as Baal the people have "changed their glory for something that does not profit" and dug out for themselves cisterns that hold no water. For that reason, their worship of other gods in itself punishes them and fills their lives with evil and bitterness (Jer 2:5-20). According to Jeremiah, the people swear by gods who are no gods, committing adultery, practicing prostitution, and neighing for

---

29. See, for example, Deut 20:18; 32:15-18; 1 Kgs 11:33; 18:18; 21:25-26; 2 Kgs 17:9-17, 29-40; 21:6-9; 2 Chr 33:4-6, 9.

their neighbor's wife like "well-fed lusty stallions" (5:7-9). At the same time, Jeremiah associates some of the same evils mentioned by Hosea with the worship of other gods and insists that such evils are entirely incompatible with the worship of Israel's God: "Will you steal, murder, commit adultery, swear falsely, make offerings to Baal, and go after other gods that you have not known, and then come and stand before me in this house, which is called by my name, and say, 'We are safe!'—only to go on doing all these abominations? Has this house, which is called by my name, become a den of thieves in your sight?" (7:9-11).

The intimate relationship between idolatry and injustice is made especially explicit in Ezekiel. Those who lift up their eyes to the idols in the high places are said to fill the land with violence and bloodshed, defile their neighbor's wife, commit robbery, and oppress the poor and needy by charging them interest and failing to feed and clothe them and restore to them the garments that they have given in pledge (Ezek 8:16-18; 18:10-18). As a result of their worship of idols, the people are said not only to commit adultery but also to have blood on their hands, including that of their own children, whom they offer up to those idols for food on the same day that they go to the Jerusalem temple to worship the God of Israel (23:37-39). The evils and injustices associated with the worship of idols are especially stressed in a passage from Ezekiel 22, where God instructs the prophet:

> You shall say, Thus says the Lord God: A city that fills itself with bloodshed! Its time has come! It pollutes itself by making idols. You have become guilty by the blood that you have shed, and polluted by the idols that you have made. . . .
>
> Look, all of the princes of Israel in your midst have used their power to shed blood. The fathers and mothers among you are treated with contempt. The alien residing within you suffers extortion; the orphan and the widow in your midst are oppressed. You have despised my holy things and profaned my Sabbaths. Dwelling in your midst are men who slander in order to shed blood, eat at the mountain shrines, and commit lewdness. There they uncover their fathers' nakedness and violate women who are unclean because they are in their menstrual periods. One man commits abomination with his neighbor's wife; another lewdly defiles his daughter-in-law; another among you defiles his sister, his father's daughter. Those dwelling in your midst take bribes to shed blood. You take interest and practice usury, and make profits from your neighbors by extortion; and you have forgotten me, says the Lord God. See, I strike my hands together at the dishonest gain you have made and at the blood that has been shed in your midst. . . .
>
> Its princes within it are like a roaring lion tearing its prey; they have devoured human lives, taken treasure and precious things, and made many widows within it. Its priests have done violence to my law and have profaned my holy things. They have made no distinction between the holy and the common, and they have not taught the difference between the unclean and the clean; they have disregarded my Sabbaths, so that I am profaned among them. Its officials within it are like wolves tearing their prey, shedding blood and destroying lives to get dishonest gain. Its prophets have whitewashed their deeds on their behalf, seeing false visions and divining lies for them, saying, "Thus says the Lord God,"

when the Lord has not spoken. The people of the land have practiced extortion and committed robbery; they have oppressed the poor and needy and have extorted from the alien without redress (vv. 3-4, 6-13, 25-29).

Other Jewish writings from the Second Temple period draw the same connection between idolatry and the practice of violence, injustice, cruelty, and oppression. Philo of Alexandria, writing in the middle part of the first century CE, associates a variety of evils with the worship of idols, which not only serves as a means of deception but also draws people away from the true God as the sole source of goodness and blessings (*Decal.* 5-9, 53-54, 72-81). Josephus chides the worshipers of idols not only for their folly and vanity but also for imitating the lewd and lascivious conduct of the gods they serve. According to Josephus, "they determine that some of the gods are to be regarded as givers of blessings but others are to be called averters of evil. They then rid themselves of the influence of the latter by means of favors and gifts, as they would the worst scoundrels of humanity, expecting that some type of mischief will befall them if they fail to pay them their price" (*Ag. Ap.* 2.249). Here the logic of *do ut des* is clearly present: the gods sell their favors and forgiveness for a price.

The most explicit statement regarding the evils that follow from the worship of idols is found in the book known as the Wisdom of Solomon, written in the first or second century BCE:

> And this became a hidden trap for humankind, because people, whether victimized by misfortune or by tyranny, bestowed on objects of stone or wood the name that ought not to belong to any other. Then, as if it were not enough for them to be in error concerning the knowledge of God, when they live in great strife due to their ignorance, they call such evils peace. For whether they kill children in their initiations, celebrate secret mysteries, or hold frenzied revels with strange customs, they no longer keep either their lives or their marriages pure. Instead, they either treacherously kill one another or grieve one another by adultery, and all is a raging riot of blood and murder, theft and deceit, corruption, faithlessness, turmoil, perjury, confusion over what is good, neglect of gratitude, defiling of souls, sexual perversion, disorder in marriages, adultery, and debauchery. For the worship of idols not to be named is the beginning and cause and end of every evil. For their worshipers either rave in exultation, or prophesy lies, or live unrighteously, or readily commit perjury; because they trust in lifeless idols they swear wicked oaths and expect to suffer no harm. But just penalties will overtake them on two counts: because they thought wrongly about God in devoting themselves to idols, and because in deceit they swore unrighteously through contempt for holiness. For it is not the power of the things by which people swear, but the just penalty for those who sin, that always pursues the transgression of the unrighteous (Wis 14:21-31; cf. 12:5-6; 14:1-20).

All of these passages describe clearly and graphically what happens when God's people dedicate themselves to serving other gods. First, they abandon his commandments. They no longer feel obliged to refrain from stealing, murdering, lying, swearing falsely, committing adultery, taking bribes, shedding blood, devouring lives, and practicing violence. Rather than caring for the weak and needy, they exploit, abuse, and scorn them. Unlike the God of Israel, the gods of the other nations not only overlook such behaviors and practices but in many cases even promote, encourage, and endorse them. What does it matter to those gods if aliens, orphans, and widows are made victims of greed, extortion, and robbery, as long as those gods receive the offerings and worship that they regard as being due to them? What do they care if the poor are charged interest at exorbitant rates? Why should they be bothered or upset if the destitute stand cold and naked because their desperate condition has left them no choice but to give their garments in pledge for loans and those garments have not been returned to them when they stand in dire need of them? These things may matter deeply to Israel's God, but they are of no concern to the type of gods worshiped by the other nations, including especially the powerful nations that seek to make smaller and weaker nations like Israel their slaves with the approval and assistance of the gods they serve.

Second, by abandoning God's good commandments that promote justice, equity, and wholeness for all, those who worship idols destroy their own lives by pursuing things that are worthless and have no value or benefit.[30] They spend the time and money that they should be using to care for their own needs and those of others who depend on them to do things such as venture into the mountains to present costly offerings to other gods there. Rather than seeking to satisfy their needs honestly through hard work, they idly prostrate themselves before pieces of wood and stone in order to implore from them the favors, blessings, and good fortune they selfishly desire for themselves and seek their help in taking from others what they covet in their greed. They weave ornate clothes to dress up their idols and pour out libations of expensive oil and wine to the queen of heaven while their children and neighbors go naked, hungry, and thirsty (2 Kgs 23:7; Jer 44:15-23). The worship of such gods thus devours their resources and deprives them of things that God has graciously provided for them in order to promote their well-being. Instead of looking to God's good commandments to direct their lives and guide their decisions, they consult sorcerers and soothsayers who not only devour their money and goods but also deceive, mislead, and manipulate them into doing things that do them great harm. As a result of practices such as these, the people are not only preyed on by those who seek only to take advantage of them but also fail to receive the instruction and orientation they need in order to live in ways that truly promote their well-being. Naturally, all of this angers God, who wishes to guide, instruct, and help his people out of love for them rather than seeing them follow down paths that lead to their ruin. For that reason, he is said not only to be provoked to anger but also to be shocked,

___

30. On this point and what follows, see especially Ps 97:7; 115:3-8; 135:15-18; Isa 44:9-20; 45:20; 46:1-2; 57:1-13; Jer 2:5-19, 26-28; 10:1-15; 11:12; 16:19-20; 51:7-18; Hos 13:1-3; Hab 2:18-19; Wis 13:10-19; 15:7-17; Ep Jer 7-72.

appalled, and dismayed when his people abandon the way of life that he has laid out for them for their own good and instead go after things that are not only worthless but also fill their lives with evil, bitterness, and vanity.

Third, and perhaps most importantly, the people's worship of other gods leads to a set of values and practices as well as a social system that destroy their well-being and that of others as well. What kind of values will people have who not only dedicate themselves to gods that demand the sacrifice of children such as Molech but even express to such gods their love and devotion by placing before them precious ornaments and perfumes, pouring out drink offerings at their feet, and singing hymns of praise and adoration in their honor? Will such people love and care for their own children and other children in their midst and reach out with kindness and compassion to assist the weak and disabled? Will they treat their spouses and loved ones with respect, affection, and tenderness rather than abusing and beating them with the same type of brutality and savagery that pleases the gods to whom they have pledged their heart and devotion? Will they speak out against those who steal, lie, and shed blood so as to decry and denounce such things or instead not only turn a blind eye to them but actually encourage and take delight in them? When they become angry and upset at others, will they seek to understand them and engage in dialogue with them in an attempt to promote peace, harmony, and tolerance or instead lash out at them in a spirit of spite and vengeance to hurt them in any way they are able?

If the gods themselves lust after wealth, power, and even blood, should not their worshipers feel compelled not only to give them what they want but also to join them in lusting after the same things? If the gods simply seek to relax and enjoy themselves in luxury and opulence while those who are subject to them break their backs waiting on them hand and foot, why should human beings not seek positions of power and prestige over others in order to act in the same ways, enjoy the same things, and treat others in the same way? If the gods love to feast on delicious meals, become drunk with fine wine, recline on beds and couches made from gold and ivory, and engage in all sorts of carnal and sexual pleasures, who is to tell the rich and powerful elites who have the ability to do the same things that they should refrain from them due to the injustices and oppression to which the common people must be subjected in order for them to take pleasure from such things? If the gods are envious, spiteful, vindictive, violent, selfish, cruel, possessive, and manipulative, why should human beings not behave in the same ways?

Prohibitions Designed to Protect

To serve and worship the pagan gods of antiquity, therefore, meant adopting the values and attitudes associated with those gods, imitating their behavior, and conforming one's life to the same ways of thinking and acting that were theirs. It also meant subjecting oneself faithfully and dutifully to whatever those gods willed and handing over control of one's life to those gods as one's lords and masters. As we have seen previously, in ancient texts such as the *Enuma Elish* it is even affirmed explicitly that the sole purpose for which human beings had been created was that they might dedicate their lives to satisfying the needs and desires of such gods.

Here it is important to stress that in antiquity to worship a deity did not simply involve spending a short time every week participating in some type of religious service, periodically lighting a candle placed in front of a statue or image, or occasionally dropping a coin in an offering box or plate. Instead, the lives of individuals, groups, and entire peoples revolved around the deities they worshiped and served. They constantly looked to their gods for the everyday decisions they made, often with regard to even trivial matters, and believed that the gods were in some way behind virtually every good or bad thing that happened to them. Those who worshiped other gods were expected to devote themselves and their possessions to them and regard them as sovereign in their life. They symbolized this devotion by doing things such as shaving their heads and the edges of their beards, dressing themselves in certain garb, making gashes in their flesh, and marking themselves with tattoos (Lev 19:26-28; 21:5; Deut 14:1). Those who worshiped pagan gods always had to be concerned whether they were acting in ways that pleased those gods and kept them content or were instead offending or upsetting them in some way, whether wittingly or unwittingly. If they wished to prosper in life and avoid tragedy, hardship, and suffering they had to devote themselves wholeheartedly to their gods, manifest their dedication to those gods through gifts and offerings that were as lavish and costly as they could afford, and invoke their favor and blessings repeatedly throughout the day.

As many of the biblical texts that condemn idolatry indicate, the worship of foreign deities was also associated with things such as divination, augury, sorcery, and the casting of spells.[31] Far from promoting a concern for justice, compassion, and the well-being of others, such practices led to abuse, deception, theft, and other evils that did tremendous damage to people's lives. In most cases, such practices were means by which some took advantage of others to obtain monetary gain for themselves and at times took control over certain aspects of their lives in order to manipulate them for their own ends. In addition, in order to make important decisions in life, God's people were to look to the Torah and the principles underlying it, including especially the concern for justice, compassion, and the good of all, rather than following the dictates of those who practiced divination and augury or claimed to have access to spiritual beings, including not only divinities and demons but also the deceased. Similarly, those who cast spells on others were generally trying to do them harm. Even if they sought to bring about some type of positive outcome or benefit for themselves or others by means of sorcery, they were doing so by using means that were not based on the practice of what was good, right, and just. The use of magic to obtain what one desired also involved attempting

---

31. See, for example, Lev 19:26, 31; 20:6, 27; Deut 18:9-14.

to manipulate and exert control over natural and supernatural forces in ways that called into question God's good and gracious sovereignty and set aside the practice of what was just, good, and right as a basis for seeking one's own well-being and that of others.

These are precisely the reasons that Philo gives for the prohibition of such practices. According to Philo, those practices subject people to deception and manipulation and lead them to base their lives on things such as the movements of birds and animals as well as the aspect of the entrails of sacrificial victims and the manner in which they are arranged in the carcasses of those victims. Thus, rather than looking to God and his commandments for guidance as to what is good, right, and just, people are easily led astray by those practices and substitute falsehood for truth (*Spec. Laws* 1.59-64).

From a biblical perspective, therefore, practices such as divination, augury, sorcery, and the casting of spells were by no means harmless or innocuous. Rather than helping people or promoting justice, true well-being, and the good of all, they often destroyed people's lives by impoverishing them, subjecting them to various forms of abuse, deception, and control, and fomenting in them a desire to do harm to others motivated by a spirit of enmity, vengeance, or hatred. For these reasons, the use of these things to obtain one's ends or to determine the course of action that one should take in life was extremely harmful. A God who was concerned for truth, compassion, justice, and well-being among his people out of love for them could hardly tolerate passively such practices among them.

Throughout the biblical texts, the worship of other gods is also frequently associated with sexual promiscuity. Among many readers of the biblical texts today it is common to regard sexual promiscuity as something that is enjoyable, gratifying, and entertaining for those who participate in it. When such a view is taken as a basis for understanding the biblical commandments and prohibitions regarding sexual promiscuity, it is easily supposed that the reason why God prohibited the sexual activities and practices condemned in them is simply that for some reason he found them displeasing or repulsive, or was even opposed to persons experiencing bodily pleasures. To interpret those commandments and prohibitions in that way is to ignore the historical contexts underlying them and to overlook realities that would have been evident to virtually any Jewish reader in antiquity. Sexual activity outside of wedlock commonly involved abuse and even violence in some form. Human trafficking and slavery meant that the weak and powerless were obliged to let others make use of their bodies in any way they saw fit. The practice of adultery destroyed marital relationships, did harm to the children within those relationships, and filled homes and living spaces with pain, tensions, strife, jealousy, divisions, and different types of violence. Women, adolescent girls, and young men and boys did not engage in prostitution, whether sacred or otherwise, because they enjoyed it, found it pleasurable, wanted to have a good time, or found it a nice and easy way to make money. Anyone acquainted with the sexual practices among peoples such as the Greeks and Romans in antiquity, who are generally regarded as "civilized," can hardly doubt that practices that were not only similar but even more inhuman and abusive also existed among other ancient peoples who worshiped the same type of gods. If the gods themselves were thought to engage in many different forms of sexual promiscuity, including not only adultery and fornication but at times even rape and incest, why should human beings not do the same?

Many of the passages that condemn Israel's idolatry use the language and imagery of sexual promiscuity to compare the people to a woman who has been unfaithful to her husband by going after other lovers and even engaging in prostitution or harlotry.[32] Such passages are often interpreted as if God were a jealous and possessive husband concerned only for himself. Once again, such interpretations ignore the logic underlying those passages. Women who abandoned their husband, house, and family in order to seek out other lovers and prostitute themselves were doing themselves great harm, abandoning the safety and well-being of their home and subjecting themselves to persons who would abuse them and take advantage of them. Undoubtedly, there were many marriages and families in which women felt unhappy and oppressed and for that reason sought to abandon those relationships for others that they hoped would represent an improvement. This is not the reality described in those passages, however, especially because the God of Israel could hardly be compared to an oppressive or abusive husband who drove his spouse away because he was seeking to manipulate and control her for his own selfish ends. Women who were promiscuous or hired out their bodies as prostitutes were hardly doing something that truly promoted their well-being and was in their best interest. If they found pleasure in such a way of life, such pleasure could hardly be considered something healthy or wholesome. In the same way, according to the logic of the biblical texts, those members of God's people who abandoned the God of Israel in order to follow other gods were doing themselves tremendous harm and letting themselves be consumed with selfish lusts and passions rather than satisfying their needs and desires in healthy ways that would bring them true happiness and well-being. If God prohibited his people from serving and worshiping other gods, it was for *their* sake rather than his own.

Due to the way in which the biblical texts associate idolatry with injustice, oppression, violence, and destructive behavior, it should also be evident why they reject as unacceptable a pluralistic approach to the worship of Israel's God. In our modern world, an increasing emphasis has been laid on the need for religious tolerance and the acceptance of diversity, especially in the area of religious beliefs and practices. The biblical perspective, however, is very different. If the God of Israel was to be worshiped and served in a manner that truly promoted the happiness and well-being of his people, he could not be placed

---

32. See, for example, Isa 1:21; 57:1-10; Jer 2:20-25; 3:1-11, 14, 20, 27; 13:27; Ezek 16:8-58; 23:1-49; Hos 2:1-20; 5:3-7; 9:1.

alongside other deities in some type of pantheon, even if he was assigned a position of superiority above those deities. To allow for the worship of other gods alongside of him among his people would mean limiting his full sovereignty in order to place certain aspects or parts of their life under the sovereignty of other gods. Because the primary concern of Israel's God was the well-being of his people, for them to subject themselves even in part to any other god who did not share that same loving concern would involve diminishing their commitment to everything that Israel's God stood for. The type of full commitment to the well-being of all that was characteristic of the God of Israel could not coexist with the lack of such a commitment on the part of other gods who sought to be served and worshiped for their own sake and on that basis promoted injustice, oppression, abuse, and violence.

For this reason, the biblical texts do not treat the worship of other gods as something that the people were to tolerate in their midst out of respect for the rights or freedom of those who chose to serve deities other than Israel's God. Undoubtedly, outside of their own territory, God's people were not to seek to impose the worship of their God on peoples who worshiped their own gods or to attempt to prevent them from worshiping those gods. Within their own territory and among themselves, however, God's people were to ban and eradicate the worship of any god other than the God of Israel, since only in that way could the blessings of justice, wholeness, and well-being that came from him alone be theirs.

It might be argued, of course, that the gods of other nations were not totally immoral and at times did in fact insist on the practice of certain virtues, such as justice, truthfulness, and kindness. In the *Iliad* and the *Odyssey*, for example, Zeus is said to punish those who do not uphold justice in legal proceedings as well as those who fail to show hospitality to others.[33] In many other ancient texts as well, the gods of other nations are presented as showing interest in the promulgation and enforcement of laws that were just and fair and as condemning things such as strife, bloodshed, and other forms of violence and injustice. Those texts often portray certain gods as being concerned for the well-being and happiness of at least some human beings and in many cases demanding that they act in accordance with what was good, right, and honest.

What was believed to distinguish the God of Israel from gods such as these, however, was that he regarded the well-being of human beings as *an end in itself* rather than as a means to some other end. In contrast, the gods of the nations were thought to regard human beings and their happiness and well-being solely as a means to another end, namely, their own happiness and well-being. If human beings were to be attentive to the needs and desires of the gods and serve them dutifully, it was necessary for there to be at least some degree of peace, order, justice, and well-being among them. In addition, even though at times gods such as Zeus and Marduk might insist on the practice of justice, honesty, and hospitality, they were generally inconsistent in their

---

33. See, for example, *Il.* 3.351-54; 13.625; 16:386-88; *Od.* 14.283-84.

demand for these things and often made exceptions when they felt that it suited their interests. They might even ignore the failure of human beings to practice such things when that failure did not affect them in any way.

Even if the gods of other nations were thought to be good in part and to desire that there be well-being and justice among human beings, therefore, the worship of those gods was thought to lead to an ethic that was fundamentally different from that associated with the worship of the God of Israel. Such gods would lead their worshipers to place their own happiness and well-being above that of others in the same way that they did themselves and to use others as means to serve their own interests. While those gods might seek the well-being of some human beings and act to promote justice among them, they would not be wholly dedicated to these things but would pursue them only when they found it convenient or conducive to their own ends and purposes. Rather than zealously caring for the needs of all, including especially those who were suffering and experiencing hardships, the worshipers of those gods would imitate them in being indifferent to those in need when they were not affected by their condition or would be inconsistent as those gods were in showing concern for the practice of things such as justice, kindness, and hospitality. Like those gods, they might show favoritism to certain people over others and either overlook or even defend injustices when it pleased or suited them to do so.

According to the logic of the biblical texts, therefore, if the God of Israel was truly concerned for the well-being of his people, he could not tolerate the worship of other gods in their midst. In one way or another, that worship would lead to inequity, injustice, and the neglect of what was good, just, honest, and compassionate. If he wished to bring into existence a people who would be fully committed to the well-being of all in the same way that he was, not only for their own sake but also for the sake of other nations who through them would be brought to think and live in the same way, it was necessary for him to insist that they love, serve, and worship him alone as the one true God over all.

Of course, the belief in such a God did not always lead the people who identified with him to live in the way he had commanded for their good, just as the belief of other peoples in their own gods did not always lead them to overlook or neglect the practice of what was just, kind, and compassionate. The only way that the God of Israel could hope and expect to bring both his own people and others to be fully committed to the well-being of all without exception, however, was to demand that they worship him alone, since none of the other gods were thought to be capable of producing in their worshipers the same type of commitment to the well-being of all without exception. Unlike the God of Israel, other gods had no choice but to concern themselves with their own needs and desires, since only by satisfying those needs and desires could they continue to exist and thrive. In contrast, because the God of Israel had no needs of his own and desired nothing but the well-being of the human beings he had created in love, he alone could promote among those who submitted obediently to him the same type of commitment and love for all of the human beings that he had created and regarded as his own.

As we shall see further on in greater detail in Chapter 10, this same concern for the good of all would have been understood as lying behind the commandment not to misuse or disrespect God's name that appears in the Decalogue and elsewhere in the biblical texts.[34] If God's people were to submit obediently to him in order to live in the way he had commanded for their own good, they had to respect and honor him as a God who was by nature good, loving, just, and committed to the well-being of all without exception. If any spoke of God in ways that communicated the idea that these things were *not* true of God, they might lead others to question or deny God's goodness, love, and sovereignty and thereby distance them not only from God but also from the way of life that he sought to bring about in all for their own good. Even greater harm would be done if the members of his people committed injustices and justified those injustices in his name or used his name to swear falsely and deceive others, since such things would convey to others the idea that the God of Israel was not actually a God who was committed to what is good, right, true, and just. Rather than offending God or depriving him of the honor to which he felt entitled, the failure to show respect for God and his name would call into question his love and his sovereignty and thereby deter people from living in the way he commanded out of love for all. Ultimately, therefore, the concern for honoring God's name was rooted in a concern for justice and wholeness. If God demanded that his name be respected and used properly, it was not primarily for *his own* sake but for the sake of those whom he sought to bless and save.

When considering the allusions to idolatry in the biblical texts, it is also important to note that even when those texts do not refer explicitly to the injustice, oppression, wrongdoing, and violence associated with idolatry, they presuppose that the readers will make that association. Among biblical interpreters, for example, it is common to observe that the narratives in the historical books of the Hebrew Bible often condemn the people of Israel and Judah and their kings for practicing or allowing the worship of idols and other gods without mentioning any other type of sins or wrongdoing in the immediate context. On that basis, these interpreters conclude that those narratives condemn idolatry alone, in isolation from other sins, as if it were the sole cause of God's anger and punishments. In response to such interpretations, it must be stressed that in the minds of those who composed, preserved, and read the biblical texts, the intimate connection between idolatry and the unjust and destructive behavior it encouraged and promoted was so obvious and self-evident that any allusions to idolatry would immediately have brought these things to mind. Those who saw or heard the commandment to serve and worship no other god but the God of Israel repeated endlessly in the

---

34. See Exod 20:7; Lev 18:21; 19:12; 20:3; 21:6; 22:32; 24:16; Deut 5:11.

Torah would have been well aware of the reasons for that prohibition and the logic underlying it, namely, that the worship of other gods inevitably led to injustice, oppression, cruelty, violence, and behavior that destroyed human well-being. When they considered the prohibition against serving other gods in the context of the Pentateuch and the Hebrew Bible as a whole, therefore, it would have been clear to them that God had prohibited the worship of idols and other gods for *their* sake rather than his own due to the pernicious effect that such worship would have, not *on him*, but *on them*.

Finally, it is important to stress as well that the passionate and fierce reaction to the worship of other gods attributed to the God of Israel in the biblical texts is not viewed in those texts as some type of petty jealousy or uncontrolled volatility on his part. On the contrary, that reaction is a rational, calculated, and controlled response to the tremendous evils that the biblical texts associate with idolatry. When Israel's God becomes incensed due to his people's insistence on worshiping gods that destroy their lives and wreak havoc on them, he was not behaving as a "loose cannon" or with "wild capriciousness," to use Walter Brueggemann's phrases.[35] Rather, he was acting out of love, demanding that his people live in ways that promoted their well-being and wholeness for their own good by avoiding and rejecting beliefs and practices that did them tremendous harm. While from our modern perspective the punishment of death that the Torah decrees for any within Israel who worship gods other than the God of Israel no doubt appears cruel and barbaric, on the basis of the logic examined here it is by no means difficult to understand why those who composed and preserved the biblical texts considered such a punishment to be justified. If it was said not only that God was a jealous God but that even his name was Jealous (Exod 34:14), that jealousy was not an expression of self-regard or selfishness but was rooted solely in a concern for the well-being of his people. That jealousy led him to command and demand that his people worship and serve no god but himself, not for *his* sake, but for *theirs*.

FINDING MEANING IN COMMANDMENTS
THAT SEEM ANYTHING BUT GOOD

While most of the laws that appear in the Torah can no doubt be understood as means by which God sought to promote the well-being of his people directly or indirectly out of love for them, there are unquestionably some laws that at first glance hardly seem to be grounded in a loving concern for their well-being. As we have just noted with regard to the prohibition of idolatry, many of the punishments prescribed for violations of certain commandments seem excessively harsh and even cruel. The provisions allowing people to acquire and own slaves from other nations also seem inhumane from a modern perspective and appear to convey the idea that it was acceptable to

---

35. Walter Brueggemann, *Theology of the Old Testament: Testament, Dispute, Advocacy* (Minneapolis: Fortress, 2005), 296, 303.

treat slaves of foreign origin more harshly than slaves who were Israelites (Lev 25:39-55). Similarly, the manner in which adolescent girls and women are to be dealt with at times seems unjust, unfair, and oppressive, especially when they are found guilty of having sexual relations outside of wedlock or are left no choice but to be wed to a man who has abused them (Exod 22:16; Num 5:11-31; Deut 21:10-14). Numerous commandments clearly seem to favor men over women, including those that allow men to put away their wives simply because they no longer find them pleasing or attractive (Deut 22:13-29; 24:1-4; 25:11-12). While the law protects authorities such as fathers, judges, and rulers from being dishonored or reviled, it does not seem to afford those under their authority the same type of protection against abusive treatment at their hands (Exod 22:28). In today's world, the commandment to put to death men who had sexual relations with other men also seems cruel and inhumane (Lev 20:13). The same is true, of course, regarding many of the other commandments that prescribe the death penalty. Above all, the command to destroy entire populations and even put innocent women and children to death under certain circumstances seems not only cruel but even barbaric.[36]

The question that must be asked regarding commandments such as these, however, is whether they were believed to have been given for God's own sake or rather for the sake of the people themselves. Among many interpreters, it has been common to maintain the first of these two alternatives. According to this interpretation of the biblical texts, God was thought to have imposed many of the commandments on the people simply because he has a personal liking for certain things or finds them pleasing. Conversely, when he prohibits certain behaviors and prescribes punishments that are extremely harsh for those behaviors, it is because he finds those behaviors displeasing or even repulsive due to the manner in which he is affected by them.

Closely related to this type of interpretation of the biblical texts is the notion that when God created the world, he designed it in a way that was intended to bring him pleasure on a personal level. On that basis, he determined that everything should be ordered in a particular manner and defined the behaviors and way of life that human beings should follow within that order to keep him satisfied and content. Thus, for example, it supposedly pleased God to establish a hierarchical system in which men should exert dominance over women and women should submit obediently to men. He also wished for the same type of hierarchical relationships to exist within families between parents and children and within societies between those whom he established as authorities and those who were to submit to those authorities. When he established marriage, he intended for it to be between one man and one woman and to last for a lifetime. The same type of personal preference led him to choose Israel as his special people and to love them more than he loved people of other nations. According to such readings of the biblical texts, like the pagan gods of antiquity, for no reason or purpose other

---

36. See, for example, Num 31:1-18; Deut 7:1-5; 20:10-18; cf. Deut 2:34; 3:6; 13:6-16.

than that of giving expression to his personal preferences, likes, and dislikes, the God of Israel commanded that human beings live and act in certain ways and showed favoritism to some people over others. On that basis, he imposed his will on people in order to please himself in a manner that must even be regarded as selfish and egotistical.

Central to this manner of conceiving of God's relation to the world is the idea that, as sovereign creator, he had a right to establish whatever order he found pleasing when he brought all things into existence. His sovereignty also gives him the right to demand that all submit obediently to the order he has established and to impose whatever punishments he desires on any who fail to comply with his demands. Thus, if wives refuse to submit to their husbands and children do not respect and obey their parents, God becomes upset and demands that they be punished severely. He is also angered if people engage in sexual relations out of wedlock and is especially repulsed if they do so with someone of the same gender. That anger and repulsion lead him to insist in his law that those who fall into such behaviors not only be punished but under certain circumstances even be put to death. Because he loves and values those who form part of his people Israel more than he does those of other nations, at times it pleases him to place foreigners under his people as their slaves. His favoritism toward Israel may even lead him to command his chosen people to destroy other nations and take their land away from them violently so as to occupy it themselves. While human beings may at times regard some of these things as unfair or unjust, they have no right to question or criticize God for imposing his will on human beings in ways such as these, precisely because as sovereign creator of all that exists he can do and command whatever he pleases and is entitled to suppress and crush any who dare to stand in his way.

This type of interpretation of God's motives for giving the law or Torah can even be applied to commandments that in themselves promote human well-being. In that case, when God commanded his people to do things that are by nature good, just, and right and prohibited them from doing things that were harmful and destructive, he did so primarily not for *their* sake but for his own. It was not the intrinsic consequences of the commandments and prohibitions promulgated by God that led him to give them to his people but rather the pleasure that God would derive from the obedience to those commandments or the displeasure that their violation would enable him to avoid.

Thus, for example, he could be thought to have commanded people to be kind and loving to one another not for *their* sake but rather for *his own*, simply because acts of kindness and love cause him pleasure but acts of self-ishness, hatred, and violence arouse disgust in him or provoke him to anger. Likewise, he wanted to see people share with one another and became upset when he observed some persons acting with malice and cruelty to others, not because of the effect that their generosity, kindness, or abusive behavior had on those directly affected by it, but rather because of the effect that their treatment of others had *on him personally*. Similarly, he might be thought to have prohibited adultery and sexual promiscuity not because of the destructive effect that such behaviors had on those who practiced them and others around them, but simply because for his own sake he found it agreeable when a man and his wife were faithful to one another but was displeased and repulsed when they had sexual relations outside of marriage. If he prohibited sexual relations between persons of the same gender, it was not due to any concern for them or the communities of which they formed part but simply because he found such relations repugnant and thus became nauseated when he saw persons engaging in them. In principle, the same type of logic could be applied to his command to observe the Sabbath: he might be seen as having given the Sabbath commandment, not to promote the well-being of those who would observe it, but simply because for some reason he found pleasure and contentment in watching people rest and relax one day a week.

According to this understanding of the law, then, God commanded certain things and called those things good simply because he found them pleasing. At the same time, he prohibited certain actions and deemed them sinful for no other reason than that they cause him discomfort, displeasure, or even disgust. In that case, rather than being grounded in a concern for his people's well-being, the commandments he gave them responded to his own personal predilections, preferences, and tastes. In other words, what moved him to command some things and prohibit others was not his love for his people but simply his penchant for some things and his dislike of others.

When the commandments of the Torah that from a modern perspective seem unjust and cruel are viewed on the basis of this understanding of God, they appear to respond to the whims of a capricious God who simply wishes to impose his personal preferences on human beings for his own sake. Like the pagan gods of antiquity, he declares certain actions to be good and right only because they are in accordance with the things he likes and enjoys, while defining other actions as sinful and even bad, wicked, or evil simply because they annoy, irritate, or anger him. When he favors and blesses those who obey his commands and punishes those who do not, he does so only to move or compel them to conform to his will for his own sake and not because he seeks to do good to people in some way or prevent them from doing themselves harm. What matters to him is not the effect of the actions and behaviors of human beings on those human beings themselves but rather the effect that their actions and behaviors have *on him.*

As already noted above in this chapter, rather than regarding the commandments and prohibitions given by God as an expression of his personal likes and dislikes, many biblical interpreters see those commandments and prohibitions as being grounded in his holy and righteous nature. In this case, what led God to dictate the commandments that today seem highly problematic and to impose punishments that at times seem excessively harsh was the need to satisfy the demands of his nature. Supposedly, his nature left God no choice but to prohibit and punish with great severity behaviors that are incompatible with that nature. Among the problems with such an understanding of God's motives for giving the law and imposing his will on human beings is that it does not address the question of why he often favors some people over others for no apparent reason and at times acts in ways that appear to be contrary to justice rather than in accordance with it. In any case, what this understanding of God's motives for what he does and commands has in common with the view that his actions and commandments are grounded solely in his own personal preferences and dislikes is that they portray God as one who imposes his will on human beings for his own sake rather than acting out of a concern for human well-being as an end in itself.

Underlying this manner of conceiving of God's actions and commandments is once again the idea that what concerns God is the effect that human actions have on him personally rather than the way in which human beings themselves are affected by their actions. This idea is commonly reflected in the interpretations given to passages from the Torah that deem certain behaviors or practices as abhorrent or refer to them as an abomination. It is said, for example, that the Hebrew term *to'ebah*, which is generally translated into English as "abomination," has "a strongly negative meaning, and in its theological use refers to things that are incompatible with God's nature and are thereby rejected by God."[37] Here the idea is clearly that God prohibits certain behaviors and practices due to the effect that they have on him personally rather than the effect that they have on human beings themselves.

This same type of interpretation is evident in the interpretation given by Old Testament scholar Thomas Kazen to the commandments regarding food purity and certain kinds of sexual relations in Leviticus 18 and 20, as well as the command for those who defecate outside the camp to cover up their excrement in Deut 23:12-14. According to Kazen, the logic underlying these commandments is that due to his holy nature God finds certain things disgusting, loathsome, or repulsive and on that basis demands that they be avoided, not for the sake of his people themselves, but for *his own* sake:

> Sexual "immorality" and "ritual" food taboos are thus combined and jointly seen as repulsive behavior causing divine disgust. . . . A different terminology is also used in Deut 23:14, where the idea is expressed of God feeling disgust at normal human defecation. . . . At the same time, the immediate argument for not offending the divine sense of taste is God's presence in the camp, which makes it necessary to keep the camp holy. The clear implication is that holiness requires the covering of human excrement. It thus has to be concluded that not only human, but also divine disgust were live issues in the social contexts reflected in these texts, and that divine holiness was thought of as no more compatible with unsavory sights than with offensive deeds.[38]

---

37. Arland J. Hultgren and Walter F. Taylor, Jr., *Background Essay on Biblical Texts for "Journey Together Faithfully, Part Two: The Church and Homosexuality"* (Chicago: Evangelical Lutheran Church in America, 2003), 6.

38. Thomas Kazen, "Dirt and Disgust: Body and Morality in Biblical Purity Laws," in *Priesthood and Cult in Ancient Israel*, ed. Gary A. Anderson and Saul M. Olyan, JSOTSup 125 (Sheffield: JSOT, 1991), 42-64 (60-61).

The question that must be addressed when considering commandments such as those mentioned here by Kazen, however, is whether they are based on a concern for the manner in which certain actions or practices affect God or if instead the concern has to do with the well-being and health of God's people. Undoubtedly, the biblical texts present God as being affected by the things that human beings do, yet his positive or negative response to those things is consistently regarded as depending on the manner in which they benefit or harm human beings rather than the manner in which they might benefit or harm him personally. While God is certainly presented as finding certain behaviors and practices disgusting and repulsive in passages such as those just considered and others in the Hebrew Bible, there is no reason to assume that he was thought to react in that manner for *his own* sake. In fact, because he was all-powerful and sovereign over all of his creation and had no needs of his own, nothing that human beings did could be said either to benefit him or do him harm. If he was present everywhere, constantly observing and experiencing all that went on even in the most remote and hidden parts of his creation, including natural processes and realities that human beings generally found disgusting and repulsive, why should he be bothered or revolted when he observed such things taking place among his people Israel? If throughout his creation he was constantly confronted with "unsavory sights" and the "offensive deeds" of countless human beings scattered across the earth, what did it matter if he observed such sights and deeds among his people Israel as well? The only plausible answer to such questions is that what displeased him was not the negative effect that such actions, behaviors, and realities had on him personally but rather the harmful effect that they had on the people he loved.

Thus, for example, if he had mandated that those who were in an encampment cover up their excrement when they defecated outside the camp, his purpose would have been seen in terms of attempting to make sure that the area immediately outside the camp was kept as clean and sanitary as possible not for *his own* sake but for the good of those within the encampment. The passage from Deut 23:12-14 does not speak of God being disgusted at uncovered excrement per se but rather being repulsed by the uncleanness of the camp as a result of that excrement. If God was concerned for his people's health and well-being, he could hardly tolerate his people living in the midst of filth and impurity that in one way or another would eventually do them harm. The all-powerful creator of the universe, however, would hardly be affected himself by human excrement, just as he would not be affected personally by any type of sexual immorality or impure food.

For the same reasons, when Leviticus 18 refers to certain sexual practices as abominable, such as the uncovering of nakedness within the family, incest, marital infidelity, sexual relationships with a menstruating woman, and sexual relationships between two males, there is no reason to suppose that God was thought to have prohibited such practices for *his own* sake. Nowhere in that chapter, in fact, is it said that such practices are abhorrent, abominable, or disgusting *for God*. On the basis of what we have seen previously and the logic reflected elsewhere in the Torah, commandments such as these would instead have been interpreted as reflecting a concern for human well-being. They served to protect people from behaviors that were considered harmful, unhealthy, unsafe, or unsound not only for them but also for the families and communities of which they formed part. These might be viewed as dangerous or risky for different reasons. The arousal of sexual passions by the uncovering of nakedness within a family might lead to incest and sexual abuse within the home and create conflict, resentment, animosity, and enmity among the family members. The same kind of conflict and dissension would result from marital infidelity and sexual relations with the spouse of a family member. While from a modern perspective sexual relations with a menstruating woman and between two males might not seem harmful to anyone, in ancient contexts it appears that people thought differently. They seem to have regarded such relations as unhealthy both for individuals and for the communities of which they formed part, perhaps due to concerns that physical contact with bodily fluids like blood and semen might cause people some type of harm. It is also possible that these prohibitions had to do in some way with relationships that were not consensual or were grounded in a concern to avoid some type of harm to people's bodies, such as the spread of sexually-transmitted diseases or lacerations that might produce internal bleeding.

The reason that God would have been thought to regard such practices as abhorrent or abominable, therefore, was that they would do some type of harm to individuals or the families and communities of which they formed part. For the members of God's people to be healthy and whole, it was important for them to avoid behaviors and practices that might lead to abuse, conflict and dissension in the home, the inhumane treatment of others, or some type of infection, illness, or disease. Within families and communities it was necessary for people to treat one another with respect instead of seeing others as objects to be used for their own ends or pleasure. Steps had to be taken to avoid arousing passions that might lead to mistreatment, conflict, or abuse. Commandments such as those found in Leviticus 18 would have been seen as having the purpose of promoting healthy, constructive, and harmonious relations within homes and communities, as well as helping avoid things that might affect those homes and communities negatively.

In that case, the reason why certain behaviors and practices are deemed abhorrent or abominable in the biblical texts is not that they affect God negatively or are incompatible with his nature but that they are regarded as undermining and destroying human well-being in some way. What is intolerable for God and incompatible with his nature is that human beings act in ways that do them harm, dehumanize them, and generate conflict, dissension, abuse, and other types of unhealthy relationships among them. Due to his love for his people, God wants them to live and act in ways that are good for them and promote their well-being and happiness.

While from a modern perspective some of the laws with regard to the treatment of young girls and women as well as slaves undoubtedly seem extremely cruel, harsh, and unfair, it must be recognized that such would not necessarily have been the case in antiquity. In contexts characterized by violence and many different types of maladies and hardships, for example, communities would constantly be under threat due to hunger, famine, plagues, and attacks from enemies. For that reason, they might be convinced that male-dominated hierarchical structures were necessary to maintain order and to defend and protect the community. The situation of women was always precarious due to the violence to which they might be subject at any moment at the hands of men who might overpower or mistreat them. In such contexts, the preservation of a certain order within marital and family relationships would need to be given high priority. Thus, while some of the commandments that appear in the Torah may seem unjust, cruel, and oppressive from a modern perspective, in their original contexts they would have been perceived quite differently. It should also be recognized that the commandments found in the Torah were formulated in contexts in which the task of defining God's will and distinguishing right from wrong and good from bad was carried out almost exclusively by males. While some of the commandments may have seemed cruel and oppressive from the viewpoint of females, therefore, it is likely that the males within the community would have thought differently, perhaps because they were not sufficiently sensitive to the legitimate concerns of the women among them. In that case, even though such laws and commandments had been given for the sole purpose of promoting human well-being rather than responding to any type of divine need, desire, or repulsion, in many cases they may not have always fulfilled that purpose in the way that they should have.

In this regard, however, it is also important to stress that all of these laws and commandments needed to be *interpreted* whenever they were applied and enforced. Furthermore, the Torah makes it clear that the basis for the interpretation of the laws and commandments it contains was to be the well-being of the members of God's people, both individually and collectively. Those who were in charge of applying and enforcing those laws and commandments, therefore, were to make sure that they did so in ways that promoted that well-being rather than undermining or destroying it.

The notion that through Israel God was attempting to form a people who would be distinct from other peoples in that they would practice justice and righteousness appears regularly throughout the Torah and is used as a basis for justifying laws that favor Israel over other nations. As we have noted above and will see further on in greater detail, God's efforts in this regard were thought to have as their ultimate goal not only the blessing of Israel but the blessing of other nations as well. According to the logic of the biblical narratives, if God was to carry out this plan, it was first necessary for Israel to be established as a people who would be set apart from other nations by a way of life that would promote well-being and wholeness among them. In order for this goal to be accomplished, it was necessary for them not only to avoid the worship of other gods but also for other aspects of their daily life to distinguish them from other peoples. Some of the practices prescribed in the Torah may have been thought to serve no other purpose than constantly reminding the people that they were to be unique among the nations and keeping them separate from those nations.

The need for God to accomplish certain objectives among his people Israel before he might accomplish those objectives among other peoples would also be seen as justifying a number of the things he commands in the Torah. As we shall see in later chapters, it was thought to be necessary for Israel to have its own land in order for those objectives to be accomplished, yet the only way that Israel could be established in its own land was by expelling other nations from that land and destroying their altars and places of worship. According to the logic of this idea, if other peoples remained in Israel's midst they might not only lead God's people to worship other gods but also might make constant war on them or harm them in other ways. Other provisions in the law that reflect preferential treatment for Israel over against the other nations might be justified on the same basis. Undoubtedly, from a contemporary perspective many of these ideas must be regarded as highly problematic, yet it must be stressed once again that the biblical texts originate from contexts and realities that in many ways were very different from our own. In any case, there is no reason to read back into the biblical texts the idea that God had given the laws and commandments that today seem problematic and objectionable for the purpose of satisfying some type of personal whim or preference. Instead, those laws and commandments would have been seen as having the purpose of enabling God to accomplish his good and loving purposes among his people Israel and human beings in general. It must also be remembered that the rampant sin, injustice, and violence that existed throughout the world were thought to leave God with no choice at times but to do and command things that might seem cruel and heartless to readers of the biblical texts both in antiquity and today.

Throughout the Torah, there are also many commandments that from a modern perspective seem pointless or senseless. It is not clear, for example, what harm there might be in wearing garments made from two different materials or using types of clothing worn by persons of the opposite sex (Lev 19:19; Deut 22:5). Many of the detailed prescriptions governing the sacrificial worship of God and the sanctuary in which that worship was to take place do not seem to respond to any apparent logic. Once again, however, these commandments would have been thought to serve some purpose in relation to God's people in their original contexts, even if that purpose was no longer evident. In fact, later generations of Jews at times concluded that such commandments also served to promote justice and righteousness among God's people by encouraging them to submit obediently to God's will even when they did not understand why he had commanded certain things.

In any case, the point that must be stressed is that despite the highly problematic nature of many of the biblical commandments, the biblical texts provide no clear basis for claiming that what was thought to have motivated God to give those commandments was a concern for himself or for his own glory, holiness, or justice or a need to satisfy the demands of his nature. While it is of course possible to read back into many of the commandments such a concern or need on the part of God, this involves interpreting them on the basis of presuppositions that are neither stated nor implied in the biblical texts. On the contrary, the distinct conception of the God of Israel in the biblical texts must be seen as excluding such interpretations, which reflect suppositions grounded in pagan modes of thought rather than than the modes of thought associated with Israel's God throughout the Hebrew Bible.

THE INHERENT GOODNESS OF THE TORAH AND ITS OBSERVANCE

Once it is clear that in biblical thought the purpose for which God had given the law or Torah was to promote the well-being of his people rather than to satisfy some need, desire, or whim of his own and that even commandments that from a modern perspective do not seem to serve such a purpose would have been viewed as doing so in biblical times, the idea that the law is exceedingly good and constitutes God's greatest blessing to his people Israel can be viewed in a new light. Precisely because the law brings life, wholeness, and happiness for God's people when they observe it, it is a means by which God fills their lives with good things.

The Torah as an Instrument of Blessing

The idea that the law is a gracious gift of God is particularly emphasized in two of the Psalms. Psalm 19 extols the Torah as a source of tremendous joy:

> The law of the LORD is perfect, reviving the soul; the decrees of the LORD are sure, making the simple wise. The precepts of the LORD are right, making the heart rejoice; the commandment of the LORD is clear, enlightening the eyes. The fear of the LORD is pure, enduring forever; the ordinances of the LORD are true and righteous altogether. They are to be desired more than gold, even much fine gold; they are also sweeter than honey and the drippings of a honeycomb (vv. 7-10).

These same ideas are echoed in Psalm 119, which is by far the lengthiest Psalm in the Psalter:

> I delight in the way of your decrees as much as in all riches. . . . My soul is consumed with longing for your ordinances at every moment. . . . Your decrees are my delight; they are my counselors. . . . Lead me in the path of your commandments, for I delight in it. . . . I find my delight in your commandments because I love them. . . . Your statutes have been my songs wherever I make my home. . . . At midnight I rise to praise you on account of your righteous

ordinances.... The earth, O Lᴏʀᴅ, is full of your steadfast love; teach me your statutes. . . . You are good and do good; teach me your statutes. . . . The law of your mouth is better to me than thousands of pieces of gold and silver. . . . If your law had not been my delight, I would have perished in my misery. I will never forget your precepts, for by them you have given me life. . . . Oh, how I love your law! It is my meditation all day long. . . . How sweet are your words to my taste, sweeter than honey to my mouth! Through your precepts I gain understanding; therefore I hate every false way. . . . Truly I love your commandments more than gold, even fine gold. . . . Your decrees are wonderful; for that reason my soul keeps them. . . . Seven times a day I praise you for your righteous ordinances. Those who love your law have great peace (*shalom*); nothing can make them stumble (vv. 14, 20, 24, 35, 54, 64, 68, 72, 92-93, 97, 103-4, 127, 129, 164-65).

The idea that the law is a good and gracious blessing given by God to Israel appears in other passages from the Hebrew Bible as well and often seems to be simply assumed.[39] The same conception of the law is found in other Jewish writings from the Second Temple period. In the books of the Maccabees, many Jews express their willingness to die for the law and in some cases even endure horrendous forms of torture rather than violate its commandments.[40] Philo repeatedly stresses the excellence of Moses' laws and insists that no other law in the world is comparable to it.[41] For Philo, this is evident from the fact that people of other nations marvel at its beauty and in many cases have themselves adopted some of the commandments contained in it. Because the commandments of the law are in perfect harmony with nature, they promote harmony in the world as well as kindness, humanity, and compassion not only toward other human beings but toward animals as well. Josephus also speaks of the law of Moses as producing admiration among other peoples and regards that law as the most excellent gift ever given by God.[42]

Behind all of these affirmations regarding the goodness of the law is clearly the idea that the law promotes human well-being by guiding and instructing people to live in ways that make that well-being possible. In other words, in and of itself, its observance allows people to enjoy the shalom or wholeness that God has always desired for all people from even before the time that he created them. While in that sense it is said to give life, the Torah also gives life and enables people to enjoy well-being and salvation because God responds to its observance by blessing that observance. Yet the reason why God blesses its observance is not that he desires that people obey his commandments for his own sake but rather that the people's commitment to a way of life that is conducive to their well-being will lead them to make use of the blessings he wishes to pour out on them in ways that will truly benefit them, since they will use what he gives them for good rather than misusing it to do harm to themselves and one another.

---

39. See Deut 4:5-8; Ps 37:31; 40:8; 94:12; Prov 28:7; 29:18.

40. See 1 Macc 1:15-38; 13:1-6; 2 Macc 6:18–7:2; 3 Macc 1:23; 4 Macc 4:21-26; 5:14–6:30.

41. On this and the points that follow, see especially Philo, *Moses* 2.12, 20-21, 25-27, 52, 79, 104; *Virtues* 113, 125, 141-42.

42. See Josephus, *Ant.* 3.223; 4.318-19; 12.110; 16.44; *Ag. Ap.* 2.175-76, 184-86, 277-80, 286.

It is precisely this idea that God gave his people Israel the commandments of the Torah for their sake rather than his own that distinguishes biblical thought regarding the law from later Western Christian interpretations of the law and God's commandments. If God is thought to have given those commandments for the purpose of obtaining from human beings what he desires for his own sake or in order to ensure that the demands of his holy and righteous nature are satisfied, the law can be good only in the sense that it enables people to know what they must do to keep God content by doing what he commands and avoiding what he prohibits. In that case, just as God gave the law and demands that his people obey it for his own sake in order to receive from them what he desires for himself or to ensure that the demands of his nature are met, so also the people will be motivated to obey it not because they truly *want* to obey it but because they *must* do so in order to enjoy God's favor and avoid his wrath.

Although this understanding of God's commandments can be reconciled with the idea that those commandments are aimed at providing the people with guidance and instruction, this guidance and instruction are no longer viewed primarily in terms of indicating to human beings the positive or negative consequences that will result naturally and intrinsically from certain actions and behaviors. Instead, those commandments guide and instruct human beings in the sense that they indicate to them the actions that are incompatible with the desires or demands of God's nature so that they can avoid bringing down on themselves his wrath and punishment, while at the same time letting them know which actions and behaviors will keep them in good graces with God and thus enable them to attain the blessings that he grants to those who obey him as a reward for their obedience.

Such an understanding of the law leads people to observe it motivated solely by the same type of self-interest that is regarded as characterizing God himself. When they obey God's commandments, they do so not because they are truly convinced that those commandments promote their well-being in and of themselves but because they have no choice but to obey what God commands if they wish to remain on his good side. What interests them is obtaining the rewards that God promises to those who obey him and being spared the punishments that God imposes on those who disobey him. If they serve others and show kindness and compassion to those in need only because God has commanded this of them, then they do so not because they truly love others or care about them but rather because they wish to obtain God's favor and avoid provoking him to anger. In fact, they may even use the needy to their own advantage by providing them with assistance in order to be able to make a claim on God or attempt to compel him to grant them what they want for their own sake. According to that logic, if they have given God what he wants, then he is obliged to give them what they want in return.

When God's commandments are viewed in this way, therefore, they become means by which people can earn his favor and blessings. Supposedly, because God has promised to reward those who observe his commandments by blessing them and showing them his favor, he is now under obligation to keep his word. Therefore, any who obey what he has commanded can not only *ask* God to keep his promise by granting them his blessings and favor as a reward for their obedience but can even *demand* that he do so. Their obedience is then seen as leaving God no choice but to fulfill his promises by granting them what they seek for themselves, since he cannot go against his word if he is to be true to it. A God who would fail to live up to his promises would be neither good nor just.

This understanding of obedience focuses exclusively on outward actions in the same way that the worship of pagan gods did in antiquity. Those gods were not able to look inside people's hearts to see the motives behind their actions, nor did they care what those motives were as long as they received from their worshipers what they wanted for their own sake. If the God of Israel acted in the same way, promising to reward people simply for observing his commandments outwardly, then he would be unconcerned about the motives behind their observance. If instead he was truly concerned that people obey him out of love, motivated by a sincere and heartfelt desire to do his will, however, then outward obedience would not be enough to obtain his favors and blessings. Those who obeyed him outwardly would have no basis for demanding that he reward their obedience with his favor and blessings, since their outward conformity to his commands would not be sufficient to obtain his rewards and favor unless it were accompanied by a sincere desire to serve him and others out of love for them. Yet because God alone could look into human hearts to determine whether this desire was truly present, people could never be sure whether their motivations had been sufficiently pure in God's sight to gain his favor. In fact, if their outward obedience had been motivated by a desire to obtain something from God in exchange for that obedience, God would regard such a motivation as self-serving and would not be pleased by it. The only behavior that would gain his favor would be behavior that was *not* motivated by a selfish desire to obtain something from him.

Furthermore, if God sought to bring people to obey him out of sincere and selfless love rather than self-interest, it would be impossible for him to attain that objective simply by rewarding them when they obeyed him, since to do so would only reinforce the self-centered behavior he wished to eradicate. He could hardly offer people rewards in order to bring them to obey him in the way he desired if his objective was that their obedience not be rooted in a desire for rewards. In biblical thought, at times God even chooses *not* to reward obedience to his will with blessings, precisely because he wants people to learn to obey him in a disinterested manner rather than out of self-interest. To demand a reward from God or claim that he was under obligation to grant some type of favor in exchange for one's obedience would involve seeking to impose one's will on God rather than submitting obediently to him, trusting in his gracious providence and goodness by accepting whatever came from his hand. If God's own behavior were based on the principle of *do ut des*, he would himself be acting out of self-interest. In that case, how could it be claimed that he did not want people to act out of self-interest when they did what he commanded? How could he demand that human beings not be self-centered in their behavior if his own behavior was self-centered?

In fact, the idea that the God of Israel might relate to his people on the basis of the principle of *do ut des* is rejected explicitly in Deut 10:17-18. There God is described as one "who does not show partiality nor take any bribe, who executes justice for the orphan and the widow, and who loves the foreigners, providing them with food and clothing." If God acts purely out of love for those in greatest need and does not show partiality or sell his favors, he clearly does not act out of a concern for himself or seek to obtain something from those whom he helps in exchange for that help. He can hardly be thought to come to the aid of orphans, widows, and foreigners out of self-interest, motivated by a desire to receive from them some type of recompense or reward for the assistance he provides for them. For the same reason, if people try to obtain his blessings and favors by offering him something in return for those blessings and favors, in effect attempting to bribe him, they provoke him to anger rather than obtaining his approval. According to the logic reflected in this passage, therefore, God does not act out of self-interest when he blesses people or commands them to do his will. In that case, the basis upon which he blesses people or withholds his blessing is not the effect that their behavior has *on him* but rather the manner in which their behavior affects *them* as well as other human beings, that is, the *intrinsic consequences* of their behavior.

In addition to leading human beings to act out of self-interest and portraying God as one who does the same, the idea that the commandments of the Torah are means by which God's people can earn his favor, keep him content, and avoid arousing his wrath in exchange for giving him what he desires or needs for his own sake turns those commandments into an oppressive burden. People end up having no choice but to obey God, because if they fail or refuse to do so, they will be subjected to his punishments. As already mentioned above, because by nature they would prefer *not* to have to obey God and would rather follow desires and interests of their own that are contrary to God's will, they constantly find themselves in a dilemma. If they choose to do their own will over that of God they will arouse his wrath, yet if they choose to do God's will rather than their own they will feel frustrated and unhappy because they are not fulfilling their own desires and wishes.

In other words, according to the traditional schemes of thought, the problem that most human beings must continually face is that God disapproves of and punishes many of the activities and behaviors that bring them pleasure and enjoyment, while at the same time commanding things that they find cumbersome, onerous, and disagreeable. If their likes and dislikes coincided with those of God, this problem would not arise, since all would want the same things that God does and thus take delight in his commandments. Unfortunately, however, human beings like many of the things that God dislikes and dislike many of the things that God likes. For that reason, they not only find it difficult to obey God's commandments but even despise those commandments. Rather than being free to pursue their own desires and interests, they feel compelled to comply with whatever God wills. They wish that they could live selfishly and behave in whatever ways they pleased without any interference or pressure from God. At the same time, they believe that if God would only allow them to live and behave in those ways, they could be truly happy. Rather than seeing God's law as something that *promotes* their happiness and is *good*, therefore, they regard it as something that *prevents* them from being happy by obliging them to do things that they would prefer to avoid and prohibiting them from doing many of the things that bring them pleasure.

In much traditional Christian thought, what makes God's law even more of a burden is that no matter how hard people may try to obey it, they can never attain a level of obedience that is acceptable to God. Supposedly, due to God's perfectly holy and righteous nature, God has no choice but to demand perfect obedience to his commandments. For mortal human beings, however, such perfection is impossible. For that reason, rather than promoting their well-being or saving them in some sense, God's law merely serves to make their sin evident to them and indicate to them that they are under his wrath and condemnation. In Lutheran theology, for example, it is said that "the law always accuses" (*lex semper accusat*). It terrifies sinners and drives them to despair by constantly threatening them with punishments. Due to their imperfection and their fallen sinful nature, they cannot deliver themselves from those punishments, since no matter how hard they may try they can never obey God's commandments perfectly. For that reason, in fact, in order for God to bless and save them, he must use some means other than the law and must even do away with the law so that it no longer condemns and accuses them. Rather than being saved from condemnation and destruction *by* God's law, they must be saved *from* it, precisely because it is the instrument by which they are condemned to destruction due to their inability to observe it perfectly.

Such an understanding of God's law, of course, only makes sense if all human beings are said to be subject to it. In biblical thought, however, the commandments of the Torah are given only to the people of Israel in the context of a covenant that God has made with them alone among all the nations of the earth. While this point is overlooked in many Christian traditions, in others it is maintained that even though the law of Moses was given to Israel alone, some of the commandments it contains are binding on all people universally. In some of those traditions, many of those commandments are said to be expressions of a natural law that God has made known to all human beings and has written on their heart or conscience. These include commandments such as those that prohibit murder, adultery, theft, false witness, and other actions that are condemned in virtually all cultures and societies, as well as those that prescribe the practice of what is just, good, and right in general terms. In other Christian traditions, the commandments that appear in the Mosaic law are divided into three different categories—civil, ceremonial, and moral—, in order to claim that only those that belong to the last of these three categories are binding on human beings as a whole. Such a division, of course, is nowhere to be found in the biblical texts or in Second Temple Jewish thought. In the centuries following the composition of the books of the Hebrew Bible, however, it became common among many Jews to claim that there are certain divine commandments that are binding on all human beings and to associate these with the commands that God is said to have given to Noah in Genesis 9 following the great flood.[43]

One other reason why the Torah or law of Moses is considered *not* to be good in much traditional Christian thought is that it is supposedly concerned only with external ceremonies and rites that in the eyes of many interpreters seem to lack any real meaning or purpose. According to this view of the Torah, it consists of many petty, inconsequential, and insignificant precepts and regulations regarding things such as purity and the sacrificial cult. This negative view of many of the commandments of the Torah not only leads to the claim that the abolishment of those commandments is fully justified but also reinforces the notion that the law given through Moses was an onerous burden rather than something good that was intended to promote life and happiness among God's people.

Lying at the heart and root of all of the negative conceptions of the Torah or law just considered is the idea that we have seen repeatedly throughout the present chapter, namely, that God gave it for his own sake. The common assumption is that God's purpose was to obtain from human beings something he desired for himself, such as the honor, glory, and worship he craved as an end in itself, or to ensure that the demands of his holy and righteous nature might not be compromised as he acted to associate with sinful human beings in order to bless and save them. When the law is understood in this fashion, it will inevitably be regarded as something oppressive and burdensome rather than a blessing that leads to life, well-being, and happiness for all who allow it to guide and instruct them. In the biblical texts and Second Temple Jewish thought in general, however, the law or Torah is good not because its observance enables one to earn God's favor or avoid his wrath and punishment but because it imparts the wisdom, knowledge, and guidance necessary to live in ways that in and of themselves lead to human well-being and wholeness. It opens people's eyes to what is good and illumines the path that leads to true life, not in a future world but in the present one. For that reason, it is to be loved as a source of delight, wonder, joy, and gladness.

---

43. See especially John Day, *From Creation to Abraham: Further Studies in Genesis 1–11* (London: T & T Clark, 2022), 155-62; Matthew P. Van Zile, "The Sons of Noah and the Sons of Abraham: The Origins of Noahide Law," *JSJ* 48 (2017): 386-417 (386-93).

This is not to deny, of course, that the Torah was also seen as good due to the promises of divine blessing that it contains for those who obey its commandments. Obedience to its commandments affords life and blessing not only due to the intrinsic and natural consequence of that obedience but also because God responds to those who obey it by pouring out on them even greater blessings. It is important to stress, however, that in biblical thought the reason that God blesses obedience to his commandments is that they are good in that in and of themselves they promote human well-being. This understanding of the commandments stands in sharp contrast to much traditional thought, which sees obedience to the commandments as good merely because God blesses that obedience. In other words, *the biblical idea is not that obedience to the law is good because God blesses it but rather that God blesses obedience to the law because it is good.* Both that obedience and the law itself are good in and of themselves and not simply because God rewards obedience to the law with blessings.

The notion that obedience to the law earns God's favor must also be considered contrary to biblical thought. In the Hebrew Bible, God's favor is always a free gift, as is his love for human beings. Because God is unconditionally committed to the well-being of all people, everything he does in relation to them has the objective of promoting that well-being and making it possible. In biblical thought, the Torah or law is itself an expression of God's favor because it is a means by which he seeks to bring his people to live in ways that will allow them to enjoy the well-being he desires for them. His demand and insistence that they obey the commandments of the Torah is also an expression of his love and favor because only by obeying those commandments can they attain that well-being. Disobedience to his commandments leads to pain, suffering, ruin, and destruction in and of itself. Those who obey those commandments, therefore, do not earn God's love or favor but merely respond to the unconditional love and favor God shows them in the way he desires for their own good.

When human beings see God's commandments as oppressive and burdensome because they oblige them to do things that they find difficult and displeasing while at the same time prohibiting them from doing things that bring them pleasure, in biblical thought the problem is not God, the law, or God's just and holy nature but the sinful nature of human beings themselves. Because they are by nature selfish and self-centered, they behave in ways that do harm not only to others but also to themselves. Many of the things that bring them pleasure in reality undermine and destroy their well-being, while many of the things that they find difficult and burdensome are actually good for them and promote their wholeness and happiness. The way in which they are made whole and find happiness, therefore, is not by following their own selfish desires and passions but by caring for one another and doing what is good, just, right, and loving in relation to one another and themselves.

The Law and the Love of God

In biblical thought, because God's law promotes the well-being of his people, it cannot be regarded as oppressive. There is a sense, however, in which it can rightly be considered a burden. For sinful and selfish human beings, at times it is indeed burdensome to live in ways that are wholesome and healthy and to avoid things that may seem good but actually are not. To use a modern analogy, for most people it is difficult and cumbersome to exercise regularly and follow a healthy diet rather than spending all of their time resting in leisure and consuming foods, beverages, and other products that they find appetizing but actually do harm to their organism over time. Nevertheless, if they wish to enjoy a long and healthy life, they must make an effort to exercise, eat well, and avoid things that are harmful to them. In the same way, due to the selfish desires and passions that tend to drive and consume them, it is difficult for most human beings to live in accordance with commandments that promote their well-being by demanding of them things that they may find difficult or unpleasant and also prohibit them from doing things that they may find gratifying and enjoyable but actually do them harm. If they truly seek to enjoy wholeness and well-being, however, they must discipline themselves to follow those commandments even when it is not easy for them to do so. In biblical thought, those who do obey those commandments will indeed find life, blessing, and happiness as a result of that obedience, despite the costs and sacrifices that it often involves.

For the same reason, what will motivate those who understand God's law in this way to obey his commandments is not primarily their desire to be rewarded by God for their obedience but their recognition that obedience to God's commandments is good in and of itself due to the intrinsic consequences of that obedience. Because they are convinced that what God has commanded promotes their well-being and happiness, out of love for both themselves and others they will submit to those commandments gladly and willingly rather than feeling forced or compelled to do so by God. Just as God is fully committed to their well-being together with that of all other human beings as well, so also will they commit themselves to living in ways that promote their well-being and that of others by obediently conforming their lives to God's law. This involves loving themselves and others in the same way that God loves them and others, since by definition to love someone is to seek that person's well-being. It is this love that will motivate them to obey God's commandments rather than a selfish desire to obtain some reward from God or the fear that God will punish them if they disobey him. They will also see the well-being that results intrinsically from their obedience to God's commandments as a reward in itself rather than seeking some other type of reward from God for their obedience. Their trust in God's goodness and sovereignty will also lead them to see anything that God does in response to their obedience as a blessing and reward. Rather than defining for themselves and for God the content and nature of the reward they seek, they will leave it up to God to define what type of response to their obedience on his part is truly in their own best interest, even if at times this may mean having to endure things that in themselves are painful or unpleasant rather than enjoyable.

While those who are motivated to obey God's commandments by genuine love for themselves and others are not acting purely out of self-interest, at the same time there is an element of self-interest involved in their obedience. Nevertheless, this self-interest is healthy rather than harmful. By living in ways that promote their well-being and happiness in accordance with God's law, they are doing what is truly in their own best interest. Yet this obedience to God's law is not only in their own best interest but that of others as well, since all benefit from it. In biblical thought, therefore, what is harmful is not to act out of self-interest per se but to place one's own interests over the interests of others and to fail to recognize that what is truly in one's best interest is to seek the interests of others together with one's own. Because they know that their own well-being is inseparable from that of others, those who obey God's commandments will be just as committed to the well-being of others as they are to their own well-being.

In addition to loving others together with themselves by committing themselves to seeking the well-being of others at the same time that they seek their own well-being, those who obey God by living in such a manner will also be acting out of love for God. The reason for this is that God himself seeks nothing but the well-being of all. Therefore, if human beings seek the same thing that God does by loving others at the same time that they love themselves, they are loving God by doing what pleases him. This means that to love God is to love oneself along with others by seeking one's own well-being and the well-being of all others in the same way that God does. It is precisely this that God's law prescribes and mandates out of love for all.

These ideas must be kept in mind when interpreting God's command for his people to love him. This command appears for the first time in Deut 6:5. There, after exhorting the Israelites to observe God's commandments and decrees so that all may go well with them in the land God is giving them, Moses continues: "Hear, O Israel: The LORD our God, the LORD is one. And you shall love the LORD your God with all your heart and with all your soul and with all your might. Keep these words that I am commanding you today in your heart" (Deut 6:4-6). The same type of exhortation appears in Deut 10:12-13: "So now, O Israel, what does the LORD your God require of you? Only to fear the LORD your God, to walk in all his ways, to love him, to serve the LORD your God with all your heart and with all your soul, and to keep the commandments of the LORD and his decrees that I am commanding you today for your own well-being." The affirmation that the people are to love God with all their heart and soul is repeated elsewhere in Deuteronomy as well, where it appears alongside injunctions to obey the commandments he has given the people.[44] In other passages, Moses exhorts the people to turn to God, seek him out, and obey him with all of their heart and soul.[45]

The idea that what God desires from his people is not merely literal or blind obedience but love, as well as an obedience that is an expression of love, can be discerned as well from the passages in Deuteronomy that speak of God's love for his people. Throughout the book, God is portrayed as a loving father or parent who carries Israel as his child, corrects and guides his people, supports them as a rock, and cares for them in the same way that a mother eagle cares for her young.[46] In the one passage from the book that speaks of God ruling as king over Israel, rather than presenting him as a self-serving ruler who demands obedience for his own sake, it is said that "he loved his people," that "all those consecrated to him were in his hand," and that he gave them instruction in order to guide and direct them (Deut 33:3-5). The most emphatic expressions of his love for the people, however, are found in the passages in which God exhorts them through Moses to obey his commandments so that all may go well with them. In Deut 4:40, for example, Moses tells the people: "Keep his statutes and his commandments, which I am giving you today for your own well-being and that of your descendants after you, so that you may live long in the land that the LORD your God is giving you for all time." In the following chapter, after Moses recalls the manner in which the people had promised to obey him at Sinai, he affirms that God had responded with pleasure to that promise by saying to him: "I have heard the words of this people, which they have spoken to you; all that they have spoken is good. Oh that they had such a heart in them to fear me and to keep all my commandments always, so that it might go well with them and with their children forever!" (5:28-29). Here God's deep desire to see the people blessed with well-being always is inseparably tied to his desire that they obey his good commandments, since these two things are inseparable from one another.

The same desires are expressed elsewhere in Deuteronomy. When God commands the people to honor their parents, he tells them to do so in order that their days may be long and they may prosper in the land he is giving them (Deut 5:16). In the opening verses of Deuteronomy 6, after exhorting the people once more to keep all of the commandments God has given them so that they may enjoy a long life, Moses adds: "Hear therefore, O Israel, and observe them diligently, so that all may go well for you and so that you may multiply greatly in a land flowing with milk and honey, as the LORD, the God of your ancestors, has promised you" (6:3). In other passages in the book, Moses reiterates repeatedly God's desire that the people may prosper and thrive for all time in the land that he is giving them.[47] At the same time, however, he not only insists that these things can happen only if the people

---

44. See Deut 11:13; 13:3; 30:6; cf. 11:1.
45. See Deut 4:29; 26:16; 30:2, 10.
46. See Deut 1:31; 8:5; 32:4-6, 10-14.
47. See Deut 6:17-19; 8:1; 11:8-9; 12:28; 19:13; 22:7; 30:16-20; 32:45-47.

obey the commandments God has given them but also stresses that God has given them those commandments *for their good*: "Then the LORD commanded us to observe all these statutes, to fear the LORD our God, for our lasting good, so that he might continue to give us life, as he does now" (6:24). As just noted above, in Deut 10:12-13 Moses also tells the people that he is giving them the commandments and exhorting them to obey those commandments for their own well-being. In this way, Deuteronomy not only expresses repeatedly God's desire for the people to enjoy perpetually the well-being that he seeks to give them due to his profound love for them but also emphasizes that the commandments that he has given them are rooted in that same love, as is his command that they diligently and carefully obey those commandments. Only as they do so will they be able to attain that well-being.

If God loves the people in this way and longs for them to enjoy well-being in all of its fullness, then in order to obey him in the way he desires, they must love themselves in the same way and be just as fully committed to their own well-being as he is. It is this that he seeks above all else when he gives them his commandments and demands that they obey those commandments. At the same time, of course, because he loves each and every one of his people with the same love, they can only love and obey God if they love all of those whom God loves, namely, themselves and others. God therefore commands that they love one another in the same way that they love themselves, seeking the well-being of all together with their own well-being. For that reason, God's command for people to love *him* with all their heart, soul, and might is at the same time a command for people to love *themselves* with all their heart, soul, and might, as well as a command for them to love one another in the same way (Deut 6:5). By loving themselves and one another, they express their love for God. However, when they fail to love themselves by seeking what is truly in their own best interest in obedience to God's command, they fail to love God as well. When God commands and demands that people love him with all their heart, soul, and might, therefore, he does so *for their sake* and not merely for his own.

Due to the sinful and selfish nature that they share with all other human beings, however, in reality it is impossible for God's people to love him with all their heart, soul, and might. Try as they may, they can never love God fully and perfectly, nor can they love themselves and others in that way. For that reason, God cannot expect them to fulfill that commandment perfectly. Certainly, he would like to see them attain an obedience that is perfect. In fact, those who truly love God would like to attain a perfect obedience to his commandments just as much as God himself would like such a thing, not for *his* sake but for *theirs*. The violent and destructive behavior into which they fall is just as odious to them as it is to God, since it makes it impossible for them to enjoy the well-being and happiness that God desires for them and that they desire for themselves. When they act in ways that do them and others harm, they arouse their own wrath at their behavior just as much as they arouse that of God.

Because it is impossible for God's people to love and obey him perfectly in the way that both he and they would like, in biblical thought God does not demand or expect perfect obedience from them. What he does demand, however, are two things. First, he insists that they be committed to loving themselves and others in the way that he has commanded in his law for their own good. Neither this commitment nor the obedience that will follow from it will ever be perfect, yet it is an indispensable condition for them to be able to attain as much as possible the well-being that God desires for them. Second, when they disobey him and his commandments so as to act in ways that do themselves and others harm, God demands that they acknowledge their wrongdoing and commit themselves to turning away from it, while at the same time asking him for the strength and ability they need to return to a life of obedience to his will. God cannot expect or demand that his people obey him perfectly, yet he can and does expect and demand that his people constantly look to him for the help and guidance they need to follow his commandments as best as possible for their own well-being and happiness.

While the law or Torah itself provides them with this help and guidance, at the same time it also points out to his people their sinfulness and wrongdoing. As they view their behavior in light of God's commandments, they realize that they are far from obeying those commandments in the way that they should. As just noted above, their failure to obey those commandments in the way God intends arouses their own anger and displeasure just as much as it arouses the anger and displeasure of God. The reason for this is that they want to live and behave in ways that promote their well-being just as much as God wants this for them. When their consideration of God's commandments leads them to the realization that they have failed to live and behave in those ways, their commitment to that objective as well as their inability to achieve it fully on their own leaves them with only one alternative, namely, to seek from God the strength, knowledge, and assistance they need to conform more fully to his commandments for their own good. Thus, while the God of Israel does not demand perfect obedience to his commandments from his people, he does insist that they constantly evaluate their conduct in light of those commandments and continually look to him for the help they need to conform their lives more fully to them. For the reasons we have seen, it is his love and his desire for their well-being that leads him to demand these things of them rather than any concern for himself, his own desires, or his own holiness, justice, and righteousness. As we have already noted repeatedly, what concerns God is not the effect that the behavior of his people has *on him* but rather the effect that it has *on them* and on others who are also the object of his love.

At the same time, the people's commitment to their own well-being and that of others will lead them not only to submit to God's commandments but also to interpret those commandments in a way that truly promotes that well-being. If the people were simply to submit to what God had commanded in a literal sense without being motivated by a sincere commitment to their own well-being and that of others, they would not be doing what God desired and commanded, nor would they truly be pursuing their own well-being. For example, if they avoided any type of work on the Sabbath yet did not do so out of a sincere concern for their own well-being and that of others, they might still do all sorts of things on the Sabbath that in reality undermined and destroyed that well-being. As they sat alongside their family members and friends in their homes on the Sabbath, they might engage in verbal violence toward one other, degrading and humiliating certain persons in their midst and mistreating them in ways that left them with deep psychological and emotional scars. They might use the time they spent together as they rested to make plans to do harm to others, deceive and extort them, or devise acts of hatred and revenge to carry out once the Sabbath had come to an end, as some of the people are in fact said to do in Amos 8:4-6. In that case, rather than promoting their well-being, the time they spent together resting on the Sabbath would actually end up doing the exact opposite of what God intended when he gave the Sabbath commandment. The time of rest would serve, not to refresh them and allow them to enjoy life, but to carry out and promote activities that filled their own lives and those of others with strife, hatred, pain, injustice, and oppression.

The same observations might be made with regard to all of the other commandments God had given them. Merchants might obey the command to have scales and balances that were just rather than weighted in their favor, yet at the same time collude among one another to drive up prices in order to generate profits that others would regard as excessive. Those who supervised the economic activity carried out at the temple related to the sacrificial worship of Israel's God might follow everything that the law commanded literally yet at the same time take advantage of their position to practice corruption and injustice, perhaps even by twisting and interpreting the laws in ways that promoted their own interests and oppressed those who came to the temple to offer sacrifice. Even a literal observance of the commandments to help the poor and needy might not actually benefit them if those commandments were not interpreted on the basis of a sincere concern for their well-being. If the poor and needy were given assistance in ways that were paternalistic or had the purpose of manipulating and controlling them, that assistance might be in accordance with what the law commanded literally yet actually do them more harm than good. As all of these examples demonstrate, the only way in which the people could truly obey God's commandments and enable their purpose to be fulfilled among them was to live in love for one another and let that love guide their interpretation and observance of those commandments.

In addition to interpreting God's commandments in a way that promoted the well-being of all, it was necessary to avoid interpretations that might do people harm rather than good. Like any law, the law given by God might at times be misused to oppress people and promote injustice. Under certain circumstances, in fact, it might be necessary to violate a commandment in order to observe the spirit of love and care for others on which it was based. When someone's life was in danger on a Sabbath day, for example, to remain at rest and do nothing to assist that person would be contrary to the concern for human well-being of which the commandment to observe the Sabbath was an expression. The same type of consideration might make it necessary at times to disobey other commandments as well in order to fulfill the good purposes for which those commandments had been given. Only by studying the law carefully so as to grasp more clearly not only what it commands but also the principles underlying its commandments would the people be able to interpret and apply the law in ways that truly promoted their own well-being and that of others. For that reason, God commanded the people and their leaders not only to *observe* the law carefully but also to *study and interpret it* with the same care.

When all of these considerations are taken into account, it becomes clear that what God ultimately wanted from his people for their own good was not simply obedience to his commandments but *love*, that is, a sincere and genuine commitment to their own well-being and that of all others as well. While they were also to love God himself with all their heart, soul, and might, by definition that love could only take the form of loving themselves and one another in the same way, which was the way that God loved them as well. God's command for his people to love him in that way, therefore, was not an expression of selfishness or a concern for himself but rather was grounded in his unconditional love for human beings. Only by truly loving him would they love themselves and one another, and only by loving themselves and one another would they truly be loving him. For that reason, even though in Deuteronomy and elsewhere in the Hebrew Bible the commandment to love God and others seems to stand alongside other commandments as one among many, in reality it must be understood as constituting the basis of all of the commandments.

At the same time, it must be recognized that the type of love that God desired to see in his people for their own good was not something that could be brought about by means of commandments alone. People cannot be brought to love God, themselves, and one another in ways that are genuine, heartfelt, and sincere merely by being commanded to do so. Much less can that type of love be brought about by means of rewards, threats, and punishments. Only genuine love itself can evoke the same type of love in others. The only way that God can bring people to love themselves and others with a love that is unconditional is by loving them with a love that is also unconditional. For that reason, it was vital for the people not only to know and become convinced of the depths of God's love for them and see that love as unconditional, but also to regard the commandments he gave them and the demands he made upon them as expressions of that love. Only in that way would they be able to love themselves and one another in the same way that God did and share fully his commitment to their own well-being and that of those around them. It is therefore no coincidence that in passages such as those from Deuteronomy just considered above, the exhortations for the people to love, obey, and serve God consistently appear in the context of allusions to the love, grace, kindness, and mercy that God has first shown for them, in spite of their unworthiness and their persistent stubbornness and disobedience to his will.

In conclusion, if both the biblical texts and the writings of the Second Temple period speak of the Torah or law as something that is not only good but a source of delight, wonder, joy, and gladness, the reason can only be that all of these writings regard the Torah as a means by which God seeks to bring his people to live and behave in ways that promote their well-being and happiness out of love for them. Because the God of Israel desired nothing but the well-being of the people he had created and chosen as his own, he had given Israel the commandments of the Torah not for *his* sake but for *theirs*, as well as for the sake of other peoples and nations whom he intended to bless through Israel. Likewise, because he had no needs that had to be satisfied by human beings and was not subject to a nature that dictated to him what he had to do or prevented him from relating to human beings in any way he chose, he was free to do whatever he considered good, right, and pleasing without any type of constraint or limitation. It was this freedom and love that had led him not only to create a world that was good in every way but also to give his people good commandments that had no other purpose than to promote the well-being of all.

The reason why people such as the Psalmists rejoiced over those commandments, therefore, was not because they responded to some need or desire on the part of God but because they enabled them and others to attain the well-being and wholeness that God desired for all people due to the intrinsic consequences that followed upon their observance. While some of the commandments were thought to contribute to the people's well-being *indirectly* rather than directly by reinforcing their identity as God's beloved people and reminding them of certain truths, such as God's unconditional love for them, ultimately all of the commandments were thought to have the purpose of enabling the people to be happy and enjoy all of the good that God desired for them. The only desire that God sought to satisfy by means of his commandments was the desire that the human beings he had created attain the happiness and well-being that he had intended for them from the start. While the people's obedience to those commandments was thought to please God greatly and make him happy, this was because he had linked his own happiness to theirs by regarding their happiness as an end in itself. For that reason, from the perspective of the biblical texts, the good commandments that God had given were not only a source of delight, wonder, and joy in themselves but also revealed a good God who was himself the source of these same things.

CHAPTER 4

Delivering Justice from the Hand of the Oppressor

In biblical thought, if there is to be well-being and wholeness in the world, there must also be justice. If justice does not exist, violent and destructive behavior will spread unchecked and fill the lives of human beings with pain and suffering. The only way that the God of Israel can accomplish his purpose of blessing the people he has chosen through Abraham and eventually blessing all of the families of the earth through that people is by demanding that they live in accordance with what is just, good, and right and put away behavior that is unjust, harmful, and destructive. At the same time, God must himself act with justice by promoting and defending what contributes to the well-being of all and being active to oppose the practice of evil and injustice, especially among those who willfully persist in doing harm to others through their oppressive behavior. Human well-being, therefore, can exist only if both God and human beings themselves are committed to practicing justice and opposing injustice.

Of course, the concern for justice is by no means unique to the biblical texts and those who composed and preserved them and embraced them as their own. Throughout history, people of all societies and cultures have recognized the need for the practice and administration of justice. The same was thought to be true in antiquity of the gods of peoples other than Israel. Even the gods who were believed to act with great cruelty were viewed as desiring and demanding justice in some sense. In fact, to a large extent it was precisely their desire and demand for justice that was thought to lead them to treat human beings in the ways that they did.

When one examines carefully the biblical texts, however, it soon becomes clear that the belief that the God of Israel was in many ways fundamentally different from the gods of other nations led to an understanding of both divine and human justice that was also fundamentally different from that of the peoples who worshiped those gods. At the same time, the failure of biblical interpreters to grasp and acknowledge these differences and their tendency to ascribe to the God of the Hebrew Bible the ways of being and behaving that characterized the pagan gods of antiquity has led to readings of the biblical texts that not only obscure the understanding of justice found in those texts but also run contrary to it. When one reads the passages in the Hebrew Bible that refer to divine and human justice on the basis of a belief in a God who is fully committed to the well-being of all as an end in itself, the problematic nature of the traditional readings of those passages becomes readily apparent.

JUSTICE, RIGHTEOUSNESS, AND THE DELIVERANCE OF THE OPPRESSED

When we turn to the passages from the Hebrew Scriptures that speak of things such as justice and righteousness, we immediately encounter a problem that appears to admit of no satisfactory solution. The Hebrew words that refer to these two concepts tend to convey certain ideas that are not reflected faithfully or adequately in the English terms generally used to translate them, while the English terms in turn convey ideas that are not entirely in accordance with the meaning of the Hebrew words. The reason for this is that there are certain assumptions and ways of viewing and judging reality that are different in the worldviews associated with each of the two languages. Of course, the basic worldview reflected in the biblical texts and Second Temple Jewish writings is also distinct from that found in other belief systems of antiquity, due especially to the idea that the God of Israel alone is truly God and is the creator of all that exists.

While there have been many scholarly studies on the differences between the Hebrew and English understandings of the terminology of justice and righteousness, a consideration of the biblical texts themselves is not only sufficient to grasp those differences but also makes it much more clear precisely what they consist of. To begin with, the fact that English uses two different groups of terms to translate the Hebrew word *tsedaqah* and its cognates suggests that neither of them can capture adequately or fully the meaning of the Hebrew. These two groups of terms are those derived from the words "just" and "righteous," including especially the nouns "justice" and "righteousness."

In English, justice is generally defined in terms of fairness, impartiality, and conformity to a legal or moral norm. To do justice in relation to others is to treat them in a way that their conduct or actions deserve in accordance with that norm. Justice also demands that those who violate the norm are to be punished in some way, whereas those who adhere to the norm are to be declared innocent or not guilty and on that basis are either to be rewarded or simply left unpunished. The legal or moral norm that is to be upheld and enforced is based on certain conceptions of what is good, right, fair, and equitable.

Righteousness in turn is generally understood in terms of a quality that is also in conformity with a norm that defines what is right and just. To be righteous is to behave in accordance with that norm and on that basis to be judged or regarded as being in the right and therefore free from sin, guilt, and blame as well, although in a sense no human being is ever entirely innocent or guiltless.

In the Hebrew Scriptures, the noun *tsedaqah* undoubtedly conveys the idea of both justice and righteousness in the sense of these terms just mentioned. In many passages, however, it also involves coming to the aid of those in need in order to deliver them from their suffering, especially when that suffering is the result of oppression and injustice. Often *tsedaqah* is paired with the term *mishpat*, which is generally translated into English as "judgment." In many cases, however, judgment is regarded as having the same objective of delivering those who are suffering and in need from their plight. While this plight is often the result of mistreatment or violence at the hands of an oppressor, it may also be due simply to natural causes or to the failure of others to care for those in need or uphold equity. Even in those cases, however, the suffering of those who find themselves in need may be considered the result of injustice, since it is expected that all of God's people should be active to search out and assist those who are unable to meet their basic needs so that they are not forced to endure hardships or affliction.

The difference between the English and Hebrew understandings of justice is particularly evident in passages such as Psalm 146. There the Psalmist rejoices:

> Happy are those whose help is the God of Jacob, whose hope is in the LORD their God, who made heaven and earth, the sea, and all that is in them; who remains faithful forever; who executes justice for the oppressed; who gives food to the hungry. The LORD sets the prisoners free; the LORD opens the eyes of the blind. The LORD lifts up those who are bowed down; the LORD loves the righteous. The LORD watches over the foreigners in the land; he upholds the orphan and the widow, but the way of the wicked he brings to ruin (vv. 5-9).

Here to do or execute justice is to help those who are oppressed, hungry, imprisoned, incapacitated, and humiliated, as well as those who are foreigners, orphans, and widows. This usage, however, is for the most part foreign to English, which sees such actions as expressions of compassion or kindness rather than expressions of justice or righteousness. This is especially the case with the idea of setting prisoners free, which would generally be understood as an act that is *contrary* to justice. Undoubtedly, it is kind and compassionate for God to do these things, yet it is also *just* in that it is fair and equitable. Because in biblical thought justice exists only when all have what they need and resources are distributed evenly and equitably, to assist those who are suffering and in need is not a voluntary act of compassion or kindness but an *obligation* on the part of those who have the power or means to do so.

The idea that to do justice is not only to do what is good and right but also to help and defend the poor and needy appears in many other passages from the Hebrew Scriptures. In Isa 1:16-17, God tells the rulers of his people: "Wash yourselves; make yourselves clean. Remove the evil of your doings from before my eyes. Cease to do evil, learn to do good; seek justice, rescue the oppressed, defend the orphan, and defend the widow's cause." A similar understanding of justice appears in Ps 82:3-4: "Give justice to the weak and the orphan; do justice to the lowly and the destitute. Rescue the weak and the needy; deliver them from the hand of the wicked." Often it is God himself who is said to do justice in this sense. In Deut 10:18, for example, it is said that God "executes justice for the orphan and the widow and loves the foreigners, providing them with food and clothing." The same concept of God is expressed in Ps 10:17-18:

"O LORD, you will hear the desire of the meek; you will strengthen their heart. You will incline your ear to do justice for the orphan and the oppressed, so that those from earth may strike terror no more."

In many passages, however, it is the ruler or those in positions of power who are expected to fulfill the role of doing justice by caring for the poor, needy, and oppressed in obedience to God. Israel's hopes and expectations regarding a king descended from David, for example, present him bringing justice in this sense.

> Give the king your judgments, O God, and your righteousness to a king's son. May he judge your people with righteousness, and your poor with justice. May the mountains yield prosperity (*shalom*) for the people, and the hills, in justice. May he defend the cause of the poor of the people, give deliverance to the children of the needy, and crush the oppressor. . . . For he delivers the needy when they call, the poor and those who have no helper. He has pity on the weak and the needy, and saves the lives of the needy. He redeems their life from oppression and violence, and their blood is precious in his sight (Ps 72:1-4, 12-14).

> He will defend the poor with justice and decide with equity for the meek of the earth; he will strike the earth with the rod of his mouth, and with the breath of his lips he will kill the wicked. Justice will be the belt around his waist, and faithfulness the belt around his loins (Isa 11:4-5).

> O house of David! Thus says the LORD: Execute justice in the morning, and deliver from the hand of the oppressor anyone who has been robbed (Jer 21:12).

> Thus says the LORD: Execute judgment and justice, and deliver from the hand of the oppressor anyone who has been robbed. And do no wrong or violence to the foreigner, the orphan, and the widow, or shed innocent blood in this place (Jer 22:3).

These passages demonstrate just how common it is for the Hebrew terms generally translated as "justice" and "righteousness" to convey the idea of a concern for the well-being and wholeness of people, especially those in need, and a commitment to delivering them from the plight they are suffering, often as a result of oppression. For that reason, to use English terms such as justice and righteousness to translate the Hebrew can often be misleading, since those English terms are not usually understood in the same way. Unfortunately, however, there is no single term in English that captures accurately the meaning of the Hebrew terms, which makes it extremely difficult to translate the Hebrew in a way that is faithful to the original.

Judging to Save

Especially associated with the idea of executing justice and righteousness is that of establishing shalom. In fact, according to biblical thought, justice can be said to exist when all the members of a people or society enjoy shalom or wholeness. When any are lacking such shalom, there is a situation of injustice. The intimate relation between shalom and justice or righteousness is evident in numerous passages from the Hebrew Bible. In the opening verses of Psalm 72, just cited above, the Psalmist affirms that as a result of the king's practice of justice the mountains will yield shalom for the people and the hills justice so that justice will flourish and shalom will abound (vv. 1-4, 7). Other passages also relate the two concepts to one another:

> Let me hear what God the LORD will speak, for he will speak peace (*shalom*) to his people, to his faithful, to those who turn to him in their hearts. Surely his salvation is near for those who fear him, that his glory may dwell in our land. Steadfast love and faithfulness will meet; justice and peace (*shalom*) will kiss each other. Faithfulness will spring up from the ground, and justice will look down from the sky (Ps 85:8-11).

> His authority will grow continually, and there will be endless peace (*shalom*) for the throne of David and his kingdom. He will establish and uphold it with justice (*mishpat*) and with righteousness (*tsedaqah*) from this time onward and forevermore (Isa 9:7).

> The effect of righteousness will be peace (*shalom*), and the result of righteousness, quietness and security forever (Isa 32:17; cf. 48:18).

> All your children will be taught by the LORD, and the prosperity (*shalom*) of your children will be great. You will be established in righteousness. You will be far from oppression, for you will not fear; and from terror, for it will not come near you (Isa 54:13-14).

Closely related to the idea that to do justice and righteousness is to help and defend those in greatest need are several other ideas that are evident in these passages. First of all, in Hebrew thought to do justice or to judge is essentially to *save* or *deliver* those who are suffering hardships or afflictions, especially as a result of injustice, oppression, or some type of violence. Second, to do justice in this sense is an act of *love*, since it is motivated by a desire to see those oppressed and in need restored to a condition in which they can experience wholeness and well-being. And third, while at times the salvation and deliverance of those in need requires acting against the oppressors who are responsible for their plight, the objective in taking such action is not simply to punish the oppressors or make them suffer but to prevent them from continuing to oppress others.

The two verbs that Hebrew most commonly uses to refer to the act of judging are *shafat* and *dan*, from the root *dyn*. While at times it is the oppressors and evildoers who are the object of these verbs, it is also common to speak of judging the oppressed and those in need. This usage is contrary to what we find in English, where judging tends to be understood in the sense of determining guilt and dictating sentences or punishments upon those found to be guilty. At times, these verbs are used to speak of judging the cause of the needy or defending their rights. Thus, for example, according to a literal translation, Jer 5:28 speaks of those who "go beyond all limits in their deeds of wickedness; they do not judge with justice the cause of the orphan to make it prosper, and the judgment of the needy ones they do not judge." Here, as in a number of the passages considered above, to judge or do justice has nothing to do with questions of guilt or innocence or the imposition of punishments. Instead, it simply involves delivering those who are suffering from their plight. The same basic idea is evident in other passages already cited above, which in Hebrew use the verb *shafat* with the weak, poor, and needy as the direct object. If the English verb "judge" is used to translate this verb, the passages would read thus:

> O LORD, you will hear the desire of the meek; you will strengthen their heart, you will incline your ear to judge the orphan and the oppressed, so that those from earth may strike terror no more (Ps 10:17-18).

> May he judge the poor of the people, give deliverance to the children of the needy, and crush the oppressor (Ps 72:4).

> Judge the weak and the orphan; do justice to the lowly and the destitute. Rescue the weak and the needy; deliver them from the hand of the wicked (Ps 82:3-4).

> Learn to do good; seek justice, relieve the oppressed, judge the orphan, and defend the widow's cause (Isa 1:17).

> He will judge the poor with justice and decide with equity for the meek of the earth (Isa 11:4).

Because this usage of the Hebrew verbs used to speak of judging is different from the English, translations must use a variety of different phrases to translate those verbs. Many translations of the passages just cited, for example, speak of doing or giving justice to the poor and oppressed, defending their cause, pleading for them, or saving and delivering them rather than judging them, as the Hebrew does. It is also important to note that in Hebrew the language of judging is frequently used in parallelism with verbs that refer to saving, delivering, rescuing, and defending. It is for this reason that the proclamation that God is coming to judge Israel, the nations, or the earth is repeatedly seen as a motive for rejoicing in the biblical texts, since his purpose is not to do harm but to save by putting an end to injustice and violence:

> Let the nations be glad and sing for joy, for you judge the peoples with equity and guide the nations upon the earth! (Ps 67:4)

> Say among the nations, "The LORD reigns! The world is firmly established; it will never be moved. He will judge the peoples with equity." Let the heavens be glad, and let the earth rejoice! Let the sea roar and all that fills it! Let the field rejoice, and everything in it! Then will all the trees of the forest sing for joy before the LORD, for he is coming, for he is coming to judge the earth. He will judge the world with justice and the peoples with his truth (Ps 96:10-13; cf. 98:7-9; 1 Chr 16:31-34).

> The LORD reigns! Let the earth rejoice; let the many coastlands be glad! Clouds and thick darkness are all around him; righteousness and justice are the foundation of his throne (Ps 97:1-2).

At times, God is expected or called on to judge people both in the sense of acknowledging that they are in the right and in the sense of saving them from those who wrongfully seek to do them harm. When the Psalmists cry out to God to judge them, they are asking him to acknowledge that they have done no wrong and to deliver them from their enemies, that is, those who wrongly persecute them and seek to do them harm:

> The Lord judges the peoples! Judge me, O Lord, according to my righteousness and according to the integrity that is in me. Let the evil of the wicked come to an end, but establish the righteous, for you test the minds and hearts, O righteous God (Ps 7:8-9).

> Judge me, Lord, because I have walked in my integrity (Ps 26:1).

> Judge me, Lord my God, in accordance with your justice, and do not let them rejoice over me (Ps 35:24).

> Judge me, O God, and defend my cause against an ungodly people; deliver me from those who are deceitful and unjust (Ps 43:1).

Numerous other passages from the Hebrew Bible reflect this same understanding of judging and judgment. The figures referred to as "judges" (*shoftim*) in the biblical book that bears that name in English are not judges in the sense in which that word is used in English but saviors or deliverers. In many passages, the terms that in Hebrew refer to justice or righteousness appear as virtual synonyms of terms that refer to salvation. Often this involves the use of parallelisms in which the same basic idea is repeated twice in different ways:

> Your righteousness is like the mountains of God; your judgments are like the great deep. You save humans and animals alike, O Lord (Ps 36:5-6).

> By awesome deeds you answer us with justice, O God of our salvation; you are the hope of all the ends of the earth and of the farthest seas (Ps 65:5).

> In your justice deliver me and rescue me; incline your ear to me and save me (Ps 71:2).

> You pronounced judgment from the heavens; the earth feared and was still when God rose up to execute judgment, to save all the oppressed of the earth (Ps 76:8-9).

> My eyes fail from watching for your salvation, and for the fulfillment of your promise of justice (Ps 119:123).

> The Lord is exalted, he dwells on high; he filled Zion with judgment and justice. He will be the stability of your times, a rich store of salvation, wisdom, and knowledge; the fear of the Lord is Zion's treasure (Isa 33:5-6).

> Shower, O heavens, from above, and let the skies rain down justice. Let the earth open, that salvation may spring up, and let it cause justice to sprout up also; I the Lord have created it (Isa 45:8).

> There is no other god besides me, a righteous God and a Savior; there is no one besides me (Isa 45:21).

Thus says the LORD: Maintain judgment and do justice; for my salvation is about to come and my justice to be revealed (Isa 56:1).

We wait for justice, but there is none; for salvation, but it is far from us (Isa 59:11).

I will greatly rejoice in the LORD; my whole being will exult in my God. For he has clothed me with the garments of salvation; he has covered me with the robe of justice, as a bridegroom decks himself with a garland, and as a bride adorns herself with her jewels (Isa 61:10).

In those days and at that time I will cause a righteous Branch to spring up for David; and he will execute justice and judgment in the land. In those days Judah will be saved and Jerusalem will live in safety. And this is the name by which it will be called: "The LORD is our righteousness" (Jer 33:15-16).

In each of these passages, of course, the translator must choose whether to employ the terminology of justice or that of righteousness in order to render into English the Hebrew word used, even though the Hebrew original itself makes no such distinction. In many cases, however, it is necessary to use English terms that refer to salvation or deliverance to translate the same Hebrew words, since in English the language of justice or righteousness does not adequately convey the meaning of the Hebrew original. This can be seen in the following passages by contemplating two possibilities of translation in each one:

But the LORD sits enthroned forever; he has established his throne for judgment/salvation. He judges/saves the world with justice/acts of deliverance; he brings justice/deliverance for the peoples with equity (Ps 9:7-8).

Posterity will serve him; future generations will be told about the LORD. They will come and proclaim his righteousness/deliverance to a people yet unborn, saying that he has done it (Ps 22:30-31).

Like your praise, O God, your name reaches to the ends of the earth! Your right hand is filled with righteousness/salvation. Let Mount Zion be glad; let the towns of Judah rejoice because of your judgments/acts of deliverance (Ps 48:10-11).

Open your mouth, judge justly/save with justice; judge/rescue the poor and the needy (Prov 31:9).

Listen to me, you stubborn of heart, you who are far from righteousness/deliverance: I am bringing near my righteousness/deliverance, it is not far off, and my salvation will not tarry. I will grant salvation to Zion, for Israel my glory (Isa 46:12-13).

My righteousness/deliverance is near; my salvation has gone out and my arms will judge/deliver the peoples! The coastlands wait for me, and for my arm they hope. Lift up your eyes to the heavens, and look at the earth beneath. For the heavens will vanish like smoke, the earth will wear out like a garment, and those who live on it will die like gnats; but my salvation will be forever, and my righteousness/deliverance will never come to an end (Isa 51:5-6).

The days are coming, says the LORD, when I will raise up for David a righteous/saving Branch, and he will reign as king and deal wisely, and will execute judgment/deliverance and righteousness/salvation in the land. In his days

Judah will be saved and Israel will live in safety. And this is the name by which he will be called: "The LORD our righteousness/deliverance" (Jer 23:5-6).

Some passages from the Hebrew Bible associate judgment or the practice of justice and righteousness with leading, guiding, and instructing people. In Ps 5:8, for example, the Psalmist tells God: "Lead me, O LORD, in your righteousness because of my persecutors; make your way straight before me." As already noted above, the author of Psalm 67:4 exclaims: "Let the nations be glad and sing for joy, for you judge the peoples with equity and guide the nations upon the earth!" In Isa 42:4, it is said that God's servant "will not grow faint or be crushed until he has established justice on the earth; and the coastlands wait for his teaching," that is, his *torah*. The same association between *mishpaṭ* and *torah* appears in Isa 51:4: "Listen to me, my people, and give heed to me, my nation; for a teaching (*torah*) will go out from me, and my justice (*mishpaṭ*) for a light to the peoples."

Often the language of reigning appears in parallelism with that of judging or executing justice and righteousness. As noted above, the task of judging in the sense of rescuing the oppressed and helping those in need is especially associated with Israel's kings and with the imagery of God as king. In a number of passages, in fact, this is considered the primary purpose for which kings are appointed by God. In 1 Sam 8:5, the people say to Samuel: "You are old and your sons do not follow in your ways; appoint for us, then, a king to judge us, like other nations." This is what David is said to do in 2 Sam 8:15: "So David reigned over all Israel; and David administered judgment and justice to all his people." In 1 Kgs 10:9, the Queen of Sheba tells Solomon: "Blessed be the LORD your God, who has delighted in you and placed you on the throne of Israel! Because the LORD loved Israel forever, he has made you king to execute judgment and justice." Of course, kings such as David and Solomon are also presented as judging the people in the sense of determining guilt and innocence, yet even in these cases the purpose of that activity is that of acting to establish wholeness, well-being, and equity among the people.[1] The hope that one day those who rule over God's people will fulfill this task faithfully is expressed in Isa 32:1, where the prophet announces: "See, a king will reign in righteousness, and princes will rule with justice."

Justice as Love and Compassion

Precisely because God's justice and righteousness are aimed at helping those in need and saving those who are suffering oppression, the Hebrew Bible sees God's justice and righteousness as expressions of his *love*. Passages from the Psalms and the prophetic writings repeatedly make use of parallelisms to present justice and righteousness as virtual synonyms with words such as mercy, compassion, faithfulness, goodness, kindness, and steadfast love or *ḥesed*. A number of these passages have already been cited above, yet the sheer

---

1. See, for example, 1 Kgs 3:9, 28; 1 Chr 18:14.

number of passages from the biblical texts that speak in these terms demonstrates how central to Hebrew thinking is this relationship between justice or righteousness and love.

He loves righteousness and justice; the earth is full of the steadfast love of the Lord (Ps 33:5).

Your steadfast love, O Lord, reaches up to the heavens, your faithfulness to the clouds. Righteousness and justice are the foundation of your throne; steadfast love and faithfulness go before you (Ps 89:14).

I will sing of steadfast love and of justice (Ps 101:1).

The Lord executes justice and judgments for all who are oppressed. He made his ways known to Moses, his acts to the people of Israel. The Lord is compassionate and gracious, slow to anger and abounding in steadfast love (Ps 103:6-8).

But the steadfast love of the Lord is from everlasting to everlasting on those who fear him, and his justice to children's children, to those who keep his covenant and remember to do his commandments (Ps 103:17-18).

His work is majestic and glorious, and his justice endures forever. He has gained renown by his wonderful deeds; the Lord is gracious and compassionate (Ps 111:3-4).

Gracious is the Lord, and righteous; our God is compassionate (Ps 116:5).

Your name, O Lord, endures forever; your renown, O Lord, throughout all ages. For the Lord will judge his people and have compassion on his servants (Ps 135:13-14).

They will celebrate the fame of your abundant goodness, and will sing aloud of your justice (Ps 145:7).

The Lord is righteous in all his ways, and kind in all his doings (Ps 145:17).

Whoever pursues justice and steadfast love will find life, justice, and honor (Prov 21:21).

Then a throne will be established in steadfast love in the tent of David, and on it will sit in faithfulness a ruler who judges, seeks justice, and is swift to do what is right (Isa 16:5).

Therefore the Lord waits to be gracious to you; therefore he will rise up to show mercy to you. For the Lord is a God of justice; blessed are all those who wait for him (Isa 30:18).

I am the Lord who practices steadfast love, justice, and righteousness in the earth; for in these things I delight, says the Lord (Jer 9:24).

And I will betroth you to me forever; I will betroth you to me in righteousness and in justice, in steadfast love and in compassion. I will betroth you to me in faithfulness; and you will know the Lord (Hos 2:19-20).

But as for you, return to your God, hold fast to steadfast love and justice, and wait continually for your God (Hos 12:6).

He has told you, O mortal, what is good; and what does the Lᴏʀᴅ require of you but to do justice, and to love kindness, and walk humbly with your God? (Mic 6:8)

According to these passages, to practice justice and righteousness is to show care and compassion for others. In Hebrew thought, therefore, what characterizes the righteous is not simply that they do not transgress God's law or are innocent of wrongdoing, as if righteousness had to do primarily with what one does *not* do, but that they actively reach out to those in need with compassion to give them the support and assistance they require. According to Ps 37:21, "the righteous are generous and keep giving." Psalm 112 repeats the same idea: "They rise in the darkness as a light for the upright; they are gracious, compassionate, and righteous. . . . They have distributed freely, they have given to the poor; their righteousness endures forever" (vv. 4, 9).

Because in biblical thought the practice of justice and righteousness involves coming to the aid of those who are in need of help out of love and compassion for them, in the Psalms it is common for those who cry to God for deliverance from injustice and oppression to appeal not only to his compassion and his steadfast love but to his justice and righteousness as well. In Hebrew, one appeals *both* to God's compassion and love *and* to God's justice and righteousness because God's justice and righteousness are *grounded* in his love and compassion and are *expressions* of these things:

Answer me when I call, oh my God of justice! You have set me at large when I was in distress. Have mercy on me and hear my prayer! (Ps 4:1)

I have not hidden your justice within my heart; I have spoken of your faithfulness and your salvation. I have not concealed your steadfast love and your faithfulness from the great congregation. O Lᴏʀᴅ, do not withhold your compassion from me; let your steadfast love and your faithfulness keep me safe forever (Ps 40:10).

For your name's sake, O Lᴏʀᴅ, preserve my life. In your righteousness bring me out of trouble. In your steadfast love cut off my persecutors, and destroy all my adversaries, for I am your servant (Ps 143:11-12).

This biblical use of the language of justice and righteousness once again runs contrary to what we generally find in English, since to appeal to God's justice or righteousness would involve affirming that one deserves to be saved or has a right to be helped. In fact, because even those who are poor and in need are sinners, for them to call out to God to judge them or do them justice might even be understood in the sense that they are asking him to dictate some sentence upon them or even punish them for their sins rather than imploring him to deliver them from their plight.

This idea that justice and righteousness are an expression of love is also reflected in the affirmation that the commandments God has given his people are just and righteous. In Psalm 119, the Psalmist rejoices and praises God for his righteous precepts and ordinances (vv. 7, 62, 106). Toward the end of the

Psalm, after affirming: "I love your law (*torah*)," the Psalmist continues: "Seven times a day I praise you for your righteous ordinances. Great peace (*shalom*) have those who love your law" (vv. 163-65). The idea here and elsewhere in the same Psalm is that the law is good and wonderful precisely because it is just and righteous. In other words, it promotes justice and righteousness because it is a means by which God saves and guides his people, promotes their well-being, and seeks to avoid oppression.

Of course, throughout the Hebrew Scriptures, there are two different aspects to God's justice or righteousness and his activity of judging and saving. The first of these is the type of caring, compassionate activity and concern for those in need to which the passages just cited refer. This aspect is evident, for example, in a very moving passage from Ezekiel, where God tells his people through the prophet: "I myself will be the shepherd of my sheep, and I will make them lie down, says the Lord God. I will seek out the lost, and I will bring back the strayed, and I will bind up the injured, and I will strengthen the weak, but the fat and the strong I will destroy. I will feed them with justice" (Ezek 34:15-16). In this case, for God to judge his people or feed them with justice is to care for them with tenderness and compassion.

According to the Hebrew text in the last part of this passage, however, God promises to feed the fat and the strong not with good and pleasant things but with judgment. The idea is clearly that some of the sheep have become fat and strong by oppressing others. This is stated explicitly in the following verses, which describe the manner in which the fat sheep tread on others and foul their drinking water (Ezek 34:17-19). Here again the two sides of judgment are evident: what God seeks is to care for those who are suffering and in need, but in order to do so he must take action against their oppressors who are responsible for their suffering and need. According to the opening verses of the same chapter of Ezekiel, the problem is that those in positions of power and authority are not taking care of the sheep or people under them as they should (34:1-10). They are not strengthening the weak, healing the sick, binding up the crippled, or seeking out the lost, but instead are eating their fat, clothing themselves with their wool, and letting them scatter so as to become easy prey for the wild beasts (vv. 3-6). For that reason, God promises to execute judgments on the rulers (vv. 10, 17, 20). The purpose of this judgment, however, is to save and rescue the people by setting a new shepherd over them (vv. 11-16, 22-31). In other words, what interests God is not punishing the oppressors as an end in itself but saving those who are suffering at their hands.

This understanding of justice and judgment is reflected in many of the same passages from the Hebrew Scriptures that we have already considered above. In order to come to the aid of the weak, needy, and oppressed, it is necessary to take action against those who are responsible for their suffering and are doing them harm:

> For he delivers the needy when they call, the poor and those who have no helper. He has pity on the weak and the needy, and saves the lives of the needy.

> He redeems their life from oppression and violence, and their blood is precious in his sight (Ps 72:12-14).

> Judge the weak and the orphan; do justice to the lowly and the destitute. Rescue the weak and the needy; deliver them from the hand of the wicked (Ps 82:3-4).

> For your name's sake, O LORD, preserve my life. In your righteousness bring me out of trouble. In your steadfast love cut off my persecutors, and destroy all my adversaries, for I am your servant (Ps 143:11-12).

> He will defend the poor with justice and decide with equity for the meek of the earth; he will strike the earth with the rod of his mouth, and with the breath of his lips he will kill the wicked (Isa 11:4).

> When the oppressor is no more, and destruction has ceased, and marauders have vanished from the land, then a throne will be established in steadfast love in the tent of David, and on it will sit in faithfulness a ruler who judges, seeks justice, and is swift to do what is right (Isa 16:4-5).

> O house of David! Thus says the LORD: Execute justice in the morning, and deliver from the hand of the oppressor anyone who has been robbed (Jer 21:12; cf. 22:3).

While God's justice and righteousness are undoubtedly often seen as expressions of his love in the biblical text, at first glance it might seem that he shows this love only for the oppressed and not for the oppressors. Many passages relate God's justice to his anger and his activity in crushing and even destroying those who practice injustice, violence, and oppression, including several of those already cited above:

> Rise up, O LORD, in your anger; lift yourself up against the fury of my adversaries! Awake, O my God; you have appointed a judgment! Let the assembly of the peoples be gathered around you, and take your seat on high over it. The LORD judges the peoples! Judge me, O LORD, according to my righteousness and according to the integrity that is in me. Let the evil of the wicked come to an end, but establish the righteous, for you test the minds and hearts, O righteous God. God is my shield, who saves the upright in heart. God is a righteous judge and a God who has indignation every day (Ps 7:6-11).

> You are to be feared. Who can stand in your presence once your anger is roused? From the heavens you proclaimed judgment; the earth feared and was still when God rose up to establish judgment, to save all the oppressed of the earth (Ps 76:7-9).

> Zion will be redeemed by justice, and those in her who repent, by righteousness. But rebels and sinners will be destroyed together, and those who forsake the LORD will be consumed (Isa 1:27-28).

As we shall see in Chapter 6 of this study, while undoubtedly there are passages that speak of God hating those who practice injustice and oppression, this should not be understood in the sense that God does not love them in the sense of seeking their wholeness and well-being. On the contrary, the Hebrew

Scriptures constantly present God as sending his prophets and messengers to call the oppressors to repent and change their ways so as to put away their wrongdoing not only for the sake of the oppressed but also for their own sake. As long as they persist in their oppressive behavior, they not only prevent others from enjoying wholeness and well-being but also deprive themselves of these things. For that reason, rather than being *contrary* to God's love, his anger and indignation at the injustice and violence of the oppressors is an *expression* of God's love for all, as is his action to prevent the oppressors from continuing to harm others.

In a sense, therefore, for those actively engaged in oppression the proclamation that God comes to reign, judge, save, and deliver the oppressed is not good news or a motive for rejoicing. In their case, such a proclamation should be a source of fear and trembling because it involves their destruction. What God would greatly prefer, however, is not to destroy them but to see them turn from their oppressive ways so as to do instead what is good, right, kind, and just for their own good as well that of others. For these reasons, rather than simply acting to destroy them, he first calls them to put away their violence and oppression. If they do not do so and as a result he does act against them to destroy them, it is not because he does not love them and want their well-being, but rather because their refusal to put an end to their oppressive ways makes it impossible for his loving purposes in relation to them to be fulfilled.

CONTRASTING JUSTICE IN HEBREW AND ENGLISH

This survey of passages from the Hebrew Scriptures makes it clear that there are significant differences between the manner in which justice and righteousness are understood in English and the manner in which these terms are used in the biblical texts. The most significant of these differences is that whereas in English justice and righteousness are commonly viewed as being *antithetical* to love, kindness, mercy, and compassion, in the Hebrew Scriptures all of these terms are often used as virtual *synonyms*, despite the differences of meaning among them. In English, in fact, to practice strict justice is generally understood in terms of being entirely impartial so as to *refrain* from showing kindness, compassion, and mercy to others, unless of course they are deserving of these things. If they are deserving of these things, however, in reality one is not showing them mercy or compassion when one treats them with kindness or offers them assistance but is merely giving them the type of treatment to which they are entitled by right.

Similarly, because in English the act of judging is usually understood to involve determining guilt and innocence in order to inflict punishments on the guilty, those who execute judgments on others are not viewed as helping them, showing them favor, or seeking their well-being. Nor is the task of a judge understood to consist of delivering people from a plight or leading, guiding, and teaching them. For that reason, it is not considered an act of love to judge people. On the contrary, judges are expected to enforce justice and adhere to what is fair and right without any type of bias, favoritism, or preference for particular persons or groups. If a judge determines that certain persons are innocent of an accusation, when the judge leaves them unpunished and lets them go free, the judge is not doing them any favor or showing them love or compassion but is simply adhering to the law and giving them what they rightfully deserve. Conversely, if a judge determines certain persons to be guilty and imposes some type of punishment on them, that judge is not attempting to save or help anyone. Nor is the judge said to be acting out of love or in a way that is contrary to love.

Among most English speakers, both justice and judgment are defined primarily in negative terms. To judge is often to condemn but never to save. For that reason, to speak of God or a human authority judging the poor and needy in the sense of delivering them from their plight or their suffering sounds extremely odd in English. As noted above, this difference between Hebrew and English makes it necessary for English translations of the biblical texts to alter the Hebrew phrases that speak of God judging those in need so as to speak instead of God defending the cause of the needy or doing justice on their behalf.

As we have also seen above, in English righteousness tends to be defined primarily in negative terms as well. To be righteous is to be blameless, innocent, or free of guilt. For that reason, even though a righteous person may show love, kindness, and compassion to others, generally it is not the practice of these things that is said to define a person as righteous but rather the avoidance of behavior that is unjust or morally wrong, that is, the things that a person does *not* do. Thus, while righteousness involves conformity to a norm, that norm usually has to do more with the absence of sinful or unacceptable behavior rather than the practice of behavior that is gracious, loving, kind, and caring.

Rather than perceiving as good news or as a cause for celebration the proclamation that God is just and righteous, many English speakers would regard such a proclamation as a motive for fear and concern. The main reason for this is that, in contrast to God, all human beings are thought to be imperfect, sinful, and unjust, at least to some extent. Because no human being is perfectly just and righteous as God is, no one can expect to be well-received or accepted by him. Instead of bringing him to save, help, or pardon them, God's justice and righteousness will lead him to condemn and punish them. The affirmation that God's law is just and righteous will be received in the same way. That law will be understood as a means by which God imposes his will on people and demands that they be perfect in their justice and righteousness as he is. At the same time, rather than benefiting anyone, a just and righteous law will lead to judgment, condemnation, and punishment for all, precisely because no one can ever measure up to God's standard of perfect justice and righteousness. In English, therefore, the notion that people should rejoice because God is just and righteous and gives people a law that is also just and righteous sounds strange.

Because in English judgment is understood primarily in terms of condemning and punishing, the biblical exhortations to rejoice because God is coming to judge his people, the earth, or the nations also come across as odd. Judgment is usually something to be feared rather than a motive for joy. Among many English speakers, in fact, the affirmation that people are to rejoice because a judge is going to execute just judgments would be understood in the sense that they should derive some type of morbid pleasure at seeing the manner in which pain and suffering will be inflicted on those who are guilty of wrongdoing in order to punish them. When people are involved in legal disputes, they may also rejoice that a judge will execute judgment, but only if the judge will decide in their favor. If the judge instead determines that justice is on the side of their adversary, rather than rejoicing that justice has been done, they will lament it.

These ways of understanding judgment and justice, therefore, stand in stark contrast to biblical thought, where judgment and justice are associated with deliverance from suffering, hardships, and oppression. When God judges, he restores the well-being and wholeness of his people and puts an end to their oppression. While this often involves acting against the oppressors to put a stop to their oppression of others, once again the emphasis is consistently on *deliverance* rather than punishment. To judge, therefore, is to act with love and concern for the well-being of those who are suffering and in need and to treat them with kindness and compassion so that their wholeness may be restored.

In English, justice is also commonly understood in terms of giving people their due, that is, making sure that they receive what they are entitled to or deserve on the basis of their actions. It therefore sounds odd to say that the needy, the oppressed, and the downtrodden *deserve* to be delivered from their plight. Such an affirmation would be understood in the sense that their behavior *merited* their receiving the assistance they need. In fact, it is common to maintain that those who are suffering or in need *deserve* to be in the condition in which they find themselves, either because they have done something that justifies their condition or has led to it, or else because they have not done what is required on their part to overcome that condition. Their suffering is therefore said to be *just* and *deserved* rather than *unjust*.

When the writings of the Hebrew Bible speak of justice, their emphasis tends to be on *distributive* justice. The aim of distributive justice is that all the members of the community or people have everything they need in order to enjoy well-being and wholeness. There is to be equity in that resources are to be divided and shared as evenly as possible. Injustice exists when some members of the community or people do not have what they need in order to experience the well-being or shalom that God desires for all. When efforts are made to ensure that their needs are met in accordance with God's will, in biblical thought this is regarded as an act of justice rather than compassion or mercy, since it involves doing what is just, fair, and right. In English, however, care for the poor and needy is generally viewed as an expression of compassion and mercy rather than justice, since it is thought to involve acting out of kindness and generosity rather than obligation. Conversely, the failure to ensure that the needs of the poor and the suffering are met is generally understood as a lack of love, kindness, and compassion rather than a breach of justice. Those who do not reach out to help those in need are not usually considered unjust or unrighteous but rather unkind and uncaring.

In contrast, among English speakers justice is understood primarily in terms of *retribution*. Justice is said to be done when wrongdoers receive the punishment due to them. Undoubtedly, in Hebrew justice is often seen as taking the form of retribution as well, since it is necessary to take action against those who oppress others in order to prevent them from doing so. This generally requires the use of force and the imposition of punishments, not only to bring the oppression to an end but also to deter any who might come to oppress others from falling into such behavior.

In biblical thought, however, retributive justice is not regarded as *an end in itself* but is instead viewed as a means to attaining the objective of distributive justice, that is, equity and well-being for all. Simply inflicting punishment on a wrongdoer does not establish or restore justice. Punishments are regarded as just only when they put an end to injustice, inequity, and oppression and contribute in some way to the well-being of the community. For this same reason, when the oppressed cry out to God for justice, in biblical thought what they are understood to be seeking is not to see their oppressors subjected to suffering and punishment as retribution for their wrongdoing but rather to be delivered from their condition of oppression. In other words, the punishment of those who oppress and do harm to others is regarded *not as an end in itself* but rather *as a means to another end*, namely, that of restoring well-being and wholeness for all. If justice were simply a matter of punishing wrongdoers, then it would be necessary to maintain that once the guilty have been punished justice has been done, even if the poor and oppressed remain in the same condition and are not helped or liberated. Such an idea runs contrary to biblical thought.

In many cases, in English justice is also thought to involve doing good to people in the sense of rewarding them for behaving in accordance with a desired norm. Those who comply with that norm are said to be deserving of the reward they receive, which is due to them on account of their righteous or just behavior. The language of merit is also used to convey the same ideas. In biblical thought, however, when justice is associated with doing good to people, the reason why they are to be treated favorably is not that their behavior merits or deserves some type of reward but rather that all people without exception deserve to be treated well, including especially those who are suffering and in need of assistance. Undoubtedly, the biblical texts speak of God rewarding just and righteous behavior, but this reward is generally not seen as something that goes beyond the well-being and wholeness that result intrinsically from living in accordance with God's will. Those who practice justice and righteousness are not doing something exceptional that deserves a special reward but are merely living in the way that God expects and demands of all people for their own good. Because they can be said merely to be fulfilling a duty or obligation, God has no reason to offer them any type of reward in addition to blessing them in the way he wishes to bless all people. Their righteous behavior, however, does make it possible for God to bless them rather than having to chastise or correct them, since that behavior makes it possible for the blessings they receive from God to do them and others good rather than harm.

When justice is understood in terms of coming to the aid of those who are suffering and in need, those who receive that assistance are not thought to have deserved or merited it as a reward for their actions. For that reason, those who are delivered from suffering and oppression are generally not said to be rewarded. If they are living righteously and obeying God's commandments, it might be said that they are rewarded for their righteousness and obedience when God comes to their aid, yet even in these cases it is God's kindness, grace, and concern for those in need that leads him to act on their behalf rather than some merit on their part. Their righteous behavior merely makes it possible for them to be restored to the well-being that God desires for them. In biblical thought, therefore, to deliver the poor and needy from their plight is to do them justice, yet this does not involve rewarding them even if they are living righteously, since what leads God to assist them is not their behavior or any merit on their part but their *need*. Similarly, in the Hebrew Bible, to do justice is not to reward good behavior as an end in itself but to ensure that all are able to enjoy wholeness and well-being. This well-being is something that all people deserve, independently of how they live, yet only those who live in accordance with God's will can attain it because any who refuse to live as God has commanded will instead bring ruin, violence, and suffering upon themselves. This understanding of justice, merit, and reward is also for the most part foreign to English, which generally does not speak of people in need deserving to be helped or meriting the help they receive, since merit and reward are generally seen as a response to *behavior* rather than to *need*.

JUSTICE IN THE PAGAN WORLDVIEWS OF ANTIQUITY

These observations raise the question of what is at the root of these differences between the way in which the Hebrew Scriptures and modern-day English define and understand justice and righteousness. To answer this question, it is necessary to consider once more the manner in which the pagan belief systems of antiquity conceive of the origin of the world as well as the gods and human beings that inhabit it.

The Justice of the Gods

As we have seen in Chapter 1 of this study, in most of the belief systems of the nations of antiquity, the gods are either equated with some primeval reality that exists from the very beginning or are said to have emerged from a primeval reality that existed prior to them. In the *Enuma Elish*, for example, the primordial gods Apsu and Tiamat are identified with the salt water and fresh water that exist from the start. Neither that water nor these two gods are said to have their origin in someone or something else. The other gods in turn derive their existence from Apsu and Tiamat. In Hesiod's *Theogony*, however, the primeval gods are identified with preexisting realities such as water, earth, the underworld, and the darkness. In belief systems such as these, other gods are either generated from the primeval gods or arise from out of the primeval reality independently of those gods.

When the gods are simply said to have existed from the beginning or to have arisen out of some reality that existed prior to them, they cannot be said to have any type of purpose or goal, since there was no one who willed them into existence for any reason or with any intention for them. Nor is there any goal, purpose, or objective to the natural order as a whole, which simply exists for its own sake.

In some of the belief systems of antiquity, human beings are viewed as having emerged from nature in the same way that the primordial gods are said to have done. In others, human beings come to exist as a result of sexual intercourse between gods or some other type of relationship or interaction among the gods that does not involve a conscious and deliberate decision on the part of the gods to create or procreate human beings. As is generally the case when human beings conceive children, the gods simply seek to satisfy their natural urges and desires and as a result they not only engender other gods but at times bring human beings into existence as well, either directly or indirectly. When human beings are said to have originated in ways such as these, they are viewed as being like the gods and the rest of nature in that they do not exist for any goal or purpose, nor are they designed to fulfill some end or accomplish some task.

In other belief systems, however, human beings are formed or fashioned by the gods deliberately. Generally, their purpose is to fulfill some task or end in relation to the gods themselves. Such is the case in the *Enuma Elish*, where Marduk decides to form human beings from the blood of his slain enemy Qingu in order that they may be devoted to the service of the gods as their slaves. To some extent, of course, human beings have freedom to decide whether or not they wish to fulfill that role and may rebel against the gods by refusing to do so. If that happens, however, the gods will certainly punish them in an attempt to force them to dedicate themselves to the service of the gods and may even destroy some or all of them if they persist in their rebellion.

According to these accounts of the origins of the gods and human beings, what both groups seek is not to fulfill some goal or purpose that lies above or beyond them but simply to survive and to thrive as much as possible so as to be able to enjoy life and avoid suffering and hardships. As we have noted previously, the gods generally like to spend their time feasting and relaxing in luxury, engaging in activities that bring them pleasure and avoiding any kind of toil or trouble. In principle, human beings would like to do the same. In any case, it is up to each individual god or human being to find ways to satisfy his or her needs and desires in order to continue to exist and to thrive as much as possible. As a result, all must regard their own existence and happiness as an end in itself. In principle, all are free to determine as well their own ends and objectives in life and to pursue those ends and objectives in whatever way they wish. To some extent, however, that freedom is limited by nature and by other beings, both divine and human, especially when these other beings are stronger and have the power to impose their will on others.

Because all those who exist are subject to nature in certain ways, there are certain natural laws that all must respect. Some of these laws are inherent to their being. Human beings, for example, must eat, drink, and sleep in order to survive and are also driven by other needs and desires. When human beings do not respect the laws of nature, nature itself can be said to punish them in the sense of causing them to endure natural consequences that are painful or harmful to them. Those who do not eat, drink, or sleep will not be able to function and will eventually die if they fail to satisfy those needs. Likewise, if they do harm to their environment or deplete the natural resources they require, human beings will not be able to survive.

At the same time, to some extent both the gods and human beings are able to exert control over nature and use it for their own ends in order to satisfy their needs and desires. They are also able to establish and exert control over other beings. The gods, of course, have much greater power than human beings and are able to control forces of nature in the sky and sea and upon the earth. They may cause it to rain, for example, or conversely may withhold the rain as they see fit. They may also cause plagues and natural disasters, just as they may also protect human beings from these things. While human beings do not enjoy the same type of power, they too are able to control both nature and other human beings in certain ways. They can use what is found in nature to build homes and cities, grow crops, and do many other things. They can also establish dominion over other people or influence them in various ways in order to obtain what is necessary to meet their needs and desires.

According to this understanding of the natural order, both the gods and human beings treat one another as means to the end of satisfying their own needs and desires. While each person inevitably regards his or her own well-being as an end in itself and regards others as means to that well-being, all are also free to regard the well-being of others as an end in itself if they wish to do so. As we have seen previously, this involves loving others unconditionally. A mother, for example, may regard her child as an end in itself and love the child unconditionally rather than simply seeing the child as a means to fulfilling her own needs and desires or attaining her own happiness. She may be willing to endure suffering and even give up her life for the well-being of the child. Yet while all are free to treat others as ends in themselves, none are obliged to do so and most in fact do not. Instead, both the gods and human beings tend to treat others merely as means to their own ends. Even when they show care and concern for them, they generally do so motivated by self-interest because they need them in some way in order to satisfy their own needs and desires or wish to receive something from them for their own sake.

While in some ways equity and equality exist naturally in the world, in other ways they do not. Nature has established the gods as superior to human beings, for example, and even among the gods there are some who are superior to others. The same is true among human beings. By nature some are stronger and possess greater intelligence, while others are weaker and less intelligent. Some are viewed as more attractive and desirable, while others are regarded as unattractive and at times even repulsive. Due to these differences, some individuals and groups gain power and supremacy over others so that they are able to bring them under their control or impose their will on them. Because this is something determined by nature, it is not regarded as unfair or unjust for those who possess greater strength, knowledge, and wisdom to establish dominance over others and to some extent impose their will on them. In the *Enuma Elish*, for example, Marduk establishes himself in a position of supremacy to all of the other gods due to his superior power, knowledge, and wisdom. In Greek mythology, the same is true of Zeus. Among human beings, powerful nations such as the Egyptians, Assyrians, and Babylonians establish their dominion over weaker nations, while powerful rulers are able to bring entire populations into subjection under their rule. These realities are considered to be fair and just since they are determined by nature, which bestows certain capabilities on some but not on others.

Because both the gods and human beings depend on nature and on one another for what they need in order to exist and to satisfy their desires, order is necessary. If there is disorder and chaos, all suffer and find it impossible to survive and thrive. Although nature has established a measure of order in the world, it is also necessary for the gods and human beings to establish and maintain order. In particular, however, the task of establishing and maintaining order corresponds to those gods and human beings who enjoy greater power, knowledge, and wisdom, since those who do not possess such characteristics or possess them to a lesser extent are not capable of establishing and maintaining order or supposedly will not do so well. In the *Enuma Elish*, for example, it is the god Marduk who carries out the task of establishing order in the world due to his superior power and wisdom. In Homer's poems, it is Zeus who is said to possess the power and wisdom necessary to maintain order among the gods and human beings, and for that reason all are to submit to him. Among human beings, those who show themselves to have been endowed with greater power, knowledge, and wisdom are given the task of establishing and maintaining order, not only by other human beings but generally by the gods as well. This gives them the *right* to rule over others.

To some extent, of course, those who have the power, ability, and right to establish order will do so in accordance with their own desires and self-interest.

While in some ways they are constrained by nature, for the most part they are free to organize the world and administer it in any way that pleases them. Because they depend on others in order to satisfy their needs and desires, however, they cannot simply abuse their power and treat others in whatever way they please, since this would destroy order and make it impossible for both those in power and those who are subject to them to live and thrive in the way necessary for order to be preserved. They must therefore establish laws, rules, and guidelines that make it possible for order to be upheld and for everything to function well for the good of all. If the gods want to receive the offerings due to them and human rulers wish to enjoy the benefits of their positions of power and privilege, they must make sure that the human beings who are subject to them can remain productive and provide them with the things that they want and need. Of course, in order to fulfill this role, human beings must also be able to provide for themselves and for one another with those things. Therefore, those in power must take care of those under them and promote relations among them that allow order to be maintained and that make it possible for everything to run smoothly and function properly.

Because the order established by those in power is contrasted with the chaos and disorder that would exist without their governance, it is claimed that the order that they have established is for the good of all and that all benefit from it. Such a claim, of course, fails to recognize that there might be other ways of ordering society and the world that might be better for certain groups or classes of people, yet because those who have actually established themselves in power have shown themselves to be superior to others in might and knowledge by doing so, they can argue that the order they have established is superior to any alternative order that others might seek to establish. On this basis, they can then demand that all submit to the order they have established for the good of all. Any who fail or refuse to do so are by definition acting contrary to the common good and are doing everyone else harm by subverting the order as its enemies. For that reason, they cannot be tolerated but must be punished or destroyed for the good of all.

When it is claimed that what matters above all else is maintaining order so as to avoid falling into chaos and therefore that whatever serves to uphold and strengthen that order is just, good, and right, that order is given priority over human beings themselves. The role and function of all human beings is defined by their place in that order so that the goal and purpose of each individual is to contribute what is necessary to it. While that order is said to exist for the common good of all within it, it takes precedence over the well-being of the particular individuals of which it is composed. In reality, however, whether it is acknowledged or not, the order exists for the sake of those at the top, since it is they who have established it in accordance with their own needs and desires. Whether they are gods or human beings, from their perspective it is their well-being that constitutes an end in itself, while the well-being of all others within the order is merely a means to that end.

Of course, in order for those at the bottom of the order to remain willingly in the position assigned to them and not seek to subvert that order, they must be convinced that the established order as it exists is also in their best interest and that they benefit from it as well. They must also be convinced that their position at the bottom of the order is justified and necessary. It is therefore generally maintained that, due to their inferiority and their lack of wisdom, knowledge, and other virtues and abilities, they *deserve* to be in the position in which they find themselves at the bottom of the order and that such a position is actually best for them. Supposedly, to place them in a superior position would involve demanding of them things of which they are not capable and thus be detrimental not only to them but to everyone else within the order as well. Therefore, for the order to function well and to prosper for the good of all, those who are more powerful and possess greater wisdom and knowledge must be at the top of the order and rule over everyone else. If those who are superior in knowledge, wisdom, and ability were to be displaced and replaced by those who are inferior in these things, chaos and disorder would ensue and all would suffer. Because the order depends on those who possess greater knowledge, wisdom, and ability being in positions of authority and superiority, supposedly for the good of all, those who are under them are said to have the duty and obligation to submit obediently to their wishes and commands. The needs of those at the top of the order are also to be given priority over those of everyone else, since if their needs are not met the order under them will fall into chaos and ruin and all others within that order will suffer or perish.

For the good of all, therefore, those who hold positions of power within the order must be active to punish and suppress any who represent a threat to the order and especially any who might seek to overthrow it. For that reason, as those of lower rank within the order dedicate themselves to doing whatever is necessary to satisfy their own needs, interests, and desires, they must seek to gain the favor and avoid the disfavor of those who are above them in the hierarchy. The same is true with regard to the relation of human beings in general to the gods. If human beings wish to prosper and avoid hardships and sufferings, their primary concern must be to keep the gods above them happy and avoid provoking them to wrath. It does not matter if what the gods demand is good, right, and just, since even if it is not, it is still necessary to do what they demand and avoid what they prohibit in order to retain their favor.

In order to preserve the order that benefits them, those who are in positions of power must not only punish any who oppose them but also find it to their advantage to bestow rewards and awards of various types on those who uphold the order as well as those who enhance, embellish, and strengthen it. When those who make important contributions to the order receive greater wealth, prestige, and privilege within the order, they are said to be *deserving* of these things because all are seen as benefiting from their contributions. Those who are in positions of lower rank within the order can also improve their lot by working hard and showing themselves to be capable of making contributions to the order for the benefit of all. In fact, those at the top of the order generally encourage those who are of lower rank to strive hard to work their way up and offer them rewards when they do so, since this strengthens the order from which they benefit. At the same time, however, those at the top of the order must be careful to make sure that those whom they allow to rise within it are not permitted to displace them at the top and much less threaten the order in any way. While individuals whose contributions and merits are exceptional may be permitted to ascend within the order, for the most part all others must be kept in their place so as to avoid altering the order in any significant way.

Often the gods and those in positions of power are said to love those who are under them and care for them as their parents, leaders, or shepherds. On that basis, those in positions of inferiority within the order are told to submit to those who are over them as their benefactors who supposedly know what is best for them and take good care of them. In most cases, however, this supposed love of the superior toward the inferior is self-interest, since what interests those in power is keeping in place the order that favors them so that those below them can serve as means for them to obtain what they need and desire for their own sake.

Although within the order or system all are free to show compassion and kindness to whomever they want, this is not demanded or expected and no one is under any obligation to treat others in this way. Among those in power, in fact, compassion and kindness are often encouraged, since these things are thought to serve as proof that they actually love and care for those under them and thus help to promote submission and obedience among them. By showing kindness to those below them, those in power keep them from rebelling and undermine any justification they may have for seeking to subvert the order, since it can then be claimed that the order is actually favorable and kind to them. The compassion and kindness of the powerful is therefore self-serving, since it constitutes a strategy to gain the support of those under them. Those in power may even come to the realization that this strategy is much more effective in maintaining their position of power and privilege than the use of force and violence, since those who regard them as good, kind, compassionate, and caring will submit to them gladly and willingly and will also encourage others to do so. In contrast, repression through the use of force and violence leads people to submit to authority *against* their will so that they *oppose* those in power rather than supporting and defending them out of gratitude toward them. Those who show compassion and kindness to those who are inferior within the order, however, must be careful to do so in ways that keep the system in place, since otherwise those who receive their assistance may use what they have received to subvert the order rather than supporting it. For the most part, therefore, the benevolence shown by those in power is not truly love for those who are subject to them but only self-interest, since it is not born out of a true concern for their well-being as an end in itself. On the contrary, it is designed as a means to maintain power and control over them so that they will continue to serve the interests of those in power.

Just as those who enjoy power and authority generally do not actually love and care for those under them but instead show kindness to them out of self-interest, so also those who are subject to them for the most part cannot truly be said to love them in return. If they do show love and reverence for those in power and authority in some sense, they generally do so out of self-interest on account of the favors and benefits they receive from them. As soon as those favors and benefits come to an end, however, whatever love can be said to have existed comes to an end as well. While many of those who express gratitude toward their superiors and praise them for their goodness and kindness may do so sincerely, others do so simply because it is a means by which they hope to bring those in power to continue to bestow on them the favors and benefits they desire and need for their own sake. If the language of love is used to describe the relations between those in power and those subject to them, therefore, such love does not generally consist of an actual concern for the well-being of the other as an end in itself and is not unconditional, since it will last only as long as both parties continue to receive from the other what they need and want for their own sake. Because relationships within the order are based on the principle of *do ut des*, people tend to seek the well-being only of those who enable them to receive what they want, either directly or else indirectly by means of the system that they support in order to obtain what they need and desire from it.

Those at the bottom of the order, therefore, are expected to show gratitude to those in power and must constantly seek to gain their approval, even though they may actually regard them as their oppressors. They cannot affirm this openly, however, since they will be punished for doing so. Instead, they must serve the gods and the powerful elites faithfully and obediently not only by providing them with what they need and upholding order but also by giving them the respect, admiration, honor, and expressions of gratitude that they desire and demand in order to remain in a position of power and superiority. It is also expected that all within the order show loyalty to the gods and those who rule over them, whom they are to regard as their benefactors. This loyalty involves supporting the rulers unconditionally in all that they do and decide, even when they do and decide things that may not actually serve the common good, since otherwise the rulers may retaliate against those who fail to show them that type of loyalty.

Within the system or order, there are also outstanding individuals who are loved by all due to the extraordinary qualities and abilities they possess. These qualities and abilities may include things such as athletic prowess, combative skills, artistic talents, or intellectual capability. As we have seen in Chapter 1, both the gods and human beings in general are also attracted to those who possess great strength and beauty or are able to perform feats that inspire awe and admiration. Those who are able to entertain them and offer them things that bring them special delight and joy enjoy the favor of the gods, the rich and powerful elites, and the masses as well. Because of the pleasure they afford to others, these individuals are regarded as being deserving of greater wealth and privilege within the system and are therefore said to merit or earn whatever benefits they obtain.

Upholding an Unjust Order in the Name of Justice

All of these ideas lie at the basis of the conceptions of justice and righteousness that are reflected in the English language and account for the differences in relation to the biblical understanding of justice and righteousness. Justice is defined in terms of that which promotes and preserves the order that supposedly exists for the good of all. While it also involves giving to each person what that person deserves, the basis for determining what any particular action or behavior deserves is the extent to which it either upholds and enhances the established order or undermines and threatens it. Justice therefore requires the establishment and enforcement of laws and rules that reward and protect those who promote and preserve order through their actions and punish those who subvert it. Because the order is identified with the common good, whatever upholds the established order is considered just, right, and good in that it contributes to the common good, whereas anything that opposes the established order is deemed unjust, wrong, and bad because it runs contrary to the good of all.

According to this understanding of justice, righteousness is understood primarily in terms of not violating the laws, rules, and norms that uphold the system or order. The righteous in turn are defined as those who abide by the rules and uphold them. They are not necessarily loving, however, because they generally obey the rules not out of care and concern for others but out of self-interest in order to avoid punishment and gain rewards and benefits for themselves. While they may show kindness and compassion to those in need, this is regarded as optional and is not considered either just or unjust, since for the most part it neither benefits nor harms the established order. If there is a sense in which righteousness and love are to be equated, it is that those who live righteously promote the common good through their submission and adherence to the order or system that has been established for the benefit of all. On this basis, it can be claimed that those who respect the laws and rules are not only righteous but loving as well.

In contrast, sin, unrighteousness, and injustice are defined in terms of actions or behaviors that are opposed to the order that exists for the common good. Any law or rule that undermines that order or does not uphold or promote it is considered unjust. The sinners and unrighteous are those who violate and subvert the laws and rules that have been established for the benefit of all. Sin and unrighteousness also tend to be defined in terms of what people *do* rather than what they *fail* to do. This is because the order or system is generally not thought to be undermined as much by the failure of people to support it and contribute to it as it is by actions and behavior that subvert and destroy it. In addition, the failure or refusal to show goodness and kindness to others is generally not considered sinful or unrighteous, since not even the righteous are required or expected to be good and kind to others. Instead, what matters is not violating the laws and rules.

In order for law and order to be maintained and for justice to be administered, of course, judges are necessary. Due to their superior knowledge and wisdom, only those who come from the educated classes are usually considered capable of carrying out properly the task of administering and enforcing justice as judges. When they judge people, they are not seeking to help, serve, or guide them or to benefit them in some other way, but instead are simply concerned about enforcing the laws. Judges are therefore not to act out of love for those whom they judge but are to adhere to strict justice, since only in that way can the order be upheld properly. If judges were to show kindness and mercy to those whom they judge, they would be allowing and even encouraging them to act contrary to justice and break the rules, since those judged would conclude that they could violate the law without being subjected to any serious consequences. Judges who do not strictly enforce the law are therefore regarded as acting unjustly and contrary to good order, in essence rewarding behavior that undermines the system. It is therefore generally preferable for judges not only to ensure that the guilty are duly punished but also to be harsh in their judgments, since this will allow them to be more effective in preventing and deterring potential wrongdoers from violating the law. Nevertheless, they must also be careful not to be overly harsh in the judgments and punishments they impose on wrongdoers, since this might foment anger and rebellion among the populace and lead people to seek to overthrow the system or order. While at times it is helpful for judges to guide, lead, and instruct people so that they follow the rules, to do so is not generally regarded as an act of love toward them, since such guidance and instruction are not designed to benefit them personally but are instead aimed at bringing them to uphold the system by enabling them to comply more fully with the law.

Because the established laws are not regarded as expressions of love for anyone but are designed solely for the purpose of maintaining order, they are not generally a motive for anyone to rejoice. This is especially true with regard to those who are needy and of lower rank within the system. Rather than seeing the law as good, fair, and just, they tend to view it as something designed to suppress them and keep them at a disadvantage. They may even regard the law as oppressive, yet the elites who have the power of definition and the resources to make their voice heard will drown out the voice of the needy, develop powerful arguments to show that they are mistaken about the law, and denounce as subversive the idea that the law is oppressive. In this way, the powerful elites are even able to convince many of those who are needy and of lower rank that the law and the system it upholds actually benefit them and therefore should constitute a motive for rejoicing and gratitude for them.

The experiences of those who suffer at the bottom of the established order, however, contradict such a claim. In addition to rejecting the idea that the established laws are just, therefore, many within the order will also reject the notion that those laws are a motive for rejoicing.

Among those at the bottom of the order, the news that a just judge is going to execute judgments will also be received with fear and concern rather than rejoicing. This is not only because those judgments are not designed to help or benefit them in any way but also because the judge's main purpose will be that of inflicting punishments on them and enforcing rules that keep them at a disadvantage. The judge does not seek to do them good or reward them for their behavior but to ensure that they are submitting fully to the order that from their perspective does not truly benefit them as it should. The best that they can hope for is that the judge will find them not guilty and leave them unpunished. In that case, their lot will not improve but will simply remain the same. They thus have no reason to rejoice that any type of judgment or justice will be carried out.

In principle, it might be expected that those who are of higher rank within the system would in fact regard as a motive for rejoicing the notion that a just judge is going to execute judgments, since it is they who are benefited most by the established laws and by judgments that uphold those laws. In reality, however, most of them would also question the notion that a judge is about to execute judgments is good news, since they already find themselves in a favorable position of power and privilege. The best that they can expect is to be permitted to remain in that position and not see it altered in any way. For that reason, like those of the lower classes, they will tend to receive with fear and concern rather than with joy the news that a just judge is going to execute judgments. Rather than improving their plight, the judge may determine that they are not abiding by the rules as they should and impose penalties on them. What they desire is not to be subjected to judgments themselves but to see those of the lower classes judged so that they may be kept in submission and punished for violating the rules that benefit those of higher rank within the order. Because they are the ones who appoint the judges and oversee the administration of justice, those in positions of power may even consider themselves to be *above* justice and therefore reject any judgments made against them. If they are those who have the responsibility of upholding and defending justice, from their perspective any judgments made against them must be regarded as *contrary* to justice, since it is they who define what is just and unjust.

According to this understanding of justice, it tends to be *opposed* to equity and equality. Justice and order require a hierarchical system in which those who are superior in knowledge, wisdom, and strength are placed over others, who are merely to submit to them. Those who possess such qualities *deserve* to be in a position of power and to be rewarded with greater privileges within the system or order because they make more significant contributions to it and will be more effective in upholding it. While those who occupy positions at the top of the order must also submit to the law, at the same time they are the ones responsible for authoring, establishing, and shaping the law, as well as those who have the task of interpreting and enforcing it. To some extent, this gives them the right to bend the rules or apply them less strictly as they see fit, since the strict and literal application of the established laws does not always promote justice and the common good. Although in principle the judges are to show no partiality in their judgments, at times justice and the common good may demand greater leniency toward the rich and powerful due to the vital contributions they make to the system and the important role they play in maintaining stability within the order.

In contrast, it is generally not considered good or right to show leniency toward those at the bottom of the order who do wrong, since this only tends to weaken the system and undermine order. Those at the bottom of the order are therefore at the mercy of those in power and authority. They do not have the right or privilege of establishing laws, interpreting them, suspending them under certain circumstances, or having any say in how they are applied and enforced. They must simply submit to those who are in power as their superiors and obey them in whatever they decide, since it is not their task but the task of their superiors to ensure order and promote justice. Those who are at the bottom of the order are also said to *deserve* the place they occupy there, since their contributions to the order are supposedly not as vital as those of their superiors and they do not possess the qualities that would justify a higher rank for them within the order. It might be argued, of course, that because it is the lower classes who provide most of the hard labor necessary to sustain the order and make it thrive, their contributions to the order are just as vital and important as those of the rich and powerful elites, if not more so. This argument, however, is generally countered by claiming that they could easily be replaced because the tasks they perform do not require great skill or knowledge.

Because both nature and the gods have assigned to those who are powerful, wise, and knowledgeable the task of establishing order and administering justice, therefore, ultimately it is up to them to decide what is just and unjust. Undoubtedly, they must respect in general terms certain accepted norms and principles regarding what is just and unjust if they hope to convince the people under them to submit willingly to their decisions, since if they violate those norms and principles blatantly the people will feel justified in opposing them and rebelling against them. Nevertheless, within certain limits, virtually anything that those in power do or dictate can be defended in the name of justice and the common good.

In the world of antiquity, for example, it is not considered *unjust* but *just* for powerful peoples such as the Egyptians, Assyrians, and Babylonians to establish their dominion over weaker and inferior peoples such as the Israelites through violence and conquest. When the Pharoah subjects the Hebrew people to slavery within his empire, he is not acting *unjustly* but *justly* because this is what they *deserve* due to their weakness, ignorance, and inferiority. Because the gods have given the Pharoah the task of promoting and preserving order, in his wisdom he is free to assign whatever role he desires to peoples such as the Hebrews in order to fulfill that task. If he determines that they are to be enslaved, it is because assigning such a position to them within the order is best for all in that it promotes the common good. And because it promotes the common good, it is best for the Hebrews as well, whose inferior capacities and capabilities require that they be subjected to the role of slaves within the order. Supposedly, if they do not accept the role assigned to them within that order, chaos will result and they will suffer even more together with everyone else, since the system will cease to be productive and will no longer be able to provide the food and resources that everyone needs, including the Hebrew slaves themselves.

Furthermore, when Moses appears before the Pharoah as the representative of the Hebrew slaves in order to demand that they be set free from their slavery, it is good, right, and just for the Pharoah not only to deny them such a demand but also to impose even harsher conditions on them as punishment for seeking to subvert the order through their demand (Exod 5:1-21). According to this logic, when the Pharoah deals with the Hebrews or Israelites in this manner, he is not *oppressing* them or acting *unjustly* toward them. On the contrary, he is acting *in accordance* with justice, since by punishing those who wish to rebel he is maintaining the order that has been established under him for the common good. He is also fulfilling faithfully the task given to him by the gods and the Egyptian people themselves, since he is not only *promoting and preserving* order but also *improving and embellishing* the order through the construction projects he is carrying out by means of the forced labor imposed on the Israelites. In fact, even when the Pharoah's taskmasters treat the Hebrew slaves with cruelty and violence, they are not acting *contrary* to justice but in reality are *supporting* it because such treatments will not only make those slaves more productive and submissive for the good of all within the order but will also help to prevent and dissuade them from subverting that order and the common good. According to the same logic, when the Hebrew people are growing in number and becoming strong, it is just and right for the Pharoah to command that the male children born among them be put to death, since they represent a threat to the system that he must uphold at all costs in the name of justice and the common good (Exod 1:8-22).

Similarly, when the gods and those in positions of power favor some human beings and reject others, this is not considered *unjust* but *just*. In Homer's epic poems, for example, the Olympian gods lend their support to certain peoples and individuals while at the same time acting in opposition to others. Although in many cases they have their reasons for favoring some over others, even when those reasons may seem unfair or arbitrary, the decisions of the gods must be considered just, not only because of their position of supremacy in relation to human beings but also because of their superior knowledge and wisdom. Nature has given them the task of overseeing and preserving order due to the qualities they possess, and therefore anything that they determine to be good, just, right, and fair is to be regarded as such.

Of course, human beings are free to question the decisions of those above them in positions of authority, such as the gods and human rulers and judges, and may attempt to convince them to alter their decisions on the basis of arguments regarding what is just and unjust. They can also ask those in authority to treat them with mercy, provide them with assistance, or deliver them from some plight. Nevertheless, they cannot *demand* any of these things from those above them, since it is ultimately up to the divine or human authorities to determine what is just and right by interpreting and applying the rules as they see fit. When those authorities deny the petitions and pleas of those who seek their kindness, support, or assistance, even when they do not appear to have good reasons for doing so, they cannot be regarded as acting unjustly or unfairly since they are upholding the order in the manner that they consider most profitable for the good of all. If there are some people who suffer poverty, hunger, and other needs and hardships within the system and the gods or human authorities choose not to assist them, therefore, no injustice can be said to exist because this is what those with authority have determined in their wisdom to be best for the order or system as a whole. To provide assistance to those in need might require diverting resources from other sectors of society that are more important or productive. In addition, because nature itself has determined that those at the bottom of the order occupy that position within the order due to their inferior qualities, to help them out of that position or deliver them from their plight through an act of kindness or generosity would be unjust and contrary to nature. If they wish to improve their lot, it is up to them to work hard and better themselves so as to demonstrate that they are deserving of a better position within the order, though of course they must act within the established rules, guidelines, and laws rather than seeking to circumvent them when seeking to move up in the ranks.

This understanding of justice therefore sets it in opposition not only to *equity and equality* but also to *mercy and compassion*. Because justice requires that greater rewards, power, and privilege be given to those who contribute most to the order that exists for the good of all and that those who do *not* contribute to that order and even subvert and threaten it be punished and marginalized, it is contrary to justice to show mercy and kindness to those who are poor, weak, unproductive, disobedient, or rebellious. To treat them with kindness would be to reward them and would be unjust in that they do not *deserve* to be rewarded. Instead, what they deserve is to be marginalized, excluded, and deprived of the benefits conferred by the system, at least until they change their ways so as to become obedient and productive elements within the system. Rather than contributing to the common good, such people diminish it not only because they do not provide any support for the system but also because they drain it of the resources that they consume. They are therefore a *burden* to the system. If they are shown kindness and mercy, this will *weaken and subvert* the system rather than strengthening and promoting it. It will also encourage them to continue to be unproductive within the system and may even lead them to believe that they can disregard the rules and not only get away with it but be rewarded for doing so. For that reason, to show them mercy must be considered *contrary* to justice.

Nevertheless, at times it may be acceptable to show mercy to such people rather than treating them with strict justice if doing so can contribute to the common good in some way. Thus, for example, while it is generally necessary to impose strict punishments on wrongdoers in order to uphold justice and order, at times it may be helpful to show them mercy by leaving their misdeeds unpunished if such mercy will enable them to be transformed into productive persons who from that point on will behave in ways that contribute to the common good. Similarly, to show mercy to the weak, the sick, the elderly, and other people who contribute little if anything to the system and instead tend to drain its resources may nevertheless promote the common good if doing so allows others within the system to be happy and productive, such as the family members and loved ones of such people who wish to see them receive the support and assistance they need.

According to the logic of this understanding of justice, because the natural order as it has been shaped and defined by those whom it has placed in power regulates the manner in which resources are distributed among the population, for the most part there is no need for the authorities to be concerned about *distributive* justice. Undoubtedly, at times the order established by nature and those in authority can be upset or altered so that resources cease to be distributed in the way that they should be, but when that happens either nature or the authorities it has established in power will generally do what is necessary to restore order and return the distribution of resources to what it should be. Because the way in which resources are distributed is deemed to be just, those who are at the bottom of the order must accept as fair and right the fact that they have less access to those resources and are therefore deprived of many of the things they want and need. Because they deserve the position within the order that they occupy, they deserve to receive less resources within that order as well.

Furthermore, if the conditions of those who have less resources become difficult for them to bear, they must not take matters into their own hands in an attempt to obtain greater resources but must continue to submit to whatever the authorities in their wisdom determine to be best for all. Due to their lack of competence and their inability to make judgments and decisions that are good, wise, and profitable, were they to assume the role of determining how resources are to be distributed in the place of the authorities, the result would be disorder and disaster for all. Even when they suffer hardships, therefore, those at the bottom of the order must accept their lot and should even be grateful to the authorities for whatever they receive from them. If anything, they may request that the authorities assist them by assigning them a greater portion of the resources available and may also appeal both to justice and to mercy when making that request, yet ultimately they must accept whatever the authorities decide, since those authorities have the knowledge, wisdom, and experience necessary to make the best decisions and for that reason have the responsibility of determining what promotes most the good of all.

Because the manner in which resources are distributed within the order is regarded as fair and just by definition and something that nature itself regulates, the main concern of those in authority must be *retributive* rather than *distributive* justice. Their most important task is not that of distributing resources fairly but rather preserving order by rewarding those who contribute to that order and punishing those who subvert and oppose it. If the authorities preserve order, the distribution of resources will for the most part take care of itself. For that reason, when it is said that those in authority are to administer justice and to judge people, this is understood primarily in the sense of *retribution*, that is, giving to all the rewards or punishments they deserve. In order to do this, of course, they must first determine guilt and innocence, which is also understood to be their primary task. As already noted above, however, administering justice and judging do not have to do with meeting people's needs or helping people. In fact, if justice demands that all be given what they deserve, helping those in need can even be seen as *contrary* to justice, not only because they must have lived or behaved in ways that led to their plight, in which case they *deserve* to be in the position in which they find themselves, but also because they must first do something to merit any help they might receive.

There can be no doubt, of course, that in many ways the system or order favors the rich and powerful, yet this too is said to be fair and just rather than unfair or unjust. Because of the superior knowledge, wisdom, and power that has allowed them to attain their position at the top, and also because it is they who uphold the order and supposedly contribute to it the most, they deserve to reap greater benefits from the system than those whose role in supporting it is less important or significant. They provide work for people and bestow many types of benefits on the populace by means of the plans and projects that they carry out. The contributions they make to the order also justify at times leaving them unpunished when they violate the established laws and rules, since were they to be punished they would no longer be able to make such contributions. In fact, because they are viewed as promoting the common good due to everything that they contribute to the order, the rich and powerful are generally regarded as the benefactors of all and therefore as just, righteous, and loving as well.

For their part, the needy and the lower classes are generally viewed as sinful, unjust, and unrighteous. In large part, this is because they tend to rebel against the system and criticize it. Because the established system or order is said to promote the common good, any who oppose it must be understood as opposing the common good as well and therefore as enemies of what is good, right, and just. The position of such people at the bottom of the order also contributes to the conclusion that they must be sinful, unjust, and unrighteous. If they were not, they would not be in the position in which they find themselves but would have moved up in the order, since the system rewards those who support it and penalizes those who do not. Because they are less supportive of the system that supposedly promotes the common good and even tend to oppose it, they also tend to be regarded as selfish, unloving, and unconcerned for the well-being of others. The fact that they have fewer resources to assist others and therefore are unable to do so also contributes to such a conclusion.

Because the rich and powerful demonstrate their care and concern for others by supporting enthusiastically the order that promotes the good of all, in contrast to the poor, they are seen as kind, generous, and loving. Even though they have many more resources than they need, they are generally not criticized for failing to share those resources if they prefer not to do so, since neither the order nor justice demands this of them. If they do share those resources with those who are in need of them, however, they are celebrated as especially compassionate and benevolent because they do so out of the kindness of their heart rather than out of any obligation to help those who are less fortunate.

The fact that those of lower rank within the order tend to be unruly and disorderly as a result of their lack of resources and the treatment they receive at the hands of the authorities contributes even further to their being characterized as sinful and unjust. Because they have great difficulty obtaining within the system the resources they need by following the established rules, they must often violate those rules in order to survive. As a result, of course, they are constantly subjected to punishments by those in charge of upholding the system and administering justice. Rather than leading them to correct or improve their behavior, however, the harsh punishments they are made to endure tend to make them even more rebellious and thus even more sinful and unjust in the eyes of others within the order. When that happens, they are subjected to even harsher punishments and condemned even more strongly as sinful and unjust. As a result, they are forced into a vicious cycle in which the punishments grow increasingly more severe while at the same time being increasingly considered justified and necessary.

In spite of these realities, according to the logic of the established order, those who are at the bottom of the order cannot rightly claim to be oppressed or to be victims of injustice. Instead of blaming those above them for their plight, they must recognize that it is they who are to blame. This is not only because nature, the gods, and the human authorities have determined that their place within the order is just and deserved but also because it is up to them to improve their lot through hard work and greater dedication. If they do not, it is their fault rather than the fault of the system or the order. For reasons already mentioned above, it would be contrary to justice to provide them with the help and resources that might allow them to move up in the order. They are not deserving of such assistance and to provide them with it would involve giving them preferential treatment, which would be unfair to others within the system. Even if they are the victims of judgments and decisions that are unfair due to an error or prejudice on the part of those who have been placed over them, from the perspective of the authorities it is generally best to uphold those judgments and decisions, since to attempt to correct them by altering them would provide a basis for people to claim that other judgments and decisions made by the authorities are wrong, unfair, or unjust. This would subvert the order that exists for the common good rather than strengthening it. For the benefit of all, then, even those who are victims of unjust judgments and decisions must accept them willingly rather than rebelling against them, just as the weak, needy, and inferior sectors of the population must accept willingly their position at the bottom of the order as a reality that is in the best interest of the system as a whole.

The Oppressive Justice of Empire

While the manner in which the rulers and powerful elites of antiquity made use of beliefs regarding the gods in order to justify their dominance over others and maintain an order that served their own interests in the name of justice and the common good can be discerned from many ancient writings, it is particularly evident in the ancient Babylonian text known as the Code of Hammurabi. Written around 1750 BCE, over a millennium before the writings of the Hebrew Bible were composed, the Code of Hammurabi contains what most scholars would regard as the closest parallel from antiquity to the collection of prescriptions and laws found in the Pentateuch or Torah.[2] Hammurabi was king during the First Dynasty of Babylon and is known from other sources to have expanded considerably the territory under Babylonian rule by conquering and subjecting other peoples in the region during his reign.

Both the Prologue and the Epilogue to the Code of Hammurabi stress very strongly the idea that the gods have not only established Babylon as their place of residence but have also designated Hammurabi as their chosen representative to do their will on account of his great virtue and capabilities. The Prologue begins:

> When Anu, the majestic, King of the Anunnaki, and Bel, the Lord of Heaven and Earth, who established the fate of the land, had given to Marduk, the ruling son of Ea, dominion over [hu]mankind, magnified him among the Igigi, and called Babylon by his great name; when they made it great upon the earth by founding therein an eternal kingdom, whose foundations are

---

2. Christine Hayes rightly notes that the Code of Hammurabi is actually not a law code but a collection of laws, since it is not exhaustive and does not exhibit much system or order (*Introduction to the Bible*, New Haven: Yale University Press, 2012, 133). Following convention, however, I will continue to use that title here.

as firmly grounded as are those of heaven and earth,—it was then that Anu and Bel called me, Hammurabi, the exalted prince, a God-fearing man, by name, to cause justice to be practiced in the land, to destroy the wicked and the evil alike, to prevent the strong from oppressing the weak, so that I might go forth like Shamash to rule over the Black-haired people, to give light to the land, and, like Anu and Bel, promote the welfare of [hu]mankind. I am Hammurabi, the prince called by Bel to pour out riches and abundance....[3]

In the remainder of the Prologue, Hammurabi describes in great detail how he provides lavishly for the sacrificial worship of the gods in order to make their hearts glad and also how he brings abundance and prosperity for the peoples under his rule thanks to his wisdom, power, and virtue. The Prologue concludes: "When Marduk sent me to rule over men [and women], to grant protection to the land, then I put law and righteousness in the mouth of the people, and brought well-being to my subjects." Here we find stated explicitly the idea that the gods have established Hammurabi on the throne as their chosen instrument to bring well-being for all and promote the practice of righteousness and justice among the people they have placed under him.

In the Epilogue, Hammurabi recounts at length all of the many benefits he provides for the people under him, not only through the just laws and pious statutes he promulgates but also through their enforcement. He affirms:

> The great gods called me, and I am the salvation-bringing shepherd, whose scepter is straight, and whose good protection extends over my city. In my breast I cherish the inhabitants of Sumer and Akkad; in my protection have I caused them to rest in peace; in my wisdom have I hidden them. That the strong might not injure the weak, and that the widow and the orphan might be safe, I have in Babylon, the city of Anu and Bel, who raised her high heads in Esagila, the temple whose foundations are firm as the heavens and the earth, in order to administer justice in the land, to decide disputes, to heal injuries, my precious words written upon my monument, before my image as king of righteousness have I set up.

Hammurabi then calls on the people whom he claims to love to respect his monument and remember his name forever, especially because he delivers the oppressed and defends what is right. He calls himself "a Lord, who is a father to his subjects," and adds: "He rejoices the heart of Marduk, his Lord; he has brought happiness to his subjects forever, and has given order to the land." He also claims to "exterminate the wicked and criminals out of his land, and grant prosperity to his subjects," and on that basis is presented as boasting: "my deeds are beyond compare, to bring low the high, to humble the proud, and to drive out insolence." Most of the second part of the lengthy Epilogue is devoted to invoking terrible and irrevocable curses from the gods on any who might alter his laws, replace his name on his monument with another, or rebel against his rule. The basis for these curses is once more that

---

3. Quotations from the Code of Hammurabi are taken from W. W. Davies, *The Codes of Hammurabi and Moses* (Cincinnati: Jennings and Graham, 1905).

the gods have chosen him as their representative and graciously pledged to protect him from any who might oppose him or wish him ill.

What is said to justify Hammurabi's rule, therefore, is not only that it has been ordained by the gods but also that it is in the best interest of all and furthers the well-being of all humankind. In addition to establishing justice and righteousness for all by destroying evildoers, protecting the weak from the strong, and bringing peace and security for the inhabitants of his reign, he cares for the needy, the weak, and the downtrodden as their loving shepherd and father. He also carries out works and projects throughout the land that enable all to enjoy the benefits of his reign. Hammurabi does all these things, however, with the help of the gods, who are said to rejoice over his rule and take great delight in the manner in which he keeps their hearts content by providing for their worship. They are also pleased at the way he upholds order by caring for his subjects and promoting reverence for Marduk and his words. Hammurabi is presented as the ideal ruler who is negligent in nothing and establishes what seems to be a perfect world by means of his benevolent rule.

If one takes all of these affirmations at face value, then it would indeed appear that Hammurabi is an extremely kind, caring, gracious, and merciful king who humbly and selflessly seeks nothing but the well-being of all of his subjects and even shows special concern for those in greatest need. There can be little doubt, however, that this portrayal of Hammurabi as the ideal king is imperial propaganda. What interests Hammurabi is justifying his reign and dominion over all. It is for that reason that he claims to promote unselfishly the good of all of his subjects, including the weak and oppressed. If he cares for the needy, the orphans, the widows, and other people at the bottom of the social order as their gracious father and shepherd, they have no reason or right to rebel against his rule or even complain about anything he does. On the contrary, they should be grateful to him and serve him with loyalty and gladness. According to this propaganda, if they do not offer Hammurabi their full and unwavering support and dedicate themselves to his service by obeying him in all things, it cannot be because Hammurabi has oppressed or neglected them or failed to do them good and show them kindness. Rather, it can only be because they are ungrateful, rebellious, and wicked people who deserve only to be punished with harshness and repressed by violence. According to the logic of the text, however, to treat them in this way would not be oppressive or unjust. On the contrary, it would involve defending what is just and good and in the best interest of all within society, including even those who are subjected to the punishments decreed by Hammurabi, since he seeks nothing but the well-being of all of his subjects as a whole. If there is to be good order, any who would threaten the order under Hammurabi must be dealt with appropriately.

Of course, the same logic applies not only to the poor and lower classes but to all of the different sectors of the population as well. Because as the ideal king Hammurabi is the benefactor of all and all of his subjects benefit greatly from his rule, they must submit to him obediently with joy and gratitude but have no reason to question or doubt anything he does or decrees. To oppose Hammurabi in any way involves not only opposing the common good that Hammurabi tirelessly and selflessly defends and promotes out of love for all, but also rebelling against the gods who have established him as lord and ruler for the benefit of all within the kingdom that they have themselves established in Babylon out of love and concern for all humanity. Supposedly, like Hammurabi himself, the gods merely wish to promote the good of humankind in general by subjecting people throughout the earth to their reign and to that of Hammurabi as their chosen instrument of blessing.

In reality, of course, what both the gods of Babylon and Hammurabi desire is to rule over a vast dominion not out of love, kindness, and consideration for the people in that dominion but for their own sake. They also wish to justify not only their rule itself but also everything that they do from their position of power and privilege so that no one will question or challenge their rule. For that reason, they must insist that they are fully dedicated to defending all that is good, just, and right and that everything they do is for the benefit of all. While the Code of Hammurabi presents the king and the gods as the defenders of justice and the staunch adversaries of wickedness, dishonesty, and oppression, in reality it is the king who defines unilaterally what is right and wrong, just and unjust, and good and evil in accordance with his own interests. By definition, an evildoer is anyone who opposes the king and the gods who put him in power as the defender of what is good, just, and right. Because the order established by the gods through Hammurabi promotes the well-being of all without exception, anyone who might challenge or upset that order is by definition posing a threat to the well-being of all of the members of society and thus must be punished or destroyed as a threat to the common good. Similarly, because the gods have established Babylon as the place from which they will rule forever for the good of humanity, any foreign power that opposes Babylon and its king is an enemy of humankind as a whole and must therefore be dealt with appropriately. In this context, to sin is to act against the system that promotes the good of all and to oppose the justice and peace that it provides for all. According to this ideology and logic, because it is the king who defines right and wrong with the authorization and support of the gods, anything that he chooses to deem as sinful, wrong, evil, and unjust must in fact be considered sinful, wrong, evil, and unjust.

By no means, however, is this to say that the laws that appear in the Code of Hammurabi are not good, just, and right in many ways. They do in fact preserve order and to a great extent promote the common good. They also help to prevent chaos, disorder, theft, dishonesty, violence, and injustice. The works and projects carried out by Hammurabi and the collection of laws established by him undoubtedly benefit many within his reign and produce wealth and abundance, at least for some. His governance ensures order and enables the production of foods and other necessities to be efficient and bountiful. All of these things may in fact be true. In fact, if they were not true to a considerable extent, Hammurabi's rule and his collection of laws would have had little popular support in Babylonia and his reign would not have lasted, unless of course it was enforced by brutal repression.

Brutal repression, however, is not the best way to maintain power over a populace. It is extremely costly for all involved, including the ruler, and always places those who practice it in imminent danger of being overthrown by rebellion or revolution. It is much better to convince the populace to submit willingly and even gladly to the rule of a king or leader. While propaganda and ideology are necessary in order to convince the populace to do so, that propaganda and ideology must be grounded at least to some extent in reality and experience in order to be credible. This means that the king and his government must indeed be active to do things that actually promote well-being, justice, equity, and peace among the population within their reign. People will not believe the propaganda and support the ruler and the ruling classes if they are in fact neglected, oppressed, hungry, or destitute. Therefore the ruler must be careful to promote and defend as much as possible the interests of all if he or she wishes to remain in power and enjoy public support. Similarly, rulers cannot simply call what is good evil and what is evil good or justify grave injustices in the name of justice and the common good if they wish to be respected as credible and supported by the general populace. Instead, they must adhere to certain principles that are universally recognized as good, right, and just, at least in general terms and within certain limits, if they are to be acknowledged by the populace as good, right, and just in their rule.

It is not necessary to consider in detail the laws contained in the Code of Hammurabi in order to observe that in general terms they do indeed promote what may be considered good, just, honest, right, and fair. In addition to protecting property and preventing falsehood, corruption, and violence, those laws regulate fairness and honesty in commerce and defend rights, relationships, and goods within the family and home. They make provisions not only to defend and support laborers and those who practice various professions but also serve to protect the populace from abuses, injury, and deception at the hands of those who are supposed to provide them with the goods and services they need. In many different ways, the laws in the Code of Hammurabi preserve good order and further peace, justice, and well-being among the people.

There are, however, certain laws in the Code of Hammurabi that favor the powerful and wealthy and preserve the privileged position of some over others.[4] In many cases, the penalties for doing harm to those in a higher social class are greater than those imposed on persons who do harm to those of lower social classes. Slaves who run away from their owners are severely punished and any who harbor escaped slaves or fail to report or denounce them

---

4. On what follows, see especially Hayes, *Introduction to the Bible*, 141-42. There she observes: "In these laws, even free persons are not deemed to be of equal value. . . and punishments are determined by the social class of both the aggressor and the victim" (142).

are liable to a death sentence. Many of the penalties prescribed are extremely harsh as well, especially from a modern perspective. They include not only the death sentence for many offenses but also drowning, burning to death, and cutting off body parts such as a tongue, an ear, a person's hands, or a woman's breast.[5] One might ask, of course, to what extent such penalties were actually administered. One would also suspect that those penalties were inflicted much more frequently on the lower classes of society and only rarely on the rich and powerful elites, if at all.

In principle, there is nothing in the Code of Hammurabi that demonstrates clearly or unequivocally that Hammurabi was not actually concerned for justice and did not truly care for the poor, the weak, and the underprivileged. Nevertheless, there are good reasons to be suspicious in this regard. Rulers who dedicate themselves to expanding their empire and conquering other peoples in order to subjugate them by force are rarely concerned for the poor and oppressed and tend to be extremely violent, unjust, and oppressive themselves. Other sources from antiquity suggest that this was probably the case with Hammurabi as well.[6]

However, when we look at what is *not* in the Code of Hammurabi, the reasons for suspecting that it did not fully promote justice and equity in the society of its day or serve as an instrument to counteract oppression and the dominance of the powerful over the weak become evident. There are no types of checks and balances to prevent the king from defining and administering justice in whatever way he pleases. He appears to be responsible only to the gods and not to any human authority that might question or criticize his actions and policies. The law collection provides no basis for reproaching or removing the king if he abuses his power or commits wrongdoing. While he presents himself as the defender of the poor and oppressed, including the widows and orphans, his laws contain no provisions aimed at supplying their needs or affording them special care. Nothing in the collection commands or encourages the inhabitants of Hammurabi's kingdom to care for one another or care for the needy and oppressed by sharing resources with them or treating them with kindness, generosity, and compassion. The collection suggests that such things are the duty of Hammurabi alone as the father to the people and shepherd of the oppressed. For that reason, the claim that he cares for those in greatest need seems to be imperial propaganda, since otherwise he would have included laws in his collection stipulating exactly how the poor, needy, and weak were to be taken care of and ensuring that a system aimed at accomplishing that objective was set in place.

Hammurabi's collection of laws, therefore, clearly seems to justify and defend a system that favors some over others and preserves a social order that in some ways is unjust and oppressive for many, even though it expressly

---

5. See sections 155, 157, 192, 194, 205, 218, 226, 253, and 282 of the Code.

6. On this point, see especially C. J. Gadd, *Hammurabi and the End of His Dynasty*, rev. ed., CAH 35 (Cambridge: Cambridge University Press, 1965), 11-17.

claims to promote the good of all. While to some extent it unquestionably promotes justice and upholds a social order that is beneficial to many, it is clearly designed to keep Hammurabi in power and thus ultimately responds to his own interests rather than those of the people in general. Although in some ways it is certainly a means by which Hammurabi seeks to benefit those who form part of the Babylonian people, it appears to be motivated not by a sincere concern for the good of all but by a desire on the part of Hammurabi to retain and consolidate his power for his own benefit.

The same observations must be made regarding the gods who according to the Code of Hammurabi have established Hammurabi in power and wish for his rule to continue and expand even further. While such gods may claim that they desire these things for the good of all, in reality like Hammurabi they are motivated by self-interest and a concern for themselves. They want Hammurabi to continue in power, not because it is truly best for the people as a whole, but because Hammurabi is devoted to serving and honoring them faithfully, providing them with the lavish and abundant offerings they desire, and demanding that all the subjects of his reign do these same things as well. Like Hammurabi, if the gods are concerned for justice and order, it is only so that the system that favors and benefits them may continue in place for all time so that they may enjoy those favors and benefits perpetually. Whatever social justice, peace, and prosperity they seek among human beings is therefore designed for their own benefit rather than the good of all, which is not truly their concern, except as it affects them. Furthermore, because it is Hammurabi who keeps the gods content on behalf of the people, his subjects have no choice but to pledge him their unswerving and unconditional loyalty if they wish to remain on good terms with the gods and avoid arousing their wrath.

There can be little doubt that most of the gods worshiped among other peoples in antiquity were believed to think and behave in the same ways as the gods described in the Code of Hammurabi. They were presented as defenders of what is good, right, and just and as the protectors of the poor and weak, yet this constituted the same type of propaganda and ideology that is evident in the Code of Hammurabi.

While legal codes and collections such as that of Hammurabi played a vital role in maintaining the social order and the position of power and privilege of rulers, priests, and other elite groups in the name of the gods, the same objective could be pursued in other ways as well. Because the members of these groups had the power and authority to make their own voice heard and to censor the voices of others, they were able to influence public opinion in their favor and present any who opposed them as a threat to the common good. They could also justify everything they did by claiming that they alone had received from the gods the knowledge and wisdom necessary to promote the welfare of all and defend what was good, right, and just. Furthermore, their control over public discourse made it possible for them to take credit for whatever prosperity and well-being existed under their reign while at the same time blaming others for any problems or hardships that the people over whom they ruled were experiencing. If the gods remained happy, it was thanks to rulers such as Hammurabi, but if they became angry and began withholding their favor and blessings from the people, it could only be the people's fault and not that of Hammurabi or other rulers like him.

In ancient Egypt, one of the ways in which the rich and powerful justified their positions of privilege in the system over which they ruled was by claiming that all those who died would be subjected to judgment in order to be either rewarded for having led a good and righteous life or punished for having failed to do so.[7] In particular, it was claimed that the dead would stand before a god or a counsel of gods, generally led by Osiris, in order to have their deeds weighed on a scale to see if they were worthy of an afterlife characterized by blessings and bliss. According to the Negative Confession associated with the Egyptian Book of the Dead, those being judged would mention one by one the wrongful deeds that they had not committed in order to gain the approval of the gods. Thus, for example, they would make claims such as the following:

> I have not committed wrongdoing against anyone. . . . I have not done evil. . . . I have not deprived an orphan. . . . I have not caused pain. . . . I am pure, I am pure, I am pure, I am pure! . . . I have not been envious. . . . I have not stolen. . . . I have not told lies. . . . I have not eavesdropped. . . . I have not been hot-tempered. . . . I have not been aggressive. . . . I have not been impatient. . . . I have not sinned; I have not done wrong. . . . I have not raised my voice. . . . Behold me; I have come before you without falsehood of mine, without guilt of mine, without evil of mine, without a witness against me, without anyone against whom I have done anything. . . . I have given bread to the hungry, water to the thirsty, clothing to the naked, and a boat to the boatless. . . . I am pure from all misdeeds.[8]

At first glance, it might seem that texts such as this one served to promote the practice of what was good, right, and just among the people who read and preserved them. Upon closer analysis, however, it becomes evident that they constitute the same type of propaganda and ideology that we find in the Code of Hammurabi. It is significant to note that the Book of the Dead and the Negative Confession were found in the tombs of the wealthy and powerful rulers and elites, who were the only ones who had the resources to be buried in such splendor and opulence. The common people rarely if ever had access to such forms of burial. Several considerations make it likely that these texts in effect served to justify the power and privilege of the ruling classes and the wealthy as well as to maintain intact the order or system from which they benefited.

---

7. On this point and what follows, see especially Jørgen Podemann Sørensen, "The Real Presence of Osiris: Iconic, Semi-Iconic and Aniconic Ritual Representations of an Egyptian God," *Religion* 47 (2017): 366-77; Erik Hornung, *The Ancient Egyptian Books of the Afterlife*, trans. David Lorton (Ithaca: Cornell University Press, 1999), 13-22.

8. The citation from the Book of the Dead 125: "The Negative Confession" is taken from *The Literature of Ancient Egypt: An Anthology of Stories, Instructions, Stelae, Autobiographies, and Poetry*, ed. William Kelly Simpson, 3rd ed. (New Haven: Yale University Press, 2003), 267-77.

In reality, no human being could truthfully claim to have never committed the type of actions described in the Negative Confession. At some point in their life, all human beings speak falsehoods, act violently and in anger, cause others pain and grief, neglect what is right and true, fail to assist the needy, and commit wrongdoing, deceit, and theft. For that reason, for any to claim that under examination by the gods they would be found to have never committed any of these things is deceitful and dishonest. Yet this was precisely what those who had such texts placed in their tombs claimed. In effect, by making such a claim, they were justifying everything they had done in life and claiming that they had never done anything wrong or acted contrary to what is good, right, and just. In most societies, such claims are made only by rich and powerful elites who regard themselves as the defenders of all that is true and virtuous and never admit any type of wrongdoing. Most scholars who have studied the Egyptian texts also recognize that few if any of the dead in whose tombs those texts were found were ever believed to have failed the examination of their deeds to which they were supposedly subjected by the gods so as to be found unworthy of the afterlife they sought. On the contrary, it would make no sense for them to have such texts in their tombs if it were thought that the life that they had led would disqualify them from attaining the blessed post-mortem existence that those texts were designed to make possible for them because their life had not been sufficiently virtuous.

It is also significant that the Negative Confession does not speak of forgiveness or describe any means by which those who have committed wrongdoing might acknowledge their faults, express remorse and repentance, and be pardoned by the gods or other human beings. Were that the basis for the dead to be judged, the idea that all or most might be judged to be righteous and admitted into the type of blessed afterlife they sought might be regarded as plausible. It appears, however, that such was not the case. Thus, rather than admitting their guilt or errors and asking to be forgiven, those who made texts such as the Negative Confession their own denied any type of guilt or error and claimed to have no need for forgiveness.

It must also be stressed that according to the Egyptian Book of the Dead the judgment of one's works was not the only condition to attain the blissful existence that was sought in the afterlife. What mattered just as much, if not more, was possessing the magic spells and incantations necessary to progress through all of the different stages on the journey to one's desired destination. Naturally, the content of these spells was known and possessed only by the rulers and the privileged elites, as well as the guardians who preserved them and kept them secret. The common people had little if any access to them and could therefore not hope to gain the same level of blessedness in the afterlife. Once it is claimed that the dead must not only have refrained from any type of wrongdoing but must also possess knowledge of the spells necessary in order to arrive at their desired destination, one's conduct in life becomes secondary. People gain access to the afterlife they desire by paying whatever it costs to obtain the spells and incantations. Even those who did in fact live virtuous lives and practice what is good and right could not hope to attain the salvation they sought without the monetary resources necessary to purchase the spells they needed.

For these reasons, it cannot be thought that texts such as the Negative Confession actually promoted justice, righteousness, and ethical behavior in ancient societies such as Egypt. On the contrary, such texts served as a basis for claiming that the rich and powerful were truly worthy of the privileges they enjoyed both in the present life and the life to come and for justifying all that they did as good, just, and right in the eyes of the gods. At the same time, these claims would be used against the common people and those of lower social classes in order to bring them to submit to the rich and powerful as the defenders of justice, given that they were faultless and just in all that they did and decreed. According to the logic of these texts, the rulers and elites would enjoy a blessed existence not only in the present life but for all eternity in the life to come, whereas such a life would be unattainable for the vast majority of human beings. Like the other writings known to us from the great empires of antiquity, rather than promoting the practice of justice, righteousness, and compassion, texts such as the Code of Hammurabi and the Negative Confession ultimately defend unjust and oppressive social and political orders by justifying the dominance of powerful elites in the name of what is good, right, just, and loving.

THE SUBVERSIVE JUSTICE OF THE GOD OF ISRAEL

This analysis of the manner in which justice and righteousness are understood within the type of belief systems found among those who worshiped pagan gods in antiquity makes it possible to distinguish much more clearly the uniqueness of the understanding of justice and righteousness that runs throughout the Hebrew Bible. This uniqueness is rooted in the beliefs regarding the creation of the world that are reflected in the biblical texts, which we have considered in Chapter 2 of this study, as well as the commitment to the well-being of all that lies at the heart of the biblical conception of God.

Establishing an Order That Is Truly Just

According to the logic of the Genesis account and other passages from the Hebrew Bible, when God created the world and the human beings who inhabit it, he was free to do so in any way he pleased. Unlike the gods of the nations, he was not subject to any type of natural order or natural laws that dictated to him what he could and could not do, nor was he limited in any way by anything external or internal to him. He did not emerge from a preexisting primeval reality, nor did that which exists emerge from him through some type of natural process. Instead, the God of the Hebrew Bible was believed to have brought the world and human beings into existence as the result of a deliberate decision and in accordance with a design that had its origin in him alone rather than anything above or beyond him.

At the same time, creation was understood as an *act of love* on the part of God. Because he had deliberately willed everything he had created to be *good*, it followed that he also wanted only good for everything he had created. This included especially the human beings to whom he had subjected his creation. When he had done so, he had chosen to give dominion over all that he had created not only to *some* human beings due to their superior power, knowledge, or wisdom but rather to *all* human beings collectively. This meant that everything in creation was to serve the needs of all human beings equally and to be distributed among them as evenly and equitably as possible. The good things in God's creation were to serve the needs of each and every person, whose well-being was *an end in itself*. According to biblical thought, God had not created human beings to serve some end or purpose that was above or beyond them, that is, to satisfy his own needs or to give him honor, reverence, obedience, or worship for his own sake. Rather, he desired the well-being of human beings *for their sake* as an end in itself. This was the end or purpose for which he was thought to have created human beings, and therefore also the end or purpose that he himself pursued and demanded that *they too* pursue collectively in their day-to-day existence. While it could be said that their well-being would constitute a source of joy for God and in that sense would satisfy a desire of his own as well, this was because from the very beginning he had linked his own happiness to theirs, as we have seen in Chapter 2. Therefore, if he was said to desire their well-being for his own sake, such a claim did not contradict the affirmation that he also desired their well-being for *their* sake as an end in itself, but rather stood alongside of it and complemented it.

These ideas are reflected in the commandments of the Torah as well. As we have seen in the previous chapter, behind many of those commandments is a concern for distributive justice. They mandate that provisions are to be made so that all without exception have what they need, including especially the weaker elements of the society, such as the poor, the widows, the orphans, the foreigners, and those with various types of disability. According to this understanding of the order that God intended to establish among his people, for example, if there was a poor, elderly widow in the community, all were to make sure that she was taken care of and that her needs were met. She was to receive the assistance she needed *not* because she was a means to the well-being of others or because of anything she might contribute to the social order, but because *her well-being was an end in itself*. She was to be valued and supported *unconditionally*, independently of any contributions she made or did not make within the order, because this was what God desired and commanded and therefore what all others within the order were also to desire and seek. The same was true of the well-being of every other person within the order. The well-being of each person was not to be regarded simply as a means to some other end or purpose but constituted an end in itself. All were to be cared for and loved unconditionally, independently of any qualities they possessed or did not possess.

This logic is evident in many of the commandments that appear in the Torah. As we have seen in the previous chapter, those who had more were to share generously what they had with the less fortunate, not closing their hand to them when they were in need of help. Provisions were to be made so that all might have the food they needed by doing things such as leaving a part of the fruits and crops unharvested so that the poor might find something to eat. The people were told not only to refrain from oppressing others but also to show special concern for those in greatest need. As Deut 15:4 states, the ideal was that there be no poor among them. The king was also to use his power and authority for the good of all and was prohibited from amassing great wealth and acquiring many wives, servants, and horses for himself. By prescribing the cancelation of debts, the return of properties to their original owner, and the liberation of slaves every fifty years, the Torah also sought to preserve and restore a certain degree of equity among the people. On the seventh day of every week, *all* were to rest and be refreshed, including the servants, slaves, foreigners, and animals. These laws and others are based on the notion that the well-being of each individual is an end in itself and that none within the system or order are to be regarded merely as a means to the happiness or well-being of others who are superior to them or of greater value and importance.

To say that the well-being of each person was an end in itself, however, was not to deny that all were also to see themselves and their own well-being as a means to the well-being of others. Because all people need others and depend on them to help satisfy their own needs and desires, it was necessary and inevitable that all regard the well-being of others not only as an end in itself but also as a means to their own well-being. Each individual was to be valued and cared for, yet was to value and care for everyone else as well. According to this same logic, all were to regard themselves and what they possessed as a means to the well-being of others rather than seeing their own well-being purely as an end in itself. As the law commanded, all were to love their neighbor as they loved themselves, caring for their neighbor's needs as they cared for their own. Any who were not dedicated to using the life and resources that God had given them to serve others and help meet their needs were sinning not only by failing to see the well-being of others as an end in itself but also by failing to see themselves as means to the well-being of others in the way that God desired and commanded. Thus, while the principle of *do ut des* is undoubtedly operative and necessary in relations among human beings, in biblical thought it does not constitute the basis for defining what is just and unjust. When one gives to others, one does so not only in order to receive something in return from them, but also in order to help satisfy their needs and promote their well-being.

Justice, therefore, was said to exist when all without exception had what was necessary for them to live and prosper. If such was not the case, then *injustice* was said to exist and it needed to be corrected. To be righteous was to be committed to the well-being of all together with one's own well-being, regarding the well-being of each individual as an end in itself, and also regarding one's own well-being as a means to that of others. For that reason, righteousness was understood as being essentially *synonymous* with terms such as kindness, compassion, mercy, and steadfast love rather than being *opposed* to these things or in conflict with them. Conversely, sin and unrighteousness were defined in terms of *not* loving and caring for others by seeking their well-being together with one's own.

Within this order, of course, there were some who had been gifted and endowed by God or nature with greater intelligence, strength, and resources of various types. Others, in contrast, might not only be less gifted in these areas but might also be weak, sickly, disabled, or disadvantaged in some way. As a result, it would be both good and inevitable that those who were stronger, wealthier, and more intelligent or gifted assume positions of leadership within the society and that others submit to them in various ways. What mattered, however, was that all use the gifts and resources they had received for the good of all and not only for their own benefit by ascribing to the well-being of others the same importance that they ascribed to their own. What God had commanded was: "You shall love your neighbor *as yourself*" (Lev 19:18). This meant not only that all were not to love others *less* than themselves but also that they were not to love others *more* than themselves by regarding the well-being of others as more important than their own. In other words, within the social order each person was to be regarded as being of equal value, to the extent that this was possible. The principle that all were to be committed to the well-being of every other person within the order was intended not only to avoid the excessive accumulation of power and wealth among a privileged few but also to prevent people from refusing to contribute to the well-being of others by being irresponsible, unproductive, or uncaring.

Because justice was understood in terms of ensuring that all without exception had what they needed, this ideal constituted the basis for defining what each person *deserved*. For that reason, it would be said that those in need *deserved* to be helped, saved, or delivered from their plight. Of course, it would also be said that the actions of each person determined what that person deserved, but the criterion for defining whether particular actions were just or unjust was the extent to which they contributed to the well-being of all as an end in itself. In biblical thought, the objective is not merely to maintain order, since any particular order may be unjust and oppressive and not truly contribute to the well-being of all. What matters is not the order itself but the well-being and wholeness of each person and group within the order. For that reason, *the criterion for defining what is just and unjust is not whether certain actions and behaviors preserve order but whether they promote the well-being of all.*

If they do not, then justice demands that the established order be replaced by a *different* order that *does* in fact serve the needs of all without exception, and to uphold the established order rather than changing or replacing it must be considered *unjust*. Whereas in pagan thought it is the established order that defines how justice is to be understood and applied, in the biblical texts it is justice in the sense of the well-being of all that defines what order must be established and preserved.

For this reason, in biblical thought there is no question that the imposition of slavery and hardships on people such as the Israelites by dominant powers such as Egypt is unjust and oppressive. The Pharoah is hardly seeking the well-being of the Hebrews as an end in itself when he subjects them to slavery. The order that the Pharoah seeks to maintain does not truly promote the well-being of the Hebrews and other enslaved peoples, since even though it allows for many of their needs to be provided for, it treats them only as means whose sole purpose is to satisfy the needs and desires of those in positions of power and privilege, such as the Pharoah himself and those Egyptians on whose behalf the order over which he rules was established. In biblical thought, there is no sense in which the Israelites *deserve* the harsh treatment they receive at the hands of the Pharoah, since what justice requires is an order or system in which the needs of all are satisfied equally and in which the well-being of the weak and the minorities is as important as the well-being of the strong and the majority. Similarly, from a biblical perspective, the gods of Homer's poems are not just but unjust and oppressive in that they favor some over others and show little if any interest in the needy and those who have nothing to offer them. They can hardly be said truly to care for all human beings collectively and be committed to the well-being of each and every human individual.

According to the biblical understanding of justice, those who judge are to seek the well-being of those whom they judge, along with the well-being of all others within the society as well. For that reason, the idea that a just judge is going to execute judgments is a motive for rejoicing for those who will be judged if they are in need or suffering hardships. In that case, the judge is indeed understood as a savior figure who acts in favor of those in need out of a desire to help and support them, since the judge establishes justice by doing what is necessary to bring their plight or suffering to an end. In principle, the coming of a just judge to execute judgments should be a motive of joy for all others as well, whether rich or poor, strong or weak, since all should be concerned for the well-being of each member of the society and therefore be glad when those who are in need of help receive that help and are delivered from their plight. The only ones who would not regard as good news the coming of a just judge to execute judgments would be those who are *not* concerned for the well-being of others as an end in itself, either because they do not care for them or else because they are acting oppressively and unjustly in relation to others and the judge will take measures to prevent them from continuing to do so. Such people are regarded as sinful, unjust, and unrighteous precisely because they are not committed to the well-being of all within the society as an end in itself. For the same reason, when speaking of sin and injustice, the biblical texts tend to view these things in terms of the refusal or failure to show care and concern for others, that is, the failure to do good to others rather than the violation of prohibitions. The sinners and unrighteous are those who neglect those in need and do not reach out to help those who are suffering, though of course the violence and harm that they do to others actively is also viewed as being sinful and unjust.

In biblical thought, those who are set over others as rulers are therefore to define their task in terms of ensuring that all have what they need to enjoy the well-being that God desires for them, including especially those in greatest need, as well as delivering those who are suffering hardships from their plight. The rulers are to do this out of *love* for such people and not simply out of obligation. Nevertheless, in order to treat the well-being of those under them as an end in itself, they must *listen* to them and attempt to discern what is necessary to establish their well-being in dialogue with them rather than defining unilaterally what they need. They must also listen to others within the society and above all submit to everything that is prescribed in the commandments that God has given. At times, both the rulers and the judges need to be flexible in the application of those commandments, yet the criterion they must use to determine when to be flexible is not merely what promotes and preserves order but what is best for the well-being of all as an end in itself. In particular, the rulers must listen to the prophets God sends to speak his word and communicate his will, most of whom come from among the common people rather than from among those who enjoy greater wealth and power. Those prophets serve as a means to prevent the rulers and the elites from arbitrarily imposing their will on the rest of the population in the name of the common good and defining unilaterally what is just, right, and fair. It is not the rulers who are ultimately to determine these things but God's good law, to which all collectively are to be subject, including especially the rulers.

Both the rulers and the judges, therefore, are accountable to the people as a whole and in that sense are subject to their judgments as well, since it is the task of all to ensure that God's commandments are respected by everyone within the society, including especially those in positions of power and authority. Rather than refusing to submit to the judgments of others, including those of the people as a whole, or doing so reluctantly, the rulers and judges should do so willingly and gladly as long as those judgments are truly just and promote the well-being of all, since this should be precisely what the rulers and judges desire above all else as well. Nevertheless, the rulers and judges also require a great deal of wisdom, knowledge, and experience in order to promote and defend justice and well-being for all. For that reason, it is important for the people to have rulers and judges who possess such qualities, as well as a genuine concern for the well-being of all and a sincere commitment to doing whatever is necessary to accomplish that objective. When such rulers and judges are in place, the people will be able to trust and respect their decisions and judgments, even when they do not fully understand them or agree with them. While the administration of justice requires authorities who are committed to the well-being of all within the society, therefore, it also demands ongoing dialogue and continuous evaluation among both the authorities and the people who are under their authority so that together they can determine whether justice is being administered properly and the needs of all are being met.

It should also be noted that in biblical thought, the purpose of the laws and their observance is not simply to promote morality in the sense in which that term is often used in English. Generally, morality is understood in terms of following rules and conforming to certain norms that are considered to be good, upright, and acceptable in themselves. What God was thought to seek through the commandments he had given, however, was not merely that all of his people be moral, upright persons who respect the rules he has established simply because it pleases him that they do so, but that all be fully committed to the well-being of everyone else within the society. The objective was not that people follow rules or adhere to norms for the sake of those rules and norms themselves or for God's own sake, but that they truly care for one another, and especially for those in greatest need.

In contrast to pagan conceptions of justice, therefore, in biblical thought the primary concern is for *distributive* justice rather than *retributive* justice. The objective is that the resources available be distributed in ways that allow all to have what they need in order to enjoy the well-being that God desires for each person within the society. Nevertheless, retributive justice is also important since it is the means by which those who prevent others from attaining the well-being that God desires for all are restrained and held in check. As we shall see in the next chapter, retribution is also necessary as a means by which people are brought to act in ways that contribute to the well-being of others, yet it is not to be regarded as an end in itself.

For the same reasons, according to biblical thought, the primary task of judges does not consist of determining innocence or guilt, assigning blame, inflicting punishments on the guilty, or rewarding those who observe the law. In itself, simply determining that certain persons are guilty of violating the law and on that basis inflicting punishments on them does not establish or restore justice, since what matters is promoting, preserving, and restoring the well-being of all, including especially those in greatest need. For the most part, punishing wrongdoers does not benefit either the victims of wrongdoing or the wrongdoers themselves, who need to be brought to put away their wrongdoing both for the sake of others and for their own sake. Similarly, simply assigning guilt and blame does not necessarily promote the well-being of anyone, since what matters is seeing that people's needs are met and that they are able to enjoy the well-being that God desires for them. If some people have suffered injustice or violence, what is necessary is not merely to determine who is responsible for their suffering in order to punish them but to see how those who are suffering can be delivered from their plight and receive the help and support they need. Likewise, rather than seeking a reward for themselves, those who observe the laws given by God for the good of all are to do so precisely because they care for one another and wish to see others enjoy the same well-being that they desire for themselves. They therefore serve and care for others not to receive some reward for their own sake but because they regard the well-being of others as an end in itself. If the language of reward is used, it should be understood in the sense that the only reward that people are to seek is that of achieving the well-being that God intends for all as a result of their commitment to the well-being of others together with their own.

At the same time, those who are in need of help due to injustice, oppression, or simply a lack of resources have a right to demand that they receive such help rather than being forced simply to depend on whatever mercy, kindness, or goodwill that those in power choose to show them. The authorities who are in charge of administering justice are under obligation to assist those in need. It is therefore not a matter of their simply being gracious, merciful, and generous if they so desire. Much less are they to use the support they give to those in need as a means to manipulate them for their own ends. For their part, rather than regarding the authorities who assist them as merciful benefactors who have done them a favor, those who receive assistance from them are to see that assistance not as an act of compassion but as something that they are entitled to in accordance with justice. Undoubtedly, they should be grateful for the love shown to them by the authorities, yet what should interest the authorities is not that people be grateful to them but rather that they be able to enjoy well-being and from that point on be able to contribute to the well-being of others as well. In this way, when the authorities assist those in need, they are seeking the well-being not only of those who receive the assistance but of the society as a whole. At the same time, those who receive assistance must also be concerned not only for themselves and their own needs but for the needs of others as well, whose well-being is to be considered just as important as their own. While all are to be committed to the well-being of others, all have a right to demand that others be committed to their own well-being in the same way.

This same concern for the well-being of all will lead both the people in general as well as the authorities to regard the just laws given by God as something *good* and thus to rejoice that in his love God has given those laws and that they are just and righteous. All will take delight in those laws because they help to ensure that everyone within the society is able to enjoy well-being and wholeness. This is something that all desire not only for themselves but also for one another in the same way that God desires well-being and wholeness for all without exception. For that reason, those who study those laws and reflect on them will find them sweeter than honey and more precious than gold, not only because those laws promote their own well-being and prosperity, but also because they serve as means by which all within society are enabled to enjoy these things (Ps 19:10; 119:72, 103, 127). God's laws will therefore be seen as an expression of his love for all, and that same love for all will characterize all the members of his people, who will rejoice just as much in the well-being that others attain through the implementation and observance of those laws as they do in the well-being that they attain themselves. By definition, then, any who do *not* love the commandments of the Torah are being selfish and are sinful and unrighteous, since they are not concerned for the good of all that comes through the study and observance of those commandments.

Of course, to affirm that the laws and commandments given by God as well as his judgments are good, just, and righteous because they promote the well-being of all of the people without exception leads to the same conclusion regarding God himself. To affirm that God is just and righteous is not to *oppose* his justice and righteousness to his love but to see his justice and righteousness as *expressions* of his love, goodness, kindness, and compassion, as the Psalms and other writings of the Hebrew Bible consistently do. Any view of God that opposes his justice and his righteousness to his love, kindness, and mercy cannot therefore be regarded as reflecting faithfully biblical thought but must instead be seen as rooted in pagan conceptions of God and his justice. In biblical thought, people do not need to be saved from God's justice or righteousness. Much less do they need God's mercy to temper his justice and hold it in check. What people must be saved from is not God's justice or righteousness but their own injustice, unrighteousness, and sin due to the harmful and destructive effect that the failure to practice what is good, right, just, and loving has on them and others. Thus, while they need to be saved *by* God in the sense of being brought to live in ways that allow them to experience the well-being he desires for them out of love for them, there is no sense in which they need to be saved *from* God.

Any reading of the Hebrew Bible that pits God's justice and righteousness against his love and mercy or that denies or rejects the notion that God is fully committed to the well-being of all human beings without exception must therefore be considered contrary to biblical thought and to reflect instead pagan conceptions regarding the gods and justice. Any God who regards as more important something other than the well-being of all human beings collectively is not the God of the Hebrew Scriptures but a pagan god. In biblical thought, what the God of Israel desires is to be served, obeyed, and worshiped, not for his own sake, but for the sake of the human beings whom he has created, because only by doing these things will they be able to enjoy wholeness and well-being by being brought to live in ways that make that wholeness and well-being possible.

Restoring a Justice That Saves

There can be little doubt that the view of God and the justice and righteousness of God that has prevailed in the West has been grounded much more in ancient pagan thought rather than the biblical texts. God is commonly presented as a strict judge whose primary concern is imposing a moral order on human beings that is in conformity with his holy and righteous nature and acting to punish any who deviate from that order. As we have noted in the previous chapter, at times that moral order is also associated with God's own personal desires and preferences, which lead him to deem certain behaviors as righteous and others as sinful. While he is undoubtedly said to be a God of love as well, that love is viewed as standing in tension and opposition to his justice and righteousness, which demand that the sins of human beings be properly punished before he can act to save and bless them. According to this mode of thought, the problem that must be resolved if human beings are to be saved is not the sinful and destructive behavior of human beings itself but the inability of God to tolerate and overlook that behavior due to his just, holy, and righteous nature. Supposedly, if God could simply leave the destructive behavior of human beings unpunished, they could enjoy peace, well-being, and happiness by pursuing a way of life in accordance with their own desires and pleasures rather than having to submit to the dictates of a holy and righteous God whose commandments they often find overbearing and even oppressive.

Because God's justice and righteousness have been understood in this manner, the affirmation that both God and the commandments he has given are just and righteous has generally been regarded as a motive for anxiety and apprehension rather than rejoicing. A just and righteous God is said to demand perfection of human beings and to stand over them constantly threatening them with punishments if they fall short of that perfection. Obviously, what moves him to relate to human beings in this way is not his love for them but the demands of his just and holy nature. While God is certainly said to love human beings and to show them mercy and kindness, his justice and righteousness are regarded as placing limits on that love, mercy, and kindness and even taking priority over them. In this way, it is not only human beings but God himself who is subject to the dictates of his just and righteous nature.

According to this understanding of God's justice and righteousness, God's primary concern is not the happiness and well-being of his creation but the satisfaction of the demands that his nature makes upon him. What his nature demands above all else is retribution for sin, which is defined as any action or behavior that is in conflict with his justice, holiness, and righteousness. For their part, human beings must give priority to obtaining God's love and favor and avoiding his wrath and condemnation by living in compliance with the demands of his justice and righteousness and making atonement whenever they violate his just and righteous commandments. The emphasis is therefore on the actions and behaviors that human beings must follow or avoid in order to remain in God's favor and be accounted as righteous in his sight rather than a life dedicated to seeking the well-being of all out of love for God, one-self, and others. What interests God is that people not break the rules he has laid down for the sake of his justice and righteousness.

Because the primary objective of God and his justice is said to be that of giving to all what their actions deserve, God tends to be presented primarily as a judge who is constantly seeking to determine guilt and innocence and ensure that the guilty are duly punished. While he is also seen as rewarding just and righteous behavior, less importance is ascribed to this aspect of God's justice because in reality no human being is considered to be truly righteous or deserving of his love. On the contrary, all without exception are imperfect sinners who deserve only to be subjected to his just punishments. The idea that some might actually be regarded as innocent or blameless is rejected out of hand, despite the fact that the Hebrew Scriptures often use such terms to refer to certain human beings, who are of course never entirely without sin.[9] If they wish to be delivered from God's righteous judgments and condemnation, human beings must find a way to be declared righteous in his sight and obtain a verdict of not guilty. Of course, in traditional Christian thought, Christ's vicarious death is said to make it possible for human beings to be accepted by God as righteous and absolved of their guilt. As we shall see in Chapter 8, this is also the role and purpose commonly ascribed to the sacrifices for sin ordained in the Mosaic law.

According to this view of God, what God demands of human beings is not only obedience to his commandments but also their loyalty and allegiance. They are to serve him alone in the sense of satisfying his personal desires and the demands of his just, holy, and righteous nature. It is also generally said that they must manifest their loyalty to God by loving and serving God will-ingly and with a sincere heart. Curiously, at the same time they are threatened with punishments should they fail to love and serve God in that way. For that reason, ultimately what motivates them to serve and obey God is fear of pun-ishment rather than a love for God that is genuine and sincere.

Among those who are accustomed to conceiving of God and his justice and righteousness in this way, the affirmation that God's primary concern is for the happiness and well-being of human beings is regarded as highly problematic and is generally rejected. From their perspective, to speak of God in those terms is to conceive of him as catering to the desires and whims of human beings as if he had made himself their servant or slave. Both divine and human love are understood in terms of fulfilling the desires of others, even when those desires are selfish and self-serving, rather than truly seeking the well-being of all and demanding that they live in ways that promote that well-being for their own good.

Such an objection to the notion that God is concerned for the happiness and well-being of his creatures above all else is rooted in a failure to grasp the

____

9. See, for example, Gen 6:9; Exod 23:7; Deut 19:10; 1 Sam 19:5; 2 Sam 22:21-25; Job 1:1; 2:3; Ps 19:13; 94:21; 119:1.

biblical understanding of God's love as well as his justice and righteousness. In biblical thought, those who live selfishly and put their own happiness and well-being above that of others in reality do harm to themselves and others, since there cannot be true happiness and well-being for some unless there is happiness and well-being for all. In giving priority to that happiness and well-being above all else, therefore, God is not catering to the selfish whims and desires of human beings but seeking what is truly in their best interest. And because God has linked his own happiness to that of human beings and his creation as a whole, as he seeks the happiness of human beings he is also thought to be seeking his own happiness. In no way, therefore, is he understood as having enslaved himself to human beings. On the contrary, he seeks their happiness and well-being by demanding that they be committed to these things themselves and commanding that they obey him by living in ways that promote that happiness and well-being. For the same reason, rather than wanting for human beings to pledge loyalty to himself personally, he asks and demands that they be loyal to the practice of what is good, just, and right out of love for them.

On the basis of these observations, it should be clear that in many ways the understandings of God and God's justice and righteousness that have prevailed in traditional Western thought have been rooted in ideas associated with the pagan belief systems of antiquity rather than biblical thought. In the Hebrew Scriptures, to speak of God's justice and righteousness is at the same time to speak of God's unconditional love for human beings and his firm and unbending commitment to do whatever is necessary to bring them to live in ways that truly promote their happiness and well-being. What God seeks in his justice and righteousness is not to uphold a moral order that is grounded solely in a concern for himself and the inviolability of his holy and righteous nature but to deliver human beings from the destructive behavior that makes it impossible for them to enjoy the well-being he desires for all and bring them instead to live in ways that are truly in their best interest. Rather than being saved *from* God's justice, therefore, human beings need to be saved *by* that justice, which seeks to deliver those who are suffering and oppressed from their plight, even when it is they who are responsible for that suffering and oppression themselves. As we have seen previously, what the God of the Hebrew Bible seeks is that the human beings whom he has created in love be just as firmly committed to their own well-being as he is. Those who do not share that commitment need to be saved, not *from God*, but *from themselves*.

CHAPTER 5

THE HEALING CHASTISEMENTS OF AN UNRELENTING GOD

In the pagan belief systems of antiquity, the way in which the gods obtained what they desired from human beings was by means of rewards and punishments. When human beings gave the gods what they wanted and acted in ways that pleased them, the gods rewarded them by blessing them in some way. These blessings might include positions of honor and privilege, wealth, victory over enemies, good health, and other forms of prosperity and good fortune. When human beings refused or failed to give the gods what they desired and instead acted in ways that displeased them, however, the gods generally became angry and responded with punishments such as defeat at the hands of enemies, disease, famine, poverty, natural disasters, and above all death and destruction.

In large part, these rewards and punishments served as means by which the gods attempted to influence human beings so that they would do their will and avoid doing whatever displeased or angered them. By rewarding those who obeyed them, the gods not only encouraged continued obedience among those who received those rewards but also communicated to human beings in general that they too could obtain the same type of rewards by submitting obediently to the gods. Conversely, when the gods punished those who disobeyed and angered them, they served notice to all other human beings that if they disobeyed the gods they would be subjected to the same type of punishments. In this way, those rewards and punishments served to promote among human beings greater submission to the gods.

According to this understanding of the relationship between human beings and the gods, it was necessary for human beings to win the approval of the gods and *merit* or *earn* the gods' favor through their deeds. If they could be said to love human beings, this love was conditional on the obedience of human beings to their will and quickly turned into rancor and hostility if that obedience came to an end. What moved the gods to respond in these ways to human behavior was a concern for their own needs and desires rather than any concern for the needs and desires of human beings themselves. If the gods wanted people to be well and to prosper, it was so that they could dedicate themselves more fully to their service and provide them with what they needed or wanted.

As we have seen in the previous chapters, biblical interpreters have often claimed that the Hebrew Bible presents the God of Israel relating to human beings in these same ways. According to these interpretations, while God wanted there to be justice and well-being among his people, ultimately he sought these things for his own sake in order that the desires or demands of his nature might be satisfied. If such was the case, then he rewarded or punished the actions of human beings for the same reasons that the gods of the other nations did. When human beings did what he wanted for his own sake, he would reward them in order to encourage both those human beings and others to continue to obey him. In that case, what would ultimately bring people to do his will was not their love for God or others but their desire to obtain for themselves the rewards he offered, that is, their own self-interest. At the same time, God's desire to attain from human beings what he needed or wanted for his own sake would lead him to punish human beings when they failed or refused to obey him. Like the pagan gods just described, he would inflict punishments for the purpose of compelling human beings to obey him by making it clear that he would fill their lives with suffering if they did not. Either way, what would motivate people to obey him was their fear of his wrath and punishments as well as their desire for the blessings he offered them in exchange for their obedience.

According to the logic of this understanding of God's rewards and punishments, if the desires and needs that are rooted in God's nature can be satisfied, there is no other impediment or obstacle that must be overcome in order for God to save and bless human beings. All that sinful human beings require in order to be saved and blessed by God is for God to forgive them their sinful behavior rather than punishing them for that behavior. What prevents them from receiving God's blessings and salvation is not their sinful behavior itself but God's inability to overlook that behavior and leave it unpunished. In that case, if they are to obtain God's blessings and salvation, what is necessary is not that they stop sinning but that God be enabled to tolerate and overlook their sinful behavior rather than punishing it.

At the same time, what motivates God to bless and save those who obey him and to punish those who do not is not his love for them but his own self-interest. If God is said to love those who obey him, this love is not unconditional but is instead rooted in a concern for his own desires and the needs imposed on him by his nature. As soon as human beings cease to give him what he wants or what his nature demands, his love for them turns into wrath and punishment. Just as his rewards are not an expression of genuine love for those who obey him, so also his punishments are motivated by a concern for himself rather than a concern for the well-being of those who disobey him. Instead of desiring the well-being of those who willfully and persistently disobey him or seeking to bless them, he wishes to make them suffer for having offended and angered him. While the punishments he inflicts on those who disobey him may serve a corrective purpose by bringing them and others to put away their disobedience to his will and instead conform to what he commands, in many cases his purpose in punishing them is simply to satisfy the demands of his just and holy nature and to give vent to his righteous wrath until it is exhausted.

When we look closely at the biblical texts that speak of God reacting favorably to behavior that is in accordance with his will but imposing suffering and hardships on those who act contrary to it, however, it becomes evident that the logic behind those texts is very different from that which we find in the pagan belief systems of antiquity. While those texts undoubtedly use the language of reward and punishment, they present a God whose response to human behavior is oriented entirely to bringing the people he loves to live in ways that will make it possible for them to enjoy the well-being he desires for all.

DEMANDING AN OBEDIENCE THAT BRINGS BLESSING

As we have observed in Chapter 2 of this study, from the very beginning of the biblical narrative, the idea that God desires to bless human beings is mentioned repeatedly. In Genesis, the blessings that God pronounces on the man and woman he has created as well as on Noah and his children immediately after the flood seem to be intended not only for those figures themselves but also for those who will descend from them (Gen 1:28; 5:2; 9:1). Subsequently, as we saw in Chapter 3, when God speaks to Abram or Abraham, from the very beginning he not only blesses him personally but repeatedly states his intention to bless his descendants and all of the families of the earth through him as well.[1] The idea that God wishes to bless Israel in a special manner yet also desires for the nations to attain his blessings runs throughout the biblical texts as a whole as well as the Jewish writings of the Second Temple period.

At the same time, however, these texts presuppose that God cannot truly bless people if they live in ways that undermine and destroy their well-being. While he may freely pour out on them blessings such as health, wealth, and prosperity and give them land, numerous descendants, and long lives, these things will not benefit them if they do not use all that he has given them for their own good. If they instead are abusive toward one another, practice injustice, oppression, and violence, and act out of greed, envy, and selfishness, they will fill their lives and those of others with pain and suffering. In that case, if God decides to withhold his blessings, it is not because he does not want to share those blessings with the human beings he created but because their behavior will not allow them to enjoy those blessings in the way they should. Rather than using the things that they receive from him for good, they will use those things for evil and do themselves and others harm.

In biblical thought, therefore, what leads God to respond favorably or unfavorably to the behavior of human beings is *the intrinsic consequences of that behavior*. When human beings behave in ways that promote their well-being for intrinsic reasons, God responds favorably to that behavior because it allows them to enjoy his blessings in the way he desires. When they act in ways that

---

1. See Gen 12:1-3; 17:16, 20; 18:18; 22:17-18; 26:3-4; 28:3-4, 14.

undermine and destroy their well-being for intrinsic reasons, however, God responds by withholding his blessings from them and imposing various types of hardships and sufferings on them in an attempt to bring them to put away that behavior and instead live in ways that are truly in their own best interest.

As we saw at the end of Chapter 2, these ideas can be clearly discerned in the Genesis narrative. When Cain kills his brother Abel and the earth subsequently becomes filled with wicked and violent behavior such as that which is described at the outset of the story of the flood and in the account of the destruction of Sodom and Gomorrah, it becomes evident that God cannot simply continue to pour out blessings such as health, long life, abundance, and prosperity on human beings if he wishes for them to attain all the good that he intended for them from the time he created them. To do so would only make things worse, since those engaged in such behavior will not only use what God has given them to do harm rather than good but will sink even more deeply into such behavior. By continuing to give them good things instead of acting to check such behavior and attempting to bring it to an end, God would be fomenting it even further and causing it to become even more widespread.

For that reason, God cannot truly bless people if he does not also lay down conditions for them to receive his blessings. These conditions, however, have nothing to do with anything that God needs or desires for his own sake. What defines those conditions is not God's nature per se but the intrinsic relationship between human behavior and the consequences of that behavior. If God is truly to bless human beings, he must at the same time demand that they live in ways that make it possible for them to enjoy those blessings and obtain the well-being he intends for them. They must do what is good and right, treating one another with love and consideration and caring for one another's needs. At the same time, God must prohibit them from acting in ways that do them harm. In addition to laying down such conditions, however, God must respond favorably when people fulfill those conditions and seek to correct them through hardships and sufferings when they do not.

Although the idea that God's blessing of well-being is conditional upon behavior that makes it possible for human beings to enjoy that well-being is evident throughout the biblical texts, it is especially prominent in a number of passages in Deuteronomy where God exhorts his people through Moses to obey all that he has commanded so that he may bless them. In the lengthy discourse of Moses that appears at the outset of the book, he tells the people: "Keep his statutes and his commandments, which I am commanding you today for your own well-being and that of your descendants after you, so that you may live long in the land that the LORD your God is giving you for all time" (Deut 4:40). Further on, God expresses to Moses his wish that the people may obey his commandments for their own good: "If only they had such a heart in them that they would fear me and keep all my commandments always, so that it might go well with them and with their children forever!" (5:29). Moses then reiterates the same idea to the people: "You must walk in all the way which the Lord your God has commanded you, that you may live, and that it may go well with you, and that you may live long in the land that you are to possess" (5:33). Then, after exhorting them once more to keep God's decrees and commandments, Moses adds: "Hear therefore, O Israel, and observe them diligently, so that it may go well with you, and so that you may multiply greatly in a land flowing with milk and honey, as the Lord, the God of your ancestors, has promised you. . . . Do what is right and good in the sight of the Lord, so that it may go well with you" (6:3, 18). The same ideas are repeated further on in Deuteronomy.[2]

In principle, these passages can be understood in two different ways. If interpreted on the basis of the logic found in the pagan belief systems of antiquity, what God wants is obedience to his commandments *for his own sake*. In that case, he is offering to bless the people in exchange for that obedience so that in that way he can get from them what he needs or desires for himself. In essence, he is telling them: "If you give me what I want for my sake, I will give you what you want for your sake. I will reward you with blessings in exchange for your obedience to my commandments." The logic would once more be that of *do ut des*: by granting the people the life of abundance and prosperity that they desired for themselves, God would obtain from the people the praise, worship, and obedient submission he desires for himself.

If these passages are instead interpreted on the basis of the idea that God seeks the well-being of his people as an end in itself, however, they must be understood very differently. By means of the Torah, God has provided his people with the guidance, knowledge, and instruction they need to live in ways that will allow them to enjoy all of the good he desires for them. To a large extent, that good results from the observance of those commandments *in and of itself* due to the natural and intrinsic consequences of that observance. Out of love for his people, therefore, God demands that they observe those commandments, not because of any benefits he derives from their observance himself, but because of the benefits that the people themselves will obtain by observing them.

At the same time, God tells the people that only if they observe those commandments faithfully will he be able to bless them in the way he desires. In other words, the blessings that will result *intrinsically* from the observance of those commandments will be complemented by the blessings that God will pour out on the people *extrinsically* because the people's way of life will make it possible for the blessings that God will grant them to contribute to their happiness and well-being rather than undermining or destroying it. Instead of having to withhold his blessings because the people will misuse what he gives them to do harm to themselves and one another, their obedience to his good commandments will allow God to pour out on them his gifts and blessings in the way he desires out of love for them, since that obedience will allow everything that God gives them to be used for good rather than for harm and evil.

---

2. See Deut 7:12-16; 11:8-21; 12:28; 30:15-20.

The contrast between these two different ways of interpreting texts like those just cited can be understood by turning once more to the distinction between ends and means. According to an interpretation that is based on pagan categories of thought, the end that God is pursuing is obedience to his commandments, while the means by which he seeks to attain that end is by promising to reward the people with blessings if they obey those commandments. According to biblical thought, however, the end that God seeks is the well-being of his people, while the people's obedience to those commandments is the means to attaining that end. In other words, *rather than offering to bless the people so that they will obey him, God commands the people to obey him so that he may bless them.* Instead of desiring their obedience for *his own* sake and promising to bless them in order to obtain that obedience, God desires their well-being for *their* sake as an end in itself and demands that they obey him because only in that way will they be able to attain and enjoy that well-being.

This, in fact, is what the passages just cited from Deuteronomy affirm explicitly. A purpose clause is used to state clearly what the objective is: Moses repeatedly tells the people to obey God's commandments "so that it may go well with you" and "so that you may live." These phrases communicate the goal or purpose of the people's obedience, namely, that things go well with them and that they be able to live in the sense of enjoying the well-being that God desires for them. The means to that end is their obedience to his commandments, the observance of which promotes that well-being in and of itself. The same idea is reflected in Josh 1:8, where Joshua tells the people: "This book of the law (*torah*) is not to depart from your mouth, but you are to meditate on it day and night so that you may be careful to act in accordance with everything that is written in it; for then you will make your way prosperous, and then you will thrive." This prosperity and thriving are therefore not something that God offers them in exchange for their obedience but rather something that will result from the observance of God's commandments for intrinsic reasons: that observance will lead to positive consequences in and of itself.

All of these passages, therefore, presuppose both an *intrinsic* and an *extrinsic* relationship between the people's obedience and the well-being that will follow upon that obedience. Although in and of itself their obedience will promote their well-being due to its natural consequences, that well-being will also result from God's *favorable response* to that obedience: he will fill their lives with blessings, confident that they will use those blessings for their good rather than for evil or injustice. In this way, their well-being will result both *intrinsically* from their obedience to God's commandments due to the natural consequences of that obedience and also *extrinsically* due to God's favorable response to that obedience, which will take the form of providing them with blessings such as long life and prosperity in the land that God has chosen to give to them.

This understanding of the relation between obedience to God's commandments and the well-being and wholeness that God is able to bring about among his people when they practice that obedience must be kept in mind when interpreting the two passages from the Pentateuch that describe at greatest length the manner in which God will respond to the obedience or disobedience of his people, namely, Leviticus 26 and Deuteronomy 28. In the opening section of both of these chapters, the people are exhorted to observe faithfully all that God has commanded them and told of the blessings that God will bestow on them if they do so. These blessings include rain for abundant harvests, prosperity, numerous descendants, peace and security in the land, protection from their enemies, and above all else the presence of God in their midst (Lev 26:1-13; Deut 28:1-14). While the language of blessing is not used in the passage from Leviticus, it appears repeatedly in the passage from Deuteronomy, which also adds that God will bless all of the people's undertakings and make them prominent among the nations (Deut 28:8, 12). In Lev 26:6, the Hebrew word *shalom* is used to describe the blessing that God will give to the people if they obey God's commandments: "I will give *shalom* in the land."

In order to understand the logic behind these passages, it is necessary not only to stress the idea that the people's obedience to God's commandments is a means to their well-being rather than an end in itself but also to consider once more both the extrinsic and the intrinsic relationship between their obedience to those commandments and their well-being. These passages clearly describe an *extrinsic* relationship between the people's observance of God's commandments and the blessings that will result from that observance. If they obey those commandments, they will be blessed because God will be active through the forces of nature and in other ways to cause good things to happen to them. He will send rain to produce abundant harvests, multiply their descendants, and deliver them from their enemies and from afflictions such as disease, pestilence, and plague. These blessings are not the automatic or intrinsic consequence of the people's obedience to God's commandments, since they do not result naturally from that obedience. In principle, the people might be very faithful in their observance of God's commandments yet nevertheless suffer things such as drought, disease, various forms of natural disaster, and defeat and destruction at the hands of their enemies. What God is promising in these passages is that he will be active in the natural order and the events of history to deliver the people from those types of hardships and afflictions and instead fill their lives with good things, such as health, wholeness, peace, long life, and prosperity.

Although these passages do not mention the intrinsic relationship between the people's obedience to God's commandments and their well-being, they clearly presuppose it. Obviously, if God promises that he will bless the people when they obey his commandments, he must have some reason for doing so. If that reason is not that he will benefit from their obedience personally by obtaining something he needs or desires for his own sake, then it must be that *they themselves* will benefit from that obedience for intrinsic reasons.

Because biblical interpreters have been accustomed to reading passages such as Lev 26:1-13 and Deut 28:1-14 on the basis of ideas and presuppositions that are grounded in the pagan worldview of the nations that worshiped many different gods in antiquity, they have generally failed to grasp the logic underlying those passages. Whether consciously or unconsciously, they have simply assumed that in the passages in which God promises to bless his people when they obey his commandments, he is presented as acting out of a concern for himself and his own needs or desires in the same way that the gods of other nations were thought to do. Interpreters therefore read back into those passages the idea that the end that God pursues is the people's obedience for his own sake and that his blessing in response to that obedience is a means to that end. In most cases, biblical interpreters never even consider the possibility that those passages instead regard the people's well-being as the end that God pursues by means of their obedience and that his blessing of that obedience is the means by which he seeks to attain that end.

The Intrinsic Consequences of Obedience

Rather than being stated explicitly, the idea that human well-being follows upon behavior that is in conformity with God's will as the intrinsic and natural consequence of that behavior is often assumed in the biblical texts. There are numerous passages, however, in which that relationship is made explicit. Many of these passages are found in the book of Proverbs. In Prov 3:1-2, the readers of the book are told that keeping the commandments brings "length of days and years of life and abundant *shalom*." While these are undoubtedly things that God grants in response to the observance of his commandments, they should also be understood as resulting naturally from a life in accordance with those commandments. The idea that loving and kind behavior produces well-being in and of itself while cruel and violent behavior destroys well-being is stated in Prov 11:17: "Those who are kind benefit themselves, but the cruel do themselves harm." A number of other passages from the same book also affirm that those who practice sin and evil bring harm upon themselves for intrinsic reasons: "The iniquities of the wicked ensnare them, and they are caught in the toils of their sin" (Prov 5:22). "The wicked are overthrown by their evildoing, but the righteous find a refuge in their integrity" (14:32). "Those who mislead the upright into evil ways will fall into pits of their own making" (28:10; cf. 17:20; 22:16). Some of these passages speak of the blessings that flow naturally from the practice of righteousness and from wisdom, which in Hebrew thought was closely associated with the Torah. They also contrast those blessings with the negative consequences that follow from practicing evil and injustice. "Wisdom is a fountain of life to those who have it, but foolishness is itself the punishment of fools" (16:22). "The righteousness of the blameless keeps their ways straight, but the wicked fall by their own wickedness. The righteousness of the upright saves them, but the treacherous are taken captive by their own schemes" (11:5-6; cf. 13:6). In Prov

8:36, God's wisdom is personified and presented as telling the readers: "those who miss me injure themselves." Here it is the behavior of people itself that saves them or does them harm rather than God's response to that behavior.

Similar ideas are stressed in the book of Jeremiah. There God tells his people that to abandon him and his good commandments is to go after "worthless things" that "do not profit" and are therefore not in the people's best interest (Jer 2:5, 8, 11; 16:19). When the people forsake God, they do themselves harm because they deprive themselves of what is good in itself: "My people have committed two evils: they have forsaken me, the fountain of living water, and they have dug out cisterns for themselves, cracked cisterns that can hold no water" (2:13). The suffering that the people endure is thus said to result from their own actions and their failure to follow God's good guidance rather than being a punishment inflicted by God: "Have you not brought this upon yourself by forsaking the LORD your God, while he led you in the way? . . . Your wickedness will punish you, and your apostasies will convict you. Know and see that it is evil and bitter for you to forsake the LORD your God" (2:17, 19). When the people suffer hardships, in large part it is because those hardships are the intrinsic consequence of their own behavior: "Your ways and your doings have brought this upon you" (4:18). "Your sins have deprived you of the good" (5:25). The idea is that the people destroy their own well-being when they choose to follow their own path rather than obey God, who knows far better than they do what is truly in their best interest.

The same ideas are repeated in passages from Hosea and Isaiah. According to Hos 8:3, by disregarding God's good commandments and failing to live in the covenant he has established with them, "Israel has spurned the good" (cf. 7:16). In the book of Isaiah, God laments that his people bring suffering upon themselves because they insist on going their own way rather than in the way he has laid out for them in love for them: "I have held out my hands all day long to a rebellious people, who walk in a way that is not good, following their own devices" (Isa 65:2).

A couple of passages from two other Jewish writings of the Second Temple period stress the same point. The book of Tobit insists that "those who commit sin and do wrong are their own worst enemies" (Tob 12:10). One passage in the Wisdom of Solomon speaks of nature or creation itself punishing those who practice injustice, thus regarding this punishment as an intrinsic consequence of wrongdoing rather than something inflicted directly by God: "For creation, serving you who made it, exerts itself to punish the unrighteous" (Wis 16:24).

At times, the English translation of certain passages tends to overlook the intrinsic relation between obedience to God's commandments and the well-being that results naturally from that obedience in order to posit a relation that is purely extrinsic. Perhaps the best example of this is found in Deut 6:25, which reads: "and there will be justice/righteousness (*tsedaqah*) for us if we diligently observe this entire commandment before the LORD our God, as he has commanded us." Most English versions translate *tsedaqah* here as "righteousness" in order to posit an *extrinsic* relationship between obedience to God's commandments and the result of that obedience. In that case, the verse would be affirming that observance of God's commandments will result in the people being accepted or accounted as righteous in God's sight, as if the goal of that observance were to obtain God's favor and approval. Such an idea is reflected in the NRSVue: "If we diligently observe this entire commandment before the LORD our God, as he has commanded us, we will be in the right." Given the context, however, in which it is explicitly stated that God gave the commandments for the people's good (6:24), it would make better sense to translate *tsedaqah* as "justice" and to see this justice as the intrinsic consequence of obedience to those commandments. The passage might then be translated: "justice will exist among us if we are careful to observe everything that God has commanded us" (6:25).

In other words, the idea in Deut 6:25 would be that the people's careful observance of all of God's commandments will result in a situation in which the people will be able to enjoy justice in the sense of attaining collectively the well-being that God desires for all. Because in themselves God's commandments promote justice in this sense, it is to be regarded as following upon the observance of those commandments as its natural consequence. In biblical thought, what concerns God is not *accounting* or *reckoning* people to be righteous but bringing people to *practice* justice and righteousness for their own good. To claim that the people should observe God's commandments simply in order that God may accept them as righteous or declare them to be "in the right" is to overlook the intrinsic relationship between the observance of those commandments and the well-being that results from that observance as its natural consequence. The idea that the people should observe God's commandments solely for the purpose of gaining his approval presupposes that God gave the commandments and demands that his people observe them for *his own* sake rather than theirs.

Rethinking Reward

Many English versions of the Bible and biblical commentaries use the language of reward when referring to the promises of blessing for obedience that appear in passages such as Lev 26:1-13 and Deut 28:1-14. The NRSVue, for example, inserts the heading "Rewards for Obedience" before Lev 26:1-13, even though the terminology of reward is never used in that passage or anywhere else in Leviticus and Deuteronomy. Such language seems to presuppose once more that the observance of God's commandments is an end in itself and that in order to get people to observe those commandments God offers them rewards. The logic would be that of *do ut des*. As we have noted previously, in that case what would motivate people to obey God's commandments would not be a love for the commandments themselves as a good gift of God that promotes their well-being for intrinsic reasons but a desire to obtain rewards for themselves from God by means of their obedience. Such an understanding of the purpose of obedience to God's commandments once more focuses exclusively on the extrinsic relationship between that obedience and human well-being and overlooks the intrinsic relationship that serves as the basis for the extrinsic relationship. In other words, the reason why God demands obedience to his good commandments and blesses those who obey them is that in and of itself such obedience promotes human well-being.

The idea that in passages such as Lev 26:1-13 and Deut 28:1-14 God is offering the people rewards in exchange for their obedience to his commandments must therefore be rejected as foreign to those passages and biblical thought in general. Undoubtedly, there are passages in the Hebrew Bible in which God is said to reward behavior that is in accordance with his will for justice and righteousness. In 1 Sam 26:23, for example, David is presented as affirming that "the LORD rewards everyone for their righteousness and their faithfulness," and similar affirmations appear elsewhere in the biblical texts.[3] The idea behind these affirmations, however, is not that God is granting people rewards in exchange for receiving from them something that he desires for his own sake. Rather, the logic is that when people live in ways that promote their own well-being and that of others by practicing justice and righteousness, God responds by blessing them in order to increase that well-being even more. What he seeks is not something *for himself* but rather something *for them*, namely, their happiness and well-being. Therefore, when they follow behaviors that contribute to their own well-being and that of others due to the intrinsic consequences of those behaviors, he is pleased for their sake and acts in various ways to promote their well-being even further. It is in that sense that he can be said to reward their obedience to his will.

While it may be said that in biblical thought God rewards or recompenses behavior that is in accordance with his will, such language should be understood in the sense that God blesses behavior that in and of itself brings blessing. What God wills is that human beings practice justice, righteousness, and love for their own sake due to the fact that such behavior promotes their happiness and well-being. That happiness and well-being therefore result both *intrinsically* from such behavior as well as *extrinsically* from God's response to that behavior. Nevertheless, the basis for the *extrinsic* relationship between behavior that is in conformity with God's will for justice and righteousness and God's favorable response to that behavior is the *intrinsic* relationship between that behavior and the well-being that follows upon it as its natural consequence. The language of reward and recompense, therefore, can be regarded as reflecting biblical thought only if it is understood on the basis of this logic and not the logic of *do ut des*. God rewards or recompenses behavior that is in conformity with his will not in order to obtain something he desires for his own sake but rather to promote the well-being of human beings, which he regards as an end in itself due to his love for them.

---

3. See, for example, 1 Sam 24:19; 2 Sam 22:21; 1 Kgs 8:32; 2 Chr 6:23; Ps 18:20; Jer 32:19.

On the basis of this same logic, the idea that God's blessings and favor can be earned by means of obedience to his commandments must also be regarded as foreign to biblical thought. Such an idea once more suggests that God desires obedience for his own sake as an end in itself and thus promises his favor and blessings to human beings in exchange for receiving that obedience from them in the same way that the pagan gods of antiquity were thought to do. In biblical thought, the purpose of obedience to God's commandments is not that of obtaining some type of blessing or favor from God in exchange for that obedience but that of attaining the well-being that follows intrinsically from that obedience as its natural consequence. Those commandments are themselves an expression of God's favor and constitute a blessing precisely because they lead, guide, and instruct the people in the path that they should follow for their own good. In biblical thought, God has given those commandments out of pure grace, mercy, and kindness to his people and not because they have earned his favor or love in any way. For the same reasons, when he responds favorably to the observance of those commandments, he is also acting out of pure grace, mercy, and kindness rather than giving the people something that they have earned by their obedience. By definition, they *cannot* earn his favor and love because that favor and love are an *unconditional gift* from God, given to them independently of anything that they might do or fail to do. In other words, one cannot earn something that one already possesses as a gracious gift.

In biblical thought, therefore, the blessings and favors that God pours out on those who obey his commandments are just as much a free and unmerited gift as those commandments themselves. Out of pure love and grace, God blesses the people's obedience not in order to obtain something from them for himself but only because that same love and grace lead him to be fully committed to their well-being. What he wants is for his people to be equally committed to the same objective. For that reason, out of love for them he demands that they obey the commandments he has given them for their own good. In essence, this involves demanding that they be just as fully committed to their well-being as he himself is. The reason that God blesses their obedience to his commandments is the same reason that he has given them those commandments in the first place, namely, his desire that they enjoy the well-being that he sought for all human beings from the moment he created them. To understand the blessings and favor that God bestows on those who obey him as something that they earn is in effect to deny God's unconditional love and to equate Israel's God with the pagan gods of antiquity, who demanded obedience for their own sake and selfishly made such obedience the condition for granting human beings their favor and blessings. Neither the commands that such gods gave human beings nor the favors and blessings that they bestowed on those who obeyed them were gracious gifts. Instead, those favors and blessings were something that human beings had to earn. Obviously, anything that must be earned is not a free gift given in love.

Furthermore, because the God of the Hebrew Bible desires that well-being for all of his people equally and has given his commandments to promote the well-being of all, any who do not share that objective by being as fully committed to their own well-being and that of others as he is are not truly obeying him. By definition, those who observe the commandments only to obtain rewards or earn blessings for themselves are violating those commandments by failing to seek the well-being of others just as earnestly as they seek their own well-being. In fact, for that reason, they cannot truly fulfill God's commandments, because those commandments can only be properly interpreted and observed if the concern for the well-being of others guides and defines their interpretation and observance. Thus, for example, any who provide assistance to the needy will not actually assist them in the way they should if they do so, not because they truly care for them, but only because they seek to obtain something for themselves from God in exchange for that assistance. Because God is fully committed to the well-being of all, any who are not fully committed to the well-being of all in the same way cannot please him. Those who seek to obey his commandments in an attempt to obtain rewards from him or earn his favor are in fact denying the unconditional nature of his love, kindness, and grace. Rather than obeying him, they are sinning against him by implying that his love for all is conditional and that he acts out of self-interest rather than sincere love for human beings. Because they are acting selfishly by seeking something only for themselves through their obedience, they cannot truly be said to be obeying God and his commandments. In biblical thought, only those who act out of genuine love for God and others are actually obeying God and fulfilling his commandments.

When people are truly committed to their own well-being in the same way that God is, therefore, if they can be said to seek or attain some reward by means of their obedience to his commandments, that reward must be understood to consist of nothing else but that well-being itself, which follows both intrinsically and extrinsically from their obedience. This desire to seek their own well-being is not selfish or self-serving, precisely because that well-being cannot be isolated or divorced from the well-being of others at the same time. Because those who truly love themselves in the sense of seeking their own well-being know that they cannot attain that well-being unless those around them attain it as well, they will be just as committed to seeking the well-being of others as they will be to seeking their own well-being. By definition, any who are not committed to the well-being of others are not committed to their own well-being. For that reason, their love for themselves will at the same time be a love for God and for others, just as their love for God will at the same time be a love for those whom God loves, namely, themselves and others. Because in his love God seeks the well-being of all without exception and demands of all the same commitment to their own well-being and that of others for their own good out of love for them, one cannot truly love oneself without loving God and loving others. If God is to accomplish his purpose of blessing all, he must not only show kindness to all but demand that all do the same in relation to one another. This means that God's gifts are inseparable from his demands, since both his gifts and his demands have the purpose of promoting the well-being of all. In a sense, in fact, his demands must themselves be viewed as a gracious gift given to all, together with the ability to fulfill those demands, because unless human beings receive and fulfill those demands, they cannot obtain well-being and wholeness.

HEALING DISOBEDIENCE THROUGH CHASTISEMENTS

According to the biblical narrative, while at times God's people Israel respond favorably to the blessings he pours out on them by living in a way that makes it possible for them to enjoy those blessings, at other times they do not. In fact, in both the biblical narratives and the prophetic writings, the people are presented as disobeying God and refusing to live in accordance with his will most of the time. When this happens, the question arises as to what God is to do. In principle, he might simply continue to pour out his blessings on them in an attempt to convince them of his love for them, yet if this does not lead them to trust and obey him it can even be counterproductive. As noted above, rather than bringing them to change their ways, their reception of those blessings will simply lead them to become even more entrenched in their destructive behavior and to do harm to themselves and others with the gifts God gives them by using them for evil rather than for good.

For that reason, it might appear that the best option open to God when his people persistently disobey him is simply to withhold his blessings from them and abandon them to the harmful and destructive way of life they have chosen for themselves until they come to realize that such a way of life is not in their own best interest. While at times this may work, the problem with such an approach is that when the people fall into destructive behavior, those who generally suffer the most are those who are weak and in greatest need. In contrast, the rich and powerful who are most responsible for the injustices, violence, and oppression that generate suffering among the people seem to prosper. If God simply abandons the people to their own ways and does nothing, therefore, in essence he is condemning the needy and marginalized to an inordinate and disproportional amount of suffering that will also last for an indefinite period of time. Such an approach tends to make the problem of injustice worse rather than resolving it. Instead of bringing the people to abandon their sinful behavior, it might even involve condemning them to go unimpeded down a path that will eventually lead to their destruction and ruin.

In principle, it might be thought that God could bring people to change their ways by producing some type of mysterious change in them, perhaps by pouring out his Spirit into their hearts. While numerous passages in the Hebrew Bible speak of God transforming the hearts of his people and sending his Spirit on them, nothing in those passages or the Hebrew Bible as a whole suggests that God can simply produce automatically in people the way of life necessary for them to enjoy the well-being and wholeness he seeks for all. While he is certainly presented as being able to influence people in many ways in order to change their hearts and bring them to live differently, the biblical texts do not speak of him accomplishing these things unilaterally, in effect acting in some hidden and mysterious way to transform those who are rebellious and disobedient into righteous and obedient people. Nor do the biblical texts present God as being able to turn those who have chosen the path of disobedience and injustice into people who gladly and willingly practice what is good, just, and right simply by pouring out his Spirit on them. In fact, those texts presuppose that the problem of human sin and disobedience cannot be resolved in this way, because if it were possible, God's love for human beings and his desire for their well-being would have led him to do so from the moment they are first said to have disobeyed him in the Genesis account. He would hardly have destroyed countless human beings in the flood in Noah's day if he had instead had the ability to transform them into people who would do what is good and right by infusing them with some mysterious power that would accomplish that objective in and of itself. Throughout the biblical texts, it is consistently assumed that in order for people to live in righteousness, obedience, and love they must desire to do so willingly and of their own accord. They may certainly receive God's help in order to be able to live in that manner and ask God to give them the strength, wisdom, and resolve necessary to do so by pouring out his Spirit upon them, yet when God responds positively to such petitions he is not bringing people to act contrary to their own will but rather enabling and empowering those who seek and desire to live in conformity with his will to do so.

If those who are disobedient must be brought to change their ways willingly, then the best option would be for God to attempt to convince them that it is in their own best interest to leave behind their destructive behavior and live in the way he has prescribed for their own good. In biblical thought, the means by which God does this is by sending the people prophets to speak to them on his behalf. These prophets may employ a variety of approaches and arguments in an attempt to convince their hearers to turn back to the way of life that will allow them to experience the wholeness and well-being that God intends for them. They may remind the people of God's love and mercies and his desire to bless them as he has in the past. They may seek to demonstrate to the people that their behavior is destroying their own well-being rather than contributing to it. The prophets may also attempt to stir up compassion in their hearers for those who are suffering due to the hearers' failure to practice justice, point out to their hearers the advantages of doing what is good and right and the disadvantages of doing harm to others, or appeal to their conscience or emotions in some way. If none of these approaches produce the desired effect, the prophets may have no choice but to proclaim to the people that God will inflict suffering and hardships on them if they persist in their disobedience and refuse to change their ways.

Such, in fact, appears to be the only option left open to God when every other course of action has failed. If God cannot bring those who persistently refuse to live in ways that will allow them to enjoy the well-being he desires for all by continuing to pour out his blessings on them, abandoning them to their own ways, or producing some type of mysterious change in them automatically and unilaterally, and if those people will not listen to the prophets he sends them, then he seems to have no choice but to inflict suffering on them. He does so in the hope that those sufferings will allow him to accomplish his loving purpose of leading them to put aside their destructive behavior and submit obediently to his will for their own good. By making it too painful for the people to continue down the same path they have been following, God seeks to compel them to abandon that path and follow instead the one he has laid out for them in his love, a path that leads to justice, wholeness, and well-being for them and for others as well.

Punishment as Chastisement, Discipline, and Correction

In English, it is common to use the language of punishment when speaking of the manner in which God inflicts sufferings and hardships on those who disobey his commandments. While that language is undoubtedly appropriate to describe God's response to disobedience to his will in the biblical texts, it can be problematic in that it tends to focus primarily on the pain and suffering inflicted by God and overlook the purpose for which he inflicts that pain and suffering or allows it to take place. As a result, the same understanding of the nature and purpose of punishment that we have noted above with regard to the pagan belief systems of antiquity tends to be read back into the biblical texts. Like the gods of those belief systems, God is thought to punish those who disobey him simply because he demands to be obeyed for his own sake or because he is compelled to uphold the system or order that he has established in order to satisfy the demands of his holiness, justice, and righteousness. Because his punishments are rooted in a concern for his own desires or for needs that are rooted in his nature, such as the need to uphold his own justice and his inability to tolerate sinful behavior, those punishments are not thought to be loving or to be aimed at promoting well-being among human beings.

In the Hebrew Bible, however, the language of punishment is not particularly common. Most of the occurrences of that language appear in the writings of the prophets, yet even there the two Hebrew terms that are usually translated as punishment in English versions are *paqad*, which literally means "to visit," and the noun *'avon*, which generally refers to wrongdoing and guilt itself rather than its punishment. Both of these terms will be examined more closely in later chapters. It is also common for English versions of the Bible to use the language of punishment when translating Hebrew verbs and nouns that refer to judging or condemning people or afflicting them with sufferings, even though that language is not used explicitly in the Hebrew text of the passages involved.

The other Hebrew term that is often translated as "punishment" is the noun *musar*, which is derived from the verb *yasar*. In reality, however, it would be more appropriate to use the language of *chastisement* to translate these two Hebrew terms. While in English chastisement is often understood as being synonymous with punishment, it focuses more specifically on the idea of correction and discipline. To chastise is not merely to inflict suffering and punishments or to reprimand, censure, or rebuke those who do wrong but to do these things for the purpose of bringing them to alter their behavior for the better.

While at times the verb *yasar* is used in the Hebrew Bible to speak of inflicting punishment on someone, its primary meaning revolves around the idea of disciplining, correcting, or even instructing.[4] In Isa 28:26, this verb appears in parallelism with the verb *yarah*, which means "to teach," to speak of God instructing his people: "For they are well instructed; their God teaches them." In Hos 7:15, *yasar* is used in the sense of training someone: "It was I who trained and strengthened their arms." The idea that chastisement has a loving purpose and is designed to guide and teach, even though it may involve inflicting suffering, is evident in passages such as Ps 94:10-12, where *yasar* appears twice in the sense of applying discipline aimed at correction and instruction: "He who disciplines the nations, he who teaches knowledge to humankind, does he not chastise? . . . Happy are those whom you discipline, O LORD, and whom you teach out of your law."

The Hebrew noun *musar* conveys the same meaning of discipline and correction.[5] In Prov 1:8, this noun is even used in parallel with the word *torah* as its virtual synonym: "Hear, my child, your father's instruction (*musar*), and do not reject your mother's teaching (*torah*)." In the Septuagint, the Greek terms regularly used to translate *yasar* and *musar* are *paideuein* and *paideia*, which also refer to instruction or correction. These terms were originally used to refer to the training and education of a child (*pais/paidion*), which was done either by the child's parents or a pedagogue (*paidagōgos*), that is, a person whose task it was to guide, instruct, protect, and care for a child. The fact that such correction was understood as an expression of God's love is evident in many of the passages that use these terms, but perhaps is stated nowhere as forcefully as in a passage from the book of 2 Maccabees. There, after describing the horrendous sufferings that the Jews were enduring at the hands of the Seleucid king Antiochus Epiphanes, the author writes:

> Therefore I exhort those who read this book not to be disheartened by these afflictions, but to consider that these punishments were aimed not at the destruction of our people but at their correction (*paideia*). For it is a sign of great kindness to punish the impious immediately rather than leaving them alone for long. For the Lord has determined not to treat us like the other nations. In their case he waits patiently for them to reach the full measure of

---

4. See, for example, Deut 4:36; 21:18; Ps 6:1; 16:7; 39:11; Prov 19:18; 29:17; 31:1; Jer 10:24; 31:18.

5. See, for example, Job 36:10; Prov 1:2-3, 7; 4:13; 6:23; 13:1, 24; 15:32-33; Jer 2:30; 5:3; 7:28; 17:23; 32:33.

their sins before punishing them, but in our case he does not wait until our sins have reached their height before inflicting punishment on us. Therefore he never withdraws his mercy from us. He does not abandon his people, but chastises (*paideuōn*) us with afflictions (2 Macc 6:12-16).

In the Hebrew Scriptures and other Second Temple Jewish writings, the manner in which God imposes suffering on his people to correct them is at times likened to that of a father who chastises or disciplines his children in order to educate and correct them. In Deut 8:5, Moses tells the people: "Know in your heart, then, that as a parent disciplines a child, so the LORD your God disciplines you." The book of Proverbs speaks of God in the same way: "My child, do not despise the LORD's discipline or be weary of his reproof, for the LORD reproves the one he loves, as a father the son in whom he delights" (Prov 3:11-12). The Psalms of Solomon, which date from the first or second century BCE, use the language of *paideia* to affirm that God "corrects the righteous as a beloved son, and his chastisement is as that of a firstborn. For the Lord spares his pious ones and blots out their errors by his chastisements" (Pss. Sol. 13:9-10). The same comparison appears further on in the same work: "Your discipline for us is as for a firstborn son, an only child, to divert the perceptive person from unintentional sins" (Pss. Sol. 18:4). Josephus similarly presents Moses warning the Israelites that when they sinned God "would exact punishment, not indeed in keeping with their misdeeds, but such as parents inflict upon their children as an admonition" (*Ant.* 3.311).

Numerous other passages from these texts convey the same ideas. For God to discipline people through suffering is seen as a blessing and an expression of God's love and favor, since it leads them to live in ways that enable them to enjoy the well-being God desires for all by guiding and teaching them. While they are painful, God's chastisements serve to heal and purify people from their destructive behavior and are therefore a motive for rejoicing:

How happy is the one whom God corrects; therefore do not despise the discipline of the Almighty. For he wounds, but he binds up; he strikes, but his hands heal (Job 5:17-18).

Whoever seeks God will accept his discipline, and those who rise early to seek him will find his good pleasure (Sir 32:14).

Therefore you correct little by little those who trespass, and you remind and warn them of the things through which they sin, so that they may be freed from wickedness and put their trust in you, O Lord (Wis 12:2).

At the heart of this understanding of the loving purpose of God's punishments or chastisements is the same idea considered above according to which there is a natural and intrinsic relationship between human behavior and the consequences that result from that behavior. Just as the practice of what is good, just, right, and loving contributes to human well-being and wholeness for intrinsic reasons, so also behavior that is self-serving, unjust, uncaring, violent, and harmful undermines and destroys such well-being and wholeness in and of itself. This is precisely the type of behavior that God prohibits in his Torah. The reason that God punishes such behavior, therefore, is that he wishes to bring his people to live in ways that promote their well-being and to avoid behavior that destroys that well-being. In other words, the *intrinsic* relationship between harmful and destructive behavior and the pain, suffering, injustice, and oppression that result naturally from it constitutes the basis for the *extrinsic* relationship between that behavior and God's response to it, namely, his chastisements or punishments. In biblical thought, when people fall into wrongdoing, what pains God is not the effect that such wrongdoing has *on him* but rather the effect that it has on human beings themselves, including especially the poor, weak, and needy.

This understanding of the reason why God prohibits and punishes disobedience to his will has made the use of the language of sin problematic and misleading when it is used to represent biblical thought. As we have seen previously, due to the influence of the modes of thought that are characteristic of the pagan worldviews of antiquity, where certain actions are deemed sinful due to the effect they have on the gods who have prohibited those actions for their own sake, biblical interpreters have generally understood sin to consist of actions and behaviors that God prohibits and punishes due to the manner in which those actions and behaviors affect *him* rather than the manner in which they affect human beings themselves. Certain actions are categorized as sinful and prohibited simply because they are thought to run contrary to God's will and to displease him on account of his holy and righteous nature, which does not allow him to tolerate those actions without punishing them. Neither those prohibitions nor the punishments he imposes on those who violate them are rooted in a concern for human well-being. Instead, they respond only to a desire or need on the part of God himself. Sin is therefore defined in terms of actions and behaviors that God prohibits *for his own sake* and for the sake of his divine nature rather than for the sake of human beings or their well-being, which is destroyed or undermined by those actions and behaviors due to the harmful consequences that follow from them intrinsically. For that reason, in contrast to biblical thought, neither God's prohibition of sin nor the punishments he imposes on sinners in response to their sins are considered to be loving. In fact, the question of *why* God prohibits and punishes sin is rarely raised or discussed among biblical scholars and theologians.

When sin is understood and defined in this way, it is regarded primarily as an *offense against God*. In English, to offend someone is to affront, irritate, or upset them, usually by doing something that dishonors and disrespects them or causes them some type of injury. On this basis, God is said to be offended by human sin for the same reasons, namely, that it diminishes his honor and glory, deprives him of something that is rightfully his, or affronts him in some other way. This is true even when the sins committed do harm to human beings due to the intrinsic consequences of those sins. Thus, for example, when people lie, cheat, practice violence, or mistreat and oppress others, such actions and behaviors are regarded as sins and offenses committed *against God*, as if what concerned God was the effect that such actions and behaviors have *on him*. It is significant that, while the Hebrew Bible often speaks of God being angered at human actions and behaviors, it is virtually impossible to find passages in which God is explicitly said to be *offended* by what human beings do, as if he were the one harmed or affronted by their wrongdoing.

As we noted briefly in Chapter 4, the same type of observations can be made with regard to the terminology of righteousness. Generally righteousness is defined in negative terms as the absence of sin. The righteous are those who do not sin or offend God. While righteousness may involve doing what is good and right, among many biblical interpreters it is understood primarily in terms of avoiding those actions and behaviors that displease God and provoke him to wrath. As a result, the righteous are defined in terms of what they do *not* do, as if what interested God is merely that people refrain from behavior that upsets and irritates him. Righteousness is thus understood to be synonymous with terms such as innocence and blamelessness. Supposedly, this is what God requires in order to accept and justify people—not that they be committed to seeking the well-being of others, including especially those in greatest need, but that they keep themselves pure and uncontaminated by sin as he is.

For the same reasons, even to speak of what is good, right, and just when considering biblical thought can be problematic. Instead of defining these terms on the basis of the intrinsic relationship between human actions and their consequences, biblical interpreters generally understand them on the basis of certain views regarding what God desires or demands for his own sake. A particular action or behavior is considered to be good, right, or just not because it promotes human well-being but simply because it pleases God and conforms to his will. Qualities such as goodness, righteousness, and justice are seen as inherent to God's nature, which compels God to demand them of human beings if he is to accept them and have fellowship with them rather than condemning them or destroying them. He therefore requires that human beings behave in ways that are good, right, and just not because he loves and cares for them but because his holy and righteous nature cannot tolerate them unless they live and act in harmony with it. If it is said to be in their best interest for them to behave in these ways, it is not because that behavior promotes their well-being for intrinsic reasons but because only by practicing that behavior can they hope to enjoy God's favor and avoid his wrath, both of which are conditional upon their conformity to his will.

Because this manner of understanding sin and righteousness is so deeply ingrained in the thought of biblical interpreters and Western culture in general, it is often preferable to substitute other words and phrases for these terms when discussing the concepts associated with them in the biblical text. When readers hear or read the word "sin" in English, they inevitably tend to think in terms of actions or conduct that God prohibits and punishes for his own sake rather than destructive and harmful behaviors that God prohibits and chastises out of love for human beings due to the manner in which those behaviors affect *them*. The same type of problem arises when people hear the word "righteousness" or read affirmations to the effect that God demands righteousness of human beings. The notion that righteousness merely involves the avoidance of behavior that God has prohibited for his own sake and therefore is virtually synonymous with guiltlessness or innocence is so deeply rooted in biblical interpretation and Western thought that readers today do not readily associate ideas such as love, compassion, and a firm commitment to seeking the well-being of others with that term.

For these reasons, throughout the present study, rather than simply using the terminology of sin when characterizing biblical thought on that subject, I have frequently preferred to speak of something such as destructive, harmful, violent, or oppressive behavior. Similarly, rather than using the terminology of righteousness, I have generally chosen to refer to behavior that promotes well-being and wholeness as well as the status that results from the loving concern for others that is behind that behavior. This type of language stresses the intrinsic relationship between human behavior and its consequences that is at the heart of the biblical understanding of those two terms. As we have seen in the previous chapter, in biblical thought righteousness is understood as being essentially *synonymous* with love in that it involves a commitment to seeking the well-being of others. Such tends not to be the case in English, however.

To affirm that in biblical thought sin and righteousness are conceived of in ways that focus on the effect that human actions and behavior have on human beings themselves is by no means to downplay or deny the idea that those actions and behaviors also affect God. On the contrary, the biblical texts speak repeatedly of God being pleased by certain behaviors and displeased by others. What must be stressed, however, is that the reason that God is pleased by certain behaviors and displeased by others is precisely his loving desire that human beings behave in ways that promote their well-being and avoid doing harm to themselves and others. Strictly speaking, what affects God is not human behavior itself but the effect that human behavior has on human beings themselves. He is pleased when they behave in ways that promote their well-being and happiness but is displeased and angered when they undermine and destroy their own well-being and happiness. In other words, while God is certainly said to be affected by the behavior of human beings, what affects him is the manner in which that behavior affects human beings themselves by benefiting them or doing them harm rather than any benefit or harm that he derives from that behavior himself.

The Return of Repentance

In the biblical texts, when the people are presented as falling into sinful and destructive behavior, the first thing that God does is to send them prophets to point out to the people their sin and call them back to the way of life he has laid out for them in his commandments. In English, the language of repentance is generally used to refer to this change of behavior. Although that language can be understood in ways that reflect faithfully biblical thought, it also tends to convey certain ideas that are not fully in accordance with the terminology used in Hebrew, where the verb *shub* is generally used to speak of repenting.

Among English speakers, repentance is commonly understood as being synonymous with contrition, remorse, or regret. These terms tend to be associated with emotions or feelings of pain and sorrow at what one has done in the past. In contrast, the Hebrew verb *shub* refers to a turning, that is, a change of direction in one's life or behavior in which one ceases to do what is contrary to God's will in order to live in accordance with it. It therefore focuses primarily on the future rather than the past and also stresses behavior rather than emotions or feelings. In essence, it involves putting away behavior that is harmful and destructive and at the same time renewing one's commitment to living in the way that God desires and commands for the good of all.

Due to the influence that pagan conceptions of the deity have had on biblical interpreters, it has been common to understand the prophets' calls to repentance primarily in terms of threats of punishment and even doom and destruction. God is typically portrayed as an ominous, menacing figure who has been moved to wrath by human sin and is anxious to vent that wrath by inflicting suffering and destruction on those who have disobeyed and offended him. Once again, the emphasis is on the manner in which God himself is affected by human behavior that is contrary to his will. In biblical thought, however, the call for people to repent and return to God is an expression of love precisely because of the intrinsic relationship between disobedience to God and the harmful consequences that follow upon that disobedience. If God calls on people to turn away from a path that is leading to their downfall and destruction and return to a path that leads to well-being and wholeness, namely, the path that he has graciously laid out for them by means of his commandments, it is because in his love he wants only what is best for them.

At the same time, the task of God's prophets goes beyond merely calling his people to repentance and warning them of the consequences they will be made to endure if they fail to turn back to him in obedience. When God acts in the life and history of his people, it is necessary for the prophets to interpret the events that take place in order to make it clear how God is at work in those events and what he is seeking to accomplish among his people through those events. If God were simply to impose sufferings and hardships on the people without letting them know his purpose for doing so, they might not understand that his intention is to bring them back to the way of life that will allow them to enjoy the blessings he desires for them. Because those events are painful for them, they might even interpret the sufferings to which they are subjected as an indication that God has rejected and abandoned them and no longer cares for them. For that reason, even when God's prophets warn the people of the punishments or chastisements that he intends to impose on them when they persist in their disobedience to his good commandments, they must also constantly remind the people of God's love for them, that is, his commitment to doing whatever is necessary for them to be brought to live in a way that truly promotes their well-being and happiness. It is that commitment that leads him to insist that they turn back to him for their own good.

Grace That Punishes as It Forgives

Among biblical scholars it is common to contrast God's wrath and punishments with his love, grace, mercy, and favor, as if these things were opposed to one another. According to this manner of thinking, when the people fall into sin and fail to repent and turn away from that sin, they also fall from God's grace and favor and he no longer treats them with love and mercy. In reality, such ideas are grounded in the pagan worldviews of antiquity and must be considered contrary to biblical thought, where God's love, grace, mercy, and favor are consistently presented as *unconditional*. There is nothing that God's people could ever do that would lead him to stop loving and caring for them and seeking to bring about in them the way of life necessary for them to enjoy the well-being and wholeness he intends for them. As the Psalmists frequently repeat, his mercy or steadfast love endures forever and knows no limits or bounds.[6]

For the same reason, as already noted above, in biblical thought God's people cannot earn, merit, or deserve his love, grace, and favor through their behavior because these things are already theirs no matter what they do or how they behave. Instead, what they merit through their behavior is *a particular form* that God's love, grace, mercy, and favor will take in response to their behavior. When they live in accordance with God's will for their own good, God's love and favor can take the form of pouring out blessings on them and granting them whatever they need to enjoy well-being and be whole. When they live in ways that are destructive and harmful to them, however, God's love, grace, and favor will take the form of chastising them in order to bring them back to the way of life that he commands and demands of them for their own good. Whether he blesses them or punishes them, therefore, in either case he is acting out of love for them and continuing to show them his grace, mercy, and favor, even when he subjects them to suffering. When viewed from this perspective, in fact, even God's punishments must be regarded as blessings, since they are manifestations of his love for his people. Were God to stop seeking to bring his people back to him in obedience through chastisements when they fall into sin, he would no longer be acting in love for them. Of course, at times he may abandon them temporarily in order to let them experience the painful consequences of their sin and disobedience, hoping that this will bring them to realize that when they live in ways that are contrary to his will and commandments, they only do themselves harm. Even when he abandons them for a time, however, sooner

---

6. See, for example, Ps 36:5; 57:10; 89:2; 100:5; 103:11; 106:1; 107:1; 108:4; 118:2-4; 136:1-26.

or later he always becomes active among them once more in order to accomplish his loving purposes for them and others.

While biblical interpreters and theologians have often recognized that in biblical thought it is not possible for people to earn or merit God's favor and grace, it has been common for them to do so on the basis of reasoning that runs contrary to that thought. According to that reasoning, what prevents human beings from earning or meriting God's love, grace, and favor is their inability to be perfectly holy and righteous as God is. Supposedly, if they could live entirely free of sin and never transgress even once any of God's commandments, they could thereby earn God's grace and favor and be deserving of his acceptance. Of course, this is regarded as possible only in theory, since mortal human beings are unable to attain that level of perfection.

Such an interpretation of the biblical texts, however, must be rejected as contrary to the logic underlying them. The reason why God's love, grace, and favor cannot be earned or merited is not that human beings can never attain perfection in God's sight but that his love, grace, and favor are already theirs as a gift given by him freely and unconditionally. One cannot earn or merit something that one already possesses as a gift.

Furthermore, even when human beings do become obedient to God's will and live in conformity with his commandments, it is only because of the love and grace that God has shown them. That obedience is not something that they produce in themselves independently of God but something that God himself brings about by instructing them as to how they should live for their own good, providing them with the knowledge and strength necessary to live in that manner, and acting to correct and discipline them when they abandon that way of life so that they may turn back to it for their own good. The life of justice, righteousness, and obedience that they attain is therefore the *consequence* of God's love and favor rather than something that *earns* or *obtains* that love and favor. The gift that God freely gives them is not merely his acceptance but also the way of life that allows them to be healed and made whole.

God's grace, mercy, and favor are often associated as well with the forgiveness of his people's sins. While such an idea is no doubt biblical, it too is often misunderstood and misinterpreted as a result of the influence of the modes of thought that were characteristic of those who worshiped pagan gods in antiquity. According to those modes of thought, forgiveness and punishment are mutually exclusive. When the gods forgive those who have offended them, they no longer inflict punishments on them. Conversely, if they inflict punishments on them, it is because they have not forgiven them.

In biblical thought, however, because the punishments that God inflicts on his people are expressions of his concern for their well-being, they stand alongside forgiveness as two of the forms that his love for his people may take. It is important to note that forgiveness can be understood in two different ways. It may involve not bearing resentment or ill will toward those who have committed some wrong or done some type of harm but instead continuing to seek their well-being and happiness. In this sense of the word, God always forgives, since nothing that his people do or fail to do can ever lead him to stop seeking their well-being and happiness. However, forgiveness can also be understood in the sense of not inflicting punishments or suffering on those who have committed wrongdoing. In this sense, God often does *not* forgive. This is not because he ceases to love those who do wrong but rather because simply leaving them unpunished may be contrary to their well-being rather than promoting it. If people are living and behaving in ways that do them harm and destroy their well-being, simply to allow them to continue unabated in such behavior without attempting to correct them would be unloving. It would involve abandoning them to the destructive consequences of that behavior rather than seeking to deliver them from those consequences by bringing them to leave that behavior behind and live in a way that instead promotes their well-being. In other words, when people live and behave in ways that do them and others harm, to ignore or overlook that behavior only reinforces it and causes it to spread and proliferate even further, thus doing them even greater harm.

Perhaps the best example of this understanding of forgiveness and punishment in the biblical texts is found in Exodus 32, which contains the account of the people's sin in making for themselves a golden calf to worship while Moses was on Mount Sinai receiving God's commandments. After Moses comes down from the mountain and sees what the people have done, he intercedes on their behalf to God, acknowledging the gravity of their sin while at the same time asking God to forgive them rather than blotting them out of his book or destroying them (vv. 31-32). Although God responds favorably to Moses' petition, he adds: "Nevertheless, when the day comes for punishment, I will punish them for their sin" (vv. 33-34). For interpreters accustomed to setting forgiveness and punishment in opposition to one another, the affirmation that God will punish the people for their sin seems to contradict the notion that he forgives them their sin. According to the logic of the narrative, however, God's forgiveness takes the form of not destroying the people or casting them off for what they have done, while his love nevertheless insists that at some point they be punished or chastised for what they have done. Simply to allow them to continue in that type of behavior without taking measures aimed at correcting it would not be loving on God's part. For their own good, the people needed to be chastised so that they might be brought to abandon their sinful behavior and instead learn to submit obediently to God's gracious will for their own good. Thus, while God forgives them in the sense of not casting them away but instead continuing to seek their well-being, he also punishes or chastises them for the same purpose of promoting their well-being by attempting to bring them to live in ways that will make that well-being possible.

This same understanding of grace and punishment is reflected in other passages as well. Two chapters later in Exodus, God describes himself as "merciful and gracious, slow to anger, and abounding in steadfast love and faithfulness, keeping steadfast love for the thousandth generation, forgiving iniquity and transgression and sin, yet by no means leaving them unpunished, but visiting the iniquity of the parents upon the children and the children's children to the third and the fourth generation" (Exod 34:6-7). Here the forgiveness of sins is explicitly distinguished from leaving sins unpunished, clearly conveying the idea that these are two different things: God is said to *forgive* iniquity, transgression, and sin, yet by no means to leave them *unpunished*. A form of this same saying appears in Numbers 14. After the Israelites doubt God's ability to deliver the land of Canaan into their hands, God threatens to disinherit them and make a great nation of Moses to take their place. When Moses rejects God's proposal and instead asks God to forgive them by reminding him of what he had promised in the saying just cited, God responds by telling Moses: "I do forgive, just as you have asked." At the same time, however, he adds: "None of the people who have seen my glory and the signs that I did in Egypt and in the wilderness and yet have tested me these ten times and have not obeyed my voice shall see the land that I swore to give to their ancestors; none of those who despised me shall see it" (Num 14:17-23).

The idea in both of these passages is that God forgives the people in the sense of not disinheriting or abandoning them on account of their sin but continuing to seek their well-being out of love for them. Yet because this well-being depends on their trusting in him and obeying what he commands for their own good, in his love he will also impose sufferings and hardships on them and their descendants in order to fashion and mold them into a people who will live as he has commanded so that they may enjoy his blessings. It is for this purpose that he will have them spend forty years in the wilderness rather than introducing them immediately into the land he had promised them. What he seeks is not to exact revenge on them for having disobeyed or offended him but to discipline and correct them.

This idea, in fact, is made explicit in Deut 8:2-5, the last verse of which we have already cited above. There Moses is presented as telling the people:

> Remember all the way in which the LORD your God has led you in the wilderness these forty years in order to humble you and test you to know what was in your heart, whether or not you would keep his commandments. He humbled you and let you endure hunger, and then fed you with manna, which neither you nor your ancestors had known, in order to make you understand that one does not live by bread alone but by every word that comes forth from the mouth of the LORD. The clothes on your back did not wear out, nor did your feet become swollen these forty years. Know in your heart, then, that as a parent disciplines a child, so the LORD your God disciplines you.

This passage makes it clear that the purpose for which God subjected the Israelites to forty years in the desert was to discipline them in the sense of teaching and instructing them, forming in them the type of humble character he wanted to see in them for their own good, and bringing about in them the obedience necessary for them to enjoy the well-being he sought for them by means of his commandments. Rather than simply seeking to make them suffer for having disobeyed him, he continued to seek their well-being, yet that well-being depended on their learning to trust in him and obey him.

The idea that God *saves* his people by *chastising* them is stated explicitly in Jer 30:11. There God tells those whom he has sent into exile: "For I am with you, says the LORD, in order to save you; I will make an end of all the nations among which I scattered you, but of you I will not make an end. I will chastise you in just measure, and I will by no means leave you unpunished" (cf. Jer 46:28). Here the chastisement inflicted by God is clearly intended to save the people from the sinful behavior that does harm both to themselves and others. For that reason, God expresses his love for the people both by saving them *and* by chastising them. To leave the people unpunished would represent a lack of love on God's part, since it would involve abandoning them to their destructive behavior rather than seeking to correct that behavior for their own good. Were God to fail to seek to correct them, it would not be possible for him to save and heal them, since their destructive behavior would prevent them from attaining salvation, well-being, and wholeness.

THE HARROWING AND HEALING CHASTISEMENTS OF LEVITICUS 26 AND DEUTERONOMY 28

Even though the language of punishment and chastisement is relatively uncommon in the narrative regarding Israel that runs throughout the historical books of the Hebrew Bible, the idea that God inflicts suffering on his people in order to bring them back to himself and his commandments must be regarded as lying at the very heart of that narrative. The two passages that speak at greatest length of the sufferings to which God subjects his people when they disobey him are the same passages that begin by describing in detail the blessings that he promises to pour out on them when they obey his commandments, namely, Leviticus 26 and Deuteronomy 28. In both of these passages, in fact, the description of the hardships and afflictions that God will impose on the people if they disobey him is much more extensive than the description of the blessings they will obtain if they keep those commandments (Lev 26:14-39; Deut 28:15-68).

A close look at the verses from Leviticus 26 and Deuteronomy 28 that describe the sufferings that God intends to impose on the people if they do not observe his commandments may initially seem to render entirely untenable the claim that God subjects his people to those sufferings for their own good out of love for them. Despite the fact that Leviticus 26 uses the language of chastisement, the sufferings and hardships described there seem excessively harsh and cruel. They include defeat and pillage at the hands of their enemies, famine and starvation, plagues, death, desolation, exile, terror, consumption, and fever, and perhaps most gruesome of all, the eating of the flesh of their children (Lev 26:14-39).

The language in Deuteronomy 28 is even more harrowing. In addition to all of the sufferings just mentioned, the passage speaks of disaster, panic, frustration, pestilence, boils, tumors, skin diseases, blindness, confusion, hunger, thirst, nakedness, and subjection to the cruelties and abuse of enemies who will enslave them and take from them not only their crops and animals but their sons and daughters as well. In response to their disobedience, God promises to make them an object of horror in the eyes of the other nations, to scatter their corpses for birds and animals to devour, to cause them to be driven mad, and to put an iron yoke around their neck until they are destroyed. The description of the manner in which they will be forced to eat the flesh of their children is much more graphic than in Leviticus 26, as are the allusions to all of the other things they will suffer (vv. 20-57). The passage especially uses the language of curse to speak of them being afflicted in all that they do. The people are told that everything they have or produce will be cursed, including not only their harvests and livestock but their children as well, and that they will be cursed both in the city and the field whether they come in or go out (vv. 15-19). At the end of the passage, Moses tells them:

> If you do not diligently observe all the words of this law that are written in this book, fearing this glorious and awesome name, the LORD your God, then the LORD will overwhelm both you and your offspring with severe and lasting afflictions and grievous and lasting maladies. He will bring upon you once again all the diseases of Egypt, of which you were in dread, and they will cling to you. Every other sickness and affliction, even though not recorded in the book of this law, the LORD will inflict on you until you are destroyed. Although you were once as numerous as the stars in heaven, you will be left few in number because you did not obey the LORD your God. And just as the LORD took delight in making you prosperous and numerous, so the LORD will take delight in bringing you to ruin and destruction; you will be torn from the land that you are entering to possess. The LORD will scatter you among all peoples, from one end of the earth to the other, and there you will serve other gods of wood and stone that neither you nor your ancestors had known. Among those nations you will find no respite, no resting place for the sole of your foot. There the LORD will give you a trembling heart, failing eyes, and a spirit of despair. Your life will hang in doubt before you; you will be in dread night and day, with no assurance of your life. In the morning you will say, "If only it were evening!," and at evening you will say, "If only it were morning!," because of the dread that your heart will feel and the sights that your eyes will see. The LORD will take you back in ships to Egypt, by a route that I promised you would never see again, and there you will offer yourselves for sale to your enemies as male and female slaves, but there will be no buyer (vv. 58-68).

Despite the severity of the sufferings described here, a careful analysis of both Leviticus 26 and Deuteronomy 28 unquestionably points to the idea that God's intention is not simply to vent his wrath on the people or to subject them to unspeakable sufferings as an end in itself but rather to chastise and purify them through the things they will suffer. This is stated explicitly, in fact, in Leviticus 26. In addition to using the terms *yasar* and *musar* to speak of chastisement, the passage makes it clear that the sufferings that God will impose on the people will increase in intensity if the people do not respond to his chastisements by returning to him in obedience. In this way, the passage leaves no doubt that the sufferings God will impose on the people when they disobey him are designed not to consume or destroy them but to refine and purify them and their land so that they will finally come to live in the way that God has commanded for their own good:

> But if you do not listen to me and observe all these commandments. . . I will set my face against you, and you will be struck down by your enemies. . . . And if *in spite of this* you will not listen to me, I will chastise you seven times more for your sins. . . . If you *continue* to walk in opposition to me, and will not listen to me, I will *continue* to plague you seven times more for your sins. . . . If *in spite of* these chastisements you are not corrected, but *continue* to walk in opposition to me, then I too will *continue* to walk in opposition to you: I myself will strike you seven times more for your sins. . . . But if, *despite this*, you do not listen to me, and *continue* to walk in opposition to me, I will *continue* to walk in opposition to you in fury; I in turn will chastise you myself seven times more for your sins. . . . Then the land shall enjoy its Sabbath years as long as it lies desolate, while you are in the land of your enemies; then the land shall rest, and enjoy its Sabbath years. As long as it lies desolate, it shall have the rest that it did not have on your Sabbaths when you were living on it (Lev 26:14, 17-18, 21, 23, 27-28, 34-35).

Here the suffering and afflictions to which God promises to subject the people when they persist in their disobedience clearly have a *corrective* purpose. In each case, the outcome that God desires is that the suffering he inflicts on them will lead them to put away their disobedience and walk in the path he has laid out for them by means of his commandments. The passage assumes that if they do so, God will put an end to the chastisements he is imposing on them, at least temporarily. If they stubbornly persist in their disobedience, however, God will increase the intensity of the sufferings he inflicts on them until eventually he acts to destroy a part of the people and to send the rest to languish in exile in a foreign land. Even this measure is said to have a constructive purpose, however, in that it will enable the land to rest and recover so that one day the people may return to it from their exile and enjoy the blessings it provides for them. This indicates that God's purpose in chastising the people is ultimately a loving one.

The idea that the objective that God pursues by means of the sufferings he inflicts on the people in response to their disobedience is that of correcting them and bringing them back to himself in obedience for their own good is also stressed in the concluding section of Leviticus 26. There God is presented as telling the people:

> But if they confess their wrongdoing and the wrongdoing of their ancestors, in the unfaithfulness that they practiced toward me, and in their walking in opposition to me, which led me also to walk in opposition to them by bringing them into the land of their enemies; if then their uncircumcised heart is

humbled and they accept the chastisement for their wrongdoing, then I will remember my covenant with Jacob. I will remember also my covenant with Isaac and my covenant with Abraham, and I will remember the land. For the land will be deserted by them, and enjoy its Sabbath years by lying desolate without them, while they accept the chastisement for their wrongdoing, because they spurned my ordinances and despised my statutes. Yet for all that, when they are in the land of their enemies, I will not cast them away nor despise them so as to destroy them entirely and break my covenant with them. For I am the LORD their God; but for their sake I will remember the covenant with their ancestors whom I brought out of the land of Egypt in the sight of the nations, to be their God. I am the LORD (vv. 40-45).

While certain parts of Leviticus 26 clearly convey the idea that Israel's blessing and well-being are conditional upon the people's obedience, these verses at the end of the chapter present God's favor as something that is *unconditional*. God tells the people that, no matter what they do, he will not spurn them definitively or forget the covenant he made with their ancestors. Even if the people do not respond to God's chastisements by turning away from their sin, God promises not to reject them, despise them, or destroy them entirely. Although it may be necessary for God to continue to chastise them repeatedly and with increasingly harsher measures, he will not give up on his objective of bringing them to live in obedience to his good commandments so that they may attain the good things that follow both intrinsically and extrinsically from obedience to those commandments.

According to this passage, therefore, nothing can bring God to put an end to his commitment to doing whatever is necessary to bring his people to live in a way that will allow them to attain the well-being he seeks for them. One way or another, he intends to accomplish that objective and promises to do whatever is necessary until it is attained, no matter how painful it may be for them or for him. If he is fully committed to their well-being, in fact, he has no choice but to act in that way, because their well-being does not depend merely *on him* but also *on them*. They cannot enjoy well-being if they do not live in a way that is conducive to that well-being.

A God Who Curses?

In contrast to Leviticus 26, the parallel passage in Deuteronomy 28 does not stress explicitly the corrective purpose of the terrible sufferings and afflictions that God promises to inflict on the people when they disobey his commandments. Nevertheless, Deuteronomy 28 must be read in conjunction with the two chapters that follow.

In Deuteronomy 29, Moses gathers the people together prior to their entrance into the land God had promised to them in order to remind them of the wonders that God performed on their behalf when he delivered them from their bondage in Egypt and led them through the wilderness for forty years. On that basis, Moses exhorts the people to live under the covenant that God is establishing with them by obeying his commandments and warns them once more of the punishments God will impose on them if they insist on going in their own stubborn way rather than obeying him. Then, at the beginning of Deuteronomy 30, we find what can be considered the continuation of Deuteronomy 28:

> When all these things have happened to you, the blessings and the curses that I have set before you, if you call them to mind among all the nations where the LORD your God has scattered you and turn back to the LORD your God, and you and your children listen to him with all your heart and with all your soul, just as I am commanding you today, then the LORD your God will put an end to your captivity and have compassion on you, gathering you again from all the peoples among whom the LORD your God has scattered you. Even if you are exiled to the ends of the world, from there the LORD your God will gather you, and from there he will bring you back. The LORD your God will bring you into the land that your ancestors possessed, and you will possess it; he will do good to you and make you more numerous than your ancestors.
>
> Moreover, the LORD your God will circumcise your heart and the heart of your descendants, so that you may love the LORD your God with all your heart and with all your soul, in order that you may live. The LORD your God will put all these curses on your enemies and on those who hated you and sought you harm. Then you will turn back and listen to the voice of the LORD, observing all his commandments that I am commanding you today, and the LORD your God will make you abundantly prosperous in all your undertakings, in the fruit of your body, in the fruit of your livestock, and in the fruit of your soil. For the LORD will again take delight in you in order to do good to you, just as he took delight in your ancestors, if you listen to the LORD your God by observing his commandments and decrees that are written in this book of the law, if you turn to the LORD your God with all your heart and with all your soul (Deut 30:1–10).

In accordance with most English versions of the Hebrew Bible, this translation makes use of the language of curse in the opening verse of the chapter, where the Hebrew noun *qalalah* appears. In this passage and others in Deuteronomy, this noun is contrasted with the Hebrew noun for blessing. The language of curse is also commonly used to translate the passive participle of the Hebrew verb *'arar* that appears repeatedly in Deuteronomy in relation to people who are said to be cursed. The problem with employing the language of curse to translate the Hebrew terms that appear in these passages is that in English that language conveys certain ideas that must be considered foreign to biblical thought. Among English speakers, a curse is generally understood as some type of mysterious, invisible force that is unleashed on someone and acts on its own to harm them in some way. For the most part, curses are uttered solely out of spite and hatred and are motivated by a desire to hurt or injure someone for no purpose other than seeing them suffer. Curses also tend to be seen as definitive, permanent, or irreversible, at least until the harm and suffering they are intended to cause is brought to pass or until some type of magical formula or spell can reverse or neutralize them. To be cursed is to be beyond hope, subject to an overwhelming maleficent power or to some type of inevitable doom from which one cannot escape. Those who pronounce a curse on others do so not in order to correct them or bring about in them some change in behavior for their own good, but simply because they wish to see them subjected to some type of evil, motivated by a desire to see them suffer to make them pay for something they have done.

Ideas such as these must be considered foreign to the logic of Deuteronomy. When the passages that use the Hebrew term *qalalah* are viewed in the context of the book as a whole, it becomes clear that the afflictions or punishments of which they speak are not curses unleashed on the people by an angry and vengeful God who wishes to see them endure horrific sufferings for having dared to disobey and offend him. Those afflictions or punishments are not permanent and irreversible, nor are they expressions of hatred or spite designed for no other purpose than to do the people harm. On the contrary, the objective that God is seeking when he afflicts the people in the ways described is to bring them to put away their destructive behavior and turn back to him so as to obey his commandments. Because his intention is ultimately to bring them to live in a manner that will make it possible for him to bless them, the punishments he imposes on them are rooted in his love for them. To use the language of curse to refer to these punishments is therefore to communicate ideas that run contrary to biblical thought, since in English curses are never pronounced on others out of love for them or due to a concern for their well-being.

The idea behind the words attributed to God in Deuteronomy 28–30 and in other passages from that book and the Hebrew Bible that speak in similar terms is that the various forms of suffering, affliction, and hardships that God promises to inflict on the people if they refuse to keep his commandments are intended to bring them back to himself in obedience for their own good. Rather than using the language of curse, it would be more faithful to the Hebrew to use terms such as scourge, blight, affliction, devastation, or calamity to describe the sufferings or punishments to which the people will be subjected if they persistently disobey what God has commanded. According to Deuteronomy 28–29, these scourges include things such as those already mentioned above, namely, pestilence, plague, famine, mental and physical illnesses, defeat and oppression at the hands of enemies, untimely death, and exile in foreign lands. Undoubtedly, such measures are extremely painful and at first glance even seem excessively harsh and cruel. However, Deuteronomy 30 leaves no doubt as to their purpose: what God seeks is not to destroy his people or do them irreversible harm but to bring them and their children back to himself so that they may obey him with their whole heart and soul for their own good. The passage refers to this transformation in terms of a circumcision of the people's heart to be brought about by God himself. Once they return to God in obedience, God will restore their fortunes with compassion and bring them back from exile so that they may enjoy his blessings once more (Deut 30:2-4). When that day comes, the people will finally love God with all their being. The passage also makes it clear that abundance and prosperity will follow upon the people's obedience as its consequence, thereby suggesting both an intrinsic and extrinsic relationship between their observance of God's commandments and their well-being: God will make them prosper not only by pouring out his blessings on them but also by acting to bring about in them the way of life that will make it possible for them to enjoy those blessings. Yet while the blessings God promises to bestow on the people are conditional upon their obedience to his commandments, God's commitment to doing everything possible to bring them to live in that obedience is *unconditional.*

The reason for which God will bring such scourges or calamities on them, therefore, is not because their disobedience to his sovereign will offends and aggrieves him, diminishes his honor and glory, or injures his pride or ego. When he allows such scourges to come upon them or even brings those scourges on them himself, he is not acting out of spite, hatred, or a spirit of revenge in the way that pagan gods were thought to do. Nor is he unleashing some type of mysterious, maleficent power upon them in order to doom them definitively and irreversibly to a future of misery and destruction. His desire is not to impose his will on them by force in order to subjugate and dominate them and oblige them to serve him against their will. On the contrary, his desire is to bring them to live in the manner necessary for them to enjoy the blessings of life, well-being, and wholeness that he intends for them. That can only happen, however, if they are brought to live in a way that promotes these things rather than preventing them from becoming a reality.

When the language of curse is avoided in the English translation of the passages from Deuteronomy that describe the afflictions to which the people will be subjected if they refuse to obey God's commandments, those passages come across very differently. This is especially evident when considering Deut 28:15-19, which in the NRSVue reads:

> But if you will not obey the LORD your God by diligently observing all his commandments and decrees that I am commanding you today, then all these curses shall come upon you and overtake you: Cursed shall you be in the city, and cursed shall you be in the field. Cursed shall be your basket and your kneading bowl. Cursed shall be the fruit of your womb, the fruit of your ground, the increase of your cattle and the issue of your flock. Cursed shall you be when you come in, and cursed shall you be when you go out.

This translation appears to convey the idea of a God who intends to inflict pain and hardships on the people if they disobey him merely for the purpose of seeing them suffer, as if he were acting out of spite and ill will. While it is of course possible to avoid the language of curse when translating these verses into English, perhaps the greatest difficulty in doing so is that there is no single word in English that can be used to translate the two Hebrew terms used in the passage. In order to capture more fully the meaning of the text, therefore, it is necessary to use a variety of words and phrases when translating these terms. To do so would result in a translation or paraphrase such as the following:

But if you will not obey the LORD your God by diligently observing all his commandments and decrees that I am commanding you today, then all these scourges and afflictions shall come upon you and overtake you: Your life shall be filled with constant suffering and unbearable pain whether you are in the city or in the field. Your basket and your kneading bowl shall remain bare and empty. The fruit of your womb, the fruit of your ground, the increase of your cattle, and the issue of your flock shall wither, decay, and die. You will experience nothing but misery, anguish, and despair both as you come in and as you go out.

Such a translation or paraphrase makes it possible to describe the enormity and intensity of the afflictions to which the people will be subjected if they refuse to obey God's commandments without implying that those afflictions are imposed by God out of spite, vengeance, or a desire simply to see the people suffer. In addition, however, it allows for the possibility that many of the hardships that the people will endure will follow upon their refusal to obey God's commandments as the intrinsic and natural consequence of that refusal. The reason that their sufferings will be so great is not only that God will inflict punishments on them but also that their unjust, violent, and destructive behavior will have devastating and disastrous consequences in and of itself. In that case, God's words to the people are not only a threat but a warning as well.

Similar observations must be made with regard to God's affirmations in Deuteronomy 28 that he will destroy the people in response to their disobedience. On multiple occasions, the passage affirms that when the people persistently refuse to obey his commandments God will afflict them with various forms of suffering until they are destroyed (vv. 20, 22, 24, 45, 48, 51, 61). While these affirmations may appear to convey the idea that God will annihilate the people entirely, the context indicates that such is not the case. This is especially evident from v. 62 of the passage. There, immediately after Moses tells the people: "Every other sickness and affliction, even though not recorded in the book of this law, the LORD will inflict on you until you are destroyed" (v. 61), he continues: "Although you were once as numerous as the stars in heaven, you will be left few in number because you did not obey the LORD your God" (v. 62). Here it is clear that the destruction of which God speaks does not involve the total annihilation of the people but rather the death of many or most of them until they become few in number. The same understanding of destruction is found earlier in the book of Deuteronomy as well. In Deut 4:26, Moses tells the people that if they serve idols and do what is evil they will "utterly perish from the land" and will be "utterly destroyed." In the very next verse, however, he continues: "only a few of you will be left among the nations where the LORD will lead you" (v. 27; cf. v. 31).

Just as the curses or scourges of which Deuteronomy 28 speaks are not regarded as permanent or irreversible, therefore, so also the destruction of the people mentioned there and elsewhere in the book should not be understood as involving their total annihilation. What God intends is not to threaten the people with some type of doom or extinction from which they will never recover if they disobey him, but to indicate to them the intensity and severity of the chastisements he will inflict on them in order to bring them to leave behind their destructive behavior and return to him in obedience for their own good. While these chastisements will undoubtedly involve the death and destruction of many of the members of his people, this death and destruction do not constitute an end in themselves but have a healing and corrective purpose in relation to those who will survive God's chastisements, as do the curses or scourges mentioned in the same context.

Finding Love and Purpose in the Depths of Despair

While both Leviticus 26 and Deuteronomy 28–30 undoubtedly present the sufferings and punishments that God promises to inflict on the people if they refuse to obey his commandments as having a corrective purpose, what makes it extremely difficult to interpret these passages in that way is the enormity, intensity, and severity of the sufferings that these passages describe. To use an analogy, when the father of a large family seeks to discipline and correct his children for their own good out of love for them, he does not willfully smite them with blindness or infect them with disease, subject them to starvation and bloodshed, or put some of them to death in the hope that the few who survive will turn back to him in obedience. Much less would he seek to drive them mad, make them an object of horror in the eyes of others, scatter their corpses for birds and animals to devour, or force them to bear an iron yoke around their neck until they fall over dead. Such measures would be considered not only cruel but barbaric, and under no circumstances would they be viewed as expressions of love. In the same way, to affirm that God is acting out of love and concern for his people and seeking their well-being when he forces them to endure the kinds of horrific sufferings described in Leviticus 26 and Deuteronomy 28 would seem not only ludicrous but revolting to most readers of the biblical texts. Starving people to death until they have no choice but to eat the flesh of their own children is no way to bring them to put away their sinful behavior and instead practice justice, righteousness, and love.

In order to grasp the logic behind passages such as these, however, it is necessary to see them in their historical context. Many biblical scholars would agree that these passages reached their present form in the period following the destruction of Jerusalem in the early sixth century BCE, either after the deportation of many of the people to Babylon or in the years following the return to the land of many of the children and grandchildren of the deportees. Both those who composed and edited these passages and those who read them were well-acquainted with the tremendous suffering that the people had endured, especially because for many that suffering had not yet come to an end. When read from that perspective, these passages would be understood as describing experiences that either the readers themselves or their parents, grandparents, and ancestors had actually been forced to endure rather than mere theoretical possibilities that had been contemplated by God or Moses centuries earlier, prior to the people's entrance into the land that God had promised to give them.

Even if parts of Leviticus 26 and Deuteronomy 28 date from a time previous to the destruction of Jerusalem by the Babylonians, it is likely that the sections that describe in graphic detail the sufferings that the people would come to endure are later embellishments. Either the Assyrians or the Babylonians seem to be in mind in the verses that allude to a particular nation whom the Israelites do not know and whose language they do not speak, which will swoop down on the people from afar like an eagle (Deut 28:32-33, 36, 49). Similarly, even though the siege in which the people will have to devour their own children to survive and endure other horrors seems to be that which took place under the Babylonians prior to the fall of Jerusalem, the passage may have in mind other sieges as well, such as those that occurred at the time of the Assyrian invasion of Israel and Judah (Deut 28:52-57). The scattering of the Israelites among other peoples from one end of the earth to the other and the return of many to Egypt mentioned in Deut 28:64-68 also appear to be descriptions of events from Israel's history either prior to the sixth century BCE or during that century. Most of the horrendous afflictions described in Leviticus 26 and Deuteronomy 28 should therefore be understood as allusions to concrete experiences that the inhabitants of Israel and Judah had endured prior to the composition of those passages, though the allusions may also be to experiences that other peoples and nations of antiquity were known to have gone through. In fact, a number of these afflictions are mentioned explicitly in the biblical narratives and some of the prophetic books.[7]

The question that would inevitably arise among those who had undergone such horrific experiences or heard them described in graphic detail by people of previous generations was why an all-powerful God who supposedly loved them had allowed such things to take place. In principle, several answers to that question were possible. It might be concluded that the God of Israel was not in fact all-powerful and that he had been unable to save and protect his people from the tremendous sufferings to which they had been subjected. If that were the case, however, then there was no sense in looking to that God for help and deliverance in times of hardships and need, since it was

---

7. Walter Brueggemann, for example, notes that Deuteronomy 28 is clearly connected to the situation described in 2 Kings 24-25, and that vv. 47-57 of this chapter "surely have reference to the Babylonian devastation of Jerusalem at the beginning of the sixth century. . . ." (*Deuteronomy*, AOTC; Nashville: Abingdon, 2001, 257). Similarly, Duane L. Christensen sees in Deuteronomy 28 repeated allusions to particular events that are described in the biblical narratives and the books of Israel's prophets (*Deuteronomy 21:10–34:12*, WBC 6B; Nashville: Thomas Nelson, 2002, 684-87). Like many other commentators, in his analysis of Deuteronomy 26:15-68 Jack R. Lundbom notes the parallels not only with sufferings described elsewhere in the Hebrew Bible but also with those mentioned in the texts of other ancient peoples, including especially those that contained similar lists of blessings and curses (*Deuteronomy: A Commentary*, Grand Rapids: Eerdmans, 2013, 766-97). On that basis, it might be concluded that both Leviticus 26 and Deuteronomy 28 are alluding not only to sufferings that the people of Israel had endured in the past but also to sufferings that other peoples of antiquity had experienced and interpreted as punishments inflicted by their gods.

impossible to depend on him due to his lack of power. To view God in such a manner would also involve rejecting the belief that as the creator of all that existed he was truly sovereign over all people and things. For these reasons, to conclude that the God of Israel had not been able to save and protect his people from the great hardships and afflictions they had endured was hardly an option. In essence, that would involve affirming that the all-powerful God in whom they had believed previously did not actually exist.

A second possible answer to the question of why God had not come to the aid of his people in the midst of the terrible sufferings that they had endured was that he had ceased to love them. In that case, he had abandoned them and rejected them as his people, perhaps because he could no longer tolerate their sinfulness. If God no longer loved them and had repudiated them definitively, however, they could have no hope for the future and it was pointless to look to him for help or deliverance in times of need. Even if they continued to believe in God and attempted to return to him in obedience, it would do them no good because he no longer cared what happened to them or had any intention of receiving and blessing them again. Such a conclusion was hardly acceptable, however, since it would make no sense for people to believe in or serve a God who had cast them off forever.

A third option was to maintain that God's love for Israel was conditional. When the people obeyed him, he responded in love, but when they refused to obey him, he responded by lashing out at them to hurt them in order to compel them to submit once again to his will. Such an idea would make sense, however, only if God was thought to be pursuing some interest or need of his own by means of Israel. This possibility was ruled out by the belief that as sovereign creator he needed nothing from his creation and did not depend on Israel to satisfy any type of personal need. While in principle it might be thought that what he sought was to be worshiped, served, and obeyed for his own sake simply because he derived pleasure from these things in the same way that the gods of the other nations did, if that were the case then he was not a good God who sought his people's well-being as an end in itself. Instead, like the other gods of antiquity, he merely wished to manipulate and control people for his own selfish ends and subject them to himself as his slaves. Because true love is unconditional in the sense that it is committed to the well-being of others independently of what they may do or fail to do, a God who offered people his favors in exchange for their submission and obedience could not truly be said to love them.

While in principle it was possible for the people to arrive at such a conclusion, the biblical texts consistently reject such an interpretation of Israel's sufferings as well as the concept of God upon which that type of interpretation is based. Instead, they posit a fourth alternative by looking to the ideas we have seen throughout the present chapter so as to conclude that the God of Israel had allowed his people to suffer the horrifying things described in Leviticus 26 and Deuteronomy 28 because he was seeking to correct them and bring them to put away their destructive behavior out of love for them. Given the intensity and brutality of the sufferings that the people had endured, this conclusion was no doubt an extremely problematic one. Nevertheless, from the perspective of those who continued to believe in the God of Israel, it was much less problematic than any of the other possible responses just considered to the question of why God had allowed his people to be subjected to such intense and unbearable sufferings. Despite the horrific nature of those sufferings, at least some of the people refused to believe that God had abandoned them definitively or that he did not love them unconditionally. The only alternative, therefore, was to maintain that he had allowed them to experience such tremendous sufferings for a purpose. If so, that purpose could only be that he sought to bring them back to himself and to the way of life that he had commanded them to follow for their own good.

This is in fact the conclusion that is stated explicitly in both Leviticus 26 and Deuteronomy 28–30. As we have seen above, in the closing verses of Leviticus 26, God is presented as affirming that he would never spurn or hate his people or destroy them utterly but would act to deliver them from the sufferings he had imposed on them and return them to the land after it had enjoyed its Sabbath rest. Similarly, in Deuteronomy 28–30, God promises that after his people have endured all of the terrible things described he will restore their fortunes, show compassion to them, and gather them back into the land he had given them in order to bless them and make them prosper there. While both of these passages mention the need for the people to turn back to God in order for these things to happen, they view both the people's recognition of their sin as well as their renewed love and obedience as something that God himself will bring about in them as a result of those experiences. In that sense, it is God himself who will circumcise their previously uncircumcised heart in order to bring them to love him with all their heart and soul (Lev 26:41; Deut 30:6). It is possible that these passages use the imagery of circumcision precisely because it involves a process that is extremely painful, as well as a definitive removal of flesh that leaves a permanent mark. According to the logic underlying both of these passages, therefore, while God may have appeared to abandon his people on account of their refusal to obey him, in reality he had been subjecting them to suffering so that they might be brought to turn away from the harmful and destructive path that they had been following and instead return to the good and life-giving path that he had laid out for them by means of the Torah, hopefully on a permanent basis.

When the horrendous sufferings and experiences described in Leviticus 26 and Deuteronomy 28 are viewed from the perspective of those who had actually endured such things and sought to find meaning and purpose in what had happened to them, therefore, it is not difficult to understand how their faith in the God of Israel left them no alternative but to interpret those sufferings and experiences as means by which God had sought to bring them to return to the way of life he had commanded for their own good. Such a conclusion was possible, however, only if they were fully convinced that God did indeed love them unconditionally and had never stopped loving them even when he had allowed them to go through such great afflictions and hardships. This conclusion is stated explicitly not only at the end of Leviticus 26, where God promises never to abandon, spurn, abhor, or utterly destroy his people (v. 44), but in Deuteronomy as well, where the same type of promise appears in the context of allusions to the utter destruction he will bring upon the people: "Because the LORD your God is a merciful God, he will not abandon you or destroy you, nor will he forget the covenant with your ancestors that he swore to them" (Deut 4:31).

The people could arrive at the same conclusion by viewing the horrific sufferings and experiences described in Leviticus 26 and Deuteronomy 28 from the perspective of God himself. If God was truly committed to the well-being of his people and that well-being could be attained only if the people lived in a manner that made it possible, then he had to be fully committed as well to doing whatever was necessary to bring them to live in that manner. When they persistently failed to do so and refused to respond favorably to the prophets he sent them, then his commitment to their well-being left him no choice but to attempt to bring about the changes necessary in their behavior by means of chastisements.

As we have noted above when considering Leviticus 26, however, at times none of the chastisements he inflicted on them would succeed in bringing them to abandon their destructive behavior and return to a life that truly promoted their well-being. In that case, if he remained committed to that objective, he had no choice but to inflict even greater sufferings on them until those sufferings became so intense and unbearable that the people would be left with no alternative but to conclude that the only way that they could survive was to heed God's call to turn back to the way of life he had laid out for them in the Torah.

In the biblical narrative, however, at times the people are presented as being so stubborn, stiff-necked, and hard-hearted that no matter how intensely they are made to suffer, they continue to refuse to mend their ways. When that happens, God sends them prophets to threaten them with sufferings and chastisements that are even more severe. The graphic descriptions of the terrible afflictions that the people will be made to endure are intended to bring them to repentance by generating shock, terror, and dismay in their hearts. When the people still refuse to listen and instead mock and persecute the prophets God sends them, the only course of action open to God is to carry out the threats he has made. If that does not work, then he may be led to destroy a portion of the people in the hope that those who remain will finally turn back to him. Even then, the survivors may still refuse to respond in the way that God desires and inexplicably may even choose to suffer destruction rather than to submit to God's will. Because God's commitment to bringing the people to abandon the path that is leading to their ruin will not allow him to relent, he must then destroy even more of the people and make that destruction even more devastating and painful. To do anything else would involve simply giving up on his loving objectives for them. For obvious reasons, however, he cannot destroy his people in their entirety, since that would put an end to any hope of bringing into existence a people who will live in ways that will enable them to enjoy the well-being he desires for them and serve as his instrument for bringing other peoples to live in those same ways.

All of this results in a tremendous paradox that can make it extremely difficult to understand the biblical texts. According to this paradox, in order for God to accomplish his loving objective of bringing the people to live in a way that will allow them to enjoy the well-being, prosperity, happiness, and wholeness that he desires for all, he must at times act in ways that seem to be anything but loving. On the contrary, in order to accomplish those objectives, he has no alternative but to do things that seem cruel and inhumane. When the sufferings he imposes on his people in an attempt to bring them back to himself repeatedly fail to accomplish that objective, eventually he must make those sufferings so unbearable that at least part of the people finally conclude that they have no choice but to return to him if they are to survive. Of course, out of love for his people, before inflicting such intense sufferings on them, he sends his prophets to announce to them what he is about to do. Yet if he is to have any hope of penetrating the hardened and unresponsive hearts of his people, he must use language that becomes increasingly violent, threatening, and ominous to describe the sufferings he intends to inflict on them. As a result, he ends up being portrayed as a God who appears to be anything but loving, since both the threats he makes and the punishments he imposes must become so harrowing as to appear barbaric if he hopes to elicit in his people any response to his pleas for them to change their ways. Yet what lies behind those horrific threats and punishments is his adamant refusal to give up on his people and hand them over to the ruin and destruction that will inevitably result from the path they have chosen for themselves. Simply stated, his love for them will not allow him to relent or capitulate but compels him to keep on trying to provoke in them the reaction he wishes to see for their own good, even though this requires that he treat them in ways that seem not only heartless but at times even monstrous.

In essence, then, there are basically two ways in which the threats and warnings of punishment for disobedience found in Leviticus 26 and Deuteronomy 28 can be read. According to the first of these, those threats and warnings are an expression of God's refusal or inability to tolerate the people's disobedience for his own sake. Either his desire to be revered, honored, glorified, and served is so powerful and overwhelming that he threatens to inflict the people with the most horrific sufferings imaginable unless they fulfill that desire in the way he demands or else his need to satisfy and safeguard his holiness and righteousness is so inflexible that he has no choice but to smite the people with unspeakable sufferings if they fail to obey him. In either case, what lies behind those threats and warnings of punishment is a concern for himself and the desires and demands of his own nature rather than a concern for the people themselves. It is this concern for his own glory, honor, holiness, and righteousness that compels him to act with such intense anger, hatred, and vehemence when the people refuse to obey him.

For the reasons we have seen here and elsewhere, however, such an interpretation of passages such as Leviticus 26 and Deuteronomy 28 must be rejected. Instead, the reason why God is presented as threatening to inflict such tremendous sufferings on the people if they persistently refuse to obey him is that he is fully and intractably committed to bringing them to turn back from behavior that makes it impossible for them to enjoy the well-being he desires for them and to live in accordance with his commandments for their own good. Precisely because his unconditional love for them will never allow him to abandon them definitively to their destructive ways or back down from his efforts to bring about in them the way of life necessary for them to attain the good he seeks for them, he will do whatever it takes to accomplish these objectives among them, even if this means inflicting suffering on them that is so severe as to become unbearable and destroying a large part of them so as to leave a small remnant that will finally have no choice but to turn back to his commandments for their own good if they wish to survive. It is as if God and his people have locked horns with one another and refuse to give in or back down until they finally break the will of the other and pin the other to the ground. In that clash of wills, in his love for his people God vows that it is not he who will finally relent and back down but his stubborn and rebellious people, no matter how long it takes or how much pain and suffering he must inflict on them. Eventually, he will prevail.

LOVING AND SERVING A GOD WHOM ONE FEARS

According to Deut 30:6, one of the main objectives that God seeks to accomplish by subjecting his people to chastisements when they have persistently failed to obey him is that they come to love him with all their heart and soul so that they may live. These words echo the ones found at the beginning of Deuteronomy 6, where God tells the people through Moses: "You shall love the Lord your God with all your heart and with all your soul and with all your might" (v. 5). God's desire that the people love him and serve him with all of their heart and soul is repeated in other passages of Deuteronomy as well.[8]

At first glance, the notion that God might lead his people to love and serve him gladly and willingly by inflicting punishments on them might seem highly problematic, especially when those punishments are as severe and horrific as those described in Deuteronomy 28. Rather than leading the people to love God and serve him with joy, it seems much more likely that such punishments would produce anger, hatred, and resentment toward God in

---

8. See Deut 10:12; 11:1, 13; 13:3; 28:47; 30:2, 10.

the people's heart. While they might serve him, they would do so reluctantly and out of fear, believing that they could not do otherwise if they wished to avoid being subjected to even greater punishments. In essence, God's punishments would force them to live as his slaves. While the people might display outwardly expressions of love and affection in order to keep him content, inwardly they would despise God for imposing his will on them by threatening them with terrible afflictions and sufferings should they fail to comply with his will in the way he desires and demands.

Both in Deuteronomy and elsewhere in the Hebrew Bible, the people are repeatedly told not only to love God but to fear him as well. In fact, the exhortation to fear God appears much more frequently in the biblical texts than the affirmation that the people are to love him. Like the love of God, the fear of God is generally equated with the careful observance of his commandments. This is evident, for example, in Deut 10:12-13, where Moses tells the people to fear God at the same time that he tells them to love and serve him: "So now, O Israel, what does the LORD your God require of you? Only to fear the LORD your God, to walk in all his ways, to love him, to serve the LORD your God with all your heart and with all your soul, and to keep the commandments of the LORD and his decrees that I am giving you today for your own good."

From the perspective of our contemporary modes of thought, the notion that the people are to obey God out of both love and fear simultaneously seems to represent a contradiction in terms. People who act out of fear of punishment are not acting out of love but under compulsion, since by definition love involves giving of oneself freely and willingly. While people can be compelled or forced to obey, they cannot be compelled or forced to love. For that reason, if they are truly to be motivated to obey God out of love, they cannot be motivated at the same time by fear of punishment, since in that case they would be acting contrary to their own will rather than in conformity with it. Furthermore, because any obedience that arises out of fear of punishment will inevitably be reluctant and half-hearted, those who are motivated by fear to obey God's commandments will not keep them in the way he desires and intends. If they attempt to relate to others in the way that God commands without actually loving them only because they wish to avoid coming under God's wrath and punishments, they will not truly be committed to doing whatever is necessary to promote their well-being in the way that God desires for the good of all. Instead, they will help and serve others as little as possible merely to comply with God's demands and will seek to avoid giving of themselves to others whenever they can do so without provoking God to anger. Because they will constantly wish to rebel against God's commandments, they will lack the inner disposition necessary to observe them in the way God intended.

If God wishes to bring his people to obey his commandments gladly and willingly in a way that will truly promote their well-being, therefore, the only way in which he can accomplish that objective is by convincing them that it is indeed in their best interest to observe those commandments because their observance promotes their well-being in and of itself. As we have noted previously, in order for them to be convinced of this truth, they must first be convinced of two other truths, namely, that the God who has given those commandments is truly committed to their well-being as an end in itself and that he knows better than they do what is best for them. If both of these things are true, then any who truly seek their own best interest and well-being will gladly and willingly submit to the commandments God has given them, because they will believe that nothing could promote their happiness and well-being more than obedience to those commandments. The same belief that God truly loves them and seeks nothing but their well-being will also lead them to trust that when he subjects them to suffering and hardships, he does so because he is attempting to bring them back into obedience to his commandments or to strengthen and confirm that obedience in them for their own good out of care and concern for them. If they regard those sufferings in that way, they will continue to love him wholeheartedly even when they go through painful and difficult times.

Nevertheless, even when they are convinced of God's love for them and that conviction leads them to love him in return, there are a couple of senses in which it can be said that they will also fear him. First, their belief that as their sovereign Lord and creator he not only seeks their well-being but also knows what is best for them will bring them to fear him in the sense of respecting him and submitting to his will, no matter what that will may be. This submission will take both the active form of doing whatever he commands as well as the passive form of accepting willingly and gratefully whatever sufferings he imposes on them for their good. Understood in this manner, fear involves both respecting God's sovereignty as well as acknowledging and accepting his sovereignty over one's life. Rather than defining God's will for themselves, opposing his will when he commands something that they do not understand, or rebelling against his will when he decides to impose some type of suffering on them, those who trust him will submit to his will obediently, confident that in all that he does and commands he is seeking only what is best for them.

This manner of understanding the fear of God runs throughout the biblical texts. When Abraham is about to offer up his son Isaac in obedience to God's command in Genesis 22, for example, the angel of the LORD tells him: "Do not lay your hand on the boy or do anything to him, for now I know that you fear God, since you have not withheld your son, your only son, from me" (v. 12). Nothing in the text indicates that Abraham was acting out of fear of punishment when he showed his willingness to do what God had commanded him. On the contrary, had he felt that God was compelling him through the use of force and threats of punishment to offer up his son, his obedience to God's command would not have provoked in God the favorable reaction that it did. What pleased God was Abraham's willingness to offer up his son freely and voluntarily, moved solely by the same trust in God that had originally led him to obey God by leaving his home for another land. When the angel of the LORD affirms that Abraham has shown that he truly fears God, therefore, the idea is that Abraham's obedience has demonstrated that he fully submits to God in all things and acknowledges God's full sovereignty over his life by doing whatever God tells him and accepting without hesitation whatever comes from his hand.

This same understanding of what it means to fear God is evident in other passages from the Hebrew Bible as well. When the Hebrew midwives are said to have disobeyed the Pharoah's command to kill the firstborn sons of the Israelites because "the midwives feared God" (Exod 1:17, 21), the idea is not that they were afraid that God would punish them if they obeyed the Pharoah but that they chose to submit to the God of Israel as their sovereign rather than the Pharoah. The prophet Samuel's words to the Israelites after God has granted their request for a king reflect the same idea: "If you will fear the LORD and serve him, and listen to his voice and not rebel against the commandment of the LORD, and if both you and the king who reigns over you will follow the LORD your God, it will be well" (1 Sam 12:14). In this passage, for the people to fear God is simply to serve and obey him and do what he commands, that is, to acknowledge his sovereignty over their lives by submitting to him in all things. Nothing in the passage suggests that Samuel is warning them to fear God's punishments. When the book of Job begins by presenting Job as "a blameless and upright man who fears God and turns away from evil" (1:8), the idea is not that he is motivated by fear of God's punishments to do what is good and right and avoid evil but that his faith in God leads him to be committed to living in the way God desires. Throughout the remainder of the book, in fact, Job demonstrates that he is *not* afraid to endure whatever sufferings or punishments come from God's hand, no matter how intense or dreadful they may be, precisely because he is convinced both of God's goodness as well as his sovereign power and wisdom. It is therefore not fear of God's punishment or wrath that leads him to submit to God in all things but rather his faith and trust in God. As in the case of Abraham, ultimately it is this absolute faith and trust in him that pleases God. What God wants is not that people *fear* him in the sense of being afraid of him but that they believe in his love for them and trust in his sovereign power so that they will submit obediently to him in all things, since this will make it possible for him to bless them in the way he desires. It is this that both Abraham and Job are said to discover.

In biblical thought, rather than contradicting the notion that people are to love God, the stress on the need to fear God serves as a necessary complement to that notion. While the people are undoubtedly commanded to love God, this love is not the same as the love they are to have for their neighbors. In part, this is because their neighbors need care, help, and support from others if they are to enjoy well-being, whereas the same cannot rightly be said of God, who stands in need of nothing that human beings might give him. If love is defined as a commitment to the well-being and wholeness of others, then by definition God cannot be the object of love in that sense, since he neither lacks well-being nor depends on human beings to be whole and complete. In addition, however, in biblical thought love for one's neighbors does not involve submitting to them in all things or giving them sovereignty over one's life. God's people are commanded to relate to him alone in that manner. For that reason, while they are to love their neighbors, they are not told to fear them. Instead, they are to fear no one but God in the sense of accepting and acknowledging him as their sovereign.

Furthermore, if left to stand alone, the affirmation that the people are to love God might be understood as implying a relationship between equals. While in biblical thought human beings are to love one another as equals, they cannot and do not relate to God as their equal. On the contrary, if they are to attain the well-being that comes through him alone, they must acknowledge his sovereignty over their life. Only when they submit fully to him can he accomplish his loving purposes in and through them. To use the language of Scripture, then, for people to attain the well-being and wholeness that God desires for them, it is not enough for them to *love* him. They must also *fear* him.

While the people are to fear God in the sense of submitting to him and acknowledging his sovereignty over their life, the biblical texts also speak of God's people fearing him in a second sense. Because the people's obedience and love for God are never perfect, God often finds it necessary to chastise them in order to correct them and bring them back to himself. While these chastisements may be motivated by love, at the same time they are of course painful. For that reason, it is both healthy and inevitable that the people should fear those chastisements and seek to avoid them as much as possible by conforming their lives to God's will. Thus, while they will wish to serve and obey God motivated by love for him, due to their sinful nature at times they will also resist God's will and wish to follow their own will instead. By indicating to them that he will subject them to chastisements when that happens, God's concern for their well-being leads him to seek to dissuade them from following their own will by instilling fear in them. This is analogous to the way in which a mother who loves her young daughter unconditionally will seek to guide her not only by orienting and instructing her but also by threatening her with punishments and when necessary inflicting those punishments on her in order to bring her to behave in ways that are truly conducive to her well-being. While God's people will similarly at times be motivated to obey him out of fear of punishment, they will remain convinced that those punishments are expressions of his love and concern for them. In effect, the purpose of those punishments and the fear that God instills through them is to help the people suppress and overcome as much as possible their tendency to rebel against God and disobey his commands. For that reason, both God and the people themselves will see that fear as a good thing and as an ally against their sinful and rebellious nature, since it helps to control and suppress that nature. Rather than regarding it negatively as something to be avoided, therefore, they will use it to their advantage.

Even when they are motivated to obey God by fear of his chastisements, however, ultimately it is not that fear but their love for God that leads the people to submit to whatever he commands. The reason for this is that deep down they *want* to do God's will due to their conviction that God loves them and knows what is best for them. While their rebellious nature may incite them to oppose God's will, that conviction leads them to battle against that nature and do everything possible to suppress and overcome it. They also implore God's help to accomplish that objective. In the same way that God does, and together with him, they seek to dominate and break their rebellious nature and may even impose chastisements on themselves for that purpose. Although they may fear the chastisements imposed by God, their love for God and their commitment to their own well-being leads them to use that fear constructively to restrain and quell whatever desires they may have to disobey God in the same way that God himself makes use of that fear. In the end, then, it is not fear that compels or forces them to obey God against their will but rather their faith and trust in his love and sovereignty that convinces them that it is truly in their best interest to do whatever he commands.

It can also be said that what motivates God's people to obey him and submit to him is their commitment to their own well-being, that is, their love for themselves. This commitment and love are rooted in God's own commitment to their well-being and his love for them. In fact, God's own commitment to their well-being and his love for them lead him not merely to *ask* or *invite* them to assume that same commitment and love for themselves but also to *demand* that they do so for their own good. Due to his love for them, he refuses to accept and tolerate their failure or refusal to love themselves by acting in ways that truly promote their well-being and wholeness. When they behave in ways that do them harm and as a result he threatens to chastise them, their fear of his chastisements ends up promoting their well-being in and of itself by leading them to turn back to him for their own good. For that reason, they can only regard that fear as something that is healthy and conducive to their well-being rather than something to be avoided as harmful or detrimental to that well-being.

In one sense, therefore, the people have no reason whatsoever to fear a God who is unconditionally committed to seeking their well-being as an end in itself or to fear his chastisements that are an expression of that same commitment. In another sense, however, the painful nature of those chastisements will lead the people to fear them while simultaneously being grateful to God for using those chastisements to correct and guide them and for instilling in them a fear that ultimately promotes their own well-being and happiness. For that reason, even though at times God may attempt to bring his people to obey him by threatening them with chastisements, in the end the way in which he seeks to produce that obedience in them is by convincing them of his love for them and his unbending commitment to their well-being. He also brings them to obey him gladly and willingly by making it clear to them that even when he chastises them, those chastisements are motivated solely by his commitment to their well-being, no matter how painful they may be.

For these same reasons, God's command that the people love him with all of their heart, soul, mind, and strength is not a selfish imposition on his part but an expression of his unconditional love for his people. Because he seeks nothing but their happiness and well-being, his demand that they love and obey him is at the same time a demand that they seek their own happiness and well-being in the same way and to the same extent that he does. In other words, his command for them to *love him* is a command for them to *love themselves and one another as he does.* Conversely, if they fail to love themselves and one another by seeking the well-being of all together with their own, they are not only doing themselves harm but also failing to love God in the way he demands for their own good. If this failure to love God by loving themselves provokes God to wrath, it is only because that wrath is an expression and consequence of his unconditional love for them.

These same ideas must be kept in mind when considering God's command to fear him and to serve him. When he commands the people to fear him, he is demanding that they acknowledge his sovereignty over their lives and submit obediently to his will by assuming the same commitment to their own well-being and that of others that is his own. Should they fail to fear him in that way, they harm no one but themselves and one another. If God threatens to punish them for failing or refusing to fear him, therefore, he does so only because he wishes to bring them to care for themselves and others rather than destroying their own well-being and happiness.

The biblical language concerning the need for the people to serve God must be understood on the basis of these same ideas. Like ancient Greek, biblical Hebrew makes no distinction between a servant and a slave. The verb *'abad* can therefore be translated both in terms of serving someone freely or doing so as their slave. Because in English slavery is invariably seen as oppressive, while the service of others is regarded as something to be valued and praised rather than avoided, English translations of the biblical texts generally prefer to speak of those who serve God as his servants rather than his slaves. There is a sense, however, in which God's people are also to be understood as his slaves. This idea is reflected in passages that speak of Israel as God's possession or as belonging to God as his own.[9] The logic behind these passages is that neither the people's lives nor their bodies and souls belong to them but are to be dedicated solely to serving God as the one who has ownership over every aspect of their existence.

At first glance, such an idea seems extremely problematic. This is especially the case when it is viewed from the perspective of the beliefs of other ancient

---

9. See, for example, Exod 19:5; Deut 4:20; 7:6; 9:26, 29; 14:2.

peoples regarding their gods, such as those reflected in the *Enuma Elish*, where human beings are said to have been created for the sole purpose of serving the gods as their slaves. Gods who demand that human beings serve them by fulfilling all of their desires and demands as their slaves are not acting out of love and concern for them but are instead treating them with cruelty and abuse. If the God of Israel is said to expect and demand that his people relate to him as his slaves, it might appear that he is just as cruel and oppressive as the pagan gods of antiquity, claiming full ownership over people's bodies and souls so as to impose his will on them by force and threatening to punish or even destroy them if they do not submit to him in all things.

Once more, however, it must be stressed that in biblical thought God seeks nothing but the happiness and well-being of all those whom he has created. He has no needs of his own that must be satisfied by human beings, nor does he have any desires related exclusively to himself. The only thing he desires and demands of human beings is that they live in ways that make it possible for them to enjoy the blessings of well-being and wholeness that he wishes for all people without exception. For that reason, just as the command for his people to love him with all their heart, soul, mind, and strength is at the same time a command for them to love *themselves* in that way by being as fully committed to their own well-being as he is, so also his command to serve him is in reality a command for them to dedicate themselves fully to seeking their own well-being and that of others in everything that they do. As they acknowledge God's sovereignty and ownership over themselves, their lives, and their bodies and souls, they commit themselves to doing his will in all things rather than their own. Yet because his will is that they use everything that he has given them in ways that promote life, wholeness, and well-being for all, to serve God as his slaves involves obeying him by seeking only what is truly good for themselves and others. Conversely, to refuse to acknowledge God's sovereignty and ownership over one's life and live as his slave is to disobey him by doing harm to oneself and others and destroying one's own well-being and that of others. In his love, this is something that God cannot accept, overlook, or tolerate, and for that reason he demands that all instead submit obediently to him so as to love and care for themselves and others in the same way that he does, not for *his* sake, but for *theirs*. That same love also leads him to threaten those who refuse to live in that way with punishments that are ultimately intended not to do them harm but to save them from their own destructive behavior.

CHASTISEMENT AND HEALING IN ISRAEL'S NARRATIVE

All of the ideas just considered serve as the basis for the interpretation of Israel's history that appears in the biblical texts. Beginning with the account of the golden calf at the foot of Mount Sinai and the forty years of the Israelites' sojourn in the wilderness, more often than not the people are presented as failing to respond to God's loving initiatives in the way that he hopes and desires. Instead, they disobey him and repeatedly rebel against him. When that happens, God responds by punishing them in various ways and calling them back to himself. According to the narrative, while at times these punishments serve to correct the people for a time, eventually they fall back into sin and God must chastise them once more in an attempt to bring about in them a change that is long-lasting rather than short-lived.

As a result of Israel's persistent disobedience and God's repeated attempts to bring his people back to obedience for their own good, a cycle emerges. When the people fall into sinful and destructive behavior, God initially points out to them their sin and calls them to turn back to him in obedience, generally by means of the prophets he sends them. If the people heed this call and return to God, he forgives them. When they do not, God then begins to inflict punishments on the people in the form of sufferings and afflictions in an attempt to correct them. At times, the people respond in the way God desires and as a result God puts an end to those punishments by delivering them from their plight and granting them his blessings once more. Sooner or later, however, the people fall back into sin and the cycle of punishment, repentance, forgiveness, and deliverance is repeated once more.

Eventually, however, the people fail to respond to the punishments God imposes on them and instead persist in their disobedience. As a result, God increases the intensity and severity of those punishments, yet even then the people generally fail to return to him in the way he desires. In fact, they are often presented as becoming even more stubborn and rebellious so as to sink even further into sin and injustice. They treat the prophets he sends them with scorn and derision and at times even mistreat, persecute, and kill them. When this happens, God is presented as taking measures that become even more drastic. These include sending the people into exile and destroying many of them so as to leave only a remnant. God's hope is that this remnant will finally acknowledge their sin and turn back to him so that he can bless, multiply, and prosper them in the way he desires. All of this is precisely what both Leviticus 26 and Deuteronomy 28–30 describe and anticipate.

The Frustrated Love of a Frustrated God

While the cycle of punishment, repentance, forgiveness, and deliverance can be discerned in numerous passages from the Hebrew Scriptures and Second Temple Jewish writings, nowhere does it appear more clearly than in the first part of the book of Judges. There, after mentioning the death of Joshua, the narrative affirms that the Israelites "did what was evil in the sight of the Lord" by abandoning him in order to worship the Baals and other gods, thus provoking him to anger (Judg 2:11-13). As a result, "he gave them over to plunderers who plundered them, and he sold them into the power of their enemies all around, so that they could no longer withstand their enemies," thereby leaving the people "in great distress" (2:14-15). The narrative then continues:

Then the LORD raised up judges, who delivered them from the hand of those who plundered them. Yet they did not listen even to their judges; for they played the harlot after other gods and bowed down to them. They turned aside quickly from the way in which their ancestors had walked in obeying the commandments of the LORD; they did not follow their example. Whenever the LORD raised up judges for them, the LORD was with the judge, and he delivered them from the hand of their enemies all the days of the judge; for the LORD would be moved to compassion by their groaning because of those who afflicted and oppressed them. But whenever the judge died, they would relapse and behave worse than their ancestors, following other gods, serving them and bowing down to them. They would not abandon any of their practices or their stubborn ways (2:16-19).

It is significant that in this first instance God is said to send judges to deliver the Israelites from their enemies even before the Israelites cry out to God for help. In the following chapters, however, this changes. When the people arouse God's anger by doing what is bad or evil once more and abandoning him for other gods, God responds by subjecting them to the king of Mesopotamia and does not act to deliver them until they cry out to him for help (Judg 3:7-8). After God liberates the people by means of the judge Othniel, the people enjoy peace for forty years (3:9-11). When Othniel dies, however, the people do what is bad or evil in God's sight once again. As a result, God subjects them to the Moabites for eighteen years until they cry out to God and he rescues them from their plight (3:15-30). Immediately the cycle repeats itself and this time the Israelites are oppressed for twenty years until God delivers them by means of Deborah (4:1-16).

When the Israelites subsequently fall into idolatry and destructive behavior once more and God responds by subjecting them to the Midianites, they cry out to God for help again. This time God sends them a prophet, who explains to them clearly why they are being subjected to suffering. The prophet does so, however, by referring first and foremost to the love that God has shown for them: "Thus says the LORD, the God of Israel: I led you up from Egypt, and brought you out of the house of slavery; and I delivered you from the hand of the Egyptians, and from the hand of all who oppressed you. I drove them out before you, and gave you their land, and I said to you, 'I am the LORD your God; you shall not fear the gods of the Amorites, in whose land you live.' But you have not listened to my voice" (Judg 6:8-10). In spite of the people's disobedience, however, ultimately God acts to deliver them from the Midianites by means of Gideon after Gideon destroys the altar dedicated to Baal that is in their midst (6:11–8:28).

Following Gideon's death, the people relapse once more into sin and idolatry and are then oppressed by the Ammonites (Judg 8:33–10:9). This time, however, when they seek God's help, initially he denies it to them:

So the Israelites cried to the LORD, saying, "We have sinned against you, because we have abandoned our God and have served the Baals." And the LORD said to the Israelites, "Did I not deliver you from the Egyptians and from the Amorites, from the Ammonites and from the Philistines? And when the Sidonians, the Amalekites, and the Maonites oppressed you, and you cried out to me, I delivered you out of their hand. Yet you have abandoned me and served other gods; therefore I will deliver you no more. Go and cry out to the gods whom you have chosen; let them deliver you in the time of your distress." And the Israelites said to the LORD, "We have sinned! Do to us whatever seems good to you, but deliver us this day!" So they put away the foreign gods from among them and served the LORD; and he could no longer bear to see Israel's misery (10:10-16).

Finally, God relents and delivers his people from their enemies once more (11:29-33).

The purpose of the sufferings that God is said to send upon the people in these passages is evident. Those sufferings are designed to bring the people back to him in repentance. After the cycle has been repeated several times, however, God is portrayed as growing weary of seeing the same thing happen over and over again. After objecting that the people have refused to heed his voice after he has acted to bless and save them from their plight on multiple occasions, he finally refuses to help them and instead tells them to cry out for help to the other gods that they have chosen to serve. Nevertheless, when the people insist and in effect ask him for one last chance, he decides to help them, moved to compassion at the suffering they are enduring. The idea that it grieves God to have to chastise his people is evident especially in Judg 2:18 and 10:16, where the suffering to which he subjects the people is said to move him to pity and even become unbearable for him. The logic behind these passages, however, is clearly that he has no choice but to inflict sufferings on the people if he wants them to turn away from their disobedience and turn back to him so that they may come to experience the blessings and well-being he desires for them by living in the way he had commanded for their own good.

The same pattern that appears in Judges is evident in the book of Amos as well. Although in most of the first part of the book God reproaches the people of Israel and Judah for their sins, he also reminds them of the fact that it was he who brought them up from Egypt and led them in the wilderness for forty years before giving them the land he had promised them (Amos 2:9-10). When God tells the people of his intentions to punish them, he stresses that he intends to do so precisely because they are his beloved chosen people: "You alone have I known of all the families of the earth; therefore I will punish you for all your iniquities" (3:2). A lengthy passage from the fourth chapter of this book makes it clear that the sufferings that God imposes on the people have the sole purpose of bringing them back to himself in obedience. The passage reflects the same logic that we have seen in Leviticus 26, where God promises to increase the intensity of the punishments he inflicts on his people when the punishments that he has imposed on them previously have not succeeded in bringing them to turn back to him:

> I gave you cleanness of teeth in all your cities, and lack of bread in all your places, yet you did not turn back to me, says the LORD. And I also withheld the rain from you when there were still three months to the harvest. I would send rain on one city, and send no rain on another city. One field would be rained upon, and the field on which it did not rain withered; so two or three towns wandered to one town to drink water and were not satisfied, yet you did not turn back to me, says the LORD. I struck you with blight and mildew. I laid waste to your gardens and your vineyards. The locust devoured your fig trees and your olive trees, yet you did not turn back to me, says the LORD. I sent among you a pestilence after the manner of Egypt. I killed your young men with the sword. I carried away your horses, and I made the stench of your camp go up into your nostrils, yet you did not turn back to me, says the LORD. I overthrew some of you, as when God overthrew Sodom and Gomorrah, and you were like a brand snatched from the fire, yet you did not turn back to me, says the LORD. Therefore thus I will do to you, O Israel; because I will do this to you, prepare to meet your God, O Israel! (Amos 4:6-12).

Here God's frustration is evident. In his love, he has tried everything possible to bring the people back to him, yet nothing he has done has been able to accomplish that objective. He has told them repeatedly: "Seek me and live," yet they have refused to do so (Amos 5:4-6). Therefore, according to the prophet, if God hopes to accomplish his purposes among his people, he must inflict on them an even harsher punishment, namely, that of exile in a foreign land (5:27). Nevertheless, the book ends in the same way that Leviticus 26 and Deuteronomy 28–30 do, with promises regarding Israel's restoration: "I will put an end to the captivity of my people Israel, and they will rebuild the ruined cities and inhabit them. They will plant vineyards and drink their wine, and they will make gardens and eat their fruit. I will plant them upon their land, and they will never again be uprooted from out of the land that I have given them, says the LORD your God" (Amos 9:14-15).

The idea that the sufferings that God inflicts on his people have the purpose of correcting them and bringing them back to himself appears in many other passages from the biblical texts and Second Temple Jewish writings as well. As in the passage from Amos 4:6-12 just cited, the Hebrew text generally uses the language of returning or turning back to God or to his commandments in order to speak of repentance. Numerous passages see such a return as the intended result of the hardships that the people are made to endure as chastisement for their sins. In Deut 4:30, for example, after affirming that God will respond to the sin of his people by sending them into exile, Moses tells them: "In your distress, when all these things have happened to you in the time to come, you will return to the LORD your God and listen to him." Similarly, in the prayer attributed to Solomon at the dedication of the temple in 1 Kings 8, he tells God:

> When your people Israel, having sinned against you, are defeated before an enemy but turn back to you, confess your name, and pray and plead with you in this house, then hear in heaven, forgive the sin of your people Israel, and bring them back again to the land that you gave to their ancestors. When heaven is shut up and there is no rain because they have sinned against you,

and then they pray toward this place, confess your name, and turn away from their sin because you have afflicted them, then hear in heaven, and forgive the sin of your servants, your people Israel, when you teach them the good way in which they should walk; and grant rain on your land that you have given to your people as an inheritance (1 Kgs 8:33-36).

Here God's purpose in subjecting the people to their enemies or to famine is clearly to chastise or discipline them in order to bring them to turn away from their sin and back to him.

The same types of affirmation appear in passages from the books of Israel's prophets. In Hos 3:4-5, the prophet anticipates a period in which the people will be deprived of the leadership and guidance they require: "For the Israelites will remain many days without king or prince, without sacrifice or pillar, without ephod or household idols. Afterward the Israelites will return and seek the LORD their God, and David their king; they will come in awe to the LORD and to his goodness in the latter days." Here, even though the prophet does not say explicitly that the situation he describes is intended to bring them back to God, that idea is clearly assumed. Likewise, a couple of chapters later, the prophet presents God as affirming: "For I will be like a lion to Ephraim, and like a young lion to the house of Judah. I myself will tear them apart and go away. I will carry them off, and no one will rescue them. I will return again to my place until they acknowledge their sinfulness and seek my face. In their distress they will earnestly seek me: 'Come, let us return to the LORD; for it is he who has torn us apart, and he will heal us; he has struck us down, and he will bind us up'" (Hos 5:14–6:1). Further on, the prophet affirms regarding Israel: "Foreigners devour his strength, but he does not know it. Gray hairs are sprinkled upon him, but he does not know it. Israel's arrogance testifies against him; yet they do not turn back to the LORD their God, or seek him, for all this" (Hos 7:9-10). The notion that God imposes sufferings on Israel in order to bring them to turn back to him is clearly reflected in all of these passages. The same relation between punishment and repentance is also assumed in Hag 2:17: "I struck you and all the products of your toil with blight and mildew and hail; yet you did not turn back to me, says the LORD."

Other passages from the prophetic writings stress even more strongly Israel's persistent refusal to respond to the chastisements God sends upon them by turning back to him. In some cases, rather than being corrected by those chastisements, they are said to sink even further into their disobedient and rebellious behavior:

The people did not turn back to him who struck them, or seek the LORD of hosts (Isa 9:13).

O LORD, do your eyes not look for truth? You have struck them, but they felt no anguish; you have consumed them, but they refused to take correction. They have made their faces harder than rock. They have refused to turn back (Jer 5:3; cf. 2:29-30).

You shall say to them: "This is the nation that did not obey the voice of the LORD their God and did not accept correction. Truth has perished; it is cut off from their lips" (Jer 7:28; cf. 32:31-33).

You have despised the rod and all discipline (Ezek 21:10).

Ah, rebellious, polluted, oppressing city! It has listened to no voice; it has accepted no correction. It has not trusted in the LORD; it has not drawn near to its God. . . . I have cut off nations; their fortified towers are in ruins. I have laid waste their streets so that no one walks in them. Their cities have been made desolate, without people and without inhabitants. I said, "Surely the city will fear me, it will accept correction; it will not lose sight of all that I have brought upon it." But they were the more eager to make all their deeds corrupt (Zeph 3:1-2, 6-7).

The word of the LORD came to Zechariah, saying: "Thus says the LORD of hosts: Execute true judgments. Show kindness and compassion to one another. Do not oppress the widow, the orphan, the alien, or the poor; and do not devise evil in your hearts against one another." But they refused to listen, and turned a stubborn shoulder, and stopped their ears in order not to hear. They made their hearts hard in order not to hear the law and the words that the LORD of hosts had sent by his spirit through the former prophets. Therefore great wrath came from the LORD of hosts. Just as they would not listen to me when I called, so would I not listen to them when they called, says the LORD of hosts. And I scattered them with a whirlwind among all the nations that they had not known. Thus the land they left behind was desolate, so that no one went back and forth, and a pleasant land was made desolate (Zech 7:8-13).

These same ideas are mentioned as well in a number of passages from the Psalms that offer summaries of Israel's history. These summaries stress the same points that appear in the passages just considered: God's goodness toward Israel, the sin and rebelliousness of the people in response to that love, God's attempts to bring the people back to himself through punishments, their persistent refusal to respond to those punishments by turning back to God, and ultimately God's promise to bless the people once those punishments have accomplished their purpose.

In Psalm 78, for example, the Psalmist beings by exhorting the people: "Give ear, O my people, to my instruction (*torah*); incline your ears to the words of my mouth" (v. 1). Then, after recalling the wonders that God performed on the people's behalf when he delivered them from their slavery in Egypt and the manner in which he cared for them in the wilderness, the Psalmist continues: "Yet they sinned even more against him, rebelling against the Most High in the desert" (v. 17). What is especially said to have provoked God to anger was that "they did not trust in God, and did not have faith in his power to save" (v. 22). Obviously, if God wanted them to trust in him and his power to save them, it was for *their* sake rather than his own. In spite of these things, God continued to bless them and care for them, yet they continued to rebel against him. This led to the same type of pattern considered above:

When he killed them, they sought for him, and they repented and sought God earnestly. They remembered that God was their rock, the Most High God their Redeemer. But they flattered him with their mouths, and they lied to him with their tongues. Their heart was not steadfast toward him; they were not faithful to his covenant. Yet he, being compassionate, forgave their iniquity, and did not destroy them. Often he restrained his anger and did not stir up all his wrath. He remembered that they were but flesh, a wind that passes and does not come back again. How often they rebelled against him in the wilderness and grieved him in the desert! (Ps 78:34-40).

This passage makes evident God's love for his people. Although here and elsewhere in the Psalm he is presented as punishing them and even killing them, his purpose is clearly to save them and bring them to change their ways for their own good. While at times they appear to do so, in reality that change is only half-hearted and temporary. For that reason, even though he repeatedly forgave them and held back his anger at their sin out of love for them, eventually it became clear that they would continue to rebel, and as a result God had to punish them even more. Nevertheless, due precisely to that love, God explicitly wishes that such punishments had not been necessary. The final phrase of this passage uses the same verbal root found in the prologue of the flood account in Gen 6:5 to speak of God being grieved by his people's sin (Ps 78:40). The remainder of the Psalm stresses the same ideas: God's goodness in saving and guiding his people Israel, their persistent rebelliousness and disobedience, and the punishments that God inflicted on them in an attempt to bring them back to himself.

After reminding the people of the manner in which God delivered his people from their bondage and rescued them when they cried out to him, Psalm 81 presents God as lamenting the fact that the people refused to listen to him and walk in the way he had laid out for them for their own good. At the same time, he laments that he had to abandon them to their own ways and was not able to bless them in the way that he desired:

"Hear, O my people, while I admonish you. O Israel, if you would but listen to me! . . . I am the LORD your God, who brought you up out of the land of Egypt. Open your mouth wide and I will fill it." But my people did not listen to my voice; Israel would not submit to me. So I gave them over to their stubborn hearts, to follow their own counsels. O that my people would listen to me, that Israel would walk in my ways! Then I would quickly subdue their enemies, and turn my hand against their adversaries. . . . I would feed you with the finest of the wheat, and with honey from the rock I would satisfy you (Ps 81:8, 10-14, 16).

God's love for his people in the midst of their stubbornness and disobedience is especially evident here. If he wishes that they would listen to him and obey him, it is clearly not *for his sake* but *for theirs*. He wishes to fill and feed them with good things and to deliver them from their enemies, yet because of their persistent disobedience, to do so would be counterproductive. What prevents him from blessing them in the way he would like is not any lack of love or favor on his part in response to their sinfulness but their refusal to listen to him and walk in the way he has laid out for them for their own good.

The same themes are stressed in the lengthy summary of the biblical narrative regarding Israel that appears in Psalm 106. The Psalm points to the kindnesses that God repeatedly showed to his people, yet also stresses their failure to acknowledge that kindness: "Our ancestors, when they were in Egypt, did not consider your wonderful works. They did not remember the abundance of your steadfast love, but rebelled against the Most High at the Red Sea" (v. 7). In spite of this, God continued to show them his favor by saving and delivering them (vv. 8-11). While initially they responded by believing his words and singing his praises, it was not long before they rebelled against him once more: "But they soon forgot his works; they did not wait for his counsel. . . . They forgot God, their Savior, who had done great things in Egypt" (vv. 12, 21). After God had graciously introduced the people into the land he had promised them, they not only continued to reject and disobey him but even sacrificed their children to demons and polluted the land with blood (vv. 23-39). The Psalm then continues:

> Then the anger of the LORD was kindled against his people, and he abhorred his heritage. He gave them into the hand of the nations, so that those who hated them ruled over them. Their enemies oppressed them, and they were brought into subjection under their hand. Many times he delivered them, but they were rebellious in their purposes and were brought low through their iniquity. Nevertheless, he regarded their distress when he heard their cry. For their sake he remembered his covenant and showed compassion according to the abundance of his steadfast love. He caused them to be pitied by all who held them captive (vv. 40-46).

Here God's ongoing and unconditional love for his people in spite of their persistent sinfulness is evident. While he becomes angry with them and chastises them for their rebelliousness, he does so in order to humble them and bring them low. At the same time, in spite of that rebelliousness, in his steadfast love for them he never forgets them or stops listening to their cries of distress. Only when they continued to rebel against him after he had repeatedly delivered them from their enemies did he hand them over to those who sought to take them captive, yet even then he continued to show them his love and mercy. For that reason, they can trust that ultimately he will save them once more and gather them together from among the nations (v. 47). It is presupposed, of course, that before that day comes they will finally acknowledge both their sin and God's undeserved love and mercy so as to be brought to live in the way he has commanded for their own good.

The idea that God does not take any delight in chastising his people and wishes that he would never have to do so is also repeated in passages from other books of the Hebrew Bible. In the book of Lamentations, which mourns the destruction of Jerusalem by the Babylonians, God is presented as inflicting chastisements against his will: "For the LORD will not cast off forever. Even though he causes grief, he will have compassion according to the abundance of his steadfast love. For he does not willingly afflict or grieve anyone" (Lam 3:31-33). God's pain at having to subject his people to suffering is especially stressed in a passage from Hosea, where he insists that he can scarcely stand to see them suffer the same type of destruction that he brought upon Sodom and Gomorrah, also known as Admah and Zeboiim: "My people are bent on turning away from me. They call out to the Most High, but he does not raise them up at all. How can I give you up, Ephraim? How can I hand you over, O Israel? How can I make you like Admah? How can I treat you like Zeboiim? My heart recoils within me; my compassion grows warm and tender" (Hos 11:7-8). The prophet Ezekiel stresses God's longing for the people to turn back to him instead of continuing down a path that leads to their death and destruction: "Do I take any pleasure in the death of the wicked?, says the Lord GOD. Am I not instead pleased when they turn from their ways and live? . . . Cast away from you all the transgressions that you have committed against me, and get yourselves a new heart and a new spirit! Why will you die, O house of Israel? For I take no pleasure in the death of anyone, says the Lord GOD. So turn, then, and live" (Ezek 18:23, 31-32; cf. 33:11). In Isaiah, God is presented as lamenting that because the people refused to obey him, he was not able to bless them as he yearned to do: "O that you had paid attention to my commandments! Then your well-being would have been like a river, and your righteousness like the waves of the sea. Your offspring would have been like the sand, and your descendants like its grains. Their name would never be cut off or destroyed from before me" (Isa 48:18-19).

Numerous passages from other Jewish writings of the Second Temple period also speak of God subjecting his people to punishments in order to bring them back to himself in obedience. In some cases, these passages use the language of correction, admonition, and discipline explicitly:

> For we are suffering because of our own sins. And if our living Lord is angry for a short while, to rebuke and discipline us, he will again be reconciled with his servants (2 Macc 7:32-34).

> When they had done this, they bowed to the ground and implored the Lord that they might never again fall into such misfortunes, but that, if they should ever sin again, they might be disciplined by him with forbearance and not be handed over to blasphemous and barbarous nations (2 Macc 10:4).

> As long as they did not sin against their God they prospered, for the God who hates iniquity is with them. But when they departed from the way he had laid out for them, they were utterly defeated in many battles and were led away captive to a foreign land. The temple of their God was razed to the ground, and their towns were occupied by their enemies. But now they have returned to their God, and have come back from the places where they had been scattered, and have occupied Jerusalem, where their sanctuary is, and have settled in the hill country, because it was uninhabited (Jdt 5:17-19).

For he has not tested us with fire, as he did them, to search their hearts, nor has he taken vengeance on us; but the Lord scourges those who are close to him in order to chastise them (Jdt 8:27).

For when they were tested, though they were being disciplined in mercy, they learned how the ungodly were tormented when judged in wrath. For you tested them as a parent does to admonish them, but you probed and condemned the ungodly as a stern king (Wis 11:9-10; cf. 12:20-22; Tob 13:1-9).

Yet you have dealt with us, O Lord our God, in all your forbearance and in accordance with all your great compassion, just as you spoke by your servant Moses on the day when you commanded him to write your law in the presence of the people of Israel, saying, "If you will not listen to my voice, this very great multitude will surely turn into a small number among the nations, where I will scatter them. For I know that they will not listen to me, for they are a stiff-necked people. But in the land of their exile they will have a change of heart and know that I am the Lord their God. I will give them a heart that obeys and ears that hear. They will praise me in the land of their exile and will remember my name and turn from their stubbornness and their wicked deeds. For they will remember the ways of their ancestors, who sinned before the Lord. I will bring them again into the land that I swore to give to their ancestors, to Abraham, Isaac, and Jacob, and they will rule over it; and I will increase them, and they will not be diminished. I will make an everlasting covenant with them to be their God, and they will be my people; and I will never again remove my people Israel from the land that I have given them" (Bar 2:27-35).

Salvaging a Righteous Remnant through Destruction

The idea that the persistent refusal of his people to abandon their violent and destructive ways leaves God no choice but to destroy many of them in an attempt to purify a remnant that will finally obey him by living in justice and righteousness appears repeatedly in the Hebrew Bible. This idea is especially stressed in a passage from 2 Kings 17, which narrates the fall of the northern kingdom of Israel under the Assyrians. While the passage particularly stresses the people's worship of gods other than the God of Israel, it also makes clear the manner in which the worship of those gods leads to the practice of violence, injustice, and evil by bringing the people to abandon God's good commandments:

These things took place because the people of Israel had sinned against the LORD their God, who had brought them up out of the land of Egypt from under the hand of Pharaoh king of Egypt. They had worshiped other gods and walked in the customs of the nations whom the LORD had driven out from before the people of Israel, and in the customs that the kings of Israel had introduced. The people of Israel did things in secret that were not right against the LORD their God. They built for themselves high places in all their towns, from watchtower to fortified city. They set up for themselves pillars and sacred poles on every high hill and under every green tree. There they burned incense on all the high places, as the nations whom the LORD carried away had done before them. They did wicked things that provoked the Lord to anger. They served idols, of which the Lord had said to them, "You must not do this."

Yet the Lord warned Israel and Judah by every prophet and every seer, saying, "Turn from your evil ways and keep my commandments and my statutes, in accordance with all the law that I commanded your ancestors and that I sent to you by my servants the prophets." But they would not listen and stiffened their neck like their ancestors, who did not believe in the Lord their God. They rejected his statutes and his covenant that he had made with their ancestors, and the warnings that he had given them. They went after false idols and became false. They followed the nations that were around them, concerning whom the Lord had commanded them that they should not do as they did. They abandoned all the commandments of the Lord their God and made for themselves cast images of two calves. They made a sacred pole, worshiped all the host of heaven, and served Baal. They made their sons and their daughters pass through fire. They used divination and augury, and they sold themselves to do evil in the sight of the Lord, provoking him to anger. Therefore the Lord was very angry with Israel and removed them out of his sight; none was left but the tribe of Judah alone (vv. 7-18).

Here God is presented as doing everything possible by means of his prophets to bring the people of the northern kingdom of Israel to turn back from their wicked ways. Instead of listening to those prophets, however, they become even more stubborn. Finally, God loses hope that he can ever bring them back to himself and his commandments and acts to destroy them.

Yet this does not mean that God gives up on his plan to bring into existence a righteous people who will do his will. According to the interpretation of Israel's history running throughout the biblical texts, the destruction of the northern kingdom was in large part aimed at bringing the southern kingdom of Judah to turn back to God in obedience. The hope was that when they saw what God had done to their sisters and brothers in the north as a result of their refusal to practice justice and righteousness by obeying his commandments, the people of Judah would realize that if they did not mend their ways they would be forced to endure the same type of destruction.

Both the historical narrative and the prophetic writings, however, present the people of the southern kingdom not only refusing to turn back from their sinful ways following the destruction of the northern kingdom but also falling even more deeply into injustice, idolatry, and destructive behavior. While occasionally they heed the voice of God's prophets and turn back to God and his commandments for a time, this change is only superficial and short-lived. They continue to worship and invoke God with their prayers and offerings, yet God rejects their worship and prayers not only because they worship other gods alongside of him but also because they actively oppose what God has commanded by oppressing the poor, practicing violence and bloodshed, and remaining mired in other forms of sin and evil.

Eventually, God is said to become weary of the people's persistent sinfulness and failure to repent, tired of holding back his anger only to see the evils continue (Isa 1:14; Jer 6:11; 15:5-7). He no longer wishes to receive their worship and sacrifices and refuses to listen to their prayers and petitions for forgiveness, since these things are expressions of a repentance that is insincere, half-hearted, and short-lived. He even tells his prophets not to intercede for the people.[10] The reason for this, however, is not that he no longer loves and cares for his people but that his love for them can no longer tolerate the harm that they insist on doing to themselves and others as well. Their evil becomes so great that the only hope for them to change is through a thorough and deep-seated cleansing that will involve destroying a large part of the people in the hope that from that destruction a righteous remnant can finally be brought into existence. Only in this way can he hope to bring about a change in their behavior that will be long-lasting rather than temporary.

While these ideas are reflected in many passages in the prophetic writings, they are especially evident in a passage from the prophet Isaiah that has often troubled biblical interpreters. This passage is Isa 6:8-13, in which Isaiah volunteers to go and speak to God's people after receiving a vision in which God appears to him on his throne, surrounded by heavenly beings called seraphim. In his response to Isaiah, rather than expressing his desire that the people repent, God indicates that he does not want the people to respond favorably to Isaiah's message but to reject it so that he may punish them:

> Then I heard the voice of the LORD saying, "Whom shall I send, and who will go for us?" And I said, "Here am I; send me!" And he said, "Go and tell this people: 'Keep on listening, but do not comprehend; keep on looking, but do not understand.' Make the mind of this people fat, and make their ears heavy, and shut their eyes, so that they may not see with their eyes, and hear with their ears, and understand with their minds, and turn and be healed." Then I said, "How long, O LORD?" And he said: "Until cities lie devastated and without inhabitant, and houses without people, and the land is utterly desolate; until the LORD sends the people far away, and the emptiness in the midst of the land is vast. And when a tenth part remains in it, it will be burned again, like a terebinth or an oak whose stump remains standing when it is felled." The holy seed is its stump.

God's response to Isaiah seems problematic for a couple of reasons. First, it seems to indicate that he no longer loves or cares for the people but simply wishes to destroy them, since he does not want them to be brought to see, hear, or understand Isaiah's message. Second, it is not clear why he should send Isaiah to speak to the people if he does not want them to comprehend what Isaiah will proclaim to them. If that is the case, why send Isaiah at all? Why not simply proceed to take action against the people and send them into exile? It might even seem that God wishes to justify the destruction he intends to bring upon them by being able to claim that he sent his messenger but the people refused to respond favorably to that messenger and therefore deserved to be punished. If it is God who prevents them from understanding Isaiah's message, however, it does not seem fair or right that God might

---

10. On this ideas, see Isa 1:10-15; Jer 7:16-20; 11:14; 14:11-12; Ezek 14:12-20.

subsequently blame the people for having rejected it and on that basis claim that he was right to punish and destroy them.

Such an interpretation of the passage fails to understand it in the context of the narrative regarding Israel that it presupposes, and especially the cycle of sin, punishment, repentance, and forgiveness that we have noted above. In the past, God has repeatedly sent his prophets to call the people to turn back to him, and while at times the people have done so, their return to him and his commandments has been half-hearted at best and in each instance has lasted only for a brief time. For that reason, God has grown weary of the cycle, since the type of profound, long-lasting change that he has sought to bring about in them has not taken place. Therefore, if he simply sends Isaiah one more time and the people respond positively to his message, only to fall back into their sinful and destructive behavior once again shortly thereafter, he will find it necessary to delay once more the type of deep-seated and thoroughgoing cleansing that he desires to carry out for the good of the people themselves.

For that reason, God does not want the people to respond favorably to Isaiah's message. Instead, what he wants is to bring about the purified remnant or "holy seed" represented by the stump mentioned at the end of the passage. In order to do so, it will be necessary for him to inflict on them a great deal of destruction and devastation, yet from God's perspective it is the only way to bring into existence the type of sanctified, obedient remnant that he wishes to see. Nothing less will be able to accomplish that objective on a long-lasting and permanent basis.

In order to achieve that remnant, however, following the destruction that God will send on the people it will be necessary for those who remain to know that God was the one who sent that destruction upon them and that he had a good purpose for doing so. For that reason, he must send Isaiah. Isaiah will proclaim a message that is aimed not at those who hear it in his own time but rather at those who will recall it *after* God has carried out the destruction described in the passage. If God were not to have told the people ahead of time what he was going to do and why he was going to do it, they might doubt that God had been behind those events and perhaps believe that the gods of their enemies had proven more powerful than the God of Israel. In addition to doubting his sovereignty, they might also question his love for them if they were not aware that he had allowed such destruction to take place for the purpose of cleansing them from their sinful and destructive behavior. Rather than being aimed at justifying God's actions to the people, therefore, the message that Isaiah is sent to speak ahead of time will make it clear to the survivors of that destruction that God's purpose was to bring about in them the type of purification and cleansing that would finally enable them to enjoy his blessings on a long-term basis.

This idea of purification appears in various forms in several of the other prophetic books as well. In Jer 15:7, the punishments imposed by God are compared to the process of winnowing, which is designed to separate the grain of wheat from the chaff: "I will winnow them with a winnowing fork in the gates of the land. I will bereave and destroy my people, since they did not turn from their ways." Although this passage speaks of God destroying his people, it is clearly referring only to a portion of the people, since otherwise the imagery of winnowing would not make sense.

Another common image is that of purifying the people in the way that metals are refined. This imagery appears in a passage from Zechariah, which presents the destruction imposed by God on his people as having the purpose of purifying them: "In the whole land, says the LORD, two-thirds shall be cut off and perish, but one-third shall be left alive. And I will put this third part into the fire to refine them as one refines silver, and to test them as gold is tested. They will call on my name, and I will answer them. I will say, 'They are my people'; and they will say, 'The LORD is our God'" (Zech 13:8-9). Similarly, in Isa 1:25, God tells the sinful people: "I will turn my hand against you; I will smelt away your dross as with lye and remove all your alloy." The prophet Ezekiel compares the punishments that God intends to impose on the people out of anger at their sins to the way in which precious metals are purified by being melted in a smelter (Ezek 22:17-22). Ezekiel also uses the imagery of removing rust from a pot after placing it on the fire: "Stand it empty upon the coals, so that it may become hot, and its copper may glow, and its filth may be melted in it, and its rust be consumed. In vain I have wearied myself; its thick rust does not depart. To the fire with its rust! Now your filthiness is lewdness. Because I tried to cleanse you but you would not be cleansed from your filthiness, you will not be clean again until I have satisfied my wrath against you" (Ezek 24:11-13). The prophet Malachi speaks of God refining people through his messenger in the same way that gold and silver are purified, yet he also adds the imagery of fullers' soap, which was used to wash cloth or clothing (Mal 3:2-3).

Ultimately, after the people of Judah refuse to turn away from their sinful ways despite God's repeated call for them to do so, God is presented as taking the drastic action of destroying Jerusalem and his temple and sending many of the people into exile under the Babylonians or Chaldeans. The biblical narrative once again presents God as having no choice but to inflict such devastation on the people due to their stubborn resistance to his attempts to correct them and bring them back to himself:

> The LORD, the God of their ancestors, sent persistently to them by his mes-sengers, because he had compassion on his people and on his dwelling place; but they kept mocking the messengers of God, despising his words, and scoff-ing at his prophets, until the wrath of the LORD against his people became so great that there was no remedy. Therefore he brought against them the king of the Chaldeans, who killed their young men with the sword in the house of their sanctuary, and had no compassion on young man or young woman, the aged or the infirm; he gave them all into his hand (2 Chr 36:15-17).

A passage from the book of Nehemiah summarizes well this interpretation of the history of God's people. According to this passage, while for a time the chastisements that God imposed on his people when they disobeyed him accomplished their objective to some degree, eventually the people's sin became so great and persistent that they no longer responded to God's calls for them to repent. God therefore had no choice but to punish them with the exile if he wished to bring about a remnant that would finally live in accordance with his commandments for their own good:

> Yet they were disobedient and rebelled against you and cast your law behind their backs and killed your prophets, who had admonished them in order to turn them back to you; and they committed great blasphemies. Therefore you gave them over into the hands of their enemies, who oppressed them. But when they cried out to you in the time of their distress, you heard them from heaven, and according to your great compassion you gave them deliverers who saved them from the hands of their enemies. But as soon as they had rest, they again did evil before you, and you abandoned them into the hands of their enemies, so that they ruled over them. Yet when they turned and cried out to you again, you heard from heaven, and many times you rescued them according to your compassion. And you admonished them in order to turn them back to your law. Yet they acted arrogantly and did not obey your commandments, but sinned against your ordinances, by the observance of which a person shall live. They turned a stubborn shoulder and stiffened their neck and would not obey. Many years you remained patient with them, and admonished them by your spirit through your prophets; yet they refused to listen. Therefore you gave them over into the hands of the peoples of the lands. Nevertheless, in your great compassion you did not make an end of them or abandon them, for you are a gracious and merciful God (Neh 9:26-31).

A number of passages from the prophetic writings state clearly the idea that the purpose for which God punished his people with exile was precisely to bring about a remnant that would finally practice the justice and righteousness God desired to see in them for their own good. Their exile is therefore understood as the means by which God intended to bring about a cleansing or purification of the people from their sinful ways:

> Whoever is left in Zion and remains in Jerusalem will be called holy, everyone who has been recorded for life in Jerusalem, when the LORD will have washed away the filth of the daughters of Zion and purged the bloodshed of Jerusalem from its midst by a spirit of judgment and by a spirit of burning (Isa 4:3-4).

> And they shall bear their punishment. . . so that the house of Israel may no longer go astray from me, nor pollute themselves any more with all their transgressions. Then they will be my people, and I will be their God, says the Lord GOD (Ezek 14:10-11).

> On that day you will not be put to shame because of all the deeds by which you have rebelled against me; for then I will remove from your midst your arrogant, exultant ones, and you will never again be haughty in my holy mountain. For I will leave in the midst of you a humble and lowly people. The remnant of Israel

will seek refuge in the name of the LORD; they will do no wrong and speak no lies, nor will a deceitful tongue be found in their mouths (Zeph 3:11-13).

These passages and others in the biblical texts express the hope that after the extremely harsh and painful chastisements to which God subjects the people, at least some of them will finally be brought to live in accordance with his commandments for their own good. For that reason, even though it grieves God greatly to see his people suffer, those chastisements are the only means by which he can bring them to follow the way of life that will finally allow them to enjoy the blessings he longs to pour out on them. For that reason, no matter how stubborn and hard-hearted his people may be, he will not relent in his efforts to heal and save them from their sinful ways until those efforts finally meet with success.

CHAPTER 6

THE WRATH OF A GOD BURNING TO SAVE

For most peoples in antiquity, the greatest obstacle to human well-being was the wrath of the gods. When they became angry at human beings, the gods made their lives unbearable by subjecting them to things such as plagues, famines, natural disasters, oppression by enemies, and other forms of death and destruction. What made the relation with the gods even more difficult was that they tended to be volatile and capricious. At any moment, often for no good or apparent reason, they might become enraged and take out their wrath on those who had done something to provoke it. If people wanted to live in peace, avoid suffering as much as possible, and either enjoy life or at least make it tolerable, keeping the gods happy and satisfied had to be their top priority.

Although at times the gods might inflict punishments on those who angered and offended them in order to compel them to alter the behavior that displeased them and make it clear to them and others that they would not tolerate such behavior, in many cases what moved them to lash out at human beings was not any particular purpose or objective that they wished to accomplish but simply their instincts and passions. When provoked to wrath, what the gods often sought was simply to vent that wrath by taking it out on human beings and exacting revenge on any who had dared to oppose them. They might even take pleasure at seeing the pain and suffering of those who had disobeyed or disrespected them and seek to make that suffering as intense and prolonged as possible. In these cases, they were simply acting out of spite, hatred, and vengeance. In fact, they might inflict suffering on people not because those people had done anything to offend or anger them but simply because for some reason they disliked and rejected those people.

For the most part, the way in which people sought to keep the gods content, avoid their wrath, and placate that wrath when it had been aroused was by presenting them with sacrificial offerings and the expressions of worship, reverence, and submission that were to accompany those offerings. As we have noted previously in this study, gods such as those described by Homer in the *Iliad* and the *Odyssey* were thought to desire these offerings and the honor and praise that went along with them for their own sake. In fact, what often provoked their wrath the most was not any type of sin or wrongdoing but simply the failure to present to them the offerings that they regarded as their due. Of course, since the gods were often capricious and behaved in ways that were unpredictable, one could never know if they would receive favorably the offerings and worship presented to them so as to afford the offerers their protection and blessings and grant them their petitions. The best that the offerers could do was to make their offerings as lavish and abundant as possible and if necessary find other means to attract the attention of the gods and obtain their favor.

According to many interpretations of the Hebrew Bible, the God of Israel was thought to behave in most of these same ways and to desire many of the same things. He too lashed out at those who dared to disobey and oppose him and inflicted punishments on them not only to compel them to submit to him but also at times simply to satisfy his rage and vent his wrath. He might even take delight at inflicting pain and suffering on those who had offended him and exacting vengeance on them. If people wished to enjoy his favor, avoid his wrath, and placate that wrath when it had been aroused, they needed to do whatever he commanded and make atonement for any sins they committed by means of sacrificial offerings, including especially those that involved the shedding of blood. While it was generally God's strict justice rather than simply passion or spite that was thought to lead God to demand that human sin be punished in the way it deserved, the satisfaction of that justice through punishment was just as essential to Israel's God as the satisfaction of the desires for vengeance and retribution was to the gods of the nations.

Some biblical interpreters, in fact, have no qualms about ascribing to the God of the Hebrew Scriptures the same type of passions and uncontrollable rage that was believed to characterize the pagan gods of antiquity. As we have seen in Chapter 1 of this study, for example, Walter Brueggemann finds in the biblical texts a God "who takes with savage seriousness Yahweh's right to be worshiped, honored, and obeyed."[1] For Brueggemann, the biblical texts speak of a God who stands over human beings as a "hovering danger" and may choose to vent his rage and fury with "savage propensity" at any moment.[2] What characterizes the God of Israel is his "strong emotional response to any affront against Yahweh's prerogative, privilege, ascendancy, or sovereignty."[3] In a passage we have seen previously, Brueggemann paints a picture of Yahweh that could just as easily apply to gods such as Marduk or Zeus:

> In the indignation and emotion that guard Yahweh's peculiar claim to honor, Yahweh is uncompromising. Yahweh acts in fury and rage, sometimes destructively.... This aspect of the character of Yahweh admits of no taming or minimalization. It witnesses to Yahweh at the extremes of love and anger. The extremity of Yahweh's passion will be turned against any who affront Yahweh, and Yahweh will act without restraint or discipline.[4]

Although there can be no doubt that the God of the Hebrew Bible is at times portrayed as an angry, jealous, and vindictive God, the question that must

---

1. Walter Brueggemann, *Theology of the Old Testament: Testament, Dispute, Advocacy* (Minneapolis: Fortress, 2005), 272.

2. Brueggemann, *Theology*, 280, 293, 296.

3. Brueggemann, *Theology*, 293.

4. Brueggemann, *Theology*, 293-94.

be addressed is whether such a portrayal is grounded in an understanding of God that was essentially the same as that which was characteristic of the pagan belief systems of antiquity. To answer that question, it is necessary to address another, namely, the motives that are said to arouse his wrath and indignation.

THE GOD WHO SEEKS NOTHING BUT JUSTICE

If the God of the Hebrew Scriptures was believed to act in the same ways and desire the same things that the gods of the other nations of antiquity did, then we should expect those Scriptures to speak of him being pleased or provoked to anger by the same things that pleased and angered other gods. When we take a close look at those Scriptures, however, what we find is a God who is very different from those gods in that regard. Not only do the biblical texts present Israel's God as being pleased or alternatively provoked to anger by things that most of the gods of antiquity cared little about, but they also portray the God of Israel ascribing virtually no importance to the things that were said to please other gods or provoke them to anger.

As we have seen in the previous three chapters, throughout the biblical texts the condition that is consistently laid down for obtaining God's blessings and avoiding his anger is the practice of justice and righteousness, that is, the commitment to seeking the well-being of others together with one's own. Those who share that commitment and act in accordance with it are presented as pleasing God, whereas those who do not are said to arouse his displeasure.

At the same time, however, the biblical texts present God commanding that his people offer sacrifices to him and usually being pleased when they do so. In this regard, he may seem to be no different than the pagan gods of antiquity. If such were the case, then those who sought to obtain blessings, favors, and assistance from him would do what virtually all people in antiquity did when they sought those things from their own gods. They would offer him sacrifices that were as lavish and abundant as possible with the hope that, by doing so, they would attract his attention and win his approval. Yet this is precisely what those who seek blessings, help, and support from Israel's God in the biblical texts do *not* do. In fact, rather than obtaining his favor, those who seek to influence or manipulate him by offering him sacrifices and gifts are thought to provoke him to wrath. In effect, they are attempting to bribe him or purchase his favor. As we have seen previously, such a *do ut des* mentality must be considered foreign to the understanding of the God of Israel that runs throughout the biblical texts.

Deserving Help That Is Undeserved

Of all the books in the Hebrew Bible, none presents human beings invoking God's protection, help, and deliverance more than the book of Psalms. If we wish to discern the basis upon which those who approached the God of Israel petitioned him to grant them such things, therefore, there is no better place in the Hebrew Bible to look. One will search in vain there for passages in which those who ask God for assistance or deliverance offer to present him with lavish sacrifices in exchange for his help or point to their faithfulness in having offered up such sacrifices in the past in the way that figures such as those in Homer's *Iliad* and *Odyssey* are said to do. The fact that the Psalmists are not presented as approaching God in that manner demonstrates not only that the God of Israel was not thought to respond to petitions for help and deliverance that were made on that basis but also that those who worshiped him *knew perfectly well* that one did not obtain his blessings, support, and assistance by offering him gifts and sacrifices in exchange for those things. This point is particularly significant in light of the widespread use of the Psalms among Jews in the Second Temple period. Like the Psalmists themselves, those Jews were fully aware that one could not obtain what one wanted from Israel's God simply by presenting him with sacrifices or offering to do so. Instead, it was plain to all that the condition upon which God came to one's aid was one's commitment to justice and righteousness, that is, the same commitment that was God's own out of love for all.

Well over a third of the 150 Psalms in the Hebrew Bible contain pleas on the part of the Psalmist for God's help in the context of a situation in which the Psalmist is experiencing some type of suffering or hardship. Many of these Psalms and others also describe the manner in which God has graciously and mercifully acted to save and deliver those in need of such help in the past. While the Psalmists often promise to praise and thank God and offer him sacrifices *in response* to the favor he has shown them, at no point do they promise to give God something that he seeks or desires for himself *in exchange* for his assistance or claim to have obtained help from God on the basis of such an exchange. Instead, the basis upon which God is consistently presented as coming to the aid of those in need is his grace and mercy as well as his justice, that is, his commitment to seeking the well-being of all of his people. In most cases, in fact, that commitment is the *only* basis upon which the Psalmists ask God to intervene on their behalf. Because they know him to be a God who is loving, caring, and compassionate and who defends what is good, right, and just, they appeal to these qualities when imploring his assistance, especially when their sufferings are the result of injustices that others are committing against them. If those who seek God's help do not offer him anything in exchange for that help, it is because they know and are fully confident that *God's primary concern is not anything that he seeks for himself but simply their own happiness, wholeness, and well-being.* For that reason, it would be not only futile but also senseless for them to offer God something in exchange for his assistance. If God values their well-being above all else as an end in itself, what need is there to attempt to sway him to be concerned for something that already *is* his primary concern?

At the same time, it is significant that the Psalmists do not seek from the God of Israel many of the things that those who worshiped gods such as

Marduk and Zeus in antiquity sought from those gods. When the Psalmists pray to God, they do not ask for things such as wealth, power, fame, glory, and dominion over others. Such things are expressions of selfishness rather than a commitment to the well-being of all. Therefore, to seek them from a God who despises selfishness would not only be senseless but also provoke his anger. Because he sees into human hearts, he knows when those who approach him for help do so with selfish motives, and when they do so he will reject them and the petitions they make.

While in principle it would not be selfish for the Psalmists to seek from God blessings such as good health, long life, many descendants, and other forms of prosperity, not only for themselves but for others as well, it is note-worthy that only rarely do they ask God to grant them such blessings. There are two reasons for this. First, in the Torah and by means of his prophets, God has already made known to his people his desire and commitment to do what-ever is necessary on his part for such blessings to be theirs. There is no point in asking God for things that he is already fully committed to giving them out of love for them. And second, in the Torah God has made it abundantly clear to his people what they need to do in order to be able to enjoy those blessings, namely, live in accordance with his good and life-giving command-ments. Those commandments promote the people's well-being and prosper-ity because these things follow naturally from the observance of those com-mandments as their intrinsic consequence. Precisely because their well-being is dependent on their living in accordance with those commandments, the people know that God can and will bless them only when they obey what he has commanded for their own good. For these reasons, the Psalmists generally feel no need to ask God to grant them his blessings, since they know that due to his unconditional love for them he is already fully committed to enabling them to attain those blessings and has indicated to them what they must do in order for those blessings to be theirs.

When the Psalmists invoke God, therefore, they generally do not seek some type of material blessing for themselves but instead ask him to deliver them from a situation in which they are suffering and in need of help. In most cases, the Psalmists have not done anything to deserve the difficulties or plight in which they find themselves. Often they are suffering and in need of help only because evildoers seek to do them harm and oppress them. On occasion, it is God who is allowing or causing them to suffer, yet when this is the case, it is because God is seeking to correct and discipline them for their own good or attempting to accomplish some other loving purpose in relation to them, such as teaching them to trust more fully in him when they experi-ence difficulties in their life. In any case, when they find themselves in such situations, all that the Psalmists can do is to entrust themselves to God and ask him to do whatever he determines to be best for them.

Even when the Psalmists are not aware of having done anything to deserve the sufferings or hardships they are enduring, they never insist that God is under some type of obligation to come to their aid. While they may point to their own justice and righteousness as evidence of their conformity with God's will, they do not claim that their practice of justice and righteousness gives them the right to demand that God help them or provides them with a basis for maintaining that if God does not give them the assistance they need he has done them an injustice. Nor do they insist that God has bound himself to some type of covenant or agreement that places him under obligation to respond to their obedience to his commandments by granting them his help. In part, the reason for this is that their obedience to God's commandments and conformity to his will are always imperfect, since no human being is capable of living without sin or conforming fully to God's will. However, the Psalmists also know that whatever help and assistance they receive from God is always an expression of his love, grace, and mercy rather than something they deserve or merit. In addition, they know that God's love, grace, and mercy at times take the form of subjecting them to correction and discipline rather than delivering them from their suffering. Therefore, if in his love and his sovereignty God has decided not to put an end to their sufferings or save them from their plight, they can only trust that he is acting for their good and accept whatever comes from his hand.

Because they believe that God is good, kind, and merciful and comes to the aid of those who are suffering not because they deserve his help but only because he cares for them, when the Psalmists seek his help they generally appeal only to his grace, love, and compassion toward those in need. Due to his reputation as a God who is concerned especially for the poor, downtrodden, weak, and oppressed, they know that he comes to the aid of those who have nothing to offer him rather than those who are able to give him something in exchange for his help. For that reason, the basis upon which they present to him their petitions for help is often not anything they have done or any quality or virtue of their own but simply his loving concern for those who suffer and are in need:

> Rise up, O Lord! O God, lift up your hand! Do not forget the oppressed. Why do the wicked revile God and say in their hearts, "You will not call us to account"? But you do see! Indeed, you take note of trouble and grief, that you may take it into your hands. The helpless commit themselves to you; you are the helper of orphans. Break the arm of the wicked and evildoers; seek out their wickedness until you find none. The Lord is king forever and ever; the nations will perish from his land. O Lord, you will hear the desire of the meek; you will strengthen their heart. You will incline your ear to do justice for the orphan and the oppressed, so that those of the earth may no longer strike terror (Ps 10:12-18).

> Rouse yourself! Why do you sleep, O Lord? Awake, do not cast us off forever! Why do you hide your face and forget our affliction and oppression? For our souls have sunk down into the dust; our bodies cling to the ground. Rise up, come to our help! Redeem us for the sake of your steadfast love! (Ps 44:23-26)

Give ear to my prayer, O God; do not hide yourself from my supplication. Attend to me and answer me; I am restless in my complaint. I am distraught by the voice of the enemy, because of the oppression of the wicked. For they bring down trouble upon me, and in anger they assail me (Ps 55:1-3).

But as for me, my prayer is to you, O Lord. At an acceptable time, O God, in the abundance of your steadfast love, answer me in your saving faithfulness. Rescue me from sinking in the mire; let me be delivered from those who hate me and from the deep waters. Do not let the floodwaters sweep me away, or the depths swallow me up, or the Pit close its mouth over me. Answer me, Lord, for your steadfast love is good; according to the greatness of your compassion, turn to me! Do not hide your face from your servant, for I am in distress; answer me quickly! Draw near to my soul and redeem it; rescue me because of my enemies! (Ps 69:13-18)

O God, the insolent rise up against me. A band of ruthless people seeks my life, and they do not set you before them. But you, O Lord, are a God of compassion and grace, slow to anger and abounding in steadfast love and faithfulness. Turn to me and be gracious to me. Give your strength to your servant, and save the son of your maidservant. Show me a sign of your favor, so that those who hate me may see it and be put to shame, because you, Lord, have helped me and comforted me (Ps 86:14-17).

But you, O Lord my Lord, act on my behalf for your name's sake; because your steadfast love is good, deliver me. For I am poor and needy, and my heart is wounded within me. I am fading like a shadow at evening; I am shaken off like a locust. My knees are weak from fasting; my body has become gaunt. I am an object of derision for my accusers; when they see me, they wag their heads. Help me, O Lord my God! Save me according to your steadfast love.... With my mouth I will give great thanks to the Lord; I will praise him in the midst of the multitude. For he stands at the right hand of the needy, to save them from those who would condemn them to death (Ps 109:21-26, 30-31).

To you I lift up my eyes, O you who are enthroned in the heavens! As the eyes of servants look to the hand of their master, as the eyes of a maidservant look to the hand of her mistress, so our eyes look to the Lord our God, until he has mercy upon us. Have mercy upon us, O Lord, have mercy upon us, for we have endured no end of contempt. Our soul has had more than its fill of the scorn of those who are at ease, of the contempt of the arrogant (Ps 123:1-4; cf. Ps 71:1-13; 142:1-7).

In Psalms such as these, the only reason that those who need help are said to hope for and expect such help from God is that they are suffering and in great need. On that basis alone, they appeal to God's grace, compassion, kindness, and steadfast love, since they know him to be a God who cares deeply for those who suffer.

There are, however, other Psalms in which those who ask God for help point out to him that they have been committed to living in conformity with his will by practicing justice, righteousness, and kindness toward others and by avoiding any type of sin or wrongdoing. At times, they also mention that they have sided with those in need in the same way that he does:

Hear a just cause, O L{\scriptsize ORD}. Attend to my cry; give ear to my prayer from lips free of deceit. Let my deliverance come from you; let your eyes discern what is right. If you try my heart, if you visit me by night, if you test me, you will find no wickedness in me; my mouth does not transgress. As for the works of others, by the instruction of your lips I have avoided the ways of the violent. My steps have kept to your paths; my feet have not slipped. I call upon you, for you will answer me, O God. Incline your ear to me; hear my words (Ps 17:1-6).

He reached down from on high; he took hold of me. He drew me out of mighty waters. He delivered me from my powerful enemy, and from those who hated me, for they were too mighty for me. They came up against me in the day of my calamity, but the L{\scriptsize ORD} was my support. He brought me out into a safe place; he delivered me because he was pleased with me. The L{\scriptsize ORD} rewarded me according to my righteousness; according to the cleanness of my hands he recompensed me. For I have followed the ways of the L{\scriptsize ORD} and have not wickedly departed from my God. For all his precepts were before me, and I did not put his statutes away from me. I was blameless before him, and I kept myself from wrongdoing. Therefore the L{\scriptsize ORD} has recompensed me according to my righteousness, according to the cleanness of my hands in his sight. With the merciful you show yourself to be merciful; with the blameless you show yourself to be blameless; with the pure you show yourself to be pure; but with the crooked you show yourself to be astute. For you deliver those who are humble, but the haughty eyes you bring down (Ps 18:16-27).

Mark those who are blameless and look upon those who are upright, for there is a future for those who are peaceable. But wrongdoers will be completely destroyed; the posterity of the wicked will be cut off. The salvation of the righteous is from the L{\scriptsize ORD}; he is their stronghold in the time of trouble. The L{\scriptsize ORD} helps them and rescues them; he delivers them from the wicked and saves them because they take refuge in him (Ps 37:37-40).

Come and hear, all you who fear God, and I will tell you what he has done for me. I cried out to him, and he was extolled with my tongue. If I had contemplated iniquity in my heart, the L{\scriptsize ORD} would not have listened. But truly God has listened; he has heard the words of my prayer. Blessed be God, who has not rejected my prayer or removed his steadfast love from me (Ps 66:16-20).

Save me, O L{\scriptsize ORD}, from my enemies; I have fled to you for refuge. Teach me to do your will, for you are my God. Let your good spirit lead me on a level path. For your name's sake, O L{\scriptsize ORD}, preserve my life. In your righteousness bring me out of trouble. In your steadfast love cut off my enemies, and destroy all my adversaries, for I am your servant (Ps 143:9-12).[5]

Among many interpreters, it is common to understand these Psalms in the sense that the Psalmists are claiming that their behavior has earned them the right to be saved by God, as if God were under obligation to help them because they had obeyed him by practicing the justice and righteousness that he asks for and demands. In that case, the basis for their petition for God's

---

5. The idea that God comes to the aid of those who refrain from wrongdoing and are committed to serving God by practicing justice and righteousness is found throughout other Psalms as well. See, for example, Ps 4:3; 7:1-11; 16:1-4; 34:15-17.

assistance would not be that he is gracious, kind, and compassionate to those who are in need but that they have given him the obedience he demands for his own sake and therefore should be rewarded for that obedience by receiving from him in exchange what they seek for their own sake. In other words, the logic would be that of *do ut des*: those who give God what he wants are entitled to receive from him what they want, since they have fulfilled their obligation to him and thus he must now fulfill his obligation to them as well. Such an interpretation of these passages would place God on the same level as the gods of the nations, who granted their favors to those who did what they desired and avoided actions that displeased them. The only difference would be that the demands made by the God of Israel in the biblical texts have to do with practicing justice and righteousness rather than simply satisfying the type of selfish desire that was thought to characterize the pagan gods of antiquity. Yet what would lead the God of Israel to seek and demand the practice of justice and righteousness would be a need or desire to satisfy the demands of his own nature rather than a concern for human well-being as an end in itself.

If this were the logic behind the Psalmists' allusions to their own righteousness when they implore God's help, then it would follow that the reason that they had been dedicated to obeying what God commanded was to be able to obtain his favor and have a basis for asking him to grant what they requested from him, or even for demanding that he do so. In that case, their practice of justice and righteousness would be motivated, not by a genuine concern for the well-being of others, but by a desire to obtain for themselves what they wanted from God. They would therefore have been acting primarily out of self-interest when they obeyed God and their behavior would be self-serving, even when they helped others, since such help would not be grounded in a genuine concern for others but rather in a desire to have a basis for making some demand upon God or convincing him to grant the petitions they presented to him.

The only way in which such behavior would be pleasing to God is if God himself were also self-serving and concerned only for his own self-interests. He would grant the requests of those who approached him with petitions in exchange for receiving from them what he sought for himself, such as their praise and recognition. The problem with such an interpretation of these passages from the Psalms would be that God would be demanding that people practice justice and righteousness for the sole reason that such conduct is pleasing to him. If he were genuinely concerned for those in need, however, he would want human beings such as the Psalmists also to be genuinely concerned for those in need rather than simply showing concern for them in order to obtain from him his blessings and favor for themselves. If they were not genuinely concerned for others, then once they had received the help they requested from God they might no longer see any reason to continue to show concern for those in need. Their practice of justice and righteousness might also be half-hearted or less committed due to the fact that it was not entirely genuine and might tend to be opportunistic as well. A God who was genuinely concerned for those in need would also want human beings to share that concern genuinely rather than simply assisting others motivated by self-interest.

Furthermore, if what interested God was receiving praise, honor, and worship from human beings and having his name extolled by them for his own sake rather than the practice of justice and righteousness, then instead of pointing to their justice and righteousness when seeking God's help and favor, the Psalmists would point to the praise and honor they had rendered to him. This is not what we find in the Psalms, however. Just as the Psalmists do not offer to present sacrifices to God in exchange for his favors and blessings or ask God to grant their petitions on the basis of the sacrifices they have offered, neither do they ever point to the praise, honor, and worship they have offered him as a basis for imploring him to grant what they asked of him. As noted briefly above, while the Psalmists frequently offer God these things *in response* to his blessings and salvation, they do not view them as *a condition* that he has laid down in order to bless and save people.

For these reasons, when the Psalmists who seek God's help and deliverance appeal to their own justice or righteousness, the logic underlying that appeal should be understood differently. Rather than attempting to manipulate God or claim that their conduct places him under obligation to respond favorably to their petitions, their purpose is to make it clear to God that they are fully committed to the same thing that he is, namely, seeking wholeheartedly the well-being of others, including especially those in need. That is what it means to practice justice and righteousness. The idea is that if God truly cares about these things and is deeply committed to them, he should come to the aid of human beings who care about them as well and share his same commitment. By helping those who are dedicated to practicing justice and promoting equity by serving those in need, God will not only show compassion to them but will also make it possible for them to continue to be involved in serving those in need. Thus his salvation of those who are dedicated to seeking the wholeness and well-being of others will serve as a means to that same end.

Confessing Sin to Seek Salvation

As we have seen in Chapter 4 of this study, in a number of passages from the Psalms, the Psalmists ask God to judge them. Many translations such as the RSV, the NRSVue, the NIV, the NASB, and the ESV use the language of vindication rather than judgment in order to present the Psalmists asking God to vindicate them. While the Psalmists' petition that God judge them undoubtedly involves asking God to vindicate them or save them from the hands of those who wrongly seek to do them harm, it also conveys the idea that God should look into their heart and evaluate their conduct to see whether they are truly committed to practicing justice and righteousness in accordance with his will:

Judge/vindicate me, O LORD, for I have walked in my integrity, and I have trusted in the LORD without wavering. Examine me, O LORD, and try me; test my heart and mind. For your steadfast love is before my eyes, and I walk in faithfulness to you. I do not sit with the worthless, nor do I consort with hypocrites. I hate the company of evildoers and will not sit with the wicked. I wash my hands in innocence and go around your altar, O LORD, singing aloud a song of thanksgiving and recounting all your wondrous deeds. O LORD, I love the house in which you dwell and the place where your glory abides. Do not sweep me away with sinners, nor destroy my life with the bloodthirsty, those in whose hands are evil devices and whose right hand is full of bribes. But as for me, I walk in my integrity; redeem me and be gracious to me. My foot stands on level ground; in the great congregation I will bless the LORD (Ps 26:1-12).

O Lord, do not be far from me! Wake up! Rouse yourself for my defense, for my cause, my God and my Lord! Judge/vindicate me, O LORD, my God, according to your righteousness, and do not let them rejoice over me (Ps 35:22-24).

Judge/vindicate me, O God, and defend my cause against an ungodly people; from those who are deceitful and unjust, deliver me! (Ps 43:1)

Search me, O God, and know my heart; test me and know my thoughts. See if there is any wicked way in me, and lead me in the way everlasting (Ps 139:23-24).

When the Psalmists ask God to judge or vindicate them, this petition should be understood once more in the sense that they are committed to seeking the well-being of all through the practice of justice and righteousness in the same way that God is. For that reason, they trust that if God examines their heart and conduct, he will see for himself that they seek the same things that he does out of love for others. While in a sense it can be said that they are deserving of God's help, this is not due to any merit of their own, since it is their own experience of God's love and grace that has led them to seek the well-being of all in the same way that God does.

At the same time, the Psalmists implicitly recognize that if God examines their heart and conduct, he may determine that they are not as fully dedicated to justice, righteousness, and mercy as they should be or believe themselves to be. In that case, they are also acknowledging that God may be subjecting them to suffering for the purpose of disciplining and correcting them. If so, then God is acting justly and they will accept the suffering they are enduring, since it is aimed at their own good and is therefore an expression of God's love for them. That suffering is therefore serving the purpose of promoting justice by helping to shape them into people who are more deeply committed to practicing it. In that case, they show their commitment to God's will by submitting obediently to God's discipline without rebelling against him.

These ideas are reflected in a number of passages in which the Psalmists openly acknowledge their sins and recognize that at times they have not been fully obedient to God's will. Curiously, in these passages, the Psalmists who seek God's help appeal not to their justice or righteousness but to their past sinfulness as well as their repentance from that sinfulness and their desire that God help them mend their ways:

> Make your ways known to me, O Lord; teach me your paths. Lead me in your truth and teach me, for you are the God of my salvation; for you I wait all day long. Be mindful of your compassion, O Lord, and of your steadfast love, for they have been from of old. Do not remember the sins of my youth or my transgressions; according to your steadfast love remember me, for the sake of your goodness, O Lord! The Lord is good and upright; therefore he instructs sinners in the way. He leads the humble in what is right and teaches the humble his way. All the paths of the Lord are steadfast love and faithfulness for those who keep his covenant and his decrees. For your name's sake, O Lord, pardon my wrongdoing, for it is great. Who are they who fear the Lord? He will teach them the way that they should choose. . . . Turn to me and be gracious to me, for I am lonely and afflicted. Relieve the anguish of my heart, and bring me out of my distress. Look upon my affliction and my trouble, and forgive all my sins (Ps 25:4-12, 16-18).

> Happy are those whose transgression is forgiven, whose sin is covered. Happy are those to whom the Lord does not reckon any wrongdoing and in whose spirit there is no deceit. While I kept silent, my body wasted away through my groaning all day long. For day and night your hand was heavy upon me; my strength was exhausted as by the heat of summer. Then I acknowledged my sin to you, and I did not hide my wrongdoing. I said, "I will confess my transgressions to the Lord," and you forgave the iniquity of my sin. Therefore let all who live in steadfast love offer prayer to you; in a time of distress, the rush of mighty waters will not reach them. You are my hiding place. You protect me from trouble; you surround me with glad cries of deliverance (Ps 32:1-7).

> Save me, O God, for the waters have come up to my neck. I am sinking in deep mire, where there is no foothold; I have come into deep waters, and the floodwaters engulf me. I am worn out from my crying; my throat is parched. My eyes grow dim with waiting for my God. Those who hate me without a cause are more than the hairs of my head; my persecutors who seek to destroy me with lies are mighty. Must I now restore what I did not steal? O God, you know my folly; the wrongs I have done are not hidden from you (Ps 69:1-5).

> Do not hold against us the iniquities of our ancestors; let your compassion come speedily to meet us, for we have been brought very low. Help us, O God of our salvation, for the glory of your name. Deliver us and forgive us our sins, for your name's sake (Ps 79:8-9).[6]

According to a *do ut des* mentality, it would be counterproductive for those who have sinned against God to acknowledge their sin when imploring his help and deliverance. Rather than convincing God that he should give them what they seek because they have given him what he wants for his own sake, their recognition of their sins would provide God with a basis for *denying* them what they seek, since it would demonstrate that they have *not* in fact given him what he wants by acting in conformity with his will. As we have

---

6. For other passages in which the Psalmists acknowledge their sinfulness when asking God for help, see Ps 38:4, 18; 51:1-9; 130:1-8.

seen in Chapter 4, this is the logic that is found in the Negative Confession of the Egyptian Book of the Dead, where those who appear before Osiris in order to be judged by him and gain his approval insist that they are innocent of any wrongdoing or injustice. Were they to confess to having sinned, they would be condemned by him and denied entry into the afterlife they seek rather than obtaining his favor.

Because in biblical thought what God seeks is the practice of what is just, kind, right, and compassionate for the good of all, however, the Psalmists' recognition of their failure to practice these things can also serve as a basis for their petition for God's help. The reason for this is that the acknowledgment of their sins conveys implicitly the idea that they are committed to living in the way God asks and demands for their own good and that of others. Were they not committed to living in that manner, they would deny their sins rather than confessing them in order to claim that their perfect obedience to God's will merits God's intervention on their behalf. Rather than leading God to help and save them, such an attitude would result in God's rejection of their petition and perhaps even provoke him to wrath, since no human being obeys him perfectly. Those who claim to be perfect in their obedience actually do others harm and displease God because they justify, overlook, and cover up their injustices rather than acknowledging them and seeking to correct them.

For that reason, what God demands from his people is not perfect obedience itself but rather a *commitment* to obeying him by practicing justice, kindness, compassion, and righteousness. Rather than claiming to be perfect and blameless in the practice of these things, his people should acknowledge their wrongdoing and ask God continually for his help, instruction, and guidance in order to be able to live out that commitment in the way that both they and God desire for the good of all. The petition for this instruction and guidance appears explicitly in Psalm 25, the first of the Psalms just quoted, as well as others in which the Psalmists ask for deliverance:

> Make your ways known to me, O Lord; teach me your paths. Lead me in your truth and teach me, for you are the God of my salvation. . . . The Lord is good and upright; therefore he instructs sinners in the way. He leads the humble in what is right and teaches the humble his way (Ps 25:4-5, 8-9).

> Teach me your way, O Lord, and lead me on a level path because of my enemies. Do not give me up to the will of my adversaries, for false witnesses have risen up against me, and they are breathing out violence (Ps 27:11-12).

> Answer me quickly, O Lord; my spirit fails. Do not hide your face from me, or I will be like those who go down to the Pit. Let me hear of your steadfast love in the morning, for in you I put my trust. Teach me the way in which I should walk, for to you I lift up my soul. Save me, O Lord, from my enemies; I have fled to you for protection. Teach me to do your will, for you are my God. Let your good spirit lead me on a level path (Ps 143:7-10).

The recognition of their sinfulness when invoking God for help and deliverance leads the Psalmists not only to ask him to guide and instruct them so that they may put away that sinfulness but also to subject themselves to whatever forms of suffering and chastisements he determines to be necessary in order to discipline, correct, and purify them for their own good. If they were not fully committed to living in accordance with God's will, they would rebel against any type of discipline and correction that God imposed on them and thus merit his reproach rather than his approval. For that reason, their petition for God's help may be accompanied not only by a request that God give them the strength to put away sin and evil but also by an expression of their willingness to be subjected to sufferings that are aimed at chastising and correcting them, even when God makes use of evildoers to inflict these sufferings on them:

> I call upon you, O LORD; come quickly to me! Give ear to my voice when I call to you! Let my prayer be counted as incense before you and the lifting up of my hands as an evening sacrifice. Set a guard over my mouth, O LORD; keep watch over the door of my lips. Do not let my heart be inclined to any evil, to take part in wicked deeds in company with those who work iniquity; do not let me eat of their delicacies. Let the righteous reprove me; it will be a kindness. Let the faithful correct me; it will be oil for my head, and let my head not refuse it, for my prayer will still be against the deeds of evildoers (Ps 141:1–5).

At the same time, by confessing their sins and accepting willingly the sufferings through which God seeks to correct and purify them, the Psalmists also communicate to God that those sufferings have accomplished their purpose, since they have now acknowledged their sin and are seeking to turn away from it. For that reason, their confession of their sins and their recognition that God was acting in accordance with love and justice in chastising them can serve as a basis for their petition to be delivered from those sufferings. The idea is that, now that God's purposes in them have been accomplished, God may act to save them from the sufferings they are enduring. Nevertheless, precisely because they acknowledge their sinfulness and their need for correction, they do not *demand* that God deliver them from their plight, since in his love God may determine that they still need further chastisements and correction. Their conformity with his will therefore leads them to accept as good, right, just, and loving whatever he determines, whether this be deliverance or further sufferings. It is this type of attitude that pleases God, since it demonstrates that they are truly conforming to his will, no matter what the cost for them may be.

In passing, it is worth noting that one would hardly expect to find such ideas in the writings of peoples of other nations that serve gods who are fundamentally distinct from Israel's God. For the most part, those who worship such gods would not ask to be subjected to suffering or any kind of trial or hardship as a means of discipline or correction, since like those gods themselves, they are concerned purely for themselves. What they seek is not to grow in the practice of what is good, right, compassionate, and just, but only to see their own desires and self-interests fulfilled. At times they may be willing to endure great hardships in order to accomplish that end and perhaps even accept sufferings imposed on them by the gods in order to test them, yet even in those cases they are motivated by a concern for themselves rather than for others. The same is true when they wound or lacerate themselves in order to gain the attention of the gods or manifest their earnest devotion to them. In those cases, their purpose is not to show that they are committed to practicing what is good and right but simply to demonstrate that they are willing to go to any extreme necessary to obtain what they seek from the gods.

The Gratitude Born out of Goodness

In many of the Psalms, the Psalmists affirm that they will give God thanks, sing his praises, proclaim his goodness to others, and offer him sacrifices when he comes to their aid. As we have already noted above, however, they do not promise these things *in exchange* for his help, as if they were operating according to the principle of *do ut des*. Rather, they merely affirm that they will do these things *as a result* of the help that he has given them when they were in need:

> The LORD is a stronghold for the oppressed, a stronghold in times of trouble. And those who know your name put their trust in you, O LORD, for you have not forsaken those who seek you. Sing praises to the LORD, who dwells in Zion! Declare his deeds among the peoples! For he who takes action against those who shed blood is mindful of them; he does not forget the cry of the afflicted. Be gracious to me, O LORD. See what I suffer at the hands of those who hate me. You are the one who lifts me up from the gates of death, so that I may recount all your praises and rejoice in your deliverance in the gates of daughter Zion (Ps 9:9-14).

> In God, whose word I praise, in the LORD, whose word I praise, in God I trust; I am not afraid. What can a mere mortal do to me? I have made vows to you, O God; I will render thank offerings to you. For you have delivered my soul from death and my feet from stumbling, so that I may walk before God in the light of life (Ps 56:10-13).

> They set a net for my feet; my soul was bowed down. They dug a pit in my path, but they have fallen into it themselves. My heart is steadfast, O God; my heart is steadfast. I will sing and make melody. Awake, my soul! Awake, O harp and lyre! I will awake the dawn. I will give thanks to you, O LORD, among the peoples; I will sing praises to you among the nations. For your steadfast love is as high as the heavens; your faithfulness extends to the clouds (Ps 57:6-10).

> Bless our God, O peoples! Let the sound of his praise be heard, who has kept us among the living and has not allowed our feet to slip! For you, O God, have tested us; you have refined us as silver is refined. You brought us to be trapped in the net; you laid an oppressive burden on our backs. You let people ride over our heads; we went through fire and through water, yet you have brought us out to a place of safety. I will come into your house with burnt offerings. I will fulfill my vows to you, those that my lips uttered and my mouth promised when I was in trouble. I will offer to you burnt offerings of fatted calves, with the smoke of the sacrifice of rams; I will make an offering of bulls and goats (Ps 66:8-15).

I will praise the name of God with a song; I will magnify him with thanks-giving. This will please the LORD more than an ox or a bull with horns and hoofs. Let the oppressed see it and be glad; you who seek God, let your hearts revive. For the LORD hears the needy and does not despise his own who are in bondage (Ps 69:30-33).

My mouth will tell of your righteous acts, of your deeds of salvation all day long, though their number is beyond my knowledge. I will come praising the mighty deeds of the Lord GOD; I will extol your righteousness, which is yours alone. O God, you have taught me from my youth, and I continue to proclaim your wondrous deeds. And even when I am old and gray, O God, do not for-sake me, until I declare your might to all the generations to come. Your power and your righteousness, O God, reach up to the high heavens. You who have done great things, O God, who is like you? You who have made me see many troubles and calamities will revive me again. You will bring me back to life again, up from the depths of the earth. You will increase my honor and sur-round me in comfort. I will also praise you with the harp for your faithfulness, O my God; I will sing praises to you with the lyre, O Holy One of Israel. My lips will shout for joy when I sing praises to you; my soul also, which you have rescued. All day long my tongue will speak of your righteous help, for those who tried to do me harm have been put to shame and disgraced (Ps 71:15-24).

Gracious is the LORD and righteous; our God is merciful. The LORD protects the simple. When I was brought low, he saved me. Return to your rest, O my soul, for the LORD has dealt bountifully with you. For you have rescued my soul from death, my eyes from tears, and my feet from stumbling. I will walk before the LORD in the land of the living. I kept my faith, even when I said, "I am greatly afflicted"; I said in my consternation, "Everyone is a liar." What shall I give back to the LORD for all his benefits toward me? I will lift up the cup of salvation and call on the name of the LORD; I will fulfill my vows to the LORD in the presence of all his people. Precious in the sight of the LORD is the death of his faithful ones. O LORD, I am your servant; I am your servant, the child of your handmaid. You have loosed my bonds. I will offer to you a sacrifice of thanksgiving and call on the name of the LORD. I will fulfill my vows to the LORD in the presence of all his people, in the courts of the house of the LORD, in your midst, O Jerusalem. Praise the LORD! (Ps 116:5-19)

In Psalms such as these, those who vow to sing God's praises and subse-quently fulfill those vows are responding to the kindnesses he has shown them with gratitude. There is no hint of the idea that they are offering God their praise and worship in exchange for his help, nor is God presented as helping them because they will offer him praises and sacrifices in return. In fact, those who are said to receive his help are those in need who have little if anything to offer God. Because of this, even if they do offer him sacrifices after receiving his help, in most cases those sacrifices will not be very lavish or abundant. Yet this does not matter to God, since his concern is not to receive sacrifices but to deliver those who require his assistance.

Furthermore, the reason why the Psalmists offer God their praise, thanks-giving, and sacrifices is that they wish to let others know that he is a good and faithful God who cares for those who are suffering and in need. By proclaiming the manner in which God has helped them, they encourage those who are in a situation in which they are being oppressed or are in need to call out to God and receive from him the help they require, not because they deserve such help but simply because God cares for the weak, lowly, and downtrodden. In other words, the Psalmists wish to make it known to other people, including those of other nations, that the God of Israel acts with justice, kindness, faithfulness, and steadfast love so that they too may draw near to him and experience his goodness and salvation. This pleases God greatly, not because he seeks worship, praise, and offerings for his own sake, but because he wants people everywhere to be brought to know him and live in accordance with his will so that in that way they may attain the well-being he desires for all out of love for them.

Those who sing God's praises and express their heartfelt gratitude toward him also grow in their love for him as they do so, while at the same time drawing others to live in that same love and be strengthened in it. The greater their love for God and their commitment to living in accordance with his will, the more they will be dedicated to serving him by seeking the well-being of others together with their own. In biblical thought, therefore, if God is content to receive expressions of praise, love, and dedication from those who have received his help, it is not because he desires these things for his own sake but because they are means by which people are brought to submit more fully to the way of life that he wants to see in all for their own good. Once more, the idea reflected in these Psalms is that God wants people to obey him, not for *his* sake, but for *theirs*.

A GOD WHO SEEKS SACRIFICE WHILE SPURNING IT

Just as the only thing that can truly please the God of the Hebrew Bible is the practice of justice, righteousness, love, and compassion, so also the only thing that arouses his wrath and displeasure is the persistent refusal of human beings to practice these things. In this regard as well, he is fundamentally different from other gods in antiquity, who were generally thought to become angry at human beings not for refusing to care for one another and do what is right and good but for failing to present them with the offerings and worship they desired for their own sake.

Desiring Sacrifice from Those Who Refuse to Give It

One will search the Hebrew Scriptures in vain for passages in which the God of Israel is presented as becoming angry at human beings for the sole reason that they have failed to offer him gifts and sacrifices. Only a few passages from those Scriptures, in fact, even seem to suggest such an idea. A close look at them, however, reveals a logic that is distinct.

In Isa 43:18-25, God is presented as telling his people:

Do not bring to mind the former things, or consider the things of old. Behold, I am about to do something new; now it springs forth, do you not perceive it? I will open up a way in the wilderness and make rivers in the desert. The wild animals will honor me, the jackals and the ostriches; for I give water in the wilderness, rivers in the desert, to give drink to my chosen people, the people whom I formed for myself. They will declare my praise. Yet you did not call upon me, O Jacob; but you have been weary of me, O Israel! You have not brought me your sheep for burnt offerings, or honored me with your sacrifices. I have not burdened you by demanding offerings, or wearied you by demanding frankincense. You have not bought me sweet cane with money, or satiated me with the fat of your sacrifices. But you have burdened me with your sins; you have wearied me with your iniquities. I, even I, am the one who blots out your transgressions for my own sake, and I will not remember your sins. Present an accusation against me, let us go to trial; set forth your case in an attempt to be proved right. Your first ancestor sinned, and your leaders transgressed against me. Therefore I profaned the princes of the sanctuary; I delivered Jacob to utter destruction, and Israel to reviling.

Here God is presented as expressing his displeasure that his people did not offer him sacrifices and honor him with their precious gifts, yet the tone and context of the passage make it clear that it is not the lack of offerings in itself that displeases God. Instead, what has exasperated him are the people's sins and iniquities. In fact, while pointing out that they have not given him sacrificial offerings, at the same time he tells them that he did not burden or weary them with the obligation of making such offerings. In that case, what he was seeking from his people was not that they offer him sacrifices but that they respond to the love he had shown for them by loving him in the same way. That love for him would have taken the form of living in the way he had commanded for their own good. Instead of acknowledging his goodness, however, they had grown weary of him and had dedicated themselves to sin and iniquity, living and acting in ways that did them harm rather than good. Even though they had burdened and wearied God in this way, out of love for them he still expresses his intention to put their sins in the past and blot them out from his sight. Yet because his love for them would not allow him to remain passive and do nothing as they followed down the destructive path they had chosen for themselves, he had subjected them to the suffering and destruction that they had endured at the hands of foreign nations. His purpose had been to cleanse and purify them of their sinfulness and bring about in them a way of life that would truly be in their own interest.

The logic behind this passage, therefore, is not that the people provoked God to wrath by not giving him the sacrificial offerings that were due to him as their sovereign, as if what interested God were those offerings themselves. Instead, the failure of the people to offer God sacrificial gifts was merely a *symptom* of a much greater problem, namely, the people's persistent sinfulness as well as their failure to respond to God's love by dedicating themselves to living in the way he had commanded for their own good. God expected that the people would respond to the love and favor he had shown them by voluntarily making offerings to thank and praise him and also by living in accordance with his will, yet the people wanted nothing to do with God and refused to live as he had commanded out of love for them. Rather than presenting a God who is angered by the lack of sacrificial offerings, the passage conveys the idea of a God who is saddened and grieved at the failure of the people to respond to his love in the way he desired so that he might accomplish his good purposes among them.

While the passage also mentions God's desire to receive honor and praise from his people, this idea must be seen in the context of the logic of the passage as a whole. In the verses immediately preceding those that are cited here, God speaks of his deep love for the people and tells them that he will never abandon them but will remain with them always: "Do not fear, for I have redeemed you; I have called you by name. You are mine. . . . Because you are precious in my sight and honored and I love you, I give people in return for you, nations in exchange for your life" (Isa 43:1-4). In the verses that follow, God also expresses his desire that the people serve as witnesses of his love, goodness, and saving power to other nations and peoples, apparently so that those peoples will be drawn to him in order to find in him the salvation he desires for all of his creatures (43:8-13).

In this context, God is presented as referring to "everyone who is called by my name, and whom I have created for my glory, whom I have formed and made" (Isa 43:7). A similar affirmation appears in v. 21 of the same chapter, where God speaks of "the people whom I formed for myself; they will declare my praise." Many English translations such as the RSV, the NRSVue, the NIV, and the ESV use a purpose clause in this verse to present God as referring to "the people whom I formed for myself that they might declare my praise," yet this involves reading back into the verse the idea that God's purpose in forming the people for himself was that they might sing his praises. Such an idea is not made explicit, however, in the Hebrew text, where no such purpose clause appears. In any case, these two verses from Isaiah 43 are often used as a basis for justifying the notion that what motivated God to create human beings and choose Israel as his people was the desire to be praised and glorified, as if this constituted his objective or goal and were an end in itself.

In light of what we have seen above, however, there is no reason to read such an idea back into the text. Both v. 7 and v. 21 of Isaiah 43 are clearly referring to Israel, as the opening verse of that chapter makes clear: "But now thus says the LORD, he who created you, O Jacob, he who formed you, O Israel" (v. 1). As a number of the Psalms considered above indicate, and as we shall see in greater detail in Chapter 10 of this study, one of God's primary objectives in choosing Israel as his people was that of drawing the other nations to himself. This idea is present in vv. 9-12 of this same chapter of Isaiah, which present Israel serving as God's witnesses to other nations and peoples. This suggests that, while God undoubtedly formed and chose Israel to live as a people who would serve him and sing his glory and praises, his purpose was to draw other nations and peoples to himself by means of the praise, glory, and worship that Israel would give to him.

In that case, God's objective is not to be praised and glorified as an end in itself but to make known to other nations and peoples through Israel his steadfast love, mercy, power, goodness, and grace. At the same time, while in biblical thought God certainly wishes to be praised, worshiped, honored, and glorified by the human beings he has created, he ultimately wants these things not for *his* sake but *for theirs*, since as they express to him their love they will be brought to grow in that love so as to grow as well in their commitment to living in the way he has commanded for the good of all. These things are therefore *means* rather than an end in themselves. Just as it might be said that God formed and chose Israel to *obey* him, not because he wanted that obedience as an end in itself but rather because he desired it for the good of all, so also can it be said that God created Israel and other nations to praise and glorify him so that as they do so they may dedicate themselves not only to him but also to the way of life that will allow them to experience the blessings of wholeness and well-being that all those who serve him and one another attain.

Instead of conveying the idea of a self-serving God who wishes to receive praise, honor, and sacrificial offerings for his own sake, therefore, this passage from Isaiah 43 once again presents a God who loves his people and desires their well-being as an end in itself. While he certainly wishes to receive praise, honor, gifts, and offerings from them, ultimately he desires these things not for his own sake but for the sake of his people Israel and for the sake of other peoples whom he wishes to bless and save through Israel as well.

Ideas based on a similar logic appear in the first chapter of Malachi. There, after stating explicitly his love for his people and referring to himself as their father (Mal 1:2), God is presented as telling them:

> A son honors his father, and servants honor their master. If then I am a father, where is the honor due to me? And if I am a master, where is the respect due to me?, says the LORD of hosts to you, O priests, who despise my name. You say, "How have we despised your name?" By offering polluted food on my altar. And you say, "How have we polluted it?" By thinking that the LORD's table may be treated with contempt. When you offer blind animals in sacrifice, is that not wrong? And when you offer those that are lame or sick, is that not wrong? Try presenting such offerings to your governor; will he be pleased with you or show you favor?, says the LORD of hosts. And now will you entreat God's favor, that he may be gracious to us? With such an offering on your part, will he show favor to any of you?, says the LORD of hosts. Oh, that someone among you would shut the temple doors, so that you would not kindle fire on my altar in vain!
>
> I have no pleasure in you, and I will not accept an offering from your hands. For from the rising of the sun to its setting my name is great among the nations, and in every place incense is offered to my name, and a pure offering; for my name is great among the nations, says the LORD of hosts. But you profane it when you say that the table of the LORD is polluted, and that the

food for it may be despised. "What a weariness this is," you say, and you sniff at me, says the LORD of hosts. You bring what has been taken by violence or is lame or sick, and this you bring as your offering! Shall I accept that from your hand?, says the LORD. Cursed be the deceiver who has a male in the flock and vows to give it, and yet sacrifices to the LORD what is blemished; for I am a great King, says the LORD of hosts, and my name is revered among the nations (1:6-14).

Like the passage from Isaiah 43, this passage from Malachi presents God as expressing his displeasure at the people's failure to honor and respect him, as well as the disdain they have shown for him. Rather than bringing him gifts that are expressions of sincere love for him, they have offered up animals that are blind, lame, and sick, that is, offerings that are of no real value. The people's disdain for God and their weariness at serving him is manifested not only in the defective quality of their offerings but also in their reluctance to bring him any offerings at all. In addition, rather than giving him of what is their own, the offerings they present to him are the fruit of what they have violently stolen from others. At the same time that they offer these defective and stolen gifts to God, they hypocritically implore him to bless them and show them his favor. For all of these reasons, God refuses to accept what they offer or respond favorably to their prayers.

Once more, however, the logic that we find here is that God loves his people and wishes to bless them, yet rather than responding to his love with a love of their own, they show him disdain and contempt. What God desires, therefore, is not sacrificial offerings themselves or expressions of praise and respect for his own sake. Rather, for their own good, he wants to see his people live in the same type of love that he has shown them, since only by doing so will they experience the well-being he desires for them. Furthermore, the repeated affirmations that his name is great and reverenced among the nations and the allusions to the pure offerings and incense presented to him elsewhere indicate once more that he is concerned not only for Israel but for the other nations whom he loves as well. Those affirmations and allusions serve to contrast the lack of love for him among his own people with the love and gratitude shown for him among the nations.

The same ideas appear in the following chapters of Malachi. God expresses his displeasure at the sacrificial worship being offered him, both because it is insincere and hypocritical and because those who are involved in that worship are engaged in violence, injustice, and oppression (Mal 2:1-16). Rather than instructing and guiding the people in the way that they should walk, Israel's leaders are causing the people to stumble and turn away from God and corrupting the covenant (2:4-9). They are even questioning God's justice and affirming that he calls those who do evil good (2:16-17). God accuses them of robbing him by not giving him their tithes and offerings, yet at the same time he promises to pour out his blessings on them if they fulfill their obligations in that regard (3:10-12). The third chapter of the book ends with further expressions of God's desire to bless and save his people once they come to understand and practice justice (3:16-18).

What has God upset in these passages, therefore, is not that the people are failing to give him the sacrificial offerings and worship that are due to him but rather that they are not truly dedicated to loving and serving him in the way he desires for their own good. In fact, in v. 10 of the passage just cited from the first chapter of Malachi, God makes it clear that he does not want their sacrifices and takes no pleasure in them precisely because they are not expressions of the type of love and genuine commitment to his will for justice and righteousness that he wishes to see in them. Once again, the insincerity and hypocrisy of their worship are symptoms of a deeper problem, namely, their lack of commitment to what is good and right. For their own good, it is this that God seeks rather than their gifts and offerings in themselves.

A third passage in which God expresses his displeasure at the lack of sacrificial worship on the part of his people appears in the book of Haggai, which describes the situation that existed following the return of God's people from their exile in Babylon. In the first chapter of the book, God tells the people through Haggai:

> Is this a time for you to live in your paneled houses, while this house lies in ruins? Now therefore thus says the LORD of hosts: Consider how you have fared. You have sown much and harvested little; you eat, but you never have enough; you drink, but you never have your fill; you clothe yourselves, but no one is warm; and you that earn wages do so to put them into a bag with holes.
>
> Thus says the LORD of hosts: Consider how you have fared. Go up into the hills and bring wood and build the house, so that I may take pleasure in it and be glorified, says the LORD. You have looked for abundance, but it amounted to little, and when you brought it home, I blew it away. Why?, says the LORD of hosts. Because my house lies in ruins, while all of you hurry off to your own houses. Therefore the heavens above you have withheld the dew, and the earth has withheld its produce. And I have called for a drought on the land and the hills, on the grain, the new wine, the oil, on what the soil produces, on humans and animals, and on all their labors (Hag 1:4-11).

Here God is presented as withholding his blessings because the people have not made an effort to rebuild the temple and resume the sacrificial worship that was interrupted when the Babylonians destroyed Jerusalem decades earlier. While it might appear that the motive for God's displeasure is simply that he is not receiving the worship and honor he desires, what the passage is actually stressing is God's desire to bless his people. The reason why God has withheld his blessings, however, is not merely that the people have not rebuilt the temple but that they have been focusing exclusively on themselves and their own needs, building houses to inhabit and working to procure food and clothing for themselves without showing any concern for God and his will. If they live in such a manner, they cannot truly be blessed, since their well-being depends on their serving God by dedicating themselves to doing what he has commanded for their own good. The problem is therefore not their lack of interest in rebuilding the temple per se but the lack of commitment to God's will that is reflected in their failure to rebuild the temple. What God wants from them is their full commitment to living in accordance with his will. This commitment should take the form of rebuilding the temple so that they may offer him their worship there. That worship will lead them to place him and his will at the center of their lives once more for their own good, since only by acknowledging his sovereignty over them as his people will they be brought to live in ways that truly promote their well-being and happiness.

In spite of the apparent similarity between these passages from the books of the Hebrew prophets and the passages from the poems of Homer in which the gods are said to become angry when they do not receive the gifts and sacrifices that they regard as their due, therefore, the idea behind them is very different. What those gods desire, demand, and command is that people offer them their sacrifices for their own sake. In the passages from the biblical prophets just considered, however, what is said to displease God is that his people are not committed to living in accordance with his will for their own good. The lack of that commitment is evident in the fact that they have no interest in presenting him with sacrificial offerings that are truly an expression of love for him and a desire to do his will with gladness. In other words, in these passages the failure of the people to offer God their sacrifices and praise is seen not as the *cause* of God's displeasure in itself but rather as a *symptom* of a deeper problem, namely, the people's failure and refusal to love and obey God by living in ways that promote their well-being and that of others as well. When God complains that his people are not offering him their sacrifices as they should, therefore, what bothers him is not the lack of sacrificial offerings per se but rather the lack of commitment to his will of which the failure to offer sacrifices is an expression or consequence.

Reclaiming Sacrifice by Rejecting It

While there are only a few passages in the Hebrew Bible that portray God as becoming displeased or angry when his people do not offer him sacrifices, numerous passages speak of God *not wanting* sacrifices if his people are not committed to practicing justice, righteousness, and mercy. In these passages, what is said to displease or anger God is not the failure of his people to offer him sacrifices but things such as injustice, violence, oppression, and disregard for those in need. These passages therefore once again present a God whose ultimate concern is *not for himself or for the worship, praises, and offerings of human beings but rather for the well-being of his people.* In fact, if his people are not committed to living in justice, righteousness, and mercy in accordance with his loving will, rather than pleasing him, their sacrifices and offerings provoke him to wrath.

These ideas are especially stressed in a number of passages from the books of Israel's prophets. In the context of allusions to the wrongdoings, bloodshed, robbery, murder, and crimes committed by the people, Hosea presents God as affirming: "For I desire steadfast love and not sacrifice, the knowledge of God rather than burnt offerings" (Hos 6:6). Similarly, in Isa 58:6-7, God tells his people who wish to obtain his favor by offering up to him their fasting:

> You fast only to quarrel and fight and to strike with a wicked fist. The type of fasting that you are doing today will not make your voice to be heard on high. Is not this the fast that I choose: to loose the bonds of injustice, to undo the straps of the yoke, to let the oppressed go free, and to break every yoke? Is it not to share your bread with the hungry, and bring the homeless poor into your house; when you see the naked, to cover them, and not to hide yourself from your own kin?

Perhaps the clearest statement of the idea that what ultimately interests God is the practice of justice rather than the offering of sacrifices is found in Mic 6:6-8:

> With what shall I come before the LORD, and bow myself down before God on high? Shall I come before him with burnt offerings, with calves a year old? Will the LORD be pleased with thousands of rams, with ten thousands of rivers of oil? Shall I give my firstborn for my transgression, the fruit of my body for the sin of my soul? He has told you, O mortal, what is good; and what does the LORD require of you but to do justice, and to love kindness, and to walk humbly with your God?

Other passages from the prophetic books stress not only God's desire for justice rather than sacrifice but also his rejection of the sacrificial worship offered to him by those who practice injustice and oppression. After insisting that God will dwell among his people at the temple only if they refrain from shedding innocent blood, worshiping other gods, and oppressing the needy, the prophet Jeremiah presents God as telling them: "Will you steal, murder, commit adultery, swear falsely, make offerings to Baal, and follow after other gods that you have not known, and then come and stand before me in this house, which is called by my name, and say, 'We are safe!'—only to go on doing all these abominations? Has this house, which is called by my name, become a den of thieves in your eyes?" (Jer 7:9-11). Several chapters later, the prophet adds: "Even though they fast, I will not hear their cry; and even though they offer burnt offerings and grain offerings, I will not accept them; but I will consume them by the sword, by famine, and by pestilence" (Jer 14:12; cf. 11:15).

In a similar manner, after claiming that the altars that the people have built in order to *expiate* sin have instead become places for *committing* sin, the prophet Hosea adds: "Though they offer choice sacrifices and eat the flesh, the LORD does not accept them" (Hos 8:11-13). In Amos 5:21-25, God tells the people: "I hate, I despise your festivals, and I take no delight in your solemn assemblies. Even though you offer up to me your burnt offerings and grain offerings, I will not accept them; nor will I look with favor on the offerings of well-being of your fatted animals. Spare me the noise of your songs; I will not listen to the melody of your harps. But let justice roll down like waters, and righteousness like an ever-flowing stream." The words attributed to God in Isa 1:11-17 are just as harsh, if not more so:

> Hear the word of the LORD, you rulers of Sodom! Give ear to the teaching of our God, you people of Gomorrah! What to me is the multitude of your sacrifices?, says the LORD. I have had my fill of burnt offerings of rams and the fat of well-fed beasts; I do not delight in the blood of bulls, or of lambs, or of goats. When you come to appear before me, who asked this from your hand? Trample my courts no more; bring no more vain offerings; incense is an abomination to me. New moon and Sabbath and the calling of convocations—I cannot endure solemn assemblies with iniquity. Your new moon feasts and your appointed festivals my soul hates; they have become a burden to me, I am weary of bearing them. When you stretch out your hands, I will hide my eyes from you; even though you make many prayers, I will not listen; your hands are covered with blood. Wash yourselves; make yourselves clean. Remove the evil of your doings from before my eyes. Cease to do evil, learn to do good. Seek justice, rescue the oppressed, defend the orphan, plead for the widow.

While some interpreters have claimed to find in passages such as these the idea that the God of Israel does not want sacrifice, the affirmation that God desires the practice of justice, righteousness, and mercy instead of sacrifices should probably be understood instead as a Hebraism. In that case, the idea is that God does not want sacrificial offerings unless they are accompanied by a commitment to justice, righteousness, and mercy and are an expression of that commitment. As we shall see in Chapter 7, in fact, in biblical thought the purpose of offering sacrifice is precisely that of strengthening the commitment to these things among God's people.

Passages from other books of the Hebrew Bible and Second Temple Jewish literature reflect the same ideas found in the prophetic writings. What interests God is not sacrifice per se but the practice of justice, righteousness, love, and compassion:

> Sacrifice and offering you do not desire, but you have given me an open ear to hear. Burnt offering and sin offering you have not required. Then I said, "Here I am; in the scroll of the book it is written of me: 'I delight to do your will, O my God; your law is within my heart'" (Ps 40:6-8).

> "Hear, O my people, and I will speak; O Israel, I will testify against you. I am God, your God. I do not reprove you for your sacrifices; your burnt offerings are continually before me. I will not accept a bull from your house, or goats from your folds. For every wild animal of the forest is mine, the cattle on a thousand hills. I know all the birds of the air, and every creature in the fields is mine. If I were hungry, I would not tell you, for the world and all that is in it is mine. Do I eat the flesh of bulls, or drink the blood of goats? Offer to God a sacrifice of thanksgiving, and fulfill your vows to the Most High. Call on me in the day of trouble; I will deliver you, and you will glorify me."
>
> But to the wicked God says: "What right have you to recite my statutes, or take my covenant on your lips? For you hate correction, and you cast my words behind you. When you see a thief, you join in with him, and you keep company with adulterers. You give your mouth over to evil, and yoke your tongue

to deceit. You sit and speak against your kin; you slander your own mother's child. These things you have done and I have remained silent; you thought that I was just like you. But now I rebuke you, and lay the charge before you. Mark this, then, you who forget God, or I will tear you apart, and there will be no one to save you. Those who bring thanksgiving as their sacrifice honor me; to those who go the right way I will show the salvation of God" (Ps 50:7-23).

For you have no delight in sacrifice, otherwise I would give it; you do not take pleasure in burnt offerings. The sacrifice that pleases God is a broken spirit; a broken and contrite heart, O God, you will not despise (Ps 51:16-17).

To do righteousness and justice is more acceptable to the LORD than sacrifice. . . . The sacrifice of the wicked is an abomination; how much more when brought with evil intent (Prov 21:3, 27).

If one sacrifices ill-gotten goods, the offering is blemished; the gifts of wrong-doers are not acceptable. The Most High is not pleased with the offerings of the ungodly, nor for their many sacrifices does he forgive their sins. Like one who kills a son before his father's eyes is the person who offers a sacrifice taken from the property of the poor (Sir 34:23-24).

When one contrasts passages such as these with what we find in the *Enuma Elish* and the poems of Homer, the difference is striking. One can hardly imagine gods such as Marduk, Zeus, or Poseidon resolutely insisting that they demand the practice of steadfast love and mercy rather than sacrifice. Much less would such gods reject the sacrifices of their worshipers because they had failed to care for the poor, the weak, and the downtrodden or because those worshipers had obtained what they were offering up by means of robbery, pillage, violence, and bloodshed. The last thing that concerned many of those gods was that those who worshiped them be dedicated to liberating the oppressed and assisting those in need. On the contrary, their primary concern was that they be given the praise, honor, worship, and offerings that they regarded as their due. If it was necessary to trample on the poor, weak, and needy in order for that to happen, then such gods would not only forgive and overlook such oppressive behavior on the part of their worshipers but at times even expect and demand it of them.

THE CAUSES OF GOD'S WRATH

As many of the passages just considered clearly demonstrate, throughout the Hebrew Bible what is repeatedly seen as provoking God to wrath is not the failure of people to offer him their worship and sacrifices but rather their persistence in living and acting in ways that undermine and destroy their own well-being and that of others. While the biblical texts often speak of God becoming angry in response to the practice of sin, injustice, violence, and oppression among his people, however, they seem to allude even more frequently to his anger at the people's insistence on worshiping other gods. Because biblical interpreters have commonly failed to recognize the relation between idolatry and injustice in biblical thought, they have tended to see these two motives of God's wrath as separate and distinct from one another. In addition, just as they have generally seen God's prohibition of sin and injustice as something that responds to a concern for himself due to the effects that these things have *on him*, they also tend to ascribe his anger at his people's worship of other gods to a desire and demand that they worship him alone *for his own sake*. For that reason, God's wrath at injustice and idolatry is consistently regarded as being rooted in motives that are self-centered and have little if anything to do with his love for human beings and his desire that they enjoy well-being. As we have noted previously, among many biblical interpreters even God's demand that his people practice justice and righteousness tends to be seen as responding to a necessity grounded in his own nature rather than a concern for the manner in which human beings themselves are affected by the practice of sin, injustice, violence, and oppression.

Before looking more closely at passages from the biblical texts that allude to God's wrath and its causes, however, it is important to note a point that has been mentioned only briefly in the preceding chapters. As we observed in Chapter 2 when analyzing the Genesis narratives regarding God's reaction to the disobedience of the first man and woman, the murder of Abel by Cain, and the destruction of Sodom and Gomorrah, many of the passages in the Hebrew Bible that speak of God imposing punishments or inflicting suffering on those who have behaved in ways contrary to his will make no allusion to any wrath or anger on his part. In fact, as we have noted in the previous chapter, God is often presented as lamenting the need to punish people or even reacting to their sinful behavior with sadness and grief rather than anger, as he does in the introduction to the flood narrative in Gen 6:5-6. The same observation applies to his calls for people to repent and turn back in obedience to him throughout the biblical texts. In many cases, these can be seen as pleas and exhortations rather than threats in that they are grounded in a deep yearning that his people recommit themselves to a way of life that promotes their well-being rather than continuing down a path that will lead only to their ruin and perdition.

It is significant, therefore, that many of the biblical passages that speak of God punishing or chastising people for their sinfulness do not make any explicit allusion to his wrath or even portray God as angry. The reason for this is that those who inflict discipline on others in order to correct their behavior are not always angry at them for that behavior, especially if they are doing so out of love for them. In fact, just as it is often painful for a parent to have to inflict punishment on a child in order to correct and discipline the child, so also in the biblical texts God is at times presented as experiencing pain when he subjects his people to his chastisements in order to bring them to change their ways.

A number of passages from the Hebrew Scriptures, including some of those we have seen in the previous chapter, also present God's wrath as something that gradually increases in the face of his repeated calls for his people to put away their sinful and destructive behavior. That wrath therefore does not constitute his initial response to sin. Only when his people not only ignore his repeated calls to repentance but willfully persist in their disobedience and injustice does he become angry at them. As this situation continues and grows even worse, God's anger and frustration increase as well and eventually take the form of rage and fury. Even in those cases, however, it is necessary to stress that what leads God to react with such passion and vehemence is his intense love for his people, which will not allow him simply to sit by passively when he sees them doing such great harm to themselves and others.

In fact, one of the phrases most commonly used in the Hebrew Bible to describe God affirms that he is "slow to anger." This affirmation appears in the context of the Sinai and wilderness narratives, in the book of Nehemiah, in several of the Psalms, and in the books of the prophets Joel, Jonah, and Nahum.[7] In many of these passages, the phrase "slow to anger" is followed by the words "and abounding in steadfast love." The contexts in which this phrase appears allude not only to the punishments or chastisements that God imposes on his people for their sins but also to his compassion and his willingness to forgive. In addition to portraying God's anger and the chastisements he inflicts on his people when they disobey him as expressions of his love, this phrase stresses that when the people fall into sin, God does not immediately become angry at them or punish them. Instead, like a loving parent, he first calls them to put away the behavior that is doing harm to themselves and others. Only when they persistently refuse to respond to this call and willfully continue in that behavior does his anger gradually become kindled.

A second phrase that stresses God's love for his people when describing the manner in which he responds to their sin is found repeatedly throughout the book of Jeremiah. There the Hebrew text speaks of God sending his servants the prophets to his sinful people "daily" and describes them as "rising up early" or at an early hour.[8] The affirmation that God sent his prophets daily underscores God's persistence in never ceasing to call the people to turn back to him when they have fallen into sin. While the allusion to God doing so at an early hour may also stress God's unwavering persistence and untiring efforts to bring the people to repent, it probably stresses as well the idea that from the very moment or hour that the people first fall into sin, God is already reaching out to them in an attempt to make them aware of their sin and calling them to turn back to him in obedience. He does not wait for the sin and disobedience to get worse, but takes action immediately. As we saw in Chapter 5, this same idea is stated explicitly in 2 Macc 6:12-16, where the author of 2 Maccabees affirms that God shows his kindness to his people by chastising them for their sins as soon as they fall into those sins rather than waiting until they have sunk more deeply into their sinful ways in order to attempt to correct them.

---

7. See Exod 34:6; Num 14:18; Neh 9:17; Ps 86:15; 103:8; 145:8; Joel 2:13; Jonah 4:2; Nah 1:3.
8. See Jer 7:13, 25-26; 11:7-8; 25:3-7; 26:4-6; 29:19; 32:33; 35:14-15; 44:4.

When the biblical texts and other Jewish writings of antiquity refer to God's wrath, therefore, what they often have in mind is not simply his anger but rather his frustration and exasperation at his people's stubborn refusal to respond to his calls to put away their destructive behavior and return to the way of life that he has laid out for them in the Torah for their own good. As several of the passages considered in the previous section demonstrate, however, what is especially said to move God to wrath is not merely his people's failure to repent and their persistence in their destructive behavior but the cruel and violent manner in which some of them oppress others. Of course, that cruelty and violence also take the passive form of failing to show kindness and compassion to those who are suffering by seeking to deliver them from their plight. In these instances, God's anger or wrath is understood as *indignation* and *outrage* at the manner in which some abuse others and trample on them or mistreat them by cold-heartedly ignoring and neglecting them when they find themselves desperately in need.

Giving Vent to God's Rage

Expressions of this indignation and outrage appear repeatedly throughout the writings of Israel's prophets. Even though in many cases the prophets do not allude explicitly to God's anger when denouncing the injustices being committed by some against others, that anger is clearly reflected in the content and tone of their words:

> Your rulers are rebels and companions of thieves. They all love a bribe and run after gifts. They do not defend the orphan, and the widow's cause does not come before them (Isa 1:23).

> The LORD enters into judgment with the elders and rulers of his people: "It is you who have devoured the vineyard; the spoil of the poor is in your houses. What do you mean by crushing my people, by grinding the face of the poor into the dirt?," says the Lord GOD of hosts (Isa 3:14-15).

> Woe to those of you who join house to house, who add field to field, until there is room for no one but you, and you are left to live alone in the midst of the land! The LORD of hosts has sworn in my ears: "Surely many houses will become desolate, large and beautiful houses, without inhabitant. For ten acres of vineyard will yield but one bath, and a homer of seed will yield a mere bushel." Woe to those who rise early in the morning to pursue strong drink, who continue to be inflamed by wine into the evening! Their feasts consist of lyre and harp, tambourine and flute and wine, but they do not regard the deeds of the LORD, or consider the work of his hands! Therefore my people go into exile for lack of knowledge; their nobles are dying of hunger, and their multitude is parched with thirst. . . .
> Woe to those who call evil good and good evil, who substitute darkness for light and light for darkness, who substitute bitter for sweet and sweet for bitter! Woe to those who are wise in their own eyes, and shrewd in their own sight! Woe to those who are heroes in drinking wine and valiant at mixing drink, who acquit the guilty for a bribe, and deprive the innocent of their rights! (Isa 5:8-13, 20-23)

Woe to those who make iniquitous decrees, who write oppressive statutes, to deprive the needy of justice and to rob the poor of my people of their right, that they may make widows their spoil, and orphans their prey! What will you do on the day of punishment, in the desolation that will come from far away? To whom will you flee for help, and where will you leave your wealth, so as not to crouch among the prisoners or fall among the slain? For all this his anger has not turned away; his hand is stretched out still (Isa 10:1-4).

For your hands are contaminated with blood, and your fingers with iniquity! Your lips have spoken lies; your tongue mutters perversity! No one brings suit justly; no one is judged with truth. They rely on empty pleas, speak falsehoods, conceive mischief, and beget iniquity. They hatch vipers' eggs, and weave spiders' webs. Whoever eats of their eggs dies, and from the crushed egg a viper is hatched. Their webs cannot serve as clothing; they cannot cover themselves with what they make. Their works are works of iniquity, and acts of violence are in their hands. Their feet run to evil, and they rush to shed innocent blood. Their thoughts are thoughts of iniquity; devastation and destruction are in their highways. They do not know the way of peace, and there is no justice in their paths. They have made their paths crooked; no one who walks in them knows peace (Isa 59:3-8).

For scoundrels are found among my people; they lurk like bird-catchers lying in wait, yet the trap they set is to catch human beings. Like a cage full of birds, their houses are filled with fraud; in that way they have become great and rich. They have grown fat and sleek. They know no limits in deeds of wickedness. They do not judge with justice the cause of the orphan, to make it prosper, and they do not defend the rights of the needy. Shall I not punish them for these things?, says the Lord, and shall I not bring retribution on a nation such as this? (Jer 5:26-29)

They bend their tongue like a bow to speak lies; they are renowned in the land, but not for truth. For they proceed from evil to evil, and they do not know me, says the Lord. Let all be on guard against their neighbors, and put no trust in any of their kin; for all your kin are usurpers, and every neighbor goes around like a slanderer. They all deceive their neighbors, and no one speaks the truth; they have trained their tongues to speak lies, and grow weary by committing iniquities. Oppression follows upon oppression, deceit upon deceit! They refuse to know me, says the Lord (Jer 9:3-6).

O house of David! Thus says the Lord: Execute justice in the morning, and deliver from the hand of the oppressor anyone who has been robbed, or else my wrath will go forth like fire and burn, with no one to quench it, because of your evil doings (Jer 21:12).

Make a chain! For the land is full of bloody crimes, and the city is full of violence (Ezek 7:23).

Ah, you who turn justice to wormwood, and cast righteousness to the ground! . . . They hate the one who reproves in the gate, and they abhor the one who speaks the truth. Therefore because you trample on the poor and take from them levies of grain, you have built houses of hewn stone, but you will not live in them; you have planted pleasant vineyards, but you will not drink their wine. For I know how many are your transgressions, and how great are your sins—you who afflict the righteous, who take a bribe, and push aside the needy in the gate (Amos 5:7, 10-12).

Ah, you who put far away the evil day, and bring near a reign of violence! Alas for those who lie on beds of ivory, and lounge on their couches, and eat tender lambs from the flock, and calves from the stall; who sing idle songs to the sound of the harp, and improvise on instruments of music like David; who drink wine from bowls, and anoint themselves with the finest oils, but do not grieve over the ruin of Joseph! (Amos 6:4-6)

Hear this, you who trample on the needy, and bring to ruin the poor of the land, saying, "When will the new moon be over so that we may sell grain; and the Sabbath, so that we may offer wheat for sale? We will make the bushel small and the shekel great, and deal deceitfully with false balances, buying the poor for silver and the needy for a pair of sandals, and selling the sweepings of the wheat" (Amos 8:4-6).

And I said: Listen, you heads of Jacob and rulers of the house of Israel! Is it not for you to know justice?—you who hate the good and love the evil, who tear the skin off my people, and the flesh off their bones, who eat the flesh of my people, flay their skin off them, break their bones in pieces, and chop them up like meat in a kettle, like flesh in a cauldron.... Hear this, you heads of the house of Jacob and rulers of the house of Israel, who abhor justice and make crooked what is straight, who build Zion with blood and Jerusalem with perversity! Its rulers give judgment for a bribe, its priests teach for a price, its prophets give oracles for money. Yet they rest in the Lord and say, "Surely the Lord is with us! No harm will come upon us" (Mic 3:1-3, 9-11).

The voice of the Lord cries to the city (it is sound wisdom to fear your name): Hear, O tribe and assembly of the city! Am I to forget the treasures of wickedness in the house of the wicked, and the false measure that is despicable? Am I to tolerate wicked scales and a bag of dishonest weights? The wealthy among you are full of violence; your inhabitants speak lies, with tongues of deceit in their mouths (Mic 6:9-12).

The faithful have disappeared from the land, and there is no one left who is upright. They all lie in wait for blood, and they hunt each other with nets. Their hands are skilled at doing evil. The official and the judge ask for a bribe, and the powerful dictate what they desire; thus they conspire together. The best of them is like a brier, the most upright of them a thorn hedge. The day that they post their sentinels, their punishment will come; their confusion is now at hand. Put no trust in a friend, have no confidence in a loved one; guard the doors of your mouth from the woman who lies in your embrace. For the son treats the father with contempt, the daughter rises up against her mother, the daughter-in-law against her mother-in-law; your enemies are members of your own household (Mic 7:2-6).

Throughout these passages, the anger and indignation of God are more than evident, as are the motives for that anger and indignation. What fills him with anger and even rage is not merely the lying, deceit, robbery, injustice, violence, and oppression that the prophets describe in graphic terms but also the disdain and contempt for the weak, the needy, and those who are suffering.

The problem is not only that some are crushing, devouring, and trampling on others but also that they are pushing aside those who are helpless and depriving them of their rights. The guilty are acquitted through the payment of bribes while the innocent are condemned. The passage from Isaiah 10 even presents the people replacing the laws and statutes that God has given them with others of their own making in order to justify and legalize their thievery and their predatory behavior toward the needy. In addition, when the righteous raise their voice to protest, speak the truth, and denounce the lies and corruption, they too are afflicted, persecuted, and even murdered. All of these things are precisely what the commandments of the Torah prohibit and are intended to prevent. For that reason, ultimately it is the failure and refusal of the people to observe those commandments that is regarded as filling the land with suffering, violence, and bloodshed.

Rather than being *opposed* to God's love, therefore, these passages make it clear that God's wrath is the *expression* of his love for his people. That love will not let him ignore or take lightly the pain and suffering that some inflict on others. While his commitment to justice certainly does not allow him to tolerate the people's sinful behavior, at the root of that commitment to justice is his deep desire that his people possess only the good and be delivered from all forms of evil, injustice, and oppression. It is his profound love for his people, including especially the weak and needy among them, that leads him to become filled with wrath and indignation when he sees the cruel and terrible things that some do to others and the heartless and inhumane manner in which they treat those whom they are to love and care for in accordance with his command. In fact, were God *not* filled with wrath and indignation upon seeing such things, he could not be considered a God of love. Instead, he would be siding with the oppressors and evildoers either by actively continuing to pour out his blessings on them when they behave in such ways or by simply looking the other way when they grind others into the dirt. For God to respond to their crimes in either of these ways would even make him complicit in those crimes.

It must also be stressed once more that the biblical texts consistently associate all of these violent and oppressive behaviors with the worship of gods other than the God of Israel. Because those gods are themselves selfish, greedy, cruel, and unjust, they not only disregard the same type of behavior among their worshipers but actually foment and promote such behavior. For that reason, the prophets frequently portray God as becoming indignant and enraged at his people when they persistently refuse to put away their idols and false gods in order to serve him alone. Once again, what moves him to react so angrily to their worship of other gods is not a concern *for himself* but a concern *for them*, and especially for the victims of the cruel and oppressive behavior that follows upon their idolatry as its inevitable consequence.

These passages from the prophetic books also reflect a number of other ideas that we considered at the outset of the present chapter and in the previous one. What makes the sin of the people so grievous is not only that they have refused to listen to the prophets whom God has sent to them in an attempt to bring them to put a stop to their oppressive and destructive behavior, but also that they have violently persecuted those prophets in order to silence them. Rather than representing a lack of love for his people, God's refusal to hear their prayers and petitions when they insist on practicing injustice and violence is the only response that his concern and passion for their well-being can take in the face of such behavior. In several of the passages just cited, God stresses that his love for the people has led to his repeated and persistent efforts to bring them to put away their wrongdoing, yet despite his persistence, those efforts have proven fruitless. For that reason, the only form that his love can now take is that of chastising them even more harshly by sending them into exile and even destroying many of them, since nothing else has worked. Once again, rather than standing *in opposition* to God's love, his intense wrath and the punishments or chastisements he imposes on the people are *grounded* in his love for all and are the *fruit* of that love. As God himself is presented as asking in Jer 5:26-29, how could he truly be said to love his people if he simply allowed such oppressive behavior to continue unabated without attempting to bring an end to it through punishments and chastisements? In fact, for God simply to *forgive* or *overlook* such behavior and leave it unpunished would be not only to accept and condone it but to prolong it and allow it to proliferate even more. Under such circumstances, to forgive the unrepentant evildoers for their sins would be an act of cruelty rather than love, since it would involve giving them free license to continue in the same behavior.

All of the passages just considered, therefore, make it clear that in biblical thought God's wrath and anger are rooted *not in a concern for himself but rather in his concern for the well-being of the human beings whom he loves.* Undoubtedly, because the biblical texts at times present God as experiencing pain and grief when he observes the manner in which some inflict suffering on others and do them harm, in a sense it can be said that God seeks to alleviate his own suffering when he acts in wrath to punish those who are causing others to suffer. Yet this is only because he has linked his own happiness to that of the human beings he has created, as we saw in Chapter 2. What leads the God of Israel to seek to put an end to the type of oppressive and destructive behavior described in these passages is not simply a concern for his own happiness but rather his concern for the happiness and well-being of those whose lives are being destroyed by that behavior. What angers and pains God is not the effect that such behavior has *on him or his divine nature* but rather the effect that it has on the human beings he loves. It is his passionate commitment to the well-being of all that leads him not only to *ask* but to *demand* and *command* that his people obey him by living in ways that promote and cultivate their well-being and that of others rather than undermining and destroying that well-being through their behavior. In other words, his love leads him to demand that his people be just as passionately committed to their own well-being and that of other human beings as he is. For that same reason, he also demands that they be filled with the same indignation and outrage that he experiences when they see some people cruelly oppressing others and neglecting those in need rather than rushing to their aid in order to defend them from those who are doing them harm. That same love and passionate commitment to the well-being of all also leads God to channel his anger in ways that must ultimately be regarded as *constructive* rather than *destructive*. What he seeks is not to do harm to those who have aroused his anger but to liberate people from behaviors that fill the world with pain and suffering.

These observations should also be kept in mind when considering passages in which God is said to vent or satisfy his wrath or fury.[9] Because God's wrath is consistently seen as being grounded in his commitment to the well-being of his people and his opposition to everything that undermines and destroys that well-being, when he acts in wrath he is not seeking to let his emotions out for his own sake or to pour out his rage simply in order to give vent to it. In that case, any actions he took in response to his anger and indignation would not accomplish any kind of constructive or salvific purpose in relation to human beings. Rather than seeking to establish justice and equity, he would merely be attempting to satisfy his own need or desire to relieve himself of pent-up rage. While the pagan gods of antiquity were thought to behave in such a manner, the biblical texts consistently present God as seeking to accomplish a clear objective when he pours out his wrath, namely, that of putting an end to injustice and oppression. When those texts speak of God venting his anger or satisfying his wrath, therefore, they should be understood in the sense that he refuses to put away his anger or wrath until his loving objectives have been accomplished as fully as possible. His anger and wrath at injustice and oppression are satisfied only when that injustice and oppression are brought to an end, either by repentance or by punishment.

The Anger and Hatred of God's Love

While the sufferings and afflictions that the God of Israel is said to impose on his people are often seen as having the purpose of bringing them to turn back in obedience to him and his commandments for their own good, this is not their only purpose. When some are oppressing others and refuse to heed God's call to put away their oppressive behavior, God may punish them not because he is attempting to bring about some change in them but only because he wishes to make it impossible for them to continue to do harm to others by means of that behavior. In that case, rather than punishing them for their own sake, God takes action against them for the sake of those who are suffering at their hands. In addition to saving the oppressed from their oppressors, God's destruction of those who insist on oppressing others also serves as a deterrent, since it is a means by which he gives notice to any who

---

9. See, for example, Ps 78:62; Lam 4:11; Ezek 5:13; 16:42; 21:17; 24:13.

would fall into such behavior that he will not tolerate it but will punish it with firmness and severity due to his commitment to the well-being of all.

According to the logic that runs throughout the biblical texts, God's destruction of those who insist on oppressing others and filling their lives with suffering is just as much an expression of his love as his persistent attempts to discipline and correct those who practice such behavior. In both cases, what he seeks is to bring sin, injustice, and oppression to an end for the good of all. Undoubtedly, when God acts to destroy those who are oppressing others, their destruction can hardly be seen as an expression of love for them. Contrary to appearances, however, it would also be a mistake to see their destruction as reflecting a lack of love for them on the part of God. In most instances, prior to destroying those who oppress others, God repeatedly exhorts and warns them to put away their oppressive behavior and instead treat others with justice, kindness, and compassion. He also warns them ahead of time of his intentions to punish and destroy them and may chastise them in various ways in an attempt to correct them before taking more drastic action.

When God has done everything possible to bring those who oppress others to change their ways, he may conclude that he has no other option but to punish them with great severity or even destroy them. This is not because he no longer loves them, however. On the contrary, he continues to desire the well-being of all people without exception, no matter what they do or fail to do. Yet when they persistently refuse to live in a way that allows God to bless them and instead fill the lives of others with pain and suffering, they cannot attain the well-being God desires for them, no matter how much God would like that well-being to be theirs. If he proceeds against the oppressors, therefore, it is not because he does not love them but because his love for them cannot accomplish its purposes in them. In that case, he must take action against the oppressors for the sake of those whom they are oppressing, who are also the objects of God's love and concern. If he cannot attain the well-being of all, he must settle for seeking the well-being of those whose way of life will allow them to enjoy that well-being. He does this by delivering them from their oppressors.

It is also important to stress that in biblical thought unjust and oppressive behavior does great harm not only to those who are regarded as the victims of that behavior but also to those who insist on practicing it. While they generally believe that they are benefited by that behavior in that it allows them to obtain the things they desire, such as wealth, power, and control over the lives of others, in reality such behavior does them harm for many different reasons. Rather than enjoying constructive and fulfilling relationships with others that are characterized by sincere love and mutual affection, their lives are filled with things such as hatred, jealousy, rivalries, greed, and selfishness. Whatever material benefits they may obtain come at a tremendous cost, since in order to attain those benefits they generate among others enmity, hostility, anger, and resentment toward themselves. They also end up living in constant fear due to the fact that others who practice the same type of behavior inevitably seek to do them harm and take away from them whatever they have obtained and accumulated. In fact, even when they appear to be loved and revered by others, it soon becomes clear to them that such love and reverence are almost always simply forms of self-interest rather than consisting of a genuine concern for their well-being. While both those who are closest to them as well as others over whom they have power may offer them praise and adulation and express their adoration and admiration for them, they do so not because they truly care for them but because they wish to obtain from them something for themselves. Rather than attaining true well-being for themselves, those who practice injustice and oppression undermine their own happiness and fill their lives and those of others with strife, rancor, and constant conflict. If God insists that they stop oppressing others, therefore, he does so not only for the sake of those whom they are oppressing but also for their own good, since their oppressive behavior does great harm not only to others but also to themselves.

At first glance, the idea that God loves and cares not only for the oppressed but for their oppressors as well may seem to run contrary to what is affirmed in many passages of the biblical texts. In particular, there are numerous passages that affirm explicitly that God hates or despises evildoers and suggest that he is pleased when the righteous hate sinners and evildoers as well.[10] These passages seem to present him taking action against evildoers and calling on others to do the same not simply for the purpose of delivering their victims from the suffering they inflict on them but also because he takes pleasure in doing evildoers harm and making them suffer.

When considering such passages, however, it is once again important to stress the difference between the biblical conception of the God of Israel and the manner in which other nations in antiquity conceived of their gods. In belief systems such as those that we encounter in the *Enuma Elish* and the poems of Homer, what leads the gods to hate certain human beings and seek to do them harm is a concern for their own desires and interests. Because the gods seek to be in positions of power and control over human beings in order to impose their will on them, they strike out in anger and hatred at any who oppose them or stand in their way. When they act in this manner, of course, they are not acting out of love for people or seeking their well-being. At times, in fact, the gods are presented as hating particular human beings for no good reason. Since they are capricious, they simply are attracted to some human beings and repulsed by others, whom they find displeasing or odious for whatever cause.

In the Hebrew Scriptures, however, those who are said to be hated by God are evildoers and those who practice injustice and oppression. The author of Psalm 5, for example, tells God: "The arrogant will not stand before your eyes;

---

10. See, for example, Lev 20:23; Deut 18:12; 25:16; Ps 31:6; 95:10; 119:13; 139:21-22; Prov 3:31-34; Hos 9:15-17; Wis 14:9; Sir 12:6; 16:8.

you hate all evildoers. You destroy those who speak lies; the Lord abhors the bloodthirsty and deceitful" (vv. 5-6). Similarly, in Ps 11:5 it is said that "the Lord tests the righteous and the wicked, and his soul hates the lover of violence." Other passages speak of God hating those who serve idols and commit other forms of injustice that God despises.[11] In biblical thought, therefore there is a *reason* why God is said to hate certain people, namely, that they do harm to others. This is true even in the case of Mal 1:2-3, where God is presented as affirming: "I have loved Jacob, but I have hated Esau." Commentators often interpret this passage in the sense that God arbitrarily chose to show favor to Jacob while rejecting Esau for no good reason, as if some type of capricious favoritism were involved. A close look at the passage, however, reveals that it is not alluding to Esau personally but to the people descended from him, Edom, and that it states clearly the reason for God's hatred of the Edomites, namely, that they have made their land a "territory of wickedness" (Mal 1:4). Neither in that passage or others from the Hebrew Scriptures, therefore, is God said to hate anyone simply out of capriciousness or spite in the way that the pagan gods of antiquity were often thought to do. On the contrary, the biblical texts repeatedly stress that God does not show partiality or favoritism to anyone and insists that human beings refrain from doing so as well.[12]

Other passages from the Hebrew Scriptures speak of God hating the evil, sin, and injustice that human beings commit rather than those human beings themselves. The author of Proverbs, for example, writes: "There are six things that the Lord hates, seven that are an abomination to him: haughty eyes, a lying tongue, hands that shed innocent blood, a heart that devises wicked plans, feet that run quickly to evil, a false witness who breathes out lies, and one who sows discord in a family" (Prov 6:16-19). In other passages, God is said to hate things such as robbery, wrongdoing, infidelity, the violence associated with idolatry, and the hypocritical worship of those who do evil.[13] Obviously, what leads God to hate the practice of all of these things is not any type of capriciousness but his love for human beings, which refuses to tolerate actions and behaviors that do them harm and destroy their lives.

When considering the passages that speak of God hating wrongdoers as well as the wrongdoing that they commit, it is important to note that in English the language of hating carries certain connotations that are not necessarily present in Hebrew. In English, hatred is generally understood as something that is permanent and excludes any desire for the well-being or happiness of the person who is the object of one's hatred. On the contrary, one desires only evil for the person whom one hates, no matter what that person may do. In Hebrew, however, one's hatred of another person

---

11. See, for example, Lev 20:23; 26:30; Deut 25:13-16; Ps 31:6; Sir 12:6; 27:22-24.

12. See Deut 10:17; 2 Chr 19:7; Job 13:10; 34:19; cf. Deut 16:19; Prov 24:23; 28:21; Mal 2:9. This idea appears in the New Testament as well: see Acts 10:34; Rom 2:9; Gal 2:6.

13. See Deut 12:31; Isa 1:14; 61:8; Amos 5:21; Mal 2:13-16.

depends on that person's actions and may come to an end if that person begins to act differently. When hatred is understood in this manner, rather than being something permanent and unconditional, it will last only as long as the person whom one hates persists in the behavior that one finds displeasing or odious. Furthermore, the objective that one seeks is not that of seeing harm done to such persons but preventing them from continuing to do harm to themselves and others. In other words, what one desires is not to see the person whom one hates *suffer*, as if that were the goal, but rather to see the harmful or oppressive behavior of that person come to an end. While this objective will be accomplished if that person is destroyed or prevented from continuing in that behavior in some other way, it can also be accomplished if that person sets that behavior aside and begins to relate to others in love and kindness.

When the biblical texts affirm that God hates those who practice evil, sin, and injustice, that hatred should be understood in the manner just described. First, it is grounded not in any dislike or rejection of persons themselves but rather in the dislike and rejection of the harmful and destructive behavior that characterizes them. In biblical thought, God loves all people unconditionally. Precisely because of that love, he refuses to accept behavior that does people harm and destroys their well-being. Second, God's hatred of evildoers lasts only as long as they persist in the harmful and destructive behavior that he rejects and condemns. If they put aside that behavior, he is no longer said to hate them. Third, the affirmation that God hates evildoers should not be understood in the sense that God wishes to see them suffer or desires them harm. In biblical thought, God does not desire suffering or harm for anyone, no matter what they do. Rather, what God desires and demands is that their harmful and destructive behavior come to an end, both for their own good and for the good of others. While ideally he would like to see them put an end to that behavior themselves by desisting from it, if they persistently refuse to do so, he will take action against them in order to bring it to an end himself. For these reasons, rather than using the language of hatred to translate the Hebrew, it may be preferable to speak of God's repudiation or rejection of evildoers and the evil that they commit, as many English versions of the Bible now do.

If God is said to derive satisfaction and pleasure at punishing or destroying evildoers, it is not their suffering or destruction itself that satisfies and pleases him. On the contrary, that suffering and destruction cause him pain and sadness. This idea is stated explicitly in Ezekiel 18, where God is presented as telling his people: "Do I take any pleasure in the death of the wicked, says the Lord God, rather than that they should turn from their ways and live? . . . Cast away from you all the transgressions that you have committed against me, and get yourselves a new heart and a new spirit! Why will you die, O house of Israel? For I have no pleasure in the death of anyone, says the Lord God. Turn back, then, and live" (vv. 23, 31-32).

In another sense, however, God can be said to derive pleasure and satisfaction from punishing and destroying evildoers. In Deut 28:63, for example, Moses tells the people: "And just as the LORD took delight in making you prosperous and numerous, so the LORD will take delight in bringing you to ruin and destruction." Rather than contradicting passages such as that just cited from Ezekiel 18, Moses' words here should be understood in the sense that God will take delight at seeing the sinful, unjust, and oppressive behavior of the people finally and decisively brought to an end. Due to their persistent sinfulness and rebelliousness, that will only happen when they have been brought to ruin and destruction, since nothing less will produce in those who survive the ordeals to which God will subject his people the type of lasting change that he wishes to see in them. What satisfies and pleases God is not inflicting suffering and destruction on those who behave in ways that do great harm to themselves and others but putting an end to that behavior so that the people can instead prosper and enjoy well-being. A God who is so passionately committed to bringing about in the people the way of life that will allow them to enjoy his blessings could hardly help but take great delight in stamping out for good the stubborn and rebellious behavior that leads to their ruin and perdition. As we have seen in the previous chapter, the idea in Deuteronomy 28–30 is that God promises to chastise the people through sufferings and hardships when they persistently refuse to live in the way that he has commanded for their own good. The purpose of these chastisements, however, is to bring them to live once more in accordance with his will so that they may enjoy the well-being he desires for them. What will delight God and fill him with joy is not inflicting pain and suffering on his people but bringing them to stop living and behaving in ways that fill their lives with the pain and suffering he detests. Because God himself is saddened, pained, and grieved when his people live in ways that fill their lives with pain and suffering, he will also experience delight and joy when the destruction and ruin he promises to bring upon the people will finally put an end not only to their pain and suffering but to his own as well by leading them to practice justice rather than injustice and violence. As Moses tells the Israelites in Deut 30:8-9, once they have been brought to turn back to God in obedience by means of the suffering and destruction they have endured, "the LORD will again take delight in prospering you, just as he delighted in prospering your ancestors."

The notion that God seeks only what is good for his people out of love for them even when he is said to hate or repudiate them appears elsewhere in the biblical texts as well. In Leviticus 26, where God conveys through Moses his intention to impose harsh sufferings and afflictions on the people if they refuse to obey him, he tells them: "I will abhor you" (v. 30). The context, however, makes it clear that this abhorrence or hatred will come to an end once those sufferings and afflictions have accomplished their purpose of bringing the people back to God in obedience. At the conclusion of the passage, in fact, when God promises to restore them to the land after they have spent time in exile outside of that land, he makes it clear that he does *not* hate or abhor them: "When they are in the land of their enemies, I will not cast them away nor abhor them so as to destroy them entirely and break my covenant with them, for I am the LORD their God; but for their sakes I will remember the covenant with their ancestors whom I brought out of the land of Egypt in the sight of the nations, to be their God" (vv. 44-45).

Similarly, in Psalm 106, after reciting a long list of sins committed by the people dating back to the time they came out of Egypt, the Psalmist affirms that God came to hate or abhor them: "Then the anger of the LORD was kindled against his people, and he abhorred his heritage; he gave them over into the hand of the nations, so that those who hated them ruled over them" (vv. 40-41). Two verses later, however, the Psalmist continues: "Many times he delivered them, but they were rebellious in their purposes, and were brought low through their iniquity. Nevertheless he regarded their distress when he heard their cry. For their sake he remembered his covenant, and showed compassion according to the abundance of his steadfast love. He caused them to be shown compassion by all who held them captive" (vv. 43-46). Here again the affirmation that God "abhorred" his people is not to be taken in a categorical sense, since God is also said to have shown them compassion and steadfast love in the midst of the punishments he inflicted on them, not in order to do them harm but to do them good.

The idea that God's love for people leads him to hate them in the sense of repudiating them when they practice sin and evil is also reflected in a couple of passages in the Wisdom of Solomon. In Wis 11:23-26, the author of the book tells God: "But you are compassionate to all, for you can do all things, and you overlook people's sins, so that they may repent. For you love everything that exists, and detest none of the things that you have made, for you would not have made anything if you had hated it. How would anything have endured if you had not willed it? Or how would anything not called into being by you have been preserved? You spare all things, for they are yours, O Lord, you who love the living." Only a few chapters later, however, in the context of allusions to the idolatrous practices of the nations, the author affirms: "For equally hateful to God are the ungodly and their ungodliness" (14:9). Here the idea is that, as long as those who worship idols and practice the evils that stem from idolatry continue to do those things, God hates them in the sense of rejecting them and standing in opposition to them. Nevertheless, as the biblical texts consistently affirm, from the moment that they turn away from their evil and wrongdoing and earnestly turn back to God in obedience and seek his forgiveness, God will receive them with joy and favor because he loves them, just as he loves all human beings. His desire for all, whether righteous or sinners, is only for good, yet for that same reason he demands that they live in ways that allow them and others to experience that good.

A GOD OF VENGEANCE?

In order for God to accomplish his objective of bringing about among his people the type of just, righteous, and loving behavior that will enable them to attain the well-being he desires for them, he must constantly determine what type of activity on his part is called for in order to promote such behavior and put a stop to behavior that undermines and destroys that well-being. This involves judging human beings in order to evaluate whether they are in fact committed to living in the way he has commanded for their own good. These judgments then serve as a basis for the decisions he makes regarding what he must do in order to accomplish his objective of bringing them to live in the way necessary for them to enjoy the wholeness he seeks for them.

Throughout the biblical texts, the God of Israel is presented as examining and judging both the *actions* of human beings as well as the *thoughts of their heart*. If God were to judge actions alone, it would not be clear to him whether those who act in accordance with his commands are doing so out of a true and sincere commitment to the well-being of others or are instead motivated by other concerns, such as a desire to gain his favor or manipulate him merely to satisfy some type of selfish desire or self-interest on their part. In that case, rewarding their behavior would not lead them to live in genuine love for others and might even result in their becoming more selfish and manipulating, since they would conclude that they can obtain what they want from God merely by doing outwardly what he commands. Conversely, if God looked only into the hearts of people when judging them, it would not be clear whether the good intentions of those he judged and their commitment to living in accordance with his will were leading them to behave in ways that actually contributed to the well-being of others. In spite of their good intentions, they might be acting in ways that do harm to others out of ignorance or a lack of understanding. In that case, they would still stand in need of correction. In addition, a commitment to doing what is good, just, and loving is insufficient if it does not actually lead to behavior that is also good, just, and loving. God must therefore determine not only whether that commitment is present in the hearts of those whom he judges but also whether it is actually leading to actions that contribute to the well-being of all.

Once God makes such a determination, he can then decide what type of response is called for on his part in order to accomplish his purposes. If he does not see the type of behavior and commitment to righteousness that he desires in those whom he judges, his love will take the form of punishments that are aimed either at correcting them or putting a stop to their destructive behavior and its consequences. In contrast, if he does see the type of behavior and commitment to righteousness that he desires in those whom he judges, he will generally respond with blessing. However, because even those who are committed and dedicated to doing his will are never perfect and always need to grow further in that commitment and dedication, at times God may subject them to suffering even when they have been obedient in order to bring them to an even greater commitment and dedication to living in the way he commands for the good of all. In that case, the suffering to which he allows them to be subjected leads them to continue to examine and evaluate their conduct to discern the changes that they still need to make. It also leads them to seek out God actively in order to ask him to continue strengthening them in their faith, obedience, and understanding.

Rediscovering the Love of Vengeance

In English, the terminology commonly used to refer to the manner in which God responds to human behavior in accordance with his judgments regarding that behavior is that of *retribution*. As we have seen in Chapters 4 and 5 of this study, when God responds to behavior that is in conformity with his will by blessing those who practice such behavior, he is generally said to *reward* that behavior. When God responds to behavior that is contrary to his will by inflicting some type of suffering on those involved in such behavior, he is said to *punish* it. Whether he rewards or punishes people, God's reaction to their behavior is based on what that behavior *deserves* or *merits*. While in principle retribution can involve rewarding people for their behavior, usually the language of retribution is used in a negative sense to refer to the punishment inflicted on those whose behavior deserves to be punished. The purpose of retribution is generally to make someone suffer or pay for having committed some type of wrong or offense. In that case, it can often be understood as a synonym for vengeance or revenge. At times the language of recompense is used to speak of rewarding people for good behavior, though recompense can also be understood in terms of restitution or requital for some type of damage or injury.

For reasons that we have also considered previously, however, terms such as these tend to convey ideas that are not fully in accordance with biblical thought and at times must even be regarded as running contrary to it. This is especially true in the case of the language of retribution. Due to the differences between the Hebrew and English understandings of justice considered in Chapter 4, in English retribution is generally not seen as being motivated out of love or a concern for others. In fact, it is often considered an end in itself. It is said that justice requires that those who have done wrong be made to pay for their conduct by being punished and made to suffer. Such retribution or punishment is not motivated by love or a desire for their well-being but rather by a concern to uphold a system or order that is said to be just. This idea of retribution is also based on the idea that justice is satisfied merely by inflicting suffering on those who are guilty of an offense.

Even more problematic, however, is the use of the terminology of vengeance in order to speak of God's response to wrongdoing in the biblical texts. In English, vengeance or revenge is not an expression of love in any sense but is instead an act of spite and even hatred. It involves seeking to inflict pain and suffering on those who have done one harm or made one suffer. The objective is merely to "get even" with such persons or make them "pay" for the harm they have done or the offense they have committed. In most cases, in fact, those who seek revenge or vengeance would like the suffering of the persons who have harmed or offended them to be as intense and severe as possible. Their suffering is even seen as a motive for rejoicing and satisfaction by those who have taken vengeance on them. It should also be noted that the opposite of vengeance or revenge is usually said to be forgiveness. To forgive is generally understood in terms of refraining from seeking retribution or taking vengeance on those who have done one harm, even though one may have a right to do so. In contrast to retribution and vengeance, therefore, forgiveness is seen as an expression of kindness, mercy, and compassion.

English translations of the Hebrew Bible regularly use the language of retribution and vengeance to refer to God's activity of inflicting suffering and punishment on those who anger him by acting contrary to his will. Most English translations of Psalm 94, for example, begin that Psalm by referring to God in this way: "O Lord, you God of vengeance, you God of vengeance, shine forth!" (v. 1).[14] The language of vengeance is also used at the beginning of the book of Nahum: "A jealous and avenging God is the Lord, the Lord is avenging and wrathful. The Lord takes vengeance on his adversaries and rages against his enemies" (Nah 1:2). The same language appears in the first chapter of Isaiah: "Therefore says the Sovereign, the Lord of hosts, the Mighty One of Israel: Surely I will pour out my wrath on my enemies and avenge myself on my foes!" (Isa 1:24). In Jer 46:10, the allusion to God's vengeance is especially violent: "That day is the day of the Lord God of hosts, a day of vengeance, to avenge himself on his foes. The sword will devour and be sated, and drink its fill of their blood." In these instances and others, English versions of the Bible regularly use the language of vengeance and retribution to translate Hebrew terms derived from the word *naqam*, which may appear either as a verb or a noun.

When one reads these passages in English, the imagery that comes across is that of a violent and vindictive God who merely seeks to inflict suffering on those whom he regards as his enemies or adversaries. What appears to motivate him is not any type of love, grace, or mercy but only spite and hatred for those who have the audacity to oppose him. A close look at the contexts in which these affirmations appear, however, reveals a very different picture. After invoking God as a "God of vengeance" in its opening verse, for example, Psalm 94 goes on to speak of God judging the arrogant evildoers who crush and afflict his people, including especially those in greatest need: "O Lord, how long will the wicked, how long will the wicked exult? They pour out their arrogant words; all the evildoers boast. They crush your people, O Lord, and afflict your heritage. They kill the widow and the stranger, and murder the orphan, and they say, 'The Lord does not see; the God of Jacob takes no

---

14. Among the translations that use the language of vengeance in this passage and the ones that immediately follow are the RSV, the NRSVue, the NASB, the NIV, and the ESV.

notice'" (vv. 3-7). The author of Psalm 94 then rejoices at the manner in which God chastises human beings out of love for them in order to save them by bringing them to practice justice and righteousness, while at the same time mercifully delivering the oppressed from their oppressors:

> He who disciplines the nations, he who teaches knowledge to humankind, does he not chastise? The LORD knows the thoughts of all, that they are but a breath. Happy are those whom you discipline, O LORD, and whom you teach out of your law, to give them respite from days of trouble, until a pit is dug for the wicked. For the LORD will not forsake his people; he will not abandon his heritage. For justice will return to the righteous, and all the upright in heart will follow it. Who rises up for me against the wicked? Who stands up for me against evildoers? If the LORD had not been my help, my soul would soon have lived in the land of silence. When I thought, "My foot is slipping," your steadfast love, O LORD, held me up. When the cares of my heart multiply within me, your consolations cheer my soul. Can wicked rulers be allied with you, those who contrive mischief by decree? They conspire together against the life of the righteous, and condemn the innocent to death. But the LORD has become my stronghold, and my God the rock of my refuge. He will repay them for their iniquity and wipe them out for their wickedness; the LORD our God will wipe them out (vv. 10-22).

In a similar manner, immediately after describing God as avenging and wrathful, the opening verses of the book of Nahum portray God as one who acts with kindness to deliver those who are being oppressed from their oppressors: "The LORD is good, a stronghold in the day of trouble; he protects those who take refuge in him, even in a rushing flood. He will make a full end of his adversaries, and will pursue his enemies into darkness" (Nah 1:7-8). After alluding further to God's destruction of those who do evil and oppress others, the same chapter ends with an expression of joy and celebration: "Thus says the LORD, Though they are at full strength and are many, they will be cut off and pass away. Even though I have afflicted you, I will afflict you no more. And now I will break off his yoke from you and tear apart the bonds that bind you. . . . Look! On the mountains the feet of one who brings good tidings, who proclaims peace! Celebrate your festivals, O Judah, fulfill your vows, for never again will the wicked invade you; they are utterly cut off!" (1:12, 14-15).

In the passage from the first chapter of Isaiah, immediately before speaking of God as one who avenges himself and pours out his wrath on his enemies, the prophet points to the corruption, injustice, violence, and thievery of the inhabitants of Jerusalem who have provoked God to anger: "How the faithful city has become a harlot! She was once full of justice, righteousness lodged in her—but now murderers! Your silver has become dross, your wine is diluted with water. Your rulers are rebels and companions of thieves. Everyone loves a bribe and runs after gifts. They do not defend the orphan, and the widow's cause does not come before them" (Isa 1:21-23). The verses that follow go on to describe God purifying the people in the same way that metals are purified through smelting in order to bring the people to practice justice and righteousness again and deliver them from those who rise up against God: "And I will restore your judges as at the first, and your counselors as at the beginning. Afterward you will be called the city of righteousness, the faithful city. Zion will be redeemed by justice, and those in her who repent, by righteousness. But rebels and sinners will be destroyed together, and those who forsake the Lord will be consumed" (1:25-28).

The allusions to God's retribution and vindication in Jeremiah 46 appear in the context of God's promise to send the Babylonians against Egypt to deliver Israel and other nations from the oppression they have endured at the hands of the Egyptians (vv. 1-26). On that basis, the passage concludes with words of encouragement for the people, who are told not to fear, since even though God chastises them, he will ultimately save them and enable them to dwell in peace:

> But as for you, my servant Jacob, have no fear, and do not be dismayed, O Israel. For I am going to save you from far away, and your offspring from the land of their captivity. Jacob will return and have peace and security, and no one will make him afraid. As for you, my servant Jacob, have no fear, says the Lord, for I am with you. I will make an end of all the nations among which I have banished you, but I will not make an end of you! I will chastise you in just measure, and I will by no means leave you unpunished (vv. 27-28).

Rather than referring to vengeance, revenge, or retribution as these terms are commonly understood in English, all four of these passages speak of God taking action against those who practice evil and oppression in order to deliver those who are suffering at their hands. In each case, the purpose of God's intervention is not to *inflict suffering*, as if that were desirable as an end in itself, but to *put an end to the injustices being committed by acting against those who are responsible for those injustices.* Undoubtedly, in order to accomplish that objective, God must inflict suffering and destruction on those who refuse to put away their unjust and oppressive behavior, and in that sense God can be said to punish them. This punishment, however, is *a means to an end which is good and loving,* namely, that of putting an end to a situation of injustice, violence, and oppression. Furthermore, it is *not the punishment itself* that restores justice, as if merely making evildoers suffer or bringing about their destruction were sufficient to set everything right, but rather *the deliverance from injustice and oppression that results from that punishment.* What satisfies God and God's justice is not that evildoers suffer for what they have done but that they no longer be able to crush and trample on others and destroy their well-being. If such punishment is a motive of rejoicing, the motive for that rejoicing is *not that of seeing evildoers suffer but that of seeing those who were suffering at their hands delivered from their plight so as to be able to enjoy peace and well-being once more.*

These ideas are expressed even more clearly in other texts in which English translations have generally used the language of vengeance to translate the Hebrew. In Isaiah 35, for example, the prophet looks forward to a day in which God will come to make the wilderness flourish, strengthen the weak, heal those with infirmities, and bring sorrow and sighing to an end by filling the earth with rejoicing and gladness. In that context, the passage affirms: "Say to those who are of a fearful heart, 'Be strong, do not fear! Here is your God. He will come with vengeance, with terrible recompense. He will come and save you'" (Is 35:4, NRSVue). Here vengeance and recompense are a means to salvation and to some extent are even synonymous with it. While the passage does not refer explicitly to any evildoers, the idea is that God will take action to put a stop to the evil and violence being committed against those who are in need of salvation and deliverance. As in the other passages just considered, God's act of taking vengeance is viewed as *an act of love* in that its purpose is to save those who are enduring oppression by restoring them to a situation in which they may once again enjoy peace, justice, and well-being.

In many passages, the language of retribution or recompense appears alongside that of vengeance or is used in its place. Nevertheless, the ideas behind that language are essentially the same. Several passages from the last chapters of Isaiah illustrate this point well. In Isaiah 59, after mentioning God's displeasure at the lack of justice among his people and the violence, corruption, and bloodshed that he sees in their midst, the prophet affirms that God "put on righteousness like a breastplate, and a helmet of salvation on his head; he put on garments of vengeance for clothing, and wrapped himself in fury as in a mantle. According to their deeds, so will he repay wrath to his adversaries, requital to his enemies; to the coastlands he will render requital.... And he will come to Zion as Redeemer, to those in Jacob who turn from transgression, says the LORD" (vv. 17-18, 20, NRSVue). Here the purpose for which God inflicts suffering and destruction on those who oppose him by trampling on the weak and vulnerable is to establish justice and righteousness by putting an end to their unjust and violent behavior so that those who are suffering at their hands may be saved. Moved by indignation at the crimes and injustices being committed by some against others, God comes as a Redeemer to restore shalom, truth, and well-being for his oppressed people. Of course, because only those who turn from their transgressions can truly enjoy the salvation he will bring and that salvation can only come to pass if those oppressing others are punished and destroyed, any who wish to be saved must repent by turning back from their destructive behavior in order to live as God has commanded out of love for all.

The language of vengeance appears particularly out of place in English translations of the opening verses of Isaiah 61, which allude to a savior figure who has been chosen by God to bring deliverance, healing, and justice to his people. In translations such as the NRSVue, this figure is presented as affirming:

> The spirit of the Lord GOD is upon me because the LORD has anointed me; he has sent me to bring good news to the oppressed, to bind up the brokenhearted, to proclaim liberty to the captives and release to the prisoners; to proclaim the year of the LORD's favor and *the day of vengeance of our God*, to comfort all who mourn, to provide for those who mourn in Zion—to give

them a garland instead of ashes, the oil of gladness instead of mourning, the mantle of praise instead of a faint spirit. They will be called oaks of righteousness, the planting of the LORD, to display his glory (vv. 1-3).

Here the prophet presents God sending his servant, not to *inflict* suffering but to *put an end to it* by delivering the oppressed, healing the brokenhearted, liberating the captives, comforting the mourning, and establishing justice and righteousness. In this context, the passage speaks explicitly of God's vengeance as an expression of his *favor*. Obviously, the reason for this is that the manner in which God intends to accomplish all of the things mentioned is by taking action against those who are responsible for the oppression, pain, captivity, and injustice that those he intends to save are enduring at their hands. A few verses later, the passage speaks of God's retribution as an expression of his commitment to what is just and right and his opposition to evil: "For I the LORD love justice; I hate robbery and wrongdoing. I will faithfully give them their recompense, and I will make an everlasting covenant with them" (Isa 61:8). The same understanding of God's recompense and retribution appears in the following chapter: "The LORD has proclaimed to the end of the earth: Say to daughter Zion, 'Look, your salvation comes; his reward is with him, and his recompense before him'" (62:11). While most English translations of this verse refer to a "reward," the context indicates that the salvation and redemption that the people are to experience is not something they have earned or merited by their own activity but a gracious gift bestowed on the oppressed simply because they are suffering and in need.

At the beginning of chapter 63, Isaiah describes a figure who comes from Edom with his robes stained in blood. The figure identifies himself by affirming: "It is I, announcing vindication, mighty to save" (v. 1, NRSVue). The Hebrew phrase translated here as "announcing vindication" is actually "speaking in justice" (*tsedaqah*). Several verses later, the figure continues to speak: "For the day of vengeance was in my heart, and the year for my redeeming work had come. I looked, but there was no helper; I was abandoned, and there was no one to sustain me, so my own arm brought me victory, and my wrath sustained me. I trampled down peoples in my anger; I crushed them in my wrath, and I poured out their lifeblood on the earth" (vv. 4-6). Here vengeance (*naqam*) is presented as being synonymous with the figure's redeeming work or activity, which is aimed at providing assistance to those in need of help by destroying their oppressors.

Other passages from the Hebrew Scriptures use the language of vengeance and retribution in the same manner. In 2 Sam 22:47-49 (= Ps 18:47-49), David joyfully refers to God as "the rock of my salvation, the God who gave me vengeance and brought down peoples under me, who brought me out from my enemies. You exalted me above my adversaries; you delivered me from the violent" (NRSVue). In Micah 5, after describing how God will send Judah a savior and shepherd to feed his flock and deliver a remnant of the people from their adversaries, God is presented as affirming: "And in anger and wrath I will execute vengeance on the nations that did not obey" (v. 15, NRSVue). The context thus indicates that the focus is once again on the deliverance of the suffering and oppressed from the people and practices that are responsible for that suffering and oppression. The "vengeance" that God brings involves acting against those who disobey God by unjustly inflicting suffering and violence on others so that those who suffer at their hands can be delivered from their plight.

Similar ideas appear in two passages from Jeremiah. In Jer 11:18-20, the prophet proclaims:

> It was the LORD who made it known to me, and I knew it; then you showed me their evil deeds. But I was like a gentle lamb led to the slaughter. And I did not know it was against me that they devised schemes, saying, "Let us destroy the tree with its fruit, let us cut him off from the land of the living, so that his name will be remembered no more!" But you, O LORD of hosts, who judge righteously, who try the heart and the mind, let me see your retribution upon them, for to you I have committed my cause.

Further on in the book, Jeremiah uses the same language of retribution or vengeance (*naqamah*) to express his hope that God will deliver him from the persecution he is enduring on account of his prophetic activity:

> For I hear many whispering: "Terror is all around! Denounce him! Let us denounce him!" All my close friends are watching for me to stumble. "Perhaps he can be enticed, and we can prevail against him, and take our revenge on him." But the LORD is with me like a mighty warrior; therefore my persecutors will stumble, and they will not prevail. They will be greatly shamed, for they will not succeed. Their everlasting disgrace will never be forgotten. O LORD of hosts, you test the righteous, you see the heart and the mind; let me see your retribution upon them, for to you I have committed my cause (Jer 20:10-12).

Undoubtedly, many of the passages that speak of the vengeance and retribution executed by God employ imagery that is extremely graphic and violent. In some cases, those passages also speak of those who have been delivered from injustice and oppression rejoicing at the punishments and destruction inflicted by God. While these passages may seem to reflect views of vengeance and retribution that are in accordance with the common understanding of these terms in English, when they are viewed in context it becomes clear that they can and should be interpreted instead on the basis of the idea that God's objective in punishing the oppressors and evildoers is to bring about the deliverance of those who suffer at their hands. Because in Hebrew the objective of retribution or vengeance is not to *inflict suffering* but to *deliver the oppressed from their oppressors*, whatever joy or rejoicing people are said to express when God takes retribution or vengeance is motivated not by seeing others suffer but rather seeing the oppressed delivered from their suffering.

In Deuteronomy 32, for example, language that is extremely graphic and violent is used to speak of God taking vengeance on those who oppose him. There the allusions to God's vengeance and punishment appear in the context of a song that describes the Israelites in the desert as a degenerate, crooked, and perverse generation who responded to God's goodness and kindness by dealing falsely with him (vv. 5-6). Despite the care and concern God showed for them out of sheer grace and mercy, they abandoned God and dedicated themselves to idols, thereby provoking him to wrath (vv. 10-22). Because of the wickedness of their deeds, God wished to destroy them, but out of concern for the other nations, he relented from doing so (vv. 23-34). The passage then continues:

> Vengeance is mine, and recompense, for the time when their foot will slip; because the day of their calamity is near, their doom will come swiftly. Indeed, the LORD will judge his people and have compassion on his servants when he sees that their power is gone, and neither bond nor free remain. Then he will say: "Where are their gods now, the rock in which they sought refuge, who ate the fat of their sacrifices and drank the wine of their drink offerings? Let them rise up and help you; let them be your protection! See now that I, even I, am he; there is no other god but me. I kill and I make alive; I wound and I heal, and no one can deliver from my hand. For I lift up my hand to heaven and swear: As I live forever, when I sharpen my flashing sword, and my hand grasps it in judgment, I will take vengeance on my adversaries, and will repay those who hate me. I will make my arrows drunk with blood, and my sword will devour flesh—with the blood of the slain and the captives, from the long-haired leaders of the enemy." Rejoice, O nations, with his people! For he will avenge the blood of his children, and take vengeance on his adversaries. He will repay those who hate him, and cleanse the land for his people (vv. 35-43).

Although these verses may seem to convey the image of a bloodthirsty, vindictive, and irate God who is anxious to slaughter and destroy his enemies, when viewed in the context of the chapter as a whole, it becomes clear that what God is eager to do is to bless and save his people. The language of vengeance, recompense, calamity, and doom appears alongside an allusion to God's compassion and his desire to judge his people in the sense of saving them. Before this can happen, however, they must be brought low and rendered powerless, since only in that way will they realize that the false gods to whom they have dedicated themselves cannot help them or give them life. The affirmation that God kills and makes alive and also wounds and heals is not intended to portray him as acting capriciously or in an arbitrary manner but instead stresses his sovereignty and his power both to destroy evildoers and to save those who suffer at their hands. The purpose of that affirmation is to let the people know that they can find life and salvation in him alone and that serving any other god will lead only to ruin and destruction for them, since those gods are not sovereign and do not possess the same power that he does. The threatening and violent words that God directs at those who act contrary to his will are intended to warn them not to stand in opposition to him and to let them know that he will defend and protect with great vigor those whom the passage refers to as his children (v. 43; cf. vv. 5-7, 10-11, 18-20). The passage concludes by affirming that the purpose for which God intends to inflict retribution on those who do evil is so that the land may be cleansed or purified for his people. This makes it clear that the violent destruction of those who oppose and hate God has the purpose of making it possible for those who will live as his people to dwell unmolested in peace, security, purity, justice, and righteousness in the land he has promised them.

The same type of graphic language appears in Psalm 58. There, after describing the depths of wickedness into which those who worship other gods fall and imploring God to destroy them by breaking the teeth in their mouths and making them vanish, the Psalmist affirms: "The righteous will rejoice when they see vengeance done. They will bathe their feet in the blood of the wicked. People will say, 'Surely there is a reward for the righteous; surely there is a God who judges on earth'" (vv. 10-11). Here again, the final allusion to God as one who judges should be understood in the sense that he *saves* by acting against the people's oppressors to establish justice for the good of all. For the reasons we have just noted above, the allusion to the people rejoicing when they see vengeance done and are able to stand in the blood of their oppressors should not be understood in the sense that they will experience a morbid sense of pleasure and satisfaction at contemplating the manner in which their enemies have been slaughtered and destroyed. Instead, what will bring them joy is seeing with their own eyes that their enemies will never be able to rise up and oppress them again. The fact that they are able to bathe their feet in the blood of their enemies is proof of this. It is not the shedding of blood that is said to cause them to rejoice but the assurance that their enemies will never be able to harm them again because their life has gone out from them for good. The idea is the same as that which appears in Nah 1:15, already mentioned above: "Never again will the wicked invade you; they are utterly cut off." Once more, the emphasis is on *deliverance and salvation* rather than punishment as an end in itself.

The idea that the oppressed will rejoice when they see their enemies defeated is also found in Psalm 149. There the Psalmist exclaims: "Let the faithful celebrate in glory; let them sing for joy on their beds! Let the high praises of God be in their throats and two-edged swords in their hands, to execute vengeance on the nations and punishment on the peoples, to bind their kings with chains and their nobles with fetters of iron, to execute on them the judgment decreed. This is glory for all his faithful ones" (vv. 5-9). What makes this passage distinct from the other passages considered above is that here it is the oppressed themselves who destroy their oppressors rather than God. Once again, however, the motive for rejoicing is that once the nations and kings who have done harm to God's people are bound with chains and fetters, their oppression will come to an end.

Translating Vengeance in a Way That Avoids It

This analysis of the biblical passages that use the term *naqam* and its cognates brings us to a problem that we have encountered previously with regard to other Hebrew terms, namely, that English lacks the vocabulary necessary to capture adequately the meaning of the Hebrew text. In English, terms such as vengeance, revenge, and retribution convey the idea of inflicting harm on another person for the purpose of making that person suffer, yet for the reasons we have just seen, this is not the idea conveyed by the Hebrew. In many contexts, the Hebrew instead focuses on the idea of taking action against those who are oppressing others for the purpose of bringing that oppression to an end. In English, however, no terminology exists to express this idea. Whereas in English the objective of vengeance is to *inflict* suffering on another person to avenge some wrong or offense, retaliate, "get even," or "settle a score," in Hebrew the objective is generally to *put a stop* to the suffering of some at the hands of others by making it impossible for those who are causing the suffering to continue to do so. According to Hebrew thought, what the wrongdoers deserve is to be prevented from continuing to harm others, whereas in English what they deserve is to suffer for the harm they have caused others in the past.

Furthermore, while in English it is those who have suffered the harm or offense who are said to take vengeance or revenge on those who have caused it, in Hebrew the person who acts against those who have been causing harm to force them to stop doing so is in many cases someone *other* than the person who has suffered the harm or injustice. Thus, for example, if a judge imposes a penalty on a murderer, in English the judge is not said to be exacting vengeance, revenge, or retribution on the murderer, since the judge herself was not affected personally by the murderer's action. If the loved ones of the person who was murdered seek to inflict harm on the murderer, however, they are said to seek vengeance or take revenge because they are the ones who were affected by the killing. In addition, when judges prescribe punishments in accordance with the law, in English they are not said to be exacting vengeance, since punishments or penalties imposed on wrongdoers in accordance with the law are not seen as having the purpose of "getting even" with them or "settling a score." In contrast to Hebrew, in English vengeance is also regarded as an act that lies *outside* the realm of the law or is *contrary* to the law rather than something that is *mandated* by the law or carried out in *conformity* with it.

In biblical thought, however, when God takes action against those who are harming others unjustly, he does so *not for his own sake* but for the sake of those who are being harmed. Those doing the harm are not hurting God in any way, especially because human beings are incapable of inflicting pain on God or doing injury to him. For the same reason, even though English translations of the Hebrew Bible often speak of God taking vengeance on his enemies or adversaries, in reality those who oppress others are not seeking to do harm to God or to oppose him personally but are only affecting other human beings by their actions. While they may be hostile to God in the sense that they are acting contrary to his will, strictly speaking they do not regard God himself as their enemy or adversary, nor does God regard them as his own enemies or adversaries, since their actions are not directed at God personally and God is not the object of their hatred or enmity.

The fact that the terminology of vengeance conveys ideas that are foreign to the Hebrew can be seen by considering the manner in which the NRSVue translates a passage from Ezekiel 25. There God is presented as intending to take vengeance on the Edomites and Philistines for their treatment of the people of Judah, which is itself described as vindictive:

> Thus says the Lord God: Because Edom acted revengefully against the house of Judah and has grievously offended in taking vengeance upon them, therefore thus says the Lord God: I will stretch out my hand against Edom and cut off from it humans and animals, and I will make it desolate; from Teman even to Dedan they will fall by the sword. I will lay my vengeance upon Edom by the hand of my people Israel, and they shall act in Edom according to my anger and according to my wrath; and they shall know my vengeance, says the Lord God.
>
> Thus says the Lord God: Because with unending hostilities the Philistines acted in vengeance and with malice of heart took revenge in destruction, therefore thus says the Lord God: I will stretch out my hand against the Philistines, cut off the Cherethites, and destroy the rest of the seacoast. I will execute great vengeance on them with wrathful punishments. Then they shall know that I am the Lord, when I lay my vengeance on them (vv. 12-16, NRSVue).

In this case, neither the people of Edom nor the Philistines had done any harm to God himself. Instead, they had acted with cruelty in relation to the people of Judah. Because it was not God who suffered personally at the hands of the Edomites and the Philistines, in English it sounds strange to speak of him taking vengeance on these nations. Such a usage implies that what moves God to take action against those who behave in ways that he deems oppressive and unjust is the effect that such behavior has *on him* rather than on the human beings who suffer the consequences of that behavior. This passage from Ezekiel also speaks of the Edomites and Philistines taking revenge or vengeance on the house of Judah, even though there is no indication in the text that the people of Judah had acted in any way against the Edomites and Philistines or done anything to provoke them to anger. While in this case the Hebrew does reflect the idea of simply seeking to make others suffer, as the Edomites and Philistines do in relation to Judah, the use of the language of revenge or vengeance here remains foreign to English in that according to English usage revenge and vengeance involve a response to a previous aggression or offense. A person who seeks to do harm to another person is not said to be taking vengeance or revenge against that person if that person has not previously injured or offended him or her in any way. For that reason, in English it is misleading to speak of the Edomites and Philistines taking revenge or vengeance on the people of Judah, since the people of Judah are never said to have done them any kind of harm or injustice.

English translations also commonly use the terminology of retaliation and repayment to speak of God taking action against those who have sinned or done evil. Like the terminology of vengeance, the language of repaying is generally understood in terms of inflicting suffering on those who have done one harm for no other purpose than seeking retaliation as an end in itself. That language is used, for example, in Deut 7:10, where it is said that God "repays in their own person those who hate him by destroying them. He does not delay but will repay in their own person those who hate him." This language also appears in the NRSVue translation of Isa 65:6-7 and Jer 16:18:

> See, it is written before me: I will not keep silent, but I will repay; I will indeed repay into their laps their iniquities and their ancestors' iniquities together, says the LORD; because they offered incense on the mountains and reviled me on the hills, I will measure into their laps full payment for their actions (Isa 65:6-7).

> And I will doubly repay their iniquity and their sin because they have polluted my land with the carcasses of their detestable idols and have filled my inheritance with their abominations (Jer 16:18).

Because in English to repay someone for some wrong that they have committed is generally understood in terms of seeking to retaliate against them in order to make them suffer out of a spirit of spite or revenge, most English readers of these passages would understand them in the sense that God is personally offended and affronted by those who hate him and instead serve other gods, and for that reason vows to take vengeance on them by doing them harm. Such a reading presupposes that God's concern is for himself and his own honor, glory, and praise. In that case, he is angry because he is being robbed or deprived of the reverence and worship to which he alone is entitled and is jealous because that reverence and worship are being given to other gods. For that reason, in his wrath he vows to inflict suffering and destruction on those who have wronged him in this way, simply to make them pay for their failure or refusal to give him what is rightfully his.

If we instead take as a starting point the idea that out of love for his people God commands his people to serve him alone and prohibits them from worshiping idols and other gods due to the injustice, violence, and other evils that result from such worship, these passages will be understood very differently. In that case, what God is seeking is not retaliation or revenge for his own sake but rather to put an end to ways of thinking, acting, and behaving that ravage the lives of countless people and do his people tremendous harm. His stated intention is to take decisive action against those who are responsible for filling the land with destructive practices and behaviors so that his people may find true life and wholeness once more by putting away those practices and behaviors and returning to a way of life that leads to justice and well-being for all. This can happen only if they love him rather than hating him or rejecting him.

The logic behind the use of the language of repayment in these passages is that God's intention to eradicate the worship of idols and other gods among his people represents a response to the actions of those who are responsible for filling the land with such worship, together with the injustice and violence that inevitably accompany that worship. God is repaying them in the sense that he is responding to their actions in a way that is appropriate to those actions, that is, doing what is necessary to put a stop to their destructive behavior by "making them pay" for that behavior. His purpose, however, is not to inflict suffering on them as an end in itself but to bring an end to the harm and damage that they are doing to themselves and others by despising and rejecting what he has commanded for the good of all and by serving gods who undermine and destroy the people's well-being rather than promoting it. While ideally he would like to put a stop to that behavior by bringing those who are practicing it to abandon it, when he sees that they refuse to do so he must respond to that behavior or "repay" it by taking action against them and perhaps even destroying them. When God becomes angry with them and "repays" them for such behavior, therefore, his concern is not *for himself* or his own glory or ego but *for those whose lives are adversely affected by that behavior.* It is his commitment to the well-being of all that leads him to make those who reject him and serve false gods "pay" for the harm they bring upon others by overthrowing or consuming them.

Unfortunately, however, it is extremely difficult to translate these passages into English in a way that reflects the logic underlying the Hebrew text. In English, to speak of God repaying the people's sins and iniquities inevitably suggests the idea of revenge and retaliation, whereas in Hebrew the idea is that God is promising to take action in response to the sins and iniquities of those who are serving other gods and idols in order to rid the land of the damage being caused by their behavior. Rather than speaking of repaying the people's sins and iniquities, it would be necessary to speak of God responding to their sinful and destructive behavior by taking action to put a stop to that behavior and doing away with those who stubbornly insist on practicing it, yet it is virtually impossible to find a single word or a brief phrase in English that would convey such an idea in the way that the Hebrew original does.

The same type of problem arises in the English translations of passages from both the Hebrew Bible and the Septuagint that use the terminology of vengeance and retribution to speak of God punishing his people for their sins or avenging himself of their wrongdoing. In several passages from the book of Jeremiah, including one that we have already seen above, after pointing out the sins of the people, God is presented as asking: "Shall I not punish them for these things, . . . and shall I not bring retribution on a nation such as this?" (Jer 5:9, 29; 9:9). Rather than using the language of retribution, English translations such as the RSV, ESV, NIV, and NASB instead present God as asking: "Shall I not avenge myself on a nation such as this?" Once again, however, the sins described by Jeremiah in these passages are not presented as affecting God in any way. Those sins consist of things such as lust, idolatry, adultery, treachery, wickedness, slander, deception, oppression, violence, and the failure to practice justice (Jer 5:7-8, 26-28; 9:4-8). If God punishes those sins, he is not exacting retribution or avenging himself for any type of harm done to himself personally, nor is his purpose that of inflicting suffering on people as an end in itself.

The idea that God acts as an avenger also appears in many English translations of Ps 99:8. This verse is preceded by allusions to the faithfulness of those who obeyed God's commandments and cried out to him when they were in need of help: "O LORD our God, you answered them; you were a forgiving God to them, but an avenger of their wrongdoings." In Hebrew, however, the idea is not that God took vengeance on his people in retaliation for their wrongdoings because he wished to see them suffer but that he chastised them through sufferings in order to correct them. This "avenging" is therefore correction of their sinful behavior. Here, as in other passages that we have considered in Chapter 5, God is said to *forgive* the people's wrongdoings at the same time that he *punishes* them (see Exod 32:31-34; 34:6-7; Num 14:18). In English, however, to inflict punishments or suffering on those who have done wrong or avenge their wrongdoings is to *deny* them forgiveness. Thus, in contrast to the Hebrew, in English the affirmation that God was a "forgiving God" at the same time that he was "an avenger of their wrongdoings" comes across as a contradiction. In biblical thought, however, God forgives his people their wrongdoing in the sense of not holding it against them or abandoning them for that wrongdoing, yet at the same time in his love he insists on taking action to chastise and correct them so that they may not continue in that wrongdoing. To use the language of avenging in this context, however, is misleading and inappropriate, since it conveys ideas that are foreign to the Hebrew.

Similar problems must be noted with regard to the manner in which the NRSVue translates 2 Macc 6:14-16 from the Septuagint: "For in the case of the other nations the Lord waits patiently to punish them until they have reached the full measure of their sins, but he does not deal in this way with us, in order that he may not take vengeance on us afterward when our sins have reached their height. Therefore he never withdraws his mercy from us. Although he disciplines us with calamities, he does not forsake his own people." In biblical thought, when God punishes his people for their sins, he does so not to take vengeance or inflict revenge on them, as if their sins have done him harm in some way, but in order to bring them to put away their sinful behavior and return to him in obedience for their own good. This is clearly the idea here, since the passage is stressing God's goodness and mercy in acting to correct the people when they fall into sin. Strictly speaking, God never takes vengeance on his people in the sense of simply inflicting suffering on them in retaliation for having angered, offended, or disobeyed him, as the NRSVue translation implies.

There are therefore very good reasons for concluding that the language of vengeance, revenge, retribution, retaliation, and repaying is inadequate and inappropriate to translate into English the Hebrew terms used in passages such as those just considered. While these English terms convey the idea of an action taken in response to some type of wrongdoing or injustice and in that regard reflect faithfully the intention of the Hebrew text, they imply that this action is intended merely to inflict suffering out of malice or spite rather than having the purpose of bringing that wrongdoing or injustice to an end out of love for those who are harmed by it. The use of the language of vengeance, retribution, and retaliation also tends to reflect the idea that justice is effected or restored merely by inflicting suffering on those who do wrong. As we have seen previously, such an idea is foreign to biblical thought, where justice is said to be accomplished only when sin, evil, and injustice are done away with so that all may enjoy peace, wholeness, and well-being. In biblical thought, if evildoers are punished but that punishment does not serve to bring about the salvation, liberation, or deliverance of those who were being harmed by those evildoers, justice has not yet been done.

Rather than using either the language of punishment or vengeance to translate passages that use the Hebrew term *naqam* or its cognates, therefore, English translations of the Hebrew Bible might simply refer to God "taking action" against those who harm others. In that case, instead of speaking of God taking vengeance on evildoers or avenging himself on his enemies, it might be said that he takes action against those who oppress others or stand in opposition to him.

In some cases, it might be preferable to use the language of deliverance rather than vengeance to translate the Hebrew. Thus, for example, the phrase "God of deliverance" might be substituted for "God of vengeance" in English translations of the opening verses of Psalm 94: "O Lord, you God of deliverance, you God of deliverance, shine forth! Rise up, O judge of the earth; take action against the proud in the way that their deeds deserve! O Lord, how long will the wicked, how long will the wicked exult? They pour out their arrogant words; all the evildoers boast. They crush your people, O Lord, and afflict your heritage" (vv. 1-5). The idea here is that when God takes action against the proud and the wicked, he is not seeking to take revenge on them but rather acting to deliver the oppressed from their hands. Likewise, in Isa 61:1-3, the phrase "day of deliverance" would communicate much more faithfully the idea reflected in the passage than the phrase "day of vengeance":

> The spirit of the Lord God is upon me because the Lord has anointed me; he has sent me to bring good news to the oppressed, to bind up the brokenhearted, to proclaim liberty to the captives and release to the prisoners, to proclaim the year of the Lord's favor and the day of deliverance of our God, to comfort all who mourn, to provide for those who mourn in Zion—to give them a garland instead of ashes, the oil of gladness instead of mourning, the mantle of praise instead of a faint spirit.

In some contexts, however, the use of the language of deliverance would fail to capture the idea that the actions that God takes are in response to the evils being perpetrated by some against others. In these cases, there is an element of retribution present in that God's activity is directed at the evildoers themselves rather than at those who are being harmed by them, even though that activity is aimed at benefiting the latter rather than making the evildoers suffer. The idea is not that God simply brings deliverance for those who are suffering but that he does so by taking action against those who are causing that suffering in order to prevent them from continuing to do so. This response to the harm being inflicted on some by others involves giving the evildoers what their actions deserve or merit, yet its purpose is to save rather than to inflict punishment as an end in itself. In other words, it is not their actions themselves that deserve reward or punishment but rather the effect that their actions are having on others. If God punishes evildoers, he does so not because they deserve to suffer for what they have done but in order to prevent them from continuing to do harm to others. His purpose is therefore not to exact revenge, "settle the score," "get even" with them, or make them "pay" for what they have done. Rather than acting out of spite, hatred, or malice in the way that the pagan gods of antiquity did, he is acting out of love by attempting to bring violence and oppression to an end. In some cases, it might even be possible to use a phrase such as "saving retribution" to translate the Hebrew word *naqamah*. This would convey the idea that God's intention is to save those who are being oppressed from their oppressors by taking action against the oppressors.

Ultimately, however, the problem of how to render into English the words and phrases used in Hebrew that have traditionally been translated with the language of vengeance, revenge, recompense, and retaliation may not admit of any solution that is entirely satisfactory. The same is true with regard to terms having to do with actions such as judging, punishing, rewarding, and repaying. The use of the terminology of vindication to refer to the manner in which God saves those who are being harmed by others by taking action against those who are doing them harm, for example, also conveys certain ideas that are foreign to the Hebrew. In English, to vindicate a person generally involves showing or proving that person to be in the right rather than delivering them from suffering or oppression. In contrast, when in Hebrew God is said to judge the poor, the needy, and the oppressed, the idea is not that he vindicates them by showing them to be "in the right" but that he delivers them from their plight. Similarly, rather than seeking to bring vindication for his people when they have been suffering at the hands of another nation, he is effecting their deliverance and salvation, since his purpose is not to exonerate them of guilt or demonstrate that their suffering has been unjustified but to bring that suffering to an end.

In whatever manner one may wish to address the problem of translating texts such as those just considered, what matters most is that the language used in English not reflect the idea of a God who acts out of spite, hatred, or malice when he takes action against those who practice injustice and oppression. To be faithful to the ideas in the Hebrew original, language that suggests that the God of Israel acts out of a concern for himself or his own ego, pride, or honor when he responds to those who are acting contrary to his will by doing harm to others must also be avoided. In one way or another, the language chosen must instead convey the idea that God is motivated solely by his love for human beings when he acts to put an end to injustice, suffering, violence, and oppression by punishing or destroying those who are responsible for perpetrating these things. Undoubtedly, the action God takes against evildoers and those who oppress others is often presented in terms that are extremely aggressive and violent, yet such language should be seen as expressing God's profound passion for the well-being of human beings, his intense hatred of anything that does them harm, and his uncompromising commitment to doing whatever is necessary to deliver them from behavior that fills their life with pain and suffering rather than the good he desires for them. While many passages from the Hebrew Bible present God as acting out of anger, fury, and rage and as being eager to pour out his wrath on those who do evil, it must always be stressed that such passions are rooted solely in his uncompromising love for human beings, a love that will stop at nothing in its efforts to save them from themselves.

VISITING SINNERS AND THEIR SINS

In most contemporary English versions, the language of punishment is commonly used to translate the Hebrew verb *paqad* and its cognates. Translations that are more literal, however, use the language of visiting. While this is the normal meaning of the Hebrew term, which can merely refer to the process of going to see a person or a place for a short time, in many contexts it is said that God visits those who have sinned or visits their sin itself. In these cases, the idea is clearly that of punishment.

This usage appears repeatedly, for example, in passages such as the following from the King James Version of the Bible (KJV) and the RSV, both of which employ the terminology of visiting when translating the verbal root *paqad*.

> I the LORD your God am a jealous God, visiting the iniquity of the fathers upon the children to the third and the fourth generation of those who hate me, but showing steadfast love to thousands of those who love me and keep my commandments (Exod 20:5; Deut 5:9-10, RSV).

> In the day when I visit, I will visit their sin upon them (Exod 32:34, RSV).

> Thou therefore, O LORD God of hosts, the God of Israel, awake to visit all the heathen: be not merciful to any wicked transgressors (Ps 59:5, KJV).

> Then will I visit their transgression with the rod, and their iniquity with stripes (Ps 89:32, KJV).

> They are vanity, and the work of errors: in the time of their visitation they shall perish (Jer 10:15, KJV).

> Behold, I am against thee, O thou most proud, saith the Lord GOD of hosts: for thy day is come, the time that I will visit thee (Jer 50:31, KJV).

While these passages undoubtedly speak of punishment, they also convey the idea that God has been absent or distant when the sins and transgressions mentioned were being committed, but now makes himself present or "visits" in order to bring those sins and transgressions to an end. He does this, of course, by taking action against the evildoers and oppressors responsible for those sins and transgressions. Although in contemporary English it is not common to use the language of visitation in this manner, the idea behind the Hebrew usage of that language is by no means difficult to comprehend.

Of course, God may also make himself present when those who are suffering or in need wish for him to help them in some way. In those instances, to visit is not to *punish* but to *save* or *deliver* people from their plight. Once again, a number of passages from the KJV and the RSV may be cited as examples of this usage:

> Then [Ruth] started with her daughters-in-law to return from the country of Moab, for she had heard in the country of Moab that the LORD had visited his people and given them food (Ruth 1:6, RSV).

> And the LORD visited Hannah, and she conceived and bore three sons and two daughters (1 Sam 2:21, RSV).

> Thou hast granted me life and favour, and thy visitation hath preserved my spirit (Job 10:12, KJV).

> What is man, that thou art mindful of him? and the son of man, that thou visitest him? (Ps 8:4, KJV)

> Remember me, O LORD, with the favour that thou bearest unto thy people: O visit me with thy salvation (Ps 106:4, KJV).

> O LORD, thou knowest; remember me and visit me, and take vengeance for me on my persecutors. In thy forbearance take me not away; know that for thy sake I bear reproach (Jer 15:15, RSV).

> They shall be carried to Babylon, and there shall they be until the day that I visit them, saith the LORD; then will I bring them up, and restore them to this place (Jer 27:22, KJV).

> For thus says the LORD: When seventy years are completed for Babylon, I will visit you, and I will fulfil to you my promise and bring you back to this place (Jer 29:10, RSV).

> The prayer of the humble pierces the clouds, and he will not be consoled until it reaches the Lord; he will not desist until the Most High visits him, and does justice for the righteous, and executes judgment (Sir 35:17, RSV).[15]

Many of these passages clearly reflect ideas that we have already seen above. At times God's visitation simply involves coming to the aid of those who are suffering or in need of his assistance. When situations of injustice and oppression arise, however, God makes himself present in order to deliver those who are suffering by acting against those who are responsible for that injustice and oppression. In these cases, there are two complementary aspects to God's visitation: saving the oppressed and either destroying the oppressors or rendering them impotent so that they may no longer do harm to others.

---

15. For other examples of this usage, see Gen 21:1; 50:24; Exod 3:16; 4:31; Ps 80:14; Zeph 2:7; Zech 10:3; Jdt 13:20; Wis 3:7; Sir 18:20; Lk 1:68, 78; 7:16; 19:44; Acts 15:14.

It must be stressed, however, that God does the latter for the sake of the former: he takes action against oppressors in order to deliver from their hand the people whom they are oppressing. While in some contexts the language of punishment is appropriate to describe the action that God takes against oppressors, the objective that God seeks is not that of inflicting suffering on the oppressors but that of preventing them from continuing to oppress others. In most cases, God is not trying to correct or discipline the oppressors but simply acts to put a stop to their oppressive behavior. For that reason, the language of punishment may often be misleading and inaccurate to describe God's activity when he "visits" contexts in which injustice and oppression exist, since his objective is not to punish anyone but rather to bring the injustice and oppression to an end.

In other contexts, however, the language of punishment is both accurate and appropriate to convey the meaning of the Hebrew text. This is especially the case in passages that speak of God visiting sin, iniquity, or transgressions. Once again, however, God's purpose is not to inflict suffering or punishment as an end in itself but either to bring those who have fallen into sin to put away their sinful behavior or else to prevent them from continuing in that behavior so that they and others may no longer be harmed by it.

It is important to keep these ideas in mind when considering passages such as Exod 20:5-6 (= Deut 5:9-10), Exod 34:6-7, and Num 14:18, all of which refer to God "visiting the iniquity" of the parents upon the children to the third and fourth generation. When this phrase is understood simply in terms of punishment as an end in itself, it appears to present God as spiteful, vindictive, and even cruel, especially because in a couple of these passages God is also described as jealous and is said to visit the iniquity of those who hate him. At the same time, however, in each instance the affirmation that God visits the iniquity of the parents upon the children is made in the context of allusions to God's love, grace, mercy, and even forgiveness:

> I the LORD your God am a jealous God, visiting the iniquity of the parents upon the children to the third and the fourth generation of those who reject me, but showing steadfast love to the thousandth generation of those who love me and keep my commandments (Exod 20:5-6; Deut 5:9-10).

> The LORD, the LORD, a God merciful and gracious, slow to anger, and abounding in steadfast love and faithfulness, keeping steadfast love for the thousandth generation, forgiving iniquity and transgression and sin, yet by no means clearing the guilty, but visiting the iniquity of the parents upon the children and the children's children to the third and the fourth generation (Exod 34:6-7).

> The LORD is slow to anger, and abounding in steadfast love, forgiving iniquity and transgression, but by no means clearing the guilty, visiting the iniquity of the parents upon the children to the third and the fourth generation (Num 14:18).

When these passages are read against the background of the idea that God seeks to correct his people when they fall into sin, it becomes evident that the allusions to God's "visiting the iniquity of the parents upon the children" are fully consistent and harmonious with the allusions to God's grace, mercy, steadfast love, and faithfulness that are also mentioned in these passages. Because God's objective is not to inflict suffering or punishment but to bring those who have fallen into sin back to himself in obedience and to strengthen them in that obedience for their own good, when he "visits" the sin of the parents upon their children, he is not acting *contrary* to love but *in accordance* with it. His purpose is to effect a thorough and profound cleansing of the people from their sin so that they may come to live in ways that make it possible for them to enjoy the well-being he desires for them.

Most of those Jews in the Second Temple period who read or heard the allusions to God visiting the iniquity of the parents upon the children to the third and fourth generation would probably have understood the passage to be referring especially to the Babylonian exile. Following the prophet Jeremiah, it was common to fix the duration of Israel's time in exile at seventy years.[16] Given that a generation was equivalent to about twenty years, a period of seventy years would be three or four generations, just as these passages affirm. It is therefore no coincidence that they speak of "the third and fourth generation" rather than specifying either the third or the fourth generation in particular, since in some of the families that went into exile the seventy years would cover three generations while in others it would cover four. Throughout the Hebrew Scriptures, the exile in Babylon is consistently presented as having the purpose of purifying the people from their sins in order to bring about a righteous remnant that might finally leave behind the idolatry that characterized both Israel and Judah prior to the exile and come to live in accordance with the commandments of God's law.

Therefore, rather than presenting the God of Israel as spiteful and vindictive and as one who maliciously makes innocent children suffer for the sins of their parents, the affirmation that he visits the iniquity of the parents upon the children and the children's children down to the third and fourth generation is intended to convey an idea that is very different: God does not merely forgive or overlook the people's sin and disobedience, which would represent a lack of love and concern for their well-being due to the harmful effects which that sin and disobedience have on them and others, but acts to correct these things. He does so by effecting a thorough cleansing that stretches across several generations in order to bring the people to put away their sinfulness and disobedience in a decisive and definitive manner. This will enable God to manifest his steadfast love for them in the way he desires by blessing them to the thousandth generation.

It is also likely that the readers of these passages would have understood them as referring to God's decision to have the Israelites spend forty years in the wilderness before entering into the land he had promised them, given

---

16. See Jer 25:11-12; 29:10; cf. Dan 9:2, 24; Zech 7:5.

the narrative context in which they appear. While this period of time would probably not cover three or four generations, God's purpose in subjecting the Israelites to those years in the wilderness was precisely to raise up a new generation of people who might trust in him, in contrast to their parents, who had doubted and rejected him when they made the golden calf and questioned his ability to introduce them into the land he had promised them due to the size of the peoples inhabiting that land (Exodus 32; Numbers 14).

While most English translations of Exod 34:6-7 and Num 14:18 speak of God as "by no means clearing the guilty," as the NRSVue does, in the Hebrew original no explicit allusion to "the guilty" appears. Nevertheless, the idea is clearly that God does not simply overlook or leave unpunished the sins of those who commit them. The reason for this is the one just mentioned: simply to overlook sinful and destructive behavior without acting to correct it would involve abandoning people to their own ways and therefore leaving them to go unhindered down a path that will lead to their ruin and perdition. For that reason, as a number of passages considered previously in this chapter affirm, when his people fall into such behavior, in his love God does not simply ignore that behavior or let it continue unchecked but immediately takes steps to bring his people back to the way of life he has laid out for them in his commandments for their own good. These verses underscore once more the fact that in biblical thought forgiveness and punishment are not mutually exclusive and that God is often said to punish those whom he forgives in order to chastise and correct them.

The descriptions of God found in these passages, therefore, are not intended to set his justice in opposition to his mercy or to present him as a God who alternates between loving and hating his people, depending on their behavior. Nor are those descriptions intended as threats, as if God were telling his people: "If you do what I have commanded you, I will show you kindness, but if you do not, I will avenge myself by pouring out my wrath and fury not only upon you but upon your children, grandchildren, and great grandchildren as well!" Rather, these passages are intended to stress the depth of God's loving commitment to the well-being of his people in the face of their sin. For that reason, they speak of God not only forgiving in the sense of not abandoning his people or rejecting them definitively when they sin but also taking whatever measures are necessary to bring them back to the way of life that is necessary for them to enjoy the well-being he desires for them when they have fallen into sin. Even if those measures involve inflicting punishments on his people that are extremely painful not only for them but for him as well, God's love for them will not hesitate to take those measures if it is the only way in which he can bring them back to himself in obedience so that his loving purposes may be accomplished among them. It was precisely for this reason that he was thought to have sent many of them into exile under the Babylonians.

THE TERRIBLE EVILS OF GOD'S LOVE AND GOODNESS

Before concluding the present chapter, it is important to return to a point raised in Chapter 2 of this study. There, after considering the Genesis account of creation, it was observed that because everything that God had created was said to be good, it seemed to follow logically that everything that God would continue to do in human history from that point on would be good as well. As we have seen in this chapter and the previous one, in a sense many of the things that God is said to do in the biblical texts can hardly be considered good. On the contrary, when God "visits" the people's sins by pouring out his wrath on them, subjecting them to the most cruel forms of suffering imaginable, and ultimately even destroying many of them, it is necessary to speak of him doing not only what is *bad* but also what is *evil*, as numerous passages from the Hebrew Bible do.[17]

On the basis of what we have seen in these two chapters, however, it must be recognized that there is also a sense in which all that God does in the world must be considered good, including those things that are rightly regarded as evil at the same time. As appalling and even obscene as it may sound, because the God of the Hebrew Bible is uncompromising and unrelenting in his commitment to doing everything within his power to enable the human beings he has created to enjoy the well-being he sought and intended for all from the very beginning, even the most intense and horrific forms of suffering and destruction that he inflicts on people or allows them to suffer must be regarded as good in the sense that they are grounded in that commitment and are an expression of it.

While such a claim is no doubt highly problematic and can even rightly be considered offensive, outrageous, and ludicrous, from the perspective of the biblical texts it must be sustained. Those texts portray a God who is fully, resolutely, and irretractably committed *only to what is good for human beings and his creation as a whole*, and therefore must be said as well *to seek only good in all that he does*, just as he is said to have sought only good when he created the world. In biblical thought, these things continue to be true of the God of Israel and have never changed. The problem and challenge he faces, however, is the presence of what is not only bad but also evil, wicked, and perverse in human beings and the world. The biblical texts do not offer any explanation as to why such great suffering, evil, and perversity exist in the world, other than insisting that God did not create or desire anything bad or evil and that suffering and evil thus exist contrary to his will and are the result of behavior that is also contrary to his will. Those texts also make it clear that God is fully committed to doing everything in his power to eradicate suffering and evil in the world and to bring human beings to join him actively in that commitment. Nevertheless, that suffering and evil are so widespread and deep-rooted that at times as he pursues that objective he must do things that

---

17. See, for example, Deut 32:23; 1 Kgs 9:9; 2 Kgs 22:20; 2 Chr 34:24; Neh 13:18; Isa 45:7; Jer 6:19; 19:3; Lam 3:38; Amos 3:6.

appear to be not only cruel and heartless but even barbaric, atrocious, and monstrous. Such things are certainly evil, therefore, yet from the perspective of the Hebrew Bible and the God of whom it speaks, they must also be seen as an expression of his unconditional love for all that exists and his passionate and burning desire that suffering and evil be brought to an end for good. In certain contexts, only by responding to the tremendous and unspeakable evils perpetrated by human beings with even greater evils can God hope to put an end to those evils in a decisive and definitive manner.

CHAPTER 7

Giving Life by Taking It

In many ways, the sacrificial worship of the God of Israel as it is described in the Hebrew Scriptures and Second Temple Jewish writings was no different than the sacrificial worship practiced among other cultures and nations in antiquity. The God of Israel had a temple dedicated to him at which those who worshiped him offered him animal victims, fruits and grains, drink offerings, monetary gifts, and other precious items. Those who made those offerings did so through priests who were believed to have been designated by God himself to serve as mediators between him and his people. Feasts to honor and celebrate God and give him thanks for the blessings he had bestowed on the people were held regularly, and whenever the people disobeyed God or acted in ways that displeased him they approached him with offerings seeking his forgiveness and renewed favor.

In spite of these similarities, however, the understanding of God reflected in the biblical texts led to an understanding of the meaning and purpose of sacrificial worship that was in important ways fundamentally distinct from that of other peoples. At the heart of this difference was the belief that the God of Israel desired and mandated the offering of sacrifice, not for *his own* sake, but for the sake of his people.

SACRIFICE IN THE PAGAN WORLDVIEWS OF ANTIQUITY

Although an extremely wide variety of beliefs and practices regarding sacrifice existed among the different peoples known to us from the Second Temple period, certain basic ideas appear to have been common in most of the belief systems of those peoples. The most important of these was that the gods were thought to desire from human beings one thing above all else, namely, sacrificial offerings. When human beings wished to obtain the favor of the gods or put away their wrath, there was virtually nothing that they could give to the gods or do for them other than presenting them some type of offering.

Because those who presented sacrificial offerings to the gods were generally seeking to obtain something from them in exchange for their offerings or to maintain their favor, those offerings were understood as embodying *petitions* or *prayers* to the gods. Those who were about to engage an enemy in warfare, for example, would offer sacrifices asking the gods to grant them victory. Those who were enduring a drought would present sacrifices to the gods asking them for rain. Individuals would offer the gods sacrifices in an attempt to obtain from them things such as healing, protection, wealth, or a position of power. In addition, it was expected that those who obtained some favor from the gods would subsequently express their gratitude by means of further sacrificial offerings and also make known publicly what the gods had done on their behalf so that others might seek the favor of those gods and honor them with their offerings as well.

This association of sacrifice with prayer runs throughout the writings of antiquity. In the *Iliad* and the *Odyssey*, those who present offerings to the gods not only make petitions for their favor and blessings but also express to them their gratitude, offer up to them their worship and praise, and at times seek to assuage their wrath. The same practice is evident in other Hellenistic writings and the allusions to sacrifice found in other ancient sources. Among the Romans, for example, it was customary for every sacrifice to be accompanied by prayers that specified clearly what those offering the sacrifice sought from the gods and on whose behalf the offering was being made.[1]

The logic behind this association of sacrifice with prayer is that words alone were insufficient to express the sentiments and motives that the offerings were intended to communicate. One could hardly give thanks to the gods without offering them a concrete sign of one's gratitude, nor could one manifest the earnestness of one's devotion and dedication to the gods without offering them something as a demonstration of that earnestness. To attempt to appease the wrath of the gods without presenting them a sacrificial offering was also unthinkable, since the offering served as the means by which those who had offended the gods manifested to them that they truly lamented having done whatever had angered them. For that reason, sacrifice and prayer were thought to be inseparable from one another. Pliny the Elder, for example, wrote that "a sacrifice without prayer is thought to be useless and not a proper consultation with the gods."[2] Three centuries later, the pagan philosopher Sallustius expressed the same idea: "Prayers divorced from sacrifices are only words, prayers with sacrifices are animated words, the word giving power to the life and the life animation to the word."[3]

The gods, of course, were free to accept or reject the sacrifices and prayers offered to them. For the most part, if they accepted the sacrifices, they were expected to grant what the offerers requested. Those who petitioned the gods for favors, therefore, generally did so either by directing the attention of the gods to the offerings they were presenting to them or by promising to present them offerings in the future.

At the outset of the *Iliad*, for example, the priest Chryses appeals to Apollo on the basis of the sacrifices he has offered him repeatedly in the past in order to ask him for help in taking revenge on the Danaans or Greeks: "Hear me, O god of the silver bow, . . . if ever it pleased you that I adorned your temple,

---

1. See John Scheid, *An Introduction to Roman Religion*, trans. Janet Lloyd (Bloomington, IN: Indiana University Press, 2003), 84, 97.

2. Pliny the Elder, *Natural History* 28.3.

3. Sallustius, *Concerning the Gods and the Universe* 16.

if ever it pleased you that I burned to you all the fat thigh pieces of bulls and goats, then grant my prayer: Let the Danaans pay for the tears I have shed with the shafts of your arrows" (*Il.* 1.37-42). The poem immediately continues: "Thus he spoke in prayer, and Phoebus Apollo heard him" (*Il.* 1.43). Further on, Agamemnon appeals to Zeus on the same basis: "In my eagerness to sack the strong-walled city of Troy, never did I pass by your richly-adorned altars in my warship on my sorrowful journey to this place without offering the fat and thigh pieces of bulls upon each one of them. Therefore, Zeus, grant me this prayer: Allow our men to get free and escape with our lives, and let not the Achaeans be utterly vanquished by the Trojans" (*Il.* 8.236-44). Immediately Zeus is said to respond favorably to Agamemnon's petition (*Il.* 8.245-46).

Toward the end of the *Iliad*, when the gods do not intervene to help the slain Hector receive an honorable burial, Apollo tells them: "You are cruel, O gods, and workers of ruin. Did not Hector burn thigh pieces of bulls and unblemished goats to you? How can you not then bring yourselves to rescue him, even though he is now but a corpse, so that his wife and mother and child may look upon him, together with Priam his father and his people, who wish to proceed without delay to burn his body in the fire and give him his burial rites?" (*Il.* 24.33-38). In the *Odyssey*, Penelope prays to the goddess Athena to protect her son Telemachus from her suitors on the same basis, namely, Odysseus's faithfulness in presenting sacrifices to Athena: "Hear me, O daughter of Zeus who bears the aegis, unwearied one: If ever the resourceful Odysseus burned to you in his palace the fat thigh pieces of a bull or a sheep, bear it in mind now, I pray you, and save for me my beloved son from the villainy of the suitors" (*Od.* 4.762-66). The goddess is then said to have heard her prayer (*Od.* 4.767).

While the gods might reject the sacrifices offered to them for any reason, their rejection usually had to do with the failure of the offerers to comply with their will in some way. Because the gods were capricious and tended to show favoritism to some human beings over others, however, at times their rejection of the sacrifices and prayers offered to them was not based on any clear logic or reason. In the *Iliad*, for example, some of the gods decide to side with the Greeks, Achaeans, or Danaans, while others support the Trojans. For the most part, nothing that the Greeks or Trojans do can bring the gods to change sides. When the Trojans look to Athena as their guardian and protector and seek her assistance by offering her lavish sacrifices at the magnificent temple they had constructed in her honor, the Trojan priestess of Athena prays: "Athena, defender of our city, you who shine among the goddesses: Break the spear of Diomedes and grant that he may be cast down before Scaea's gates. Do this, and we will immediately sacrifice in your temple twelve young heifers that have never been broken, if only you will take pity on the city of the Trojans and their wives and little children" (*Il.* 6.305-10). Despite the devotion that the Trojans have shown for Athena, however, the priestess is unable to gain her favor: "Thus she prayed, but Pallas Athena denied her prayer" (*Il.* 6.311).

Subsequently, it is said of the people of Troy, also known as Ilios, and their king Priam that "they rushed to bring cattle and fattened sheep from the city, brought sweetened wine and bread out from their houses, and heaped up abundant firewood. They then offered up hecatombs of unblemished victims to the immortal gods, and the winds carried up to heaven from the plains below the sweet savor of their sacrifices. But the blessed gods did not partake of what was offered or receive it favorably, for their hatred for sacred Ilios and for Priam and his heavily armed people was exceedingly great" (*Il.* 8.544-52). Likewise, in the *Odyssey*, Odysseus recalls how he sacrificed a ram to Zeus and burned its thigh-pieces, but then says of Zeus: "He paid no heed to my sacrifice, and instead pondered how he might destroy all my warships together with my trusty companions" (*Od.* 9.550-55). Later on, an elderly woman who had nursed Odysseus in his infancy tells him: "Surely Zeus hated you more than all other men, even though you had a god-fearing heart. For never did any mortal burn to Zeus, the hurler of thunderbolts, as many fat thigh pieces or choice hecatombs as you did, as you prayed that you might reach a sleek old age and raise your glorious son to adulthood. But now he has prevented you from ever returning to your home" (*Od.* 19.363-68).

The gods of Homer's poems not only demand that human beings present them sacrifices but also desire those sacrifices to be as lavish and bountiful as possible. The greater the offering, the greater the favor obtained by it. Conversely, the greater the favor sought from the gods or granted by them, the more lavish and abundant the sacrifice was expected to be. The most precious offerings mentioned are hecatombs consisting of a hundred oxen or fattened bulls that have never been used for labor in the fields and whose horns are gilded. These offerings are often accompanied by drink offerings and grain offerings as well.

In addition to making their offerings as appealing as possible to the gods and celebrating feasts, festivals, and games in their honor, those who sought to obtain the gods' favor or placate their wrath might at times attempt to sway them in other ways. They might dedicate songs and dances to them or perform other actions that honored, amused, or entertained them.[4] They might also seek to manifest the sincerity of their devotion and submission to the gods by fasting or doing some type of bodily harm to themselves, as the priests of Baal are said to have done by cutting themselves and covering themselves with their blood in the account of their confrontation with Elijah in 1 Kgs 18:28. Because the gods were always free to accept or reject the sacrifices and prayers offered to them for any reason, however, those offerings were not thought to work automatically or *ex opere operato*. One could not obtain what one wanted from the gods simply by performing sacrificial rites or following prescribed rituals. In this regard, the presentation of sacrificial offerings and worship was distinct from the practice of magic, by means of which people sought to obtain what they desired by manipulating forces that were thought to function on their own independently of the gods and other spiritual beings.

---

4. See, for example, *Il.* 1.436-74; 10.292-98; *Od.* 3.273-75, 379-84, 418-63.

While the gods of antiquity might lay down virtually any condition they pleased for accepting favorably the sacrifices and petitions offered to them, for the most part the conditions they established had little to do with morality or the practice of justice, kindness, and compassion. Naturally, both the gods and the human authorities who served them as their representatives demanded that people respect certain rules of behavior and obey their laws and commands, yet in many cases they cared about these things only when they were affected by them directly. They might also insist that those who presented them offerings submit obediently to other human beings whom they had designated as their representatives, such as the priests who oversaw the worship offered to them or the rulers whom they had placed in power. As we have seen in Chapter 4, however, what particularly concerned the gods and their designated representatives was that order be maintained so that they could enjoy peace and tranquility and receive what they desired from the human beings who were devoted to them. Strictly speaking, therefore, they were not promoting or defending the practice of morality but simply imposing on human beings the type of behavior that benefited them in some way.

At the heart of all of these practices and beliefs regarding sacrifice, of course, is the principle of *do ut des* that we have seen previously: sacrifices serve as means by which human beings seek to obtain what they need or want from the gods by offering the gods something that those gods need or want from them in exchange. The only reason that human beings can influence the gods by means of their sacrificial offerings is that the gods have needs and desires that such offerings are able to satisfy. Were that not the case, it would be pointless for human beings to present sacrificial offerings to the gods, since those offerings would not benefit the gods in any way or attract any favorable response from them.

SACRIFICING TO THE GOD OF ISRAEL

While many passages from the Hebrew Bible speak of people offering sacrifices to the God of Israel and prescribe in detail the type of sacrifices that were to be offered up to him, nowhere do the biblical texts ever enter into any type of discussion regarding the purpose for which sacrificial offerings were presented to God or the meanings ascribed to those offerings and the rites that accompanied them. In general terms, of course, it is clear that those who presented sacrificial offerings to God did so as an expression of thanks, praise, and devotion to him and at times in order to seek his favor or forgiveness. Any clear explanation as to why they felt it important or necessary to do these things by means of sacrificial offerings or why they thought that God had commanded his people to present him such offerings, however, is lacking in the Hebrew Scriptures and for the most part in the Jewish writings of the Second Temple period as well. All of these texts simply presuppose that those who would read them already understood the reasons why sacrificial offerings were to be presented to God and why he had mandated those offerings in the Torah. The fact that those texts never discuss the purpose of the various rites involved also indicates that those who composed and redacted them either assumed that the readers already knew what the purpose of those rites was or did not consider it important or necessary for the readers to know their purpose.

Almost from the beginning of the narrative they present, the Hebrew Scriptures refer to sacrifices of various types being offered to God. In the first part of Genesis, figures such as Cain, Abel, and Noah present sacrificial offerings to God (Gen 4:3-7; 8:20-21), and throughout the rest of the book the patriarchs do the same. In Genesis 14, Abraham is said to have offered to God by means of the high priest Melchizedek the tithe of all the goods he had taken from the kings he had defeated in battle (vv. 17-21). Abraham also sacrifices a ram to God after God's angel had stopped him from slaying his son Isaac to offer him up as a burnt offering (Gen 22:9-13). Several other passages from Genesis present Jacob offering sacrifice to the God of Abraham and Isaac (Gen 31:54; 35:14; 46:1). Subsequently, in the book of Exodus, Moses asks the Pharaoh to let the Israelites go so that they may go to a place where they can worship God with their sacrifices.[5] After God frees the Israelites from the Pharoah's hand, Moses' father-in-law Jethro is said to present a burnt offering and sacrifices to God in the presence of Moses, Aaron, and the elders of Israel as an expression of his joy at the people's deliverance (Exod 19:8-12).

All of these passages allude only briefly to the offering of sacrifice without mentioning explicitly any motive or purpose behind the offering other than that of worshiping God and giving him thanks. Those who offer the sacrifices are not presented as seeking any type of favor or blessing from God in exchange for their offering, nor are they imploring God for forgiveness or attempting to assuage his wrath, since in no case are they said to have acted contrary to his will or provoked him to anger prior to offering their sacrifice.[6] None of these passages, therefore, can be said to reflect the principle of *do ut des* that was thought to lie at the heart of pagan conceptions of sacrifice. Nor do those who offer God sacrifice do so out of obligation or in response to some type of demand on God's part that they give him what is due to him. Instead, the sacrificial offerings appear to be spontaneous expressions of devotion and gratitude toward God, motivated only by a desire to thank and praise him for his goodness and blessings.

---

5. See Exod 7:16; 8:1, 20; 9:1, 13; 10:3, 26; 12:31.

6. Some scholars such as Gordon J. Wenham have claimed that Noah's sacrifice following the flood in Gen 8:21 is presented as placating God's wrath, yet there is no evidence of such an idea in the passage ("The Akedah: A Paradigm of Sacrifice," in *Pomegranates and Golden Bells: Studies in Biblical, Jewish, and Near Eastern Ritual, Law, and Literature in Honor of Jacob Milgrom*, ed. David P. Wright, David Noel Freedman, and Avi Hurvitz; Winona Lake, IN: Eisenbrauns, 1995, 93-102 [94-95]). The passage contains no allusion to God's wrath, and the reason why God is said to promise never to curse the ground again is not that Noah has offered a sacrifice but that he realizes that the heart of human beings is evil from its youth. In that case, for God to flood the earth again would be pointless, since such a measure would still not resolve the problem that is at the root of the destructive behavior that God would like to eradicate.

The first sacrifice that the God of Israel commands of his people in Exodus is that of the Passover lamb immediately prior to their departure from Egypt. The prescriptions God gives through Moses include not only the manner in which the people are to sacrifice the lamb, smear its blood on the doorposts and lintels of their houses, consume its flesh, and dispose of its remains but contemplate as well the celebration of the Passover feast in the future, which is also referred to as the Festival of Unleavened Bread (Exod 12:1–13:10). At the same time, God commands that the firstborn of all of the people's animals be offered to him and that their firstborn sons be redeemed by a payment (13:1-2, 11-16).

When God gives his commandments to Moses at Sinai and makes his covenant with the people there, initially he has Moses tell them that they can present him burnt offerings and offerings of well-being at any of the places he causes his name to be remembered among them, simply by making a rudimentary altar of earth and uncut stones (Exod 20:22-26). In the same passage, God affirms that he will come to the people and bless them (v. 24). Shortly thereafter, the command for the people to present to God the first fruits of their harvest and produce is added to the command for them to present to him the firstborn males of their children, oxen, and sheep (22:29-30). Through Moses God also invites the Israelites to offer him gold, silver, bronze, and other items of value in order to construct his sanctuary, which is referred to as the tabernacle or tent of meeting (25:1-9).

In the remainder of Exodus, God gives further instructions regarding the offerings that the priests and people are to present to him, the sanctuary that they are to build for him, the consecration of the priests, and other matters related to the sacrificial worship that was to be given to him (Exodus 25–30, 35–40). According to Exod 26:33-34, the innermost part of the sanctuary was designated as the Most Holy Place or Holy of Holies. It contained the ark of the covenant, which was lost following the destruction of the First Temple by the Babylonians in 586 BCE. The lid covering the ark of the covenant was known as the *kapporet*, which is commonly referred to as the mercy seat in English translations of the Bible. The *kapporet* was made of gold and decorated with two winged figures that the Hebrew text calls cherubim. Often it is portrayed as God's throne. The only person allowed access to the Most Holy Place was the high priest, who entered there once a year on *Yom Kippur* or the Day of Atonement carrying incense and sacrificial blood, which he was to sprinkle on the mercy seat and in front of it (Lev 16:1-17).

Outside of the Most Holy Place was another area known as the Holy Place. A decorated veil or curtain separated these two areas from one another. A second veil hung at the entrance of the Holy Place, thus shielding its interior from the view of those outside of the sanctuary in the outer court. No one but the priests were allowed to enter into the Holy Place. Inside this area there was a golden lampstand as well as an incense altar and a table upon which bread was offered to God daily together with the incense. In the outer court was another altar for burnt offerings as well as a brazen laver. According to the biblical texts, any violation of the prescriptions regarding access to these places and objects was to lead to death.

In the first seven chapters of Leviticus, God lays out in detail the manner in which the different kinds of offerings are to be presented to him. These include the burnt offering or holocaust (*'olah*), the grain offering (*minhah*), the offering of well-being, also known as a peace offering or communion offering (*zebah shelamim*), the purification or sin offering (*hatta't*), and the reparation or guilt offering (*'asham*).[7] The most common of these offerings were the burnt offerings and the offerings of well-being, both of which are mentioned repeatedly throughout the Hebrew Bible. In contrast, outside of the passages that contain prescriptions for the purification and reparation offerings in Leviticus, Numbers, and Ezekiel, these two kinds of offering are mentioned explicitly in only a handful of passages.[8] This clearly indicates that most sacrifices were not offered in order to seek the forgiveness of sins. It is also important to stress that many of these offerings did not involve animals but consisted of things such as grain, flour, fruit, incense, and liquids given as libations or drink offerings.

What distinguished the various types of animal sacrifice from one another was not merely the motive or occasion for which they were to be presented but also what was to be done with the animal's remains and its blood after it had been slaughtered. In each case, after the slaughter, the blood of the animal victim was drained from it. In the burnt offerings, the blood was poured out around the altar and the skin was removed from the carcass before the rest of it was offered to God by being burnt on the altar. In the case of the offerings of well-being, after the blood had been extracted from the animal and poured out around the altar, the flesh and organs of the animal were divided, with certain parts being offered to God and others being given to the priests and those who presented the offerings. In contrast, those making purification offerings and reparation offerings did not receive any part of the animal sacrifice. In the purification offerings, the animal's blood was also handled differently: a portion of it was sprinkled before God and rubbed on the corners of the altar of incense in front of the curtain that separated the Holy Place from the Most Holy Place, while the rest was poured out at the base of the outside altar. The different types of animals that might be used for presenting sin or purification offerings included not only larger animals such as bulls, sheep, and goats but also turtledoves and pigeons. Those who were so poor that they could not even afford these birds were allowed to offer as their purification offering a measure of flour instead (Lev 5:7-13).

---

7. On the biblical prescriptions regarding these offerings and the similarities and differences among them, see especially Roland de Vaux, *Ancient Israel: Its Life and Institutions*, vol. 2: *Religious Institutions*, trans. John McHugh (New York: McGraw-Hill, 1965), 415-23, 426-32.

8. See 2 Kgs 12:16; 2 Chr 29:23-24; Ezra 8:35; Neh 10:33; Prov 14:9; Isa 53:10; cf. 1 Sam 6:1-17.

Other passages from Leviticus and parts of Exodus, Numbers, and Deuteronomy contain further prescriptions regarding the offerings that the people were to present to God and mention other aspects of the sacrificial worship and rites ordained by God.[9] The most important of these prescriptions have to do with *Yom Kippur* as well as the three annual festivals or feasts that the people were to celebrate, namely, the Festival of Passover or Unleavened Bread, the Festival of Weeks (Pentecost) or First Fruits (Harvest), and the Festival of Tabernacles (Booths) or Ingathering. In addition to the sacrificial offerings prescribed for these occasions, the Torah mandates animal offerings that were to be presented on a daily, weekly, and monthly basis. Many of the prescriptions found in the Pentateuch have to do with things such as the dimensions, layout, and adornment of the sanctuary, the sacred objects that were to be placed within the sanctuary and outside of it, different types of oaths and vows, the consecration and responsibilities of the priests, the high priest, and the Levites, and rites designed to purify a variety of people, places, and objects.

Although the book of Deuteronomy anticipates a time when all of the offerings presented to God will be given in one particular location, according to the historical writings the people offered sacrifices to God in a number of different places until David and Solomon established Jerusalem as the place in which all of the Israelites were to offer God their sacrificial worship. When the monarchy was divided following Solomon's death, sacrifices to the God of Israel continued to be offered in the northern kingdom of Israel, yet the narrative appearing in the books of Kings, Chronicles, Ezra, and Nehemiah regards the sacrificial worship of Israel's God in any place other than the temple built by Solomon in Jerusalem as illegitimate and contrary to God's will. That sacrificial worship was suspended following the destruction of Solomon's temple by the Babylonians, yet it was resumed once more when the Persian kings Cyrus and Darius allowed the Jewish people to rebuild their temple in the latter part of the same century, around 515 BCE.

For reasons we shall consider in the next chapter, scholarly discussions regarding the meaning and purpose of sacrifice in biblical thought and the need for the sacrificial death and blood of animal victims have focused almost exclusively on the sacrifices involving animals that were offered for sin or for purification. As a result, biblical scholars and interpreters have tended to ascribe less importance to other types of offerings and other aspects of the sacrificial worship of Israel's God mentioned in the Hebrew Bible. As we have noted above, most of the sacrificial offerings mentioned in the biblical texts were burnt offerings and offerings of well-being rather than sin or purification offerings. This means that most of the offerings presented to God were not a response to sins that people had committed and did not have the purpose of attaining God's forgiveness or purifying people from their sins and impurities. Furthermore, the biblical evidence suggests that most of

---

9. On this subject and the discussion that follows, see especially de Vaux, *Ancient Israel*, 2:468-74, 484-510.

the people participating in the sacrificial worship of God did not understand its primary purpose in terms of assuaging God's wrath. In the prescriptions regarding sacrificial offerings in the book of Leviticus, in fact, there is not a single allusion to God's wrath, and much less to the idea of appeasing or placating God's wrath.

Throughout the biblical texts, the offering of sacrifice instead tends to be seen as an expression of praise and thanksgiving to God for his blessings and as an occasion to feast and celebrate before God with joy. Whatever offerings were presented for sin or purification merely served as a prelude for other forms of sacrificial worship and for the communal celebrations of God's people in general. For this reason, discussions regarding the need for sacrifice or the meaning and purpose of sacrificial offerings in biblical thought must not be limited to the offerings that were presented for sin or purification or even focus primarily on sin and purification offerings. Instead, any attempt to grasp the meaning and purpose of the sacrificial practices described in the biblical texts and the various aspects of the sacrificial worship offered to Israel's God must take into consideration all of these different sacrificial practices and aspects of sacrificial worship if it is to reflect faithfully biblical thought on the subject.

SACRIFICE AS OFFERING AND PRAYER

Perhaps the most important point to note when considering the question of the meaning and purpose of the sacrificial worship of Israel's God as it is described and prescribed in the biblical texts is that it revolves around the idea of *presenting offerings to God*. Throughout the Hebrew Bible, the terms used most frequently to refer to sacrificial offerings are *qorban*, *minḥah*, and *mattanah*, each of which means "gift," "present," or "offering." The Septuagint consistently translates these terms with *dōron* and *prosphora*, which also refer to gifts and offerings. The two verbs generally employed in the Hebrew to speak of the act of presenting an offering are the hiphil forms of *qarab* and *ba'*, both of which convey the idea of presenting something to God by bringing it near to him or taking it into his presence. This is also the meaning of the Greek verbs *prosagein*, *pherein*, and *prospherein*, which are used in the Septuagint to translate the two Hebrew verbs. The use of the term *'olah* to refer to the burnt offerings reflects the same basic idea, since it refers to something that rises up in the air, that is, to heaven or to God.

Given that the idea behind all of these terms is that of presenting an offering or gift to God, the use of the terminology of sacrifice to refer to the worship of Israel's God with offerings and gifts must even be regarded as misleading to some extent, since in English sacrifice is generally understood in the sense of killing or slaughtering. Because of this, in English it can sound somewhat odd to speak of sacrificing fruits, grains, oil, or wine, for example, since no type of killing or slaughter is involved. In Hebrew, however, the same terms are used to refer to all of these different types of offering and to animal offerings as well, since the basic idea underlying them was not that of *killing* or *slaughtering* but that of *offering*.

Most of the offerings that people presented, in fact, did not involve animals. As noted above, the Pentateuch and other books of the Hebrew Bible mention offerings that consisted not only of fruits and vegetables, grains, oils, and wine but also things such as incense, jewelry, spices, wood, linen, precious metals and stones, and even hair.[10] When animals were sacrificed, in most cases the offerings presented to God did not include the entire animal but only parts of it, in particular its fat and blood. The exception, of course, was the burnt offering or holocaust, which involved presenting the entire animal to God by burning it entirely once it had been skinned and its blood had been drained and dashed against the sides of the altar.

The biblical texts and Second Temple Jewish writings also regularly speak of God receiving, accepting, and at times rejecting the offerings presented to him. In a number of passages, God is said to send down fire to consume the offerings being presented to him.[11] This was seen as a sign that God had been pleased by the sacrifices and had accepted them. The reason why those who offered sacrifice raised up or elevated their gifts before God and then placed them upon altars that were generally located in high places was that all of these practices conveyed the idea that the offerings presented to God would ascend to him. Similarly, the purpose for which the offerings were burned on the altar was not that they might be destroyed but rather that they might be transformed into smoke in a manner that would allow them to rise up to God and enter into his presence. What the offerers sought, therefore, was that God receive and accept what they were presenting to him.[12]

Although the biblical texts rarely speak explicitly of prayers being offered up to God together with sacrificial offerings, this practice is generally assumed. The texts that prescribe the different types of sacrifice in the Pentateuch presuppose that prayers would be offered together with those sacrifices by the priests and in many cases by the offerers as well. Even if the offerers did not pronounce their own prayers, they undoubtedly joined themselves to the prayers offered by the priests so as to make those prayers their own. Offerings presented for sin were accompanied by prayers of confession in which those making the offering were to acknowledge whatever they had done wrong, ask God for forgiveness, and commit themselves anew to living in accordance with God's commandments (Lev 4:5; 5:1-5; Num 5:7). Such prayers of confession are also mentioned in Leviticus 16 in association with the offerings for sin and the rite carried out with the goat for Azazel on *Yom Kippur*. When sacrifices were offered out of a spirit of thanksgiving, the motives for which the offerers gave thanks were clearly articulated, even if those motives had to

---

10. See, for example, Exod 35:20-35; Num 6:18.

11. See 1 Kgs 18:38; 1 Chr 21:26; 2 Chr 7:1; 2 Macc 2:10; Josephus, *Ant.* 3.210-12; 4.33, 54-56; 8.118, 342; Philo, *Heir* 251; *Moses* 2.154-55.

12. See, for example, Gen 4:4-5; 1 Kgs 8:10-11; 2 Chr 5:13-14; Amos 5:22; cf. Josephus, *Ant.* 3.214-15; 7.327-39; 8.106, 126; Philo, *Spec. Laws* 1.221.

do simply with acknowledging God's goodness in general terms. The sacrifices that were offered daily were similarly accompanied by prayers and intercessions for the people as a whole as well as for the people's leaders and often for other nations and their leaders as well. If God manifested his acceptance of the sacrifices in some way, he was manifesting at the same time his acceptance of the prayers and petitions that were being offered up to him together with those sacrifices.

Thus, even though the Mosaic law does not explicitly command the people to present prayers to God when offering sacrifices to him, it was generally expected that they should do so. If those prayers were heartfelt and sincere, however, it was thought that words alone were not sufficient to express the sentiments and motives which they were intended to express. Those who were truly thankful to God for the blessings he had bestowed on them, for example, could hardly manifest their gratitude to God without presenting him an offering as a concrete and palpable sign of that gratitude. How could one thank God for what one had received from his hand while at the same time keeping one's own hand closed by refusing to share with him and others a portion of what he had graciously given? Similarly, if one was truly repentant for having sinned against him, it was expected that one demonstrate the sincerity of that repentance by presenting him an offering. Both the praise and adoration his people offered him as well as the petitions with which they came before him were also to be accompanied and articulated by means of sacrificial gifts and offerings. In certain contexts, in fact, the Hebrew word commonly translated as "worship" or "serve" in reality means to present a sacrificial offering or carry out sacrificial rites (*'abad*).[13] Sacrifice was thus seen as an integral and essential part of worship.

The idea that sacrifice was a means by which God's people offered up to him their prayers is reflected elsewhere in the biblical texts and Second Temple Jewish writings as well. The reason why the idea that God or his name dwelled at the sanctuary was considered important is that his presence there meant that he was near to the people in order to hear and receive their prayers and petitions. Because this was its main purpose, the temple was known primarily not as a house of *sacrifice* but as a house of *prayer* (Isa 56:7; 1 Macc 7:37). In fact, in the lengthy prayer attributed to Solomon on the occasion of the dedication of the Jerusalem temple in 1 Kgs 8:22-53 and 2 Chr 6:12-42, not once does he mention the sacrificial offerings that would be presented there. Instead, what he asks God over a dozen times in each of these two passages is that God *hear the prayers* that will be addressed to him there. The idea that to offer up sacrifice is to offer up prayers to God is simply presupposed in 2 Sam 24:25, where the author of the book affirms: "David built there an altar to the Lord and offered burnt offerings and offerings of well-being. So the Lord answered his supplication for the land." Here the author of the passage assumes that the readers know perfectly well that to offer up a *sacrifice* is to

---

13. See, for example, Exod 4:23; 7:16; 8:1, 20; 9:1, 13; 10:3, 7-11, 24-26; 12:31; Isa 19:21; Ezek 20:40; Zeph 3:9-10.

offer up a *prayer* or *supplication*. Numerous other passages from the historical books of the Hebrew Bible, the Septuagint, and Second Temple Jewish writings relate the offering of sacrifice with the offering of prayers as well.[14]

For the author of Psalm 20, when God accepts the sacrifices presented to him, he is also responding favorably to the prayers of the offerer: "May he remember all your offerings, and receive with favor your burnt sacrifices. May he grant you what your heart desires, and fulfill all your intentions. . . . May the LORD grant all your petitions" (vv. 3-5). In Ps 27:6-7, David is presented as crying out and singing to God as he offers him sacrifice with shouts of joy. According to the author of Ps 116:17, to offer a sacrifice of thanksgiving is to "call on the name of the LORD." When Job's friends are required to present a burnt offering for having spoken wrongly of God, they are said to be forgiven not because of their offering but on account of the prayer that Job offers up to God together with their sacrifice (Job 42:8-9). The antithetical parallelism used in Prov 15:8 in essence views sacrifice as synonymous with prayer: "The sacrifice of the wicked is an abomination to the LORD, but the prayer of the upright is his delight." The prophet Isaiah portrays God as rejecting not only the multitude of sacrifices, offerings, and incense that the people present to him but also the multitude of prayers that they offer up to him due to the injustices and violence that they commit (Isa 1:10-17). The same idea appears in Amos 5:21-25, where God refuses to accept not only the people's sacrifices but also their songs and praises due to their failure to practice justice and righteousness. The book of Sirach presents the priests, the high priest, and the people as a whole offering God prayers and singing hymns of praise as they present him their offerings and sacrifices at the temple (Sir 50:1-19). These and other passages clearly convey the idea that, when God accepts or rejects the sacrifices offered to him, he is also accepting or rejecting the prayers and petitions that accompany those sacrifices.

Elsewhere in the biblical texts and Second Temple Jewish writings, the daily sacrifices and the incense that arose to heaven together with the smoke of those sacrifices are associated with prayers. In Ps 141:2, the Psalmist prays: "Let my prayer be counted as incense before you, and the lifting up of my hands as an evening sacrifice." In the book that bears her name, Judith is presented as offering up a lengthy prayer at the time that the evening incense and sacrifices were being offered at the temple (Jdt 9:1-14). The Wisdom of Solomon similarly mentions the practice of offering up prayers at the hour at which the morning sacrifices were presented to God and speaks of "prayer and propitiation by incense" (Wis 16:28; 18:21).

At certain times and for different reasons, it was not possible for certain people or groups to offer up sacrifice. Under these circumstances, it was

---

14. See, for example, 1 Kgs 18:24-26, 36-37; 2 Kgs 16:15; 2 Chr 20:5-20; Jdt 4:13-15; 2 Macc 1:8, 21-30; 10:3-4; 14:30-36. For other references and further discussion on this subject, see David A. Brondos, *Jesus' Death in New Testament Thought*, vol. 1: *Background* (Mexico City: Theological Community of Mexico, 2018), 145-50.

common to claim that the prayers that were otherwise offered up together with sacrifice could serve as a substitute for it. The book of Daniel presents him as praying to God at the same hours that the daily sacrifices had been presented prior to the temple's destruction (Dan 6:10; 9:20-21). In a passage known as the Prayer of Azariah from the Septuagint version of Daniel, the three young men who are about to be cast into a fiery furnace as a result of their refusal to worship the gods of Babylon pray to the God of Israel: "At present we have no ruler, or prophet, or leader, no burnt offering, or sacrifice, or oblation, or incense, no place to make an offering before you and to find mercy. Yet with a contrite heart and a humble spirit may we be accepted, as though we were presenting burnt offerings of rams and bulls or tens of thousands of fat lambs; so may our sacrifice be in your sight today" (Pr Azar 15-17). When the community at Qumran found the sacrificial worship being offered at the Jerusalem temple unacceptable, they maintained that prayer alone was sufficient to obtain God's forgiveness for their sins: "They shall atone for guilty rebellion and for sins of unfaithfulness that they may obtain loving-kindness for the land without the flesh of holocausts and the fat of sacrifice. And prayer rightly offered shall be an acceptable fragrance of righteousness, and perfection of way a delectable free-will offering" (1QS 9:4-5). The author of Psalm 69 even goes so far as to affirm that God prefers prayers of praise and thanksgiving to sacrifice: "I will praise the name of God with a song; I will magnify him with thanksgiving. This will please the LORD more than an ox or a bull with horns and hoofs" (vv. 30-31).

No Jewish author of the Second Temple period emphasizes the relation between sacrifice and prayer more frequently than Philo of Alexandria. He refers to sacrifices explicitly as "a medium of prayer and thanksgiving" (*Spec. Laws* 1.195). In one passage after another, he uses the phrase "prayers and sacrifices," as if the two were inseparable.[15] For Philo, the offerings of individuals are petitions for health and well-being (*Spec. Laws* 1.167-68). The offering of incense represents prayers of thanksgiving, as does the offering of blood (*Spec. Laws* 1.171). The soul of the person who seeks spiritual healing is to "come to the altar as a suppliant, beseeching grace with prayers and vows and sacrifices, by which alone it can obtain forgiveness" (*Dreams* 2.299). Philo understands the daily sacrifices offered at the temple as prayers on behalf of the nation and humankind in general and interprets the fire that is said to have consumed the offerings presented to God on the altar as a sign of God's acceptance of the prayers presented to him (*Moses* 2.5, 153-55, 159).

Many of these same ideas are found in the writings of Josephus, who also repeatedly ties prayer to sacrifice, speaks of prayers being offered up together with the sacrificial offerings, and affirms that when God accepts the sacrifices presented to him he accepts and grants the prayers that accompany them as

---

15. See, for example, *Drunkenness* 66; *Moses* 1.219; 2.133, 147, 153-54; *Spec. Laws* 1.97, 113, 224; *Unchangeable* 8.

well.[16] For Josephus, the sacrifices offered to God at the temple in Jerusalem are prayers for the well-being of all the people, as well as the leaders of Israel and the other nations that rule over them.[17] Josephus also regards the sacrifices offered at the time of the festivals as prayers (*Ant.* 4.203). When he offers his own retelling of the narratives that appear in Genesis, he interprets the sacrifices of both Cain and Noah as supplications made to God (*Ant.* 1.58, 96). In Josephus's version of Genesis 22, when Abraham is about to sacrifice Isaac his son, he is also said to offer a prayer to God (*Ant.* 1.230-31). Subsequently, when Josephus paraphrases Solomon's prayer at the dedication of the temple, he stresses the idea that the temple is not merely a place of sacrifice but above all else a house of prayer:

> I have built this temple to your name so that from it we may send up our prayers into the air when we sacrifice and seek your favor, constantly convinced that you are present and not far distant. For just as you look down to see and hear all things, you do not cease to be near to all as you dwell here continually. Instead, you are present night and day to come to the aid of all who seek you (*Ant.* 8.108).

While some passages from the biblical texts speak of God dwelling at the sanctuary dedicated to him and receiving there the prayers and sacrificial offerings presented to him, others speak of both the people's prayers as well as the incense and smoke of the offerings burnt on the altar rising up to God in heaven. The altar stood outside of the sanctuary so that what was burnt on it might ascend into the air freely and unimpeded, thereby making its way up to heaven. Thus, while in one sense God was thought to be present in the sanctuary, at the same time it was recognized that in another sense he remained in heaven, which was his true abode. These ideas are reflected in Solomon's prayer of dedication, where he tells God:

> But will God truly dwell on the earth? If the heavens and the highest heavens cannot contain you, how much less this house which I have built! Have regard to your servant's prayer and his plea, O LORD my God, heeding the cry and the prayer that your servant prays to you today; may your eyes be open night and day toward this house, the place of which you said, 'My name shall be there,' that you may listen to the prayer that your servant prays toward this place. Hear the plea of your servant and of your people Israel when they pray toward this place. O hear in heaven your dwelling place; pay heed and forgive (1 Kgs 8:27-30; cf. 2 Chr 6:18-21).

Here God's dwelling place is said to be in heaven, while the sanctuary is the place in which God makes his name dwell. The affirmation that God's eyes and ears are open "toward this house" expresses the idea that his attention is focused there and therefore that he is especially attentive toward the prayers presented to him there. The allusions to God's name in relation to the worship offered him in this passage and others in the Hebrew Bible respond to

---

16. See *Ant.* 3.100; 4.243; 5.256; 6.19, 25, 102; 7.331-34; 11.17; 14.260-61; 18.1.
17. See *Ant.* 7.331; 11.17; *J.W.* 2.197, 409; *Ag. Ap.* 2.77, 196.

a concern to avoid the idea that God's presence was actually confined to the sanctuary. He was said to have put his name there in the sense that he had provided the people with a place in which they might invoke his name in prayer and be heard by him. Nevertheless, this understanding of God's presence at the sanctuary dedicated to him did not lead to the conclusion that he did not heed prayers made to him by those who were far away from the sanctuary. On the contrary, this same passage speaks of God hearing the prayers of his people when they have been taken away in exile to foreign lands but turn toward the temple to ask his forgiveness (1 Kgs 8:44-51). The temple was seen as a place that God had established as a visible sign or symbol that he had promised to hear the prayers and receive the offerings that his people presented him. He did not need to be present there in a literal sense in order to do these things, nor did he need to be in close proximity to those who prayed to him.

All of these texts and passages reflect the same basic understanding of the meaning and purpose of the sacrificial offerings and worship presented to the God of Israel by his people. According to biblical thought, the sacrificial offerings presented to Israel's God by his people served above all else as concrete and palpable means by which they offered up to him their prayers and petitions, thanking and praising him for his goodness, expressing to him their repentance and their desire for his forgiveness, asking him to continue to bless and assist them, and committing themselves to living in accordance with his will as he had made it known to them. While of course the meaning and purpose that the people ascribed to their sacrificial worship of God cannot be reduced to these ideas, there can be little doubt that they lay at the heart and center of the people's understanding of that worship as it is known to us from the biblical texts.

It is also important to note that this basic understanding of the meaning and purpose of sacrifice was by no means exclusive to the people of Israel. On the contrary, as we have seen at the outset of this chapter, virtually all of the peoples known to us from antiquity understood sacrifice as a means by which people offered up to the gods they worshiped the same type of prayers and petitions just mentioned. While they may have viewed in different terms the manner in which their sacrificial offerings obtained from the gods the types of response they desired and certainly conceived of their gods in ways that distinguished those gods from the God of Israel, there can be little doubt that the reasons for which they offered up sacrifice were essentially the same as those that can be discerned from the biblical texts and the Jewish literature of the Second Temple period in general.

Undoubtedly, among people of other nations there were certain beliefs with regard to the meaning and purpose of sacrificial offerings that were foreign to the understanding of sacrificial worship reflected in the biblical texts. Those texts reject the idea that the God of Israel actually ate or drank of the things offered to him and never mention ideas such as entering into some type of mysterious union with God by eating of what had been offered to him or seeking to assimilate the life force of a sacrificial animal by consuming its flesh.[18] In virtually every culture of antiquity known to us, however, sacrifice was not primarily about *killing* but about *presenting offerings to the gods*, as well as accompanying those offerings with prayers and petitions of different types. In this regard, the biblical understanding of sacrifice is in full continuity with the beliefs of other peoples in antiquity.

THE OFFERING OF GIFTS AS THE OFFERING OF ONE'S SELF

While the biblical texts no doubt reflect many ideas regarding the practice of sacrifice that were common to other peoples in antiquity, there is one idea above all else that made the biblical understanding of sacrificial worship unique in the ancient world as we know it. That was the idea that the God of Israel did not desire or command sacrifice *for his own sake* but only *for the sake of his people*, that is, to promote among them a way of living and behaving that would make it possible for them to enjoy the well-being he desired for them. Unlike other gods, the God of Israel neither needed the offerings that were presented to him nor sought the honor, praise, and worship that people manifested through their offerings as an end in itself.

For this reason, as already mentioned above, the principle of *do ut des* that lies at the heart of ancient pagan beliefs regarding the meaning and purpose of sacrifice must be regarded as foreign to biblical thought. Because God did not have any needs that human beings needed to satisfy and had no desire other than seeing human beings enjoy happiness and well-being together with the rest of his good creation, there was nothing that he sought to receive purely for his own sake from those who offered him sacrifice in exchange for their offerings. In biblical thought, sacrificial offerings were not means by which people could manipulate God, purchase his favor and blessings, or coerce him into doing what they desired.

As we have seen in the previous chapter of this work, what ultimately interests the God of the Hebrew Bible is not receiving sacrificial offerings or the worship, honor, and praise associated with those offerings but the practice of what is good, just, right, and loving among his people. What the God of Israel desires and demands is not sacrifice but justice, righteousness, and mercy. These things alone can please him and obtain his approval. Conversely, the biblical texts do not present God as becoming angry or upset at the failure of his people to present to him sacrificial offerings, except when that failure is an expression of a lack of a commitment to living in accordance with his will by obeying his commandments.

If Israel's God had desired sacrificial worship for his own sake, simply because his ego was pleased when human beings ascribed honor and glory to

---

18. On these understandings of the meaning and purpose of sacrifice in antiquity, see Jacob Milgrom, *Leviticus 1–16: A New Translation with Introduction and Commentary*, AB 3 (New York: Doubleday, 1991), 440-43; de Vaux, *Ancient Israel*, 2:447-50.

him and sang his praises, he would have had no reason ever to reject the sacrificial offerings and worship presented to him, unless of course he perceived that those who offered him sacrifices were attempting to manipulate him in some way or place him under obligation to grant what they desired of him. Even in those cases, however, he might still accept the sacrificial offerings presented to him while nevertheless refusing to grant the offerers what they sought, as pagan gods were at times thought to do. As noted above, because it was the offerings themselves that interested such gods, they rarely rejected the gifts that human beings presented to them.

In contrast, passages such as those that we have seen from the biblical texts and other Second Temple Jewish writings in the previous chapter consistently present God as rejecting the sacrificial offerings and worship of those who disobey his command to do what is good and right. In fact, those texts and writings speak not only of God rejecting sacrificial offerings but also approving of the destruction of his own temple when his people have persistently refused to put away their sinful and destructive behavior. The book of Lamentations, composed in response to the temple's destruction at the hands of the Babylonians, even presents God as carrying out that destruction himself: "He has broken down his place of dwelling as if it were a garden; he has destroyed his tabernacle. The Lord has abolished in Zion festival and Sabbath and in his fierce indignation has spurned king and priest. The Lord has scorned his altar, disowned his sanctuary; he has delivered into the hand of the enemy the walls of her palaces. A clamor was raised in the house of the Lord as on a day of festival" (Lam 2:6-7). One can hardly imagine gods such as Marduk or Zeus participating actively in the destruction of their own sanctuary simply because the people who worship them have not practiced what is good, right, and just.

What is also lacking in the biblical texts is the idea that God is especially pleased when his people offer him lavish and ornate sacrifices involving large numbers of costly animals. Outside of the passages that narrate the dedication of the Jerusalem temple by Solomon, the Hebrew Bible does not present the people offering sacrifices of that type to God. Instead, the offerings that are said to please God tend to be relatively simple and austere. These are the types of offering prescribed in Leviticus and elsewhere in the Mosaic law. As we have seen repeatedly, what is consistently said to interest God is not the size or lavishness of the offerings but the dedication of the offerers to living in conformity with his will for justice and righteousness.

What distinguished more than anything else the understanding of the meaning and purpose of sacrifice found in the Hebrew Scriptures from that of other ancient peoples, therefore, was the conviction that any sacrificial offering that was not an expression of a sincere and heartfelt dedication to living in accordance with the core values of justice, righteousness, compassion, and love reflected in the Mosaic law was not only unacceptable to God but even displeasing to him. Multiple passages from the Hebrew Scriptures and Jewish writings of the Second Temple period stress this idea, not only by claiming that what interests God is justice, righteousness, and steadfast love rather than sacrifice but also by stressing that only the sacrificial offerings of those who are committed to practicing these things are pleasing to him.

As we have seen in Chapter 6, this idea appears repeatedly in the Psalms, the books of Job and Proverbs, and the writings of Israel's prophets. However, it is also emphasized in the biblical narratives that allude to the practice of sacrifice. In 1 Sam 15:22, after Saul has displeased God by offering him sacrifices from the spoil he has taken in warfare contrary to God's command, the prophet Samuel tells him: "Has the LORD as great delight in burnt offerings and sacrifices, as in obedience to the voice of the LORD? Surely, to obey is better than sacrifice, and to heed than the fat of rams." In his commentary on this passage, Josephus stresses at length the understanding of sacrifice just considered above:

> But the prophet said that the Deity did not take pleasure in sacrifices, but in those who are good and righteous. Such are those who follow God's will and commands, and consider no action of theirs to be good unless it is done at his bidding rather than at their own initiative. For contempt for God is shown not by failing to offer him sacrifice but by appearing to disobey him. Even if one sacrifices many fat victims or offers up precious offerings made of silver and gold, if one does not obey God or offer him the true worship that alone is acceptable to him, God does not receive such offerings favorably but rejects them and regards them as expressions of iniquity rather than godliness. Only those who bear in mind nothing but that which God has spoken and commanded and would prefer to die rather than transgress any of his commands are truly pleasing to God. From such persons God does not require sacrifices, and if they do offer any, no matter how modest they may be, he welcomes more gladly the honor given him out of poverty than that given him by the most wealthy (*Ant.* 6.147-49).

The same ideas are reflected in the prayers attributed to David and Solomon in connection with the construction and dedication of the temple in Jerusalem. After procuring most of the materials that would be used to build the temple, David tells God that all that he has provided has been done out of a sincere desire to serve God willingly and joyfully: "I know, my God, that you search the heart and take pleasure in uprightness; in the uprightness of my heart I have offered all these things freely, and now with joy I have seen your people, who are present here, offering freely to you as well. O LORD, God of our ancestors Abraham, Isaac, and Israel, keep such purposes and thoughts in the hearts of your people forever, and direct their hearts toward you" (1 Chr 29:17-18). Were Israel's God like the gods of the nations, who were interested in receiving gifts, honor, and adulation purely for their own sake, it would not have mattered to him what he saw in the heart of David and others who presented him offerings or whether those offerings were a sincere expression of devotion to him. What would have interested him were those offerings themselves.

In the prayer that Solomon offers up on the occasion of the temple's dedication in 1 Kings 8, he stresses the same ideas. He asks God that whenever he finds it necessary to chastise the people as a result of their sinful behavior, he forgive them when they acknowledge their sins and return to the good path that he has laid out for them (vv. 33-40). According to this passage, what will lead to God's forgiveness is not the sacrificial offerings themselves, which as noted above are not even mentioned in the passage, but the people's return to God in obedience. More importantly, however, Solomon asks God to look into the hearts of his people to see their affliction at their sins and to judge them according to their ways (vv. 38-40). Several verses later, he asks God to treat the people with compassion and forgiveness if they confess their sins sincerely and "repent with all their heart and soul" as they pray in the direction of the temple from the lands to which they have been exiled (vv. 46-50). The fact that these petitions to God are made in the context of the dedication of the temple underscores once more the idea that the sacrifices that were to be presented there were to be expressions of a heartfelt commitment to doing God's will.

A number of Jewish writings from the Second Temple period stress the same ideas. The book of Judith affirms: "For every sacrifice presented as a fragrant offering is a small thing, and the fat of all burnt offerings presented to you is a very little thing; but whoever fears the Lord is great forever" (Jdt 16:16). The author of 2 Enoch similarly claims that it is purity of heart rather than sacrifice that pleases God: "Does the Lord demand bread or lambs or sheep or oxen or any kind of sacrifices at all? That is nothing, but he demands pure hearts, and by means of all those things he tests people's hearts" (2 En. 45:3; cf. 46:1). A passage from the book of Sirach underscores these same points:

> Those who keep the law make many offerings, and those who observe the commandments make an offering of well-being. Those who return a kindness make an offering of choice flour, and those who give alms present a thank offering. To abstain from wickedness is pleasing to the Lord, and to forsake unrighteousness is an expiation. Do not appear before the Lord empty-handed, for all that you offer is in accordance with the commandment. The offering of the righteous enriches the altar, and its pleasing odor rises before the Most High. The sacrifice of the righteous is accepted, and it will never be forgotten.... Do not offer God a bribe, for he will not accept it; and do not rely on a dishonest sacrifice. For the Lord is the judge, and with him there is no partiality (Sir 35:1-9, 14-15; cf. 7:7-10).

The writer who especially stresses the idea that what interests God is not the sacrificial offerings themselves but the commitment to living in accordance with his will is Philo. According to Philo, "God does not delight in the fleshiness or fatness of animals, but in the blameless intention of the votary" (*Spec. Laws* 2.35).[19] If God sees any type of selfishness or self-interest on the part of the offerers, he does not accept their offerings (*Spec. Laws* 1.196). In his *Life*

---

19. Citations from the writings of Philo of Alexandria are taken from volumes 247, 261, 275, 289, 320, 341, and 380 of the Loeb Classical Library (Cambridge, MA: Harvard University Press, 1911–). In many cases I have made modifications to the text to make it conform to modern English usage.

of Moses, after affirming that what interests God is not the parts and limbs of the victims placed on the altar but the intention of the offerer, Philo continues:

> For, if the worshiper is hard of heart or unrighteous, the sacrifices are no sacrifices, the consecrated oblation is desecrated, and the prayers are words of ill omen with utter destruction waiting upon them. For, when to outward appearance they are offered, it is not a remission but a reminder of past sins which they effect. But, if the worshiper is pure of heart and just, the sacrifice stands firm, even if the flesh is consumed; or rather, even if no victim at all is brought to the altar. For the true oblation, what else can it be but the devotion of a soul which is dear to God? (*Moses* 2.106-8).

Similarly, when he addresses the question of why God accepted the offering presented by Abel but rejected Cain's offering, Philo answers that when God looked into the heart of each of the two, he saw the goodness of Abel but the wickedness of Cain:

> He turned toward the good man, looking upon him because he is a lover of goodness and virtue, and first seeing him to be more inclined toward that side in the order of nature, he deprecates and turns away from the evil man. Accordingly, it is said in a most excellent manner not that God saw the offerings but that he first saw those who were offering gifts before the gifts themselves, for men look at the quantity of gifts and approve them; but God looks at the truth of the soul, turning aside from arrogance and flattery (*QG* 1.61).

Philo also insists that the purification to which those who offer sacrifice are to subject themselves prior to presenting their offerings has to do not merely with their body but also their soul. He writes that "the best and most perfect form of purification" is "never even to admit into one's mind any heinous thoughts" but to live in peace with others and abstain from lying, perjury, slander, and any other type of conduct aimed at doing harm to others (*Names* 240; cf. *QG* 2.52). After stressing that those who make offerings to God merely give back to him what is already his own, he adds that they are to be

> pure from wrongdoing and wash away the filthiness which defiles [their] lives in thought and word and deed. For it is absurd that a man should be forbidden to enter the temples unless he has first bathed and cleansed his body, and yet should attempt to pray and sacrifice with a heart still soiled and spotted. . . . Whoever is resolved not only to commit no further sin, but also to wash away the past, may approach with gladness; but let any who lack this resolve keep far away, since they shall hardly be purified. For they shall never escape the eye of him who sees into the recesses of the mind and treads its inmost shrine (*Unchangeable* 7-9).

While Philo alludes frequently to the subject of sacrifice throughout his writings, by far his most extensive treatment of the sacrificial practices prescribed in the Mosaic law appears in the first two books of his work known as *De Specialibus Legibus* or *Special Laws*. There he examines in minute detail virtually every aspect of the sacrificial worship offered to God in accordance with the biblical prescriptions. In a number of passages from the first book of this work, he especially stresses the point just mentioned, namely, that what interests God is not the sacrificial offerings themselves but the commitment to living in accordance with his will of those who present them:

> For the law desires, first, that the mind of the worshiper be sanctified by the exercise of good and profitable thoughts and judgments; second, that his life should be a consistent course of the best actions, so that as he lays his hands on the victim, he can boldly and with a pure conscience affirm, "These hands have taken no gift as a bribe to commit injustice, nor shared in the proceeds of plunder or avarice, nor been soiled with innocent blood. They have not maimed or wounded anyone, nor have they done anyone harm or violence. They have performed no action of any other kind that might be liable to accusation or censure, but have made themselves humble ministers of excellent and profitable things that are held in honor in accordance with wisdom and the law and among persons who are wise and law-abiding" (*Spec. Laws* 1.203-4).

> How then is the soul purified? "Note, friend," says the lawgiver, "how perfect and utterly free from blemish is the victim that you bring. . . . For if you observe this with your reason rather than with your eyes, you will proceed to wash away the sins and defilements with which you have soiled your whole life. . . . For you will find that all this careful scrutiny of the animal is a symbol representing figuratively the reformation of your own conduct, for the law does not give prescriptions for unreasoning creatures but for those who have mind and reason. It is concerned not that the victims be without flaw but that those who offer them should not suffer from any corroding passion" (*Spec. Laws* 1.259-60).

> So we see that those who intend to frequent the temple to take part in sacrifice must have their bodies made clean and bright, and before their bodies their souls. The mind is cleansed by wisdom and the truths of wisdom's teaching, which guide its steps to the contemplation of the universe and all that is in it, and by the sacred company of the other virtues and the practice of them shown in noble and highly praiseworthy actions. Whoever, then, is adorned with these may come with confidence to the sanctuary as his true home, the best of all mansions, there to present himself as victim. . . . God does not rejoice in sacrifices even if one offer hecatombs, for all things are his possessions. Yet though he possesses them, he needs none of them, but he rejoices in the will to love him and in those who practice holiness. From these he accepts plain meal or barley, and the things that cost the least, regarding them as more precious than those that are most costly. And indeed even if the worshipers bring nothing else, when they bring themselves, they offer the best of sacrifices, the full and truly perfect oblation of noble living (*Spec. Laws* 1.269-72).

> [E]ven the least morsel of incense offered by a devout man is more precious in the sight of God than thousands of cattle sacrificed by men of little honor. . . . What is precious in the sight of God is not the number of victims immolated but the true purity of a rational spirit in the person who makes the sacrifice. Do you think that a judge whose heart is set on giving righteous judgments will take gifts from any of the litigants? And if he does take them, will he not be open to the charge of bribery? Or do you think that a good man will receive gifts from one who is bad, though both are men, even if the one is in

need and the other is rich? In the same way, do you think that it is possible to corrupt God, who is absolutely sufficient to himself and has no need of anything created? Will not the God who is the primal good, the consummation of perfection, and the perennial fountain of wisdom and justice and every virtue turn his face from the gifts of the unjust? Are not those who would offer such gifts the most shameless of human beings, especially when they give to God a share of the profits they have obtained through theft or robbery, or by denying a just debt or refusing pay it, thereby treating him as a partner in their wickedness and greed?

To such a person I would say: "Most miserable of wretches. . . . When you should hide your face in shame for the sins you have committed, you make an open show of the outward signs of your iniquity and, priding yourself on them, assign a portion of them to God. You bring him the first fruits of unholiness and have not considered that the law does not admit of lawlessness, just as sunlight does not admit of darkness". . . . So those who intend to sacrifice must consider not whether the victim is unblemished but whether their own mind stands free from defect and imperfection. Furthermore, let them examine the motives that lead them to make the offering (*Spec. Laws* 1.275, 277-79, 283).

All of these passages clearly reflect the idea that it is not the sacrificial offerings themselves that please God but the commitment to a way of life in accordance with his will. As Philo insists, when sacrificial offerings are not an expression of such a commitment, neither the offerings nor those who present them are acceptable to Israel's God. At the same time, those who are sincerely committed to living in accordance with God's will for justice and righteousness are acceptable to God even if for some reason they are unable to present sacrificial offerings to him. This means that what obtains God's acceptance and forgiveness is not sacrificial offerings but the commitment to living in the way God has commanded out of love for all. What interested God was not the offering of gifts in itself but the offering of one's self by means of one's gifts.

The Transforming Power of Sacrificial Offerings and Rites

To affirm that what interests God is not the sacrificial offerings themselves but the hearts and lives of those who present them is not to deny, of course, that the Hebrew Bible generally portrays God as being pleased when his people offer him their worship, praises, and sacrifices. What must be stressed, however, is not merely that the sacrificial worship of God is pleasing to him only when it is an expression of a sincere commitment to a life in accordance with his will but also that his desire to receive worship and praise is rooted *in a concern for human beings themselves rather than a concern for himself.* Because he wishes to bless and save human beings, it brings him joy when some human beings proclaim to others that he is a good and gracious God who blesses and saves people, since this proclamation will lead even more people to seek and find blessing and salvation in him. He wishes for his sovereign power, steadfast love, and commitment to justice to be made known to all people so that they may look to him to guide, strengthen, and accompany them. When people thank him for his goodness, acknowledge his sovereignty over their lives, confess to him their wrongdoings, and seek his blessing and favor by means of sacrificial offerings, their commitment to living in accordance with his will is reinforced in the way that he desires for their own good. The reason why he is pleased by sacrificial worship and offerings that are sincere expressions of love for him and a desire to serve him, therefore, is that these things promote among his people the kind of life that leads to their well-being.

For the same reason, while God may not demand sacrificial offerings that are lavish and ornate, he is pleased by such offerings when they are an expression of sincere love for him. When his people go out of their way to manifest to God their love for him and their desire to thank, praise, and serve him by means of their sacrificial offerings, as they are said to have done at the dedication of the Jerusalem temple in Solomon's day, it brings God joy precisely because that type of love and devotion for him will lead them to be firmly committed to living in accordance with his will for their own good. In that way, it will result in their well-being. The greater their love for him, the greater the expression of that love will be. At the same time, the more they express that love both through sacrificial offerings and through their obedience to his will, the more it will be strengthened in them.

These same ideas must be kept in mind when considering the passages in which God is said to be pleased by the sweet smell or pleasant odor of the sacrifices being offered to him. In Gen 8:20-22, for example, Noah is said to build an altar to God and present him with burnt offerings there after he has descended from the ark together with his family and the animals that had been in the ark with him during the flood. When God smells the pleasing odor of these offerings, he is moved in his heart to promise never again to curse the ground or destroy his creatures by means of another flood, even though from their youth human beings are inclined to do what is bad (v. 21). Neither here nor elsewhere in the biblical texts should passages such as this one be understood in the sense that it is the sweet smell of the offerings presented to God in itself that pleases God and obtains his approval. If such were the the case, it would follow that human beings could behave in ways that provoked God to wrath and then appease that wrath merely by presenting him with sweet-smelling burnt offerings, without repenting of their behavior and seeking to amend it. For reasons we have seen repeatedly, the biblical texts firmly condemn such an idea. What must be seen as bringing God joy is that people such as Noah choose to express their love for him by taking the time and effort to present him with sacrifices that they attempt to make as pleasing as possible to him, since they will live out that love for him through behaviors that promote their own well-being and that of others. The affirmation that God determined not to destroy human beings again after recognizing that from their youth they inevitably tend toward behaviors that are bad and harmful should be understood in the sense that, despite the sinful tendency in them, there is still much that is good in them and they are still capable of living in love for him and one another. According to this understanding of the passage, the sweet smell of Noah's offering reminded God of this truth and thus led him to promise never to bring such destruction on human beings again.

If it was the practice of justice, righteousness, mercy, and love that truly interested God rather than sacrificial offerings per se, it might be asked why there was any need for people to present him such offerings or why he was interested in receiving them. The answer to these questions lies in the intimate relationship between the spiritual and the physical or material in biblical thought, that is, the attitudes and ways of thinking that are internal to human beings and the outward expressions of those attitudes and ways of thinking by means of concrete actions and behaviors. Within the Christian tradition, in large part because of the influence of certain Hellenistic modes of thought, it has often been claimed that what really matters to God is that which is in the heart, the spiritual rather than the physical. The body is seen as being of secondary importance in relation to the soul or spirit. The words attributed to Jesus in his conversation with the Samaritan woman in the fourth chapter of the Gospel of John are commonly understood in this manner. There, after telling the woman that a day will come when those who will worship God in the way he desires will do so neither at the site dedicated to him on Mount Gerizim in Samaria nor at the Jerusalem temple, Jesus adds: "the hour is coming and is now here when the true worshipers will worship the Father in spirit and in truth, for these are the kind of worshipers that the Father seeks. God is spirit, and those who worship him must worship in spirit and in truth" (John 4:23-24). Interpreters of this passage often overlook the fact that nowhere does it affirm or imply that the worship of God through external or material means is to be rejected. It simply affirms the same idea that runs throughout the biblical texts as a whole and the writings of Jews such as Philo, namely, that all worship of God must be done "in spirit and truth."

This tendency to value the spiritual and the internal over the physical and the external has often led Christians to condemn as outmoded, superficial, meaningless, or even displeasing to God the practice of outward rites having to do with bodily and physical realities such as those described in the biblical texts and practiced among most Jews throughout history. Such ways of thinking among Christians overlook the fact that Christians also ascribe great importance to the same type of rite by means of their practice of baptism and the Lord's Supper. In principle, Christians might receive a child or an adult into their community of faith through a ceremony that consisted solely of an exchange of words, without using water or any other material substance. They could also recall the love that Jesus manifested for them in his death, reflect on the forgiveness that they receive from God through Jesus, and express their commitment to living in love, unity, and fellowship as Jesus commanded without eating and drinking together in the way that they do when they celebrate the Lord's Supper. These actions would be much less meaningful and powerful, however, if they were limited exclusively to the use of words and did not involve bodily actions and material realities such as water, bread, and wine. Furthermore, both these material realities as well as the actions performed with them convey ideas and symbolisms that could never be expressed by words alone.

The same observations should be made with regard to the sacrificial practices described and prescribed in the Hebrew Bible. In principle, people could manifest their love for God by telling him that they loved him with words alone, without making use of their body or any physical or material element. They might express their gratitude to him in the same way, merely by pronouncing their words of thanksgiving out loud or in their heart. When they had done something that was contrary to God's will and were filled with remorse as a result of the pain that their action had caused God and others, they might likewise simply use words to tell him that they were sorry and that they were making a commitment not to repeat such an action again in the future.

By using physical and material elements and substances to perform actions with their body in the presence of others, however, those Jews who lived in the period of the Second Temple were able to express in a much more meaningful and powerful manner the sentiments and intentions that were in their heart. The material offerings that they presented to God served as means by which they manifested to him their love, praise, and gratitude in ways that went far beyond anything that words alone could communicate. The same was true when they were profoundly sorry for something they had done and wished to do something to give expression to that sorrow in a concrete and visible manner. Just as a person who loves another wishes to express that love through physical contact such as embraces and caresses and is not satisfied with the use of words alone, so also those who sought to manifest their sentiments toward God found it much more fulfilling and satisfying to do so through sacrificial offerings and the type of rites and rituals mentioned in the biblical texts.

In addition to allowing people to express in a visible, palpable, and concrete manner the sentiments and intentions that were in their heart, the sacrificial offerings and rites that the biblical texts describe and prescribe served to reinforce those sentiments and intentions and to strengthen them even more. Those who traveled long distances and spent a considerable amount of time, effort, and money to present an offering at the sanctuary in order to express their love, gratitude, and dedication to God tended to grow immensely in that love, gratitude, and dedication as a result of that experience. When those who had done something that God had prohibited out of love for his people manifested their repentance by slaughtering an animal and watching as a priest sprinkled its blood toward the symbols of God's presence and burned part of its remains on the altar, they were brought to reflect more deeply on the consequences of their actions and become even more resolved to avoid disobeying God's commands in the future. Those who presented an animal as an offering of well-being to God and subsequently sat down with their fellow

Israelites and family members in the place that symbolized God's presence to eat of what they had offered grew even further in their commitment to live in communion and fellowship with God and one another and felt their bond with God and others become even stronger.

The gestures and rites involved in the sacrificial worship of Israel's God also afforded experiences that went far beyond anything that might have been accomplished by words alone. All of the senses were involved in those rites as they laid their hand on the animal, saw its blood being sprinkled, dashed, or poured out at the altar, and listened to the crackling of the fire as they observed its remains rising up in smoke together with the sweet aroma of incense. It is likely that they listened to singing and chanting and united their voices to those of others, not only in what was sung but in the prayers earnestly offered up and perhaps in outbursts of joy, devotion, zeal, or contrition as well. Even those who could afford nothing but a turtledove or a pigeon must have felt an enormous satisfaction at seeing their gift to God being consumed on the altar as a heartfelt expression of their love for him and their gratitude for his mercies and his forgiveness.

The experience of offering sacrifice was therefore an extremely powerful one and evoked deep sentiments and intense emotions in those who participated in the rites involved. They not only expressed verbally their gratitude, dedication to God, or compunction at their sin but were able to feel these things in body and spirit down to the core of their being. These rites possessed a power to touch and transform their lives profoundly, and it was for that reason that God had commanded them. They not only served as channels by which people were able to express what was in their heart but also inflamed and aroused the attitudes, sentiments, convictions, and behaviors that God wished to see in them for their own good and that of others.

The symbolisms conveyed by the people's participation in these rites served to contribute to the same objective. The offering of a portion of what belonged to them symbolized the offering to God of everything they had received from him in his grace and mercy. Their entrance into the area outside of the sanctuary with their gift in their hands was symbolic of their desire to draw near to the God whom they adored in order to serve him and dedicate their lives to doing his will. The fat of the animal victims that was burnt on the altar symbolized the offering to God of what was most precious, pleasing, and desirable in life.

Furthermore, like any symbolic action, the rites and rituals performed could convey a wide variety of meanings that went beyond anything that words alone could ever express. The different types of food and drink that were placed before God could serve as a symbol of God's care and compassion in giving his people what they needed to sustain their life, the goodness of his gifts, and the manner in which God fed them spiritually and not only materially. Their offerings might also bring to mind their dependence on God and symbolize the work of their hands, their growth and transformation, and the manner in which they had been brought together as a single people in the same way that the things they had harvested had been combined into a single offering that was placed before the God who had given them life. The slaughter of an animal and the shedding and sprinkling of its blood might symbolize the gravity and cost of disobedience to God's commandments, the manner in which the offerers were to die to themselves and their sinful behavior, the renewed offering of their life up to God, and a recognition that all life belonged to God, among other things.

Although ideas such as these are not stated explicitly in the prescriptions regarding animal sacrifice in the Mosaic law, they clearly seem to be presupposed. As noted above, the most complete type of animal sacrifice was the burnt offering or holocaust, precisely because the animal in its entirety was presented to God after its blood had been drained and its skin removed. Because the offerers kept nothing for themselves, the burnt offerings represented their total commitment to God and his will and the dedication of their entire lives to God. In contrast, the offerings of well-being were seen as means by which God and the offerers gave themselves to one another by sharing the gift that was placed before God. After offering up to God that which they had received from his hand, the people partook of a meal in which they shared not only what they had offered but also their lives with God and one another. The offerings for sin and guilt in turn were means by which those who had sinned consecrated their lives to God once more by offering him something that expressed and embodied their renewed commitment to putting away their wrongdoing and serving others in the way he desired and commanded. They manifested these things not only by means of their offering, which they forfeited in its entirety rather than having some part returned to them, but also by the restitution they made in cases in which they had wronged someone else.

At the heart of all of these sacrificial rites and symbolic actions was the idea that those who offered up gifts and sacrifices to God were at the same time offering up to him their own selves and lives. As we have stressed above, this is what interested God: that his people offer themselves up to him together with everything that they had in order to serve him and do his will, not for *his* sake but for *theirs*. By means of their sacrificial offerings they expressed their commitment to dedicating their bodies, souls, minds, possessions, talents, time, and energies to doing what was good, right, just, and kind in the way that God had commanded out of love for all. Any offering that was not a sincere expression of this kind of offering of oneself or was not presented in that spirit was unacceptable to God. Conversely, no matter how large or small the offering, if it was a sincere expression of one's commitment to God's will and was presented in that spirit, it was pleasing and acceptable to him. In fact, even if one was unable to present a material offering for some reason, such as illness, a lack of material resources, or captivity in a foreign land, the offering of nothing but one's own self, mind, soul, and body was thought to be just as pleasing and acceptable to God as the lavish and abundant sacrifices of those who had the resources to express their love, devotion, and dedication to God in that manner.

Under normal circumstances, however, it was unthinkable that one might offer oneself up to God without offering up some type of material gift or sacrifice at the same time. For that reason, the Mosaic law includes the command that no one appear before God with empty hands (Exod 23:15; 34:20; Deut 16:16). If one withheld from God the good things that one had received from him and refused to share them with God and others, one could hardly be said to be offering oneself and one's being up to God out of love and devotion for him. The people's love and devotion for God was to take concrete and palpable forms not only through acts of obedience but also through gifts and offerings that served as means by which they dedicated their lives to him.

Finding Meaning and Purpose in the Offering of Sacrifice

As has already been noted above, for the most part neither the biblical texts nor the Jewish writings of the Second Temple period enter into discussions regarding the meaning and purpose of the sacrificial offerings and rites they describe. There is one exception, however. Writing around the year 40 CE, only about three decades before the temple's destruction at the hands of the Roman army, Philo not only considers the question of the meaning and purpose of the sacrificial offerings, rites, and worship prescribed in the biblical texts but does so at great length.

Despite Philo's careful and painstaking examination of the many different aspects of the biblical prescriptions concerning the sacrificial worship of Israel's God, his writings have tended to be virtually ignored by biblical scholars who have written on this subject. There are primarily two reasons for this. The first is that the question that interests most scholars who write on the subject of biblical sacrifice is that of its *modus operandi*, that is, the manner in which the sacrificial rites were thought to "work" to "effect" something such as atonement, purification, or reconciliation and communion with God. Philo does not address this question in his writings, however. A second reason why scholars writing on the subject of biblical sacrifice often pay little attention to Philo is that throughout his writings he interprets the Hebrew Scriptures allegorically. Because this type of interpretation of the biblical texts tends to disregard questions related to their literal meaning and the intention of their authors, and also because outside of Philo's writings there is little evidence of the same kind of allegorical approach to the Hebrew Scriptures in the Second Temple period, it is thought that Philo's understanding of sacrifice was unique in his day and reflected Hellenistic modes of thought that were otherwise foreign to the Judaism of antiquity.

When we look closely at Philo's interpretations of the sacrificial rites and worship prescribed in the Hebrew Bible, however, it becomes evident that it revolves around the same kinds of ideas just considered above. For Philo, all of the various aspects of the sacrificial worship of Israel's God contribute in some way to promoting the practice of righteousness among God's people, whether directly or indirectly. They do this by reminding the people of certain ideas and truths, bringing them to reflect on their way of life and behavior, and reinforcing certain fundamental convictions regarding God, human life, and the world in general. The ceremonies, celebrations, and rites involved also serve as means by which those who participate in them consecrate themselves more fully to God and grasp more clearly his will for their life.

Most of Philo's discussion regarding the meaning and purpose of the various aspects of Israel's sacrificial worship of God is found in the first two books of *Special Laws*. As mentioned above, in these two books he examines in great detail the prescriptions regarding that worship that are found in the Mosaic law. As he does so, however, Philo also offers an explanation regarding the purpose for which God gave each of those prescriptions and discusses the meanings that those who participated in the sacrificial worship at the sanctuary were to ascribe to each of the various aspects of that worship.

In the latter part of Book 1, for example, Philo argues that each of the three basic forms of sacrifice commanded in the law of Moses is intended to convey certain truths that are to be reflected in the lives of the offerers. The various rites associated with the holocaust serve to remind the offerers that their lives are to be pure and blameless, that their minds should be "sanctified by exercise in good and profitable thoughts and judgments," and that their lives should be "a consistent course of the best actions," devoid of injustices, deceit, and violence (*Spec. Laws* 1.198-204). These offerings also stress that God's people are to dedicate themselves entirely to doing what is excellent and profitable in accordance with the law and avoid any action that might be censurable (1.204). By means of the commandment to pour out in a circle around the altar the blood of the animals offered in order to present it as a libation, God "teaches in this symbol that the mind, whole and complete, dancing in a circle through every phase of word and intention and deed, is to show its willingness to do God's service" (1.205). The washing of the animal victim's belly and feet and the division of its limbs illustrates the manner in which the offerers are to be cleansed from sinful desires, focus on heavenly truths, and give thanks for all of the different parts of God's good creation (1.206-11). The use of animals that are free of any defect stresses the need for the offerers to be free of any type of spiritual blemish: "For it would be a strange inconsistency if, while each of the victims consumed in the burnt offering is only dedicated when found to be free from defect and blemish, the mind of the worshiper should not be purified in every way and washed clean and fair by the ablutions and lustrations, which the right reason of nature pours into the souls of those who love God through ears that are sound in health and free from corruption" (1.191).

In similar fashion, when considering the various rites associated with the offering for well-being, Philo argues that participation in these rites teaches the offerers not to follow the path of injustice or turn away from the road that leads to virtue and noble conduct. Those rites also stress to the offerers that they are to share freely and generously with all who are in need, remembering that they are merely stewards of what they offer, since it belongs not to them but to God (*Spec. Laws* 1.212-15, 220-21). The praise offering, which is a form of the offering of well-being, reminds the offerers of God's benefits and brings them to give thanks to God for his blessings (1.224-25).

For its part, the sin or purification offering leads the offerers to reproach themselves for their errors and to seek a blameless life as their goal (*Spec. Laws* 1.226-28). As they present this offering, they are to acknowledge their wrong-doing, seek pardon for it, make restitution to those whom they have wronged, and change their lives for the better (1.235-38). In fact, Philo states explicitly that the sin offering has the purpose of reminding the offerers not to continue in sin (1.193). Thus each of the three main types of offering contributes in a different way to a life that is in greater conformity with God's will: the holo-caust teaches them to honor God alone, the offering for well-being promotes betterment in human affairs, and the sin offering leads their souls to be healed from their faults and errors (1.197).

The prescriptions regarding the vow of the Nazirite that appear in Numbers 6 include the command for those who make that vow to present all three of the basic forms of sacrificial offering. According to Philo, this vow serves as a means by which the offerers "dedicate and consecrate themselves, thus showing an extraordinary sanctification and a surpassing devotion to God" (*Spec. Laws* 1.248). This vow also promotes temperance and piety, reminds the offerers of their sin, brings them to surrender their lives to God, and encour-ages them to press forward to "that perfect and wholly sound frame of mind of which the whole burnt offering is a symbol" (1.251-52). Due to the pro-hibition against offering human blood on God's altar, those making this vow offer up some of their hair rather than their own blood in order to symbolize the offering up of their life to God (1.254).

For Philo, the prescriptions that are common to all the various types of sacrifice fulfill the same purposes. The rite in which the offerers laid hands on the victim to be sacrificed was to symbolize their commitment to refrain from corruption, plunder, and bloodshed, all of which are committed with the hands (*Spec. Laws* 1.203-4). The purificatory rites that all those who present sacrificial offerings are to carry out prior to presenting those offerings serve not only to cleanse the bodies of the offerers but also to purify their souls from all passions and vices in word and deed (1.257-61). The ashes combined with water that are used in purification rites remind the offerers that they too are composed of earth and water, and thus their use leads the offerers to put away conceit and arrogance by stressing to them that they will some day return to the elements from which they were created (1.262-66). These rites also lead those who participate in them to cleanse their souls and minds so that they may present their own selves to God as sacrificial victims and put away covetousness and sinful desires (1.269-70). The prohibition against the use of honey and leaven in the offerings is "a symbol of the utter unholiness of excessive pleasure," which initially tastes sweet but later produces bodily pain, and the need to avoid becoming "uplifted or puffed up by arrogance" so that one may practice justice, goodwill, and equity in relation to others (1.291-95).

According to Philo, the prescriptions regarding the parts of the animal that are assigned to the priests and for the altar were given for the purpose of "promoting personal and public welfare alike" by means of the symbolisms they convey (*Spec. Laws* 1.145-50). In general, the people's participation in the sacrifices and the hymns and prayers that accompanied them encouraged the people to "make themselves pure by curbing the appetites for pleasure" and also helped to "make them enamored of self-control and piety" (1.193).

Philo sees other prescriptions related to the objects found in the sanctuary and the vestments that the high priest was to wear as having the same type of purpose. The loaves of bread that were to be set out on a table are "emblematic of that most profitable of virtues, self-control, which has prudence and good temper and moderation for its bodyguard against the harmful assaults engineered by licentiousness and covetousness" (*Spec. Laws* 1.172-73). The frankincense that is to accompany the offering of the bread serves "as a symbol that in the court of wisdom no relish is judged to be more sweet-savored than moderation and self-control," whereas the salt used symbolizes "the permanence of all things, since it preserves whatever it is sprinkled on" (1.174-75; cf. Lev 24:5-9). By training the people "to disregard the pleasures of the flesh" and reflect on the truths of the nature of the created order, these things promote the service of God among them (1.176). The fire burning on the altar day and night reminds the people that "the gracious gifts of God granted every day and night to all people are everlasting, unfailing, and unceasing," thus bringing about in them a spirit of thankfulness and promoting an appreciation of the eternal quality of wisdom so that they are constantly illuminated by it (1.285-88). The light from the lamps that burned from evening until morning in the sanctuary reminds the people that thanks should be given to God in every time and season and that God continues to pour out his blessings even on those who slumber (1.296-98).

According to Philo, the observance of the special days and festivals prescribed in the law similarly promotes a way of life in greater conformity with God's will by reminding the people of truths that are vital to their well-being and leading them to dedicate themselves more fully to God. The Feast of the New Moon that is celebrated at the beginning of every lunar month, when the sun begins to illumine the moon and reveal its beauty once more, serves as "an obvious lesson inculcating kindness and humanity and bidding men never grudge their own good things, but imitating the blessed and happy beings in heaven banish jealousy from the confines of the soul, producing what they have for all to see, treat it as common property, and give freely to the deserving" (*Spec. Laws* 2.140-41). The fact that the moon completes a monthly cycle in which it "ends its course at the starting-point at which it began is honored by the law, which declares that day a feast, again to teach us an admirable lesson, that in the conduct of life we should make the ends correspond with the beginnings" (2.142). The Festival of Passover reminds those who participate in it to give thanks to God and to love wisdom and virtue by crossing over from the passions of the body (2.147). Because it is celebrated in the spring, it also serves to remind the people that God is the creator of all good things: "So every year God reminds us of the creation of the world by setting before our eyes the spring when everything blooms and flowers" (2.152). The Feast of Sheaves associated with the Passover serves to check sinful impulses, promote a spirit of fellowship and goodwill to all people everywhere, and to remind the people of God's kindness in providing for the needs of all created beings so that they may give him thanks (2.162-75, 180-82). The Festival of Tabernacles similarly teaches two morals: "The first is that we should honor equality and hate inequality, for the former is the source and fountain of justice, the latter of injustice. The former is akin to open sunlight, the latter to darkness. The second moral is, that after all the fruits are made perfect, it is our duty to thank God, who brought them to perfection and is the source of all good things" (2.204).

For Philo, the offering of the first fruits accomplishes the same type of objectives. It reminds the people that all that they have is a gift from God and is therefore to be used in the way he has commanded for the good of all. It brings them to recall not only God's blessings in general but also God's kindness in giving them a good and fertile land not only for their own benefit but also for the benefit of other peoples (*Spec. Laws* 2.162, 167-68). The offering of first fruits thus promotes an attitude of thanksgiving in relation to God (2.171, 175). This attitude of thanksgiving leads the offerers to consecrate and offer themselves up to God as they offer him the best portion of what they have received from his hand (2.248; cf. 252). The dedication of first fruits to God thus "teaches us a high truth," namely, that the beginning of all things is to be found in God (*Heir* 114)

Both in his *Special Laws* and the *Life of Moses*, Philo sees the layout of the sanctuary as reminding the people and priests of certain truths as well. The woven curtains symbolized the elements of which the world was made, thereby reminding the worshipers of God's act of creation, while the altar of incense served as "a symbol of the thankfulness for earth and water which should be rendered for the benefits derived from both" (*Moses* 2.84-88, 101). The design of the vestment to be worn by the high priest also served to symbolize different aspects of the created order and thus reinforce among the people and the priests certain truths regarding God's sovereignty, the beauty of all that he has created, and God's kindness, mercy, and grace not only toward Israel but toward all peoples (*Spec. Laws* 1.84-97; *Moses* 2.109-35). The manner in which the ark of the covenant was decorated served to emphasize the same truths and symbolized the gracious power of God (*Moses* 2.95-100).

Reflection upon all of these truths thus served to promote a spirit of love and thanksgiving in relation to God and to lead the worshipers to consecrate themselves to the type of life that God had commanded for the good of all.

PROMOTING JUSTICE AND RIGHTEOUSNESS THROUGH SACRIFICE

There can be little doubt that many of the interpretations that Philo gives to the Mosaic prescriptions regarding the sacrificial worship of Israel's God are unique to him rather than being common among other Jews in antiquity or grounded in the Jewish tradition of his day. Philo himself acknowledges as much, often commenting that he is speculating or offering opinions that are his alone. At times his interpretations also draw heavily on Platonic ideas, such as the superiority of the soul to the body. Nevertheless, what can scarcely be doubted is that his attempts to find deeper meanings in the Mosaic prescriptions and discern some purpose behind them were common among Jews in antiquity, including those who put the biblical texts into the form in which they now exist and brought them together in a single collection. At some point or another, those who considered those prescriptions must have asked themselves why God had ordained many of the things they contained and what purpose those things fulfilled.

It might have been supposed, of course, that Israel's God had no purpose in prescribing in such great detail the many different aspects of the sacrificial worship that was to be offered to him, other than that of satisfying some type of desire or whim on his part. He simply found pleasure in defining with great precision and in great detail each and every aspect of that worship and then seeing everything that he had commanded carried out precisely as he had ordained. In that case, the only reason why he had designed the sacrificial worship that the people were to offer him in the way that he had and demanded that the priests and people perform all of the different rites and procedures exactly in the way that he had prescribed was that he found that form of worship entertaining, gratifying, or appealing. What had led him to give those commandments was not any concern for his people but pure capriciousness.

For reasons we have seen repeatedly, however, it is highly unlikely that those who examined the Mosaic prescriptions regarding the offering of sacrifice would have thought in such terms. Unlike the gods of other nations, the God of Israel was not interested in satisfying his own whims and fancies and being worshiped in certain ways purely for his own sake, simply because he took pleasure at watching the things he had commanded being carried out down to the last detail. Nor was he attempting to satisfy some type of personal need, since as sovereign creator he needed nothing from human beings. Because there is nothing in the biblical texts to suggest that sacrificial offerings were thought to have some type of magical or mysterious effect on God or the offerers that would benefit them in some way, there was no reason to suppose that God had prescribed those offerings for the purpose of producing such an effect. If he had given such detailed prescriptions, therefore, it could only be concluded that he had done so in order to bring about something he desired to see in his people themselves for their own sake. Each of the different prescriptions must have been designed to fulfill some particular purpose related to a more general objective. And when that objective was viewed in the context of the story that appears in the Hebrew Scriptures as a whole, it could only be related in some way to the well-being of his people as well as the practice of justice, righteousness, love, and mercy that was necessary for them to enjoy that well-being.

This assumption is clearly present in Philo's interpretation of the prescriptions regarding the sacrificial worship of Israel's God that appear in the Mosaic law. While the original purpose of many of those prescriptions would have been just as much a mystery to Philo as it was to other Jews in antiquity and his interpretations of their meaning tended to be based on mere speculation, he would by no means have been alone in assuming that in some way those prescriptions had been designed to promote a particular way of life and certain behaviors among those who would put them into practice. In most cases, those prescriptions would be thought to fulfill this purpose indirectly by reminding the offerers of certain ideas and reinforcing certain basic truths and beliefs that would in some way contribute to the objective of leading them to live in the way that God had commanded for their own good. The commandments regarding the offering of sacrifice would also have been seen as promoting the fulfillment of that same objective by making it possible for the people to experience in concrete and palpable ways different aspects of their relationship to God, one another, and the world in general. Due to the rich symbolisms inherent in the rites and ceremonies that God had prescribed and the profound manner in which the people's participation in those rites and ceremonies touched and transformed them in body, soul, and spirit, the observance of those prescriptions served to deepen and strengthen the people's commitment to living as God's people and obeying all of the other things he had commanded of them for their own good.

Such an understanding of the meaning and purpose of the prescriptions regarding sacrificial worship that God had given his people would have been especially evident to them when they considered God's commands regarding the celebration of the three annual festivals of Passover, Weeks, and Tabernacles. These festivals clearly had the purpose of bringing the people to recall key moments in their history, especially from the period of their exodus from Egypt and their sojourn in the wilderness. Each of these feasts was also associated with an agricultural celebration, namely, the gathering of the first fruits as well as the spring and autumn harvests. At each of these festivals, sacrifices were offered and the people celebrated by eating of what had been sacrificed.

Virtually all Jews in antiquity would have recognized that these festivals had been designed to contribute to the practice of justice and righteousness among them in several ways. Above all, they reminded the people of their identity as God's chosen people whom he had redeemed from slavery in Egypt to be his own possession. As such, the people were to live in conformity with his will as he had made it known in the commandments, which promoted justice and righteousness. As they celebrated these festivals, the people were not only to remember the events of the past but also to reflect on their meaning. At Passover, they were to recite anew the story of the exodus of their ancestors from Egypt, while at the Festival of Tabernacles they were to recall the time their ancestors had spent in the wilderness by dwelling in the same type of tents or booths that their ancestors had inhabited during that time. Because the three major festivals were associated with the harvest of fruits and crops, they were also to be an occasion for the people to reflect on the kindness and mercy that God had shown them by providing them with the things they needed to sustain life. As they were reminded of God's gracious activity in their history and in his creation as a whole, they would be brought to dedicate their lives more fully to serving him by doing his will.

There can be little doubt that those who contemplated the commandments regarding things such as the high priest's vestments, the layout and adornment of the sanctuary, the ark of the covenant, the lampstand, the showbread, and the altar of incense understood their meaning and purpose in much the same way that Philo did, even if their interpretation of the meaning and symbolism of these things differed from his. All of these symbolic objects and realities served to remind the people of certain truths regarding God, in particular his sovereignty and his love as the creator and sustainer of all that existed and of his people Israel in particular. While those objects and realities might fulfill this function in regard to the people as a whole, they especially served to remind the priests and Levites dedicated to God's service in the sanctuary of these and other truths, thus underscoring for them their unique and special role in promoting among the people the type of life he desired and commanded for the good of all.

In a number of passages in the biblical prescriptions regarding sacrifices, it is said explicitly that certain aspects of those prescriptions are to serve as a memorial or reminder of particular beliefs and truths. The Festival of Passover is called a memorial, as is the unleavened bread that the Israelites were to eat during the festival (Exod 12:14; 13:9; Deut 16:3). Other of the feasts that God prescribes are also said to serve as memorials or reminders for the people (Lev 23:24, 42-43; Deut 16:12). In Num 10:10, the sacrifices are referred to as a memorial explicitly. A number of texts also speak of a "memorial portion" in relation to the sacrificial offerings, which suggests that this portion was to serve as some type of reminder, though precisely what the people were to recall is not entirely clear in the texts.[20] The stones on the ephod, a linen apron which formed part of the high priest's vestments, were to serve as a memorial, similar to the way in which the stones on the breastplate worn by the high priest served as reminders of the twelve tribes of Israel (Exod 28:12, 17-21,

---

20. See Lev 2:2, 9, 16; 5:12; 6:15; 24:7; Num 5:26.

29; 39:7). The half shekel paid by all Israelites is called a memorial as well (Exod 30:16). According to Deut 26:1-11, those who brought their offerings of first fruits before the priests were to recite a summary of the story of Israel's redemption as they did so. In this way, their identity as God's chosen people dedicated to doing his will with everything that he had given them was reinforced once more.

Many other aspects of the sacrificial worship prescribed in the Mosaic law had the same purpose of reminding the people that they were his chosen possession and promoting in them a spirit of gratitude and loving service. Virtually all of the sacrificial offerings were seen as expressions of thanksgiving to God. The logic of these offerings is expressed in the prayer attributed to David in 1 Chr 29:10-19. There he tells God:

> Yours, O LORD, are the greatness, the power, the glory, the victory, and the majesty; for everything that is in the heavens and on the earth is yours; yours is the kingdom, O LORD, and you are exalted as head above all. Riches and honor come from you, and you rule over all. In your hand are power and might, and the power to make great and to give strength to all is in your hand. . . . For all things come from you, and what we have given to you is from your own hand. . . . O LORD our God, all this abundance that we have provided to build you a house for your holy name comes from your hand and is your own (vv. 11-12, 14, 16).

In this prayer of David, we see the stress on God's sovereignty as Lord of all and the recognition that, because all things belong to him, those who make offerings to him are simply giving to him what is already his own. As they recalled that not only their possessions but also their very lives and existence were God's own, those who presented God with their offerings acknowledged his loving and gracious lordship over their lives and became strengthened in their commitment to doing his loving and gracious will.

As we have already noted above, these same ideas were stressed by means of the burnt offerings or holocausts. Because the animal victim in its entirety was presented to God by being burnt on the altar, there could be no self-interest on the part of the offerers, since they retained nothing of the victim's remains for their own use or consumption. While in many cases the offerers were undoubtedly hoping to receive some type of blessing from God in response to their offering, it was stressed to them that they could not purchase God's favor or bribe him with gifts (Deut 10:17; 2 Chr 19:7; Sir 35:14). Any who viewed their offering in that manner would be provoking God to anger rather than obtaining his favor. According to the beliefs reflected in the biblical texts, when God looked into the hearts of the offerers, what interested him was determining whether they were truly committed to living in accordance with his will for their own good. If that was the case and their petition involved something that might promote their well-being and that of others as well, it was expected that in most cases God would grant them their petition. However, it was also recognized that God might deny their petition in order to accomplish some purpose or objective that he regarded as more important or more conducive to their well-being than that which they sought. When he did choose to respond in that manner, God was not rejecting them or withholding from them what was good for them. On the contrary, he was acting in their best interest, since at times he had a better plan for them or wished to strengthen or correct them by means of some type of hardship, want, or affliction. Therefore, what God sought in the offerers was that they simply trust in his love, sovereignty, and goodness by accepting whatever response he gave to their petition as a means by which he sought their well-being and the well-being of his people as a whole. It was this spirit and attitude that he sought to see in the hearts and minds of the offerers, not for his own sake but for theirs.

The offerings of well-being reinforced some of these same ideas as well as others. The fact that the offerers dedicated a portion of their offering to the priests and divided the rest among themselves in a meal served to emphasize the idea that the blessings of shalom and well-being that they received from God were to be shared with others and to be a motive for rejoicing and celebration in their lives. This type of sharing was of course a central component of the commitment to justice, righteousness, and mercy that God sought to bring about in all of his people. The rejoicing and celebration that were to be reflected in the sacrifice and meal reinforced the idea that true joy was to be found in this type of sharing and in serving God and others rather than in a life of selfishness and avarice. The offerings of well-being might also be understood not only as an expression of gratitude for the blessings received from God but also as a petition for continued well-being for oneself and others in the future. To make such a petition was to acknowledge God as the source of well-being. Yet because the condition upon which God granted such petitions was that those who made them be committed to doing his will by practicing justice, righteousness, mercy, and solidarity with others, those offerings also served as means by which such a commitment was reinforced. The fact that many of the sacrificial offerings were presented by the people and priests on behalf of others rather than on their own behalf also made those offerings an expression of love for others and thus helped that love to grow and extend out further. In these ways and others, the offerings of well-being served to strengthen the bonds that united the members of the community to one another and increase their commitment to sharing with others the blessings that God had given them.

As Philo stressed, the offering of the first fruits served as a reminder that everything came from God's hand and was therefore to be dedicated to his service. For that reason, not only were the people to give back to God a portion of what they had received from him, but they were also to give him the first and best of all that he had provided. Because the first fruits and tithes were kept by the priests and Levites in order to sustain them, these offerings also contributed to the ongoing worship of God at the sanctuary that promoted justice and well-being among the people by constantly reminding them of the truths associated with that worship. Like the other offerings, the first fruits provided the people with a concrete and palpable means by which they might express their gratitude to God and also served to reinforce not only their faith in God as sovereign creator and provider but also the spirit of gratitude and commitment to obeying his will that God wished to see in them for their own sake.

The idea that the people belonged to God as his possession, together with all that he had given them, was reinforced as well by the practice of redeeming the firstborn.[21] In the case of clean animals that were fit for sacrifice, the firstborn was to be given to God in the form of a sacrificial offering. If the animal had a defect or if it was an animal that was not fit for sacrifice, it still belonged to God but was in essence to be purchased back from him through the payment of a monetary amount (Lev 27:11-13, 27; Num 18:15-16). In the case of donkeys, if the firstborn male was not purchased back from God, it was to be destroyed in order to prevent it from being kept as a possession by the animal's owner as his own (Exod 13:13; 34:20). Of course, the firstborn male children were not to be sacrificed to God, yet because they belonged to God they needed to be purchased back from him by means of a payment as well (Exod 13:12; Num 3:46-47; 18:15-16). While in a sense this may be understood as a form of substitution, it is important to stress that a firstborn son was not under any type of death penalty or subject to death if he was not purchased back from God. Much less was any type of redemption from sin or guilt thought to be involved. Instead, the idea was that those who belonged to God were to be dedicated fully to God's service, as the child Samuel was in 1 Samuel 1:20-28. Thus, when people purchased back from God a firstborn male child, this was understood not in terms of redeeming the child from a death penalty on account of someone's sins but rather in terms of making it possible for the child to remain with his parents so as to live as part of his family. Obviously, even though that child would not be dedicated to God's service at his sanctuary, it was expected that he would be dedicated to God's service elsewhere and in other ways, together with the other members of his family.

In Exod 13:14-16, it is emphasized that the commandment to redeem the firstborn served as a sign to remind the Israelites of the manner in which God had put to death the firstborn of the male animals and human beings in Egypt before delivering the Israelites from their bondage there, although of course the firstborn of the Israelites who had smeared the blood of sheep on the doorways of their homes had been spared. This commandment therefore represents one more example of a practice designed to remind the people of fundamental truths, such as God's sovereignty over all life as well as their identity as the people whom God had made his own by electing them through Abraham and subsequently redeeming them from their slavery in Egypt.

---

21. See Exod 13:11-16; 22:29-30; 34:19-20; Lev 27:26; Num 8:17; 18:15-18; Deut 12:6.

In addition to mandating the redemption of the firstborn male children in every Israelite family, the Mosaic law speaks of God taking the Levites for himself in the place of the Israelites' firstborn (Num 3:40-45; 8:14-18). In Num 8:17-18, God's election of the Levites is also said to serve as a reminder that God struck down all the firstborn in Egypt. Once again, when the Levites are said to be taken in the place of the Israelites' firstborn sons, this was not thought to involve any type of substitutionary death. Instead, the idea was that God took for his service at the sanctuary only a portion of the people, even though in principle the people as a whole were to be dedicated to serving him there. While *all* of the people belonged to God and were to be a "kingdom of priests" (Exod 19:6), the Levites took the place of the other Israelites and their firstborn by consecrating themselves fully to God's service and carrying out the tasks associated with the priesthood.

In Exod 30:11-16, God tells the Israelites through Moses that all of them are to give a half shekel as an offering to support the sacrificial worship carried out at the sanctuary. While many English translations of this passage refer to this payment as a ransom for the lives of those who make it, such a translation can be misleading if it is understood in the sense that by paying the half shekel the people avoided having to forfeit their lives by being put to death. Because the idea is simply that each individual Israelite is expected to provide support for the sacrificial worship offered at the sanctuary, the allusion to ransoming or purchasing one's life or soul should be interpreted in the sense that each Israelite male is to make the necessary payment on his own behalf. If any idea of substitution is thought to be present, this substitution should be understood once more in terms of being excused from the obligation to dedicate one's life to God's service at the sanctuary. The payment of the half shekel, which as noted above is explicitly called a memorial, reminded the people that their life, their body, and their being as a whole had been given to them by God and thus belonged to him as his possession. In essence, by means of the half shekel they were purchasing themselves and their lives back from God so that they might belong to themselves in a sense, even though they would continue to belong to God as well.

The common people's support for the priests and Levites and for the temple service as a whole was also a means by which God was thought to strengthen his people's commitment to living in justice, love, and solidarity. Because the sacrificial worship carried out at the sanctuary had this as its objective, all of the support that the people provided for that worship contributed either directly or indirectly to the fulfillment of that objective. Those who gave of their time and resources to make that worship possible and to sustain and embellish it were therefore expressing their love for God and one another. The more the people participated in that worship, the more they would grow in their love for God and others. By using their gifts and energies to make that worship more attractive and appealing to others and bringing greater honor and glory to God, they would also bring more people to love and serve God so as to find in him the happiness and well-being he desired for all.

Because the worship of Israel's God at his sanctuary was one of the primary means by which he sought to bring about in all of his people the way of life that would allow them to be blessed, it was important for the people to support the persons and activities related to that worship through their gifts and offerings. Of course, it was important for them not to neglect the poor and needy as they presented their resources as gifts and offerings to God, yet even their efforts to adorn and enhance the worship of God at his sanctuary could be seen as an act of love for the poor and needy, since those who would participate in that worship would be strengthened in their commitment to serving those who needed their help. By supporting the priests and Levites through their monetary contributions and by giving them the share of their offerings that the law prescribed, the common people made it possible for them not only to carry out the rites that made the people grow in their love for God and others but also to instruct the people in God's good law and fulfill other duties aimed at accomplishing that same objective.

The offerings that the people provided for the priests and the temple service as well as the payment of the half shekel that the law mandated also served as a means by which the people made the public sacrifices offered at the sanctuary their own. Because their contributions made those sacrifices possible, they were means by which individual Israelites became joined to the rest of God's people in order to thank and praise God for his goodness and acknowledge his sovereignty over their lives and the world as a whole. The prayers that were offered up to God by means of the daily, weekly, and monthly offerings were thus those of the people themselves and not merely those of the priests who pronounced them, since it was the people's support for the temple service that made those prayers and offerings possible. By contributing to the temple service, the common people made it their own.

Furthermore, because the prayers that were offered up together with the public sacrifices invoked God's blessings not only for Israel but for all the nations of the world and their leaders, the support that the people provided for those prayers and sacrifices was an expression of love not only for their fellow Israelites but for people of all other nations as well. When people pray for others and ask God to bless them, they are strengthened in their own commitment to living and acting in ways that benefit others and enable them to enjoy God's blessings. For that reason, the people's support for the public offerings led them to grow in their love not only for God but for all of the peoples of the earth, no matter what their nationality or ethnic background. Of course, the people made the public sacrifices and the prayers that accompanied them their own not only by their financial support for those offerings but also by turning toward the temple to join themselves to the prayers and sacrifices being offered to God at the hour in which they were being presented. Every day, both at morning and at night, they were thereby brought to offer up with their fellow Israelites petitions that invoked God's blessing on themselves as a people and on every other people throughout the world as well. As noted above, these ideas are repeated frequently by Philo, who insists that the sacrificial worship of Israel's God at the Jerusalem temple is offered not only on Israel's behalf but also on behalf of human beings as a whole. As such, the worship in which every individual Israelite was to participate constituted an expression of love for all people everywhere, whether those people acknowledged it as such or not, at the same time that it served to reinforce such love in each of the Israelites who joined in that worship.

Above all, the offering of sacrifice promoted the type of values that God wished to see instilled in his people. The command for them to present him their offerings encouraged generosity and sharing among them. By bringing the people together not only to celebrate God's gifts and recall the story that united them but also to acknowledge together their sins and implore God's forgiveness, the offering of sacrifice helped generate the kind of solidarity and mutual love that was vital to the people's well-being. The simplicity of much of the sacrificial worship fostered humility and temperance. The concessions to the poor that allowed them to offer birds and measures of flour rather than costly animals taught the people that in their daily life they were to make the same type of concessions and allowances for those less fortunate. The commandment that all were to redeem themselves by paying the same price of a half shekel independently of whether they were rich or poor stressed that all human lives were of equal value and thus that all people were to be valued equally, no matter what their social status. The prohibition against the consumption of blood and the commandment that all blood was to be offered to God or disposed of on the ground similarly emphasized the value of all life and reinforced the idea that no life was ever to be taken lightly (Lev 17:10-14; Deut 12:16, 23-25; 15:23). The offering of the blood and fat of the sacrificial animals to God underscored not only the idea that all life belonged to God but also that he was to be given that which was most prized and precious in life. The offering or redemption of the firstborn and the offering of the first fruits communicated the same idea. The care and concern that the people were to show for the needs of the priests and Levites were also to lead the people to show the same care and concern for those who served God in other ways, as well as other members of the community who depended on the kindness and generosity of their sisters and brothers in order to meet their needs.

By instilling greater love and dedication to God, therefore, the sacrificial worship prescribed in the law also stimulated greater love among the people themselves as well as a greater commitment to the practice of justice and righteousness. Because the God they worshiped with their sacrifices needed and desired nothing for himself but was dedicated entirely to the well-being of his people as a whole, to love and serve him by definition meant loving and serving those whom he loved. One could not be consecrated to the God who was committed above all else to the well-being of all without sharing fully that same commitment. Similarly, to respect as holy not only God but also the people, places, and objects dedicated to his worship was by definition also to accept as holy his command that all be cared for and treated with dignity, respect, and kindness. Any who did not treat others in this manner were failing to treat God in that manner as well. By continually reminding the Israelites of their identity as God's chosen and holy people and the manner in which God had acted throughout their history, the sacrificial worship God had prescribed reminded them as well of the task and purpose for which he had chosen them, namely, to be a "kingdom of priests" in relation to all other peoples (Exod 19:5).

In all these ways, then, the biblical prescriptions regarding the sacrificial worship of God promoted a life of justice, love, and righteousness among his people and strengthened them in their commitment to living in accordance with the commandments he had given them to promote their happiness and well-being. It was for that purpose that he commanded that his people offer him sacrifice and took delight when they did so in the way he intended, expressing to him their love and dedication and renewing their commitment to obeying his commandments for their own good. By receiving from their hand the gifts and offerings that transformed their hearts and lives, God gave them life. If he desired and demanded sacrificial offerings of them, it was not for *his* sake but for *theirs*.

CHAPTER 8

Purging a Paganized God
from the Sins of His Interpreters

Among the different types of sacrificial offerings that God had commanded of his people in the Torah were those that were to be presented for the sins they committed. When the people sinned, they were expected to confess and acknowledge their sin, ask forgiveness of God, compensate for any harm they had done to others in order to be reconciled with them, and commit themselves once more to living in accordance with God's commandments. In addition, however, under certain circumstances they were also to offer up sacrifices for sin and participate in sacrificial rites and ceremonies that served as means by which they made manifest their repentance and renewed commitment to observing God's law.

Although the books of Leviticus and Numbers describe in considerable detail the different rites associated with the sacrifices for sin that God was said to have prescribed, they never state clearly the reasons or purpose for which God had commanded for those rites to be carried out. As a result, it has been common for biblical scholars and interpreters to assume that the God of Israel demanded that his people offer him sacrifices for sin for the same basic reason that the gods of the nations demanded sacrificial offerings when human beings had disobeyed and offended them: like those gods, the God of Israel found the sinful behavior of human beings intolerable for his own sake and insisted not only that such behavior come to an end but also that those responsible for it make atonement or reparation for the sins they had committed. They were to do so by compensating him for what they had done, reversing the effects of their actions in some way, or submitting to the punishments that those actions deserved.

According to this understanding of the sacrifices for sin prescribed in the Torah, those sacrifices were not only desirable but also necessary if the God of Israel was to remain present among his people in order to bless and save them. Without those sacrifices, God's holy and righteous nature made it impossible for him to dwell in the midst of sin, injustice, and impurity.

When we examine the biblical prescriptions regarding sacrifices for sin on the basis of the concept of God that we have seen throughout the present work, however, it becomes clear that such an understanding of the meaning and purpose of those sacrifices must be regarded as foreign to biblical thought. Rather than being a God who is wholly committed to the happiness and well-being of the people he loves, a God whose justice, righteousness, and holiness leave him no choice but to demand sacrifices if he is to forgive and accept sinful human beings and dwell in their midst is a God whose nature proves oppressive not only for them but for him as well.

SEEKING FAVOR AND FORGIVENESS FROM THE PAGAN GODS OF ANTIQUITY

In virtually all of the belief systems of antiquity, one of the primary concerns of human beings had to be that of seeking the forgiveness of the gods when one had offended or angered them. The reason for this was that the gods were thought to have power and control over virtually all aspects of human life. They controlled many of the forces of nature on which human beings depended and might strike people, animals, and crops with disease, plague, or drought at any time. They also gave victory and dominance to some peoples and nations while abandoning others to slavery, submission, destruction, and doom. Because they influenced daily life in many other ways as well, their favor was absolutely indispensable if human beings were to enjoy happiness, well-being, and prosperity.

The primary means by which human beings sought forgiveness from the gods, of course, was by presenting them with sacrificial offerings. While some gods might be content with offerings such as fruits and vegetables, drink offerings, or monetary gifts, others demanded animal offerings of different types. Gods such as Molech even demanded the life and blood of human beings, including especially children. These offerings were thought to make reparation to the gods by restoring to them not only any material goods that they had been deprived of but also the honor and respect owed to them. For the gods, it was vital that human beings continue to revere them and hold them in high esteem, since otherwise those human beings would not submit to them as they should or give them what they regarded as being due to them by right. For that reason, the reparations made by those who had angered and offended the gods were viewed as means by which they restored to the gods what was rightfully theirs and indicated their intention to submit obediently to those gods once more in order to give them what they desired and demanded. Furthermore, if one had robbed or deprived the gods of something that was rightfully theirs, it was not enough simply to give back to them what one had taken. One had to pay a penalty as well by giving them an additional amount as reparation or satisfaction for the offense committed.

In many cases, the actions and behaviors that angered and offended the gods had nothing to do with questions of morality but simply involved a failure to give them what they wanted or needed for their own sake. For that reason, as we noted briefly in Chapter 1, it would not be entirely accurate to refer to those actions and behaviors as sins in the biblical sense of the word. Those who disobeyed the gods were undoubtedly committing offenses against them, but strictly speaking they were not transgressing ethical norms that had been established by the gods out of concern for human well-being. Whatever moral principles or ethical norms that existed were thought to be grounded in nature rather than the will of the gods, even though the gods might demand that those principles and norms be respected so that order might be preserved as much as possible. Although at times the gods became angry at those who violated those principles and norms and punished them, what motivated them was not a concern to uphold moral or ethical behavior as an end in itself but rather a desire to avoid the negative consequences that resulted intrinsically and naturally from the violation of those principles and norms, since their violation might adversely affect not only human beings but the gods themselves.

Because the actions and behaviors that generally angered and offended the gods were not sins in the biblical sense of the word, it is also problematic to speak of those who offered them sacrifices in order to regain their favor making atonement for their sins through those sacrifices. While they certainly sought to assuage the wrath of the gods by means of their offerings, what interested the gods was not that those who had angered and offended them recommit themselves to living in accordance with moral principles or ethical norms but simply that they do whatever the gods commanded and avoid whatever they prohibited. The offering of prayers, gifts, and sacrifices was the means by which those who had disobeyed the gods manifested visibly and concretely their renewed commitment to obeying them in all things. Nevertheless, it was not the repentance or remorse of the offerers in itself that appeased the gods but rather the fact that as a result of that renewed commitment they would once again dedicate themselves to giving the gods what they wanted and demanded for their own sake.

For these same reasons, what led the gods to put away their anger at those human beings who had acted in ways that displeased and upset them was not the sentiments that lay behind the offerings presented to them but those offerings themselves. Throughout the poems of Homer, for example, human beings are repeatedly presented as propitiating the gods merely by means of the sacrifices that they offer them.[1] For the most part, the spirit in which the offerers presented their gifts to the gods mattered little to them. What interested the gods was simply receiving the gifts and offerings they desired as well as the honor, worship, recognition, and respect of which those gifts and offerings were to be an expression.

In addition to desiring and demanding sacrificial offerings and requiring that those who had angered and offended them make reparation for their actions, the gods of antiquity often were thought to have need of a place to dwell. While in principle they might dwell in the heavens or in some place that was distant from their worshipers, generally those who worshiped the gods wanted them to be in close proximity to them so that they might receive

---

1. See, for example, *Il.* 1.99-100, 146-47, 442-44; 6.379-80; *Od.* 3.143-45, 418-20; 4.581-84; cf. 1.60-62; 8.508-10.

their offerings, hear their prayers, and pay attention to their needs and desires. For that reason, they provided the gods with a sanctuary, shrine, or temple that was devoted to their worship. Of course, the worshipers also sought to make the dwelling place of the gods as pleasant and appealing as possible for them. This involved constructing buildings for them that were spacious and attractive, adorning them in various ways, burning offerings and incense that the gods found pleasing, and entertaining them with music, hymns, and games in their honor. The idea was to keep the gods content and avoid arousing their wrath or displeasure.

Naturally, it was expected that those who presented themselves before the gods wear their finest clothes and be as appealing as possible for them in other ways as well. It was important for them to be washed and bathed and in many cases to use perfume and wear make-up.[2] To fail to be presentable when offering a sacrifice would be an offense to the gods since it would represent a failure to show them the proper honor and respect. The gods could hardly be pleased if those who stood before them offering prayers and sacrifices were unwashed, disheveled, or dressed in shabby clothes. They demanded cleanness and purity, however, not for the sake of the offerers themselves but for their own sake, since they did not wish to gaze on anything or anyone that was unpleasant to their sight.

The sanctuaries dedicated to the gods also had to be kept clean and pure. If a sanctuary or temple was dirty, polluted, or smelled unpleasant, the deity who dwelled there might be led to abandon it. In that case, the people would no longer be able to have the deity in their midst to bless them, protect them from harm, and grant them their prayers and petitions. In fact, the images and statues of the deities themselves were to be treated in the same way. As Roy Gane notes, for example, the statues of the ancient gods of Egypt were purified, anointed, clothed, and adorned every day, while the gods of other nations received similar treatment from their priests and worshipers: "daily service to a Mesopotamian god, represented by his or her idol, entailed elements such as fumigations and purifications with water at mealtimes, when various foods (grain products, fruit, meat) and beverages (beer, wine, milk) were served. Other regular, but not necessarily daily, care included ritual washing of the image and arraying it in magnificent clothing with jewelry...."[3]

Of course, the presence of the gods in the midst of the people could also be dangerous if those gods became angry or violent. Since the gods were often thought to be capricious, even the slightest provocation or offense might provoke their anger and lead them to lash out at the human beings that were within reach of them. Nevertheless, if human beings wished to enjoy the blessing and protection of the gods, it was necessary to remain in close

---

2. See, for example, *Il.* 1.312-17; 10.570-79; 24.281-314; *Od.* 3.464-68; 4.750-67; 17.45-60.

3. Roy E. Gane, "Worship, Sacrifice, and Festivals in the Ancient Near East," in *Behind the Scenes of the Old Testament: Cultural, Social, and Historical Contexts*, ed. Jonathan S. Greer, John W. Hilber, and John H. Walton (Grand Rapids: Baker Academic, 2018), 361-67 (362).

proximity to them. For that reason, they had no choice but to risk the danger of keeping the gods in their midst by providing them with a place in which they could dwell and doing everything possible to fulfill their needs, desires, and demands.

At times it was thought that the gods themselves needed to be protected from supernatural forces that might do them harm or upset them in some way. According to Jacob Milgrom, in the polytheistic belief systems of antiquity, "the realm of the gods is never wholly separate from or transcendent to the human world. Natural objects such as specific trees, rivers, stones and the like are invested with supernal force. But this earthbound power is independent of the gods and can be an unpredictable danger to the latter as well as to people."[4] These mysterious forces, whether personal or impersonal, could penetrate into the sanctuary where a particular deity was worshiped and either do some type of harm to that deity or lead the deity to abandon the sanctuary. For that reason, it was necessary to purify the sanctuary to keep it free from such forces and also to purify the particular objects that these hostile forces would strike at first: "In the ancient Near East, temples were periodically smeared with magical substances at precisely the same vulnerable points, in order to expel the malefic power from the object and to protect it against future incursions."[5] This was often done with the use of sacrificial blood taken from an animal victim, since such blood was considered to be especially effective against those forces due to the power inherent in it. It was the task of the priests who were dedicated to the service of these gods to apply the blood to the sacred objects and places by sprinkling it on them or smearing them with it to cleanse them from their impurity or drive the demonic and malefic forces out of the sanctuary.[6]

The concern for the purity not only of those who drew near to the gods to worship them but also of the places in which they dwelt was thus common in many of the pagan belief systems of antiquity. This concern was intimately related to the gods' desire to receive the sacrificial offerings that pleased them and their insistence that their worshipers adhere to all of the rules, procedures, and conditions that they had laid down either for their own pleasure or their own protection. As John H. Walton explains, the failure to keep the gods happy by satisfying their demands and maintaining the purity of the sanctuaries dedicated to them was thought to bring disaster and chaos in its wake:

> Because of the deity's residence in the temple, it was the center of order in the cosmos. Different cultures had different ways of portraying the temple as cosmic nexus, but because of this role, if the temple was not maintained and its

---

4. Jacob Milgrom, "The Changing Concept of Holiness in the Pentateuchal Codes with Emphasis on Leviticus 19," in *Reading Leviticus: A Conversation with Mary Douglas*, ed. John F. A. Sawyer, JSOTSup 227 (Sheffield: Sheffield Academic Press, 1996), 65-75 (65).

5. Jacob Milgrom, *Leviticus 1–16: A New Translation with Introduction and Commentary*, AB 3 (New York: Doubleday, 1991), 279.

6. Jacob Milgrom, *Leviticus: A Book of Ritual and Ethics*, CC (Minneapolis: Fortress, 2004), 164-65.

god sustained, the cosmos would be in jeopardy and subject to collapse.... In the temples the gods were pampered. No expense was spared to ensure that the gods would not become angry and strike out at the people, become offended and abandon the people to demonic forces or to their enemies, or, worst of all, become so dissatisfied that they would leave altogether. The god's presence was essential, and thus the temple became the locus for divine-human interrelationship, a fragile and often unpredictable relationship of mutual need and dependence.... Purity in the ancient Near East is associated with the elitist attitudes of the gods and the prerogatives to which they felt entitled. They deserved the very best and could easily grow offended at any carelessness in performance or at any lapse in quality of what was provided for them. They were persnickety and petty. Purity was designed to meet their exacting demands so that they would not express their inherently temperamental nature.[7]

SACRIFICES FOR SIN IN THE HEBREW BIBLE

Although a great deal of research has been done on the subject of Hebrew sacrifice since the rise of biblical scholarship in the nineteenth century, it is the sacrifices for sin prescribed in the Hebrew Bible that have particularly occupied the attention of biblical scholars. The main reason for this has to do with the interpretations given to Jesus' death in the New Testament and in Christian teaching, especially in the West since the time of the Protestant Reformation. Scattered throughout the writings of the New Testament are brief formulas that speak of Jesus dying for others and for their sins, obtaining God's forgiveness on their behalf by means of his death and blood, and giving up his life to redeem them and reconcile them to God.[8] Many of the passages in which these formulas appear use sacrificial language and imagery explicitly. Due to the influence that these passages have had in Christian thinking over the centuries, the idea that through his sufferings, death, and blood Jesus made atonement for the sins of humanity and restored fallen human beings to God's favor is regarded by most Christians as one of the central tenets of the Christian faith.

Despite the centrality and importance of that belief for Christians, however, it raises difficult questions that Christian theologians have long struggled to answer. Why was it necessary for Jesus to suffer, die, and shed his blood in order for human beings to be saved? Why could God not simply have forgiven human beings their sins freely, without Jesus' death on the cross? And precisely how do his sufferings, death, and blood result in the salvation, justification, and redemption of those who believe in him and obtain God's forgiveness and acceptance on their behalf?

Because the New Testament writings never address such questions or provide the background information necessary to answer them, Christian scholars and biblical interpreters have felt the need to turn to the Hebrew

---

7. John H. Walton, "The Temple in Context," in *Behind the Scenes*, ed. Greer, Hilber, and Walton, 349-54 (349, 351, 353).

8. See Matt 20:28; 26:28; Rom 3:24-25; 5:6-10; Gal 1:4; Eph 1:7; 2:13; Col 1:21-22; 1 Tim 2:5-6; Heb 9:26; 1 Pet 1:2; 1 John 1:7; Rev 1:5; 5:9.

Bible or Old Testament in an attempt to reconstruct the beliefs regarding sacrifice, atonement, and forgiveness that led Jesus' earliest followers to make use of sacrificial language and imagery to interpret his sufferings and death. These scholars and interpreters make the logical assumption that Jesus' earliest followers, all of whom were Jewish, had a clear understanding of the manner in which the sufferings, death, and blood of a sacrificial victim were believed to obtain God's forgiveness and restore people to his favor. In that case, when they associated Jesus' death and blood with the forgiveness of sins, they would have known why it had been necessary for Jesus to suffer and die in order for God to forgive and save sinful human beings and would also have had a clear understanding of the manner in which his sufferings and death resulted in human salvation.

The problem, however, is that just as the New Testament writings never address the question of why Jesus needed to suffer and die in order for human beings to be forgiven and saved or offer any explanation as to the manner in which his sufferings, death, and blood make that forgiveness and salvation possible, so also the passages from the Hebrew Bible that relate the offering of sacrifice to the forgiveness of sins and God's acceptance of sinners offer few if any insights into the nature of that relationship in biblical thought. As a result, biblical scholars have engaged in endless debates in an attempt to define the precise manner in which the sacrifices for sin prescribed in the Hebrew Bible were thought to obtain God's forgiveness and effect purification from sin, just as New Testament interpreters have struggled to reach any type of consensus regarding the manner in which Jesus' death and blood were believed to have made it possible for God to forgive human beings and save them from their sins.

Due to the centrality and importance that the subject of sin and its atonement has had in both Jewish and Christian thought and the key role that it plays in defining the manner in which God is conceived of in both of these traditions, any consideration of biblical thought regarding the nature and character of God cannot neglect or gloss over this subject but must examine it at length. In order to do that here, it will be necessary to refer in some detail to the scholarly literature on the subject, including especially the work of Jacob Milgrom (1923-2010), whose thought on the subject has been particularly influential among biblical interpreters for over half a century. Precisely because the discussions and debates regarding the manner in which sacrifices for sin were thought to make it possible for God to forgive those who had sinned and continue to dwell among them strike at the very heart of the understanding of God that runs throughout the biblical texts, this examination of the scholarly literature will also serve to demonstrate the extent to which biblical scholars have embraced modes of speaking and conceiving of Israel's God that are more deeply rooted in the pagan belief systems of antiquity than they are in the Hebrew Scriptures.

Purification and Expiation through Sacrificial Rites

The opening chapters of the book of Leviticus prescribe two types of offerings that are to be made for sin, namely the *ḥaṭṭa't* or sin offering and the *'asham* or guilt offering (Lev 4:1–6:7; 6:24–7:7). As we noted briefly in the previous chapter, because in many cases the *ḥaṭṭa't* was to be offered not in response to any type of sin that had been committed but only for the purpose of declaring a person or object to be clean or pure from a physical impurity, many scholars today prefer to refer to the *ḥaṭṭa't* as a purification offering rather than a sin offering. It is also common to refer to the *'asham* as a reparation offering rather than a guilt offering, since it was often to be accompanied by a monetary payment given to the priest or to the person who had been affected by the sin that the offerer had committed (Lev 5:14-16; 6:1-7; Num 5:5-8). The texts are not entirely clear as to what distinguished these two offerings from one another, other than the rites involved and the conditions under which each was to be offered.[9] For our purposes here, however, it is not necessary to go into further detail regarding the differences between these two types of offering or look more closely at the rites associated with each of them. Instead, it will be sufficient to refer to both types of offering in general terms as sacrifices for sin.

In the passages from Leviticus that contain the prescriptions for purification and reparation offerings, the description of the rites to be carried out concludes with the statement that by means of those rites atonement or expiation is made on behalf of the offerers.[10] In most cases, this statement is followed by the affirmation that the offerers will be forgiven. The Hebrew verb that appears in these passages is *kipper*. While most English versions of the Bible use the language of atonement or expiation when translating this verb, some scholars have proposed that terms such as purification or purgation be used instead. Thus, for example, when a purification offering was presented on behalf of a person who had been cured of a skin disease, a man who had had an emission of semen, or a woman who had given birth or had a discharge of blood, its purpose was not to atone for sin but to purify or purge from impurity those on whose behalf it was presented.[11] A purification offering involving a red heifer was also to be presented by those who came into contact with a corpse (Num 19:1-19; cf. 6:9-17). The same Hebrew verb is used to speak of sacred objects such as the altar or the sanctuary being purified or purged from impurity by means of the rite, as well as houses that had become impure as the result of the growth of some type of fungus.[12] In Lev 1:4, a burnt offering or holocaust is said to make atonement or expiation for the offerer as well, even

---

9. On the rites involved in these two offerings for sin and the circumstances under which each was to be offered, see especially Roland de Vaux, *Ancient Israel: Its Life and Institutions*, vol. 2: *Religious Institutions*, trans. John McHugh (New York: McGraw-Hill, 1965), 418-21, 429-30.

10. See Lev 4:20, 26, 31, 35; 5:6, 10, 13, 16, 18; 6:7.

11. See, for example, Lev 5:13-15, 29-30; 12:1-7; 14:10-32.

12. See Exod 29:36-37; 30:10; Lev 8:14-15; 15:33-53; 16:16-18, 33; cf. Num 8:10-12.

though it was not offered in response to any sins that had been committed and thus did not have the purpose of obtaining forgiveness for those on whose behalf it was presented. Similarly, in Num 31:50, articles of gold and jewelry are said to make atonement or expiation for the people who presented them.

There were several ways in which someone or something that had become impure or unclean might be restored to a state of purity or cleanness. In some cases, it was simply necessary to let some time pass in order for that impurity to go away on its own. Those who became impure as a result of contact with a corpse or with certain bodily fluids simply needed to wait for a specified period of time before entering into certain places or being in the presence of other people once again. In other cases, impurity was removed by washing or bathing. It was generally expected that the priests and people who were to participate in the sacrificial rites at the sanctuary, for example, purify themselves in this way ahead of time. It is important to note, however, that in these instances the sacrificial rites themselves were not thought to purify people, since those who had become impure needed to be purified or made pure *prior* to participating in those rites. According to Lev 12:1-8, for example, a woman who had given birth to a child was to wait for a specified period of time and then bring an offering to the priest for him to offer up on her behalf. In this way, she was pronounced "clean from her flow of blood" (v. 7). Likewise, because those who had been healed of a skin disease needed to be declared clean or pure by a priest *before* they presented a sacrificial offering to God, the sacrifice itself was not thought to effect their purification (Lev 14:1-32). Rather, it served as an indication to the other members of the community that the individual was pure or clean once more and could therefore be accepted in their midst without any restrictions.

In this regard, it is also important to note that the sacrificial rites associated with the purification of people who had become physically impure or unclean according to the Mosaic prescriptions were not aimed at obtaining forgiveness for them, since it was not a sin to become impure or unclean. In many cases, in fact, it was good or necessary. Those who became unclean by burying the corpse of a loved one were not sinning but doing something that was considered good and necessary. Similarly, women who became impure by giving birth to a child were doing something wonderful rather than sinful when they brought a new life into the world. At times, people became impure due to no fault of their own, such as when they were stricken with a skin disease or had some type of discharge. While at times it was thought that God had caused or allowed certain persons to be afflicted with a disease or disorder that made them unclean due to some type of sin or wrongdoing into which they had fallen, the rites by which they came to be declared clean or pure after they had recovered from that disease or disorder were not believed to obtain the forgiveness of sins on their behalf in themselves. Those rites simply served to restore them to a state of purity within their community so that they might be accepted there once more.

These observations must be kept in mind when considering the manner in which people were thought to be declared pure from the sins that they had committed. Biblical scholars generally make a distinction between physical or ritual purity and moral purity. In contrast to ritual purity, which has to do primarily with physical realities and conditions, moral purity is associated with behavior that is in conformity with what is good, just, and right. Those who fell into behavior that was unjust and harmful for them and others might be said to become morally impure, yet such behavior did not in itself make them ritually or physically impure. While they might be required to present a sacrifice for sin, they were to do so only after they had purified and cleansed their hearts, minds, and lives by acknowledging their sin, repenting of it, and committing themselves once more to living in accordance with God's commandments. Strictly speaking, it was this repentance and renewed commitment to doing God's will that cleansed them and made them pure once again rather than the sacrificial offering that was presented or the rites that were performed on their behalf. The offering and rites merely served as means by which they gave expression to what was in their heart, experienced God's forgiveness, and were restored to a condition or status that allowed them to be accepted by others within the community once again.

This cleansing from moral impurity was especially associated with the observance of *Yom Kippur* or the Day of Atonement. Once a year on that day, the people were to fast, refrain from work, and manifest their contrition and repentance for their sins in other ways (Lev 16:29-31; 23:27-32; Num 29:7-11). According to the ritual prescribed in Leviticus 16, after purifying himself in the way that God had prescribed and donning the high priestly vestments, the high priest was to enter the Most Holy Place with incense and the blood of sacrificial victims that he had offered for himself and for the people. The smoke from the incense that the high priest offered there served to shroud the mercy seat of the ark of the covenant, over which God had promised to appear as a cloud. The priest was to sprinkle the sacrificial blood on the mercy seat and in front of it with his finger.

After the high priest had carried out the prescribed rites within the sanctuary, he was to place his hands on the head of a goat known as the goat for Azazel. As he did so, he was to confess over it all of the iniquities, transgressions, and sins of the people, thereby putting them on the goat in some sense. The goat was then led out to the desert and left to die there. This is the only passage in the Hebrew Bible that speaks of sins being put upon an animal victim and associates the rite of placing hands on an animal victim with such an idea. In Lev 16:10, it is said that the goat is presented "to make expiation with it." Other verses in Leviticus 16 also use the Hebrew verb *kipper* to speak of the high priest making expiation or purification for himself and his house, the sanctuary, the altar, and the people as a whole by means of the rites carried out on *Yom Kippur*.[13]

---

13. See Lev 16:6, 11, 16-18, 24, 30, 32-34.

When considering the rites prescribed in all of these passages, it is important to note that the slaughter of the animal victims that were to be used in many of those rites was not regarded as a central element. What is said to make atonement, expiation, or purification is not the killing of the animal victim but the rites carried out with the blood that was drained from it after its death. When an offering involving a sacrificial victim was made by an individual, the actual slaughter was done by the offerer rather than the priest.[14] Rather than ascribing importance to the death of the animal victims presented, the texts repeatedly stress the offering of the victim's remains to God and the use of its blood in the rites. The slaughter of the animal was therefore not an end in itself but was a necessary precondition to the other rites that were to be carried out.

This observation is important in order to stress once more the point that in Hebrew thought the idea lying at the heart of both animal and non-animal sacrifices was not that of inflicting death but rather that of *presenting gifts and offerings to God*, along with the prayers and petitions that accompanied those gifts and offerings. In the case of offerings that were presented to make expiation for sin or to effect the purification of persons or objects that had become impure, it was the use of the victim's blood in the prescribed rites rather than its death that was regarded as the means by which these things were accomplished.

Distinguishing Holiness from Purity

Many passages from the Pentateuch mention sacrificial rites being carried out in relation to the dedication or consecration of persons such as the priests as well as spaces and objects that are to be used for the worship of Israel's God. These persons, spaces, and objects were to be regarded as holy in the sense that they had been set apart for God and his worship. In some cases, the rites prescribed for consecration included the offering of sacrificial victims and the use of sacrificial blood or anointing oils.[15] At times, people are said to consecrate or sanctify themselves without carrying out any rite but simply by abstaining from certain foods and activities and by washing and cleaning themselves up.[16]

In this regard, it is important to note that holiness and purity were not simply equated with one another. When persons or objects that had been consecrated to God and set apart for his worship as holy became impure, they did not cease to be consecrated or holy.[17] A priest who came into contact with a corpse, for example, became impure and needed to be purified, yet even then

---

14. See de Vaux, *Ancient Israel*, 2:416: "The man making the sacrifice would himself cut the throat of the victim at some distance from the altar. The priests and the Levites slaughtered only the animals offered in public sacrifices (2 Ch 29:22, 24, 34; Ez 44:11)."

15. See, for example, Exod 29:1-37; 30:22-30; 40:9-15; Lev 8:10-15; 16:19; Num 6:13-21; 7:1-11.

16. See, for example, Exod 19:9-15; 22:31; Lev 20:6-7; Num 11:18.

17. See, for example, Lev 5:2; 7:21; 11:24-39; 15:5-12, 19-23, 27; 22:4-6; Num 5:2; 19:11-22; 31:19.

he remained holy in the sense that he had been set apart for God's service. Conversely, people and objects that had not been set apart for God might be in a state of purity or become impure and need to be purified, yet this did not make them holy. Generally, however, anyone or anything that was to be involved in rites or procedures related to the worship of God at the sanctuary dedicated to him was to be both holy and pure at the same time.

According to the biblical prescriptions, some people, objects, and spaces were to be considered more holy than others. Persons such as the priests and Levites were regarded as being holy and consecrated to God in a way that distinguished them from the rest of the Israelites, even though the people of Israel as a whole are repeatedly said to be holy and consecrated to God as well. The Holy Place and Most Holy Place within the sanctuary were, of course, to be regarded as especially holy by those who worshiped Israel's God, yet according to the biblical prescriptions certain areas immediately outside of the sanctuary were also to be marked off as holy. Access to each of the different areas in and around the sanctuary depended on the degree of holiness that the law assigned to particular individuals and groups that formed part of God's people.

FINDING A NEED FOR SACRIFICES FOR SIN

Throughout the Hebrew Scriptures, whenever people commit any type of sin by disobeying God's commandments or acting contrary to his will, what is said to matter most is that they repent. As we observed in Chapter 5 of this study, in Hebrew the verb *shub* is used to speak of turning *away* from one's wrongdoing and turning *back* to God and his commandments at the same time. What interests God is not merely that people feel remorse for the sins they have committed but that they commit themselves once again to living in conformity with God's will as he has made it known in the Torah and ask God and one another for the assistance and strength they need in order to live out that commitment.

If God's only concern is that his people live in a manner that allows them to attain the well-being he desires for them, then as long as they turn back to him and his commandments whenever they go astray, it might seem that there is no reason why he should demand or require anything else of them. Their renewed commitment to living in accordance with his will should be sufficient to obtain his forgiveness and acceptance, as long as that commitment is firm and sincere, since there is nothing further that God could ask or demand of them that would lead them to conform more fully to his will or enable them to become more obedient to his commandments. All that God can expect of people is that they strive to the best of their abilities to understand and fulfill the commandments he has given them, look to him and one another for the strength, knowledge, and wisdom necessary to obey those commandments properly, and turn back to him any time they slip or fail in their efforts and commitment to follow faithfully the good path he has laid out for them.

If such is the case, however, then it must be asked why God commanded his people to present the offerings for sin that appear in the Torah and to participate in rites that are aimed at their purification and the expiation of their sins. The fact that God gave such commandments to his people suggests that when the people fell into sin, for some reason it was not sufficient for them simply to repent and turn back to him. Clearly he demanded something more, but why?

Biblical scholars and interpreters have traditionally answered this question by positing some type of need on God's part. This need is not absolute in the sense that God's existence depends on it being satisfied or fulfilled. Rather, it exists in relation to human beings and is grounded in his nature. If God is to bless and save human beings, he must act in conformity with the dictates of his nature. In general, biblical scholars and theologians have spoken of three types of needs to which God is subject: the need to be honored, respected, and obeyed, the need to act in conformity with justice and righteousness, and the need to maintain intact his holiness and purity. Supposedly, these needs make it impossible for him to tolerate sin, guilt, injustice, and impurity.

In accordance with this understanding of the needs that are grounded in God's nature, several different answers have been offered to the question of why the God of the Hebrew Bible demands sacrifices for sin in addition to the repentance and renewed commitment to his will of those who sin. On occasion, it is claimed that the sins of human beings deprive God of the honor, respect, glory, and obedience that is due to him by right. In that case, it is not enough for those who have sinned to turn back to him in order to honor, worship, and obey him once more, since they must also restore or pay back to God what they have taken away from him in the past. For that reason, they must make satisfaction to his honor and justice by offering him something to compensate for that which they have wrongfully taken away from him or stolen from him.

Although since the time of Anselm of Canterbury (†1109) this argument has been used to explain why it was necessary for Jesus to suffer and die on the cross as a sacrifice for the sins of the world, it is rarely found in the work of biblical scholars who write on the subject of the meaning and purpose of Hebrew sacrifice.[18] Perhaps the main reason for this is that the sacrifices for sin prescribed in the Pentateuch are quite simple and austere. They involve a single animal rather than multiple animals, and in most cases that animal is not a large bull but a goat, a sheep, or even a turtledove or pigeon, all of which are relatively small in comparison. In fact, as noted in Chapter 7, those who were poor might even present a measure of flour as a sin offering. Given the simplicity and austerity of most of these offerings, it is difficult to imagine that those who presented them in biblical times believed that they were restoring

---

18. On the thought of Anselm regarding the need for human beings to make satisfaction to God's justice and restore to him the honor they have deprived him of through their sin, see David A. Brondos, *Fortress Introduction to Salvation and the Cross* (Minneapolis: Fortress, 2007), 80-85.

to God the honor, respect, and obedience that their sins had deprived him of or stolen from him. In addition, there is nothing in the biblical texts to suggest that the sacrifices for sin commanded by God were thought to make satisfaction to his honor. On the contrary, such medieval and Western categories and modes of thought appear to be foreign to the Hebrew worldview reflected in those texts.

For these reasons, those scholars who have claimed that in biblical thought the need for sacrifices for sin was grounded in God's nature have instead looked to a particular understanding of God's justice or his holiness as a basis for making that claim. Scholars and interpreters who base the need for sacrifices for sin on God's justice have traditionally argued that God's justice and righteousness prevent him from overlooking or ignoring human sin and guilt. Because it would not be just but *unjust* for God to forgive sins freely without punishing them in the way they deserve, God demanded sacrifices for sins as a means by which those who had sinned might be spared from having to endure themselves the punishment that their sins rightly deserved. That punishment or penalty, which was death and the suffering associated with it, was inflicted on an animal victim in their stead. According to this understanding of sacrifices for sin, they involved penal substitution: the life of the animal victims substituted for the life of the offerers, who were spared from the penalty of having to forfeit their own life and endure the suffering that their own death would have entailed by means of their sacrifices.

While proponents of penal substitution views often appeal to a similar understanding of God's holiness to argue that it was not only God's strict justice but also his holiness that demanded punishment for all sins committed, other scholars ground the need for sacrifices for sin in a different understanding of God's holiness. These scholars conceive of God's holiness as an active force or ontological reality that cannot coexist with anything that is unholy, impure, or contaminated. According to these scholars, the sacrifices for sin prescribed in the biblical texts had the purpose of purifying or cleansing people, places, and objects that had become impure or unclean as a result of the sins of those on whose behalf they were offered. As noted above, it is this understanding of the purpose of sacrifices for sin that leads many scholars to prefer to speak of purification offerings rather than sin offerings.

Although there are many similarities between the interpretations of sacrifices for sin that are based on the notion of penal substitution and those that instead revolve around the notion of purification from sin and impurity, the significant differences between these interpretations make it preferable to examine each of them separately. Despite the fact that both of these interpretations ground the need for sin or purification offerings in God's inability to tolerate sin, injustice, and impurity, the manner in which they resolve the problem posed by God's intolerance of human sinfulness distinguishes them clearly from one another.

SATISFYING THE DEMANDS OF
GOD'S JUSTICE THROUGH SACRIFICE

For scholars and interpreters who look to the idea of penal substitution to interpret the biblical prescriptions regarding sacrifices for sin, the claim that by nature God is perfect in his justice and holiness is of fundamental importance. This perfection not only makes it impossible for him to tolerate anything or anyone that is not perfectly just, righteous, and holy as he is but also makes it necessary for him to demand the same perfection of human beings in order to accept them and have any type of communion or fellowship with them. Even though in his love and mercy he would like to bless and save sinful human beings without demanding that their sins be punished in the way that they deserve, his nature will not allow it. If he were simply to overlook the sins committed by human beings or not take them into account, he would be acting contrary to his nature. By definition, it is impossible for him to do such a thing. A just God cannot act unjustly.

According to many biblical interpreters, God's holy and righteous nature not only makes it necessary for him to judge sin in order to punish it but also leads him to become angry when human beings sin against him. Thomas R. Schreiner, for example, writes:

> *God's judgment of sin represents his personal anger against sin.* The Lord judges sin because of his holiness—the beauty of his goodness that separates him so radically from human beings. . . . [I]n the biblical worldview judgment represents the personal response of the holy Lord to human sin. . . . God's wrath and judgment are personally directed against sinners who have failed to praise, honor and thank him. . . . God is angry, then, because of human rejection of his lordship. . . . The wrath of the true God flows from his holiness—from the perfection of his character and the beauty of his goodness.[19]

Because human beings cannot avoid sinning and disobeying God, all stand under his judgment, condemnation, and wrath. At the same time, however, due to his love for humanity, God does not want to punish and condemn sinful human beings but instead wishes to save them from his righteous wrath and condemnation. The sacrifices for sin that he has prescribed make it possible for him to do so without compromising his justice, righteousness, and holiness. By allowing those who are guilty of sin to present an animal victim in their place and offering up its life instead of their own, God satisfies the demands of his justice and holiness while at the same time making it possible for the sinners whom he loves to be saved from the punishment that their sins deserve. Their sins are punished in accordance with his justice, yet the sinners are spared from having to endure that punishment themselves.[20]

---

19. Thomas R. Schreiner, "Penal Substitution View," in *The Nature of the Atonement: Four Views*, ed. James Beilby and Paul R. Eddy (Downers Grove, IL: InterVarsity, 2006), 67-98 (79-80).

20. On this understanding of sacrifices for sin, see especially David A. Brondos, *Jesus' Death in New Testament Thought*, vol. 1: *Background* (Mexico City: Theological Community of Mexico, 2018), 128-39.

Those who defend this understanding of animal sacrifice interpret a number of the sacrificial rites prescribed in the Pentateuch as means by which the sin and guilt of the offerers and the punishment to which they were subject were transferred to the animal victim that was to die in their place. Once this transfer has taken place, that sin, guilt, and punishment are said to be taken away when the animal is put to death. According to many interpreters, this idea is reflected most clearly in the rite carried out with the goat for Azazel on *Yom Kippur*. Supposedly, when the priest laid his hands on the head of the goat and confessed the sins of the people over it, the goat became subject to the penalty that those who had committed those sins deserved, which was death. This penalty was inflicted on the goat when it was led out to the desert and abandoned there to die. As a result, the sins of the people were removed far from God's presence in definitive fashion and he no longer found it necessary to exact punishment for those sins.

Even though the goat for Azazel was not offered up in sacrifice, those who interpret the sacrifices for sin on the basis of the idea of penal substitution generally understand the rites involved in those sacrifices in the same basic manner. Supposedly, those who laid their hand on the animal that they were about to sacrifice were thought to be transferring to the animal the sins that they had committed or the guilt that resulted from those sins, together with the penalty that those sins and that guilt deserved. In this case, however, rather than sending the animal out into the desert to endure the death that God's justice demanded, the offerers put those animals to death in the courtyard of the sanctuary. After their blood was drained from them, the priest sprinkled some of it before the symbols of God's presence or smeared it upon the altar before pouring out the rest of it at the base of the altar. These rites with blood are often understood as a means by which the priest and offerers provided God with evidence that the penalty to which the offerers had been subject on account of their sins had in effect been carried out by being inflicted on the animal victim as their substitute. In this way, God was given assurance that the demands of his justice had been fulfilled.

Scholars who interpret the biblical prescriptions regarding sacrifices for sin on the basis of these ideas traditionally have used terms such as atonement, expiation, and propitiation to refer to the manner in which those sacrifices were thought to take away the sins of those on whose behalf they were offered. The English word "atone" was coined in the sixteenth century by combining the words "at" and "one." Originally atonement was understood in terms of the restoration of a relationship between two persons who had become estranged from one another. For that reason, atonement was essentially synonymous with reconciliation. In the course of the seventeenth century, however, atonement came to be understood in terms of making reparation, compensation, or satisfaction for sins or offenses. Among English speakers, therefore, it became common to speak of sacrificial offerings atoning or making atonement for sins.

The language of expiation is generally understood in the same manner. To expiate one's sins is to make amends or reparation for those sins, often by expressing remorse and repentance for them and accepting the punishment that is due to them. Originally, however, the Latin term *expiatio* conveyed the idea of cleansing or purification as well.

Most English versions of the Bible have traditionally used the language of atonement or expiation to translate the Hebrew verb *kipper* and its cognates. Some scholars have argued that *kipper* was originally understood to involve removing something from view by washing it away or rubbing it off from a surface to which it had adhered. In that case, in sacrificial contexts the term was used to refer to the manner in which sin and guilt were taken away and those who had sinned were restored to a state of purity by means of the sacrifices offered. In some contexts, however, *kipper* has the sense of covering something up from view by placing something over it. On that basis, many scholars have preferred to speak of sins being covered up as a result of the sacrificial rites performed. According to this idea, the death of the animal victims and the rites performed with their blood covered up from God's sight the sin and guilt of those on whose behalf those victims had been sacrificed. Because the same Hebrew root is used to form the noun *kofer*, which referred to a payment made as a ransom or in exchange for something of value such as a human life, it has also been common to see the sacrifices presented for sin in terms of a payment made to God or his justice. By paying the price of the life of an animal victim, those who had sinned obtained God's forgiveness in exchange for that life and were delivered from the penalty of death to which they were subject on account of their sins.

All of these terms tend to be associated with the idea of propitiation as well. Propitiation is generally understood in the sense of appeasing or placating the wrath of a person or deity, often by means of a gift or offering. As a result, one is restored to the favor of that person or deity. According to this understanding of Hebrew sacrifice, the death and blood of the animal victims offered to God put away God's wrath at the sins that had been committed by satisfying the demands of his justice, which required that those sins receive the punishment due to them. It can also be said that God's wrath at the sins committed was appeased because those sins had been washed away or covered up from his view by means of the sacrificial rites carried out. As a result, those who had sinned became pure and holy in his sight once more and were restored to his favor.

In Lev 17:11, what is explicitly said to make atonement or expiation is blood rather than suffering or death per se. Most English translations use the language of atonement to translate the form of the verb *kipper* that appears in this verse: "For the life of the flesh is in the blood, and I have given it to you for making atonement for your lives on the altar, for, as life, it is the blood that makes atonement." Proponents of a penal substitution understanding of sacrifice generally associate this blood with death. According to this view of sacrifice, it is the shedding of blood that is of primary importance rather than the offering of the blood to God, since it is death and perhaps the suffering that was associated with it as well that was thought to atone for sins.

When the offering of sacrifices for sin is understood on the basis of these ideas, those sacrifices are said to purify those on whose behalf they are offered and make them righteous in a *forensic* sense. This term is taken from a legal context and refers to a declaration made by a judge or jury in a court of law. While in reality those whose sins are expiated and atoned for are not innocent or righteous but are instead guilty of wrongdoing, as a result of the sacrifices offered on their behalf they are acquitted of their guilt and *declared* innocent and righteous so as no longer to be liable to the penalty that their sins deserve. Their restoration to a state of purity and holiness is therefore *forensic* in that they are not *actually* righteous, holy, pure, and free of sin but are only reckoned or considered to be so in the sight of God. In a sense, however, it might be said that once God has *declared* them to be righteous, holy, pure, and innocent, they actually *become* so, since whatever God declares to be true actually *becomes* true by means of that declaration.

Once the people's sins had been washed away, covered up, or atoned for by means of the sacrificial death and blood of animal victims, supposedly it was possible for a perfectly just and holy God to forgive them those sins, receive and accept them once more, and look upon them with favor rather than wrath. Even though in a sense they continued to be guilty of the sins they had committed, God no longer regarded them as such because their guilt and punishment had been transferred to an animal victim that had suffered and died in their place as their substitute. By means of the sacrifices offered, therefore, all obstacles to their salvation, blessing, and forgiveness were removed.

While proponents of this understanding of Hebrew sacrifice generally regard the expiation or removal of sin as forensic in nature, it is also common for them to conceive of sin as some type of actual force or substance that exists as an ontological reality. Biblical interpreters who conceive of sin in this way claim that when those who had sinned laid their hands on an animal victim that was about to be sacrificed, they were thought to be transferring to the animal not only their guilt or the punishment that their sins deserved but also some type of toxic or deadly force or substance that was identified with those sins or had been generated by them. It is not always clear precisely how this understanding of sin and impurity as ontological realities is to be combined with the idea that the condition of righteousness, purity, and holiness that was attained by means of the sacrifices for sin was forensic in nature. Some interpreters suggest that rather than being viewed as a *penalty* or *punishment* that was inflicted on the sacrificial victims as a result of the transfer of the sin and guilt of the offerers to those victims, death was seen as the natural consequence of the toxic and deadly substance or forces that were passed on to the animal victims when the sins of the offerers were laid upon them.

The allusions to bearing sin or guilt that appear in the context of the biblical prescriptions regarding sacrifice are often understood on the basis of both of these conceptions of sin. The sacrificial victim is said to bear the sin or guilt of the offerers in the sense that it becomes subject to the punishment or penalty of death which that sin or guilt deserve. At the same time, the victim bears the sin of the offerers by receiving into its body the toxic or malefic substance or force that is associated with that sin. When it is then put to death or abandoned to die in the desert, as the goat for Azazel was, that substance or force is destroyed or made to disappear together with the victim to which it had adhered. In this way, the animal victim can be said to have borne the sin or guilt of those on whose behalf it is put to death in both a forensic and an ontological sense.

Most of the scholars who interpret the biblical prescriptions regarding sacrifice on the basis of ideas such as these look to the same ideas to interpret passages that speak of atoning or expiating sins or propitiating God's wrath by means other than the sacrificial offerings for sin prescribed in the Mosaic law. In Exodus 32, for example, after the Israelites have sinned by means of the golden calf, Moses tells them that he will seek to make atonement or expiation for them. As we have seen previously, Moses then proceeds to intercede to God on their behalf and asks to die together with the people if God chooses to destroy them rather than forgiving them. When the Israelites begin to abandon God in order to yoke themselves to the god Baal of Peor in Numbers 25, Aaron's grandson Phinehas is said to have expiated the people's sin and to have appeased God's wrath by slaying one of the people's leaders who had fallen into idolatry, together with the Midianite woman whom he had taken as his companion (Num 25:10-13). While the language of atonement and forgiveness is not used explicitly in Isa 52:13–53:12, the servant of which this passage speaks is said to be crushed by God, endure God's chastisement on behalf of others, bear their iniquities, suffer for their sins, and offer up his life as a guilt offering. In a couple of passages from the book of 4 Maccabees, sacrificial language is used in relation to the willingness of a Jewish priest named Eleazar as well as a mother and her seven sons to endure tortures and a violent death rather than transgress the Mosaic law. Their blood and deaths are said to bring about the purification and redemption of the Jewish people who have been subjected to the same type of sufferings and persecution at the hand of the Seleucid king Antiochus Epiphanes (4 Macc 6:28-29; 17:20-22). Many biblical interpreters understand the sacrifice of the Passover lamb in Exod 12:1-10 on the basis of some of these same ideas. Those who obeyed God's command to put a lamb to death and smear its blood on the doorposts and lintels of their homes are said to have been spared from the death that was inflicted on the firstborn throughout the land of Egypt by means of God's angel.

In various ways, all of these passages seem to associate atonement, expiation, and propitiation with suffering, death, blood, and sacrifice. They thus appear to provide support for the idea that in the Hebrew Bible and Second

Temple Jewish thought, sacrificial death and blood were believed to make atonement for sins, put away God's wrath, and obtain his forgiveness. In the mind of many biblical interpreters, sacrifices for sin were therefore the primary means by which it became possible for a righteous and holy God to dwell in the midst of a sinful people without compromising his demand that they be free of sin and perfectly righteous in the same way as he is.

Questioning Punishment and Propitiation

The claim that the purpose of sacrifices for sin was to deliver those who had sinned from the punishment their sins deserved by inflicting that punishment on an animal victim in their place is so problematic from both a biblical and theological standpoint that it is a wonder that there are still biblical scholars who insist on maintaining such a claim. In addition to reading back into the biblical texts ideas that are foreign to them, such an interpretation of the biblical prescriptions regarding sacrifices for sin pits God's justice against his love, subjects God to his own nature in a way that makes his nature oppressive not only for human beings but for God himself, and undermines the practice of justice and righteousness rather than promoting it.

According to the logic underlying interpretations of biblical sacrifice that are based on the idea of penal substitution, what concerns God above all else is that the sins committed by human beings receive the punishment they deserve. Only in this way can he uphold justice and satisfy the demands of his just, holy, and righteous nature. This concern takes precedence over every other consideration, including his desire to bless and save human beings. No matter how much he may love human beings and wish for them to be saved, he cannot allow for the sins they commit to be left unpunished. If he is to deliver them from the punishment and condemnation that their sins deserve and his justice demands, therefore, his only option is to provide them with a means by which they can put forward a substitute who will endure that punishment and condemnation in their place. Supposedly, this is the purpose for which he has instituted the sacrifices for sin that are prescribed in his law.

When we examine the biblical texts, however, it becomes clear that the claim that each and every sin deserved punishment, and especially the punishment of death, goes far beyond anything found in those texts in general and the Mosaic law in particular. Among the many actions that are prohibited in that law, only a small handful are said to be punishable by death. The same is true with regard to actions that are mandated as obligatory: in most cases, those who failed to fulfill what was commanded were not sentenced to death. Even those individuals who blatantly rejected God's commandments and refused to submit to them were for the most part simply expelled from the community rather than being put to death.

Conversely, those who did commit acts that were deserving of the penalty of death were not given the option of offering up an animal victim in order to avoid having to endure that penalty themselves. Instead, it was necessary for the sentence prescribed to be carried out by having them executed in the way that the law stipulated. While in some instances individuals might be spared from a death penalty by paying a price to compensate for the harm that they had caused, especially through their negligence, this did not involve offering up a sacrifice (Exod 21:28-31). Certain commandments explicitly prohibit putting an innocent person to death in the place of a guilty one, and there is no reason to think that the same logic would not have applied to the substitution of an innocent animal for a guilty person as well (Lev 27:29; Num 35:31). Furthermore, nowhere in the biblical texts are people who have committed sins but have failed to offer up a sacrifice for sin ever put to death for that failure, as they would need to be if God's justice required that sins that were not expiated by sacrifice be punished with death. Sacrifices for sin were therefore not means by which people were thought to be spared from being subjected to a penalty or punishment of death for the sins they committed.

For several reasons, the common claim that it was impossible for God to forgive sins without the death and blood of sacrificial victims must also be regarded as contrary to biblical thought. Numerous passages from the Hebrew Bible speak of God forgiving people their sins without offering up any type of sacrifice or demanding bloodshed.[21] As we have noted above, in fact, according to Lev 5:11-13, those who could not afford to pay for an animal sacrifice could obtain God's forgiveness by offering up a measure of flour as a sin offering. Throughout the biblical texts, the condition that those who have sinned must fulfill in order to be forgiven by God is simply that they repent of their sins and commit themselves anew to living in conformity with his will. Sacrifices for sins were merely a means by which they manifested this repentance and commitment in a concrete and palpable manner. To insist that God demanded that all sins be atoned for by means of a sacrificial offering so as to ensure that no sin was left unpunished is in effect to deny that God ever forgave sins freely.

The idea that sins constantly had to be punished by putting animal victims to death as substitutes for the guilty also requires that some type of equivalence be established between the sins committed and the quantity of sacrifices required to atone for those sins. Thus, for example, if it was truly believed that God's justice demanded that all of the sins that people committed on a daily basis be punished by means of atoning sacrifices, numerous questions would arise for which no answers would be entirely satisfactory: How often did the sacrificial rites aimed at delivering them from that punishment need to be performed? Would not endless sacrifices for sin need to be presented every day and hour in order to make sure that each and every sin that the people committed received its due punishment? And how serious did a sin or a series of sins have to be in order to require the death of a sacrificial victim? Was there a list of more serious sins that needed to be atoned for by sacrifice, in

---

21. See, for example, Num 11:1-2; 2 Chr 32:24-26; Neh 9:16-17; Ps 32:1-5; 85:1-3; 103:1-5; 130:3-4; Prov 16:6; Isa 27:9; 33:22-24; 55:6-7; Jer 31:31-34; 33:7-8; Dan 4:27; Jonah 3:8-10; Mic 7:18-19.

contrast to lesser sins that did not require a sacrifice? If so, why is there no evidence for any such list in the biblical texts? If the rule was "a life for a life," as many biblical interpreters claim, would not the death of one sacrificial animal be required for each individual who had sinned, and perhaps for every sin committed by each individual as well? How could the death of a single animal atone for the innumerable sins of large numbers of people? Was there a limit to the number of people whose sins could be atoned for by a single animal? Who could make the determination regarding all of these questions, and on what basis were they to do so?

The prescriptions regarding *Yom Kippur* raise similar problems for this interpretation of biblical sacrifice. If all of the sins that the people had committed over the course of the previous year were taken away by being transferred to the goat for Azazel or scapegoat, why was it necessary for a sin offering for the people's sins to be presented on that day as well? Were some of the sins of the people taken away by the sin offering and others taken away by the goat? In either case, how could the sins that countless individuals had committed over the course of an entire year be taken away by the sacrifice or death of a single animal? If the punishment that all of those sins deserved was taken away by the *Yom Kippur* rites, why was it also necessary to present sin offerings for the sins that people committed at other moments during the year? Could not those who had sinned simply wait for *Yom Kippur* for their sins to be taken away instead of offering up sacrifices for sin repeatedly over the course of the previous year? If not, why not?

The claim that the idea of propitiating God's wrath by putting animals to death was central to the biblical understanding of sacrifice is particularly problematic in that it suggests that the people in biblical times believed that God was constantly angry with them because of their sins and therefore needed to be placated continually by the death of one sacrificial animal after another. Sacrificial offerings were acts of love, worship, and adoration by means of which people expressed their devotion to God and their gratitude for his gifts and mercies. Undoubtedly, at times they believed that God was angry with them because of their sins, but this was not the central or dominating concept of the biblical conception of God. Even when they had sinned and offered God sacrifices for sin out of repentance and a desire for a restored relationship with him, those who were truly committed to living in accordance with his will were not simply trying to appease his wrath but to draw near to him in love, confident that in his mercy and grace he would receive them favorably so that they might continue to live in peace and communion with him and rejoice over the blessings that he graciously poured out on them. In fact, not once do the texts in the Pentateuch that prescribe the offering of sacrifice ever speak of those offerings appeasing God's wrath.

Interpretations of sacrifices for sin that understand their purpose in terms of propitiating God by satisfying the demands of his justice also suggest the mistaken idea that in biblical thought what appeases or exhausts God's wrath is simply pouring out or venting that wrath by having an animal victim put to death. If what arouses God's wrath in the first place is behavior that undermines and destroys human well-being, then the only thing that can appease that wrath is that people put away such behavior in order to live in conformity with his loving will. In biblical thought, what God's wrath seeks is not to vent itself until it is exhausted but rather to correct those who insist on practicing destructive behavior. As long as that behavior persists, God's wrath is *not* put away, no matter how much he may pour out that wrath on those who persist in that behavior or how many sacrifices for sin they may offer him. As we have noted previously, in fact, throughout the biblical texts the idea that people can placate God's wrath merely by offering up sacrifices for sin is thoroughly rejected and condemned. What interests God is not sacrifice but the practice of justice, righteousness, love, and solidarity.

A God Held Captive by His Nature

Virtually all biblical scholars recognize that it was not enough to present God with sacrificial offerings or carry out sacrificial rites in order to obtain his favor and forgiveness. Repentance and a renewed commitment to living in accordance with his commandments were also necessary. Among those commandments, of course, were the commandments to offer up sacrifices for sin under certain circumstances and to participate in other rites such as those prescribed for *Yom Kippur*. It was therefore necessary for his people to obey those commandments simply because God had commanded that they do so.

As we have noted above, however, scholars who maintain that sacrifices for sin were necessary in order for those who had sinned to obtain God's forgiveness generally argue that the reason why they were necessary was that repentance and obedience alone were not sufficient to satisfy the demands of God's justice. Supposedly, because God is perfectly just, even when people repent of their sins and strive their best to obey him, they cannot obtain his approval and favor, since nothing less than perfection is acceptable for him. God's justice therefore leaves him no choice but to demand that the sins that human beings inevitably commit receive the punishment due to them. Supposedly, however, God's love for human beings moves him to allow for that punishment to be inflicted on a sacrificial victim in their place.

According to this understanding of the need for sacrifices for sin, therefore, those sacrifices make it possible for sinful human beings to be saved *from God himself and the demands of his justice.* By means of those sacrifices, God's love and mercy save sinners from his righteous wrath and the punishment demanded by his just and holy nature. Strictly speaking, the obstacle that must be overcome in order for those sinners to be saved is not their sinful and destructive behavior per se but rather God's inability to tolerate and overlook that behavior. This is what sacrifices for sin are said to accomplish: they make it possible for God to tolerate and forgive the sinful behavior of human beings without inflicting on them the penalty that their sins deserve.

When God's demand for the death and blood of sacrificial victims is understood on the basis of these ideas, it can be said that he commands that his people present him with sacrificial offerings both for *his* sake and for *theirs*. It is important to grasp clearly, however, the sense in which both of these things are true. Because God can bless and save those who sin only if the demands of his holiness, justice, and righteousness are satisfied by means of the sacrificial rites he has prescribed, God can be said to require sacrifice for *their* sake. His purpose and motive is not to obtain something for himself but to be able to forgive and accept his sinful people without compromising his justice and righteousness. At the same time, however, because God's demand for sacrificial death and blood responds to a need that is found *in him* by virtue of his holy and righteous nature, it can be said that he commands animal sacrifices from his people for *his own* sake. That nature leaves him no choice but to demand sacrificial death and blood if he is to save sinful human beings.

The reason why God must demand sacrifices for sin, therefore, is that *he is subject to his own nature*. This nature defines what he can and cannot do. In that sense, it is not God who defines his nature but his nature that defines him. It imposes certain needs and conditions on God and forces him to act in certain ways while preventing him from acting in others. Although this nature forms part of his being and is inherent to it rather than existing prior to him or independently of him, he must nevertheless obey whatever it dictates in the same way that the pagan gods of antiquity had no choice but to submit to the forces and demands of nature that set limits on them and dictated what was possible and impossible for them. By definition, God cannot do or even desire anything that is incompatible with his just, holy, and righteous nature.

When this understanding of God and God's nature is taken as a starting-point for arguments that posit the necessity of animal sacrifices, those sacrifices are then regarded as responding to a divine need that is similar to the need that the pagan gods of antiquity had for sacrificial offerings. Undoubtedly, unlike many of those pagan gods, the God of Israel was not thought to need sacrificial offerings in order to nourish himself or to continue to exist. If he had need of sacrifices, this need existed only in relation to his desire to save human beings from the punishment and condemnation that his justice demanded on account of their sins. That justice could be satisfied only by means of death, which was the penalty that it dictated for sin. While the God of Israel therefore did not need sacrifices in order to exist, he did have need of the death and blood of sacrificial victims if he was to save sinful human beings from the suffering and death that their sins deserved.

Furthermore, just as the pagan gods of antiquity found it oppressive to be subject to the demands of their own nature, which constantly had to be satisfied if they were to continue to exist, so also the just, holy, and righteous nature of the God of Israel proves oppressive for him due to the demands it makes upon him. In his love, ideally he would like to be free to bless, save, and forgive sinful human beings without demanding sacrificial death and blood from them. His holy and righteous nature, however, will not allow him that freedom. Instead, his nature holds him captive to its demands by preventing him from relating to human beings in the way that he would like. His love is therefore held captive by his justice and limited by it. Only when the demands of his justice are satisfied through punishment, suffering, and death can he manifest his love for sinful human beings by accepting and receiving them into his favor.

Even when God receives the sacrificial death and blood that his perfect justice demands, however, he still cannot love human beings in the way that he would like. Because he has no choice but to demand that his people give him the sacrifices that will allow him to tolerate and overlook their sins if he is to save and bless them, he must oppress them by continually demanding that they present him with the sacrificial offerings necessary to atone for all of the sins they commit on a daily basis. This demand is extremely costly and onerous for them. A considerable portion of the limited resources that they have for their own support and sustenance must be dedicated to providing God with the animal victims and other offerings that he needs if the demands of his justice are to be satisfied. If it costs his people the death and blood of countless animal victims to make it possible for him to forgive and save them and as a result many among them are forced to endure poverty and hunger, that is the price that both God and the people must pay. His needs must take priority over theirs, since if his need to punish their sins is not satisfied by means of those sacrifices, he will have no alternative but to deny them his forgiveness and inflict on them the punishment and condemnation that their sins deserve. Like the pagan gods of antiquity, God may desire to bless those who draw near to him, yet without their sacrifices that desire must be left unfulfilled. Similarly, while he may not wish to lash out in anger at them in order to punish them for their sins, his holy and righteous nature will not allow for that anger to be placated unless its demands are met by means of the death and blood of sacrificial victims.

In addition to oppressing God by means of the demands it makes on him, then, God's holy and righteous nature also oppresses human beings due to the demands it makes on them as well. They must constantly be carrying out sacrificial rites that require the death and blood of animal victims, since otherwise God's nature will make it necessary for him to punish them for their sins. Try as they might, they cannot avoid sinning, and for that reason they cannot avoid having to offer him the sacrifices he needs in order for them to be delivered from his righteous wrath. If they wish to be acceptable to God and obtain his blessings, they have no choice but to slaughter one animal victim after another continuously in order to carry out the rites that will enable him to look favorably upon them. Their need to provide God with the animal victims and offerings that he needs in order to forgive them their sins is insatiable. Even if they wish to love one another and take care of the needs of others along with their own, their need to fulfill the demands of God's nature absorbs them. They cannot share with the needy or show kindness and compassion to others in the way that they would like because their time, energy, and resources are limited. They must give priority to God's needs not only over their own needs but over those of others as well.

While in a sense God's demand for sacrificial death and blood is rooted in his love for human beings and his desire to bless them, therefore, ultimately it is not *his love* that leads or obliges him to command sacrificial offerings from them but *his holy and righteous nature*. That nature stands *in opposition to his love* and constitutes an *obstacle* or *impediment* to it. For the same reason, his love for his people can never be unconditional. On the contrary, he cannot express his love for his people unless the conditions that are rooted in his holy and righteous nature are first met. This must be his primary concern. He must ensure that his *own* need for the sins of the people to receive the punishment that is due to them is satisfied before he can satisfy the needs of his people, since it is impossible for him to disregard or dismiss the demands made upon him by his perfect justice, righteousness, and holiness.

By maintaining that God's primary concern must be for himself and the demands of his own nature, which take priority over the needs of the human beings he wishes to save and bless, interpretations of sacrifice that are based on the idea of penal substitution make the God of Israel similar to the pagan gods of antiquity in another way as well. What those gods desired above all else was to dwell unmolested in peace so as to be able to enjoy a blissful existence. For that reason, they simply wished to be served by human beings while at the same time demanding that those human beings avoid any actions that might upset, bother, or irritate them. In a similar manner, what the God of Israel is thought to desire is that his people do all that he commands so that he may be undisturbed and at peace in his heavenly abode or his earthly dwelling at his sanctuary. If he demands that they practice justice and righteousness, it is not so much for *their* sake as it is for *his*, because the practice of sin, injustice, and unrighteousness bothers and upsets him. Like the god Apsu in the *Enuma Elish*, he cannot help but become angry if the activities and behavior that he finds disagreeable prevent him from being content and at peace. It is for that same reason that he commands sacrifices for sin, which serve to cover up or remove sin and guilt from his sight and assuage his righteous wrath.

According to this understanding of God, both the obedience that he commands of human beings as well as the sacrifices that he requires from them when they fail to obey him are ultimately rooted in a concern for himself. Once again, what matters to him is not the effect that their obedience or disobedience to his commandments has *on them* but rather the effect that it has *on him*, whether directly or indirectly. For the same reason, what moves him to command that they offer sacrifices to him when they sin against him is the manner in which their fulfillment of that command or their failure to fulfill it affects *him*. Those sacrifices are designed not to make the people more obedient to his commandments or bring them into greater conformity with his will but to satisfy the demands of his holy and righteous nature.

Substituting Sacrifice for Obedience

One of the arguments commonly employed by those who defend interpretations of sacrifice that are based on the idea of penal substitution is that if God left human sins unpunished, he would be giving human beings license to sin. Supposedly, if people were allowed to sin freely and not threatened with punishment, they would have no reason to obey God and submit to his will. For that reason, by demanding that those who sin present sacrifices in order to be spared the punishment that their sins deserve, God dissuades them from sinning by making it clear to them that their sinful behavior will have consequences and that they will have to pay a price when they fail to obey what he has commanded.

The idea that God's nature demands perfection, however, ultimately undermines such an argument. In reality, it is pointless for people to strive to avoid God's punishments by obeying him, since it will never be possible for them to attain the perfect obedience he demands. They will always fall short of perfection and as a result will always be liable to his punishments. The only way in which they can avoid those punishments is not by doing their best to obey his commandments but by putting animals to death and shedding their blood in order to carry out the sacrificial rites God has prescribed so that the demands of his justice and holiness may be satisfied and his righteous wrath may be appeased.

By allowing his people to substitute sacrifice for obedience, therefore, God frees them from the necessity of having to obey his commandments, except of course the commandment to offer up sacrifices whenever they sin. What ultimately interests God is not that people practice justice and righteousness but that they satisfy the demands of his holy and righteous nature by presenting him with sacrificial offerings to atone for their inevitable *failure* to practice justice and righteousness. When they fall into sinful behavior, what God's justice requires is *not* that they put away that sinful behavior so as thereby to become pure in their conduct once more but rather that they slaughter animal victims and present him with the blood of those victims. God demands sacrificial offerings not because they promote the well-being of human beings by bringing them to live in justice, righteousness, and love but only because he cannot tolerate their sinfulness and impurity without those offerings.

For these reasons, it is futile not only for human beings to attempt to live in justice, love, and righteousness but also for God to demand such a life of them. In the end, what will obtain God's favor and acceptance is not their manner of life but the sacrificial offerings that they will present to him. Rather than leading human beings to put away the sinful way of life that makes them unacceptable to him, therefore, God's demand for sacrificial offerings does the opposite: it allows them to continue freely in their sinful behavior and simply to make use of sacrificial death and blood to cover up or remove that behavior from his sight in order to avoid the punishments that his justice would otherwise demand for that behavior. Their efforts must therefore be aimed, not at putting an end to their sinful ways so as no longer to endure the harmful consequences of their sins, but at appeasing God through sacrifices and acts of atonement so that he is no longer angry at them and no longer insists on punishing them. If by means of the death of sacrificial victims they can bring God to withhold punishment for their sins, they can have assurance of salvation even if they continue in those sins, since it is not those sins themselves that do them harm but rather the fact that God's justice demands punishment for those sins. There is thus no need for them to be overly concerned about the sins they commit or fear any type of punishment for those sins, since as long as they offer up sacrifices for those sins, God will simply overlook them.

Instead of communicating to human beings that God does not and will not tolerate sin, then, interpretations of sacrifice that are based on the idea of penal substitution lead them to conclude that God *can* and *will* tolerate their sin and leave it unpunished as long as they give him the offerings he desires and demands. Likewise, instead of bringing them to seek to *avoid* sin, the idea that they can atone for their sins through sacrifice can be seen as giving them license to sin. In principle, they might even conclude that they can sin deliberately and then offer up a sacrifice for sin to avoid facing any type of punishment or consequence for their sin.

Of course, biblical scholars and interpreters generally insist that it was not acceptable for people to sin deliberately with the idea that after they had sinned they could simply offer up a sacrifice to atone for their sin and be restored to God's favor. Those who took such an approach to sacrificial offerings were not thought to obtain God's forgiveness but were instead believed to arouse his wrath. Only those who sought to avoid sin and were truly repentant for any sins that they had committed could make atonement for their sins by means of sacrificial offerings and receive forgiveness from God.

In reality, however, once it is claimed that any and all sins committed could be expiated and obtain God's forgiveness by means of sacrificial offerings, then this must be said with regard to sins that were committed deliberately as well, as long as those guilty of those sins repented of them. To affirm otherwise would mean that certain sins could never be forgiven or expiated under any circumstances. Once again, however, if forgiveness ultimately depended on repentance, then it is not clear why sacrifices for sin were also necessary. In any case, as long as their repentance was sincere, those who had sinned deliberately could always satisfy the demands of God's justice by means of more atoning sacrifices that would free them from the punishment which their behavior deserved, no matter how often they fell into such sins.

Trying to Make Sacrifice Work

The recognition that in biblical thought sincere repentance and a renewed commitment to obeying God's commandments were necessary to obtain God's favor and forgiveness has led most biblical scholars and interpreters to insist that sacrifices were not thought to atone for sins automatically. Many of these scholars and interpreters speak of sacrificial rites making atonement by means of some type of *modus operandi* or "mechanics." Thus, for example, Milgrom alludes explicitly to "the *modus operandi* of the *ḥaṭṭāʾt*" and the "mechanism of the purgation" involved in the purification offerings,[22] while Stephen Finlan refers to the scapegoat as "a sin-bearing mechanism" and affirms that the sacrificial rites were thought to involve "an impersonal atoning mechanism" that worked on its own independently of any divine intervention.[23]

According to this manner of understanding the sacrificial rites, when those rites were performed in the way that God had commanded, they "worked" to produce their salvific "effects," atoning for sin and obtaining God's forgiveness and acceptance. Biblical interpreters who look to the idea of penal substitution to interpret sacrifices for sin generally posit a *modus operandi* that is fairly simple and straightforward. Following the transfer of the sin and guilt of the offerers to the animal they brought for sacrifice as their substitute, the animal was put to death and its blood was presented before God. Once this had taken place, the fact that in his law God had made the promise and commitment to grant forgiveness to any who offered up a sacrifice for sin in that manner with a sincere heart meant that they could have full assurance that as a result of that rite God's forgiveness and favor were theirs once again.

Such an understanding of sacrifice, however, raises multiple problems. If God had imbued the sacrificial offerings and rites with the power to obtain his forgiveness and acceptance, then the people were to seek these things not from God directly or by means of a life lived in accordance with God's will but by slaughtering animals and presenting their blood to God in the way he had commanded. They would be led to place their trust and confidence not in God himself but in the rites to which he had irreversibly attached his promises of blessing. Any assurance of forgiveness that they might have would come from the belief that those rites had "worked" to atone for their sins because they had been carried out properly in accordance with God's command.

Of course, in order to have such assurance, they would need to be certain that those rites had in fact been carried out in the way that God had commanded. For different reasons, however, it would be difficult for them to attain such certainty. Thus, for example, among the requirements that God had laid down for sacrificial offerings to be acceptable was that the animals

---

22. See Jacob Milgrom, "The *Modus Operandi* of the *ḥaṭṭāʾt*: A Rejoinder," *JBL* 109 (1990): 111-17 (113); *Studies in Cultic Theology and Terminology*, SJLA 36 (Leiden: Brill, 1983), 87.

23. Stephen Finlan, *The Background and Content of Paul's Cultic Atonement Metaphors*, AcBib 19 (Atlanta: SBL, 2004), 42, 81.

chosen for sacrifice be free from any blemish or defect.[24] If people offered up an animal that they initially believed to be without any type of blemish but later discovered on its carcass a small blemish that had escaped their view, they would have to conclude that the offering had actually been unacceptable to God and had not actually "worked" to obtain his forgiveness due to that blemish. In fact, it was even possible that they might fail to discover the small blemish it had and mistakenly believe that the sacrifice had worked to make atonement for their sins when such was not actually the case because of the blemish. Similarly, if the priest was not in a state of purity in the way that the law prescribed when he performed the rites on behalf of the offerers and the offerers were unaware of the priest's impurity, they might believe that the rite had been properly carried out when such was not actually the case. The priest himself might not even realize that he had acquired some type of impurity and thus had not performed the rite in accordance with the law. In these cases, God's forgiveness would need to be denied to the offerers and they would continue to be subject to his wrath and punishments. Rather than having full assurance that the sacrificial rites in which they had participated had made atonement for their sins, therefore, the offerers might always be left with lingering doubts as to whether every aspect of the rite had been performed precisely in the way that God had commanded.

The idea that the sacrificial offerings and rites did not obtain forgiveness automatically but only restored the offerers to God's favor when they were truly repentant of their sins would also have undermined any assurance of forgiveness on the part of the offerers. Even if God had conferred some power on the rites he had prescribed, ultimately what would determine whether he would forgive and accept the people once more was not the performance of the rite but that which he saw when he looked into their hearts. Unless they could be certain that their hearts were sufficiently pure and free from sin to obtain God's approval, they could never know whether or not those rites had produced the effect they desired. Because the determining factor was not the performance of the rite but the spirit of repentance and obedience in which it was to be carried out, in fact, the rite itself would become superfluous, unless of course it is claimed that God could not and would not forgive those who repented and renewed their commitment to obey him unless they also carried out the sacrificial rites he had prescribed. Such a claim, however, would raise once more the question of why God had found it necessary to prescribe those rites and whether he had done so for his own sake or that of the people themselves.

The notion that repentance was necessary in order for sacrifices for sin to work in order to obtain God's forgiveness would therefore raise other questions as well. How sincere did that repentance need to be in order for the sacrifice to effect atonement? Would not God have to make some determination or judgment as to whether that repentance was sufficiently sincere

---

24. See, for example, Lev 1:3, 10; 3:1, 6; 4:23, 28, 32; 5:15, 18; 6:6; Num 6:14.

and profound to make atonement by means of the sacrifices presented? If so, then forgiveness would depend, not on the sacrifice or the rite, but on that which God saw when he looked into the hearts of the offerers. If God had to determine whether their repentance was sufficient to satisfy his demands, those who presented sacrifices for sin could never be sure whether or not their sacrifice had actually secured God's forgiveness and made atonement.

This problem is compounded even further in the case of sacrifices for sin offered for more than one person, such as the sin offering presented for the sins of the entire people on *Yom Kippur*. If repentance was necessary for the sin offering on that day to attain God's forgiveness but many of the people were not sufficiently repentant for their sins, did the sin offering obtain forgiveness only for the portion of people that were truly repentant? If so, did the people who were not sufficiently repentant remain liable to the punishment that their sins deserved? Or did God instead forgive the people as a whole for their sins if a sufficient portion of them were repentant? If so, what percentage of the people had to be truly repentant in order for the *Yom Kippur* rites to take away the people's sins? Was fifty or fifty-one percent sufficient, or was the number higher? How could anyone ever know? Did the sins for which people were not truly repentant actually get placed on the scapegoat when the high priest laid his hands on the goat to transfer sins to it? If the sins of the unrepentant were not taken away by the rite, what happened to those sins? Did they remain on the priest who had supposedly taken up all of the sins committed by the people as a whole when he confessed those sins over the goat or did they instead revert back to the unrepentant individuals who had committed them? On what basis could any of these questions be answered?

These observations also make it clear why it is problematic to maintain that God had promised to grant forgiveness whenever the rites were carried out properly. If that were the case, then God had placed himself under the obligation to forgive the people their sins when they presented him with the sacrifices for sin that he had prescribed. In essence, he had given the people and the rites some power over himself that he now had no choice but to respect and had established a system in which people could simply purchase his forgiveness by means of an offering. The idea that sacrifices for sin were ransom payments made to God in exchange for his favor and forgiveness is based on this same type of logic. What people sought and obtained by means of their sacrifices was deliverance from his wrath and punishments. Supposedly, once their sacrifices had appeased his wrath and satisfied his demand for punishment, those who had sinned could enjoy peace and no longer be fearful of divine punishment, no matter how much damage their sins had done to themselves or others. They could also attain salvation independently of the manner in which they lived or behaved, since their salvation was not thought to result intrinsically from their conduct but was instead said to be brought about by God alone, simply by leaving their sins unpunished.

Such a view of salvation can hardly be regarded as representing faithfully biblical thought. Instead, it is essentially pagan in nature, since it merely involves being spared from the wrath of the deity. The plight that human beings face is not that their sinful behavior destroys their happiness and well-being but that it arouses God's anger, condemnation, and judgment. In contrast, in the Hebrew Bible salvation involves being made whole and experiencing well-being both individually and collectively. That wholeness and well-being can be attained only by means of a life in accordance with God's will. Such a life is not brought about merely by being spared from God's punishments. On the contrary, the belief that as a result of a person's sacrifice that person is no longer subject to punishment for the sins that he or she has committed may lead people to sin even more, confident that their sin will not be taken into account.

Of course, it is commonly maintained that those who have received God's forgiveness should strive to live in conformity with his will out of gratitude for that forgiveness. In reality, however, they are under no obligation to do so. To affirm the contrary would be to claim that the sacrifice for sin that they presented in accordance with God's command was *not* truly effective and thus did *not* actually make atonement for their sins, since they must still obtain God's forgiveness and atone for their sins by means of their obedience to his commandments. The idea that one should obey God out of gratitude also implies that God wants obedience from human beings for *his* sake rather than theirs. In that case, what should motivate human beings to live in accordance with God's will is once more the effect that their actions will have, not on them directly, but *on God.* Conversely, what should lead them to avoid sinful behavior is not that such behavior will do them harm and undermine their wholeness and well-being but simply that it is not pleasing to God. Whatever negative consequences their sin may have do not follow intrinsically from that sin itself but instead are the result of God's wrath and punishments.

The claim that sacrificial offerings and rites were thought to work by means of some type of *modus operandi* or mechanics not only leads to an understanding of salvation that is foreign to biblical thought but also runs contrary to the idea of justice that runs throughout the biblical texts. As we have seen in Chapter 4 of this study, justice was not thought to be achieved merely by meting out punishments on those who were guilty of sin. In the Hebrew Bible, justice can be said to exist only when all enjoy wholeness and well-being. For that reason, the notion that God's justice could be satisfied simply by inflicting punishments on those who had sinned or on the animal victims that they presented as their substitutes cannot be regarded as reflecting faithfully biblical thought.

In fact, critics of penal substitution views of sacrifice have often pointed out that the idea of substitutionary punishment in itself represents a denial of justice in that it involves subjecting an innocent victim to a punishment which that victim does not deserve in order to let the guilty who actually do deserve to be punished go free. In that way, justice is supposedly satisfied by an *injustice*. The conception of God associated with such an idea is problematic for the same reason. Rather than taking care to ensure that those who are guilty of sin receive the punishment they deserve, God is simply concerned that their sin not be left unpunished for his own sake. It does not matter to him whether those who are made to endure the punishment that his justice requires are those who have actually sinned or not, as long as that punishment is carried out. Ultimately, what concerns him is not justice but the need for the demands of his nature to be satisfied.

Similarly, once God's wrath at sin is said to be taken away by the death or blood of sacrificial offerings, that wrath ceases to be an expression of love and concern for human beings and instead is rooted in a concern for God's own self. Like the pagan gods of antiquity, what interests him is merely venting his wrath by inflicting punishment for the sins that have been committed in order that his demand for retribution may be satisfied. He does not care if that wrath is poured out on the persons who are guilty themselves or on an animal victim in their place, as long as someone or something is made to endure the punishment of suffering and death that his justice requires. Once that punishment has been inflicted, he can be at peace with himself and his justice once more, at least until the sins of human beings begin to arouse his wrath once again. When that happens, however, the solution is always the same: to slaughter another animal victim to provide him with the blood he needs to satisfy the demands of his justice. As long as sinful human beings continue to do that, in principle they can live in peace and do whatever they desire. While it may be advantageous to them to turn away from their sins and stop offending God by their behavior, since that will delay the onset of his wrath as well as the need to offer up an atoning sacrifice, in reality they can commit sin and injustice freely as long as they are willing to offer up sacrifices more frequently and tell God that they sincerely repent of what they have done.

Reconsidering Atonement as a Biblical Concept

Once it is recognized that it was not the death or blood of sacrificial victims that obtained God's forgiveness or appeased his wrath at sin but the commitment to turn away from one's sin and return to the way of life that God commanded for the good of all, the idea that those who had sinned were thought to make atonement for their sins by means of the sacrificial offerings and rites prescribed in the Torah must be called into question. Such an idea implies that what interested God was that those who had sinned make amends for their sin or compensate in some way for their wrongdoing.

To affirm that the suffering and death of sacrificial victims or the rites performed with their blood made atonement for sins is to maintain that what satisfies God's justice, puts away his wrath, and obtains his forgiveness is *something other* than the practice of what is good, right, and just. Rather than demanding such behavior of those who have sinned, God accepts a sacrifice *in the place* of that behavior. Their sacrifice compensates for their failure to obey God, in effect constituting a payment to him for their disobedience to his will. While initially God demanded obedience, he puts away that demand in order to accept a sacrifice instead. In that case, what interests God is not that people practice justice and righteousness but that they present him with something that will make amends for their *failure* to practice justice and righteousness.

The language of atonement also conveys the idea that what God or God's justice demands is that people perform some act that will restore to him something that is rightfully his or make reparation to him for having offended him or disobeyed his law. The purpose is to make amends *for the past*. What interested the God of the Hebrew Bible, however, was not that people do something to compensate or make amends for past actions or offer him something as payment and reparation for having sinned against him, but that his people commit themselves anew to living in accordance with his loving will in the *present* and the *future*. This commitment was something that God desired, not for *his own sake* or for the sake of his honor and justice, but for *their* sake. While under certain circumstances those who had wronged others were required to make reparation to them, generally by means of a monetary payment, that reparation was not an atoning sacrifice or sacrificial offering made to God but simply a means by which the harm that they had caused to others might be undone or mitigated to the extent that this was possible. God's forgiveness and acceptance could not be bought.

Although in principle it might be said that repentance atoned for sins, such an affirmation can be misleading if it is understood in the sense that it compensated for the wrongs that one had committed or made amends for one's sins. Repentance was not something that people offered up to God in exchange for his forgiveness. If God demanded that those who had sinned turn away from their sin and turn back to him in obedience, it was not because he wanted them to make up for what they had done but because only in that way could they attain the well-being that resulted from putting away behavior that did them harm.

In biblical thought, therefore, those who offered God sacrifices for sins were not seeking to atone for their sins. They did not think that putting an animal victim to death or presenting sacrificial blood to God made satisfaction or restitution to God for having violated his law. Unlike the gods of the nations, the God of Israel had no interest in receiving offerings or acts of worship in themselves. He was not demanding compensation or reparation for actions that people had committed in opposition to his will or seeking to regain something that they had wrongfully taken from him. For that reason, neither sacrificial offerings nor the death of animal victims were thought to make atonement for sins. The notion that one had to atone for one's sins by suffering, death, or sacrifice instead reflects a way of thinking that was associated with the pagan gods of antiquity, who merely wanted to make those who had offended and angered them pay for what they had done.

For the same reasons, the language of expiation and propitiation can also convey ideas that do not reflect faithfully biblical thought. Strictly speaking, sacrificial offerings did not expiate sins or propitiate God's wrath. They simply served as means by which people manifested to God their sincere repentance as well as their intention to return to a life of obedience to his commandments. This was the only thing that could bring God to forgive them their wrongdoing and put away his wrath at the destructive behavior into which they had fallen, precisely because it was the only means by which they could attain the well-being that he desired for them out of love for them.

As long as people remained committed to living in accordance with his will, therefore, there was nothing that prevented God from forgiving their sins freely. No type of atonement, propitiation, expiation, or ransom was necessary. Of course, because the people's obedience to his will was always imperfect and it was impossible for them to live without sin, God had to remain active among them constantly to correct and discipline them through various means so as to bring them into greater conformity with his will. If they responded to this activity in the way that he desired, however, he simply overlooked their past sins, since they were fulfilling the demands of his justice to the best of their abilities for their own good. That was all that God could ask or expect of them. As we have seen in the previous chapter and will see in greater detail in the next chapter as well, while God did command sacrifices of those who had sinned, the sole purpose of those sacrifices was to strengthen their commitment to the way of life he had laid out for them in his love and to bring about in them a greater conformity to his will for the good of all.

SATISFYING THE NEED OF A HOLY GOD FOR PURITY

In contrast to those scholars who have argued that the God of Israel was thought to have prescribed the offering of sacrifices for sin in order to satisfy the demands of his justice, many scholars have claimed that the biblical prescriptions regarding sacrifices for sin are grounded instead in a concern for God's holiness. According to these scholars, actions and behaviors that ran contrary to God's will were believed to generate some type of impure substance or force that God was unable to tolerate due to his holiness and purity. This impure substance or force was said to adhere either to human beings themselves or to the sanctuary and the sacred objects associated with it. While some scholars have argued that this substance or force had to be eliminated by being transferred to an animal victim that was then put to death, others insist that its elimination was brought about through contact with the blood of sacrificial animals. According to this view, sacrificial blood was believed to possess the power to absorb or neutralize the impure substance or force generated by human sins. When applied to the people, places, or objects that had been contaminated with that substance or force as a result of the sins committed by human beings, they became clean and pure and thus acceptable to God once more.

It is this type of interpretation regarding the manner in which the sacrificial offerings and rites prescribed in the Torah effected purification that is especially associated with Jacob Milgrom. While Milgrom's reading of the biblical texts was grounded in his Jewish tradition, many of the assumptions that are evident in his work are commonly found in the writings of Christian biblical interpreters as well.

Pollution, Purification, and the Power of Sacrificial Blood

Throughout the Hebrew Bible, the idea that people become unclean or impure as a result of the sins they commit is fairly common. Although the passages that speak in these terms can be understood purely in a figurative or metaphorical sense, many biblical scholars have argued that sinful behavior was thought to make people unclean or impure in a literal sense as well. In some mysterious manner, the sins that people committed were transformed into some type of invisible and pernicious substance or force that could affect them adversely if they did not take action to rid themselves of that substance or force in some way. As we have noted above, it is common to claim that when those who presented an animal victim as a sacrifice for sin laid their hands upon the animal, they were thought to be transferring that substance or force to the animal in the same way that the high priest was said to lay the sins and transgressions of the people upon the goat for Azazel on *Yom Kippur*. According to this understanding of the offerings for sin, when the sacrificial victim was slaughtered and its remains were burned on the altar, those who had sinned were cleansed from the impurity that their sins had generated, delivered from the harmful consequences of those sins and the punishment that they deserved, and restored to God's favor.

Although the same basic understanding of sin and impurity runs throughout the work of Milgrom, the manner in which he conceives of that sin and impurity affecting those who had violated God's commandments is very different. Rather than seeing the purpose of the sin or purification offerings in terms of ridding human beings themselves from the impurity or pollution that resulted from their sins, Milgrom argued that those offerings were intended to purify the sanctuary in which Israel's God was believed to dwell. According to Milgrom, the prescriptions regarding sin and sacrifice in the book of Leviticus establish a distinction between two categories of commandments, "performative and prohibitive," that is, "dos and don'ts": "The performative commandments are violated by refraining from or neglecting to do them," in contrast to the prohibitive commandments, which are violated by performing deeds and actions that God has forbidden. While the violation of performative commandments or sins of omission affect the sinner, they carry "no impact upon his environment." Any violation of the prohibitive commandments, however, "sets up reverberations that upset the divine ecology" and "generates impurity, which impinges upon God's sanctuary and land."[25]

Milgrom argues that this impurity was conceived of as an actual substance that traveled through the air in order to adhere to the sanctuary and some of the sacred objects found there, that is, the "sancta": "for both Israel and her neighbors impurity was a physical substance, an aerial miasma that possessed magnetic attraction for the realm of the sacred."[26] This substance possessed a "dynamic and malefic power" and polluted different areas of the sanctuary in three stages. The courtyard altar was polluted by the impurity generated by an individual's inadvertent sin, the shrine and its inner altar were polluted by the inadvertent sin of the high priest or the community as a whole, and all of these places together with the adytum or Most Holy Place were polluted by "wanton unrepented sin." According to Milgrom, in this way "the severity of the sin or impurity varies in direct relation to the depth of its penetration into the sanctuary."[27] The impurity caused by more serious sins "is powerful enough to penetrate into the shrine and adytum" and is "dangerously contagious."[28] The biblical texts "are grounded in the axiom, common to all ancient Near Eastern culture, that impurity is the implacable foe of holiness wherever it exists; it assaults the sacred realm even from afar."[29] The book of Leviticus thus "propounds a notion of impurity as a dynamic force, magnetic and malefic to the sphere of the sacred, attacking it not just by direct contact but from a distance."[30]

Milgrom maintained that if the pollution and impurity generated by these various types of sin was allowed to accumulate, eventually it became intolerable for God, who was thought to dwell in the sanctuary. Because "the impure and the holy are mutually antagonistic and irreconcilable," when that happens God's holiness will lead him to abandon the polluted sanctuary, thereby depriving his people of his presence there as well as the blessings associated with that presence.[31] In Milgrom's words, "the God of Israel will not abide in a polluted sanctuary. The merciful God will tolerate a modicum of pollution. But there is a point of no return. If the pollution continues to accumulate, the end is inexorable: 'Then the cherubs raised their wings' (Ezek 11:22). The divine chariot flies heavenward, and the sanctuary is left to its doom."[32] Milgrom uses the analogy of electromagnetism to explain what happens when impurity builds up in the sanctuary: "the contracted impurity, be it even so slight at the outset, will grow in force until it has the power to pollute the sanctuary from afar.... Let electromagnetism serve, mutatis mutanda, as

---

25. Milgrom, *Leviticus 1–16*, 229; cf. 1055.
26. Milgrom, *Leviticus 1–16*, 257.
27. Milgrom, *Leviticus 1–16*, 257.
28. Milgrom, *Leviticus 1–16*, 263.
29. Milgrom, *Leviticus 1–16*, 257.
30. Milgrom, *Leviticus 1–16*, 257.
31. Milgrom, *Leviticus 1–16*, 261.
32. Milgrom, *Leviticus 1–16*, 258.

an illustrative analogy. The minus charge of impurity is attracted to the plus charge of the sanctuary, and if the former builds up enough force to spark the gap, then lightninglike it will strike the sanctuary."[33] For Milgrom, the incompatibility of God's holiness and the pollution caused by human sin and impurity not only places human beings at risk but God himself. In the priestly writings, "impurity is virulent, dangerous to humans and God alike. However, the threat to God is not from nonexistent demons but from humans who willfully or inadvertently violate the divine commandments and ultimately drive YHWH out of the sanctuary."[34]

According to Milgrom's interpretation of the biblical texts, the solution to this problem is provided by the blood of the *ḥaṭṭa't*, that is, the sin or purification offering. Once the blood of the animal victim has been extracted from it and has been consecrated by being sprinkled toward the altar, it can then function as a "purging element" or "ritual detergent."[35] The impurities generated by the sins of the people and the priests are "absorbed by the blood detergent" when the blood is applied to the surfaces to which those impurities have adhered.[36] Milgrom explains: "By daubing the altar with the *ḥaṭṭā't* blood or by bringing it inside the sanctuary (e.g., 16:14-19), the priest purges the most sacred objects and areas of the sanctuary on behalf of the person who caused their contamination by his physical impurity or inadvertent offense."[37] Because the people continually sin, it is necessary to carry out the purification of the sanctuary periodically: "it is the continuous pollution of the sanctuary by Israel's moral and physical impurity that mandates its indispensable purgation by means of the *ḥaṭṭā't* offering."[38]

Once a year, however, it is necessary to purge the innermost part of the sanctuary as well as the sancta on *Yom Kippur*. This is the only day of the year that the high priest enters into the Most Holy Place to purge the *kapporet*, "the very seat of the Godhead," from the impurity that has polluted it.[39] He does this by sprinkling the blood of the bull he has offered up as a purification offering for himself on and in front of the *kapporet* (Lev 16:14). Once the blood of the purification offerings for the high priest and the people has cleansed the holy places and objects associated with the sanctuary from the impurity that has accumulated there over the previous year, the people can rest assured that God will continue to dwell in their midst in order to bless them. "God would continue to reside with Israel because his temple and people were once again pure."[40]

According to Milgrom, the rite performed with the goat for Azazel on *Yom Kippur* in Leviticus 16 is also related to the purification of the sanctuary.

---

33. Milgrom, *Leviticus 1–16*, 271.

34. Jacob Milgrom, "Impurity is Miasma: A Critical Response to Hiram Maccoby," *JBL* 119 (2000): 729-46 (730).

35. Milgrom, *Leviticus 1–16*, 254.

36. Milgrom, *Leviticus 1–16*, 1036.

37. Milgrom, *Leviticus 1–16*, 256.

38. Milgrom, *Leviticus 1–16*, 1052.

39. Milgrom, *Leviticus 1–16*, 1034.

40. Milgrom, *Leviticus 1–16*, 51.

Once the pollution has been purged from the sanctuary and the sacred objects within it, it must be carried away by the goat: "all of the sanctuary's impurities must first be released by the blood rite before the high priest can transfer them onto the head of the live goat."[41] This transfer is accomplished when the high priest lays his hands on the goat and confesses the people's sins. After this transfer has taken place, the sins and impurities of the people are banished to the wilderness when the goat is led out there to die.[42] Although strictly speaking it is the sanctuary that is purged from impurity rather than the people themselves, according to Lev 16:30 they too are purified in a sense: "The purgation rites in the sanctuary purify the sanctuary, not the people. Yet as the sanctuary is polluted by the people's impurities, their elimination, in effect, also purifies the people."[43]

While this summary of the main points of Milgrom's interpretation of the biblical prescriptions regarding the offerings for purification does not do justice to many of the intricacies of his thought, it is sufficient to make evident a number of the presuppositions on which his interpretation is based. Chief among these is the notion that human sin generates impurity, which is understood as some type of malefic substance or dynamic force that can be transmitted from one person, place, or object to another. While impurity can cause harm to human beings, it is also incompatible with God's holy nature and thus must be removed or kept away from God's presence if God is to dwell among his people. For that reason, it is important for them to keep God's sanctuary pure by means of the sacrificial rites he has prescribed. These rites enable their sin and impurity to be purged or eliminated, either by the application of blood as a ritual detergent or else by the transfer of that sin and impurity to the goat that is led out to the desert to die.

These ideas are repeated in the works of other biblical scholars as well. Baruch Schwartz, for example, follows Milgrom in affirming that sinful actions were thought to generate some type of pernicious force or substance that required purification: "throughout the biblical literature transgressions, once committed, are often objectified. They are depicted not as past events or actions but rather as odious, foul objects that come into present existence. Numerous biblical metaphors speak of how these objectified sins behave, affect man and his world, and need to be disposed of in some fashion."[44] Elsewhere Schwartz speaks of the "metaphysical spontaneous generation of impurity" and claims to find in the biblical texts the idea that "sins metamorphose into impurity."[45] Baruch Levine understands impurity in the same

---

41. Milgrom, *Leviticus 1–16*, 1040.

42. Milgrom, *Leviticus 1–16*, 1042-43.

43. Milgrom, *Leviticus 1–16*, 1056.

44. Baruch J. Schwartz, "The Bearing of Sin in the Priestly Literature," in *Pomegranates and Golden Bells: Studies in Biblical, Jewish, and Near Eastern Ritual, Law, and Literature in Honor of Jacob Milgrom*, ed. David P. Wright, David Noel Freedman, and Avi Hurvitz (Winona Lake, IN: Eisenbrauns, 1995), 3-21 (7).

45. Schwartz, "Bearing of Sin," 19.

way: "Impurity was viewed as an external force which entered the person or attached itself to him. The primary purpose of expiation was, therefore, to rid one's self of this external force."[46] Roy Gane regards the rite with the goat for Azazel prescribed for *Yom Kippur* as "the means by which the sins of the entire nation are transformed from abstraction, as if out of the air, into a concentrated, quasi-spatially containable form, gathered to the high priest, and channeled through his hands to the goat."[47] Jonathan Klawans distinguishes between moral and ritual impurity, yet conceives of both as the same type of contagious force just described:

> Moral impurity is best understood as a potent force unleashed by certain sinful human actions. The force unleashed defiles the sinner, the sanctuary, and the land. . . . In the case of ritual impurity, a real, physical process or event (e.g., death or menstruation) has a perceived effect: impermanent contagion that affects people and certain objects within their reach. . . . In both cases, the impurity is conveyed by contact: ritual impurity is conveyed by direct and indirect human contact, and moral impurity is conveyed to the land by sins that take place upon it.[48]

On the basis of this manner of understanding impurity, the expiatory rites prescribed in the Mosaic law are understood as having the purpose of making it possible for a holy God to dwell among human beings whose sin and impurity are incompatible with his nature. Echoing Milgrom's claim that impurity is a danger not only to human beings but to God as well, Levine writes: "Implicit in all expiatory rites is the assumption that ritual offenses endanger the deity in some way, since they threaten to diminish the purity of his earthly dwelling. . . . Yahweh demanded that the forces of impurity, unleashed by the offenses committed, be kept away from his immediate environment. There is a reason for Yahweh's wrath. It was not mere displeasure at being disobeyed. His wrath was a reaction based on a vital concern for his own protection."[49] The manner in which this incompatibility between God's holiness and the impurity associated with human sin is said to be resolved is by the application of the blood of sacrificial victims, which possesses the power to eliminate or absorb the toxic impurity. Christian Eberhart describes "the modus operandi of blood application rites" in the following terms: "Sacrificial blood actually purifies the sanctuary from sin and impurities (Lev 16:16, 19, 20; cf. 8:15). Likewise, it purifies and/or consecrates humans (Lev 8:23-24, 30; 14:14)."[50]

---

46. Baruch A. Levine, *In the Presence of the Lord: A Study of Cult and Some Cultic Terms in Ancient Israel*, SJLA 5 (Leiden: Brill, 1974), 77.

47. Roy Gane, *Cult and Character: Purification Offerings, Day of Atonement, and Theodicy* (Winona Lake, IN: Eisenbrauns, 2005), 245-46.

48. Jonathan Klawans, *Impurity and Sin in Ancient Judaism* (Oxford: Oxford University Press, 2000), 29, 34.

49. Levine, *In the Presence*, 76, 78.

50. Christian A. Eberhart, "Atonement: Amid Alexandria, Alamo, and Avatar," in *Atonement: Jewish and Christian Origins*, ed. Max Botner, Justin Harrison Duff, and Simon Dürr (Grand Rapids: Eerdmans, 2020), 10.

Like Milgrom, scholars often conceive of this incompatibility between holiness and impurity as similar to the manner in which substances and forces in nature are repelled by one another. On this basis, they conceive of the sacrificial rites prescribed for purification functioning by means of a *modus operandi* or mechanics that are distinct from those associated with penal substitution interpretations of sacrifice. Richard Nelson finds in the biblical texts the idea that "human sin defiled holy space and holy things and, unless cleaned off or covered over, threatened to generate the 'holy-unclean fusion reaction' and bring on Yahweh's wrath."[51] Finlan uses the same type of analogy offered by Milgrom to explain the purifying effect produced by the application of sacrificial blood to the objects that have been contaminated by sin and impurity: "The positive life-charge in the blood neutralizes the negative death-charge in the pollution, wherever it has penetrated into the temple. Another analogy would be the Midas touch: the blood transforms and purifies the defiled symbols."[52] At times this purification process is even regarded as magical in character. Finlan has no qualms about speaking of "the magical power of blood,"[53] while Levine asserts that "biblical expiation, conveyed by *kippēr*, involved acts of a magical character, specifically the magical utilization of sacrificial blood."[54]

According to all of these conceptions of the sacrificial rites prescribed for purifying people, places, and objects from sin and impurity, the primary purpose of these rites was to make it possible for a holy God to remain in the midst of a sinful and unholy people. Many biblical scholars, however, combine the idea of the purification of the sanctuary through sacrificial rites with the forensic understanding of atoning sacrifice that we have considered above. Thus, for example, Old Testament scholar Gordon Wenham writes:

> The idea that man is always in danger of angering God runs through the whole Pentateuch. Fierce judgments and sudden death stud its pages. Sacrifice is the appointed means whereby peaceful coexistence between a holy God and sinful man becomes a possibility. . . . Sin not only angers God and deprives him of his due, it also makes his sanctuary unclean. A holy God cannot dwell amid uncleanness. The purification offering purifies the place of worship, so that God may be present among his people.[55]

A similar understanding of the need for expiatory sacrifices is maintained by William Lane Craig: "The sacrificial system functioned to facilitate the juxtaposition of the holy and the unholy. It did this, not merely by purging the Tabernacle and its paraphernalia of impurity but also by propitiating God and so averting his wrath upon the people."[56]

---

51. Richard D. Nelson, *Raising Up a Faithful Priest: Community and Priesthood in Biblical Theology* (Louisville: Westminster John Knox, 1993), 75.

52. Finlan, *Background and Content*, 42.

53. Finlan, *Background and Content*, 95.

54. Levine, *In the Presence*, 60.

55. Gordon J. Wenham, *The Book of Leviticus*, NICOT (Grand Rapids: Eerdmans, 1979), 56, 89.

56. William Lane Craig, *Atonement and the Death of Christ: An Exegetical, Historical, and Philosophical Exploration* (Waco, TX: Baylor University Press, 2020), 19.

When biblical interpreters such as Wenham and Craig allude not only to the need to maintain the purity of God's dwelling place but also to appease his wrath, it is evident that they are combining the idea that the sacrificial rites prescribed for sin were intended to meet the demands of God's holiness with the idea that those rites were thought to be necessary to satisfy the demands of God's justice as well. For that reason, in the passage just cited Wenham alludes explicitly to God's judgments and affirms that sin angers God because it "deprives him of his due."

It is by no means evident, however, that these two understandings of the manner in which sacrifices for sin were thought to benefit those for whom they were offered are entirely compatible with one another. To remove or eliminate impurity by applying sacrificial blood to a polluted surface or object is not the same as placating God's wrath by slaughtering an animal and presenting its blood to God to satisfy his demand that sin receive the punishment due to it. Nevertheless, despite the conceptual problems and inconsistencies involved, many biblical scholars see the biblical prescriptions regarding sacrifices for sin as having the purpose of satisfying both the demands of God's holiness for *purity* and the demands of God's justice for *punishment* or *reparation*.

The Dangers of a Holy God

Many of the biblical scholars who conceive of impurity as some type of invisible and mysterious substance or force claim that the biblical texts reflect a similar understanding of God's holiness. According to these scholars, holiness was thought to emanate from God as its source and to define the manner in which it was necessary for God and human beings to relate to one another. This idea is stated explicitly by Cana Werman: "All biblical documentary sources share the view that God is holy, and that holiness emanates from God to persons and things that are connected or belong to him."[57] Similarly, Menahem Haran claims that the biblical texts speak of a "contagious holiness" that "is conceived of as being virtually tangible, a physical entity, the existence and activity of which can be sensorially perceived. Any person or object coming into contact with the altar (Exod. 29:37) or any of the articles of the tabernacle furniture (30:29) becomes 'holy', that is, contracts holiness and, like the tabernacle appurtenances themselves, becomes consecrated."[58] This same conception of holiness is developed further by Schwartz:

> It has a unique, magical quality to it. It is transferable ritually, and it can even be contracted contagiously. As can be seen even from non-priestly texts, contagious holiness is dangerous, potentially fatal if it comes into close contact

---

57. Cana Werman, "The Concept of Holiness and the Requirements of Purity in Second Temple and Tannaic Literature," in *Purity and Holiness: The Heritage of Leviticus*, ed. M. J. H. M. Poorthuis and J. Schwartz, JCPS 2 (Leiden: Brill, 2007), 163-79 (163).

58. Menahem Haran, *Temples and Temple-Service in Ancient Israel: An Inquiry into the Character of Cult Phenomena and the Historical Setting of the Priestly School* (Oxford: Clarendon Press, 1978), 176.

(even by sight or mere proximity) with what it should not. It is dynamic, essentially magical, because it is basically an emanation, a radiation or effusion of energy. But unlike similar emanations present in pagan religions, it inheres in no natural forces or objects; rather, it originates and flows only from the Presence of YHWH. . . . Holiness is an emanation from the Godhead outward, radiating from the divine abode to whatever is in range and tuned in to receive it. Impurity is what is exuded by earthly death and its manifestations, moving inward towards the divine abode and accumulating there, unless it is not cleansed. . . . As pictured by the priestly myth, the abiding presence of God in Israel's midst will remain as long as the Israelites prevent, as much as possible, sins and impurities from accumulating in his abode; if they do not he will leave, abandoning them to their doom.[59]

When holiness is conceived of in this manner, its incompatibility with impurity is commonly understood as being analogous to the manner in which two natural forces that are mutually opposed to one another react when brought together. As already noted above, Nelson speaks of a "holy-unclean fusion reaction," while Finlan sees sacrificial blood neutralizing pollution in the same way that a positive electrical charge neutralizes a negative one. Milgrom's use of the "vocabulary of electromagnetism" leads him to affirm that "opposites attract, and in the Priestly system holiness is opposite in charge to the impure. If either the holiness or the impurity source is strong enough or the distance between them small enough, impurity will become airborne, spark the gap, and impinge on the sanctum. . . ."[60] John Hartley's explanation of the relation between God's holiness and impurity follows along the same lines:

> Yahweh, the true God, is holy. His holiness is powerful, affecting all that comes into his presence. It cleanses, consumes, or transforms. Its power might be compared to electricity. Electricity is a useful, wonderful source of energy, but in order to work with it safely one must be very careful and astute. Whoever touches uninsulated, hot wires is severely shocked, burned, or depending on the voltage, instantly killed. When a person approaches God properly, his holiness imparts life (cf. Isa 57:15) and inspires wonder (cf. Exod 3:3-4). But should anything that is profane or unclean enter God's presence, it is consumed.[61]

This conception of God's holiness leads many scholars to argue that the presence of God among his people in his sanctuary not only represented a blessing for them but also constituted a constant threat. Craig, for example, writes: "God was conceived to be specially present in the innermost sanctum of the Tabernacle, which therefore had to be approached with utmost care. It was a dangerous business to have a holy God dwelling in the midst of a sinful and impure people. . . ."[62] The same idea is repeated by Old Testament

---

59. Baruch J. Schwartz, "Israel's Holiness: The Torah Traditions," in *Purity and Holiness*, ed. Poorthuis and Schwartz, 48-59 (54, 59).
60. Milgrom, *Leviticus 1–16*, 981.
61. John E. Hartley, *Leviticus*, WBC 4 (Dallas: Word, 1992), 133.
62. Craig, *Atonement*, 19.

scholar John Goldingay: "Now Yhwh's dwelling stands in the people's very midst, which is a new privilege, but also a new danger. That was implicit in the awareness of danger involved in approaching Yhwh on Sinai, a danger recognized both by Yhwh and by Israel. How much more danger as well as privilege lies in having Yhwh living in the midst of the people."[63] Hartley argues that the reason for this danger was the manner in which God's holiness reacted to the presence of impurity: "The power and the danger lay not with the unclean, but with the holy. The holy would consume anything unclean that came into its presence."[64] On the basis of these same ideas, Milgrom claims that the entrance of the high priest into the Most Holy Place on *Yom Kippur* was "fraught with peril" and that for that reason no one else was to draw near: "The shrine is just too dangerous a place for anyone but the high priest."[65] As Levine affirms, however, if God's people wished to have the blessings and privilege of having his holiness in their midst, they had to accept the dangers that came with that holiness: "The Israelites were willing to risk the dangers of God's nearness to them for the blessings they believed would be forthcoming from him."[66]

According to the biblical texts, God's desire for holiness and purity led him to command that his people keep themselves holy and pure not only by carrying out the sacrificial rites he had prescribed in the Torah but also by means of other practices and behaviors. In addition to being holy and pure in their thoughts, words, and actions in a moral sense, they were to refrain from certain foods that God had declared to be impure and avoid coming into contact with other forms of impurity that were thought to exist. When people did become impure in some way, it was necessary for them to take action to purify themselves if they were to approach God at his sanctuary or be in close contact with others in the context of their families and communities. As noted briefly above, while in a sense all of the people were to regard themselves as holy and to live as such, the priests and Levites were to be holy in a special sense and to keep themselves pure in order to serve God at his sanctuary. They alone were to have access to certain areas of the sanctuary and to come into contact with certain objects and substances that the law designated as holy. Places and objects outside of the sanctuary might also be regarded as holy, as were certain days such as *Yom Kippur* and the Sabbath. While at times the failure to observe what the law prescribed with regard to holiness and purity could be corrected or forgiven through the performance of rites or procedures, under certain circumstances it was necessary to punish the offenders in some way. These punishments might even include death.

---

63. John Goldingay, *Old Testament Theology*, vol. 1: *Israel's Gospel* (Downers Grove, IL: Inter-Varsity, 2003), 446.

64. Hartley, *Leviticus*, lix; cf. 142.

65. Milgrom, *Leviticus 1–16*, 1036.

66. Levine, *In the Presence*, 71.

Protecting Israel's God from the Perils of Pollution

Although the claim that the God of Israel was thought to have prescribed the sacrificial offerings and rites for sin that appear in the Pentateuch out of a concern for his holiness is problematic for a number of reasons, the most serious difficulty raised by such a claim has to do with the concept of God associated with it. Like the interpretations of the biblical prescriptions regarding sacrifices for sin that regard those sacrifices as means by which God sought to satisfy the demands of his justice, interpretations of the sacrificial offerings and rites prescribed for sin that are based on the idea that God's holiness will not allow him to tolerate the impurity generated by the sins of his people ground the need for those offerings and rites in God's concern for himself and the demands of his nature. While he undoubtedly commands that his people present him with those offerings and carry out those rites because he wishes to bless, forgive, and save them, ultimately he demands these things for *his own* sake, since the problem that must be resolved is not their sin and impurity per se but rather his inability to *tolerate* that sin and impurity.

According to the views of Milgrom and other scholars whose work reflects the same ideas, the primary purpose of the purification offerings and rites with blood that God had prescribed in the Torah was that of maintaining the sanctuary clean and pure so that God would not abandon it. Such an understanding of those offerings and rites is based on several assumptions that are highly questionable not only because they appear to have no biblical basis but also due to the theological and conceptual difficulties they raise.

The first of these assumptions is that, in order for God to bless people, he must dwell in their midst and be in close proximity to them. While such an idea was common in the pagan worldviews of antiquity, it can hardly be considered to reflect faithfully the conception of God found in the biblical texts. The God of the Hebrew Bible is present throughout his creation and is free to act at any time and in any place that he desires. Although in a sense he was thought to make himself present at his sanctuary, by no means were his presence and activity thought to be confined there. In the prayer attributed to Solomon at the dedication of the temple, he speaks repeatedly of heaven as the place where God dwells and states no less than eight times that it is from heaven that God will hear the people's prayers (1 Kgs 8:22-54; 2 Chr 6:12-42; cf. 7:14). In 2 Chr 7:1, the fire that is said to consume the offerings after Solomon finishes his prayer is also said to come from heaven rather than from somewhere inside the temple. As we have seen in the previous chapter, throughout the biblical writings it is common to speak of God making his name dwell at the temple to communicate the idea that he made himself present there without denying that at the same time he remained present both in heaven and throughout the earth. Many other passages from the Hebrew Bible also speak of God hearing, speaking, and acting from heaven.[67]

---

67. See, for example, Exod 16:4; 20:22; Deut 4:36; 26:15; Josh 10:11; 2 Sam 22:14; 2 Kgs 1:10-14; 1 Chr 21:26; Neh 9:13-15, 27-28; Job 1:16; Ps 57:3; 102:18-20.

A second assumption closely related to the first is that God's presence in the midst of his people guarantees his blessing. For reasons we have seen repeatedly, people can be blessed only if they live in the way that God has commanded for their own good. If they instead live in ways that undermine and destroy their well-being, God cannot bless them, no matter how near he is to them. He must first seek to correct and purify them, and for him to do so often involves "visiting" them in the sense of punishing and chastising them in order to accomplish that objective. In the biblical texts, in fact, God's presence among the people is often said to depend on their living in accordance with his will. In that case, the idea is not so much that God's presence brings blessing but rather that obedience to God's will brings both his loving presence as well as his blessing. Of course, even when God acts to correct and chastise people through punishments, it can be said that he is at the same time acting to bless them in the sense of attempting to bring about in them the way of life that will make it possible for them to enjoy the well-being he desires for them. Thus, while in a sense it can be said that God's presence always brings blessing, this blessing may at times take the form of chastisements and punishments. At the same time, God can bless his people from afar just as easily as he can when he is near to them.

A third assumption reflected in the idea that the purpose of the sacrificial offerings and rites prescribed for sin was to enable a holy God to dwell in the midst of a sinful people is that what mattered to God was not the sinful behavior of the people in itself nor the harmful effect which that behavior had *on them*, but rather the impure substance or force that their sins generated and the manner in which that substance or force affected *him*. This assumption may be considered the most problematic of all. Strictly speaking, what God is said to find impossible to tolerate due to his holiness and purity is not the practice of sin and injustice among his people but rather the *impurity* or *pollution* that is generated by that sin and injustice. According to this logic, rather than demanding that his people put a stop to their sin and injustice, what interests God is that they keep his sanctuary clean so that he may dwell there unmolested.

This is the logic reflected in Milgrom's work. What ultimately concerns God is not that people refrain from destructive behaviors that do them and others harm but that they carry out the rites that he has ordained in order to rid his sanctuary of the impurity generated by their sins. The logical conclusion that follows from such an idea is that as long as the priests keep the pollution at tolerable levels by repeatedly cleansing the sanctuary with sacrificial blood as a ritual detergent, the people can persist in that behavior without any consequences and God will remain in their midst to bless them with security, prosperity, and well-being *in spite of* that behavior. "Because God dwells in the land as well as in the sanctuary," it is necessary for all who live in the land "to keep the land holy by guarding against impurity and following the prescribed purificatory procedures. . . . Without the commitment of every individual to eschew impurity and purify if necessary, YHWH would be driven from the land and would not bless the land and its inhabitants with fertility and security (Lev 26:3-11)."[68] The condition for attaining God's blessings is not that the people stop generating pollution by sinning but that they make sure that the level of pollution that their sins generated in the sanctuary does not reach "the point of no return" and exceed the "modicum" that God can safely tolerate. The way in which the people are to avoid the doom and disaster caused by the accumulation of that pollution is not by changing their behavior but by performing the rites with blood that are necessary to wash that pollution away after they have acknowledged those sins and told God that they repent of them. Rather than having the purpose of promoting pure conduct among his people, those rites are aimed at making it possible for God to tolerate their impure conduct without having to withdraw from their presence or impose some other measure that they would find painful or disagreeable.

In fact, according to Milgrom's interpretation of the rites prescribed for *Yom Kippur* in Leviticus 16, those rites can bring about the cleansing of the sanctuary and the people every year independently of the number of sins they have committed and the quantity of pollution that those sins have generated. In that case, there is no need for them to be concerned about these things. The prescriptions for *Yom Kippur* never state that there is a limit to the number of sins that can be expiated through the rites to be performed. Nor do those prescriptions imply that if the people sin more frequently or commit sins that are more grievous in nature, they should offer up a greater number of sacrifices for sin over the course of the year to atone for those sins. This means that, no matter how much the people had sinned or how much pollution their sins had generated, as long as the rites that God had prescribed were performed in the way he had commanded, the result would be the same: "God would continue to reside with Israel because his temple and people were once again pure."[69]

The problems raised by Milgrom's views are especially evident in his consideration of the passages in which God prohibits his people from sacrificing their children to the god Molech or Molek. According to Milgrom, what led God to regard such practices as atrocious and abominable was not primarily his concern for his people's well-being but rather his concern for the purity of his dwelling place: "The sin of the Molek worshiper is exceptionally grievous because of its severe consequence: pollution of the sanctuary and desecration of the name YHWH. The sinner must be killed immediately; any delay jeopardizes the welfare of the entire nation."[70] If such is the case, what threatens the people's well-being and should fill them with abhorrence and fear is not the practice of human sacrifice itself but the pollution of God's sanctuary that is generated by that practice, since it is not that practice but the pollution generated by it that will lead to God's departure from the

---

68. Milgrom, *Leviticus: A Book of Ritual and Ethics*, 252.
69. Milgrom, *Leviticus 1–16*, 51.
70. Milgrom, *Leviticus: A Book of Ritual and Ethics*, 253.

sanctuary and the land. The threat that his people face is not from the cruelty and violence associated with the sacrifice of children to gods such as Molech but from God's refusal to dwell in a sanctuary polluted by such sacrifices. Ultimately, rather than needing to be saved from their own injustice, cruelty, and inhumanity, the people need to be saved from God's inability to tolerate that injustice and inhumanity.

According to views such as those of Milgrom, while the God of the biblical texts undoubtedly wishes to be near to his people in order to bless them, what ultimately concerns him is that he be allowed to dwell in his sanctuary in peace, unmolested by anything unclean or polluted. In that case, his priority is himself and his own comfort. His needs and desires take priority over those of his people. If he must choose between dwelling in a polluted sanctuary in order to bless his people or departing from the sanctuary when it becomes polluted in order to distance himself from the impure substance or force that he finds intolerable, he will invariably choose the latter alternative, even if it means depriving his people of his blessings and abandoning them to their doom.

Here again, we find the idea that God's holy and righteous nature is oppressive for both God and his people. In this case, what makes it necessary for God to demand that one animal victim after another be put to death is not his need to ensure that the sins that his people commit receive their due punishment but rather his inability to tolerate substances or forces that irritate and upset him or cause him to react adversely. If he is to remain in their midst, he therefore has no choice but to demand constant sacrifices from his people and to tolerate the modicum of pollution that gradually builds up in his sanctuary in the time between one cleansing and the next.

For their part, the people also find the obligation to provide the sacrificial victims necessary to keep God's sanctuary pure burdensome and oppressive. Nevertheless, they have no choice but to procure those victims and offer them up in sacrifice if they wish for God to dwell among them in order to bless them. In principle, the people might do their best to avoid sinning so as not to generate the impurity that will require that the sanctuary be cleansed with sacrificial blood, yet this too would represent a burden and a challenge for them, given the sinful desires and tendencies that they must constantly attempt to keep under control and repress. At the same time, their concern for the purity of God's sanctuary must outweigh the concern for their own well-being and take priority over it. If the people want to prevent God from abandoning them, they must dedicate themselves, their time, their energy, and their resources to supplying the priests with the animal victims necessary to obtain the blood that will allow the impurity generated by their sins to be washed away. Ultimately the God of Israel becomes akin to a pagan god whose thirst for sacrificial offerings and blood must continually be satiated. Both God and the temple are converted into an idol that demands death and blood and threatens to abandon the people to their doom if they fail to meet those demands.

The notion that God might be driven away from the sanctuary as a result of the accumulation of the impurity generated by the people's sins is problematic for other reasons as well. Such a notion reflects a conception of God that is strongly at odds with that which we find in the Hebrew Bible, where God is consistently presented as the sovereign and all-powerful creator of all that exists. In biblical thought, God can never be endangered by anything within his creation. While gods such as those worshiped by other nations might be subject to forces that were more powerful than they, the same could not be said of the God of Israel as he is portrayed in the Hebrew Scriptures. Just as he created all things with his word, so also was he thought to be able to destroy anything that existed with nothing more than a word. Nothing in his creation was thought to be able to cause him harm or injury, and much less threaten his existence or cause him to grow weak or die. Nor does anything that takes place in that creation have the power to drive him away or require that he take measures to protect himself. Such ideas reflect pagan modes of thought rather than the manner of conceiving of God that runs throughout the biblical texts.

In fact, nowhere in the context of the passages from the Pentateuch that prescribe the offering of sacrifice is it ever stated or implied that God will abandon his sanctuary if the expiatory rites that he has prescribed are not carried out there. The only passages to which Milgrom is able to point to justify his claim that God will depart from the sanctuary if the pollution generated by the people's sins reaches "a point of no return" are not in the Pentateuch but in the books of Ezekiel and Lamentations.[71] These passages speak of God's glory and the cherubim departing from the Jerusalem temple and present God abandoning his altar (Ezek 10:18-19; 11:22-23; Lam 2:7). Nowhere, however, do these passages state or imply that the reason for which God departs from the sanctuary is that he finds the impurity or pollution that has accumulated there intolerable or that the sacrificial rites aimed at purifying the temple have not been carried out in accordance with his command. Instead, what leads God to abandon the sanctuary is that he will no longer tolerate the sinful, violent, oppressive, and destructive behavior that the people refuse to turn away from. Furthermore, passages from other books of the Hebrew Bible make it clear that if the people persistently refuse to put away that behavior, no matter how many sacrificial offerings they present to God or how frequently and meticulously they perform the sacrificial rites he has prescribed, they will not obtain his blessing but will remain subject to his wrath.

Although the Mosaic prescriptions insist that those who are unclean as a result of contact or proximity with someone or something that might pollute or contaminate them must not enter into the area in and around the sanctuary, they give no reason for this prohibition. Nothing in the texts, however, ever suggests that God himself was thought to be harmed, endangered, or affected adversely by impurities or by persons or things that are spoken of as impure. There is therefore no reason to suppose that such a prohibition is grounded in

---

71. Milgrom, *Leviticus 1–16*, 258.

some type of concern for God himself. This makes it likely that the concern lying behind that prohibition is for the health and well-being of those gathering within the confines of the temple, who might be harmed or infected by any who bore some type of contagious illness or uncleanness.

Giving Substance to the Metaphor of Impurity

One of the claims that is fundamental for interpretations of sacrifices for sin that see their purpose in terms of cleansing people, places, and objects from the impurity or pollution caused by sin is that the sins that people committed were believed to be transformed into some type of actual substance or force, such as the "miasma" of which Milgrom speaks or the "odious, foul objects" to which Schwartz refers. Independently of whether this impure substance or force is said to affect God or human beings, such a conception presupposes once more that the problem that must be addressed is not sinful behavior as such but the pollution or contamination that it generates. In that case, the solution is not to put an end to that behavior but to carry out some type of rite or ritual that will enable the impure substance or force to be covered up, neutralized, absorbed, washed away, or carried off to a place where it can no longer do anyone harm.

There can be little doubt that in the biblical texts and the contexts in which they arose some forms of impurity were conceived of in this manner. Just as visible forms of dirt, filth, pollution, and contamination could have adverse effects on people and cause illness and disease, so also was it evident to all that there were invisible substances and forces that could harm people in various ways. Even though people in antiquity did not know of the existence of microbes such as bacteria or viruses, they would have learned from experience that sicknesses and diseases can be transmitted by contact or close proximity with people or things that are unclean or impure. It was also obvious that many things might enter into states of decay or decomposition and cause aversion and repulsion by the way they smelled, looked, tasted, or felt to the touch. Such things also made people sick. It is therefore natural that the biblical texts declare certain things unclean and affirm that in many cases those who come into close contact with what is unclean or impure are to be considered unclean or impure as well.[72]

Not everything that the Mosaic prescriptions declared impure was thought to contain some substance or force that made it impure or unclean, however. There is nothing in the commandments that declare certain foods and animals to be impure to suggest that those foods or animals were thought to have some unclean or impure substance or force within them that could adversely affect human beings. In fact, in the passages from Leviticus 11 and Deuteronomy 14 in which the distinctions between clean and unclean foods appear, the people are repeatedly told that certain meats and foods shall be

---

72. See, for example, Lev 5:2-3; 7:19-21; 11:24-39; 15:5-27; 22:4-6; Num 9:6-10; 19:11-22.

"unclean *for you.*" In other words, these commandments refer to things that are to be *regarded* as impure rather than things that are inherently or intrinsically impure. Likewise, when it is said that certain persons or things are to be considered unclean or impure for a particular period of time, such as prior to nightfall or during a certain number of days, the idea is not that whatever harmful substance or force has made them impure will magically disappear the moment in which the specified period of time comes to an end but rather that after a certain amount of time has passed the impure substance or force will have disappeared naturally by itself. In these cases, persons or things could continue to be considered impure for a period of time even when the substance or force that was thought to make them impure was no longer present in them. They *became* pure or clean before they were *accepted* as pure or clean.

For this reason, when it is said in the biblical texts that certain persons or things become impure when they come into contact or proximity with impurity in some form, it cannot be concluded that this is because they were actually thought to become impure in the sense of being infected or penetrated by some type of unclean substance or force. In many cases, what is involved is merely a precautionary measure aimed at ensuring that the person or thing has not been contaminated. People who touch a corpse or come into contact with someone who has a contagious skin disease may be infected or contaminated by some type of harmful substance or force, for example, yet it is also possible that no such infection or contamination occurs. If they show no signs of illness or contagion after a certain period of time, then in most cases it can be concluded that they never were actually infected or contaminated. This means that at times persons and objects that were not *actually* impure were nevertheless to be *regarded* as impure in accordance with certain commandments. When the biblical laws declare certain persons or things to be impure, therefore, this is not always an *observation* about what *actually happened* to them but in many cases is merely a *prescription* regarding how they are *to be regarded.*

At the same time, it is important to stress the distinction between physical and moral impurity. When people became physically impure, it was generally not because they had committed any kind of sin but due to some reason that had nothing to do with sinful behavior, such as contracting a skin disease, coming into contact with a corpse, or giving birth to a child. Conversely, for the most part immoral behavior did not make one physically unclean or impure. While such behavior was certainly unacceptable, the biblical texts never speak of it generating any type of mysterious substance or force that was harmful or dangerous for God or human beings.

There is no reason to suppose, therefore, that the passages from the Hebrew Bible that speak of people becoming impure as a result of behavior that was contrary to God's will were intended to be understood in a literal, physical, or ontological sense. Instead, such language should be regarded as *metaphorical.* In passages such as the following, for example, the allusions to both purity and impurity are clearly not to be taken literally:

The LORD has dealt with me according to my righteousness; according to the cleanness of my hands he has recompensed me (Ps 18:20).

Who shall ascend the mountain of the LORD? And who shall stand in his holy place? Those who have clean hands and pure hearts, who do not lift up their souls to what is false and do not swear deceitfully (Ps 24:3-4).

Wash me thoroughly from my iniquity, and cleanse me from my sin. . . . Purge me with hyssop, and I shall be clean; wash me, and I shall be whiter than snow. . . . Create in me a clean heart, O God, and put a new and right spirit within me (Ps 51:2, 7, 10).

They sacrificed their sons and their daughters to the demons; they poured out innocent blood, the blood of their sons and daughters, whom they sacrificed to the idols of Canaan, and the land was polluted with blood. Thus they became unclean by their acts and prostituted themselves in the things they did (Ps 106:37-39).

Who can say, "I have made my heart clean; I am pure from my sin"? (Prov 20:9)

Wash yourselves; make yourselves clean. Remove the evil of your doings from before my eyes. Cease to do evil, learn to do good. Seek justice, rescue the oppressed, defend the orphan, plead for the widow. Come now, let us argue it out, says the LORD: though your sins are like scarlet, they shall be like snow; though they are red like crimson, they shall become like wool (Isa 1:16-18).

We have all become like one who is unclean, and all our righteous deeds are like a filthy rag (Isa 64:6).

Though you wash yourself with lye and use much soap, the stain of your iniquity is still before me, says the Lord GOD (Jer 2:22).

The word of the LORD came to me: Son of man, when the house of Israel lived on their own land, they polluted it with their ways and their deeds; their conduct in my sight was like the uncleanness of a menstrual period (Ezek 36:16-17).[73]

Clearly, righteous behavior does not lead people to have clean hands or pure hearts in a literal or physical sense, just as sinful behavior does not actually pollute or contaminate hands, hearts, human bodies, or the land on which people live. Those who become unacceptable to God as a result of sinful behavior do not regain his acceptance or obtain his forgiveness merely by washing themselves, their hearts, or their hands with lye or soap, nor do they become sparkling clean or whiter than snow in a literal sense by repenting of their sins and turning away from actions and behaviors that are contrary to God's will.

The use of metaphorical language to refer to sinful behavior is common elsewhere throughout the Hebrew Scriptures as well. In passages such as the following, such behavior is described as something that is conceived and born like a child, plowed like land, or sown like seed:

---

73. For other examples of the metaphorical use of the language of purity, impurity, and cleansing to refer to moral behavior and its correction, see Job 4:17; 8:6; 22:30; 33:9; Jer 13:27; 33:8; Lam 1:8-9; 4:13-15; Ezek 24:12-13; 36:23-29; 39:24; Dan 12:10; Zech 13:1; Mal 3:2-3.

As I have seen, those who plow iniquity and sow trouble reap the same (Job 4:8).

They conceive mischief and bring forth evil, and their belly prepares deceit (Job 15:35).

See how they conceive evil and are pregnant with mischief and bring forth lies (Ps 7:14).

Whoever sows injustice will reap calamity, and the rod of anger will perish (Prov 22:8).

To interpret these passages in the sense that sinful behavior actually generates some type of mysterious substance or force that might proceed forth from a human body or be implanted in the ground clearly runs contrary to their intended meaning.

The same type of metaphorical language is also used throughout the Hebrew Scriptures to refer to the forgiveness of sin. Sins and transgressions are said to be covered, blotted out, removed, cast far off, swept away, and tread upon under foot:

Do not cover their iniquity, and do not let their sin be blotted out from your sight, for they have raged against the builders (Neh 4:5).

Happy are those whose transgression is forgiven and whose sin is covered (Ps 32:1).

As far as the east is from the west, so far does he remove our transgressions from us (Ps 103:12).

You have cast all my sins behind your back (Isa 38:17).

I alone am the one who blots out your transgressions for my own sake, and I will not remember your sins (Isa 43:25; cf. Ps 85:2; 109:14; Jer 18:23).

I have swept away your transgressions like a cloud and your sins like mist (Isa 44:22).

He will again have compassion upon us; he will tread our iniquities under foot. You will cast all our sins into the depths of the sea (Mic 7:19).

Many passages in the biblical texts from the Hebrew Scriptures speak of people or the land becoming polluted or contaminated as a result of sinful behavior. There is no reason, however, to interpret what these passages affirm literally:

Thus the land became contaminated, and I punished it for its iniquity, and the land vomited out its inhabitants (Lev 18:25; cf. Num 35:33-34; Deut 21:23; Ps 106:38).

For your hands are contaminated with blood and your fingers with iniquity (Isa 59:3).

I brought you into a bountiful land to eat of its fruits and its good things. But when you entered you polluted my land and made my heritage an abomination (Jer 2:7).

You have polluted the land with your prostitutions and wickedness (Jer 3:2).

And I will repay them double for their iniquity and their sin because they have polluted my land with the carcasses of their detestable idols and have filled my inheritance with their abominations (Jer 16:18).

Ah, rebellious, polluted, oppressing city! It has listened to no voice; it has accepted no correction. It has not trusted in the LORD; it has not drawn near to its God (Zeph 3:1-2).

There you will remember your ways and all the deeds by which you polluted yourselves, and you will loathe yourselves for all the evils that you committed (Ezek 20:43; cf. 14:11; 20:31; 22:4; 23:30; Hos 5:3).

To take these passages in a literal sense would involve affirming that the sinful behavior mentioned had actually produced some type of dirt or filth that covered the people's bodies or hands. If such were the case, all that would be necessary to deal with such dirt or filth would be to use water together with some type of cleansing agent to remove it. In that case, people who had sinned could undo the effects of their sin through physical processes that had nothing to do with repentance or a change in their behavior and way of life. Similarly, while certain forms of sinful and destructive behavior may certainly have harmful effects on the environment, there is no need to understand the affirmations that the land is polluted by such behavior in a literal, physical, or ontological sense, just as the allusions to the land vomiting out its inhabitants are clearly not to be taken literally.

In light of passages such as these, it should be clear that when the biblical texts speak of people, places, or objects becoming impure, unclean, or polluted as a result of sinful behavior, such language is generally intended to be taken figuratively or metaphorically. When people disobeyed God so as to act in ways that did them and others harm, their actions were not thought to be converted into some type of impure physical or material entity that from that point forward existed independently of them, as if it took on a life of its own. The sins that the people committed were not "objectified" or "metamorphosed" in the sense of being transformed into actual objects, substances, or forces that then had to be dealt with by being washed away, neutralized, covered up, or cast off into the distance. Instead, the allusions to sin as impurity or pollution in the biblical text should be understood as metaphorical.

The same must be said with regard to the passages that speak of people, places, and objects being purified or cleansed from the sins and transgressions committed by the people, including those that associate this purification or cleansing with sacrificial rites. Whatever damage was caused by sinful and destructive behavior could not be undone, reversed, or taken away by sacrificing animals or using their blood in rites carried out in the sanctuary. Just as neither lye nor soap could actually wash away sinful actions or purify people from behaviors and attitudes that did them harm, no amount of sacrificial blood could make the hearts and minds of God's people pure and clean or make them pleasing to God once more after they had sinned. When they had disobeyed God, what was necessary in order for them to obtain his forgiveness was not that they remove some actual stain that their sin had caused or cover up some type of dirt or filth from his sight but that they repent of what they had done and renew their commitment to living in accordance with his will.

These observations should make it clear just how problematic many of the claims made by Milgrom and other scholars who share his views are. Milgrom's assertion that the violation of certain commandments was thought to generate impurity as a "physical substance" that took the form of "an aerial miasma that possessed magnetic attraction for the realm of the sacred" represents the type of baseless and unsubstantiated assumption that is characteristic of the work of many interpreters of the biblical prescriptions regarding sacrifice. Milgrom cannot cite a single text from the Hebrew Bible or Second Temple Jewish writings that speak of the impurity or pollution associated with sinful behavior in that manner, simply because there are none. Nor is there anything in the biblical texts to support Gane's affirmation that the people's sins were thought to be "transformed from abstraction, as if out of the air, into a concentrated, quasi-spatially containable form," or Schwartz's claim that the "metaphysical spontaneous generation of impurity" was thought to take place as the result of a process in which "sins metamorphose into impurity."

Such interpretations of the passages that associate sin with impurity and pollution not only involve taking metaphorical language in a literal sense and reading back into the biblical texts ideas that are foreign to them but also raise questions and problems that from a biblical perspective would have been impossible to answer. How could concrete actions materialize into actual substances or forces? Would not sins of omission or the "performative" sins of which Milgrom speaks, such as the failure to observe the Sabbath or help a neighbor in need, also take material form? How could sinful actions then be gathered together from many different locations as an "aerial miasma" or assume a "concentrated, quasi-spatially containable form"? How could they fly or float through the air, at times for hundreds or even thousands of miles? How could the sanctuary serve as a magnet to attract them from such faraway places? Or how could countless sins committed over the course of an entire year throughout the world come to be concentrated together in a substance small enough to penetrate into the high priest's hands and then be transmitted to a goat?

Such a conception of sin also presupposes the existence of some type of impersonal power or mechanism that could automatically define an action or a failure to act as a sin and on that basis generate the impure substance, force, miasma, or pollution that would travel through the air to adhere to the sanctuary. How was this supposed to take place? Were there not, for example, differences of interpretation regarding precisely what actions were permitted on the Sabbath? In that case, who or what could determine whether a particular action had violated the Sabbath commandment? When emergencies arose, was it not acceptable to set aside the literal observance of the Sabbath commandment? Other commandments from the Decalogue could be equally problematic to interpret. Who or what could determine whether particular individuals had actually failed to honor their father and their mother? If one failed to honor one's grandparents or a step-parent, had one also broken that commandment, or did it apply only to one's biological father and mother? If one accidentally took the life of another person out of no fault of one's own, had one violated the commandment not to kill? Under certain circumstances, was it not permissible to kill another person, such as when one was engaged in warfare or acting in self-defense in the face of a life-threatening attack? If a man became intimate with a woman who was married to another man but did not actually have sexual relations with her, had the two of them actually committed the sin of adultery? If a witness had doubts about the veracity of his or her testimony but chose to give that testimony anyway and it later proved to be false, was he or she guilty of bearing false witness? And how could it be known whether a person had coveted something or someone that belonged to his or her neighbor without examining what was in that person's heart?

In all of these cases, how could anyone but God judge whether a sin capable of generating the malefic substance or miasma had been committed? Would certain sins generate a greater quantity of miasma than others? If one person wrongly killed one man and another person wrongly killed twenty men, did the second person's sin generate twenty times as much miasma as the sin of the first person? Milgrom's claim that "the severity of the sin or impurity varies in direct relation to the depth of its penetration into the sanctuary" raises the same type of problems, as does his affirmation that "wanton unrepented sin" and the sin committed by the community as a whole penetrated furthest into the Most Holy Place or adytum. Who but God could determine if a sin that had been committed was "wanton unrepented sin"? What if that sin had been committed collectively by a group of people, but some of them had sinned inadvertently and others wantonly? How much of that sin would generate the "dynamic and malefic" miasma of which Milgrom speaks, and how far would it penetrate into the sanctuary? Would only part of that miasma enter into the Most Holy Place to adhere there and the rest of it remain outside? Did the miasma generated by sins have a mind of its own so that it would know how far to penetrate or which areas and objects of the sanctuary it should adhere to? Or did the severity of the sin determine the strength of the magnetic force that would draw the miasma into the sanctuary? How exactly did the mechanism or process by which miasma was generated work?

Similar questions could be asked regarding the supposed use of blood as a "ritual detergent." Did the amount of blood used have to be proportional to the amount of miasma that the people's sins had generated? Why is this not specified in the texts? If an entire surface had been covered with the miasma that had adhered to it but only a few drops of blood fell on that surface, how would that blood take away all of the miasma that did not come into direct contact with it? If the people or the priest who offered the sacrificial animal whose blood was being used were not truly and sincerely repentant for the sins they had committed, did the blood still work, or did their lack of repentance instead deprive it of its cleansing power? If only a part of the people who offered the sacrifice was truly repentant, was the cleansing power of the blood diminished in proportion to the percentage of the people who remained unrepentant?

Questions such as these demonstrate just how untenable and even nonsensical many aspects of the interpretations of the biblical prescriptions regarding sacrifices for sins put forward by scholars such as Milgrom are. The biblical texts offer no basis for answering questions such as these, yet the reason is not that they fail to provide the details and information necessary to address them but that the type of scheme proposed by Milgrom is so radically at odds with biblical thought that such questions would never have arisen in the first place.

Milgrom's attempt to ground his interpretations in the biblical text are just as problematic. Because the biblical texts never speak of impurity as a physical substance, a magnetic and malefic dynamic force, or as an aerial miasma that possessed electromagnetic properties, Milgrom looks to a handful of ancient Mesopotamian and Egyptian texts that describe rites aimed at expelling demonic beings from pagan temples to claim that impurity was thought to be demonic as well and to constitute a threat to the gods.[74] On that basis alone, he then argues that the rites prescribed in Leviticus 16 for *Yom Kippur* must be understood as reflecting the same *modus operandi* for the purification of the altar and sacred spaces devoted to Israel's God. His distinction between performative and prohibitive commandments and his claim that the miasma generated by different types of sin penetrated into different areas and objects within the sanctuary are based solely on the observation that Leviticus 16 prescribes several different blood rites that are to be carried out in different areas of the sanctuary on behalf of the high priest himself and his household as well as the people in general. Such an observation hardly justifies the conclusions that Milgrom draws from it.

In addition, Milgrom claims that some of the rites with blood prescribed in Leviticus 16 serve to consecrate the blood while others have "a purgative effect" and that only certain types of sins could be purged by means of the prescribed rites.[75] These distinctions hardly seem to be grounded in the biblical text. In Lev 16:30, the people themselves are said to be cleansed or purified from all of their sins on *Yom Kippur* even though they never come into contact with any blood on that day. In that case, their purification cannot be attributed to the use of blood as a ritual detergent or cleansing agent. Although rites in which blood is used are said to purify people and objects in a few passages from the biblical texts, nowhere is blood spoken of as a ritual detergent or said

---

74. Milgrom, *Leviticus 1–16*, 256-57. For a critique of Milgrom's thought on this subject, see Hyam Maccoby, *Ritual and Morality: The Ritual Purity System and its Place in Judaism* (Cambridge: Cambridge University Press, 1999), 182-92.

75. Milgrom, *Leviticus 1–16*, 1038-43.

to cleanse or purify anyone or anything in itself.[76] All of these interpretations and others proposed by Milgrom are based purely on speculation and involve reading back into the texts ideas that are nowhere stated explicitly or even implied in them. Some of the distinctions he makes are equally arbitrary and based purely on conjecture rather than any type of solid evidence.

More importantly, however, Milgrom's interpretations of the biblical prescriptions regarding sacrifice are based on an understanding of sin and impurity that not only overlooks and ignores the concerns reflected in the biblical texts but also reflects a logic that is foreign to them. As we have seen repeatedly throughout the present study, in the biblical texts the problem that must be addressed is the destructive behavior that prevents people from attaining the happiness and well-being that God in his love desires for all. What is necessary is that people be brought to leave that behavior behind and instead live in ways that promote that well-being and make it possible.

In biblical thought, therefore, the problem is *not* that sinful behavior generates some type of dynamic and malefic substance or force that represents a danger to human beings or to God himself. Nor does the problem faced by God and sinful human beings have to do with their physical proximity to one another or the need for Israel's God to dwell in the sanctuary dedicated to him in order for his people to receive his blessings. The God of the Hebrew Bible can act in any way he wishes among human beings located anywhere on the earth. He has also made it clear that the condition that must be fulfilled in order for people to receive his blessings is that they live and behave in ways that are conducive to their well-being and abandon the ways of living and behaving that undermine and destroy that well-being. What harms human beings is their failure to live in the way God has commanded for their own good rather than any type of malefic substance or force that suddenly and mysteriously materializes out of nowhere every time they break some rule that God has laid down. In order to attain God's blessings, what his people need is not the performance of sacrificial rites aimed at purging the sanctuary dedicated to him from some type of physical pollution through the application of sacrificial blood but their adherence to the way of life that he has graciously laid out for them in the Torah.

The logic behind the passages in the Hebrew Bible that speak of the sins of the people being taken away, therefore, is that once they have been cleansed of their destructive behavior and have been purified in their hearts and minds, God will forgive and forget what they had done in the past and no longer take it into account. Because they will have stopped doing themselves and others harm, God will no longer hold against them the sins, transgressions, and iniquities that they had committed previously. Those sins, transgressions, and iniquities will be washed away, covered up, buried, and cast far from his sight. The reason that God will forgive and forget the past, however, is not that the people will have carried out some type of rite or offered him sacrifices

---

76. See Lev 14:52; 16:19; 17:11; cf. Ezek 43:18.

but that they will have put away the ways of thinking and behaving that were doing them and others harm. This is the only condition for God's forgiveness and also constitutes the *basis* for that forgiveness. God will overlook the past because of the new present and future that is resulting from the change in the people's behavior, a present and future characterized by justice, righteousness, mercy, solidarity, and a way of life that promotes the well-being of all. It is in that sense that the people, their lives, and their land will be cleansed and purified from the pollution and contamination that their sinful behavior has brought about in the way that the texts describe.

All of these problems are what make interpretations of the biblical prescriptions regarding sacrifice such as those of Milgrom so objectionable. In addition to the conceptual difficulties they raise, they suggest that what people needed to obtain God's blessings was not ultimately to avoid sin and injustice but to make sure that they performed the rites necessary to avoid allowing the pollution generated by their sin and injustice to accumulate to the extent that it would drive God away from the sanctuary. In that case, God's concern is not that the people put away their sin and injustice but that they cover it up from his sight or remove it from his presence with sacrifices, blood, and death so that he does not see it and it can no longer bother him. As in penal substitution interpretations, the purpose of the offering of sacrifice becomes, not that of promoting righteous behavior, but making it possible for God to tolerate *unrighteous* behavior.

Attempting to Reconcile Symbol with Reality

Milgrom's writings leave no doubt that he was well aware of many of the problems raised by his interpretations of the biblical prescriptions regarding sacrifices for sin, including the kinds of problems just mentioned. He attempted to address them in several different ways, yet those attempts can hardly be considered successful. Thus, for example, in order to avoid the idea that the sacrificial rites produced their desired effect automatically or mechanically, he often stresses that it was necessary for the people participating in the sacrificial rites to be truly repentant in order for those rites to bring about purification and forgiveness.[77]

As we have noted above, however, such a claim is highly problematic in that it suggests that the rites in themselves were thought to produce certain effects by means of some type of *modus operandi*. In biblical thought, it is not the performance of rites that effects purification or obtains God's forgiveness and acceptance but repentance and a renewed commitment to obeying his will. While this repentance and commitment were expressed by means of the rites, those rites were not thought to function mechanically or magically, even if those who performed those rites or participated in them repented of their sins, since the only thing that mattered to God was what he saw in people's hearts

---

77. See, for example, Milgrom, *Leviticus 1–16*, 50: "Expiation by sacrifice depends on two factors: the remorse of the worshiper (verb *'āšam*) and the reparation (noun *'āšām*) he brings to both man and God to rectify his wrong."

and lives. If people thought that they could oblige God to bless and forgive them by means of rites, by definition they were thinking and acting contrary to his will rather than approaching him in a spirit that pleased him. Furthermore, if they thought that those rites themselves could obtain blessings and benefits for themselves in mechanical or magical fashion, they were attempting to sidestep God in order to manipulate on their own forces that they thought would produce some desired effect independently of God's intervention.

Milgrom attempts to avoid ideas such as these by claiming that the prescribed rites were thought to be effective only because God graciously granted them such power: "though the priest performs the rituals, it is only by the grace of God that they are efficacious."[78] Similarly, he writes: "Ritual substances have no intrinsic force: they are powered by the will of God. Thus blood can act as a detergent."[79] "Blood is life. Hence it is powerful, but only God can activate it."[80] According to these affirmations, the sacrificial rites work only because God in his grace *makes* them work. In addition to presupposing that the rites themselves produced certain effects magically or mechanically, however, such affirmations raise theological and conceptual problems. If God could bring about certain desired results by causing rituals and ritual substances to be "efficacious" or "powered," why should he not be able to bring about the same results without such rituals or substances? If he was truly almighty and the sovereign creator of all, why could he not make the impure forces, substances, or miasma generated by the people's sins disappear by an act of omnipotence, simply by *fiat* or by pronouncing a word in the same way that he had when he created everything that existed in the first place? What need did he have for sacrificial blood or any other type of "ritual detergent" to protect him from substances and forces over which he already possessed complete power?

Another way in which Milgrom attempts to avoid the difficulties raised by his interpretations of the biblical prescriptions regarding sacrifices for sin is by insisting that the rites carried out were merely symbolic. Thus, for example, he writes that "the blood of the purification offerings symbolically purges the sanctuary by symbolically absorbing its impurities" and speaks of the symbolic removal of Israel's impurities by the sacrificial rites prescribed in Leviticus.[81] Milgrom's repeated use of the language of symbolism clearly seems to be grounded in his awareness of the problems involved in taking his interpretations of the texts literally.

To affirm that the purification from impurity effected by the sacrificial rites and the application of sacrificial blood was symbolic rather than literal, however, requires understanding everything else in the sacrificial rites prescribed in the Mosaic law in a symbolic rather than literal sense as well. If the impurities generated by Israel's sins are only symbolic, they cannot consist

---

78. Milgrom, *Leviticus 1–16*, 1084.

79. Milgrom, *Leviticus 1–16*, 279.

80. Jacob Milgrom, *Leviticus 17-22: A New Translation with Introduction and Commentary*, AB 3A (New York: Doubleday, 2000), 1479.

81. Milgrom, *Leviticus 1–16*, 46, 625; *Leviticus: A Book of Ritual and Ethics*, 97.

of actual substances or forces. Yet in that case, how can Milgrom speak of impurity as "a physical substance, an aerial miasma that possessed magnetic attraction for the realm of the sacred," or as "a dynamic force, magnetic and malefic to the sphere of the sacred"? How can a substance be physical yet at the same time be only symbolic? How can impurity be "virulent, dangerous to humans and God alike" if it is merely symbolic? If the cleansing of the sanctuary is not to be understood literally but only symbolically, is it not also necessary to understand God's presence in the sanctuary, his departure from it, and the supposed doom that Israel will experience as a result of that departure as purely symbolic as well? Are we to believe that the people's sins were thought to generate a miasma that was not real but merely symbolic and traveled through the air only symbolically in order to penetrate into the sanctuary and adhere there not in a literal sense but only a symbolic one? Was "the threat to God" arising "from humans who willfully or inadvertently violate the divine commandments" that made it necessary for the blood of countless sacrificial victims to be shed literally and physically only symbolic?

Clearly, Milgrom cannot resolve the conceptual problems raised by his interpretations of the biblical prescriptions regarding sacrifices for sin by reducing everything to mere symbolism. In fact, many aspects of those interpretations simply make no sense if they are understood only symbolically and even exclude meanings that are purely symbolic. One can hardly claim that impurity and pollution were believed to be actual substances or forces while at the same time arguing that the rites whose purpose was to cleanse people, places, and objects from them functioned only symbolically.

The idea that one could undo or reverse the effects of one's sin by means of sacrificial offerings and rites also suggests that people could sin freely or deliberately and then simply carry out the rites necessary to eliminate the impurity that their sin had caused and obtain God's forgiveness. Biblical scholars generally reject such an idea, claiming that God's forgiveness and acceptance would be denied to any who thought and acted in that manner. If that was the case, however, then no forgiveness would ever be possible for sins committed deliberately, and the impurity generated by them could never be cleansed from the sanctuary. Those who sinned deliberately would remain liable to death or some other punishment, in essence being placed under a curse for the rest of their lives, no matter what they did. Even if they made a radical change in their behavior and ceaselessly dedicated the rest of their lives to doing what is good, right, and just, they could never be restored to God's favor. Such is the conclusion that Schwartz derives from the priestly writings of the Pentateuch: "there are inexpiable offenses: sins from which one can never be disencumbered. In these cases, sin-bearing is never alleviated. It is a permanent state. The sin remains with the offender forever."[82] In that case, it

---

82. Schwartz, "Bearing of Sin," 15. Several pages later, however, Schwartz argues that although deliberate sins cannot be eradicated, they can be driven off into the wilderness by means of the rite with the goat for Azazel on *Yom Kippur* (21).

would be senseless for God to demand that these offenders repent and practice justice and righteousness, since the possibility that they could obtain his blessings once more by doing so would cease to exist. Were God to behave in such a manner, he would simply be condemning countless people to an irreversible doom and would not be promoting the practice of justice and righteousness among those who had fallen into such sins. Instead, he would be discouraging it, since it would be pointless and nothing could be gained by it.

Milgrom attempts to resolve this difficulty by claiming that through confession and repentance it was possible for sins that had been committed deliberately to be reduced to inadvertent sins that could be expiated by means of a sacrificial offering: "For a deliberate sin, the remorse must be verbalized, the sin articulated, and responsibility assumed.... The repentance of sinners, through remorse (*'ašam*) and confession, reduces intentional sin to an inadvertence, which is then eligible for sacrificial expiation. Confession is then the legal device fashioned by Israel's priesthood to transform deliberate sins into inadvertencies, thereby qualifying them for sacrificial expiation."[83] If such is the case, however, then those who have sinned deliberately with the intention of subsequently seeking God's forgiveness by means of a sacrificial offering can obtain that forgiveness without any difficulty. They may pay a higher price for committing an intentional or deliberate sin and then making expiation for it, yet if they are willing to pay that price there is nothing else preventing them from doing so. Needless to say, for God to allow people to behave in that way does not promote among them the practice of justice and righteousness. Instead, it gives them free rein to do as they please, as long as they atone for what they have done by means of the sacrificial offerings necessary to be restored to God's favor and obtain his forgiveness once again.

The same type of problems that plague Milgrom's interpretation of the biblical prescriptions regarding sacrifices for sin run throughout the work of other biblical scholars who read back into the biblical texts the idea that sin, impurity, and pollution were thought to consist of invisible and mysterious substances or forces that the sacrificial rites were designed to dispose of or eliminate. Such interpretations inevitably conceive of those rites as having the purpose of dealing not with sinful behavior itself but with some type of reality generated by that behavior that supposedly affects human beings and at times even God himself negatively. They also view the sacrificial rites as working mechanically or magically through some type of *modus operandi* that operates on its own independently of God or any type of divine decision or intervention. At the same time, such interpreters claim that the rites do *not* work if those participating in them are not sufficiently repentant and committed to obeying God's commandments. They thus affirm the efficacy of the rites while at the same time denying that efficacy by affirming that ultimately God's forgiveness, acceptance, and blessings depended on the repentance of those participating in them rather than the rites themselves.

---

83. Milgrom, *Leviticus: A Book of Ritual and Ethics*, 46.

DEFUSING THE DANGERS OF GOD'S HOLINESS

According to most proponents of views of sacrifice that regard its purpose as enabling a holy God to dwell in the midst of a sinful people, it was necessary not only for sin and impurity to be removed from God's presence but also for the people and priests to keep a safe distance from God due to his holiness. As we have noted above, many scholars regard God's holiness as a dangerous force that emanates out from him and may kill or harm any who draw too near to him. At times scholars understand God's anger in the same way. It is common to claim that this manner of conceiving of God's holiness and wrath is reflected in passages from the biblical narratives that describe the sudden death of persons who disobey what God had commanded with regard to the worship given him at his sanctuary as well as sacred objects such as the ark of the covenant. Two passages in particular are especially said to convey this conception of God's holiness and wrath, namely, the story of the fire that came out from God's presence to consume Aaron's sons Nadab and Abihu in Lev 10:1-3 and the account of the death of Uzzah, who was killed when he reached out to prevent the ark of the covenant from falling to the ground as it was being transported (2 Sam 6:1-9). A couple of passages from Numbers similarly speak of people being struck dead by God or threatened with death or plagues at the sanctuary (Num 8:19; 16:1-49). There are also passages in the Pentateuch that command that people who enter into areas that are regarded as holy be put to death, yet in these passages their death is not caused directly by God or his holiness but is to result from their execution at the hands of others.[84] In some cases, it is simply said that people will die if they draw near to the holy things, yet it is not clear whether this means that God will strike them dead or that they are to be put to death by others (Num 4:19; 17:13; 18:3).

On the basis of passages such as these, for example, Levine affirms that "Yahweh's wrath will be unleashed against all who fail to take proper precautions when entering into his immediate presence, or against all who were not permitted to stand in sacred precincts, to start with."[85] According to this manner of conceiving of God, at any moment he may lash out at those who provoke his wrath for any reason, especially if they transgress the boundaries he has fixed around himself or violate some other commandment that he regards as sacred. In these cases, what leads him to react in such a manner is not that those who arouse his anger have done anything unjust, immoral, or oppressive but simply that they have not respected the rules he has established to safeguard his holiness and to ensure that he is treated with the honor and respect that are due to him. This involves acting in the same way that was thought to be characteristic of the pagan gods of antiquity.

---

84. See Exod 19:9-12; Num 1:51; 3:10, 38; 18:7; 19:13-20.
85. Levine, *In the Presence*, 70. On this idea, see also Milgrom, *Leviticus 17–22*, 1438.

This manner of conceiving of God's holiness is highly problematic for several reasons. Chief among these is that the Hebrew Bible never speaks of God's holiness as some type of substance, force, or energy. In fact, as Schwartz has noted, nowhere in the Hebrew Bible is the term "holiness" ever used in an abstract sense to refer to something that has existence in itself. The only noun formed from the root *q-d-sh* that is used in the Hebrew texts is *qodesh*, which refers to "a sacred object, something which belongs to the divine sphere."[86] This means that in biblical thought people, places, and objects may be regarded as holy, but holiness is not something that they are said to possess, nor is holiness objectified so as to be conceived of as some type of tangible, physical entity that inheres in persons or objects and can radiate or emanate out from them.

Throughout the Hebrew Bible, to be holy is to be separated from what is common or profane and to be dedicated to God so as to belong to him in some sense. Because what defines something as holy is that it is set apart for God or for some role or use pertaining to God, if the noun "holiness" is used it should be understood in the sense of what we might refer to as "set-apartness." In that case, to speak of a particular place or object as holy is not to conceive of it as being pervaded or imbued with some type of divine substance or force but to see it as something that has been set apart and dedicated to God.

Of course, God himself is also repeatedly said to be holy in the sense that he is distinct from human beings and relates to his creation in a manner that is in many ways unique, not only because he possesses a sovereign power that sets him far above all other beings but also because he invariably acts in accordance with what is good, right, just, and loving. For that reason, when holiness is attributed to God as a quality, it should also be understood in terms of his "set-apart-ness," that is, a manner of existing, acting, and relating to others that sets him apart from all other persons and beings rather than some type of mysterious energy or force that he possesses.

This understanding of holiness leads to a very different reading of the biblical passages that speak of certain things becoming holy by contact with something else that is holy. In reality, there are only four such passages in the Hebrew Bible. In Exod 29:37 and 30:29, it is said that anything that touches one of the altars or the objects pertaining to it shall be holy, while in Leviticus 6 it is said that anything that comes into contact with the offerings mentioned in the passage shall be holy (vv. 18, 27). If this holiness is understood merely in terms of being set apart for God or dedicated to him, then all four of these passages are simply affirming that things that come into contact with other things that have been dedicated to God are also to be dedicated to him. The fact that in the immediate context of Exod 29:37 and 30:29 the people are told that certain things shall be holy *to* them or *for* them suggests that the idea in these passages is that they are to *consider* and *treat* as holy those things that come into contact with one of the altars or that which pertains to it (Exod 30:32, 36). In other words, the idea is not that some mysterious transformation takes place when

---

86. Schwartz, "Israel's Holiness," 49.

those things come into contact with what is set apart as holy but rather that those things are to be set apart in the same way.

The same type of observations must be made with respect to other passages that threaten with death those who enter into areas that have been designated as holy or touch holy objects contrary to God's command. There is no reason to read back into these passages the idea that those areas or objects are permeated with some type of holy substance or force that automatically strikes out against any impure person or thing that comes into contact or close proximity with it, as if some type of electrical charge or "holy-unclean fusion reaction" were involved. The most natural reading is instead that those areas and objects have simply been set apart for the worship or service of Israel's God or for some other sacred purpose. God therefore demands that human beings respect and obey what he has commanded regarding those areas or objects and will either take action himself against any who disobey his command or will have those whom he has chosen to serve him at the sanctuary do so on his behalf.

While a number of passages speak of people being struck down and dying as a result of their failure to respect what God has commanded with regard to areas and objects that he has designated as holy, a close look at those passages reveals that they do not attribute the deaths of these individuals to God's holiness as if it were some type of deadly force or energy emanating from him but to God himself. In Exodus 19, after God commands Moses to set limits around Mount Sinai to mark it off as holy and commands that any who so much as touch the edge of the mountain are to be put to death, he adds: "Do not let either the priests or the people break through to come up to the Lord; otherwise he will strike out against them" (Exod 19:24). In the same context, God tells Moses that if the priests who approach him have not consecrated themselves, he will strike out against them as well (v. 22). The same Hebrew verb used in these verses appears in the passages in which Uzzah is said to have been struck dead after he touched the ark of the covenant (2 Sam 6:8; 1 Chr 13:11; 15:13). Many other passages from the Hebrew Bible use this verb to refer to God or human beings breaking down something such as a wall or gate, breaking into an area, or simply acting with violence.[87] In all of these passages, that verb does not refer to any type of energy or force acting on its own but describes a personal agent striking out at something violently in order to break or destroy it.

This observation is especially pertinent when considering the account of Uzzah's death in 2 Sam 6:7-8 and 1 Chr 13:10-11. Both of these passages explicitly affirm that it was not the ark itself or anything radiating out from it that killed Uzzah but God himself: "The anger of the Lord was kindled against Uzzah; and *God* struck him there." The same affirmation appears in 1 Chr 15:13.

---

87. See, for example, 2 Kgs 14:13; 1 Chr 14:11; 2 Chr 20:37; 24:7; 25:23; 26:6; 32:5; Job 16:14; Ps 60:1; 80:12; 89:40; Eccl 3:3; 10:8; Isa 5:5; Hos 4:2; Mic 2:13. The Hebrew verb that appears in all of these passages is *parats*.

There, after he recalls the incident with Uzzah, David tells the priests who are about to carry the ark: "Because you did not carry it the first time, *the LORD our God* burst out against us, because we did not give it proper care."

Many biblical interpreters have claimed to find in other passages that allude to the ark of the covenant the idea that some type of mysterious energy or force was thought to radiate out from it either to benefit people in some way or to do them harm. Often they identify this energy or force with God's holiness. In the book of Joshua, for example, the waters of the Jordan River are parted and then return to their normal levels after the priests who are carrying the ark lead the people across the river bed (Josh 3:10-17; 4:15-18). In 2 Sam 6:10-14 and 1 Chr 13:13-14, the family and possessions of Obed-edom the Gittite are blessed when he receives the ark into his house for three months in order to care for it. Conversely, when the Philistines capture the ark in the time of Eli and Samuel and place it in the temple of their god Dagon, during the night Dagon's statue is toppled and later they are struck with a plague of tumors that causes some to die (1 Sam 5:1-12). In the following chapter of 1 Samuel, seventy men from Beth-shemesh are said to have died at God's hand, either because they looked into the ark or because they did not rejoice when the ark was returned to Israel (1 Sam 6:19-20).[88]

None of these passages, however, ever attribute any type of mysterious power to the ark of the covenant itself. Instead, as in the account of Uzzah's death, they speak of God himself acting to bless or do harm to the people mentioned in the narrative. In Josh 4:23, for example, the people are told that it was God himself who parted the waters of the Jordan River rather than the ark of the covenant: "*the LORD your God* dried up the waters of the Jordan for you until you crossed over." Similarly, in 2 Sam 6:11-12 it is explicitly said that "*the LORD* blessed Obed-edom and all his household." The same affirmation appears in 1 Chr 13:14: "*the LORD* blessed the household of Obed-edom and all that he had." When the seventy men who look into the ark or do not rejoice at its return are struck dead in 1 Sam 6:19-20, their deaths are attributed not to the ark but to God: "*he* slew some of the men of Beth-shemesh, because they looked into the ark of the LORD; *he* slew seventy men of them, and the people mourned because *the LORD* had made a great slaughter among the people." The tendency to ascribe some mysterious power to the ark in and of itself is particularly evident in most English translations of 1 Sam 5:11, which presents the Philistines as affirming: "Send away the ark of the God of Israel, and let it return to its own place, that it may not slay us and our people." In reality, however, the Hebrew verb can be understood as referring to God himself, in which case the verse would be translated: "Send away the ark of the God of Israel, and let it return to its own place, that *he* may not slay us and

---

88. On the basis of a few Hebrew manuscripts, translations such as the NRSVue, NIV, and ESV refer to the death of seventy men rather than the 50,700 mentioned in the Masoretic text. Some English versions also follow the Septuagint text in ascribing to the men killed the sin of not rejoicing at the ark's return rather than looking into the ark. For our purposes here, these differences are not significant.

our people." The fact that the verses immediately preceding and following 1 Sam 5:11 repeatedly speak of the hand of God afflicting the Philistines with tumors and death makes it clear that it is not the ark itself that is doing them harm but God personally (5:6-12; 6:5).

Although the ark of the covenant is undoubtedly associated with God's presence, the texts never speak of God actually dwelling inside the ark. When the ark is in the Most Holy Place, God is said to make himself present by appearing over the mercy seat or *kapporet*, yet this does not suggest that God was thought to have imbued the ark with some type of mysterious divine power associated with his holiness or that he actually resided in or upon it.[89] Rather, like the sanctuary itself and the Most Holy Place, the ark served as a symbol of God's presence. If God was said to make himself present in a special way at his sanctuary or in proximity to the ark, he nevertheless continued to dwell in heaven at the same time. The question of how he could remain in heaven and yet be present at particular times and places on earth is never addressed in the biblical texts. Even when he acted on earth, however, he could be said to be acting from heaven as well.

While many scholars claim to find in the account of the death of Nadab and Abihu in Lev 10:1-7 the idea that God's holiness can suddenly strike out at those who draw near to him against his will, in reality the passage never suggests such an idea. According to the narrative, the reason that Nadab and Abihu are struck dead by God is not that they draw near to him but that they offer him incense in a way that he had not prescribed or approved of: "each took his censer, put fire in it, and laid incense on it, and they offered unholy fire before the LORD, such as he had not commanded them" (v. 1). Rather than affirming that Nadab and Abihu were struck dead by God's holiness, the passage states that "fire came out from the presence of the LORD and consumed them" (v. 2). The people are then told that God's wrath will come upon the whole community if Aaron and his other sons mourn the death of Nadab and Abihu (vv. 2, 6). There is nothing in the passage, therefore, that would support the idea that God's holiness was conceived of as some type of mysterious power or force that endangered anyone who came too close to him. What strikes Nadab and Abihu dead is not God's holiness but the fire that comes out of his presence, and the reason that God is angered with them is not that they have come too near to him but that they offered him incense in a manner that ran contrary to his will.

A similar account appears in Numbers 16. There a group of Levites led by Korah challenge the leadership of Moses and Aaron and in particular their position as mediators between God and the people because the members of this group desire that position for themselves. Moses tells Korah and those who have sided with him to present themselves the following day with their censers of incense at the entrance of the sanctuary alongside Aaron and Moses so that God can "make known who is his and who is holy and who will be

---

89. See Exod 25:22; 30:6; Lev 16:2; Num 7:89.

allowed to draw near to him" (v. 5). When they do as Moses has commanded, God tells Moses and Aaron to stand apart from Korah and his group and the earth opens up and swallows the latter together with all of their families and belongings (vv. 20-32). Immediately thereafter fire is said to come out from the LORD and consume the other Levites who had joined themselves to Korah's rebellion. In the following chapter, after God makes it clear that he has chosen Aaron and the Levites to serve him by producing buds and ripe almonds on Aaron's staff, the other Israelites express their fear that "everyone who draws near to the tabernacle of the LORD will die" (Num 17:12-13).

Here, as in the passage from Leviticus 10 just considered, the sin of those who are destroyed by the fire that is said to proceed from God's presence consists not of drawing nearer to God than his holiness would allow but rather disobeying what God has commanded regarding the leadership of Moses and Aaron. Similarly, the reason why it is affirmed that Israelites who are not Levites will die if they approach the tabernacle is not that they pose some threat to God's holiness but that God has not chosen them to serve him in that capacity. Although the passage speaks of the need for those who approach God to be holy, the idea is that they must have been chosen and designated by God himself in order to enter into his presence and serve as mediators between him and the people. Furthermore, Korah and those who die are not struck by God's holiness but are instead swallowed up by the earth or consumed by the fire that comes out from God's presence. Passages such as this one from Numbers therefore provide no basis for scholars to affirm that the Levites were thought to "protect the people as a whole by occupying the danger zone around God's dwelling" or to serve as "a lightning rod, whereby God's wrath was turned away from the whole people and concentrated on them."[90]

In several passages from the Hebrew Bible, it is said to be dangerous to look upon God. When the prophet Isaiah has a vision in which he sees God sitting on his throne with seraphim in attendance above him, for example, he exclaims: "Woe is me! I am lost, for I am a man of unclean lips, and I live among a people of unclean lips, yet my eyes have seen the King, the LORD of hosts!" (Isa 6:5). Other passages speak of God appearing to persons such as Hagar, Jacob, Moses, Aaron, the elders of the people, and an Israelite man named Manoah.[91] While in some of these passages it is said that any who see God will die as a result, those who gaze upon God are *not* said to die. For that reason, these passages do not see death as an automatic consequence of contemplating God but instead suggest that God was generally thought to cause the death of any who saw him, though he might also decide to allow them to live. In any case, the logic underlying such passages is not that God's presence or holiness represents a danger for those who draw near to him, but that under most circumstances he does not allow sinful human beings to look

---

90. Goldingay, *Israel's Gospel*, 446; Wenham, *Leviticus*, 64.
91. See Gen 16:13; 32:30; Exod 24:9-11; 33:17-23; Judg 13:19-23; cf. Exod 19:21; Judg 6:22-23.

at him. Other passages speak of those who hear God fearing for their lives, yet what arouses that fear is not God's holiness per se but his sovereign power and greatness (Exod 20:19; Deut 4:33; 5:23-26). None of these passages, therefore, provide any basis for the claim that God's holiness was thought to be dangerous in and of itself.

From a biblical perspective, the notion that a particular object or place could bring blessing to people by means of some positive substance or force that radiated out from it is problematic not only because the Hebrew Scriptures never speak in such terms but also because such a notion would have been fundamentally at odds with the understanding of God and God's will that runs throughout those Scriptures. If such a substance or force had been thought to exist, then what would have mattered was obtaining access to it or gaining power over it in order to use and manipulate it for one's own ends. In that case, what would bring blessings and well-being would be that substance or force in itself rather than behavior that is in accordance with God's will. Instead of acting personally in relation to human beings in order to do whatever he believed would be most conducive to their well-being and promote among them ways of living and behaving that contributed to that well-being, God would have imbued certain objects and places with a mysterious power that could benefit people automatically, independently of how they lived or behaved. Their blessing would no longer depend on God's activity in their life or his favorable response to their obedience to the commandments he had given them for their good, but on their access to the object or place that contained such a power.

Furthermore, rather than promoting the people's well-being, any place or object that might bring blessing by means of some type of divine energy, substance, or force that radiated out from it would undermine the practice of justice and righteousness and become a source of conflict. Instead of seeking God's blessings by obeying the commandments he had given to promote justice and righteousness, people would instead selfishly seek wealth, power, good fortune, and other things that they desired for themselves by attempting to gain access to the place or object that might confer these things on them. They would also fight to gain possession over the place or object and control access to it, thereby doing harm to one another. Instead of promoting greater love and solidarity among the people, therefore, the sacred place or object would encourage the pursuit of selfish desires and interests and lead to conflict and strife.

Of course, it might be claimed that the sacred places and objects associated with God's presence or power would bring blessings only for those who were dedicated to doing his will by obeying his commandments. Even in that case, however, those places and objects would promote selfishness and injustice rather than the practice of righteousness and solidarity. If God were thought to have imbued the ark of the covenant with some mysterious, inherent power to bless and prosper those who kept it in their midst as long as they obeyed his commandments, for example, he would have been encouraging among his people an obedience that would be motivated purely by self-interest rather than a sincere love for him and others. Instead of striving to do his will out of a conviction that *in and of itself* a life of obedience to all that he had commanded was in their best interest due to the intrinsic consequences of such a life, people would merely practice an outward obedience to his commandments in an effort to procure for themselves the benefits afforded magically or mysteriously by the ark's presence among them. As a result, they would *not* truly live in accordance with God's will, since by definition any who obey God only in order to receive something they selfishly seek for themselves in exchange for that obedience will not obey him in the way he desires. Furthermore, instead of making God the object of their love, trust, and devotion, people would seek out the ark or the object that imparted blessings to them for its own sake and in essence make an idol of it by loving it, placing their trust in it, and devoting themselves to it as the source of the blessings they sought. In that case, God would be promoting idolatry through the idolatrous worship of the object that he had endowed with mysterious powers.

The same type of problems would arise if the sanctuary dedicated to the God of Israel was thought to impart blessings to people by means of some inherent power that he had bestowed on it. People would be led to believe that God's blessings depended not only on obedience to his commandments but also on their proximity to the place at which he was thought to dwell. In effect, they would see the sanctuary as something akin to an amulet or talisman, mysteriously or magically radiating out to those near to it some type of substance or force that would bring them good fortune in and of itself. Such a belief would once again lead people to the conclusion that what brought them blessing was not the life of justice, righteousness, and mercy that God demanded of them for their own sake but their proximity to the sanctuary. In that case, those who practiced justice and righteousness from a location near the sanctuary would be thought to obtain a greater blessing from God than those who did so from far away. Once people began to view proximity to the sanctuary as an end that was to be pursued alongside the practice of justice and righteousness, their commitment to living in accordance with God's will would be compromised to some extent by their selfish pursuit of the personal gain to be obtained by proximity to the sanctuary due to the mysterious benefic power flowing out of it.

For all of these reasons, both the claim that God's holiness might prove dangerous for people as well as the claim that his holiness might bring blessing in and of itself must be rejected as contrary to the logic that runs throughout the biblical texts. Such claims not only reflect modes of thought that are characteristic of the pagan belief systems of antiquity rather than the faith associated with the God of the Hebrew Bible but also result in conceptions of God that deny both his justice and his holiness.

CHAPTER 9

Consecrating a People Set Apart for Solidarity

As we have seen in the previous chapter, the notion that the God of Israel had commanded his people to present sacrificial offerings and carry out sacrificial rites in order that he might be enabled to tolerate their sin, guilt, and impurity as he dwelled among them to bless them must be rejected as foreign to biblical thought. Nothing in the world he had created prevented or impeded him from acting in any way he desired at any time or making himself present anywhere he wished among sinful, impure, and imperfect human beings. What stood in the way of his efforts and commitment to fill the lives of his people with the good things he intended for them was not anything in him or his nature but rather their failure and refusal to practice justice, righteousness, love, and solidarity in accordance with his will.

In biblical thought, therefore, the challenge that God constantly faces is that of bringing his people to be as fully dedicated and consecrated to their wholeness and well-being as he is. It was this that he sought to accomplish by means of the sacrificial worship he had ordained in the Torah. The many different aspects of that worship were designed to contribute to that objective by reinforcing among his people certain key beliefs and practices and reminding them that he had chosen them and set them apart as his own out of love for them. At the same time, because it was important for them to put away the behaviors that undermined and destroyed their well-being, he had given them prescriptions that would lead them to examine and evaluate their conduct continuously so as to identify and correct anything that might cause them harm. Above all else, however, what he sought was that they might consecrate themselves to a way of life that would enable them not only to obtain the blessing he had pronounced on them in Abraham's day but also to serve as his instrument for blessing all of the families of the earth. In order for that to happen, it was necessary for all to be brought to look to him as a God who was like no other, fully consecrated to nothing else but the well-being of all of his creatures without exception.

PUTTING AWAY SIN THROUGH SACRIFICE

Once it is recognized that in biblical thought the objective of Israel's God was to bring about in his people the way of life necessary for them to enjoy the well-being and wholeness he desired for all, the offering of sacrifice in general as well as the offering of sacrifices for sin in particular must be understood as having the same objective. Rather than being designed to satisfy the demands of God's justice or holiness in order to make it possible for God to bless, forgive, and save people, the sacrificial worship prescribed in the Torah was thought to have the purpose of promoting among God's people the commitment to living in the way he had commanded for the good of all. Like all of the other commandments God had given, the commandments regarding sacrifices for sin and the prescriptions regarding purity were viewed as an expression of God's love for his people rather than being rooted in a concern for himself or the desires and needs of his holy and righteous nature. That love had led him to prescribe a series of sacrificial practices and rites aimed at keeping their commitment to obeying him firm and strong as well as restoring and renewing that commitment in them when they fell into ways of thinking and behaving that did them and others harm.

The commandments regarding sacrifices for sin and the regulations regarding purity helped accomplish that objective in several ways. Like the system of sacrificial worship in general, those commandments and regulations led the people to reflect continually on certain truths regarding God, his loving intentions for them, their identity as his people, and the manner in which they were to relate to him and one another for their own happiness and well-being. They also served as a means by which the people were regularly brought to examine and evaluate their ways of thinking and behaving so as to see if they were observing carefully all that God had commanded. If they had committed some type of injustice or wrongdoing, for their own good and that of others it was important for them to acknowledge their fault, ask for forgiveness, do what was necessary to rectify the harm they had done to the extent that this was possible, and commit themselves anew to obeying the good commandments given by God. Because these things promoted justice and well-being for all, they benefited both the persons who had acted contrary to God's will by bringing them back into conformity with God's commandments as well as those who had been harmed by their injustice or wrongdoing. At the same time, they benefited and strengthened the community as a whole by restoring healthy relationships within it. In addition, those sacrifices allowed the people to express in concrete and palpable ways their renewed commitment to living in the way that God had commanded so that they might enjoy God's blessings of life and well-being.

God's command for the people to offer up sacrifices for unintentional or inadvertent sins made it especially important for the people to pay close attention to their behavior. In order to determine whether or not they had fallen into some type of sin without realizing it, they not only had to examine themselves individually but also had to look to one another for help. In this way, the commandments regarding purification and reparation offerings also served to promote a greater sense of community and solidarity among the people. Because at times these offerings were to be presented not only by individuals but by larger groups of people and entire communities, they brought the people to reflect on individual violations of God's commandments as well as the collective behavior of communities and the people as a whole.

The prescriptions regarding the reparation offerings also promoted the practice of justice and righteousness among the people. According to these prescriptions, those who had wrongly taken money or property from another person were not only to restore what they had taken but also to add further compensation (Lev 5:14–6:7). This practice not only served as a deterrent but also reinforced the idea that sincere repentance for wrongdoing had to take the form of doing whatever one could to undo the damage caused by that wrongdoing. People could hardly be considered to be truly repentant for the wrongs and injustices they had committed and seek God's forgiveness for those wrongs and injustices if they did not act to correct them when they had the opportunity to do so.

Sacrifices for sin were thus a means that God had graciously prescribed for his people to be strengthened in their obedience to God's commandments for their own good. By presenting an offering for sin, those who had sinned acknowledged openly their sin as well as their repentance and their renewed commitment to returning to the way of life that God had commanded. Obviously, there was a cost involved in presenting such an offering. Those who showed themselves willing to assume that cost were at the same time recognizing that they had sinned and manifesting concretely their petition for forgiveness and acceptance within the community of God's people again, as well as their intention to avoid sinning in the same way in the future. It was therefore not the offerings themselves that were thought to please God or obtain his approval and forgiveness but rather the acknowledgment of wrong-doing, the spirit of repentance, the willingness to make reparation, and the renewed commitment to God's will that those who had sinned expressed by making the effort and assuming the cost to present a sacrifice for sin.

According to the prescriptions in Leviticus, in some cases the transgression for which a purification offering was to be presented had to do with the violation of a prescription related to the sacrificial rites themselves or some regulation regarding purity rather than any type of moral wrongdoing. While it might appear that such offenses were of less importance, it must be remembered that everything related to the sacrificial worship of Israel's God contributed to the practice of justice and righteousness among the people not only directly but also indirectly by reminding them of certain truths and reinforcing certain beliefs and practices. If the prescribed rites were to convey properly the truths, ideas, and symbolic meanings associated with them, it was important to observe them in the way that God had commanded. While in some cases the precise meanings of certain aspects of these rites may not have been evident or clear to those participating in them, in those cases their faithful adherence to those rites manifested a willingness to submit obediently to what God had commanded out of faith in him even when they did not fully comprehend the reasons for which God had given certain commandments.

Like the other sacrificial rites that God had prescribed in the Torah, the rites associated with the sacrifices for sin were thought to be full of symbolic meanings and to convey many important truths. Although the rite in which the offerers laid their hand on the head of an animal that they were presenting for sacrifice was prescribed for all of the different types of sacrificial offerings, when it was carried out in connection with sacrifices for sin it may have had a significance or symbolism that was tied to these sacrifices in particular. In addition to indicating that the animal was theirs, those who laid their hands on the animal may have understood themselves to be identifying in some way with its death, perhaps to symbolize that they too were putting to death their sinful self or the sins they had committed. The animal's slaughter at the hands of the offerers and the burning of part of its remains on the altar as an offering to God may similarly have symbolized some type of death to their sin or to the way of being that had led to the sin they committed, as well as a recognition of the gravity of failing to act in accordance with God's commandments and the price that one paid for that failure. The offering of the animal's blood before the symbols of God's presence as well as its disposal at the base of the altar may have represented the rededication of the life of the offerers to God as well as an acknowledgment that their life belonged to him, as did the life of all living beings. The rites with blood may even have symbolized the purification of the sanctuary from the pollution of the people's sins in the way that Jacob Milgrom proposed, even though this purification would not have been thought to be effected by sacrificial blood in a literal or physical sense. In fact, there is no reason to suppose that all of these rites meant exactly the same thing for all of the different people who participated in them or that the meanings ascribed to them remained constant over time. As symbolic acts, they could have had many different meanings for different people at different times.

What must be stressed, however, is precisely that these rites were *symbolic* in nature. Their power and impact was due, not to the manipulation or transmission of invisible substances or forces, but to the truths, ideas, and meanings that they conveyed to those who participated in them, as well as the manner in which they allowed the participants to experience and express in tangible and concrete ways different aspects of their relationships with God and one another. It was one thing for the offerers to ask God for forgiveness verbally and another to do so by means of an offering that manifested palpably and visibly the sincerity and earnestness of their petition. It was one thing to rededicate their lives to God in thoughts and words and another to do so by offering up to God a costly animal victim and watching as its blood was drained from its carcass, sprinkled toward the symbols of God's presence, and poured out at the base of the altar. It was one thing to hear or believe that one had been cleansed of one's sins and forgiven by God and another to experience the sensation of having that cleansing and forgiveness pervade throughout one's body as well as one's soul as a result of having involved one's whole being in the sacrificial rites performed. Such rites had a profound impact on those who participated in them because of the symbolisms they communicated and the transformative power inherent in those symbolisms. It was precisely their transformative power and the impact that they had on the offerers that was thought to have led God to prescribe such rites for his people as a means to strengthening them in their commitment and dedication to all that he had commanded them out of love for them.

Of course, the sacrifices for sin served other purposes as well. Because the priests and Levites retained certain portions of the offerings presented, those offerings were means by which the people provided them with the support they needed to continue to carry out their ministry on behalf of others. The participation of the priests in the rites emphasized their role as mediators between the people and God and reinforced their authority among the people so that they might lead and guide the people in their daily life. In addition to strengthening observance of the commandments among the people in general, those rites served as a deterrent to their falling into sins that might require similar sacrifices in accordance with the law. In fact, it would be impossible to state in any exhaustive manner the meanings associated with the various rites involved and the different ways in which those rites served to bring about in the people a greater commitment to living as God's own and to renew in them the obedience necessary for them to attain the blessings that God desired to pour out on them.

Reconsidering Expiation, Propitiation, and Atonement

The Hebrew verb *kipper* as well as the concepts of purification, expiation, and propitiation should be understood against the background of all of the ideas just considered. While those on whose behalf a purification offering was presented to God were said to be cleansed or purified, it must be stressed that it was not the sacrifice itself or the rites associated with it that were seen as resulting in their cleansing or purification but rather their repentance and renewed commitment to the way of life laid out in God's commandments. Just as those who presented purification offerings after they had been cleansed of skin diseases or some other type of physical impurity had to be clean or pure *before* the offering was presented on their behalf, so also those who presented sacrifices for sin had to be cleansed and purified from their sinful manner of thinking and acting before their sacrifices were offered.

It was therefore not the offering itself that cleansed or purified those on whose behalf it was presented. Rather, the offering was a means by which those who had been cleansed and purified from their sinful conduct and their disobedience to God's will were accepted as clean and pure within the community of God's people once again and were declared to be forgiven. The offerings were not thought to produce some type of salvific "effect" by means of the "mechanics" involved or their *modus operandi*. Rather, the offerings for sin constituted *a petition to God* for forgiveness, acceptance, cleansing, and purification. And the basis upon which God was thought to grant these things was precisely what he saw in the hearts and lives of those on whose behalf those offerings were presented, namely, the intention to turn back to him in loving obedience that the offerers were expressing visibly and concretely by means of their offerings.

Because the cleansing and purification that were associated with sacrifices that were offered for actions that ran contrary to God's will for justice and righteousness did not have to do with questions of bodily purities and impurities, in a sense they were to be understood metaphorically or spiritually. What was involved was a cleansing or purification of people's hearts, minds, lives, and behavior. These things had not become polluted in a literal or physical sense. Nevertheless, it is important to stress that biblical thought is not characterized by the type of marked distinction between the physical and the spiritual that was common in Hellenistic thought. The cleansing or purification of people's hearts, minds, and souls was at the same time understood in terms of a cleansing and purification of their bodies and their entire being. It was *the whole person* that was thought to be cleansed by means of the repentance that they expressed by means of their sacrificial offering. For this reason, it was customary for those who were going to enter into the temple precincts to wash or bathe themselves. This washing and bathing represented not only an outward cleansing but a purification of one's heart and soul as well.

By means of the sacrifices for sin, therefore, those who had done something that had made them unacceptable within the community or had become physically impure in some manner manifested publicly that they had been cleansed from whatever had made them impure or unclean in order to be reincorporated into the community. This was true whether an individual's impurity or uncleanness was physical or bodily or instead involved actions or behaviors that violated what God had commanded. The willingness to present a sacrifice manifested one's acknowledgment that one had been unclean in either a physical or spiritual sense as well as one's desire to be accepted as pure and clean by others within the community once more. Before those who had become unclean in either of these senses were allowed to present their offering, it was necessary for the priest to determine whether they had in fact been purified of their uncleanness, whether in body or in soul. If the priest determined that such was the case, he gave his approval to the offering. The rite thus constituted a petition for acceptance on behalf of those who presented the offering while also signifying the acceptance of that petition on the part of the community as represented by the priest.

At the same time, the fulfillment of the rite under the priest's supervision signified God's acceptance of that petition as well. For that reason, in the prescriptions found in Leviticus it is repeatedly affirmed that when the priest has made purification for the offerers, they shall be forgiven.[1] This forgiveness included both that of God as well as that of the community. The basis for

---

1. See Lev 4:20, 26, 31, 35; 5:10, 13, 16, 18; 6:7; 19:22; Num 15:25-28.

this forgiveness, however, was not the rite itself but the inward and outward purification that had taken place in the offerers. Ultimately, the condition for their acceptance by God and the community was not the sacrificial offering or rite itself but that which it expressed, namely, the cleanness and purity in body and soul to which they had been restored.

According to this understanding of the sacrifices for sin, the basic idea expressed by means of the rites involved was that of becoming acceptable once again after something had happened to render one *unacceptable* in some way. Obviously, the practice of sin and injustice made one unacceptable, independently of whether it was intentional or not, because sin and injustice undermine and destroy human well-being. However, some type of malady or physical impurity could also render one unacceptable within the community, especially when that impurity might affect the members of the community or do them harm. Those who had contracted some type of skin disease that was contagious needed to be isolated from others for their sake, while a woman who had given birth had to be isolated from others for her own sake, so that her body might heal after the trauma it had endured. In these cases, it was not acceptable for certain persons to be in contact with others, not because those persons had done anything wrong, but simply because such contact might be harmful in some way to them or to others.

No matter what had happened to make a person unacceptable, therefore, something had to be done in order to make that person acceptable once again. If some type of wrongdoing or injustice had been committed, those who had committed it were required to acknowledge it, do whatever they could to make it right—especially by making reparation if possible—, and commit themselves to avoiding such behavior in the future so as to live in ways that would permit them and others to enjoy the well-being that God desired for all. However, for the good of the community of which they formed part, they were to do these things not simply in their heart but *publicly*, so as to manifest to the other members of the community their repentance and their renewed commitment to living in conformity with God's commandments. They did so by offering a sacrifice and carrying out the prescribed rites at the sanctuary in the sight of others *after* they had taken all of the steps necessary to be cleansed of the impurity or uncleanness that had resulted from their sin in a figurative or metaphorical sense. In the same way, when they had contracted some type of physical impurity, after they had become cleansed by allowing a natural or physical process of cleansing to take place on its own or by taking steps to cleanse themselves actively in the way that the law prescribed, they then offered a sacrifice of expiation so that they might be accepted within the community once more. Strictly speaking, however, it was not the sacrificial offering or the rite itself that was thought to cleanse them or render them acceptable, but that which had taken place *prior* to the offering and rite and which was subsequently expressed by means of the offering and rite.

When properly understood, the terminology of expiation can be regarded as reflecting accurately the biblical understanding of the process of purification through sacrificial offerings and rites, as long as the idea that those offerings and rites in themselves made atonement or amends for sin is avoided. In a sense, of course, those who made expiation for their sins were making amends or reparation for their sins and transgressions in that they were putting them in the past and doing what was necessary to set things right and restore their relationships with God and others within the community of which they formed part. If the language of atonement is understood in this sense, it may be considered to reflect faithfully biblical thought as well. It is important to stress, however, that what set things right was not the offering itself or the sacrificial rites performed but the willingness of those who had sinned or transgressed to acknowledge their sin or transgression and divorce themselves from it, as well as their promise to avoid sinning or transgressing in the same manner in the future and their commitment to submit obediently once more to God's commandments.

For this reason, it would be a mistake to understand the sacrifices for sin in terms of the payment of some type of penalty or ransom for the sins that had been committed. What set things right was not the sacrificial offering itself but the renewed spirit of obedience to God's will of which it was an expression. What interested God was that justice and wholeness be restored in the community and not simply that some penalty be inflicted on those who had sinned or that some ransom payment be made by them or on their behalf. That objective could be accomplished only by means of the renewed spirit of obedience of which the sacrifices for sin were to serve as a visible and concrete expression. When that spirit was manifested by means of a sacrifice for sin, the sacrifice might be said to make expiation or perhaps even atone for sin, yet strictly speaking this was not true of the sacrifice itself but only of the spirit with which it was offered. What made the offerers pure and clean in God's sight was not the sacrificial offering or rite but the fact that they had purified themselves and their lives from the uncleanness that had been a threat to their own well-being and that of others within the community. Furthermore, this purification and cleansing was not something that they offered God in order to expiate or atone for their sins, since it was not intended to compensate or make up for the sin they had committed. Because it was the community that concerned God rather than his own justice or holiness, the purification and cleansing of the offerers was something that he desired and demanded *not for his own sake but for theirs and for that of the community as a whole.* The same was true of the offering for sin that was to symbolize that purification and cleansing and serve as a means by which the offerers manifested that it had truly taken place.

Ultimately, then, what expiated sin was the repentance and renewed commitment to obedience on the part of those who offered sacrifices for sin. The same must be said with regard to the concept of propitiation. Strictly speaking, what propitiated God or appeased his wrath was not the sacrificial offering or rite itself but the spirit of repentance and renewed obedience of which it was to serve as a visible and tangible expression. Of course, this spirit was manifested not only by means of the offering but also in the form of the spoken or unspoken prayer that accompanied it. It was this idea that led those who composed the Septuagint to use the verbs *exilaskesthai* and *hilaskesthai* to translate the Hebrew *kipper* and led St. Jerome to translate this term with the Latin verbs *orare, rogare, propitiare*, and *expiare* in the Vulgate, since these terms communicate the idea of presenting prayers and petitions to God seeking his favor and forgiveness. In this regard, it is significant to note that when Josephus summarizes in his own words the prayer that Solomon presented to God on the occasion of the dedication of the temple, he attributes to Solomon the idea that it is the prayer or voice of the offerers that propitiates God rather than their sacrificial offerings per se: "For with what else is it more appropriate for us to put away your wrath when you are angry and displeased and be restored to your favor than by the voice that we have from the air and that we know ascends through the air again?" (*Ant.* 8.112). What put away God's wrath was the prayer that was articulated by means of a sacrificial offering and together with it, as long as that prayer was sincere and heartfelt.

It is also important to stress that sacrifices for sin were not intended to address the problem of *guilt* in relation to God in the manner that this has traditionally been understood. According to the pagan conceptions of justice that we have considered in Chapter 4, the obstacle that prevented human beings from enjoying the favor of the gods was guilt, and the manner in which this obstacle was removed was by means of its punishment. To understand sacrifices for sin in that manner would involve claiming that the God of Israel acted in the same way and for the same reasons that the pagan gods of the nations did, demanding that those who had disobeyed him offer him a sacrifice as a penalty or payment for having angered or offended him. When those who had offered up a sacrifice for sin were forgiven, they were not thought to be declared free of guilt or "not guilty." In reality, they *were* guilty of having acted contrary to God's will, and nothing could change this, yet what interested God was not assigning or addressing guilt but rather seeing people cleansed of their sinful behaviors. The basis upon which people sought to be declared and accepted as clean and pure by God was not the sacrifice for sin that they had presented but the cleansing and purification of their hearts, minds, souls, and bodies of which their sacrifice was to be an expression. Similarly, the purpose of sacrifices for sin was not to make it possible for God to tolerate the people's sinfulness or declare them clean in a forensic sense but rather to bring and enable them to be cleansed and purified from the sinful behavior that God refused to tolerate for their own good out of love for them.

Biblical scholars have often debated the question of whether all sacrifices were thought to make expiation and obtain the forgiveness of sins. In the prescriptions found in the Pentateuch, the only sacrifices that are said to be presented in response to sinful actions and to require that a confession of sin or guilt be made prior to their presentation are the offerings for sin. In Lev 1:4 and 9:7, however, burnt offerings are also said to make expiation. According to Lev 16:10, the same was true of the rite with the goat for Azazel, even though the goat was not sacrificed to God.

In order to address that question, it must be remembered that in biblical thought all who approach God by means of their prayers and offerings are sinful and imperfect. For that reason, it is necessary for them to acknowledge their sin and to ask him for forgiveness at the same time that they ask him to accept and grant their petitions in spite of their sinfulness and unworthiness. Of course, because what mattered to God was not their guilt for the sins they had committed but their transformation and their cleansing from the sinful behavior that did them and others harm, as they approached him with their prayers and offerings they not only sought his forgiveness but also asked that he cleanse and purify their hearts, minds, and lives.

In this sense, then, every sacrificial offering was intended to be expiatory. This was not because the offerings presented obtained God's favor, grace, or mercy by satisfying the demands of his righteousness and holiness, however, since by definition his favor, grace, and mercy were a free and unconditional gift given to all people. Whether God granted one's petition or rejected it, he was acting in love, since he was doing what he had determined to be in one's best interest and that of others as well. The reason that all sacrificial offerings were intended to be expiatory is that they were to be a means by which the offerers became cleansed of their sinfulness. What was to cleanse and purify them, however, was not the offering itself but the spirit in which they were to present it as well as their petition to God for him to do what was necessary in their life to enable them to put away their sinfulness and grow in their obedience to his will for their own good.

It is also important to stress once more that nothing prevented God from forgiving people their sins even when they did not offer up sacrifices for sin. All that was necessary to obtain God's forgiveness was to acknowledge and repent of one's sins, commit oneself once more to obeying his good commandments, and ask him for the strength, knowledge, and guidance necessary to live in accordance with his will. Out of love for his people, however, God had commanded that they offer him sacrifices for sin because he desired that the cleansing of the hearts and minds of his people be as profound and thoroughgoing as possible when they had fallen into sinful and destructive behavior. For reasons we have mentioned in the previous two chapters, the rites that God had prescribed contributed to that goal by means of the effect they had, not on God, but on those who participated in them.

For that very reason, it was regarded as important and as necessary for those who had fallen into certain forms of sinful behavior to offer up sacrifices for sin in the way that God had prescribed if they were able to do so. To fail to present an offering when the law commanded it was to act contrary to what God had ordained for the good of all. By definition, those who had sinned could hardly manifest their renewed commitment to obeying all that God had commanded if they failed or refused to offer up the sacrifices that were included among his commandments. The same was true if they did not follow all of the procedures that he had prescribed when they presented their sacrifices. If it was said that the offering of sacrifices for sin or the shedding of blood was necessary to obtain God's forgiveness, therefore, this would have been understood in the sense just affirmed. While it would not be accurate to affirm that God was thought to have commanded such sacrifices or the shedding of sacrificial blood because these things were necessary for the demands of his holy and righteous nature to be satisfied, the fact that God had commanded that his people offer him those sacrifices and carry out the rites with sacrificial blood in the way that he had prescribed when it was possible for them to do so did make it necessary for his people to obey his command if they wished to obtain his forgiveness and acceptance once more.

The Cleansing of Yom Kippur

In general terms, the rites prescribed for *Yom Kippur* were thought to fulfill the same purpose as the sacrifices for sin that were offered when people had violated some commandment of the Torah. By setting apart an entire day to examine their behavior over the previous year, acknowledge their wrongdoing, ask God for forgiveness, and participate in rites that symbolized their repentance and contrition as well as their cleansing from all of the sins that they had committed, that cleansing became a reality in the lives of the people. While they focused on the past as they reflected on their conduct and acknowledged their failure to fulfill God's good intentions for them, they did so with the future in mind, since the primary purpose was not to rid themselves of guilt but to commit themselves to putting their wrongdoing behind them in order to return more fully to the way of life that God commanded of all for their own good.

According to the prescriptions found in Leviticus 16, before carrying out any rites on behalf of others, the high priest was to make expiation for his own sins and those of his household (vv. 6-14). The idea seems to be that before the high priest intercedes for others by means of the sacrifice for sins that he is to present, he must first ask God to forgive and cleanse him from his own sins. The high priest can hardly serve as God's instrument to bring his people to acknowledge their sin and commit themselves to turning away from it if he does not first do so himself. Nor can he represent the people before God imploring his forgiveness for the people's sins with sincerity and dedication if he is not truly repentant for his own sin and wrongdoing. The priority of the high priest's offering on his own behalf no doubt had to do as well with his responsibility as the one designated by God to guide and instruct his people in the path that he had laid out for them. The purification offering that he presented for himself and his household was to symbolize the same things mentioned above in relation to the purification offerings in general, namely, his own repentance, his renewed commitment to living in accordance with God's commandments, and the cleansing of his heart, mind, soul, and body from sin and disobedience.

The commandment for the high priest to present a purification offering for his own sins may have served to stress another idea as well. Among most peoples in antiquity, those who were in the most elevated positions of leadership, such as the rulers and the high priests, often claimed to be infallible and without fault as those who represented the gods and stood in their place. Rather than recognizing their own errors, wrongdoings, injustices, and violations of the law, they justified everything they did as good, just, and right and considered themselves to be above the law. In this way, they became oppressive figures who identified their own will with the will of the divinity. By mandating that the high priest first present a purification offering for his own sins, the Mosaic law emphasized that he was just as sinful and imperfect as the rest of the people and therefore had no right to place himself above them as the sole arbiter of God's will, as if he alone spoke for God or represented him in relation to the people. It is also worth noting that the prescriptions for *Yom Kippur* do not assign any role to Israel's king in the rites to be performed and therefore suppose that the king was to stand alongside the rest of the people as the rites were carried out. Those rites thus communicated the idea that all were to be subject equally to God as the sole sovereign among the people and were to submit equally to God's commandments as well. No one, including especially the leaders of the people, was above the law or was morally superior to the rest. On the contrary, all were sinful and unjust and constantly in need of God's mercy and forgiveness.

After the high priest presented the purification offering for himself and his household, he was to present a second purification offering on behalf of the people. In both cases, he was to go before the symbols of God's presence to sprinkle the blood of the purification offerings there. He was also to go out to the altar of burnt offerings at the entrance of the sanctuary to make expiation with the sacrificial blood on its behalf. In Lev 16:16-19, it is said that the high priest makes expiation for the sanctuary and the altar because of the impurities, sins, transgressions, and iniquities of the people and that the rite with blood at the altar cleanses and sanctifies it from the people's impurities. On the basis of all that we have seen previously, these affirmations should be understood in a metaphorical or figurative sense rather than a literal one.

The basic meaning that was to be ascribed to these rites seems fairly self-evident and straightforward. They served as a reminder to the people that they were far from living in the way that God had commanded for their own good and that they constantly needed to evaluate and amend their behavior. At the same time, those rites stressed the grace and mercy of God, who continued to dwell among his people to hear their prayers and receive their offerings in spite of their sinfulness and unworthiness. Those who drew near to God at the sanctuary and presented their offerings to him on the altar over the course of the previous year had indeed polluted his temple in a figurative sense, since they were never entirely free of sin nor fully consecrated to God in the way that they should be. In addition, by bringing to mind their sinfulness, the rites reminded the people that if God did not respond favorably to their petitions by granting them what they sought when they offered up sacrifices to him on the altar throughout the year, it was not due to a lack of love for them but rather due to their ongoing need for cleansing, purification, and correction. If he chose to deny them what they asked of him, it was because in his love for them he considered that such a response was in their best interest. The petitions embodied by the offerings they presented to him, therefore, were to be understood in terms of asking him to do what was necessary to cleanse and purify their hearts and minds as well. The sacrificial rites carried out on *Yom Kippur*, then, conveyed all of these meanings and many more, thus leading the people to reflect on many different aspects of their relation to God and to one another.

As in other rites associated with the ideas of cleansing and purification, what was actually thought to cleanse and purify the people of their sins on *Yom Kippur* was not the rites themselves but the repentance and renewed commitment to obedience that they expressed by means of the rites. In that sense, it was not God or the high priest who purified the people but the people themselves, especially by humbling themselves in the manner prescribed (Lev 16:29-31; 23:27-29; Num 29:7). In the words of Philo, the people's participation in the rites prescribed for *Yom Kippur* conveyed the idea that those who had sinned were "purified by conversion to the better life, and through their new obedience washed away their old disobedience to the law" (*Spec. Laws* 1.188). Nevertheless, the rites also played a role in that purification by leading the people to reflect on their behavior and purify and cleanse their hearts. The symbolisms communicated and the various stimuli that the people experienced by means of the rites also contributed to that end. It is important to stress once more, however, that God wanted them to be clean and pure in their ways of thinking, acting, and behaving not for *his* sake but for *theirs*.

The rite with the goat for Azazel reinforced many of these same ideas. Because it conveyed symbolic meanings rather than effecting any type of actual elimination of the people's sins, there is no reason to suppose that it was thought to deal with sins that were in some way distinct from those for which the purification offering for the people had been presented a short while earlier. It simply involved expressing in a different way the same basic ideas and truths associated with the purification offering, as well as others. In particular, the rite communicated the idea that in response to their contrition and repentance as well as their renewed commitment to living in accordance with all that God had commanded for their own good, he put his people's sins in the past and cast them far off so as to eliminate them definitively from his consideration and memory.

After the goat had been led out to the wilderness, the high priest was to bathe and then offer up two burnt offerings, one for himself and one for the people (Lev 16:23-25). As was the case in other contexts, these sacrifices were means by which the high priest and the people were to symbolize and express the offering up to God of themselves and all that they had as well as their full consecration to him and his will. As we have noted previously, the burnt offerings represented the most complete expression of dedication to God, since no part of the offering was left for the priests or offerers. The person who had led the goat out to the wilderness as well as those who disposed of the remains of the animal victims that had been presented as a purification offering and whose blood had been sprinkled before God were also to bathe (16:26-28). This bathing would also have been understood as a symbolic act, though the contact with animal carcasses and other aspects of the rite may have been thought to make those persons impure in a physical sense as well.

As we have observed previously, nothing in the biblical texts suggests that the rites prescribed for *Yom Kippur* were necessary for God to forgive the people's sins, refrain from punishing or abandoning them, or continue to bless them with his presence among them. There is a sense, however, in which those rites can be spoken of as necessary. They were necessary for the people to grasp and experience the ideas and truths that they were designed to convey, precisely because they communicated those ideas and truths in a way that went far beyond anything that might be accomplished by words alone. A simple verbal pronouncement by a priest that God had forgiven them their sins in light of their acknowledgment and repentance of those sins could never have the same impact as the type of rites carried out at the tabernacle or temple before the people's eyes. When the high priest emerged from the Most Holy Place after he had entered there to sprinkle the blood of a sacrificial animal before the symbols of God's presence while bowing reverently and fervently imploring God's mercy and forgiveness, the impact on those who stood observing would have been extremely powerful. The idea that through the high priest they had sought God's forgiveness with all of their heart and had been granted that forgiveness in light of their repentance would not simply be something that the people imagined abstractly in their minds but something that was impressed deeply on them through their participation in the rite. Many would be deeply moved and touched by the solemnity of the rite carried out by the high priest in a stunning and elegant vestment with a bowl full of the blood that had been drained from two animals that had been slaughtered before their eyes. These rites would touch the people present in both body and soul and be charged with a significance and a power that words alone could never capture or express. Not only would they be told verbally that God had forgiven them all of their sins and wrongdoing on account of their repentance and renewed commitment to obeying his commandments, but they would actually *feel* and *experience* that forgiveness in their entire being after they had expressed that repentance and commitment by means of the rites carried out by the high priest.

In a similar manner, the rite carried out with the goat for Azazel would allow the people to express outwardly and concretely by means of powerful symbolisms the idea that they wished to be rid of their sins and transgressions permanently and to experience in the depth of their being the sensation of having their sins forgiven and put out of God's sight for good. One can only imagine the profound impact that such a rite would have had on all who participated in it, or even on those who had not been present but imagined it being carried out in their mind from afar. No doubt as the priest confessed audibly the sins of the people over the goat with passion and conviction, those present made that confession their own by joining in with verbal exclamations and bodily expressions such as beating their breast. In this way, they put their whole being into the confession that was made. As the goat was led away, they would almost certainly have heaped upon it expressions of revulsion and contempt through shouts and cries, perhaps waving their fist in the air and making other gestures that symbolized a loathing, not for the goat itself, but for the sins and transgressions that it was figuratively carrying and embodying and that they wished to put away from themselves for good. As the goat disappeared from sight, there must have been expressions of joy and celebration among the people, despite the solemnity of the occasion. The rite communicated the idea that, just as assuredly as the goat had gone out to the wilderness to perish there and never return, so also had God put their sins out of his sight for good. What gave them this assurance, however, was not the rite itself or the fact that it had been done properly down to the last detail, but rather the sincerity of the repentance and renewed commitment to obedience that they had manifested by means of their participation in the rite.

BEARING SIN AND INIQUITY

Throughout the Pentateuch, a number of passages speak of certain individuals bearing sin, including especially the priests and those who have violated some commandment. Because this phrase is used in Lev 16:20-22 to affirm that the goat for Azazel bore the people's sins when it was led out to the desert after the high priest had confessed those sins while placing his hands on the goat's head, many interpreters have claimed that other passages that use the language of bearing sin in the context of allusions to sacrifice are to be understood on the basis of the same basic idea. It is also common to understand the phrase in the sense of bearing the punishment or penalty for sin rather than sin itself.

A close look at the Mosaic prescriptions, however, reveals that outside of Lev 16:20-22 they never refer to people or sacrificial victims bearing sins in the same sense that the goat for Azazel was said to bear the sins and iniquities of the people on *Yom Kippur*. The animals presented as offerings for sin are never said to bear sins, nor are those who present animals for sacrifice ever said to transfer their sins to them. In many passages, to bear sin or iniquity simply means to be guilty of some action contrary to God's command and on that account to be required to offer up a sacrifice for sin or to be subject to some type of punishment.[2] In some cases, to bear sins involves being cut off from the community, though this is obviously not equivalent to being put to death.[3] When the sin involved is considered more serious, however, to bear sin may involve being sentenced to a death penalty (Lev 22:8-9; 24:15-16). In Num 14:33-35, after the Israelites have sinned by not trusting in God's ability to deliver the land he had promised them into their hands, he tells them through Moses that before they enter that land they will need to bear their iniquity by spending forty years in the wilderness. While this involves being subjected to God's chastisements, neither in this context nor in any other context are people said to bear the sin or sins of others in the sense of enduring some type of punishment that they deserve in their place.

In this regard, it is important to stress once more that the offering of sacrifice was not thought to be equivalent to the payment of a penalty or fine. Such an idea is suggested by English versions of the Bible such as the NRSVue, which refers to those who have sinned being "subject to punishment" instead of bearing their iniquity when translating the Hebrew phrase *nasa' 'avon* in Lev 5:1 and 5:17.[4] The same idea is reflected in the NRSVue translation of Lev 5:6, where the command to present an offering for the sin one has committed is replaced by an allusion to a "penalty for the sin." In these cases, what was required of those who had violated some commandment of the law was not that they be penalized by having to offer up a sacrifice but that they acknowledge their sin and manifest their intention to submit once more to God's commandments by purifying their hearts and asking God for forgiveness by means of the offering they were to present. What interested God and satisfied his justice was not imposing penalties on sinners as an end in itself but bringing them to repent of their sin and put it behind them by returning to him in obedience. The offerings for sin were means by which people were to manifest their intention to do these things. In these passages, then, to bear sin is not to be subject to punishment or a penalty but to assume one's responsibility for the sin that one has committed and carry out the rites prescribed, while at the same time imploring God's forgiveness with a sincere heart.

Although in some contexts to bear sin or iniquity can be said to involve bearing guilt, the use of the language of guilt in sacrificial contexts must be considered problematic. Many English versions of the Hebrew Bible use the word "iniquity" to translate the Hebrew *'avon*, yet at times this Hebrew term can refer not to the act itself but to the condition or state resulting from the act.[5] In these cases, it is common to translate the Hebrew phrase in terms of bearing guilt rather than bearing iniquity. Because in English guilt is generally seen as something that requires some type of punishment or penalty, this idea tends to be read back into the Hebrew text when the language of

---

2. See Lev 5:1-3; 22:15-16; cf. 7:18; 19:17.

3. See Lev 17:14-16; 19:5-8; 20:17-20; Num 5:27-31; 9:13.

4. On this translation, see also Lev 19:8; 20:17, 19.

5. See, for example, Exod 28:38, 43; Lev 5:1, 17; 7:18; 10:17; 17:16; 22:16; Num 5:31; 14:34; 15:31.

guilt is used. In Hebrew, however, those who are said to bear iniquity are not necessarily subject to punishment on account of their guilt but are simply required to acknowledge their sin and deal with it in some way. When they do so by means of a sacrificial offering, that offering serves as an expression of their contrition and repentance and constitutes a petition for forgiveness. Because sacrificial offerings were not viewed as penalties or punishments, in these cases the guilt is taken away not by being punished but by being assumed by the one who is guilty and dealt with by means of a rite that serves as a concrete manifestation of the intention of the offerer to turn back to God in obedience to his will.

In several passages from Leviticus and Numbers, priests or Levites are said to bear the sin of the people in the sense of offering up sacrifices for sin on their behalf (Lev 10:16-18; Num 18:1-7, 22-24). This does not involve any type of substitution, penalty, or punishment, however. The cost of such sacrifices was to be borne by the guilty or by the community as a whole, and the priests or Levites were not being subjected personally to any type of penalty by means of the requirement to carry out the sacrificial rite on behalf of those who had sinned. In fact, they were to receive for themselves a portion of what they offered up as a sacrifice. In these cases, the priests or Levites bore the sins of the people in the sense of assuming the task and responsibility of seeking and obtaining forgiveness for those who had sinned by interceding for them and carrying out the prescribed sacrificial rites on their behalf.

When the Mosaic prescriptions speak of bearing sin, therefore, they do not have in mind any type of substitution or transfer of sin or guilt. Those prescriptions also provide no basis for the claim that those who laid their hand upon an animal before it was sacrificed were thought to be transferring sin and guilt or some type of penalty to it. As noted above, the only passage that speaks in such terms is Lev 16:20-22, yet this passage is unique not only in that it associates the rite of laying hands on the head of an animal with the confession of sins but also in that it mandates that two hands are to be placed upon the animal's head. The fact that those who offered up burnt offerings and offerings of well-being were to lay their hand on the animal before it was sacrificed also suggests that this action was not understood in terms of transferring sin to the animal to be sacrificed, since those offerings were not presented for sin or guilt. Likewise, when those who were poor presented a measure of flour for their purification offering, they did not lay hands upon it or do anything that might be understood in terms of a transfer of their sins to it. Obviously, they were not subjecting the flour to any type of vicarious punishment. There is therefore no reason to read back into the prescriptions to lay one's hand on an animal to be sacrificed the idea of any type of transfer of sin.

The biblical texts also provide no support for the idea that those who offered up sacrificial animals were thought to be designating those animals as their representatives in order to be joined in some mysterious way to their death or to die together with them in a mystical sense. Such an interpretation once again assumes that what interested God was that the sins people committed be borne in the sense of receiving the punishment they deserved. In sacrificial contexts, to bear sin was not to bear punishment or a penalty but to acknowledge one's sin and assume responsibility for doing what was necessary to deal with that sin and the harm it had done in the way that God had commanded.

THE SERVANT WHO TAKES AWAY SIN BY BEARING IT (ISAIAH 53)

Among many interpreters of the Hebrew Scriptures, the idea that to bear the sin or guilt of others involves enduring the punishment that their sin deserves in their place has especially been associated with Isaiah 52:13–53:12 (hereafter simply Isaiah 53). This passage has played an important role in Christian thought due to the claim that it foretold what would happen to Christ. There, after describing the sufferings and afflictions of a figure who is referred to as God's servant, the Hebrew text speaks of the servant suffering for the transgressions of others, offering up his life as a guilt offering, bearing the iniquities of those whom he makes righteous, and bearing the sin of many while pouring himself out to death (Isa 53:5, 10-12). Due to the influence of this passage in Christian thought as well as the interpretations of Christ's death that are based on the idea of penal substitution, it has been common to claim that the passage represents the clearest statement in the Hebrew Bible of the idea that bearing the sin, iniquity, and guilt of others involves offering up to God as a sacrifice the life of a victim who endures in the place of the guilty the punishment that their sins deserve.

A careful consideration of the main ideas found in the passage, however, indicates that such a reading is entirely foreign to it. There is no need to address here the question of the identity of the servant mentioned in the passage in order to grasp what it affirms concerning the servant and his suffering and death on behalf of others. Nor is there any need to examine any of the traditional interpretations of the passage to see that it does not contain many of the ideas that have been read back into it.[6] There can be little question that the servant is a prophetic figure. This means that his relation to the people who are mentioned in the passage and are presented there as the speakers is that of a prophet sent to call them to repentance. For that very reason, he is referred to as God's servant, since he serves God by carrying out among the sinful people the prophetic task given to him.

At its outset, the passage describes the manner in which the servant's marred and grotesque appearance startles and astonishes those who gaze upon him (Isa 52:14–53:2). These onlookers include kings and people of other nations. It refers to him as one who "was despised and rejected by others, a man of sorrows and acquainted with infirmity. He was despised

---

6. For a more complete consideration of the text of Isaiah 53 and the scholarly discussion on the interpretation of this passage, see David A. Brondos, *Jesus' Death in New Testament Thought*, vol. 1: *Background* (Mexico City: Theological Community of Mexico, 2018), 203-22.

as one from whom others hide their faces, and we held him of no account" (53:3). The passage then continues:

> Surely he has borne our infirmities and carried our diseases, yet we accounted him stricken, struck down by God, and afflicted. But he was wounded for our transgressions, crushed for our iniquities; upon him was the chastisement that made us whole, and by his bruises we have been healed. We have all gone astray like sheep; we have all turned to our own way, and the LORD has laid on him the iniquity of us all. He was oppressed and afflicted, yet he did not open his mouth; like a lamb that is led to the slaughter and like a sheep that is silent before its shearers, so he did not open his mouth. By a perversion of justice he was taken away (53:4-8).

These verses attribute the servant's suffering to the people and their sins. The sins of the speakers can be regarded as responsible for the servant's suffering in two different ways. First, the passage clearly describes the servant being mistreated and abused by others. He is bruised, oppressed, and afflicted by at least some of the people, who lead him to the slaughter like a sheep and take him away by a perversion of justice. When he was treated in this way, he did not protest or strike out at his abusers but remained silent. In order to understand the logic of this passage, it is important to stress that much of the servant's suffering is caused by some of the people themselves, who treat him with violence due to no fault of his own. The servant can therefore be said to suffer as a result of the people's sins in the sense that the sins they commit against him and the violence they inflict on him lead him to be bruised, disfigured, and afflicted.

At the same time, the passage refers to sufferings that result from infirmities and diseases. The people who observe the servant are presented as concluding that God himself is also responsible for his sufferings, since he struck down the servant and subjected him to afflictions. The passage relates God's treatment of the righteous and innocent servant to the people's sins: he is wounded and crushed for *their* transgressions and iniquities rather than any of his own. They affirm that "the LORD has laid on him the iniquity of us all." This affirmation, in combination with the allusion to the punishment that made the people whole being laid upon the servant, has led interpreters to understand the passage in terms of penal substitution: the punishment that the people deserved and that God's justice demanded was inflicted on the servant rather than the guilty people themselves, and as a result they were healed and made whole in the sense of being forgiven.

There is no reason to believe, however, that the readers of this text in antiquity would have understood it in that manner. Instead, they would have related the sufferings of the servant to the people's sins on the basis of their understanding of his prophetic task and role. Because the people had fallen into sin and injustice and were going astray like sheep, in order for them to be restored to wholeness it was necessary for God to do something to correct them and bring them back to himself. Only by abandoning their sinful and destructive behavior could they be healed and made whole. As we have seen repeatedly in the present study, this is the understanding of the plight of God's people that runs throughout the Hebrew Scriptures as a whole. Readers of the passage in antiquity familiar with the biblical texts would therefore have presupposed these ideas and looked to them as a basis for interpreting the passage. They would also have seen the servant as one who had been sent by God to carry out the same task that he gave to all of his prophets, namely, that of calling the people to put away their sinful and unjust behavior and turn back to him in repentance and obedience. In biblical thought, this is the indispensable condition for people to be made whole.

According to the logic of the passage, therefore, it was the people's sinfulness that had made it necessary for God to send his servant to turn them away from their sin and bring them back to himself. Rather than heeding the servant's call to repentance, however, the people mistreated, oppressed, wounded, bruised, and abused him. In that regard, they were responsible for his sufferings. At the same time, however, there is a sense in which God was also responsible for the servant's sufferings. It was God who not only sent the servant into the people's midst but also willed for him to remain there when the people were mistreating and abusing him. Even if the infirmities and diseases that the servant endures are seen as resulting from an act of God, they are also related in some way to the servant's activity and presence in the midst of the sinful, unjust, and violent people. This may be because he becomes sick and diseased as a result of the mistreatment he receives at the hands of the people.

However, God may also have afflicted the servant with the infirmities and diseases mentioned for some other reason. He may have allowed for the servant's appearance to be especially gruesome in the eyes of others in order to make an even stronger impression on them, or he may have wished to test the servant in order to increase his resolve by making the performance of his prophetic task even more difficult for him. What must be stressed is that the infirmities and diseases that the servant suffers are those of the people as well: "he has borne *our* infirmities and carried *our* diseases." It might even be concluded that his presence among the sick and diseased people led him to become infected with the same sicknesses and diseases that they were suffering. In any case, it is important to note that the passage does not speak of him enduring the people's infirmities and diseases *in their place* but rather bearing their infirmities and diseases *together with them*. It is also possible that these infirmities and diseases are intended to be understood in a spiritual sense rather than a physical one. In that case, the passage would be characterizing the people's sinful behavior as infirm and diseased.

Once these ideas are understood, the second sense in which the servant is being wounded and crushed for the people's transgressions and iniquities and bearing their sins becomes clear. He is suffering not only because of the sins, injustice, and violence that he is enduring at the people's hands but also because he remains faithful to his task of calling on the people to abandon their sinful behavior and turn back to God. It is the people's sins that have made it necessary for God to send him into the people's midst in order to carry out that task, as well as their stubborn persistence in their sins and transgressions that requires that he continue to be active among them if he is to succeed in that task. In other words, if the people are to be saved from their sins in the sense of being delivered from their sinful behavior, the servant has no choice but to continue to carry out his prophetic activity among them in spite of the tremendous suffering that he must endure as a result of doing so.

To whatever extent God is directly responsible for the servant's ailments, therefore, he is also responsible for the suffering that the servant endures because he is the one who has sent the servant into the midst of the sinful, unjust, and violent people and wills that he remain there, despite the suffering that this entails for the servant. At the same time, the people's sins are responsible for that suffering both in the sense that they sin by means of the suffering that they inflict on the servant and in the sense that it is their sinfulness and their need to be saved from that sinfulness that has made it necessary for God to send the servant as his prophet into their midst. He is being wounded and crushed because of his faithfulness to his God-given task of saving the people from the sins, iniquities, and transgressions into which they have fallen and which they continue to commit. For the reasons already mentioned, the servant's presence and prophetic activity among the people has resulted in all of the infirmities, diseases, wounds, bruises, and afflictions that he is said to endure. Because it is the sins that the people are committing as well as God's desire to save the people from their sinful behavior by means of the servant that have made the servant's presence and prophetic activity among the people necessary, the servant is said to bear the people's infirmities and diseases and to be wounded and crushed for their transgressions and iniquities. Yet because he has been sent by God and God insists that he continue to carry out his work among the people in spite of the intense suffering that this entails, it can also be said that God himself is subjecting the servant to afflictions.

The affirmation that "the LORD has laid on him the iniquity of us all" would have been understood against the background of these same ideas. God laid the people's iniquity on the servant in the sense that he assigned to the servant the task of bringing the people to turn away from their iniquity and abandon their sinful behavior. In other words, what God laid on the servant was not the iniquity of the people per se, as if that iniquity could be objectified or materialized into some type of mysterious substance or force and subsequently transmitted to the servant. Nor did God lay the people's guilt on the servant and on that basis make the servant suffer for that guilt. Rather, what God laid on the servant was the task of bringing the people to put away their iniquity as well as the suffering that resulted both from his faithfulness to that task and his mistreatment at the people's hands.

In this regard, it is important to stress that the Hebrew word translated as "chastisement" or "punishment" in the passage is *musar*, the same term we considered in Chapter 5. As we saw there, this Hebrew term refers to correction or discipline rather than simply punishment per se. When people fall into sinful behavior, as the speakers in the passage have done, what God seeks is not to inflict punishment on them to satisfy his justice and make them pay for that behavior but to correct them by subjecting them to sufferings that will bring them to repent of their sinful behavior and turn back to him in obedience. The sufferings he inflicts on those who sin are therefore to serve as a means to their correction.

In this case, however, it is not the people who endure the sufferings of which the passage speaks but the servant. This means that rather than subjecting the people themselves to the suffering necessary to chastise and correct them, God subjects the servant to that suffering by sending him into the midst of the sinful and violent people and having him remain there. In other words, it is the servant who suffers the chastisement aimed at bringing the people to repent of their sins rather than the people themselves. In this sense, it can be said that the servant is suffering what the people deserve in their place or stead. Because God's purpose is not to inflict punishment for its own sake but to bring about correction, however, this does not involve penal substitution. The idea is not that God is inflicting the punishment that his justice demands on the servant instead of the people and that, once he has done so, the demands of that justice will have been satisfied and as a result the people can be spared from having to endure that punishment themselves. Instead, the idea is that the means that God is employing to bring the people back to himself in repentance and obedience is that of subjecting the servant rather than the people themselves to the sufferings and chastisements that are necessary to correct the people's behavior.

The sufferings that the servant endures enable that objective to be accomplished in a couple of ways. First, his willingness to endure the sufferings that result from his presence and prophetic activity among the sinful people makes it possible for him to continue to call them to repentance. Eventually, his persistence in his prophetic task despite the suffering it entails leads at least some of the people to turn away from their sinful and destructive behavior. Second and more importantly, however, the patient resolve that he demonstrates in the midst of the suffering and rejection he experiences as well as his willingness to endure the mistreatment that leads to his disfigured and ghastly appearance make a profound impression on the people. What astonishes and startles them and leaves them speechless is not merely his appearance but his persistent willingness to endure all of the pain and suffering to which he has been subjected in order to carry out in their midst his prophetic task of bringing them back to God in repentance. Ultimately, it is this persistent willingness to endure the suffering that results from his prophetic task that leads to him being marred, disfigured, diseased, and crushed in the way that the passage describes, since he would endure none of these things if he chose to renounce that task and go elsewhere, thereby leaving the people to continue in their sinful behavior and to suffer the destructive consequences of that behavior.

At the same time, however, both the servant's willingness and resolve to persist in the task given him by God as well as the physical disfigurement and gruesome appearance that result from that persistence impress the people so much that they come to their senses and turn away from their sinfulness. The servant's patience and willingness to endure suffering, abuse, and rejection at their hands cuts them to the heart, revealing to them the utter depravity and inhumanity into which they have fallen. What makes such a profound impression on them is not merely the servant's horrendous appearance but the fact that they and their sins are responsible for that appearance, both because they are the ones who mistreated him and because it was their sinfulness that necessitated his presence and activity in their midst if there was to be any hope that they might be brought to turn away from that sinfulness.

More than his patience, persistence, and disfigured appearance, however, it is the servant's *love* for the people that astonishes them and leaves them dumbfounded, as well as the love, patience, and persistence of God himself, who not only sent the servant to them out of pure mercy, grace, and compassion but willed for him to remain in their midst despite the suffering that this would entail not only for the servant but for God himself. Due to God's immense love for his faithful and beloved servant, he too would be struck to the heart as he saw the servant being subjected to such enormous pain and suffering and having to endure such wicked, unjust, and atrocious behavior at the hands of the sinful people. Obviously, the people are not deserving of the tremendous love and compassion that both God and the servant have shown them by calling them so patiently and persistently to repentance, despite the suffering that this has entailed. On the contrary, the only thing that their behavior has deserved is God's immense wrath and their judgment and destruction at his hands. By remaining firm in their love for the sinful and wicked people, therefore, both the servant and the God who sent him bring the people to acknowledge the depth of their sin and to turn away from their wickedness.

These ideas are reflected in the fact that the passage presents the speakers referring to "our transgressions," "our iniquities," and "the iniquities of us all," in addition to comparing themselves to sheep that have gone astray and turned to their own way. Prior to the coming of the servant, the people would not have acknowledged their sinfulness, transgressions, and iniquities or viewed themselves as persons who had gone astray. Now that they have seen the patience and love of the servant as well as the depravity of their own sin as it was reflected in the servant's appearance, however, the speakers have come to acknowledge their sinfulness and wickedness and have turned away from these things.

At the same time, it is this repentance and turning back to God that has made the people whole and healed them. It is important not to equate this wholeness and healing with divine forgiveness, as interpretations of the passage that are based on the idea of penal substitution do. If the people have merely been forgiven but have not turned away from their destructive behavior, they cannot be said to have been healed or made whole. What makes the people whole and heals them is their acknowledgment of their sin and the fact that they have now turned away from that sin in order to live in accordance with God's will once more. The passage implies that they have stopped going astray like sheep and turning to their own way. They have now been brought back into God's fold in order to follow him as their shepherd. Of course, now that they have turned back to God, he undoubtedly forgives them all of the sins that they had committed, yet here as elsewhere throughout the Hebrew Bible the basis for this forgiveness is their renewed obedience to his will. What the servant patiently sought, and what God persistently sought through him, was not merely to *forgive* the people their sins but to bring them to *abandon* those sins so that they might attain the wholeness and healing that results from living in the way he has commanded out of love for all. It is this that the servant accomplishes through his patience in suffering and his refusal to give up on the sinful people when they persist in mistreating him so viciously.

According to the passage, however, the servant not only suffered and became disfigured but was also taken away to his death. After referring to the manner in which he was led like a lamb to slaughter and taken away by a perversion of justice, the passage continues:

> Who could have imagined his future? For he was cut off from the land of the living, stricken for the transgression of my people. They made his grave with the wicked and his tomb with the rich, even though he had done no violence and there was no deceit in his mouth. Yet it pleased the LORD to crush him with affliction. When you make his life an offering for sin, he shall see his offspring and prolong his days; through him the will of the LORD shall prosper. Out of his anguish of his soul he shall see and find satisfaction; through his knowledge my righteous servant shall make many righteous, and he shall bear their iniquities. Therefore I will allot him a portion with the great, and he shall divide the spoil with the strong, because he poured out his life to death and was numbered with the transgressors. He bore the sin of many and made intercession for the transgressors (Isa 53:7-12).

What is seen as making such a profound impression on the people in the passage is not only the servant's willingness to endure persecution and suffering as he carried out his prophetic task but also his willingness to offer up his life for others by submitting to a violent and unjust death at the hands of his persecutors. When those who wished to kill him led him away to his death, he did not lash out at them, revile them, or speak out against them. Instead, he allowed himself to be led away in silence, like a lamb led to the slaughter or a sheep before its shearers. At the same time, in this way his innocence and righteousness became evident to all. The servant allowed himself to be numbered or reckoned with the transgressors and to be treated as if he himself were a transgressor, even though there was no deceit or sin in him.

According to the passage, in fact, he did more than this. He also made intercession for the transgressors. The allusion to him becoming an *'asham* or offering for sin should be understood in this sense. Because sacrificial offerings were in essence petitions offered up to God by means of the animal or gift that was presented to him, the servant became an offering for sin in the sense that he offered himself or his life up to God interceding on behalf of the transgressors who were responsible for his cruel and unjust death. While this intercession would have been understood as a plea for their forgiveness, it would also have been viewed as a petition that God continue to be active to bring the sinful people to abandon their violent and destructive behavior, since both their well-being and God's forgiveness were thought to depend on such a change in them. The love that the servant demonstrates not only by refraining from striking out at those who unjustly led him to his death but also by interceding on their behalf makes a deep impression on the speakers in the passage and contributes to their being brought to acknowledge their sins and turn away from them.

The servant can therefore be said to bear the people's iniquities in this sense as well. Like Israel's priests, he bears their iniquities by interceding on their behalf, asking God not only to forgive them but to purify their hearts and minds as well. At the same time, he offers up a sacrifice for sin, though in this case it is not an animal victim but his own life. His objective is to "make many righteous" by leading the people to put their sinful and unjust behavior behind them and instead live in accordance with righteousness in the way that God commands. It is his efforts to accomplish that objective that lead to his suffering and death, yet he embraces that suffering and death rather than seeking to avoid it because only by remaining faithful to the end to the prophetic task given to him by God can he fulfill that task and bring about in the people the change of behavior that God desires to see in their lives for their own good.

The affirmation that the servant bore the iniquity and sin of the people, then, would be understood in several ways. First, he bore their sin in the sense of enduring rejection, violence, and death at their hands. Their treatment of the servant was sinful and unjust, given his innocence as well as his efforts to do them good by bringing them to change their ways. Second, he bore their sins in the sense that, in obedience to God, he took it upon himself to do what was necessary to deliver them from their sinful behavior as well as the harmful consequences of that behavior. This entailed suffering, afflictions, and in the end a violent death, which he freely accepted out of faithfulness to his prophetic task, since had he abandoned that task instead of giving up his life it would not have been accomplished and the objectives he sought among the people would not have been fulfilled. In other words, the servant assumed the burden and responsibility of bringing the people to put away their sins, in spite of the suffering he had to endure on account of his faithfulness and commitment to that goal. And third, he bore the people's sins and iniquities in the sense that he offered up his life to God asking him to allow his efforts aimed at delivering the people from their sinful behavior to be successful, in addition to asking him to forgive the people their sins and accept them once more on that basis.

Thus the servant was wounded and crushed for the people's transgressions and iniquities in the sense that he suffered enormously as a result of his commitment to bringing them to put away those transgressions and iniquities so that they might be saved from their consequences and forgiven by God. He endured the chastisement that made them whole by accepting his suffering at the hands of the people as well as God himself, who willed that he continue to carry out his prophetic activity in the midst of the people in spite of the afflictions that this involved for the servant. The servant's willingness to remain faithful to his prophetic task in obedience to God led to his being crushed, bruised, and wounded, yet his willingness to endure these things resulted in the people being made whole and healed by means of their acknowledgment of their sins and their renewed obedience to God's will. The impact that the persistence, patience, faithfulness, and love of the servant had on the people was the means by which they were healed and made righteous. Because it was God who had sent the servant into the midst of such a sinful and violent people and had him remain there even when this meant enduring tremendous suffering and an unjust death, it could be said that God himself had afflicted the servant and made him suffer, since only in that way would the servant be able to accomplish his objective. It was in that sense that God had laid upon the servant the iniquity of the people: he subjected the servant to suffering at the hands of the sinful people by sending him into their midst to carry out his prophetic activity, but also by laying upon him the task and responsibility of delivering the people from their sinful behavior, despite the cost that this involved for the servant.

While in a sense it could be said that it pleased God to see the servant suffer, since God allowed this to happen rather than acting to prevent it, strictly speaking what pleased God was the manner in which the servant remained faithful all the way to his death to the prophetic task given him, precisely because it was this faithfulness that made it possible for the people to be brought to turn away from their sins and return to him. The servant thus bore the people's sins and iniquities by enduring everything that had been necessary to save them from continuing in those sins and iniquities. He also bore those sins and iniquities in the sense of interceding for the people in the midst of his suffering and death, asking God to make all that he was enduring a means by which the people might be brought back to him so as to be saved from their sins and transgressions.

Given that the servant is presented as being put to death and buried, it is not entirely clear how the affirmations that God exalted the servant and made him prosper would have been understood (Isa 52:13; 53:10-12). What is clear, however, is that in biblical thought the only way that sinful people such as the speakers in the passage can be made whole and righteous and obtain God's forgiveness and acceptance is by being brought to abandon their sinful and destructive behavior and return to God in repentance and obedience. This is always the condition for salvation, healing, wholeness, forgiveness, and blessing, since as long as people stubbornly persist in sinful behavior they cannot be helped, saved, and blessed. Simply inflicting punishment either on the people themselves or on someone else in their place, including especially a person who is innocent and righteous, would not make them righteous or restore them to the obedience necessary for them to enjoy the well-being and wholeness God desires for all. For that reason, the claim that the idea of penal substitution is present in Isaiah 53 must be rejected in no uncertain terms. Such an idea runs contrary to the logic of this passage as well as the Hebrew Scriptures as a whole.

SACRIFICIAL BLOOD AND THE OFFERING OF LIFE

In many passages from the Mosaic law, the use of the blood of animal victims is prescribed in rites that are said to make expiation for people, places, and objects. As we have noted in the previous two chapters, in the prescriptions regarding the different types of sacrifice for sin and guilt in Leviticus 4–7, the priest is commanded to sprinkle the blood with his finger toward the veil of the sanctuary or the side of the altar, smear some on the horns of the altar of incense, and pour out the remainder at the base of the altar of burnt offerings, depending on the particular rite involved.[7] On *Yom Kippur*, the high priest was not only to sprinkle blood on and in front of the mercy seat of the ark in the Holy of Holies but also to smear some of the blood on the horns of the altar of burnt offerings before sprinkling some blood upon the altar itself as well (Lev 16:14-15, 18-19). The prescriptions for *Yom Kippur* do not mention what was to be done with the sacrificial blood of the victims that remained after the rites had been carried out, but it is likely that it was to be poured out at the base of the altar. In the prescriptions for holocausts and offerings of well-being in Leviticus 1 and 3, the blood of the animal victims offered was also to be dashed or drained out on the side of the altar (Lev 1:5, 15; 3:2, 8, 15-16). Other passages speak of sacrificial blood being applied not only to sacred places and objects but also to the priests and their vestments at their consecration (Exod 29:20-21), to those cleansed from skin diseases (Lev 14:14, 17, 25, 29), to the interior of a house that is to be cleansed (Lev 14:51-52), and in one instance to the people as a group (Exod 24:8). Although in several of these passages some type of purification is said to be involved, in others there is no allusion to purification or expiation.

It would be a mistake to assume that the meaning ascribed to the rites with blood associated with each of these different types of sacrificial offerings

---

7. See Lev 4:5-7, 16-18, 25-26, 30, 34; 5:9; 7:2.

was the same. When it was poured out at the base of the altar or into the ground elsewhere, it is likely that the blood was merely being returned to the earth. This idea appears in the book of Deuteronomy, though the allusion there is not to the disposal of blood from a sacrificial victim offered to God.[8] In other instances, such as when it was sprinkled on objects, places, or persons, the blood no doubt had some symbolic significance. It seems clear that in many cases this significance had to do with the consecration or dedication of those objects, places, or persons to God. In some sense, they were being set apart as holy for his service. It is also likely that the application of blood was often understood as symbolizing the purification of the objects, places, or persons upon which it was sprinkled, smeared, or poured.

There are a number of passages in the biblical texts and Jewish writings of the Second Temple period, however, in which sacrificial blood is explicitly said to be *offered to God*. In the opening verses of Leviticus, the prescriptions given for burnt offerings use the verb form *hiqrib* to speak in these terms: "The bull shall be slaughtered before the LORD; and Aaron's sons the priests shall offer the blood, dashing the blood against the sides of the altar that is at the entrance of the tent of meeting" (Lev 1:5). If this is the meaning ascribed to the dashing of blood against the altar in this passage, then the other passages throughout Leviticus that speak of dashing the blood against the altar should probably be understood in the same way: it is a means by which the blood is offered to God.

Allusions to the offering of sacrificial blood to God also appear in Exod 23:18 and 34:25, as well as Lev 7:33, where the sons of Aaron are said to offer up the blood and the fat of the offering of well-being. The idea that the priests offer to God the blood and the fat of the animals is also stated explicitly twice in Ezekiel 44 (vv. 7, 15). A couple of other passages in the Pentateuch associate the dashing of blood against the altar with the offering of the fat of the sacrificial animal to God (Lev 17:6; Num 18:17). This suggests that the blood was being offered to God together with the fat. Philo refers to the sacrificial blood as a libation in several passages of his works, which indicates that he also understood it as an offering presented to God: "the blood is poured upon the altar as a libation" (*Spec. Laws* 4.125; cf. *Spec. Laws* 1.171, 205; *Moses* 2.150). The book of Jubilees seems to understand the blood as something offered to God as well. After recalling God's prohibition against consuming blood, the author of Jubilees alludes to the use of blood in the sacrificial rites prescribed in the Mosaic law in the following terms: "They shall keep it for their generations so that they might make supplication on your behalf with blood before the altar on every day. And at the hour of daybreak and evening they will seek forgiveness on their own behalf continually before the Lord so that they might guard it and not be rooted out" (Jub. 6:14). Here the offering of blood is viewed as a means by which prayers and petitions are offered up to God.

---

8. See Deut 12:16; 15:23, cf. 12:27; Lev 17:13.

The passages that speak of smearing blood on the altar and sprinkling blood on and in front of the mercy seat as well as in front of the sanctuary and the veil covering it should probably be understood as conveying the idea that the blood was being offered to God as well, especially because the blood is said to be sprinkled "before the LORD" (Lev 4:6-7, 17-18). Undoubtedly, in all of the sacrifices, the blood is handled differently than the flesh, fat, and other parts of the animal that are offered to God by being placed upon the altar in order to be burnt there. The reason that blood could not be offered up to God in the same manner, however, is simply that blood cannot be burned upon an altar in the same way as the other parts of the animal, especially because blood is not flammable. This made it necessary to offer it to God in some other way, such as by sprinkling it toward the symbol of his presence, smearing it upon the altar, or dashing it against the side of the altar. It is possible that the blood that was poured out at the base of the altar was also thought to be offered to God. Even if it was being returned to the earth, this could have been understood in terms of returning it to God as well. The general idea in all of these passages is that the blood of an animal victim, like its fat, belongs to God and therefore must be presented to him (Lev 3:16-17).

Although the idea that all blood belongs to God is not stated explicitly in Lev 17:10-14, it clearly seems to be presupposed in the passage. There, in the context of prohibitions regarding the consumption of blood, God is presented as telling the people through Moses: "For the life of the flesh is in the blood; and I have given it to you for making expiation for yourselves on the altar. For it is the blood that makes expiation, by reason of the life" (v. 11). A few verses later, the passage adds: "for the life of all flesh is its blood" (v. 14).

These verses are extremely difficult to translate, and certain translations can convey ideas that are not necessarily present in the Hebrew text. The Hebrew term translated here as "life" is *nefesh*, which is often rendered "soul." Most biblical scholars would maintain that it refers to the whole being or totality of a person rather than simply a person's soul. Due to the tendency of biblical scholars to interpret passages such as Lev 17:10-14 in a literal or ontological sense, the affirmation that the life of the flesh is in the blood has often been understood as conveying the idea that some type of life force or substance is present in blood. There is no reason to read this idea back into the text, however. The Hebrew can be understood as affirming that one's existence as a living being is in one's blood in the sense that it depends on one's blood or is tied to it. In that case, the Hebrew phrase could be loosely translated "it is the blood that gives life to the flesh." The idea would be that the blood animates the flesh or body of a living being. This same idea may be present in v. 14, which in essence equates the blood with the *nefesh*. Translated literally, the Hebrew there affirms that "the *nefesh* of all flesh is its blood in its *nefesh*." What makes these verses so difficult to translate is not only the grammatical considerations but the Hebrew concept of the *nefesh*, for which no exact equivalent exists in English.

In whatever manner these Hebrew phrases are understood, there is no reason to read back into them the idea that blood possesses some intrinsic power to make atonement, obtain forgiveness, ransom lives, or wash away impurities. For reasons we have seen in the previous chapter, the idea that God has bestowed such power on blood must also be regarded as foreign to the passage. If expiation is not a mechanical process but instead involves offering up a prayer to God seeking his acceptance and forgiveness by means of an offering, the affirmation that he has given the blood to the people so that they can make expiation for themselves on the altar should merely be understood in the sense that he allows and commands them to make use of blood in the rites he has prescribed in the law by sprinkling, smearing, or pouring it on the altar or dashing it against the altar as they offer up to him their prayers there. In other words, the only use that the people are to make of blood is in the expiatory rites by means of which they implore God to forgive and accept them once more.

The passage therefore provides no basis for the idea that sacrificial blood obtains God's forgiveness or atones for sins simply by being brought into contact with the altar, as if it possessed atoning power by virtue of the life-force present in it or because God had conferred on it that power. As we have seen above, what purified people and obtained God's forgiveness was not the performance of rites or manipulation of substances but the repentance and renewed commitment to obedience that those who had sinned expressed and manifested by means of those rites. When the priests presented the blood on the altar, they were not purchasing God's forgiveness or paying God some type of ransom on behalf of the offerers in order that they might not be put to death for the sin that they had committed. God's forgiveness could not be bought, nor did his justice demand any type of ransom payment to revoke a death sentence. Those who offered up sacrifices for sin were not seeking to avoid being put to death as a penalty for their sins. Nor were they attempting to use blood as a ritual detergent to wash away some type of pollution that had been mysteriously generated by their sins and had adhered to the altar. Instead, they were expressing by means of a sacrificial rite their desire and intention to put their sinful behavior behind them and return to a life of obedience to God's commandments and asking him to forgive and accept them once again on that basis.

Milgrom interprets Lev 17:11 in the sense that those who slaughter an animal are guilty of taking a life, which is a capital offense, and are therefore liable to the penalty of death. According to Milgrom, "the function of the blood on the altar is to ransom the life of the one who offered it."[9] The problem with such an interpretation is that it implies once more that those who presented sacrificial offerings to God were paying a penalty or a ransom price in order to avoid being put to death. It is possible, however, that the general

---

9. See Jacob Milgrom, *Leviticus 17–22: A New Translation with Introduction and Commentary*, AB 3A (New York: Doubleday, 2000), 1474.

idea behind Milgrom's interpretation was in fact associated with the rite with blood. In essence, those who had taken the life of an animal in order to offer it up to God were giving its blood back to God, the author of life, since the blood as the life of the animal belonged to God and was not to be consumed or used by human beings. If understood in this manner, the presentation of the blood on the altar would not involve the payment of a penalty or ransom price but rather an offering. Furthermore, the blood would not be offered up to God *in exchange* for the life or souls of the offerers but on their behalf.

Many biblical interpreters have claimed to find the idea of penal substitution in God's command in Exod 12:1-13 for the Israelites to smear the doorposts and lintels of their homes with the blood of the Passover lamb in order for the lives of their firstborn to be spared. Such an interpretation is based on ideas that are foreign to the passage. The firstborn of the Israelites were not guilty of any sin and were therefore not subject to the penalty of death. In fact, the same is true of the firstborn of the Egyptians in general, who are not said to have sinned in the narrative. God's purpose in afflicting the firstborn of the Egyptians with death was to compel the Pharoah to let the Israelites go. While the death of the firstborn may be viewed as a punishment on the Pharoah, it was not a means by which God sought to satisfy the demands of his justice for the sins that the Pharoah had committed, and much less for any sins that had been committed by the Egyptians as a whole. As the passage itself affirms, the use of blood on the doorposts and lintels of the Israelites' homes simply constituted a sign for the angel of death to know that the persons that were dwelling there were Israelites rather than Egyptians.

The idea that sacrificial blood appeases God's wrath at sin must also be seen as foreign to that passage as well as others in the biblical texts. Those texts provide no basis for the claim of Baruch Levine that in the biblical cult "Yahweh accepts the blood as an apotropaic agent, and contains his wrath,"[10] or for interpretations such as that of Gordon Wenham: "The sprinkling of the animal's blood within the sanctuary protected the sinner from the holiness of God expressing itself in righteous anger."[11] What provoked God to wrath was not that sinful human beings draw near to him at the sanctuary dedicated to his name but that they persistently disobey the commandments he had given them for the purpose of promoting justice, righteousness, and solidarity among them. Similarly, what put away his wrath was not sacrificial blood but the people's repentance and their renewed commitment to observing those commandments once again.

As we observed in the previous chapter, the Hebrew Bible offers no basis for the common claim that the death and blood of sacrificial victims was necessary to make expiation for sins and obtain God's forgiveness. In addition to containing many passages that speak of God forgiving sins freely without

---

10. Baruch A. Levine, *In the Presence of the Lord: A Study of Cult and Some Cultic Terms in Ancient Israel*, SJLA 5 (Leiden: Brill, 1974), 68.

11. Gordon J. Wenham, *The Book of Leviticus*, NICOT (Grand Rapids: Eerdmans, 1979), 93.

receiving any type of sacrificial offering, the biblical texts refer to expiation being made by means of offerings that consisted of things such as flour and articles of gold jewelry (Lev 5:11-13; Num 31:50). The account of the golden calf also speaks of Moses making expiation for the people independently of any sacrificial offering, simply by intercession (Exod 32:30). In Lev 14:29, the priest is presented as making expiation before the LORD on behalf of a person being cleansed from a skin disease by rubbing oil on that person's head. When the people arouse God's anger in Num 16:41-48, Aaron is said to make expiation for the people by offering up incense. In Exod 30:15, the half shekel that all male Israelites are to pay is said to be "an offering to make expiation for your lives" or yourselves. Once again, it is common to read into this verse the idea of substitution, as Baruch Schwartz does when he claims that in the phrase used here and in passages such as Lev 17:11 and Num 31:50, "the meaning 'ransom' is intended: 'to act as a ransom for your lives', as payment in place of your lives, which would otherwise be forfeit."[12] The idea in these texts is not that those who offer up the blood of a sacrificial victim, present God with articles of jewelry, or pay the half shekel avoid having to forfeit their lives by means of a ransom payment but simply that they are made pure or acceptable to God by means of that which they give to him on their own behalf. Once again, because in Hebrew the term used in all of these passages is *nefesh*, the idea is not that they pay a ransom for their lives or souls but simply that they make expiation on their own behalf by means of an offering or payment.

A number of passages outside of the Pentateuch also speak of expiating sin independently of any type of sacrifice or shedding of blood. In Isa 27:9, the prophet affirms that the sinfulness of God's people will be expiated by destroying the altars dedicated to the worship of other gods. According to Prov 16:6, the practice of kindness and faithfulness is said to make expiation for iniquity. The author of the book of Sirach affirms that "those who honor their father expiate for sins" and that "almsgiving expiates sin," in addition to writing that "to forsake injustice is to make expiation" (Sir 3:3, 30; 35:5; cf. Tob 12:9). Other Second Temple Jewish writings such as the Psalms of Solomon speak of making expiation by fasting and humbling oneself (Pss. Sol. 3:7-8). A passage from the Sybilline Oracles calls on people to make expiation by offering praise to God (Sib. Or. 4.166-68). The Community Rule from Qumran speaks of sins being expiated "through the spirit of true counsel concerning the ways of man" and "by the spirit of uprightness and humility" (1QS 3:7-10). It also affirms that prayer properly offered, righteousness, and perfection of way can expiate sins without sacrificial offerings (1 QS 9:4-6).

In spite of the apparent differences among them, in reality all of these passages from the biblical texts and Second Temple Jewish writings are based on the same understanding of expiation. Ultimately, what makes expiation is not

---

12. Baruch J. Schwartz, "The Prohibitions Concerning the 'Eating' of Blood in Leviticus 17," in *Priesthood and Cult in Ancient Israel*, ed. Gary A. Anderson and Saul M. Olyan, JSOTSup 125 (Sheffield: Sheffield Academic Press, 1991), 34-66 (55).

that which is offered to God in itself, but the renewed commitment to living in accordance with God's will for the good of all. This renewed commitment can be manifested in many different ways and through many different means: by offering to God the blood of a victim that one has dedicated to him, by means of the half shekel, or by presenting him with some other type of material gift, such as flour, gold, jewelry, oil, or incense. Strictly speaking, however, in all of these cases what expiates sin is the offering of oneself to God of which those gifts are a concrete and palpable expression. If one can also expiate sins by putting away idolatry and injustice, fasting, honoring one's parents, assisting the needy, humbling oneself, glorifying God, embracing the truth, and practicing kindness, faithfulness, mercy, and righteousness, it is precisely because all of these things are means by which one purifies oneself from sin by offering up to God all that one is and has in order to do his will. It is this that truly interests God and obtains his forgiveness, acceptance, and blessing. These things do not therefore *substitute* for sacrifice but are simply other ways in which people might express the same dedication to God and his will that they did by means of their sacrificial offerings.

There is a sense, however, in which it can be said that sacrificial blood was thought to be necessary to make expiation for sins. God's desire to bring people to examine their behavior, acknowledge their sin, and turn away from that sin had led him to command that they present him with sacrifices for sin, since those sacrifices served as a means by which he sought to accomplish those objectives. Furthermore, due to the symbolisms involved, he had prescribed that the blood of the animal victims offered up in those rites be presented to him on the altar. Because God had commanded these things in order to promote the practice of justice and righteousness among his people, it was necessary for them to obey him by offering up sacrifices for sin when their actions called for it and by presenting to him the blood of the animals sacrificed in the way he had prescribed. Because of God's command, therefore, it was necessary for those whose sinful behavior placed them under the obligation to present him with a sacrifice for sin to do so, provided they had the means, and for the rites to be carried out in the way that God had prescribed. Only in that way could those rites fulfill the purpose for which God had given them.

The notion that blood made expiation for sins, then, should be understood in the sense that its presentation to God served as a means by which the people were to express their repentance for their sins and their earnest intention to put away those sins and return to a life of obedience. Because of its association with life, blood could be considered more precious than anything else that existed in the world, in which case there was nothing more fitting or valuable that human beings could offer to God. Due to its profound significance for human life and the many rich symbolisms that it conveyed, it was especially suited for the uses that the Mosaic law assigned to it in the sacrificial rites. What interested God was that his people offer up their lives to him for their own good and that they turn away from everything that destroyed their lives and those of others. It was this that he desired rather than sacrificial blood per se. If God had commanded that blood be used in certain ways in the sacrificial rites he had prescribed for his people, it was due not to any type of power or effect that the blood had on him, but rather due to the power and effect that its use in the rites had on the people themselves by virtue of the symbolic meanings it conveyed and the deep impression that it caused on those who observed what was done with it when those rites were performed.

The commandment to avoid the consumption of blood, regard it as holy, and return it to God by pouring it out at the base of the altar or on the ground promoted the people's well-being in other ways as well. It led them to regard life as sacred and taught them that the shedding of blood was acceptable only under certain circumstances. It also reminded them that all life belonged to God and therefore that all life was to be dedicated to him as the sovereign creator of all that exists. To dedicate life to God, however, was not understood in terms of satisfying God's own needs and desires but seeking the well-being and wholeness of all of his creatures as well as everything in his creation as a whole. God's commandment regarding the use of blood therefore promoted the well-being of all by leading his people to care for all living beings and show them kindness. Even when it was necessary for human beings to take life in order to feed themselves or satisfy other needs, this was to be done in a humane manner that avoided unnecessary suffering as much as possible.

A HOLINESS TO BE EMBRACED

According to the most common interpretations of the Hebrew Scriptures and the biblical prescriptions regarding sacrifices for sin that we have considered in Chapter 8, both God's justice and God's holiness were thought to constitute the primary obstacle to human salvation, wholeness, and well-being. Supposedly, God's strict justice and his perfect righteousness made it necessary for him to demand that the sins committed by human beings receive the punishment due to them. At the same time, his perfect holiness made it impossible for him to tolerate anything or anyone that was impure or unclean. If he was to forgive, save, and bless human beings, therefore, it was necessary for him to ensure that the demands of his justice were satisfied and that the impurity generated by human sin was kept out of his presence at his sanctuary. It was for these reasons that he had commanded that his people offer him sacrifices for sin. Those sacrifices made it possible for the obstacle presented by his perfect justice and holiness to be overcome.

As we have seen in Chapter 4 of this study, the idea that justice is satisfied merely by ensuring that wrongdoing receives the punishment due to it must be considered contrary to biblical thought. Throughout the Hebrew Scriptures, justice can be said to exist only when there is wholeness and well-being for all. If this is what God's justice seeks, then rather than constituting an *obstacle* to human salvation, his justice is the means by which that salvation is brought about. Only by pursuing justice in the sense of doing everything possible to ensure that human beings and his creation as a whole are able to enjoy the well-being he desires for them can he make that salvation a reality. Yet because that well-being and salvation cannot be brought about unless human beings are committed to justice and righteousness in the same way that he is, God must not only demand the same commitment of human beings but must also provide them with the guidance, instruction, and correction that they need to make that commitment theirs. In biblical thought, it was for this purpose that he had given his people Israel the commandments of the Torah, including the commandments to offer him sacrifice and to present sacrifices for sin when they fell into behaviors that undermined and destroyed their well-being rather than promoting it.

In order to understand the manner in which the biblical texts conceive of God's holiness, these same ideas must be taken as a starting point. If the concept central to the biblical understanding of holiness is that of being set apart and distinct from what is common or profane, and if the defining characteristic of the God of the Hebrew Bible is his unbending commitment to justice, wholeness, and well-being for all, then his holiness must be defined primarily in terms of this commitment above all else. What makes the God of the biblical texts holy is that he is fully and unreservedly committed to seeking the well-being and wholeness of all without exception and will not let anything stand in the way of his efforts to enable that objective to be achieved.

According to this understanding of God's holiness, it is essentially synonymous with his love. At the same time, however, the language of holiness stresses certain aspects of that love, in particular its uncompromising and demanding nature. In biblical thought, God's holiness is his intractable, obdurate, and resolute commitment to the well-being of all. To refer to God as holy is to affirm that he will not compromise, desist, or relent in his pursuit of that objective and will not tolerate anyone else compromising, desisting, or relenting in their pursuit of that objective either. What God's holiness demands is that human beings be as fully and resolutely committed to their own well-being as he is and that they be just as persistent, tenacious, and unwavering as he is in their efforts to make that well-being a reality for all without exception. For that reason, rather than constituting an *obstacle* or *impediment* to human salvation, God's holiness is a *means* to that objective. Instead of constituting something that human beings should fear, avoid, or attempt to keep their distance from, God's holiness is something that they should embrace and desire above all else. Rather than standing against them and threatening them, God's holiness seeks to bless them and therefore stands entirely in their favor.

Throughout the biblical texts, God's holiness is also closely associated with his sovereignty, power, and glory. Numerous passages describe God as holy in the sense that he is the sovereign creator and Lord of everything that exists and manifests his might by working wonders that are magnificent and awe-inspiring.[13] At the same time, many passages relate God's holiness to his acts of redemption and salvation, which also display his might, power, and sovereignty.[14] Precisely because God's holiness seeks to redeem and save, the biblical texts also associate it with his love, justice, and faithfulness as well as his special concern for the poor, needy, and downtrodden.[15] It is all of these things that set God far above human beings and make him so radically distinct from them. While human beings are undoubtedly to react to God's holiness with admiration, respect, and even fear, they are also called to rejoice in that holiness because it is something that seeks to do them good rather than harm.[16] When they contemplate God's glory and greatness as the one who is sovereign over all that exists, they may be overwhelmed and moved to keep silent or even tremble in awe, yet this is not because he is capricious, vengeful, or wrathful but because he is so exceedingly good and wonderful in every way.[17]

In biblical thought, therefore, the affirmation that God is not only committed to justice, wholeness, and well-being for all but is also highly exalted in power and might above all people and all things is *good* news to be received with joy and celebration. When God's people praise and glorify him for his holiness, they do so not out of compulsion or fear of retribution and punishment but gladly and spontaneously, because that holiness is synonymous not only with his steadfast love and commitment to their well-being but also the power and might he possesses to achieve that objective, no matter what obstacles may stand in his way. To say that God is holy is to say that he will stop at nothing to accomplish his loving purposes and that no power or force in the world can dissuade or deter him in his attempts to bring those purposes to pass.

At the same time and for the same reasons, however, for those who are opposed to God's loving purposes and willingly stand in the way of his commitment to well-being and wholeness for all, God's holiness does indeed constitute a threat and a motive for fear and trembling. In many passages from the Hebrew Bible, God's holiness is presented as something that may in fact do people harm. In Josh 24:19-20, for example, after the Israelites have promised to forsake all other gods and serve the God of Israel alone, Joshua's awareness that they have shown themselves time and again to be a rebellious people who forsake the God of Israel for other gods leads him to tell them: "You will not be able to serve the LORD, for he is a holy God. He is a jealous God; he will not forgive your transgressions or your sins. If you forsake the LORD and serve foreign gods, then he will turn and do you

---

13. See, for example, Exod 15:11; Ps 77:13-14; Isa 40:25-26; 47:10; Jer 25:30; Hab 3:2-4.

14. See, for example, Ps 111:9; Isa 41:14; 43:14-17; 45:11-12; 47:4; 48:17; 54:5.

15. See, for example, Ps 22:3-6; 68:5; 71:22; 102:18-22; Isa 5:16; 63:15-16.

16. See, for example, 1 Sam 2:1-2; 1 Chr 16:9-12; Ps 103:1-5; 105:3-5; 138:2; 145:21; Isa 12:6; 29:19.

17. See, for example, 1 Chr 16:29-31; Ps 5:7; 96:9-13; 99:1-5; Isa 55:5; 56:6-7; 60:9; Hab 2:20; Zech 2:13.

harm and consume you, after he has done you good." Because of his holiness, God refuses to be mocked, reviled, questioned, or treated with pride and haughtiness.[18] That holiness leads him to take action against those who call evil good and good evil and who exalt themselves in his presence (Isa 5:18-21; Jer 50:29-32). It also leads him to strike out in anger against those who persistently reject and despise him and refuse to put away their unjust and oppressive treatment of others.[19] Because he is sovereign and holy, he may burn and devour like a flame all that stands in opposition to him and at times destroy both body and soul (Ps 11:4-6; Isa 10:16-18; Mic 1:2-4). Those who insist on walking contrary to his will and conspire against him, therefore, should indeed tremble before his holiness: "But the LORD of hosts, him you shall regard as holy; let him be your fear, and let him be your dread" (Isa 8:11-13; cf. Joel 2:1-2; Hab 3:2-6).

Viewed out of context, these passages appear to present a vindictive, unforgiving, proud, and domineering God who simply wishes to impose his will on human beings by force and threatens to crush or destroy any who dare to oppose him. Such is especially the case if these passages are read on the basis of the idea that God's concern is for himself. If he is angry and jealous and demands to be obeyed *for his own sake*, then he is hardly a good and loving God. When viewed in context and in the light of the other passages that allude to God's holiness just considered above, however, these passages convey a very different idea. They present a God who is uncompromising and unrelenting in his love and commitment to human beings. In that case, if he refuses to be mocked, reviled, questioned, challenged, resisted, and disobeyed, it is *not for his own sake but for the sake of the human beings he loves*. For their own good, he will not allow those who have promised to serve him alone to follow other gods, practice injustice, or stand up to him in a spirit of pride and arrogance. On the contrary, he will take action against them in decisive manner, using all of his power and might, precisely because he will not let anything or anyone stand in the way of his efforts to bring people to practice the same justice, righteousness, mercy, and compassion that he does as the sovereign Lord and creator of all. Nor will he tolerate any kind of opposition or resistance to his will, which demands of human beings the same type of unconditional love that characterizes him and will settle for nothing less.

There is no denying, however, that this poses a problem for human beings. Even if they wish to be as firmly committed to their own well-being as God is and share fully God's concern for justice and wholeness for all, their inherent sinfulness and the limitations that their nature places on them will not allow them to attain the same level of commitment and concern for these things that characterizes God. If God refuses to tolerate sin, injustice, apathy, selfishness, and destructive behavior, then no human being can ever be acceptable to him

---

18. See, for example, 2 Kgs 19:22; Isa 37:23; 45:9-11; Ezek 39:7.
19. See, for example, Isa 1:4; 5:24; 30:9-14; 31:1-12; Jer 25:30-31; Ezek 43:7-8.

because all people inevitably fall into these things and no one can avoid them. In that case, to some extent all must come under his wrath and judgment.

This, then, is the dilemma. If God truly loves human beings and desires their well-being, he must demand perfection of them. To accept anything less than perfection would be unloving, since it would involve ignoring or overlooking behavior that does them harm and regarding even a minimal amount of that behavior as acceptable. Harmful and destructive behavior is *never* acceptable under any circumstance, and if God is committed to human well-being he must always reject and condemn such behavior and do everything possible to eradicate it. At the same time, however, because human beings cannot avoid falling into such behavior, if God did not tolerate and accept it to some extent, he would have no choice but to destroy human beings altogether. Obviously, he cannot save human beings and seek their well-being and wholeness if he destroys them. In a sense, then, he must accept their sinful and destructive behavior at the same time that he *refuses* to accept it. He must tolerate that behavior at the same time that he *refuses* to tolerate it. He must demand that they be perfect in their practice of justice, righteousness, and solidarity while at the same time accepting their lack of perfection and their failure to practice these things as they should and must in order to attain the well-being and wholeness he desires for all.

It is for this reason that God's holiness is both a source of rejoicing and celebration for his people as well as a motive for fear and trembling. That holiness leads God to be fully and resolutely committed to doing whatever is necessary to bring about their well-being and wholeness and to make use of all of his sovereign power and might in pursuit of that end. In that regard, his holiness is an expression of his steadfast love for his people and should fill them with joy and a deep desire to praise and glorify him for being holy, as the Psalmists often do. Yet because God's holiness also demands that his people avoid any type of behavior that undermines and destroys their well-being and does them harm, it is a motive for fear and trembling at the same time, precisely because it is impossible for sinful human beings to fulfill that demand perfectly. This results in situations such as that described in Isaiah 6, where after seeing God sitting on a throne attended by seraphim who chant: "Holy, holy, holy is the LORD of hosts; the whole earth is full of his glory," the prophet exclaims: "Woe is me! I am doomed, for I am a man of unclean lips, and I live among a people of unclean lips, yet my eyes have seen the King, the LORD of hosts!" (vv. 1-5). After one of the seraphim touches the prophet's lips with a hot coal, he tells him that his iniquity is taken away and his sin is purged (vv. 6-7).

This passage is often read on the basis of the assumption that God's justice and holiness demand that sin be punished and that sinners be consumed, destroyed, or cast far from his presence. Many read back into it the idea that God's holiness is dangerous for human beings as well. Such interpretations tend to set God's justice and holiness in opposition to his goodness and his love for human beings. On the basis of what we have seen above, however, this passage can and should instead be read in the sense that God's demand that those who enter into his presence be clean and pure is rooted not in a concern for God himself but rather in his concern for the human beings he loves. In that case, God refuses to tolerate any type of impurity or sinfulness in the thoughts and actions of human beings such as the prophet Isaiah and the people among whom he lives *not for his own sake but for theirs*, since his steadfast love for them and his uncompromising commitment to their well-being prevent him from accepting ways of thinking and behaving that do them harm.

As the passage indicates, however, in the end God *does* accept the prophet in spite of his uncleanness and impurity while at the same time acting to purify him by means of the seraph's touch. When God asks: "Whom shall I send, and who will go for us?," the prophet responds: "Here am I; send me!" (Isa 6:8). While God then indicates to the prophet his intention to execute judgments on the sinful people and entrusts to him the task of preparing the people to receive those judgments, he ends by referring to a "holy seed" that will be left as a remnant (6:9-13). The idea in the passage is not that God wishes to destroy the people or inflict punishments on them in retribution for their sins, therefore, but that he intends to purify them through judgments so that those who remain will be holy and can thus constitute the basis for a new beginning.

While this passage from Isaiah alludes to the incompatibility and conflict between God's holiness and the impurity, sin, and iniquity of human beings, it also points to the manner in which that incompatibility and conflict are resolved. By means of the seraph, God both forgives and purifies the prophet. He announces his intention to purify the people through judgment as well. These two ideas must not be divorced from one another. As we have seen previously, if God wishes to accomplish his purposes among human beings, he cannot simply forgive and overlook their sinfulness, since that alone would not bring about in them the change of life necessary for them to attain the well-being he desires for them. He must also cleanse and purify them of their sinfulness and the destructive ways of thinking and behaving that make that well-being impossible. This means that rather than giving up on his demand that they abandon the ways of thinking and living that do them harm, he must persist adamantly in that demand if his loving objectives are to be accomplished in them. At the same time, he must do everything in his power to enable them to fulfill that demand by purifying their hearts and lives and enabling them to be brought into conformity with his will.

Because he is sovereign over all, however, God alone can determine when it is best to forgive and overlook the sinful behavior of human beings and when it is best to purify them through judgments and chastisements. Whether he does one or the other, in biblical thought he is acting in love. Once again, this situation leads human beings to react to his holiness, justice, and righteousness both with joy and celebration as well as with fear. On the one hand, they will rejoice when God forgives and accepts them in spite of their sinfulness and disobedience to his will. On the other, however, they know that they are in constant need of cleansing and transformation through discipline and chastisements, and that at times this process can be painful and difficult for them. This knowledge generates fear in them, even though at the same time they are grateful to God for his efforts and commitment to purifying them of the sinful and destructive behavior that does them harm. Although they fear his judgments and chastisements, therefore, they submit to them gladly and willingly since they know that in his love and sovereignty he is doing what he considers to be best for them.

In this regard, it is important to stress that those who truly know the God of Israel and are convinced of his unconditional and uncompromising love for them desire the same things for themselves that he desires for them. Like him, they wish to be perfect and blameless in their justice, righteousness, and love. Out of love for themselves and a concern for their own well-being, they find their sinful and destructive behaviors and attitudes just as detestable and intolerable as God does. Like him, they refuse to accept, overlook, or ignore their own imperfection and impurity and for that reason insist on doing everything in their power to overcome and eradicate their practice of sin and injustice. Yet at the same time, like God himself, they have no choice but to accept and tolerate their imperfection to a great extent, since in this life they can never attain the perfection that God desires for them and that they desire for themselves. Most importantly, however, they constantly ask God not only for forgiveness but also for the cleansing necessary to leave behind the ways of thinking and acting that do them harm so as to be brought into conformity with God's will in the way that the author of Psalm 51 does. After acknowledging his sins and transgressions and imploring God's mercy and forgiveness, the Psalmist continues:

> Wash me thoroughly from my iniquity, and cleanse me from my sin. . . . Therefore teach me wisdom in my secret heart. Purge me with hyssop, and I shall be clean; wash me, and I shall be whiter than snow. . . . Create in me a clean heart, O God, and put a new and right spirit within me. Do not cast me away from your presence, and do not take your holy spirit from me. Restore to me the joy of your salvation, and sustain in me a willing spirit (vv. 2, 6-7, 10-12).

These observations must be kept in mind when considering God's command for his people to be holy as he is holy.[20] Because God's holiness has traditionally been understood as standing in opposition to his love, among many interpreters it is common to see this command as a threat or warning. In biblical thought, however, it is an expression of God's love. In effect, God is demanding that his people consecrate themselves fully to the same thing to which he is fully consecrated, namely, their well-being and wholeness. This involves being committed to the way of life he has laid out for them for their

---

20. See Lev 11:44-45; 19:2; 20:7, 26; Num 15:40.

own good by means of the instruction and commandments he has given them. If they truly love and care for themselves in the way that God does, they will value holiness and strive for it with all their being in the same way that they pursue justice and righteousness, since out of a concern for their own well-being they will want nothing more than to be perfectly holy, just, and righteous in their thinking and conduct. If holiness involves an unconditional and uncompromising commitment to that well-being and a rejection of anything that undermines it or stands in opposition to it, they will see God's demand for them to be holy as an expression of his immense love and concern for them rather than any type of oppressive threat or harsh imposition. Out of love for themselves and others, they will also regard any type of apathy, indifference, or failure to strive for what is good, right, just, and holy as something that is unacceptable.

For the same reasons, they will understand God's command for them to sanctify him and his name in the same manner. Rather than viewing that command as selfish or oppressive on God's part, they will regard it as an expression of his steadfast love for them. They *rejoice* that God is holy because they understand his holiness in terms of his unwavering and unshakable commitment to their well-being and wholeness. They also want to sanctify him both in the sense of conforming their lives to the holiness of God that seeks nothing but what is best for them and in the sense of making known to others that he is holy and is to be regarded as such for the good of all. Just as God reacts in anger when people belittle, mock, or reject him or call into question his holiness—not for *his* sake but for *theirs*—, so also those who live as his people defend God's goodness and holiness with the same passion and vigor, precisely because his goodness and holiness are synonymous with his commitment to the well-being of all people everywhere. Only if people are convinced that God is holy will they look to him for help, deliverance, healing, and salvation.

Setting Apart a People for Justice

In biblical thought, God's holiness makes him different from all other gods. None of the gods of the nations can be considered holy, not only because those gods are not sovereign over all people and things as their creator like the God of Israel is, but also because unlike him they are not dedicated above all else to the objective of making it possible for human beings everywhere to enjoy wholeness and well-being. It is for this reason that the biblical texts associate God's holiness with his jealousy and his demand that his people have no other gods. Only the God of Israel can bring about the well-being of all precisely because of his sovereignty as well as his unconditional and uncompromising commitment to that objective.

It is therefore God's love and concern for human beings that leads him to seek and demand that people regard him and his name as holy. He wishes all people to know and be convinced that he is holy and thus is greatly pleased when he is proclaimed and acclaimed as such, since this will allow him to be active among them in the way he desires in order to accomplish his loving purposes in the world. The prophet Ezekiel especially speaks of God's desire to be sanctified or regarded as holy in the eyes of the nations: "I will display my greatness and my holiness and make myself known in the eyes of many nations. Then they will know that I am the LORD" (Ezek 38:23; cf. 20:40-41; 28:25). God's desire that all people come to know him leads him to become angry when the people who are called and known by his name live and act in ways that place his holiness in doubt. For that reason, he is so anxious to defend his holiness: "My holy name I will make known among my people Israel, and I will not let my holy name be profaned any more; and the nations will know that I am the LORD, the Holy One in Israel" (39:7). While God wants all people to know that his holiness will not allow him to tolerate sin, evil, injustice, and oppression, he also wishes to make it clear that the reason why he refuses to tolerate these things is that they destroy the well-being and wholeness that he desires for all due to his love for them.

In biblical thought, God's election of Israel as his chosen people and his establishment of the covenant with them is the means by which he seeks for all people to come to know him as holy. This involves sanctifying Israel in the sense of setting Israel apart as a holy people consecrated to him. Immediately after bringing the Israelites to Sinai, God tells them through Moses: "Now, therefore, if you obey my voice and keep my covenant, you shall be my treasured possession out of all the peoples. Indeed, the whole earth is mine, but you shall be for me a kingdom of priests and a holy nation" (Exod 19:5-6). The idea that God has chosen them to be a holy people and that for that reason they belong to him is stressed throughout the biblical texts, but especially in the Pentateuch: "You shall be holy to me, for I the LORD am holy, and I have separated you from the other peoples to be mine" (Lev 20:26; cf. Deut 14:2; 26:18-19; 28:9). The affirmation that God sanctifies the people should be understood in the same way (Exod 31:13; Lev 22:9). However, this sanctification, consecration, or setting apart involves not only choosing Israel to be special but also bringing his people to live in a manner that distinguishes them from all other people. God will be sanctified and regarded as holy only when the people who are called by his name are sanctified and behave in ways that reflect his holiness.

What is to distinguish Israel from the other nations is not merely that they serve the one true God, therefore, but that they manifest to all the holiness of that God by being fully committed to what is good, right, just, and loving in the same way that he is. While God desires and demands that Israel serve him alone and reject all other gods, he does so not for *his* sake but for the sake of Israel and the other nations as well, since only by abandoning gods who promote injustice, violence, and oppression and dedicating themselves to a holy God whose sovereign love seeks their well-being above all else can people be saved and made whole. The affirmation that the people of Israel are to be a "kingdom of priests" or "priestly kingdom" points to a special role for

Israel among the nations, namely, that of mediating the knowledge and love of God to other peoples and serving as a means by which those peoples will be brought to worship God and consecrate their lives to him for their own good. This can happen, however, only if his people Israel sanctify him by living in accordance with what is good, just, loving, and right.

In addition to sanctifying the people of Israel as a whole, God is said to sanctify particular groups and individuals within Israel. These include especially the priests and Levites and on occasion the prophets he has chosen to speak on his behalf.[21] All of these groups and individuals play a vital role in leading the people to live as holy by dedicating themselves to God and his will. God also declares the land he has given Israel to be holy and sanctifies or consecrates the sanctuary dedicated to him as well as the objects it contains (Exod 29:43-44; 2 Chr 7:16, 20). His purpose is that the people who live on that land and worship him in that sanctuary be holy, consecrating themselves and all that he provides for them to his service so that his goodness, justice, love, and mercy may be manifested to all.

The commandments God gives to his people regarding clean and unclean foods in Leviticus 11 must be understood against the background of these ideas. The biblical texts do not explain why some foods are to be regarded as unclean. What those texts do make clear, however, is that the observance of a diet that was distinct from that of other people served to set Israel apart as holy. At the end of Leviticus 11, after God has finished defining through Moses the foods that are to be considered clean and unclean, he adds: "For I am the LORD your God; sanctify yourselves, therefore, and be holy, for I am holy.... For I am the LORD who brought you up from the land of Egypt to be your God; you shall be holy, for I am holy" (vv. 44-45). These words relate the prescriptions regarding clean and unclean foods to the idea that Israel is to be holy in the sense that the people are to be separate and distinct from other peoples.

Like the practice of circumcision, however, the prescriptions regarding foods that were clean and unclean would not only identify Israel as a special people but would also serve as a constant reminder regarding what was truly to make them distinct from other peoples, namely, the practice of justice and righteousness. Just as the sign of circumcision reminded the people that God had chosen them to live in righteousness like their forefather Abraham so as to have the "circumcision of the heart" of which Moses had spoken (Deut 10:16; 30:6), so also the consumption of foods that were to be regarded as clean and the avoidance of foods that were unclean might be thought to promote purity of heart and life as well as the rejection of thoughts, words, and behaviors that were impure and unclean. These were the things that were truly to distinguish Israel from other peoples.

While the idea that the prescriptions of Leviticus 11 have the purpose of promoting righteous living among the people of Israel by keeping them distinct from people of other nations is never stated explicitly in the biblical

---

21. See Exod 13:2; 29:1, 21; 30:30; 40:9-13; Lev 21:8; Num 3:13; 8:17; 16:9; Jer 1:5.

texts, it does appear in the Letter of Aristeas, a Jewish work that was probably composed in the second century BCE. There, referring to Moses as "the legislator," the author writes:

> In his wisdom the legislator, in a comprehensive survey of each particular part, and being endowed by God for the knowledge of universal truths, surrounded us with unbroken palisades and iron walls to prevent our mixing with any of the other people in any matter, being thus kept pure in body and soul, preserved from false beliefs, and worshiping the only God omnipotent over all creation. . . . So, to prevent our being perverted by contact with others or by mixing with bad influences, he hedged us in on all sides with strict observances connected with meat and drink and touch and hearing and sight, after the manner of the Law. In general everything is similarly constituted in regard to natural reasoning, being governed by one supreme power, and in each particular everything has a profound reason for it, both the things from which we abstain in use and those of which we partake. . . . The fact is that everything has been solemnly set in order for unblemished investigation and amendment of life for the sake of righteousness. . . . [God] has thereby indicated that it is the solemn binding duty of those for whom the legislation has been established to practice righteousness and not to lord it over anyone in reliance upon their own strength, nor to deprive him of anything, but to govern their lives righteously. . . . The symbolism conveyed by these things compels us to make a distinction in the performance of all our acts, with righteousness as our aim. . . . I have therefore given a brief résumé of these matters, indicating further to you that all the regulations have been made with righteousness in mind, and that no ordinances have been made in Scripture without purpose or fancifully, but to the intent that through the whole of our lives we may also practice justice to all [hu]mankind in all our acts, remembering the all-sovereign God (Let. Aris. 139, 142-44, 147, 151, 168).

Here it is clear that the author of this text regards the prescriptions regarding purity and impurity as promoting the practice of justice and righteousness among God's people by reinforcing their identity as a people set apart for God. The symbolisms associated with these distinctions thus reminded the people that they too were to be clean and pure in their conduct in a metaphorical sense by doing what is good and right.

A couple of centuries later, Philo of Alexandria similarly writes that God did not give the people "full liberty" with regard to food and drink "but bridled them with ordinances most conducive to self-restraint and humanity and what is chief of all, piety" (*Spec. Laws* 4.97). According to Philo, the reason why God prohibited the people from eating pork and the aquatic species of animals that do not have scales is that these foods are the most delicious. This prohibition thus teaches the people to practice self-control and to avoid gluttony and extravagance (*Spec. Laws* 4.100-101). In this way, God instills greater virtue in his people. By prohibiting them from eating of those animals that are carnivorous and obtain their food by attacking other animals or human beings and devouring their flesh, God also teaches his people that it is not acceptable for them to retaliate against those who do them harm or act out of anger in relation to others (*Spec. Laws* 4.103-5). Philo offers similar reasons for God's prohibition against eating the flesh of other animals that the law declares impure, often resorting to allegory in order to do so (*Spec. Laws* 4.106-18). The prohibition against eating the fat and the command to offer it instead to God serve the same purpose (*Spec. Laws* 4.124-25). While these interpretations of the biblical prescriptions regarding clean and unclean foods may have been unique to Philo, what is important is that he sees those prescriptions as having the same general purpose as that which is ascribed to them in the Letter of Aristeas, namely, teaching the people certain truths and instilling in them a pious and righteous way of life.

It is quite likely that other Jews in antiquity would have understood the purpose of the regulations regarding food in the same manner. If so, they would have believed that God had commanded that his people eat only what he had designated as pure or clean in order to promote among them a commitment to what was good, just, and right. Eating only of certain foods would contribute to such a commitment, as would the observance of purity in other contexts. The need for the people to make sure that they were physically pure as they drew near to the symbols of God's presence in the sanctuary, for example, would stress to them the idea that they were to be pure of heart as well. By carrying out rites of purification before approaching God at his sanctuary, they were showing respect not only for the signs and symbols of his presence but also for his will in their lives. The observance of the regulations regarding purity promoted greater love and respect for God and therefore furthered the practice of justice, righteousness, and solidarity with others, since these things were inseparable from one another.

In some passages from the Hebrew Bible, the idea that God sanctifies his people appears in conjunction with the affirmation that his people are to sanctify themselves as well. When God commands that the people observe as holy the Sabbath or day of rest, he also has Moses tell them: "I, the LORD, sanctify you" (Exod 31:13). As we have seen above, this sanctification involved separating the people out from the other nations to be his (Lev 20:26). At the same time, however, God commands the people to sanctify themselves in the same way that he has sanctified them: "Consecrate yourselves, therefore, and be holy, for I am the LORD your God. Keep my statutes and observe them: I am the LORD; I sanctify you" (Lev 20:7-8). "You shall not profane my holy name, that I may be sanctified among the Israelites: I am the LORD; I sanctify you" (Lev 22:32). The idea in passages such as these is that God has sanctified the people in terms of setting them apart from other peoples, though he may be said to sanctify them in the sense of acting among them to enable them to be holy by living in justice and righteousness as well. For that reason, they are to sanctify and consecrate themselves in the same way that God does by regarding themselves as distinct from other peoples. Once more, however, what is to distinguish them from other peoples is their commitment to living in accordance with what is good, right, and just by observing his statutes. As this last passage indicates, as they do this they will also be sanctifying God in the sense of making evident from their behavior that he is holy, precisely because he has brought into existence a people who are to be holy like him.

On special occasions, especially when drawing near to God or receiving the ark of the covenant in their midst, the people are told to sanctify or consecrate themselves in the sense of putting on clean clothes, abstaining from certain activities, and preparing themselves in other ways.[22] While the priests and Levites were set apart for God in the sense of being dedicated to his service in general terms, they were also to sanctify themselves or consecrate themselves to God in the sense of making special preparations before carrying out some type of activity related to his worship.[23] Those who took a vow as Nazirites consecrated themselves to God as well (Num 6:18-19). In a number of passages, God tells the people that the firstborn of every creature that opens the womb, whether of human beings or of animals, is also to be set apart and dedicated to him.[24] In the place of the firstborn children, however, God takes the Levites as his own in a special sense (Num 8:16-19).

Both God and the people are said to sanctify certain objects as well. God sanctifies the sanctuary dedicated to him as well as the altar and other objects consecrated to his worship, but the people and priests are also to do so.[25] The incense and offerings that the people present to God are consecrated to God by being dedicated to him (Exod 30:34-37; Lev 27:30-33; Ezek 43:26). The area around the sanctuary is to be set apart as holy, as are the animal victims consecrated to God and the portions of the animal that are set apart for the priests and Levites.[26] The people may also consecrate to God their homes and possessions (Lev 27:14-22).

Numerous passages from the Torah call on the people to sanctify or regard as holy certain days and times. In addition to the Sabbath, these include *Yom Kippur*, the three annual festivals, and the year of Jubilee.[27] At the same time, God himself can be said to consecrate or sanctify days such as the Sabbath, since he is the one who has set them apart as holy (Exod 20:11).

In all of these passages, to be holy, sanctified, or consecrated involves being set apart and regarded as special or distinct. God is holy and is to be regarded as such in that he is unlike any other god and is to be served and worshiped exclusively. The Israelites are to be holy and are to sanctify and consecrate themselves to God by regarding themselves as his own special people and living as such by practicing the justice and righteousness that characterize him as their Lord. They are also to consecrate to God all that they have received from him and to regard as holy everything that he has declared to be holy.

---

22. See Exod 19:10-14; Num 11:18; Josh 3:5; 7:13; 1 Sam 16:5; 2 Chr 29:31; Joel 2:16.
23. See Exod 19:22; Num 11:18; 1 Chr 15:12; 2 Chr 29:5, 17, 34; 35:6.
24. See Exod 13:2, 11-12; 34:19-20; Num 3:13; 18:15; Deut 15:19.
25. See Exod 29:37, 44; 30:22-30; 40:9-13; Lev 8:10-11, 15; Num 7:1; 2 Chr 7:16; 30:8.
26. See Exod 29:30-34; Lev 2:10; 6:26-27; 14:13; Num 18:8-29.
27. See Exod 20:8; 31:14-15; Lev 23:1-43; 25:12.

What is entirely absent from all of these passages that speak of holiness, sanctification, and consecration is any hint or suggestion that holiness was thought to consist of some type of mysterious, invisible force or substance that might radiate out from God or be transmitted through contact or proximity between one person or object and another. For that reason, as we have noted in the previous chapter, the affirmation in Exod 29:37 that whatever touches the altar shall be or become holy should not be understood in the sense that the altar is imbued with some mysterious divine substance or force that is transmitted to anything that touches it. Rather, the passage is simply prescribing that whatever touches the altar is to be set apart and treated as holy in that it is to be consecrated to God.

The same observations must be made with regard to Exod 30:22-33. There God commands Moses to elaborate a special oil for anointing things as holy and then to use that oil to anoint the sanctuary, the objects found in it, and the priests. Nothing in the text suggests that, by mixing together the contents of the anointing oil, Moses is concocting some type of mysterious potion or infusing the oil with some sacred power that will then be transmitted through anointing to the things and people to which it will be applied. Rather, by anointing those things and people with the oil in accordance with God's command, Moses will merely carry out a solemn symbolic act by means of which he will dedicate them to God and his service. In that context, when God tells Moses: "You shall consecrate them, so that they may be most holy; whatever touches them shall be holy" (Exod 30:29), the idea is that both those objects and the things that come into contact with them are to be treated as special rather than profane, since they are to be set apart exclusively for God's service. This idea is reflected a few verses later, where God says of the oil: "it is holy, and it shall be holy *to you*" (v. 32). Because the oil has been set apart for a sacred use, it is to be *regarded* and *treated* as holy. God's command in Lev 6:18 and 6:27 to set apart as holy anything that comes into contact with the offerings should be understood in the same way.

This understanding of sanctification is also evident in the command for the people to set apart certain days and feasts as holy. Because the times designated as holy do not consist of material realities, objects, or places, they cannot be said to be imbued or penetrated by any type of mysterious substance or force. The times set apart are holy only in the sense that they are to be considered special due to the commandments God has given with regard to the manner in which they are to be observed.

Commanding Respect for the Symbols of God's Presence

Among the most problematic passages in the Hebrew Bible are those in which God threatens with death any who do not respect what he has commanded with regard to the holiness of objects such as the ark of the covenant as well as the places that he has designated as holy, including especially the sanctuary itself. At first glance, those commandments and the penalty of death associated with them hardly seem to respond to any concern on the part of God for the practice of justice and righteousness or the well-being of human beings. On the contrary, they appear to be rooted in a concern to keep human beings at a distance for his own sake, either because he sees them as a threat in some way or because he simply cannot tolerate them due to their sinfulness and impurity.

In order to understand the logic behind such passages, however, it is necessary to grasp the significance of the objects and places that are designated as holy in the biblical texts. In different ways, those objects and places served as signs or symbols of God's presence and activity among his people. Of course, just as God could be said to be present at his sanctuary while nevertheless remaining in heaven, at times he might also choose to manifest himself to people visibly or audibly in connection with the objects and places that he had designated as holy, as he was said to do when he appeared to the high priest over the mercy seat in the Most Holy Place every year on *Yom Kippur* and when he made his voice heard at Sinai. Even when he made himself present in some way in relation to those objects and places, however, his presence was in no way confined to them, nor did they cease to be symbols in order to become means by which his presence might remain constant or be assured. The sovereign creator of the universe could not be manipulated by human beings or tied to any particular object or place, since he transcended all that existed and remained free to make himself present whenever and wherever he chose to do so.

Although the objects and places that God had designated as holy served as symbols of his presence, at the same time they symbolized the attributes that were associated with him, such as his holiness, his power, his glory, and his sovereignty. By means of these symbols, therefore, God not only reminded his people of his constant presence among them but also reinforced certain core beliefs and convictions that were considered to be of primary importance for their life and well-being. These beliefs and convictions had to do not only with his own nature and character but also his relation to his people. As they contemplated symbols such as the sanctuary and the sacred objects that it contained, they were moved not only to reflect on his power, greatness, and majesty as creator and sustainer of all that existed but also to recall that he had set them apart to be his people and to serve him as their sovereign Lord. They were to regard their lives as his and remember all that he had done for them in the past and had promised to do for them in the future. Because he had made them his own, not only by creating them together with the rest of humanity but also by redeeming them from their bondage in Egypt and taking them to the land he had given them, everything they had was to be dedicated to his service and used in the way that he desired and commanded. The fact that he had sanctified them in that way meant that they were to consecrate themselves to him and consider themselves holy as he did. His sovereignty over their lives was therefore to be absolute, total, and complete. They were to regard his will as sacred and treat it with the utmost respect in everything they did in their daily life. Nothing was to compare in value or importance to him or to the instruction and guidance that he had provided for them in the Torah, the instrument through which he graciously sought to fill their lives with goodness and blessing.

The various symbols of God's presence were to remind the people not only of his sovereign power and might but also of his love, that is, his unbending and uncompromising commitment to their well-being. From God's perspective, nothing took precedence over that commitment or was equal to it in importance. In a sense, he had made that commitment sovereign alongside himself and consecrated it as holy by making it his own. It was that commitment that had led him to make use of his power to free his people from their bondage in Egypt with signs and wonders and to accompany them through the wilderness until he introduced them into a land of their own. At times, for his people this had meant conflict and warfare with other peoples who stood in opposition to his intentions for them, yet when his people trusted and obeyed him he had enabled them to overcome those who sought to do them harm. He had done all of these things not because he wished to show favoritism for them as a people but because through them he sought to bring people of all nations to know him as a holy God who was implacably opposed to anything that undermined and destroyed human well-being. His desire and demand that he be honored and revered as holy was grounded in his longing that not only Israel but all the nations of the earth come to know him as a God who would not tolerate ways of thinking and living that filled people's lives with pain, suffering, injustice, and oppression and would not relent or back down in his insistence that people conform to his justice, holiness, and love for their own good.

If God had chosen to establish his dwelling among his people Israel at the sanctuary dedicated to him, it was not because he needed to be in close proximity to the people to receive things from them for his own sake but because in his love he wanted them to have a physical, visible symbol of his presence among them. He had no need to be near to them if he was to hear their prayers and receive their offerings, since he could observe and hear anything that went on anywhere in the world he had created. Nevertheless, he had chosen to give them a visible sign or symbol of his presence so that they might *know* and *remember* that he desired to be present among them constantly, day and night, to hear their prayers, pour out his blessings on them, and accompany them in all that they did and experienced. Symbols of his presence such as the ark, the oil lamps that shone day and night, and the smoke of incense that was continually to rise up to him reminded the people of these things as well.

What God wished to convey through the symbols of his presence, therefore, was that he was holy and that he demanded to be regarded as such precisely due to his love for all. There could be no compromising on this demand, nor was it to be questioned or challenged in any way, since to question or challenge what he had commanded was to question and challenge both his absolute sovereignty as well as his unconditional love for his people. While it was important for the people to recall his love for them, it was also important for them to remember that this love had led him to command that they submit fully to him in every way and in all things, and that he refused to take it lightly or look the other way when they did not. That love would not tolerate any kind of willful disobedience or rebellion and demanded nothing but the very best from them, not for *God's* sake, but for *theirs*. Only by consecrating themselves fully to a holy God could they be fully consecrated to their own well-being and wholeness in the same way that he was.

When considered against this background, all of the prescriptions given in the Mosaic law that were designed to stress God's holiness by means of the symbolic realities he had ordained had the sole purpose of bringing the people to live in love, justice, and righteousness for their own well-being and happiness. When the people regarded the symbols of God's presence, his love, his promises, his goodness, and his will as holy, they would place his will above their own and commit themselves to doing everything that he had commanded. By respecting all that he had commanded as inviolable and sacrosanct, they would be brought to offer themselves not only to him but also to one another with a love that was inviolable and sacrosanct as well. They would see their commitment to God and one another as unconditional and non-negotiable in the same way that God's demand for all to respect, revere, and honor the symbols of his holiness and presence was.

When these things are understood, it becomes clear why in the biblical texts God is so zealous for the symbols of his presence. The chief symbol of God's holiness and his presence, of course, was the sanctuary itself. Its layout and design as well as the objects and adornments within it conveyed the idea that he was distinct and set apart, especially because only the priests were to enter into the sanctuary itself. By commanding that people remain outside the sanctuary in which he was said to dwell in some sense and that only a designated few whom he had sanctified or set apart to serve him enter into the special areas that he had designated as holy, he made it clear to his people that he was to be held in awe by them and shown the utmost respect in every way and at every moment. He was unlike any other god, infinitely more powerful and wise than other gods were and committed to justice and righteousness in a way that none of them could ever be. The fact that no divine or human beings could rival him or compare to him in glory, might, power, and strength was conveyed by his insistence that no one approach the symbols of his presence except those to whom he had given his permission, as well as his command that any who dared to disobey him in this regard be put to death. While from a modern perspective this command is no doubt highly problematic, it emphasized in no uncertain terms that he was holy and demanded that all respect him and treat him as holy.

When those whom God did allow into his presence drew near, they were to make sure that they prepared themselves by sanctifying and purifying themselves in ways that in some regards were also symbolic. The bathing, washing, changing of clothes, and other preparations made by those who approached him at the sanctuary were to be the outward and visible expressions of the cleansing and purification of their thoughts, hearts, and lives. Ultimately, it was this that mattered to God. If God was concerned that the symbols of his presence be treated as holy, it was because only by laying stress on his holiness could he hope to have a holy people who would live in ways that would make their well-being possible and serve as his instrument for bringing others to live in those ways as well.

In their own way, the sacred objects associated with the sanctuary, including especially the ark of the covenant, served as symbols of God's holiness and presence as well. For that reason, they were to be treated with the same care, respect, and reverence. Only certain individuals whom God had consecrated to his service were to touch and handle them, and out of respect for the sanctity of those objects, anything that came into contact with them was to be set apart as holy as well. As we have noted in Chapter 8, the biblical texts provide no evidence that this command had anything to do with a belief that some type of mysterious force or substance was contained in these objects or transmitted by them. Rather, it was grounded in the same demand for absolute respect for everything associated with God and dedicated to his worship. What had been made holy by being consecrated to God was not to be treated as common or ordinary but was to be removed from the realm of everyday life so as to be devoted exclusively to him. The same was true with regard to the days that he had set apart for his people to observe as holy. By sanctifying those days, they sanctified themselves as well in the sense of dedicating themselves, their time, their energies, and their resources to his service. Yet because the only thing that God desired and sought was the well-being of all of his people, for them to sanctify themselves and dedicate themselves to his service meant being fully committed to their own well-being in the same way that God himself was.

By demanding that the common people remain outside the sanctuary and keep their distance from the other symbols of his presence and holiness, God was promoting the holiness of his people at the same time by leading them to sanctify and purify themselves from all the things that did them and others harm and to dedicate themselves to ways of thinking and behaving that brought life and well-being for all. The distance that the people were to keep in relation to those symbols promoted the type of respect, reverence, and awe that was necessary for them to submit fully to his will as their sovereign Lord. He was the one who was to reign supreme in their lives and dictate how they were to live, yet he insisted on doing so not for *his* sake but for *theirs*. They were not to live in any manner they desired but in the way he had commanded for their own good. Their distance from the symbols of his presence reinforced among them the idea that God was above them as one who was infinitely superior to them and utterly distinct from them. In no way were they ever to see themselves as being equal to him or on the same level with him. No one, not even the priests or the high priest, could claim to stand in his place, nor were those whom he had placed in positions of leadership to equate their own word with his. Any who did so were usurping his authority. No one but God was to stand above the people and dictate to all what was to be done. The people as well as the priests were simply to obey.

God's demand that the people show the same type of reverence for the other symbols of his holiness and presence served the same purpose. Respect for these symbols helped promote justice and righteousness because it promoted respect for God and God's will as well. Conversely, to fail to show respect for the signs and symbols that God had established communicated the idea that it was also acceptable to fail to show respect for God and his will. For that reason, such disrespect could not be tolerated. Because what God desired and sought was the practice of justice, righteousness, and solidarity for the good of all, any who did not treat the things dedicated to honoring him as holy would treat his will for the good of all with the same contempt and disdain.

In order to grasp the logic behind God's zeal for the symbols of his holiness and presence as well as his refusal to tolerate any type of disrespect for those symbols, we might imagine what would take place if his commands to show reverence and respect for his sanctuary and the sacred objects associated with it were not observed carefully. For example, if anyone might trod into his sanctuary at any time, soiling and debasing it, dropping trash or debris, scribbling graffiti, or speaking and acting there in ways that evidenced a lack of reverence and respect, the symbols of his holiness that God had given his people as a gift out of love for them could not fulfill their purpose. Those symbols would no longer be able to remind the people of God's sovereignty and goodness. Instead, all would receive the impression that one could treat God's gifts with indifference and disdain and that there was nothing special or worthy of admiration not only about the symbols of God's presence but also about God himself. If that were the case, then it made little difference if one treated his word and his commandments with the same lack of respect and reverence. Furthermore, if people could treat the symbols of God's presence with contempt and the almighty God simply allowed them to do so, they would be led to conclude that he did not care whether his people acknowledged and respected him as sovereign Lord over their lives and that it did not matter to him if they treated the symbols he had given them as if they were of no value or importance.

This type of logic can be seen in the account of the events surrounding Israel's arrival at Mount Sinai found in Exodus 19. There, after God states his intention to make his covenant with Israel and the people accept, God tells Moses to have the people consecrate themselves by washing their clothes and preparing themselves in other ways to receive his commandments. He commands Moses to set limits around the mountain and to prohibit any person or animal from crossing those limits or even touching the mountain except at the time he appoints. He also adds that any who disobey are to be put to death. God then descends upon the mountain in the midst of an intense fire that covers it in smoke and causes it to shake violently. He speaks to Moses with a voice that thunders and strikes the mountain with bolts of lightning while at the same time shrouding himself in darkness. These things cause such great fear among the people that they beg Moses to ask God to speak through him rather than speaking to them directly (Exod 19:10-23; 20:18-21). It is important to note the words with which Moses responds to their petition: "Do not be afraid, for God has come only to test you and to put the fear of him upon you so that you do not sin" (20:20).

Here there can be no doubt that God wishes to impress upon the people his power, glory, sovereignty, and might. While in a sense he clearly seeks to instill fear in them, Moses' words also indicate his true purpose: not that they be afraid of him but that they be brought to obey him. Once again, by imagining an alternative scenario, the reasons why God acts in this way become evident. If God had not made such a public display of his power, glory, and transcendence but had simply encountered Moses privately to give him the commandments there out of their sight, the people might not feel any need to respect those commandments in the way God desired. Instead, they might treat them with disdain and treat Moses in the same way, perhaps even doubting that God had actually spoken with Moses or given him any commandments at all. According to the logic of the text, therefore, what God intended was to impress on the people in a convincing and overpowering manner the idea that he was holy and sovereign over all things so that they would take the commandments he was giving with utmost seriousness and recognize that he would not tolerate their failure or refusal to submit fully to those commandments for their own good.

Similar observations can be made with regard to the limits God sets around the mountain. According to the logic underlying the passage, if God had allowed the people to stand, sit, or lie idly upon the mountain as he made himself present there to give Moses his commandments, perhaps laughing, playing, or even acting with indifference to what was taking place there, their disrespect for his presence among them might lead to the same disrespect for him and his commandments. If the people were trampling and treading all over the mountain, perhaps urinating or defecating there, allowing their animals to graze on it, and carrying on as if nothing special was taking place, they would hardly view the commandments he was giving Moses as an expression of his sovereign will that they were to receive with utmost seriousness. If they were to subject every aspect of their lives fully to those commandments from that day on, it was necessary for God to manifest to them the overwhelming greatness of his sovereign power so that they would be overcome with awe and commit themselves to respecting and observing everything that he was commanding them in his wisdom as Lord and creator of all. At the same time, however, they were to be made aware that the same power, magnificence, and might that he was displaying before their eyes would be there to accompany, protect, defend, and prosper them if they submitted to his covenant and his commandments so as to live as his people. He wanted them to know that as their sovereign Lord he would refuse to let anything or anyone stand in his way of fulfilling his loving objectives among them. His will to bring them to live in ways that would enable them and others to attain the well-being and wholeness he desired for them was sacrosanct and non-negotiable. He would not be stopped until he had fashioned them to become the holy, just, and righteous people he intended them to be for their own good and that of the other nations as well.

The commandments that God gives with respect to the care and handling of the ark of the covenant as well as his reaction when Uzzah reaches out to the ark to prevent it from falling when it is being transported should be seen as reflecting the same logic (2 Sam 6:1-9; 1 Chr 13:5-12). The ark symbolized in a special and unique way God's holiness and presence and was therefore to be kept not only at a distance from the people but also out of their sight, except when it was necessary to transport it prior to the construction of the temple. If the purpose for which God had given his commandments regarding the ark was that it serve as a symbol and expression of his power, grace, transcendence, and love and remind his people of the manner in which he had accompanied them with signs and wonders in the wilderness in order to make his will known to them, it could not fulfill that purpose if it were treated simply as a common object that anyone might touch, handle, or gaze inside of. That could happen only if it was treated with utmost care and reverence.

While at first glance the manner in which God strikes Uzzah dead after he touches the ark to keep it from falling certainly seems excessively harsh and cruel, as it did even to David himself, there can be little doubt that God's reaction is seen as being rooted in a concern for the sanctity of the ark as a symbol of his presence. The narrative does not explain why God reacts so drastically, but while Uzzah may have been seeking to protect the ark, it is possible that he was thought to have been at fault in some way for what had happened. Perhaps he had not secured the ark properly to the cart on which it had been placed or was negligent in some other way with regard to the manner in which the cart and the oxen pulling it had been prepared for the ark's transportation. It is also possible that Uzzah was not watching carefully to make sure that the cart stayed in the correct path or did something else that made the oxen that were pulling the cart lurch. A more likely explanation is suggested in 1 Chr 15:11-15, where David's words seem to indicate that the reason why God had reacted in the way that he had was that the Levites had not been carrying the ark on their shoulders with poles. In that case, the fault or oversight that had led to Uzzah's death was not that of Uzzah alone but that of all of the Levites, apparently because they should have been carrying the ark rather than placing it on a cart. Had the Levites been transporting the ark properly in the first place, there would have been no need for Uzzah to reach out to prevent it from falling.

In any case, according to the logic underlying the account, if God had not responded in a visible and forceful manner that shook and impacted all those present when Uzzah grasped the ark, the onlookers and eventually the people in general would have come to the conclusion that anyone might touch the ark without suffering any type of consequence. If so, then in the future it might be treated disrespectfully in other ways as well. All sorts of persons might approach it to open the lid and gaze into it, purely out of curiosity. People might even doubt that God had actually given the ark as a sign or symbol of his presence, since when someone such as Uzzah touched it in a way that God had not authorized, nothing happened. Undoubtedly, many who read or heard this account would have reacted negatively in the same way that David is said to have done. God's reaction to Uzzah, however, left no doubts in anyone's mind regarding God's sovereignty and the need to respect both him and the symbols of his presence that he had given. To respect God's sovereignty also meant respecting his right to respond in any way he saw fit when his commands regarding the ark had been disobeyed. If he did not make it clear that he demanded to be obeyed under any circumstance, then people might be led to believe that they could disobey him without suffering any consequences under other circumstances as well.

At times, however, if it suited his purposes, God might choose to make exceptions regarding what he had commanded with regard to the symbols of his presence. An excellent example of this is found in 1 Sam 21:1-6, where David is allowed to eat of the consecrated bread that was placed in the sanctuary to symbolize God's presence there. Because God was with David and wished for him to be saved from harm at the hands of those who were seeking his life, at that moment God considered that it was acceptable for David to eat of that bread and therefore did not punish him in any way for doing so. As sovereign Lord, God was free to respond to what people did in any way he saw fit, not only when they disobeyed him but when they obeyed him as well. For that reason, no one was to question or challenge anything he did or commanded. On the contrary, all were to accept whatever came from his hand and to acknowledge and trust that in his wisdom and his love he knew what was best for all.

If God was so zealous and uncompromising in his demand that all respect the symbols of his holiness and presence and reacted so harshly when any disobeyed him in this regard, therefore, ultimately it was not for his sake but for theirs. Only by insisting that what he had commanded be obeyed down to the last detail could he demonstrate to his people the need for them to submit fully to his will in every way for their own good. Of course, what really interested him were not the symbols themselves but the life of justice and righteousness that those symbols were intended to promote, as well as the unconditional love of his people not only for himself but for one another as well. By demanding that his people treat the symbols of his presence with respect and reverence, he was also demanding that they treat one another with the same respect and reverence by caring and loving others in the same way that he did as the sovereign Lord and creator of all. Those symbols were aimed at bringing about in his people the same commitment to the well-being of all of his creatures that was the primary characteristic of God himself. By constantly reinforcing among them the idea that he was holy and that his will was also to be regarded as such, he reminded them that he would not tolerate behaviors that did harm to others, undermined their well-being, or disrespected them in any way. If one was truly to treat God with respect, one could not treat others with disrespect and a lack of love, because this involved disobeying God and not respecting his will. Conversely, if one respected others and treated them in the way that God desired and commanded, one was respecting God and his holiness at the same time. For that reason, love for others would necessarily take the form of showing reverence for the symbols of God's presence so that others might also do the same. In that way they would bring others to live in the same type of love for God and one another.

God's demand that people respect the symbols of his holiness and presence also led him to command that they participate faithfully and regularly in the sacrificial worship dedicated to him at his sanctuary. Those symbols could fulfill their purpose only if the people constantly contemplated them and reflected on them to the extent that this was possible for them. Even when they found themselves at a distance from the temple and could not gaze upon it, as they turned at least twice a day to pray in its direction, they were inevitably brought to visualize in their mind the many symbolisms associated with it and the sacred things that it contained. In this way, God brought about in them a greater love not only for himself but for others, as well as for his creation as a whole.

While the sanctuary and the symbols it contained stressed the holiness and sovereignty of God, curiously at the same time they expressed his simplicity and humility. This was especially the case with regard to the tabernacle he had commanded the Israelites to build for him, which was basically little more than a portable tent. When David offers to build a temple to replace the tabernacle, God tells him that he had never aspired to have a temple in which to dwell and was satisfied with the portable tent that he had commanded Moses to construct. In the same context, he also reminds David that he had taken him from the pasture when he was nothing more than a lowly shepherd, evidently to stress David's humble origins and present himself as a God who was humble and simple in the same way (2 Sam 7:1-9). This humility and simplicity are also expressed in the fact that the offerings that God commands of his people in the Torah are in no way ornate or excessively lavish or abundant. On the contrary, rather than demanding large hecatombs of costly animals, he simply commanded that his people offer him one ram or lamb in the morning and another in the afternoon on a daily basis and for other occasions prescribed offerings that were for the most part extremely modest as well (Exod 29:38-43; Num 28:1–29:39). The only offerings that were presented to him continually were incense and twelve loaves of bread that were to be replaced once a week. Because all of these offerings were relatively austere and inexpensive, they did not become an onerous burden for the people or consume their resources to any considerable extent. While on occasion God is said to be pleased by offerings that are much more lavish and abundant, such as at the dedication of the temple by Solomon, those offerings were entirely voluntary rather than something that he had demanded of the people (1 Kgs 8:62-66). He received them gladly, not because he wished to be honored for his own sake, but because he was pleased to see in his people the expressions of deep love and devotion that such offerings symbolized, since that love and devotion would lead them to submit more fully to his will for their own good.

God's humility and concern for the lowly and needy was reflected as well in the special provisions he had made in the Torah for those who were poor. He allowed them to give offerings that were less costly and elaborate, yet he valued those offerings just as much as he did those that were more lavish. God's command that animals as well as individuals who had some type of physical defect not be dedicated or consecrated to him or to his service should therefore not be understood as a lack of care and concern for the weak and disabled or those who were impaired in other ways.[28] Instead, the logic behind that command was that those animals and individuals were not able to symbolize his power and sovereignty in the way he desired due to their disability or imperfection. As numerous passages from the Torah demonstrate, however, he had taken care to ensure that provisions were made for such individuals and that the other members of his people care for them and afford them special attention.

Interestingly, God's command for the common people not to enter the sanctuary and his demand that the priests who approached him there be fully sanctified in both body and soul also communicated two ideas that at first glance might seem to be in conflict with one another, namely, his transcendence as well as his nearness and accessibility. By reminding the people of his greatness and transcendence as sovereign Lord of all through the symbols he had established, at the same time he reminded them that he was present throughout all of his creation and thus was close at hand and available to them no matter where they might find themselves or how far away from his sanctuary they might be. By emphasizing his hiddenness, therefore, the sanctuary also reinforced the idea that he made himself present throughout the world to hear and answer any who called out to him or sought to approach him.

---

28. See Lev 21:16-23; 22:17-25; Deut 15:19-21; 17:1.

Finally, it is important to stress that when his people came to forget that the sanctuary and the objects contained within it were merely symbols designed to promote a life of justice and righteousness among them and instead ascribed to the sanctuary and those objects some type of mysterious or magical power to bless and protect them due to their association with God's presence there, God was thought to react in anger and make it clear through his prophets that such was not the case. This is the situation described in Jeremiah 7, for example:

> The word that came to Jeremiah from the LORD: Stand in the gate of the LORD's house and proclaim there this word, and say: Hear the word of the LORD, all you people of Judah, you who enter these gates to worship the LORD. Thus says the LORD of hosts, the God of Israel: Amend your ways and your doings, and I will let you dwell in this place. Do not trust in these deceptive words: "This is the temple of the LORD, the temple of the LORD, the temple of the LORD." For if you truly amend your ways and your doings, if you truly execute justice with one another, if you do not oppress the foreigner, the orphan, and the widow or shed innocent blood in this place, and if you do not go after other gods to your own ruin, then I will cause you to dwell in this place, in the land that I gave to your ancestors forever and ever. Look, you trust in deceptive words to no avail. Will you steal, murder, commit adultery, swear falsely, make offerings to Baal, and go after other gods that you have not known, and then come and stand before me in this house, which is called by my name, and say, "We are safe!"—only to go on doing all these abominations? Has this house, which is called by my name, become a den of thieves in your sight? I, too, am watching, says the LORD. Go now to my place that was in Shiloh, where I made my name dwell at first, and see what I did to it for the wickedness of my people Israel. And now, because you have done all these things, says the LORD, and did not listen when I spoke to you persistently, and did not answer when I called you, therefore I will do to the house that is called by my name, in which you trust, and to the place that I gave to you and to your ancestors just what I did to Shiloh. And I will cast you out of my sight, just as I cast out all your kinsfolk, all the offspring of Ephraim (vv. 1-15).

As we have stressed repeatedly elsewhere, the condition for the people to be blessed was not that God be present at the temple or dwell there but that they practice what was good, right, and just. They were not to place their trust in the temple but in God, yet by definition to trust in God was to live in the way he had commanded, since any who disobeyed him could hardly be said to be trusting in him. If they placed their trust in the temple itself, then they were no longer looking to God but making of the temple an idol, since they were ascribing mysterious powers to it and devoting themselves to it as if it were itself divine.

As this passage from Jeremiah indicates, when that happened God would not hesitate to destroy the temple dedicated to him, precisely because it was promoting injustice, exploitation, violence, and wrongdoing rather than the practice of what was good and right. While in one sense he might be seen as withdrawing his presence from the temple, in another sense God could be seen as making himself present or "visiting" the people by taking action to put a stop to the abuses and corruption that his temple was promoting rather than preventing. When the people who associated themselves with the temple fell into sin and injustice and refused to repent, he made it a special point to remove from them the gracious signs and symbols of his presence, since under those circumstances to leave the temple standing and allow his people to continue to present offerings to him there would convey to all the idea that he remained pleased by those offerings and had no reservations about calling those people his own.

CHAPTER 10

THE GOD WHO PLANS TO BLESS

Although the Hebrew Scriptures never speak explicitly of God having a plan for the world and the human beings that he created, they clearly presuppose such an idea. As we noted in Chapter 2 of this study, those Scriptures not only present God as the creator of all that exists but also consistently stress his sovereignty over all the people and things that he has created. Because there are no powers or beings that are superior to him, he was not subject to any type of force or compulsion when he created the world and the human beings he placed over his creation but was free to order and fashion all that exists in any way that pleased him. If such was the case, then he must have had some type of objective or purpose in mind and therefore some type of plan as well. Without such a plan, he would have had no basis for creating the world and human beings in the way that he had.

The same observation must be made with regard to God's election of Israel as his special people or "treasured possession" (Exod 19:5). That election presupposes a plan of some kind, that is, some purpose or objective that God intended to carry out from the time he decided to choose Israel as a people, even before they existed as such. While in the previous chapters we have already examined in detail many aspects of that plan as it is presented in the biblical texts, what we have seen up to this point will make it possible to contemplate and spell out that plan even more clearly in the present chapter.

THE INTENTIONS OF THE GODS
IN ANCIENT PAGAN THOUGHT

Because the gods of most of the nations in antiquity were believed to have emerged from nature and had not been brought into existence for any purpose, they were not thought to be attempting to direct history toward any type of goal or objective. If they were thought to have any objective themselves, it was the same as that which most human beings have: simply to spend their existence in as much comfort and pleasure as possible without suffering any type of need or hardship. To the extent that the gods cared about human beings, they merely wanted human beings to do whatever contributed to their comfort and pleasure by serving and honoring them, doing their will, and offering them the gifts and sacrifices they desired for their own sake. Since the gods regarded human beings as a means to their own ends rather than seeing their well-being as an end in itself, they were not thought to be pursuing some objective in relation to human beings themselves, other than ensuring that they might continue to serve them perpetually.

Because virtually all of the gods of antiquity were associated with a particular people or nation, they were not thought to be concerned for all human beings equally. Instead, they cared for the people and nations that gave them what they wanted by offering them their worship and sacrifices. They were especially concerned for the rulers and the elites among these people and nations, since the wealthy and powerful leaders ensured that the people under them would continue to serve the gods loyally and faithfully. For the same reasons, the gods also sought to protect and care for the people and nations who were dedicated to their worship and service. This too, however, responded to their own self-interest, since if those people and nations suffered some type of misfortune or disaster they would no longer be able to give the gods what they needed and desired. It was also in the gods' best interest to associate with great and powerful nations rather than those that were small, weak, and insignificant, since nations that were inferior would inevitably be forced to serve other nations that were superior to them and to adopt the gods of those nations as their own.

Among many peoples, the worship of their gods was not voluntary but obligatory. Those gods would bless the people and nations under them only if they received the offerings and worship that were regarded as their due. If they did not, it was thought that those gods would punish not only the individuals or groups that refused to serve them but the entire nation or people. For that reason, it was necessary for all of the people and their leaders to pressure or oblige those individuals or groups that were not serving the gods faithfully to do so in order to avoid provoking the wrath of the gods and bringing down their punishment on the people as a whole.

Because what concerned the gods was simply receiving the worship and offerings they desired for their own sake, as long as the rulers and people who were dedicated to serving them satisfied their desires, the gods were for the most part content with them. It was extremely important, however, for those who worshiped them to remain loyal to them and submit to them fully. In exchange for that loyalty and submission, the gods would themselves remain loyal to their worshipers even when they acted in ways that were morally reprehensible. The gods especially continued to defend and side with those who were most dear to them, no matter what they did. Thus, for example, as we have noted in Chapter 1, even though the manner in which Polyphemus treated Odysseus and his men in the *Odyssey* was cruel, reprehensible, and unjust, the god Poseidon sided fully with Polyphemus against Odysseus because Polyphemus was his son. That type of loyalty and faithfulness to one's own kin or people was thought to be more important than a concern for the practice of what was good, just, and right and thus to override such a concern.

Because most gods in antiquity were said to be immortal, it was generally claimed that the position they occupied in relation to human beings was intended to last indefinitely or forever. This enabled the people associated with those gods to regard themselves in the same way. In the *Enuma Elish* and the Code of Hammurabi, for example, it is not only Marduk and the other great gods of Babylon who are expected to remain in power forever but also the Babylonian people, as well as the city of Babylon that those gods had established as their dwelling place. Such a view justified subjugating other peoples not only to the Babylonian gods but to the Babylonian people and their rulers as well. To affront or attack the Babylonian people or their rulers, therefore, was also to affront or attack their gods. Gods such as Marduk would not tolerate any such opposition and would act through the Babylonian people and their rulers to quash any type of rebellion or resistance to their dominion.

For the same reasons, it was not generally thought that the gods had any intention to bring about a reality that was different in any significant way from that which existed in the present. On the contrary, as is evident from the Prologue and Epilogue to the Code of Hammurabi considered in Chapter 4, the people and rulers who claimed to have been chosen by the gods to subject other peoples to themselves tended to maintain that the prosperity and well-being of all depended on their submitting unquestioningly and unreservedly to them as the representatives of those gods. To criticize the existing order and express hopes regarding an alternative order that might replace it was seen as unacceptable and subversive, since it involved an implicit rejection of the rulers in place as well as the gods who had chosen those rulers as their representatives.

THE BLESSING OF ISRAEL IN GOD'S PLAN

As we have seen in Chapter 2 of this study, the opening chapters of Genesis stress several points that are key for understanding the Hebrew Scriptures as a whole. First, they affirm that God desired only the good for the human beings and the world he created. From the beginning, he pronounced his blessing on human beings collectively and not merely on one of the nations or peoples in particular that would come into existence. Second, the Genesis account makes it clear that human beings can attain the blessing and the good that God desires for them only if they live in accordance with God's will by doing what is good, right, just, and loving. When they instead practice injustice, violence, and oppression, they destroy their own well-being and fill the earth with pain and suffering. And third, the story of the flood in Noah's day assumes that God cannot force human beings to abandon their destructive behavior so as to live instead in ways that allow them to enjoy the well-being he desires for them. If God could bring human beings to alter their behavior unilaterally, he would have done so after they had became violent and corrupt instead of destroying them through the flood.

The narrative in the opening chapters of Genesis also assumes another important point, namely, that God holds out hope that eventually he can bring human beings to change their ways and commit themselves to living in accordance with his will so that they may attain the happiness and well-being he intended for them. Such a hope, of course, is possible only if God remains committed to doing everything in his power to bring them to abandon their violent and destructive behavior. If God no longer held out such a hope or were no longer committed to doing everything possible to see that hope fulfilled, it would make no sense for him to allow human beings to continue to live and multiply across the earth. Instead, he would simply destroy them or abandon them definitively so as to let them destroy themselves.

Only when we bring together all that we have seen in the preceding chapters of this study is it possible to grasp more fully the manner in which the biblical texts conceive of God acting to accomplish his objective of bringing human beings to live in ways that will enable them to enjoy the well-being he desired for them from the start. Despite the diversity of perspectives and emphases that we encounter in those texts, they share a common vision regarding the manner in which the God who created all that exists intends to accomplish his purposes in the world he has fashioned, just as they reflect a common vision regarding that God himself.

The Challenge of Bringing Blessing

By affirming that God had chosen to create all things as good and that he had blessed all that he had created, the opening chapters of the Genesis account presuppose that the reason and purpose for which God had created the world and human beings was a loving one. The biblical account of creation, however, also presupposes another idea. According to that account, God had not created separate groups of people or nations when he had made human beings, nor had he divided them into distinct groups or nations. Of course, once human beings began to multiply, it was inevitable that they eventually form different families, peoples, and nations. Even when that took place, however, there was no reason why they might not all continue to live as a single family, people, or nation in some sense. If instead the families and peoples of the earth had come to be divided among themselves and at enmity with one another, it had been due to the sin, evil, jealousy, and lust for power and dominance that are described in passages such as the account of Abel's murder by Cain in Genesis 4 and the story of the tower of Babel in the opening verses of Genesis 11.

Therefore, if God had created human beings as a unified whole and if the divisions that had come to exist among them were not his work but that of human beings themselves, then from the start God must have desired the well-being of *all* human beings without exception and not just certain groups or peoples among them. Because all descended from the same man and woman, all were equally to be considered the work of his hands and in some sense were also to be regarded as sisters and brothers and as fellow children of the one God who had made them.

As we have seen in previous chapters of this study, however, beginning in Genesis 12 with the account of God's calling of Abram or Abraham, God is presented as choosing for himself a particular individual together with the people that will descend from him. From its very outset, the narrative regarding Abraham makes it clear that God's intention is not merely to bless him and his offspring but to bless all of the peoples and nations of the world: "in you all the families of the earth shall be blessed" (v. 3). The idea that God wishes for all of the families to be blessed is not only repeated elsewhere in key passages from the book of Genesis but also appears both explicitly and implicitly in other passages from the Hebrew Scriptures, especially in the Psalms and the prophetic writings, as we shall see below. At the same time, however, the blessing of other peoples is tied to the blessing of Abraham and the people descended from him. In biblical thought, therefore, these two blessings are inseparable from one another.

When considering these ideas, it is important to stress once more a point that we have seen repeatedly throughout this study, namely, that by definition *those who are not committed to living in accordance with God's will for justice and righteousness cannot be blessed.* Their failure or refusal to live in ways that will allow them to enjoy the well-being that God desires for all makes it impossible for them to be blessed, since rather than using whatever they receive from God's hands for good, they will use it in ways that do them harm and promote injustice and oppression. As we have seen in Chapter 3 of this study, according to the logic of the Genesis narrative, what made it possible for God to bless Abraham was Abraham's faith and trust in God and his commitment to practicing righteousness and obeying God in all that God commanded him.

The biblical account, therefore, presupposes that if the people descended from Abraham as well as the other families of the earth are to be blessed through Abraham and together with him, *they must be brought to live in accordance with justice and righteousness in the same way that Abraham did.* For that reason, God's promise to Abraham must be understood in terms of a commitment not merely to pour out blessings on the descendants of Abraham and the other families of the earth but also to bring them to practice the justice and righteousness that will enable them to attain the well-being associated with those blessings. In that case, what concerns and interests God is not the election of a particular people for its own sake but rather the existence of a people who will practice justice and righteousness and bring others to do the same. In other words, God's concern for the well-being of the people descended from Abraham and the other families of the earth who will be blessed through them is inseparable from his intention and insistence that all of these nations and peoples come to obey him as Abraham did by practicing justice and righteousness. If they fail or refuse to do so, God simply will not be able to bless them, no matter how much he may wish to do so.

Further on in the biblical narrative that begins in Genesis, of course, it becomes clear that the "great nation" to which God is referring in Gen 12:1-3 is the people descended from Abraham through Isaac and Jacob, that is, the people of Israel. God's intention to bless Israel is, of course, stressed repeatedly elsewhere throughout the biblical texts. At the same time, however, those texts consistently maintain that if Israel does not obey God and live as his people by practicing the justice and righteousness he demands of them, God will remove them from the land he promised to Abraham, deliver them into the hands of their enemies, and even destroy a large part of the people so as to leave behind only a remnant. Numerous passages add that ultimately this remnant will come to live obediently in the way God demands for their own good so as to attain the blessings he intended for them from the moment he chose them as his own through Abraham.

While in a sense God's promise to bless the people descended from Abraham is unconditional, therefore, since God intends to do whatever is necessary to make that blessing a reality for them, in another sense that promise is conditional upon the people's living in faith, obedience, and righteousness in the same way that Abraham did. The biblical account makes it clear that many of those descended from Abraham will *not* be blessed and will even be subjected to hardships, punishments, and destruction due to their refusal to follow in Abraham's footsteps. Although God will do everything in his power to enable them to attain the blessing he desires for them by providing them with instruction and guidance, pouring out his Spirit on them, calling them to turn back to him when they stray, and seeking to correct them through chastisements when necessary, many of Abraham's descendants will *not* attain that blessing because their conduct will prevent them from doing so.

These ideas must be kept in mind when interpreting God's promise to bless those who bless Abraham and curse those who curse him or make light of him in Gen 12:3. The logic behind this promise is not that God has chosen to bless Abraham simply because for no good or apparent reason he determined to show preference for one individual over all others, as if some type of arbitrary favoritism were involved on God's part. If Abraham has been blessed by God and should be blessed by others, it is because of his commitment to doing God's will. To refuse to bless him or to curse him and speak ill of him would be to belittle or make light of his commitment to doing God's will and serving as God's instrument to bless others. In contrast, to bless Abraham would involve valuing his commitment and obedience to God and attempting to live in the same commitment and obedience.

Blessing a People to Be a Blessing for All

Because the people descended from Abraham through Isaac and Jacob will not always practice justice and righteousness but will frequently fall into sinful behavior that is willful and persistent, to bless them must not be understood in terms of offering unconditional support for everything they do or speaking with approval of them when they act in ways that are contrary to God's will. While all people are to desire that Abraham's offspring be blessed rather than cursed, when the people descended from him fall into destructive behavior that does them and others harm, this desire for them to be blessed will take the form of expressing disapproval for that behavior and exhorting them to change their ways. The reason why God wants Abraham's offspring to be blessed is that like Abraham they are his chosen instrument for blessing others as well. For the same reason, God promises to curse any who show contempt for Abraham's offspring, since in order for them to be a blessing to others they must themselves be blessed rather than cursed and rejected. Behind God's promise to bless those who bless Abraham and curse those who curse him or make light of him, therefore, is not the kind of arbitrary favoritism that was characteristic of the pagan gods of antiquity but rather a concern to see both Israel and the other nations of the world blessed by practicing the same type of justice and righteousness seen in Abraham. That would happen only as his people Israel were blessed, yet for Israel to be blessed the people needed to be committed to living in accordance with God's will.

Such a vision regarding the blessing of Israel stands in stark contrast to interpretations of the passage that imply that God loves Israel more than he loves other nations and desires a blessing for Israel that is greater than the blessing he desires for others on a permanent basis. According to such an understanding of God's election of Israel, what really matters to God is that Israel be blessed as the people whom he prefers and cares about over all others. Any blessing that the other nations may receive from God is secondary and should in some way contribute either directly or indirectly to the blessing of Israel, which is of much greater importance to God than the blessing of any other nation. In that case, God has assigned to the nations an auxiliary role in relation to Israel. Their primary purpose is to serve Israel so that Israel may be the most blessed of all peoples on the earth.

If God's intention for the nations is reduced to that of fulfilling such a role, then the needs and desires of Israel are to be given priority over the needs and desires of all the other nations of the world. Undoubtedly, in order for Israel to be blessed, the needs and desires of the nations must also be met, yet this is not an end in itself but only a means to the end of ensuring that Israel's needs and desires are satisfied. In that case, the people of Israel are to be concerned primarily for themselves and only secondarily for others, while the nations are expected to put the needs and desires of Israel above their own. Such a relationship would make of God's chosen people an instrument of oppression for other nations. They would be justified in treating those nations as their slaves in order to be served by them and would even have God's approval for relating to them in that way. In the eyes of those nations, the God of Israel would be an oppressive God rather than a liberating one, since he would demand that all people dedicate themselves to serving Israel rather than concerning themselves primarily with their own needs. At the same time, that God would make of Israel a selfish and egotistical people who subjected other nations to themselves for their own sake. He would also show himself to be the same type of God, namely, a selfish and egotistical God who imposed his will on the nations by force in the same way that his people Israel were to do. While his love for Israel would be unconditional, his love for the nations would be conditional upon their loving Israel more than they loved themselves.

Were the God of Israel to behave in that way, he would be acting in the same manner that the pagan gods of antiquity were thought to do. As we have seen above, one of the primary characteristics of those gods was that they sought to be served purely for their own sake and were ultimately concerned only for themselves. Their only interest in attending to the needs and desires of the people who worshiped them consisted in bringing those people to satisfy their own needs and desires as gods. If such gods served human beings, it was only to be served by them. Furthermore, rather than caring about human beings in general, they cared only for those who were dedicated to providing them with the things they needed and desired for their own sake.

The people who worshiped such gods inevitably came to relate to people of other nations in the same way. With the support and approval of their gods, they sought to subjugate and dominate those people and compel them to live as their servants or slaves. If the people of Israel viewed the God whom they worshiped in the same way, therefore, they too would seek to impose their will on the other nations of the world with his help and bring them into submission so that those nations might be dedicated to their service.

If this was what God intended for Israel, however, then rather than seeking his people's well-being he was doing them tremendous harm. The reason for this is that any who relate to others by seeking to impose their will on them and subjugate them by force can never truly enjoy well-being and wholeness. In order for people to be happy and whole, they must live in solidarity with one another. Because all depend on others for what they need in order to enjoy well-being and no person or group of people can attain that well-being on their own without the assistance and support of others, those who seek to enjoy well-being for themselves must seek the well-being of others at the same time. If they do not, they will be undermining their own well-being and acting in ways that are contrary to it. Furthermore, this concern for others must be *genuine* and *sincere*, since it must involve regarding the well-being of others as an end in itself rather than solely as a means to one's own well-being. If that concern is not genuine or sincere, it will inevitably end up being selfish and self-serving and others will perceive it as such, since they will realize that they are merely being used and manipulated. In that case, there will not truly be solidarity, that is, a sincere commitment on the part of all to seeking the well-being of others together with their own. Where there is not a true and sincere commitment to solidarity, by definition there cannot be wholeness, well-being, and justice for all.

A further reason why those who live in ways that are selfish and self-serving cannot enjoy true well-being and wholeness is that the manner in which they will relate to others will generate tensions, conflict, enmity, and violence. When they show disregard and indifference for the well-being of others and either trample upon them or oppress and mistreat them by seeking to use them for their own ends, they will generate anger, hatred, and enmity among those whom they treat in that manner. As a result, those others will seek to do them harm and they will be forced to be constantly on the defensive, concerned for their own safety. They will inevitably live in fear of the aggressions and attacks of others and will have to dedicate much of their time, energy, and resources to implementing measures aimed at protecting themselves from others as well as keeping them in subjection and under control. As a result, they will never be able to enjoy peace and security. Their lives will instead be full of unrest, anxiety, fear, and hostility. Those who live under such conditions cannot experience well-being and wholeness.

For these reasons, if God truly seeks to bless Israel, he cannot give preference to the well-being of Israel over that of the nations or allow Israel to do so, since that would involve promoting the type of injustice and oppression that makes it impossible for people to enjoy the well-being he desires for all. The only way in which God can bless Israel is by seeking the blessing of the other nations at the same time and demanding that Israel do likewise. If God ascribes greater importance to the well-being of Israel than he does to that of the nations and commands that the nations give greater priority to the needs and desires of Israel than they give to their own needs and desires, then he not only makes of himself an oppressor in relation to those nations but he makes of Israel an instrument of oppression in the world as well.

If Israel is to enjoy well-being, wholeness, and justice in accordance with God's will, therefore, neither Israel's God nor the people themselves can be concerned primarily or exclusively for the welfare of Israel. Instead, both for the sake of others *and for their own sake*, the people must be genuinely concerned for the welfare of other nations, and both God and the people themselves must be just as committed to seeking the well-being of others as they are to seeking that of Israel. In essence, this involves striving to live *in solidarity* with other peoples and nations so that all together are equally committed to doing whatever is necessary to promote the well-being of all people without exception. Ultimately, this must be the goal or objective pursued not only by God but by Israel: a world in which all seek the well-being of one another by genuinely caring for one another, looking out especially for the weak and suffering, and seeking to ensure that the needs of all are met. Only when such a world exists will all within it be able to enjoy true well-being, peace, and prosperity. In contrast, if any particular people or group of people lives selfishly and seeks to serve only its own needs by disregarding, manipulating, dominating, or subjugating others, that people will undermine and destroy not only the well-being and happiness of others but its own well-being and happiness as well.

The problem, of course, is that for such a world to exist, not only Israel but the other nations and peoples must be committed to that type of solidarity. This means that if God and Israel are to seek such a world, they must be dedicated to doing what is necessary for those nations and peoples to be brought to care for one another and do everything possible to combat injustice and oppression in the world. From the perspective of the biblical writings, however, as long as human beings continue to serve gods of their own making rather than the one true God, it is impossible for a world characterized by such solidarity and mutual concern to exist. As long as people continue to worship and submit to gods who promote violence and injustice out of selfishness and self-regard, they will never be able to live in ways that truly promote their well-being and for that reason will never be able to attain that well-being. The world will continue to be filled with suffering, hatred, injustice, violence, strife, and discord as long as those who inhabit it do not come to know and serve the one true God who created them so as to live in the way that he commands, not for *his* sake but for *theirs*.

In biblical thought, this is the challenge that God faces. The only way in which he can bless the nations along with Israel is by bringing them to know and serve him for their own good. However, because those nations have no desire to know and serve him but are instead committed to serving their own gods, whose worship leads them to live in ways that make it impossible for them to enjoy well-being, there appears to be no way for God to bless them. His only hope is first to establish through Israel a people that will acknowledge and serve him alone as their God so as to live in justice and righteousness. Only when the other nations see how such a way of life leads to blessing will they choose to abandon their own gods to serve the God of Israel alone alongside Israel.

In light of these considerations, the idea that God has chosen Israel as his special people and desires to bless them above all other nations cannot be viewed in isolation from God's intention to bring all of the families of the earth to attain the same blessing that he desires for Israel. In biblical thought, while God's blessing of Israel is undoubtedly an end in itself, it is also a means toward the end of eventually bringing people of all nations to live as his people together with Israel. In other words, God first intends to bless Israel, yet once that has happened he will then seek to use the blessing of Israel to bring other nations to be blessed in the same way.

If the passages in which God speaks of his intention to bless all of the families of the earth through Abraham and his offspring are understood in this way, then the plan that God intends to carry out becomes clear. First, God must bless his people Israel not only by multiplying them, giving them the land he promised them, and making them prosper, but also by guiding and instructing them through the Torah so that they live in a way that promotes their well-being. He must also take whatever measures are necessary to discipline and correct his people when they depart from the good path he has laid out for them. Then, when the people are blessed as a result of their righteous conduct and God's response to that conduct, those from among the nations who observe how richly Israel is blessed will be attracted to Israel's God and will also want to live as his people in order to obtain the same blessings. In this way, they too will be brought to live in accordance with God's will for justice and righteousness and God will respond by making them prosper together with Israel.

A GOD FOR THE NATIONS

Although God's desire and intention to bless all of the families of the earth through Abraham and the people who will descend from him is affirmed explicitly only once in the narratives regarding Isaac and Jacob that follow upon the account of the life and death of Abraham in Genesis (Gen 26:2-5), a number of passages from the other books of the Pentateuch hint at the same idea. As we shall see further in the following chapter, when God works wonders in order to deliver the Israelites from their bondage in Egypt and then seeks to bring them to live faithfully as his people, he is presented as doing so not only for the sake of Israel but also for the purpose of bringing the nations to see and know what kind of God he is. The clearest expression of this idea in these books can be found in Deut 4:5-8. There, in the context of an exhortation for the Israelites to submit obediently to God's commandments when they enter into the land God has promised to them, Moses tells them:

> See, just as the LORD my God has commanded me, I have now taught you statutes and ordinances for you to observe in the land that you are about to enter and occupy. Keep them and do them, therefore, for this will demonstrate your wisdom and understanding in the eyes of the peoples, who, when they hear all these statutes, will say, "Surely this great nation is a wise and discerning people!" For what other nation is so great as to have a god as near to it as the LORD our God is whenever we call to him? And what other nation is so great as to have statutes and ordinances that are as just as this entire law that I am setting before you today?

Although this passage does not speak explicitly of people from the nations surrounding Israel being drawn to worship and serve Israel's God, such an idea is clearly implied. The hope that the other nations will marvel at the goodness of Israel's law as well as the kindness and proximity of Israel's God makes little sense unless it is understood as a desire that those nations also be brought to know Israel's God so that they may be blessed by living in accordance with the justice that his commandments serve to promote. It is in this sense that the statutes and ordinances of God's law are said to be just: they are means by which God will bring about justice and well-being among his people so that the other nations will marvel at the manner in which obedience to that law brings blessing.

The idea that the other nations of the world should be brought to love and serve the God of Israel by means of Israel's testimony regarding his goodness is particularly stressed in the Psalms. In many passages from the Psalms, the Psalmists call on people and nations throughout the world to praise God and celebrate the wonders that he works throughout his creation as well as his love and care for all of his creatures. In Psalm 36, for example, the Psalmist speaks of God's love for all people and all the other living beings he has created, as well as his desire to save them: "Your steadfast love, O Lord, reaches up to the heavens, your faithfulness to the clouds. Your righteousness is like the mountains of God, your judgments are like the great deep; you save humans and animals alike, O Lord. How precious is your steadfast love, O God! All people may take refuge in the shadow of your wings" (Ps 36:5-7). Similar ideas are expressed in Psalm 145:

> The Lord is good to all, and extends his compassion over all that he has made. All your works will give thanks to you, O Lord, and all your faithful people will bless you. They will speak of the glory of your kingdom and tell of your power, to make known to all people your mighty deeds and the glorious majesty of your kingdom. Your kingdom is an everlasting kingdom, and your dominion endures throughout all generations. The Lord is faithful in all his words and gracious in all his deeds. The Lord upholds all who are falling and raises up all who are bowed down. The eyes of all look to you, and you give them their food in due season. You open your hand and satisfy the desire of every living thing. The Lord is just in all his ways and kind in all his doings (vv. 9-17).

Other passages from the Psalms present God as a source of joy for the nations and call on them to praise him and give him thanks. According to Ps 22:27, "All the ends of the earth will remember and turn to the Lord; and all the families of the nations will worship before him." In Ps 67:4-5, the nations are to rejoice at the fact that God establishes justice and equity among them and guides them: "Let the nations be glad and sing for joy, for you judge the peoples with equity and guide the nations upon earth! Let the peoples praise you, O God! Let all the peoples praise you!" The same exhortation appears in other Psalms: "Bless our God, O peoples! Let the sound of his praises be heard!" (Ps 66:8). "Sing to God, O kingdoms of the earth! Sing praises to the Lord!" (Ps 68:32). "Praise the Lord, all you nations! Glorify him, all you peoples!" (Ps 117:1). The hope that other nations will come to love and serve God appears in Ps 86:9: "All the nations you have made will come and bow down before you, O Lord, and will glorify your name." The author of Psalm 102 envisions a day when "peoples gather together, and kingdoms, to serve the Lord" (v. 22). All of these ideas are especially stressed in Psalm 96:

> Ascribe to the Lord, O families of the peoples, ascribe to the Lord glory and strength. Ascribe to the Lord the glory of his name; bring an offering, and come into his courts. Worship the Lord in the splendor of his holiness; tremble before him, all the earth. Say among the nations, "The Lord reigns! The world is firmly established; it will never be moved. He will judge the peoples with equity." Let the heavens be glad, and let the earth rejoice! Let the sea roar, and all that fills it; let the field be jubilant, and everything in it! Then will all the trees of the forest sing for joy before the Lord, for he is coming; for he is coming to judge the earth. He will judge the world with justice and the peoples with his truth (vv. 7-13).

In passages such as these, people from among the nations are invited and exhorted to serve God, not because he threatens to punish them if they do not, but because he provides for all their needs and is committed to their well-being. Similarly, when the Psalmists call on the nations to rejoice because God is coming to judge the world, this can only be because that judgment involves delivering those who suffer injustice and oppression from their plight and establishing justice in the world for the good of all. Those who truly seek well-being for themselves and others, therefore, will be blessed by God's coming and the deliverance he brings. People from among the nations, however, can be brought to know of this God and come to love and serve him for their own good only if his people Israel proclaim to those nations in both word and deed his steadfast love, mercy, grace, and sovereignty.

Numerous passages from the prophetic books also express the hope that the nations will come to know God and his goodness through Israel and its prophets. In Isaiah, God tells the nations through his prophet: "Turn to me and be saved, all the ends of the earth! For I am God, and there is no other" (Isa 45:22). God's desire for the nations to experience his salvation is also stressed in Isa 42:1-6, where God promises to bring justice to the nations through his servant, whom he calls to be "a light to the nations," as well as Isa 49:6, where God tells his prophet: "I will give you as a light to the nations, that my salvation may reach to the ends of the earth." Further on in Isaiah, God speaks of bringing justice, guidance, deliverance, and hope to other peoples along with Israel by sharing with them his teaching or *torah*: "For a teaching will go out from me, and my justice for a light to the peoples. I will bring near my deliverance swiftly. My salvation has gone out and my arms will judge the peoples; the coastlands wait for me, and for my arm they hope" (51:4-5). In Isa 60:3, the people are told: "Nations will come to your light and kings to the brightness of your dawn." The blessing of the nations is tied explicitly to Israel's repentance and the people's practice of justice in Jer 4:1-2: "If you return, O Israel, says the LORD, then return to me. If you remove your abominations from my sight and do not waver, and if you swear, 'As the LORD lives!' in truth, in justice, and in righteousness, then nations will be blessed by him, and in him they will glory."

Perhaps the passage from the Hebrew Scriptures that describes most graphically God's desire to bless and save people of all nations is found in Isa 25:6-9. There the prophet affirms:

On this mountain the LORD of hosts will make for all peoples a lavish banquet, a feast of well-aged wines and rich food filled with marrow, of well-aged wines strained clear. And on this mountain he will destroy the shroud that is cast over all peoples, the veil that is spread over all the nations. He will swallow up death forever. Then the Lord GOD will wipe away the tears from all faces, and he will take away the disgrace of his people from all the earth, for the LORD has spoken. It will be said on that day, "Look, this is our God! We have waited for him, so that he might save us. This is the LORD for whom we have waited; let us be glad and rejoice in his salvation!"

The idea that other nations will be drawn to know and serve God so as to experience his salvation by means of his people Israel is repeated in a number of other passages in the prophetic books as well:

And the foreigners who join themselves to the Lord, to minister to him, to love the name of the Lord and to be his servants, all who keep the Sabbath and do not profane it, and hold fast my covenant—all these I will bring to my holy mountain, and make them joyful in my house of prayer. Their burnt offerings and their sacrifices will be accepted on my altar, for my house will be called a house of prayer for all peoples (Isa 56:6-7).

At that time Jerusalem will be called the throne of the Lord, and all nations will gather to it, to the presence of the Lord in Jerusalem, and they will no longer follow the stubbornness of their evil heart (Jer 3:17).

O Lord, my strength and my stronghold, my refuge in the day of trouble, to you will the nations come from the ends of the earth and say: "Our ancestors have inherited nothing but lies, worthless things in which there is no benefit" (Jer 16:19).

In the last days the mountain of the Lord's house will be established as the highest of the mountains, and it will be raised up above the hills. Peoples will stream to it, and many nations will come and say: "Come, let us go up to the mountain of the Lord, to the house of the God of Jacob, that he may teach us his ways and that we may walk in his paths." For instruction (*torah*) will go forth from Zion, and the word of the Lord from Jerusalem. He will judge between many peoples, and will settle disputes among strong nations far away. They will beat their swords into plowshares, and their spears into pruning hooks. Nation will not lift up sword against nation, neither will they train for war any more; but they will all sit under their own vines and under their own fig trees, and no one will make them afraid; for the mouth of the Lord of hosts has spoken (Mic 4:1-4; cf. Isa 2:2-4).

Sing and rejoice, O daughter Zion! For look, I will come and dwell in your midst, says the Lord. Many nations will join themselves to the Lord on that day, and they will be my people; and I will dwell in your midst (Zech 2:10-11).

Thus says the Lord of hosts: Peoples will yet come, the inhabitants of many cities. The inhabitants of one city will go to another, saying, "Come, let us go to entreat the favor of the Lord, and to seek the Lord of hosts; I will go as well." Many peoples and strong nations will come to seek the Lord of hosts in Jerusalem, and to entreat the favor of the Lord. Thus says the Lord of hosts: In those days ten people from nations of every language will take hold of a Jew, clutching his garment and saying, "Let us go with you, for we have heard that God is with you" (Zech 8:20-23).

Other passages from the books of Isaiah, Jeremiah, and Ezekiel look forward to a day in which God will restore the fortunes of particular nations such as Egypt, Assyria, Moab, Ammon, and Elam along with Israel (Jer 48:47; 49:6, 39; Ezek 29:13-14). The most surprising of these passages is no doubt Isa 19:19-25, where God seems to place the Egyptians and Assyrians on a par with Israel and even to show them preference. After referring to God's intentions to save and heal the Egyptians so that they may turn to him, the passage concludes: "On that day Israel will be the third with Egypt and Assyria, a blessing in the midst of the earth, whom the Lord of hosts has blessed, saying, Blessed be Egypt my people, and Assyria the work of my hands, and Israel my heritage!"

Implicit in all of these passages is the idea that Israel is to serve as the means by which other nations will be drawn to God for their own good. Of course, this will happen only if Israel lives in the way that God commands, since otherwise Israel will not be able to enjoy God's blessings and attract people from other nations to God. In Jer 33:9, for example, it is said that all the nations of the earth will "hear of all the good" that God does for Israel and be stricken with awe at "all the good and all the prosperity" that God provides for his people. Israel is also called to serve as a witness to God's love and kindness and to share with others its testimony regarding all of the wonderful things God has done for them as his people.[1] By means of Israel and God's activity among his people, the nations will come to know that Israel's God alone is the true God.[2]

All of these passages, therefore, leave no doubt that the nations are the object of God's love. The nations would hardly be told to worship, bless, and glorify God and give thanks to him if God did not care for them or seek their salvation and wholeness along with that of Israel. Precisely because of God's love for them, however, these passages also express the hope that those nations will abandon their own gods and idols and turn exclusively to the God of Israel. Unlike Israel's God, the gods of the nations do not truly love those who serve them or seek their well-being as an end in itself. Nor do they demand that the people who worship them practice the core values associated with the Torah in the way that Israel's God does. If the nations do not put away their worship of their own gods and turn to Israel's God to serve him alone, they cannot be blessed with the well-being that God desires for them. This is not because God will refuse to bless them but because their own unjust and destructive behavior will make it impossible for them to be benefited by his blessings.

Because by its very nature the way of life necessary to enjoy well-being is possible only when people desire and choose to adopt it voluntarily, however, God cannot force or compel the nations to live as he desires and commands. Instead, he must convince them by means of Israel that it is in their own best interest to live in accordance with his will and acknowledge him alone as God. Only God's love can accomplish that objective. Because love for God and others must be heartfelt, sincere, and genuine if it is truly to be love, the only way in which the nations can be brought to abandon their own gods and dedicate themselves to serving him exclusively is by experiencing God's love in the same way that Israel does. If they are not brought to love God, their obedience to him will be a servile obedience, motivated purely by self-interest and a desire to keep God content and avoid his wrath. True love for others cannot be grounded solely in self-interest or motivated by a concern only for oneself, nor can it be brought about by threats of punishment or promises of rewards. Those who act out of fear or selfishness cannot truly love others.

---

1. See Ps 9:11; 96:3; 108:3-4; Isa 12:3-4; 43:10; 44:8; 66:19-20.
2. See Jer 16:20-21; Ezek 36:23; 38:16; 39:7.

For these reasons, if God seeks to bless the nations with wholeness and well-being, he must attempt to draw them to himself in some way so that they submit to his loving will voluntarily and with gladness. According to many passages from the Hebrew Scriptures, Israel is his chosen servant to accomplish that objective as a light and a witness to the nations. When his people fulfill that role faithfully by living in accordance with his will, God is able to pour out his blessings on them, since they use those blessings for good rather than for harm. As a result, the nations who desire the same blessings for themselves are attracted to Israel's God, who brings about in them the way of life necessary for them to enjoy those blessings by guiding and instructing them as well.

In biblical thought, then, the obedience of Israel is fundamental to God's plan. The nations will be drawn to him only if his people live in a way that allows them to be blessed. For that reason, when Israel fails to obey God, that failure harms not only Israel but the other nations as well, since they cannot be drawn to Israel's God unless Israel is able to attain the blessings that will enable the other nations to seek the same blessings. When God chastises his people Israel and responds to their persistent disobedience in wrath and judgment, he does so not only for their sake but also for that of the nations. Only by purifying his people from their sin can he hope to see other nations purified from their sin as well, since if Israel persists in sin and disobedience the nations will not be drawn to him.

For that reason, throughout the Hebrew Scriptures the passages that hold out hope that the nations will be drawn to Israel's God to attain the blessings of salvation that come from worshiping and serving him alone are generally found in the context of other passages that speak of Israel itself attaining God's blessings through obedience. The blessing and obedience of Israel are a precondition to the blessing and obedience of other nations. Furthermore, just as God promises by pure grace to do everything possible to bring his people Israel to live in accordance with his will for their own good, so also by pure grace does he promise to do everything in his power to bring other nations to do the same so that they may be blessed together with Israel by living under him as his people alongside Israel.

At the same time, it is important to recognize that the passages that speak of God judging and destroying the other nations rather than saving them are much more common throughout the Hebrew Scriptures than those that refer to the nations attaining God's blessing. The reason for this, however, is that the nations of the world persistently refuse to abandon the practice of evil, injustice, and oppression, as well as the worship of false gods that leads to these things. This constitutes a cause of consternation for God and for the prophets whom he sends to speak to the nations on his behalf and to censure and rebuke the people of those nations for their own good. For the most part, the biblical texts hold out little if any hope that the nations will actually turn away from their oppressive gods unless something radically new and drastic takes place. On the contrary, both the biblical narratives and passages from the Psalms and the prophetic books present the nations as being irremediably and hopelessly immersed in the worship of false gods and in the harmful, destructive, and oppressive conduct that is associated with that worship. History had seemed to show that this situation was not going to change on its own. Only some type of dramatic intervention on God's part would bring the nations to abandon their false gods and to love and serve him alone for their own good. It is for this reason that most of the passages that speak of the nations turning to Israel's God regard this turning as something that will take place only at some decisive moment in the future, an end time when the renewal and restoration of Israel and the creation as a whole will come to pass. Only then will the nations be convinced that the gods they worship are no gods at all and that life and salvation are to be found in the God of Israel alone as the creator and Lord of all.

If the nations are to be blessed, then, they must become convinced of the same basic truths of which Israel must be convinced, namely, that the God of Israel is the sovereign creator and Lord of all and that he loves all people unconditionally in the sense of seeking their well-being as an end in itself. God must also make his will known to the nations in the same way that he has made it known to Israel. Only by doing so can he hope to bring the nations to live in ways that truly promote their well-being. The nations must also be brought to realize that the God of Israel is fundamentally distinct from their own gods, precisely because he is fully committed to their well-being above all else and is not using them for his own selfish ends in an attempt to satisfy needs or desires of his own. It is this conviction that will lead them to submit gladly and willingly to whatever he commands, since like Israel they will know that all that he commands is only for their good and is truly in their best interest. In this way, they will be brought to serve and obey him, not for *his* sake, but *for theirs*.

At the same time, it is important to stress that to affirm that the blessing of Israel is to serve as a means by which the other peoples of the earth will be blessed is by no means to question or deny that the blessing of Israel is an end in itself. On the contrary, in biblical thought God wishes to bless his people Israel *for their own sake* out of love for them and not merely for the sake of the nations who will be brought to know him through Israel. In fact, only by truly loving Israel and treating the people's well-being as an end in itself could God hope to attract others to himself, since if he were to treat Israel only as a means to some greater end it would soon become apparent to all that he was merely using them for some ulterior motive. In that case, he would bless them and seek to bring them to obey him not primarily out of love for them but because he was attempting to accomplish through them some objective that he regarded as more important than their own well-being and happiness. There would be no reason for other peoples to be attracted to Israel's God if he simply used human beings for his own ends, since that is the manner in which the pagan gods of antiquity were thought to behave. Only if God was truly committed to Israel's well-being as an end in itself would Israel be able to attain that well-being and be able to serve as a means for other peoples to attain it as well.

Conversely, to affirm that God has a special and unique love for Israel as his chosen people and relates to them in a way that is distinct from the way in which he relates to all other nations is by no means equivalent to saying that he loves the people of other nations less and is less concerned with their well-being than he is with that of Israel. In biblical thought, ideally God would like to enjoy the same type of relationship with *all* the nations of the world, who are just as much his creation as Israel and therefore should be understood as being just as dear to his heart. However, because those nations do not know him and are not interested in knowing him, it is impossible for him to enjoy such a relationship with them at present. They have no interest in living as his people or identifying with him in any way. Instead, they wish to subjugate, dominate, and control other peoples and look to their own gods for everything they need in order to accomplish that objective, since those gods seek the same things for themselves. What those people and their gods desire is to establish their rule over other peoples in the way that imperial powers such as Egypt, Assyria, and Babylon are said to do in the biblical texts. This is not what the God of Israel seeks for his people, however. His objective is not to dominate the nations of the world and subjugate them to himself or to his people Israel but to establish peace, wholeness, and justice throughout the earth for the good of all. Such peace, wholeness, and justice will become a reality only when all submit willingly and obediently to his own rule as a God who is committed to the well-being of all people without exception.

This background makes it possible to understand why many passages from the Hebrew Scriptures portray God as loving Israel more than other nations and seeking to bless them above all others. For all of the reasons mentioned above, if God is to accomplish his purposes in the world, at present he must show a special concern for Israel as his chosen people and relate to them differently than he does to the other nations of the world. This involves giving priority to their well-being over that of all others and establishing a close and intimate relationship with them as their God and Lord. He must make himself known to them as fully as possible and allow them to experience his love and commitment to their well-being so that they are brought to love him in the same way. Only if they truly love him will they obey him so as to live in ways that make it possible for them to experience the well-being he desires for them.

Finally, it is important to stress once more that because of the intrinsic relation between human well-being and a way of life that makes that well-being possible, God's desire to bless Israel as his chosen people cannot be divorced or viewed in isolation from his commitment to bringing about in them that way of life. As noted above, behind God's election of Abraham and the people descended from him through Isaac and Jacob is not merely a concern or love for *a particular people* but rather a concern for *the practice of a way of life that will enable that people to enjoy the well-being that God desires for all.* In fact, because all of God's blessings depend on the people living in a way that promotes their well-being, that way of life must itself be regarded as his greatest blessing.

A COVENANT DESIGNED FOR BLESSING

According to the biblical narrative, in order to carry out his plan of blessing not only for Israel but for all of the families of the earth as well, God establishes a covenant with Abraham and his descendants. The first allusion to this covenant appears in Gen 15:18, where in the context of a covenant ritual with Abraham God promises to give to Abraham's descendants the land to which he had led him. Two chapters later, God is presented as elaborating further on the promises he has made to Abraham by means of the covenant he establishes with him. He tells Abraham that a multitude of nations will come forth from him and that he will be God to Abraham and his offspring for all of their generations (Gen 17:1-8). In addition to describing this covenant as everlasting, God tells Abraham that he is giving to him and to his offspring the land he had promised to them as a "perpetual holding" (vv. 7-8). As a sign of this everlasting covenant, God orders Abraham to have all the males of his household circumcised together with himself and ordains that in the future all of Abraham's male descendants be circumcised from infancy as well (17:9-14).

After the people descended from Abraham through Isaac and Jacob fall into slavery in Egypt, God is said to remember his covenant with them. On that basis, he determines to fulfill the promises he had made by freeing them and taking them to the land he had vowed to give them (Exod 2:24; 6:2-8). Once he has delivered the Israelites from the hand of the Pharoah, he directs them to Sinai, where he has Moses tell them: "If you obey my voice and keep my covenant, you shall be my treasured possession out of all the peoples. Indeed, the whole earth is mine, but you shall be for me a kingdom of priests and a holy nation" (19:5-6). After Moses receives the commandments that God initially gives him and reads them to the people, they respond: "All the words that the LORD has spoken we will do" (24:3). Moses then writes down those commandments on a scroll that is referred to as the book of the covenant and carries out a rite in which he sprinkles sacrificial blood both on the book and on the people before telling them: "This is the blood of the covenant that the LORD has made with you in accordance with all these words" (24:8).

Although the covenant God establishes here with Israel can be seen as essentially the same covenant that he had made previously with Abraham, in some ways it is also distinct, primarily because it involves a detailed list of stipulations that lay out the manner in which God and Israel will relate to one another from that point on. No matter how the covenant God makes with Israel at Sinai is understood as relating to the covenant he had made previously with Abraham, the ideas that are central to it remain the same: God promises to bless the people by giving them the land he had promised to Abraham and making them his own so as to be their God forever. Of course, this can happen only if the people descended from Abraham consent to live under that covenant and under the God who has established that covenant with them. As God's words in Exod 19:5-6 indicate, this covenant will set Israel apart from all of the other peoples of the earth as God's special possession. Nevertheless, when God immediately adds: "indeed, the whole earth is mine," he makes it clear that all of the other nations of the world are his possession as well, thus reminding the Israelites that they are not unique in that regard. While in certain ways his relation with Israel will be special and unique, God's words to Moses leave no doubt that he intends to continue to relate to all of the other peoples of the earth as his own possession as well, since they too are his creation.

Although the centrality of God's covenant with Israel in the biblical narrative is recognized by virtually all interpreters of the Hebrew Scriptures, the precise nature and purpose of that covenant have been understood in many different ways. What is common to many of these understandings of the covenant, however, is the idea that it was based on the principle of *do ut des*. According to this idea, the reason that God established the covenant with Israel was so that he might receive from Israel what he desired or needed for his own sake. This understanding of God's covenant with Israel is especially reflected in the comparisons that are often made between it and other pacts and treaties from antiquity known to us.

For over half a century, scholars of the Hebrew Bible have compared the covenant between God and Israel as it is presented in the biblical texts with ancient treaties between great kings known as suzerains and the vassal kings who ruled under them. In these treaties, the suzerain committed himself to conferring certain benefits on the vassal king in exchange for the vassal's loyalty and obedience. Many of these treaties use the language of love to speak of the suzerain loving his vassals by caring for their needs, while at the same time placing the vassals under the obligation to love the suzerain in return by doing everything that he commanded of them and remaining faithful and loyal to him at all times and under all circumstances. This love of the vassals for the suzerain was to be exclusive of any type of similar relationship with other sovereigns or rulers. These treaties generally concluded with a list of witnesses together with promises of blessing for the vassals if they fulfilled the conditions established in the treaty as well as threats of curses and punishments if they did not. As Jon Levenson has noted, the curses and punishments mentioned in these treaties included things such as "annihilation, epidemic, sterility, drought, famine, dethronement, and exile."[3]

---

3. Jon D. Levenson, *Sinai and Zion: An Entry into the Jewish Bible* (Minneapolis: Winston, 1985), 30. On the ideas associated with the suzerainty treaties and the history of the comparison between these treaties and the covenant between God and Israel as it is presented in the Hebrew

The fact that Leviticus 26 and Deuteronomy 28 present a list of blessings for obedience to the commandments given to Israel by God and curses for disobedience to those commandments has led many biblical scholars to interpret these passages on the basis of the ideas associated with the suzerainty treaties of antiquity. Supposedly, what God sought by means of his covenant with Israel was that the people submit obediently to him and that they be faithful and loyal to him alone. If they did so, God promised to bless them, yet if they failed or refused to be faithful, loyal, and obedient to him, God would bring down on them the curses that were associated with disobedience.

According to such an understanding of God's covenant with Israel, that covenant was in essence a treaty by means of which God promised to grant his people Israel the blessings they wanted for themselves for their own sake in exchange for receiving from them the obedience and devotion that he desired for *his* own sake. In Levenson's words, the relationship between God and Israel was to be one of "mutual service" and "mutual benefit."[4] Like the great rulers of antiquity, what God sought were devoted vassals, servants, or even slaves who would submit to everything he commanded them so that he might obtain from them the things he sought for himself. His objective was to have a people who would be committed to him under any and every circumstance, not because he sought their well-being as an end in itself but because this brought him satisfaction and pleasure. This satisfaction and pleasure might derive simply from being loved, served, and obeyed by the people. In that case, this was the "benefit" he obtained. Many biblical interpreters presuppose that what interested God was receiving the people's adoration and worship. He wished to have a people who would be dedicated to singing his praises and ascribing to him the honor and glory that he regarded as his due. By means of the covenant, God imposed his will on the people as their superior or sovereign and promised to treat them well if they gave him what he desired, yet at the same time he threatened to punish them severely if they failed to submit obediently to his will and were unfaithful and disloyal to him.

The comparisons that the Hebrew Bible repeatedly makes between God's relationship to Israel and the relationship between a husband and a wife have often been interpreted as reflecting a similar understanding of God's covenant with Israel. According to these interpretations, God's love for Israel was thought to be like that of a man who takes a wife because he wishes to be loved and served by her. While he undoubtedly can be said to love and serve her as well, at the same time he is jealous and possessive in the sense that he demands that her love for him be exclusive and that she remain faithful, loyal, and obedient to him at all times and in all things. While God appears to be

---

Bible, see 26-30. Levenson offers a more detailed analysis of these ideas and comparisons in his more recent work *The Love of God: Divine Gift, Human Gratitude, and Mutual Faithfulness in Judaism* (Princeton: Princeton University Press, 2016); see especially 6-15, 36-38, and 48-51. On the scholarly critique of these comparisons, see especially Bruce C. Birch, *Let Justice Roll Down: The Old Testament, Ethics, and Christian Life* (Louisville: Westminster John Knox, 1991), 146-48.

4. Levenson, *Love of God*, 6

kind and caring toward Israel when the people live in this type of relationship with him, as soon as they are unfaithful to him and disobey him he becomes angry, violent, and abusive. As a result, the people must live in constant fear of God and be careful to avoid doing anything that might upset him. Such an understanding of the covenant relationship between God and his people Israel once again makes that relationship an extremely oppressive one. Rather than truly caring for Israel, God establishes the covenant because he wishes to use and manipulate Israel for his own ends and obtain some benefit that he desires for his own sake.

While there are no doubt many significant parallels between the covenants, pacts, and treaties that ancient peoples made with their gods and rulers in antiquity and the covenant that God is said to make with Israel in the Hebrew Bible, these parallels must not be allowed to obscure the fact that the biblical understanding of God's covenant with Israel is fundamentally at odds with the ideas just considered. As we have seen repeatedly throughout this study, in biblical thought there is one thing alone that interests and concerns the God of Israel: the well-being of the human beings and creatures that he has made, including especially the people to whom he has chosen to make himself known.

This distinguishes the God of Israel radically from any type of suzerain or king of old. What he sought were not faithful and submissive vassals who would do his bidding for his own sake but a people who would be as fully committed to their own well-being and that of others as he was. Rather than seeking to control his people and impose his will on them, he sought to guide and instruct them in the way that they were to go for their own good. What God desired and demanded of the people was the same thing that they were to desire and demand for themselves, namely, a life characterized by justice, righteousness, compassion, and solidarity that would enable them to enjoy the well-being that God desired for all.

None of the other nations in antiquity understood themselves to be living in any type of covenant or pact with a God like the God of Israel. The gods whom they worshiped and served were not believed to have created all that existed, nor did any of them claim to be the one and only true God. Just as importantly, however, those other nations did not believe in gods who loved them unconditionally and were concerned for their well-being as an end in itself in the way that Israel's God is said to be in the biblical texts. For that reason, the demand of their gods for loyalty and obedience was a selfish and self-serving one rather than an expression of love and concern for them. Like the suzerains and rulers of old, those gods merely wished to have vassals and slaves who would do their bidding dutifully and submissively without questioning them or rebelling against them. According to many biblical interpreters, however, rather than conceiving of the God of Israel in terms that were radically different, the biblical texts present him as acting in the same ways and for the same reasons as the gods of the other nations of antiquity.

This pagan conception of the God of the Hebrew Bible and his covenant with Israel is reflected in many of the translations of the biblical texts. In the NRSVue translation of Lev 26:40-41, for example, after speaking of the diverse chastisements to which God will subject the people if they fail to obey his commandments, God is presented as referring to "their treachery against me and also their continued hostility to me" and as treating them with hostility as well. In English, treachery is generally understood in terms of an act of subversion or betrayal against a ruling authority to whom one is obliged to be loyal. In biblical thought, however, the possibility that his people might betray him or commit treason against him is not a concern of God, since he does not seek to be served and obeyed for his own sake but for theirs. If his people disobey him, they do no harm to him but only to themselves. What the God of Israel desires from his people is not loyalty but that they be faithful to him in the sense of pursuing the same objective he seeks, namely, their own well-being and that of others as well through obedience to his will.

For similar reasons, the use of the language of hostility to describe the relation between God and the people in Lev 26:40-41 must be regarded as reflecting ideas that are not present in the Hebrew text. In English, hostility generally implies enmity, that is, a desire to do harm to another person. A vassal who is hostile to a king or at enmity with him seeks to subvert his reign and overthrow him. In the case of the God of Israel, however, human beings can never threaten his reign or do him any type of harm. The Hebrew original in these verses speaks of God and the people walking contrary to one another or in opposition to one another rather than being hostile to one another. In biblical thought, the problem is not that God's people regard him as their enemy and wish to do him harm but that they insist on walking in a path of their own that runs contrary to the path that God has laid out for them for their own good. When God sets himself in opposition to them in order to prevent them from walking down the path they have chosen for themselves and attempts to bring them to walk instead in the path that he has graciously laid out for them in the Torah, strictly speaking he is not being hostile to them or behaving as their enemy. Much less is he attempting to do them harm or being jealous and possessive. Rather, he is merely seeking to stop the people from continuing to walk in a way that is not good for them and seeking their well-being by insisting that they walk instead in accordance with his commandments for their own good.

God's covenant with Israel as well as the mutual love that is to characterize that covenant should be understood on the basis of these same ideas. In biblical thought, God establishes the covenant because in his love he wishes to bring the people to live in a way that will make it possible for them to enjoy the well-being he desires for them. For the same reason, he commands that they love him by obeying him for their own good. By loving him, they will also be loving themselves in the sense of doing what is best for them. This understanding of God's covenant love is therefore at odds with affirmations such as that of Levenson: "Positively, the covenantal love of God means heeding the LORD's commandments and walking in his ways. Negatively, it means scrupulously avoiding actions that signal disloyalty. . . ."[5] According to Levenson, what God sought was the same thing that suzerains sought from their vassals, namely, "the complete fidelity of the vassal and his wholehearted reliability as an ally."[6] In biblical thought, however, what God's covenantal love seeks is not loyalty or "reliability as an ally" but the well-being of his people. If there is a sense in which Israel is to be his ally, it is that the people are to ally themselves with God in committing themselves to seeking their own well-being along with that of the other peoples and nations that he loves by living in the way that he has commanded for the good of all.

For all of these reasons, the claim that the relationship that God sought with Israel by means of the covenant was essentially the same as the relationship that rulers in antiquity sought with their vassals by means of the suzerainty treaties known to us must be firmly rejected. While many of those treaties use the terminology of love to describe that relationship, any such love is fundamentally distinct from the love that God had for his people Israel and the love that he expected and demanded of them as well. Unlike the suzerains and rulers of old, God was genuinely concerned with the well-being of his people as an end in itself and out of love for them demanded that they love both him and themselves by being just as firmly committed to their own well-being as he was. If God were to relate to his people in the ways that the gods and rulers of antiquity did, treating them as a means to his own self-centered ends rather than viewing their well-being as an end in itself and seeking to satisfy his own needs and desires by using his superior power to impose his will on them, he could never hope to be truly loved by them. On the contrary, they would relate to him in the same way that he related to them, acting purely out of self-interest and attempting to get from him what they wanted for *their* own sake. Rather than consisting of a relationship based on mutual love, God's covenant with Israel would be reduced to a relationship of mutual manipulation in which both God and his people would use one another for their own ends and seek to derive some personal benefit from the other by means of the principle of *do ut des*.

God's covenant with Israel, therefore, must be viewed in the context of his plan to bring about the well-being of Israel together with the nations that he hopes to bless through Israel as well. That covenant is an expression of unconditional love rather than any type of self-interest. What God seeks are not loyal and faithful vassals who submit to him for his own sake but a people committed to loving themselves and others in the same way that he does.

Just as it is contrary to biblical thought to conceive of God's relationship to Israel as analogous to that of a suzerain or ruler who seeks to impose his will on his vassals for his own sake, so also is it problematic to conceive of

____

5. Levenson, *Love of God*, 13.
6. Levenson, *Love of God*, 13.

that relationship in terms of a jealous and possessive husband who takes a wife simply because he wishes to derive pleasure from her and be loved, served, and obeyed by her. A husband who acts in that manner does not truly love his wife but instead wishes to exploit and dominate her. His jealousy and demand for loyalty and faithfulness are not motivated by any genuine concern for her well-being as an end in itself but are self-serving and aimed at controlling her for his own ends.

Rather than focusing primarily or exclusively on God's desire to receive from his people something that he desires for his own sake when considering the manner in which the biblical texts conceive of the covenant between God and Israel, many interpreters see that covenant as having the purpose of ensuring that the demands of God's justice, righteousness, or holiness might be satisfied. As we have seen in previous chapters of this work, according to this conception of the covenant, while God loves Israel and wants only to bless his people, the demands of his just and holy nature make it necessary for him to lay down certain conditions that the people must fulfill if he is to be able to dwell in their midst and bless them as he desires. In this case, the commandments that he gives have the purpose of communicating to them what they must do to remain on good terms with him and avoid actions and behaviors that his justice, righteousness, and holiness will not allow him to tolerate. Some of those commandments also indicate what the people must do to be restored to his good graces if they fall into any of the actions and behaviors that his nature finds intolerable. By means of the covenant, God makes his people aware of the conditions that they must fulfill in order for him to bless them and the people commit themselves to fulfilling those conditions. On that basis, God assures the people that if they do in fact fulfill the conditions he has laid down, he will indeed bless them. However, he also warns them that if they do not fulfill those conditions, he will subject them to his punishments and may even eventually reject or destroy them, at least in part.

All of these ways of conceiving of the covenant between God and Israel ground that covenant in God's own desires or the needs of his nature. The covenant is then viewed either in terms of some type of pact or deal in which both parties promise to "keep their end of the bargain" in order to obtain from the other what each party wants for its own sake or else in terms of a series of conditions that God imposes on Israel in order to satisfy the demands of his holy and righteous nature. In both cases, lying at the heart of the covenant is the idea that Israel can obtain certain rewards in exchange for giving God the obedience he desires for his own sake but will be subjected to God's punishments if they fail to obey him as they should. What God demands from Israel is faithfulness, loyalty, and submission to himself, and if the people give him what he demands, he promises that he will bless them and be loyal and faithful to them as well.

Just as the idea that God entered into a covenant with Abraham and his descendants for his own sake in order to receive from them something he desired only for himself must be considered foreign to biblical thought, the same must be said of the notion that he established his covenant with Israel for the purpose of ensuring that the demands of his holy, just, and righteous nature might be satisfied. Although by means of the covenant prescriptions God undoubtedly lays down conditions for the people to obtain the blessings he desires for them, those conditions are rooted not in God's nature but rather in the need for the people to live in ways that promote their well-being and avoid behaviors that undermine and destroy that well-being. God commands that the people live and behave in certain ways not *for his sake* or for the sake of his nature but *for theirs*, since only by living and behaving in those ways can they enjoy the well-being he desires for them.

The Covenant as Faithfulness and Commitment

While God committed himself to blessing Israel by means of the covenant he established with the people, the fact that it was necessary for the people to obey his commandments for their own good in order to obtain that blessing meant that God's commitment to the people would not always take the form of giving them abundance and prosperity in the land he had promised to them. As Leviticus 26 and Deuteronomy 28 make clear, God certainly intended to pour out his blessings on his people if they lived in accordance with his commandments, yet if they insisted on disobeying those commandments, his love for them and his commitment to their well-being would take the form of doing whatever was necessary to bring them back to himself in obedience for their own good. As we have seen previously, at times this meant imposing sufferings and chastisements on them in order to discipline and correct them. If the people repeatedly failed to respond to those chastisements in the way God desired, God might inflict even greater sufferings on them and if necessary even send the people into exile or destroy them in part until a righteous and obedient remnant was brought into existence.

God's commitment to the people's well-being, therefore, took the form of refusing to abandon them or give up on them until he might accomplish in them his loving purpose of bringing them to live in ways that would allow them to enjoy the blessings he wished to pour out on them. While he might abandon the people for a time so as to let them experience the negative consequences that followed intrinsically from disobeying his good commandments, he promised never to abandon them definitively but to keep attempting to do whatever was necessary to bring them into conformity with his loving will until that objective was accomplished.

At the same time, however, because the people could obey God and live in conformity with justice and righteousness only if they were genuinely and sincerely committed to doing what he commanded for their own good, God could not achieve that objective by imposing his will on them by force. According to the biblical narrative, at no point does God ever compel or oblige the Israelites to submit to him as their God so as to obey him and live in his covenant. Instead, through Moses he merely makes clear to them the manner in which it will be necessary for them to live if they wish to be his people and asks them whether they will commit themselves to living in that manner under him as their God.

This understanding of God's covenant with Israel is especially evident in the words that God speaks to the people through Moses in Exod 19:5-6, which we have already cited above. After reminding them of the manner in which he had delivered them from the Egyptians and bore them on eagles' wings in order to bring them to himself, God tells them: "Now, therefore, if you obey my voice and keep my covenant, you shall be my treasured possession out of all the peoples" (v. 5). By means of the imagery of the mother eagle, God points to the love and care that he has shown to the people by pure grace and mercy. At the same time, the allusion to their deliverance from their slavery in Egypt serves to remind them of his sovereign power. He also expresses to them his desire that they live as his own and become a kingdom of priests and holy nation in his service (v. 6). He makes it very clear to them, however, that these things can happen only if they obey his voice and keep his covenant. According to the narrative, when the people respond by promising: "Everything that the LORD has spoken we will do" (v. 8), God had not yet even given them any commandments. In essence, the people had merely told God that they were willing to do whatever he commanded, even though the contents of God's commandments had not yet been revealed to them.

While both God and the people of Israel were making a commitment to one another by means of the covenant, therefore, both the commitment that God made to the people and that which the people made to God were aimed at the well-being of the people themselves and not at anything God needed or desired purely for his own sake. By means of the covenant, God manifested his commitment to blessing the people in the sense of doing whatever was necessary to bring about their well-being. He did this first and foremost by means of commandments that instructed and guided them in a way of life that would promote their well-being for intrinsic reasons. Obviously, however, those commandments could only contribute to the people's well-being if they observed them faithfully and carefully. For that reason, the covenant also stipulated that the people were to commit themselves to learning, studying, and implementing to the best of their ability everything contained in those commandments.

Because the people were sinful and imperfect in the same way that all human beings are, it was recognized that their obedience to the commandments given to them by God would be deficient in many ways. For that reason, as we have seen in the previous three chapters of this work, from the very beginning the covenant also included commandments that were aimed at bringing the people to acknowledge their wrongdoing when they fell into sin and to take steps to correct it. Those commandments thus anticipated the people's disobedience and included provisions through which they might manifest their commitment to turning away from their wrongdoing and seek

God's forgiveness on that basis. While these provisions included sacrificial rites, the condition for the people to obtain God's forgiveness was not simply the performance of those rites but a renewed commitment to living in accordance with his will. What God demanded from the people was not perfect obedience, therefore, but a sincere commitment to observing the commandments he was giving them for their own good. As long as the people remained firm in that commitment, God would accept and forgive them even when they stumbled and fell into sin. Of course, this commitment to obeying God's commandments was also by definition a commitment to seeking their own well-being, since that well-being constituted the purpose for which God had given those commandments.

It is especially important to stress, however, that from the start God tells the people that when they fall into disobedient and destructive behavior he will chastise them in different ways in an attempt to bring them back to himself in obedience for their own good. In passages such as Leviticus 26 and Deuteronomy 28, he also makes it clear that if those chastisements do not accomplish their objective, he will not give up on them but will instead chastise them even further and in ways that will become even more painful for them. The alternative would be simply to abandon the people to their own fate by letting them follow whatever path they desire. To treat them in that manner would not be loving on God's part, however, since it would involve handing them over to their own self-destruction. Any path other than the good one that God had laid out for them would eventually lead to their ruin and perdition.

According to biblical thought, therefore, when God chastises the people in order to purify and correct them, he is being faithful to the covenant he made with them and keeping that covenant, even though in a sense this involves doing them harm and evil. That harm and evil must actually be considered something good, however, precisely because when the people are persistently rebellious his painful chastisements are the only means by which God can hope to bring them to return to a way of life that will allow them to enjoy the well-being he seeks for them. Were he not to chastise them in an attempt to purify and correct them, it would be necessary to affirm that he was *not* fulfilling the covenant he had made with them or observing it faithfully.

In a sense, it may similarly be said that God shows the people compassion, kindness, and favor even when he treats them in ways that are *not* compassionate or kind and withholds his favor from them. Such an affirmation does not represent a contradiction in terms. His compassion, kindness, and favor consist of seeking nothing but what is truly best for his people, yet at times what is best for them is that he refuse to show them compassion, kindness, and favor in the sense of subjecting them to suffering and hardships. Only in that way can he bring them to abandon their destructive behavior and obey him for their own good.

Likewise, it can be said that when the people persist in their stubbornness and rebelliousness, God blesses them by withholding his blessings from them and subjecting them instead to the scourges or curses mentioned in the covenant. Those scourges have the sole objective of molding them into a people who will be fully committed to practicing justice, righteousness, compassion, and love for their own good and for the good of others as well, even though at times they involve hardships and afflictions that can only be described as horrific and harrowing. While God is a "devouring fire" and "a jealous God" (Deut 4:24), his ultimate purpose is not to do harm to the people but to purify them from the behaviors that destroy their life and well-being. This is clear from the words that Moses speaks only a few verses after he has described God in those terms and has alluded to the scourges, afflictions, and utter destruction that God will bring upon them when they disobey him: "In your distress, when all these things have happened to you in the time to come, you will turn back to the Lord your God and listen to him. Because the Lord your God is a compassionate God, he will not abandon you or destroy you, nor will he forget the covenant with your ancestors that he swore to them" (4:30-31). When it is said that God does not forget that covenant, this should be understood not only in the sense that he remains committed to blessing and saving his people but also in the sense that he remains committed to chastising and punishing them when their behavior does not allow him to bless and save them. In other words, he blesses and saves them not only by granting them good things but at times also by subjecting them to the scourges, afflictions, and hardships that most English translations of the book of Deuteronomy refer to as curses.

It is also important to stress that when the people assented to living in accordance with God's covenant and the commandments it contained, they also gave their assent to the punishments or scourges that God promised to bring upon them if they refused to live within that covenant and submit obediently to its commandments. They did not only pledge to obey everything that God commanded them through Moses, as they are said to have done in passages such as Exod 19:8, Exod 24:3-8, and Deut 5:27, but they also subjected themselves to whatever measures God might regard as necessary in order to bring them to live faithfully under his covenant by obeying his commandments for their own good. Through Moses, God had told the people ahead of time that if they promised to obey his commandments but did not fulfill that promise as they should, the chastisements he would inflict on them would be extremely painful and difficult to bear. According to the book of Deuteronomy, he had told the new generation of Israelites again of those chastisements as they prepared to cross the Jordan River into the land he had promised them. For that reason, when God subsequently subjected his people to those chastisements following their entrance into the land, they had no right to complain that they were excessive or overly harsh. From the start, God had made it clear to them just how dire the consequences for disobedience would be. By agreeing to live in the covenant not only at Sinai but also a short time before taking possession of the land God was giving them, they agreed at the same time to the chastisements that God said he would inflict on them if they disobeyed him.

While God's faithfulness to the covenant and to the people's well-being would take the form of imposing sufferings on them when he considered that they needed to be corrected, therefore, the people's faithfulness to the covenant and to their own well-being had to take the form of submitting willingly to any disciplinary measures God might take in order to accomplish his purposes in them. Even when the people acknowledged their wrongdoing and sought God's forgiveness, their faith and trust in God and their faithfulness to the covenant were to be manifested by accepting whatever chastisements God might deem to be necessary in order to correct them without complaining or rebelling against him. Those chastisements were not an imposition on his part, nor were they something that in principle ran contrary to the will of those who had agreed to live under the covenant. On the contrary, even though God's chastisements were painful and were therefore to be feared, the people were to regard those chastisements as an expression of God's love for them and his faithfulness to his covenant commitment of bringing them to live in the way that was in their own best interest. Because he was seeking only their well-being when he chastised them, the people were even to be grateful for those chastisements, since for God to fail to seek to correct them would involve handing them over to behavior that would lead to their ruin and destruction rather than doing them good.

At the same time, because the covenant was an expression of God's love for the people and his desire for their well-being rather than something that he imposed on them against their will for his own sake, at no point does God threaten to punish the people if they choose not to live in that covenant. If they rejected the covenant, however, they would forfeit the blessings promised to them in it, including especially the blessing of a land that they would be able to call their own. In essence, by electing not to live in the covenant, they would reduce themselves to the same condition in which all the other nations of the earth found themselves. Just as God was not thought to punish those nations for serving other gods but for the most part merely let them live in whatever way they desired, so also would he allow the people of Israel to go their own way should they so choose. Because they were a small, weak, and insignificant people who would have no land of their own, however, and also because following in their own ways would do them harm rather than good, for God simply to abandon them to their own fate would almost certainly involve handing them over to hardships such as those that they had experienced in Egypt, and perhaps to their own destruction at some point as well. Nevertheless, according to the logic of the biblical account, if that is what the people desired, God would respect their decision.

For that reason, after the people initially indicate their willingness to live in the covenant that God sought to establish with them in Exodus 19, in chapters 20–23 of the book God defines more precisely for them what it will mean to live in that covenant. There, after giving them the Decalogue, God gives them commandments that have to do with sacrificial worship, social justice and equity, the Sabbath rest, and the celebration of the annual festivals. The people are then asked to confirm their intention to submit to the covenant two more times before Moses ratifies it with sacrificial blood (Exod 24:3-8).

Forty years later, after Moses' death, Joshua reminds them once more of the need for them to obey all that God had commanded immediately before guiding them across the Jordan River into the land God had promised them (Josh 1:10-15). Only when they have reiterated their promise to obey God's commandments are they finally allowed to enter: "They answered Joshua, 'All that you have commanded us we will do, and wherever you send us we will go. Just as we obeyed Moses in all things, so we will obey you'" (1:16-17). Then, after the conquest of the land under Joshua has been completed, he asks the people one more time whether they intend to live under the covenant. Joshua's words, however, leave no doubt that they are under no obligation to do so: "Now if you are not willing to serve the LORD, choose this day whom you will serve, whether the gods your ancestors served in the region beyond the River or the gods of the Amorites in whose land you are living; but as for me and my household, we will serve the LORD" (24:15). When the people indicate their intention to serve YHWH as their God and live under his covenant, Joshua tells them: "You are witnesses against yourselves that you have chosen the LORD, to serve him," and the people respond: "We are witnesses" (24:22). The passage clearly conveys the idea that the people are accepting the consequences of their decision, in essence giving their consent to whatever measures and chastisements God may impose on them if they fail to fulfill their word.

According to the prescriptions that God gives to Moses in Deut 31:9-13, shortly before his death, once the people had entered the land to possess it they were to renew their commitment to observing the covenant every seven years. On the Festival of Tabernacles, they were to gather together to hear the covenant read to them so that they might continue to adhere to it. Such a provision presupposes that the people were not under obligation to continue in the covenant relationship with God. Individuals or even groups of people might simply decide either then or at some other point in time that they no longer wished to submit to the covenant. Any who made such a decision, however, would be viewed as having divorced themselves from his people. As a result, they would be understood to have forfeited the blessings God had promised to his people on the condition that they obey his commandments, including especially the blessing of living in the land he had promised to make theirs on the condition that they submit to his covenant.

To affirm that the people always remained free to abandon the covenant, of course, is also to affirm that they remained free to reject the commandments that formed part of that covenant and no longer commit themselves to living under them. Those who made such a choice would not be subjected to divine punishment but would simply no longer be regarded as forming part of

God's covenant people, despite their ethnic origin as descendants of Abraham. What the biblical texts repeatedly condemn, therefore, is not the failure of human beings in general to live in accordance with the commandments that appear in the Torah but only the failure of those who have committed themselves to observing those commandments to fulfill that commitment.

The notion that the commandments given by God through Moses were binding only on those who willingly submitted to them and to the covenant of which they formed part may also be reflected in the fact that those commandments generally appear in the text in the form of indicatives in the future tense rather than imperatives. Thus, for example, what Moses is instructed to tell the people is not: "Do not have other gods before me," but rather: "You shall have no other gods before me" (Exod 20:3; Deut 5:7). This use of the future indicative rather than the imperative is characteristic of the prescriptions that appear in the remainder of the Decalogue and throughout most of the Pentateuch as well.

Although biblical interpreters often ascribe little significance to the use of future indicatives in the formulation of the prescriptions that God is said to have given Israel through Moses, their use may be seen as conveying the idea that those commandments are conditions that those who accept the covenant commit themselves to fulfilling. In that case, God is not imposing commandments on them but is instead telling them that if they choose to enter into the covenant relationship that he seeks to establish with them, they will be expected to observe certain prescriptions and behave in certain ways. In a sense, therefore, it might be said that God is communicating expectations to the people rather than giving them commandments. In essence, he is not giving them orders by means of imperatives but is instead indicating to them what living in that covenant will entail. By giving their consent to the covenant, the people give their consent to the conditions laid down in it as well and commit themselves to living in accordance with the expectations that God makes clear to them. It must be stressed once more, however, that what God expects of the people is simply that they be as firmly committed to their own well-being as he is. He thus tells them all that he will expect and demand of them if they choose to live in his covenant, not for *his* sake, but for *theirs*.

In this regard, it is important to note that in a number of passages in the Pentateuch, rather than referring to the prescriptions that God gives to the people for them to obey as commandments, the Hebrew describes them simply as "words." Thus, for example, after the account of the golden calf and God's response to the people's sin in Exodus 32–33, God tells Moses to make new tablets to replace those that he had smashed on the ground when he had contemplated the people's sin with the golden calf after descending from the mountain. What he tells Moses to engrave on those tablets, however, are not *commandments* but *words*: "The Lord said to Moses, 'Cut two tablets of stone like the former ones, and I will write on the tablets the words that were on the former tablets that you broke'" (Exod 34:1). After God tells Moses what he is to write on the tablets, he adds: "Write these words, for in accordance with these words I have made a covenant with you and with Israel" (34:27). The passage then continues by affirming that Moses "was there with the LORD forty days and forty nights; he did not eat bread or drink water. And he wrote on the tablets the words of the covenant, the ten words" (34:28). The reason why the Hebrew text speaks of words rather than ten commandments may have to do with the same idea reflected in the use of the future indicative to refer to those words: strictly speaking, they are not commandments that God is imposing on the people contrary to their will but words that describe the manner in which the people will be expected to live if they choose to submit to the covenant that God is making with them.

This is not to deny, of course, that in some sense the prescriptions or words of which the text speaks are also commandments. In fact, the Hebrew text uses several different terms to refer to them. These terms are reflected in English translations that speak of things such as precepts, decrees, statutes, ordinances, and laws.[7] What is important, however, is that all of these terms be understood in the context of a covenant relationship that God has established with Israel as his people. While God undoubtedly commands certain actions and behaviors in the Torah, he does not impose anything on the people by force or against their will. Instead, out of love for those who desire to attain the blessings he graciously wishes to pour out on them by living as his covenant people, God demands that they act and behave in ways that will make it possible for them to attain all the good he seeks for them, trusting that the only thing that interests him is their well-being and that he knows better than they do what is necessary for that well-being to be theirs.

At the same time, it must be stressed that the instruction or Torah that God gives to Israel cannot be reduced to a series of legal prescriptions, commandments, ordinances, and precepts. The narratives that form part of the Torah play an equally important role in instructing the people and guiding them in the way they should go for their own good. Those narratives not only tell God's people who they are, where they come from, and what God desires for them but also provide the background and framework necessary to understand and interpret properly the prescriptions and precepts God gives to his people. It is not only by means of commandments or ordinances, therefore, that God seeks to bring his people to live in the way he desires for their own good but by means of *all* of the activity he has carried out in the past and will continue to carry out in the future in relation to them and the world he has created.

Although the biblical texts refer to the covenant as something that God establishes with the people of Israel as descendants of Abraham, they also reflect the idea that people of other nations are free to join themselves to Israel so as to live alongside of the Israelites as part of God's covenant people. In fact, from the moment that the Israelites depart from Egypt after the final

---

7. See, for example, Deut 6:20; 11:1; 26:17; 30:16; 1 Kgs 2:3; 6:12; 2 Kgs 17:37; 2 Chr 19:10; 33:8; Neh 9:13.

plague involving the death of the firstborn, other peoples are said to have made the decision to accompany them: "The Israelites journeyed from Rameses to Succoth, about six hundred thousand men on foot, in addition to the little ones. A mixed multitude also went up with them and livestock in large numbers, both flocks and herds" (Exod 12:37-38). While the precise meaning of the phrase "mixed multitude" in Hebrew is not entirely clear, there seems to be a solid basis for affirming that "the group here mentioned is distinct from the people Israel."[8] As we have noted above, other passages from the biblical texts also speak of non-Israelites joining themselves to Israel. These include individuals such as Rahab and Ruth, from whom King David was said to descend (Ruth 4:13-17; Matt 1:5), as well as larger groups of people. As we have noted above, the prophet Isaiah alludes explicitly to "the foreigners who join themselves to the LORD, to minister to him, to love the name of the LORD, and to be his servants" (Isa 56:6). In principle, there was no reason why any persons or groups of non-Israelite origin might not join themselves to God's people Israel by submitting to the covenant and the commandments associated with it.

While people of other nations might join themselves to Israel and its God, however, it is important to stress once more that the commandments or prescriptions that form part of the covenant are viewed as having been given to Israel alone. Those commandments are not presented as universal divine laws imposed on human beings of all times and places, nor are they given to any nation or people other than Israel. Undoubtedly, the biblical texts present God as desiring that all people everywhere live in accordance with what is good, right, just, and loving and often speak of him punishing those of other nations who practice injustice, violence, and oppression. Some passages from those texts may also be read as expressing the hope that one day people of other nations may come to live as God's people simply by practicing justice and righteousness, yet without submitting fully to all of the commandments found in the Torah. Nevertheless, those texts consistently speak of Israel alone as the people with whom God has chosen to enter into the covenant he established through Moses. For that reason, the commandments contained in that covenant apply only to those who have agreed to live under that covenant as members of God's people Israel.

Israel as God's Treasured Possession

The idea that God does not impose the covenant and its commandments on Israel against the people's will must also be kept in mind when considering God's election of Israel to be his "treasured possession out of all the peoples" (Exod 19:5). This passage and many others in the Hebrew Bible present Israel as a people who belong to God as his own. This idea is affirmed explicitly

---

8. Joel N. Lohr, *Chosen and Unchosen: Conceptions of Election in the Pentateuch and Jewish-Christian Interpretation*, SLTHS 2 (Winona Lake, IN: Eisenbrauns, 2009), 88; see 86-89 for Lohr's full discussion of the phrase.

whenever God refers to Israel as "my people." While in a sense all people belong to God, as this verse from Exodus 19 makes clear ("indeed, the whole earth is mine"), there is also a sense in which Israel alone is God's people. The main reason for this is that Israel alone has *agreed* to live as God's people by accepting the covenant that God has chosen to establish with them. Because of this, there is also a sense in which the people are to regard themselves as belonging to God rather than as belonging to themselves: *they are not their own but God's.* The same is true of their lives and everything they have and are. Throughout the biblical texts, in fact, the Hebrew term *'ebed* is used repeatedly to refer to the people of Israel as God's servants or slaves.[9] Slaves are people who do not belong to themselves but to someone else as their owner. They are therefore obliged to do what their owner wills rather than simply acting in accordance with their own will.

As we have noted briefly in Chapter 5 of this study, at first glance the idea that the people are God's possession and are to live as his servants or slaves might seem highly oppressive. Such an idea might be understood as placing the people of Israel in a relation to God that is the same as that described in the *Enuma Elish*, where the gods create human beings so that they may be dedicated to their service as their slaves. It might also seem to conflict with the notion that by delivering the people from their bondage in Egypt and giving them a land of their own, God has given them their freedom. If God took them out of Egypt merely to make them his own slaves for his sake, then rather than freeing them from slavery he has simply taken the Pharoah's place as the new taskmaster and overlord whom they are now under obligation to serve.

For a couple of reasons, however, such a conception of God's relationship with Israel must be regarded as foreign to the biblical texts. The first of these reasons is that which we have just considered above: after God has freed the people from their bondage in Egypt and taken them to Sinai, he does not *oblige* them to enter into the covenant with him but lets them decide for themselves whether they wish to live in that covenant. His words indicate to them that they will be his special people and his treasured possession only if they choose to live as his own by serving him and doing what he asks: "*if you obey my voice and keep my covenant*, then you shall be my treasured possession out of all the peoples" (Exod 19:5). In contrast to the *Enuma Elish*, where human beings have no choice but to serve the gods as their slaves, here the people are free to determine for themselves whether they wish to live as God's own and obey his commands.

It is therefore not simply *God* who makes the people his treasured possession but *the people themselves* by presenting themselves, their lives, and their souls and bodies to God as his own. Undoubtedly, it is God who has chosen them from out of all the peoples to be his treasured possession, as Moses affirms in Exod 19:4, Deut 7:6, and Deut 14:2, but that election in

---

9. See, for example, Lev 25:55; Deut 32:36; Ps 90:13; 102:14; 135:14; 136:22; Isa 41:8-9; 43:10; 44:21; Jer 30:10; 46:27; Ezek 37:25.

itself does not make the people his own. If they refuse to *live* as God's own people and do not accept him as their God, they will not *be* his own people. This is clear from Moses' words to the people in Deut 26:17-18: "Today you have declared that the LORD will be your God and that you will walk in his ways, keep his statutes, commandments, and ordinances, and listen to his voice. And today the LORD has declared that you will be his treasured people, as he promised you, by keeping all his commandments." According to this passage, what makes Israel God's special people and treasured possession is not only God's election of them as his people but also their declaration that they will *live* as his special people and treasured possession by observing his commandments. Of course, they will do so only in response to the grace, love, and mercy he has shown them in electing them to be his own, delivering them from their bondage in Egypt, giving them his good commandments, and blessing them in other ways. Thus, while in one sense it is God's election of Israel that makes them his people, in another sense it is their favorable response to that election that will make them his people. Were they not to respond favorably to God's election, they would *not* be God's special people or treasured possession, no matter how much God wished to regard them as such or desired for them to live as such.

The second reason why it is liberating rather than oppressive for the people to live as God's possession and serve him is that *he is dedicated entirely and exclusively to their happiness and well-being rather than selfishly seeking something from them for his own sake*. His purpose is in no way to control or manipulate them for his own ends. Nor does he wish for them to live as his exclusive possession and serve him purely out of self-interest. Rather, he wishes for them to submit fully to him and obey him in all things *for their own sake* out of love for them. In this regard, it must be stressed once again that affirmations such as that made by the Dutch Reformed theologian Hermann Bavinck must be regarded as entirely contrary to biblical thought: "Obedience in love or subjection by force is the final destiny of all creatures."[10] While pagan gods such as those of which the *Enuma Elish* speaks may wish to subject human beings to themselves by force in that manner and even demand that those human beings love them as they serve them—an idea which is actually a contradiction in terms, since true love can never be coerced or compelled by the use of force—, the God of Israel does not treat human beings in that way, and much less his people Israel. On the contrary, he makes it clear to them that he desires nothing but their happiness and well-being and reminds them that, as their creator, he alone truly knows what is in their best interest and will contribute to that happiness and well-being. Then, on that basis, he asks them to submit to him and obey him for their own good. For the people of Israel to live as God's possession and as his servants thus involves being *dedicated entirely and exclusively to their own happiness and well-being in the same way*

---

10. Herman Bavinck, *Reformed Dogmatics*, vol. 2: *God and Creation* (Grand Rapids: Baker Academic, 2004), 434.

that God is. To submit to him and obey him is to seek only what contributes to their wholeness and well-being and avoid anything that undermines or destroys that wholeness and well-being, since this is what God commands of them as their lord and master.

It is these convictions that are to lead Israel to accept the covenant that God determines to establish with them and to submit to the commandments contained in that covenant. God does not *oblige* the people to become his treasured possession or live as a kingdom of priests and a holy nation. Nor does he force them to serve him as his own possession so as to do *his* will rather than their own. Instead, on the basis of their belief in his sovereignty and his unconditional love for them, the people decide to enter into the covenant relationship with him voluntarily. They become God's treasured possession not merely because all people are already his by nature as their creator but because they choose freely to live as his own, since they are convinced that only in that way will they attain the happiness and well-being that God in his love desires for them. For the same reason, they also choose to obey him in all things so as to do his will rather than their own. In reality, however, they make his will their own so that when they do *his* will they are doing *their own* will as well. What *they* will is the same thing that *God* wills, namely, that they enjoy wholeness or shalom in its fullness. They are to be confident that everything that God commands and demands of them is for their own good and is motivated solely by his desire for their happiness and well-being. What will compel them to submit fully to God is not the use of force on God's part but their convictions regarding his love for them and his sovereign wisdom as the creator of all that exists. When God is presented as describing the people as his own treasured possession and commands them to serve him alone, therefore, he does so out of a desire not to *control* them or *enslave* them but to *bless* them.

Even though the people must respond favorably to God's election in order to be his treasured possession, however, ultimately it is not their response that makes them God's people but God's unconditional love for them. If God treasures them, it is not because they do his bidding faithfully and serve him loyally. In fact, for the most part, they do neither of these things, since they are a rebellious and stiff-necked people who constantly disobey him. Instead, God treasures them simply because he loves them unconditionally. At the same time, even though it no doubt sounds extremely odd, it is precisely that unconditional love for his people that leads God to demand that they serve him as his slaves. The service that he demands and commands of them is not like that imposed by the Pharoah or other rulers in antiquity, who wished to be obeyed for their own sake. Instead, what God demands and commands of his people is that in everything they do they seek their own well-being with all their heart, soul, and might in the same way that he does. The love that he seeks from them *for himself* is a sincere and genuine love *for themselves*, that is, a commitment to their own happiness and wholeness together with that of others. Because the Torah is the means by which he has indicated to them what such a commitment is to consist of and the things that it is to involve, out of love for his people he commands and demands that they submit fully to that Torah and obey everything in it *for their own sake.* This involves striving to practice justice, kindness, and compassion in all of their dealings with others and avoiding any type of behavior that might be harmful and destructive for them or anyone else.

In other words, for the people to live as God's servants or slaves involves loving themselves and others unconditionally in the same way that God loves them and all people. If the only thing that interests and concerns God is that all people enjoy well-being and wholeness, then what he must be said to desire and demand is that his people dedicate themselves to seeking their own well-being and that of others with the same passion, dedication, and commitment that he does. It is this and this alone that God desires and demands of them out of love for them as their sovereign king, lord, and master. According to this understanding of God's relationship to his people, they serve God as his faithful slaves and loyal subjects when they obey him by caring for themselves and one another in the same way that he cares for them. These ideas are reflected in the only passages in the Pentateuch that portray God as Israel's king and speak of the people as God's servants or slaves. When Lev 25:55 and Num 23:20-22 refer to the Israelites as God's servants or slaves and present God as Israel's king, the only thing that they mention in connection with these ideas is God's commitment to blessing the people and their deliverance from their bondage in Egypt by his hand. Similarly, when Moses describes God as Israel's king in Deut 33:3-5, he states that God "loves his people," that all those consecrated to him are in his hand, and that he gives them instruction in order to guide and direct them. In the only passage from the same book in which he uses the Hebrew term *'ebed* to refer to the people as God's servants or slaves, Moses affirms that "the LORD will deliver his people and have compassion on his servants when he sees that their power is gone and neither bond nor free remain" (Deut 32:36).

According to these passages and others in the biblical texts, therefore, neither the kingship of God nor the submission of his people to him as his servants or slaves is oppressive for them. On the contrary, as their king God seeks nothing but their happiness and well-being and demands nothing of them as his servants or slaves but that they seek the same thing for themselves. In this regard, he is nothing at all like the kings and suzerains of antiquity, nor does he treat the people who belong to him as his vassals or slaves in the way that those rulers did. Rather than attempting to control, manipulate, or use them for his own ends or for his own pleasure, he loves them unconditionally and seeks only what is best for them, even when they disobey him, are unfaithful to him, and rebel against him. The faithfulness that he demands of them is not faithfulness to himself but faithfulness to the practice of what is good, just, right, and merciful for their own sake. When they live in this manner, it might even be said that they are being faithful to him by being faithful to themselves in the same way that he is faithful to them. Similarly, the loyalty he expects of them is not merely loyalty to himself but rather the same loyalty to their own well-being that is his as well. When the people are unfaithful and disloyal to him by being unfaithful and disloyal to themselves and as a result he is moved to anger, he becomes angry only because he is grieved, saddened, and frustrated that they insist on undermining and destroying their own well-being rather than living in a manner that promotes that well-being. While he demands and commands that his people obey him, he does not want or expect them to do so out of *fear* but out of *love*, since the obedience he seeks from them is for *their benefit* rather than his own.

Paradoxically, then, only as the people live as God's servants or slaves and submit fully to everything that he commands will they be free. Only as they cease to regard themselves and all that they have as their own possession and instead understand their lives and their possessions as belonging to God will they be able to enjoy the well-being that he desires for them and that they desire for themselves. While true freedom involves choice, it also exists and is to be desired solely for the purpose of doing what truly contributes to one's own happiness and well-being. In that sense, those who live and act in ways that do them harm are not free but are slaves to their own ignorance and selfish desires. They believe themselves to be acting in accordance with their best interest but in reality are deceived. In biblical thought, only those who willingly seek to conform to the way of life commanded by God out of love for all are truly free. Only those who act in accordance with what is good, right, and just and refrain from practicing injustice, violence, oppression, and other forms of selfish and destructive behavior will enjoy a freedom that truly grants them well-being.

For the same reason, the worship of any god other than the God of Israel leads to death and destruction rather than life. Because the gods of the nations do not seek the well-being of human beings but merely seek to control and manipulate them for their own selfish ends, they reduce human beings to their slaves and seek to impose their will on them by force. Any who conform their lives to the way of being that is characteristic of such gods make themselves their slaves and destroy their own well-being rather than contributing to it. Likewise, any who relate to those gods on the principle of *do ut des* in an attempt to obtain something from them in exchange for giving them what they desire for themselves are not truly acting in their own best interest but contrary to it.

These observations also provide the basis necessary for understanding why God demands that his people Israel set themselves apart from other peoples as a "holy nation" and remain distinct from them (Exod 19:6). What God desired by means of the covenant was that his people relate to him and to one another in the same way that he related to them, that is, with a love that was to be genuine, sincere, heartfelt, and unconditional. The people were to regard their own well-being and that of others as an end in itself rather than treating others merely as means to their own ends in order to pursue self-interests that were not actually in their best interest. That could happen only as they lived in the covenant that God was establishing with them, loving and serving him alone. From the moment they broke with that covenant and began to serve other gods, they would inevitably begin to relate to others in harmful, selfish, and destructive ways in the same manner that those gods and their worshipers did. The worship of those gods and the adoption of the ways of thinking and behaving that characterized the peoples who worshiped them would thus destroy the people's well-being.

For that reason, God demanded that if the people chose to live in the covenant he was establishing with them, they not only worship and serve him alone as their God but also separate themselves from other peoples. He tells them not to imitate those peoples, make pacts with them, or follow their practices, since any of these things would do them great harm for the reasons just considered.[11] He also imposes extremely harsh punishments for those who violate his commands in this regard and especially for those of his people who worship other gods or lead others to do so. From God's perspective, such things are not to be taken lightly but instead are to be dealt with severely. God's command that his people be holy or set apart is therefore not grounded in any kind of concern for himself or his own nature but is given solely *out of a concern for them and their well-being*. As we have seen in the previous chapters, rather than being an attempt to maintain at a distance some type of pollution or contamination for his own sake or safeguard himself from something that might do him harm, God's command for Israel to be holy is rooted in his insistence that those who were to live as his people do whatever was necessary to avoid falling under the influence of those who would lead them to live in ways that would make it impossible for them to enjoy the well-being he desired for them. God's command for the people to be holy and to remain separate from others was designed not to protect *him* from what was dangerous but to protect *them* from behaviors that would do them and others harm. At the same time that he separates his people from other nations, however, God also places them in the midst of those nations so that they may be a means to drawing those nations to himself: "I will give you as a light to the nations, that my salvation may reach to the end of the earth" (Isa 49:6).

For the same reasons, what God sought from his people was not that they be loyal or faithful to him personally but to the covenant he was establishing with them for their own good. In a sense, as just noted above, by being loyal and faithful to that covenant they would be loyal and faithful to their own well-being and thus to themselves as well. They would be acting in accordance with their own self-interest, yet this would be healthy and good for them rather than selfish and harmful. What was truly in their self-interest was their own well-being. This well-being would result from their faithfulness to the

---

11. See especially Lev 18:24-30; Deut 7:1-6; 12:29-32; 14:1-2; 18:9-14.

covenant, both because of the positive consequences that would follow intrinsically from their obedience to the commandments contained in that covenant and because their obedience would make it possible for God's actions on their behalf to contribute to their happiness and well-being.

Conversely, if God is said to have promised to be loyal and faithful to Israel as his people, this should be understood in the sense that no matter what Israel did or failed to do, he would not back down from his efforts to bring them to live in ways that enabled them to experience the well-being he desired for them in his love. For that reason, God's loyalty and faithfulness to his people did not take the form of simply approving of anything they did and defending their actions even when they fell into wrongdoing. He did not behave in the way that the god Poseidon is said to have done in relation to his son Polyphemus in the *Odyssey*, standing by him even when he behaved with great cruelty and lashing out at any who opposed him even when they had good reason to do so. On the contrary, God's loyalty and faithfulness to his people took the form of demanding that they act in accordance with his will for what was good, right, just, and loving and attempting to bring them back to such a way of life when they departed from it, even if this meant punishing and chastising them with sufferings that were extremely painful for them.

For this reason as well, it is foreign to biblical thought to view God's relation to Israel as reflecting the kind of favoritism that was characteristic of the pagan gods of antiquity and many of the rulers and powerful figures that worshiped those gods. In reality, rather than showing them favoritism, the demands he made on his people Israel were much greater than those he made on the other peoples of the earth. The biblical texts often repeat that God shows no favoritism or partiality to anyone, including Israel as well as its rulers and leaders, and demands that his people refrain from showing favoritism or partiality to others as well.[12] God also makes it very clear to the people that if they behave in the same way as the peoples that previously inhabited the land he is giving to them, he will expel them from the land just as he expelled those peoples from it before them.[13] Out of love for his people and for their own good, his insistence that they live in accordance with what is good, right, just, and compassionate is just as firm and unbending as it is for human beings as a whole.

In fact, in biblical thought the reason why God is so uncompromising in his demand that his people obey his commandments and practice justice and righteousness is that he is concerned not only for their own well-being but for that of others who are affected by their behavior as well. These include not only certain groups that form part of his people Israel, such as the poor, the weak, and those in greatest need, but also those who do not form part of his people. In addition to seeking to protect and defend the foreigners in their midst, he desires that other peoples come to know him so as to live in

---

12. See, for example, Deut 10:17; 16:19; cf. 2 Chr 19:7; Mal 2:9.
13. See especially Lev 18:24-28; 20:22-23; Deut 4:25-26.

accordance with his will for justice, love, and righteousness and thereby obtain his blessings as well. Therefore, if his people fail to obey him and instead practice injustice, violence, and oppression, they not only deprive themselves of the well-being God desires for them but also prevent other peoples from being drawn to him as their God so that they too may attain that well-being. Those peoples will hardly be drawn to him if the people who are said to be his own live and act in ways that do tremendous harm to themselves and others rather than promoting the good of all.

Strictly speaking, therefore, God's commitment is not to Israel per se but to the existence of a people who will live in the way necessary for them to enjoy the well-being he desires for all and be able to serve as his instrument to bring others to live in the same way. While he certainly wants to bless Israel and will do everything in his power to make that blessing a reality, his concern is not for Israel alone but for all the peoples of the earth. The other nations will attain the blessing he desires for all only if Israel attains that blessing first, since those other nations will be attracted to Israel's God only if they become convinced that there is no greater blessing or happiness than living under that God and serving him by obeying what he commands for the good of all. If God's people Israel fail to live in that way themselves, however, they will undermine and destroy not only their own well-being but that of the other nations of the earth as well, since they will no longer be able to serve as a means to draw those other nations to serve and obey the God of Israel.

While there is a sense in which God's blessing of Israel is conditional upon the people's living in accordance with his commandments, there is also a sense in which God is committed to blessing Israel no matter what the people do. As we have noted above, because he cannot bless them with well-being and prosperity if they do not obey his commandments, when necessary his blessing will take the form of chastisements aimed at correcting them for their own good. What he promises his people, therefore, is that he will do everything in his power to accomplish his goal of bringing them to live in conformity with his commandments, even if he must take the drastic step of destroying a part of the people and sending another part into exile in foreign lands. Given that Israel is his chosen instrument to draw the other peoples of the earth to himself so that they may live under him and be blessed by him as well, to give up on his efforts to bring his people Israel to live in the way he has commanded for their own good would be to give up on the rest of the nations of the earth as well. Due to his love for all, he refuses to put an end to those efforts.

In biblical thought, therefore, God's election of Israel as his special people is not an expression of favoritism toward one people above all others but rather is a means by which he wishes to bless both Israel and all of the other peoples of the world. While it involves treating Israel differently from the other nations and showing them special consideration, God does these things not only for Israel's sake but for the sake of the other nations as well. In other words, in biblical thought what led God to choose Israel as his people and establish his covenant with them was his love not only for Israel but for all of the families of the earth as well.

Until the day comes when other nations can be drawn to him by means of Israel, of course, God must bless Israel more than the other nations, even though at times this blessing must take the form of chastisements. Although in Deut 7:14 God promises to make Israel "the most blessed of all peoples" if they obey his commandments, this promise should not be understood as describing a permanent situation. The reason that Israel will be blessed more than all other nations is that their reception and acceptance of the instruction and guidance God gives them through the Torah will lead them to live in ways that will allow them to enjoy blessings that the other nations who have not received and accepted the same instruction and guidance will not be able to attain. In addition to the well-being that the people will attain as a result of the intrinsic consequences of obedience to the commandments of the Torah, they will be blessed by God with things such as long life, prosperity, abundance, health, and deliverance from their enemies in response to their obedience, precisely because that obedience will allow them to use the blessings that God will give them for good rather than in destructive ways. Yet while their obedience to God's commandments will enable them to become the most blessed of all peoples, God's intention is that other peoples eventually be brought to live in the same manner so that they may obtain the same type of blessings that he promises to give to his people Israel if they obey him.

A GOD CONCERNED FOR HIS NAME

Throughout the Hebrew Scriptures, one of the things that is said to concern most YHWH the God of Israel is his name and reputation. The importance of this idea for biblical thought is evident from the fact that it appears in the opening section of the Decalogue: "You shall not use the name of YHWH your God lightly, for YHWH will not regard as innocent anyone who misuses his name" (Exod 20:7; Deut 5:11). The prohibition against profaning God's name appears repeatedly in Leviticus as well.[14] The most emphatic of these prohibitions is found in Lev 24:16: "One who blasphemes the name of YHWH shall be put to death; the whole congregation shall stone the blasphemer. Aliens as well as the native-born, when they blaspheme the Name, shall be put to death." Among the other writings of the Hebrew Bible, none stresses the idea that God is concerned for his name more than the book of the prophet Ezekiel.

As we have seen in Chapter 1 of this work, scholars such as Walter Brueggemann interpret the passages that speak of God's command for his name to be honored and respected as being rooted in a concern for God himself. According to Brueggemann, God's concern for his name is in essence a

---

14. See Lev 18:21; 19:12; 20:3; 21:6; 22:2, 32.

concern for his identity and reputation. What God desires and demands is that Israel act in ways that are congruent with Yahweh's name and his holiness:

> When Israel acts in ways that are congruent with Yahweh's name, then Yahweh's name is made holy; or perhaps we should say, intensified in holiness. Whenever Israel as Yahweh's visible partner acts in ways that are incongruous with Yahweh's holy character, however, Yahweh's name is debased, profaned, and diminished in the eyes of the nations. Israel's actions decisively and substantively affect the quality of Yahweh's holiness. In the end, the notion of Yahweh's holiness suggests that Yahweh cares most about Yahweh's own name, reputation, and character—even more than Yahweh cares for Israel. Yahweh does indeed penultimately care about Israel, and so the Holy One comes to save Israel. Some texts—the more decisive texts, I believe, related to this notion of holiness—make clear that finally Yahweh cares most about Yahweh's own self.[15]

Commenting on Ezek 39:7, where God affirms that he will no longer allow the people to profane his holy name any more as they have in the past, Brueggemann adds:

> Yahweh will act decisively for Yahweh's own name. There is something stubborn and toughly determined about Yahweh's resolve to recover Yahweh's own name, in light of Israel's debasing of it in the eyes of the nations. . . . Yahweh must act for Israel in order to act for self and for the recovery of Yahweh's holy but now profaned name. Ezek 36:22-32 is an amazing account of the way in which Yahweh's self-regard is now maddeningly enmeshed with the well-being of Israel. As a result, this text must (a) promise Yahweh's good act for Israel, but (b) make it clear that the motivation for such good acts on the part of Yahweh is not love for Israel but Yahweh's self-regard. . . .[16]

According to this type of interpretation of the passages in which God is said to show a concern for his name, that concern is rooted in his desire to be honored, respected, and obeyed for his own sake. Due to his intense self-regard, what he cares most about is himself. Like the gods of the nations, Israel's God wants his name to be revered, glorified, and worshiped because these things bring him pleasure and satisfaction.

In light of what we have seen throughout the present work, however, the passages that speak of God's concern for his name should be understood on the basis of ideas that are very different. Because throughout the Hebrew Bible the primary concern of the God of Israel is the well-being of all, his concern for his name must be understood as a secondary concern that is derived from that primary concern. In that case, the reason that God wishes for all to hold him and his name in high regard and acknowledge his sovereignty and saving power is that their well-being depends on their doing so. In other words, he desires for his name to be respected and held in high regard, not for *his own* sake, but for *the sake of human beings themselves.* Behind this desire is the hope that, when human beings hear of his love for the world and his saving power, they will

---

15. Walter Brueggemann, *Theology of the Old Testament: Testament, Dispute, Advocacy* (Minneapolis: Fortress, 2005), 290.

16. Brueggemann, *Theology*, 291.

abandon their destructive ways and their worship of false gods so as to come to find in him the healing and wholeness he desires for all people. In that case, his concern that his name be held in high regard and that all acknowledge his sovereignty and saving power is not an end in itself but a means toward another end, namely, the salvation and well-being of the human beings he loves.

This, in fact, is precisely what we find in the passages from the prophetic writings that speak of God's concern for his name. In the first chapter of Malachi, for example, God tells his people: "A son honors his father and a servant his master. If then I am a father, where is the honor due me? And if I am a master, where is the respect due me?, says the LORD of hosts to you, O priests, who despise my name" (Mal 1:6). After expressing his displeasure that the people have offered him sacrifices of polluted, defective, and sick animals, God adds: "For from the rising of the sun to its setting my name is great among the nations, and in every place incense is offered to my name, and a pure offering; for my name is great among the nations, says the LORD of hosts. But you profane it when you say that the LORD's table is polluted, and that the food for it may be despised" (1:11-12). As we have seen in Chapter 6 of this study, the idea in the passage is that the people profane God's name among the nations because their defective offerings suggest that the people do not truly respect or honor God but regard him as being worthy only of gifts that are of little value. When the people's actions convey this idea to the other nations around them, those nations lose any interest they may have had in serving such a God. This displeases God precisely because he wants to be served by Israel and the nations, not for *his* sake, but *for theirs*.

In the following chapter of Malachi, God denounces the injustices and violence that his people commit while at the same time stressing his desire to bless them. He speaks of the covenant he made with Levi in the following terms: "My covenant with him was a covenant of life and well-being, which I gave him; this called for reverence, and he revered me and stood in awe of my name. True instruction was in his mouth, and no wrong was found on his lips. He walked with me in integrity and uprightness, and he turned many from iniquity" (Mal 2:5-6). Here God's desire for the members of his people to enjoy life and well being by living in integrity and justice and avoiding iniquity is not only made explicit but is also tied to their reverencing him and his name. Similarly, in the final chapter of Malachi, God tells the people through the prophet: "But for you who revere my name the sun of righteousness will rise, with healing in its wings. You will go out leaping like calves from the stall. And you will tread down the wicked, for they will be ashes under the soles of your feet, on the day when I act, says the LORD of hosts" (4:2-3). In these verses, revering God's name is associated with justice or righteousness and healing, as well as joyfulness and salvation from oppression. These passages thus indicate that the reason that God wishes for the people to revere him and his name is so that they may live in the way he has commanded for their own well-being and that on that basis he may bless them.

The first allusions to God's concern for his name in Ezekiel appear in chapter 20 of the book. There God affirms that he has acted for the sake of his name so that it might not be profaned among the nations while at the same time complaining that the people have profaned his name in the sight of the nations by not observing the statutes and ordinances he gave them in order that they might find life in them (vv. 8-14). In particular, the passage stresses that God brought them out of Egypt in the sight of the nations, hoping to bless them in a land of milk and honey and hoping as well that the nations would come to know him (vv. 15-17). In v. 22, after mentioning the disobedience and rebellion of the people, God tells them: "I withheld my hand, and acted for the sake of my name, so that it should not be profaned in the sight of the nations, in whose sight I had brought them out." The clear implication is that God wanted the nations to see how he saved and blessed Israel, no doubt so that they too might be drawn to him. Israel's sin and disobedience, however, have prevented this from happening.

Nevertheless, in the latter part of the same chapter, God promises that he will become king over the people and enter into judgment with them to purge out the rebels and transgressors (Ezek 20:33-38). In that day, they will no longer profane his name with their idols and the offerings they present him but will turn away from those idols and the evils they practice in order to serve him faithfully (20:39-43). At the end of the passage, God tells the people: "And you will know that I am the LORD, when I deal with you for my name's sake, not according to your evil ways or corrupt deeds, O house of Israel, says the Lord GOD" (20:44). The idea that God will do these things for the sake of his name clearly implies that he wishes to see the people whom he has chosen to bear his name practicing justice and righteousness both for their own well-being and also in order that other nations might come to know him as a good God who is committed to justice and righteousness.

These ideas are made explicit in Ezekiel 36. In vv. 16-19, God is said to have judged the people in his wrath by scattering them among the nations after they had polluted the land by worshiping idols and shedding blood upon it. God then tells the people:

> But when they came to the nations, wherever they went, they profaned my holy name, because it was said of them, "These are the people of the LORD, and yet they had to go out of his land." But I was concerned for my holy name, which the house of Israel had profaned among the nations where they went. Therefore say to the house of Israel, Thus says the Lord GOD: It is not for your sake, O house of Israel, that I am about to act, but for the sake of my holy name, which you have profaned among the nations where you went. I will sanctify my great name, which has been profaned among the nations, and which you have profaned among them; and the nations will know that I am the LORD, says the Lord GOD, when through you I make manifest my holiness before their eyes. I will take you from among the nations, and gather you from all the lands, and bring you into your own land.

I will sprinkle clean water upon you, and you will be clean from all your impurities, and from all your idols I will cleanse you. I will give you a new heart, and I will put a new spirit within you; and I will remove from your flesh the heart of stone and give you a heart of flesh. I will put my spirit within you, and will cause you to walk in my statutes and observe my ordinances carefully. Then you will live in the land that I gave to your ancestors; and you will be my people, and I will be your God. I will save you from all your impurities, and I will call forth the grain and make it abundant so that no famine comes upon you. I will multiply the fruit of the tree and the produce of the field, so that you may never again suffer the disgrace of famine among the nations. Then you will remember your evil ways, and your actions that were not good; and you will loathe yourselves for your iniquities and your abominable deeds. It is not for your sake that I will act, says the Lord God; let that be known to you. Be ashamed and dismayed for your ways, O house of Israel.

Thus says the Lord God: On the day that I cleanse you from all your iniquities, I will cause the towns to be inhabited, and the places that lie in ruin will be rebuilt. The land that was desolate will be tilled, instead of lying in desolation in the sight of all who pass by. And they will say, "This land that was desolate has become like the garden of Eden; and the waste and desolate and ruined towns are now inhabited and fortified." Then the nations that are left all around you will know that I, the Lord, have rebuilt the places that were in ruins and replanted that which was desolate. I, the Lord, have spoken, and I will do it (vv. 20-36).

According to this passage, God's concern for his name has to do with the fact that Israel bears that name as "the people of YHWH" (Ezek 36:20). This means that other nations know of him through Israel. Therefore, if Israel lives faithfully, practicing justice and righteousness, as a consequence God will be able to bless his people in the way he desires. When the other nations see this, they will be attracted to Israel's God as a God who brings justice, equity, and well-being. In that way, they will come to hold his name in high regard as a good God who blesses those who worship him with well-being.

When God's people practice sin, injustice, and oppression, however, the opposite occurs. Because Israel bears God's name as his people and the other nations identify YHWH with Israel, when they see Israel's impure, unjust, and sinful behavior, they associate the God whom Israel worships with the same type of behavior. Then, when God chastises them as a result of that behavior by sending them into exile in order to discipline and correct them, the nations who do not know the type of God that YHWH is conceive of him in terms that are even less favorable: not only does he allow and perhaps even promote unjust and immoral behavior among the people he calls his own, but he also fails to assist them when they are in need. Instead of doing them good, he sends them into exile. In this way, their impression of Israel's God becomes a very negative one. Far from being attracted to him, they want nothing to do with him.

For that reason, if God is to restore honor to his name so that the nations might be attracted to him again, he must act on behalf of Israel in two ways.

First, he must restore the people to obedience so that they practice justice and righteousness once more. The passage speaks of God cleansing them from their impurities and putting a new heart and spirit into them so that they live in accordance with his good will and commandments. Second, he must restore their fortunes by bringing them back into the land and pouring out abundant blessings on them. In this way, they will live once more as his people and he will be known through them as a God who does good and promotes justice and well-being. By restoring Israel to obedience and to their land, his name or reputation will also be restored in the sight of the nations so that they too will know of his goodness and be drawn to him.

The same basic ideas appear in Ezekiel 39. In v. 7 of that chapter, God is presented as affirming: "I will make known my holy name among my people Israel; and I will not let my holy name be profaned any more; and the nations will know that I am the LORD, the Holy One in Israel." Further on in the chapter, this idea is developed further:

> I will make my glory manifest among the nations; and all the nations will see my judgment that I have executed, and my hand that I have laid on them. The house of Israel will know that I am the LORD their God, from that day forward. And the nations will know that the house of Israel went into captivity for their iniquity, because they were unfaithful to me. Therefore I hid my face from them and gave them into the hand of their adversaries, and they all fell by the sword. I dealt with them according to their uncleanness and their transgressions and hid my face from them.
>
> Therefore thus says the Lord GOD: Now I will bring the captivity of Jacob to an end and have mercy on the whole house of Israel, and I will be jealous for my holy name. They will forget their shame, and all the unfaithfulness that they showed toward me, when they live securely in their land with no one to make them afraid, when I have brought them back from among the peoples and gathered them from their enemies' lands, and through them have made manifest my holiness in the sight of many nations. Then they will know that I am the LORD their God because I sent them into exile among the nations, and then gathered them again into their own land. I will leave none of them in captivity; and I will never again hide my face from them, when I pour out my spirit upon the house of Israel, says the Lord GOD (vv. 21-29).

Here God promises to do the same things just mentioned above, restoring Israel to its land and bringing the people to live obediently so that they may enjoy his blessings. In this way, God will reveal his nature and character not only to Israel but to the other nations as well. Both Israel and the nations will also be brought to understand why God treated Israel as he did. It will become clear that he had not been acting out of cruelty or malice but was merely chastising them so that they might be brought back to obedience and live in a way that would make it possible for them to enjoy his blessings in their land once again.

The affirmation that God seeks to act in this way for the sake of his name rather than for the sake of Israel must be understood against the background of these ideas. In his reading of these passages from Ezekiel 36 and 39, Brueggemann presents a false alternative when he affirms that "the motivation for such good acts on the part of Yahweh is not love for Israel but Yahweh's self-regard."[17] It is certainly an act of love on the part of Israel's God to restore the people to a way of living that will enable them to enjoy his blessings and to bring them back to their land in order to bless them with abundance there. To question such an idea would involve affirming that what ultimately interests God is not blessing Israel but only having his name held in high regard by human beings. In that case, God's blessing of Israel and the nations would not be an end in itself but a means toward a greater end, namely, gaining greater recognition and honor in the eyes of human beings.

Clearly, in the thought of Ezekiel, God wants his name or reputation to be held in high regard for the sake of Israel and the nations, since when his people hold it in high regard they live in a way that enables them to experience the well-being he desires for them. The affirmation that God's act of restoring Israel to obedience and blessing is done for the sake of his name rather than for the sake of Israel in Ezek 36:22, therefore, can be understood in a couple of different ways. The phrase may imply that God's aim goes beyond merely restoring Israel, since he wishes not only to restore Israel but also to restore honor to his name for the sake of the nations as well. In that case, the idea would be that God will restore Israel and bring the people to obey him so that he may bless them once again *not only* for their sake but also so that other peoples may be brought to see what kind of God he is and hold his name in high regard so that they may be drawn to him. Because the Hebrew preposition in the first part of the phrase used in this verse can be translated "on account of" and not only "for the sake of," it can also be understood in the sense that what will lead God to act to restore his people Israel is not the manner in which they have behaved, since their sinful behavior does not merit God's intervention on their behalf, but rather his desire to bring honor to his name once again for the sake of Israel as well as the nations. In either case, however, God's concern for his name must be understood not as a selfish concern for his honor and glory for his own sake, but as a concern that all the peoples of the earth come to know him as a God who is committed to giving life to human beings by bringing them to live in justice and righteousness for their own good. Only in that way will they be drawn to him as he desires.

REJOICING IN THE BLESSINGS SURE TO COME

As we have seen in Chapter 5, throughout most of the Hebrew Bible, the history of Israel is interpreted on the basis of the ideas found in Leviticus 26 and Deuteronomy 28. While God seeks to fill his people's lives with the blessings described in the opening verses of both of these passages, their sinful and destructive behavior prevents him from doing so. When they persistently

---

17. Brueggemann, *Theology*, 291.

refuse to listen to the prophets God sends them and fail to respond as they should to the chastisements he imposes on them, he has no choice but to increase the intensity and severity of those chastisements in the manner that both of those passages anticipate. Because his love will not let him simply abandon the people definitively or give up on them, when none of the terrible sufferings and hardships he inflicts on them succeed in producing in them the results he desires, he sends foreign powers upon them to destroy many of them and take others into captivity and exile.

According to the biblical account, following the rise to power of the Persian king Cyrus and his conquest of the Babylonian empire, many of the Jews who had been living in exile in Babylon and elsewhere returned to Jerusalem and Judea with the hope that God would bless them with the type of abundance and prosperity described at the outset of the two passages just mentioned. The reality they encountered, however, was very different. Although in some ways they were blessed, their lives continued to be filled with struggles and hardships. On the basis of the logic reflected in passages such as Leviticus 26 and Deuteronomy 28, they could only conclude that even though they had been purified of much of the sinful behavior that had led to their exile in foreign lands, they had not yet attained the level of obedience God desired to see in them. For that reason, rather than fulfilling all of the promises of blessing he had made to them in the way they had hoped, God was continuing to chastise and discipline them in order to correct them further. If such was the case, then they needed to strive even more earnestly to conform their lives to God's will by observing his commandments with greater care and diligence and identifying the behaviors and attitudes that they still needed to put away in order to achieve the type of wholeness and well-being that God had promised to give them.

On the basis of their faith and hope in the God of whom their sacred Scriptures spoke, however, both the Jewish people living in the land of their ancestors and those who remained scattered among the other nations of the earth continued to look forward to the day when the promises that he had made to them would be fulfilled in the way that those Scriptures anticipated. Among many Jews it became common to speak of a new age in order to refer to the blessings of peace, well-being, and prosperity that those Scriptures describe. That age stood in contrast to the present age, which was associated with the sin, suffering, and hardships that continued to characterize the people's existence. Many of the passages that portray the glories of the awaited new age reflect a hope that when that age arrived it would last indefinitely.

Often the promises regarding the new age that God intends to bring to pass are seen as revolving around the restoration of Jerusalem or Zion. All those who had been scattered throughout the world would return to the land and the city of David so as to enjoy God's blessings there once more. God would dwell in their midst in order to bless and accompany them, respond to their prayers, and show them his favor. His presence among his people would bring them to worship him with joy and gladness in their hearts and experience firsthand his abundant goodness, grace, and mercy.

Many of the descriptions of the coming new age that appear in Israel's Scriptures are extremely graphic and moving. They include not only prosperity and long life but also rest from all of their toils and afflictions and salvation from all those who would seek to do them harm:

> Therefore the LORD is waiting to be gracious to you; therefore he will rise up to show you mercy. For the LORD is a God of justice; blessed are all those who wait for him. O people in Zion, inhabitants of Jerusalem, you will weep no more. He will be gracious to you beyond measure at the sound of your cry; when he hears it, he will answer you. Even though the LORD may give you the bread of adversity and the water of affliction, yet your Teacher will not hide himself any longer, but your eyes will see your Teacher. And when you turn to the right or to the left, your ears will hear a word from behind you, saying, "This is the way; walk in it."
>
> Then you will desecrate your silver-covered idols and your gold-plated images. You will scatter them like filthy rags; you will say to them, "Away with you!" He will give rain for the seed which you sow in the ground, and grain, the produce of the ground, will be rich and plenteous. On that day your cattle will graze in broad pastures, and the oxen and donkeys that till the ground will eat silage that has been winnowed with shovel and pitchfork. On every lofty mountain and every high hill there will be streams running with water on the day of the great slaughter, when the towers fall. Moreover, the light of the moon will be like the light of the sun, and the light of the sun will be sevenfold, like the light of seven days, on the day when the LORD binds up the injuries of his people and heals the wounds inflicted by his blow (Isa 30:18-26).

> Then justice will dwell in the wilderness and righteousness will abide in the fruitful field. The effect of justice will be peace, and the result of righteousness, quietness and security forever. My people will abide in a peaceful habitation, in secure dwellings, and in quiet resting places (Isa 32:16-18).

> See, the Lord GOD comes with might, and his arm rules for him; his reward is with him and his recompense before him. He will feed his flock like a shepherd; he will gather the lambs in his arms and carry them in his bosom and gently lead the mother sheep (Isa 40:10-11).

> So the people redeemed by the LORD will return and come to Zion with rejoicing; everlasting joy will be upon their heads. They will obtain joy and gladness, and sorrow and sighing will flee away (Isa 51:11; cf. 35:1-10).

> For you will go out in joy and be led back in peace. The mountains and the hills before you will break forth in song, and all the trees of the field will clap their hands. Instead of the thorn bush, the cypress will grow; instead of the brier, the myrtle will come up, and it will be a memorial to the LORD, an everlasting sign that will not be cut off (Isa 55:12-13).

> Look! I am about to create new heavens and a new earth; the former things will not be remembered or come to mind. But be glad and rejoice forever in what I am creating, for I am about to create Jerusalem to be a delight and

its people to be a joy. I will rejoice in Jerusalem and delight in my people; no more will the sound of weeping or the cry of distress be heard in it. No more will there be in it an infant who lives but a few days or an old person who does not live a full lifetime, for one who dies at a hundred years will be considered a youth, and one who falls short of a hundred will be considered accursed. People will build houses and inhabit them; they will plant vineyards and eat their fruit. They will not build for another to inhabit; they will not plant for another to eat, for like the days of a tree will the days of my people be, and my chosen will long enjoy the work of their hands. They will not labor in vain or bear children for calamity, for they will be the offspring blessed by the Lord, as will their descendants after them. Before they call I will answer, and while they are still speaking I will hear. The wolf and the lamb will feed together; the lion will eat straw like the ox, but the food of the serpent will be dust! They will not cause harm or destruction on all my holy mountain, says the Lord (Isa 65:17-25).

I have loved you with an everlasting love; therefore I have drawn you with steadfast love. Again I will build you, and you will be built, O virgin Israel! Again you will take up your tambourines, and go forth to the dancing of mer-rymakers. Again you will plant vineyards on the mountains of Samaria; those who plant them will enjoy their fruit. . . .

Look, I am going to bring them from the land of the north and gather them from the farthest parts of the earth. Among them will be the blind and the lame, those with child and those in labor; together, as a great company, they will return. They will come with weeping, but with consolations I will lead them back. I will bring them to walk by streams of water, on a straight path in which they will not stumble; for I am a father to Israel, and Ephraim is my firstborn. Hear the word of the Lord, O nations, and declare it in the coastlands far away; say, "He who scattered Israel will gather his people and will keep them as a shepherd does a flock". . . .

They will come and sing for joy on the height of Zion, and they will be radiant over the goodness of the Lord, over the grain, the wine, and the oil, and over the young of the flock and the herd; their life will be like a watered garden, and they will never languish again. Then will the young women rejoice in the dance, together with the young men and the old. I will turn their mourning into joy. I will comfort them and give them gladness instead of sorrow (Jer 31:3-5, 8-10, 12-13).

In that day the mountains will drip sweet wine, the hills will flow with milk, and all of the streambeds of Judah will flow with water. A fountain will come forth from the house of the Lord and water the valley of Shittim. Egypt will become a wasteland and Edom a desolate wilderness, because of the violence done to the people of Judah, in whose land they have shed innocent blood. But Judah will be inhabited forever and Jerusalem to all generations (Joel 3:18-20).

Therefore, thus says the Lord: I have returned to Jerusalem with compassion; my house will be built in it, says the Lord of hosts, and a measuring line will be stretched out over Jerusalem. Proclaim further: Thus says the Lord of hosts: My cities will again overflow with prosperity; the Lord will again comfort Zion and again choose Jerusalem (Zech 1:16-17).

On that day the Lord their God will save them, for they are the flock of his people; for like the jewels of a crown they will sparkle in his land. How great are his goodness and his beauty! Grain will make the young men flourish, and new wine the young women (Zech 9:16-17; cf. 10:6-12).

Take courage, my children, cry out to God, and he will deliver you from the power and the hand of the enemy. For I have put my hope in the Everlasting One to save you, and joy has come to me from the Holy One, because of the compassion that will soon come to you from your everlasting Savior. For I sent you out with sorrow and weeping, but God will give you back to me with everlasting joy and gladness. For as Zion's neighbors have now seen you taken captive, so they soon will see your salvation by God, which will come to you with great glory and with the splendor of the Everlasting One. . . . Look toward the east, O Jerusalem, and see the joy that is coming to you from God! Look, your children whom you sent away are coming; they are coming at the word of the Holy One, gathered from east and west, rejoicing in the glory of God (Bar 4:21-24, 36-37).

Take off the garment of your mourning and affliction, O Jerusalem, and put on forever the beauty of the glory that comes from God. Drape yourself in the robe of the righteousness that comes from God; put on your head the diadem of the glory of the Everlasting One, for God will make manifest your splendor everywhere under heaven. God will give you evermore the name, "Peace of Righteousness and Glory of Godliness."

Arise, O Jerusalem, stand upon the high place; look toward the east, and see your children gathered from west and east at the word of the Holy One, rejoicing that God has remembered them. For they departed from you on foot, led away by their enemies, but God will bring them back to you, as if carried in glory on a royal throne. For God has ordered that every high mountain and the everlasting hills be made low and that the valleys be filled in to make level ground, so that Israel may walk securely in the glory of God. The woods and every fragrant tree have given shade to Israel at God's command. For God will lead Israel with joy, in the light of his glory, with the compassion and justice that come from him (Bar 5:1-9).

Of course, in order for the happiness, joy, and well-being described in passages such as these to exist among the people, it was necessary for them to live in ways that promoted justice and equity. Only if that happened could poverty, oppression, injustice, and violence be brought to an end. To some extent, God's purification of the people through the sufferings they had endured was viewed as a means by which the obedience that God sought to bring about in them would be accomplished. At the same time, God needed to continue to act among his people to bring about in them the way of life necessary for them to enjoy the well-being he sought to make theirs. A number of passages from the books of Israel's prophets speak of God bringing about in his people the change of heart that would enable them to be blessed:

I will set my eyes upon them for good, and I will bring them back to this land. I will build them up and not tear them down; I will plant them and not pluck them up. I will give them a heart to know me and know that I am the Lord, and they will be my people, and I will be their God, for they will return to me with their whole heart (Jer 24:6-7).

See, the days are coming, says the LORD, when I will make a new covenant with the house of Israel and the house of Judah. It will not be like the covenant that I made with their ancestors when I took them by the hand to bring them out of the land of Egypt, the covenant that they broke, even though I was a husband to them, says the LORD. But this is the covenant that I will make with the house of Israel when those days come, says the LORD: I will put my law within them, and I will write it on their hearts, and I will be their God, and they will be my people. No longer will they teach one another or say to each other, "Know the LORD," for they will all know me, from the least of them to the greatest, says the LORD, for I will forgive their iniquity and remember their sin no more (Jer 31:31-34).

See, I am going to gather them from all the lands to which I drove them in my anger and my wrath and in great indignation; I will bring them back to this place and will cause them to dwell in safety. They will be my people, and I will be their God. I will give them one heart and one way, that they may fear me always, for their own good and the good of their children after them. I will make an everlasting covenant with them, never to cease to do good to them, and I will put the fear of me in their hearts so that they may not turn away from me. I will rejoice at doing good to them, and I will plant them in this land in faithfulness, with all my heart and all my soul. For thus says the LORD: Just as I have brought all this great evil upon this people, so will I bring upon them all the good that I now promise them (Jer 32:37-42).

I am going to bring this city health and healing; I will heal them and grant them an abundance of prosperity and security. I will bring an end to the captivity of Judah and the captivity of Israel and will rebuild them as they were formerly. I will cleanse them from all of their iniquity by which they sinned against me, and I will forgive all of the iniquities by which they sinned and transgressed against me. And this city will be to me a name of joy, praise, and glory before all the nations of the earth who will hear of all the good that I do for them; they will fear and tremble because of all the well-being and prosperity I provide for it. Thus says the LORD: In this place of which you now say, "It is a wasteland without humans or animals," in the towns of Judah and the streets of Jerusalem that are desolate, without humans or animals inhabiting them, there will once more be heard the voice of gladness and the voice of rejoicing, the voice of the bridegroom and the voice of the bride, the voices of those who sing as they bring thank offerings to the house of the LORD: "Give thanks to the LORD of hosts, for the LORD is good, for his steadfast love endures forever!" For I will restore the fortunes of the land as it was formerly, says the LORD (Jer 33:6-11).

I will give them one heart and put a new spirit within them; I will remove the heart of stone from their flesh and give them a heart of flesh, so that they may walk in my statutes and follow my ordinances and observe them. Then they will be my people, and I will be their God (Ezek 11:19-20; cf. 36:25-27).

I will heal their rebellion; I will love them freely, for my anger has turned away from them. I will be like the dew to Israel. They will blossom like a lily;

they will cast down roots like the forests of Lebanon. Their shoots will spread out; their beauty will be like the olive tree and their fragrance like that of Lebanon. They will again live beneath my shadow; they will flourish like a garden. They will blossom like the vine; their fragrance will be like the wine of Lebanon (Hos 14:4-7).

A day will come when I will pour out my spirit on all flesh; your sons and your daughters will prophesy, your old men will dream dreams, and your young men will see visions. In those days I will pour out my spirit even on the male and female slaves (Joel 2:28-29).

On that day you will not be put to shame because of all the deeds by which you have rebelled against me; for then I will remove from your midst your arrogant, exultant ones, and you will never again be haughty in my holy mountain. For I will leave in the midst of you a humble and lowly people. The remnant of Israel will seek refuge in the name of the Lord; they will do no wrong and speak no lies, nor will a deceitful tongue be found in their mouths (Zeph 3:11-13).

Blessing David to Bless Israel

While many passages from the Hebrew Bible seem to present God as acting to bring about the salvation, justice, and wholeness that he has promised his people directly, others speak of him accomplishing these things through certain human beings whom he has chosen as his instruments. In particular, they express the hope that a descendant of David will be established in power and become God's agent to restore the people's fortunes:

For the Lord has chosen Zion; he has desired it for his habitation: "This will be my resting place forever; here I will reside, for that is my desire. I will abundantly bless its provisions; I will satisfy its poor with bread. I will clothe its priests with salvation, and its faithful people will shout for joy. There I will make a horn to sprout up for David; I have prepared a lamp for my anointed one. I will clothe his enemies with disgrace, but on him, his crown will gleam" (Ps 132:13-18).

For a child has been born for us, a son has been given to us; and the government will rest upon his shoulders. He will be called Wonderful Counselor, Mighty God, Everlasting Father, Prince of Peace. There will be no end to the expansion of his government and the peace of David's throne and kingdom. He will establish and uphold it with judgment and with justice from this time forward and forevermore. The zeal of the Lord of hosts will do this (Isa 9:6-7).

A shoot will spring up from the stump of Jesse, and a branch from his roots will blossom. The spirit of the Lord will rest on him, the spirit of wisdom and understanding, the spirit of counsel and strength, the spirit of knowledge and the fear of the Lord. His delight will be in the fear of the Lord. He will not judge by what his eyes see, or decide by what his ears hear; but he will judge the poor with righteousness and decide with equity for the meek of the earth. He will strike the earth with the rod of his mouth, and with the breath of his lips he will kill the wicked. Righteousness will be the belt around his loins, and faithfulness the belt around his waist. The wolf will dwell with the lamb; the leopard will lie down with the young goat. The calf and the lion and the fatling will dwell together, and a little child will lead them. The cow and the bear will graze; their young will lie down together, and the lion will eat straw like the ox. The nursing child will play over the hole of the viper, and the weaned child will put its hand on the serpent's den. They will not do harm or cause destruction on all my holy mountain; for as the waters cover the sea, so will the earth be full of the knowledge of the Lord (Isa 11:1-9).

When the extortioner is no more, and destruction has ceased, and oppressors have vanished from the land, then a throne will be established in steadfast love in the tent of David, and on it will sit in faithfulness a ruler who judges, seeks justice, and is swift to do what is right (Isa 16:4-5).

Then I will gather the remnant of my flock out of all the lands where I have driven them, and I will bring them back to their fold, and they will be fruitful and multiply. I will raise up shepherds over them who will care for them, and they will no longer fear or be dismayed, nor will any be missing, says the Lord. The days are coming, says the Lord, when I will raise up for David a righteous Branch, and he will reign as king and deal wisely, and will execute justice and establish righteousness in the land. In his days Judah will be saved and Israel will dwell securely. And this is the name by which he will be called: "The Lord is our righteousness." Therefore the days are coming, says the Lord, when it will no longer be said, "As the Lord lives who brought the people of Israel up out of the land of Egypt," but, "As the Lord lives who brought the descendants of Israel up out of the land of the north and out of all the lands where he had driven them." Then they will dwell in their own land (Jer 23:3-7).

The days are coming, says the Lord, when I will fulfill the promise I made to the house of Israel and the house of Judah. In those days and at that time I will cause a righteous Branch to sprout up for David, and he will execute judgment and establish justice in the land. In those days Judah will be saved, and Jerusalem will dwell securely. And this is the name by which it will be called: "The Lord is our righteousness" (Jer 33:14-16).

Therefore, thus says the Lord God to them: See, I myself will judge between the fat sheep and the lean sheep. Because you pushed away with your side and shoulder and butted at all the weak animals with your horns until you scattered them far and wide, I will save my flock; they will no longer be ravaged, and I will judge between one sheep and another. I will set up over them one shepherd, my servant David, and he will care for them; he will care for them and be their shepherd. And I the Lord will be their God, and my servant David will be prince among them; I the Lord have spoken.

I will make with them a covenant of peace and banish wild animals from the land, so that they may live in the wilderness and sleep in the forest securely. I will make them and the region around my mountain a blessing, and I will send down the showers in their season; they will be showers of blessing. The trees of the field will yield their fruit, and the earth will produce its increase. They will dwell securely on their land, and they will know that I am the Lord when I have broken the bars of their yoke and have saved them from the hands of those who enslaved them. They will no longer be prey for the nations, nor will the animals of the land devour them. They will dwell in safety, and no one will make them afraid. I will provide for them a place renowned for its fertility so that they will no more be consumed with hunger in the land and no longer suffer the insults of the nations. Then they will know that I, the LORD their God, am with them and that they, the house of Israel, are my people, says the Lord GOD. You are my sheep, the sheep of my pasture, and I am your God, says the Lord GOD (Ezek 34:20-31).

Thus says the Lord GOD: I will take the people of Israel out from among the nations to which they have gone and will gather them from all sides and bring them to their own land. I will make them one nation in the land on the mountains of Israel, and a single king will reign over them all. Never again will they be two nations, and never again will they be divided into two kingdoms. They will never again contaminate themselves with their idols and their detestable things or with any of their transgressions. I will save them from all the rebellions into which they have fallen and will cleanse them. Then they will be my people, and I will be their God.

My servant David will be king over them, and they will all have one shepherd. They will walk in my ordinances and follow my statutes and observe them. They will dwell in the land that I gave to my servant Jacob, in which your ancestors lived; they and their children and their children's children will live there forever, and my servant David will be their prince forever. I will make a covenant of peace with them; it will be an everlasting covenant with them, and I will bless them and multiply them and will set my sanctuary among them forever. My dwelling place will be over them, and I will be their God, and they will be my people. Then the nations will know that I the LORD sanctify Israel, when my sanctuary is among them forever (Ezek 37:21-28).

For the Israelites will remain many days without king or prince, without sacrifice or pillar, without ephod or household idols. Afterward the Israelites will return and seek the LORD their God, and David their king; they will come in awe to the LORD and to his goodness in the latter days (Hos 3:4-5).

On that day I will raise up the booth of David that is fallen and repair its breaches. I will raise up its ruins and rebuild it as in the days of old, in order that they may possess the remnant of Edom and all the nations who are called by my name, says the LORD who does this. The time is coming, says the LORD, when the one who plows will overtake the one who reaps and the treader of grapes will overtake the one who sows the seed. The mountains will drip sweet wine, and all the hills will flow with it. I will bring back my people Israel from their captivity, and they will rebuild the ruined cities and inhabit them. They will plant vineyards and drink their wine, and they will make gardens and eat their fruit. I will plant them upon their land, and they will never again be plucked up out of the land that I have given them, says the LORD your God (Amos 9:11-15).

Although passages such as these present David and the kings descended from him as God's chosen instrument to bless and save his people, it must be stressed that God's objective is not simply to bless David or his descendants but to bless his people Israel and eventually other nations of the world as well through him. Yet because this can happen only if David and his descendants practice and promote justice and equity, God insists that he will chastise David and the rulers descended from him when they disobey in order to bring them back to himself in obedience (2 Sam 7:14-15). Furthermore, because David and his descendants are to seek the well-being of all in everything they do, God wants his people to submit to them not for his sake or for the sake of David but for *their own* sake. Should any of David's descendants depart from the path of justice, righteousness, and equity, however, the people are to disobey them in order to obey God instead. This does not involve rebelling against their rulers or attempting to overthrow them but rather demanding that those rulers submit obediently to God's will for the good of all. They leave it up to God as to whether he wishes to remove any particular ruler from the throne in order to replace him with another.

Strictly speaking, therefore, God does not tie himself to David or the rulers descended from him in the same way that the gods of antiquity tied themselves to certain individual monarchs. God's commitment is not to any particular individual or his descendants but to justice and wholeness for all. His promise to David is not to accept him and give him his stamp of approval no matter what he does but to use him and his descendants as his instruments to accomplish his loving purposes in relation to Israel and the rest of the world. When he makes his covenant with David and promises him that a descendant of his will remain on the throne perpetually, he establishes with him and his descendants the same type of relationship that he established with Abraham and his offspring, namely, that he will bless them if they obey him but will punish and chastise them if they do not. He will not spurn David's descendants definitively, however, but will continue to do everything in his power to bring them back to himself when they persistently disobey him, even if at times this involves removing them from the throne in the same way that he will remove Israel from the land if they do not observe his covenant with them.

Judging the Nations for Good

As several of the passages just considered make clear, if the people are to enjoy God's blessings of peace, well-being, and prosperity, it is not enough for them to obey him and for God to multiply them and provide abundant harvests and other material blessings. As long as there are other peoples who seek to oppress Israel and do the people harm, they will be unable to live in peace and tranquility. Instead, they will be under constant threat of violence and must live in fear and anxiety. Even if they trust that God will give them the victory over other nations that rise up against them, as long as they have to defend themselves against those nations, they will have to suffer the loss of lives, goods, and other resources as they wage war against them. This will make it impossible for them to live entirely at peace and enjoy the blessings God gives them unimpeded.

For that reason, God must deal in some way with the nations that pose an obstacle to Israel's well-being and must do so definitively if his people are to attain the salvation he desires for them. Basically, there are two ways in which those nations can be prevented from doing Israel harm. The first of these is that they put away their sinful ways and enmity toward Israel by committing themselves to living in accordance with God's will for justice and righteousness. If they do so and seek the assistance of Israel's God in order to live in that way, then they can dwell alongside Israel in peace and even enjoy the same blessings that Israel will receive from God's hand. As we have seen previously in this chapter, there are numerous passages from the Hebrew Scriptures that anticipate a day when the nations will turn to God and serve him alongside of Israel so that they too may obtain the blessings of wholeness, peace, and justice that he desires for them.

Nevertheless, because many people from among the nations reject God's will and refuse to turn to him in obedience in the same way that some of the members of God's people Israel do, God must take action against those who persist in injustice, violence, and oppression. Just as he does with Israel, he does not immediately take action against the nations that refuse to submit to him but first calls them to repentance through his prophets. Only after they refuse to heed his repeated calls for them to put away their violent and destructive ways does God take action against them.

Many of the prophetic writings contain oracles that simply announce God's intention to inflict suffering and punishment on the nations that stand in opposition to his will and to destroy them.[18] Because they contain no call for those nations to repent and turn back to God, it may seem that they are not aimed at bringing those nations to turn to the God of Israel in order to live under him and obey him by practicing justice and righteousness. In many cases, however, this idea is presupposed.

Perhaps the best example of this unstated and implicit call to repentance is found in the book of the prophet Jonah. Initially, the message proclaimed by Jonah simply announces the destruction of Niniveh: "Jonah began to go into the city, going a day's walk. And he cried out, 'Forty days more, and Nineveh will be overthrown!' And the people of Nineveh believed God. They proclaimed a fast, and everyone, great and small, put on sackcloth" (Jonah 3:4-5). Here there is no call for the people to change their ways but simply an announcement of destruction. However, the fact that God's objective was to bring the people to repent is evident from the narrative that follows:

> When the news reached the king of Nineveh, he arose from his throne, took off his robe, covered himself with sackcloth, and sat in ashes. Then he issued a proclamation in Nineveh: "By the decree of the king and his nobles: No human or animal, no herd or flock, will taste anything. They will not eat, nor will they drink water. Humans and animals will be covered with sackcloth, and they will cry in a loud voice to God. All will turn from their evil ways and from the violence that is in their hands. Who knows if God may perhaps relent and change his mind; he may turn from his fierce anger, so that we do

---

18. See, for example, Deut 9:5; Ps 59:5; 79:6-7; Isa 10:5; 44:29; Mic 4:13; 5:15.

not perish." When God saw what they did, and that they turned from their evil ways, he changed his mind about the evil that he had said he would bring upon them, and he did not do it (3:6-10).

Passages such as this one suggest that others in which the nations are threatened with punishments and destruction may also be intended to bring them to abandon their destructive ways and turn to God. If so, the harsh, aggressive, and violent language they contain can be interpreted as an attempt to jar the nations into responding in the same way that the people of Nineveh did so that they may be saved from God's intentions to stamp out the injustice and oppression that they practice. Those threats of punishment may have another purpose as well. If God forewarns the sinful nations of the manner in which he will punish their unjust and oppressive behavior before inflicting punishment on them, when he subsequently carries out those threats of punishment, the other nations who observe what has happened will know that when he calls them to repentance and threatens them with punishment if they refuse to repent, they will suffer the same fate. They thus learn to take seriously the message that God speaks to them through his prophets. Of course, the threats of judgment against the nations that oppress Israel also provide God's people with hope that at some point he will deliver them from those nations.

It is important to stress, however, that God's judgments against the nations must not be understood in terms of any kind of desire to do them harm as an end in itself. Like Israel, all the nations of the world are objects of God's unconditional love. When that love is unable to accomplish its purposes and those nations instead persist in their violent and oppressive behavior in relation to other nations such as Israel, what motivates God to take action against them is not any type of hatred or resentment toward them but his intense desire to put an end to the suffering that they cause others. For that reason, if he acts to destroy some of those nations in definitive fashion, he does so only so that they may never again cause harm to Israel or other people who desire to live in peace and justice. This is the hope expressed in passages such as Isa 29:19-21:

> The meek will obtain fresh joy in the LORD, and those in greatest need will rejoice in the Holy One of Israel. For the tyrant will be no more, and the scoffer will cease to be; all those who intend to do evil will be cut off: those who with a word make someone out to be guilty, those who set a trap for the one who adjudicates at the gate, and those who undermine justice for the one in the right.

As is the case with regard to Israel, therefore, the obstacle to the blessing and salvation of the nations is found not in God but in those nations themselves. Because those nations are also God's good creation, he longs to save and bless them just as he longs to save and bless his people Israel. That can happen, however, only when he succeeds in carrying out his plan to bless Israel in the sight of all of the other nations of the world by bringing his people to live in a manner that will finally enable that blessing to be theirs.

CHAPTER 11

A Stubborn Love for a Stubborn People

Although the Hebrew Scriptures never address explicitly the question of what God envisioned when he created the heavens and the earth and placed his creation under the human beings he made in his image, they seem to leave no doubt that things did not turn out in the way he had hoped and expected. As we have seen in Chapter 2, only a few chapters into the Genesis narrative it is said that "the LORD was sorry that he had made humans on the earth, and it grieved him to his heart" (Gen 6:6). When he decides to make a fresh start by means of the great flood, hoping that such a measure will resolve the problem of the wickedness, corruption, and violence that have filled the earth, God seems to end up disappointed and frustrated once more. Almost immediately, the human beings who survive turn back to their sinful and destructive ways and it is not long before they cover the earth once again with the same evils. Clearly, if God still hopes to accomplish the objectives that led him to create the world, he must implement a different plan.

According to the narrative that runs throughout the Pentateuch, the plan that God conceives and decides to carry out through the descendants of Abraham, Isaac, and Jacob was a fairly simple one. After they had fallen into bondage and slavery in a foreign land, he would manifest to them his unconditional love and sovereign power by liberating them from their oppressors with great signs and wonders that would convince them to trust fully in him and do everything he asked of them. He would then take them to a mountain he had chosen to instruct them in the manner of life that would allow them to be happy and blessed and lay out for them a series of rules, regulations, and guidelines that would ensure their well-being. Once they had understood his good intentions for them and on that basis had committed themselves gladly and gratefully to obeying him in all things, he would introduce them immediately into a land of their own overflowing with milk and honey, where they would enjoy peace and prosperity in abundance. When all of the other nations of the earth saw how happy and blessed this people was under the God who had made them his own, they would eagerly and enthusiastically join with that people in adopting that God as their own and in that way attain the same blessings and prosperity for themselves.

If all of this was what God hoped and expected, as the biblical narrative clearly seems to indicate, it would not be long before his hopes would be dashed to the ground once more. Virtually nothing that he had envisioned would turn out as planned. Once again, however, rather than admitting defeat and giving up on his intentions to bless the human beings he had created, he stubbornly chose to move forward with his plan, vowing that in one way or another he would make it work. While the people he had chosen as his own would do everything in their power to prevent him from filling their lives with the blessings he desired and intended for them, he refused to let them have the last word. That word would instead be his alone.

SETTING THE STAGE FOR SINAI

Although in Chapter 3 of this study we have already considered in general terms the narrative of the events stretching from the creation of the world to the giving of the commandments at Sinai, the ideas that we have explored in Chapters 4–10 shed new light on certain aspects of that narrative. Viewed in the context of the biblical narrative as a whole, the first eleven chapters of Genesis lay out the problem of the persistent disobedience and sinfulness of human beings and make clear the dilemma that God faces. While God desires only what is good for human beings, their seemingly incorrigible tendency to fill their lives with suffering, violence, injustice, and oppression makes it necessary for him to make extremely difficult decisions. His love for them will not allow him simply to abandon them and let them go their own way, since this would only lead to greater suffering and destruction. Because they insist on practicing evil, however, the only way God can take action against evil in the world is by taking action against those human beings who practice it. If he wishes to do good to the human beings he has created in love, therefore, he has no choice but to tolerate to a certain degree their persistent evil, sinfulness, and injustice, yet at times these things become so intolerable that he must act to punish and destroy those who refuse to stop practicing them.

According to the Genesis account, after God determines to make a fresh start through the righteous Noah and his family, he realizes that the destruction that he has brought about by means of the flood has not resolved the problem that lies at the root of the violence, injustice, and corruption that characterize human life on earth, namely, that from the time of their youth the inclination of the heart of human beings is bad or evil (Gen 8:21). Nevertheless, God's decision not to destroy human beings entirely but to spare Noah and his family indicates that he will continue to pursue the same objective that led him to create human beings in the first place, namely, that they be enabled to enjoy the wholeness and well-being he originally intended for them by living in a manner that makes these things possible. As we have seen in the previous chapters, God's election of Abram or Abraham and his offspring is the means by which he seeks to accomplish that objective. Both the multiplication of Abraham's descendants as well as God's gift to them of a land of their own will allow them not only to attain God's blessings themselves but also to serve as God's instrument to attract the other families of the earth to himself so that those blessings may be theirs as well.

Following the account of the life of Abraham, the biblical narrative presents the period of time between the era of the patriarchs and God's appearance to Moses in the burning bush in Exodus 3 as one in which God is relatively inactive. Other than acting at various moments to influence events in the lives of Isaac, Jacob, and their children, including especially Jacob's son Joseph, God does not do anything that seems particularly spectacular or noteworthy. To a large extent, the narrative that appears in the second half of Genesis has the purpose of setting the stage for the story that will begin in the book of Exodus by explaining how Abraham came to have descendants through Isaac and Jacob and how those descendants came to reside in Egypt. Once they settle there, they begin to grow and multiply, yet God disappears from the scene as this takes place.

When the descendants of Abraham, Isaac, and Jacob fall into slavery and begin to groan and cry out due to the harsh measures imposed on them by the Pharoah and their Egyptian overlords, however, the situation changes drastically. From the moment that God hears their cries and looks upon their condition, he remembers the covenant that he had made with their ancestors and becomes intensely active among them to carry out a plan (Exod 2:23-25). This plan goes far beyond merely liberating the people from their bondage in Egypt. In fact, it embraces Israel's history as a whole and the fulfillment of the promises that God had made to Abraham from the time he called him to leave his home and depart for the land that he would show him. Everything is oriented to the purpose of establishing Israel in that land so that they may enjoy there the wholeness and well-being that God desires for them not only for their own sake but for the sake of the nations who will come to know him through Israel as well.

One of the questions that arises when considering the biblical narrative is why God chose to have Abraham's descendants through Isaac and Jacob depart from the land that he had promised to give them and instead have them grow and multiply in Egypt before allowing them to fall into slavery there. There might seem to be no reason why God could not simply have left Abraham's descendants where they were in Canaan in order to carry out there whatever was necessary to bring them to live in accordance with his will and attain his blessings. God might have given them the Torah from a place such as Mount Zion instead of Sinai and had the people occupy more and more of the land gradually as they became more numerous. In that case, the people descended from Jacob or Israel and his twelve sons would never have had to leave the land that God had promised them in order to take possession of it.

If the God of Israel has the power to exert control over the events of history in the way that the biblical texts assume, then if he had chosen to accomplish his purposes in relation to Israel in the way that the biblical narrative describes rather than sparing them from the ordeal of enduring a harsh slavery in Egypt and then journeying to Canaan through a hostile desert, he must have done so for a reason. Clearly, in order for God to accomplish his purposes and fulfill what he had promised, something more was necessary than merely multiplying Abraham's descendants, establishing them in the land he had promised them, giving them commandments, and pouring out his blessings on them. What was necessary was for them to be brought to live in accordance with God's will. For reasons we have seen previously, the people could be truly blessed only if they committed themselves to the practice of what is good, right, just, and loving and put away the sinful and destructive behavior that makes human well-being impossible. God's primary concern, therefore, had to be that of bringing about in them such a way of life. According to the logic of the biblical narrative, the people's descent into Egypt and their liberation from slavery there as well as their time wandering in the Sinai desert played an important role in God's plan to accomplish that objective.

Engendering Trust to Beget Obedience

In biblical thought, if God is to accomplish his objective of bringing Abraham's descendants through Isaac and Jacob to live in conformity with his will for their own good, the first thing that he must do is make himself and his will known to them. He must also, however, gain their trust. As we have seen previously in this study, according to the logic of the biblical texts, if the people of Israel are to trust in God so as to be committed to doing his will, they must be convinced of his unconditional love for them as well as his sovereign power over all that exists. If they are convinced of his sovereign power but do not believe that in his love he seeks nothing but their well-being, they will have no reason to trust that he will use that power only for their good. Instead, they can only expect that he will try to control and manipulate them for his own ends and pursue interests that are distinct from theirs. In that case, if they obey him, they will not do so willingly and enthusiastically out of a conviction that he seeks only what is best for them but will instead be motivated purely by a fear of punishment, thinking that he wishes to impose his will on them by force for his own sake rather than theirs. If that is their motivation, they will not truly commit themselves to practicing justice and righteousness in the way God desires but will do what God commands reluctantly and half-heartedly, out of obligation rather than conviction.

Alternatively, if the people are convinced of God's unconditional love but do not believe that he possesses the sovereign power and wisdom necessary to accomplish his loving purposes among them, they cannot trust that his good intentions for them will be sufficient to deliver them when they are in need and fill their lives with the blessings he has promised them. They cannot be brought to depend on him to help them and care for them if they believe that he might be overpowered or subdued by the gods of other nations or by forces of nature that are more powerful than he is. The only way that God can convince the people to trust fully in him, therefore, is by manifesting to them both his love and his sovereign power through actions that leave them with no doubt that he truly does love them unconditionally and is in fact capable of bringing to pass all the good things that he has promised them.

Once the people have become convinced that in his love God can and will take care of them, deliver them from the hardships and afflictions that they experience, and provide for their every need, they will submit gladly to his will and do whatever he commands. Their trust in him will take the form of obedience. They will rest assured that everything he asks and demands of them is solely for their own good and that he insists that they obey him not for *his own* sake but for *theirs*. Their trust in his goodness and his loving commitment to care for them in all their needs will also allow them to live in freedom. They will be able to live without fear, confident that their life is in God's hands. At the same time, this freedom and confidence in God's care will enable them to give of themselves to one another and care for the needs of others, since they will not have to be concerned that they will lack the resources they need and as a result can share generously what they have with those around them. For that reason, the people's total trust in God and his goodness and sovereignty is an absolute necessity in order for God to accomplish his purposes of blessing them with well-being and bringing them to live in ways that will make it possible for them to enjoy that well-being in the way that both he and they desire.

If the people are to enjoy well-being and wholeness, however, it is not enough for them to trust in God's loving commitment to care for them and his power to provide for all their needs. They must also commit themselves to doing everything in their own power to promote well-being and wholeness among themselves. That means caring for one another in the same way that they care for themselves, as God tells them in Lev 19:18: "You shall love your neighbor as yourself." Once again, if they are truly to live in this manner, they must *want* to do so. Their love for others must be heartfelt and sincere, since by definition true love for others cannot be imposed by force through commandments and threats of punishment. In order for such love to exist among the people, they must realize that the well-being of each person depends on the well-being of all others and is inseparable from it. Particular individuals can experience wholeness only when those around them are whole. Conversely, any community of people can be whole only when the individuals who form part of it enjoy wholeness and well-being. For that reason, it is not possible for people to be committed to their own wholeness and well-being without being committed to the wholeness and well-being of those around them at the same time.

All of these ideas are essential for understanding the logic underlying the narrative in the book of Exodus. By having Jacob's sons and their families settle in Egypt, multiplying their descendants there, and then allowing them to fall into slavery under the Pharoah, God places them in a desperate situation. That situation grows even more desperate when the Pharoah orders the male children born to the Israelites to be put to death (Exod 1:15-21). After God reveals himself to Moses and sends him back to Egypt to demand that the Pharoah let the Israelites go, their suffering grows even more unbearable. The Pharoah imposes even harsher conditions upon the Israelites by forcing them to produce the same number of bricks without being given the straw that had been provided for them previously (5:1-19). As a result, rather than trusting in God and Moses, the people become angry at them (5:20-21). Instead of benefiting them, God's intervention thus seems only to have made things worse for the Israelites. According to the logic of the narrative, however, before God can make known to the Israelites the full extent of his sovereign power and his love for them, it is necessary for them first to sink to the lowest depths of desperation and helplessness. Only when they have nowhere else to turn will they feel compelled to trust in the God who has chosen Moses as his spokesperson.

When Moses initially addresses himself to the Israelites after his encounter with God at Sinai, the people know very little about the God of whom Moses speaks. Like Moses, they are ignorant of his name until he reveals it to them and tells them that he is the god of their ancestors, in particular Abraham, Isaac, and Jacob (Exod 3:6, 13-15; 6:2-4). Because they are for the most part unacquainted with God and up to that point he has done little to demonstrate to them that he is worthy of their trust, the people initially have no reason to expect much of anything from him. In fact, because he has allowed them to become subjected to slavery and endure great hardships under the Egyptians, he seems to have neglected or forgotten them. There thus seems to be no reason why the Israelites should look to God or trust in him. All that they have received from him is the promise that he will bless and multiply them some day in another land that they have not yet known, yet that promise remains unfulfilled and their dire situation in Egypt makes it seem unlikely that he will be able to bring what he has promised to pass.

Beginning in Exodus 6, however, God makes himself known more fully to the Israelites and gains their trust by means of the miraculous deeds he performs on their behalf. When he manifests his power over the forces of nature by turning the waters of the Nile into blood, striking the livestock with pestilence, and afflicting the land and the people with frogs, lice, flies, boils, hail, locusts, and darkness, he leaves the Israelites with no doubts regarding his sovereignty (Exodus 7–10). The slaying of the firstborn of the Egyptians' children and animals by means of his angel accomplishes the same purpose (Exodus 11). Subsequently, by parting the sea in order for the Israelites to escape from the Egyptian army and then drowning that army in the sea once the Israelites have passed to safety, God assures the people that they can depend fully on his strength and might to save them (Exodus 14). While in principle any one of the ten plagues or the miraculous deliverance of the Israelites from the Pharoah's army might have been sufficient to convince the people of his sovereign power, by performing all of these deeds God chooses to provide the Israelites with evidence that is so overwhelming and compelling that there should be no reason for them ever to harbor any doubts about that power in the future. He shows himself to be greater not only than the most powerful and exalted gods of Egypt but also those of empires that have yet to arise in the biblical account, such as Assyria and Babylonia. Those gods have nowhere near the control over history and the forces of nature that the God of Israel displays in the events surrounding the exodus of the Israelites from Egypt.

Of course, the liberation of the Israelites from their bondage in Egypt also provides evidence to the Israelites of God's love for them. Throughout the biblical narrative, this liberation is seen as the supreme manifestation of God's grace and compassion for his people. In addition to delivering them from their bondage, God shows his favor to the Israelites by having the Egyptians give them gifts of silver and gold jewelry as well as clothing prior to their departure from the land (Exod 12:35-36; cf. 3:21-22; 11:2). The manner in which God guides the Israelites by a pillar of cloud during the day and a pillar of fire during the night also manifests to them both his power and his love (13:21-22). Once they find themselves out in the desert, his provision of food by means of the manna he gives them and the water that he makes flow from a rock convince the people of these things as well, as does the victory he gives them when they are attacked by the Amalekites (Exodus 16–17).

At first glance, these expressions of love for Israel may appear to be no different than the miraculous acts that the gods of other nations performed on behalf of the people and armies whom they favored. Thus, for example, in Book 1 of the *Iliad*, the god Apollo defends the Trojans by unleashing a plague on the Achaeans or Greeks when they are attacking Troy, striking many of them dead with his arrows. Subsequently the Olympian gods are active in other ways to support those on both sides of the conflict by making use of the supernatural powers they possess. Similar accounts of the intervention of the gods on behalf of the people whom they favor when they find themselves in need appear in many other writings from antiquity. In principle, therefore, the miraculous deeds that God performs on behalf of the Israelites might be seen merely as a sign of his favoritism rather than an expression of unconditional love for them.

What makes God's interventions on behalf of the Israelites different is precisely their existence as a lowly, weak, endangered, and enslaved people who find themselves in desperate straits and have nothing to offer God. They have done nothing to earn or merit his love and favor, nor do they promise to give God something he desires for his own sake in exchange for his assistance and deliverance. The initiative is taken by God alone. At no point do the people even cry out to him to ask for his help until they are caught between the Egyptian army and the sea (Exod 14:10). When God acts to save them, he never lays down any condition for doing so or attempts to exact some promise from them regarding what he would like from them in the future in exchange for his deliverance. His actions make it abundantly clear that the only thing he seeks is to bless and protect this people for their sake rather than his own and that their safety and well-being are his only concern.

By allowing the people to be subjected to bondage, slavery, and other hardships in Egypt before coming to their aid when their situation becomes unbearable, therefore, God is able to demonstrate to them not only that he loves them but also that his love for them is unconditional. Precisely because they are nothing but a nation of downtrodden slaves who are insignificant and irrelevant not only in the eyes of others but also in their own eyes, if God looks upon them with favor, his only reason for doing so must be that he has chosen to love them by pure grace. Likewise, because they are so frail and powerless and possess no virtues or qualities that might make them deserving or worthy of God's attention and love, when he intervenes on their behalf they can only interpret that intervention as an expression of unconditional love. Were they a larger and more powerful nation, they might conclude that God had chosen them to be his people because they were deserving of his election.

From the very outset of the narrative that appears in Exodus, then, the notion that the relationship between God and his people Israel will be based on the principle of *do ut des* is excluded. The people have nothing to offer God that might be of value or worth in his eyes and move him to grant them some type of favor, kindness, or blessing in exchange. For the same reason, God can hardly be thought to be pursuing some type of self-interest or seeking some personal benefit when he delivers them from the Pharoah's hand, not only because anything they might offer him is already his but also because the only thing he gains for himself by liberating them is a group of oppressed, abused, and humiliated slaves. By showering his love on those who have no quality, attribute, or virtue on the basis of which they might believe themselves to be deserving or worthy of that love, God leaves them with no doubt that his love for them is unconditional and undeserved.

What is implicit in the Exodus narrative is made explicit in two passages from Deuteronomy. In Deut 7:7-8, Moses is presented as telling the people: "It was not because you were more numerous than any other people that the LORD set his heart on you and chose you, for you were the fewest of all peoples; but because the LORD loved you and kept the oath that he swore to your ancestors, the LORD brought you out with a mighty hand and redeemed you from the house of slavery, from the hand of Pharaoh the king of Egypt." Here God's love for the people is made explicit, as is the fact that as a small group of lowly slaves they possessed no qualities that might make them deserving of that love.

A couple of chapters later, after mentioning that God will defeat and subdue the nations that would prevent Israel from occupying the land he has promised them, Moses makes it clear that the people have done nothing to deserve the kindness and favor God is showing them:

> When the LORD your God casts them out from your presence, do not say to yourself, "It is because of my righteousness that the LORD has brought me into this land to possess it." Rather, it is because of the wickedness of these nations that the LORD is driving them out from your presence. It is not because of your righteousness or the uprightness of your heart that you are entering in

to possess their land; rather, it is because of the wickedness of these nations that the LORD your God is driving them out before you, in order to fulfill the promise that he swore to your ancestors, to Abraham, Isaac, and Jacob. Know, then, that the LORD your God is not giving you this good land to possess because of your righteousness, for you are a stiff-necked people. Remember and do not forget how you provoked the LORD your God to wrath in the wilderness; from the day you came out of the land of Egypt until you came to this place, you have been rebellious against the LORD (Deut 9:4-7).

This passage stresses the people's unworthiness both prior to their exodus from Egypt and in the years they spent in the wilderness. They were undeserving of God's love not only because they were neither righteous nor upright in their thoughts and behavior but also because by nature they are stiff-necked and rebellious. If anything, what they deserved was God's wrath, rejection, and condemnation rather than his favor. Despite their lack of any qualities that might make them suitable to be chosen by God as his people and their stubborn resistance to his will, however, out of pure grace and kindness God adopts them as his own.

The idea that God chooses those who are small, lowly, and weak over those who are great and powerful is therefore central to the narrative. In fact, this idea is stressed from the very beginning of the narrative in Genesis that revolves around Abraham and his descendants. Abraham is a common man of no great significance or distinction when he is called by God, and by following God's call he leaves behind whatever status he had in his own land to go to another in which he is treated as a foreigner. His wife Sarah is barren and is not able to give Abraham the heir God has promised to him until she miraculously conceives as an old woman of ninety years (Gen 17:15-19; 18:9-15; 21:1-7). When their son Isaac takes Rebekah as his wife, initially she too is barren until God gives her twin sons, and when he does so God chooses the younger Jacob over the elder Esau as the one through whom he will fulfill the promises he made to Abraham (25:21-26). God then acts primarily through Joseph, the next-to-last of Jacob's sons, to deliver the entire family from famine after Joseph has been attacked and sold into slavery by his brothers, declared to be dead, and cast into prison (Genesis 37–46). When Jacob takes his family and household to Egypt in order to survive the famine, he is a fragile old man whose life has been filled with hardships (47:8-9). He and his sons take up residence there as foreigners and must live in the land of Goshen because as keepers of livestock Jacob's sons would be abhorrent to the Egyptians (46:28-34). While they enjoy a degree of favor once they have settled there thanks to their kinship with Joseph, whom the Pharoah has placed in a position of authority over his house and the land, the situation of Joseph's brothers and their families clearly remains precarious at the end of the Genesis account.

In Exodus, of course, the idea that God shows special concern for those who are lowly, insignificant, and seemingly unworthy of his love and attention lies at the heart of the narrative regarding the deliverance of the Hebrew slaves from their oppression at the hands of the mighty Pharoah and his army. However, that idea is present elsewhere in the narrative as well. It is particularly evident in the story of Moses, whose life is in danger from the time he is born until he is adopted by the Pharoah's daughter after his mother protects him by hiding him in a basket among the reeds on the bank of the Nile (Exod 2:1-10). When he grows up, Moses has to flee to the wilderness to reside there as a fugitive after he kills an Egyptian for mistreating one of his fellow Hebrews, since the Pharoah seeks his life (2:11-15). When God calls Moses as a lowly shepherd to be the man through whom he will deliver the Israelites from their bondage, Moses initially rejects that call, insisting that neither the Egyptians nor the Israelites will bother to listen to him and protesting that he is "slow of speech and slow of tongue" as well (4:1-15). Neither the Israelites nor Moses himself, therefore, seem to be worthy of God's love and election or to have any qualities that might merit his attention. Much less do they seem to be the type of people through whom the almighty God who created the heavens and the earth would choose to carry out his plan aimed at bringing blessing upon all of the nations and families of the earth. In fact, this band of oppressed slaves and their leader would appear to be the exact opposite of the type of people whom God would choose for that task.

According to the logic of the narrative, however, it is precisely this unworthiness that will convince the Israelites and Moses of God's unconditional love for them and in that way bring them to trust in his grace and goodness so as to obey and follow him in all that he commands. What will also bring them to trust in God is their condition of helplessness and the desperate situation in which they find themselves. Because they are so weak and powerless and find themselves in such great peril, they have no choice but to trust God and do whatever he asks and commands of them. Even if they wanted to deliver themselves from their plight on their own and become self-sufficient, they cannot do so because they lack the strength, wisdom, and resources necessary to do so. By allowing the people to fall into an existence that is extremely difficult and precarious and then reaching out to them to save and accompany them, God not only demonstrates that his love for them knows no conditions or limits but also teaches them that they have no other alternative than to look to him and depend on him if they are to survive and go forward. In this way, he attains their trust and confidence, even though it is painful for him to see them reduced to slavery and hardships before he acts on their behalf.

Hopefully, once God has gained the people's trust, he will be able to carry out his purposes in them. That trust will lead them not only to live in justice and righteousness but also to do anything he asks of them. As just noted above, this is another central element in the narrative: God accomplishes his purposes not through the strong and mighty but through those who are weak, powerless, and seemingly insignificant. In contrast, those who consider themselves to be self-sufficient and capable of existing independently of God generally see no need for him and thus have no interest in living in accordance with his will rather than their own. They also see themselves as worthy of God's love and favor. As a result, rather than trusting in God and submitting obediently to him, they feel they have a right to make demands on him and obtain what they want from him in exchange for the things they offer him. Their love for God will be conditional rather than unconditional, as will their love for others. Because such "love" must be earned, in addition to believing that they have earned God's love, they will expect God to earn their love as well by granting them what they seek from him. They will also expect those around them to earn their love and favors in the same way. They will disdain and disregard others unless they are capable of giving them what they seek and thus will especially fail to show regard for the needy, the weak, and those who have nothing to offer them. People who relate to others in that manner cannot serve as God's instruments to accomplish his purposes in the world, since their way of thinking and living leads them to mistreat, neglect, and oppress others. They therefore destroy human well-being rather than contributing to it.

For this same reason, God cannot accomplish his purposes among human beings by means of a great and powerful people such as the Egyptians. In the world of antiquity, a nation could become great and powerful only by subduing and oppressing others and imposing its will on them by force and violence. By definition, any people who would treat other nations in that way could never be committed to what is good, right, just, and loving. Alternatively, people who are committed to treating others in accordance with what is good, right, just, and loving will tend to be oppressed and mistreated by other nations, given that in antiquity the powerful dominated the weak and nations that did not have the means or power to rule over other peoples were almost invariably subjected to the rule of the strong and mighty. Those who seek to live in solidarity with others rather than attempting to dominate and manipulate them will instead be a kind, humble, caring, and generous people. In a sinful and violent world, however, any who live in that manner are at a disadvantage. They are generally trampled on by the powerful and tend to remain weak and marginalized. The only way they can resist, survive, and thrive is by looking to some greater power for the strength, wisdom, and resources they need to protect and sustain themselves. In biblical thought, the only greater power to which the persecuted and oppressed can look for help and strength is the God of Israel, since neither other nations nor the gods they serve are fully committed to helping those in need or truly care for them in an unconditional manner.

The system of values found among the great and powerful nations that seek to dominate others is also reflected in the gods whom they serve. Those gods justify and legitimate the rule of the strong and mighty over the weak and thus promote injustice and oppression. Rather than pursuing what is truly in the best interest of all, the gods worshiped by imperial powers such as Egypt, Assyria, and Babylon wish to receive the worship, obedience, and offerings of human beings for their own sake and thus expect that the nations who serve them subjugate, exploit, and enslave other peoples so as to obtain what they desire. The same is true of the gods of peoples such as the Moabites, Midianites, Ammonites, and Edomites. Even though for the most part these nations were not particularly great or powerful and did not establish large empires, they too worshiped gods who promoted the same system of values as those of the imperial powers of antiquity. Such nations would never abandon their own gods in order to worship a god such as the Lord God of Israel, who represents values and ideals that are radically at odds with their own gods.

By allowing the Israelites to fall into hardships and slavery and Egypt, therefore, God also lets them discover for themselves that the type of system or order that exists in Egypt under the Pharoah and the Egyptian gods is unjust, violent, and oppressive. A system that favors some over others, mistreats foreigners, exploits the poor and the weak, and reduces entire groups and nations of people to slavery destroys human lives and cannot bring well-being and wholeness for anyone, in spite of any claims to the contrary. Such a system does great harm not only to the oppressed but to the oppressors as well. As a people who are brought to learn firsthand what it is to suffer under such a system, the Israelites become convinced that the gods who legitimate it and keep it in place in the name of the common good must also be rejected as false, cruel, and oppressive. Such gods not only disdain the poor, weak, and marginalized in order to show favor to the strong and mighty but also lead their worshipers to behave in the same way.

The fact that in the opening chapters of Exodus the Israelites are never presented as serving the gods of Egypt or any other nation suggests that they have realized that those gods will not bless or benefit them in any way but instead are responsible for their oppression and suffering. The harsh conditions that the Israelites are made to endure thus serve as a means by which God convinces them not to worship such gods, since their worship results in ways of living and behaving that are harmful and destroy human well-being. At the same time, by showing himself to be a god who stands radically opposed to those gods, the God of Israel makes it clear to the people that he alone is a god who is truly committed to their well-being and wholeness and therefore that only by serving and worshiping him can they attain these things.

Such is the logic behind God's election of Israel to be his people. Because they are a people who are oppressed not only by another nation but also by the gods in whose name that nation justifies their oppression, the Israelites are led to reject any god other than their own. As they reject other gods, they will also reject the values associated with them and instead adopt the values of their own God. If they are to practice justice, righteousness, compassion, and love for others, they must not seek to dominate and exploit others or have the strength to do so, since that strength might tempt them to impose their will on others by force in the same way that the powerful people and nations around them did. They must also worship God alone, since the worship of other gods will not only lead them to neglect the values associated with the

God of Israel but also make it impossible for them to serve as his instrument in the world to bring others into conformity with those values.

The hardships and slavery that the Israelites endure in Egypt should also be seen as having the purpose of instilling in the people a sense of solidarity and empathy with those who suffer unjustly at the hands of others. Throughout the Pentateuch, in fact, the reminder that the Israelites were abused and mistreated as slaves and foreigners in Egypt serves as a basis for exhorting them to show kindness to such people once they have been established in a land of their own.[1] In order for an oppressed people to survive, they must learn to band together and support and defend one another, as the Hebrew midwives do at the beginning of Exodus and as Moses does when he kills the Egyptian who was mistreating a Hebrew slave (Exod 1:15-21; 2:11-13). By experiencing in their own lives what it is like to be weak, needy, and oppressed, they will be drawn to care for others who share their same condition and live in solidarity with them.

For all of these reasons, then, God appears to have had good reasons for allowing the Israelites to be subjected to the harsh conditions of slavery in Egypt and persecuted by the Pharoah before acting to liberate them and take them to the land he had promised them. Once this logic is understood, it would appear that God had not in fact forgotten about the descendants of Abraham, Isaac, and Jacob or the covenant he had made with them, as the narrative might be read as suggesting (Exod 2:24-25). Rather, God had chosen to guide the course of events in the way that he did because in his wisdom he had determined that it was the best way to accomplish his purposes of blessing Israel by acting to bring about in them the way of life necessary for them to enjoy the well-being he desired for them, while at the same time molding them into the type of people who would be able to serve as his instrument for blessing others.

According to the logic underlying the biblical narrative, therefore, if God was going to fulfill the promises he had made to Abraham to bless his descendants together with all of the families of the earth through them, before introducing them into the land he had promised them he needed to mold them into a people who would look to him in faith and trust and depend entirely on him rather than on their own strength, wisdom, or power. In addition, it was necessary for him to bring them to be committed to practicing the justice, righteousness, and love that are necessary in order for people to enjoy wholeness and well-being before they might be established in that land, since only in that way would it be clear to them that the condition upon which he was giving them a land of their own was that they live in conformity with his will for their own good. God's decision to subject them to the experiences that they were made to endure in Egypt was made with these objectives in mind. As a weak, enslaved, and powerless people, they will have no choice but to depend on him and his love and sovereignty in order to survive. They will also be made

---

1. See Exod 22:21; 23:9; Lev 19:33-34; Deut 5:15; 10:17-19; 15:15; 16:11-12; 23:7; 24:17-22.

aware of the fact that God's love for them is unconditional and undeserved. When God acts to save and deliver them and gives them his commandments, it will be clear to them that he is not seeking something for himself but only for them, since they have nothing to offer him of value or worth other than themselves and their love and devotion. The fact that they are a small, insignificant, and marginalized people will also make it possible for them to be brought to live in accordance with justice, righteousness, and compassion, since they will have no pretensions about dominating other peoples or subjecting them to their will by the use of force and violence. All of these things make them the ideal people for God to use as his instrument to accomplish his objective of bringing them and other nations through them to live in ways that will allow them to attain the well-being and wholeness he desires for all once he has established them in the land that he promised to their ancestors.

Hardening Hearts in Pursuit of Justice

While the Exodus narrative is undoubtedly intended to stress above all else the love and concern that God shows for the Israelites as the people he has chosen as his own, there can be little doubt that it also seeks to convey certain ideas about the Egyptians and especially the Pharoah as their king. Although the image it presents of the Pharoah is almost exclusively a negative one, one of the questions that the narrative would raise in the minds of many of those who read or heard it is why God treated the Pharoah and the Egyptians in the way that he did. In fact, to many it might appear that God's treatment of the Pharoah and his people was unjust and cruel. Not only did God repeatedly harden the Pharoah's heart and incite him to send his horses and chariots after the Israelites so that he might destroy the Pharoah's army in the sea, but he also subjected the Egyptian people as a whole to the plagues he sent upon them, including the final plague in which he took the lives of all of their firstborn.

Although these aspects of the narrative are no doubt problematic, it is important to see them in the context of the narrative as a whole. If God's primary concern is to bring into existence a people who will be committed to practicing justice and righteousness so that they may then serve as his instrument for bringing others to live in the same way, then in each situation that arises he must make a determination as to what actions on his part will contribute best to that end. After the Egyptian Pharoah decides to enslave and oppress the Israelites, God must clearly act to liberate the Israelites from his hand if he is to accomplish his purposes in and through them. As noted above, when Moses first tells the Pharoah to let the Israelites go, the Pharoah not only refuses to do so but oppresses the people even more by requiring them to make bricks without providing them with straw, as he had done previously (Exod 5:1-20). It is therefore very clear that the Pharoah has no intention of freeing the Israelites from their slavery.

By hardening the Pharoah's heart, God simply delays the liberation of the Israelites that he already intends to carry out so that he may manifest his power to all by means of the plagues. Initially, it is not God who makes the Pharoah's heart hard but the Pharoah himself, since it is the Pharoah who chooses to enslave the Israelites of his own accord. What God does is merely to harden the Pharoah's heart further by moving him not to grant the Israelites their freedom when the plagues that God inflicts on the land should have been sufficient to convince the Pharoah that it was in his best interest to let the Israelites go. Because it is clear that the Pharoah wants to keep the Israelites in bondage, sooner or later God will have to defeat the Pharoah and destroy his army if he is to liberate the Israelites. What God accomplishes by hardening the Pharoah's heart, which is already hard, is to prolong the period in which the Israelites remain in slavery so that he may have the opportunity to demonstrate to all his power in a manner that is progressively more convincing by means of the plagues. As we have seen above, his purpose is to gain the confidence and trust of the Israelites.

There is also another reason why God does not want the Pharoah to respond favorably to his demand that he release the Israelites from their slavery. Were the Pharoah to do so, it would appear to the Israelites that *he* is their liberator rather than God. In that case, they would have no good reason to submit to God and do whatever he asks them, since he would have done nothing to convince them that he loves them and seeks their well-being other than sending Moses to ask the Pharoah to liberate them. Rather than being grateful to God as their benefactor, they might even be grateful to the Pharoah instead. If that happened, the liberation of the Israelites would not have been able to serve God's purposes in the way he intended and desired.

It must also be stressed that this hardening of the Pharoah's heart has nothing to do with the Pharoah's eternal destiny in the afterlife. In biblical thought, what interests God is not saving people's souls in another world but accomplishing his purposes in the present world. As is evident elsewhere in the biblical narratives, the reason why God chooses at times to harden further the hearts of people such as the Pharoah so that they continue to oppose his will is that this allows him to make his sovereign power known to all and to carry out in the world his plans and purposes through Israel as his chosen people.[2]

While God undoubtedly subjects the Egyptian people as a whole to great suffering by means of the ten plagues and in contrast shows favor to the Israelites, it must be remembered that this is not because the Israelites are more righteous or deserving of his favor than the Egyptians. Even though the Israelites are an oppressed people, like the Egyptians they too are sinful. To some degree, many of the Egyptian people as well as the soldiers forced to serve in the Pharoah's army are also victims of the Pharoah's oppression. The system or order imposed by the Pharoah is an unjust, violent, and oppressive one not only for the Israelites but also for many other people and nations who live under his rule. If God treats the Israelites differently, it is not because they are worthy of such treatment but because his plan is to bring into existence

---

2. For this idea outside of the Exodus narrative, see Deut 2:30; Josh 11:20; Dan 5:17-20.

through them an alternative system or order that will eventually be able to benefit other peoples and nations as well by drawing them to look to him as the only true God and live under his loving rule. Until that happens, however, God must act in ways that do not always seem to be fair and just. On occasion, he must inflict suffering, death, and destruction on some people who are no more deserving of his punishments than others in order to carry out a plan that is ultimately aimed at drawing other people throughout the world to himself so that he might save and bless them as well. This logic will be evident in many other passages further on in the narrative as well.

At the same time, even if many of those who are serving in the Egyptian army have been conscripted by the Pharoah against their will and may not wish to do any harm to the Israelites of their own accord, if God is to liberate the Israelites in order to accomplish his plan and purposes through them, he must protect them from the Egyptian army when it pursues them after they have left Egypt. In principle, it may not have been necessary for God to drown the Egyptian army in the sea or destroy them in order to accomplish that objective. In his sovereignty and wisdom, however, God determined that this was the best alternative to accomplish his purposes. Perhaps the powerful Egyptians would have pursued or persecuted the Israelites at a later point in time after they had left the land and God chose to do away with the Pharoah's army in the present to prevent that from happening in the future. In theory, God may also have wished to weaken the Pharoah by destroying his army so that other oppressed peoples living in Egypt might have some reprieve from the difficulties and hardships to which the Pharoah had been subjecting them. In particular, God appears to have drowned the Pharoah's army in the sea in the way that he did in order manifest to the Israelites and others one more time in an emphatic manner the extent of his power so that they might become even more convinced that he was worthy of their trust.

When considering this portion of the biblical narrative as well as that narrative as a whole, therefore, it is important to recognize that in order to accomplish his plans and purposes the God of Israel cannot always treat people fairly or equitably. The unjust, oppressive, and violent systems that human beings construct for themselves and impose on one another generate countless victims, many of whom are relatively innocent in comparison to others. In most cases, those who suffer the most under those systems are not the ones responsible for creating them or ensuring that they are kept in place. In biblical thought, if God is to weaken, dismantle, or destroy those systems in order to establish an alternative order, he must often act in ways that appear to be unjust or unfair in relation to many simply because at times the nature of reality and the oppressive systems that human beings create will not allow him to do otherwise if the good that he seeks to accomplish is to be attained. In fact, as the Exodus account of the Israelites' deliverance from slavery in Egypt makes clear, God must himself make use of violence in order to combat and overcome the violence generated by human beings. In a sense, he does so against his will, since he would prefer never to do harm to any of the human beings he has made. Yet when those human beings create systems that themselves do tremendous harm to people, God can act to oppose those systems and seek to put an end to them only by inflicting harm on human beings as well, often in an indiscriminate manner that in principle he would have preferred to avoid.

According to the logic of the biblical text, those who believe in the God of Israel as a good and loving God must simply trust that in his sovereignty and wisdom he knows what is best in any given situation and will act in the ways that are the most loving and least harmful and painful for the human beings he cares for. The harsh reality of evil, injustice, and suffering that has come to predominate throughout the world makes it necessary for God to make decisions that from a human standpoint are extremely difficult and complex and may often appear to be unfair, unjust, and even cruel and heartless. As the book of Jeremiah stresses, if God is to carry out his plan to bless all of the families of the earth with well-being and wholeness, he cannot build and plant a new and alternative order without also plucking up and pulling down, destroying and overthrowing (Jer 1:10). Rather than questioning or challenging the destructive manner in which he often behaves, especially with regard to nations and peoples such as the Egyptians, all who look to him as their God must trust in his judgment and accept whatever comes from his hand.

SIN, SEDUCTION, AND SEDITION AT SINAI

Although the liberation of the Israelites from their bondage in Egypt is a central element in God's plan to bring blessing upon all of the families of the earth through his people, viewed in light of the biblical narrative as a whole, it is merely a precondition to God's objective of establishing a people who will practice justice and righteousness so as to serve as his instrument for bringing other peoples to do the same for their own good. To some degree, what God does after he has guided the people to Sinai is even more vital to that plan. While God seeks to introduce his people Israel into a land of their own in order to bless them there, they can only be blessed if they live in a manner that allows them to enjoy the well-being he desires for them. For that reason, the guidance and instruction that he will provide for them by means of the Torah or law that he gives them at Sinai through Moses is indispensable for the fulfillment of his purposes among them. In a sense, therefore, the biblical narrative points just as much to Israel's time at Sinai as it does to the people's exodus from Egypt and their entrance into the land that God had promised to their ancestors.

Before the people even arrive at Sinai, they begin to question and challenge both God and Moses. Once they are out in the wilderness, they complain to Moses that the only water that they have to drink is bitter. When Moses cries out to God, God provides him with a piece of wood that makes the water sweet and drinkable (Exod 15:22-25). At the same time, God is said to begin to put the people to the test and tells them through Moses that they must listen to his voice and do what is right by obeying his commands if they wish for him to bless and heal them (15:25-26). From the very outset, then, God makes it clear to the people that they will be able to attain the good things he desires to give them only if they submit obediently to the guidance and instruction he gives them through everything that he commands of them.

In the following chapters of Exodus, however, the Israelites are presented as continuing to question and challenge God's goodness and his intention to bless them. In particular, they accuse Moses of leading them out into the desert in order to have them die there (Exod 16:1–17:7). Even when God responds to the people's complaints by giving them manna to eat and water to drink, the people continue to doubt and disobey him. The narrative thus makes it clear that from the moment that the people left Egypt, they are stubborn and rebellious.

This point must be kept in mind when considering the manner in which God strikes fear into the people once they arrive at Sinai. After threatening them with death for touching the mountain and manifesting his presence by means of thunder, lightning, smoke, trumpet blasts, and an earthquake, God speaks with a voice that is so loud and overpowering that the people cannot bear to hear it (Exod 19:9-25; 20:18-21). These manifestations of God's sovereign power seem to communicate anything but a loving desire to bless and prosper the people.

According to the logic of the narrative, however, God has good reasons for manifesting himself in this way. If the people are to follow and obey him in all things, they must be convinced that he is a great and powerful God for whom nothing is impossible and that he stands far above all other gods in glory and might. The people's behavior in the desert up to that point has demonstrated that in spite of all of the wonders he performed on their behalf in Egypt and at the sea, they still do not trust him as they should. This is what God has learned by testing them on their way to Sinai (Exod 15:25; 16:4). In biblical thought, when God is said to test people, his purpose is not simply to see how they will respond to a particular situation but also to determine how best to continue to relate to them in the future in order to accomplish his purposes among them. By not immediately providing the people with food and water and subsequently giving them instructions with regard to the gathering and the consumption of the manna he provides for them, God is able to determine the extent to which his efforts to fashion them into an obedient people for their own good have been successful. When it becomes clear to him that they are still far from becoming the type of people he intends for them to be, he chooses to impress upon them once more his power and might at Sinai in an attempt to convince them of the need for them to submit to him in trust and obedience if they are to attain his blessing as his people. If the manifestations of love that he has provided for them up to that point have not accomplished that objective, then he must manifest more emphatically to them his sovereign power in order to bring them into submission for their own good.

As we have seen in Chapter 9 of this study, the manner in which God manifests to the Israelites his sovereign power and might following their arrival at Sinai should also be understood as a means by which he seeks to bring them to value and respect the commandments that he is about to give them through Moses. Once again, this is something that he desires not for *his* sake but for *theirs*. Because those commandments lie at the very heart and core of his plan to bless Israel and the other families of the earth, it is necessary for him to impress on the people the supreme importance of listening to those commandments and obeying them, since the failure of the people to do so would make it impossible for them to be brought to live in a way that would enable them and others to enjoy the blessings he desired to pour out on them. If the people took those commandments lightly or ascribed relatively little importance to them, that objective would not be accomplished.

While the manner in which God manifests himself at Sinai is undoubtedly intended to strike fear and awe into the people, this too is something that God wishes to do for their sake rather than his own. If the people are to obey him, they must not only love him but must also fear his chastisements and punishments. Just as parents who love their small children unconditionally nevertheless need to be strict with them and to some extent instill fear and respect in them in order to bring them to obey for their own good, so in biblical thought God must do the same with Israel. As we have seen previously, when God seeks to bring about obedience to his commandments among his people by instilling fear in their hearts, his intention is not that this fear constitute the sole motivation for that obedience but that by obeying what he commands they learn from experience that those commands are designed to promote their well-being and that their fulfillment in and of itself brings life and wholeness.

This idea is made clear in the words Moses speaks to the people after they tell him: "You speak to us, and we will listen, but do not let God speak to us, or else we will die" (Exod 20:19). Moses responds: "Do not be afraid, for God has come only to test you and to put the fear of him within you so that you do not sin" (20:20). According to Moses, God's purpose is not to do the people harm but rather to see if the people will respond to the manifestations of his glory and power by obeying him and respecting his will for them for their own good. Only if they do these things will the guidance and instruction he is giving them through the commandments of the Torah be able to benefit them.

Bordering on the Edge of Destruction

According to the narrative in Exodus, even before God finishes giving Moses the commandments, the people begin to rebel against God by making for themselves a golden calf (Exodus 32). It is not entirely clear from the account what the sin of the people is thought to consist of. Because they ask Aaron to make the calf as a result of Moses' delay on the mountain (v. 1), they may have doubted whether God was in fact still revealing his commandments to Moses and were thinking that they were now on their own to fend for themselves in the desert, perhaps because God had abandoned them. Alternatively, their sin may have consisted of consciously rejecting the God of their ancestors in order to make a god or gods of their own. It is also possible that they were not actually rejecting God but simply constructing a physical representation of him, contrary to his command. The affirmations that the people "rose up to revel" and were "running wild" or "out of control" suggest that they were sinning as well by engaging in the type of immoral activities and festivities associated with the worship of the pagan gods of antiquity (vv. 6, 25; cf. v. 18).

God's immediate response to the people's action is to command Moses to descend from the mountain to see what the people have done (Exod 32:7). After observing that the people "have been quick to turn aside from the way that I commanded them," God tells Moses: "I have seen this people, and look, they are a stiff-necked people. Now therefore let me alone, so that my wrath may burn against them and I may consume them; but of you I will make a great nation" (32:9-10). According to the logic of God's words, in all that has taken place from the time of the plagues and the exodus to the people's arrival at Sinai, God has manifested repeatedly and concretely through many signs and wonders his love for them and his absolute sovereignty over the Egyptians and the forces of nature. If in spite of these things the people still do not trust in him and his love and sovereignty but instead immediately turn away from him the very first time they set up camp, it would seem that all that God has done is in vain. From God's perspective, what more could he have done to gain the people's trust and convince them that it is in their own best interest to follow and obey him in all things? If they are already turning away from him to their own ways when they have scarcely finished observing all the wonders he has performed and the magnificent manifestations of his power and love, what hope can there be that they will ever live faithfully as his people? There seems to be no point in continuing to attempt to carry out his plan and purposes through them.

For that reason, God concludes that if the Israelites will reject his lordship and practice idolatry in spite of all that he has just done for them in an attempt to bring them to live as his people for their own good, there is no point in going forward with the plan as he had laid it out previously. They are so stubborn and "stiff-necked" that, try as he might, he will not be able to bring them to change their ways. In that case, it will be useless to take them to Canaan and give them the land he had promised them, as he had originally intended. They will not become a people committed to living in accordance with his own will, nor will they be able to serve as his instrument to bring people of other nations to do the same. The logic of God's response, therefore, is that if they will simply persist in their destructive ways and engender more and more descendants who will do the same, he might as well do away with them in the present before the situation grows even worse and becomes uncontrollable.

Because Moses himself has shown himself to be faithful and obedient, however, if God wishes to continue forward in his attempts to bring into existence a people who will live in ways that will make it possible for them to enjoy his blessings, the best option may be to make a new beginning with Moses' descendants. The logic here is the same that we have seen with regard to figures such as Noah and Abraham in Genesis: if God wishes to start over to carry out his plan of bringing into existence a people who will live in ways that will enable them to enjoy the well-being he desires for all, his best option is to attempt to do so through an individual who has shown himself to be obedient to his will, since it is more likely that the descendants of that individual will do the same.

Of course, according to the narrative, God has already attempted this strategy twice, and now it appears to have failed for a second time. While both Noah and Abraham were righteous men, it was not long before the offspring descended from them turned back to the same type of violent and unjust behavior that characterizes humanity as a whole. God's eventual decision not to attempt that strategy a third time may be due not only to Moses' intercession on behalf of the people but also in part to God's realization that if it has not worked previously with the descendants of Noah and Abraham, that strategy will probably not work with the descendants of Moses either. While it may be helpful for the people to have a righteous ancestor whom they can emulate and look to for inspiration in order to live righteously themselves, they already have this in Abraham.

Rather than accepting God's offer to make of him a great nation on that basis, however, Moses attempts to dissuade God from destroying the people by directing his attention to the manner in which the Egyptians might respond to God's destruction of the Israelites. He tells God: "Why should the Egyptians say, 'It was with evil intent that he brought them out to kill them in the mountains and wipe them off from the face of the earth'? Turn away from your burning anger; change your mind, and do not bring evil on your people!" (Exod 32:12). At the same time, Moses reminds God of the promises he had made: "Remember your servants Abraham, Isaac, and Israel, to whom you swore by your own self, telling them, 'I will multiply your offspring like the stars of heaven, and I will give to your offspring all this land so that they may inherit it forever'" (32:13). The logic behind Moses' words to God may be not only that God should remain true to his promises but also that if he does not fulfill those promises he will give the Israelites as well as other nations such as the Egyptians the impression that his word is unreliable. In any case, God is presented as responding favorably to Moses' argument. The narrative affirms that "the Lord changed his mind about the evil that he planned to bring on his people" (32:14).

Undoubtedly, this passage is problematic for a number of reasons. Above all, it presents Moses as the calm voice of reason in contrast to God, who is extremely upset and seems not to have thought through what would happen if he destroys the Israelites. Many of the readers of this passage would also have found it surprising that a mere mortal such as Moses is said to have changed God's mind. Here and elsewhere, however, the biblical texts have no hesitation in presenting a God who in many respects is very human and is willing to consider the petitions and arguments of human beings who think differently than he does and wish to convince him to think as they do. While such a conception of God is no doubt problematic, it does emphasize his love and concern for human beings over against his sovereignty. Rather than being inflexible with regard to what he intends to do in the future, he is willing to listen to human beings and even to enter into dialogue with them before acting definitively on his intentions or imposing his will on them. This willingness must be understood as an expression of care and consideration for them.

The affirmation that God changed his mind after listening to Moses might also have seemed problematic for many in that it conveys the idea that the future is undetermined and that God may alter his plans and intentions for the future at any time. If such is the case, then to at least some extent the future is unknown not only to human beings but to God as well, since he may initially determine to do one thing and then change his mind in order to do something else. As we have seen in Chapter 2 of this study, the idea that God does not have knowledge of everything that will happen in the future has already appeared in the biblical narrative in Genesis 6. There it is said that God became sorry and grieved that he had created human beings after he observed that "every inclination of the thoughts of their hearts was only evil continually" (Gen 6:5). This passage thus suggests that God did not anticipate that human beings would turn out to be so unjust, violent, and oppressive in their behavior. The narrative in Exodus 32 seems to convey the same basic idea. Apparently, when God took the Israelites out of Egypt and brought them to Sinai, he had not known that they would be such a stiff-necked, rebellious, and idolatrous people. For that reason, after they have made the golden calf and have begun to worship it, God initially intends to destroy them, just as in Genesis he decided to destroy most of the human beings he had created when he came to realize how strong their inclination to evil was.

The idea that God has only a limited knowledge of the future because it remains open and depends not only on God but on decisions that human beings will make, in fact, runs throughout the biblical texts as a whole. As later philosophical reflection would demonstrate, both the idea that God knows the future fully in all of its details and the idea that he does not are problematic, each for its own reasons. The biblical texts never enter into a discussion of that subject, just as they never address explicitly the question of why God created human beings with the capacity to sin and do evil or the question of whether he could have created a world that would be better than the present one. As we have seen, however, the texts do offer implicit answers to these last two questions by maintaining that in his love and sovereignty God has chosen to leave human beings and the world essentially as they are rather than destroying all that he has created in order to start over. The fact that God has not in fact destroyed the world and the human beings he created even though he possesses the power to do so leads to the conclusion that he is convinced that he could not have created a better world or made human beings in such a fashion that they might have been preserved from coming to practice sin and evil in the way that the biblical texts describe.

Even when God initially indicates his intention to destroy the Israelites and to make a new start with Moses and his descendants, however, he does not waver in his commitment to the same purpose he has had from the time of Abraham. That purpose is to bring into existence a people who will live in accordance with his will for their own good and serve as his instrument in the world to bring other peoples to do the same. What he proposes, therefore, is not to abandon his plan but to carry it out through Moses and his descendants rather than the people of Israel as a whole. In reality, of course, any descendants of Moses would also be descendants of the patriarchs and therefore in theory God would still be carrying out his original plan if he destroyed the Israelites in order to make a great people of Moses instead. However, many of the descendants of Abraham, Isaac, and Jacob would be excluded from the promises God had made to those descendants. This appears to be the reason why destroying the Israelites would run contrary to the plan. The idea is not that those who would descend from Moses would not be descendants of the patriarchs, but rather that many of the descendants of the patriarchs would not participate in the fulfillment of the promises that God had originally made to them, including especially the members of the tribes other than Levi, since this is the tribe to which Moses belongs and from which all of his off-spring would be descended.

The affirmation that God initially intended to destroy the people after they had made the golden calf seems problematic for another reason as well. To many readers it might imply that the love that God had shown for the people when he brought them out of Egypt had turned into hatred and rejection as a result of their sin. In that case, from the very beginning God's love for Israel was not unconditional but instead depended on the manner in which the people would behave. If God's objective was merely to obtain for himself a people who would obey or worship him for his own sake, then his anger at the sin they had committed with the golden calf would be seen as rooted in a concern for himself rather than for the Israelites or the plan he intended to carry out through them.

According to the logic just mentioned above, however, God's original intention to destroy the Israelites must be understood differently. If God had come to the conclusion that it was pointless for him to continue to attempt to carry out his plan by means of this stiff-necked people, it was not clear what he should do with them now that they were out in the middle of the desert. As he tells Moses in Exod 33:1-6, if he continues to accompany them on their journey, they will only continue to provoke him to wrath by means of their failure to trust in him. He might let them continue to Canaan on their own and guide them there by means of an angel, as in fact he initially proposes to Moses, yet even in that case their rebelliousness and the excessive burden that they will represent for Moses once God has left the people on their own will continue to spell disaster (33:12-16). In addition, they will hardly be able to conquer the powerful inhabitants of the land of Canaan without God's help.

In principle, God might also allow the Israelites to return to Egypt. Throughout the narrative, the comparisons that the people repeatedly make between the hardships they are being forced to endure in the desert and the conditions that they had experienced when living in Egypt suggest that many of them would in fact prefer to return. Were they to do so, however, it is likely that their situation would be worse than it was previously. The Pharoah might seek to make an example of them either by destroying many of them or by imposing even harsher conditions on them after their return. If they were in danger of disappearing as a people prior to their exodus from Egypt, that danger will only increase if they return. This option, therefore, hardly seems to be viable.

For that reason, from God's perspective, the destruction of the people at Sinai might appear to be the least of all possible evils. If the people will simply continue in the same type of behavior they have manifested up until that point, it might seem more kind and gracious for God to put an end to their existence before they bring even greater suffering and disasters upon themselves and their descendants. In the end, however, God decides against destroying the Israelites. This decision indicates that, despite the people's persistent stubbornness and rebelliousness, he still holds out hope that eventually he will be able to carry out his plan and purposes in and through them.

Although this hope seems to constitute the primary grounds for God's decision not to destroy the Israelites after they have sinned with the golden calf, the narrative offers another reason for that decision as well. As already noted above, when God indicates to Moses his intention to destroy the Israelites, the concern that Moses raises in his response has to do with the manner in which the Egyptians will react if God destroys the people: "Why should the Egyptians say, 'It was with evil intent that he brought them out to kill them in the mountains and wipe them off from the face of the earth'?" (Exod 32:12). Here Moses makes an important supposition, namely, that God has brought Israel out of Egypt in the way that he did not only for the sake of Israel but also for the sake of the Egyptians and perhaps other peoples as well. In fact, God's desire for the Egyptians to know who he is by means of the wonders he performs on behalf of the Israelites has already been stated in the narrative (14:4, 18). If God were not concerned for his name and reputation among other peoples, it would not matter to him in the least what the Egyptians might think if he destroyed the Israelites. In that case, the argument employed by Moses would bear no weight whatsoever with God.

The fact that God responds favorably to this argument, however, makes it clear that God does indeed care very much about his name and reputation among the Egyptians. In principle, there may be different reasons for this. It may be that he holds out hope that once the Egyptians see both his sovereign power and his steadfast love for those who submit to him as their god, at some point they will join themselves to the Israelites so as to live as his people as well. It is also possible that the concern raised by Moses and reflected in God's response to him has to do not with the Egyptians as a whole but only with those among them who are marginalized and oppressed in the same way that the Israelites had been before God liberated them. In that case, God hopes that other enslaved and oppressed peoples will look to him as their god. In fact, the affirmation in Exod 12:38 that a "mixed multitude" joined themselves to the Israelites when they departed from Egypt suggests that this may already have taken place prior to the people's arrival at Sinai, since this multitude would probably have consisted of other peoples enslaved and oppressed by the Pharoah.

In either case, according to the logic of the narrative, what concerns God is that he be known among the Egyptians as a good god who cares for oppressed people such as the Israelites. In principle, were he to destroy the Israelites, the only thing that the Egyptians might conclude was that he no longer cared for the Israelites, perhaps because they had disobeyed him and fashioned for themselves a different god contrary to his will. It would not make sense for God to be concerned only that the Egyptians might think that he no longer cared for Israel as his people, however, because after he has freed them from their bondage in Egypt the manner in which he chooses to relate to them would not affect the Egyptians in any way. It would make no difference to the Egyptians if God loved the Israelites or spurned them.

The concern expressed by Moses has to do instead with the possibility that the Egyptians might think that God is a cruel and capricious god. If he had liberated the Israelites only to lead them out into the wilderness and then destroy them there, he was not a good god but an evil or mischievous one. In effect, he had been toying with the Israelites and leading them to believe that he cared for them when such was not actually the case. God's positive response to the argument presented by Moses indicates that this is what he wishes to avoid: he does not want the Egyptians to have that opinion of him. Instead, he wants them to know that he is a good, faithful, and trustworthy god who cares for oppressed peoples such as the Israelites and forgives them even when they sin against him by abandoning him for gods of their own making. Were he to destroy the Israelites, he would be demonstrating to the Egyptians that these things were not actually true of him.

The argument attributed to Moses in Exod 32:11-12, therefore, seems to assume that God wishes for the Egyptians to know what kind of god he is so that at least some of them may come to believe and trust in him in the future. Because of the signs and wonders he has performed in Egypt, they already know him to be a powerful god. However, they have also seen that he is a god who sides with weak and oppressed people such as the Israelites. His concern, therefore, is that they continue to think of him in this way. It is for that reason that he spares the Israelites rather than destroying them, though it would appear that he has other reasons as well, as we have noted above.

Putting God's Wrath to Rest

Immediately after convincing God not to destroy the Israelites in response to their sin with the golden calf, Moses is said to descend from the mountain carrying the tablets upon which God had inscribed the commandments that Moses was to give to the people. When Moses sees for himself what the people are doing, he smashes the tablets to the ground and then burns the golden calf with fire, grinds it into powder, mixes the powder with water, and forces the Israelites to drink it (Exod 32:19-20). Moses then commands those who are on God's side to come to him and orders them to slay their brothers, companions, and neighbors. Those who do so are Levites. Moses subsequently tells these Levites: "Today you have consecrated yourselves to the service of the LORD, each one at the cost of his son and of his brother, that he may bestow a blessing upon you this day" (32:25-29).

At first glance, God's command for the Levites to kill their brothers, companions, and neighbors seems not only cruel but barbaric. Several observations are in order, however. First, the passage seems to assume that all those who were put to death had engaged in the worship of the golden calf and that those who remained faithful to God were spared. If this is in fact the case, then the passage is simply reflecting the same punishment for the worship of gods other than the God of Israel that is found throughout the biblical texts as a whole, namely, death. While from a modern perspective such a drastic punishment is unthinkable, such was apparently not the case when the biblical texts were composed. Furthermore, those texts make very clear the logic behind the command to put to death any of the members of God's people who worship other gods: such worship cannot be tolerated because it inevitably leads to injustice, corruption, and immorality among the people and does them tremendous harm. This truth is made evident in the lewd, unbridled behavior of those who worship the golden calf. Only the worship of the God of Israel promotes true justice, wholeness, and well-being for all. For that reason, if God simply allows the people to worship gods of their own making without taking decisive action to put an end to such worship, he will be doing them harm rather than good.

Second, in the chapters that immediately follow upon the account regarding the golden calf, the people express remorse for what they have done and subsequently rededicate themselves to God by offering up their possessions so that they may be used to build the tabernacle and the sacred objects associated with it (Exod 33:4-6; 35:4-29). This response on the part of the people suggests that the punishment prescribed by God and carried out by the Levites initially produced among them the result that God desired. In that case, the severity of the punishment that followed upon the people's sin with the golden calf might be considered justified. It is possible that a lighter punishment would not have led the people to rededicate themselves to God's service in the same way. At the same time, when the narrative picks up again with the people's departure from Sinai, they immediately begin to provoke God to wrath once more by rebelling against his will and failing to trust him as they should (Num 10:11–11:15). Because the repentance brought about in the people by the punishment imposed on them by God was short-lived and shallow, it might be concluded that instead of being overly severe, that punishment was not severe enough.

And third, in addition to provoking at least a temporary change in some of the people, the command for those faithful to God to kill their brothers, friends, and neighbors is said to have accomplished two other objectives. By eliminating many of those who were not faithful to Israel's God, the Levites' obedience to that command served to purify the people by removing those who were particularly rebellious and disobedient from their midst. At the same time, by ordering those who chose to remain faithful to him to kill their brothers, companions, and neighbors, it became possible for God to determine which members of his people were truly dedicated to serving and obeying him at any cost, no matter what the circumstances. Any who lacked such dedication would not have been willing to obey God's command. For that reason, Moses says that the Levites have consecrated themselves to God's service at the cost of their sons and brothers and as a result will be blessed by God (Exod 32:29). Their obedience to God's command leaves no doubt that they truly have dedicated their lives to his service, and in biblical thought God responds to such dedication with blessing. Of course, many readers of the passage both in antiquity and today would no doubt find ideas such as these highly problematic, to say the least. Nevertheless, the logic behind that passage seems quite clear.

On the day after these things take place, Moses tells the Israelites: "You have committed a great sin, but I will go up to the LORD now; perhaps I can make expiation for your sin" (Exod 32:30). Most English versions use the language of atonement here to present Moses as affirming that he will make atonement for the people's sin. Such a translation is problematic in that it suggests that Moses will do something to make amends for the people's sin, such as present an offering to God or perform some other act that will make up for what the people have done and appease his wrath.

In reality, however, all that Moses does is to intercede and ask for God's forgiveness. According to standard English usage, simply to ask for forgiveness is not to atone for sin. For that reason, the language of atonement must once again be considered inappropriate to convey the idea behind the biblical text. What Moses does in the following two verses is to acknowledge the gravity of the people's sin, ask God to forgive them, and tell God that if he refuses to forgive them he should blot Moses out of his book as well (Exod 32:31-32). As we have seen in Chapter 5, God responds by rejecting the possibility of blotting Moses out of his book and in essence tells Moses that while he does forgive the people their sin, he will also punish or "visit" them when the day comes to do so (32:33-34). While God's words seem to suggest that the "day of punishment" of which he speaks lies in the future rather than in the immediate present, in the very next verse God is said to have inflicted a plague on the people because of the sin that they had committed with the golden calf (32:35). This is how the account ends.

When considering this passage from Exodus, it is important to stress that it does not say that either the slaughter of those who had sinned with the golden calf or the plague that God subsequently inflicted upon the people expiated the people's sin. Nor does Moses' request to be blotted out of God's book make expiation in any sense. Instead, what is said to expiate the people's sin is simply Moses' intercession on their behalf. Contrary to many interpretations of the passage, therefore, it provides no support for the idea that suffering or death expiates sin or atones for it.

In order to understand the logic behind this passage, it is important to understand properly Moses' function as a mediator in the narrative. The reason that Moses can make expiation for the people and put away God's anger at their sinfulness is that they have been placed under his leadership. If he asks God to forgive them and God responds favorably to that petition, the unstated basis for that favorable response is that as the one who has been placed over the people as their leader, Moses will assume the responsibility of doing everything within his power to bring the people back into conformity with God's will. For that reason, Moses can make expiation for the people and obtain God's forgiveness. The same would not be true of other members of the people, since because they are not in the same type of position of leadership that Moses is, they cannot offer God assurance that they will be able to exert any significant influence on the people in order to alter their behavior in the way that Moses can.

It is important to stress this point in order to grasp the understanding of forgiveness found in this passage. Just as the idea that sin can be expiated by suffering or death is entirely foreign to the passage, so also is the idea that God might grant the people forgiveness by accepting the righteousness of Moses in lieu of the righteousness of the people themselves. The idea that in and of itself Moses' petition for God to forgive the people's sin leads God to grant them his forgiveness must be rejected as well. In biblical thought, God forgives only when he has reason to believe or hope that the sinful and destructive behavior that he regards as unacceptable will come to an end. If such is not the case, then it is not only pointless for him to forgive those who have sinned but also counterproductive. If they will simply continue in their sin, God is not doing them any favor by forgiving them, since that forgiveness will not promote their well-being and may in effect undermine it by leading them to think that they can continue in their destructive behavior without being concerned that God will do anything about it. In this instance, for God simply to have forgiven the people their sin in the sense of overlooking what they had done and leaving them unpunished would have done the Israelites harm rather than good, since God would have done nothing to correct the people's behavior.

For these reasons, it must be concluded that the basis upon which God responds favorably to Moses' petition that he forgive the people's sin is that he trusts that as their leader Moses will do everything in his power to bring them to put away the type of behavior mentioned in the passage and not fall into such behavior again in the future. The fact that Moses bothers to intercede for the people communicates to God the idea that Moses is committed to that objective and thus provides God with a basis for hoping that it will be attained. Of course, Moses cannot offer God any definitive assurance that his efforts to modify the people's behavior will be effective, since ultimately it will be up to the people to avoid sinning in the same way again in the future.

God's favorable response to Moses' petition, as well as his affirmation that he forgives the people but will still punish them in an effort to correct them, make it clear that God continues to love the Israelites. In arriving at his decision to forgive and punish them rather than destroying them, God also seems to take into account once more the promises he had made to Abraham, Isaac, and Jacob (Exod 32:12). Nevertheless, in light of what we have seen here, that decision must be seen as an expression of God's continued love for the Israelites rather than a reluctant concession made to Moses, Abraham, Isaac, and Jacob on the basis of promises that he felt obliged to keep in relation to a people that he no longer cared for as a result of their persistent sinfulness.

After God responds favorably to Moses' petition to continue to accompany the people on their journey to Canaan, Moses also asks God to show him his glory (Exod 33:18). Once again, God grants Moses his petition, though he tells Moses that he will not allow him to see his face but only his back (33:20-23). When God responds to Moses, however, he also tells him: "I will be gracious to whom I will be gracious, and I will show compassion on whom I will show compassion" (33:19). At first glance, these words might be understood in the sense that God is capricious in the way that other gods in antiquity were thought to be. Like Zeus is said to do in the *Iliad* and the *Odyssey*, he may simply assign good fortune to some while filling the lives of others with pain and suffering for no good reason other than that it pleases him to do so.[3]

When viewed against the background of God's commitment to blessing his people with the well-being he desires for them, however, his words to Moses must be understood differently. As the account of the golden calf has demonstrated, while God wishes to be gracious and show kindness and favor to his people, at times his commitment to their well-being must take the form of harsh chastisements and even death and destruction. Such is the case when they refuse to submit to him and stubbornly insist on going their

---

3. *Il.* 24.525-33; *Od.* 4.236-37; 6.188-89.

own way, which will lead to their ruin. At each step of the way, therefore, in his sovereignty God must determine the best course of action in order to accomplish his purpose of bringing the people to live in a manner that will allow them to attain the well-being that he seeks for them. At times, this involves being compassionate and forgiving, while at other times it must involve inflicting suffering and refusing to overlook sinful and destructive behavior. Precisely because he is sovereign and can see and know things that are hidden to human beings and beyond their understanding, his people must trust his judgments and recognize that they may not always comprehend the reasons behind his decisions and actions. For that reason, rather than demanding certain things or seeking to impose their will on him, they must accept what he decides and decrees. As they do so, however, they must also trust that in his grace, love, and mercy he consistently does what he determines to be in the best interest of all and remains committed to placing the well-being of all over any other concern.

In the end, God's response to the people's sin with the golden calf is intended to bring the people to realize that, because he is committed to their well-being and that well-being depends on them doing his will by living in the way he has commanded for their own good, he will not tolerate or look lightly upon the worship of gods of their own making that lead them to abandon the path he has laid out for them in his love. While for the time being they have learned their lesson, eventually the people will fall back into idolatry once more and need further chastisements. The account of the golden calf thus anticipates the ongoing rebelliousness and hard-heartedness of the people, which will continue to make itself evident throughout their time in the wilderness and following their entrance into the land that God had promised them. It also raises the question of how God will ever succeed in bringing this persistently stiff-necked and stubborn people to obey him and understand that, because he alone is God, true life and blessing are to be found in him alone. If God cannot bring them to obey his commandments by doing them good, then he will have no choice but to continue to impose chastisements on them and make those chastisements increasingly more severe if he is ever to accomplish that objective among them.

DELVING FURTHER INTO DISTRUST AND DISASTER

While there are some narrative elements in the final six chapters of Exodus, the book of Leviticus, and the opening chapters of Numbers, most of the material in those sections of the Pentateuch consists of the commandments and prescriptions that we have already examined previously. Beginning in Numbers 9 and 10, however, the narrative resumes with the departure of the people from Sinai. Almost from the start, the people fall back into the same sins that had characterized them from the time they left Egypt. They murmur and complain constantly about the hardships they are having to endure. Rather than believing in God and subjecting themselves to everything he ordains, trusting that he seeks nothing but what is best for them and that all that he does has the purpose of shaping them into a people who will live in the way he desires for their own good, they constantly question and disobey him and rebel against his will.

Because of God's love for the people, this behavior arouses his anger and frustration and he responds by disciplining and chastising the people in various ways. Their persistent hard-heartedness and their stubborn and stiff-necked resistance to his will forces him at times to continue to resort to measures that are extremely harsh in an attempt to correct the people, yet even when those measures succeed in producing a change in the people, that change is only short-lived and it is not long before they are back at their ways.

Pushing a Patient God to the Limits

According to Num 11:1-3, the people have barely left Sinai when they start to complain once more about the hardships they are being forced to endure. This provokes God to anger and as a result he sends fire to consume the outlying parts of their camp. The people respond by crying out to Moses, who intercedes for them, and God extinguishes the fire. The fire has scarcely abated when the people tell Moses that they are tired of eating nothing but manna and begin lamenting the fact that they no longer have access to meat and a number of other foods that they supposedly enjoyed in Egypt (11:4-9).

Readers of this text in antiquity would probably have believed the Israelites to be making up the claim that they enjoyed such a rich and diverse diet during their existence as slaves in Egypt, given that in most places the consumption of meat and other of the foods that the people mention was a luxury that only the most privileged could regularly afford.[4] If so, the readers would have understood the Israelites to be pining for a past that never existed, as they are said to do elsewhere in the narrative. Here and elsewhere they idealize their former life in Egypt in order to claim that they were better off living in slavery than they will be under God's good guidance and protection, despite God's promises to the contrary. In any case, God becomes angry with the people once again and Moses himself protests that he cannot satisfy the people's demand for meat (Num 11:10-15). As a result, God has Moses tell the people that he will give them so much meat that it will come out of their nostrils and become loathsome to them. The narrative presents the people's complaint as a rejection of God (11:16-23). When God finally sends quails for them to eat, the people do indeed get sick (11:31-33).

In the following chapters, the acts of rebellion and the failure to trust in God continue. In a couple of instances, those who rebel are individuals. First, Aaron and Miriam protest that God speaks not only through Moses but through them as well. This arouses God's anger and he strikes Miriam

---

4. See George V. Pixley, *On Exodus: A Liberation Perspective*, trans. Robert R. Barr (Maryknoll, NY: Orbis, 1987), 100.

with leprosy, though as a result of Moses' intercession on her behalf the leprosy is lifted after seven days (Num 12:1-15). Subsequently, Korah leads a group of people who criticize Moses and Aaron for exalting themselves over the rest of the assembly. As we have seen in Chapter 8, Moses has Korah and his group stand before God together with Aaron to see whom God accepts. Even though Moses intercedes for Korah and all of his household, the earth opens up and swallows them all, while others who have sided with Korah are consumed by fire (16:1-35). When the people see this, they become angry at Moses and Aaron, blaming them for what has happened. Once again, God becomes incensed and sends a plague upon the people, but Moses and Aaron intervene to make expiation for the people. The plague then stops, but not before over fourteen thousand have died (16:41-50).

As in the account of the golden calf, the chastisements that God is said to impose on those who rebel against him in these passages at first glance seem to be exceedingly harsh and cruel. Once again, however, the fact that those punishments do not succeed in bringing about any real change in the people's behavior suggests that, from the perspective of the narrative, rather than being overly harsh, those chastisements are not harsh enough. In some cases, those chastisements seem to accomplish nothing at all. Thus, for example, the sin attributed to Korah and the men who side with him in Numbers 16 is essentially the same as that which is attributed to Aaron and Miriam in Numbers 12: in both cases, it consists of questioning and opposing the leaders that have been appointed by God. The narrative seems to assume that Korah and the men who join him have seen how Miriam was struck with leprosy when she sinned in this manner, yet this does not stop them from following in her footsteps so as to replicate her same sin. God therefore responds by inflicting an even harsher penalty on Korah and his men by having the earth swallow them up. The question that the narrative keeps raising in the mind of the reader, therefore, is this: What more must God do in order to convince the people to stop rebelling against his will and instead to submit obediently to him? If measures that are as extreme and severe as those he has already taken do not succeed in accomplishing that objective, to what other measures is he to resort?

In between these two accounts, God has Moses send spies to scout out the land he has promised the Israelites (Numbers 13). When they return after forty days, one of the spies named Caleb calls on the people to trust God and go take the land, yet all of the other spies with the exception of Joshua inform the Israelites that the inhabitants of the land are too powerful for the Israelites to defeat. The people then cry out in fear and desperation and complain that Moses had simply led them out to the desert in order for them to die there (Numbers 14). They also express once more their intention to return to Egypt. Moses and Aaron respond by pleading with the people not to rebel against God but instead to trust him and the promises he has made regarding the land. When Caleb and Joshua assure the Israelites that they will indeed be able to take the land, rather than believing them, the people threaten to stone them. At that point, God intervenes by manifesting his glory at the tent of meeting or tabernacle. He complains to Moses: "How long will this people scorn me? And how long will it take for them to believe in me, in spite of all the signs that I have done among them? I will strike them with pestilence and disinherit them, and I will make of you a nation greater and mightier than they" (14:11-12).

When God speaks these words to Moses, Moses responds in the same way that he did in the account of the golden calf in Exodus 32. Rather than accepting God's offer, he intercedes on behalf of the people, asking God to forgive them, and points to the manner in which the Egyptians will react if God destroys the Israelites in order to convince him not to do so (Num 14:13-19). Moses also reminds God of the words that God had spoken previously in Exod 34:6-7 shortly after the incident with the golden calf: "The Lord is slow to anger, and abounding in steadfast love, forgiving iniquity and transgression, but by no means clearing the guilty, visiting the iniquity of the parents upon the children to the third and the fourth generation" (Num 14:18). Moses then implores God: "Forgive the iniquity of this people according to the greatness of your steadfast love, just as you have pardoned this people from Egypt even until now" (14:19).

God responds by telling Moses: "I have forgiven, as you have asked; but as I live, and as all the earth will be filled with the glory of the Lord, none of these people who have seen my glory and my signs that I did in Egypt and in the wilderness, and in spite of this have tested me these ten times and have not obeyed my voice, shall see the land that I swore to give to their ancestors; none of those who have scorned me shall see it" (Num 14:20-23). In the following verses, God expresses even more emphatically his displeasure at the ongoing complaining and murmuring of the Israelites and tells Moses that he will make them bear their iniquity by spending forty years in the desert, where those who rebelled against him will die and be buried (14:26-35). After the ten spies who had failed to trust God are struck down by a plague and the people acknowledge their sin, they seek to demonstrate to God that they have come to trust in his ability to give them victory over the inhabitants of the land by attacking the Amalekites and the Canaanites in accordance with God's original plan. Because God's plan has changed as a result of the people's lack of faith in him, however, their initiative to take the land in this way is contrary to God's will and they are badly defeated (14:36-45).

Although in his petition to God in Num 14:13-19 Moses points to the manner in which the Egyptians and other nations will react if he destroys the people in the same way he had done following the incident with the golden calf, in this passage the argument he employs is slightly different. Instead of arguing that the Egyptians might conclude that the God of Israel is a cruel and capricious god who toys with people such as the lowly Israelites by first showing them kindness and then crushing them, Moses says that the Egyptians will tell the other nations that Israel's God was unable to introduce the Israelites into the land he had promised them. Because Moses' petition is based once more on the question of what other nations might say if God destroys the people, it reflects the same idea that we have considered previously: what God is doing in relation to the Israelites is not for the sake of the Israelites alone but also for the sake of other nations whom God wants to come to know him and believe in him.

In this case, however, what Moses affirms that the Egyptians will call into question is not God's care and concern for peoples such as the Israelites but rather his power to accomplish his will by enabling the Israelites to enter and possess the land (Num 14:15-16). Given the dominance of the Egyptians in the region, Moses seems to be claiming that they see the God of Israel as a threat to their interests. If other nations in the region see that the God of Israel is one who delivers out of the hand of powerful nations such as Egypt those who have been forced to submit to them and are oppressed by them, they might look to the same God for help in order to seek to be liberated by him. By telling the other nations in the region that God was not able to introduce the Israelites into the land he had promised them, the Egyptians would hope to prevent this from happening.

This interpretation of the words attributed to Moses in Numbers 14 may help explain why he is also presented as mentioning the Egyptians in Exodus 32 when he seeks to dissuade God from destroying the Israelites. If the concern of Moses in Exodus 32 is the same as in Numbers 14, then when he affirms that the Egyptians will claim that the God of Israel is cruel and capricious if he destroys the Israelites, he has in mind the idea that God's destruction of the Israelites would enable the Egyptians to discourage other segments of the population whom they have enslaved and oppressed from looking to the God of Israel for help and liberation. In that case, the argument that Moses presents to God in Exodus 32 does not have to do with the possibility that the Egyptians themselves might be dissuaded from adopting the God of Israel as their own if God destroys the Israelites, but rather the possibility that the peoples whom they oppress might do so. These passages, then, suggest not only that Israel's God wishes other nations to come to know him but also that he is especially interested in other oppressed peoples of the world coming to faith in him so that he might liberate them from their oppressors, as he has the Israelites.

While in Chapter 6 we have already examined in detail the saying found in Exod 34:6-7 and Num 14:18, here it is important to note the context in which Moses reminds God of what he had told the people previously, namely, that he is "slow to anger" and "abounding in steadfast love" and that he forgives iniquity while nevertheless "visiting" or punishing it. As we have stressed previously, the purpose for which God "visits the iniquity of the parents upon the children" is not to take vengeance on the parents by venting his wrath on their children but to bring about in the people a thorough cleansing from their sinfulness. In effect, this is what Moses is asking God to do in Numbers

14. He implores God to forgive the sinful people but recognizes the need for God to discipline them thoroughly in accordance with his promise to "visit" them and their sins when they disobey. Although it is the parents who have sinned, it is not only the parents who will be disciplined and chastised during the forty years in the desert but their children as well. In fact, once God has determined that the Israelites are to spend forty years in the desert and that the parents will not be allowed to enter the land he promised to their ancestors, there would apparently be no point in attempting to discipline and correct them, since they will all end up dying in the desert during those forty years. Rather, those who are to be disciplined in the sense of being trained and taught to obey will be the children, so that when they come to settle in the land they will have learned to obey God faithfully. Undoubtedly, in order to educate their children in God's ways, the parents also need to be disciplined and learn to obey God, yet this is not simply an end in itself but is rather a means by which the children will be taught to obey God under the guidance and instruction of their parents.

The affirmation that God forgives sins but does not "clear the guilty" must be understood on the basis of these ideas. God forgives the people in the sense that he does not reject them, abandon them, or act to destroy them. Nevertheless, it would not be in their best interest for him simply to clear them of their wrongdoing by overlooking what they had done, since unless he acts to correct and discipline them they will continue in that wrongdoing. Thus, while he forgives them out of love for them, that love also takes the form of chastising them for their own good.

In the context of Numbers 14, then, the affirmation that God visits the iniquity of the parents upon the children is intended to point to his loving commitment to do everything possible to prevent the children from falling into the same type of sinful behavior that has characterized their parents, since such behavior would prevent them from coming to live in ways that will allow them to enjoy the blessings that God desires for them. In essence, Moses is asking God to remain patient with the sinful and stiff-necked people and to continue to seek to correct and purify them rather than destroying them. In this same context, Moses also rejects once more God's offer to make of him a great nation so as to bless his descendants alone rather than the Israelites as a whole.

Underlying this narrative are the same basic ideas we have examined previously. There are two aspects to the people's sin. First, they fail to believe in God and trust him in spite of all the wonders he has performed on their behalf. Second, when he subjects them to hardships, they complain and rebel rather than submitting willingly to whatever he determines. It is important to note once more that neither of these sins affects God directly or does any harm to him. If the people do not trust in God but remain in the desert or return to Egypt, it is not God who will suffer but the people themselves, since they will fail to attain the good land that God wishes to give to them and perhaps return to a life of slavery as well. Similarly, when they complain about their hardships, in principle it would be no trouble for the God who has sent the plagues, parted the sea, and fed them with meat to provide them with some type of food other than manna. Thus, if God chooses not to do these things and becomes upset at their complaining, it is once again not because he is affected personally by their complaints but because the people are not responding in the way he desires to the chastisements and hardships he is imposing on them for their own good. In other words, behind God's displeasure at the people's behavior and attitudes is a concern *not for himself but for the people themselves.*

Although the book of Numbers does not use the language of testing or disciplining to describe God's purpose in subjecting the people to forty years in the desert prior to the entrance of their children into the land he has promised them, this idea seems to be assumed in the narrative. By subjecting the people to hardships, God is attempting to teach them that they have no choice but to depend on him and follow him wherever he leads them if they are to survive. At the same time, by miraculously providing them with food and water in the desert, he is also manifesting to them his power as well as his care and concern for their needs. While they would prefer to have something to eat other than manna, they must learn to be content with whatever God provides for them and accept even the simple food he gives them as a sign of his grace. If he chooses to shape and discipline them by giving them nothing but manna to eat, they must trust that he is doing so for their good. Their time in the wilderness thus serves to make it clear to them that if they wish to enjoy God's protection and blessings, they have no choice but to place their lives in his hands and do whatever he asks and commands of them.

This understanding of God's purpose in forcing the Israelites to spend forty years in the desert before entering the land he has promised them also explains why at the end of Numbers 14 God does not assist the Israelites when they go up to fight the Amalekites and the Canaanites but instead lets them suffer defeat at their hands. In principle, the people seem to have acknowledged that they were mistaken when they failed to trust in God's power to introduce them into the land. By deciding to attack the Amalekites and the Canaanites in the way that God had initially intended for them to do, the people apparently wish to demonstrate that they now trust in God's ability to give them the victory over these peoples. According to the logic of the narrative, however, the problem is that the people have not yet learned to submit fully to God and to obey him in the way he desires. Their initial failure to believe what Moses, Caleb, and Joshua told them makes it clear to God that they are still not ready to enter the land because they have not yet learned to trust in his power and obey him. For that reason, God determines that they need further correction and chastisements before he will allow them to take possession of the land. Even when they finally come to trust in God's ability to give them victory over the powerful inhabitants of the land, they still need to learn to trust in God in the sense of doing only what he tells them to do rather than taking initiatives of their own.

After God enables the Israelites to defeat a group of Canaanites in the Negev desert in Numbers 21, the Israelites begin to complain once again about their hardships in the wilderness and the fact that the only thing they have to eat is manna. In response, God sends poisonous serpents upon them to bite them. After the people acknowledge their sin and ask Moses to pray for them, God tells Moses to make a bronze serpent and raise it up on a pole so that those who gaze upon it may be healed (Num 21:1-9). Here the same cycle is evident once more. God shows his love and sovereign power to the Israelites by saving them from those who sought to do them harm, yet rather than trusting him and submitting obediently to whatever measures he determines to be in their best interest, they go back to questioning him and rebelling against him. He then inflicts punishments on them in order to bring them to repentance, and once they respond in the way he desires he brings those punishments to an end.

Breaking the Yoke of a People Bent on Rebellion

Although the sins attributed to the people in the passages from Numbers already considered are regarded as serious, none of those sins are viewed as comparable to that which they commit in Numbers 25. While camped in the area of Moab following their passage through the wilderness, the Israelites begin to have sexual relations with the Moabite women, join in their sacrificial feasts, and bow down to their gods (vv. 1-2). The Hebrew text indicates that the Moabite or Midianite women were actively calling on the Israelite men to join them in these things and seems to refer not merely to sexual relations but acts of prostitution or harlotry.[5] The narrative then affirms that the Israelites provoke God to wrath by joining, yoking, or binding themselves to the god Baal of Peor (v. 3). This language conveys something stronger than simply participating in the sacrificial worship of the god, since it implies actually pledging themselves to the service of that god.[6] In other words, the people are not merely adopting the worship of Baal in order to serve him alongside the God of Israel but are dedicating themselves to Baal as the god whom they will serve above all others and regard as sovereign, thereby rejecting the God of Israel. Obviously, if the people have forsaken God for Baal, everything that God has sought to accomplish up to that point will have been in vain. His project and plan of bringing into existence a people who will live in a way that

---

5. According to Baruch A. Levine, it is not entirely certain that the Hebrew verb used in the passage refers to sexual activity or harlotry (*Numbers 21–36: A New Translation with Introduction and Commentary*, AB 4A; New York: Doubleday, 2000, 295-96). In any case, it is clear that the allusion is to some form of enticement of the Israelite men by the Moabite women.

6. According to Philip J. Budd, "Clearly some formal recognition by the Israelites of the Baal localized at Peor is implied" (*Numbers*, WBC 5; Waco, TX: Word, 1984, 279). David L. Stubbs similarly understands the terminology of yoking in terms of establishing "a formal association with a particular god," in this case Baal of Peor (*Numbers*, BTCB; Grand Rapids: Brazos, 2009, 462).

will bring them wholeness and well-being and attract people of other nations to live under him in the same way will no longer be able to go forward. The years that the people have spent in the wilderness will have been a waste of time. If God does not take action, everything that he has so patiently and persistently been seeking to accomplish since the time he called Abraham to leave his home for the land he would show him will have been for naught.

Further on in the same chapter, it is said that the Midianites were harassing or attacking the Israelites with enmity by deceiving and seducing them (Num 25:18). The same idea appears in Num 31:16, where it is said that the Midianite women had been advised by Balaam to lure the Israelite men into committing apostasy against God. These affirmations give a better idea of what is being described at the outset of Numbers 25: the Midianites had sent their women out to the Israelites not only to seduce the men into having sexual relations with them but also to entice them into participating in the worship of their gods in order to draw them away from the worship of the God of Israel. The sexual relations were not merely aimed at providing pleasure to the Israelite men but were intimately related to the worship of the Midianite gods through the sacrifices and feasting mentioned in the passage. In effect, the Midianites were attempting to erase or destroy the Israelites' identity as a people by integrating them into their own midst and leading them to abandon the God of Israel so that they might follow the Midianite gods instead. The problem was therefore an extremely serious one.

God responds to the situation by telling Moses to impale publicly in the light of day the leaders who have encouraged or allowed the rest of the Israelites to dedicate themselves to Baal of Peor (Num 25:4).[7] Moses also orders the judges of Israel to slay any of their people who have yoked themselves to the Midianites' gods (25:5). When one of the Israelites brings a Midianite woman into the midst of the people in the plain sight of Moses and the people gathered by the tabernacle, Aaron's grandson Phinehas takes a spear and kills both the Israelite man and the Midianite woman by stabbing them through the belly (25:6-8). The man and woman are later identified as members of prominent households of the Israelites and Midianites: the man is said to have been the head of an ancestral house of the tribe of Simeon, while the woman is the daughter of the head of a Midianite clan (25:14-15). According to the narrative, as a result of Phinehas's act, a plague in which twenty-four thousand Israelites are killed comes to a halt (25:8-9). God then tells Moses: "Phinehas, the son of Eleazar, the son of Aaron the priest, has turned away my wrath from the Israelites by manifesting such great zeal among them on my behalf, so that in my jealousy I did not consume the Israelites. Therefore say, 'I hereby give to him my covenant of peace. It shall be a covenant of perpetual

---

7. There is some doubt as to whether the punishment described was impaling or some other form of execution. According to Martin Noth, "The type of punishment is not clear, but is at any rate unusual. . . . One has the impression of a cruel method of putting to death which, however, probably had behind it a particular significance which is unknown to us" (*Numbers: A Commentary*, trans. James D. Martin; Philadelphia: Westminster, 1968, 197).

priesthood for him and for his descendants after him, because he was zealous for his God, and made expiation for the Israelites'" (25:11-13).

While the punishments that God is said to impose on the Israelites for their sin in this passage are greater in severity than any he has decreed previously, the narrative clearly suggests that the reason for this is that the sin they have committed is much more serious than any of those into which they have fallen in the past. Of course, the people had already been told that any who engaged in the worship of other gods were to be put to death: "Whoever sacrifices to any god other than the LORD alone shall be handed over to destruction" (Exod 22:20). This was a law that applied to the Israelites alone and not to people of other nations living in their own land, such as the Midianites. According to the Exodus narrative, this commandment was included among those that Moses had read out loud to the people and put in writing when the covenant between God and Israel had been instituted at Sinai. The people who had heard Moses read those commandments out to them had responded twice: "All that the LORD has spoken we will do" (24:3, 8). On that basis Moses had carried out the rite by means of which that covenant was formalized. In effect, what the people had agreed to—under no force or compulsion—was that they would serve the God of Israel alone, and that if they entered into this covenant with God, any from among them who would worship and sacrifice to other gods would accept the consequences stipulated for doing so, namely, the penalty of death.

This is precisely the understanding of the covenant that we have considered in Chapter 10. God's intention was to bring into being a people who would practice justice and righteousness in the land that he had promised to give to them. Because there was no other god among the nations in the region who demanded such a commitment on the part of his worshipers, if the Israelites abandoned the God of Israel in order to worship other gods, God's plan to constitute a nation that might be blessed and be a blessing to others would be thwarted entirely. For this reason, as God told the people from the very beginning, if the people entered into the covenant with him in order to attain his blessings, he would not tolerate it if they came to serve other gods, and any who did so would be put to death. According to the logic of the biblical narrative, this was not because he was a vindictive or self-serving God, but rather because only in this way could he accomplish among them his good purposes. The people had been made aware of this condition for living under the covenant and of their own free will had chosen to accept God's offer to be their God and to live as his people.

When it is viewed in this context, even though the punishment in Numbers 25 is indeed extremely harsh, it is in full conformity with what the people had agreed to. The command to execute publicly in the light of day those who had devoted themselves to Baal has the purpose of placing before the eyes of the people as a whole the punishment for serving another god. This measure is no doubt intended to serve as a deterrent by reminding the people that they too will be put to death if they do not desist from their worship of the Midianites' gods. The punishment imposed as chastisement on the rest of the people is the plague that results in the death of twenty-four thousand Israelites. Of course, these punishments must once again be seen in the context of a narrative that has stressed time and time again the people's persistent refusal to submit to God's will and their continual rebelliousness, despite all of the harsh punishments that God had already inflicted on them.

It is also important to understand the logic behind the words that God is said to have spoken concerning Phinehas. The reason why God was inflicting such harsh punishments on the people was the same one we have seen previously, namely, that there was no point in bringing the Israelites into the land God had promised them if they were going to abandon him for false gods such as Baal, since in that case God would be unable to accomplish his purposes among them. The narrative suggests that even though it was primarily the Midianite women who were enticing the Israelites to yoke themselves to Baal of Peor, the Israelite leaders were also responsible for the people's sin in some way. Among these leaders was the Israelite man slain by Phinehas. By bringing the Midianite woman into the area outside of the tabernacle where many of the people had gathered and then introducing her into the tent, he appears to have been encouraging other Israelite men not only to take Midianite women for themselves but also to follow both him and the woman in yoking themselves to Baal.

By slaying the Israelite man and the Midianite woman who had enticed and seduced that man, Phinehas had demonstrated that there was at least one Israelite who was still fully dedicated to God—so dedicated, in fact, that he was willing to put to death one of his kinsmen who had blatantly fallen into sin. It is significant that elsewhere Phinehas is not only said to be the grandson of Aaron, who according to the narrative had already died by this time, but also was later to become high priest himself (Judg 20:27-28). His action thus provided God with hope regarding the Israelites, not only because he had shown that there were at least some Israelites who were fully dedicated to the God of Israel alone, but also because as a priest he showed himself to be fully committed to defending and promoting the exclusive worship of Israel's God among his people. It is on that basis that God is said to have put away his wrath at the Israelites and to have refrained from consuming them entirely (Num 25:11). In effect, the zealous act of Phinehas demonstrated to God that there was still hope that the Israelites as a nation might be turned away from their adhesion to Baal of Peor and commit themselves once more to serving the God of Israel alone.

The affirmation that Phinehas "made expiation for the children of Israel" must be understood against the background of these ideas (Num 25:13). Nothing in the text suggests that God was demanding that someone be put to death to satisfy the demands of God's justice or appease his wrath at the people's sins. The Israelite man who was slain was not an innocent substitute offered up to God to atone for the people's sins but one who was guilty of idolatry and was apparently leading others into the same type of idolatry. He died for his own sins, not for the sins of anyone else. In addition, what is said to have made expiation for the people's sins was not the death of the idolatrous Israelite or the blood he shed but the zeal shown by Phinehas in slaying the Israelite man. What interested God was not that someone die or be killed as punishment for the people's idolatry. God himself inflicted punishment by putting to death many of the Israelites who had yoked themselves to Baal, both by commanding that the people's leaders be executed and by sending a plague on the people. Had God merely wished to inflict punishment on the people or exact vengeance on them for their sin, both the execution of the leaders and the plague sent by God would have accomplished that objective, independently of any action on the part of Phinehas.

According to the logic of the narrative, however, what interested God was seeing whether there were still any Israelites who were zealously committed to serving him alone, and especially any leaders from among the people who might influence the remainder of the people to turn back to him. When Phinehas slayed the Israelite man and the Midianite woman, in effect he demonstrated to God that such was indeed the case. On that basis, God was willing to put away his anger at the people who survived the plague, since what Phinehas had done provided him with hope that his purposes among the people might still be accomplished. The fact that as Aaron's grandson and eventual successor Phinehas would some day assume a position of leadership over the people and thus be able to influence them to be faithful to God in the future should also be seen as an important factor in God's decision to put away his wrath at what the people had done. Phinehas thus expiated the people's sins in the sense that he provided God with a basis for accepting the people once more by means of the zeal he showed for God, since that zeal gave God good reasons to suppose that there was still hope for the people in the future. Of course, what Phinehas did also prevented the idolatry among the people from spreading further and in that regard put away God's wrath as well by dealing with the causes of that wrath.

At the end of the account, God tells Moses to attack and destroy the Midianites for having attempted to entice the Israelites away from him with guile and deception and bring them to serve Baal of Peor instead (Num 25:17-18). This destruction and its aftermath are described in Numbers 31, where God repeats to Moses the command to attack the Midianites. The narrative there employs terms derived from the Hebrew verb *naqam*, which we considered in Chapter 6 of this work (vv. 2-3). As they do elsewhere, most English versions of the Bible use the language of vengeance to translate these terms so as to speak of the Israelites exacting revenge on the Midianites. For reasons we have seen previously, however, such a translation must be considered problematic, especially because it implies that the purpose for which the Israelites attacked and destroyed the Midianites was simply to make them pay for what they had done by inflicting suffering and death on them, as if this in itself restored justice or set things right.

Such an interpretation of the passage, however, must be regarded as running contrary to the logic of the narrative as well as the Hebrew Bible as a whole. What interested God was not inflicting punishment on the Midianites as an end in itself but preventing the same thing from happening again in the future. The main reason why the Midianites had attempted to entice the Israelites away from God in order to bring them to worship Baal of Peor was that they wished to weaken them by destroying their identity and turning them away from the god who had been guiding, protecting, and strengthening them since they had left Egypt. They saw the Israelites and their god as a threat to their own interests. Furthermore, the Midianites had shown themselves to be clever and cunning in their attempts to alienate the Israelites from God and bring them to worship Baal instead, as the allusions to their trickery and deception in Num 25:18 make clear. For these reasons, if the Midianites were allowed to continue to live in the region as Israel's neighbors, they would continue to pose a serious threat to the Israelites by attempting to draw them away from God, perhaps by means of the same type of trickery and deception that they had already manifested. In addition to seeking to destroy the Israelites' identity, they might also lead the Israelites to practice the type of injustice, violence, and bloodshed associated with gods such as Baal of Peor. The reason that God tells Moses to destroy the Midianites, therefore, is not that he seeks some kind of vengeance against them but simply because his love for his people Israel and the other nations—including the Midianites themselves—cannot allow the Midianites to stand in the way of carrying out the plan he has designed to bring into existence a people who will be fully dedicated to living in accordance with God's will for justice and righteousness and eventually serve as his instrument to bring others to do the same.

God's command to destroy the Midianites, therefore, would have been understood as a means to prevent the Midianites from continuing to pose a threat to God's plan by doing harm to the Israelites. Of course, that command would have been thought to have other objectives as well, such as serving as an example to other peoples in the region who might attempt to deceive and harm the Israelites in the same way that the Midianites had. Undoubtedly, while God's command to exterminate most of the Midianites is extremely troubling and problematic, it responds to the same logic we have seen elsewhere in the biblical texts.

Even when this logic is understood, the manner in which Num 31:2-3 should be translated into English remains a problem. Rather than presenting God as commanding Moses to avenge the Israelites on the Midianites or take vengeance on them, it would be preferable to understand God's command in terms of having the Israelites take action against the Midianites to address the evil they had done and prevent the same type of thing from happening again in the future. In that case, rather than having God tell Moses in v. 2: "Avenge the Israelites on the Midianites," the English translation might read: "Have the Israelites strike the Midianites in response to the evil they have committed." Similarly, in the following verse, instead of phrasing Moses' command to the Israelites in terms of attacking the Midianites "to execute the LORD's vengeance on Midian," as many English versions of the Bible do, the English translation might present Moses as telling the Israelites to attack the Midianites "to strike Midian in response to the evil they have done in the way that the LORD desires." Undoubtedly, alternative translations such as these are problematic and do not convey fully the original meaning of the Hebrew, but the same is true with regard to the English translations that use the terminology of vengeance. As we have seen in Chapter 6 of this study, there simply is no way in which any English translation can convey adequately and faithfully the meaning of the Hebrew verb *naqam* and its cognates without resorting to phrases that are somewhat lengthy, and even then those phrases cannot be regarded as communicating accurately the idea reflected in the Hebrew original. Translations such as those just proposed, however, convey the idea that the action taken is in response to an evil that has been committed and has the purpose of putting a stop to that evil or preventing it from being repeated in the future without implying that the purpose of the action taken is simply to exact revenge for its own sake.

Although God's command for the Israelites to destroy the Midianites in Numbers 31 gives the impression that he had the Israelites annihilate the Midianites completely, with the exception of the young virgin women mentioned in v. 18 of that chapter, it should be noted that the book of Judges offers a different perspective. There the Midianites are said to be "thick as locusts," together with other peoples in the region, and to possess innumerable camels (Judg 7:12). In Judges 7 and 8, the Midianites are also presented as continuing to fight against the Israelites. These passages thus present the Midianites as continuing to thrive after the events described in Numbers 25. Readers who sought to reconcile the narrative that appears in Numbers with the narrative found in Judges might conclude that God had commanded the Israelites to destroy only those Midianites mentioned in Numbers who had sought to trick and deceive the Israelites into adopting Baal of Peor as their god. In that case, God had not ordered the Israelites to exterminate the Midianites in their entirety. Of course, even if God's command to annihilate the Midianites in Numbers 31 contemplated only those who had sought to do the Israelites harm rather than the nation as a whole, it remains highly problematic. In spite of this problem, however, the logic behind God's command is in accordance with what we have seen elsewhere in the Hebrew Bible: just as God must save and deliver Israel in order to fulfill his purpose of bringing into existence a people whom he can bless and make a blessing for others, so also must he oppose and destroy any people or nation that stands in the way of bringing that purpose to pass.

The fact that great importance was ascribed to the story of Israel's fall into idolatry at Beth-Peor and the zeal of Phinehas is evident from the repeated allusions to that story elsewhere in the biblical texts.[8] The account is also mentioned in numerous Jewish writings from the Second Temple period. The reason why the story continued to be held in high regard no doubt had to do with the fact that it stressed not only the depravity of those Israelites who rejected God in favor of Baal but also the need for those who remained faithful to the God of Israel to be zealous for him in the same way that Phinehas had been.

In the remainder of the narrative from Numbers, it is significant that the people are no longer presented as sinning against God in the ways that they did prior to the account in Numbers 25. While in Numbers 32 Moses initially becomes upset when the tribes of Reuben and Gad ask to settle in the land east of the Jordan rather than crossing over the river with their fellow Israelites, he looks favorably upon their request and grants it when they agree to accompany and assist the other tribes in their conquest of the land west of the Jordan before returning to their own land. The Israelites' apparent willingness to obey Moses not only in the final chapters of Numbers but throughout Deuteronomy and Joshua suggests that the forty years they spent in the wilderness and the harsh punishments to which God has subjected them at various points in the narrative have accomplished their purpose, at least temporarily. For the most part, those who are about to enter into the land that God has promised them have finally learned to trust God and obey his commands. As the book of Judges makes clear, however, they will not be in the land for long when they begin to rebel against God and disobey him once more.

A FINAL PLEA FOR DEAF EARS TO HEAR

The book of Deuteronomy picks up the narrative where it ends in the final chapters of Numbers, with the people in the plains of Moab, poised to cross the Jordan River into the land that God has promised them in order to take possession of it. In fact, with the exception of the account of Moses' death and burial in its final chapter, Deuteronomy as a whole consists of a lengthy series of discourses by Moses in which he reflects on all that has taken place up to that point, reiterates and supplements many of the commandments that God had given the people previously, and contemplates the future of the people in the land. In this way, the book not only interprets Israel's narrative as a whole from beginning to end but also provides the basis necessary for interpreting many of the particular events that make up that narrative.

Several key themes run throughout the book and lay the basis for the interpretation of the narrative that it presents and summarizes. For the most part, these are the same themes that are emphasized throughout the biblical texts as a whole. The most important of these themes is no doubt God's love, grace, and compassion for his people Israel and his intense desire to bless them. From the very outset of the book, Moses reminds the Israelites

---

8. See Deut 4:3-4; Judg 22:13-18; Ps 106:28-31; Hos 9:10.

that God has fulfilled his promise to multiply them and accompany them to the land that they are about to enter. He also tells them that God will fight on their behalf against any who would oppose or resist them (Deut 1:8-11, 19-21, 30-31). According to Moses, even though God had subjected the people to a period of forty years in the wilderness in order to discipline them on account of their sinfulness, he continued to manifest his love for them during this time by carrying them in the same way that one carries a child (1:31; cf. 8:5; 32:6). Moses stresses the same idea in the second chapter of the book: "Surely the LORD your God has blessed you in all that you have done; he has watched you go through this great wilderness. These forty years the LORD your God has been with you; you have lacked nothing" (2:7). While God's love is evident in all that he has done for the people during their time in the wilderness, it is especially associated with his liberation of the people from their bondage in Egypt and his gift to them of a land of their own. Moses makes this point clear in Deut 4:37-38: "And because he loved your ancestors, he chose their offspring after them. He brought you out of Egypt with his own presence by his great power, driving out from before you nations greater and mightier than yourselves, to bring you into their land and give it to you for a possession, as it still is today."

Other passages in the opening chapters of the book stress the ways in which God has manifested his love for the people as well.[9] In the same contexts, however, Moses reminds the people of their persistent rebelliousness and their failure to trust in God.[10] His purpose is not simply to point out to the people their sin and guilt but also to underscore to them the unconditional nature of God's love: even when they repeatedly rejected that love and God found it necessary to chastise and discipline them, he never stopped loving them and caring for them. If God has continued to love and care for them, therefore, it is due not to any quality, characteristic, or virtue that the people possess of themselves but only to his grace and mercy.

As we have seen above in the present chapter, in Deut 7:7-8 and 9:4-7 Moses also stresses to the people that God is giving them the land he had promised to them not because they are a large and powerful nation or because they are any more righteous or deserving than its previous inhabitants but only because out of love for them he intends to carry out the promises he had made to their ancestors. In fact, he makes it a point to remind them once more that they are a stubborn people who have rebelled against God from the moment that they came out of Egypt (9:6-7). By doing so, he once again makes it clear that God has chosen to bless and favor them out of pure grace, mercy, and compassion and that his love is therefore unconditional, since it does not depend on anything that they do or fail to do.

The same basic ideas are behind Moses' words to the people in Deut 8:11-18. There he tells them that when they come to prosper in the land as a result

---

9. See especially Deut 8:2-4, 14-16; 10:21-22; 11:2-7.
10. See especially Deut 1:26-45; 4:3-4; 6:16; 9:7-29.

of the abundance and blessings God will provide for them, they must not exalt themselves but must instead remember the manner in which God provided for their every need as they journeyed through the wilderness over the previous forty years. He then concludes: "Take care that you do not say in your heart, 'My power and the strength of my own hand have gotten me this wealth.' Instead, remember the LORD your God, for he is the one who enables you to obtain wealth, so that he may confirm his covenant that he swore to your ancestors, as he has done to this day" (vv. 17-18). By means of these words, Moses not only reminds the people of God's goodness and grace but also exhorts them to depend wholly on God's love, power, and strength rather than their own abilities or capacities.

While all of these passages stress the enormity of God's unconditional and unmerited love for his people, that love is also evident in the repeated exhortations for the people to obey the commandments he is giving them so that all may go well with them and that they may live long in the land once they have entered there.[11] As we have seen in Chapter 5 of this study, those exhortations are not to be understood on the basis of the principle of *do ut des*, as if God were attempting to bring the people to do what he desires and demands for his own sake by means of the promise of rewards and the threat of punishments. Instead, the basis for those exhortations is the intrinsic relationship between obedience to his commands and the well-being that results from that obedience as its natural consequence. This is reflected in Moses' words to the people that God has commanded observance of his precepts and ordinances "for our lasting good" and "for your own well-being and that of your descendants after you" (Deut 4:40; 6:24; 10:13). His exhortation for the people to observe everything that God has commanded so that all may go well with them is therefore an expression of the same love, care, and concern that led God to give the people the commandments of the Torah.

As we have also noted in Chapter 5 of this study, in his words to the people Moses points to God's chastisements and discipline as an expression of God's love. In Deut 8:2-5, after affirming that the people's time in the wilderness had the purpose of humbling them and putting them to the test for their own good, Moses adds: "Know in your heart, then, that as a parent disciplines a child, so the LORD your God disciplines you" (v. 5). In two other passages, Moses uses the same terminology in Hebrew to speak of God disciplining the people by making them to hear his voice from heaven and by means of the signs and wonders he performed on their behalf when he brought them out of Egypt (Deut 4:36; 11:2-7). In these instances, the allusion is clearly not to any type of chastisement in response to Israel's sin but rather to the manner in which God sought to instruct his people and bring them to trust in him by making manifest to them his power, might, and glory. These passages thus underscore once more the point that when the Hebrew verb *yasar* and the noun *musar* are used in other contexts in the Hebrew Bible to speak of

---

11. See Deut 5:16, 28-29, 32-33; 6:1-3, 17-19; 8:1; 11:8-9; 12:25-28; 19:13; 22:7; 32:45-47.

God chastising or punishing the people in response to their disobedience, the emphasis falls on his intention to instruct them and mold them into a people who will obey him for their own good rather than any desire to inflict suffering on them for its own sake.

While throughout Deuteronomy Moses repeatedly reminds the people of their persistent stubbornness and hard-heartedness, he also reproaches them for their failure to trust in God. In Deut 1:19-33, after recalling how they had refused to go up to take possession of the land that God had promised them out of fear of the powerful nations that were occupying it, he reminds them that he had exhorted them not to be afraid but to remember how God had fought for them in Egypt and had carried them like a child during their time in the wilderness. He then adds: "But in spite of this, you still have not trusted in the LORD your God" (v. 32). Further on in the book, Moses reiterates the same accusation: "When the LORD sent you from Kadesh-barnea and told you, 'Go up and take possession of the land that I have given you,' you rebelled against the command of the LORD your God and did not trust him or listen to him. You have been rebellious against the LORD from the day I have known you" (9:23-24). In these passages, therefore, Moses points to the root of the people's persistent failure to obey God, namely, their lack of trust in him, despite all the marvelous works he had repeatedly performed on their behalf.

This persistent stubbornness and rebelliousness must be kept in mind when considering Moses' recollection of the manner in which God had responded when the people were badly defeated after they had disobeyed God by attempting to take possession of the land on their own following his decree that they spend forty years in the wilderness before entering it. He tells the Israelites: "When you returned and wept before the LORD, the LORD would neither listen to your voice nor pay any attention to you" (Deut 1:45). Although at first glance this response on God's part may seem heartless and cruel, the idea behind it is that because the people had refused to trust in him in spite of the manner in which he had repeatedly demonstrated to them both his love for them and his sovereign power, he had determined that for their own good they needed to spend those forty years in the wilderness in order to be taught to trust in him. The idea is the same as that just mentioned above in connection with Deut 8:2-5, where Moses affirms explicitly that the purpose of the people's forty years in the desert was to discipline them by humbling them and teaching them to trust that God would provide for their needs, as he had done by satisfying their hunger and taking care of them in other ways. The reason that God had refused to listen or pay attention to the people when they wept following the defeat they had suffered when attempting to take possession of the land on their own, therefore, was not that God did not love them or care for them but that their previous failure to trust in him had led him to conclude that for their own good they needed to be thoroughly disciplined in the wilderness before entering the land. There was no point in introducing them into the land if they had not yet learned to trust him and obey him in all things, since without their trust and obedience he would not be able to fulfill the purposes for which he was giving them that land in the first place. Despite their tearful pleas for mercy and forgiveness, therefore, God had determined that it was best to continue to chastise them rather than pardoning them for their failure to trust and obey him.

God's response to the people's failure to trust him also exemplifies the saying that Moses cites in Deut 5:9-10: "I the LORD your God am a jealous God, visiting the iniquity of the parents upon the children to the third and the fourth generation of those who reject me, but showing steadfast love to the thousandth generation of those who love me and keep my commandments." As in Exod 20:5-6, here in Deuteronomy that saying appears in the context of God's command for the people to have no gods other than him at the beginning of the Decalogue. Moses' repeated exhortations against the worship of other gods throughout Deuteronomy as well as the repeated allusions to that sin throughout the biblical narrative as a whole stress the fact that in biblical thought the worship of other gods rather than the LORD God of Israel is considered to be the root of all other evils. The saying attributed to God in Exod 20:5-6 and Deut 5:9-10 thus anticipates the sin that will be the primary cause of Israel's exile and ruin throughout the remainder of the biblical narrative, as we shall see in the following chapter. It should also be noted that up to that point of the narrative the two sins that have by far been the most grievous are those that the Israelites committed when they made the golden calf and when they yoked themselves to Baal of Peor (Exodus 32; Numbers 25). In both instances, God responded by having many of the people put to death and sending a plague upon the people to kill others.

As we have seen previously, in biblical thought God is jealous in the sense that he adamantly refuses to tolerate the people's worship of other gods, not for *his* sake, but for *theirs*. The same must be said with regard to God's "visiting the iniquity of the parents upon the children to the third and the fourth generation" of those who reject or hate him. Clearly, the allusion is to God's chastisements or punishments. While the sin that led God to chastise and discipline the people by having them spend forty years in the wilderness was not that of idolatry but rather their failure to trust him, God's response to that sin is the same as it will be centuries later when Israel's persistent sinfulness and worship of other gods will result in the destruction and exile of many of his people under the Assyrians and Babylonians: it is not only the parents who will be subjected by God to sufferings and chastisements for their sins but their children and grandchildren as well. In this case, God denies entrance into the land to the generation that left Egypt in order to raise up a new generation that he intends to teach to trust him in the way that their parents and grandparents did not by means of their sojourn in the wilderness. God's purpose is not to inflict suffering on the people for its own sake but to mold them into the type of trusting and obedient people that they will need to be if they are to prosper and be blessed in the land God has promised them. In this regard, it is worth noting that both when God decrees that the people are to spend forty years in the wilderness and when he sends them into exile centuries later, the children and grandchildren are made to suffer not *in the place* of their parents and grandparents but *together with them*, even though they were not guilty of the sins of their parents and grandparents. It is this that the saying attributed to God in Deut 5:9-10 anticipates when it speaks of God visiting the iniquity of the parents upon the children: not that the chastisements that the sins of the parents call for will be inflicted on the children in their stead but that the children who did not commit those sins will nevertheless suffer the chastisements imposed by God *together with* their parents.

After expounding for the people once more many of the commandments that they had already received at Sinai and giving them other instructions and ordinances in chapters 12–26 of Deuteronomy, Moses exhorts the people once again to observe carefully and diligently all that God has commanded with all their heart and soul (Deut 26:16). He then reiterates that both God and the people have committed themselves to living in the covenant relationship with one another and commands them to write the words of the Torah on large stones and to set them up on Mount Ebal once they have entered into the land across the Jordan (26:17–27:10). In chapters 28–32 of the book, he looks ahead to the future by anticipating what will happen after the people enter the land, establishing Joshua as his successor, renewing the covenant once more, and exhorting the people to choose life by committing themselves to observe everything in that covenant. In addition, God has Moses compose a song that he commands to be taught to the Israelites to serve as a witness against them in the future (31:16–32:47). The idea behind the song is that when the people fall into sin in the future as a result of their stubborn and rebellious nature and God responds by sending terrible afflictions and troubles upon them to chastise them, the song will provide them with a basis for interpreting all that has taken place and will remind them of God's good intentions for them in the midst of their pain and sorrow. In Deut 33:1-29, Moses pronounces a final blessing on all of the tribes of Israel.

LAYING TO REST A PROPHET LIKE NO OTHER

The last chapter of Deuteronomy relates Moses' death and burial. It mentions that prior to his death Moses was allowed to look into the land that God had promised to Israel's ancestors but not to enter it (Deut 34:4). The reason for this is given in Deut 32:50-52, where God commands Moses to go up Mount Nebo and then tells him: "You shall die there on the mountain that you ascend and shall be gathered to your kin, as your brother Aaron died on Mount Hor and was gathered to his kin, because both of you broke faith with me among the Israelites at the waters of Meribath-kadesh in the wilderness of Zin, because you did not treat me as holy in the midst of the children of Israel."

The allusion here is to the account that appears in Numbers 20. There, in response to the people's complaint that they have no water, God says to Moses: "Take the rod and assemble the congregation, you and your brother Aaron, and command the rock before their eyes to yield its water. Thus you shall bring water out of the rock for them; thus you shall provide drink for the congregation and their livestock" (Num 20:8). The account then continues:

> So Moses took the rod from before the LORD, just as he had commanded him. Moses and Aaron gathered the assembly together before the rock, and he said to them, "Listen now, you rebels, shall we bring forth water for you from out of this rock?" Then Moses lifted up his hand and struck the rock twice with his rod; water came out abundantly, and the congregation and their livestock drank. But the LORD said to Moses and Aaron, "Because you did not trust in me, to sanctify me in the eyes of the Israelites, therefore you shall not bring this assembly into the land that I have given them." These are the waters of Meribah, where the people of Israel contended with the LORD, and by which he made manifest his holiness (vv. 9-13).

Interpreters of this passage have long struggled to understand what Moses did that might be regarded as a lack of trust in God and a failure to show God's holiness before the Israelites. The answer to that problem may lie in v. 10, where Moses asks the people: "Shall we bring forth water for you from out of this rock?" The way in which Moses frames that question suggests that it is he and Aaron who will make water come forth from the rock rather than God. In that case, rather than presenting God as the one who is coming to the aid of the people by performing a wonder on their behalf, the words attributed to Moses imply that Moses and Aaron are their helpers and deliverers, as well as those responsible for working the wonder that enables the Israelites to obtain water. While in principle Aaron does not do anything wrong, Moses' words appear to implicate him as well. Rather than raising his voice to correct Moses or point out that the wondrous deed is in no way his own, Aaron remains silent and thus becomes complicit in giving the Israelites the impression that he too is responsible for the miraculous deed. In this way, Moses failed to sanctify God in the sense that he did not make it clear to the people that it was God rather than he or Aaron who had brought forth water from the rock.[12]

If the passage is interpreted in this manner, then it provides the basis necessary for understanding why God does not allow Moses and Aaron to enter the promised land. According to the logic underlying the narrative, God is not punishing Moses and Aaron out of spite because he is angry and offended

---

12. This idea is suggested by Budd, among others: "Moses and Aaron have failed to 'believe in' Yahweh, by claiming that they themselves can bring water from the rock. In so doing, they fail to 'sanctify' him in the eyes of Israel, and thereby deprive him of his due honor" (*Numbers*, 220; cf. 218-19). Such a reading, however, seems to presuppose that what interests God is receiving his "due honor" for his own sake. For other proposals regarding what is said to lead God to accuse Moses and Aaron of not trusting him and not sanctifying him in the eyes of the Israelites, see Baruch A. Levine, *Numbers 1-20: A New Translation with Introduction and Commentary*, AB 4 (New York: Doubleday, 1993), 489-90; Stubbs, *Numbers*, 338-43.

that the glory, honor, and gratitude that should have been given to him as his due are instead being given to Moses and Aaron, as if his concern were merely for himself or his own worship, praise, and reputation among the people. While God is certainly concerned about these things, it is not for *his own* sake but for the sake of the people, since for their own good they are to follow and trust *in him* rather than in Moses or Aaron independently of him. For the same reason, it is important for the Israelites to know that it is not Moses or Aaron who will bring them into the land God has promised to them but God alone. Throughout their generations, the people are to view God rather than Moses or Aaron as their savior and deliverer. Moses and Aaron were simply God's servants whom he used as his instruments. Furthermore, neither of them were deserving of such a role by virtue of any merit of their own. While the people are certainly to hold Moses and Aaron in high esteem, they are not to idolize or venerate them in any way.

According to this interpretation of the narrative, therefore, the reason that God does not allow Moses to enter the land he had promised to Israel is not that Moses accidentally phrased his question about bringing forth water from the rock in the wrong way or that he committed some type of trivial sin at Meribah that God's strict justice could not leave unpunished. Rather, the logic seems to go much deeper. In large part, it has to do with a concern that the people of Moses' own generation and perhaps those of later generations as well might attribute to Moses certain actions or qualities that were to be attributed to God alone and even come to divinize Moses in some way. However, that logic also has to do with a desire to convey to the people as a whole a message that reminded them of certain fundamental truths. Throughout the narrative, Moses has repeatedly placed himself in full solidarity with the people, not only in the way that he has faithfully led them in accordance with all that God has asked of him but also in his intercessions on behalf of the people when they have fallen into sin. Rather than rejecting the people who have caused him such heartaches and troubles, Moses has loved them even more than his own life. When God threatened to destroy the people as a result of their stubbornness and rebellion and offered instead to make of Moses a great people who would inherit all of his blessings, Moses refused. He even told God that if God were going to destroy the people, he would prefer to be destroyed along with them rather than continuing to live on his own without them. No solidarity could ever be greater than that which Moses has expressed in relation to the people in both his words and his actions.

In a sense, it may even be said that throughout the narrative Moses has borne the people's sins. He has put up with their constant complaints, their persistent stubbornness and disobedience, and their rebellion and aggressions against God and against him personally. He has also endured patiently and willingly the consequences of all of their sinful and destructive behavior. He too has had to spend forty years wandering in the desert, enduring countless hardships and afflictions. In some ways he has had to suffer even more than the people have, since whenever their disobedience led God to inflict punishments on them to chastise them, Moses has had not only to endure those punishments together with them but also to intercede on their behalf and attempt to convince God to bring those punishments to an end. In the words of Moses himself, he has taken this burdensome, rebellious, and exasperating people on his back for forty years and carried them through the desert, despite the fact that rather than thanking him for doing so the people constantly criticize and reject him and make all sorts of accusations against him (Deut 31:27; cf. 9:6-27). He has therefore loved them beyond measure, purely out of grace, kindness, and compassion and not because of any merit on their part or self-interest of his own.

In several passages in Deuteronomy, Moses tells the people that it was on *their* account that the LORD became angry with him and determined not to allow him to enter into the land God had promised to his people (Deut 1:37; 3:26; 4:21). This affirmation should not be understood in the sense that Moses is claiming that he is innocent of any wrongdoing and that it is solely the people's fault that he will be prohibited from entering the land. The narrative makes it clear that it was Moses' own action that led to this prohibition. However, it was the people's sin of failing to trust God and instead complaining against God that had put Moses in the position in which he found himself when they were in Meribah. Of course, what had put Moses in that position was also his own decision to remain in solidarity with the people and seek to assist them in their needs both at Meribah and throughout the forty years. While Moses had acted wrongly at Meribah in some way, the reason that he was at Meribah in the first place and was finding it necessary to produce water for the people was that they had been sinful and rebellious from the time he had led them out of Egypt. Had the people not rebelled against God, neither they nor Moses would have been in the desert needing water in the first place, nor would Moses have had to take upon himself the responsibility of finding water at Meribah if the people had trusted God in the way that they should have.

It can therefore be said that Moses was prevented from entering the promised land due not only to what he did at Meribah but also to the sinfulness and disobedience of the people as a whole, as well as the love he showed for them in remaining in solidarity with them despite their persistent rebellion both against God and his own person. While they had not caused him to sin at Meribah, through their lack of trust in God and their sinfulness they had put him in the position in which he found himself when he sinned against God, apparently by failing to point to God as the people's helper and deliverer and instead putting himself and Aaron in that role.

Precisely why Moses did not make it clear to the people that it was God who was bringing forth water from the rock rather than he and Aaron is not entirely clear from the narrative. Nothing in the account indicates that Moses actually wanted to usurp God or ascribe to himself attributes such as power, honor, or glory that belong solely to God. Instead, it appears that Moses has simply become fed up with the people and wants to get them off his back. It is worth noting that at the beginning of the account in Numbers, the people are said to gather against Moses and Aaron and express their anger at Moses for bringing them and their herds of cattle out to the desert to die of thirst (Num 20:2-5). The people's words indicate that they are still not acknowledging that it was God who brought them out of Egypt and recognizing that the reason why they are in the desert enduring thirst and other hardships is that God is seeking to break their rebellious spirit and discipline them so that they may become obedient to his will. Because Moses does not reinforce these points to them but simply brings forth water from the rock, perhaps because he is weary of dealing with the people and simply wishes for them to stop bothering and blaming him, the incident does not serve any type of constructive or corrective purpose among the people. They are not led to look to God as their helper. Instead, the idea that Moses must solve their problems is reinforced and left uncorrected. Nor are the people reminded that God is testing and disciplining them for their own good by subjecting them to the hardships in the desert, in which case the incident would have served to bring them to reflect on what God was attempting to accomplish in relation to them.

In any case, whatever sin Moses has committed at Meribah seems relatively minor rather than consisting of something more serious that was deserving of the rather harsh decree on the part of God that Moses would not be allowed to enter the land he had promised to Israel. It is possible, however, that this is precisely the point of the story. Moses seems to have been perfect and obeyed God in all things from the time God first appeared to him in the burning bush. Nevertheless, while he may be very close to perfection, he is *not* actually perfect, since only God is perfect. Despite all of the admirable things he has done, the tremendous faith he has shown in God, and the extraordinary love and solidarity he has demonstrated in relation to the people, he still has flaws because he is a sinful human being like every other human being that has ever existed.

For that reason, if God were to let Moses enter the land while prohibiting the Israelites who had sinned in the desert from doing so, God might be giving the impression that Moses had *earned the right* to enter the land because of his obedience, righteousness, and perhaps even perfection. God would appear to be rewarding Moses, in which case his entrance into the land would no longer be a manifestation of God's grace, mercy, and kindness. In addition, the link of total solidarity between Moses and the sinful people would be broken, since Moses would no longer be enduring alongside the people the same chastisements to which God had subjected them in order to bring them to live obediently. It might appear as if throughout the time in the desert, Moses had not really been pursuing the interests of the people themselves and making endless sacrifices on their behalf out of love for them but had instead been pursuing his own interests, serving the people primarily to obtain for himself a reward, namely, a place in the promised land that would be denied to them.

By denying Moses entry into the promised land, therefore, God under-scores a couple of fundamental truths, as mentioned above. First, he makes it clear that no one is deserving of his love and gifts and that, if he is giving the Israelites the land he has promised them, it is purely out of grace. Were God to act in some way that might lead the people to think that they or their leaders such as Moses could earn his kindness and favors, they would no longer serve him out of love but purely out of self-interest. For reasons we have seen previously, that would have made it impossible for them to fulfill God's commandments in the way that he desired. No matter how obedient or righteous one may be, every human being is an imperfect sinner and will be treated as such by God. Were this point to be forgotten or denied, some people might come to claim that they were deserving of God's love and set themselves above others, while others whose faults and imperfections were evident to them might despair of ever attaining the perfection necessary to obtain God's approval, love, and favor. Once again, this would represent a denial of God's grace and mercy. Such a denial would in turn undermine the type of love God wished to see among his people and the values he wished to instill in them. The reason for this is that once love and favors are thought to be earned, love becomes conditional upon the actions of others rather than being a free and unmerited gift. Such a belief would lead the people not only to place conditions on their love for others but also condemn them to having to live constantly trying to earn the love of God and others.

Second, by not allowing Moses to enter the land promised to Israel, God preserves the solidarity between Moses and the people. They learn that those in positions of authority such as Moses are to give themselves fully to the people and serve them for their own sake rather than seeking their own per-sonal ends or interests or using their position for their own benefit. Had God allowed Moses to enter the promised land, the message he would have con-veyed to the people was that those whom he places over the people as leaders need not enter into full solidarity with them but are justified in breaking ranks with them and abandoning them when they do wrong rather than sticking with them in both good times and bad, no matter what they do, as Moses did. Those in positions of authority and leadership are thus to bear the sins of the people in the way that Moses did and even be willing to die for the people out of love for them.

There may also have been a third reason why it would have been prob-lematic for Moses to enter into the land promised to Israel. Once they had entered, the people were going to need someone to lead them in warfare and destroy entire towns, cities, and peoples. This was the role assigned to Joshua. Were Moses to have assumed such a role, his reputation as one who had been dedicated solely to seeking the well-being of others at whatever the cost would have been damaged severely. Instead, he would be thought to have blood on his hands, even if he had merely directed and overseen the killing and destruction carried out by the people rather than participating directly in their actions.

Just as God later deemed it inappropriate for David to build him a temple because of all the blood he had shed (1 Chr 22:6-8), so also God might have deemed it inappropriate for his servant Moses to be involved in the type of bloodshed that the narrative associates with the conquest of the promised land under Joshua. Moses' task was that of serving as God's instrument to bring the people to live in love, justice, and righteousness rather than leading them in warfare. Undoubtedly, at other moments in the narrative Moses commands the Israelites to put people to death and directs them to attack and kill those of other nations (Exod 17:8-13; 32:25-29; Num 31:1-18). At no point, however, does he engage in any of the fighting or killing himself in the way that Joshua is said to do. In any case, it may have appeared inappropriate for Moses to lead the people in the conquest and destruction of the peoples that had been inhabiting the land of which the Israelites were to take possession.

In the end, just as both the narratives and the commandments that appear throughout the Pentateuch serve to instruct the people in the will of God and guide them in the way they should go for their own good, the person of Moses must be seen as fulfilling the same role. Moses is regarded as an exemplary figure who embodies the type of love, commitment, and dedication that God desires to see in all of his people. He teaches them not only through the words he communicates to them on behalf of God but also through his actions and behavior. For that reason, the narrative stresses the loving, generous, and self-less character of Moses not only by means of the behavior it attributes to him but also by the descriptions of Moses that it provides explicitly. In Num 12:3, for example, it is said that "the man Moses was very humble, more so than anyone else on the face of the earth." As the context in which that affirmation appears makes clear, this humility involves loving and serving the people under him with all his heart, mind, soul, and strength, despite the price he must pay for doing so and the humiliations and aggressions he constantly had to bear. Moses' greatness is also stressed in the final verses of Deuteronomy: "Since that time there has never arisen in Israel a prophet like Moses, whom the LORD knew face to face, and who was equal to him in all the signs and wonders that the LORD sent him to perform in the land of Egypt, against Pharaoh and all his servants and his entire land, and in all the mighty deeds and all the terrifying acts of power that Moses performed in the sight of all Israel" (Deut 34:10-12). What made him great was not simply the manner in which he related to God and the signs and wonders that God had him perform, but the fact that he had been totally dedicated to serving God as his instrument to accomplish his purposes, in spite of the many sacrifices and afflictions he had to endure as a result of that dedication. It was this dedica-tion that made it possible for God to accomplish his purposes through him.

CHAPTER 12

Bringing a Stiff-Necked People to Their Knees

In one of the strangest and most surprising passages in the Hebrew Bible, at the end of chapter 32 of the book of Genesis, a man is said to appear suddenly to Abraham's grandson Jacob and engage him in a wrestling match. After the two struggle throughout the night until daybreak, the man strikes Jacob's hip and puts it out of joint. He then tells Jacob to let him go, but Jacob refuses to do so until the man pronounces a blessing on him. The man responds by telling Jacob that he has been struggling with God and on that basis changes his name from Jacob to Israel, "the one who contends with God." When Jacob asks the man his name, he refuses to give it to him and simply blesses Jacob before departing from his presence. Following this encounter, Jacob calls the place Peniel, "the face of God," because of what has taken place there: "For I have seen God face to face, but my life has been preserved." He then limps away as the sun rises (Gen 32:22-32).

To whatever extent this passage is intended to anticipate what will take place in the remainder of the biblical narrative, it unquestionably foreshadows in an extremely accurate manner the relationship that will characterize God and his people Israel throughout that narrative. From the moment that God delivers them from their bondage in Egypt, that relationship is a constant struggle. After contending with the people endlessly as they rebel against him in the desert and stubbornly refuse to listen to him, God finally succeeds in bringing them to the bountiful land he had promised them and enables them to drive out the previous inhabitants of that land in order to take possession of it for themselves. Once they have been established there, however, the struggles between God and Israel resume and grow even more vicious and violent. Even when God removes ten of the twelve tribes permanently from the land he had given them and subjects the people who remain to hardships and afflictions that are scarcely bearable, they refuse to give in. As a result, he wreaks destruction on their land as well and scatters most of them among foreign nations in distant lands before graciously allowing some of their children and grandchildren to return to their own land once more. At the end of the narrative, while a small remnant of the people is left standing, like their ancestor Jacob those who survive their struggle with God can only limp about, hoping that at some point their pain and misery will give way to something better.

Although there are no doubt important parallels between the story of Jacob's struggle with God at Peniel and the history of God's relationship to his people Israel, however, there is one significant difference. Whereas at Peniel it is Jacob who insists on receiving a blessing from a God who seems reluctant to give it, in the narrative regarding Israel in the biblical texts it is God who tenaciously seeks to give blessing to a people who just as tenaciously refuse to receive it. Even though the narrative ends without offering a clear resolution regarding what is to follow, the hope that it seems to hold out is that after all is said and done, God will finally get his way.

A FRESH START FOR A POLLUTED LAND

Both prior to the death of Moses and immediately after it under the leadership of Joshua, God commands the Israelites to wage war on other peoples who stand in the way of his intentions to give his people Israel the land he had promised to their ancestors. These peoples include not only the previous inhabitants of that land but also some of the surrounding nations, who either seek to prevent the Israelites from entering into the land or else pose a threat to them once they have arrived there.

As God directs the Israelites to engage in battle the peoples in and around the land he is giving them, he also gives them instructions regarding the manner in which they are to treat those peoples and indicates to them what they are to do with their possessions after they have defeated them. These instructions and indications appear both in the book of Deuteronomy and in the book of Joshua. In many cases, God commands the Israelites to put entire populations to death, including women, children, and the elderly. At other times, they are told to spare some of the people, often to take them as slaves or to take their women as wives. On occasion, the Israelites are instructed to allow certain nations and groups of people to remain in the cities or lands they had inhabited previously, with the condition that they either submit to the Israelites or else simply refrain from molesting them. When the Israelites conquer the peoples and cities that stand in their way, in some instances God allows them to keep all or part of the spoils, while in others they are told either to destroy the possessions of those whom they conquer or to offer them up to God.

Contending with the Carnage of a Conquest

Without a doubt, the passages from the Pentateuch and from the book of Joshua that describe the conquest and destruction of these other peoples so that the Israelites may take possession of the land that God has chosen to give them are some of the most problematic and troubling in the Hebrew Bible. Viewed in the light of the claim that God is not partial to anyone and is concerned not only for the well-being of the Israelites but also that of widows, orphans, and foreigners (Deut 10:17-19), at first glance his commands to destroy entire populations in order to take their land and possessions seem both incongruous and inhumane. Readers of the Hebrew Bible in antiquity would no doubt have considered such passages to be just as disturbing as they are for readers today.

The biblical narrative, however, leaves no doubt as to the purpose of God's command. If the Israelites are to occupy the land, the previous inhabitants must be removed from it. Because the nations and peoples dwelling in the land will not accept a peaceful coexistence with Israel in the land or be willing to depart from it in order to hand it over to Israel and go live elsewhere, if Israel is to occupy it, those nations and peoples must be removed from it forcibly. Rather than allowing Israel to occupy the land or share it with them, they would fight relentlessly against the Israelites and attempt to destroy them or drive them out. Even if God were to leave many of those peoples in place and simply protect the Israelites from them by allowing the Israelites to defeat them whenever they came under attack from them, the Israelites' existence would be characterized by constant conflict and fighting with them. While in principle some of the peoples dwelling in the land might be willing to live in peace alongside the Israelites, such an arrangement might threaten Israel's identity as a separate and distinct people dedicated to God, since various forms of intermingling would eventually take place between the Israelites and the other peoples. Under those circumstances, were God to bless Israel with abundance and prosperity throughout the land, he could hardly do so without blessing at the same time the other peoples dwelling in their midst who would continue to worship their own gods. In that case, it would not be evident to Israel or the other nations and peoples in the land that the blessings being enjoyed by Israel were coming from God's hand in response to Israel's obedience to his commandments, since those who did not form part of Israel would enjoy the same blessings in spite of their failure to acknowledge Israel's God and live in accordance with his will. Both those peoples and the Israelites themselves might even believe that the blessings they were receiving came from the gods of those peoples rather than the God of Israel.

A further reason why the biblical narrative considers it necessary for the other nations and peoples to be destroyed or driven out of the land that God is giving Israel is that their worship of their own gods would present a threat to Israel. In addition to enticing the Israelites to join them in serving gods other than the God of Israel, those nations would practice the injustice, violence, and oppression associated with the worship of their gods. As a result, the Israelites would not only suffer these things at the hands of those nations but might also be drawn to practice such things themselves. Rather than living in accordance with what is good, right, and just, they would be tempted to adopt the system of values associated with those nations and their gods. This would make it impossible for them to enjoy the well-being and prosperity that God desires and intends for them. For all of these reasons, then, if God is to give Israel the land he has promised them and Israel is to live at peace in that land, the previous inhabitants cannot be allowed to remain in the land.

These ideas are stated explicitly in the opening chapters of Deuteronomy. At the beginning of chapter 7, Moses tells the people to destroy entirely the seven nations that inhabit the land God is giving to Israel so that those nations may be cleared out from that land (vv. 1-2). The Israelites are told not to make any type of treaty or agreement with those nations, spare any of them, or intermarry with them, since this would turn the Israelites away from following God (vv. 3-4). The Israelites are also instructed to destroy entirely the sacred objects and places of worship of these nations, as well as their altars and idols (v. 5). In addition to preventing the Israelites from adopting the practices of those nations, these measures will also allow them to be a people set apart entirely to Israel's God as holy and distinct from all other peoples (v. 6).

Further on in the same chapter, Moses tells the Israelites that the destruction of these other peoples and their gods will prevent them from being a "snare" to Israel (Deut 7:16). While the Israelites themselves are to destroy these peoples and their places and objects of worship, God himself will also send signs, wonders, plagues, and panic upon those peoples so as to clear them from the land (vv. 17-24). The Israelites are told not to covet the silver and gold from which the idols of these nations are made but are to destroy them completely so that they might not be ensnared by the worship of those idols (vv. 25-26). Several verses in the preceding chapters of Deuteronomy repeat these ideas as well and point to the manner in which God has already destroyed other peoples who stood in the way of Israel's entrance into the land in order to assure the Israelites that God will continue to give his people the strength necessary to overcome nations that seem more powerful than they.[1]

In Deut 9:4-5, a passage that we have already considered in the previous chapters, Moses also makes it clear that God is removing those peoples from the land due to their violent, unjust, and oppressive ways. In these verses, Moses tells the people twice that "it is because of the wickedness of these nations that the LORD is driving them out from your presence." What God wants to see in the land is the practice of justice and righteousness. Because the nations that have been occupying the land will never abandon their destructive behavior due to their insistence on worshiping gods who promote such behavior, the only way in which God can establish a people who will be committed to what is good, right, and just in the land is by removing those nations from the land and replacing them with a nation that will serve him instead.

Readers of the biblical text might wonder why God chose to command the Israelites to destroy the previous inhabitants of the land rather than acting entirely on his own to bring about their destruction by means of some type of plague or similar disaster. While that question is not addressed in Deuteronomy or Joshua or anywhere else in the Hebrew Bible, in theory several answers might be given. According to the logic underlying the narrative, God may have thought that by having his people carry out much of

---

1. See Deut 2:21-36; 4:38; 6:18-19; cf. 12:2-4.

that destruction instead of doing so himself, he would be able to see to what extent they had come to trust him and perhaps even increase that trust as they learned to depend on him to give them the strength and power necessary to defeat the other nations. In this case, God would learn whether the forty years in the wilderness had taught the people to believe in him, in contrast to their parents, who had doubted his ability to give them the victory over the inhabitants of the land after most of the Israelite spies sent by Moses had returned from their trip into Canaan with an unfavorable report (Numbers 13–14). God may also have wanted to bring the surrounding nations to fear Israel so that they would refrain from attacking the Israelites in the future. Had he simply destroyed the previous inhabitants of the land through a plague or some other type of natural disaster, the other nations would not have learned that he had been the one who had introduced his people Israel into the land by enabling them to defeat peoples who appeared to be superior in size and strength. For these or other reasons, according to the logic underlying the biblical narrative, God had chosen to accomplish his plan by having Israel destroy many of the previous inhabitants of the land he was giving to his people rather than destroying all of them himself. Of course, one might also question such a decision, given that asking the people to commit acts of savagery and brutality would affect them negatively in some ways and even do them harm. In this regard, then, the narrative must be regarded as highly problematic, despite the logic underlying it.

While the destruction of the nations and peoples that had been occupying the land that God had promised to Israel is unquestionably barbaric and inhumane, it is important to view that destruction within the context of the biblical narrative as a whole, as well as the divine plan that is presupposed in that narrative. Ironically, what God ultimately seeks by having the nations that had been dwelling in the land destroyed so that Israel may be established in that land is the blessing not only of Israel but of all of the nations and families of the earth. Although this destruction is extremely cruel, according to the logic of the biblical texts it would be even more cruel for God simply to let the nations of the earth continue unimpeded in their destructive, unjust, and violent ways. For that reason, God instead chooses to implement through Israel a plan that is aimed at eventually bringing the families and nations of the earth to live in ways that will allow them to enjoy the well-being he desires for all of the human beings he has created, even though this plan requires the destruction of a handful of those nations.

Of course, one of the questions that arises when considering the passages in which the Israelites are commanded to destroy entire populations is why it would be necessary to kill not only the men but also the women and children belonging to those populations. In principle, the women and children might not seem to represent a threat to the Israelites. According to the logic underlying the text, however, if the women were to be spared, they would need to be incorporated among the Israelites in order to survive, since it would be thought that they could hardly exist on their own in the places in which they had dwelled previously without any men forming part of their community. If Israelite men took them as wives, the fact that the women would want to continue to dedicate themselves to the gods they had served previously would create a situation in which many of the men of Israel would be drawn to those gods. If the Israelites attempted to prohibit those women from worshiping their gods by the use of force, many of them would do everything possible to resist those attempts and it is likely that those attempts would not be entirely successful. In addition, those women would harbor strong feelings of animosity and resentment toward the Israelites for having slaughtered their husbands, fathers, brothers, and sons and also for prohibiting them from continuing to serve their own gods and living in whatever manner they pleased.

Similar problems would arise if the children were spared together with the women. The mothers would teach their children to worship and serve their traditional gods rather than the God of Israel, unless they were forced to do otherwise. They would also probably tell and remind their children that the Israelites had slaughtered the men among them and thereby instill in the children the same type of hatred and resentment that they harbored for the Israelites themselves. In addition, because they spoke their own language and did not identify as Israelites, it would not be easy for other peoples to assimilate into the communities of Israel or even communicate with the Israelites. They would instead preserve their own identity and pass that identity on to their children and descendants. Attempts to integrate them into the Israelite population would therefore be resisted and tend to be unsuccessful or tedious at best. Furthermore, both the women and the children who were spared would need to be cared for by the Israelites. This would represent a considerable burden for the Israelites, who would have to use their limited resources to satisfy not only their own needs but also the needs of the large numbers of foreign women and children that they had allowed to live.

In principle, of course, the Israelites might put only the women to death and spare the children, yet even in that case many of the problems just mentioned would arise. The children who were old enough to remember what the Israelites had done to their parents and relatives would harbor strong feelings of hatred toward the Israelites and probably strive to maintain their own identity as well. They might resist assimilation and seek to preserve the traditions they had learned from their parents when young, including those traditions related to the worship of the gods their parents had served. Adopting large numbers of foreign children into Israelite families would also generate many problems. In addition to having to feed, clothe, and educate those children, the treatment that those children would receive within the families and homes that adopted them would not be the same as that given to the native Israelite children. The presence of foreign children in Israelite homes would generate tensions and conflicts among the Israelites for other reasons as well.

According to the biblical texts, then, there was a clear logic behind God's command for the Israelites to slay not only the men from among the nations and populations that had been occupying the land previously but at times the women and children as well. To acknowledge this point is by no means to deny that the type of destruction and annihilation described in the texts is extremely problematic as well as barbaric and inhumane. As we have seen when considering the story of the flood in Noah's day and other difficult passages from the Hebrew Bible, however, in biblical thought God must often do or command things that are extremely cruel and unfair in order to accomplish his purposes in a world that is already filled with behaviors and practices that are equally violent, barbaric, and inhumane. At times, this involves choosing which of the alternatives that are open to him is less evil, given that all of the possible alternatives are in some ways evil. In this case, while it is undoubtedly cruel for God to command the extermination of entire populations in the land that he is giving to Israel, he evidently considers it necessary in order to accomplish his purposes in the way he desires.

From the perspective of the biblical texts, therefore, in spite of the apparent cruelty and even barbarity of many of God's actions and determinations, those who know him as the one true God will remain convinced that in all that he does and commands he is seeking what is best for all of the peoples of the earth as a whole and that he alone is able to discern how best to accomplish his loving purposes in the world. Because in biblical thought the peoples of the earth are so deeply and helplessly mired in the destructive behavior that does them such great harm, at times God has no choice but to do things that are extremely painful not only for them but for him as well. For that reason, those who believe God to be both all-knowing and all-loving will accept whatever he determines rather than questioning it. They must be aware of their own ignorance and limitations as creatures whom he alone has brought into being. On that basis, they must also simply submit to his will as he reveals it to them without supposing that they know how to deal with the tremendous problems and challenges raised by the persistent sinfulness and rebelliousness of human beings better than God does.

At the same time, it must be remembered that God's purpose of blessing all of the families of the earth through Israel can be accomplished only if he is able to form Israel into a people who will be committed to living in a manner that will make it possible for them to enjoy the well-being he desires for them. Only as the Israelites are brought to live in that manner can they serve as God's instrument to draw other nations and peoples to himself so that they too may be blessed together with Israel by living in the same manner. However, unless the Israelites are given a land of their own, this plan cannot be accomplished in the way God intends. Part of that plan involves granting Israel prosperity, freedom from disease and sickness, and other blessings that will allow the people to enjoy well-being and wholeness in their land so that other nations and peoples may see how God loves and cares for Israel and thereby be drawn to him as well. If that is to happen, Israel must be set apart from the other nations in a land that is capable of producing bounty and abundance. At the same time, those nations can observe the manner in which Israel is blessed in that land only if they remain in close proximity to it, as the peoples surrounding Israel's territory do.

As we have noted in the previous chapter, the idea that God wishes to draw other nations to himself by establishing Israel in the land he promised to the people's ancestors appears in the narrative itself. In Deut 4:5-8, after exhorting the people to keep God's commandments rather than worshiping other gods as they did when they yoked themselves to Baal of Peor, Moses tells the people that their observance of those commandments will demonstrate their wisdom and understanding in the eyes of the surrounding peoples and lead those peoples to marvel at the greatness of Israel and Israel's God. In particular, those peoples will see how the statutes and ordinances of the Torah promote justice in a way that their own laws and customs do not (v. 8). If this is what God seeks, what must interest him is not that those nations simply look upon Israel with envy on account of the good law he has given them but that they be drawn to him and his law so that they too may attain the blessings that result from serving him and obeying his law.

In this regard, it is also important to note that God commands the Israelites to leave many of the surrounding peoples undisturbed in the land he has assigned to these peoples rather than destroying them. Such is the case, for example, with respect to the Moabites, the Ammonites, and the descendants of Esau (Deut 2:4-5, 9, 19). This command seems to reflect not only God's love for these nations, despite the fact that they do not regard themselves as his people, but also a hope that eventually they may be among the nations drawn to serve and worship him along with the Israelites. It also indicates that God intends to give Israel only the land that the people need for themselves. They are not to subject other peoples outside of the land given to them by God or take their land from them. God does not wish to make of Israel an empire that dominates, subdues, and enslaves the surrounding nations, since that would turn the Israelites into oppressors rather than a people committed to practicing what is good, right, and just.

It must be recognized, however, that the commandments given to Israel regarding warfare against other peoples both in and around the land he is giving them do not always adhere to these principles. In Deut 20:10-16, for example, God tells the people that when they wage war with particular cities, they are first to offer terms of peace to the inhabitants of those cities. If they accept the terms of peace and surrender, then the Israelites are to make the people of the city serve them at forced labor. If the inhabitants refuse to accept the terms of peace and instead fight against Israel, then the Israelites are to kill the males but take the women, children, and livestock as plunder after they besiege and conquer the town. While this passage speaks of reducing the people of those cities to forced labor if they surrender rather than fighting, the idea seems to be that the city is to be left standing but that its inhabitants are to pay tribute to the Israelites. Obviously, such an arrangement seems to be less cruel than destroying the people of the city entirely, yet it is still highly problematic.

When considering God's command for the Israelites to destroy the inhabitants of the land he is giving to them, it is important to stress that this command is never presented as a general principle that may be applied to other times and places. God's command is given only with regard to particular peoples and places and applies only to a specific historical context. The destruction of the peoples mentioned forms part of a concrete plan that is unique to the situation described, namely, the entrance of the Israelites into the land that God is giving them in the time of Moses and Joshua. The Israelites therefore are not given permission by God to destroy or annihilate other peoples in other contexts at other times at their own initiative. Even when the foreign peoples around and among them practice sin, evil, and injustice or seemingly pose a threat to God's plan and purposes, no one but God as sovereign LORD can determine how best to carry out his plan and purposes or decide which peoples should live or die. God never delegates to anyone else the power to make such determinations, much less the authority to carry out the destruction of a community or people without an express command to do so on his part. It is significant, for example, that when Deuteronomy speaks of the people's future return to the land following a period in which they have been scattered among the other nations of the world, it never affirms that they are to attack or destroy any of the people who have come to inhabit that land during their absence. The same observation can be made with regard to the narratives that appear in the books of Ezra and Nehemiah. Nowhere in those narratives are the people who return to the land from their exile in Babylonia ordered or given permission to do harm to any of the other peoples who have become established in that land while they were in exile.

While God's command for the Israelites to destroy the inhabitants of the land in order to take possession of it may seem to be an expression of partiality and favoritism toward Israel over against the other nations in the region, a careful consideration of the biblical texts suggests that this is true only to a certain extent. As we have noted elsewhere, according to those texts God's primary concern is not for a particular people or nation per se but for the practice of justice and righteousness among all the peoples and nations of the world. His election of Israel as his people is aimed at blessing not only the Israelites as descendants of Abraham but all of the other families of the earth as well. According to his plan, however, in order to bring people from all of the nations of the world to live in a manner that will make it possible for his blessings of well-being and wholeness to be theirs, he must first bring Israel to live in that manner. Only then can Israel serve as his instrument to draw other peoples to himself.

Although initially God desires to bless Israel more than the other nations, therefore, he also makes it clear to the people that if they do not practice justice and righteousness, he will treat them just as harshly as he has treated the previous inhabitants of the land. As already noted above, in Deuteronomy Moses emphasizes this point repeatedly to the people. Just as God had the nations that inhabited the land utterly destroyed and expelled from the land because of their wickedness, violence, and injustice, so also will he do the same to Israel if his people fill the land with the same type of wickedness, violence, and injustice. In this sense, God is not showing any type of partiality or favoritism toward Israel. If anything, he is even more demanding toward Israel and will treat his people with even greater severity than he treated the previous nations. While those nations were ultimately destroyed, in most cases they were not subjected to the same type of scourges and afflictions mentioned in Deut 28:15-68 that his people Israel will be forced to endure if they persistently refuse to obey the commandments God has given them. Even though utter destruction is a terrible fate to suffer, many might regard it to be just as terrible to be subjected to the type of sufferings mentioned in Deuteronomy 28, especially if those sufferings end up constituting a mere prelude to the utter destruction that will follow in their wake.

The destruction of the nations that had been dwelling in the land God had promised to his people prior to their entrance into that land also reflects a logic that we have seen elsewhere in the biblical texts with regard to Israel. At times, in order to save and bless Israel, God must subject a part of the people to destruction. This becomes necessary when God's repeated calls for the people to return to him and to his commandments are not only rejected but also met with mockery and derision. When the people become hopelessly entrenched in the type of behavior that destroys their well-being and that of others in spite of all of God's efforts to bring them to abandon that behavior, the only way in which God can hope to accomplish his purposes among them is to destroy a large part of the people in order to bring into existence a small remnant that will finally be committed to living in justice and righteousness. In biblical thought, while God would always prefer to avoid having to take such a measure, at times he has no choice if he is to accomplish his objective of bringing at least some of the people to live in a way that makes it possible for them to enjoy the well-being he desires for all. Once he has established this small remnant, it can then constitute the basis for a new beginning.

According to the logic of the biblical narrative, the same basic idea is reflected in God's command for the Israelites to destroy the previous occupants of the land that God is giving them. In order to implement his plan aimed at blessing people from all of the nations of the earth, God must first destroy some of those nations. The reason for this is that those nations refuse to put away the same type of unjust, violent, and oppressive behavior that the biblical texts often associate with Israel as well. Simply to allow those nations to continue in that behavior and see it spread further will not resolve the problem. On the contrary, it will only make it worse. As long as those nations stubbornly persist in that behavior, there is no hope for them. This is the manner in which the nations that are resolutely attached to their own gods are consistently described in the biblical texts. Because they are so deeply entrenched in the worship of gods who promote injustice and violence and there is no hope that they will ever abandon those gods for the God of Israel, they cannot be brought to live in ways that will enable them to enjoy the well-being and wholeness God desires for all the peoples he has created. The only course of action that God can follow to change this situation is to destroy some of those peoples in order to establish in the midst of those who remain a just and righteous people whose way of life will allow them to enjoy his blessings. It is this that he hopes and intends to do through Israel. What will draw these peoples to God is that they will see that obedience to his commandments brings blessing and well-being not only due to the intrinsic consequences of such obedience but also because God responds to that obedience by blessing those who observe his commandments even further.

Taking Possession of a Promise

At the beginning of the book of Joshua, when God instructs Joshua to lead the Israelites across the Jordan in order for them to take possession of the land he had promised to give them, he impresses on Joshua several of the same points that have appeared previously in the biblical narrative. Joshua is to trust fully in God and in his promise to be with him, reflect continually on all that God has commanded in the Torah, and obey God's commands with care and diligence (Josh 1:6-9). At the same time, the opening section of the book stresses the purpose of that obedience: only by obeying God in all things will Joshua and the people be able to prosper and thrive in the way God desires in the land he is giving them (vv. 7-8). As we have seen elsewhere, the reason why obedience to God's commandments will bring blessing is not merely that God will act from heaven to grant the people abundance and prosperity but that in and of itself that obedience will allow them to enjoy well-being due to its natural and intrinsic consequences.

Throughout the book, for the most part both Joshua and the people are said to fulfill what God has commanded. As a result, with God's help they generally succeed in defeating the peoples who stand in their way and are able to take possession of the land.

In Josh 6:17-21, however, prior to the conquest of Jericho, the people are told not to take any spoil but to devote everything in the city to destruction, except for the items and vessels of precious metals that are to be dedicated to God for use at his sanctuary. After the Israelites take the city, one of the men named Achan sins by secretly taking some of the things that were to be devoted to God and hiding it under his tent (7:1-26). Immediately after Achan commits this sin, to the surprise of Joshua and the people under him the Israelites are defeated at the city of Ai. Initially, they wonder why God has not kept his promise to be with them and give them victory over the peoples he commands them to conquer. When God explains to Joshua that the reason for their defeat is that some of them have disobeyed him by taking some of the spoils from Jericho for themselves and subsequently reveals that the one guilty of this sin is Achan, at God's command the Israelites stone to death not only Achan himself but his family and animals as well. They then burn their corpses and all of their possessions. Undoubtedly this punishment is extremely harsh, especially because it includes Achan's family members. The narrative does not make it clear whether they are put to death because they knew of Achan's sin and said nothing, thereby becoming complicit in Achan's deed, or simply because the severity of the punishment inflicted on him would constitute an even stronger deterrent to any who might consider sinning in the same way that Achan had, since everyone would learn that if they disobeyed God in that way their families would be subjected to the same type of destruction. In any case, the severity of the punishment makes it clear that God does not take lightly what Achan did and will not tolerate any of his people doing the same.

The logic behind this account seems to be that the Israelites are not to enrich themselves at the expense of the peoples they defeat in the way that other nations of antiquity did when they conquered a city or people in order to subjugate them to themselves, enslave them, and take their possessions as plunder. Such was the practice of the great empires of antiquity, such as the Assyrians and the Babylonians, as well as the objective that the Achaeans or Greeks are said to have been pursuing when they attacked the city of Troy. If God's purpose is not that his people Israel subjugate, enslave, and oppress other peoples in that way but instead simply take possession of their land in order to practice justice and righteousness in that land once they have been established there, then in principle it would seem inappropriate for the Israelites to treat the peoples whom they conquer in the same way that other peoples of antiquity treated those whom they conquered. What appears to have made Achan's sin more serious is that what he took was to be devoted to God. Because Jericho was the first city that the Israelites were to take, it is possible that God's command for the Israelites not to take any plunder but to devote part of the spoils to God was thought to reflect the same logic underlying the commandments for the people to dedicate to God the firstborn of their children and animals as well as the first fruits of their harvest. Such a practice reinforced the idea that everything that they had and received came from God and continued to belong to him. For that reason, it was to be dedicated to his service and to be used in the way he commanded.

Elsewhere in the book of Joshua, however, God does allow the people to take as spoil the animals and other goods of the inhabitants of the cities that they exterminate and destroy.[2] In these instances, the logic seems to be that God is providing the people with the livestock and possessions that will enable them to have what they need to make a new start in the land into which they are entering.

---

2. See Josh 8:2; 11:14; 22:7-8; cf. Num 31:9-11; Deut 2:35; 3:7.

In Josh 11:20, God is said to have hardened the hearts of the inhabitants and kings of many of the cities and towns that the people conquer: "For it was the LORD himself who hardened their hearts so that they might go against Israel in battle, in order that they might be utterly destroyed and receive no mercy, but be exterminated, just as the LORD had commanded Moses." The logic underlying this passage is that which we have seen above, namely, that the people of those cities and towns must be destroyed if they are not to become a thorn in Israel's side or a "snare" by enticing the Israelites to worship their gods and adopt their customs.[3] If some of those cities and towns were to make treaties with the Israelites so as to continue to occupy the land, however, either of those things might happen. For that reason, as he states in this passage, God does not want the Israelites to show those peoples any mercy, even though they might feel compelled to do so out of compassion for them. Furthermore, while the destruction of these peoples is cruel enough as it is, for the Israelites to attack and destroy peoples who are not actively fighting against them and may even be asking for peace would be even more cruel. By hardening the hearts of these peoples and their kings so that they actively fight against the Israelites, therefore, God justifies their destruction at the hands of the Israelites and avoids making their destruction even more appalling than it already is. Of course, these peoples are already opposed to the Israelites taking their land and in that sense their hearts are already hard. By hardening their hearts even further, however, God simply makes them even more obstinate in their opposition to the Israelites, apparently so that the Israelites will feel less averse to attacking and destroying them in order to take their land.

At the end of the book, Joshua gathers together the people of Israel with their leaders and reminds them of all that God has done for them from the time of the patriarchs up until that moment (Josh 24:1-13). On that basis, Joshua exhorts them to put away all other gods in order to serve the God of Israel alone, as he will continue to do together with his own household (24:14-16). When the people promise to do what Joshua has mentioned, he responds to them: "You will not be able to serve the LORD, for he is a holy God. He is a jealous God; he will not forgive your transgressions or your sins. If you forsake the LORD and serve foreign gods, then he will turn and do you harm, and consume you, after having done good to you" (24:19-20). The people then insist once more in even stronger terms that they will serve the LORD God of Israel, and Joshua answers: "You are witnesses against yourselves that you have chosen the LORD, to serve him" (24:22). After the people promise once again to serve the God of Israel alone, Joshua writes the words of the covenant on a stone and sets it up in their presence as a monument before telling them: "See, this stone will be a witness against us; for it has heard all the words of the LORD that he spoke to us. Therefore it will be a witness against you, if you deny your God" (24:27).

---

3. On the idea that the other peoples in the land might constitute a "snare" for the Israelites, see especially Exod 23:33; 34:12; Deut 7:16; 12:30; Josh 23:13; Judg 2:3.

This dialogue clearly anticipates what will take place later on in Israel's history. Because both the redactors of the text and its readers know that in fact Israel will not remain faithful to the God of Israel but will abandon him for other gods, the narrative wishes to stress that following the conquest and settlement of the land the people had promised to be faithful to God and serve him alone. They had done so voluntarily, under no compulsion or obligation. Joshua's words make it clear that they are free *not* to serve the God of Israel if they instead wish to serve other gods, though of course if they abandon him he will no longer remain active among them to bless them in the ways that he has up until that moment. Nor will he give them the assistance and support they need to remain in the land that he has given them and prosper there, since the condition for giving them that land was that they commit themselves to living as his people.

Joshua's affirmation that the people will not be able to serve God because he is holy and jealous and will not forgive them when they sin is both a warning and a prophecy. Viewed in their context, his words are not simply a warning that God will punish the people if they abandon him for other gods because he is holy and jealous. Rather, they are a warning that *if the people commit themselves to serving him alone as God*, he will punish them for abandoning him. It is important to stress this distinction. In the biblical texts, God does not punish the nations that do not submit to him as their God for serving gods other than him. He lets them go their own way, and thus if Israel wishes to go its own way as well, the people are free to do so. In that case, however, God will no longer stand by the people and lend them his support, since they will have chosen to go down a path that is not good for them and will eventually lead to their ruin. If they commit themselves to serving him alone as God, however, he will demand that they continue to follow him in all that he commands because only in that way will he be able to accomplish his loving purposes among them. If they make such a commitment, therefore, they will be blessed, but it will also be necessary for God to punish and chastise the people if they begin to go astray and follow paths other than the one he has laid out for them.

Joshua's words thus anticipate what will happen once the people have settled in the land. If they pledge to follow and worship no god other than the LORD God of Israel, he will be able to bless them, yet he will also need to punish and chastise them when they break that pledge. In order to remind the people of this, at God's command Joshua sets up the stone monument to serve as a witness both of Israel's pledge as well as God's intention to hold Israel to that pledge, especially if the people begin to abandon him for other gods and break their pledge. The stone monument will therefore serve as a constant reminder not only of the commitment that the Israelites have made to God but also of the commitment that God has made to them, a commitment that he will not abandon the people no matter what they do.

What this section of the biblical narrative accomplishes, therefore, is to make it clear that whatever suffering that will come upon the people for their failure to serve and follow God is something to which they had given their consent from the time that they took possession of the land God was giving them. They had been warned of what would happen if they agreed to serve God alone and then failed to keep that promise, and they had agreed ahead of time to the consequences or chastisements that would follow upon that failure. When they are later subjected to sufferings in chastisement for their unfaithfulness, they have no one to blame but themselves. Of course, it must not be overlooked that God does not wish to impose anything on them against their will or force them to serve him. Instead, he desires to bring them to live under his loving guidance so that he may continue to be active to bless them as he has up to that point. The reason that God is holy and jealous and will not tolerate their serving other gods is that, as soon as they begin to do so, they will fall into the destructive behavior associated with the worship of those gods and as a consequence will no longer be able to experience the well-being that comes from serving him alone. Yet precisely because he loves the people and is committed to them, God will not relent in his efforts to accomplish his loving purposes among them if they commit themselves to him as he has to them.

SINKING BACK INTO A CYCLE OF CHAOS

Almost from the very beginning of the book of Judges, even before Joshua dies and is buried, the Israelites begin to disobey God. First, God accuses them of entering into pacts with the inhabitants of the land and failing to drive them out and destroy their altars (Judg 2:1-4). Immediately following Joshua's death, they abandon God and begin to serve the Baals (2:11-12). The people are also said to have "turned aside quickly from the way in which their ancestors had walked in obeying the commandments of the LORD" (2:17). Clearly, what Joshua had anticipated is taking place.

While the book of Joshua gives the impression that all of the other peoples in the land have been driven out or destroyed, the book of Judges affirms that God responds to the people's disobedience by allowing some of those peoples to remain in the land in order that through them he might continue to test and chastise the Israelites. God is presented as announcing: "Because this nation has transgressed my covenant that I commanded their ancestors and has not obeyed my voice, I will no longer drive out from their presence any of the nations that Joshua left when he died." The narrative then continues: "In order to test Israel, to see whether or not they would keep the way of the LORD to walk in it as their ancestors did, the LORD let those nations remain rather than driving them out at once, and had not handed them over to Joshua" (Judg 2:20-23). The same idea is repeated at the beginning of the following chapter, which mentions the names of the nations that God left in the land before affirming: "They were for the testing of Israel, to know whether Israel would obey the commandments of the LORD that he had commanded their ancestors through Moses" (3:4).

The use of the language of testing in these verses might seem to imply that God simply wished to see how Israel would respond to the ongoing presence of the other nations, almost as if he were driven by curiosity. As we have noted previously, however, according to the logic of the narrative God's purpose is not merely to find out whether or not the people will obey him. Rather, the testing of which the narrative speaks must be seen in relation to God's objective of bringing the people to obey him for their own good. If the people respond to the ongoing presence of the nations who are hostile to them by returning to him in obedience, then God may decide to deliver them from those nations by removing them from the land. If not, then he will not only continue to leave those nations in the land but will also take other measures in an attempt to bring his people to obey him. Were God to remove those nations from the land prior to finding out whether or not Israel will obey him, he would no longer be able to use them to accomplish his purposes in relation to Israel.

Furthermore, even if the Israelites became obedient to God and as a result he blessed them and saved them from the peoples who were hostile to them, in the past the people's obedience had been inconstant and short-lived. If they came to obey God simply because he was blessing them and delivering them from every hardship and adversity, he could not know how firm their obedience was or how long it would last. According to the logic of the text, therefore, in order to discern whether the Israelites have attained the level of obedience he desires to see in them for their own good, God must leave the other nations and peoples in place in order to be able to use them to continue to test Israel by subjecting Israel to suffering at their hands when he considers it necessary to do so. Only when he is convinced that the Israelites have finally been fashioned and molded into a people who will obey him under all circumstances and remain firm in that obedience on a long-term basis will he remove the other peoples from the land. In the meantime, however, he must continue to test and chastise Israel through those nations. This testing, therefore, has the purpose of allowing God to determine how best to proceed with his people in order to accomplish his objectives among them.

After God delivers the Israelites from the Canaanites at the hand of Deborah and Barak in Judges 4, the two of them raise a song of thanksgiving and praise to God. In this context, they rejoice that the people will recount the judgments of the LORD (Judg 5:11). Rather than speaking of God's judgments, most English versions of the Bible use words and phrases such as "victories," "triumphs," "righteous acts," or "righteous deeds" to translate the Hebrew plural noun *tsidqoth* that appears in this verse. As we have seen previously, however, such translations fail to capture adequately the meaning of the Hebrew. The allusion is instead to the manner in which God acts to deliver the oppressed from their oppressors. Because it has no exact English equivalent, the translation of the Hebrew term poses a problem. While the phrase "acts of deliverance" may be the best option, it fails to communicate clearly the idea that

God's purpose is to put an end to the oppression that the Israelites are enduring at the hands of those who are doing them harm. In any case, the motive for rejoicing is not merely that God has given the Israelites victory in battle or that he has shown himself to be righteous but that he has delivered the people from those who were abusing and mistreating them with great cruelty so that they may enjoy peace, well-being, and prosperity once more (4:3).

In a sense, the oppression that the Israelites endure is both just and unjust. It is just in that God subjects the Israelites to suffering at the hands of other nations in order to chastise and correct them and bring them back to the practice of justice and righteousness that is associated with serving the God of Israel alone. In this regard, it is important to stress once more that in biblical thought justice does not have to do with simply inflicting punishments on wrongdoers in order to make them pay for their sins by subjecting them to suffering. While the chastisements to which Israel is subjected are deserved, the objective is *not to give the Israelites what their actions deserve*, as if this in itself would establish justice, but *to bring them back to God in obedience for their own good* so that they may practice justice and righteousness in the way that is necessary for them to enjoy the well-being that God desires for them. As we have seen elsewhere, what interests God and satisfies his justice is not inflicting punishments for their own sake but correcting his people when they go astray by bringing them back to a way of life that will enable them to attain the good that he wishes to be theirs.

At the same time, the afflictions that the Israelites endure at the hands of other nations are *unjust*. Those nations are not seeking Israel's well-being or attempting to establish the practice of justice and righteousness among the Israelites when they afflict Israel. They are not liberators or defenders of what is good and right but cruel oppressors. They seek to harm and destroy the Israelites, not to help, guide, or correct them. For that reason, when Israel's judges deliver the people from these nations, they are saving them from injustice and oppression, even though the injustice and oppression to which Israel is subjected are in a sense ordained by God as a means of disciplining and correcting his people. Throughout the biblical narrative as a whole, in fact, we repeatedly find these same ideas. God uses other nations such as the Assyrians and the Babylonians to chastise Israel, yet those nations are regarded as practicing injustice and oppression and are therefore condemned for their activity even as God acts through them to accomplish his purposes in relation to Israel. Thus, for example, in Isa 10:5-19, God refers to Assyria as "the rod of my wrath," a nation commissioned by him to chastise Israel for his people's sins, yet at the same time he pronounces judgment and condemnation upon the Assyrians for their arrogant boasting and haughty pride and promises to destroy them as well.

The manner in which God is presented as delivering the Israelites from those who oppress them and seek to do them harm in Judges also stresses another theme that we have seen previously in the biblical narratives. Rather than accomplishing his purposes by means of individuals and peoples who are mighty and powerful, God manifests his power and greatness through those who are regarded as small, weak, and insignificant. As just noted above, in Judg 4:1-23 God chooses Deborah, a woman judge, to deliver the Israelites from the Canaanites. In that context, for a man to be overcome by a woman is considered to be so shameful that when Gideon's son Abimelech is crushed by a stone thrown by a woman, he has a young man put him to death so that it will not be said that he died at the hands of a woman (9:53-54). Elsewhere in Judges, when God calls Gideon to deliver the Israelites from the Midianites, Gideon initially responds: "How can I deliver Israel? My clan is the weakest in Manasseh, and I am the youngest in my family" (6:14-15). In the account that follows, rather than sending Gideon out to conquer the Midianites with an army of twenty-two thousand Israelites, God has him reduce the size of the army to three hundred in order to manifest to all his power (7:1-8). These stories and others in Judges thus illustrate once more the biblical truth that God acts to carry out his saving purposes not through individuals and peoples who appear to be strong and mighty and deserving of his favor and support, but rather through those who seem to be powerless and of little esteem in the eyes of the world.

As we have seen in Chapter 5 of this study, throughout the first part of the book of Judges God's relationship with his people Israel is defined by a cycle of sin, chastisement, repentance, and deliverance. When the people fall into sin by serving other gods, God subjects them to suffering at the hands of other nations in an attempt to correct and discipline them. As a result, the people eventually acknowledge their sin and turn back to God. On that basis, God acts to deliver them from their oppressors. It is not long, however, before the people return to their sinful ways and God finds it necessary to chastise them once more.

By presenting the history of Israel in this fashion, the book of Judges emphasizes not only the people's persistent stubbornness and rebelliousness but also God's unconditional love for them. It is clear that God wishes to bless his people with well-being and prosperity in the land that he has given them, yet their insistence on abandoning him and his commandments in order to serve other gods makes it impossible for him to do so in the way he desires. By serving other gods, they fill their lives with violence, injustice, and suffering, contrary to God's will. In his love, he cannot simply allow them to continue unabated in the destructive behavior that results from their devotion to other gods. Yet when the people fail to respond in the way he desires to his repeated efforts to correct them and bring them back to himself and his commandments through the sufferings and chastisements that he imposes on them, it is not clear what else God can do. His only option appears to be that of subjecting them to even greater pain and hardships. When that consistently fails to produce in them the changes that he desires to see for their own good, however, he must resort to measures that are even more extreme, unless of course he chooses to abandon the people definitively. In that case, he would be handing them over to their own destruction. His unconditional love for his people would never allow him to do such a thing. Therefore, that love leaves him with no choice but to continue in his efforts to bring them into conformity with his will rather than giving up on them.

In the face of his people's persistent disobedience and hardness of heart, throughout Judges God is presented as becoming increasingly angry and frustrated with them. Eventually, God becomes so exasperated that when the people cry out to him for help in Judg 10:6-16, he refuses to come to their aid. He tells them instead to cry out to the other gods that they have chosen for themselves. In this context, he also reminds them that he has repeatedly saved them from the nations that oppressed them in the past, yet each time they have responded by turning away from him to serve those other gods once more. When the people put away those gods and in essence ask God to give them one last chance, however, he finally relents and acts to deliver them from the Ammonites who have been oppressing them. God's unconditional love for the people is evident from the affirmation that he decided to save the people because "he could no longer bear to see Israel suffer" (v. 16).

Although this account might appear to give the impression that God had reached a point at which he was ready to give up definitively on his people and abandon them for good, the fact that he is said to be unable to bear the pain of seeing them continue to suffer indicates clearly that he continues to love them and desire nothing but their well-being. The idea that God saves the people because he is moved to pity when they suffer has already been stated in the narrative in Judg 2:18, which affirms that when God subjected them to punishment at the hands of their enemies, he was repeatedly "moved to compassion by their groaning because of those who afflicted and oppressed them." These passages make it clear that God's love for the people is constant and unchanging. While he may abandon them for a time in order to allow them to endure the consequences of their destructive behavior and their failure to trust in him, he can never give up on them or destroy them entirely. If he becomes increasingly angry and frustrated with them, it is not because their actions have offended or harmed him personally but because he is deeply pained and grieved at seeing them continually do themselves such great harm by abandoning him for other gods whose worship promotes injustice and violence rather than justice, equity, and well-being for all. For that reason, the people's stubbornness and rebelliousness must be seen as causing pain not only to them but to God as well. Nevertheless, what leads God to experience this pain is not a concern *for himself* but his concern *for the people whom he loves.*

Although for the most part throughout the last half of the book of Judges the people refrain from worshiping other gods, they continue in other forms of disobedience. Even when they pledge themselves to serving the God of Israel, they do so in ways that are contrary to his will. They also fall into behavior that is increasingly destructive, cruel, and even barbaric. After God gives Gideon the victory over the Midianites, for example, Gideon has the earrings of the Midianites made into an ephod that entices the Israelites and his own descendants to engage in acts of idolatry (Judg 8:22-28). Subsequently, when God raises up Jephthah as judge to deliver the Israelites from the Ammonites, Jephthah makes a vow that if God gives him victory, when he returns home he will sacrifice to God whatever comes first out of his house. Upon his return, his daughter is the first to come out, and rather than renouncing his vow, Jephthah offers her up to God (11:29-40). In Judges 17 and 18, an Ephraimite named Micah makes an idol and a shrine of his own for Israel's God and then hires a Levite to serve as his own personal priest at the shrine, thus violating explicit commandments of the Torah. At the end of the book, a group of inhabitants of the Benjaminite town of Gibeah rape and abuse the concubine of a Levite throughout the night, leaving her dead. When the Levite discovers her corpse the next morning, he cuts it up and sends the pieces to the other tribes of Israel, who are shocked and remark that nothing so perverse and wicked had ever been done since the Israelites came into the land (19:1-30). The Israelite tribes then join together and virtually exterminate the tribe of Benjamin before deciding not to destroy the Benjaminites entirely (20:1–21:5). Because the Benjaminites need wives in order to generate offspring, the tribes then turn on one of the Israelite towns named Jabesh-Gilead and massacre the population, sparing only four hundred young virgins who are then given to the men from Benjamin (21:6-24).

When considering these passages, it is important to stress that the narrative nowhere states or implies that God approves of things such as those just mentioned. Nothing in the account of the story of Jephthah's daughter, for example, indicates that God was pleased when she was offered up to him in sacrifice, and much less that it was God who demanded that Jephthah keep his vow. On the contrary, God's strict prohibition of human sacrifice throughout the Hebrew Bible clearly suggests that he would have been extremely displeased with what Jephthah had done. The same could be said with regard to the account of the Levite and his concubine as well as the other stories just mentioned. The God who up to this point in the narrative has made himself known to the Israelites in Egypt, at Sinai, in the wilderness, and during the conquest under Joshua hardly can be thought to look with approval on the manner in which his people behave in passages such as these, even when in some cases they appear to be acting out of dedication and devotion to him.

By the end of the book, it also becomes evident that if God is going to accomplish his purposes in and through Israel, some other type of leadership will be necessary. For the reasons just seen, judges such as Gideon and Jephthah, who is described as the son of a prostitute and an outlaw (Judg 11:1-3), are certainly not the kind of leaders that the people need. The same is true of Samson, whose attraction to a foreign woman who manipulates and deceives him ends up ruining him (Judges 14–16). The manner in which the book concludes makes it clear that during the period of the Judges the Israelites have fallen into depravity and utter chaos. Rather than living together as a single people, the tribes of Israel remain divided and dispersed. They do not join together to fight alongside one another until they attack their own flesh and blood, the Benjaminites. Both in Judg 17:6 and in the final verse of Judges, it is said that "in those days there was no king in Israel" and therefore that "all the people did what was right in their own eyes," that is, whatever they pleased (21:25). These verses thus imply that the chaos, division, and depravity into which the Israelites have fallen will continue as long as the people do not have a king to lead them and rule over them.

THE ASCENT AND DESCENT OF ISRAEL'S KINGS

Several of the themes that are stressed in Judges are prominent in 1 Samuel as well. In particular, the idea that God cares especially for those who are weak, downtrodden, and marginalized is stressed at the very outset of the book. Because she has not been able to conceive a child, Hannah is berated and treated with scorn. In her helplessness and distress she begs God to give her a child, promising to dedicate the child to God's service should he do so (1 Sam 1:1-18). God answers her prayer and as a result Samuel is born (1:19-28). In the song of thanksgiving attributed to Hannah, she rejoices that God comes to the aid of those who are poor, feeble, hungry, barren, and at the point of extinction, raising them up and filling them with good things (2:1-10). The same basic idea runs throughout other passages in the book. The first king chosen by God is Saul, who works in the fields with donkeys and oxen and belongs to "the least of all the families of the tribe of Benjamin," which is also "the smallest of the tribes of Israel" (9:1-21; 11:5). When God tells Samuel to anoint another king as a result of Saul's failures, he sends Samuel to the tiny and insignificant village of Bethlehem and has him pass over the older brothers of Jesse in order to choose the youngest, David, who is only an adolescent (16:1-13). Then, when all the Israelites cower in fear at the possibility of confronting the Philistine giant Goliath, David volunteers to fight against him and kills him with a rock cast from his sling (17:20-54). In this way, he demonstrates to all that God "does not deliver by sword or spear" but simply through the faith of those who trust in him (17:45-47).

The idea that the tribes of Israel are in a state of chaos and disorder and suffering injustice and oppression due to a lack of the type of leadership they need is also stressed at the outset of 1 Samuel. The sons of the frail and elderly judge and high priest Eli engage in acts of corruption and immorality as they serve at the sanctuary in Shiloh, thus tainting the worship offered to Israel's God there (1 Sam 2:12-17, 22-36). The Israelites fall under the power of the Philistines, who not only defeat and slaughter them in battle but also humiliate them by taking the ark of the covenant from them (4:1-11). When Eli hears that his two sons have been killed in the battle and that the ark has been taken, he keels over dead (4:13-18). While the ark is subsequently recovered and the Israelites are able to drive the Philistines out of their territory under the leadership of Samuel, who brings them to put away their other gods and serve the God of Israel alone, the situation of the people continues to be precarious (6:1–7:14). Although the people experience forty years of peace under Samuel, when he grows old and approaches his death it is not clear where the religious and political leadership that the people need will come from, especially since Samuel's own sons become just as corrupt as those of Eli were (8:1-5).

In this context, the elders of Israel ask Samuel to appoint a king over them (1 Sam 8:5). In the narrative that follows, this petition is portrayed as a rejection of Israel's God, yet at the same time the appointment of a king seems to be necessary and to serve as a means by which God intends to bless the people and save them from their enemies. On the one hand, by asking for a king, the people are said to be rejecting God himself as the only true king who is to reign over them (1 Sam 8:67; 10:19; 12:12; cf. Judg 8:22-23). The people's affirmation that having a king will allow them to become like the other nations is ironic and tragic, given that they have been chosen by God to be *different* from all other nations. The same is true of God's instruction to Samuel to "listen to the voice of the people in all that they say," since it implies that it is now God who is obeying the people rather than the people obeying God (1 Sam 8:5-9, 19-20). Samuel also warns the people that the king will become an oppressive figure, since he will take for himself their sons and daughters and the harvest of their fields (8:10-17). He adds that when they cry out to God as a result of the difficulties and hardships they will endure under the kings placed over them, God will not listen to them, obviously because they had been forewarned and God will require that they submit fully to the consequences of their decision to demand a king (8:18).

On the other hand, however, God himself promises to do good to the people by means of the kings he places over them. When the people request a king, they are presented as defining the purpose of the king in terms of judging them, that is, delivering them from their enemies and establishing justice among them: "Give us a king to judge us" (1 Sam 8:5-6, 19-20). While in one sense it will no longer be God himself who will act as their king by leading them in battle and delivering them from their enemies as he has in the past, in another sense God will use the king as his instrument in order to continue to do these same things through him. When he reveals to Samuel that he has chosen Saul to be king, God tells Samuel: "You shall anoint him to be ruler over my people Israel. He will save my people from the hand of the Philistines; for I have seen the affliction of my people, because their out-cry has come to me" (9:16). Here the language of the narrative echoes that of Exodus, where God is said to take pity upon the people as a result of their cries for help (Exod 2:23-25; 3:7-9). Thus, while the narrative presents the people's demand for a king as a lack of trust in God and an expression of their wickedness, at the same time God has Samuel tell them:

Do not be afraid. You have done all this evil, yet do not turn aside from following the Lord, but serve the Lord with all your heart; and do not turn aside to go after useless things that cannot profit or save, for they are useless. For on account of his great name the Lord will not abandon his people, because it has pleased the Lord to make of you a people for himself. Moreover, as for me, far be it from me that I should sin against the Lord by ceasing to pray for you; but I will instruct you in the way that is good and right. Only fear the Lord, and serve him faithfully with all your heart; for consider what great things he has done for you. But if you still do wickedly, both you and your king will be swept away (1 Sam 12:20-25).

Here the idea is that, even though the people have sinned, as long as they serve and obey God under their king, God will bless them.

Earlier in the same chapter, Samuel is presented as telling the people: "If you fear the Lord and serve him and heed his voice, and do not rebel against the commandment of the Lord, and if both you and the king who reigns over you follow the Lord your God, it will be well; but if you do not heed the voice of the Lord, but rebel against the commandment of the Lord, then the hand of the Lord will be against you and your king" (1 Sam 12:14-15). Here the obedience of the people is tied to the obedience of the king. This idea is central to the narrative that runs throughout the remainder of the books of Samuel, Kings, and Chronicles. If the king is faithful to Israel's God, he will lead the people as a whole to be faithful as well. However, if the king fails to serve Israel's God in the way that the Torah prescribes and instead allows for the worship of other gods, he will lead the people as a whole to fall into sin and idolatry. If that happens, God will need to inflict suffering upon the people in order to chastise them and attempt to bring them back to himself. Yet if the king himself is not brought back to serve Israel's God exclusively in the way that he commands, the people will also fail to turn back to Israel's God to serve him. For that reason, it is of utmost importance that the king obey God in all things so that the people may be brought to do the same.

According to the narrative of 1 Samuel, Saul disobeys God almost from the start. First, when Samuel delays in coming to Gilgal, where Saul and the Israelite army are waiting in order to engage the Philistines, rather than waiting any longer for Samuel to arrive in order to offer up the sacrifices imploring God's favor prior to the battle, Saul offers up the sacrifices himself (1 Sam 13:5-10). Upon his arrival, Samuel condemns what Saul has done: "You have acted foolishly. You have not kept the commandment of the Lord your God, which he gave you. The Lord would have established your kingdom over Israel forever, but now your kingdom will not endure. The Lord has sought out a man after his own heart; and the Lord has appointed him to be ruler over his people, because you have not obeyed what the Lord commanded you" (13:13-14). While in principle Saul's intentions may have been good, in the eyes of God and Samuel what matters is that he obey God in all things, trusting that if God commands for things to be done in a certain way, he has a reason for doing so.

A couple of chapters later, Saul disobeys God's command to exterminate the Amalekites fully and spares the best of the sheep and oxen that his army has captured in order to sacrifice them to God (1 Sam 15:1-21). God responds to Saul's disobedience by telling Samuel: "I regret that I made Saul king, for he has turned back from following me, and has not carried out my commands" (15:11). In a passage we have seen previously, Samuel tells Saul that what pleases God is not burnt offerings and sacrifices but obedience to his commands (15:22-23). Samuel then adds: "Because you have rejected the word of the LORD, he has also rejected you from being king" (15:23). Even when Saul acknowledges his sin and begs forgiveness, Samuel tells him once more: "You have rejected the word of the LORD, and the LORD has rejected you from being king over Israel. . . . The LORD has torn the kingdom of Israel from you this very day, and has given it to one of your neighbors, who is better than you" (15:26, 28). The allusion here is clearly to David, whom Samuel anoints as Israel's next king in the following chapter (16:1-13).

Throughout the remainder of 1 Samuel, Saul is presented almost exclusively in a negative light, in contrast to David, who is said to have been "successful in all that he did, for the LORD was with him" (1 Sam 18:14). Saul seeks to kill David, but David repeatedly escapes and on a couple of occasions even has the opportunity to kill Saul (1 Sam 24:1-22; 26:1-25). As a result, Saul tells David: "You are more righteous than I am; for you have repaid me good, whereas I have repaid you evil" (24:17). The narrative presents Saul as falling increasingly into erratic behavior and continuing to arouse God's anger and displeasure. As a result of Saul's persecution, David is forced to take refuge among the Philistines. When God will no longer have anything to do with Saul and has become his "enemy," he consults Samuel through a medium who brings Samuel back from the dead, and Samuel tells Saul that the next day he and his sons will die in battle (28:3-19).

Behind God's rejection of Saul is a clear logic. Saul's behavior makes it evident that he will not be able to serve as God's instrument to bring his people to obey him and serve him faithfully so that he may bless them, since Saul himself does not trust in God and obey him as he should. God's rejection of Saul and his refusal to forgive him in the sense of overlooking his persistent disobedience are therefore not an expression of hatred or animosity for Saul but are instead grounded in God's realization that he will never be able to carry out his plan to bless Israel and the other nations of the world by means of Saul and his descendants.

A King after God's Own Heart

At first glance, the narrative that appears in the last part of 1 Samuel and throughout all of 2 Samuel appears to portray David in an extremely favorable manner. Undoubtedly, it mentions two grave sins committed by David, namely, the killing of Uriah the Hittite after David has committed adultery with Uriah's wife Bathsheba and David's order to take a census among the

Israelites (2 Sam 11:1-27; 24:1-17). Even in these instances, however, David is presented as confessing his sin without hesitation, submitting willingly to the punishments imposed by God while implicitly acknowledging that those punishments are just and well-deserved, and manifesting openly his repentance by humbly carrying out acts that demonstrate his renewed dedication to God (12:1-23; 24:10-25). Even when David sins, therefore, he is presented as responding to God's chastisements in ways that please God greatly and even move God to alleviate the chastisements imposed (12:13-14; 24:16).

When the narrative regarding David in 1 and 2 Samuel is read carefully, however, it becomes evident that the narrator has presented David in a much more favorable light than his actions and reputation may have warranted.[4] At times David appears to act in ways that are underhanded, devious, and double-dealing in order to consolidate his power and impose his will by force and violence on those who oppose him and stand in his way. Certain passages even suggest that he may have usurped Saul's throne and that he may not have been as loved and revered among the people as the narrative suggests (2 Sam 15:13; 16:5-14; 20:1-2). Even when David mourns the death of figures such as Saul, Abner, and Absalom, the overt and exaggerated manner in which he does so seems to suggest that his grief may not be entirely sincere and that he is seeking to convince the populace that he played no role in their deaths, when such may not actually have been the case (2 Sam 1:1-27; 3:31-39; 18:33–19:7). Similarly, when David shows kindness to figures such as Shimei and Mephibosheth, the reader may get the impression that he does so for ulterior motives that are not as altruistic and selfless as they may seem (2 Sam 9:1-13; 16:5-14; 19:18-30; 21:1-9; 1 Kgs 2:8-9).

While this tendency to cover over David's flaws and misdeeds and portray him in ways that are much more favorable than his conduct may have merited is not as obvious in 1 and 2 Samuel as it is in 1 and 2 Chronicles, one cannot help but wonder whether it would have been as apparent to readers of the narrative regarding David in antiquity as it is to those who read that narrative with a measure of suspicion today. In fact, one may even wonder whether the narrator or the final redactors of the narrative in 1 and 2 Samuel intentionally left in the text certain hints for the readers that David had not been as righteous and exemplary of a figure as a cursory reading of the narrative would suggest. If so, they would probably have been intending to convey to the readers some truth that they regarded as important, such as the conviction that God can accomplish his good purposes through leaders and figures whose conduct is at times unacceptable and reprehensible or the belief that sin, evil, hypocrisy, and duplicity are present even in those who are most dedicated to doing God's will.

In any case, the biblical narrative regarding David makes it abundantly clear that he is greatly favored by God in spite of any defects and flaws he has and that the basis for this favor is his tremendous love for God and his

---

4. On what follows, see especially James L. Kugel, *How to Read the Bible: A Guide to Scripture, Then and Now* (New York: Free Press, 2007), 482-84.

commitment to doing whatever God asks and desires. What especially seems to please God is the spontaneity and heartfelt sincerity of the love and devotion that David displays for him. Just as the trust he shows in God when he goes out to meet Goliath is like that of a small child whose blind faith in his father's power to protect him is unshakable, so also the unbridled joy and exhilaration that David displays when singing and dancing before the ark of the covenant as the symbol of God's presence remind one of a child whose adoration for his father knows no bounds (1 Sam 17:31-47; 2 Sam 6:5, 14-16, 21-23). David's petition to God to allow him to build him a house or temple is also presented as something that arises spontaneously at his own initiative out of the deep love and devotion that he feels for God (2 Sam 7:1-7). It is in response to that petition that God promises to bless David, treat him always with steadfast love as a father treats a son who is dear to him, and establish his throne permanently, even though God ultimately rejects David's request to build him a temple (2 Sam 7:8-16). David in turn reacts to the promises God has made to him by heaping thanksgiving and praise upon God for the magnitude of the grace, kindness, and mercy he has shown both to David personally and to his people Israel as a whole (2 Sam 7:18-29). In spite of David's faults and flaws, therefore, he clearly takes great delight in God, and God takes great delight in David as well. As the meaning of his name in Hebrew indicates, David is truly beloved by God.

The fact that the narrative refers repeatedly to David singing and playing music and even includes the texts of several of the songs he composed is also significant.[5] There can be little doubt that most Jews in the Second Temple period who read the narrative regarding David in 1 and 2 Samuel were well-acquainted with many of the songs or psalms attributed to him in the book of Psalms. If so, they knew that most of these songs were expressions of love, dedication, praise, and thanksgiving to God. By means of these songs, David had not only proclaimed his own sincere and profound devotion to Israel's God but had also provided a means by which God's people as a whole might do the same. While it was Solomon who ultimately built the temple in Jerusalem, the initiative had been entirely that of David, as the narrative in 1 Chronicles 28–29 later sought to stress. In 1 Chronicles 22–29, in fact, it is David who provides all of the material for the temple and makes all of the preparations necessary for its construction. In this way, he too is presented as building the temple in a sense, even though strictly speaking that task falls to Solomon. Both through the psalms he wrote and the planning and construction of the temple, David had therefore established two of the most important means by which God's people would express their love and devotion to him and be constantly inspired and aroused to grow stronger in that love and devotion. The immense love and favor that God shows to David in the narrative and elsewhere in the biblical texts would therefore be seen as a response not only to David's own personal devotion to God but also and especially to

---

5. See, for example, 1 Sam 16:14-23; 18:10; 19:9; 2 Sam 1:19-27; 3:33-34; 22:1–23:7.

the manner in which David had influenced God's people as a whole to love and serve him with the same joy, passion, conviction, and heartfelt sincerity that he had himself shown for God throughout his life.

The narrative regarding David stresses not only David's love for God but also his unbending trust in God and his mercy, kindness, and forgiveness. Of course, this is a primary theme in the book of Psalms as well. From the very beginning of the narrative in 1 and 2 Samuel, David is presented as constantly inquiring as to God's will and seeking God's guidance and direction in all that he does.[6] This same trust also leads David to obey God in all things, with the exceptions noted above. He also looks to God for the strength necessary to overcome his enemies and to do what God commands of him.[7] For that reason, all that he accomplishes is seen not only as his own work but the work of God through him. Furthermore, just as David's own love for God serves to generate the same type of love in the people as a whole, so also his own unwavering and resolute trust in God influences those over whom he rules to trust in God in the same way and with the same conviction.

For these reasons, in spite of David's flaws, the narrative consistently extols David for his goodness and righteousness and presents him as Israel's greatest king. He not only leads the people to love and serve God by practicing justice and righteousness but also serves as God's instrument to guide his people and care for them as their shepherd (2 Sam 5:2). Thus, while in one sense it is God himself who shepherds his people, in another sense it is David who does so as the one whom God has placed over the people to care for them as his sheep. In a similar manner, while in one sense God's appointment of a king means that it is no longer God himself who rules over Israel, in another sense as a result of David's faithfulness and obedience to God and his trust in God's guidance, God can be said to rule over Israel through David as the rock on whom David stands (22:2-3, 47; 23:3-4). What God ultimately seeks to accomplish through Israel's king is to allow his people to thrive and be blessed by practicing justice and righteousness in the way that is necessary for them to enjoy the well-being he seeks for them. It is this that God is said to accomplish through David: "So David reigned over all Israel; and David administered justice and equity to all his people" (8:15). David accomplishes this objective not only by judging the people as their king but also by leading and inciting them to practice justice and righteousness themselves in the ways mentioned above. In addition, David acts as God's instrument to save the people from their enemies so that they may live in peace and prosperity, free from fear and oppression (3:18; 7:10-11). He thus rules as king, *not for his own sake*, but *for the sake of the people whom God desires to bless through him*: "David then perceived that the LORD had established him as king over Israel and that he had exalted his kingdom *for the sake of his people Israel*" (5:12).

---

6. See, for example, 1 Sam 23:2-5; 30:8; 2 Sam 5:19, 23, 25.
7. See, for example, 1 Sam 17:37, 45-47; 30:6; 2 Sam 22:33, 40.

Toward the end of the narrative regarding David that appears in 2 Samuel, David's relationship to God is expressed by means of a psalm that also appears in the book of Psalms as Psalm 18. The Psalm not only underscores David's trust in God as the one who protects and delivers him but also mentions the delight that God takes in David (2 Sam 22:2-20, 29-51). David also affirms that God has saved and blessed him as a result of his righteousness, purity, and blameless obedience (22:21-27). According to the narrative itself, of course, David was not actually blameless or perfectly righteous. It must be remembered, however, that in biblical thought what characterizes those who are called blameless and righteous is not that they are without sin but that, when they sin, they sincerely repent of that sin and consecrate themselves anew to God's service.

Although many English translations use the language of reward and recompense in 2 Sam 22:21-27 to speak of the blessings and favor that God bestows on David in response to his righteousness, as we have seen in Chapters 4 and 5 of this study, this should not be understood in the sense that David has earned God's blessings and favor through his own merits and righteous behavior. According to biblical thought, had David been attempting to obtain personal rewards by means of righteous behavior and obedience to God's will, that behavior would not truly have been righteous, nor would he truly have been obeying God. The reason for this is that, by definition, to practice justice and righteousness and to obey God involves seeking the well-being of others for their own sake rather than pursuing personal interests and benefits. Any who do the latter are behaving *unrighteously* and *failing* to obey God. Rather than meriting God's blessings, those who behave in that manner merit his censure and condemnation. If God has responded favorably to David's behavior, therefore, it is because through that behavior David has committed himself fully to seeking the well-being of others by promoting justice and equity among them in the way that God desires. According to the logic of David's words, God has saved and delivered David precisely because he is dedicated to doing God's will in this regard. Furthermore, if David has done what is good and right, it is only by God's grace, since God is the one who chose David without regard to any merit on his part—as the story of his anointing by Samuel makes clear—and has instructed, guided, strengthened, and empowered David to do all that he has done. For that reason, to use the language of reward and recompense in this context may be misleading, since it might be seen as implying that David behaved in the way he did simply to gain some reward from God and that God grants his love and favor to those who obey him because he desires such obedience for *his own* sake rather than for *their* sake and the sake of those whom they serve.

While affirmations of God's approval for David appear throughout the narrative of 1 and 2 Samuel, they appear even more frequently and explicitly in the books of 1 and 2 Kings. There the kings of Israel and Judah are constantly compared to David, generally in order to contrast their sin and disobedience with David's righteousness and faithfulness. In 1 Kgs 3:6, Solomon is presented as telling God at the very beginning of his reign: "You have shown great and steadfast love to your servant my father David, because he walked before you in faithfulness, in righteousness, and in uprightness of heart toward you; and you have kept for him this great and steadfast love, and have given him a son to sit on his throne today." Toward the end of the narrative that recounts Solomon's reign, however, it is said that "his heart was not true to the Lord his God, as was the heart of his father David" and that "Solomon did what was evil in the sight of the Lord, and did not completely follow the Lord, as his father David had done" (1 Kgs 11:4, 6).

In a similar manner, when God appoints Jeroboam to be king over Israel, he tells him: "If you listen to all that I command you, walk in my ways, and do what is right in my sight by keeping my statutes and my commandments, as David my servant did, I will be with you, and I will build for you an enduring house, as I built for David, and I will give Israel to you" (1 Kgs 11:38). Toward the end of Jeroboam's reign, however, God tells him: "You have not been like my servant David, who kept my commandments and followed me with all his heart, doing only that which was right in my sight" (14:8). In 1 Kings 15:3, it is said of king Abijam of Judah that "his heart was not wholly devoted to the Lord his God, like the heart of his father David." A couple of verses later, Abijam is reminded that "David did what was right in the sight of the Lord, and did not turn aside from anything that he commanded him all the days of his life, except in the matter of Uriah the Hittite" (15:5). David's righteousness and obedience to God are stressed in several other passages in the narrative regarding the kings of Israel and Judah as well.[8] It is worth noting that several of these passages speak not only of David's righteousness and obedience but the fact that he followed God with his whole heart.

This favorable view of David is stressed even more strongly in 1 and 2 Chronicles. There the narrative omits mention of David's act of adultery with Bathsheba and his murder of Uriah and also suppresses or alters other affirmations from 1 and 2 Samuel that are unfavorable to David. His commitment to serving God and practicing justice and righteousness is also stressed in the prayer attributed to him in 1 Chr 29:10-19. There, after blessing God for his greatness and goodness, David tells God:

> I know, my God, that you search the heart and take pleasure in uprightness; in the uprightness of my heart I have offered all these things willingly, and now I have seen your people, who are present here, offering willingly and joyously to you. O Lord, the God of Abraham, Isaac, and Israel, our ancestors, keep such intentions in the hearts of your people forever, and direct their hearts toward you. Grant to my son Solomon a heart wholly dedicated to keeping your commandments, your decrees, and your statutes, fulfilling all of them, and grant that he may build the temple for which I have made provision (vv. 17-19).

Here David points not only to his own sincere love and devotion to God but the fact that the temple for which he has made all the necessary preparations will

---

8. See 1 Kgs 11:33-34; 15:11; 2 Kgs 14:3; 16:2; 22:2.

serve as a means for the people to make their own offerings to God "willingly and joyously." David also asks God to keep the hearts, purposes, and thoughts of the people and his son Solomon directed toward God, thus making clear his desire to see in others the same type of love and devotion for God that he has manifested in his own lifetime. It is all of this that greatly pleases God.

The Glories of a Kingdom Soon to Fade

At its outset, the narrative regarding Solomon that appears in 1 Kings reflects the same ideas regarding what God desires and demands of a king. Initially, it is said that "Solomon loved the LORD, walking in the statutes of David his father," except for the fact that he sacrificed to God in the high places (1 Kgs 3:3). When God offers to give Solomon whatever he would like, he is extremely pleased that Solomon asks for wisdom and the ability to discern right and wrong so that he may judge the people, that is, execute justice among them for their own well-being (3:9-12). When Solomon begins to judge the people with great wisdom, they too respond favorably (3:16-28). His wisdom soon becomes known throughout the world (4:29-34).

From the beginning of his reign, Solomon is said to offer God lavish offerings out of love for him (1 Kings 3:3-4, 15). When God responds by bestowing even greater riches on Solomon and extending his kingdom far beyond its previous boundaries, Solomon's offerings become even more bountiful (4:21-28). The people too are greatly blessed: "Judah and Israel were as numerous as the grains of sand by the sea; they ate and drank and were happy" (4:20). Solomon himself comments to King Hiram of Tyre: "Now the LORD my God has given me rest on every side; there is neither adversary nor misfortune" (5:4).

With the help of Hiram, Solomon also begins to build the temple. Even though Hiram is presented very favorably in the narrative, given that the Phoenician inhabitants of Tyre like Hiram himself were known to worship other gods and that the Phoenicians were reputed to have practiced child sacrifice, it is not clear whether the narrative intends to portray the influence of Hiram solely in positive terms. In any case, almost from the start, the account of the temple's construction provides hints that it will in some ways prove to be oppressive when it reports that "King Solomon conscripted forced labor out of all Israel; the levy numbered thirty thousand men" (1 Kgs 5:13). While the biblical text describes at great length the ornate beauty and majesty of Solomon's construction, it is not entirely clear that this is a good thing, given the tremendous cost involved in raising up and maintaining such a building and the corruption, injustice, and oppression that tend to be associated with great wealth in Israel's Scriptures. It would also have been well-known to the readers of the narrative that the grandiose and ostentatious buildings and monuments constructed by kings tend to be used to justify and promote their domination and subjugation of the peoples over whom they rule through force and imposition.

The narrative of Solomon's dedication of the temple in 1 Kings 8 seems to display the same ambiguity and ambivalence regarding the temple. On the one hand, the fact that Solomon sacrifices "so many sheep and oxen that they could not be counted or numbered" can be seen as an expression of the depth and enormity of his love and devotion to God (1 Kgs 8:5, 62-64). The affirmation that "the glory of the LORD filled the house of the LORD" in the form of a cloud so thick that the priests could not bear to minister to God in the holy place suggests that God looked extremely favorably upon the temple Solomon was dedicating to him (vv. 10-12). On the other hand, however, there may be some irony involved in the claim that the glory was so great that the priests were unable to carry out their duties aimed at honoring God there. The central and prominent role that Solomon assumes in the ceremony of dedication also seems to raise the question of the extent to which his aim is that of glorifying God or alternatively that of glorifying himself as God's representative and the benefactor that God has placed over his people. In his prayer of intercession on behalf of the people, he also casts himself as mediator between God and the people, thus assuming a role generally assigned to the priests and high priest (8:28-53). When Solomon stands before the altar affirming that it is he who has built God a house and provided a place for the ark, telling God that "there is no God like you in heaven above or on earth below" and reminding God of his promise to keep David's sons on the throne perpetually, many readers could not help but wonder if Solomon's words are intended only to exalt God or to exalt himself as well as the one who has provided such a great God with a house or dwelling of his own (8:14-26, 43-44, 48).

For the same reasons, even though the petitions that Solomon offers up in his prayer of dedication are in conformity with justice and righteousness and stress God's love, mercy, grace, and forgiveness, the fact that it is Solomon who presents those petitions rather than the high priest or the people as a whole suggests that, if God does respond favorably to the prayers that the people will offer up to him while at the temple or facing toward it, it will be in large part thanks to Solomon's intercession on their behalf. It is also worth noting that in his prayer Solomon does not allude to prayers and offerings presented to God purely out of a spirit of devotion, praise, and thanksgiving but instead refers almost exclusively to the prayers that the people will present when they have sinned and as a consequence have been subjected to chastisements at God's hands. The prayer also anticipates that God will send the people into exile on account of their sins (1 Kgs 8:33-34, 46-51). This emphasis on the fact that the people will repeatedly fall into sin and require God's forgiveness seems to suggest that what will result from the construction of the temple is not an increase in the practice of righteousness and a greater obedience to God's commandments among the people but instead a descent into the sin that will bring God to banish them from the land.

Of course, both the prayer and the blessing that Solomon pronounces upon the people at the end of his prayer stress the need for the people to obey God's commandments, practice righteousness, and turn back to God when they sin. Nevertheless, Solomon's words can also be interpreted in the sense that if the people do all of these things, it will be thanks at least in part to Solomon's leadership and the plea he has presented to God on their behalf. Similar observations can be made concerning Solomon's petition that God receive favorably the petitions of the foreigners from distant lands who come to pray at or toward the temple after hearing of the greatness of God's name and the power of his hand and arm (1 Kgs 8:41-43). When Solomon tells God: "hear in heaven your dwelling place, and do according to all that the foreigner calls to you, so that all the peoples of the earth may know your name and fear you, as do your people Israel, and so that they may know that your name has been invoked on this house that I have built," his words can be understood as expressing the hope that the temple he has built will lead people of all nations to acknowledge and fear not only God but also the king who has made God's glory and power known to all by building such a magnificent temple.

Immediately following the account of the temple's dedication, God appears to Solomon to tell him that he has received favorably the prayer that Solomon has offered up (1 Kgs 9:1-3). God then adds that, in accordance with the promise he made to David, he will establish Solomon's throne forever. Unlike the promise God originally made to David in 2 Sam 7:11-16, however, the promise God makes to Solomon is conditional:

> As for you, if you will walk before me as David your father walked, in integrity of heart and uprightness, doing all that I have commanded you and keeping my statutes and my ordinances, then I will establish your royal throne over Israel forever, as I promised David your father, saying, "You will never fail to have a successor on the throne of Israel." But if you or your children turn aside from following me, and do not keep my commandments and my statutes that I have set before you, but go and serve other gods and worship them, then I will cut Israel off from the land that I have given them; and the house that I have consecrated for my name I will cast out of my sight; and Israel will become a proverb and a byword among all peoples. This house will become a heap of ruins; everyone passing by it will be astonished and will hiss; and they will say, "Why has the LORD done this to this land and to this house?" Then they will say, "Because they abandoned the LORD their God, who brought their ancestors out of the land of Egypt, and embraced other gods to worship and serve them; therefore the LORD brought this disaster upon them" (1 Kgs 9:4-9; cf. 2:4).

This passage clearly anticipates precisely what will happen as a result of the failure of Solomon to remain obedient to God until the end of his reign. Israel will indeed be cast out of the land so as to be humiliated in the eyes of the nations and the beautiful temple that Solomon has built will indeed become a heap of ruins. The passage also implies that the throne of David and Solomon will *not* be established forever due to Solomon's failure to walk in the way of his father David. Of course, the passage attributes the disasters that will fall upon the people to their own abandonment of God as well, yet the clear implication is that they will forsake God because Solomon will lead them to do so by forsaking God himself.

In the remainder of chapter 9 and in chapter 10, the narrative in 1 Kings stresses the tremendous wealth and power accumulated by Solomon and the great admiration he inspires throughout the world (1 Kgs 9:1–10:29). In particular, the Queen of Sheba travels from afar to witness for herself the wisdom and accomplishments of Solomon (10:1-8). She tells Solomon: "Blessed be the LORD your God, who has taken pleasure in you and set you on the throne of Israel! Because the LORD loved Israel forever, he has made you king to execute judgment and justice" (10:8-9). In reality, by means of this latter affirmation, the Queen of Sheba provides the reason for which Solomon will provoke God's anger and lead both his descendants and the people down a path that will end in tragedy and destruction. God made Solomon king in order that he might execute judgment and justice, yet he will soon cease to fulfill this task as a result of his desire to expand his dominion, wealth, and power even further, since this desire will lead him to take foreign wives and accept the worship of their gods in Israel.

This is the reality described in 1 Kgs 11:1-8. There it is said that Solomon's wives "turned away his heart after other gods" so that it was no longer "true to the LORD his God," and that "Solomon did what was evil in the sight of the LORD, and did not follow the LORD fully, as his father David had done" (vv. 4, 6). Solomon is even said to have erected high places for the gods Chemosh and Molech, who were associated with the practice of child sacrifice (1 Kgs 11:7; 2 Kgs 3:26-27; 23:10-13). According to the narrative, God appeared to Solomon twice to command him to turn away from following the gods of his wives, yet he did not obey (1 Kgs 11:9-10). As a result, God tells Solomon that he will tear the kingdom away from his son, though for the sake of David and Jerusalem he will give Solomon's son one tribe over which to rule, namely, Judah (11:11-13). God also raises up adversaries who harass Solomon during the rest of his reign and provokes Solomon by choosing Jeroboam as the one who will reign over the ten northern tribes of Israel, which from that point on will constitute a kingdom that is distinct from Judah (11:14-40).

Although the narrative of 1 Kings never criticizes Solomon explicitly or overtly for the wealth and power he accumulates, it clearly points back to the passages in Deuteronomy and 1 Samuel that foresee the manner in which the people will be oppressed by their king (Deut 17:14-17; 1 Sam 8:11-18). No subsequent king of Israel or Judah is presented as conscripting for his own service the sons and daughters of the Israelites, acquiring many wives and vast treasures of silver and gold, or gathering for himself large numbers of chariots, horses, and other animals in the way that Solomon does (1 Kgs 10:14–11:3). According to the biblical narrative, therefore, the monarchy can be both a means of blessing the people and promoting justice and righteousness as well as a means of oppressing the people and promoting injustice, inequity, idolatry, and corruption. Obviously, in order for the monarchy to be the former, the king must submit fully to the God of Israel alone, obey his commandments, and listen to the prophets he sends.

Dragging a People Down to Destruction

According to the biblical narrative, throughout the remainder of the period of the monarchy in Israel and Judah, both the king and the people in general fall more and more deeply into sin, due primarily to their failure to serve the God of Israel alone, and the result is disaster for both kingdoms. The ten tribes of the northern kingdom are removed permanently from the land after the Assyrians conquer them and deport and disperse many of them throughout the Assyrian empire. The Assyrians also bring new peoples into the land that those tribes had inhabited and have them mix with the Israelites who are left there, thereby destroying their identity as a distinct people (2 Kgs 17:24). While many of the inhabitants of the land that comes to be known as Samaria will continue to worship the God of Israel, they will do so while also worshiping other gods at times and will not submit fully to the God of Israel in the way necessary for them to enjoy the well-being he desires for all. While the kingdom of Judah in the south will endure longer, eventually many of its inhabitants will also go into exile at the hand of the Babylonians.

For the most part, the biblical narrative regarding this period focuses on the kings of Israel and Judah rather than the people themselves. The reason for this has already been mentioned above. Because the kings are set over the people as their leaders, the people's behavior as well as their well-being depend primarily on the decisions taken by their king. If the king is faithful to Israel's God, cleanses the land from the worship of any other god, and enforces the observance of God's good commandments among the people, the people will be able to live in accordance with God's loving will so as to thrive and prosper. They will enjoy well-being not only because God will respond favorably to their behavior by blessing them but also because, in and of itself, that behavior will lead to their well-being due to the intrinsic consequences that follow naturally upon doing what is good and right. If the king disobeys or abandons the God of Israel, however, and promotes the worship of other gods among the people or even allows for such worship to take place, he will undermine and destroy not only his own well-being but that of the people as a whole, since the worship of gods other than the God of Israel inevitably leads to injustice, inequity, violence, corruption, and suffering.

These are the ideas that are repeatedly stressed throughout the narrative. Several kings are presented as following Israel's God faithfully, although these are all confined to Judah. These kings include Asa, Jehoshaphat, Uzziah, Jotham, and especially Hezekiah and Josiah. They remove from their territory the idols and high places devoted to other gods and seek to bring the people to worship the God of Israel alone and keep his commandments.[9] Above all, they dedicate themselves fully to the God of Israel and serve him with their whole heart (1 Kgs 15:14; 2 Kgs 20:3; 23:25).

---

9. See 1 Kgs 15:11-14; 22:43; 2 Kgs 18:3-7; 23:1-24.

The vast majority of the kings of Israel and Judah, however, are said to have done what was bad or evil in God's sight. While at times they serve Israel's God, they do not act to put an end to the worship of other gods among the people and at times fall back into idolatry themselves. The kings of the tribes of Israel in the north are also judged negatively for allowing Israel's God to be worshiped in places other than Jerusalem. In large part, what is unacceptable is not merely that the Israelites of the northern kingdom worship God in places other than Jerusalem but especially that this worship is tied to the golden calves erected by Jeroboam in Dan and Bethel (1 Kgs 12:26-33; 2 Kgs 10:29; 17:16). By representing Israel's God in this way, contrary to what he had commanded, in effect they were making of him an idol or a god of the same type that the nations served. Another reason why in biblical thought God was to be worshiped in Jerusalem alone was that by definition those serving him were to live as one among themselves. If the people of Israel were his children and they were divided among themselves, he could hardly be pleased. Throughout the biblical texts, the ideal is that the people of Israel live out their identity as a single people by worshiping God together. According to the narrative that runs throughout most of the Hebrew Bible, the place in which God had chosen for this worship to take place was the sanctuary at Jerusalem.

In virtually all of the passages in which the kings of Israel and Judah are evaluated negatively, it is said that they caused the people to sin.[10] While this undoubtedly involves leading the people to serve gods other than the God of Israel, it should also be understood in the sense that the people's worship of other gods led them to disregard and disobey the commandments given by God in general. In a number of passages, the relation between abandoning the God of Israel for other gods and abandoning the observance of God's commandments as a whole is made explicit.[11] Other passages refer to the violation of specific commandments contained in the Mosaic law. Thus, for example, when King Ahab and his Phoenician queen Jezebel plot to steal Naboth's vineyard, they violate several of the commandments of the Mosaic law by making up false charges against Naboth and having him stoned so that they may take possession of it (1 Kgs 21:1-26). This account and others make it clear that the worship of gods other than the God of Israel leads to the practice of injustice and violence that is associated with the failure to observe the good and righteous commandments that God gave to Israel.[12]

The biblical narrative speaks of a number of prophets who were sent to the kings of Israel and Judah to speak God's word to them. The most important of these prophets are Elijah and his successor Elisha. These prophets utter a wide variety of messages given to them by God. In many cases, they simply provide guidance to the kings or tell them what to do in a particular situation. They

---

10. See, for example, 1 Kgs 15:26, 30, 34; 16:2, 13, 19, 26; 22:52; 2 Kgs 10:31; 13:2, 11; 15:24; 21:9, 16.

11. See 1 Kgs 18:18; 2 Kgs 10:31; 17:13-17; 18:11-12; 21:7-9.

12. On this point, see also 2 Kgs 14:6; 21:6-10; 24:3-4.

also speak words of judgment foretelling disasters that will come upon the kings or the people as a result of their sins. In some cases, what they prophesy can be avoided if the kings or the people turn from their sinful ways. Even when that does not happen, those prophecies fulfill the function of making it clear that the disasters or hardships that come upon the kings or the people are brought by God in response to their sinful behavior. Those prophecies thus enable the kings and people to interpret after the fact the events that have taken place and to warn them of what will happen to them as well if they do not turn away from their sin and submit obediently to God.

Many of the narratives of the period of the monarchy contain elements that readers in antiquity would probably have found as troubling as most readers today do. Once again, acts of tremendous violence and cruelty are justified in the name of Israel's God and at times are even carried out by Israel's God himself. Elijah, for example, orders the mass slaying of four hundred fifty prophets of Baal after he has shown the God of Israel to be the true Lord in Israel (1 Kgs 18:20-40). Similarly, in 2 Kgs 10:18-30, after Israel's king Jehu uses deception to draw together all of the priests and worshipers of Baal in his kingdom and then has them all slaughtered by his soldiers, God tells him: "You have done well in carrying out what is right in my eyes." When God wishes to see King Ahab die in battle, he intentionally puts a lying spirit into the mouths of his prophets so as to entice Ahab to attack the Arameans, and as a result Ahab is killed (1 Kgs 22:20-37). In perhaps the most disturbing story of all, Elisha curses in God's name forty-two small boys who are making fun of him for being bald and two she-bears come out of the forest to rip the boys apart (2 Kgs 2:23-24).

The logic behind these passages, of course, is clear. The priests and worshipers of Baal are regarded as doing great harm to the people of Israel both by drawing them away from the God of Israel and by leading them to practice the type of injustice and violence associated with the worship of Baal. This violence is evident in the account of Elijah's encounter with the prophets of Baal. There, in an attempt to get Baal to respond to their pleas, "they cried aloud and, as was their custom, they cut themselves with swords and lances until the blood gushed out over them" (1 Kgs 18:28). A god who will listen to people and respond favorably to them only when they mutilate themselves is clearly a god who takes pleasure in violence and bloodshed for its own sake. In that case, from the perspective of the biblical text, there are good reasons to exterminate the worship of Baal throughout the land, since that worship is itself generating violence, injustice, and bloodshed. Similarly, given that Ahab is said to have done more evil than any other king of Israel, God's desire to see him dead so that the evil and suffering he is causing may come to an end might seem to justify the means God uses to accomplish that end. The killing of the boys by the she-bears is no doubt intended to stress the importance of showing respect for God's prophets, though the punishment imposed on them clearly seems excessive and inhumane.

Throughout the narrative stretching from Deuteronomy to 1 and 2 Kings, the idea that God blesses those who obey him and chastises those who do not in an effort to bring them into conformity with his will for their own good or to stamp out evil and injustice is used as a basis for interpreting the major events that take place in Israel's history. As we have seen above, when the people endured terrible sufferings and hardships, this idea led them to interpret those sufferings and hardships as a means by which God was seeking to correct and purify them from their sins. When atrocities were committed against the people, the same idea led them to conclude that God had allowed them to suffer those atrocities for the same purpose, thus making God responsible for them to some extent. It is possible that something similar happened with regard to the account regarding the she-bears that attacked the young boys. If such a tragedy had in fact taken place, those who observed it might have sought to find a reason why God had allowed it. On the basis of the idea that misfortunes are often a response on the part of God to sinful behavior, they may have drawn a connection between the death of the boys and their mocking of Elisha's baldness, even though this involved ascribing to God an act that seemed exceedingly cruel.

At times the biblical narrative covering the period of the monarchy seems to attempt to force the history of Israel and Judah and their kings into the same scheme. Thus, for example, even though Ahab is presented as the king who did the greatest evil, some explanation was required as to why God allowed his son Ahaziah to succeed him as king instead of cutting off his line of succession entirely. According to the account in 1 Kgs 21:27-29, the reason that God did so was because Ahab repented of his sin and expressed that repentance through concrete acts. In this way, the narrative justifies the fact that Ahab's dynasty continued for one more generation rather than coming to an end with his own death.

Similarly, the king of Judah who is said to have practiced the greatest evil was Manasseh, yet Manasseh was also the king who had the longest reign in Judah, namely, fifty-five years (2 Kgs 21:1-9). His grandson Josiah, however, was considered by many Judah's greatest king due to the fact that he promoted the worship and service of Israel's God among the people more than any other king before him (2 Kgs 23:2-3, 25; cf. 2 Chr 34:31-33). When a long-lost scroll of the Mosaic law is found at the temple, Josiah has the scroll read publicly and presides over a ceremony in which all the people and their leaders recommit themselves to obeying God's commandments and living under his covenant (2 Kgs 22:3–23:3). In spite of Josiah's faithfulness and his success in reestablishing faithfulness to God among the people after the harm done by Manasseh, the narrative claims that God had already determined to send Judah into exile prior to Josiah's reign in response to the evils perpetrated by Manasseh (2 Kgs 23:26-27). The book of 2 Chronicles attempts to offer a partial solution to the problem of why God allowed Manasseh to reign so long by claiming that he repented and corrected the wrongs he had committed

(2 Chr 33:10-20). In these passages, the narrative clearly seems to be attempting to reconcile what actually took place in the history of these kings with the notion that God blesses obedience and righteousness and punishes disobedience, injustice, and idolatry. Some justification had to be given as to why God had allowed the most wicked of Judah's kings to enjoy the longest reign and why the reign of one of Judah's best kings was considerably shorter.

A Wrath with No Remedy

By far the two most important events in the accounts of the period of the monarchy following the construction of the temple by Solomon are the destruction of the northern kingdom by the Assyrians and the conquest of Jerusalem by the Babylonians, which resulted in the destruction of Solomon's temple and the deportation of many of the inhabitants of Judah to Babylon under the Babylonian king Nebuchadnezzar. The narrative that appears in 2 Kings 17 appeals to the interpretation of Israel's history just considered to explain why God allowed the Assyrians to destroy the northern kingdom, while a brief passage near the end of 2 Chronicles appeals to the same type of interpretation to justify the tragic events that took place in Jerusalem under Nebuchadnezzar (2 Chr 36:15-17).

Although we have considered both of these passages in Chapter 5 of this work, here it is important to stress once more the role that they play in the biblical narrative. According to that narrative, from the time that the Israelites left Egypt they have been a stubborn and stiff-necked people. While their rebelliousness was held in check to some extent during the conquest under Joshua and during the reign of kings such as David, Hezekiah, and Josiah, for the most part the sin and depravity of the people and their kings have only grown worse. God has done everything possible to bring them back to himself, sending them one prophet after another and subjecting them to harsh punishments in an attempt to correct them, but to no avail. Rather than responding to the prophets in the way that God desired, the people have despised and mocked those prophets and have become even more entrenched in their violent and destructive behavior.

For that reason, if God is ever to accomplish his purposes among the people by bringing them to practice justice and righteousness for their own good, he has to take measures that are much more drastic. He begins by destroying the ten tribes of the northern kingdom, whose behavior had been especially wicked and perverse, hoping that this would serve as a warning to those of the southern kingdom of Judah and thereby lead them to turn back to him and his commandments. Eventually, however, the people in Judah become just as wicked and perverse as a result of the influence of kings such as Manasseh and those who occupy the throne following Josiah's death. When God comes to the conclusion that it is pointless to continue sending the people prophets and imposing lesser chastisements on them, he decides to subject them to the most intense sufferings imaginable by acting through the Babylonians to destroy their land, their capital, and the temple dedicated to him and to send many of the people into exile, while having others killed by the sword, by starvation, and by disease. According to 2 Kgs 24:14 and 25:12, only the poorest of the land are left in it to carry out forced labor in the fields. The narrative interprets the disaster that the people were made to endure by affirming that "Jerusalem and Judah so angered the LORD that he expelled them from his presence" and that "the wrath of the LORD against his people became so great that there was no remedy" (2 Kgs 24:20; 2 Chr 36:16).

Although the narratives at the end of 2 Kings and 2 Chronicles do not elaborate on the intense sufferings that the inhabitants of Jerusalem and Judah experienced at the hands of the Babylonians, other passages from the Hebrew Bible describe their pain, heartache, and distress as well as the cruelties and atrocities that they were made to endure. These include passages such as Leviticus 26 and Deuteronomy 28, which anticipate the destruction and devastation associated with the fall of Jerusalem and Judah long before it takes place, as well as the book of Lamentations and several of the Psalms, which portray in graphic terms the people's anguish, torments, and despair.[13]

In some of these passages, the people express the belief that God has abandoned them definitively and that as a result they no longer have any future. While those passages acknowledge the people's sin and recognize that God was justified in punishing them so severely, at times they also express doubts as to whether God's anger will ever subside. For the most part, however, they still hold out hope that at some point in the future at least a portion of the people will be restored to God's favor and attain his blessings once more by being brought to live in a manner that will allow them to experience the well-being he intended for them from the time he chose them as his own. Yet before that can happen they must be utterly devastated, crushed, and broken. Only then can God begin to fashion them anew and finally bring them to practice justice and righteousness in the way he desires for their own good.

In the closing verses of 2 Chronicles, it is said that it was necessary for the people to remain in exile "until the land had enjoyed its Sabbaths," lying desolate for seventy years (2 Chr 36:20-21). The idea appears to be that the wickedness of the people had also done great harm to the land, perhaps not only in a figurative sense but a literal sense as well. The imagery is similar to that found in Lev 18:24-28 and 20:22, which speak of the land vomiting out its inhabitants due to the manner in which it is polluted by their sins and abominations.

By affirming that the land must enjoy its Sabbaths, the book of 2 Chronicles makes it clear that what God seeks by subjecting the people to the humiliation and devastation associated with the destruction of Jerusalem and the exile in foreign lands is not to annihilate his people but to carry out a thorough purification and radical transformation in them. Once the land has rested and recovered, it will be possible for the people to return to it and inhabit it once more. Of course, if God allows them to do so, it will first be

---

13. See especially Psalms 74, 79, and 137.

necessary for them to undergo a radical transformation so that they cease to be the stubborn and stiff-necked people that have persistently rebelled against God since the time they came out of Egypt and finally commit themselves to loving and serving the God of Israel alone with all of their heart and soul.

As we have seen in Chapter 5 of this study, while the accounts of the deportation and exile of many of the people of Israel and Judah might seem to portray God as a cruel and despotic figure who chooses to subject the people to great suffering and destruction simply to avenge himself on them for having abandoned him for other gods, such a portrayal does not reflect the logic underlying the biblical narrative. Faced with the people's stubborn and persistent refusal to live in accordance with his will and serve him alone as their God for their own good, God is left with only two alternatives. He must either give up on his efforts to bring the people back to himself by abandoning them definitively to their own fate or else inflict on them sufferings and punishments that are so severe that they too will be left with only two alternatives: either to submit to God in the way he desires and commands for their own good or be destroyed. If God chooses to abandon the people, they will destroy themselves and fall into ruin. If he instead chooses to continue in his efforts to bring them back to himself, the only way that will happen is if the people become so utterly broken and devastated that they have no choice but to acknowledge their sin, cry out to God for help, and do whatever God tells them.

According to the biblical texts, God's love for Israel will never let him destroy his people entirely or abandon them definitively. Therefore, the only alternative is for him to continue to do everything possible to convince them to turn back to him for their own good. To accomplish that objective, he will have to destroy a part of the people and subject another part to intense and unbearable sufferings until at least some of them are ultimately so crushed and despondent that they finally turn away from their disobedience and rebelliousness and turn back to him. Furthermore, as strange and objectionable as it may sound, when the people finally are brought to change their ways and live in accordance with God's will for their own good, *they will finally realize that all of the horrific and unbearable sufferings and devastation that God has brought upon them have been an expression of his unconditional love, a love that will never give up on them or cease to seek their well-being.* While the terrible sufferings to which God subjects them seem to be anything but loving, gracious, and merciful on God's part and instead appear to be an expression of great hatred and hostility toward them, in reality those sufferings manifest the extent to which God is willing to go in order to accomplish his loving purposes among them. *Nothing* that his people Israel or other human beings do can ever make God put away his love for them or abandon the loving purposes for which he created them. Despite the intense pain and suffering that it causes not only human beings but also God himself, he will never stop seeking to do everything in his power to bring them to live in accordance with his will for justice and righteousness, since only in that way will they ever be able to enjoy the well-being and happiness that he sought for them even before he brought them into existence.

PUTTING A BROKEN PEOPLE BACK ON THEIR FEET

The book of 2 Chronicles ends by mentioning the decree emitted by the Persian King Cyrus in the first year of his reign in which he allows the Jews in exile to return to Jerusalem in order to rebuild the temple. The narrative of the people's return and the rebuilding of the temple in Jerusalem appears in the books of Ezra and Nehemiah. Both of these books present the people putting away definitively the worship of any gods other than the God of Israel and dedicating themselves fully to God by submitting to all the commandments of the Mosaic law. In addition to rebuilding the temple and presenting offerings to God in accordance with the prescriptions found in the law, the people reinstitute the observance of the Sabbath, begin to offer their tithes once more, abolish usury, resume the celebration of the sacred feasts, and establish judges who will judge them in conformity with all that the law commands.[14] They also put away the foreign wives they have taken (Ezra 9:1–10:44; Neh 13:23-31). Undoubtedly, this measure seems extremely cruel in that it involves dissolving marriages that were otherwise legitimate and apparently leaving the women destitute or forcing them to find some other means to support themselves. The logic, however, is clearly that the survival of the Jews as a people depends on their continuing to intermarry only among themselves in order to preserve their identity and also avoiding entirely the worship of the gods of the nations from which their wives came. Should the people be led once more to allow the worship of those gods within their land and homes, the exile that had just come to an end might end up being for naught, since eventually the people would fall back into the same sins.

Both Ezra and Nehemiah also contain lengthy prayers in which the people confess their sins and implore God's forgiveness and blessings. In Ezra 9, after sacrifices for sin have been offered up on behalf of all of the people (Ezra 6:17), Ezra is said to have gotten up from his fasting at the time of the evening sacrifice and prostrated himself before God, dressed in garments that he has torn as an expression of repentance (9:5). He then prays:

> O my God, I am too ashamed and embarrassed to lift up my face to you, my God, for our iniquities have risen higher than our heads, and our guilt has mounted up to the heavens. From the days of our ancestors to the present day we have been deep in guilt, and because of our iniquities we, our kings, and our priests have been handed over to the kings of the lands, to the sword, to captivity, to plundering, and to utter shame, as it is to this day. But now for a brief moment grace has been shown to us by the LORD our God, who has left us a remnant and given us a secure hold in his holy place, in

---

14. See Ezra 3:1-13; 5:1–6:22; 7:25-26; Neh 5:1-13; 8:1-18; 10:28-39; 13:15-22.

order that he may enlighten our eyes and grant us some relief in our captivity. For we are slaves; yet our God has not abandoned us in our slavery, but has extended to us his steadfast love in the eyes of the kings of Persia, to restore our life so that we may set up the house of our God, repair its ruins, and give us a wall in Judea and Jerusalem.

And now, our God, what shall we say after this? For we have forsaken your commandments, which you commanded by your servants the prophets, saying, "The land that you are entering to possess is a land unclean with the pollutions of the peoples of the lands, with their abominations. They have filled it from one end to another with their uncleanness. Therefore do not give your daughters to their sons, neither take their daughters for your sons, and never seek their peace or prosperity, so that you may be strong and eat the good of the land and leave it for an inheritance to your children forever." After all that has come upon us for our evil deeds and for our great guilt, seeing that you, our God, have punished us less than our iniquities deserved and have given us such a remnant as this, shall we break your commandments again and intermarry with the peoples who practice these abominations? Would you not become so angry with us as to destroy us without remnant or survivor? O Lord, God of Israel, you are just, but we have escaped as a remnant, as it is this day. Here we are before you in our guilt, though no one can stand before you because of this (9:6-15).

In addition to explaining why the people are putting away their foreign wives, this prayer stresses several key themes mentioned above. Ezra not only acknowledges the sin of the people but also recognizes that their sinfulness has been persistent and deep-seated. On that basis, he affirms that they have deserved the chastisements and sufferings that God has imposed on them and even states that, despite their severity, these chastisements and sufferings have been lighter than the people's sins deserved. Therefore, while those punishments have been just, they have also been gracious and merciful, not only because they have been less harsh than they might have been but also because they had the purpose of bringing about in the people the type of change that is now being manifested in Ezra and others for their own good. Ezra's words suggest that those chastisements have in fact accomplished their objective.

The prayer attributed to Ezra also reflects and reinforces the idea that God's destruction of Israel and his partial destruction of Judah had as its goal the establishment of a remnant that would finally live in faithfulness and obedience to God in the way he desired from the start. Since the people have barely reestablished themselves in the land God had given to their ancestors, it remains to be seen whether the change that has taken place in the people will be definitive and permanent. For that reason, they have not been fully redeemed or restored but still remain in slavery under the Persians. Although their situation is much better than it was under the Babylonians, especially because they are allowed to live in their own land once more and serve the God of Israel there, Ezra contemplates the possibility that if they fall back into disobedience God might destroy them entirely and leave them with no remnant or survivor. The implication of Ezra's words is that, because that possibility still exists, God will not act to redeem and restore the people fully until he can have some assurance that they have in fact put away their sinful and destructive behavior fully and permanently.

These same ideas are evident in the prayer of confession attributed to Ezra in Neh 9:6-38, a portion of which we have seen at the end of Chapter 5. The prayer begins by recalling God's activity as sovereign creator, the promises he made to Abraham, his miraculous deliverance of the Israelites from their bondage in Egypt, his gracious gift of commandments that are good and just at Sinai, and the manner in which he cared for the Israelites in the wilderness (vv. 6-15). In spite of these kindnesses, however, the people disobeyed God and abandoned him. Even then, however, God did not abandon them but out of pure grace, mercy, and compassion continued to lead and guide them and care for them:

> But they, our ancestors, acted presumptuously and stiffened their necks and did not obey your commandments; they refused to obey and were not mindful of the wonders that you performed among them, but they stiffened their necks and appointed a leader to return to their slavery in Egypt. But you are a God ready to forgive, gracious and merciful, slow to anger and abounding in steadfast love, and you did not forsake them. Even when they had cast an image of a calf for themselves and said, 'This is your God who brought you up out of Egypt,' and had committed great blasphemies, you in your great mercies did not forsake them in the wilderness; the pillar of cloud that led them in the way did not leave them by day nor the pillar of fire by night that gave them light on the way by which they should go. You gave your good spirit to instruct them and did not withhold your manna from their mouths and gave them water for their thirst. Forty years you sustained them in the wilderness so that they lacked nothing; their clothes did not wear out, and their feet did not become swollen. And you gave them kingdoms and peoples and allotted to them every corner, so they took possession of the land of King Sihon of Heshbon and the land of King Og of Bashan. You multiplied their descendants like the stars of heaven and brought them into the land that you had told their ancestors to enter and possess. So the descendants went in and possessed the land, and you subdued before them the inhabitants of the land, the Canaanites, and gave them into their hands, with their kings and the peoples of the land, to do with them as they pleased. And they captured fortress cities and a rich land and took possession of houses filled with all sorts of goods, hewn cisterns, vineyards, olive orchards, and fruit trees in abundance; so they ate and were filled and became fat and delighted themselves in your great goodness (vv. 16-25).

According to Ezra's prayer, however, rather than responding in the way that God desired when he showered them with blessings and abundance, they rebelled against him and his commandments, killing the prophets he had sent to them to call them to turn back to him and committing "great blasphemies" (Neh 9:26). When he gave them into the hands of their enemies in order to chastise them, they would often turn back to him and cry out to him for help in their distress, and in his great compassion he would send deliverers to save them (9:27). Each time this happened, however, soon afterwards they would fall back into the same evils they had committed previously, yet even then God's love and compassion for them would lead him to rescue them once more (9:28). Nevertheless, after he had shown great patience and had continued to admonish them through his prophets for many years, their persistent refusal to put away their arrogance and rebelliousness led God to give them over into the hands of other peoples (9:29-30). Even then, however, in his grace and mercy he did not make an end of them or abandon them (9:31).

Ezra ends his prayer by acknowledging the people's sin and God's just chastisements of that sin and by asking God to continue to show his grace, mercy, and goodness to the people in spite of their sinfulness:

> Now therefore, our God, the great and mighty and awesome God, you who keep covenant and steadfast love, do not look lightly upon all the hardship that has come upon us, upon our kings, our officials, our priests, our prophets, our ancestors, and all your people, since the time of the kings of Assyria until today. You have been just in all that has come upon us, for you have acted faithfully and we have acted wickedly; our kings, our officials, our priests, and our ancestors have not kept your law or heeded the commandments and the warnings that you gave them. Even in their own kingdom, and in the great goodness you bestowed on them, and in the vast and fertile land that you set before them, they did not serve you and did not turn from their wicked deeds. Today we are slaves—slaves in the land that you gave to our ancestors to enjoy its fruit and its good gifts. Its abundant yield goes to the kings whom you have set over us because of our sins; they have power also over our bodies and over our livestock to do as they please, and we are in great distress. Because of all this we are making a firm agreement in writing, and on that sealed document have inscribed the names of our officials, our Levites, and our priests (Neh 9:32-38).

Similar to what we find at the end of 2 Kings, the narrative presented in 1 and 2 Chronicles, Ezra, and Nehemiah ends without any clear conclusion or resolution. While the people have returned to their land, and in that sense have finished enduring the worst of the chastisements God has imposed on them, they are still subject to a foreign power, living in a form of servitude. They are thus in need of further deliverance, yet that deliverance will depend on their continuing to submit faithfully to God and his good commandments. The future is therefore open. While the people can be sure that God still loves them and desires to see all of his gracious promises fulfilled in them, those promises can be fulfilled only if they remain faithful and obedient to him due to the intrinsic relationship between their behavior and their well-being. All that they can do, therefore, is strive to live in accordance with God's will and wait for God to fulfill completely the promises of blessing he has made to them. At the same time, they must also depend on God to bring about in them the obedient way of life he desires to see in them for their own sake, since they cannot attain that way of life on their own. For that reason, they must ask God not only to redeem them from their ongoing subjection to foreign powers but also to bring about in them the obedience, justice, and righteousness necessary for that redemption to take place. In other words, they must look to God in faith, depending fully on him for all that they need to experience his blessings and salvation and leaving it up to him to answer the questions of when, where, and how he will fulfill his gracious promises.

Many of the same themes and ideas mentioned in the prayer of Ezra appear elsewhere in the Hebrew Bible and in the Jewish writings that were composed in the centuries following the return of many of the people of Judah from Babylon and prior to the destruction of the Second Temple in 70 CE. These include especially a number of the Psalms as well as passages from the books of Daniel, Tobit, Baruch, Jubilees, and the Psalms of Solomon, all of which contain summaries of the history of God's dealings with Israel throughout their existence as a people.[15] These passages stress God's love and grace toward Israel, the people's persistent rebelliousness and failure to observe the good commandments God had given them, and God's response to their sinfulness and disobedience. While that response often consisted of showing them patience and forgiving them, finally it became necessary for God to punish them by scattering them among the nations. Nevertheless, he will not abandon them but will gather them together in the land he had given them once they have been brought to return to him so that they may enjoy his blessings there once more. As we shall see in detail in the next chapter, those same themes and ideas are especially prominent in the books of Israel's prophets.

While most of the writings we have examined in the present chapter anticipate in one way or another a future in which Israel will finally attain the blessings that God intends for his people, it should also be noted that scattered throughout many of those writings are brief allusions to the hope that by means of Israel the other nations of the earth may come to know Israel's God. When Joshua orders the people to set up twelve stones as a memorial to remind their descendants how God had parted the waters of the Jordan River to allow them to cross it by foot, he tells them that they are to recount that event to their children by telling them: "For the LORD your God dried up the waters of the Jordan for you until you had crossed over, as the LORD your God did to the Red Sea, which he dried up for us until we had crossed over, so that all the peoples of the earth may know that the hand of the LORD is mighty and so that you may fear the LORD your God forever" (Josh 4:23-24). As we have seen above, in the prayer attributed to Solomon at the dedication of the temple, he also looks forward to the day when foreigners of distant lands will become convinced of God's greatness and come to the temple to offer up their prayers to him or turn in the direction of the temple as they pray to him from afar (1 Kgs 8:41-43; cf. 2 Chr 6:32-33). When he blesses the people after finishing his prayer, Solomon expresses his desire that God may bless him and his people Israel "so that all the peoples of the earth may know that the LORD is God; there is no other" (1 Kgs 8:60). Subsequently, when Judah's king Hezekiah prays to God asking for deliverance from the Assyrian king

------

15. See especially Psalms 78–81, 105–106; Dan 9:1-19; Tobit 13; Baruch 1–5; Jub. 1:4-25; Pss. Sol. 7–9, 17.

Sennacherib, he tells God: "So now, O Lord our God, I pray you, save us from his hand so that all the kingdoms of the earth may know that you alone, O Lord, are God" (2 Kgs 19:19). All of these passages suggest that the hope that people of other nations might come to know and serve the God of Israel was a vital part of the faith and self-understanding of those who composed and preserved the biblical texts, since that hope is articulated both explicitly and implicitly throughout the biblical narratives.

Although in one sense the narrative regarding Israel in the historical books of the Hebrew Bible ends with the account of the return of many of those deported to Babylon in the time of Ezra and Nehemiah, in another sense it does not end but continues on. Throughout the historical books, there are numerous passages that allude to the things that God intends to bring to pass in the future. As we have just noted, these passages include the restoration and blessing of Israel in the land God has given them after the people are brought back from the nations among whom they have been scattered and the acknowledgment of the God of Israel as the one true God among the nations.

Perhaps the most important of these passages are those that are found in the closing chapters of Deuteronomy. There, after Moses tells the people of the terrible afflictions and scourges that they will be made to endure when they persistently fail to obey the commandments God has given them in chapters 28 and 29 of the book, including especially their exile in other lands, Moses looks ahead to the day when those who survive the devastation and destruction that God will bring upon his people will understand why he allowed such terrible things to happen to them (Deut 29:22-28). At the same time, Moses anticipates the day when God will have compassion on them and bring all of them back to the land from the peoples among whom they have been scattered in order to bless them there (30:1-5). According to Moses, God will circumcise the people's heart and the heart of their descendants so that they may love and obey him with all of their heart and soul. This obedience will enable them to enjoy the abundance that God will pour out on them and to prosper in all that they do (30:6-10).

In a similar manner, the song that God has Moses compose for the people of later generations to recite not only interprets the past but also anticipates the future. Toward the beginning of the song, Moses portrays God as a faithful rock and loving father who sustained, shielded, and cared for the people in the desert as "the apple of his eye" (Deut 32:4-15). At the same time, his song describes the Israelites as "degenerate children" who have "dealt corruptly" with God and are perverse, crooked, foolish, and senseless (vv. 5-6). When God fed them with the finest produce and the choicest food and drink, they "grew fat, thick, and bloated," abandoned God and scoffed at him, and provoked him to anger by serving strange gods (vv. 15-21). Moses also refers to the Israelites as "a nation void of sense" who have no understanding (v. 28).

After contrasting God's unconditional love with Israel's ungratefulness and infidelity in this way, Moses presents God as spurning the Israelites in anger, hiding his face from them, and heaping disasters, hunger, consumption, pestilence, and death on both old and young (Deut 32:19-25). He affirms that God was at the point of blotting out the memory of his people from humankind by making an end of them, but that ultimately he decided not to do so because their adversaries would claim that it was they rather than God who had destroyed them (vv. 26-27). As we have noted in Chapter 6 of this study, while many English versions of the Bible use the language of vengeance and recompense in vv. 35 and 43 of Deuteronomy 32 to speak of the calamities that God will bring upon the people when they provoke him to anger, the context indicates that his intention is not to destroy his people but to bring them back to himself in obedience. This is evident from the allusions to the compassion that he will show them after he has brought justice and seen them reduced to a condition in which they are weak and helpless (v. 36). By subjecting them to suffering and the sword, God will demonstrate to them that there is no other god on earth and that no one can deliver from his hand (vv. 37-42). While he kills and wounds, therefore, he also makes alive and heals (v. 39). Because he acts on behalf of his children to cleanse their land by delivering them from those who shed their blood and taking action against those who hate and oppose him, the Hebrew text of the song ends by calling on the nations to rejoice that God will deliver his people from their adversaries and show mercy to them and to their land (v. 43).

This song thus serves not only to summarize the narrative that appears throughout the historical books of the Hebrew Bible but also indicates how God intends for that narrative to continue into the future. As God promises two chapters earlier in Deut 30:1-10, in one way or another he will accomplish the objective that he has pursued from the time he created human beings and chose Abraham in order to bless his descendants together with all of the families of the earth. While it will be necessary for God to subject both Israel and the nations to harsh punishments and afflictions that are extremely painful and even to destroy many among them in order to bring into existence a righteous remnant that will finally be able to enjoy his blessings of well-being, wholeness, and prosperity, God will not yield or relent in his efforts to make that remnant and those blessings a reality until they meet with success, no matter how long it may take him.

CHAPTER 13

Proclaiming a Passion That Refuses to Die

Nowhere in the Hebrew Bible is the God of Israel depicted in terms that are more moving, tender, and affectionate than in the books of Israel's prophets. Those prophets repeatedly emphasize the goodness, kindness, patience, and compassion of Israel's God as one who comforts, strengthens, and lifts up his people and graciously provides for all their needs. He is a God who is deeply in love with his chosen people and waits with open arms for them to return to him any time they turn away from him. Nothing they do can ever put a stop to that love or lead him to reject them as his people and abandon them to their own fate.

Just as frequently, however, those same prophets present the God of Israel acting in ways that are anything but loving and compassionate. He lashes out at his people with uncontrollable rage and fury and threatens to reduce the land he gave them to ashes and rubble. He calls them children of a harlot and the offspring of evildoers and vows that he will not rest until he has covered his sword with their blood and littered the streets of their cities with the corpses of young and old alike. Rather than showing them mercy and compassion, he insists that he will exact vengeance on them and have no pity on them as he uproots them from their land and sends them off into captivity and slavery under their enemies in faraway places.

These portrayals of God in the books of Israel's prophets can be read in two different ways. They can be seen as descriptions of a volatile, erratic, and temperamental God who constantly fluctuates between love and wrath, blowing hot one moment and cold the next. In that case, he is a god just like Marduk, Poseidon, or Zeus, treating those who submit obediently to him and express enthusiastically their affection for him with charity and kindness but threatening to crush and annihilate any who oppose him or stand in his way. For many readers of the Hebrew Bible, this is the only way in which it is possible to make sense of the striking contrasts in the depictions of God that run throughout the prophetic writings.

There is, however, a second way to make sense of those contrasts. The God of whom the prophets of Israel speak is so fiercely and passionately committed to the well-being of the people he loves that he will not stop or rest until he has brought them to put away the ways of being and behaving that fill their lives with pain and suffering in order to follow the good and life-giving path in which he seeks to guide them. If at some times he appears warm and tender but at others is filled with anger and indignation, it is not because his love for his people is fickle or depends on how they behave but rather because in his love he adamantly refuses to let them destroy their own happiness and bring down ruin on themselves and others.

PINING FOR A WAYWARD PEOPLE

Although the books of Israel's prophets speak repeatedly of God's steadfast and unconditional love for Israel as his people, a number of passages from those books in particular recall God's gracious and compassionate election of Abraham's descendants when they were as yet an insignificant and oppressed people. Among these passages are those that portray Israel as God's beloved son or child. In the book of Hosea, for example, God is presented as recalling fondly the time of his people's youth: "When Israel was a child, I loved him, and out of Egypt I called my son" (Hos 11:1). At the outset of the book of Isaiah, God makes a similar affirmation regarding his people Israel: "I reared children and brought them up" (Isa 1:2). Near the end of the same book, the people explicitly address God as their father and as one who fashioned and formed them from the very beginning: "O LORD, you are our father! We are the clay, and you are our potter; we are all the work of your hand" (Isa 64:8). Other passages in Isaiah make use of imagery that portrays God relating to the people as a mother. In Isa 49:15, God asks his people: "Can a woman forget her nursing child, or have no compassion for the child of her womb? Even these may forget, but I will not forget you." Likewise, near the end of the book, after promising to make the people prosper and comparing his relationship with them to the way in which a mother nurses her child in her arms and bounces the child on her lap, God tells them: "As a mother comforts her child, so I will comfort you; you will be comforted in Jerusalem" (Isa 66:12-13). The same type of imagery appears in Isa 46:3-4: "Listen to me, O house of Jacob, all the remnant of the house of Israel, who have been borne by me from birth and carried from the womb. Even to your old age I am he; even when your hair turns gray I will carry you. I have made you and will bear you; I will carry you and deliver you."

Elsewhere in the Hebrew Bible the prophets compare God's love for Israel with that of a husband for his wife: "For your Maker is your husband, the LORD of hosts is his name; your Redeemer is the Holy One of Israel, who is called the God of all the earth. For the LORD has called you like a wife forsaken and grieved in spirit, like the wife of a man's youth when she has been cast off, says your God" (Isa 54:5-6). "For as a young man marries a young woman, so will your children be united with you; and as the bridegroom rejoices over the bride, so will your God rejoice over you" (Isa 62:5).[1] Toward the beginning of the book of Jeremiah, God speaks to Israel in the same terms: "I remember the devotion of your youth, your love as a bride, when you followed me in the wilderness, in a land not sown" (Jer 2:1-2).

---

1. On this translation of the verse, see Joseph Blenkinsopp, *Isaiah 56–66: A New Translation with Introduction and Commentary*, AB 19 (New York: Doubleday, 2003), 232-33.

The passage from the prophetic writings that describes at greatest length the grace and mercy shown by God for Israel when Israel was still an insignificant, downtrodden, and oppressed people appears at the outset of Ezekiel 16. This chapter, which is by far the longest of the book, uses metaphorical and figurative language to recount the history of God's people from their lowly and humble beginnings all the way to their exile in foreign lands and the restoration that God ultimately intends to bring about for them. The opening verses of the chapter portray God's initial dealings with the people in the following terms:

> Thus says the Lord GOD to Jerusalem: Your origin and your birth were in the land of the Canaanites; your father was an Amorite and your mother a Hittite. As for your birth, on the day you were born your navel cord was not cut, nor were you washed with water to make you clean; you were not rubbed with salt or even wrapped in cloths. No eye looked on you with pity to do any of these things for you out of compassion for you, but you were cast out into the open field; for you were abhorred on the day you were born. I passed by you and saw you flailing about in your blood. As you lay in your blood, I said to you, "Live! Grow up like a plant in a field!" You grew up and became tall and fully adorned; your breasts were formed and your hair grew long, yet you were naked and bare.
>
> Then I passed by you again and looked at you, and I saw that you were at the age for love. I spread the edge of my cloak over you and covered your nakedness: I pledged myself to you and entered into a covenant with you, and so you became mine, says the Lord GOD. After that I bathed you with water, washed off the blood from you, and anointed you with oil. I also clothed you with embroidered cloth and put sandals of fine leather on your feet. I wrapped you in fine linen and covered you with costly garments. I adorned you with jewelry. I put bracelets on your arms, a chain around your neck, a ring in your nose, earrings in your ears, and a beautiful crown upon your head. So you were adorned with gold and silver, while your clothing was of fine linen, costly fabric, and embroidered cloth. You had choice flour and honey and oil for food. You grew exceedingly beautiful and became fit to be a queen. Your fame spread among the nations on account of your beauty, for it was perfect because of my splendor that I bestowed on you, says the Lord GOD (vv. 3-14).

In this passage, the imagery of Israel as an abandoned child adopted by God out of grace and compassion gives way to the imagery of Israel as a young wife taken by God in marriage. Among many readers today, such imagery may seem highly problematic since it is suggestive of an older man compelling a young girl in her adolescence to become his bride so that he may possess her as his own, perhaps motivated purely by selfish desires or lust. When this passage is read against the background of the concept of God that we have considered throughout the present work, however, such a reading of the passage must be ruled out as contrary to its intention. As we have seen repeatedly, the God of Israel was not thought to need or desire anything of human beings for his own sake. The biblical texts do not portray him as a God who seeks to take advantage of people in order to obtain some type of personal satisfaction or pleasure for himself at their expense in the way that a lustful man, jealous lover, or possessive husband might seek to gain control over the life or body of a young woman. For that reason, there is no reason to suppose that the author of Ezekiel 16 intended to describe the God of Israel in such a manner. Instead, what he wished to stress was God's tender, compassionate, and selfless love for Israel as a people whom he chose to be his own out of pure grace and mercy. God's intention was not to satisfy some self-centered desire or need on his part but simply to fill the lives of his people with blessings and good things in the same way that the man in the passage seeks to bestow on the bride he loves his splendor and adorn her life with precious gifts.

While passages such as those just considered employ language and imagery that is extremely moving and tender, they often do so for the purpose of contrasting the kindness and compassion shown by God for Israel when the people were nothing but a small and insignificant group of oppressed outcasts with the people's ungratefulness, disobedience, and rebellious spirit. In Hosea 11, immediately after presenting God as affirming: "When Israel was a child, I loved him, and out of Egypt I called my son," the author of the book contrasts God's ongoing love for Israel with the people's rejection of God and even compares them to the inhabitants of Sodom and Gomorrah, which were also known as Admah and Zeboiim:

> The more I called them, the more they turned away from me; they kept sacrificing to the Baals and burning incense to idols. Yet it was I who taught Ephraim to walk; I took them in my arms, but they did not know that it was I who healed them. I led them with cords of kindness, with bands of love. I was to them like those who lift infants to their cheeks. I bent down to them and fed them. . . . My people are bent on turning away from me. They call out to the Most High, but he does not lift them up. How can I give you up, Ephraim? How can I hand you over, O Israel? How can I make you like Admah? How can I treat you like Zeboiim? My heart recoils within me; my compassion grows warm and tender. I will not pour out my fierce anger; I will not destroy Ephraim again, for I am God and not a man, the Holy One in your midst, and I will not come in wrath (Hos 11:1-4, 7-9).

Earlier in the same book, Hosea also presents God as complaining that Israel behaved like an unfaithful wife who takes the good things she receives from her husband to dedicate them to her lovers: "She did not know that it was I who gave her the grain, the new wine, and the oil, and who lavished upon her the silver and the gold that was used for Baal" (Hos 2:8). Further on, God's gracious treatment of Israel is contrasted with Israel's infidelity and lack of understanding: "It was I who trained them and strengthened their arms, yet they plot evil against me. They turn to that which does not profit; they are like a defective bow" (7:15-16). A few verses later, the prophet adds: "Israel has spurned the good" (8:3).

The same type of contrast appears in the opening verses of the book of Isaiah. There, after portraying God as a loving father who "reared children and brought them up," the prophet continues: "The ox knows its owner and the donkey its master's crib, but Israel does not know; my people do not understand. Ah, sinful nation, people laden with iniquity, offspring of evildoers, children who act corruptly! You have forsaken the LORD; you have despised the Holy One of Israel, and are utterly estranged!" (Isa 1:2-4).

Several of the other passages from Isaiah cited above present the same contrast. After speaking of God as one who has carried Israel from the time that the people were born and will continue to bear them in his arms even in old age, the prophet contrasts that imagery with that of the sinful people fabricating their own gods in order to bear those gods up in their arms and carry them on their shoulders. In that context, he refers to them as transgressors who are "stubborn of heart." Rather than looking for help and deliverance to God as the incomparable creator of all that exists, they cry out to idols made of perishable gold and silver that cannot answer or save anyone (Isa 46:5-13). In the same context in which he refers to God as the people's father and to Israel as clay in the hands of God as a potter, the prophet has the people confess their persistent sinfulness and justifies God's anger at their sin: "You were angry, and we sinned; we continued in our sins a long time, yet shall we be saved? We have all become like one who is unclean, and all our righteous deeds are like filthy rags. We all wither like a leaf, and our iniquities carry us away like the wind. There is no one who calls on your name or rises up to take hold of you, for you have hidden your face from us and have handed us over to our iniquity" (64:5-7). In the following chapter of the book, the prophet continues to contrast God's love for his people and his desire to bless them with their rebelliousness and their refusal to follow in the path he laid out for them for their own good: "I was ready to be sought out by those who did not ask for me, to be found by those who did not seek me. I said, 'Here I am, here I am!' to a nation that did not call on my name. All day long I held out my hands to a rebellious people, who walk in a way that is not good, following their own devices" (65:1-2).

In Isaiah 5, the prophet compares the love, concern, and care God showed to Israel from the time he adopted them as his people with the manner in which a man builds a vineyard for his beloved, only to see the vineyard then produce rotten grapes. For that reason, despite his love for the vineyard, the man ends up tearing it down:

> I will sing for my beloved my love song concerning his vineyard: My beloved had a vineyard on a very fertile hill. He dug it out and cleared it of stones and planted it with choice vines; he built a watchtower in the midst of it and hewed out a wine vat in it. Then he expected it to yield grapes, but the grapes it yielded were rotten. So now, inhabitants of Jerusalem and people of Judah, judge between me and my vineyard. What more was there to do for my vineyard that I have not done in it? When I expected it to yield good grapes, why did it yield rotten grapes? Now I will tell you what I will do to my vineyard: I will remove its hedge, and it will be devoured; I will break down its wall, and it will be trampled down. I will lay waste to it; it shall not be pruned or hoed, and it will be overgrown with briers and thorns. I will also command the

clouds not to send rain upon it. For the vineyard of the LORD of hosts is the house of Israel, and the people of Judah are the garden in which he delighted. He looked for justice, but saw only bloodshed; for righteousness, but heard only a cry of distress! (vv. 1-7).

Similar ideas appear in the book of Micah. There the prophet presents God reminding the people of all the good that he did for them when he brought them out of Egypt, while at the same time asking why they have grown weary of his goodness rather than valuing and appreciating it: "O my people, what have I done to you? In what have I wearied you? Answer me! For I brought you up from the land of Egypt and redeemed you from the house of slavery; and I sent Moses, Aaron, and Miriam to go before you" (Mic 6:3-4).

The idea that God is grieved when his people do harm to themselves by rejecting his love is particularly stressed in the book of Jeremiah. Both God's goodness as well as his sadness and frustration are expressed in the verses that appear at the beginning of Jeremiah 2, where God recalls the people's devotion to him in their youth and their love for him as his bride when they followed him in the wilderness (vv. 1-2). God then asks the people: "What wrong did your ancestors find in me that they went far from me and went after worthless things, and became worthless themselves? They did not ask, 'Where is the LORD, who brought us up from the land of Egypt, who led us in the wilderness, a land of deserts and pits, a land of drought and deep darkness, a land that no one passes through and where no one lives?' I brought you into a bountiful land to eat its fruits and its good things. But when you entered you polluted my land and made my inheritance an abomination" (vv. 5-7). In the remainder of the same chapter, God laments that the people "have changed their glory for that which is worthless" and insists that it is they who do themselves harm by abandoning him and showing contempt for his love and kindnesses:

> For my people have committed two evils: they have forsaken me, the fountain of living water, and dug out cisterns for themselves, cracked cisterns that cannot hold water. . . . Have you not brought this upon yourself by forsaking the LORD your God while he led you in the way? . . . Your own wickedness will chastise you, and your faithlessness will reprove you. Know and see that it is evil and bitter for you to forsake the LORD your God (vv. 11, 13, 17, 19).

Other passages from Jeremiah similarly describe God's pain and sorrow at seeing his beloved people suffer the consequences of their sinful and destructive behavior, as well as his deep longing that they return to him for their own good so that he might save them from those consequences. In some of these passages, it is not entirely clear if the one presented as speaking is God himself or the prophet, yet the expressions of sadness and frustration that appear in them must be regarded as something that both God and the prophet share:

I contemplated how I would set you among my children and give you a pleasant land, the most beautiful inheritance of all the nations. And I thought, "You will call me 'my father' and will not turn away from following me." But instead, as an unfaithful wife leaves her husband, so you have been unfaithful to me, O house of Israel, says the Lord. A cry is heard on the bare heights, the disconsolate weeping of Israel's children, because they have perverted their way; they have forgotten the Lord their God. Return, O rebellious children! I will heal your rebelliousness (Jer 3:19-22).

Your ways and your deeds have brought this upon you. This is your downfall; how bitter it is! It has pierced your heart! My anguish, my anguish! I writhe in pain! Oh, the walls of my heart! My heart is pounding wildly; I cannot keep silent, for I hear the sound of the trumpet, the call of war. Disaster follows disaster; the whole land lies in ruins. My tents are suddenly destroyed, and my curtains torn down in an instant. How long must I see the standard and hear the sound of the trumpet? For my people are foolish; they do not know me. They are stupid children and have no understanding. They are skillful in doing evil but do not know how to do good (Jer 4:18-22).

How can I forgive you? Your children have forsaken me and have sworn by those who are not gods. When I fed them to the full, they committed adultery and went off to the houses of prostitutes (Jer 5:7).

But this people has a stubborn and rebellious heart; they have turned aside and gone away. They do not say in their hearts, "Let us fear the Lord our God, who gives the rain in its season, the autumn rain and the spring rain, and keeps the weeks appointed for the harvest for us." Your iniquities have turned these things away, and your sins have deprived you of what is good (Jer 5:23-25).

Is it I whom they provoke?, says the Lord. Is it not themselves, to their own ruin? (Jer 7:19)

My joy is gone; grief is upon me. My heart is sick. Listen! The cry of the daughter of my people from far and wide in the land: "Is the Lord not in Zion? Is her King not in her?" Why have they provoked me to anger with their carved images and their foreign idols? "The harvest has passed, the summer has ended, and we have not been saved." On account of the brokenness of the daughter of my people I am broken; I mourn, and horror has taken hold of me. Is there no balm in Gilead? Is there no physician there? Why then has the health of the daughter of my people not been restored? O that my head were a spring of water and my eyes a fountain of tears, so that I might weep day and night for the slain of the daughter of my people! (Jer 8:18–9:1)

Woe is me because of my hurt! My wound is severe. But I said, "Truly this is my punishment, and I must bear it." My tent is destroyed, and all my cords are broken. My children have gone from me and are no more; there is no one to spread out my tent again and set up my curtains. For the shepherds are stupid and do not inquire of the Lord; therefore they have not prospered, and all their flock is scattered (Jer 10:19-21).

The same tone of sadness and frustration is evident throughout Ezekiel 16. After recalling how God had showered his blessings upon the people after he had saved them from extinction like a man who rescues a newborn baby that has been abandoned and left to die, the prophet accuses the people of behaving like an ungrateful woman who has experienced only kindness from her husband but then seeks out other lovers who do nothing but abuse her and take advantage of her:

> But you trusted in your beauty and played the harlot because of your fame; you lavished your favors on any who passed by. You took some of your garments and made for yourself colorful high places and prostituted yourself on them. Nothing like this has ever happened or will happen again. You also took your beautiful jewels of my gold and my silver that I had given you and made for yourself male images in order to play the harlot with them, and you took your embroidered garments to cover them and offered up my oil and my incense before them. You also took my bread that I had given you, the choice flour and oil and honey that I fed you with, and you set it before them as a pleasing aroma; so it was, says the Lord GOD. You even took your sons and your daughters, whom you had borne to me, and you offered them up in sacrifice to be devoured. As if your harlotries were not enough! You slaughtered my children and offered them up by making them pass through fire. And in all your abominations and your harlotries you did not remember the days of your youth, when you were naked and bare, flailing about in your blood.
>
> After all your wickedness—Woe, woe to you!, says the Lord GOD—, you built yourself a house of prostitution and made yourself a high place in every square; at the head of every street you built your high place and prostituted your beauty, offering yourself to all who passed by and multiplying your harlotries. You prostituted yourself with the Egyptians, your lustful neighbors, multiplying your harlotry, to provoke me to anger. Therefore I stretched out my hand against you, reduced your rations, and delivered you up to the desire of your enemies, the daughters of the Philistines, who were astonished by your lewd behavior. You also prostituted yourself with the Assyrians because you were insatiable; but even when you prostituted yourself with them, you were still not satisfied. You multiplied your prostitution with Chaldea, the land of merchants, but even with this you did not have your fill.
>
> How sick is your heart, says the Lord GOD, that you did all these things, the deeds of a shameless harlot, building your house of prostitution at the head of every street and making your high place in every square! Yet you were not like a prostitute because you scorned payment. You adulterous wife who receives strangers instead of her husband! Gifts are given to all prostitutes, but you instead gave your gifts to all your lovers, bribing them to come to you from all around for your prostitutions. So you were different from other women in your harlotries: no one solicited you to prostitute yourself, and you gave payment, while no payment was given to you; in that you were different (vv. 15-34).

Similar imagery of Israel as an unfaithful and adulterous wife or as a prostitute or harlot appears elsewhere in the prophetic writings. It is particularly prominent in the book of Hosea, where God commands the prophet: "Go, take for yourself a wife of prostitution and have children of prostitution, for the land commits great prostitution by forsaking the LORD" (Hos 1:2). In Hosea, as in Ezekiel 16 and other passages from the prophetic books, this imagery is combined with that of God as Israel's husband. When considering these passages, it must be stressed once again that they conceive of God as a husband who is kind and good to his wife rather than as a possessive or abusive figure who seeks only to obtain something for himself from her. Like the figure in Ezekiel 16, in Hosea God is portrayed as a husband who cares deeply for his wife and gives her only what is good. In Hos 2:7, the adulterous wife comes to the realization that her life is better alongside of her husband, yet she is still not fully conscious of all of the kindnesses he shows for her: "Then she will say, 'I will go and return to my first husband, for it was better with me then than now.'" At the same time, as is generally the case when women prostitute themselves, the lovers to whom the adulterous wife in Hosea sells her favors do not seek her happiness and well-being but merely wish to abuse her and take advantage of her for their own selfish and lustful ends. For that reason, the woman needs to be rescued and saved from the hands of those lovers, just as God seeks to rescue and save Israel from the sufferings that the worship of other gods brings into the lives of his people (2:10, 14-23).

Throughout the books of Israel's prophets, therefore, the portrayal of Israel as a prostitute, harlot, or adulterous wife must be understood on the basis of the idea that only the God of Israel truly loves and cares for his people and seeks their well-being. In contrast, the other nations and the gods they serve simply wish to exploit, oppress, and take advantage of the people and thus do them tremendous harm. Although they may appear to obtain certain things that are desirable as a result of their alliance with other nations and the worship of their gods, in reality the things that the people obtain are worthless and unprofitable and ultimately destroy their well-being rather than promoting it. For that reason, rather than doing themselves any type of good or favor, when the people are unfaithful to God or "play the harlot," they do themselves great harm and exchange a life that is conducive to their happiness and well-being for one that is inevitably filled with pain, violence, injustice, suffering, and oppression.

One other image that appears repeatedly throughout the prophetic books, often in conjunction with that of the image of Israel as an adulterous wife or a prostitute, is that of Israel as a people who forget not only God's love, grace, and kindnesses but God himself. In Hosea, God is presented as lamenting that Israel "chased after her lovers and forgot me," in addition to forgetting his law (Hos 2:13; 4:6; 8:14). Near the end of the same book, God reminds the people that he has been their God and Savior from the time they came out of Egypt, yet they have persistently failed to acknowledge and appreciate his goodness toward them: "It was I who cared for you in the wilderness, in the land of drought. When I fed them, they were satisfied; they were satisfied, and their heart became proud. Therefore they forgot me" (13:4-6).

The same complaint appears in the books of Isaiah, Jeremiah, and Ezekiel: "For you have forgotten the God of your salvation; you have not remembered the Rock of your refuge" (Isa 17:10). "You have forgotten the LORD your Maker, who stretched out the heavens and laid the foundations of the earth"

(Isa 51:13). "Can a young woman forget her jewelry or a bride her attire? Yet my people have forgotten me for days without number" (Jer 2:32; cf. 3:21). "This is your lot, the portion I have measured out for you, says the LORD, because you have forgotten me and trusted in lies" (Jer 13:25). "My people have forgotten me; they burn incense to worthless idols. They have stumbled in their ways, in the ancient paths, and have gone on the byways instead of the highway, making their land a horror, an object of perpetual hissing" (Jer 18:15-16; cf. 23:26-27). "One man commits abomination with his neighbor's wife; another lewdly defiles his daughter-in-law; another man among you defiles his sister, his father's daughter. There are those among you who take bribes to shed blood; you take interest and practice usury, and make profits from your neighbors by extortion; and you have forgotten me, says the Lord GOD" (Ezek 22:11-12). "Therefore thus says the Lord GOD: Because you have forgotten me and cast me behind your back, therefore bear the consequences of your lewdness and harlotry" (Ezek 23:35).

All of these passages make it clear that the idea that from the very beginning God sought nothing but the well-being of his people Israel and wished only to fill their lives with good things out of love and compassion for them is central to the thought of Israel's prophets. At the same time, however, many of these passages contrast God's grace, kindness, and compassion with the ingratitude, unfaithfulness, and destructive behavior of Israel as a people who fail to acknowledge, appreciate, and treasure God's unconditional and unfailing love. Rather than looking to him as the sole source of all that is good and life-giving, the people turn to gods and idols whose worship is not only senseless and unprofitable but also does them great harm.

PURSUING THE LUSTS OF AN ADULTEROUS HEART

As we have seen repeatedly throughout the present study, the biblical prophets consistently accuse the people of Israel and especially their rulers of two sins that are intimately tied to one another, namely, idolatry and injustice. The worship of false gods leads the people to abandon the good commandments that God has laid out for them in the Torah and instead adopt ways of thinking, living, and behaving that are based on values that are contrary to what is good, just, and right. These are the values associated with other nations and the gods and idols that they serve.

As is evident from several of the passages just cited above, one of the most common criticisms of the worship of false gods and the idols associated with them is that they cannot actually help, save, or benefit those who serve them and pray to them. Those idols are merely pieces of wood, stone, or metal and have no life. The idea that such gods are unable to do anything in favor of those who invoke them is particularly stressed in passages such as the following:

> All who fashion idols are nothing, and the things they delight in are worthless. Those who testify to them do not see or know anything, and so they will be put to shame. Who would fashion a god or cast an image that is of no use

to anyone? . . . From the wood that is left over he makes a god, his idol; he bows down to it and worships it. He prays to it and says, "Save me, for you are my god!" They do not know or comprehend; for their eyes are shut so that they cannot see, and their minds are closed so that they cannot understand. . . . "Shall I fall down before a block of wood?" He feeds on ashes; a deluded mind has led him astray, and he cannot save himself or say, "Is not this that I hold in my right hand a fraud?" (Isa 44:9-10, 17-20).

As a thief is shamed when caught, so the house of Israel will be shamed: they, their kings, their leaders, their priests, and their prophets. They say to a tree, "You are my father," and to a stone, "You gave me birth." For they have turned their backs to me instead of their faces. But in the time of their trouble they say, "Rise up and save us!" But where are the gods that you made for yourself? Let them rise up if they can save you in your time of trouble! For you have as many gods as you have towns, O Judah! (Jer 2:26-28; cf. 11:12; 51:17-18)

Of what use is an idol once its maker has fashioned it, a cast image and a spouter of lies? For its maker trusts in his own creation when he produces an idol that cannot speak! Woe to you who say to the wood, "Rise up!," and to silent stone, "Rouse yourself!" Can it give guidance? See, it is plated with gold and silver and there is no breath whatsoever in it (Hab 2:18-19).

Because the worship of false gods and idols is senseless, those who abandon the all-powerful and eternal God who in love created all that exists in order to seek instead the assistance of gods and idols of their own making are regarded as ignorant and foolish. They deprive themselves of what is good and life-giving and in exchange obtain what is worthless and useless. At the same time, their abandonment of the one God and the truth associated with him leads the people to base their lives on what is false so as to practice injustice, violence, and oppression:

For our transgressions before you are many, and our sins testify against us. Our transgressions are with us, and we know what our iniquities consist of: rebellion, denying the LORD, turning away from following our God, planning oppression and revolt, and uttering lying words conceived in the heart. Justice is turned back, and righteousness stands far off; for truth stumbles in the streets, and uprightness cannot enter. Truth is lacking, and whoever turns from evil is preyed upon (Isa 59:12-15).

The children gather wood, the fathers kindle fire, and the women knead dough to bake cakes for the queen of heaven; and they pour out drink offerings to other gods to provoke me to anger. Is it I whom they provoke?, says the LORD. Is it not themselves, to their own confusion? (Jer 7:18-19)

Why does the land lie in ruin and waste like a wilderness, so that no one passes through it? The LORD replies: Because they have forsaken my law that I set before them, and have not obeyed my voice or walked in accordance with it. Instead, they have followed their own stubborn hearts and have gone after the Baals, as their ancestors taught them (Jer 9:12-14).

Because the people have forsaken me and have profaned this place by making offerings in it to other gods whom neither they nor their ancestors nor the kings of Judah have known, and because they have filled this place with innocent blood and built the high places of Baal to burn their children in the fire as offerings to Baal—something which I did not command or decree and which never even entered my mind—, therefore days are coming, says the LORD, when this place will no longer be called Topheth or the valley of Ben-hinnom, but rather the valley of Slaughter (Jer 19:4-5; cf. 2:33-35; 3:1-3).

Then he said to me, Son of man, have you seen what the elders of the house of Israel are doing in the dark, each in his room of carved images? For they say, "The LORD does not see us; the LORD has forsaken the land." He also said to me, You will see even greater abominations that they are committing. . . . Have you seen this, O son of man? Is it not bad enough that the house of Judah commits the abominations done here? Must they also fill the land with violence and provoke my anger still further? (Ezek 8:12-13, 17)

For they have committed adultery and have blood on their hands; they have committed adultery with their idols. They have even offered up to them for food the children whom they had borne to me. Moreover, they have done this to me: they have polluted my sanctuary on the same day and profaned my Sabbaths. For when they slaughtered their children for their idols, on the same day they came into my sanctuary to profane it. That is what they did in my house (Ezek 23:37-39).

Hear the word of the LORD, O people of Israel, for the LORD has an indictment against the inhabitants of the land. There is no faithfulness or kindness and no knowledge of God in the land. There is swearing, deception, murder, theft, and adultery; bloodshed follows upon bloodshed. Therefore the land mourns, and all who live in it languish together with the animals of the field and the birds of the sky; even the fish of the sea are disappearing. . . . My people consult a piece of wood, and a diviner's rod gives them oracles. For a spirit of harlotry has led them astray, and they have prostituted themselves, forsaking their God. They sacrifice on the tops of the mountains and burn offerings on the hills, under oak, poplar, and terebinth, because their shade is good. Therefore your daughters play the harlot, and your daughters-in-law commit adultery. I will not punish your daughters when they play the harlot, nor your daughters-in-law when they commit adultery; for the men themselves go aside with harlots and sacrifice with temple prostitutes. In this way a people devoid of understanding comes to ruin. . . . Ephraim is joined to idols—let him alone. When their drinking is ended, they indulge in sexual orgies; they love lewdness more than their glory (Hos 4:1-3, 12-14, 17-18).

Closely related to the worship of false gods and idols is the practice of divination and the activity of false prophets who claim to speak in the name of the God of Israel yet in reality merely deceive the people. These things also lead the people to turn away from God and fall into behaviors that do them great harm:

The righteous perish, and no one takes it to heart; the devout are taken away, while no one understands. For the righteous are taken away from calamity and enter into peace; those who walk in integrity will rest in their beds. But as for you, come here, you children of a sorceress, you offspring of an adulterer and a harlot! Whom are you mocking? Against whom do you open your mouth wide and stick out your tongue? Are you not children of transgression, the offspring of deceit? You burn with lust among the oaks, under every green tree; you slaughter your children in the valleys, under the clefts of the rocks. Among the smooth stones of the valleys is your portion; they are your lot. To them you have poured out a drink offering and have brought a grain offering. Should I be pleased with these things? On a high and lofty mountain you have made your bed, and there you went up to offer sacrifice. Behind the door and the doorpost you have set up your symbols. For as you have deserted me you have uncovered your bed; you have climbed into it and made it spacious. You have made a pact with them and have loved their bed; you have gazed on their nakedness. You journeyed with oil to Molech and multiplied your perfumes; you sent your envoys far away, and even sent down to Sheol (Isa 57:1-9).

I have heard what the prophets who prophesy lies in my name say: "I have had a dream, I have had a dream!" How much longer? Will the hearts of the prophets who utter lies and prophesy the deceit of their own heart ever turn back? They seek to make my people forget my name by their dreams that they tell to each other, just as their ancestors forgot my name for Baal. Let the prophet who has a dream tell the dream, but let the one who has my word speak it truthfully. What does straw have in common with wheat?, says the Lord. Is not my word like fire, says the Lord, and like a hammer that breaks a rock in pieces? Therefore, says the Lord, I am against the prophets who steal my words from one another. I am against the prophets, says the Lord, who say with their own tongues, "Thus says the Lord." I am against those who prophesy false dreams, says the Lord, and make them known, and those who lead my people astray by their lies and their falsehoods, when I did not send them or commission them; so they do nothing at all to benefit this people, says the Lord (Jer 23:25-32).

As for you, son of man, set your face against the daughters of your people, who prophesy from out of their own imagination. Prophesy against them and say, Thus says the Lord God: Woe to the women who sew magic bands on every wrist and make veils for the heads of persons of every height in order to ensnare human lives! Will you ensnare lives among my people and yet preserve your own? You have profaned me among my people in exchange for handfuls of barley and pieces of bread, putting to death persons who should not die and keeping alive persons who should not live, by lying to my people who listen to your lies. Therefore thus says the Lord God: I am against your magic bands with which you ensnare lives; I will tear them from your wrists and will set free the lives of those whom you ensnare like birds. I will tear off your veils and save my people from your hands; they will no longer be prey in your hands, and you will know that I am the Lord. Because you have disheartened the righteous with lies, although I have not disheartened them, and you have encouraged the wicked not to turn from their wicked ways and save their lives, you will no longer see false visions or practice divination; I will save my people from your hand. Then you will know that I am the Lord (Ezek 13:17-23).

Although Israel's prophets speak out against the idolatry and injustices of the people as a whole, they especially hold Israel's rulers responsible not only for practicing these things themselves but also for promoting them among the people over whom God has placed them. Instead of leading and guiding the people as their shepherds, the rulers and powerful elites devour and destroy them:

For the shepherds are stupid and do not inquire of the LORD; therefore they have not prospered, and all their flock is scattered (Jer 10:21).

For thus says the LORD concerning Shallum son of King Josiah of Judah, who succeeded his father Josiah but has gone away from this place: He shall never again return here, but in the place to which they have carried him captive he shall die, and he shall not see this land again. Woe to him who builds his house with injustice and his upper rooms with unrighteousness, who makes his neighbors work for nothing and does not pay them their wages, who says, "I will build myself a large house with spacious upper rooms," and who cuts out windows for it, paneling it with cedar and painting it with vermilion! Are you a king because you compete in cedar? Did not your father eat and drink and practice justice and righteousness? Then all went well with him. He judged the cause of the poor and needy; then all was well. Is not this to know me?, says the LORD. But your eyes and heart are fixed only on your dishonest gain, and on shedding innocent blood and practicing oppression and violence (Jer 22:11-17).

The princes of Israel among you, each in accordance with his power, have been bent on shedding blood. Father and mother are treated with contempt among you; the foreigner residing in your midst suffers extortion; the orphan and the widow among you are wronged. You have despised my holy things and profaned my Sabbaths. Among you are those who slander to shed blood and eat upon the mountains, those who commit lewdness in your midst (Ezek 22:6-9).

The word of the LORD came to me: Son of man, prophesy against the shepherds of Israel! Prophesy and say to the shepherds: Thus says the Lord GOD: Ah, you shepherds of Israel who have been feeding yourselves! Should not shepherds feed the sheep? You eat the fat and clothe yourselves with the wool; you slaughter the fattened ones but you do not feed the sheep. You have not strengthened the weak and healed the sick; you have not bound up the injured and brought back the strayed. You have not sought out the lost, but have ruled them with force and violence. So they were scattered, because there was no shepherd; and once scattered, they became prey for all the wild animals. My sheep were scattered; they wandered upon all the mountains and on every high hill. My sheep were scattered all over the face of the earth with no one to search or look for them (Ezek 34:1-6).

When reading these and similar passages from the prophetic books, it is important to note the deep sense of outrage, consternation, and indignation that is expressed in them. Only when the violence and atrocities that Israel's prophets describe are fully appreciated and given their due stress can readers of these books grasp the reasons why they make use of language that at times is extremely harsh, vicious, fierce, and damning to condemn the tremendous injustices committed by some against others. Such passages seek to portray vividly the extent of the harm, destruction, and chaos that prevail when the people and their rulers abandon the good and just law that God has given them and instead devote themselves to serving gods and idols whose worship promotes bloodshed, greed, deception, thievery, exploitation, physical and sexual abuse, and countless other evils.

THE STRUGGLE TO SAVE
A PEOPLE FROM THEMSELVES

As we have seen in Chapter 5 of this study, when the people and their leaders fall into sin, injustice, and destructive behavior, God's first response is to send them prophets to call them to turn back to him in repentance for their own good. Because this call involves an insistence that the people return to a way of life that is in their own best interest in that it promotes justice and well-being for all, it is an expression of profound love and concern for them. While the prophets' call for the people to repent is often accompanied by words of condemnation and threats of judgment, in reality it is rooted in God's love for the people and his desire to bless them.

In a number of passages from the prophetic writings, expressions of love for the people appear explicitly alongside calls for them to repent. God makes it clear to the people that he wishes them to turn back to him and his commandments not for *his* sake but for *theirs*, because only in that way can they attain the good that he desires for them and wishes to grant them:

> Remember these things, O Jacob, and Israel, for you are my servant. I formed you; you are my servant. O Israel, you will not be forgotten by me. I have swept away your transgressions like a cloud, and your sins like a mist. Return to me, for I have redeemed you! (Isa 44:21-22)

> Listen up, everyone who thirsts! You who have no money, come to the waters! Come, buy and eat! Come, buy wine and milk without money and without cost! Why do you spend your money on that which is not bread, and your labor for that which does not satisfy? Listen carefully to me, and eat what is good, and delight yourselves in abundance. Incline your ear and come to me; listen, so that you may live! ... Seek the LORD while he may be found; call on him while he is near! Let the wicked forsake their ways and the unrighteous their thoughts. Let them return to the LORD so that he may show compassion to them, and to our God, for he will abundantly pardon (Isa 55:1-3, 6-7).

> Return, unfaithful Israel!, says the LORD. I will not look on you in anger, for I am gracious, says the LORD; I will not be angry forever. Only acknowledge your wrongdoing, that you have rebelled against the LORD your God, and scattered your favors among strangers under every leafy tree, and have not obeyed my voice, says the LORD. Return, O faithless children, says the LORD, for I am your master! I will take you, one from a city and two from a family, and I will bring you to Zion. I will give you shepherds after my own heart who will feed you with knowledge and understanding. And when you have multiplied and become numerous in the land, in those days, says the LORD, they will no longer say, "The ark of the covenant of the LORD." It will not come to mind, or be remembered or missed; nor will another one be made. At that time Jerusalem will be called the throne of the LORD, and all nations will flock to it, to the presence of the LORD in Jerusalem; and they will no longer stubbornly follow their own evil heart. In those days the house of Judah will walk alongside the house of Israel, and together they will come from the land of the north to the land that I gave to your ancestors as an inheritance (Jer 3:12-18).

While in principle God might bring his sinful people to repent by promising to do them good and pour out his blessings on them if they turn back to him, the prophetic writings give the impression that for the most part such a message does not evoke in the people the desired response. When God blesses the people and shows them kindness, as he did when he took them out of Egypt and introduced them into the fertile land he had promised to their ancestors, rather than responding with gratitude and submitting obediently to the way of life he has graciously laid out for them, they quickly turn away from him so as to go their own way. For that reason, it is generally regarded as futile and pointless for God to attempt to bring his people to turn back to the obedient way of life that is truly in their own best interest by promising them further blessings if they do so.

When the people fail to respond to God's repeated calls for them to return to him and put away the ways of thinking and behaving that are doing them and others great harm, he is left with no alternative but to threaten the people with hardships and afflictions. Only by doing so can he hope to bring them to change their ways. Even then, however, the prophets often stress that God does not wish to chastise and punish the people and will refrain from doing so if they respond in the way he desires.

> Thus says the LORD: Stand in the court of the LORD's house, and speak to all the cities of Judah that come to worship in the house of the LORD the words that I command you; do not leave out a word! It may be that they will listen, and all of them will turn from their evil way, that I may change my mind about the evil that I intend to bring upon them because of their wicked deeds (Jer 26:2-3).

> Say to them, As I live, says the Lord GOD, I take no pleasure in the death of the wicked, but that the wicked turn from their ways and live. Turn back, turn back from your evil ways; for why will you die, O house of Israel? (Ezek 33:11; cf. 18:23, 31-32)

> Yet even now, says the LORD, return to me with all your heart, with fasting, weeping, and mourning. Rend your hearts and not your clothes. Return to the LORD your God, for he is gracious and compassionate, slow to anger and abounding in steadfast love, and relents from punishing. Who knows whether he may turn and relent and leave behind him a blessing, a grain offering and a drink offering for the LORD your God? (Joel 2:12-14)

> Seek good and not evil, that you may live; then the LORD, the God of hosts, will be with you, just as you have said. Hate evil and love good, and establish justice in the gate; it may be that the LORD, the God of hosts, will be gracious to the remnant of Joseph (Amos 5:14-15).

> Return to me, says the LORD of hosts, and I will return to you, says the LORD of hosts. Do not be like your ancestors, to whom the former prophets proclaimed, "Thus says the LORD of hosts, Turn back from your evil ways and from your evil deeds." But they did not listen to me or pay attention to me, says the LORD. Your ancestors, where are they now? And the prophets, do they live forever? But did not my words and my statutes, which I commanded my servants the prophets, overtake your ancestors? So they repented and said,

"The Lord of hosts has dealt with us according to our ways and deeds, just as he planned" (Zech 1:3-6).

For I, the Lord, do not change; therefore, O children of Jacob, you have not been consumed. Ever since the days of your ancestors you have turned aside from my statutes and have not kept them. Return to me, and I will return to you!, says the Lord of hosts (Mal 3:6-7).

As in the historical books of the Hebrew Bible, for the most part the calls to repentance that God makes through his prophets in the prophetic writings go unheeded. Not only do the people fail to take seriously God's threats to inflict chastisements on them in order to bring them back to the way of life he has graciously laid out for them, but they also become even more entrenched in their violent and destructive behavior. Rather than listening to the prophets whom God sends them, they persecute them and seek to silence them. This leads the prophets to repeat the same accusation found throughout the historical writings: the people are stubborn, stiff-necked, and hard of heart. They persistently reject God, persecute the prophets he sends them, and fall even more deeply into sin and injustice:

For they are a rebellious people, deceitful children, children who will not listen to the instruction of the Lord. They say to the seers, "Do not see," and to the prophets, "Do not prophesy the truth to us. Tell us pleasant things, prophesy illusions. Do not stand in our way; move out of our path. Let us hear no more about the Holy One of Israel" (Isa 30:9-11; cf. 5:24).

I allowed myself to be sought out by those who did not ask, to be found by those who did not look for me. I said, "Here I am, here I am!," to a nation that did not call on my name. I held out my hands all day long to a rebellious people who walk in a way that is not good, following their own designs; a people who continually provoke me to my face, sacrificing in gardens and offering incense on bricks. They sit among the graves, and spend the night in secret places; they eat swine's flesh, and the broth of abominable things is in their pots. They say, "Keep away! Do not come near me, for I am too holy for you!" These people are like smoke in my nostrils, a fire that burns all day long (Isa 65:1-5).

I will also choose to afflict them and bring down on them what they fear; because, when I called, no one answered, and when I spoke, they did not listen; but they did what was evil in my sight, and chose what displeased me (Isa 66:4).

I gave them this command: "Obey my voice, and I will be your God, and you will be my people; and walk only in the way that I command you, so that all may be well with you." But they did not obey or incline their ear. Instead, they walked in their own counsels and in the stubbornness of their evil heart, and looked backward rather than forward. From the day that your ancestors came out of the land of Egypt until this day, I have persistently sent all my servants the prophets to them, day after day; yet they did not listen to me or pay attention. Instead, they stiffened their necks; they behaved worse than their ancestors. So you shall speak all these words to them, but they will not listen to you. You shall call to them, but they will not answer you. You shall say to them: "This is the nation that did not listen to the voice of the Lord their

God and did not accept correction; truth has perished; it has been cut off from their lips" (Jer 7:23-28).

Thus says the LORD: When people fall, do they not get up again? If they go astray, do they not turn back? Why then has this people turned away in perpetual rebellion? They cling to deceit; they refuse to return. I have listened and paid attention, but they do not speak truthfully; no one repents of wickedness, saying, "What have I done!" All of them pursue their own course, like a horse charging into battle. Even the stork in the heavens knows its seasons, and the turtledove, swallow, and crane observe the time of their migration; but my people do not know the ordinance of the LORD (Jer 8:4-7).

For I solemnly warned your ancestors from the day that I brought them up out of the land of Egypt until this day, warning them persistently, saying, Obey my voice! But they did not obey or incline their ear. Instead, they all walked in the stubbornness of an evil heart. So I brought down on them all the words of this covenant, which I commanded them to do, but they refused (Jer 11:7-8; cf. 6:28; 9:14).

This evil people, who refuse to listen to my words and walk in the stubbornness of their hearts, going after other gods to serve and worship them, shall be like this loincloth, which is good for nothing. For as the loincloth clings to one's loins, so I made the whole house of Israel and the whole house of Judah cling to me, says the LORD, in order that they might be for me a people, a name, a praise, and a glory. But they would not listen (Jer 13:10-11).

And when you speak all these words to this people, and they say to you, "Why has the LORD pronounced all this great evil against us? What is our iniquity? What is the sin that we have committed against the LORD our God?," then you shall say to them: It is because your ancestors have forsaken me, says the LORD, and have gone after other gods to serve and worship them; they have forsaken me and have not kept my law. And it is because you have behaved worse than your ancestors, for here you are, each one of you, following your stubborn evil heart and refusing to listen to me (Jer 16:10-13; cf. 17:23).

Now, therefore, say to the people of Judah and the inhabitants of Jerusalem: Thus says the LORD: Look, I am a potter crafting evil against you and devising a plan against you. Turn now from your evil ways, all of you, and amend your ways and your doings! But they say, "It is no use! We will follow our own plans, and each of us will act according to the stubbornness of our evil heart" (Jer 18:11-12; cf. 19:15; 23:17).

For twenty-three years, from the thirteenth year of King Josiah son of Amon of Judah to this day, the word of the LORD has come to me, and I have spoken to you persistently, but you have not listened. And though the LORD has continually sent you all of his servants the prophets, you have neither listened nor inclined your ears to hear when they said, "Turn now from your evil ways and wicked doings, each one of you, and you will continue to dwell in the land that the LORD has given to you and your ancestors from of old and forever! Do not go after other gods to serve and worship them, and do not provoke me to anger with the work of your hands! Then I will not do you any harm." But you did not listen to me, says the LORD, and so you have provoked me to anger with the work of your hands to your own harm (Jer 25:3-7; cf. 29:19).

I have spoken to you persistently, but you have not listened to me. And I have persistently sent to you all my servants the prophets, saying, "Turn now from your evil ways and amend your doings, each one of you, and do not go after other gods to serve them. Then you shall live in the land that I gave to you and your ancestors." But you did not incline your ear or listen to me (Jer 35:14-15; cf. 36:30-31).

He said to me, Son of man, I am sending you to the people of Israel, to a rebellious people who have rebelled against me; they and their ancestors have transgressed against me to this very day. The descendants are obstinate and stubborn. I am sending you to them, and you shall say to them, "Thus says the Lord God." Whether they hear or refuse to hear (for they are a rebellious house), they will know that there has been a prophet among them. And you, O son of man, do not be afraid of them, and do not be afraid of their words. Even though briers and thorns surround you and you sit among scorpions, do not be afraid of their words or be dismayed at their glances, for they are a rebellious house. You shall speak my words to them, whether they hear or refuse to hear; for they are a rebellious house (Ezek 2:3-7; cf. 12:1-3; 20:5-8).

But the house of Israel will not listen to you, for they are not willing to listen to me; because all the house of Israel have a hard forehead and a stubborn heart (Ezek 3:7).

Like a stubborn heifer, Israel is stubborn; can the Lord now feed them like a lamb in a broad pasture? (Hosea 4:16; cf. 7:10)

When the stubborn and hard-hearted people refuse to listen to the prophets whom God sends them and persist in their violent, unjust, and destructive behavior, God's love for them leaves him no choice but to seek to correct them and bring them back to himself through chastisements and afflictions. As we have seen above and elsewhere in this study, on occasion the prophets present God expressing his dismay, sadness, and pain at having to inflict suffering on his people. At the same time, however, he recognizes that he has no choice but to do so if he is to accomplish his good purposes among them by bringing them back to himself:

Therefore thus says the Lord of hosts: I will refine and test them, for what else can I do with my sinful people? Their tongue is a deadly arrow; it speaks deceit. With their mouth they all speak friendly words to their neighbors, but in their hearts they set traps for them. Shall I not punish them for these things?, says the Lord; and shall I not bring retribution on a nation such as this? (Jer 9:7-9)

What shall I do with you, O Ephraim? What shall I do with you, O Judah? Your love is like a morning cloud, like the dew that disappears early. Therefore I have cut them in pieces by the prophets. I have killed them with the words of my mouth, and my judgments go forth like the light. For I desire steadfast love and not sacrifice, the knowledge of God rather than burnt offerings (Hos 6:4-6).

While occasionally the people respond favorably to God's calls to repentance and the chastisements he imposes on them bring about in them the changes he desires to see, these things are by far the exception rather than the rule. Even when the people do turn back to him, their obedience tends to be half-hearted and lasts only for a short time. As a result, God must inflict even greater sufferings and hardships on them. In a number of passages, God expresses his frustration that his attempts to correct the people through chastisements have had no lasting effect:

> Why do you seek further beatings? Why do you continue to rebel? The whole head is sick and the whole heart is faint. From the sole of the foot all the way to the head, there is nothing healthy in it, but only bruises and sores and open wounds; they have not been drained or bandaged or soothed with oil (Isa 1:5-6).

> Why do you contend with me? You have all rebelled against me, says the LORD. In vain have I struck down your children; they did not accept correction. Your own sword devoured your prophets like a ravenous lion (Jer 2:29-30; cf. 5:3; 7:28).

> For the people of Israel and the people of Judah have done nothing but evil in my sight from their youth; the people of Israel have done nothing but provoke me to anger by the work of their hands, says the LORD. This city has provoked me to anger and wrath, from the day it was built until this day. Therefore I will remove it from my sight because of all the evil that the people of Israel and the people of Judah did to arouse my anger—they, their kings and leaders, their priests and prophets, the citizens of Judah, and the inhabitants of Jerusalem. They have turned their backs to me instead of their faces; though I have taught them persistently, they would not listen and would not accept correction (Jer 32:30-33).

> Thus says the LORD of hosts, the God of Israel: You yourselves have seen all the evil that I have brought down on Jerusalem and on all the towns of Judah. Look at them; today they are in ruins and are uninhabited because of the wickedness they committed, and because they provoked me to anger by continuing to make offerings and serve other gods that they had not known, neither they, nor you, nor your ancestors. Yet I persistently sent to you all my servants the prophets, saying, "Do not do this abominable thing that I hate!" But they did not listen or incline their ear to turn from their wickedness and cease to make offerings to other gods. Therefore my wrath and my anger were poured out and kindled in the towns of Judah and in the streets of Jerusalem; and they became a waste and a desolation, as they still are today. And now thus says the LORD God of hosts, the God of Israel: Why are you doing such great harm to yourselves by cutting off from Judah man and woman, child and infant, so as to leave yourselves without a remnant? Why do you provoke me to anger with the works of your hands, making offerings to other gods in the land of Egypt where you have come to dwell, so as to be cut off and become an object of scorn and ridicule among all the nations of the earth? Have you forgotten the wickedness of your ancestors and the kings of Judah and their wives, as well as your own wickedness and that of your wives, which they committed in the land of Judah and in the streets of Jerusalem? To this day they have shown no contrition or fear, nor have they walked in my law and my statutes that I set before you and your ancestors (Jer 44:2-10).

A LOVE THAT WILL NOT BE SCORNED

All of the realities just considered make it clear why throughout the prophetic books God is so frequently portrayed as being filled with intense anger, indignation, and rage and as acting in accordance with such powerful emotions. What provokes him to become so upset and even furious is not only the harm and destruction that his people bring upon themselves, but also their repeated refusal to put away their harmful and destructive behavior when he calls on them to repent and inflicts harsh sufferings on them in an attempt to correct and discipline them. In the face of their persistent stubbornness, rebelliousness, and hardness of heart, God must be just as stubborn and unrelenting in conveying to them through his prophets his indignation and outrage at their behavior and threatening them with punishments that are even more terrifying and severe. As a result, the prophets are led to speak of God's wrath in ways that can come across to readers as heartless and inhumane unless their words are viewed in the context of the realities just described:

> And to this people say: Thus says the LORD: Look, I am setting before you the way of life and the way of death. Those who remain in this city will die by the sword, by famine, and by pestilence; but those who go out and surrender to the Chaldeans who are besieging you will live and will have their lives as a prize of war. For I have set my face against this city for evil and not for good, says the LORD; it will be given into the hands of the king of Babylon and he will burn it with fire. And to the house of the king of Judah say: Hear the word of the LORD, O house of David! Thus says the LORD: Execute justice in the morning, and deliver from the hand of the oppressor anyone who has been robbed, or else my wrath will go forth like fire and burn, with no one to extinguish it, because of your evil doings! (Jer 21:8-12)

> For the land is full of adulterers! The land mourns because of the scourge, and the pastures of the wilderness are dried up. The course that they follow is evil, and their might is used unjustly. Both prophet and priest are godless; even in my house I have found their wickedness, says the LORD. Therefore their way will be like slippery paths in the darkness for them, paths into which they will be driven and fall; for I will bring evil upon them in the year of their punishment, says the LORD. Among the prophets of Samaria I have seen a disgusting thing: they prophesied by Baal and led my people Israel astray. But among the prophets of Jerusalem I have seen something even more horrible: they commit adultery and walk in lies; they strengthen the hands of evildoers so that no one turns from wickedness. All of them have become like Sodom to me, and its inhabitants like Gomorrah. Therefore thus says the LORD of hosts concerning the prophets: I will make them eat wormwood and give them poisoned water to drink; for from the prophets of Jerusalem godlessness has spread throughout the land (Jer 23:9-15).

> Then my anger will be spent, and I will exhaust my wrath on them and satisfy myself; and they will know that I, the LORD, have spoken in my jealousy, when my anger is spent on them. Moreover, I will make you a desolation and an object of derision among the nations around you and in the sight of all who pass by. You will be the object of mockery and taunting, a warning and a horror for the

nations around you when I execute judgments on you in anger and indignation, and with furious punishments—I, the Lord, have spoken—, when I rain down on you my deadly arrows of famine, arrows for destruction which I will let loose to destroy you, and when I bring more and more famine upon you and break your supply of bread. I will send famine and wild animals against you, and they will take your children from you; pestilence and bloodshed will also pass through you, and I will bring the sword upon you. I, the Lord, have spoken (Ezek 5:13-17).

Numerous passages from the prophetic books present God as being eager and anxious to pour out his wrath on the stubborn and rebellious people and even taking delight in doing so. Rather than seeing these passages as expressions of intense hatred toward his people or a desire to inflict suffering on them in a spirit of spite and revenge, however, they must be read against the background of God's intense longing to put an immediate end to the violent and destructive behavior that is doing the people such tremendous harm and wreaking such great havoc among them. The more that God delays or relents in taking the type of decisive action necessary to bring about a profound change in his people and in the situation in which they find themselves as a result of their behavior, the more prolonged the suffering, chaos, and despair that reigns among them will be. For that reason, he expresses his intention to act not only decisively but also swiftly:

Look, the day of the Lord is coming, a cruel day with wrath and fierce anger, to make the land a desolation and to destroy from it its sinners. For the stars of the heavens and their constellations will not give their light; the sun will be dark when it rises, and the moon will not shed its light. I will punish the world for its evil, and the wicked for their iniquity; I will bring to an end the pride of the arrogant, and lay low the haughtiness of tyrants (Isa 13:9-11).

Look, the Lord is about to lay waste to the land and make it desolate, and he will tear up its surface and scatter its inhabitants. And as it is with the people, so will it be with the priest; as it is with the slave, so will it be with his master; as it is with the maid, so will it be with her mistress; as it is with the buyer, so will it be with the seller; as it is with the lender, so will it be with the borrower; as it is with the creditor, so will it be with the debtor. The earth will be laid to waste completely and utterly despoiled; for the Lord has spoken this word (Isa 24:1-3).

You have forsaken me, says the Lord. You are going backward, so I have stretched out my hand against you to destroy you; I am weary of relenting. I will winnow them with a winnowing fork in the gates of the land. I will bereave and destroy my people, because they did not turn from their ways. I will make their widows more numerous before me than the grains of sand on the seashore; I will bring up against the mothers of youths a destroyer at midday. I will bring down anguish and terror upon her suddenly. She who bore seven children has grown feeble; she is unable to breathe. Her sun has gone down while it was still day; she has been disgraced and humiliated. And I will put those who survive to the sword in the presence of their enemies, says the Lord (Jer 15:5-9).

In many of the passages that speak in terms such as these, God insists that he will show the people no compassion or pity when pouring out his wrath on them. While this no doubt sounds extremely cruel, the idea is that the wrong-doings and injustices being committed by the people have become so grievous, persistent, and widespread that any compassion or pity that God might show to them would ultimately do them harm rather than good. Were God to show mercy or let up in his attempts to eradicate fully the evil and violence that have taken hold among the people, there would be sectors or pockets of evil and violence that would persist and survive the thorough cleansing that he intends to bring about in their midst. As a result, that evil and violence would begin to sprout up once again in the land as soon as his punishments had come to an end:

> For this is a people who have no understanding; therefore their Maker will not have compassion on them; their Creator will not be gracious to them (Isa 27:11).

> Soon I will pour out my wrath on you and exhaust my anger against you. I will judge you according to your ways and punish you for all your abominations. My eye will show you no pity and I will not spare you! I will punish you for your ways, while your abominations are in your midst. Then you will know that it is I the LORD who strikes you. Look, the day! Look, it is coming! Disaster has broken out! The rod has blossomed; arrogance has sprouted. Violence has grown into a rod of wickedness. None of the people will be left, none of their wealth nor anything of value among them. The time has come; the day is drawing near. Let the buyer not rejoice and the seller not mourn, for wrath is coming on all their multitude (Ezek 7:8-12; cf. Hos 1:6).

> Because I tried to cleanse you but you would not be cleansed from your filthiness, you will not be clean again until I have satisfied my wrath against you. I the LORD have spoken. The time is coming, and I will act. I will not hold back; I will not have pity; I will not relent. According to your ways and your doings I will judge you, says the Lord GOD (Ezek 24:13-14).

Closely related to the idea that God will show no compassion, pity, or mercy for his sinful people is the affirmation that God will not forgive them. As we have seen previously when considering passages such as Exod 32:30-35 and Num 14:17-23, when the people have fallen into grave sins that do them and others tremendous harm, it would be contrary to their well-being for God simply to ignore and overlook their sinful behavior without making any attempt to correct it. To do so would lead them to persist unabated in that behavior and become even further entrenched in it.

For that reason, even though God always forgives his people when they sin in the sense of not casting them away from himself definitively, at times his concern for the people's well-being leads him to insist that he will punish them severely. In that sense, he denies them his forgiveness. Only by subjecting them to suffering and chastisements can he cleanse and purify them from their destructive behavior:

> On that day the Lord GOD of hosts called for weeping and mourning, for shaven heads and sackcloth; but instead there was gaiety and gladness, the killing of cattle and the slaughtering of sheep, the eating of meat and the

drinking of wine. "Let us eat and drink, for tomorrow we will die." The LORD of hosts has revealed himself to me: This iniquity will surely not be forgiven you until you die, says the Lord GOD of hosts (Isa 22:12-14).

We have transgressed and rebelled, and you have not forgiven. You have wrapped yourself in anger and pursued us, killing us without pity; you have wrapped yourself in a cloud so that no prayer can pass through. You have made us filth and rubbish in the midst of the peoples. All our enemies have opened their mouths against us; panic and pitfall have come upon us, devastation and destruction. Rivers of tears flow from my eyes because of the destruction of my people (Lam 3:42-48).

As we have seen in Chapters 5 and 6 of this work, a number of passages from the prophetic writings insist that God will not hear the people's prayers when they cry out to him. In many cases, the logic is the same as that just considered: when the people's sinfulness, stubbornness, and rebelliousness have become so great that they need to be subjected to chastisements that are severe and prolonged in order to be thoroughly corrected and purified, God will not heed their pleas for clemency or leniency but will instead insist on effecting their cleansing and purification to whatever extent he considers necessary to accomplish his purposes in them.

At first glance, it may seem surprising that at times God also refuses to respond favorably when the people acknowledge their sins and repent of them, given that this is precisely what he seeks when he chastises them. In many cases, however, as he looks into the people's hearts he may see that their repentance is not a sincere recognition of their wrongdoing or an expression of heartfelt remorse at that wrongdoing but is instead motivated only by a desire to be spared further punishment due to the pain involved. In that case, if he were to put an end to the sufferings he is imposing on them, they would quickly revert back to their sinful and destructive behavior. Even when their acknowledgment of their sin and their repentance are sincere and heartfelt, however, God may choose to continue to subject them to further sufferings and chastisements in an attempt to make their purification from their sinfulness more complete and thorough and also to deepen their renewed commitment to living in accordance with his will.

For these reasons, as we noted briefly in Chapter 5 of this study, at times God not only refuses to listen to his people's prayers but also commands his prophets not to pray on behalf of the people or express any type of lamentation for the suffering that they are enduring. Any such lamentation would involve an implicit petition or desire that their suffering be brought to an end independently of whether or not God's purposes have been accomplished in them as fully as he would like. Such a lamentation might also be seen as an expression of disapproval for the chastisements that God has deemed necessary to impose on them:

When you spread out your hands in prayer, I will hide my eyes from you. Even though you offer many prayers, I will not listen. Your hands are covered with blood (Isa 1:15).

As for you, do not pray for this people. Do not raise a cry or prayer on their behalf, and do not intercede with me, for I will not hear you. Have you not seen what they are doing in the towns of Judah and in the streets of Jerusalem? (Jer 7:16-17)

As for you, do not pray for this people or raise a cry or prayer on their behalf, for I will not listen when they call out to me in the time of their trouble. What right has my beloved in my house when she has done many vile deeds? Can the flesh of sacrifices save you from punishment and allow you to rejoice? The LORD once called you "a green olive tree, flourishing with lovely fruit"; but with the roar of a great tempest he will set fire to it and its branches will be consumed. The LORD of hosts, who planted you, has decreed evil for you because of the evil that the house of Israel and the house of Judah have done, provoking me to anger by offering sacrifice to Baal (Jer 11:14-17).

The LORD said to me: Do not pray for the well-being of this people. Even if they fast, I will not hear their cry; and even if they present burnt offerings and grain offerings, I will not accept them; I will consume them by the sword, by famine, and by pestilence (Jer 14:10-11).

I will act in wrath; my eye will not show pity, nor will I spare. Even if they cry in my ears with a loud voice, I will not listen to them (Ezek 8:18).

In a couple of passages from the books of Jeremiah and Ezekiel, God insists that even if figures such as Moses and Samuel or Noah, Daniel, and Job were to intercede on behalf of the people, he would not forgive them or turn away his wrath from them (Jer 15:1-7; Ezek 14:12-20). In biblical thought, the intercession of a righteous person on behalf of those who have sinned is at times said to obtain God's forgiveness for them, yet the reason for this is that all those who identify with the intercession of a righteous person on their behalf will be expected to identify with that person's righteousness as well in order to be committed to living in the same way. In other words, even when a righteous person intercedes on behalf of people who have sinned, the basis upon which God grants their intercession is the commitment of the sinful people to return to him in obedience. In these passages from Jeremiah and Ezekiel, however, the idea is that the sinfulness of the people is so great and so deeply ingrained into them that God feels that he has no choice but to inflict on them chastisements that are severe enough to bring about in them the lasting change he wishes to see in them. He would not be doing either the people themselves or the righteous persons interceding on their behalf any favor by putting away his anger and refraining from the chastisements he deems necessary in order to cleanse and purify them, since to do so would only lead them to continue in their sinful ways to their own harm and ruin.

Peering into Eyes Fixed for Evil

In some passages from the prophetic books, God is presented as doing his people harm in ways that hardly seem aimed at correcting or chastising them through sufferings. The prophet Amos, for example, speaks of God seeking out those who are attempting to escape his chastisements by hiding in the most remote places they can find in order to send them into captivity and kill them with a sword (Amos 9:2-4). In that context, he affirms: "I will fix my eyes on them for evil and not for good" (v. 4). As we have seen previously in this study, when God is said to do evil to the people in the sense of bringing misery and disaster upon them, the idea is not that he wishes to inflict suffering on them for its own sake out of spite or vengeance, but rather that he must do harm to them in order to bring about in them the reaction he desires to see for their own good. In a sense, of course, when God brings evil on them he is doing something that must be considered bad, yet his purpose is ultimately to do them good rather than harm.

Elsewhere in the writings of Israel's prophets, God is said to do other things that may be considered bad or evil. He gives the people statutes that are not good (Ezek 20:23-26), places them under shepherds or leaders who will do them harm rather than caring for them (Zech 11:15-17), gets the people drunk until they vomit, stagger, and go out of their minds so that he can then slay them (Jer 13:12-14; 25:15-38), and exposes them publicly to shame them in the same way that an adulterous wife or prostitute might be stripped naked and made to stand in the midst of her lovers (Ezek 16:35-43; Hos 2:2-13). Passages such as these, however, must be understood in the context of God's repeated attempts to bring the people back to the way of life that he has laid out for them out of love for them and their persistent refusal to return to that way of life.

Thus, for example, when the prophet Ezekiel presents God as affirming: "I gave them statutes that were not good and ordinances by which they could not live," he does so in the context of allusions to their rejection of his commandments as well as their offering up of themselves, their possessions, and even their firstborn children to false gods and idols (Ezek 20:23-26). According to the logic of the passage, this destructive behavior made it necessary for God to impose on them commandments that were "not good" in the sense that those commandments would make their lives difficult and even unbearable as long as they persisted in that behavior. The "ordinances by which they could not live" were commandments designed to prevent them from continuing down paths that destroyed their well-being rather than promoting it and to bring them to the realization that they needed to submit to God's will rather than following their own. At the end of this passage, God states explicitly his intention in terms of devastating the people and leaving them utterly desolate "in order that they may know that I am the LORD." In other words, at times he not only allows the people to follow paths and practices that will do them great harm but occasionally even leads and commands them to go down those paths and follow those practices so that they will realize just how harmful and destructive they are. What leads him to act in this way is his people's stubbornness and rebelliousness, since only by bringing them to endure the painful consequences of that stubbornness and rebelliousness will they realize that they need to abandon those paths and practices and instead submit to God as the only one who in his love and sovereignty can truly give them life and well-being.

For the same reasons, God may subject the people to shepherds, leaders, or rulers who will do them harm rather than good. When he had placed them under shepherds and leaders such as Moses and Samuel who cared for them and sought to guide them in the way that he had laid out for them for their own good, the people had repeatedly rebelled against those shepherds and leaders. Not only had they refused to submit to them and obey them, but they had at times even sought to overthrow or replace them. For that reason, God may intentionally subject his people to the type of shepherds, leaders, and rulers that they choose for themselves, that is, wicked and egotistical authorities who will fill their lives and their land with injustice, violence, suffering, and oppression, in order to force them to endure the consequences of their stubbornness and rebelliousness. In that way, they will hopefully be brought to the realization that they should follow shepherds, leaders, and rulers who are truly committed to serving God and seeking the well-being of the people as a whole in accordance with his will. Those are the type of authorities that God seeks to place over them for their own good.

Similarly, when the people choose for themselves a life of drunkenness, debauchery, licentiousness, and depravity and persistently refuse to heed God's command to abandon such a life, rather than continuing to call them to repent and turn back to him, God may choose to encourage them to sink even further into that way of life until it becomes unbearable for them. If they wish to get drunk, God will force them to drink even more until they vomit, stagger, and pass out. If they insist on practicing other destructive behaviors, rather than persisting in his unsuccessful calls for them to abandon those behaviors, God may simply let many of them destroy themselves by means of those behaviors until their destructiveness becomes evident to all. When they reach such a weakened state, he may even send their enemies upon the people to vanquish and kill them so that those among them who are left alive are brought to see the ruinous and disastrous consequences of such lewd and degenerate behavior. Only by doing harm to the people in this way can God hope to convince them to abandon that behavior.

The public exposing of an adulterous wife or prostitute who has been stripped naked and forced to stand before her lovers and other persons would be seen as having the same purpose. In biblical thought, both men and women were expected to live in the context of healthy marriage and family relationships that promoted the well-being of all, including not only spouses and parents but their offspring and other family relations as well. Those who willingly abandoned those relationships in order to live in ways that were contrary to God's will did harm not only to themselves and their families but also to the community as a whole. If they were not confronted with their destructive behavior and its consequences but were instead allowed to live undisturbed within the confines of home and family and continued to enjoy the same privileges and protection as other members of the community, their presence there would become toxic and would gradually undermine and subvert the well-being, happiness, and unity of those around them. For that reason, it was necessary to expose them and make public what they were doing in an attempt to put an end to their destructive behavior. Of course, this was true not only for women but for men as well. The law therefore commanded that both men and women endure the same penalty for adultery, though it can hardly be doubted that in a society dominated by males the laws tended to be interpreted and applied in ways that favored men over women and resulted in the treatment of women and girls that at times was not only unjust but even cruel and inhumane.

It is important to recognize, however, that the passages from the prophetic books that portray God as stripping naked and exposing publicly his people Israel in the same way that a man would treat his adulterous and unfaithful wife who has prostituted herself among many lovers do not conceive of him doing such a thing for *his own* sake, as if he were some type of abusive and possessive husband who merely sought to shame and embarrass his wife out of spite and jealousy. Rather, the idea behind such passages is that his people are pretending outwardly to be living in faithfulness and submission to him in order to enjoy his blessings and protection when in private they are dedicating themselves and their lives to false gods and idols in order to pursue their own selfish desires and interests, contrary to God's will. For that reason, God wishes to expose publicly what they are doing privately in order to make it clear to all that they are in fact acting in ways that destroy their own well-being and that of others who form part of their same family and community as a result of their devotion to other gods and their unfaithfulness to the one true God to whom they belong. By bringing their infidelity and licentiousness out into the open, God not only wishes to shame them but also seeks to force them to make a decision as to whether they will continue to abandon him for other gods or instead return to a life of faithfulness and commitment to him and to everything he desires and commands of them for their own good.

While the vast majority of people today would rightly condemn as cruel, inhumane, and entirely unacceptable the practice of exposing publicly the nakedness of adulterous wives or women who prostitute themselves in the way that the biblical texts describe, it is important not only to take into consideration the original contexts in which those texts were composed when reading and interpreting them but also to seek to grasp their logic within those contexts. A woman who had voluntarily chosen to bare herself and have sexual relations with men who had no commitment to her within the confines of a home and family simply to satisfy an unhealthy or selfish desire on her part for pleasure, money, or other favors was not acting in ways that promoted her own good and that of the other members of her family and community. To expose her publicly in the eyes of the lovers she sought out was not only a means by which her husband attempted to bring out into the open her decision to behave in such a manner and force her to choose between those lovers and himself but also placed her at the disposal of those lovers. In principle, one of those lovers might even receive her and take her into his home in order to care for her and do good to her. It would be much more likely, however, that the lovers she had chosen for herself would continue to use her and abuse of her in order to satisfy their own selfish and lustful desires. Thus to expose her publicly in front of those lovers was to hand her over to the consequences of the decisions she had made by subjecting her to the whims, passions, and mistreatment of the men to whom she had chosen to give herself, unless of course she repented of what she had done, renounced her infidelity and adultery, and committed herself to being a faithful wife to her rightful husband once more.

The imagery of God exposing publicly his people Israel to make manifest to all their infidelity and lustful pursuit of other gods as their "lovers" should be understood against the background of these ideas. In addition to making it clear for all to see that, contrary to appearances, his sinful people were not serving him in righteousness and obedience but had instead fallen into injustice, falsehood, lewdness, and violence as a result of their worship of other gods, God was in essence handing them over to the gods they had chosen for themselves as well as the people who served those gods. Rather than preventing the people from prostituting themselves with such gods, God was delivering them up to those gods and the nations associated with them and forcing the people to endure the consequences of their decision to dedicate their lives to such gods. God was, of course, aware that those consequences would be disastrous. For that reason, in passages such as Ezekiel 16, it is not God himself who does harm to the people when they serve the gods of the nations but those nations themselves. He does so by handing them over to those gods and nations:

> I will judge you as women who commit adultery and shed blood are judged and bring blood upon you in wrath and jealousy. I will deliver you into their hands, and they will throw down your houses of prostitution and break down your high places. They will strip you of your clothing and your precious jewels and leave you naked and bare. They will bring up a large host against you and will stone you and pierce you through with their swords. They will burn down your houses and execute judgments on you in the sight of many women. I will stop you from playing the harlot, and you shall prostitute yourself no more. So I will satisfy my fury on you and my jealousy will be turned away from you. I will be calm once more and no longer be angry. Because you have not remembered the days of your youth but have provoked me to anger with all of these things, I will bring down on your head what you have done, says the Lord God (vv. 38-43).

While this passage clearly speaks of God's intense anger at Israel, the manner in which he satisfies that anger is not by inflicting suffering and punishments on his people personally but by handing them over to the nations and peoples to whom they have joined themselves by dedicating themselves to their gods. The passage also states clearly his intention, however: what he seeks is to stop his people from continuing to prostitute themselves and make payments to their lovers by subjecting them to suffering at the hands of others that are so intense that they will be compelled to return to him and live once more as his own, as they did in the time of their youth.

The same logic is present in other passages that employ the same imagery. The prophet Ezekiel repeats the accusation of adultery and prostitution against Israel and Judah in chapter 23 of the book, yet once more presents God as handing the idolatrous people over to their lovers rather than punishing them himself: "I will stir up against you your lovers from whom you have turned away in disgust, and I will bring them against you from every side. . . . They will also strip you of your clothing and your precious jewels. So I will put an end to your lewdness and your prostitution that you brought from the land of Egypt" (Ezek 23:22, 26-27). In Jer 13:12-27, where God threatens to make the people drunk and says he will lift their skirts over their faces in order to expose them to shame, the prophet likewise portrays the suffering to which Israel will be subjected as something that will be brought on not by God personally but by the nations with whom his people have allied themselves. After affirming that those nations will come from afar to take them captive and carry them off into exile, God tells the people: "And if you ask in your heart, 'Why have these things come upon me?,' it is for the magnitude of your iniquity that your skirts have been lifted up and you have been violated" (Jer 13:22). Here it is not God but the nations who lift up Israel's skirt to violate her. While God is also presented as responding to Israel's persistent pursuit of other lovers by uncovering her nakedness in their presence in Hosea 2, there he seeks to convince Israel that it is he rather than those lovers who provides her with the good things she treasures. At the same time, he promises to allure her back to himself with tenderness, steadfast love, and mercy so that she will choose to live as his wife in justice and righteousness (Hos 2:1-23). Once again, therefore, his purpose in exposing and shaming Israel is ultimately to deliver the people from the mistreatment and abuse that they experience at the hands of others and to reestablish them as his beloved people so that they may enjoy his blessings and goodness. While such imagery obviously remains highly problematic from a modern perspective, as is the case with other images used in the biblical texts, the logic underlying it has to do with God's intentions to do his people good, even though at times this requires that he also do them harm or evil.

The Ravages of a Wrath Unleashed

While many of the passages from the prophetic books that speak of God subjecting his people to suffering and hardships for the purpose of chastising and correcting them are fairly easy to reconcile with the idea that ultimately he is seeking to bring them back to himself and his commandments for their own good out of love for them, others are not. In particular, there are numerous passages that describe God imposing on the people forms of suffering, death, and destruction that seem not only cruel and heartless but even horrific, hideous, and barbaric. Many of these even go beyond the type of scourges, plagues, calamities, and other afflictions with which God is said to threaten the people in the second part of Deuteronomy 28. In some of these passages, in fact, the extreme violence with which God is said to treat both guilty and innocent alike seems not only inhumane but monstrous and perverse.

Such passages use a wide array of images to portray God intentionally doing harm to the people and causing them tremendous pain and suffering. In Isaiah, God is said to attack his people like a warrior filled with rage and fury to lay waste to the land and destroy all who stand in his way (Isa 42:13-15). In his anger he stretches out his hand to smite them until their corpses lie like refuse in the streets (5:25). The prophet tells the people that God will become a trap and a snare for the inhabitants of Jerusalem and then ominously adds: "Let him be your fear, and let him be your dread!" (8:13-15). Isaiah also presents God as failing to show pity on children, orphans, and widows and making the people become "like fuel for the fire" in his burning wrath (9:17-19). In his fury God will come in fire and whirlwind to fill the land with the dead bodies of those who rebel against him: "their worm will not die, their fire will not be extinguished, and they will be an abhorrence to all flesh" (66:15-24).

In the book of Jeremiah, God has the prophet tell the people: "I am full of the wrath of the Lord; I am weary of holding it in. Pour it out on the children in the street, and on the gatherings of young men as well! Both husband and wife shall be taken, the aged and the very old. Their houses will be handed over to others, together with their fields and wives; for I will stretch out my hand against the inhabitants of the land, says the Lord" (Jer 6:11-12). After telling Jeremiah that he is about to fill the inhabitants of the land with drunkenness to inflict tremendous suffering on them, he adds: "I will dash them one against the other, parents and children together, says the Lord. I will not show pity or mercy or compassion when I destroy them" (13:14). In a passage from Jeremiah 15 already cited above, God tells the inhabitants of Jerusalem that he will make their widows more numerous than the grains of sand on the seashore and fill the lives of mothers with anguish, panic, and terror (vv. 8-9).

In the very next chapter of Jeremiah, the prophet continues: "They shall die of deadly diseases. They shall not be mourned, nor shall they be buried. They shall become like dung covering the ground. They shall perish by the sword and by famine, and their dead bodies shall become food for the birds of the air and for the wild animals of the earth" (Jer 16:4-5; cf. 21:3-10). In Jer 25:33, the prophet describes in similar terms the outcome of the day of disaster and tempest that God has determined to bring upon Israel and other nations as well: "Those slain by the Lord on that day will be strewn from one end of the earth to the other. They will not be lamented or gathered up or buried; they will become like dung covering the ground." The fate of those whom God will send into exile is described in much the same way: "Thus says the LORD of hosts: I am going to let loose on them sword, famine, and pestilence, and I will make them like rotten figs that are so bad they cannot be eaten. I will pursue them with the sword, with famine, and with pestilence, and will make them a horror in the sight of all of the kingdoms of the earth, an object of cursing and scorn and contempt, and a derision among all the nations where I have driven them" (29:17-18).

The imagery used to describe the destruction of Jerusalem by the Babylonians in the book of Lamentations is even more horrific. God is said to have destroyed Israel as if he were the people's enemy, leaving the land and even his sanctuary in ruins, littering the streets with the corpses of the young, the old, and even infants, and leaving mothers with no choice but to boil and eat the flesh of their own children in order to survive (Lam 2:5-12, 15-21; 4:10). "Their skin has shriveled on their bones; it has become as dry as wood. Happier were those pierced by the sword than those pierced by hunger; they wasted away, pierced through by the lack of the produce of the field" (4:8-9). In addition to the imagery that is extremely violent and gruesome, the book describes graphically the laments, despair, pain, and weeping of the survivors of the slaughter: "Our skin is black as an oven from the scorching heat of famine. Women are raped in Zion, young virgins in the towns of Judah. Princes are hung up by their hands; the elderly are shown no respect. Young men are forced to grind grain, and boys stagger under loads of wood. The old men have left the city gate, the young men their music. The joy of our hearts has ceased; our dancing has been turned to mourning" (5:10-15).[2]

Ezekiel speaks not only of parents eating their children but children eating their parents and subsequently scattering any who survive to the winds (Ezek 5:10). God tells the people that he will spend his fury on them by slaying them with the sword, with famine, and with pestilence until they are made a desolation and their land is laid to waste:

> Thus says the Lord GOD: Clap your hands, stamp your feet and say, Ah, because of all of the evil abominations of the house of Israel, they will fall by the sword, famine, and pestilence; those who are far away will die of the pestilence, and those who are near will fall by the sword, and those who remain and are spared from these things will die of famine. Thus I will satisfy my anger against them. Then you will know that I am the LORD, when their slain lie among their idols around their altars, on every high hill and mountaintop, under every green tree and leafy oak, in every place where they offered fragrant incense to their idols. And I will stretch out my hand against them and the places where they dwell, and will make the land more desolate and deserted than the wilderness toward Riblah. Then they will know that I am the LORD (6:11-14).

Several chapters later, God is presented as sending executioners on the people to kill them. He instructs them: "Your eye shall not spare, and you shall

---

2. For other examples of similar imagery, see especially Lam 1:2-4, 8-9, 11-13, 16-17, 20-21; 3:1-6, 15-20, 48-51.

show no pity. Slaughter old men, young men and young women, little children and women" (Ezek 9:5-6). According to the prophet, when God draws from out of its sheath his sword sharpened for slaughter, both righteous and wicked will moan in agony and will cry and wail: "Every heart will melt and every hand grow feeble; every spirit will faint and every knee will turn to water" (21:3-12). Further on in the book Ezekiel is called to proclaim to the people:

> Therefore, as I live, says the Lord God, I will give you over to bloodshed, and bloodshed will pursue you; since you did not hate bloodshed, it shall pursue you. I will make Mount Seir a wasteland and a desolation; and I will cut off from it all who come and go. I will fill its mountains with the slain; on your hills and in your valleys and in all your ravines those killed by the sword shall fall. I will make you a perpetual desolation, and your cities shall never again be inhabited. Then you will know that I am the Lord (35:6-9).

In the book of Hosea, the words that God speaks to his people through the prophet are equally harsh and gruesome. Near the end of the book, God says of those who have rebelled against him: "They shall fall by the sword; their little ones will be dashed in pieces, and their pregnant women will be ripped open" (Hos 13:16). Several chapters earlier, God tells the people:

> Even if they bring up children, I will take them away until none are left. Woe to them indeed when I depart from them! Once I saw Ephraim planted in a pleasant meadow as a young palm, but now Ephraim must bring his children out for slaughter. "Give something to them, O Lord; but what will you give? Give them a womb that miscarries and breasts that are dry!" All of their wickedness began at Gilgal; it was there that I came to hate them. Because of the evils they have done I will drive them out of my house. I will love them no more; all their leaders are rebels. Ephraim has been struck down; their root is dried up, they will bear no fruit. Even though they bear children, I will kill the cherished offspring of their womb. Because they have not listened to him, my God will cast them away; they will become wanderers among the nations (9:12-17).

The books of the other prophets of the Hebrew Bible contain imagery that reflects the same type of violence and terror. The prophet Amos tells those who oppress the poor and crush the needy: "The Lord God has sworn by his holiness: The time is surely coming when they will take you away with meat hooks, and the last ones left among you with fishhooks" (Amos 4:1-2). In Mic 3:12 the rulers and leaders of the people are told: "Zion will be plowed up like a field; Jerusalem will become a heap of ruins, and the mountain of the temple will be turned into a forest." The prophet Malachi presents God as becoming so incensed when the priests and the people refuse to listen to him that he promises to curse both them and their blessings: "I will rebuke your offspring, and spread dung on your faces, the dung of your sacrificial victims, and I will banish you from my presence" (Mal 2:2-3). From its very beginning, the book of Zephaniah presents God vowing that he will "utterly sweep away everything from the face of the land," including not only humans and animals but also the birds of the air and the fish of the sea (Zeph 1:2-3). Further on in the opening chapter of Zephaniah, the prophet continues:

> That day will be a day of wrath, a day of anguish and distress, a day of devastation and destruction, a day of darkness and gloom, a day of clouds and thick darkness, a day of trumpet blasts and battle cries against the fortified cities and against the high battlements. I will bring such distress upon people that they will walk like the blind, because they have sinned against the LORD; their blood will be poured out like dust, and their flesh like dung. Neither their silver nor their gold will be able to save them on the day of the LORD's wrath. In the heat of his passion the whole earth will be consumed; for he will make a full and terrible end of all of the inhabitants of the land (vv. 15-18).

Striving to Make Sense of Terror and Torment

While it may seem that passages such as those just considered are impossible to reconcile with faith in a God who desires nothing but the well-being of his people, it is important to see them in context and grasp the logic underlying them. This logic, in fact, is essentially the same as that found in the account of the flood in Genesis 6–8. According to that account, the wickedness, injustice, and violence among the people of the earth had reached such great heights that there appeared to be no remedy. God came to the conclusion that there was nothing that he might do to bring about any kind of change in human beings, and for that reason he chose to bring upon all but the righteous Noah and his family the destruction of the flood.

In the books of Israel's prophets, however, God is also said to have sent his people one prophet after another in an attempt to bring the people to put away their sinful behavior, which is often portrayed not only as oppressive and unjust but even ruthless, savage, and murderous. These repeated and persistent efforts on God's part to bring his people back to him have not only proven fruitless but have consistently been met with even further wickedness, injustice, and violence. For that reason, from the perspective of the biblical texts as well as the God of whom they speak, the only possible hope for the people is for God to subject them to such tremendous suffering and destruction that those who survive the carnage that he will bring upon them are so broken, humiliated, and driven to despair that they will have no choice but to abandon their ruinous and reprehensible behavior. They must be brought so low and become so thoroughly devastated, ravished, and despondent that they can do nothing but cry out to God for mercy and beg him to put an end to the unbearable afflictions and hardships to which he will subject them. Only by creating such tremendous anguish, distress, and misery among them can God hope to bring about any deep and lasting change in them.

For the same reason, when God addresses himself to the people by means of his prophets, he has them make use of language that leaves no doubt as to the intensity and ferocity of his anger and indignation at their wicked behavior, as well as his intention to take decisive action against them to put a stop to it. That language is designed to evoke shock, horror, fright, and dismay in the hearers by means of the violent imagery and threats that it conveys. Precisely because the prophets wish to evoke such a response in their hearers, at times they may be said to go to extremes in their use of such language and imagery. Likewise, the tremendous outrage, revulsion, anger, and horror that the injustices, atrocities, and crimes being committed evoke in the prophets lead them to make threats that describe those guilty of such behaviors being subjected to the same type of brutal and savage treatment that they have displayed against others. It must be stressed, however, that such violent language and imagery must be understood not as an expression of hatred for those who have perpetrated such great evils on others but rather of a deep and burning desire to see such injustices, violence, atrocities, and crimes brought to an end. This will happen as those responsible for these things are either utterly destroyed and devastated or else brought to change their ways, though the prophets generally hold out little hope for the latter to happen.

In order to illustrate this point, it is helpful to consider a passage that many would consider one of the most violent and disturbing in all of the Hebrew Bible. In Psalm 137, the Psalmist recalls the violence done to the people by the Edomites and the Babylonians during the destruction of Jerusalem. That Psalm begins by describing the survivors of the destruction weeping while their tormentors taunt them by asking them to sing songs for them in the land to which they have been taken captive. It then concludes: "O daughter of Babylon, you devastator! Happy will be those who do to you what you have done to us! Happy will be those who take your little ones and dash them against the rocks!" (vv. 8-9). The clear implication of these words is that the speaker and his people were forced to watch the skulls of their own infant children being crushed as they were dashed against rocks by the Babylonian soldiers who were in the process of destroying Jerusalem and taking the parents of those children into captivity and exile.

At first glance, the words of the Psalmist appear to be an expression of nothing but hatred, spite, and a desire for vengeance. Yet while there can be little doubt that those who saw their infant children killed in this manner experienced intense feelings of hatred and anger toward those responsible for their murder, the wish expressed in this passage must not be reduced simply to a desire to see those who had inflicted such great suffering on them made to endure the same type of horrendous experience as an end in itself, as if it were motivated purely by spite and a longing for revenge. Rather, that wish may also be understood as a desire that their Babylonian captors be subjected to such an experience so that they may learn what it is like to be forced to endure such atrocities and in that way be brought to stop inflicting the same type of atrocities on others, including especially innocent people such as small children and their parents. In addition, by being subjected to such a horrifying experience themselves, those who perpetrated those atrocities might even be brought to feel sympathy and compassion for those who are subjected to such violence and bloodshed at the hands of others, since they would come to know what it feels like to see their loved ones treated with such brutality. That sympathy and compassion would lead them to enter into solidarity with those who suffer such violence rather than continuing to treat others with the same cruelty. By no means, therefore, must the wish that the infant children of the Babylonians be seized and dashed against the rocks in the same way that the infant children of the inhabitants of Jerusalem were killed at their hands be understood purely as a desire for vengeance as an end in itself.

The same type of observations should be made with regard to the crude and violent language and imagery used in many of the passages from the prophetic books to describe the sufferings and destruction that God is said to pour out on his people when they have fallen into sins that are particularly grievous and heinous. That language and imagery need not and should not be understood as conveying the idea that God actually hates the people and seeks to inflict revenge on them as an end in itself. On the contrary, such passages must be read in conjunction with the other passages in those same books that make it clear that God's commitment to bless and prosper the people remains fully intact. If that commitment is to be fulfilled, however, in the minds of the prophets the evils that must be eradicated and expunged among the people are so widespread and deep-seated that nothing less than a total devastation of the people and their land will be sufficient to lay the basis for a radical, thoroughgoing, and long-lasting change in the behavior of those who survive that devastation. In essence, in order for them to be healed of the wickedness that has become so deeply ingrained in them, God must make their existence so wretched and unbearable that they are left with no other choice but to turn back to him and submit to whatever measures he may impose on them if they wish to have any hope of surviving. They must be so badly bruised, battered, and beaten as to be left desperate and despondent, because only in that way can God do away in definitive fashion with their hardness of heart and begin to form a new people out of them.

It is likely, of course, that many of the terrifying images that appear in passages from the prophetic writings such as those just considered above describe experiences that people had actually lived through some time before those passages were written. In that case, the gruesome experiences portrayed by means of those images represent memories of the past rather than prophetic threats regarding the future. In fact, these two possibilities by no means exclude one another. The prophets may be describing many of the unspeakable things that the people had experienced or observed in the past or even in previous generations in order to communicate to the people that they will go through such horrendous experiences once again unless they change their ways. This would explain why that imagery is often so crude and graphic. While in our own day the extreme violence that these passages describe is relatively rare, at least in the Western world, in biblical times such was not the case.

Many of these passages speak of righteous persons and even innocent children and infants being subjected to horrific forms of suffering and death along with the guilty and wicked who are regarded as deserving such a fate. Because the notion that the innocent might suffer such great cruelties together with the guilty and wicked appears to contradict the idea that Israel's God consistently acts in conformity with what is fair and just, it is no doubt highly problematic. According to the logic of the biblical texts, however, when God brings down destruction and devastation upon his people in order to chastise them or do away with the evil and destructive behavior that has arisen in their midst, he generally deals with them not as individuals but collectively as a group. In these instances, it is the people as a whole who must be chastised and purified or in some cases subjected to forms of destruction that do away with a large part of the people in order to leave only a small remnant that will submit obediently to him. These collective forms of chastisement and destruction do not allow for any kind of selective separation between the righteous and the sinners or the innocent and the guilty in order to spare those individuals or groups that are relatively righteous and innocent. Because they are intermingled with the sinners and evildoers and to some extent are inseparable from them, the righteous and innocent are subjected to suffering and destruction together with the guilty and the wicked when God acts to punish and purify the people.

In biblical thought, when the people's evil and destructive behavior has become so firmly entrenched among them that God must take drastic measures in order to purge them of that behavior in a way that is thoroughgoing, comprehensive, and long-lasting, those measures must also be taken against the righteous and the innocent because they too tend to be implicated in that behavior in some ways. While they may not be engaged in that behavior themselves, they often overlook it or implicitly give their consent to it by not doing anything to correct or change it. In that way, they become complicit in such behavior. Even when they stand up to it and oppose it, their love for others may bring them to choose to remain in solidarity with them even when they must suffer together with them as a result of that solidarity. In those cases, rather than seeking to distance themselves from the rest of the people, they prefer to stand by their side and endure together with them the same sufferings that they do in order to accompany them and give them strength and hope.

In contexts in which the evil and violence have grown particularly rampant and widespread, all of the people come under pressure either to join in that evil and violence themselves or else to tolerate it and overlook it. As a result, all are in constant danger of being brought to adopt that behavior themselves and need to be warned of the consequences for doing so. In these cases, the punishments that the people are made to endure collectively are preventative: even though many of them have not yet fallen into sinful behavior, by being made to suffer together with the guilty, they will be brought to avoid it in the future. The death and destruction to which their family members and loved ones are subjected will produce a change even in those who have not fallen into sinful behavior, since they will be dissuaded from adopting such behavior themselves and will hopefully be formed into people who will actively discourage and suppress such behavior among others. Because God is attempting to bring about a change in the people as a whole and not merely in isolated individuals, the sufferings that the people endure collectively transform in profound ways all of the individuals that make up that people and thus result in significant changes among them as a group. In various ways, the suffering that they endure alongside one another serves not only to change the people on an individual level but also to generate greater solidarity among them.

The punishments that God inflicts on innocent persons such as children and infants may also be preventative in the sense that the things they suffer will lead them to avoid destructive behaviors when they become older. As they see the manner in which God responds to those behaviors among others, they are forewarned not to adopt such behaviors in the future. At the same time, as they accompany their family members, loved ones, and neighbors in their suffering, they learn to live in solidarity with them as well and are brought to feel sympathy and empathy for those who suffer. In this way, the sufferings that even the innocent endure serve to transform both them and others.

To some extent, of course, it is simply not feasible for God to inflict suffering only on the isolated individuals who are particularly guilty of evil and wrongdoing rather than on the people as a whole. Often it is virtually impossible to make a determination as to which persons are more deserving of punishment than others, since the guilt is not only individual but is shared among all. In many cases, the evils have become so pervasive and deeply ingrained among the people that it is impossible to root out those evils without taking action against all of the people collectively. As in Jesus' parable of the wheat and the tares or weeds in the Gospel of Matthew in the New Testament, the good and the bad have become so inseparably intertwined with one another that it is not possible to do away with the bad without doing away with the good, righteous, and innocent at the same time (Matt 13:24-29).

The idea that at times the cruel and severe sufferings that God inflicts on people are designed to impact those who observe those sufferings rather than those who are actually subjected to them is actually fairly common in the Hebrew Bible. In the prophetic books, for example, God is said to have destroyed the northern kingdom of Israel at the hands of the Assyrians in order to bring the people of the southern kingdom of Judah to repent of their ways. In Jer 3:6-10, God is presented as reminding Judah of the manner in which he had sent away her sister Israel after she "played the harlot" and then accusing Judah of the same behavior: "her false sister Judah did not fear, but she too went and played the harlot.... She did not return to me with her whole heart, but only feigned repentance." Several chapters later God promises to do to the people of Jerusalem what he did to the city of Shiloh, where the Israelites of the northern kingdom had dedicated a sanctuary to him, casting them out of his sight because of their wickedness (Jer 7:12-15). Similarly, in Ezek 16:45-52 and 23:1-34, the people of Jerusalem are said to have fallen into sins that were worse than those of the Israelites of the northern kingdom. For that reason, they are to expect to be subjected to an ever harsher judgment than their sister Israel in the north was made to endure. In the second of these passages, God tells the people: "You shall drink your sister's cup, deep and wide; you shall be scorned and mocked, since it holds so much. You shall be filled with drunkenness and sorrow. The cup of your sister Samaria is a cup of horror and desolation; you shall drink it down to the last drop and gnaw on its broken pieces and tear out your breasts; for I have spoken, says the Lord God" (Ezek 23:31-34).

In the case of this last passage, in order to impress upon his hearers the idea that the suffering and punishments to which God will subject them will be even greater than those he had inflicted on the people of the northern kingdom, the prophet Ezekiel must use imagery that is particularly graphic in nature. Other passages from the prophetic writings use the same type of graphic language to depict the sufferings and destruction that God promises to inflict upon other nations as well. Isaiah speaks of God being "enraged against all the nations" and as a result giving them over to slaughters and sating his sword with blood until the land is soaked and flooded in that blood and the stench of the corpses of those slain becomes unbearable (Isa 34:2-7). He also promises to make Israel's oppressors eat their own flesh and become drunk with their own blood as if it were wine (Isa 49:25-26). Jeremiah speaks in similar terms regarding the manner in which God intends to slaughter the Egyptians and portrays the destruction of other nations in extremely harsh terms as well.[3] In some cases, the prophets are merely describing the type of terror and bloodshed that these nations have inflicted on Israel and other nations so as to promise that they will be subjected to sufferings that are either just as intense or even greater. Even in these cases, however, God's purpose is not understood in terms of exacting vengeance for its own sake but rather of humbling and bringing low the powerful nations that oppress others or putting a complete end to their violence and oppression. While his main purpose is that of delivering the oppressed from their hands, he also seeks to make them an example for other peoples throughout the world so that those peoples may be made to know that if they fall into the same type of oppressive behavior, they will be subjected to sufferings and destruction that are just as devastating.

In some cases, language and imagery that is extremely violent is used to assure those who have been subjected to great suffering at the hands of others that they will be liberated and delivered in a dramatic and decisive manner. The oppressors who have crushed and decimated them will not only be

---

3. See Jer 46:10-12; 48:8-10, 25-26; 50:11-16; 51:37-44.

overthrown but will be so utterly destroyed and ravished that they will never again be able to do any type of harm to others. One such passage is Isa 42:10-17, which combines expressions of rejoicing and celebration with allusions to God going forth in fury as a mighty warrior in order to lay waste to the land:

> Sing to the LORD a new song; sing his praises from the end of the earth! Let the sea roar, and all that fills it, the coastlands and those who dwell in them! Let the desert and its towns lift up their voice, the villages that Kedar inhabits! Let the inhabitants of Sela sing for joy and shout from the tops of the mountains! Let them give glory to the LORD and declare his praise in the coastlands! The LORD goes forth like a warrior; like a man of war he stirs up his fury. He utters a shout and raises a war cry. He shows himself to be mighty against his foes. For a long time I have held my peace; I have kept still and restrained myself, but now I will cry out like a woman in labor, gasping and panting. I will lay waste to mountains and hills and dry up all their vegetation; I will turn the rivers into islands, and dry up the pools. I will lead the blind along a road they do not know and guide them down paths they have never walked. I will turn the darkness before them into light and the rough places into level ground. These are the things I will do, and I will not abandon them. Those who trust in idols and say to cast images, "You are our gods" will be turned back and utterly put to shame.

Like this passage, many of the texts that describe people being subjected to horrific forms of suffering and destruction speak of God blessing and prospering those whose lives he has filled with afflictions in the same immediate context. In some cases, the reason why these two apparently conflicting ideas or images are combined with one another is that the prophets wish to speak of a new beginning for the people that will be radically different from anything they have experienced previously. In order for that new beginning to be brought about, God must act to sweep away definitively and decisively every form of sinfulness, evil and wrongdoing. Only by utterly laying waste to the people and their land can God root out the terrible evils that have arisen among them and bring about something new. It is as if that which has existed up to that time must be burned to the ground and reduced to ashes so that from those ashes a reality unlike anything ever known previously may arise. This is the process described in Jer 31:28, for example: "And it shall come to pass that just as I have watched over them to root up and tear down, to demolish and destroy and bring down evil, so I will watch over them to build and to plant, says the LORD." The same type of threat and promise of blessing are found later in the same book with regard to the Ammonites:

> Therefore, the days are surely coming, says the LORD, when I will cause the battle cry to be heard against Rabbah of the Ammonites; it shall be reduced to a desolate mound, and its villages shall be burned with fire. Then Israel shall dispossess those who dispossessed him, says the LORD. Wail, O Heshbon, for Ai is laid waste! Cry out, O daughters of Rabbah! Gird yourselves with sackcloth and mourning, and run to and fro among the hedges! For Milcom shall go into exile, with his priests and his princes.... See, I will bring down terror on you from all sides, says the Lord GOD of hosts, and you shall be driven out

straightaway, with no one left to gather those who escape. But afterward I will restore the fortunes of the Ammonites, says the Lord (Jer 49:2-3, 5-6).

The same combination of utter destruction and hope for the future is found in Isa 10:16-23. There in the same context in which God threatens to burn, devour, and lay waste to the people and their land and even make a full end of them, he also promises to bring into existence a small remnant of righteous persons who will look to him in faith:

> Therefore the Lord, the Lord of hosts, will send a debilitating illness among his stout warriors, and in the place of his splendor a burning will be kindled, like the burning of fire. The light of Israel shall become a fire, and his Holy One a flame; and it will burn and devour his thorns and briers in a single day. He will destroy in both soul and body the glory of his forest and his fertile land, and it will be like a sick man who wastes away. The trees that are left in his forest will be so few that a child could write them down. In that day the remnant of Israel and the survivors of the house of Jacob will no longer lean on those who struck them, but will lean upon the Lord, the Holy One of Israel, in truth. A remnant shall return, the remnant of Jacob, to the mighty God. For though your people Israel be as numerous as the grains of sand on the seashore, only a remnant of them will return. The destruction decreed will be overflowing with justice. For the Lord, the Lord of hosts, will consume all that is within the land, as it is decreed.

While there is certainly a great deal of language and imagery in the prophetic books that evokes horror and consternation, therefore, it is important to see this language and imagery in the context of the books as a whole and also in the context of the forms of extreme violence and bloodshed that often characterized the world of antiquity. Such language and imagery reflects the intense passion of Israel's prophets as well, and especially their tremendous outrage and fierce indignation at the depths of injustice, oppression, and depravity into which the people to whom they address their words have descended. According to the logic of the texts, if those prophets hope to effect any type of change or see the evil and injustice swept away for good so that a new beginning can be made, they must attempt to sow shock and dismay among their hearers and threaten them with sufferings that are so unspeakable and hideous that they will either be overcome by fear and horror or else left with no choice but to turn back to God after they have been battered and broken in the manner in which those prophets describe.

Finally, it is also important to stress the ideas that are *not* behind the prophetic passages that employ such graphic imagery to describe the sufferings that God intends to bring upon the people. As we have seen throughout this study, when the God of the Hebrew Bible is said to impose tremendous sufferings and harsh punishments upon his people, it is not because he is a selfish or self-centered God who acts out of spite, hatred, or revenge for his own sake simply to inflict pain on people for having offended or angered him in some way. Much less is he a God who takes delight in seeing acts of great cruelty carried out against people whom he has come to despise or even loathe for some capricious or selfish reason. The God of Israel is not a god like Molech who demands that human beings or innocent babies be put to death in order to quench his thirst for blood. Nor is his holy and righteous nature thought to demand that those who blatantly persist in acting contrary to his will be subjected to atrocities and acts of savagery and brutality in order to ensure that they receive a retribution that is proportional to the heinous nature of their deeds. Images of God as a "loose cannon" who simply explodes in anger and strikes down the righteous and innocent with the guilty as he flails away wildly at his people in order to give vent to his pent-up fury and rage must also be rejected as contrary to the portrayal of God found throughout the biblical texts. When the God of Israel is said to inflict suffering on his sinful people, what he seeks is not to satisfy his justice or wrath by striking down sinners or making them pay for their sins but to effect some type of profound and lasting change in them and their behavior for their sake rather than his own.

SOWING HOPE IN THE MIDST OF HEARTACHE

Despite their continual stress on Israel's persistent sinfulness and the people's refusal to turn back to God even when he inflicts harsh sufferings on them to chastise them, virtually all of the prophetic writings hold out hope that eventually God's efforts to form a people who will live in justice and righteousness for their own good will be successful. Both for the people themselves as well as God, this involves a process that is extremely painful, especially because it can be accomplished only by condemning a large portion of the people to destruction and subjecting another part to exile among the nations. As a result, the remnant of people who ultimately turn back to God in obedience so as to enjoy his blessing in the land he promised to them is relatively small in number. Yet in spite of its reduced size, this remnant provides hope for the future since it constitutes a seed or sprout from which a nation that will finally practice justice and righteousness will grow, develop, expand, and prosper.

Before this can happen, however, the people must be broken and humiliated. A passage near the beginning of the book of Isaiah particularly stresses this point. After pointing out how the land has been filled with idols and riches that have been obtained through injustice and violence, the prophet affirms that this situation will change only when the people have been made to suffer:

> The eyes of the haughty will be brought low, and all arrogance will be humbled; and the LORD alone will be exalted on that day. For the LORD of hosts has fixed a day to put down the proud and lofty and to bring low all that is elevated and held high.... The idols will be utterly abolished. People will enter the caves in the rocks and the holes in the ground to flee from the terror of the LORD and from the glory of his majesty when he arises to make the earth tremble. On that day people will throw to the moles and to the bats the idols of silver and gold that they made for themselves to worship (Isa 2:11-12, 18-20; cf. 27:7-10).

Elsewhere in the prophetic books God is presented as telling the people that before he can save and redeem them and restore their fortunes, they must endure fully the punishments that he is imposing on them in order to correct and purify them. It is necessary for this purification to be thorough and complete so that it will be long-lasting and bring about a definitive change in their behavior. The prophet Ezekiel especially stresses this idea:

> And they shall bear their punishment—the punishment of the prophet and the punishment of the diviner will be the same—so that the house of Israel may no longer go astray from me, nor pollute themselves any more with all their transgressions. Then they will be my people, and I will be their God, says the Lord God (Ezek 14:10-11).

> I will bring you back from among the peoples and gather you out of the lands where you have been scattered with a mighty hand and an outstretched arm, with the full extent of my fury; and I will bring you into the wilderness of the peoples, and there I will enter into judgment with you face to face. Just as I entered into judgment with your ancestors in the wilderness of the land of Egypt, so I will enter into judgment with you, says the Lord God. . . . I will purge out from among you the rebels and those who transgress against me; I will bring them out of the land where they reside as foreigners, but they will not enter the land of Israel. Then you will know that I am the Lord (Ezek 20:34-36, 38).

> Therefore thus says the Lord God: Because you have all become dross, I will gather you into the midst of Jerusalem. As one gathers silver, bronze, iron, lead, and tin into a smelting furnace to blow fire upon them in order to melt them, so I will gather you in my anger and in my wrath, and I will put you in and melt you. I will gather you together and blow upon you with the fire of my wrath, and you will be melted within it. As silver is melted in a smelter, so you will be melted in the midst of it; and you will know that I the Lord have poured out my wrath on you (Ezek 22:19-22).

Once this process of purifying and refining the people is complete, the people who remain will finally turn back to God. They will acknowledge their sinfulness and come to understand that the sufferings that God imposed on them were for their own good, precisely because they were designed to bring them to put away the sinful and destructive behavior that was doing them and others great harm. At the same time, they will put away the idols whose worship led them to practice sin and injustice and dedicate themselves to serving the God of Israel alone:

> Therefore by this the guilt of Jacob will be expiated, and this will be the full price for the pardoning of his sin: when he makes all the stones of the altars like chalkstones crushed to pieces, and no sacred poles or incense altars are left standing (Isa 27:9).

> Turn back to him whom you have so grievously betrayed, O people of Israel! For on that day all of you will throw away the idols of silver and gold that your sinful hands have made for yourselves (Isa 31:6-7).

> Therefore thus says the Lord God: How much more when I send upon Jerusalem my four deadly acts of judgment—sword, famine, wild animals, and

pestilence—to cut off humans and animals from it! Yet some survivors will be left in it, sons and daughters who will be brought out; they will come out to you and you will see their ways and their deeds. Then you will find consolation for the evil that I have brought upon Jerusalem, for all of the things that I brought down upon it. They will console you when you see their ways and their deeds, and you shall know that it was not without cause that I have done all that I did to it, says the Lord God (Ezek 14:21-23).

As for you, O house of Israel, thus says the Lord God: Every one of you, go serve your idols now and hereafter if you will not listen to me; but you will no longer profane my holy name with your gifts and your idols. For on my holy mountain, the high mountain of Israel, says the Lord God, all the house of Israel shall serve me in the land, every one of them. There I will accept them and demand from you your offerings and the choicest of your gifts, with all your holy sacrifices. As a pleasing aroma I will accept you when I bring you out from among the peoples and gather you out of the lands where you have been scattered; and I will manifest my holiness among you in the sight of the nations. You shall know that I am the Lord when I bring you into the land of Israel, the land that I swore to give to your ancestors. There you shall remember your ways and all the deeds by which you polluted yourselves; and you shall loathe yourselves for all the evils that you committed (Ezek 20:39-43; cf. 36:29-31).

See, I am sending my messenger to prepare the way before me, and the Lord whom you seek will suddenly come to his temple. Look, the messenger of the covenant in whom you delight is coming, says the Lord of hosts. But who can endure the day of his coming, and who can stand when he appears? For he is like a refiner's fire and like fullers' soap; he will sit as a refiner and a purifier of silver, and he will purify the descendants of Levi and refine them like gold and silver until they present to the Lord offerings of righteousness. Then the offering of Judah and Jerusalem will be pleasing to the Lord as it was in the days of old and in the years gone by (Mal 3:1-4).

The idea that the remnant that will be left will be relatively small in comparison to the population that existed prior to God's actions to purify them is stressed in a number of passages. While in one sense God will bring an end to Israel as it had existed previously, that end will be only partial but not full:

The remnant of the house of Judah that will survive shall again establish roots downward and bear fruit upward; for from Jerusalem a remnant shall go out, and from Mount Zion a band of survivors. The zeal of the Lord of hosts will do this (Isa 37:31-32; cf. 4:2-4).

I looked at the earth and it was without form and void; and to the heavens, and they had no light. I looked at the mountains and they were quaking, and all the hills shook to and fro. I looked and there was no one left, and all the birds of the air had flown away. I looked at the earth, and the fertile land had become a desert, and all its cities lay in ruins before the Lord, in the presence of his fierce anger. For thus says the Lord: The whole land shall be a desolation; yet I will not consume it completely (Jer 4:23-27; cf. 5:18).

In all the places where you live, your towns shall be laid to waste and your high places destroyed, so that your altars will be destroyed and lie in ruins;

your idols will be broken and shattered, your incense altars torn down, and the things you have made demolished. The slain will fall in your midst; then you will know that I am the LORD. But I will spare some from among you. Some of you will escape the sword among the nations and be scattered throughout foreign lands. Those of you who escape will remember me among the nations where you have been taken into captivity, calling to mind how I was crushed by their adulterous hearts that turned away from me and their wandering eyes that lusted after their idols. Then they will be loathsome in their own sight for the evils that they committed, for all their abominations. And they will know that I am the LORD; it was not in vain that I threatened to bring this disaster upon them (Ezek 6:6-10).

And they will know that I am the LORD when I scatter them among the nations and disperse them throughout foreign lands. But I will allow some of them to escape from the sword, from famine, and from pestilence so that they may acknowledge all their abominations among the nations where they go; then they will know that I am the LORD (Ezek 12:15-16; cf. Zeph 3:8-13; Zech 13:8-9).

A Return to Rejoice In

At the heart of the hopes of Israel's prophets for their people is the idea that God will gather those who have been scattered throughout the nations so that they may live once more on the land promised to them. This return to the land is seen as inseparable from a turning back to God in justice, righteousness, and obedience to his will. At times, this return is regarded as taking place alongside the punishment and destruction of the nations who have oppressed Israel and have served as God's instruments to chastise them and purify them from their sinful behavior. All of these things are seen as expressions of God's love and concern as well as a motive for rejoicing, despite the tremendous pain that the people have been made to endure:

On that day the root of Jesse will stand as a signal to the peoples; the nations will look to him, and his dwelling place will be glorious. On that day the LORD will once again raise his hand to recover the remnant that is left of his people from Assyria, from Egypt, from Pathros, from Cush, from Elam, from Shinar, from Hamath, and from the coastlands of the sea. He will raise up a signal for the nations and will assemble the outcasts of Israel and gather the dispersed of Judah from the four corners of the earth. The jealousy of Ephraim will leave him and the hostility of Judah shall be cut off; Ephraim will no longer be jealous of Judah, and Judah will not be hostile toward Ephraim. But they will swoop down on the slopes of the Philistines in the west and will take possession of the riches of the people of the east. They will subdue Edom and Moab, and Ammon will be subject to them. And the Lord will dry up the tongue of Egypt's sea and wave his hand over its river with his scorching wind. He will split it into seven channels and make a path to cross it on foot; so there shall be a highway from Assyria for the remnant that is left of his people, as there was for Israel when they came up from the land of Egypt (Isa 11:10-16).

On that day the LORD will thresh from the channel of the Euphrates to the Wadi of Egypt, and you will be gathered up one by one, O people of Israel.

And on that day a great trumpet will be blown, and those who were perishing in the land of Assyria and those who were scattered in the land of Egypt will come and worship the LORD on Jerusalem's holy mountain (Isa 27:12-13).

On that day the LORD of hosts will be a garland of glory and a diadem of beauty for the remnant of his people; he will be a spirit of justice for the one who sits down to judge, and give strength to those who turn back the battle at the gate (Isa 28:5-6).

Woe to the shepherds who destroy and scatter the sheep of my pasture!, says the LORD. Therefore thus says the LORD, the God of Israel, concerning the shepherds who shepherd my people: You have scattered my flock and driven them away, and you have not attended to them. So now I will attend to you for your evil doings, says the LORD. I myself will gather the remnant of my flock out of all the lands where I have scattered them, and I will bring them back to their fold, and they will be fruitful and multiply. I will raise up shepherds over them who will shepherd them, and they will no longer live in fear or be dismayed, nor will any be missing, says the LORD (Jer 23:1-4; cf. 16:14-15; 30:10-11).

For thus says the LORD: Sing aloud with gladness for Jacob, and raise shouts of joy for the head of the nations! Make your praises heard and say, "O LORD, save your people, the remnant of Israel." See, I will bring them from the land of the north and gather them from the ends of the earth. The blind and the lame, those with child and those in labor, will return here together with a great company. They will come with weeping, and with consolations I will bring them back. I will lead them by brooks of water, in a straight path on which they will not stumble; for I am a father to Israel, and Ephraim is my firstborn (Jer 31:7-9).

Then I fell down on my face, cried out with a loud voice, and said, "Ah, Lord GOD, will you make a full end of the remnant of Israel?" Then the word of the LORD came to me: Son of man, your kinsfolk, your own kin, the whole house of Israel, every one of them, are those of whom the inhabitants of Jerusalem have said, "They have gone far away from the LORD; this land has been given to us for a possession." Therefore say: Thus says the Lord GOD: Though I removed them far away among the nations, and though I scattered them among foreign lands, I have nevertheless been a sanctuary to them for a short while in the lands where they have gone. Therefore say: Thus says the Lord GOD: I will gather you from among the peoples, and assemble you out of the lands where you have been scattered, and I will give you the land of Israel. When they come there, they will remove from it all the detestable things and abominations. I will give them one heart and put a new spirit within them. I will remove the heart of stone from their flesh and give them a heart of flesh so that they may follow my statutes and observe my ordinances and obey them. Then they shall be my people, and I will be their God (Ezek 11:13-20).

I will surely gather all of you together, O Jacob; I will gather up the survivors of Israel. I will set them together like sheep in a fold, like a flock in its pasture; it will be filled with the noise of many people (Mic 2:12).

Then the remnant of Jacob will be surrounded by many peoples, like dew from the LORD, and like showers on the grass that do not depend on anyone to fall or require someone to make them descend. And the remnant of Jacob will dwell among the nations in the midst of many peoples, like a lion among the animals of the forest, like a young lion among the flocks of sheep, which tramples down and tears in pieces when it passes through, with no one to deliver. Your hand will be lifted up over your adversaries, and all your enemies will be cut off (Mic 5:7-9).

The seacoast will belong to the remnant of the house of Judah, and they will pasture on it. They will lie down in the houses of Ashkelon in the evening. For the LORD their God will care for them and restore their fortunes (Zeph 2:7).

Sing aloud, O daughter Zion! Shout for joy, O Israel! Rejoice and be jubilant with all your heart, O daughter Jerusalem! The LORD has taken away his judgments against you; he has turned away your enemies. The king of Israel, the LORD, is in your midst; you will fear disaster no more. On that day it will be said to Jerusalem: "Do not fear, O Zion; do not let your hands grow weak. The LORD your God is in your midst, a mighty warrior who will save you. He will rejoice over you with gladness; he will give you rest in his love. He will celebrate over you with loud singing." I will gather up those who are afflicted among you due to the loss of your appointed festivals, so that you will no longer suffer reproach for it. See, I will deal with all your oppressors at that time; I will save the lame and gather the outcast, and I will bring them to be acclaimed and celebrated in every land where they have been put to shame. At that time I will bring you home, at the time when I gather you together; for I will make you to be celebrated and acclaimed among all the peoples of the earth, when I restore your fortunes before your eyes, says the LORD (Zeph 3:14-20).

Thus says the LORD: I will return to Zion and dwell in the midst of Jerusalem. Jerusalem will be called the faithful city, and the mountain of the LORD of hosts will be called the holy mountain. Thus says the LORD of hosts: Old men and old women will sit once more in the streets of Jerusalem, each with staff in hand because of their advanced age. And the streets of the city will be full of boys and girls playing in them. Thus says the LORD of hosts: Even though it may seem impossible to the remnant of this people in these days, should it also seem impossible to me, says the LORD of hosts? Thus says the LORD of hosts: I will save my people from the lands of the east and the lands of the west, and I will bring them to dwell in Jerusalem. They will be my people and I will be their God, in faithfulness and in righteousness (Zech 8:3-8).

God's unconditional love for his people and his deep desire to bless them are also evident in a number of passages that speak of him consoling and comforting those whom he has subjected to hardships and sufferings in order to correct them. He is even said to heal and bind up the wounds that have resulted from the chastisements he imposed on them. These passages make it clear that all of the sufferings to which he subjected them were an expression not of hatred or rejection but rather of his loving commitment to bring about in them the way of life necessary for them to enjoy the well-being and wholeness that he seeks for them:

He will give rain for the seed with which you sow the ground, and the grain that the ground will yield will be rich and plentiful. On that day your cattle will graze in broad pastures; and the oxen and donkeys that till the ground will eat seasoned fodder that has been winnowed with a shovel and a fork. On every high mountain and lofty hill there will be streams running with water on the day of the great slaughter, when the towers fall. Moreover the light of the moon will be like the light of the sun, and the light of the sun will be seven times greater, like the light of seven days, on the day when the Lord binds up the wounds of his people and heals the injuries caused by his blows (Isa 30:23-26).

Comfort, O comfort my people!, says your God. Speak tenderly to Jerusalem, and proclaim to her that the time of her affliction has come to an end, that her punishment is complete, that she has received from the Lord's hand double for all her sins (Isa 40:1-2).

For you will spread out to the right and to the left, and your descendants will possess nations and will inhabit towns that were desolate. Do not be afraid, for you will not be put to shame again. Do not be discouraged, for you will not be disgraced. For you will forget the shame of your youth, and will remember the disgrace of your widowhood no more. For your Maker is your husband, the Lord of hosts is his name; your Redeemer is the Holy One of Israel, who is called the God of all the earth. For the Lord has called you like a wife forsaken and grieved in spirit, like the wife of a man's youth when she has been cast off, says your God. For a brief moment I abandoned you, but with great compassion I will gather you up. In an outburst of anger I hid my face from you for a moment, but with everlasting love I will have compassion on you, says the Lord, your Redeemer (Isa 54:3-8).

For thus says the Lord: Your wound is incurable, and your injury is grievous. There is no one to defend your cause, no remedy for your wound, no healing for you. All your lovers have forgotten you; they do not care for you. For I have wounded you with the blow of an enemy, the punishment of a merciless foe, because your iniquity is great and your sins are so numerous. Why do you cry out over your affliction? Your pain is incurable. I have done these things to you because your iniquity is great and because your sins are so numerous. Therefore all who devour you will be devoured, and all of your foes will go into captivity, every one of them. Those who plunder you will be plundered, and I will make a prey of all those who prey on you. For I will restore you to health and heal your wounds, says the Lord, because they have called you an outcast: "It is Zion, whom no one cares about!" (Jer 30:12-17).

For thus says the Lord God: I myself will search for my sheep and will seek them out. As shepherds seek out their flocks when they are among their sheep that have been scattered, so I will seek out my sheep. I will rescue them from all the places to which they have been scattered on a day of clouds and thick darkness. I will bring them out from among the peoples and gather them together from foreign lands and bring them into their own land, and I will feed them on the mountains of Israel, by the ravines and in all the inhabited regions of the land. I will feed them with good pasture, and the heights of the mountains of Israel will be their pasture; there they will lie down in good grazing land and feed on rich pasture upon the mountains of Israel. I myself will be the shepherd of my sheep, and I will make them lie down, says the Lord God. I will seek out the lost, and I will bring back the strayed, and I will bind up the injured, and I will strengthen the weak, but the fat and the strong I will destroy. I will feed them with justice (Ezek 34:11-16).

Pondering a Future for Israel and the Nations

In many passages from the prophetic writings, the wrath and anger that God displayed when chastising his people is contrasted with his forgiveness and the love and compassion that he will show them once those chastisements have accomplished their purpose. Both God and the people look forward to a time when it will no longer be necessary for God to discipline and correct his people through sufferings because they will abandon their sinful and destructive behavior for good in order to practice justice and righteousness in conformity with his loving will.

> On that day you will say, "I give thanks to you, O Lord, for although you were angry with me, your anger has turned away and you have comforted me" (Isa 12:1).

> Thus says the Lord concerning all of my evil neighbors who seize the inheritance that I have given my people Israel: I am about to uproot them from their land, and I will uproot from among them the house of Judah. And after I have uprooted them, I will again have compassion on them and bring them to their inheritance and to their land, every one of them. And then, if they diligently learn the ways of my people and come to swear by my name, "As the Lord lives" in the same way that they taught my people to swear by Baal, then they will be built up in the midst of my people (Jer 12:14-16).

> Therefore thus says the Lord of hosts, the God of Israel: I am going to punish the king of Babylon and his land, just as I punished the king of Assyria. I will bring Israel back to its pasture, and it will feed on Carmel and in Bashan; and on the hills of Ephraim and in Gilead its hunger will be satisfied. In those days and at that time, says the Lord, iniquity will be sought in Israel, but there will be none, and sins in Judah, but none will be found; for I will pardon the remnant that I have spared (Jer 50:18-20).

> The punishment for your iniquity, O daughter Zion, is complete; he will keep you in exile no longer (Lam 4:22).

> Who is a God like you, pardoning iniquity and passing over the transgression of the remnant of his possession? He does not retain his anger forever because he delights in showing steadfast love. He will have compassion on us once again; he will tread our iniquities under foot. You will cast all of our sins into the depths of the sea. You will show Jacob your faithfulness and Abraham your steadfast love, as you swore to our ancestors in the days of old (Mic 7:18-20).

> Then the angel of the Lord said, "O Lord of hosts, how long will you hold back your mercy from Jerusalem and the cities of Judah, with which you have been angry these seventy years?" Then the Lord replied with kind and comforting words to the angel who talked with me. So the angel who was talking with me said, "Proclaim this message: Thus says the Lord of hosts: I am exceedingly jealous for Jerusalem and for Zion. And I am extremely angry with the nations that feel secure; for while I was only a little angry, they made the disaster worse. Therefore, thus says the Lord, I will return to Jerusalem with compassion; my house shall be built there, says the Lord of hosts, and a measuring line shall be stretched out over Jerusalem. Proclaim

this as well: Thus says the LORD of hosts: My cities will overflow with prosperity once again; the LORD will comfort Zion again and choose Jerusalem once more" (Zech 1:12-17).

But now I will not deal with the remnant of this people as in days past, says the LORD of hosts. For there will be a sowing of peace; the vine will yield its fruit and the ground will give its produce. The skies will give their dew, and I will cause the remnant of this people to possess all these things. Just as you have been an object of scorn among the nations, O house of Judah and house of Israel, so I will save you and you will be a blessing. Do not be afraid, but let your hands be strong. For thus says the LORD of hosts: Just as I determined to bring evil upon you when your ancestors provoked me to wrath, and I did not change my mind, says the LORD of hosts, so again I have determined in these days to do good to Jerusalem and to the house of Judah. Do not be afraid! These are the things that you shall do: Speak the truth to one another; render in your gates judgments that are just and make for peace; do not devise evil in your hearts against one another, and do not love false oaths; for these are all things that I hate, says the LORD (Zech 8:11-17).

I will strengthen the house of Judah and save the house of Joseph. I will bring them back because I have compassion on them, and it will be as if I had never rejected them; for I am the LORD their God, and I will answer them. Then the people of Ephraim will become like warriors, and their hearts will be glad as with wine. Their children will see it and be glad; their hearts will rejoice in the LORD. I will send out a signal for them and gather them in, for I have redeemed them, and they will be as numerous as they were before. Even though I scattered them among the nations, in distant lands they will remember me, and they will rear up their children and return. I will bring them back from the land of Egypt and gather them from Assyria; I will bring them to the land of Gilead and to Lebanon until there is no more room for them. They will pass through the sea of distress, and the waves of the sea will be struck down, and all the depths of the Nile will dry up. The pride of Assyria will be laid low, and the scepter of Egypt will depart. I will make them strong in the LORD, and they will walk in his name, says the LORD (Zech 10:6-12).

Many of these ideas are brought together at the conclusion of the lengthy summary of Israel's history that appears in Ezekiel 16. There, after recalling how God had rescued Israel as an abandoned newborn and taken the people to himself as his beloved wife, only to see them take the rich blessings he had bestowed on them and give them to other lovers as they played the harlot, God promises to restore and bless his people once again. The conclusion to this passage stresses both the need for the people to be humiliated in order for them to be brought to change their ways as well as God's intention to forgive them and gather them up once again. Only by subjecting them to shame, disgrace, mockery, and suffering is it possible for a definitive change to be brought about in their behavior:

I will restore their fortunes, the fortunes of Sodom and her daughters and the fortunes of Samaria and her daughters, and I will restore your own fortunes together with theirs, so that you may bear your disgrace and be ashamed of all that you have done and be a consolation to them. As for your sisters, Sodom and her daughters, they will be restored to their former state; Samaria and her daughters will also return to their former state, as will you and your daughters. Was not your sister Sodom an object of scorn for you in the days of your arrogance, before your wickedness was uncovered? Now you are an object of mockery for the daughters of Edom and all her neighbors and for the daughters of the Philistines; those all around you ridicule you. You must bear the punishment for your lewdness and your abominations, says the LORD.

For thus says the Lord GOD: I will do with you as you have done, you who have despised the oath you made by breaking the covenant. Nevertheless, I will remember the covenant I made with you in the days of your youth, and I will establish with you an everlasting covenant. Then you will remember your ways and be ashamed when you receive your older and younger sisters; I will give them to you as daughters, but not on account of my covenant with you. I will establish my covenant with you, and you will know that I am the LORD, so that you may remember and be confounded and never open your mouth again because of your shame, once I have forgiven you all that you have done, says the Lord GOD (Ezek 16:53-63).

By means of the great hardships and sufferings he imposes on his people, therefore, God breaks the people's stubborn resistance to his will and brings about in them by pure grace the righteous and obedient way of life that is necessary for them to enjoy his goodness and blessings. If he is to accomplish fully his purposes in the world, however, he must also deal with the nations in the same way that he deals with Israel. In order to bring to an end their cruelty, injustice, violence, and oppression, he must not only subject them to suffering and hardships but also destroy them to some extent. Only in that way can he break their resistance to his will and bring into existence a remnant of peoples who will be committed to justice and righteousness in the same way that the remnant of Israel will be.

While some passages speak of the nations serving Israel, this should not be understood in the sense that Israel will become an oppressor to those nations, since this would promote injustice and enmity rather than peace and justice. Rather, as the nations live alongside Israel, they will be brought to love and serve Israel's God for their own good in order to attain the blessings that God desires for them as well. If Israel is to rule over the nations, therefore, it is not to do them harm but to serve as God's instrument to destroy evil, violence, and oppression for good and to incorporate within its midst the foreigners who wish to join themselves to God's people in order to live as his own. For this reason, many of the passages that look forward to the blessing of many people from the nations alongside Israel also anticipate the destruction of many of those nations. Like Israel, they too must be subjected to ruin in order for a new world to be brought about in which all who remain will live as one with Israel and Israel's God:

For the LORD will have compassion on Jacob and will again choose Israel and settle them in their own land; and foreigners will join them and attach themselves to the house of Jacob. And other peoples will take them up and bring them to their place, and the house of Israel will make them their possession as male and female servants in the Lord's land; they will take captive those who were their captors and rule over those who oppressed them (Isa 14:1-2).

Break forth in singing! Shout together for joy, you waste places of Jerusalem! For the Lord has comforted his people; he has redeemed Jerusalem. The Lord has bared his holy arm in the sight of all the nations, and all the ends of the earth will see the salvation of our God (Isa 52:9-10).

They will build up the ancient ruins; they will raise up that which was made desolate. They will repair the ruined cities and all that was devastated for many generations. Strangers will stand and feed your flocks; foreigners will till your land and dress your vines, but you will be called priests of the Lord; you will be named ministers of our God. You will enjoy the wealth of the nations and glory in their riches. Instead of your shame you will receive a double portion, and instead of disgrace you will rejoice in your inheritance; everlasting joy will be theirs. . . . Their descendants will be known among the nations and their offspring among the peoples; all who see them will acknowledge that they are a people whom the Lord has blessed. . . . For as the earth brings forth its sprouts and as a garden causes what is sown in it to spring up, so the Lord God will cause righteousness and praise to spring up in the sight of all the nations (Isa 61:4-7, 9, 11).

I am coming to gather together all nations and tongues, and they will come and see my glory, and I will set a sign among them and send survivors from them to the nations, to Tarshish, Put, and Lud, who draw the bow, to Tubal and Javan, and to the coastlands far away that have not heard of my fame or seen my glory; and they will declare my glory among the nations. And they will bring to my holy mountain all your brothers and sisters from all the nations as an offering to the Lord, on horses, in chariots and wagons, and on mules and camels, says the Lord, in the same way that the Israelites bring their grain offering in a clean vessel to the house of the Lord. I will also take some of them to serve as priests and Levites, says the Lord. For just as the new heavens and the new earth that I will make will remain before me, says the Lord, so will your offspring and your name remain. From one new moon to the next and from one Sabbath to the next all flesh will come to worship in my presence, says the Lord. And they will go out and look at the dead bodies of those who rebelled against me; for their worm will not die nor will their fire be extinguished, but they will be an abhorrence to all flesh (Isa 66:18-24).

Is it not from the Lord of hosts that people labor only to feed the flames and that nations weary themselves for nothing? But the earth will be filled with the knowledge of the glory of the Lord, as the waters cover the sea (Hab 2:13-14).

For my decision is to gather nations, to assemble kingdoms, to pour out upon them my indignation and all the heat of my anger; for in the fire of my passion all the earth will be consumed. At that time I will make the speech of the peoples pure so that all of them may call on the name of the Lord and serve him with one accord. From beyond the rivers of Cush my worshipers, my scattered ones, will bring me my offerings (Zeph 3:8-10).

Finally, it is important to note that in many cases the vision of Israel's prophets regarding the future is not clearly defined. While they express hopes and expectations with regard to the new reality that God will bring about, in many cases there is ambiguity and a great deal of uncertainty as to what they expect that new reality to look like. For the most part, they continue to anticipate that human life will remain much the same and that human beings will continue to be born, grow old and die. It is also difficult for them to imagine a world that may some day be entirely free of evil, suffering, and injustice. In fact, rather than projecting a single and uniform vision with respect to the future, Israel's prophets express a wide variety of hopes that are not always consistent with one another. What they do share in common, however, is the hope that eventually the intentions and purposes that led God to create the heavens and the earth and subject his creation to the human beings he made in his own image will be fulfilled, if not entirely at least to a considerable extent. Such a hope is rooted not in their confidence regarding human beings but rather in their trust in a God who will simply not give up, back down, or relent in his efforts to see all the good that he has always sought for human beings and his creation as a whole become a reality for all.

Conclusion

"Not for *his* sake, but for *theirs*." Perhaps to the chagrin of many readers, this phrase has been repeated endlessly throughout the present work. There is a good reason for that, however: this phrase holds the key to the rereading of the Hebrew Scriptures that has been put forward here.

The idea that the primary concern of the God of Israel as he is portrayed in the Hebrew Bible is that of the happiness and well-being of all of his creatures, including especially the human beings he created in his image, is a very simple one. By no means is it difficult to grasp. That idea, however, stands in stark contrast to the conceptions of the deity that are characteristic of all of the other worldviews known to us from antiquity. The primary reason for this is the nature of those deities themselves: because those gods depended on the world for their existence and were not fully sovereign over the world in the way that the God of Israel was thought to be as its creator, their primary concern *could not* be for other beings. Instead, it had to be *for themselves*, since if their own needs were not satisfied they could not exist.

This means that by necessity, all of the gods of antiquity other than Israel's God had no choice but to give priority to their own needs over those of others, including not only the other gods but human beings as well. For that reason, they inevitably saw human beings simply as a means to meeting their own needs rather than regarding their well-being as an end in itself. If they wanted human beings to thrive and prosper, they did so *not for the sake of human beings themselves but for their own sake*, since only if human beings were able to satisfy their own needs would they be able to satisfy the needs of the gods as well.

At the same time, however, what the gods were said to desire was simply to spend their days in luxury and splendor, enjoying all the things that brought them pleasure and receiving the honor, praise, and gifts of human beings. In most cases, they wished to be amused and entertained by human beings as well and for that reason became engrossed in human affairs. While they tended to favor some nations and groups of human beings over others, this was simply because in their consideration those nations and groups served their needs, interests, and self-centered desires better than others or brought them pleasure in ways that others did not.

This manner of understanding the gods led to a similar understanding of the meaning and purpose of human life. Like the gods, human beings had to be concerned primarily for themselves and their own needs in order to exist. Because the gods had control over many of the forces of nature and exerted influence over human life in other ways as well, however, human beings had to give priority to the needs and desires of the gods over their own. Only if they kept the gods happy and avoided arousing their wrath could they survive and prosper and hope to satisfy their own needs and desires. Thus, while their service and dedication to the gods was a constant burden for them, they had no choice but to provide the gods with all that they needed and desired if they wanted to enjoy their favor and do well in life. Just as the gods attended to the needs and desires of human beings *for their own sake* rather than for the sake of human beings themselves, so also human beings dedicated themselves to attending to the needs and desires of the gods for *their* own sake rather than for the sake of the gods per se. And just as the gods did not regard the well-being of human beings as an end in itself but purely as a means to satisfying their own needs and desires, so also human beings regarded the happiness of the gods as a means to attaining what they needed and desired for themselves rather than an end in itself.

For many centuries, the God of Israel and the Hebrew Bible has been understood as relating to human beings in the same way that the other gods of antiquity were thought to do. Like those gods, what concerned him above all else was his own happiness and pleasure. The purpose for which he had created human beings was that they might serve as a means to that end. Undoubtedly, the God of Israel was distinct from other gods in that he did not have the same type of needs that they had and did not derive pleasure from the same things that they did. What pleased him was that human beings treat one another with justice and kindness and avoid doing harm to one another, yet he ultimately sought that they live and behave in certain ways not for *their* sake but for *his own*, since such behaviors made him happy while the practice of injustice and violence bothered and upset him. He therefore commanded that human beings obey him for *his own* sake, to keep him content and satisfied. Undoubtedly, he wanted them to enjoy well-being and be happy as well, but only because this made *him* happy and brought him pleasure. He also wanted to receive their praises, honor, obedience, and offerings *for his own sake*, since these things also brought him pleasure and satisfaction. The well-being of human beings was therefore not *an end in itself* but was rather a means to *his own happiness*. Furthermore, if it did *not* make human beings happy to serve and obey him, this did not matter to him. Because they had been created as a means to *his own* happiness, *their* happiness was of secondary importance. What mattered was that *he* be kept happy. If human beings found that bothersome or burdensome, that was not *his* problem but *theirs*.

According to what I have argued throughout the present study, however, while this may be the God of most biblical scholars and interpreters, it is not the God of the Hebrew Bible. Instead, the God of the Hebrew Bible is consistently presented as seeking the happiness of human beings *as an end in itself*. He wanted them to enjoy well-being for *their own* sake and not merely for his. Undoubtedly, as we have seen in Chapter 2, their happiness and well-being would also bring him happiness, but this was because he had inseparably linked his own happiness to theirs. Unlike other gods in antiquity who could be perfectly happy and pleased even if human beings were miserable, the creator God of Israel would be happy only if human beings were also happy, healthy, whole, and well.

What made it possible for this God to be fully committed to seeking the well-being of human beings as an end in itself was that he did not depend on the world he created in any way for his own existence. In this regard, he was distinct from all of the other gods known to us from antiquity. Because he did not depend on the world for his existence as they did, even if the world ceased to exist, he would continue to exist.

Perhaps because this manner of understanding God is so unlike anything known to us from the belief systems of peoples other than Israel in antiquity, for centuries biblical scholars and interpreters have failed to grasp it. As a result, they consistently conceive of the God of the Hebrew Scriptures doing everything that those Scriptures ascribe to him *for his own sake*. He creates the heavens and the earth for his own glory and fashions human beings from the earth so that they may serve, honor, praise, and obey him. While he undoubtedly loves them and wants them to be content, satisfied, and at peace with themselves and the rest of creation, ultimately he desires these things *for his own sake* since they allow him to be content, satisfied, and at peace as well. When he dictates laws and commandments and demands that human beings obey them, his purpose is to satisfy the needs and desires of his own nature, which cannot tolerate anything that might contradict, upset, or threaten it. If he is jealous and strictly prohibits human beings from showing devotion to any god other than him, it is because he selfishly desires and demands all of their love, honor, and praise for himself and becomes angry when they rob and deprive him of what is rightfully his. If he punishes them for disobeying him and acting in accordance with their own will rather than his, he does so not for *their* sake but because his own happiness and pleasure take priority over theirs. When he chooses a people as his own and enters into a covenant with them, it is so that he can place them under the obligation to give him what he seeks for his own sake by pledging to give them what they seek for themselves in exchange for his favors. Should they fail to live up to their end of the bargain, however, he will fill their life with suffering and if necessary even destroy them in part until they go back to making him happy by giving him what he wants and craves.

To use the word "love" to characterize such a relationship is to attribute to that word a meaning that must be regarded as foreign to the worldview found in the Hebrew Scriptures. A God who "loves" in that manner does not seek the well-being of others as an end in itself but instead seeks to manipulate and control human beings for no purpose other than that of satisfying his own self-centered desires and interests. Like the pagan gods of antiquity, if they give him what he desires for his own sake, he will reward them with kindness and benevolence. The moment they rebel against him and his will, however, that "love" will turn into wrath and seek to impose its will on them once more by means of vicious punishments. His calls to repentance must be understood as threats of condemnation and curses designed to strike terror into any who fail to submit to him. Because what matters to him is simply being obeyed and worshiped for his own sake, inwardly he will take great delight when human beings acclaim him as a God of vengeance, since their fear of that vengeance will lead them to do whatever he tells them. Yet because he wants to receive expressions of love, adulation, praise, and thanksgiving from human beings for his own sake, outwardly he shows himself to be gracious, forgiving, kind, and charitable in the way that all tyrants and dictators do. One way or the other, however, he will do whatever is necessary to make his will prevail.

Such is the God that biblical scholars and interpreters have consistently found in the biblical texts. Undoubtedly, they clothe him in white and plate him with gold, extolling his immense goodness and celebrating the magnitude of his love and mercy while at the same time directing attention away from his volatile temper and keeping his violent character and vindictive nature under wraps. Deep down, they insist, he really *is* kind and gracious. But when it is in their interest or his, they allow him to come out from behind the curtain and reveal himself for who he really is, an implacable avenger of anything that he has vilified as wicked and evil, though only for a few moments until his true nature can be concealed from sight once more so as to avoid sending his terror-stricken worshipers into too much of a panic.

While most biblical scholars and interpreters today would deny that this is the God of whom they write and speak, their own words betray them and show that denial to be an illusion. They speak of a God who is filled with anger when human beings fail to give him the praise and honor they owe him and refuse to acknowledge his lordship, while claiming that his justice and holiness make it impossible for him ever to forgive sins freely: "God's wrath and judgment are personally directed against sinners who have failed to praise, honor and thank him. . . . God is angry, then, because of human rejection of his lordship. . . . God would deny his very being as God if he forgave us and violated his justice and holiness."[1] They portray him as a God who is "jealously *for God's own self* and takes with dreadful seriousness every threat of profanation to God's own life," a God "who takes with savage seriousness Yahweh's right to be worshiped, honored, and obeyed," and a God "who will brook no rival, who practices intense self-regard, and who will not tolerate any who detract from this self-regard. . . . The extremity of Yahweh's passion will be turned against any who affront Yahweh, and Yahweh will act without restraint or discipline. . . . This is a God who will be taken seriously, who will

---

1. Thomas R. Schreiner, "Penal Substitution View," in *The Nature of the Atonement: Four Views*, ed. James Beilby and Paul R. Eddy (Downers Grove, IL: InterVarsity, 2006), 67-98 (79-80, 94).

be honored and obeyed, and who will not be mocked."[2] If any refuse to bend the knee before him, he will make sure to bend it for them: "Voluntarily or involuntarily, every creature will someday bow his knee before him. Obedience in love or subjection by force is the final destiny of all creatures."[3] If any dare to cross him, he will not delay in making them pay the price: "The idea that man is always in danger of angering God runs through the whole Pentateuch. Fierce judgments and sudden death stud its pages."[4] His holiness places those who seek to approach him in constant peril: "Yahweh's wrath will be unleashed against all who fail to take proper precautions when entering into his immediate presence, or against all who were not permitted to stand in sacred precincts, to start with."[5] "It was a dangerous business to have a holy God dwelling in the midst of a sinful and impure people...."[6] If they defile his dwelling place and fail to undo the damage they have caused it, disaster will come swiftly: "the sinner may be unscarred by his evil, but the sanctuary bears the scars and, with its destruction, he too will meet his doom."[7] Examples of such depictions of Israel's God among biblical scholars and theologians could be multiplied to no end.

Protests against such portrayals of God are quickly met with objections that include ample citations from the Hebrew Scriptures. Is he not a God who threatens those who reject him with fierce wrath and fearsome punishments? Does he not strike down sinners, consume them with famine and plagues, and litter the streets with their corpses? Does he not mandate that those who violate his commands be stoned to death or put to the sword? Is he not said to strike out against those who fail to respect his holiness and consume them in anger? Is he not the God who has Moses tell his people, "the LORD your God is a devouring fire, a jealous God" (Deut 4:24)? Does he not describe himself as one who refuses to clear the guilty and vows to visit the iniquity of the parents upon the children and the children's children down to the third and the fourth generation (Exod 34:7)?

Certainly, the Hebrew Scriptures affirm all of these things to be true. Yet those Scriptures make such assertions in the context of an overarching narrative from which they cannot be divorced if the logic underlying them is to be understood properly, and also do so from within a historical context that in many ways is very different from our own. More importantly, however, all of these assertions regarding God as well as others that have been

---

2. Walter Brueggemann, *Theology of the Old Testament: Testament, Dispute, Advocacy* (Minneapolis: Fortress, 2005), 193, 272, 283, 294-95.

3. Herman Bavinck, *Reformed Dogmatics*, vol. 2: *God and Creation* (Grand Rapids: Baker Academic, 2004), 434.

4. Gordon J. Wenham, *The Book of Leviticus*, NICOT (Grand Rapids: Eerdmans, 1979), 56.

5. Baruch A. Levine, *In the Presence of the Lord: A Study of Cult and Some Cultic Terms in Ancient Israel*, SJLA 5 (Leiden: Brill, 1974), 70.

6. William Lane Craig, *Atonement and the Death of Christ: An Exegetical, Historical, and Philosophical Exploration* (Waco, TX: Baylor University Press, 2020), 19.

7. Jacob Milgrom, *Leviticus 1–16: A New Translation with Introduction and Commentary*, AB 3 (New York: Doubleday, 1991), 260.

mentioned above raise a question that biblical scholars and interpreters consistently ignore due to their assumption that the answer is self-evident: Does the God of the Hebrew Scriptures do all of the things attributed to him in those Scriptures *for his sake* or *for the sake of the human beings he has created and chosen to be his own*? All of the gods and deities known to us from the texts of antiquity act first and foremost out of a concern for themselves and take into account the needs and desires of others only as the fulfillment of those needs and desires allows for their own to be fulfilled as well. Therefore the same must be true of the God of the Hebrew Bible. How could it be otherwise?

Everything that I have argued throughout the present work can be reduced to the simple claim that it *is* otherwise. At some point many centuries ago, a community of people who will forever remain unknown to us came to believe in a God who was not only the sovereign creator of all that exists but also acted purely out of a concern for his creation and the creatures he had made in all that he did. When he brought those creatures into existence and gave them life, he did so just as much for *their* sake as he did for his own. When he placed the man and woman he had made in a garden and surrounded them with delightful and pleasant things, it was not so much for *his* sake as it was for *theirs*. He wanted nothing for them but what was good and saw their happiness as an end in itself. When he gave them and their offspring commands and told them to obey him, his concern was not *for himself* but *for them*. When they began to fill their lives with violence, corruption, and other things that were bad for them, rather than being offended or becoming angry and upset because he had been robbed of the honor, respect, and obedience due to him, his reaction was one of sadness, pain, and grief. What pained and grieved him was not the effect that their violent and destructive behavior had *on him* but the effect that it had *on them*. His only desire was that they be well and prosper and enjoy all the good he intended for them, but the way of life they insisted on following made it impossible for that desire to be fulfilled.

In spite of that insistence, however, he determined not to give up on his good intentions for the human beings he had created but to continue to do everything in his power to enable those intentions to be fulfilled, not merely for *his* sake but above all for *theirs*. In order to carry out the plan he devised, he chose for himself a band of oppressed slaves who had nothing to offer him, hoping to fashion them into a people who would live as his own treasured possession, not because *he* would benefit in any way from his election of this people but because *they* would, as would others throughout the earth who would eventually come to know him through them. Despite his repeated and persistent efforts to bring them to trust in his sovereign power as well as his unconditional love, however, he struggled to gain their confidence and obedience, which he sought to obtain not because he desired these things for his own sake but because only by trusting and obeying him as he instructed and guided them could they ever be happy and prosper.

For no other reason than that he wished to bless them and others through them, he determined to give them a land of their own and enter into a covenant with them. While this covenant included a long list of commandments, he gave them those commandments and told them to obey them not because by doing so they would do him any favor or allow him to obtain something he sought for his own sake but only because their observance of those commandments would enable them to experience the wholeness he intended for them. Although the manner in which some of those commandments actually promoted the people's well-being was not always clear and from a modern perspective many of those commandments must be regarded as problematic, the community of people who made all of those commandments their own believed that they had been given by God purely out of a concern for their happiness and well-being. That same concern had led him not only to insist that they observe those commandments carefully but also to indicate to them that if they wandered from the good path he had laid out for them he would do whatever he deemed necessary to correct and discipline them in order to bring them back to that path. While this would often involve subjecting them to hardships and afflictions that would be painful for them, his purpose was in no way to do them harm. On the contrary, he sought only what was good for them and for that reason demanded that they follow him alone, since if they abandoned him for other gods they would only fill their lives with the suffering, injustice, and violence that the worship of those gods promoted. He alone could bring about among them the justice, peace, and well-being that would allow them to enjoy a blessed and blissful existence in the land he was giving them.

Perhaps because this manner of understanding God and his intentions for them was so novel and revolutionary that even many of the members of the people who had adopted this God as their own could not fully grasp or accept it, they doubted that he truly sought their well-being as an end in itself and for that reason did not submit to all that he had commanded of them for their own good. They attributed to him the same type of selfish and self-centered motives and interests that characterized all of the other gods of antiquity and thus began to serve and worship those other gods alongside of him and even came to abandon him for those gods. In this way, they filled their lives and their land with the suffering, injustice, and violence that followed from adopting the values and ways of thinking and behaving that the worship of such gods promoted and deprived themselves of all the good that their own God sought for them.

As he had promised, out of love for them and the firm commitment he had made to their well-being, God refused to abandon them to such a life and to let them continue unimpeded down a path that would lead only to their ruin and destruction. For that reason, he sent them prophets who called them to turn back to the path he had laid out for them for their own good, but despite their persistent calls and pleas for the people to do so, the people continued to insist on going their own ways instead. As a result, God allowed them to suffer the consequences of their failure to trust him and their destructive behavior and was even thought to inflict sufferings and hardships on them himself, not out of spite or hatred for them but only because he desperately wanted to see them brought to live in ways that promoted their well-being rather than destroying it. At the same time, his unconditional love for them led him to be filled with anger and frustration when they stubbornly refused to listen to him and turn back to him so that the good he sought for them might be theirs. In addition, he became not only angry but even outraged and incensed when he saw the tremendous violence and evils that their behavior brought upon themselves and others as well as their persistent refusal to acknowledge that behavior as evil and turn away from it. As that anger, frustration, and outrage intensified and his repeated attempts to bring them to abandon their destructive ways were met not only with rejection but with mockery and derision as well, his pleas and warnings to them grew more and more desperate, ominous, and threatening, and the sufferings and calamities that were understood as means by which he sought to chastise and correct them became so harsh and intense that the people could scarcely bear them. Yet no matter what he said and did, the situation did not improve but only grew worse.

When the people who believed in this God as a God who loved them unconditionally and sought nothing but their well-being came to be subjected to experiences that could only be described as hellish and horrific due to the unspeakable atrocities and devastation they were made to endure, they struggled to understand why this God would have allowed them to suffer such things. Those who continued to believe and trust in that God could only come to one conclusion: he had not abandoned or rejected them but instead had considered it necessary to leave them so utterly broken, battered, and humiliated that those among them who had survived the slaughter and destruction would have no choice but to return to the way of life that he had commanded of them for their own good. While such a conclusion was extremely difficult to accept due to the severity and brutality of the sufferings they had endured, it was the only way they could make sense of what had happened and continue to hold out hope that the good and gracious God in whom they had believed and trusted might restore them and fill their lives with his blessings. What gave them that hope was their firm conviction that there was nothing in the world that could ever bring that God to put an end to his efforts to accomplish that objective in the way he had intended from the start, and that even if he considered it necessary to do or allow things that human beings would consider evil and atrocious in pursuit of that objective, he would prefer that alternative to that of giving up on those intentions and abandoning his creation and creatures to their own fate. He was a God who stubbornly and adamantly refused to relent, surrender, or back down in his efforts to bring his will for the good of all to prevail, no matter what obstacles stood in his way.

As they told and retold the stories and narratives that previous generations had passed down to them and tried to make sense of all that had happened in their past, the people who continued to believe in this God of whom their ancestors had spoken interpreted and shaped those stories and narratives on the basis of their convictions regarding him and his goodness and love. While at times it was extremely difficult to reconcile those convictions with the stories and narratives passed down to them as well as the customs and traditions that they also inherited, their faith in this God who was so fundamentally and radically distinct from any other god known to them not only gave meaning and purpose to their lives but also filled them with the hope that some day they, their descendants, and other peoples of the earth would come to experience in their fullness the happiness, wholeness, and well-being which that God had intended for all of his creation and creatures from the very beginning.

Over the period of many centuries, these stories, narratives, traditions, customs, convictions, and hopes were shared and recited orally, put in writing, edited and reworked, harmonized and shaped into a consistent whole, and eventually brought together in a collection of books that we now call the Hebrew Bible, Tanakh, or Old Testament. While this collection of books was intended to fulfill a variety of purposes, the most important of these was to preserve and promulgate the belief in the unique and revolutionary God of whom they spoke, a God who was like no other god ever known or imagined in human history.

From the time of my youth, the God of whom I have spoken throughout the present work is the only God I have ever seen or found in the biblical texts. As I have insisted above, this conception of a God who from the very beginning sought nothing but the happiness and well-being of all of his creation and creatures is very simple and by no means difficult to grasp or understand. As I have worked with the biblical texts over the decades, the fact that those texts portray the God of whom they speak in that manner as a God whose love for human beings is unending, unconditional, uncompromising, and unrelenting has always seemed to me to be obvious and self-evident: "his steadfast love endures forever." In my own mind, I have only grown in the conviction that those texts can be regarded as coherent and make sense only if they are read and interpreted on the basis of the understanding of God that I have presented here.

At the same time, however, I have struggled to understand why I cannot find other biblical scholars and interpreters who find in those texts the same God that I do. Instead, as the tiny but representative sample of Christian and Jewish authors whose work I have cited here demonstrates, those biblical scholars and interpreters consistently speak of a God who has been paganized, which is precisely the kind of god that the Hebrew Scriptures sought to reject as false. Undoubtedly, he is concerned for what is good, just, and right in the way that was not characteristic of most of the pagan gods known to us from antiquity, yet like those gods his primary concern is *for himself*, for the demands and desires of his own nature that take precedence over the well-being of his creatures and prevent him from pursuing their well-being as an end in itself and giving priority to that well-being over all else.

As I have worked with other Jewish writings of the Second Temple period, I have found that the depaganized God of whom the Hebrew Bible speaks appears throughout most of those writings as well. At times, however, those writings give evidence that in some circles certain traits that were thought to characterize the pagan gods of antiquity were already beginning to be ascribed to the God of Israel. I unquestioningly find the same depaganized God that runs throughout the books of the Hebrew Bible in all that I read in the teachings of Jesus, the letters of Paul, and the writings of the New Testament in general, although those writings also provide evidence that there were some Jews who had begun to adhere to a conception of God that was in important ways foreign to the God of the Hebrew Scriptures, that is, the God whose commitment to the well-being of all people without exception is unbending, unconditional, and uncompromising. As I have argued elsewhere, for the most part I also find the same God of the Hebrew Bible in the Christian writings of the early second century, yet by the end of that century there were also Christian authors such as Melito of Sardis and Irenaeus of Lyons who were portraying the God of the Hebrew Scriptures in ways that were foreign to those Scriptures.[8]

While I am not sufficiently familiar with the rabbinic writings that began to circulate in the second century CE to come to any conclusions regarding the extent to which those writings continue to reflect the conception of God that I consistently find throughout the Hebrew Bible, in the little that I have read of these writings I have encountered evidence that this conception of God continued to predominate in at least some Jewish circles. The clearest example of this evidence that I can cite is a passage from the Babylonian Talmud that recalls the manner in which God delivered the Israelites from the army of the Pharoah by parting the waters of the sea in order for them to cross it. After describing the manner in which the Egyptians were drowned when God made those waters return to their place, the text affirms: "In that hour the ministering angels wanted to sing a song before God, but God rebuked them, saying, 'My handiwork is drowning in the sea and you want to sing to me?'" (*Sanh.* 39b). Here is unquestioningly the God who loves all people and desires nothing but the well-being of all of his creatures without exception. For that reason, he is deeply pained and saddened when he must bring any kind of harm or destruction upon the human beings he has created, including even those who seek to do evil to his chosen people Israel as their enemies.

Beginning with the writings of the church fathers in the third and fourth centuries and in both the Western and Eastern Christian traditions that have developed out of their thought, I struggle to catch anything more than occasional glimpses of the depaganized God that I find in the Hebrew Scriptures. Instead, in the writings of Christian and Jewish biblical interpreters today and in those that date back at least to the sixteenth century, I repeatedly

---

8. See David A. Brondos, *Jesus' Death in New Testament Thought*, vol. 2: *Texts* (Mexico City: Theological Community of Mexico, 2018), 1109-1242.

and consistently encounter the paganized conceptions of God that I have described and critiqued throughout the present work. The God of whom these interpreters speak is a God who is subject to the dictates of his nature and held captive by it, a God whose primary concern must be that of satisfying the demands and desires of that nature and therefore a God who has no choice but to insist that human beings also place that concern above all others if he is to save, bless, and forgive them in the way that both he and they desire. This God does *not* love unconditionally but places conditions on his love and rejects in anger any who fail or refuse to fulfill those conditions. His steadfast love is not *truly* steadfast love, nor does it endure forever. Instead, that "steadfast love" is the same type of self-centeredness and self-interest that was thought to characterize all of the gods of antiquity known to us, except of course the God of the Hebrew Bible.

The fact that the conception of God that runs throughout the Hebrew Bible is so fundamentally at odds with the pagan conceptions of God that are characteristic of the other worldviews known to us is also evident from the difficulties I have pointed out with regard to the translations of the biblical texts into English. Because the worldview that is reflected and preserved in English and other modern European languages has its origins in the pagan worldviews of antiquity, it is extremely difficult to translate into English many of the key terms and concepts found in the Hebrew Bible, and at times in fact it may not even be possible to do so. English terms such as "justice," "righteousness," "reward," and "punishment" convey many ideas that are foreign to the Hebrew worldview found in the biblical texts, while at the same time failing to capture important aspects of the meanings of the Hebrew terms corresponding to those translations. The idea that God "visits" and "judges" human beings in order to save them, correct and discipline them, or deliver the oppressed from the hand of their oppressors is also difficult to articulate in modern English, as is the distinction between what is "bad" and what is "evil" in biblical thought. Above all, the use of terms such as "curse," "retribution," and "vengeance" in English translations of the Hebrew Scriptures inevitably leads to an understanding of God that is not only foreign to those Scriptures but radically at odds with the God of whom they speak. From my perspective, the precise manner in which these problems of translation should be addressed in order to avoid conveying ideas that run contrary to the logic and worldview found in the biblical texts is not entirely clear. What is evident, however, is that translations that are based on a one-to-one correspondence between the Hebrew terms in the texts and the terms chosen to render them into English will inevitably fail to capture adequately many of the most important meanings of those texts and will also reflect ideas that are not only foreign to them but clash with them.

Perhaps the most important conclusion to be derived from the present work, however, has to do not only with the need for a thoroughgoing critique and reappraisal of the manner in which the biblical texts must be read in order to represent faithfully the conception of God that runs throughout them but also the question of their normativity for those who continue to regard them as authoritative for their faith and life as Jews or Christians. For centuries, both Jews and Christians have struggled to define the precise manner in which the biblical writings are to be understood as authoritative. While many believers of both traditions continue to insist that the reason that the biblical texts must be regarded as authoritative is that they are entirely accurate as portrayals of past history and that everything found in them was communicated directly by God in the form in which it appears in those texts, many others no longer find such claims to be tenable. If those texts are not regarded as historically accurate in all that they convey and the God of whom they speak is not thought to have been the only one responsible for everything they contain, however, it is not entirely clear in what sense or to what degree they are to be considered authoritative and normative for believers in that God today. If to a large extent those texts are human creations rather than narrations of historical fact or direct revelations from God, the question arises as to precisely which parts or aspects of those texts are to be viewed as authoritative and normative and how their normativity and authority are to be interpreted and reflected in the lives of those who look to them for guidance, truth, meaning, and hope.

Following the proposal of scholars such as Walter Brueggemann, I would argue that the normativity and authority of the biblical texts among those who continue to regard them as sacred scripture should be understood on the basis of the idea that they give *testimony* or *witness* to the faith of those who composed and preserved them.[9] While to some extent this testimony has to do with historical events and facts, from a modern perspective not all of the testimony that they provide can be considered factual or historically accurate. Readers of those texts are of course free to regard as historical anything that they find in them on the basis of their own criteria regarding what is credible or not, yet their faith need not depend on the historical accuracy of all that is in those texts or the credibility they ascribe to the things of which those texts speak. Rather, the testimony that may be said to constitute the object of faith is the testimony that those texts provide regarding an ancient people's belief in a God like no other who is concerned above all else for the happiness, wholeness, and well-being of all of his creation and the creatures in it and regards that shalom, wholeness, or well-being as an end in itself.

In that case, what matters is not the historical accuracy of everything that the biblical texts and narratives recount, but rather the faith of the ancient communities to which those texts and narratives bear witness. Those communities interpreted the stories, narratives, traditions, and practices that were handed down from one generation to the next on the basis of their faith in the God of whom the biblical texts speak. They did so, of course, from within their own particular historical contexts on the basis of a worldview very different from our own and to some extent even an understanding of what is

---

9. See Brueggemann, *Theology*, 117-22.

good and bad, right and wrong, acceptable and unacceptable that in some ways is distinct from ours today. Their contexts also differed greatly from our own with regard to many other aspects of daily life, including especially the hardships and violence that were much more widespread and commonplace in their time. When they experienced those hardships and violence, as they did when they experienced good things as well, they interpreted the realities they encountered on the basis of their faith in the God of sovereign power and unconditional love to which the biblical texts bear witness.

When the normativity and authority of the biblical texts are understood on the basis of this understanding of the faith to which they testify, it is not necessary to believe in everything they contain as historical fact or direct revelation from the God of whom they speak, nor is it necessary to adhere to all of the interpretations of the events and beliefs found in them. Questions as to whether or not God actually commanded all of the things those texts ascribe to him or intervened at certain moments of history either to save and bless people or inflict punishments, suffering, death, and destruction on them can for the most part be left for readers of those texts to answer in whatever way they see fit or find convincing.

In that case, what will join those who continue to regard the biblical texts as sacred scripture both to one another and to all of the past generations of those who also made those texts their own is the belief they share in the sovereign power, unconditional love, and infinite goodness of the God of whom those texts speak. Both their belief in that God and their conviction that in all that he does he seeks nothing but the well-being of all as an end in itself will constitute the measure of all things and the criterion by which they define his will for their lives and the world as a whole. This understanding of God and his will for all people will set those who share that faith apart from those who choose to believe instead either in him or any other deity or power as one who acts and behaves like the pagan gods of antiquity known to us, all of whom placed their own needs and desires over those of all others and pursued interests that led them to regard the well-being of human beings merely as a means to their own self-centered ends rather than as an end in itself. By definition, to believe in a God who is fully, resolutely, and intractably committed to the happiness and well-being of all of his creatures as an end in itself must involve rejecting belief in any god whose primary characteristic is something other than that commitment. At the same time, any who call that God their own but do not share his same commitment to the happiness and well-being of all people without exception cannot truly be said to believe in him but must be regarded as having replaced him with a false god and an idol of their own making, a god who is someone other than the God of the Hebrew Bible.

ABBREVIATIONS

AB	Anchor Bible Commentary
AcBib	Academia Biblica
AIL	Ancient Israel and Its Literature
AOTC	Abingdon Old Testament Commentaries
BSac	*Bibliotheca Sacra*
BBR	*Bulletin for Biblical Research*
BTCB	Brazos Theological Commentary on the Bible
CAH	Cambridge Ancient History
CBQ	*Catholic Biblical Quarterly*
CC	Continental Commentaries
ESV	English Standard Version of the Bible
FAT	Forschungen zum Alten Testament
HTR	*Harvard Theological Review*
JBL	*Journal of Biblical Literature*
JCPS	Jewish and Christian Perspectives Series
JLT	*Journal of Literature and Theology*
JSJ	*Journal for the Study of Judaism in the Persian, Hellenistic and Roman Period*
JSOTSup	*Journal for the Study of the Old Testament* Supplement Series
LCC	Library of Christian Classics
MC	Mesopotamian Civilizations
NASB	New American Standard Bible
NICOT	New International Commentary on the Old Testament
NIV	New International Version of the Bible
NRSV	New Revised Standard Version of the Bible
NRSVue	New Revised Standard Version Updated Edition of the Bible
RSV	Revised Standard Version of the Bible
SJLA	Studies in Judaism in Late Antiquity
SLTHS	Siphrut, Literature, and Theology of the Hebrew Scriptures
WBC	Word Biblical Commentary

Bibliography

PRIMARY SOURCES

Biblia Hebraica Stuttgartensia. Edited by K. Elliger and W. Rudolph. Stuttgart: Deutsche Bibelstiftung, 1977.

Davies, W. W. *The Codes of Hammurabi and Moses*. Cincinnati: Jennings and Graham, 1905.

Lambert, W. G. *Babylonian Creation Myths*. MC 16. Winona Lake, IN: Eisenbrauns, 2013.

The Old Testament Pseudepigrapha. Vol. 1: *Apocalyptic Literature and Testaments*. Edited by James H. Charlesworth. Garden City, NY: Doubleday, 1983.

The Old Testament Pseudepigrapha. Vol. 2: *Expansions of the "Old Testament" and Legends, Wisdom and Philosophical Literature, Prayers, Psalms and Odes, Fragments of Lost Judeo-Hellenistic Works*. Edited by James H. Charlesworth. Garden City, NY: Doubleday, 1985.

Septuaginta. Edited by Alfred Rahlfs. 2nd rev. ed. Edited by Robert Hanhart. Stuttgart: Deutsche Bibelgesellschaft, 2006.

The Literature of Ancient Egypt: An Anthology of Stories, Instructions, Stelae, Autobiographies, and Poetry. Edited by William Kelly Simpson. 3rd ed. New Haven: Yale University Press, 2003.

SECONDARY SOURCES

Bavinck, Herman. *Reformed Dogmatics*. Vol. 2: *God and Creation*. Grand Rapids: Baker Academic, 2004.

Birch, Bruce C. *Let Justice Roll Down: The Old Testament, Ethics, and Christian Life*. Louisville: Westminster John Knox, 1991.

Blenkinsopp, Joseph. *Isaiah 56–66: A New Translation with Introduction and Commentary*. AB 19. New York: Doubleday, 2003.

Brondos, David A. *Fortress Introduction to Salvation and the Cross*. Minneapolis: Fortress, 2007.

——————. *Jesus' Death in New Testament Thought*. 2 vols. Mexico City: Theological Community of Mexico, 2018.

Brueggemann, Walter. *Deuteronomy*. AOTC. Nashville: Abingdon, 2001.

——————. *Theology of the Old Testament: Testament, Dispute, Advocacy*. Minneapolis: Fortress, 2005.

Budd, Philip J. *Numbers*. WBC 5. Waco, TX: Word, 1984.

Caldwell, Richard. *The Origin of the Gods: A Psychoanalytic Study of Greek Theogonic Myth*. Oxford: Oxford University Press, 1989.

Calvin, John. *Calvin: Theological Treatises*. Translated by J. K. S. Reid. LCC 22. Philadelphia: Westminster, 1954.

Chapman, Stephen B. "Collections, Canons, and Communities." Pages 28-54 in *The Cambridge Companion to the Hebrew Bible/Old Testament*. Edited by Stephen B. Chapman and Marvin A. Sweeney. New York: Cambridge University Press, 2016.

Christensen, Duane L. *Deuteronomy 21:10–34:12*. WBC 6B. Nashville: Thomas Nelson, 2002.

Cottrell, Jack. *What the Bible Says about God the Ruler*. Vol. 2: *The Doctrine of God*. Eugene, OR: Wipf and Stock, 2000.

Craig, William Lane. *Atonement and the Death of Christ: An Exegetical, Historical, and Philosophical Exploration*. Waco, TX: Baylor University Press, 2020.

Day, John. *From Creation to Abraham: Further Studies in Genesis 1–11*. London: T & T Clark, 2022.

de Kroon, Marijn. *The Honour of God and Human Salvation: A Contribution to an Understanding of Calvin's Theology according to His Institutes*. Edinburgh: T & T Clark, 2001.

de Vaux, Roland. *Ancient Israel: Its Life and Institutions*. Vol. 2: *Religious Institutions*. Translated by John McHugh. New York: McGraw-Hill, 1965.

Eberhart, Christian A. "Atonement: Amid Alexandria, Alamo, and Avatar." Pages 3-20 in *Atonement: Jewish and Christian Origins*. Edited by Max Botner, Justin Harrison Duff, and Simon Dürr. Grand Rapids: Eerdmans, 2020.

Finlan, Stephen. *The Background and Content of Paul's Cultic Atonement Metaphors*. AcBib 19. Atlanta: SBL, 2004.

Fredriksen, Paula. "Philo, Herod, Paul, and the Many Gods of Ancient Jewish 'Monotheism'." *HTR* 115 (2022): 23-45.

Gadd, C. J. *Hammurabi and the End of His Dynasty*. Rev. ed. CAH 35. Cambridge: Cambridge University Press, 1965.

Gane, Roy E. *Cult and Character: Purification Offerings, Day of Atonement, and Theodicy*. Winona Lake, IN: Eisenbrauns, 2005.

—————. "Worship, Sacrifice, and Festivals in the Ancient Near East." Pages 361-67 in *Behind the Scenes of the Old Testament: Cultural, Social, and Historical Contexts*. Edited by Jonathan S. Greer, John W. Hilber, and John H. Walton. Grand Rapids: Baker Academic, 2018.

Goldingay, John. *Old Testament Theology*. Vol. 1: *Israel's Gospel*. Downers Grove, IL: InterVarsity, 2003.

Haran, Menahem. *Temples and Temple-Service in Ancient Israel: An Inquiry into the Character of Cult Phenomena and the Historical Setting of the Priestly School*. Oxford: Clarendon Press, 1978.

Hart, George. *Egyptian Myths*. The Legendary Past. Austin, TX: University of Texas Press, 1990.

Hartley, John E. *Leviticus*. WBC 4. Dallas: Word, 1992.

Hayes, Christine. *Introduction to the Bible*. New Haven: Yale University Press, 2012.

Heiser, Michael S. "Monotheism, Polytheism, Monolatry, or Henotheism? Toward an Assessment of Divine Plurality in the Hebrew Bible." *BBR* 18 (2008): 1-30.

Hensel, Benedikt. "Who Wrote the Bible? Understanding Redactors and Social Groups behind Biblical Traditions in the Context of Plurality within Emerging Judaism." Pages 11-23 in *Social Groups behind Biblical Traditions: Identity Perspectives from Egypt, Transjordan, Mesopotamia, and Israel in the Second Temple Period*. Edited by Benedikt Hensel, Bartosz Adamczewski, and Dany Nocquet. FAT 167. Tübingen: Mohr Siebeck, 2023.

Hesselink, John I. *Calvin's First Catechism: A Commentary*. Louisville: Westminster, 1997.

Holladay, William L., editor. *A Concise Hebrew and Aramaic Lexicon of the Old Testament*. Leiden: Brill, 1971.

Hong, Koog P. "Synchrony and Diachrony in Contemporary Biblical Interpretation." *CBQ* 75 (2013): 521-39.

Hornung, Erik. *The Ancient Egyptian Books of the Afterlife*. Translated by David Lorton. Ithaca: Cornell University Press, 1999.

Hultgren, Arland J., and Walter F. Taylor, Jr. *Background Essay on Biblical Texts for "Journey Together Faithfully, Part Two: The Church and Homosexuality"*. Chicago: Evangelical Lutheran Church in America, 2003.

Hurtado, Larry W. *Ancient Jewish Monotheism and Early Christian Jesus-Devotion: The Context and Character of Christological Faith*. Waco, TX: Baylor University Press, 2017.

Jeon, Jaeyoung. "Introduction: The State of Pentateuchal Research." Pages 3-27 in *The Social Groups Behind the Pentateuch*. Edited by Jaeyoung Jeon. AIL 44. Atlanta: SBL, 2021.

Johnston, Gordon H. "Genesis 1 and Ancient Egyptian Creation Myths." *BSac* 165 (2008): 178-94.

Kazen, Thomas. "Dirt and Disgust: Body and Morality in Biblical Purity Laws." Pages 42-64 in *Priesthood and Cult in Ancient Israel*. Edited by Gary A. Anderson and Saul M. Olyan. JSOTSup 125. Sheffield: JSOT, 1991.

Kittel, Gerhard, and Gerhard Friedrichs, editors. *Theological Dictionary of the New Testament*. Translated by Geoffrey W. Bromiley. 10 vols. Grand Rapids: Eerdmans, 1964–1976.

Klawans, Jonathan. *Impurity and Sin in Ancient Judaism*. Oxford: Oxford University Press, 2000.

Kugel, James L. *How to Read the Bible: A Guide to Scripture, Then and Now*. New York: Free Press, 2007.

Levenson, Jon D. *Sinai and Zion: An Entry into the Jewish Bible*. Minneapolis: Winston, 1985.

—————. *The Love of God: Divine Gift, Human Gratitude, and Mutual Faithfulness in Judaism*. Princeton: Princeton University Press, 2016.

Levin, Christoph. "The Pentateuch: A Compilation by Redactors." Pages 579-87 in *The Formation of the Pentateuch: Bridging the Academic Cultures of Europe, Israel, and North America*. Edited by Jan C. Gertz, Bernard M. Levinson, Dalit Rom-Shiloni, and Konrad Schmid. FAT 111. Tübingen: Mohr Siebeck, 2016.

Levine, Baruch A. *In the Presence of the Lord: A Study of Cult and Some Cultic Terms in Ancient Israel*. SJLA 5. Leiden: Brill, 1974.

—————. *Numbers 1–20: A New Translation with Introduction and Commentary*. AB 4. New York: Doubleday, 1993.

——————. *Numbers 21–36: A New Translation with Introduction and Commentary*. AB 4A. New York: Doubleday, 2000.

Lohr, Joel N. *Chosen and Unchosen: Conceptions of Election in the Pentateuch and Jewish-Christian Interpretation*. SLTHS 2. Winona Lake, IN: Eisenbraums, 2009.

López-Ruiz, Carolina. *When the Gods Were Born: Greek Cosmogonies and the Near East*. Cambridge, MA: Harvard University Press, 2010.

Lundbom, Jack R. *Deuteronomy: A Commentary*. Grand Rapids: Eerdmans, 2013.

Maccoby, Hyam. *Ritual and Morality: The Ritual Purity System and its Place in Judaism*. Cambridge: Cambridge University Press, 1999.

Milgrom, Jacob. *Studies in Cultic Theology and Terminology*. SJLA 36. Leiden: Brill, 1983.

——————. "The *Modus Operandi* of the *Ḥaṭṭā't*: A Rejoinder." *JBL* 109 (1990): 111-17.

——————. *Leviticus 1–16: A New Translation with Introduction and Commentary*. AB 3. New York: Doubleday, 1991.

——————. "The Changing Concept of Holiness in the Pentateuchal Codes with Emphasis on Leviticus 19." Pages 65-75 in *Reading Leviticus: A Conversation with Mary Douglas*. Edited by John F. A. Sawyer. JSOTSup 227. Sheffield: Sheffield Academic Press, 1996.

——————. "Impurity is Miasma: A Critical Response to Hiram Maccoby," *JBL* 119 (2000): 729-46.

——————. *Leviticus 17-22: A New Translation with Introduction and Commentary*. AB 3A. New York: Doubleday, 2000.

——————. *Leviticus: A Book of Ritual and Ethics*. CC. Minneapolis: Fortress, 2004.

Nelson, Richard D. *Raising Up a Faithful Priest: Community and Priesthood in Biblical Theology*. Louisville: Westminster John Knox, 1993.

Noble, Paul R. "Synchronic and Diachronic Approaches to Biblical Interpretation." *JLT* 7 (1993): 130-48.

Noth, Martin. *Numbers: A Commentary*. Translated by James D. Martin. Philadelphia: Westminster, 1968.

Pixley, George V. *On Exodus: A Liberation Perspective*. Translated by Robert R. Barr. Maryknoll, NY: Orbis, 1987.

Pritchard, James B. *Ancient Near Eastern Texts Relating to the Old Testament*. 2nd ed. Princeton: Princeton University Press, 1955.

Römer, Thomas. *The Invention of God*. Translated by Raymond Geuss. Cambridge, MA: Harvard University Press, 2015.

Scheid, John. *An Introduction to Roman Religion*. Translated by Janet Lloyd. Bloomington, IN: Indiana University Press, 2003.

Schmid, Konrad. *The Scribes of the Torah: The Formation of the Pentateuch in Its Literary and Historical Contexts*. AIL 45. Atlanta: SBL, 2023.

Schreiner, Thomas R. "Penal Substitution View." Pages 67-98 in *The Nature of the Atonement: Four Views*. Edited by James Beilby and Paul R. Eddy. Downers Grove, IL: InterVarsity, 2006.

Schwartz, Baruch J. "The Prohibitions Concerning the 'Eating' of Blood in Leviticus 17." Pages 34-66 in *Priesthood and Cult in Ancient Israel*. Edited by Gary A. Anderson and Saul M. Olyan. JSOTSup 125. Sheffield: Sheffield Academic Press, 1991.

——————. "The Bearing of Sin in the Priestly Literature." Pages 3-21 in *Pomegranates and Golden Bells: Studies in Biblical, Jewish, and Near Eastern Ritual, Law, and Literature in Honor of Jacob Milgrom*. Edited by David P. Wright, David Noel Freedman, and Avi Hurvitz. Winona Lake, IN: Eisenbrauns, 1995.

——————. "Israel's Holiness: The Torah Traditions." Pages 48-59 in *Purity and Holiness: The Heritage of Leviticus*. Edited by M. J. H. M. Poorthuis and J. Schwartz. JCPS 2. Leiden: Brill, 2007.

Sørensen, Jørgen Podemann. "The Real Presence of Osiris: Iconic, Semi-Iconic and Aniconic Ritual Representations of an Egyptian God." *Religion* 47 (2017): 366-77.

Stubbs, David L. *Numbers*. BTCB. Grand Rapids: Brazos, 2009.

Ursinus, Zacharias. *The Commentary of Dr. Zacharias Ursinus on the Heidelberg Catechism*. Translated by G. W. Williard. Grand Rapids: Eerdmans, 1954.

Van Zile, Matthew P. "The Sons of Noah and the Sons of Abraham: The Origins of Noahide Law." *JSJ* 48 (2017): 386-417.

Vos, Johannes G. *The Westminster Larger Catechism: A Commentary*. Edited by G. I. Williamson. Phillipsburg, NJ: R & R Publishing, 2002.

Vriezen, T. C., and A. S. van der Woude. *Ancient Israelite and Early Jewish Literature*. Translated by Brian Doyle. Leiden: Brill, 2005.

Walton, John H. "The Temple in Context." Pages 349-54 in *Behind the Scenes of the Old Testament: Cultural, Social, and Historical Contexts*. Edited by Jonathan S. Greer, John W. Hilber, and John H. Walton. Grand Rapids: Baker Academic, 2018.

Wenham, Gordon J. *The Book of Leviticus*. NICOT. Grand Rapids: Eerdmans, 1979.

——————. *Genesis 1-15*. WBC 1. Waco, TX: Word, 1987.

——————. "The Akedah: A Paradigm of Sacrifice." Pages 93-102 in *Pomegranates and Golden Bells: Studies in Biblical, Jewish, and Near Eastern Ritual, Law, and Literature in Honor of Jacob Milgrom*. Edited by David P. Wright, David Noel Freedman, and Avi Hurvitz. Winona Lake, IN: Eisenbrauns, 1995.

Werman, Cana. "The Concept of Holiness and the Requirements of Purity in Second Temple and Tannaic Literature." Pages 163-79 in *Purity and Holiness: The Heritage of Leviticus*. Edited by M. J. H. M. Poorthuis and J. Schwartz. JCPS 2. Leiden: Brill, 2007.

Index of Scripture and Ancient Literature

HEBREW BIBLE

Genesis
1:1-2 — 53-54
1:1–2:4 — 53-65, 78
1:22 — 57
1:26-27 — 38, 55, 60
1:28 — 54, 57-58, 223
2:5-25 — 57-58
2:9, 17 — 78-81, 88
2:18 — 57, 59-60
3 — 78-90
3:8-9 — 59, 64
3:17-19 — 58
3:22-24 — 38, 54, 81, 87
4:1-16 — 91-92, 224
4:3-7 — 354
4:4-5 — 359
4:23-24 — 92
5:2 — 58, 223
6–9 — 93-96, 155, 525, 720
6:5 — 275, 604
6:5-6 — 85, 99-103, 275, 311, 583
6:9 — 218
6:11-13 — 93, 103
8:20-22 — 96, 103, 354, 372, 584
9:1 — 223
11:1-9 — 96, 104, 526
12 — 103-5, 107-9
12–14 — 105
12–26 — 109
12:1-3 — 107-9, 223, 526-29
13:13 — 97
14:17-21 — 105, 354
15:6 — 106
15:18 — 541
16:13 — 460
17 — 105, 108
17:1-14 — 541
17:9-19 — 124
17:15-19 — 591
17:16, 20 — 223
18:1-15 — 105
18:9-15 — 591
18:14 — 55
18:16-33 — 97-98, 106
18:17-19 — 105, 108, 223
19 — 97-98
20:1-13 — 108
21:1 — 343
21:1-7 — 591
21:8-14 — 108
21:33 — 55
22 — 105-7, 223, 363
22:9-13 — 354
22:12 — 263
25:21-26 — 591
26:2-5 — 105, 107, 223, 533
28:3-4 — 223
28:14 — 105, 223
31:54 — 354
32:22-32 — 105, 639-40
32:30 — 460
35:14 — 354
37–46 — 591
46:1 — 354
46:28-34 — 591
47:8-9 — 591
50:24 — 343

Exodus
1:8-22 — 194
1:15-21 — 587, 595
1:17, 21 — 264
2:1-15 — 592
2:11-13, 24-25 — 595
2:23-25 — 585, 660
2:24 — 541
3:3-4 — 435
3:6, 13-15 — 588
3:7-9 — 660
3:16 — 343
3:21-22 — 589
4:1-15 — 592
4:23 — 360
4:31 — 343
5:1-21 — 194, 588, 596
6–11 — 588-89
6:2-8 — 541
6:30 — 124
7:16 — 354, 360
8:1, 20 — 354, 360
9:1, 13 — 354, 360
10:3, 26 — 354, 360
10:7-11, 24-26 — 360
12:1-10 — 411
12:1-13 — 493
12:1-27, 43-49 — 125
12:1–13:10 — 355
12:14 — 384
12:31 — 354, 360
12:35-36 — 589
12:37-38 — 556
12:38 — 607
13:1-2, 11-16 — 125, 355
13:2 — 505, 508
13:9 — 384
13:11-16 — 387, 508
13:21-22 — 589
14 — 588-89
14:4, 18 — 606
15:11 — 498
15:22-26 — 599-600
16–17 — 589, 600
16:4 — 437
17:8-13 — 637
18:4 — 60
19 — 514-15
19:3-5 — 115-16
19:4-5 — 41, 267, 391, 523, 556-57
19:5-6 — 504, 541-42, 549
19:6 — 388, 561
19:8 — 549, 551
19:8-12 — 354, 455
19:9-15 — 403, 508
19:10-23 — 515

19:9-25 600
19:10-14, 22 508
19:21 460
19:22, 24 457
20–23 552-53
20:3-6 126, 554
20:5-6 342, 344-46, 630
20:7 39, 139, 565
20:8-11 120, 508
20:11 508
20:12-17 116-17
20:18-21 461, 515, 600-601
20:22-26 355, 437
20:23 126
21:2 121
21–23 116-21
21:28-31 413
22:16, 28 141
22:20 126, 621
22:21 595
22:29-30 125, 355, 387
22:31 121, 403
23:7 218
23:9 595
23:13-17, 24, 32-33 125-26
23:15 377
23:18 490
23:33 651
24:3-8 489, 541, 551-53, 621
24:9-11 460
25–30 355
25:22 459
28:12, 17-21, 29 384-85
28:38, 43 478
29:1 505
29:1-37 405
29:20-21 489, 505
29:30-34 508
29:36-37 400, 434, 456, 508-9
29:38-43 519
29:43-44 505, 508
30:6 459
30:10 400
30:11-16 385, 388, 494
30:22-30 403, 508-9
30:29 434, 456-57
30:30 505
30:32, 36 456-57
30:34-37 508
31:12-18, 21 120
31:13 504, 507
31:14-15 121, 508
32 411, 601-16, 630
32:25-29 637
32:30 494
32:30-55 709
32:31-34 245, 339
32:34 342
32–33 554-55
33:1-6 604-5, 608
33:12-16 606
33:17-23 460, 611
34:1 554
34:6 312
34:6-7 6, 49, 246, 339, 344-46, 616-17
34:7 745

34:12 651
34:13-18, 22-26 125-26
34:14 47, 140
34:19-20 377, 387, 508
34:21, 26 120
34:25 490
34:27-28 555
35–40 355
35:2-3 120-21
35:4-29 608
35:20-35 359
39:7 385, 566
40:9-15 403, 505, 508

Leviticus
1–7 125
1:3, 10 422
1:4 400, 472
1:5, 15 489-90
2:2, 9, 16 384
2:10 508
3:1, 6 422
3:2, 8, 15-16 489
3:16-17 491
4–8 400, 468, 489
4:5 359
4:6-7, 17-18 491
4:23, 28, 32 422
5:1-3, 6, 17 478
5:1-5 359
5:2-3 121, 403, 442
5:6 400, 478
5:7-13 356
5:11-13 413, 494
5:12 384
5:14–6:7 400, 465
5:15, 18 422
6:2-3 117
6:6 422
6:15 384
6:18, 27 456, 509
6:26-27 508
7:18 478
7:19-21 121, 403, 442
7:33 490
8:10-15 403, 508
8:23-24, 30 432
9:7 472
10:1-3 455
10:1-7 459
10:16-18 478-79
11:24-39 403, 442
11:27-28, 39-40 121
11:44-45 502, 505
12:1-8 400-401
12:3 124, 637
13–15 121
14:1-32 400-401
14:13-14 432, 489, 508
14:17, 25, 51-52 489
14:29 489, 494
14:52 450
15:5-27 403, 442
15:33-53 400
16 125, 355, 359, 402, 430-32, 439, 449, 473-77, 489
16:2 459

16:10 472
16:16-18, 33 400
16:19 403, 450
16:20-22 408, 428, 477, 479
16:30 431, 449
17:1-9 125
17:6, 13 490
17:10-14 390, 491-92
17:11 409-10, 450, 492-94
17:14-16 121, 478
18 126, 144-46
18:6-20 116
18:21 126-27, 139, 565
18:23 120
18:24-28 563, 677
18:24-30 126, 562
18:25 445
19 116-21
19:2 502
19:4 126
19:5-8 125, 478
19:12 139, 565
19:14 119
19:17 478
19:17-18 118, 587
19:19 120, 148
19:22 468
19:26-31 126, 134
19:33-34 118, 595
20 116-21, 127, 134, 144
20:3 139, 565
20:6-7 134, 403
20:7-8 502, 507
20:13 141
20:17-20 478
20:22-23 320-21, 563, 677
20:22-27 124, 134
20:26 502, 504, 507
21:5-6 134, 139, 565
21:8 505
21:10 126
21:16-23 519
22:2, 32 565
22:3-8 121
22:4-6 403, 442
22:8-9, 15-16 478
22:9 504
22:17-25 519
22:32 139, 507
23 120, 125, 508
23:22 118
23:24, 42-43 384
23:27-32 402, 475
24–25 117-21
24:5-9 380
24:7 384
24:15-16 139, 478, 565
25:12 508
25:39-55 140-41
25:55 557-58, 560
26 126, 227-31, 247-50, 255-61, 269-72, 543-50, 571-72, 677
26:1-13 227-31, 439
26:2 120
26:30 323
26:40-41 124, 258, 545
26:40-45 249-50, 259, 323-24

27:1-33   125
27:11-13, 26-27   387
27:14-22, 30-33   508
27:29   413

Numbers
1:51   455
3:10, 38   455
3:13   505, 508
3:40-47   387-88
4:19   455
5:1-10   120-21, 125, 403
5:5-8   117, 400
5:7   359
5:11-31   141
5:26   384
5:27-31   478
6:1-21   125, 403
6:9-17   400
6:14   422
6:18-19   359, 508
7:1-11   403, 508
7:89   459
8:10-12   400
8:14-19   387-88, 505, 508
8:19   455
9–10   612-14
9:1-3   125
9:6-10   442
9:13   466
10:10   384
10:11–11:15   609
11:1-2   413
11   613
11:18   403, 508
12–14   613-16, 643
12:3   637
14:11-12, 19-21   49
14:17-23   246, 709
14:18   6, 312, 339, 344-46, 615-17
14:33-35   478
15:1-31   125
15:25-28   468
15:31   478
15:40   502
16   455, 459-60, 614
16:9   505
16:41-48   494
17:12-13   455, 460
18:1-7, 22-24   479
18:3, 7   455
18:8-29   508
18:15-18   387, 508
18:17   490
19:1-19   400
19:11-22   121, 403, 442, 455
20   632, 635
21   619
23:20-22   560
25   117, 411, 619-26, 630
28–29   125, 519
29:7-11   402, 475
30:2   117
31   621-26
31:1-18   141, 637
31:9-11   650
31:16   620
31:19   403

31:50   400, 494
32   626
35:9-33   117, 121
35:31   413
35:33-34   445

Deuteronomy
1   627
1:19-33, 45   629
1:31   159
1:37   634
2:4-5, 9, 19   646
2:7   627
2:21-36   642
2:30   597
2:34-35   141, 650
3:6   141
3:7   650
3:26   634
4:3-4   626-27
4:5-8   150, 533, 646
4:9-20   124-25
4:20   267
4:21   634
4:23-24   126
4:24   1, 551, 745
4:25-26   563
4:29   159
4:30-31   259, 272, 551
4:33   461
4:36   237, 437, 628
4:37-38   627, 642
4:40   159, 224, 628
5:6-10   126
5:7   554
5:9-10   342, 344-45, 630-31
5:11   39, 139, 565
5:12-15   120, 595
5:16   159, 628
5:20   117
5:23-26   461
5:27   551
5:28-29   159, 628
5:29-33   224-25, 628
6:1-3   159, 225, 628
6:4-6   158, 160
6:7-15   56, 124-26
6:16-19   159, 225, 627-28, 642
6:20   555
6:20-25   125
6:24-25   160, 229-30, 628
7:1-6   141, 562, 642
7:5, 25-28   126
7:6   267, 557-58
7:7-8   590, 627
7:10   337
7:12-16   225
7:14   41, 565
7:16   651
7:16-26   642
8:1   159, 628
8:2-5   246, 627-29
8:5   159, 238
8:11-18   125, 627
9:4-7   590-91, 627, 642
9:5   581
9:6-29   267, 627, 634
9:23-24   619

10:12-13   158, 160, 261-62, 628
10:16   124
10:17   321, 385, 563
10:17-18   153, 167
10:17-19   118, 595, 640-41
10:21-22   627
11:1   159, 261, 555
11:2-7   627-28
11:8-9   159, 628
11:8-21   225
11:13   159, 261
11:18-21, 26-28   124-26
12:1-4   126, 642
12:6   387
12:7, 12, 18   120
12:16   390, 490
12:23-25   390
12:25-28   490, 628
12:28   159, 225
12:29-32   126, 321, 562, 651
12–26   631
13:1-17   126
13:3   159, 261
13:5, 10   121
13:6-16   141
14:1-2   126, 134, 562
14:2   267, 508, 557-58
14:21-29   118, 120
15:1-18   118, 120-21
15:15   595
15:19-21   125, 508, 519
15:23   390, 490
16:1-17, 21-22   125-26
16:3, 12   384
16:11, 14   120
16:11-12   595
16:16   377
16:18-20   117, 321, 563
17:1-7   117, 121, 126, 519
17:14-20   120, 671
18:9-14   126, 134, 320, 562
19:1-21   117
19:10   218
19:13   159, 628
20:5-7   120
20:10-18   129, 141, 646
21:10-14   141
21:18-23   116, 121, 237
21:23   445
22–24   116-21
22:5   148
22:7   159, 628
22:13-19   141
23:7   118, 595
23:12-14   144-45
24:1-4   141
24:17-22   595
25:2-3, 13-16   117
25:4   120
25:11-12   121, 141
25:13-16   320-21
26:1-15   118, 125, 385
26:15   437
26:16   159, 631
26:17-19   504, 555, 558
26:17–27:10   631
27:1-8, 15   125-26
27:7   120

27:16-25   116-18
28   247-61, 543, 548-50, 571-72, 677, 717
28–30   252, 255, 258, 269, 272, 323
28–33   631
28:1-14   227-31
28:9   504
28:15-68   247-61, 648
28:63   323
29   250-51, 684
29:18-19   126
29:23   97
30:1-10   159, 251-53, 261, 684-85
30:6   124, 159, 258
30:8-9   323
30:15-20   159, 225, 555
31:9-13   125, 553
31:27   634
32   159, 332-34, 684-85
32:6   627
32:15-21   126, 129
32:23   347
32:36   557, 560
32:45-47   159, 628
33:3-5   159, 560
33:7, 26, 29   60
34:4   631
34:10-12   637

Joshua
1:6-9   649
1:8   226
1:10-17   553
3:5   508
3:10-17   458
4:15-18   458
4:23-24   458, 683
6–8   649-50
7:13   508
10:11   437
11:14   650
11:20   597, 651
22–24   650-51
24:15, 22   553
24:19-20   498-99

Judges
2–7   653-56
2:3   651
2:11-19   269-71
3:7-11, 15-30   270
6–8   270, 625
6:22-23   460
8:22-23   658, 660
8:33–10:16   270-71
9–21   656-59
11:29-33   271
13:19-23   460
20:27-28   622
22:13-18   626

Ruth
1:6   343
4:13-17   556

1 Samuel
1–30   659-65
1:20-28   387

2:1-2   498
2:21   343
5:1-12   458-59
6:1-17   356
6:5, 19-20   458-59
8:5   173
8:11-18   671
12:14   264
15:22   367
16:5   508
16:7   70
19:5   218
21:1-6   517
24:19   231
26:23   231

2 Samuel
1–24   662-66
6:1-14   455-59, 516-17
7:1-9   518
7:11-16   670
7:14-15   580
8:15   173, 665
22:14   437
22:21-25   218, 231
22:47-49   331
24:25   360-61

1 Kings
2–8   668-70
2:3   555
2:8-9   663
3:6   666-67
3:9, 28   173
6:12   555
8:10-11   359
8:22-54   360, 368, 437
8:27-30   363
8:32   231
8:33-36   272-73
8:39   70
8:41-43, 60   683
8:44-51   364
8:62-66   519
9–15   667, 670-71
9:9   347
10:9   173
11:33   129
12–18   672-74
18:18, 28   128-29
18:38   359
18:24-26, 36-37   361
21:25-26   129
21–22   672-75

2 Kings
1:10-14   437
2–25   667, 671-77
12:16   356
14:13   457
16:15   361
17:7-18   127, 278-79
17:9-17, 29-40   129
17:37   555
19:19   683-84
19:22   499
21:6-9   127, 129
22:20   347

23:7   132
23:10   127
24–25   256

1 Chronicles
13:5-12   516-17
13–15   457-58
15:12   508
16:9-12, 29-31   498
16:31-34   170
16:36   55
21:26   359, 437
22–29   664
22:6-8   637
28:9   70
29:10-19   62, 385, 667
29:17-18   367

2 Chronicles
5–6   359-60
6:12-42   437
6:18-21   363
6:23   231
6:32-33   683
7:1   359, 437
7:14   437
7:16   508
7:16, 20   505
19:7   321, 385, 563
19:10   555
20:7   106
20:5-20   361
20:37   457
24:7   457
25:23   457
26:6   457
29–30   508
29:23-24   356, 403
32:5   457
32:24-26   413
33–36   675-77
33:4-9   127, 129, 555
34:24   347
35:6   508
36:15-17   282, 676

Ezra
3–10   679-81
8:35   356

Nehemiah
4:5   445
5–13   679-81
9:5   55
9:13   555
9:13-15, 27-28   437
9:16-17   312, 413
9:26-31   283
10:33   356
13:18   347

Job
1:1   218
1:8   264
1:16   437
2:3   218
4:8   445
4:17   444

5:17-18	238	39:11	237
8:6	444	40:6-8	150, 309
10:12	343	40:10	175
13:10	321	41:13	55
15:35	445	43:1	171, 295
16:14	457	44:21	70
22:30	444	44:23-26	290
33:9	444	47:5-9	67
34:19	321	48:10-11	172
36:10	237	50:7-23	309-10
42:2	55	51:1-9	296
42:8-9	361	51:2, 6-7, 10-12	444, 502
		51:16-17	310
Psalms		55:1-3	291
4:1	175	56:10-13	299
4:3	292	57:3	437
5:5-6	320-21	57:6-10	299
5:7	498	57:10	65, 243
5:8	173	58:10-11	334
6:1	237	59:5	342, 581
7:1-11	292	60:1	457
7:6-11	177	65:5-13	66, 171
7:8-9	171	66:1-4	67
7:9	70	66:8-15	299, 534
7:14	445	66:16-20	292
8	58, 63	67:4-5	170, 173, 534
8:4	343	68:5	498
9:7-8	172	68:32	534
9:9-14	299	69:1-5	296
9:11	537	69:13-18	291
10:12-18	290	69:30-33	300, 362
10:17-18	167-68, 170	70:5	60
11:4-6	321, 499	71:1-13	291
16:1-4	292	71:2	171
16:7	237	71:15-24	300
17:1-6	292	71:22	498
18	666	72:1-4, 7	168-70
18:16-27	292	72:12-14	168, 176-77
18:20	231, 444	74	677
18:47-49	331	76:7-9	171, 177
19:1, 4	66	77:13-14	498
19:7-10	149, 216	78:1, 17, 22	274
19:13	218	78-81	683
19:14	70	78:34-40	275
20:3-6	361, 478	78:62	318
22:27	534	79	677
22:30-31	172	79:6-7	581
24:1-2	62	79:8-9	296
24:3-4	444	80:12	457
25:4-12, 16-18	296-97	80:14	343
26:1-2	70, 171	81:8, 10-14, 16	275
26:1-12	295	82:1	38, 54
27:6-7	361	82:3-4	167, 170, 177
27:11-12	297	85:1-3	413
29:1-2	67	85:2	445
31:6	320-21	85:8-11	169
32:1	445	86:8-10	54, 66, 534
32:1-7	296, 413	86:14-17	291, 312
33:5	65, 174	89:2	243
33:20	60	89:5-16	67
34:15-17	292	89:11	62
35:22-24	171, 295	89:14	174
36:5-7	171, 243, 533-54	89:32	342
36:5-10	65	89:40	457
37:21	175	90:2	55
37:31	150	90:13	557
37:37-40	291	93:1-2	55, 67
38:4, 18	296	94:1-7	327-28, 340

94:10-12	150, 237
94:10-22	218, 327-28
95:1-5	54, 62, 67
95:10	320
96:1-3	67, 537
96:7-13	498, 534
96:10-13	67, 170
97:1-2	67, 170
97:6-7	66, 132
98:4, 8	67
98:7-9	170
99:1-5	67, 498
99:8	338-39
100:1-3	67
100:5	67, 243
101:1	174
102:14	557
102:18-22	437, 498, 534
103:1-5	413, 498
103:6-8	174, 312
103:11	243
103:12	445
103:17-18	55, 174
103:19-22	67
104	66
104:31	62
105:3-5	498
105-106	683
106:1	243
106:4	343
106:7-12, 21-29	276
106:28-31	626
106:36-39	127, 444-45
106:40-48	55, 276, 324
107:1	243
107:8, 15, 21, 31	67
107:8-9	66
108:3-4	243, 537
109:14	445
109:21-26, 30-31	291
111:2-7	66, 174
111:9	498
112:4, 9	175
113:1-9	67
115:3-8	55, 62, 132
115:9-11	60
116:5-19	174, 300
116:17	361
117	67, 534
118:2-4	243
119	149-50
119:1	218
119:7, 62, 106	175
119:13	320
119:64	65
119:72, 103, 127	216
119:123	171
119:163-65	175-76
121:1-2	60
123:1-4	291
124:8	60
130:1-8	296
130:3-4	413
132:13-18	577
135:6	55
135:13-14	174, 557
135:15-18	132
136:1-26	243

136:4-9	65
136:22	557
137	677, 721-22
138:2	498
138:4-5	66-67
139:1-14	66, 70
139:21-24	70, 295, 320
141:1-5	298
141:2	361
142:1-7	291, 298
143:7-12	292, 297
143:11-12	175, 177
145:1-13	67
145:7-9	66-67, 174, 312
145:9-17	174, 534
145:21	498
146:5-9	60, 66, 167
147:7-9	66
148:1-14	67
149:5-9	334

Proverbs

1:2-3, 7-8	237
3:1-2	228
3:7	79
3:11-12	238
3:31-34	320
4:13	237
5:22	228
6:16-19	321
6:23	237
8:22-31	62-63
8:36	228-29
11:5-6, 17	228
13:1, 24	237
13:6	228
14:9	356
14:16	79
14:32	228
15:8	361
15:32-33	237
16:6	413, 494
16:22	228
17:3	70
17:20	228
19:18	237
20:9	444
21:2	70
21:3, 27	310
21:21	174
22:8	445
22:16	228
24:23	321
28:7	150
28:10	228
28:21	321
29:17	237
29:18	150
31:1	237
31:9	172

Ecclesiastes

3:3	457
10:8	457

Isaiah

1:2-4	499, 688, 690-91
1:5-6	705
1:10-17	280, 309, 361
1:14	279, 321
1:15	710
1:16-18	167, 170, 444
1:21-24	136, 313, 327-28
1:25-28	177, 282, 328-29
2:2-4	536
2:11-12, 18-20	728
3:14-15	313
4:2-4	283, 730
5:1-7	457, 691-92
5:8-13, 20-23	313
5:16, 18-21	498-99
5:24-25	499, 705, 717
6:1-13	280-81, 500-501
6:5	460
8:11-15	499, 717
9:6-7	169, 577
9:13	273
9:17-19	717
10:1-4	314
10:5-19	581, 655
10:16-23	499, 727
11:1-9	578
11:4-5	168, 170, 177
11:10-16	731
12:1	735
12:3-6	498, 537
13:9-11	708
14:1-2	738
16:4-5	174, 177, 578
17:10	695
19:19-25	360, 536-37
22:12-14	710
24:1-3	708
25:6-9	535
27:7-10	728
27:9	413, 494, 729
27:11	709
27:12-13	732
28:5-6	732
28:26	237
29:19-21	498, 582
30:9-14	499, 703
30:18-26	174, 573
30:23-26	733-34
31:1-12	499
31:6-7	729
32:1	173
32:16-18	169, 573
33:5-6	171
33:22-24	413
34:2-7	725
35:1-10	573
35:4	329-30
37:23	499
37:31-32	730
38:17	445
40:1-2	734
40:10-11	573
40:25-26	498
40:28	55
41:8-9	106, 557
41:14	498
42:1-6	535
42:4	173
42:8	46
42:10-17	717, 726
43:1-25	301-4
43:10	537, 557
43:14-17	498
43:25	445
44:8	537
44:9-20	129, 132, 696-97
44:21-22	445, 557, 701
44:29	581
45:7	347
45:8, 21	171
45:9-12	498-99
45:20-25	50, 75-77, 132, 535
46:1-2	132
46:3-4	688
46:5-13	691
46:12-13	172
47:4, 10	498
48:11	46
48:17-19	169, 277, 498
49:6	535, 562
49:15	688
49:25-26	725
51:4-6	172-73, 535
51:11	573
51:13	695-96
52:9-10	738
52:13–53:12	411, 480-89
53:10	356
54:3-8	498, 688, 734
54:13-14	169
55:1-3	701
55:5	498
55:6-7	413, 701
55:12-13	573
56:1	172
56:6-7	360, 498, 536, 556
57:1-10	127, 129, 136, 699
57:1-13	132
57:15	435
58:6-7	308
59:3-8	314, 445
59:11	172
59:12-15	697
59:17-18, 20	330
60:3	535
60:9	498
61:1-3	330-31, 340
61:4-7, 9, 11	738
61:8	321, 331
61:10	172
62:5	688
62:11	331
63:1, 4-6	331
63:15-16	498
64:5-7	444, 691
64:8	688
65:1-5	129, 229, 691, 703
65:6-7	337
65:17-25	574
66:4	703
66:12-13	688
66:15-24	537, 717, 738

Jeremiah

1:5	505
1:10	599
2:1-2	688, 692
2:5-20	129, 132, 229, 692

2:7 445
2:20-25 136
2:22 444
2:26-30 132, 237, 273, 697, 706
2:32-35 696, 698
3:1-3 446, 698
3:1-11, 14, 20, 27 136
3:6-10 724
3:12-18 701
3:17 536
3:19-22 693, 696
4:1-2 535
4:4 124
4:18-22 229, 693
4:23-27 730
5:3 237, 273, 706
5:7-9 129-30, 338, 693
5:18 730
5:23-25 229, 693
5:26-29 314, 317, 338
5:28 169-70
6:11-12 279, 717
6:19 347
6:28 704
7:1-15 520-21
7:9-11 130, 308
7:12-15 724-25
7:13, 25-26 312
7:16-20 280, 711
7:18-19 693, 697
7:23-28 703-4
7:28 237, 274, 706
8:18–9:1 693
8:4-7 704
9:3-6 314
9:4-8 338
9:7-9 705
9:12-14 697, 704
9:24-26 124, 174
10:1-15 132, 342
10:19-21 693, 700
10:24 237
11:7-8 312, 704
11:12 132, 697
11:14-17 280, 308, 711
11:18-20 70, 332
12:14-16 735
13:10-11 704
13:12-14 712, 717
13:12-27 716
13:25 696
13:27 136, 444
14:10-12 280, 308, 711
15:1-7 711
15:5-9 279, 708, 717
15:7 281-82
15:15 343
16:4-5 127, 717
16:10-13 704
16:14-15 732
16:18 337, 446
16:19-21 132, 229, 536-37
17:10 70
17:23 237, 704
18:11-12 704
18:15-16 696
18:23 445
19:3 347

19:4-5 127, 697-98
19:15 704
20:10-12 70, 332
21:3-10 717
21:8-12 707
21:12 168, 177, 314
22:3 168, 177
22:11-17 700
23:1-4 732
23:3-7 172-73, 578
23:9-15 707
23:17 704
23:25-32 696, 699
24 78
24:6-7 576
25:3-7 312, 704
25:11-12 345
25:15-38 712
25:30-31 498-99
25:33 717
26:2-3 702
26:4-6 312
27:22 343
29:10 343, 345
29:17-18 718
29:19 312, 705
30:10-11 247, 557, 732
30:12-17 734
31:3-5, 8-10, 12-13 574
31:7-9 732
31:18 237
31:28 726
31:31-34 413, 576
32:17, 27 55
32:19 231
32:30-33 274, 706
32:33 237, 312
32:35 127
32:37-42 576
33:6-11 413, 444, 576
33:9 537
33:14-16 172, 578
35:14-15 312, 705
36:30-31 705
44:2-10 706
44:4 312
44:15-23 132
46:1-28 329
46:10-12 327, 725
46:27-28 247, 557
48:8-10, 25-26 725
48:47 536
49:2-3, 5-6 726-27
49:6, 39 536
50:11-16 725
50:18-20 735
50:29-32 499
50:31 342
51:7-18 132
51:17-18 697
51:37-44 725

Lamentations
1:2-21 718
1:8-9 444
2:5-12, 15-21 718
2:6-7 366, 441
3:1-6, 15-20, 48-51 718

3:31-33 277
3:38 347
3:42-48 710
4:8-10 718
4:11 318
4:13-15 444
4:22 735
5:10-15 718

Ezekiel
2:3-7 705
3:7 705
5:10 718
5:13-17 318, 707-8
6:6-10 730-31
6:11-14 718
7:8-12 709
7:23 314
8:12-13, 17 698
8:16-18 130
8:18 711
9:5-6 718-19
10:18-19 441
11:5 70
11:13-20 576, 732
11:22-23 429, 441
12:1-3 705
12:15-16 731
13:17-23 699
14:10-11 283, 446, 729
14:12-20 280, 711
14:21-23 729-30
16:3-14 689-90
16:8-58 136
16:15-34 694
16:35-43 318, 712, 715
16:45-52 725
16:53-63 736-37
18:10-18 130
18:23, 31-32 277, 322, 702
20:5-8 705
20:8-17, 22 568
20:23-26 712-13
20:31 127, 446
20:33-44 568, 729-30
20:40-44 49, 360, 504
20:43 446
21:3-12 719
21:10 274
21:17 318
22:3-4, 6-13, 25-30 130-31
22:3-12 127
22:4 446
22:6-9 700
22:11-12 696
22:17-22 282, 729
23:1-34 725
23:1-49 136
23:22, 26-27 716
23:30 446
23:35 696
23:37-39 127, 130, 698
24:11-13 282, 444
24:13-14 318, 709
25:12-16 336
28:25 504
29:13-14 536
33:11 277, 702

33:25-26 — 127
34:1-6 — 700
34:1-31 — 176
34:11-16 — 734
34:14 — 47
34:20-31 — 578-79
35:6-9 — 719
36:16-17, 23-39 — 444
36:16-36 — 568-69
36:22-23 — 47, 537, 571
36:22-32 — 49, 566
36:25-27 — 576
36:29-31 — 730
37:21-28 — 557, 579
38:16 — 537
38:23 — 504
39:7 — 499, 504, 537, 566, 570
39:21-29 — 49, 444, 570-71
43:7-8 — 499
43:18 — 450
43:26 — 508
44:7, 9 — 124
44:7, 15 — 490

Daniel
4:27 — 413
4:35 — 55
5:17-20 — 597
6:10 — 362
9:1-19 — 683
9:2, 24 — 345
9:20-21 — 362
12:10 — 444

Hosea
1:2 — 694-95
1:6 — 709
2 — 136, 695, 712, 716
2:8 — 690
2:19-20 — 174
3:4-5 — 273, 579
4:1-18 — 129, 698
4:2 — 457
4:6 — 695
4:16 — 705
5:14–6:1 — 273
5:3-7 — 136, 446
6:4-6 — 308, 705
7:9-10 — 273, 705
7:15-16 — 229, 237, 690
8:3 — 229, 690
8:11-14 — 308, 695
9:1 — 136
9:10 — 626
9:12-17 — 320, 719
11:1-9 — 688-90
11:7-8 — 277
12:6 — 174
13:1-3 — 132
13:4-6 — 695
13:16 — 719
14:4-7 — 577

Joel
2:1-2 — 499
2:12-14 — 312, 702
2:16 — 508
2:28-29 — 577
3:18-20 — 574

Amos
2:9-10 — 271
3:2 — 271
3:6 — 347
4:1-2 — 719
4:6-12 — 271-72
5:4-6, 27 — 272
5:7, 10-12 — 314-15
5:14-15 — 702
5:21-25 — 308-9, 321, 361
6:4-6 — 315
8:4-6 — 162, 315
9:2-4 — 712
9:11-15 — 272, 579

Jonah
3:4-10 — 581-82
3:8-10 — 413
4:2 — 312

Micah
1:2-4 — 499
2:12-13 — 457, 732
3:1-3, 9-11 — 315
3:12 — 719
4:1-4 — 536
4:13 — 581
5:7-9 — 732-33
5:15 — 331-32, 581
6:3-4 — 692
6:6-8 — 175, 308
6:9-12 — 315
7:2-6 — 315
7:18-20 — 413, 445, 735

Nahum
1:2-15 — 327-28
1:3 — 312
1:15 — 334

Habakkuk
2:13-14 — 738
2:18-19 — 132, 697
2:20 — 498
3:2-6 — 498-99

Zephaniah
1:2-3, 15-18 — 720
2:7 — 343, 733
3:1-2 — 274, 446
3:6-7 — 274
3:8-13 — 360, 731, 738
3:11-13 — 284, 577
3:14-20 — 733

Haggai
1:4-11 — 306-7
2:17 — 273

Zechariah
1:3-6 — 703
1:12-17 — 574, 735-36
2:10-11 — 536
2:13 — 498
7:5 — 345
7:8-13 — 274
8:3-8 — 733
8:11-17 — 736

8:20-23 — 536
9:16-17 — 575
10:3 — 343
10:6-12 — 575, 736
11:15-17 — 712
13:1 — 444
13:8-9 — 282, 731

Malachi
1:2-4 — 304, 321
1:6-14 — 304-5, 567
2:1-17 — 305-6
2:2-3 — 719
2:5-6 — 567
2:9 — 321, 563
2:13-16 — 321
3:1-4 — 282, 444, 730
3:6-7 — 703
3:10-12, 16-18 — 305-6
4:2-3 — 567

APOCRYPHA AND
PSEUDEPIGRAPHA

Tobit
4:12 — 106
12:9-10 — 229, 494
13 — 278, 683

Judith
4:13-15 — 361
5:18-19 — 277
8:27 — 278
9:1-14 — 361
13:20 — 343
16:16 — 368

Wisdom of Solomon
3:7 — 343
11:9-10 — 278
11:23-26 — 66, 324
12:2 — 238
12:3-6 — 127, 131
12:20-22 — 278
13:10–14:31 — 131-32
14:9 — 320, 324
14:23-25 — 127
15:7-17 — 132
16:24 — 229
16:28 — 361
18:21 — 361

Sirach
3:3, 30 — 494
7:7-10 — 368
12:6 — 320-21
16:8 — 320
18:20 — 343
27:22-24 — 321
32:14 — 238
34:23-24 — 310
35:1-9, 14-15 — 368
35:5 — 494
35:14 — 385
35:17 — 343
44:19-20 — 106
50:1-19 — 361

Baruch
1–5 — 683
2:27-35 — 278
4:21-24, 36-37 — 575
5:1-9 — 575

Epistle of Jeremiah
7-72 — 132

Prayer of Azariah
15-17 — 362
28-65 — 67

Prayer of Manasseh
8 — 106

1 Maccabees
1:15-38 — 150
2:52 — 106
7:37 — 360
13:1-6 — 150

2 Maccabees
1:8, 21-30 — 361
2:10 — 359
6:12-16 — 237-38, 339
6:18–7:2 — 150
7:32-34 — 277
10:3-4 — 277, 361
14:30-36 — 361

3 Maccabees
1:23 — 150

4 Maccabees
4:21-26 — 150
5:14–6:30 — 150
6:28-29 — 411
17:20-22 — 411

Jubilees
1:4-25 — 127, 683
6:14 — 490
11:4-6 — 127
17:17-18 — 106
18:16 — 106
23:10 — 106

Psalms of Solomon
3:7-8 — 494
7–9 — 683
13:9-10 — 238
17 — 683
18:4 — 238

2 Enoch
45:3 — 368
46:1 — 368

Letter of Aristeas
139-51, 168 — 506

Sybilline Oracles
4.166-68 — 494

QUMRAN

Community Rule (1 QS)
3:7-10 — 494
9:4-6 — 362, 494

PHILO OF ALEXANDRIA

On the Change of Names
240 — 369

On the Decalogue
5-9, 54-54, 72-81 — 131

On Dreams
2.299 — 362

On Drunkenness
66 — 362

On the Life of Abraham
225-44 — 106

On the Life of Moses
1.219 — 362
2.5, 133, 147-59 — 359, 362
2.12-27, 52, 79, 104 — 150
2.64 — 96
2.84-135 — 381-82
2.106-8 — 369
2.150 — 490

Questions and Answers on Genesis
1.61 — 369
2.52 — 369

On the Special Laws
1.59-64 — 135
1.84-97, 145-298 — 378-81
1.97, 113, 167-68, 195, 224 — 362
1.171 — 362, 490
1.188 — 475
1.196 — 368
1.203-4, 259-83 — 370-71
1.205 — 378, 490
1.221 — 359
1.312-13 — 127
2.35 — 368
2.140-252 — 380
4.97-125 — 506-7
4.125 — 490

That God is Unchangeable
7-9 — 362, 369

On the Virtues
113, 125, 141-42 — 150

Who is the Heir?
114 — 381
251 — 359

JOSEPHUS

Against Apion
2.77, 196 — 363
2.175-86, 277-86 — 150
2.249 — 131

Jewish Antiquities
1.41-42, 46-47 — 90
1.58, 96 — 363
1.256 — 106
3.100 — 363
3.210-15 — 359
3.223 — 150
3.311 — 238
4.33, 54-56 — 359
4.203, 243 — 363
4.318-19 — 150
5.256 — 363
6.19, 25, 102 — 363
6.147-49 — 367
7.327-39 — 359, 363
8.106, 118, 126, 342 — 359
8.108 — 363
8.112 — 471
11.17 — 363
12.110 — 150
14.260-61 — 363
16.44 — 150
18.1 — 363

Jewish War
2.197, 409 — 363

NEW TESTAMENT

Matthew
1:5 — 556
13:24-29 — 724

Luke
1:68, 78 — 343
7:16 — 343
19:44 — 343

John
4:23-24 — 373

Acts of the Apostles
10:34 — 321
15:14 — 343

Romans
2:9 — 321

Galatians
2:6 — 321

Index of Authors

Bavinck, H., 43-44, 75-77, 558, 745
Birch, B. C., 543
Blenkinsopp, J., 688
Brondos, D. A., 361, 405, 407, 480, 750
Brueggemann, W., 45-51, 69, 75, 82, 140, 256, 286, 565-66, 571, 745, 752
Budd, P. J., 619, 632

Caldwell, R., 18
Calvin, J., 43
Chapman, S. B., 11
Christensen, D. L., 256
Cottrell, J., 56
Craig, W. L., 433-35, 745

Day, J., 53, 155
de Kroon, M., 43
de Vaux, R., 356-57, 365, 403

Eberhart, C. A., 432

Finlan, S. 421, 433, 435
Fredriksen, P., 13

Gadd, C. J., 204
Gane, R. E., 396, 432, 447
Goldingay, J., 436, 460

Haran, M., 434
Hart, G., 18
Hartley, J. E., 435-36
Hayes, C., 199, 203

Heiser, M. S., 38
Hensel, B., 4
Hesselink, J. I., 43
Hong, K. P., 17
Hornung, E., 206
Hultgren, A. J., 144
Hurtado, L. W., 13

Jeon, J., 4
Johnston, G. H., 18

Kazen, T., 144-45
Klawans, J., 432
Kugel, J. L., 663

Levenson, J. D., 542-43, 546
Levin, C., 4
Levine, B. A., 431-33, 436, 455, 493, 619, 632, 745
Lohr, J. N., 556
López-Ruiz, C., 18
Lundbom, J. R., 256

Maccoby, H., 449
Milgrom, J., 365, 397, 399, 421, 428-42, 447-55, 466, 482-93, 745

Nelson, R. D., 433, 435
Noble, P. R., 17
Noth, M., 620

Pixley, G. V., 613

Pritchard, J. B., 22

Römer, T., 38

Scheid, J., 350
Schmid, K., 4
Schreiner, T. R., 407
Schwartz, B. J., 431, 434-35, 442, 447,
    453, 456, 494
Sørensen, J. P., 206
Stubbs, D. L., 619, 632

Taylor, W. F., Jr., 144

Ursinus, Z., 43-44

van der Woude, A. S., 11
Van Zile, M. P., 155
Vos, J. G., 44
Vriezen, T. C., 11

Walton, J. H., 397-98
Wenham, G. J., 104, 354, 433-34, 460,
    493, 745
Werman, C., 434

Index of Subjects

Abraham, 103-9, 263-64, 354, 526-29,
541-42, 584-86, 591
faith/righteousness of, 105-9, 505,
527, 603
age to come, 572-80, 728-39
ark of the covenant, 355, 381, 402, 455-62,
489, 513, 516-17, 659, 669
atonement, 395, 398-401, 408-14, 419-27,
467-73, 492, 609-10

Bible, formation of, 3-11, 13-14, 748-49
blood. *See* sacrificial blood

chastisement. *See* divine punishment/
chastisements
circumcision, 105, 108, 124, 258, 505, 541
clean/unclean. *See* purity; impurity
Code of Hammurabi, 199-208, 525
conquest of Canaan, 637, 640-51
covenant, 49, 108, 154, 250-51, 504,
541-65, 621, 747
creation, 23-25, 40-44, 53-78, 98-101, 164,
208-9, 303-4, 347, 523, 526, 583-84,
604-5, 741-43
curse, 91-92, 104, 248-55, 528-29, 542-43,
551, 744, 751

David, 168-74, 361, 367, 516-18, 577-80,
662-71. *See also* Israel, kings/rulers of
Day of Atonement. *See Yom Kippur*
divine plan, 55, 104-9, 279, 523-41, 582-86,
597-606, 615, 624, 643-48, 746

divine punishment/chastisements, 44-45,
70-72, 82-85, 95, 114, 142-43, 178-81,
190-94, 198, 217-23, 236-52, 260-286,
311, 317-19, 325-30, 338-46, 406-25,
477-79, 484, 547, 551-53, 562-63, 582,
608-11, 614, 619-24, 652, 709-11, 723-
29, 743-45

Egyptian Book of the Dead, 18, 206-8, 297
Enuma Elish, 18, 22-28, 50, 57, 89, 134,
183, 185, 268, 310, 320, 525, 557-58
expiation, 400-403, 408-11, 427, 432-33,
467-74, 489-95, 610, 622-23

festivals, 24-25, 125-26, 357, 380-84, 553
forgiveness, 2, 6, 99-100, 207, 243-47, 269,
317, 327, 339, 345-46, 362-64, 368,
371, 394-402, 409-27, 450-53, 464-81,
486-93, 501-2, 550, 609-12, 615-17,
709-11, 744

goat for Azazel, 402, 408, 411, 414, 421,
423, 430-32, 475-77
God,
as creator, 37-44, 53-81, 96, 141-42, 208-
9, 257, 347, 441, 604-5, 741-43, 746
as father/parent, 159, 238, 312, 664,
688, 690-91
as husband to Israel, 136, 543, 547,
688-90, 694-95, 714
as judge, 6, 171, 294-95, 325-26, 501-2,
534-35, 580-82

cruelty/violence of, 247-61, 325-42, 347-48, 603-15, 619-25, 640-49, 674-75, 705-28, 737

desires/objectives of, 41-51, 59-78, 148-56, 217-19, 223-34, 246-68, 303-10, 318, 344-48, 404-8, 497-98, 558-71, 599-601, 654-55, 746-48

fear of, 77, 83, 114-15, 259-67, 498-502, 515, 561, 586-87, 600-601

foreknowledge of, 99, 583, 604-5

glorification/glory of, 42-51, 58, 66-71, 74, 126, 253, 260-61, 303-4, 337-38, 405, 498, 515, 566

goodness of, 57-62, 66-67, 70-71, 75-77, 347-48, 587, 744, 753

hatred of, 1, 258-59, 320-24, 722, 727-28

holiness of, 45-51, 111-12, 260-61, 405-7, 427-38, 455-62, 496-503, 512-21, 566, 744-45

jealousy of, 1, 45-49, 126, 136, 140, 286-87, 337, 498-99, 543, 547, 551, 630, 743-45

justice/righteousness of, 2-3, 40-45, 50-51, 111-12, 167-82, 208-19, 297-301, 307-24, 406-20, 425-27, 484, 496-98, 547, 744

kingship of, 159, 173, 544-45, 560-61

love of, 1-3, 6-8, 48-49, 64-78, 93-94, 115-19, 157-64, 173-82, 209-19, 232-80, 288-301, 311-48, 497-503, 549-65, 586-93, 626-31, 656-57, 678-85, 688-96, 731-39, 746-48

name of, 13, 39-40, 47-49, 111, 139-40, 363-64, 503-4, 565-71, 606

nature of, 45, 99, 111-12, 131, 143-51, 217-24, 239-40, 405-20, 431-33, 440, 547-48, 743

perfection of, 154, 160-61, 244, 407, 415-19, 496, 500-503

praise/worship of, 43-51, 57-58, 66-77, 126-27, 299-307, 543, 741-44

preexistence of, 53-54, 208-9

presence/proximity of, 40, 364, 395-97, 436-38, 450, 459, 462, 511, 519, 745

sovereignty of, 39-40, 45-50, 53-56, 75-76, 80-89, 115, 263-68, 497-503, 510-12, 515-19, 586-88

transcendence of, 510, 515-19

wrath/anger of, 45-51, 55-56, 66-67, 97-98, 115-19, 286-87, 291-97, 307-24, 414-18, 423-27, 455-56, 470-71, 586-88, 605-8, 676-85, 707-28, 744-45

gods. *See* pagan gods

holiness, concepts of, 403-4, 434-35, 455-56, 497-504, 509

idolatry, 126-40, 316-17, 622-23, 671-73, 696-700, 728-31

and injustice, 128-34, 139-40, 310-11, 321, 324, 699-700

Iliad and *Odyssey*, 22, 28-37, 83, 137, 350-52, 524, 563, 589, 611

impurity, 45-46, 145, 400-406, 427-55, 467-69, 496, 505-7, 569-70. *See also* purification/purity

Israel,

and the nations, 104-9, 147-48, 303-5, 463, 504-5, 525-41, 562-71, 640-57, 684-85, 731-39

as God's possession, 116, 267, 384-88, 541-42, 556-65

blessing of, 104-9, 116, 149-64, 223-34, 525-65, 595-96, 647-48

election of, 107-9, 303-4, 504-5, 527-29, 540, 556-59, 564-65, 590-94, 688, 746

exile of, 46, 249, 252, 272, 282-83, 317, 345-46, 569-72, 630-31, 675-79

holiness of, 124-25, 503-9, 561-62

hopes for, 571-80, 728-39

kings/rulers of, 120, 168, 173, 210, 213-15, 474, 577-80, 659-79, 699

salvation of, 256-57, 268-71, 275-84, 331-34, 571-80, 657, 701-6, 728-39

sinfulness of, 234-36, 259-84, 549-52, 562-64, 600-634, 653-59, 676-85, 687-727, 747

justice,

and compassion, 48-49, 134-35, 173-81, 188, 215-16, 550-51, 708-9

and judgment, 166-80, 191-99, 212-14, 217-18, 294-95, 325-37

distributive/retributive, 121-22, 180-81, 196-97, 209, 214

in pagan thought, 182-208

in Western Christian thought, 178-82,
216-19, 236-39

law/Torah,
and human well-being, 113-26, 138-64,
209-19, 227-30
as blessing, 109-16, 149-59, 234-36
as burden, 110, 115, 153-57
fulfillment of, 161-63, 233-34, 547, 601
goodness of, 109-12, 125-26, 138-64,
228-34
in Western Christian thought, 111-12,
141-45, 227-28

Marduk, 23-28, 183, 185, 199-201, 525
Moses, 245-46, 354-55, 459-60, 553-56,
587-88, 596-637, 684
intercession/mediation of, 245, 411,
603, 609-15, 633-34, 711

nations,
as God's creation, 526, 539-42
blessing of, 104-9, 511, 532-41, 564-65,
580-82, 647-48, 737-38
condemnation/destruction of, 580-82,
637, 640-51, 737-39
salvation of, 76-77, 533-41, 580-82,
737-38
sinfulness of, 128-33, 525-27, 580-82,
590-91
nature. *See* God, nature of; pagan gods
and nature

Odyssey. See Iliad and *Odyssey*

pagan gods,
and nature, 18, 36-37, 40, 183-86, 394-
95, 741
desires of, 19-21, 24-37, 127-28, 352-
53, 394-98, 523-25, 530
love of, 30-31, 188-90, 202-6
needs of, 30-33, 394-98, 657
wrath of, 26-27, 30-37, 221, 285-86,
310, 395-97
Passover, 125, 355, 357, 384, 411, 493
penal substitution, 387-88, 406-27, 433,
451, 479-89, 493-95, 744
propitiation, 30-34, 361, 372, 395, 408-15,
419, 423, 427, 433-34, 467-73, 493
punishment. *See* divine punishment/
chastisements

purification/purity, 44-47, 123-26, 155,
281-83, 356-58, 369, 379, 396-411,
421-22, 427-55, 464-76, 489-92,
501-2, 507, 513. *See also* impurity

redemption of firstborn, 125-26, 355, 387-90
repentance, 37, 241-43, 269-73, 312-13,
360, 402, 404-5, 420-23, 426-27,
446-51, 454, 465-86, 492-93, 581-82,
701-5, 710, 744
retribution, 92, 122, 181, 197, 214, 217,
326-42, 728, 751. *See also* justice,
distributive/retributive
reward, 71-72, 151-53, 157, 181-82, 190-
92, 195-98, 214-15, 221-23, 230-34,
628, 666, 751

Sabbath, 120-25, 143, 162-63, 447-48, 507-8
sacrifice,
and idolatry, 128-29, 133, 568-69,
619-21, 696-700
and justice/righteousness, 287, 305-10,
365-73, 378-91, 407, 415-27, 450-
51, 463-77, 495-97
and prayer, 350-53, 359-64, 380, 389,
395-96, 403, 471-73, 487, 490-94,
511, 572
and purification, 401, 427-54, 464-76,
489-92
as offering, 350-53, 357-59, 367, 381,
389-91, 403, 489-96, 512
for sin, 356, 376, 393-94, 398-452,
463-80, 492, 495-97
in Christian thought, 155, 218, 373-74,
398-99, 405-6
in pagan thought, 19-37, 127-28, 200,
285-88, 307, 349-53, 393-98, 416-
18, 426-27, 471, 523-24
meaning and purpose of, 357-58, 364-
91, 405-6, 411-12, 427-28, 437-39,
442, 451-55, 464-67, 473, 507, 512
mechanical views of, 377, 421-25, 432-
36, 451-54, 467-68
necessity of/need for, 404, 413-19,
427-28, 433-42, 476, 493-96
to God of Israel, 123-26, 288,
299-310, 353-91, 400-452,
463-80, 489-97, 658
sacrificial blood, 127-28, 286, 355-59,
374-78, 390, 397-403, 408-40, 448-53,
466, 473-76, 489-96

as ritual detergent, 430-31, 438, 448-52,
    492
sanctuary, 355, 363-66, 374-75, 386-89,
    396-97, 404, 428-41, 448-55, 462, 507-
    14, 518-20. *See also* tabernacle; temple
scapegoat. *See* goat for Azazel
shalom, 113-16, 168-69, 227-28, 752
sin,
    bearing of, 411, 421, 453, 477-80, 487,
        615, 636
    conceptions of, 21, 35-36, 80-83, 190-99,
        238-41, 395, 410-11, 428-49, 454
slavery, 119-21, 140-42, 147, 194, 203-4,
    212, 267-68, 557-61, 585-86, 590-98
suzerainty treaties, 542-47, 560

tabernacle, 355, 433-35, 518, 608. *See also*
    sanctuary
temple, 306-8, 357, 360-72, 430, 433, 437-
    42, 462, 518-21, 664-70, 676-79, 683.
    See also sanctuary
theogony, 17-18, 182-84
Torah. *See* law/Torah

vengeance, 1, 33-35, 117-19, 252-54,
    285-86, 325-42, 623-25, 685, 721-22,
    744, 751

Yom Kippur, 125, 355-59, 402, 414-15, 423,
    430-32, 439, 449, 473-77, 489

Zeus, 28-37, 64, 82, 137, 185, 351-52,
    611, 687